Saint Thomas Aquinas

Commentary on the Gospel of John
Chapters 1-8

Translated by Fr. Fabian R. Larcher, O.P.
Edited by The Aquinas Institute

Biblical Commentaries

Volume 35
Latin/English Edition of the Works of St. Thomas Aquinas

AQUINAS INSTITUTE | EMMAUS ACADEMIC
GREEN BAY, WI | STEUBENVILLE, OH

This printing was funded in part by donations made in memory of:
Marcus Berquist, Rose Johanna Trumbull, John and Mary Deignan,
Thomas and Eleanor Sullivan, and Fr. John T. Feeney and his sister Mary.

The printing was also made possible by a donation from Patricia Lynch,
and by a donation made in honor of Fr. Brian McMaster.

Published with the ecclesiastical approval of
The Most Reverend Paul D. Etienne, DD, STL
Bishop of Cheyenne
Given on July 16, 2013

Printed in the United States of America

Second Printing 2021

Publisher's Cataloging-in-Publication data

Thomas Aquinas, Saint, 1225?-1274
  Commentary on the Gospel of John, chapters 1-8 / Saint Thomas Aquinas; edited by The Aquinas Institute;
  translated by Fr. Fabian R. Larcher, O.P.
  p. 504 cm.
  ISBN 978-1-62340-017-0

1. Bible. N.T. John--Commentaries--Early works to 1800. I. Title. II. Series

BS2615.T5312 2013
226'.5'07--dc23   2013942433

Notes on the Text

Sacred Scripture

The text of Sacred Scripture presented at the beginning of each lecture is given in Latin, English, and Greek. Since St. Thomas appears to be familiar with more than one translation, quotes from memory, and often enough paraphrases, it has proven difficult to reconstruct the version of Scripture St. Thomas was working with. However, the closest available version of Scripture to St. Thomas's text was found to be the Clementine Vulgate of 1598, and this version of the Vulgate is the one found at the beginning of each lecture. The choice of an English version of Scripture to parallel to the Vulgate was therefore the Douay-Rheims. Both of these versions have been slightly modified to fit the text of St. Thomas. The Greek text is from the Nestle-Aland, Novum Testamentum Graece, 27th Revised Edition, edited by Barbara Aland, Kurt Aland, Johannes Karavidopoulos, Carlo M. Martini, and Bruce M. Metzger in cooperation with the Institute for New Testament Textual Research, Münster/Westphalia, © 1993 Deutsche Bibelgesellschaft, Stuttgart. Used with permission. The numbering of Scripture in the lecture headings and the English translation of the commentary is taken from the Nestle-Aland 27th Revised Edition and the RSV, while the numbering St. Thomas uses in the Latin text has been kept intact.

Latin Text of St. Thomas

The Latin text used in this volume is based on the 1972 Marietti edition, which is presently the best edition of the text. The text was scanned and edited by The Aquinas Institute.

English Translation of St. Thomas

The English translation used in this volume is based on the text prepared by Fr. Fabian R. Larcher, O.P. (1864-1947). It has been edited and revised by The Aquinas Institute.

The Aquinas Institute requests your assistance in the continued perfection of these texts.
If you discover any errors, please send a note to us by e-mail: editor@theaquinasinstitute.org.

Dedicated with love to
Our Lady of Mt. Carmel

Contents

COMMENTARY ON THE GOSPEL OF JOHN
CHAPTERS 1-8

Prologue

Isaiah 6:1

6:1 Vidi Dominum sedentem super solium excelsum et elevatum, et plena erat omnis terra maiestate eius, et ea quae sub ipso erant, replebant templum.

6:1 Καὶ ἐγένετο τοῦ ἐνιαυτοῦ, οὗ ἀπέθανεν Οζιας ὁ βασιλεύς, εἶδον τὸν κύριον καθήμενον ἐπὶ θρόνου ὑψηλοῦ καὶ ἐπηρμένου, καὶ πλήρης ὁ οἶκος τῆς δόξης αὐτοῦ.

6:1 I saw the Lord seated on a high and lofty throne, and the whole house was full of his majesty, and the things that were under him filled the temple.

---

1. Verba proposita sunt contemplantis, et si capiantur quasi ex ore Ioannis Evangelistae prolata, satis pertinent ad declarationem huius Evangelii. Ut enim dicit Augustinus in libro *de Consensu evangelist.*, *caeteri Evangelistae informant nos in eorum Evangeliis quantum ad vitam activam; sed Ioannes in suo Evangelio informat nos etiam quantum ad vitam contemplativam.*

In verbis autem propositis describitur contemplatio Ioannis tripliciter, secundum quod Dominum Iesum est tripliciter contemplatus. Describitur autem alta, ampla et perfecta. Alta quidem, quia *vidi Dominum sedentem super solium excelsum et elevatum*; ampla quidem, quia *plena est omnis terra maiestate eius*; perfecta, quia *ea quae sub ipso erant replebant templum*.

2. Circa primum sciendum quod altitudo et sublimitas contemplationis consistit maxime in contemplatione et cognitione Dei; Is. XL, 26: *levate in excelso oculos vestros, et videte quis fecit haec.* Tunc ergo homo oculos contemplationis in excelso elevat, quando videt et contemplatur ipsum rerum omnium Creatorem. Quia ergo Ioannes transcendit quicquid creatum est, scilicet ipsos montes, ipsos caelos, ipsos angelos, et pervenit ad ipsum Creatorem omnium, ut dicit Augustinus, manifestum est, quod contemplatio sua altissima fuit; et ideo *vidi Dominum*. Et quia, sicut ipse Ioannes dicit: **haec dixit Isaias quando vidit gloriam eius**, scilicet Christi, **et locutus est de eo**, ideo Dominus sedens super solium excelsum et elevatum, Christus est.

In hac autem contemplatione Ioannis circa verbum incarnatum quadruplex altitudo designatur. Auctoritatis, unde dicit *vidi Dominum*, aeternitatis, cum dicit *sedentem*, dignitatis, seu nobilitatis naturae, unde dicit *super solium excelsum*, et incomprehensibilis veritatis, cum dicit *et elevatum*.

Istis enim quatuor modis antiqui philosophi ad Dei cognitionem pervenerunt.

3. Quidam enim per auctoritatem Dei in ipsius cognitionem pervenerunt; et haec est via efficacissima.

Videmus enim ea quae sunt in rebus naturalibus, propter finem agere, et consequi utiles et certos fines; et cum intellectu careant, se ipsa dirigere non possunt, nisi ab aliquo dirigente per intellectum dirigantur et

1. These are the words of a contemplative, and if we regard them as spoken by John the Evangelist they apply quite well to showing the nature of this Gospel. For as Augustine says in his work *On the Agreement of the Evangelists: the other evangelists instruct us in their Gospels on the active life; but John in his Gospel instructs us also on the contemplative life.*

The contemplation of John is described above in three ways, in keeping with the threefold manner in which he contemplated the Lord Jesus. It is described as high, full, and perfect. It is high: *I saw the Lord seated on a high and lofty throne*; it is full: *and the whole house was full of his majesty*; and it was perfect: *and the things that were under him filled the temple.*

2. As to the first, we must understand that the height and sublimity of contemplation consists most of all in the contemplation and knowledge of God. *Lift up your eyes on high, and see who has created these things* (Isa 40:26). A man lifts up his eyes on high when he sees and contemplates the Creator of all things. Now since John rose above whatever had been created—mountains, heavens, angels—and reached the Creator of all, as Augustine says, it is clear that his contemplation was most high. Thus, *I saw the Lord*. And because, as John himself says below: **Isaiah said this because he had seen his glory**, namely, of Christ, **and spoke of him** (John 12:41), therefore the Lord seated on a high and lofty throne is Christ.

Now a fourfold height is indicated in this contemplation of John. A height of authority; hence he says, *I saw the Lord*. A height of eternity; when he says, *seated*. One of dignity, or nobility of nature; so he says, *on a high throne*. And a height of incomprehensible truth; when he says, *lofty*.

It is in these four ways that the early philosophers arrived at the knowledge of God.

3. Some attained to a knowledge of God through his authority, and this is the most efficacious way.

For we see the things in nature acting for an end, and attaining to ends which are both useful and certain. And since they lack intelligence, they are unable to direct themselves, but must be directed and moved by one directing them, and

moveantur. Et hinc est quod ipse motus rerum naturalium in finem certum, indicat esse aliquid altius, quo naturales res diriguntur in finem et gubernantur. Et ideo cum totus cursus naturae ordinate in finem procedat et dirigatur, de necessitate oportet nos ponere aliquid altius, quod dirigat ista et sicut dominus gubernet: et hic est Deus. Et haec gubernandi auctoritas in Verbo Dei demonstratur, cum dicit *Dominum*; unde in Ps. LXXXVIII, 10 dicitur: *tu dominaris potestati maris; motum autem fluctuum eius tu mitigas*; quasi dicat: *tu es Dominus et universa gubernas.*

Hanc cognitionem manifestat Ioannes se habere de Verbo, cum dicit: **in propria venit**, scilicet in mundum; quia totus mundus est suus proprius.

4. Alii vero venerunt in cognitionem Dei ex eius aeternitate. Viderunt enim quod quicquid est in rebus, est mutabile; et quanto aliquid est nobilius in gradibus rerum, tanto minus habet de mutabilitate: puta, inferiora corpora sunt secundum substantiam et secundum locum mutabilia; corpora vero caelestia, quae nobiliora sunt, secundum substantiam immutabilia sunt; secundum autem locum tantum moventur. Secundum hoc ergo evidenter colligi potest, quod primum principium omnium rerum, et supremum et nobilius, sit immobile et aeternum.

Et hanc aeternitatemVerbi propheta insinuat, cum dicit *sedentem*, idest absque omni mutabilitate et aeternitate praesidentem; Ps. c. XLIV, 7: *sedes tua, Deus, in saeculum saeculi*; Hebr. ult., 8: *Iesus Christus heri et hodie, ipse et in saecula*. Hanc aeternitatem Ioannes ostendit dicens: **in principio erat Verbum**.

5. Quidam autem venerunt in cognitionem Dei ex dignitate ipsius Dei: et isti fuerunt Platonici.

Consideraverunt enim quod omne illud quod est secundum participationem, reducitur ad aliquid quod sit illud per suam essentiam, sicut ad primum et ad summum; sicut omnia ignita per participationem reducuntur ad ignem, qui est per essentiam suam talis. Cum ergo omnia quae sunt, participent esse, et sint per participationem entia, necesse est esse aliquid in cacumine omnium rerum, quod sit ipsum esse per suam essentiam, idest quod sua essentia sit suum esse: et hoc est Deus, qui est sufficientissima, et dignissima, et perfectissima causa totius esse, a quo omnia quae sunt, participant esse. Et huius dignitas ostenditur, cum dicitur *super solium excelsum*, quod, secundum Dionysium, ad divinam naturam refertur; Ps. CXII, 4: *excelsus super omnes gentes Dominus*. Hanc dignitatem ostendit nobis Ioannes, cum dicit: **et Deus erat Verbum**, quasi: Verbum erat Deus, ut ly **Verbum** ponatur ex parte suppositi, et **Deus** ex parte appositi.

6. Quidam autem venerunt in cognitionem Dei ex incomprehensibilitate veritatis.

who possesses an intellect. Thus it is that the movement of the things of nature toward a certain end indicates the existence of something higher by which the things of nature are directed to an end and governed. And so, since the whole course of nature advances to an end in an orderly way and is directed, we have to posit something higher which directs and governs them as lord; and this is God. This authority in governing is shown to be in the Word of God when he says, *Lord*. Thus a Psalm says: *you rule the power of the sea, and you still the swelling of its waves* (Ps 88:10), as though saying: *you are the Lord and govern all things.*

John shows that he knows this about the Word when he says below, **he came unto his own** (John 1:11), i.e., to the world, since the whole universe is his own.

4. Others came to a knowledge of God from his eternity. They saw that whatever was in things was changeable, and that the more noble something is in the grades of being, so much the less it has of mutability. For example, the lower bodies are mutable both as to their substance and to place, while the heavenly bodies, which are more noble, are immutable in substance and change only with respect to place. We can clearly conclude from this that the first principle of all things, which is supreme and more noble, is changeless and eternal.

The prophet suggests this eternity of the Word when he says, *seated*, i.e., presiding without any change and eternally. *Your throne, O God, is forever and ever* (Ps 44:7); *Jesus Christ is the same yesterday, today, and forever* (Heb 13:8). John points to this eternity when he says below, **in the beginning was the Word** (John 1:1).

5. Still others came to a knowledge of God from the dignity of God; and these were the Platonists.

They noted that everything which is something by participation is reduced to what is the same thing by essence, as to the first and highest. Thus, all things which are fiery by participation are reduced to fire, which is such by its essence. And so since all things which exist participate in being and are beings by participation, there must necessarily be at the summit of all things something which is its existence through its own essence, i.e., whose essence is its existence. And this is God, who is the most sufficient, the most eminent, and the most perfect cause of the whole of existence, from whom all things that are participate in existence. This dignity is shown in the words, *on a high throne*, which, according to Denis, refer to the divine nature. *The Lord is high above all nations* (Ps 112:4). John shows us this dignity when he says below, **the Word was God** (John 1:1), with **Word** as subject and **God** as the predicate.

6. Yet others arrived at a knowledge of God from the incomprehensibility of truth.

Omnis enim veritas quam intellectus noster cape-re potest, finita est; quia secundum Augustinum, *omne quod scitur, scientis comprehensione finitur,* et si finitur, est determinatum et particularizatum; et ideo necesse est primam et summam veritatem, quae superat om-nem intellectum, incomprehensibilem et infinitam esse: et hoc est Deus. Unde in Ps. VIII, 2 dicitur: *elevata est magnificentia tua super caelos,* idest super omnem intel-lectum creatum, angelicum et humanum. Et hoc ideo, quia, ut dicit Apostolus, *lucem habitat inaccessibilem,* I Tim. ult. 16.

Huius autem incomprehensibilitas veritatis ostendi-tur nobis, cum dicit *et elevatum,* scilicet super omnem cognitionem intellectus creati. Et hanc incomprehensi-bilitatem insinuat nobis Ioannes, cum dicit: **Deum nemo vidit unquam.**

Sic ergo contemplatio Ioannis alta fuit et quantum ad auctoritatem, et quantum ad aeternitatem, et quantum ad dignitatem, et quantum ad Verbi incomprehensibi-litatem, quam nobis in suo Evangelio tradidit Ioannes.

7. Fuit etiam ampla. Tunc enim contemplatio ampla est, quando in causa potest aliquis considerare omnes effectus ipsius causae; quando scilicet non solum essen-tiam causae, sed etiam virtutem eius, secundum quam se ad multa diffundit, cognoscit. De qua diffusione dici-tur Eccli. XXV, 35: *qui implet quasi Phison sapientiam, et quasi Tigris in diebus novorum;* Ps. LXIV, 10: *flumen Dei repletum est aquis,* quia divina sapientia altitudinem ha-bet quantum ad cognitionem omnium rerum; Sap. IX, 9: *ab initio est tecum sapientia quae novit opera tua.*

Quia ergo Ioannes Evangelista elevatus in contem-plationem naturae divini Verbi et essentiae est, cum dicit: **in principio erat Verbum, et Verbum erat apud Deum,** statim virtutem ipsius Verbi secundum quod dif-fundit se ad omnia, nobis insinuat, cum dicit: **omnia per ipsum facta sunt.** Ideo contemplatio sua ampla fuit. Et ideo in auctoritate praemissa, postquam dixerat Prophe-ta *vidi Dominum sedentem,* subiungit de virtute eius *et plena erat omnis terra maiestate eius,* idest tota plenitudo rerum et universi est a maiestate eius, et virtute Dei, per quem omnia facta sunt, et cuius lumine omnes homines venientes in hunc mundum illuminantur; Ps. XXIII, 1: *Domini est terra, et plenitudo eius.*

8. Fuit etiam contemplatio eius perfecta. Tunc enim contemplatio perfecta est, quando contemplans perduci-tur et elevatur ad altitudinem rei contemplatae: si enim remaneret in infimis, quantumcumque alta ipse contem-plaretur, non esset contemplatio perfecta. Ad hoc ergo quod sit perfecta, oportet quod ascendat et consequatur ipsum finem rei contemplatae, inhaerendo et assentien-do per affectum et intellectum veritati contemplatae. Iob XXXVII, 16: *numquid nosti semitas nubium,* idest

All the truth which our intellect is able to grasp is finite, since according to Augustine, *everything that is known is bounded by the comprehension of the one knowing*; and if it is bounded, it is determined and particularized. Therefore, the first and supreme truth, which surpasses every intellect, must necessarily be incomprehensible and infinite; and this is God. Hence a psalm says, *your greatness is above the heavens* (Ps 8:2), i.e., above every created intellect, angelic and human. The Apostle says this in the words, *he dwells in unapproachable light* (1 Tim 6:16).

This incomprehensibility of truth is shown to us in the word *lofty,* that is, above all the knowledge of the created intellect. John implies this incomprehensibility to us when he says below, **no one has ever seen God** (John 1:18).

Thus, the contemplation of John was high as regards au-thority, eternity, dignity, and the incomprehensibility of the Word. And John has passed on this contemplation to us in his Gospel.

7. John's contemplation was also full. Now contempla-tion is full when someone is able to consider all the effects of a cause in the cause itself, that is, when he knows not only the essence of the cause, but also its power, according as it can extend out to many things. Of this flowing outward we read, *it overflows with wisdom, like the Pishon, and like the Tigris in the days of the new fruits* (Sir 25:35); *the river of God is full with water,* since the divine wisdom has depth in relation to its knowledge of all things (Ps 65:9). *With you from the beginning is wisdom, who knows your works* (Wis 9:9).

Since John the Evangelist was raised up to the contem-plation of the nature of the divine Word and of his essence when he said, **in the beginning was the Word; and the Word was with God** (John 1:1), he immediately tells us of the power of the Word as it extends to all things, saying, **through him all things came into being** (John 1:3). Thus his contemplation was full. And so after the Prophet had said, *I saw the Lord seated,* he added something about his power, *and the whole house was full of his majesty,* that is, the whole fullness of things and of the universe is from the majesty and power of God, through whom all things were made, and by whose light all the men coming into this world are enlightened. *The earth and its fullness are the Lord's* (Ps 23:1).

8. The contemplation of John was also perfect. For con-templation is perfect when the one contemplating is led and raised to the height of the thing contemplated. Should he remain at a lower level, then no matter how high the things which he might contemplate, the contemplation would not be perfect. So in order that it be perfect it is necessary that it rise and attain the end of the thing contemplated, adher-ing and assenting by affection and understanding to the truth contemplated. Job says, *do you not know the path of*

contemplationes praedicantium, *quod perfectae sint?* Inquantum firmiter per affectum et intellectum inhaerent summae veritati contemplatae.

Quia ergo Ioannes non solum docuit quomodo Christus Iesus, Verbum Dei, est Deus super omnia elevatus et quomodo omnia per ipsum facta sunt, sed etiam quod per ipsum sanctificamur, et ei per gratiam quam nobis infundit, inhaeremus, dicit: **de plenitudine eius omnes accepimus gratiam pro gratia**. Ideo apparet, quod sua contemplatio perfecta fuit. Et haec perfectio ostenditur, cum subdit *et ea quae sub ipso erat, replebant templum.* Nam, sicut dicitur I Cor. c. XI, 3, *caput Christi Deus.* Quae ergo sub Christo sunt, sacramenta sunt humanitatis, per quae fideles replentur plenitudine gratiae. Sic ergo *ea quae sub ipso erant, replebant templum,* idest fideles qui sunt templum Dei sanctum, sicut dicitur I Cor. III, 17 inquantum per ipsius sacramenta humanitatis, fideles Christi omnes de plenitudine gratiae ipsius accipiunt.

Fuit ergo Ioannis contemplatio ampla, alta et perfecta.

9. Sed notandum quod diversimode diversae scientiae istos tres modos contemplationis sortiuntur. Perfectionem namque contemplationis habet scientia moralis, quae est de ultimo fine; plenitudinem autem scientia naturalis, quae res a Deo procedentes considerat; altitudinem vero contemplationis inter scientias physicas habet metaphysica. Sed Evangelium Ioannis, quod divisim scientiae praedictae habent, totum simul continet, et ideo est perfectissimum.

10. Sic ergo ex praemissis colligitur materia huius Evangelii; quia cum evangelistae alii tractent principaliter mysteria humanitatis Christi, Ioannes specialiter et praecipue divinitatem Christi in Evangelio suo insinuat, ut supra dictum est: nec tamen praetermisit mysteria humanitatis; quod ideo factum est, quia postquam alii evangelistae sua Evangelia scripserunt, insurrexerunt haereses circa divinitatem Christi, quae erant quod Christus erat purus homo, sicut Ebion et Cerinthus falso opinabantur. Et ideo Ioannes Evangelista, qui veritatem divinitatis Verbi ab ipso fonte divini pectoris hauserat, ad preces fidelium, Evangelium istud scripsit, in quo doctrinam de Christi divinitate nobis tradidit, et omnes haereses confutavit.

Patet ergo ordo istius Evangelii ex verbis praemissis. Primo enim insinuat nobis *Dominum sedentem super solium excelsum et elevatum,* in prima parte, cum dicit: **in principio erat Verbum**. In secunda vero parte insinuat quomodo *omnis terra plena est maiestate eius,* cum dicit: **omnia per ipsum facta sunt**. In tertia parte manifestat

the clouds, that is, the contemplation of those preaching, *how perfect they are?* (Job 37:16), inasmuch as they adhere firmly by affection and understanding to contemplating the highest truth.

Since John not only taught how Christ Jesus, the Word of God, is God, raised above all things, and how all things were made through him, but also that we are sanctified by him and adhere to him by the grace which he pours into us, he says below, **of his fullness we all have received—indeed, grace upon grace** (John 1:16). It is therefore apparent that his contemplation is perfect. This perfection is shown in the addition, *and the things that were under him filled the temple.* For *the head of Christ is God* (1 Cor 11:3). The things that are under Christ are the sacraments of his humanity, through which the faithful are filled with the fullness of grace. In this way, then, the *things that were under him filled the temple,* i.e., the faithful, who are the holy temple of God (1 Cor 3:17) insofar as through the sacraments of his humanity all the faithful of Christ receive from the fullness of his grace.

The contemplation of John was thus full, high, and perfect.

9. We should note, however, that these three characteristics of contemplation belong to the different sciences in different ways. The perfection of contemplation is found in moral science, which is concerned with the ultimate end. The fullness of contemplation is possessed by natural science, which considers things as proceeding from God. Among the physical sciences, the height of contemplation is found in metaphysics. But the Gospel of John contains all together what the above sciences have in a divided way, and so it is most perfect.

10. In this way then, from what has been said, we can understand the matter of this Gospel. For while the other evangelists treat principally of the mysteries of the humanity of Christ, John, especially and above all, makes known the divinity of Christ in his Gospel, as we saw above. Still, he does not ignore the mysteries of his humanity. He did this because, after the other evangelists had written their Gospels, heresies had arisen concerning the divinity of Christ, to the effect that Christ was purely and simply a man, as Ebion and Cerinthus falsely thought. And so John the Evangelist, who had drawn the truth about the divinity of the Word from the very fountain-head of the divine breast, wrote this Gospel at the request of the faithful. And in it he gives us the doctrine of the divinity of Christ and refutes all heresies.

The order of this Gospel is clear from the above. For John first shows us *the Lord seated on a high and lofty throne,* when he says below, **in the beginning was the Word** (John 1:1). He shows second how *the house was full of his majesty,* when he says, **through him all things came into being** (John 1:3). Third, he shows how *the things that were*

quomodo *ea quae sub ipso erant, replebant templum* cum ipse dicit: **Verbum caro factum est.**

Patet etiam finis huius Evangelii, qui est ut fideles templum Dei efficiantur, et repleantur a maiestate Dei; unde et ipse Ioannes XX, 31: **haec autem scripta sunt, ut credatis quia Iesus est Christus Filius Dei.**

Patet etiam materia huius Evangelii, quae est cognitio divinitas Verbi. Patet ordo, patet et finis.

11. Sequitur conditio auctoris, qui quidem describitur in praemissis quantum ad quatuor: quantum ad nomen, quantum ad virtutem, quantum ad figuram, et quantum ad privilegium.

Quantum ad nomen, quia Ioannes, qui huius Evangelii auctor fuit, Ioannes autem interpretatur *in quo est gratia*, quia secreta divinitatis videre non possunt nisi qui gratiam Dei in se habent; unde I Cor. II, 11 dicitur: *quae sunt Dei nemo cognovit, nisi Spiritus Dei.*

Ioannes ergo vidit Dominum sedentem, quantum ad virtutem, quia fuit virgo: talibus enim competit videre Dominum; Matth. c. V, 8: *beati mundo corde.*

Quantum ad figuram, quia Ioannes figuratur per aquilam. Et hoc quia cum alii tres evangelistae circa ea quae Christus in carne est operatus, occupati, designentur per animalia, quae gradiuntur in terra, scilicet per hominem, vitulum et leonem; Ioannes vero, supra nebulam infirmitatis humanae sicut aquila volans, lucem incommutabilis veritatis altissimis atque firmissimis oculis cordis intuetur, atque ipsam deitatem Domini nostri Iesu Christi, qua Patri aequalis est, intendens, eam in suo Evangelio, quantum inter omnes sufficere credidit, studuit praecipue commendare. Et de hoc volatu Ioannis dicitur Iob c. XXXIX, 27: *numquid ad praeceptum tuum elevabitur aquila?* Idest Ioannes; et infra: *oculi eius de longe prospiciunt,* quia scilicet ipsum Verbum Dei in sinu Patris oculo mentis intuetur.

Quantum ad privilegium, quia inter caeteros discipulos Domini Ioannes magis fuit dilectus a Christo: **iste est enim discipulus ille quem diligebat Iesus,** sicut ipsemet non exprimens nomen suum dixit; et ideo, quia amicis revelantur secreta, ut dicitur ibid. XV, 15: **vos autem dixi amicos, quia omnia quaecumque audivi a patre meo, nota feci vobis,** secreta sua huic discipulo specialiter dilecto specialiter commendavit. Unde Iob XXXVI, 32 dicitur: *immanibus,* idest superbis, *abscondit lucem,* Christus scilicet divinitatis suae veritatem, *et annuntiat de ea amico suo,* scilicet Ioanni, *quod possessio eius sit* etc., quia ipse est, qui lucem Verbi incarnati excellentius videns, ipsam nobis insinuat, dicens: **erat lux vera** etc.

Patet ergo materia, ordo, finis et auctor huius Evangelii beati Ioannis, quod prae manibus habemus.

under him filled the temple, when he says, **the Word was made flesh** (John 1:14).

The end of this Gospel is also clear, and it is that the faithful become the temple of God, and become filled with the majesty of God; and so John says below, **these things are written so that you may believe that Jesus is the Christ, the Son of God** (John 20:31).

The matter of this Gospel, the knowledge of the divinity of the Word, is clear, as well as its order and end.

11. Then follows the condition of the author, who is described above in four ways: as to his name, his virtue, his symbol, and his privilege.

He is described as to name as John, the author of this Gospel. John is interpreted as *in whom is grace,* since the secrets of the divinity cannot be seen except by those who have the grace of God within themselves. *No one knows the deep things of God but the Spirit of God* (1 Cor 2:11).

As concerns his virtue, John saw the Lord seated, because he was a virgin; for it is fitting that such persons see the Lord: *blessed are the pure in heart* (Matt 5:8).

He is described as to his symbol, for John is symbolized by an eagle. The other three evangelists, concerned with those things which Christ did in his flesh, are symbolized by animals which walk on the earth, namely, by a man, a bull calf, and a lion. But John flies like an eagle above the cloud of human weakness and looks upon the light of unchanging truth with the most lofty and firm eyes of the heart. And gazing on the very deity of our Lord Jesus Christ, by which he is equal to the Father, he has striven in this Gospel to confide this above all, to the extent that he believed was sufficient for all. Concerning this flight of John it is said: *will the eagle,* that is, John, *fly up at your command?* (Job 39:27) And further on it says, *his eyes look far away,* because the Word of God is seen in the bosom of the Father by the eye of the mind.

John is described as to privilege since, among the other disciples of the Lord, John was more loved by Christ. Without mentioning his own name John refers to himself below as **the disciple whom Jesus loved** (John 21:20). And because secrets are revealed to friends, **I have called you friends because everything I have heard from my father I have made known to you** (John 15:15), Jesus confided his secrets in a special way to that disciple who was specially loved. Thus it says in Job: *from the savage,* that is, the proud, *he hides his light,* that is, Christ hides the truth of his divinity, *and shows his friend,* that is, John, *that it belongs to him* (Job 36:32), since it is John who sees the light of the incarnate Word more excellently and expresses it to us, saying **he was the true light** (John 1:19).

Now the matter, order, end and author of this Gospel of the blessed John are clear.

Prologue of Saint Jerome

I. *Hic est Joannes Evangelista, unus ex discipulis Domini, qui virgo a Deo electus est, quem de nuptiis, volentem nubere, vocavit Deus.*

II. *Cui virginitatis in hoc duplex testimonium datur in Evangelio; et quod prae caeteris delectus a Deo dicitur: et huic matrem suam pendens in cruce commendavit Dominus, et virginem virgo servaret.*

III. *Denique manifestans in Evangelio, quod erat ipse incorruptibilis Verbi opus inchoans, solus Verbum carnem factum esse, nec lumen a tenebris comprehensum fuisse, testatur, primum signum ponens quod in nuptiis fecit Dominus: ostendens quod ipse erat: ut legentibus demonstraret, quod ubi Dominus invitatus sit, deficere nuptiarum vinum debeat: et veteribus immutatis nova omnia, quae a Christo instituuntur, appareant. Hoc autem Evangelium scripsit in Asia, posteaquam in Pathmos insula Apocalypsim scripserat: ut cui in principio Canonis incorruptibile principium pranotatur in Genesi, ei etiam incorruptibilis finis per virginem in Apocalypsi redderetur; dicente Christo: Ego sum α et ω.*

IV. *Et hic est Joannes, qui sciens supervenisse diem recessus sui, convocatis discipulis suis in Ephaso, per multa signorum experimenta promens Christum, descendens in defossum supulturae suae locum, facta oratione positus est ad patres suos: tam extraneus a dolore mortis, quam a corruptione carnis invenitur alienus.*

V. *Tamen post omnes Evangelium scripsit: et hoc virgini debebatur. Quorum tamen vel scriptorum temporis dispositio, vel librorum ordinatio, ideo a nobis per singula non exponitur, ut sciendi desiderio collato, et quaerentibus fructus laboris, et Deo magisterii doctrina servetur.*

I. *This is John the Evangelist, one of the disciples of the Lord, who was chosen by God as a virgin, whom God called from his wedding, when he wished to marry.*

II. *A twofold testimony of his virginity is given in this Gospel: both that he is called beloved above all the others by God; and that to him the Lord entrusted his mother when he was hanging on the cross, so that a virgin should protect a virgin.*

III. *Finally revealing in the Gospel, that he was an inaugurating work of the incorruptible Word, he alone bears witness that the Word became flesh, and the light was not comprehended by the darkness, setting down the first sign that the Lord did at a wedding: showing that he himself was there: so that he could demonstrate to his readers that where the Lord was invited, the wedding wine had to run out: and that to the unchanged old ones, all the new things that are instituted by Christ would appear. But he wrote this Gospel in Asia, after he had written the book of Revelation on the island of Patmos: so that to him to whom in the beginning of the canon the incorruptible beginning is predicted in Genesis, to him also the incorruptible end through a virgin in Revelation would be rendered; by Christ's saying: I am the alpha and omega.*

IV. *And this is John, who knowing that the day of his passing away was upon him, having called together his disciples in Ephesus, and presenting Christ through many experiences of signs, and descending into the place dug out for his tomb, having made his prayer was placed with his fathers: he is found as much a stranger to the sorrow of death as he was a foreigner to the corruption of the flesh.*

V. *But he wrote his Gospel after everyone else: and this was owing to the Virgin. However the disposition of these writings in time or the ordering of the books, will not then be explained in detail by us, so that having granted the desire to know, both for those seeking the fruit of labor, and for God, the teaching of a master may be preserved.*

Exposition of St. Thomas

12. In quo duo intendit Hieronymus exprimere, scilicet auctorem Evangelii, et ostendere quod ei scribere hoc Evangelium competebat.

Dividitur ergo in duas partes. Primo ergo describit Ioannem quantum ad vitam; secundo quantum ad mortem, ibi *hic est Ioannes.*

Circa primum duo facit. Primo describit auctorem operis, quantum ad dona in vita sibi collata; secundo

12. In this Jerome aims to express two things, namely the author of the Gospel, and to show that he was qualified to write it.

Therefore it is divided into two parts. First he describes John as to his life; second, as to his death, where it says, *this is John.*

Concerning the first point, he does two things. First he describes the author of the work, as to the gifts conferred

ex illis ostendit idoneitatem ad Evangelium conscribendum, ibi *denique manifestans in Evangelio.*

Circa primum duo facit. Primo ostendit praeconia auctoris; secundo probat, ibi *cui virginitatis in hoc duplex testimonium datur in Evangelio.*

13. Describit enim auctorem quantum ad nomen, dicens *hic est Ioannes,* in quo gratia; I Cor. XV, 10: *gratia Dei sum id quod sum.* Secundo quantum ad officium, cum dicit *Evangelista*; Is. XLI, 27: *primus ad Sion dicet: ecce adsum, et Ierusalem Evangelistam dabo.* Tertio quantum ad dignitatem, cum dicit *ex discipulis Domini*; Is. LIV, 13: *ponam universos filios tuos doctos a Domino.* Quarto quantum ad castitatis virtutem, cum dicit *qui virgo.* Quinto ab electione *est electus a Domino*; infra XV, 16: **non vos me elegistis.** Sexto a modo vocationis, cum dicit, quod *de nuptis vocavit,* ab illis scilicet nuptiis ad quas est invitatus Iesus cum discipulis suis, ubi mutavit aquam in vinum.

14. Sed contra est, quod dicitur Matth. c. VI, 21, quod vocatus est cum Iacobo fratre suo de navi, non autem de nuptiis.

Ad quod dicendum est quod diversae fuerunt vocationes apostolorum. Primo enim vocati fuerunt ad familiaritatem Christi, sed ultimo vocati ad discipulatum, quando scilicet relictis omnibus, secuti sunt Iesum. Quod ergo Hieronymus dicit, intelligendum est de prima vocatione, qua Ioannes ad familiaritatem Christi de nuptiis est vocatus; quod vero Matthaeus dicit, intelligendum est de ultima vocatione, qua de navi vocavit cum Iacobo fratre suo, quando scilicet relictis omnibus, secutus est Christum.

15. Consequenter cum dicit *cui virginitatis in hoc duplex testimonium datur,* probat praeconium virginitatis Ioannis duplici signo.

Primo, signo maioris dilectionis. Et quantum ad hoc dicit *cui,* scilicet Ioanni, *in hoc,* scilicet Evangelio, *duplex testimonium virginitatis datur in Evangelio,* idest ex verbis Evangelii, sive quae continentur in Evangelio, *quod et prae caeteris discipulis a Deo dilectus dicitur*; infra XXI, 24: **hic est discipulus ille qui testimonium perhibet de his et scripsit haec.** Causa autem huius specialis dilectionis fuit munditia, quae ad dilectionem provocat, ut dicitur Prov. XXII, 11: *qui diligit cordis munditiam propter gratiam labiorum, habebit amicum regem.*

Secundo probat idem signo commendationis matris, cum dicit: *et huic,* scilicet Ioanni, *Dominus,* scilicet *in cruce pendens, matrem commendavit,* ut dicitur Io. XIX, 27, *ut virgo,* scilicet Ioannes, *virginem* matrem congrue *servaret.*

on him in life; second, he shows by them his fittingness for composing a Gospel, where he says, *finally revealing in a Gospel.*

Concerning the first, he does two things. First, he shows the illustriousness of the author; second, he proves it, where he says, *of whose virginity in this a two-fold testimony is given in the Gospel.*

13. For he describes the author according to his name, saying *this is John,* in whom there is grace: *by the grace of God I am what I am* (1 Cor 15:10). Second, according to his office, when he says, *the Evangelist*: *the first shall say to Zion, behold, I am here, and I will give an Evangelist to Jerusalem* (Isa 41:27). Third, according to his dignity, where he says, *one of the disciples of the Lord*; *I will make all your children to be taught by the Lord* (Isa 54:13). Fourth, according to the virtue of chastity, where he says, *who was a virgin.* Fifth, by election, at *was chosen by the Lord*; as it says in: **you have not chosen me** (John 15:16). Sixth, by the manner of his calling, where it says that *he called him from his wedding,* namely that wedding to which Jesus was invited with his disciples, where he changed the water into wine.

14. But to the contrary is what is said in Matthew, that he was called with his brother James from their boat, not from a wedding (Matt 4:21).

To this it should be said that there were several callings of the apostles. For first they were called to the acquaintance of Christ, but finally they were called to discipleship, namely, when having left everything, they followed Jesus. Therefore what Jerome says is to be understood concerning John's first calling, when John was called from his wedding to the aquaintanceship of Christ; but what Matthew says is to be understood as to his final calling, in which he called him from his boat with his brother James, which was when he left everything and followed Christ.

15. Accordingly, when he says *of whose virginity in this a two-fold testimony is given,* he proves the illustriousness of John's virginity by two signs.

First, by the sign of his greater love. And as to this he says, *whose,* that is, John's, *in this,* namely, this Gospel, *a two-fold testimony of virginity is given in the Gospel,* that is, by the words of the Gospel, or else those that are contained in the Gospel, *because he is also said to be loved by God above the other disciples*: **this is that disciple who gives testimony of these things and has written these things** (John 21:24). But for the sake of this special love was his purity, which further provoked him to love: *he who loves cleanness of heart shall have the king for a friend on account of the grace of his lips* (Prov 22:11).

Second, he proves the same thing by the sign of entrusting him with his mother, where he says: *and to him,* that is, to John, *the Lord,* that is, *hanging on the cross, entrusted his mother, so that a virgin,* that is, John, *might protect a virgin mother fittingly* (John 19:27).

16. Deinde cum dicit *denique manifestans in Evangelio*, etc. ostendit quod Ioanni competebat Evangelium scribere; et hoc quantum ad quatuor.

Primo quantum ad principium Evangelii, quod incipit a Verbo incorruptibili, de quo non nisi incorruptum tractare oportuit. Et quantum ad hoc dicit *denique manifestans*, scilicet Ioannes, *in Evangelio, quod ipse erat incorruptibilis Verbi opus inchoans, solus Verbum carnem factum esse, nec lumen a tenebris comprehensum fuisse testatur.*

17. Secundum quantum ad miraculorum exordium.

Incipit enim miraculorum ordinem texere a miraculo quod Deus in nuptiis ostendit, quando scilicet aquam mutavit in vinum, ut patet Io. II, 1–11, in quibus vinum nuptiarum defecit, vino novo, scilicet virginitatis, restituto. Et quantum ad hoc dicit *primum signum*, id est miraculum, *quod in nuptiis facit Dominus, ponens*, scilicet in principio aliorum miraculorum, *ostendens quod ipse erat*, scilicet virgo, *ut legentibus demonstraret quod ubi dominus invitatus sit, deficere vinum nuptiarum*, idest coniugii delectatio, *debeat; et veteribus immutatis*, idest antiqua aqua in novum vinum, *nova omnia quae a Christo instituuntur, appareant*; quia scilicet homines conversi ad Christum, debent exuere veterem et induere novum hominem, ut dicitur Col. c. III, 10, et Apoc. XXI, 5: *dicit qui sedebat in throno: ecce nova facio omnia.*

18. Sed contra. Videtur per hoc quod dicit, quod *ubi dominus invitatus est debeat deficere vinum nuptiarum*, quod quicumque Deum amat, et diligit, debet cessare a coniugio: non ergo licet uxorem ducere.

Respondeo dicendum quod homo invitatur a Deo dupliciter: quantum ad communem gratiam et sic non est necesse deficere vinum nuptiarum; et quantum ad speciale contemplationis fastigium: et sic oportet deficere vinum nuptiarum. Cuius rationem Apostolus assignat I Cor. VII, 34: *quia mulier, quae nupta est, cogitat quomodo placeat viro*, et ideo oportet quod ab actu contemplationis impediatur, *quae autem nupta non est, cogitat quomodo placeat Christo.*

Vel dicendum quod diligentibus Deum, et habentibus ipsum per gratiam, deficere debet vinum nuptiarum ab effectu vini, ut scilicet non inebrientur delectatione carnali, quae tanta posset esse, et cum tanta libidine exerceri, quod etiam in coniugatis esset peccatum mortale.

19. Tertio quantum ad ordinem descriptionis libri.

Nam post omnes alios libros Sacrae Scripturae, hoc Evangelium est scriptum. Cum enim canonica Scriptura incipiat a libro Genesis et terminetur in Apocalypsim, Evangelium istud conscriptum fuit postquam Ioannes revocatus est a Pathmos insula Asiae, ubi ad

16. Next, when he says, *finally revealing in the Gospel*, he shows that John was qualified to write the Gospel; and this for four reasons.

First, as to the beginning of the Gospel, which begins with an incorruptible Word, whom it was only fitting that an incorrupted man should discuss. And as to that, he says, *finally revealing*, that is, John, *in the Gospel, because he himself was an inaugurating work of the incorruptible Word*, he testifies that the Word was made flesh, and the light was not comprehended by the darkness.

17. Second, as to the prelude to miracles.

For he begins to weave the order of miracles from the miracle that God shows at the wedding, when he changed water into wine, as is clear from John 2:1–11, where the wedding wine ran out, and was replaced with new wine, that is, virginity. And as to this, he says, *the first sign*, that is, miracle, *which the Lord did at the wedding, setting forth*, namely, in the beginning of all the other miracles, *showing that he himself was*, namely, a virgin, *so that he might demonstrate to those reading that where the Lord was invited, the wine of the wedding*, that is, the enjoyment of conjugality, *had to run out*; and to the *unchanged old ones*, that is, the old water into new wine, *all the new things that were instituted by Christ would appear*; because namely men converted to Christ should cast off the old man and put on the new man (Col 3:10), and *the one who was sitting on the throne, says, behold, I make all things new* (Rev 21:5).

18. But to the contrary. It seems by the fact that he says that *where the Lord is invited the wine of marriage must run out*, that whoever loves God, and loves him rationally, must quit marriage: and then it would not be permitted to take a wife.

I answer that a man is invited by God in two ways: with regard to the shared grace and in that way it is not necessary for the wine of marriage to fall short; or with regard to the special zenith of contemplation: and in this way it is necessary for the wine of marriage to fall short. The reason for this the Apostle designates: *for the woman who is married thinks how to please her husband*, and thus she is necessarily hampered from the act of contemplation, *but the one who is not married, thinks how to please Christ* (1 Cor 7:34).

Or it may be said that for those loving God, and possessing him by grace, the wine of marriage must fall short in the effect of wine, that is, so that they are not drunk with fleshly enjoyment, which can be so great and can be practiced with so much sexual desire that even between spouses there can be mortal sin.

19. Third, as to the order of description of the book.

For after all the other books of Sacred Scripture, this Gospel was written. For although the canon of Scripture begins with the book of Genesis and ends in Revelation, this Gospel was composed after John was recalled from the island of Patmos to Asia, where he wrote this Gospel at

preces episcoporum Asiae hoc scripsit Evangelium. Non tamen ordinatur ultimo, licet ultimo scripserit. Ex quo congruentia scribendi Evangelium ostenditur *ut cui in principio canonis*, idest Sacrae Scripturae, ubi dicitur: *in principio creavit Deus caelum et terram, incorruptibile principium praenotatur in Genesi ei etiam incorruptibilis finis per virginem in Apocalypsi redderetur*, quantum ad ordinem librorum, non quantum ad ordinem Scripturae.

20. Deinde cum dicit *et hic est Ioannes*, describitur auctorem: et circa hoc duo facit.

Primo ponit praeconia suae laudis quantum ad mortem; secundo concludit ex his congruentiam ordinis huius Evangelii, ibi *tamen post omnes Evangelium scripsit.*

21. Privilegium autem mortis admirabile et speciale est, quia nullum dolorem sensit in morte; et hoc Deo faciente, ut qui a corruptione carnis extitit penitus alienus, esset a dolore mortis extraneus.

22. Congruentiam auctoris ad fidem ostendit, dicens *tamen post omnes Evangelium scripsit.*

In libris Sacrae Scripturae duplex ordo consideratur, unus scilicet temporis quo scripti fuerunt, et alius dispositionis, quo in Biblia ordinantur.

the request of the bishops of Asia. But nevertheless it is not ranked last, although he wrote it last. From this the fittingness of his writing the Gospel is shown *so that for the one for whom in the beginning of the canon* of Sacred Scripture, where it is said: *in the beginning God created the heaven and the earth* (Gen 1:1), *an incorruptible beginning is set down in Genesis, to him also an incorruptible end is rendered by a virgin in the book of Revelation*, as regards the order of the books, not as to the order of Scripture.

20. Next when he says *this is John*, he is described as author: and concerning this he does two things.

First he sets forth the illustriousness of his praise as regards his death; second he concludes from these things the fittingness of the order of this Gospel, at *yet he wrote a Gospel after everyone else.*

21. But the privilege of his death is wondrous and unique, for he experienced no suffering in death; and God did this so that someone who stood out as almost a stranger to the corruption of the flesh, should be a foreigner to the suffering of death.

22. He shows the fittingness of this author for our faith, saying *yet he wrote a Gospel after everyone else.*

In books of Sacred Scripture a two-fold order is considered, namely, the one of the time in which they were written, and the other of the disposition to which they are ordered in the Bible.

CHAPTER 1

Lecture 1

1:1 In principio erat Verbum, et Verbum erat apud Deum. Et Deus erat Verbum. [n. 24]

1:2 Hoc erat in principio apud Deum. [n. 60]

1:1 Ἐν ἀρχῇ ἦν ὁ λόγος, καὶ ὁ λόγος ἦν πρὸς τὸν θεόν, καὶ θεὸς ἦν ὁ λόγος.

1:2 οὗτος ἦν ἐν ἀρχῇ πρὸς τὸν θεόν.

1:1 In the beginning was the Word, and the Word was with God, and the Word was God. [n. 24]

1:2 He was in the beginning with God. [n. 60]

---

23. Evangelista Ioannes, sicut dictum est, intendit principaliter ostendere divinitatem Verbi incarnati; et ideo dividitur istud Evangelium in partes duas.

Primo enim insinuat Christi divinitatem;

secundo manifestat eam per ea quae Christus in carne fecit, et hoc II cap. *et die tertia*.

Circa primum duo facit.

Primo proponit Christi divinitatem;

secundo ponit modum, quo Christi divinitas nobis innotuit, ibi *et vidimus gloriam eius* etc.

Circa primum duo facit.

Primo agit de divinitate Christi;

secundo de Verbi Dei incarnatione, ibi *fuit homo missus a Deo*.

Quia vero in unaquaque re sunt consideranda duo, scilicet esse et operatio, sive virtus ipsius, ideo

primo agit de esse Verbi quantum ad naturam divinam;

secundo de virtute, seu operatione ipsius, ibi *omnia per ipsum facta sunt*.

Circa primum quatuor facit.

Primo ostendit quando erat Verbum, quia *in principio erat Verbum*;

secundo ubi erat, quia *apud Deum*; unde dicit *et Verbum erat apud Deum*;

tertio quid erat, quia Deus; unde subiungit *et Deus erat Verbum*;

quarto quomodo erat, quia *hoc erat in principio apud Deum*.

Prima duo pertinent ad quaestionem, an est: secunda vero duo pertinent ad quaestionem quid est.

24. Circa primum autem videndum est quid sit hoc quod dicitur *in principio erat Verbum*. Ubi tria diligenter inquirenda concurrunt, secundum tres dictiones huius orationis. Et primo quid sit hoc quod dicitur

23. John the Evangelist, as already indicated, makes it his principal object to show the divinity of the incarnate Word. Accordingly, his Gospel is divided into two parts.

In the first he states the divinity of Christ;

in the second he shows it by the things Christ did in the flesh, at *and on the third day* (John 2:1).

In regard to the first, he does two things.

First he shows the divinity of Christ;

second he sets forth the manner in which Christ's divinity is made known to us, at *and we saw his glory, the glory as it were of the only begotten* (John 1:14).

Concerning the first he does two things.

First he treats of the divinity of Christ;

second of the incarnation of the Word of God, at *there was a man sent from God, whose name was John* (John 1:6).

Because there are two items to be considered in each thing, namely, its existence and its operation or power,

first he treats the existence of the Word as to his divine nature;

second of his power or operation, at *all things were made through him* (John 1:3).

In regard to the first he does four things.

First he shows when the Word was: *in the beginning was the Word*;

second where he was: *and the Word was with God*;

third what he was: *and the Word was God*;

fourth, in what way he was: *he was in the beginning with God*.

The first two pertain to the inquiry of whether something exists; the second two pertain to the inquiry of what something is.

24. With respect to the first of these four we must examine the meaning of the statement, *in the beginning was the Word*. And here three things present themselves for careful study according to the three parts of this statement.

Verbum; secundo quid sit hoc quod dicitur *in principio*; tertio quid sit hoc quod dicitur *Verbum erat in principio*.

25. Ad intellectum autem huius nominis *Verbum*, sciendum est quod, secundum Philosophum ea quae sunt in voce, sunt signa earum, quae sunt in anima, passionum. Consuetum est autem in Scriptura quod significata nominantur nominibus signorum, sicut illud I Cor. X, 4: *petra autem erat Christus*. De necessitate autem oportet quod illud intrinsecum animae nostrae, quod significatur exteriori verbo nostro, verbum vocetur. Utrum autem per prius conveniat nomen 'verbi' rei exteriori voce prolatae, vel ipsi conceptioni mentis, nihil refert ad praesens. Planum est tamen quod illud quod voce significatur, interius existens in anima, prius est quam ipsum verbum exteriori voce prolatum, utpote causa eius existens.

Si ergo volumus scire quid est interius verbum mentis, videamus quid significat quod exteriori voce profertur.

In intellectu autem nostro sunt tria: scilicet ipsa potentia intellectus; species rei intellectae, quae est forma eius, se habens ad ipsum intellectum, sicut species coloris ad pupillam; et, tertio, ipsa operatio intellectus quae est intelligere. Nullum autem istorum significatur verbo exteriori voce prolato.

Nam hoc nomen 'lapis' non significat substantiam intellectus, quia hoc non intendit dicere nominans; nec significat speciem, quae est qua intellectus intelligit, cum etiam hoc non sit intentio nominantis; non significat etiam ipsum intelligere, cum intelligere non sit actio exterius progrediens ab intelligente, sed in ipso manens. Illud ergo proprie dicitur verbum interius, quod intelligens intelligendo format.

Intellectus autem duo format, secundum duas eius operationes. Nam secundum operationem suam, quae dicitur indivisibilium intelligentia, format definitionem; secundum vero operationem suam, qua componit et dividit, format enunciationem, vel aliquid huiusmodi. Et ideo, illud sic formatum et expressum per operationem intellectus, vel definientis vel enunciantis, exteriori voce significatur. Unde dicit Philosophus quod ratio, quam significat nomen, est definitio. Istud ergo sic expressum, scilicet formatum in anima, dicitur verbum interius; et ideo comparatur ad intellectum, non sicut quo intellectus intelligit, sed sicut in quo intelligit; quia in ipso expresso et formato videt naturam rei intellectae. Sic ergo habemus significationem huius nominis 'verbum.'

Secundo, ex his quae dicta sunt, concipere possumus, quod verbum semper est aliquid procedens ab intellectu in actu existente. Iterum quod verbum semper

First it is necessary to investigate the name **Word**; second the phrase **in the beginning**; third the meaning of **the Word was in the beginning**.

25. To understand the name **Word** we should note that according to the Philosopher (*On Interpretation* 16a3), vocal sounds are signs of the affections that exist in our soul. It is customary in Scripture for the things signified to be themselves called by the names of their signs, as in the statement, *and the rock was Christ* (1 Cor 10:4). It is fitting that what is within our soul, and what is signified by our external word, be called a word. But whether the name 'word' belongs first to the exterior vocal sound or to the conception in our mind, is not our concern at present. However, it is obvious that what is signified by the vocal sound, as existing interiorly in the soul, exists prior to the vocal expression inasmuch as it is its actual cause.

Therefore if we wish to grasp the meaning of the interior word, we must first look at the meaning of that which is exteriorly expressed in words.

Now there are three things in our intellect: the intellectual power itself, the species of the thing understood, which is its form, and this form being to the intellect what the species of a color is to the eye; and third, the very activity of the intellect, which is to understand. But none of these is what is signified by the exterior vocal word.

For, the name 'stone' does not signify the substance of the intellect because this is not what the one naming intends; nor does it signify the species, which is that by which the intellect understands, since this also is not the intention of the one naming; nor does it signify the act itself of understanding since to understand is not an action proceeding to the exterior from the one understanding, but an action remaining within. Therefore, that is properly called an interior word which the one understanding forms when understanding.

Now the intellect forms two things, according to its two operations. According to its operation which is called the understanding of indivisibles, it forms a definition; while according to its operation by which it unites and separates, it forms an enunciation or something of that sort. Hence, what is thus formed and expressed by the operation of the intellect, whether by defining or enunciating, is what the exterior vocal sound signifies. So the Philosopher says that the notion that a name signifies is a definition. Hence, what is thus expressed, i.e., formed in the soul, is called an interior word. Consequently it is compared to the intellect, not as that by which the intellect understands, but as that in which it understands, because it is in what is thus expressed and formed that it sees the nature of the thing understood. Thus we have the meaning of the name 'word.'

Second, from what has been said we are able to understand that a word is always something that proceeds from an intellect existing in act; and furthermore, that a word is

est ratio et similitudo rei intellectae. Et si quidem eadem res sit intelligens et intellecta, tunc verbum est ratio et similitudo intellectus, a quo procedit; si autem sit aliud intelligens et intellectum, tunc verbum non est similitudo et ratio intelligentis, sed rei intellectae: sicut conceptio quam aliquis habet de lapide, est similitudo lapidis tantum, sed quando intellectus intelligit se, tunc huiusmodi verbum est similitudo et ratio intellectus. Et ideo Augustinus ponit similitudinem Trinitatis in anima, secundum quod mens intelligit seipsam, non autem secundum quod intelligit alia.

Patet ergo quod in qualibet natura intellectuali necesse est ponere verbum: quia de ratione intelligendi est quod intellectus intelligendo aliquid formet; huius autem formatio dicitur verbum; et ideo in omni intelligente oportet ponere verbum.

Natura autem intellectualis est triplex, scilicet humana, angelica et divina: et ideo triplex est verbum. Scilicet humanum, de quo in Ps. XIII, 1: *dixit insipiens in corde suo: non est Deus.* Est et angelicum, de quo Zac. I, 9 et in multis locis Sacrae Scripturae dicitur: *dixit angelus* etc. Tertium est verbum divinum, de quo Gen. I, 5: *dixit Deus: fiat lux* etc.

Cum ergo Evangelista dicit **in principio erat Verbum**, non intelligi potest de humano vel angelico verbo: quia utrumque istorum verborum est factum, cum homo et angelus habeant sui esse et operationis principium et causam; verbum autem hominis vel angeli non potest praeexistere eis. De quo autem verbo intellexerit Evangelista, declarat per hoc quod dicit, hoc verbum non esse factum, cum omnia sint facta per ipsum; hoc autem est Verbum Dei, de quo Ioannes hic loquitur.

26. Sciendum est autem, quod hoc Verbum differt a nostro verbo in tribus.

Prima differentia est, secundum Augustinum, quia verbum nostrum prius est formabile, quam formatum: nam cum volo concipere rationem lapidis, oportet quod ad ipsam ratiocinando perveniam; et sic est in omnibus aliis, quae a nobis intelliguntur, nisi forte in primis principiis, quae cum sint simpliciter nota, absque discursu rationis statim sciuntur.

Quamdiu ergo sic ratiocinando, intellectus iactatur hac atque illac, nec dum formatio perfecta est, nisi quando ipsam rationem rei perfecte conceperit: et tunc primo habet rationem rei perfectae, et tunc primo habet rationem verbi. Et inde est quod in anima nostra est cogitatio, per quam significatur ipse discursus inquisitionis, et verbum, quod est iam formatum secundum perfectam contemplationem veritatis. Sic ergo verbum nostrum primo est in potentia quam in actu; sed Verbum Dei semper

always a notion and likeness of the thing understood. So if the one understanding and the thing understood are the same, then the word is a notion and likeness of the intellect from which it proceeds. On the other hand, if the one understanding is other than the thing understood, then the word is not a likeness and notion of the one understanding but of the thing understood, as the conception which one has of a stone is a likeness of only the stone. But when the intellect understands itself, its word is a likeness and notion of the intellect. And so Augustine (*On the Trinity* IX, 5) sees a likeness of the Trinity in the soul insofar as the mind understands itself, but not insofar as it understands other things.

It is clear then that it is necessary to have a word in any intellectual nature, for it is of the very nature of understanding that the intellect in understanding should form something. Now what is formed is called a word, and so it follows that in every being which understands there must be a word.

However, intellectual natures are of three kinds: human, angelic and divine; and so there are three kinds of words. The human word, about which it is said: *the fool said in his heart: there is no God* (Ps 13:1). The angelic word, about which it is said in Zechariah, and in many places in Sacred Scripture, *and the angel said to me: I will show you what these are* (Zech 1:9). The third is the divine word, of which it is said, *and God said: let there be light* (Gen 1:3).

So when the Evangelist says, **in the beginning was the Word**, we cannot understand this as a human or angelic word, because both these words have been made since man and angel have a cause and principle of their existence and operation, and the word of a man or an angel cannot exist before they do. The word the Evangelist had in mind he shows by saying that this word was not made, since all things were made by it. Therefore, the word about which John speaks here is the Word of God.

26. We should note that this Word differs from our own word in three ways.

The first difference, according to Augustine, is that our word is formable before being formed, for when I wish to conceive the notion of a stone, I must arrive at it by reasoning. And so it is in all other things that are understood by us, with the sole possible exception of the first principles, which, since they are known in a simple manner, are known at once without any discourse of reason.

So as long as the intellect, in so reasoning, casts about this way and that, the formation is not yet complete. It is only when it has conceived the notion of the thing perfectly that for the first time it has the notion of the complete thing and a word. Thus in our mind there is both a cogitation, meaning the discourse involved in an investigation, and a word, which is formed according to a perfect contemplation of the truth. So our word is first in potency before it is in act. But the Word of God is always in act. In consequence,

est in actu: et ideo nomen cogitationis Verbo Dei proprie non convenit. Dicit enim Augustinus, XV de Trinit., ita dicitur *Verbum Dei, ut cogitatio non dicatur, ne quid quasi volubile credatur in Deo.* Id autem quod Anselmus dicit, scilicet dicere *summo Spiritui nihil aliud est, quam cogitando intueri*, improprie dictum est.

27. Secunda vero differentia verbi nostri ad Verbum divinum est, quia verbum nostrum est imperfectum, sed Verbum divinum est perfectissimum.

Quia enim nos non possumus omnes nostras conceptiones uno verbo exprimere, ideo oportet quod plura verba imperfecta formemus, per quae divisim exprimamus omnia, quae in scientia nostra sunt. In Deo autem non est sic: cum enim intelligat, et seipsum etiam et quicquid intelligit per essentiam suam, uno actu, unicum Verbum divinum est expressivum totius quod in Deo est, non solum personarum, sed etiam creaturarum: alias esset imperfectum. Unde dicit Augustinus: *si quid minus esset in Verbo, quam in dicentis scientia continetur, Verbum imperfectum esset. Sed constat quod est perfectissimum; ergo est tantum unum.* Iob XXXIII, 14: *semel loquitur Deus.*

28. Tertia differentia est, quod verbum nostrum non est eiusdem naturae nobiscum, sed Verbum divinum est eiusdem naturae cum Deo: et ideo aliquid subsistens in natura divina.

Nam ratio intellecta, quam intellectus videtur de aliqua re formare, habet esse intelligibile tantum in anima nostra; intelligere autem in anima nostra non est idem quod est natura animae, quia anima non est sua operatio. Et ideo verbum quod format intellectus noster, non est de essentia animae, sed est accidens ei. In Deo autem idem est intelligere et esse; et ideo Verbum intellectus divini non est aliquid accidens, sed pertinens ad naturam eius: quia quicquid est in natura Dei, est Deus. Unde, dicit Damascenus, quod Deus verbum substantiale est, et in hypostasi ens, reliqua vero, verba nostra scilicet, virtutes sunt animae.

29. Ex praemissis etiam patet quod Verbum, proprie loquendo, semper personaliter accipitur in divinis, cum non importet nisi quid expressum ab intelligente.

Item quod Verbum in divinis sit similitudo eius a quo procedit; et quod sit coaeternum ei a quo procedit, cum non prius fuerit formabile quam formatum, sed semper in actu; et quod sit aequale Patri, cum sit perfectum, et totius esse Patris expressivum; et quod sit coessentiale et consubstantiale Patri, cum sit substantia eius.

Patet etiam quod cum in qualibet natura illud quod procedit, habens similitudinem naturae eius a quo procedit, vocetur filius, et hoc Verbum procedat in similitudine et identitate naturae eius a quo procedit,

the term cogitation does not properly speaking apply to the Word of God. For Augustine says (*On the Trinity* XV): *the Word of God is spoken of in such a way that cogitation is not included, lest anything changeable be supposed in God.* Anselm was speaking improperly when he said: *for the supreme Spirit to speak is for him to look at something while cogitating.*

27. The second difference is that our word is imperfect, but the divine Word is most perfect.

For since we cannot express all our conceptions in one word, we must form many imperfect words through which we separately express all that is in our knowledge. But it is not that way with God. For since he understands both himself and everything else through his essence, by one act, the single divine Word is expressive of all that is in God, not only of the persons but also of creatures; otherwise it would be imperfect. So Augustine says: *if there were less in the Word than is contained in the knowledge of the one speaking it, the Word would be imperfect; but it is obvious that it is most perfect; therefore, it is only one. God speaks once* (Job 33:14).

28. The third difference is that our word is not of the same nature as we; but the divine Word is of the same nature as God. And therefore it is something that subsists in the divine nature.

For the understood notion which the intellect is seen to form about some thing has only an intelligible existence in our soul. Now in our soul, to understand is not the same as the nature of the soul, because our soul is not its own operation. Consequently, the word which our intellect forms is not of the essence of our soul, but is an accident of it. But in God, to understand and to be are the same; and so the Word of the divine intellect is not an accident but belongs to its nature. Thus it must be subsistent, because whatever is in the nature of God is God. Thus Damascene says that God is a substantial word, and a hypostasis, but our words are concepts in our mind.

29. From the above it is clear that the Word, properly speaking, is always understood as a person in the divinity, since it implies only something expressed, by the one understanding;

also, that in the divinity the Word is the likeness of that from which it issues; and that it is co-eternal with that from which it issues, since it was not first formable before being formed, but was always in act; and that it is equal to the Father, since it is perfect and expressive of the whole being of the Father; and that it is co-essential and consubstantial with the Father, since it is his substance.

It is also clear that since in every nature that which issues forth and has a likeness to the nature from which it issues is called a son, and since this Word issues forth in a likeness and identity to the nature from which it issues, it is

convenienter et proprie dicitur filius, et productio eius dicitur generatio.

Sic ergo patet primum, scilicet quod sit hoc quod dicitur **Verbum**.

30. Circa hoc autem quatuor quaestiones occurrunt. Duae sunt Chrysostomi.

Prima est cur Ioannes Evangelista Patrem dimittens, confestim incepit a Filio, dicens **in principio erat Verbum**.

Ad hoc autem est duplex responsio. Una est, quia Pater omnibus innotuerat in Veteri Testamento, quamvis non in ratione Patris, sed ut Deus; Filius autem ignorabatur: et ideo in Novo Testamento, in quo agitur de cognitione Verbi, incipit a Verbo, sive Filio.

Alia est, quia per Filium ducimur in notitiam Patris; infra XVII, 6: **Pater, manifestavi nomen tuum hominibus, quos dedisti mihi**. Volens ergo fideles in notitiam Patris ducere Evangelista, decenter incepit a Filio, statim subiungens de Patre cum dicit **et Verbum erat apud Deum**.

31. Secunda quaestio est etiam Chrysostomi.

Cum enim, sicut dictum est, Verbum procedat ut Filius, quare dixit **Verbum**, et non *Filius*?

Ad hoc etiam dupliciter respondetur. Primo quia *Filius* dicit aliquid genitum, et cum audimus generationem Filii, posset quis cogitare generationem illam talem esse, qualem comprehendere potest, scilicet materialem et passibilem; ideo ergo non dixit *Filius* sed **Verbum**, quod importat intelligibilem processum, ut non intelligatur materialem et passibilem generationem illam fuisse. Ostendens igitur Filium ex Deo impassibiliter nasci, destruit vitiosam suspicionem per **Verbi** nuncupationem.

Aliter potest dici sic: Evangelista tractaturus erat de Verbo, inquantum venerat ad manifestandum Patrem. Unde cum ratio manifestationis magis importetur in nomine **Verbi** quam in nomine *Filii*, ideo magis est usus nomine **Verbi**.

32. Tertia quaestio est Augustini in Lib. *LXXXIII Quaest.*, quae talis est: in Graeco, ubi nos habemus **Verbum**, habetur **Logos**. Cum ergo *Logos* significet in Latino rationem et verbum, quare translatores transtulerunt **Verbum**, et non *rationem*, cum ratio sit quid intrinsecum, quemadmodum etiam verbum?

Respondeo. Dicendum quod ratio proprie nominat conceptum mentis, secundum quod in mente est, etsi nihil per illam exterius fiat; per verbum vero significatur respectus ad exteriora: et ideo quia Evangelista per hoc, quod dixit **Logos**, non solum intendebat significare respectum ad existentiam Filii in Patre, sed etiam operativam potentiam Filii, qua **per ipsum facta sunt omnia**,

suitably and appropriately called a son, and its production is called a generation.

So now the first point is clear, the meaning of the term **Word**.

30. There are four questions on this point, two of them from Chrysostom.

The first is: why did John the Evangelist omit the Father and begin at once with the Son, saying, **in the beginning was the Word**?

There are two answers to this. One is that the Father was known to everyone in the Old Testament, although not under the aspect of Father, but as God; but the Son was not known. And so in the New Testament, which is concerned with our knowledge of the Word, he begins with the Word or Son.

The other answer is that we are brought to know the Father through the Son: **Father, I have manifested your name to the men whom you have given to me** (John 17:6). And so wishing to lead the faithful to a knowledge of the Father, the Evangelist fittingly began with the Son, at once adding something about the Father when he says, **and the Word was with God**.

31. The second question is also from Chrysostom.

Why did he say **Word** and not *Son*, since, as we have said, the Word proceeds as Son?

There are also two answers to this. First, because *Son* means something begotten, and when we hear of the generation of the Son, someone might suppose that this generation is the kind he can comprehend, that is, a material and changeable generation. Thus he did not say *Son*, but **Word**, which signifies an intelligible proceeding, so that it would not be understood as a material and changeable generation. And so in showing that the Son is born of the Father in an unchangeable way, he eliminates a faulty conjecture by using the name **Word**.

The second answer is this. The Evangelist was about to consider the Word as having come to manifest the Father. But since the idea of manifesting is implied better in the name **Word** than in the name *Son*, he preferred to use the name **Word**.

32. The third question is raised by Augustine in his book *Eighty-Three Questions*; and it is this. In Greek, where we have **Word**, they have **Logos**; now since *Logos* signifies in Latin both notion and word, why did the translators render it as **Word** and not *notion*, since a notion is something interior just as a word is?

I answer that notion, properly speaking, names a conception of the mind precisely as in the mind, even if through it nothing exterior comes to be; but word signifies a reference to something exterior. And so because the Evangelist, when he said **Logos**, intended to signify not only a reference to the Son's existence in the Father, but also the operative power of the Son, by which, **all things were made**

magis antiqui transtulerunt **Verbum**, quod importat respectum ad exteriora, quam *ratio*, quae tantum conceptum mentis insinuat.

33. Quarta quaestio est Origenis, quae talis est. Scriptura in pluribus locis loquens de Verbo Dei, nominat ipsum non absolute **Verbum**, sed cum additione, scilicet *Dei*, cum dicit Verbum Dei, vel Domini: Eccli. I, 5: *fons sapientiae Verbum Dei in excelsis*, et Apoc. XIX, 13: *et nomen eius Verbum Dei*. Quare ergo Evangelista, cum loqueretur hic de Verbo Dei, non dixit: *in principio erat Verbum Dei*, sed dixit tantummodo **Verbum**?

Respondeo. Dicendum, quod licet sint multae veritates participatae, est tamen una veritas absoluta, quae per suam essentiam est veritas, scilicet ipsum esse divinum, qua veritate, omnia verba sunt verba. Eodem modo est una sapientia absoluta supra omnia elevata, scilicet sapientia divina, per cuius participationem omnes sapientes sunt sapientes. Et etiam unum Verbum absolutum, cuius participatione omnes habentes verbum, dicuntur dicentes. Hoc autem est Verbum divinum, quod per seipsum est Verbum super omnia verba elevatum.

Ut ergo Evangelista hanc supereminentiam divini Verbi significaret, ipsum Verbum absque ulla additione nobis absolute proposuit; et quia Graeci, quando volunt significare aliquid segregatum et elevatum ab omnibus aliis, consueverunt apponere articulum nomini, per quod illud significatur sicut Platonici volentes significare substantias separatas, puta bonum separatum, vel hominem separatum, vocabant illud ly per se bonum, vel ly per se hominem ideo Evangelista volens significare segregationem et elevationem istius Verbi super omnia, apposuit articulum ad hoc nomen **Logos**, ut si dicatur in Latino, ly **Verbum**.

34. Secundo considerandum est, quid significet hoc quod dicitur **in principio**.

Sciendum est autem quod 'principium,' secundum Origenem, multis modis dicitur. Cum enim 'principium' importet ordinem quemdam ad alia, necesse est invenire principium in omnibus, in quibus est ordo.

Invenitur autem ordo in quantitatibus; et secundum hoc dicitur principium in numeris et longitudine, puta lineae.

Invenitur etiam ordo in tempore; et secundum hoc dicitur principium temporis, vel durationis.

Invenitur ordo in disciplinis, et hic est duplex: secundum naturam, et quoad nos; et utroque modo dicitur principium. Hebr. V, v. 12: *deberetis esse magistri propter tempus*. Et hoc modo, secundum naturam quidem, in disciplina Christiana initium et principium sapientiae nostrae est Christus, inquantum est sapientia et Verbum Dei, idest secundum divinitatem. Quoad nos vero

through him: and without him was made nothing, our predecessors preferred to translate it **Word**, which implies a reference to something exterior, rather than *notion* which implies merely a concept of the mind.

33. The fourth question is from Origen, and is this. In many passages, Scripture, when speaking of the Word of God, does not simply call him the **Word**, but adds *of God*, saying, *the Word of God*, or *of the Lord: the Word of God on high is the foundation of wisdom* (Sir 1:5); *his name is the Word of God* (Rev 19:13). Why then did the Evangelist, when speaking here of the Word of God, not say, *in the beginning was the Word of God*, but said **in the beginning was the Word**?

I answer that although there are many participated truths, there is just one absolute truth, which is truth by its very essence, that is, the divine act of being; and by this truth all words are words. Similarly, there is one absolute wisdom elevated above all things, that is, the divine wisdom, by participating in which all wise persons are wise. Further, there is one absolute Word, by participating in which all persons having a word are called speakers. Now this is the divine Word which of itself is the Word elevated above all words.

So in order that the Evangelist might signify this supereminence of the divine Word, he pointed out this Word to us absolutely without any addition. And because the Greeks, when they wished to signify something separate and elevated above everything else, did this by affixing the article to the name, as did the the Platonists, wishing to signify the separated substances, such as the separated good or the separated man, called them the good *per se*, or man *per se*, so the Evangelist, wishing to signify the separation and elevation of that Word above all things, affixed an article to the name **Logos**, so that if it were stated in Latin we would say **the Word**.

34. Second, we must consider the meaning of the phrase, **in the beginning**.

We must note that according to Origen, the word '*principium*' has many meanings. Since the word '*principium*' implies a certain order of one thing to another, one can find a *principium* in all those things which have an order.

First of all, order is found in quantified things; and so there is a principle of number and lengths, as for example, a line.

Second, order is found in time; and so we speak of a beginning of time, or of duration.

Third, order is found in learning; and this in two ways: as to nature, and as to ourselves, and in both cases we can speak of a beginning. *By this time you ought to be teachers* (Heb 5:12). As to nature, in Christian doctrine the beginning and principle of our wisdom is Christ, inasmuch as he is the wisdom and Word of God, i.e., in his divinity. But as to ourselves, the beginning is Christ himself inasmuch as

principium est ipse Christus, inquantum *Verbum caro factum est*, idest secundum eius incarnationem.

Invenitur etiam ordo in productione rei; et secundum hoc principium dicitur ex parte generati, scilicet ipsa prima pars generati seu facti: sicut fundamentum dicitur principium domus. Vel ex parte facientis: et sic est triplex principium, scilicet intentionis, quod est finis, quod movet agentem; rationis, quod est ipsa forma in mente artificis; et executionis, quod est potentia operans.

His igitur modis de principio inquirendum est, quomodo sumatur hic *principium*, cum dicit **in principio erat Verbum**.

35. Dicendum est igitur quod potest sumi tripliciter.

Uno modo, secundum quod *principium* supponit pro persona Filii, quod principium est creaturarum secundum rationem virtutis activae, et per modum sapientiae, quae est ratio eorum quae fiunt; unde dicitur I Cor. I, 24: *Christum Dei virtutem et Dei sapientiam.* Unde et Dominus de se dicit infra VIII, 25: **ego principium, qui et loquor vobis.**

Sic ergo accipiendo *principium*, intelligendum est quod dicitur **in principio erat Verbum**, ac si diceret *in Filio erat Verbum*, ut sit sensus: ipsum Verbum est principium, ex modo loquendi, quo dicitur vita esse in Deo, quae tamen non est aliud, quam ipse Deus. Et haec est expositio Origenis.

Dicit ergo hic Evangelista **in principio**, ut statim in principio divinitatem Verbi ostenderet, ut Chrysostomus dicit, dum asserit ipsum esse principium; quia secundum determinationem omnium principium est honoratissimum.

36. Secundo modo potest accipi *principium*, prout supponit pro persona Patris, quod est principium non solum creaturarum, sed omnis divini processus; et sic accipitur in Ps. CIX, 3: *tecum principium in die virtutis tuae.*

Secundum hoc ergo dicitur **in principio erat Verbum**, ac si diceretur: *in Patre erat Filius*. Et haec est expositio Augustini, et etiam Origenis.

Dicitur autem Filius esse in Patre, quia eiusdem essentiae est cum Patre. Cum enim Filius sit sui essentia, in quocumque est essentia Filii, est Filius. Quia ergo in Patre est essentia Filii per consubstantialitatem, conveniens est quod Filius sit in Patre. Unde infra XIV, 10 dicitur: **ego in Patre, et Pater in me est.**

37. Tertio modo potest accipi *principium* pro principio durationis, ut sit sensus **in principio erat Verbum**, idest Verbum erat ante omnia, ut Augustinus exponit, et

the Word has become flesh (John 1:14), i.e., by his incarnation.

Fourth, order is found in the production of a thing. In this perspective there can be a *principium* on the part of the thing generated, that is, the first part of the thing generated or made; as we say that the foundation is the beginning of a house. Another is on the part of the generator, and in this perspective there are three principles: of intention, which is the purpose, which motivates the agent; of reason, which is the idea in the mind of the maker; and of execution, which is the operative faculty.

Considering these various ways of using the term, we now ask how *beginning* is used here when it says, **in the beginning was the Word.**

35. We should note that this word can be taken in three ways.

In one way so that *principium* is understood as the person of the Son, who is the principle of creatures by reason of his active power acting with wisdom, which is the conception of the things that are brought into existence. Hence we read: *Christ the power of God and the wisdom of God* (1 Cor 1:24). And so the Lord said about himself: **the source, who also speaks to you** (John 8:25).

Taking *principium* in this way, we should understand the statement, **in the beginning was the Word**, as though he were saying, *the Word was in the Son*, so that the sense would be: the Word himself is the principle, in the sense in which life is said to be in God, when this life is not something other than God. And this is the explanation of Origen.

And so the Evangelist says **in the beginning** here in order, as Chrysostom says, to show at the very outset the divinity of the Word by asserting that he is a principle because, as determining all, a principle is most honored.

36. In a second way *principium* can be understood as the person of the Father, who is the principle not only of creatures, but of every divine process. It is taken this way in, *yours is princely power in the day of your birth* (Ps 110:3).

In this second way one reads **in the beginning was the Word** as though it means, *the Son was in the Father*. This is Augustine's understanding of it, as well as Origen's.

The Son, however, is said to be in the Father because both have the same essence. Since the Son is his own essence, then the Son is in whomsoever the Son's essence is. Since, therefore, the essence of the Son is in the Father by consubstantiality, it is fitting that the Son be in the Father. Hence it is said: **I am in the Father, and the Father in me** (John 14:10).

37. In a third way, *principium* can be taken for the beginning of duration, so that the sense of **in the beginning was the Word** is that the Word was before all things, as

designatur per hoc Verbi aeternitas, secundum Basilium et Hilarium.

Per hoc enim quod dicitur *in principio erat Verbum*, ostenditur quod quodcumque principium durationis accipiatur, sive rerum temporalium, quod est tempus, sive aeviternarum, quod est aevum, sive totius mundi, sive quodcumque imaginatum extensum per multa saecula, in illo principio iam erat Verbum. Unde Hilarius dicit VII *de Trinitate*: *transeuntur tempora, transcenduntur saecula, tolluntur aetates. Pone aliquid quod voles tuae opinionis principium; Verbum iam erat, unde tractatur.* Et hoc est quod dicitur Prov. VIII, 22: *Dominus possedit me in initio viarum suarum, antequam quicquam faceret a principio.* Quod autem est ante durationis principium, est aeternum.

38. Sic igitur secundum primam expositionem, asseritur Verbi causalitas; secundum autem secundam, Verbi consubstantialitas ad Patrem, qui Verbum loquitur; secundum vero tertiam, Verbi coaeternitas.

39. Considerandum est etiam hic, quod dicitur *Verbum erat*, quod est temporis praeteriti imperfecti, et hoc maxime videtur competere ad designandum aeterna, si attendamus naturam temporis et eorum quae sunt in tempore. Quod futurum est, nondum est actu; praesens autem actu est, et per hoc quod est actu praesens, non designatur fuisse: praeteritum autem perfectum designat aliquid extitisse, et esse iam determinatum, et iam defuisse; sed praeteritum imperfectum significat aliquid fuisse, et non esse adhuc determinatum, nec defuisse, sed adhuc remanere. Ideo signanter Ioannes ubicumque ponit aliquid aeternum, dicit *erat*; ubi vero dicit aliquid temporale, dicit *fuit*, ut infra patebit.

Sed quantum ad rationem praesentis competit maxime ad designandum aeternitatem praesens tempus, quod signat aliquid esse in actu, quod semper convenit aeternis: et ideo dicitur Ex. III, 14: *ego sum qui sum*; et Augustinus dicit, *quod ille solus vere est, cuius esse non novit praeteritum et futurum.*

40. Est etiam considerandum quod hoc verbum *erat*, secundum Glossam, non sumitur hic inquantum significat temporales motus, more aliorum verborum, sed secundum quod signat rei existentiam: unde et verbum substantivum dicitur.

41. Sed potest aliquis quaerere, cum Verbum sit genitum a Patre, quomodo possit esse Patri coaeternum: homo enim filius a patre homine genitus, est eo posterior.

Ad quod dicendum est quod principium originis invenitur esse prius duratione, eo quod est ex principio, propter tria. Primo quidem quia principium originis alicuius rei praecedit tempore actionem, qua producit rem cuius est principium; sicut non statim quando homo est,

Augustine explains it. According to Basil and Hilary, this phrase shows the eternity of the Word.

The phrase **in the beginning was the Word** shows that no matter which beginning of duration is taken, whether of temporal things, which is time, or of aeviternal things, which is the aeon, or of the whole world or any imagined span of time reaching back for many ages, at that beginning the Word already was. Hence Hilary says (*On the Trinity* VII): *go back season by season, skip over the centuries, take away ages. Set down whatever you want as the beginning in your opinion: the Word already was.* And this is what Proverbs says: *the Lord possessed me in the beginning of his ways, before he made anything* (Prov 8:23). But what is prior to the beginning of duration is eternal.

38. And thus the first explanation asserts the causality of the Word; the second explanation affirms the consubstantiality of the Word with the Father, who utters the Word; and the third explanation affirms the co-eternity of the Word.

39. Now we should consider that it says that **the Word was**, which is stated in the past imperfect tense. This tense is most appropriate for designating eternal things if we consider the nature of time and of the things that exist in time. For what is future is not yet in act; but what is at present is in act, and by the fact that it is in act what is present is not described as having been. Now the past perfect tense indicates that something has existed, has already come to an end, and has now ceased to be. The past imperfect tense, on the other hand, indicates that something has been, has not yet come to an end, nor has ceased to be, but still endures. Thus, whenever John mentions eternal things he expressly says **was**, but when he refers to anything temporal he says **has been**, as will be clear later.

But so far as concerns the notion of the present, the best way to designate eternity is the present tense, which indicates that some thing is in act, and this is always the characteristic of eternal things. And so it is said: *I am who am* (Exod 3:14). And Augustine says: *he alone truly is whose being does not know a past and a future.*

40. We should also note that this verb **was**, according to the Gloss, is not understood here as indicating temporal changes, as other verbs do, but as signifying the existence of a thing. Thus it is also called a substantive verb.

41. Someone may ask how the Word can be co-eternal with the Father since he is begotten by the Father: for a human son, born from a human father, is subsequent to his father.

I answer that there are three reasons why an originative principle is prior in duration to that which derives from that principle. First of all, if the originative principle of anything precedes in time the action by which it produces the thing of which it is the principle; thus a man does not begin

incipit scribere, et ideo tempore praecedit Scripturam. Secundo per hoc quod actio successionem habet, et ideo etiam si simul cum agente incipiat, tamen terminus actionis est post agentem: sicut simul cum generatus est ignis in istis inferioribus, incipit sursum tendere; prius tamen est ignis quam sit sursum, quia motus quo sursum tendit, quodam tempore mensuratur. Tertio modo eo quod ex voluntate principii determinatur initium durationis eius quod est in principio, sicut ex voluntate Dei determinatur initium durationis creaturae: unde prius fuit Deus quam creatura.

Nihil autem horum trium in generatione divini Verbi invenitur. Non enim Deus primo fuit quam inceperit generare Verbum: cum enim generatio Verbi nihil aliud sit quam intelligibilis conceptio, sequeretur quod Deus esset prius intelligens in potentia quam in actu, quod est impossibile. Similiter non potest esse quod ipsa Verbi generatio sit successiva: sic enim divinum Verbum prius esset informe quam formatum, sicut accidit in nobis, qui cogitando verba formamus; quod est falsum, ut iam dictum est. Similiter non potest dici quod Pater sua voluntate initium durationis Filio suo praestiterit; quia Deus Pater non generat Filium voluntate, ut Ariani dixerunt, sed naturaliter: Deus enim Pater seipsum intelligendo, Verbum concepit, et ideo non ante fuit Deus Pater quam Filius.

Huius aliqualis similitudo apparet in igne, et in splendore procedente ab igne: procedit enim splendor naturaliter et sine successione. Item si ignis esset aeternus, splendor eius coaeternus esset: propter quod Filius dicitur splendor Patris; ad Hebr. I, 3: *qui cum sit splendor gloriae* etc. Sed in hac similitudine deficit connaturalitas, et ideo nominamus eum Filium, cum tamen in humana filiatione deficiat coaeternitas: oportet enim ex multis similitudinibus sensibilium in divinam cognitionem pervenire, quia una non sufficit; et hoc est quod dicitur in libro Ephesini Concilii, coexistere semper Patri Filium: *splendor* enim denunciat impassibilitatem, *nativitas* ostendit Verbum, consubstantialitatem vero *Filii* nomen insinuat .

42. Nominamus ergo Filium diversis nominibus, ad exprimendum perfectionem eius, quae uno nomine non potest exprimi. Ut enim ostendatur connaturalis Patri, dicitur *Filius*; ut ostendatur in nullo dissimilis, dicitur *imago*; ut ostendatur coaeternus, dicitur *splendor*; ut ostendatur immaterialiter genitus, dicitur **Verbum**.

43. Deinde dicit **et Verbum erat apud Deum**.

Hic ponitur secunda clausula, quam Evangelista ponit in sua narratione. Ubi prius consideranda est significatio duorum verborum quae in prima clausula posita non fuerunt, scilicet **Deum** et **apud**. Quid enim sit

to write as soon as he exists, and so he precedes his writing in time. Second, if an action is successive; consequently, even if the action should happen to begin at the same time as the agent, the termination of the action is nevertheless subsequent to the agent. Thus, as soon as fire has been generated in a lower region, it begins to ascend; but the fire exists before it has ascended, because the motion by which it tends upward requires some time. Third, by the fact that sometimes the beginning of a thing depends on the will of its principle, just as the beginning of a creature's coming-to-be depends on the will of God, such that God existed before any creature.

Yet none of these three is found in the generation of the divine Word. God did not first exist and then begin to generate the Word: for since the generation of the Word is nothing other than an intelligible conception, it would follow that God would be understanding in potency before understanding in act, which is impossible. Again, it is impossible that the generation of the Word involve succession: for then the divine Word would be unformed before it was formed, as happens in us who form words by cogitating, which is false, as was said. Again, we cannot say that the Father pre-established a beginning of duration for his Son by his own will, because God the Father does not generate the Son by his will, as the Arians held, but naturally: for God the Father, understanding himself, conceives the Word; and so God the Father did not exist prior to the Son.

An example of this, to a limited degree, appears in fire and in the brightness issuing from it: for this brightness issues naturally and without succession from the fire. Again, if the fire were eternal, its brightness would be coeternal with it. This is why the Son is called the brightness of the Father: *the brightness of his glory* (Heb 1:3). But this example lacks an illustration of the identity of nature. And so we call him Son, although in human sonship we do not find coeternity: for we must attain our knowledge of divine things from many likenesses in material things, for one likeness is not enough. The Council of Ephesus says that the Son always coexists with the Father: for *brightness* indicates his unchangeability, *birth* points to the Word himself, but the name *Son* suggests his consubstantiality.

42. And so we give the Son various names to express his perfection, which cannot be expressed by one name. We call him *Son* to show that he is of the same nature as the Father; we call him *image* to show that he is not unlike the Father in any way; we call him *brightness* to show that he is coeternal; and he is called the **Word** to show that he is begotten in an immaterial manner.

43. Then the Evangelist says, **and the Word was with God**.

This is the second clause which the Evangelists posits in his narration. The first thing to consider is the meaning of the two words which did not appear in the first clause, that is, **God**, and **with**; for what is signified by **Verbum** and

Verbum, et quid *principium*, iam expositum est. Haec ergo quae in hac secunda clausula ponuntur de novo, scilicet *Deum* et *apud*, investigantes, diligentius prosequamur.

Et ut melius expositionem huius secundae clausulae intelligamus, dicendum est aliquid de significatione utriusque, quantum pertinet ad propositum.

44. Sciendum est ergo in primis quod hoc nomen *Deus* significat divinitatem, sed in supposito et concrete; hoc vero nomen 'deitas' significat deitatem in abstracto, et absolute: et inde est quod non potest supponere pro persona ex naturali virtute et ex modo significandi; sed supponit solummodo pro natura. Hoc vero nomen *Deus* habet naturaliter ex modo significandi quod supponat pro aliqua personarum, sicut hoc nomen 'homo' supponit pro supposito humanitatis, et ideo quandocumque veritas locutionis, vel ipsum praedicatum exigit ut hoc nomen 'Deus' supponat pro persona, tunc supponit pro persona ut cum dicimus, *Deus generat Deum*. Et ita cum hic dicitur *apud Deum*, necesse est quod Deus pro persona Patris supponat, quia haec praepositio *apud* distinctionem significat Verbi, quod esse dicitur *apud Deum*; et licet significet distinctionem in persona, non tamen in natura, cum eadem sit natura Patris et Filii. Evangelista igitur significare voluit Patris personam per hoc quod dixit *Deum*.

45. Sciendum est autem circa hoc quod haec praepositio *apud* quamdam coniunctionem rei significatae per rectum, ad rem significatam per obliquum importat, sicut haec praeposito 'in'. Sed differenter, quia haec praeposito 'in' significat quamdam coniunctionem intrinsecam; haec vero praepositio *apud* quodammodo extrinsecam coniunctionem importat. Et utrumque dicimus in divinis: scilicet Filium esse in Patre, et esse *apud* Patrem; et intrinsecum quidem ad consubstantialitatem pertinet, extrinsecum vero (ut sic loqui liceat, cum improprie in divinis dicatur extrinsecum) non nisi ad distinctionem personalem refertur, cum Filius a Patre solum per originem distinguatur. Et ideo per utrumque istorum, et consubstantialis in natura designatur, et distinctio in personis: consubstantialitas quidem, inquantum coniunctionem quamdam importat; distinctio vero, inquantum distinctionem quamdam significat, ut superius dictum est.

Et quia haec praepositio *in*, ut dictum est, principaliter consubstantialitatem designat, inquantum importat coniunctionem intrinsecam, et ex consequenti distinctionem personarum, inquantum omnis praepositio est transitiva; haec autem praepositio *apud* distinctionem personalem significat principaliter, consubstantialitatem vero, inquantum quamdam coniunctionem significat quasi extrinsecam, ideo Evangelista in hoc loco specialiter ista praepositione *apud* usus est, ut distinctionem

---

principium has already been related. Therefore, let us diligently continue investigating that which is new in the second clause, namely **God** and **with**.

And to better understand the explanation of this second clause, we must say something about the meaning of each so far as it is relevant to our purpose.

44. At the outset, we should note that the name **God** signifies the divinity concretely and as inherent in a subject, while the name 'deity' signifies the divinity in the abstract and absolutely. Thus it cannot naturally and by its mode of signifying stand for a divine person, but only for the divine nature. But the name **God** can, by its natural mode of signifying, stand for any one of the divine persons, just as the name 'man' stands for any individual possessing humanity. Therefore, whenever the truth of a statement or its predicate requires that the name 'God' stand for the person, then it stands for the person, as when we say, *God begets God*. Thus, when it says here that **the Word was with God**, it is necessary that God stand for the person of the Father, because the preposition **with** signifies the distinction of the Word, which is said to be **with God**. And although this preposition signifies a distinction in person, it does not signify a distinction in nature, since the nature of the Father and of the Son is the same. Consequently, the Evangelist wished to signify the person of the Father when he said **God**.

45. Here we should note that the preposition **with** signifies a certain union of the thing signified by its grammatical antecedent to the thing signified by its grammatical object, just as the preposition 'in' does. However, there is a difference, because the preposition 'in' signifies a certain intrinsic union, whereas the preposition **with** implies in a certain way an extrinsic union. And we state both in divine matters, namely, that the Son is in the Father and **with** the Father. Here the intrinsic union pertains to consubstantiality, but the extrinsic union (if we may use such an expression, since extrinsic is improperly employed in divine matters) refers only to a personal distinction, because the Son is distinguished from the Father by origin alone. And so these two words designate both a consubstantiality in nature and distinction in person: consubstantiality inasmuch as a certain union is implied; but distinction, inasmuch as a certain otherness is signified as was said above.

The preposition *in*, as was said, principally signifies consubstantiality, as implying an intrinsic union and, by way of consequence, a distinction of persons, inasmuch as every preposition is transitive. The preposition **with** principally signifies a personal distinction, but also a consubstantiality inasmuch as it signifies a certain extrinsic, so to speak, union. For these reasons the Evangelist specifically used here the preposition **with** in order to express the distinction of the person of the Son from the Father, saying, **and**

personae Filii a Patre insinuaret, cum dixit *et Verbum erat apud Deum*, idest Filius apud Patrem, ut alia persona apud aliam.

46. Sciendum est autem quod per hanc praepositionem *apud* quatuor significantur, per quae obiectiones quatuor contrariae excluduntur.

Significat enim haec praepositio *apud* primo subsistentiam in recto; quia ea quae subsistentiam per se non habent, non dicuntur proprie esse apud aliquid: sicut non dicimus albedinem esse apud corpus, et similiter de aliis quae per se non subsistunt. Ea autem quae per se subsistunt, dicuntur proprie esse unum apud aliud; sicut dicimus hominem esse apud hominem, et lapidem apud lapidem. Secundo significat auctoritatem in obliquo, non enim proprie dicitur rex esse apud militem sed proprie dicitur miles apud regem. Tertio dicit distinctionem: non enim proprie dicitur aliquis esse apud seipsum, sed unus homo est apud alium. Quarto significat coniunctionem et societatem quamdam: cum enim dicitur aliquis esse apud alium, insinuatur nobis inter eos quaedam socialis coniunctio. Secundum autem istas conditiones importatas in significatione huius praepositionis *apud* convenienter Evangelista hanc clausulam, scilicet *Verbum erat apud Deum*, subiungit primae clausulae, scilicet *in principio erat Verbum*.

Praetermissa namque una illarum trium expositionum huius quod est *in principio erat Verbum*, illa scilicet secundum quam *principium* ponitur pro Filio, ad quamlibet aliarum expositionum, scilicet ad illam quae *principium* dicit idem quod *ante omnia*, et ad illam secundum quam principium sumitur pro Patre, duplex obiectio fit ab haereticis; et sic sunt quatuor obiectiones, quas per quatuor conditiones huius praepositionis *apud* supra positas excludere possumus.

47. Quarum prima talis est: tu dicis quod Verbum erat in principio, idest ante omnia; sed ante omnia nihil erat; ubi ergo erat Verbum, si ante omnia nihil erat?

Haec autem obiectio procedit secundum imaginationem eorum qui ponunt, omne quod est, esse alicubi et in loco. Quae quidem excluditur a Ioanne, cum dicit *apud Deum*. Et designat coniunctionem secundum ultimam dictarum conditionum, ut sit sensus, secundum Basilium: ubi ergo erat Verbum? Respondet *apud Deum*, non in aliquo loco, cum incircumscriptibile sit, sed apud Patrem, qui nullo comprehenditur loco.

48. Secunda quaestio ad idem, est talis: tu dicis quod Verbum erat in principio, idest ante omnia. Sed ea quae sunt ante omnia, a nullo videntur procedere; cum illud a quo procedit aliquid, prius esse videatur eo quod procedit ab ipso; ergo Verbum non est procedens ab alio.

the Word was with God, that is, the Son was with the Father as one person with another.

46. We should note further that this preposition *with* has four meanings, through which four contrary objections are eliminated.

First, the preposition *with* signifies the subsistence of its antecedent, because things that do not subsist of themselves are not properly said to be with another; thus we do not say that a color is with a body, and the same applies to other things that do not subsist of themselves. But things that do subsist of themselves are properly said to be with another; thus we say that a man is with a man, and a stone with a stone. Second, it signifies authority in its grammatical object. For we do not, properly speaking, say that a king is with a soldier, but that the soldier is with the king. Third, it asserts a distinction. For it is not proper to say that a person is with himself but rather that one man is with another. Fourth, it signifies a certain union and fellowship. For when some person is said to be with another, it suggests to us that there is some social union between them. Considering these four conditions implied in the meaning of this preposition *with*, the Evangelist quite appropriately joins to the first clause, *in the beginning was the Word*, this second clause, *and the Word was with God*.

For if we omit one of the three explanations of, *in the beginning was the Word*, namely, the one in which *principium* was understood as the Son, certain heretics make a twofold objection against each of the other explanations, namely, the one in which *principium* means the same as *before all things*, and the one in which it is understood as the Father. Thus there are four objections, and we can answer these by the four conditions indicated by this preposition *with*.

47. The first of these objections is this. You say that the Word was in the beginning, i.e., before all things. But before all things there was nothing. So if before all things there was nothing, where then was the Word?

This objection arises due to the imaginings of those who think that whatever exists is somewhere and in some place. But this is rejected by John when he says, *with God*, which indicates the union mentioned in the last four conditions. So, according to Basil, the meaning is this: where was the Word? The answer is: *with God*; not in some place, since he is unsurroundable, but he is with the Father, who is not enclosed by any place.

48. The second objection against the same explanation is this. You say that the Word was in the beginning, i.e., before all things. But whatever exists before all things appears to proceed from no one, since that from which something proceeds seems to be prior to that which proceeds from it. Therefore, the Word does not proceed from another.

Haec autem obiectio excluditur cum dicit **Verbum erat apud Deum**, ut ly **apud** accipiatur secundum secundam conditionem, secundum quam importat auctoritatem in causali, et sit sensus secundum Hilarium: a quo est Verbum si ante omnia? Evangelista respondet **Verbum erat apud Deum**; quasi dicat: licet Verbum careat initio durationis, non tamen caret principio vel auctore: erat enim apud Deum, ut apud auctorem.

49. Tertia quaestio est ad aliam expositionem secundum quam **principium** supponit pro Patre; quae talis est: tu dicis **in principio erat Verbum**, idest Filius erat in Patre; sed illud quod est in aliquo, non videtur esse subsistens, ut hypostasis: sicut albedo quae est in corpore, non subsistit.

Sed haec obiectio solvitur per hoc quod dicit **Verbum erat apud Deum**; ut ly **apud** sumatur secundum primam conditionem per quam importat subsistentiam in recto; et sic, secundum Chrysostomum, est sensus **Verbum erat in principio**, non ut accidens: sed **erat apud Deum**, ut subsistens, et hypostasis divina.

50. Quarta quaestio ad idem est talis: tu dicis quod Verbum erat in principio, idest in Patre; quod autem est in aliquo, non est distinctus a Patre.

Sed haec obiectio excluditur per hoc quod dicit **et Verbum erat apud Deum**; ut ly **apud** sumatur secundum tertiam conditionem, secundum quam significat distinctionem: ut sit sensus, secundum Alcuinum et Bedam, **Verbum erat apud Deum**, et sic erat in Patre per consubstantialitatem naturae, quod tamen est apud ipsum per distinctionem personae.

51. Sic ergo per hanc clausulam **et Verbum erat apud Deum**, ostenditur coniunctio Verbi ad Patrem in natura, secundum Basilium; distinctio autem in persona, secundum Alcuinum et Bedam; substantia Verbi in natura divina, secundum Chrysostomum; auctoritas Patris ad Verbum, secundum Hilarium.

52. Notandum autem, secundum Origenem, quod per hoc quod dicit **Verbum erat apud Deum**, ostendit Filium semper fuisse apud Patrem. In Veteri enim Testamento dicitur factum esse Verbum Domini ad Ieremiam, vel quemcumque alium, ut patet in multis Scripturae locis, non autem dicitur: Verbum Domini erat apud Ieremiam vel apud alium; quia ad illos fit Verbum, qui incipiunt habere Verbum, postquam non habuerunt. Unde Evangelista non dixit, Verbum factum esse apud Patrem, sed **erat apud** Patrem: quia ex quo Pater erat, Verbum apud eum erat.

53. Deinde dicit **et Deus erat Verbum**. Haec est tertia clausula narrationis Ioannis, quae quidem secundum ordinem doctrinae congruentissime sequitur. Quia enim Ioannes dixerat de Verbo quando erat et ubi erat; restabat quaerere, quid erat Verbum; idest **Verbum erat**

This objection is rejected when he says, **the Word was with God**, taking **with** according to its second condition, as implying authority in what is causing. So the meaning, according to Hilary, is this: from whom is the Word if he exists before all things? The Evangelist answers: **the Word was with God**, i.e., although the Word has no beginning of duration, still he does not lack a beginning or author, for he was with God as his author.

49. The third objection, directed to the explanation in which **principium** is understood as the Father, is this. You say that **in the beginning was the Word**, i.e., the Son was in the Father. But that which is in something does not seem to be subsistent, as a hypostasis; just as the whiteness in a body does not subsist.

This objection is solved by the statement, **the Word was with God**, taking **with** in its first condition, as implying the subsistence of its grammatical antecedent. So according to Chrysostom, the meaning is this: **in the beginning was the Word**, not as an accident, but he **was with God**, as subsisting, and a divine hypostasis.

50. The fourth objection, against the same explanation, is this. You say that the Word was in the beginning, i.e., in the Father. But whatever is in something is not distinct from it. So the Son is not distinct from the Father.

This objection is answered by the statement, **and the Word was with God**, taking **with** in its third condition, as indicating distinction. Thus the meaning, according to Alcuin and Bede, is this: **the Word was with God**, and he was with the Father by a consubstantiality of nature, while still being with him through a distinction in person.

51. And so, **and the Word was with God**, indicates: the union of the Word with the Father in nature, according to Basil; their distinction in person, according to Alcuin and Bede; the subsistence of the Word in the divine nature, according to Chrysostom; and the authorship of the Father in relation to the Word, according to Hilary.

52. We should also note, according to Origen, that **the Word was with God** shows that the Son has always been with the Father. For in the Old Testament it says that the Word of the Lord was with Jeremiah or someone else, as is plain in many passages of Sacred Scripture. But it does not say that the Word of the Lord was with Jeremiah or anyone else, because the Word comes to those who begin to have the Word after not having it. Thus the Evangelist did not say that the Word came to the Father, but **was with** the Father, because, given the Father, the Word was with him.

53. Then he says, **and the Word was God**. This is the third clause in John's account, and it follows most appropriately considering the order of teaching. For since John had said both when and where the Word was, it remained

Deus, ut ly *Verbum* ponatur ex parte subiecti, et ly *Deus* ex parte praedicati.

54. Sed cum prius quaerendum sit de re quid est, quam ubi et quando sit, videtur quod Ioannes hunc ordinem pervertat, insinuans primo de verbo ubi et quando sit.

Ad hanc autem quaestionem respondet Origenes, quod aliter dicitur esse Verbum Dei apud hominem, et aliter apud Deum. Nam apud hominem est ut perficiens ipsum, quia per illud homo efficitur sapiens et bonus, Sap. c. VII, 27: *amicos Dei et prophetas constituit.* Apud Deum vero non ita dicitur esse Verbum, quasi Pater perficiatur per Verbum et illustretur ab ipso; sed sic est apud Deum, quod accipiat naturalem divinitatem ab ipso, qui Verbum loquitur, a quo habet ut sit idem Deus cum eo. Ex eo ergo quod est per originem apud Deum, necesse fuit primum ostendere quod Verbum erat in Patre et apud Patrem, quam quod Verbum erat Deus.

55. Sciendum est autem quod per hanc clausulam *Deus erat Verbum*, responderi potest duabus obiectionibus, quae ex praecedentibus insurgunt.

Quarum una insurgit ex nomine *Verbi*, et est talis: tu dicis quod *Verbum erat in principio, et apud Deum*; constat autem quod 'verbum' secundum communem usum loquendi significat vocem aliquam et enuntiationem necessariorum, manifestationem cogitationum; sed ista transeunt et non subsistunt; posset ergo credi quod de tali verbo Evangelista loqueretur.

Sed ista quaestio satis per praedicta excluditur, secundum Hilarium et Augustinum, Hom. prima *super Io.*, qui dicit, manifestum esse, *Verbum* in hoc loco non posse pro locutione accipi, quia cum locutio sit in motu et transeat, non posset dici quod *in principio erat Verbum*, si Verbum esset quid transiens et in motu. Item cum dicit *et Verbum erat apud Deum*, datur idem intelligi; satis enim patet quod aliud est inesse, et aliud est adesse. Verbum enim nostrum, cum non subsistat, non adest, sed inest; Verbum autem Dei est subsistens, et ideo adest. Et idcirco Evangelista signanter dixit *Verbum erat apud Deum*. Sed tamen, ut obiectionis causa tollatur totaliter, naturam et esse Verbi subdit, dicens *et Verbum erat Deus*.

56. Alia quaestio insurgit ex hoc quod dixerat *apud Deum*. Cum enim ly *apud* dicat distinctionem, posset credi quod *Verbum erat apud Deum*, scilicet Patrem, ab ipso in natura distinctum. Et ideo ad hoc excludendum statim subdit consubstantialitatem Verbi ad Patrem, dicens *et Verbum erat Deus*; quasi dicat: non separatus a Patre per diversitatem naturae, quia ipsum Verbum est Deus.

57. Nota etiam specialem modum significandi, quia dicit *Verbum erat Deus*, absolute ponendo *Deum*; ut

to inquire what the Word was, that is, *the Word was God*, taking *Word* as the subject, and *God* as the predicate.

54. But since one should first inquire what a thing is before investigating where and when it is, it seems that John violated this order by discussing these latter first.

Origen answers this by saying that the Word of God is with man and with God in different ways. The Word is with man as perfecting him, because it is through him that man becomes wise and good: *she makes friends of God and prophets* (Wis 7:27). But the Word is not with God as though the Father were perfected and enlightened by him. Rather, the Word is with God as receiving natural divinity from him, who utters the Word, and from whom he has it that he is the same God with him. And so, since the Word was with God by origin, it was necessary to show first that the Word was in the Father and with the Father before showing that the Word was God.

55. It is to be noted however, that this clause also enables us to answer two objections which arise from the foregoing: *the Word was God*.

The first is based on the name *Word*, and is this. You say that *in the beginning was the Word*, and that *the Word was with God*. Now it is obvious that 'word' is generally understood to signify a vocal sound and the statement of something necessary, a manifesting of thoughts. But these words pass away and do not subsist. Accordingly, someone could think that the Evangelist was speaking of a word like these.

According to Hilary and Augustine, this question is sufficiently answered by the above account. Augustine says (Homily I *On John*) that it is obvious that in this passage *Word* cannot be understood as a statement because, since a statement is in motion and passes away, it could not be said that *in the beginning was the Word*, if this Word were something passing away and in motion. The same thing is clear from *and the Word was with God*: for to be in another is not the same as to be with another. Our word, since it does not subsist, is not with us, but in us; but the Word of God is subsistent, and therefore with God. And so the Evangelist expressly says, *and the Word was with God*. To entirely remove the ground of the objection, he adds the nature and being of the Word, saying, *and the Word was God*.

56. The other question comes from his saying, *with God*. For since *with* indicates a distinction, it could be thought that *the Word was with God*, i.e., the Father, as distinct from him in nature. So to exclude this he adds at once the consubstantiality of the Word with the Father, saying, *and the Word was God*. As if to say: the Word is not separated from the Father by a diversity of nature, because the Word itself is God.

57. Note also the special way of signifying, since he says, *the Word was God*, using *God* absolutely to show that he

ostendat non eo modo Deum esse, quo nomen deitatis attribui dicitur creaturae in Sacra Scriptura; quia cum additione aliqua aliquando hoc nomen creatura participat. Sicut illud Ex. VII, 1: *ego constitui te Deum Pharaonis*, ad designandum quod non erat Deus simpliciter, nec per naturam, quia constituebatur Deus alicuius determinate; et illud Ps. LXXXI, 6: *ego dixi, dii estis*, quasi dicat: per meam reputationem, non secundum rei veritatem, dii estis: aliud enim est Deum reputari, et aliud esse Deum. Unde Verbum absolute dicitur Deus, quia est secundum essentiam suam Deus, et non participative, sicut homines et angeli.

58. Sciendum est etiam quod circa hanc clausulam Origenes turpiter erravit, ex modo loquendi, qui in Graeco habetur, sumens occasionem sui erroris.

Consuetudo enim est apud Graecos, quod cuilibet nomini apponunt articulum, ad designandum discretionem quamdam. Quia ergo in Evangelio Ioannis in Graeco, huic nomini quod est **Verbum**, cum dicitur **in principio erat Verbum**, et similiter huic nomini quod est **Deus**, cum dicitur **et Verbum erat apud Deum**, apponitur articulus, ut dicatur ly **Verbum**, et ly **Deus**, ad designandum eminentiam et discretionem Verbi ad alia verba, et principalitatem Patris in divinitate; ideo, cum in hoc quod dicitur **Verbum erat Deus**, non apponatur articulus huic nomini **Deus**, quod supponit pro persona Filii, blasphemavit Origenes quod Verbum non esset Deus per essentiam, licet sit essentialiter Verbum; sed dicitur per participationem Deus: solus vero Pater est Deus per suam essentiam. Et sic ponebat Filium Patre minorem.

59. Quod autem non sit verum, probat Chrysostomus per hoc quod si articulus positus huic nomini **Deus**, importaret maioritatem in Patre respectu Filii, numquam apponeretur huic nomini **Deus**, cum de alio praedicatur, sed solum quando praedicatur de Patre, et semper cum dicitur de Patre, apponeretur articulus.

Invenimus autem contrarium per duas auctoritates Apostoli, qui notat Christum *Deum* cum appositione articuli, dicens in Epist. ad Titum, II, 13: *expectantes beatam spem, et adventum gloriae magni Dei*. Ibi enim *Deus* supponit pro Filio, et apponitur ei articulus in Graeco; ergo Christus est Deus magnus. Item idem Apostolus, Rom. IX, 5, dicit: *ex quibus Christus, qui est super omnia Deus benedictus in saecula*. Ibi similiter ad ly *Deus* ponitur in Graeco articulus. Praeterea I Io. ult., 20: *ut simus in vero Filio eius Christo Iesu; hic est verus Deus, et vita aeterna*. Christus ergo non est Deus per participationem, sed verus. Patet igitur esse falsum quod Origenes finxit.

Ratio autem quare Evangelista non apposuit articulum huic nomini **Deus**, assignatur a Chrysostomo; scilicet quia iam bis nominaverat Deum cum appositione

is not God in the same way in which the name of the deity is given to a creature in Sacred Scripture. For a creature sometimes shares this name with some added qualification, as when it says, *I have appointed you the God of Pharaoh* (Exod 7:1), in order to indicate that he was not God absolutely or by nature, because he was appointed the god of someone in a qualified sense. Again, it says in a psalm: *I said: you are gods* (Ps 81:6) as if to say: in my opinion, but not in reality. Thus the Word is called God absolutely because he is God by his own essence, and not by participation, as men and angels are.

58. We should note that Origen disgracefully misunderstood this clause, led astray by the Greek manner of speaking and this was the occasion of his error.

It is the custom among the Greeks to put the article before every name in order to indicate a distinction. In the Greek version of John's Gospel the name **Word** in the statement, **in the beginning was the Word**, and also the name **God** in the statement, **and the Word was with God**, are prefixed by the article, so as to read the **Word** and the **God**, in order to indicate the eminence and distinction of the Word from other words, and the principality of the Father in the divinity. But in the statement, **the Word was God**, the article is not prefixed to the noun **God**, which stands for the person of the Son. Because of this Origen blasphemed that the Word, although he was Word by essence, was not God by essence, but is called God by participation; while the Father alone is God by essence. And so he held that the Son is inferior to the Father.

59. Chrysostom proves that this is not true, because if the article used with the name **God** implied the superiority of the Father in respect to the Son, it would never be used with the name **God** when it is used as a predicate of another, but only when it is predicated of the Father. Further, whenever it would be said of the Father, it would be accompanied by the article.

However, we find the opposite to be the case in two statements of the Apostle, who calls Christ *God*, using the article. For he says, *the coming of the glory of the great God and our savior Jesus Christ* (Titus 2:13), where *God* stands for the Son, and in the Greek the article is used. Therefore, Christ is the great God. Again he says: *Christ, who is God over all things, blessed forever* (Rom 9:5), and again the article is used with *God* in the Greek. Further, it is said: *that we may be in his true Son, Jesus Christ; he is the true God and eternal life* (1 John 5:20) . Thus, Christ is not God by participation, but truly God. And so the theory of Origen is clearly false.

Chrysostom gives us the reason why the Evangelist did not use the article with the name **God**, namely, because he had already mentioned God twice using the article, and so

articuli, et ideo non oportebat reiterare tertio, sed subintelligitur.

Vel dicendum est et melius, quod *Deus* ponitur hic in praedicato, et tenetur formaliter; consuetum est autem quod nominibus in praedicato positis non ponitur articulus, cum discretionem importet. Si vero Deus poneretur hic ex parte subiecti, pro quacumque persona supponeret, sive pro Filio sive pro Spiritu Sancto; et tunc non est dubium quod in Graeco ibi apponeretur articulus.

60. Deinde dicit *hoc erat in principio apud Deum*.

Hic ponitur quarta clausula, quae introducitur propter clausulam praecedentem. Ex hoc enim quod Evangelista dixerat quod *Verbum erat Deus*, duplex falsus intellectus accipi poterat a non recte sentientibus. Unus a gentilibus, qui ponunt pluralitatem et diversitatem deorum, et eorum contrarias dicunt esse voluntates; sicut illi qui fabulantur Iovem pugnasse cum Saturno; et sicut Manichaei, qui ponunt duo contraria principia naturae. Contra hunc errorem Dominus dixit, Deut. VI, 4: *audi Israel, Dominus Deus tuus, Deus unus est*.

Quia ergo Evangelista dixerat *Verbum erat apud Deum*, *et Deus erat Verbum*, possent isti in fulcimentum sui erroris istud adducere, intelligentes alium esse Deum, apud quem est Verbum, et alium ipsum Verbum, et cum hoc alterius, sive contrariae voluntatis; quod est contra legem Evangelii.

Ad hoc ergo excludendum dicit *hoc erat in principio apud Deum*; quasi dicat, secundum Hilarium: ita dico quod Verbum est Deus, quod tamen non est habens divinitatem, sed est apud Deum, scilicet in una natura et eadem in qua ipse est. Item per hoc quod dicit, *Verbum erat Deus* ne intelligeretur quod haberent contrariam voluntatem, addidit hoc, quod scilicet *Verbum erat in principio apud Deum* scilicet Patrem; non divisum ab ipso, non contrarium, sed habens cum eo identitatem naturae et concordiam voluntatis: quae quidem unio fit per communionem divinae naturae in tribus personis, et per nexum naturalis amoris Patris et Filii.

61. Alius error poterat ex praemissis verbis elici ab Arianis, qui ponunt Filium minorem esse quam Pater, propter hoc quod dicitur: *Pater maior me est*. Dicunt enim Patrem maiorem Filio, et quantum ad aeternitatem, et quantum ad naturae divinitatem. Ut ergo Evangelista excluderet, addidit *hoc erat in principio apud Deum*.

Arius enim primam clausulam, scilicet *in principio erat Verbum*, admittit: non tamen vult quod ibi *principium* accipiatur pro Patre, sed pro principio creaturarum. Unde dicit quod Verbum erat in principio creaturarum, et ideo nequaquam Patri est coaeternus. Sed hoc excluditur, secundum Chrysostomum, per illam clausulam *hoc erat in principio*, non quidem creaturarum, sed *in principio apud Deum*; idest ex quo Deus fuit.

it was not necessary to repeat it a third time, but it was implied.

Or it could be said, and this is a better reason, that **God** is used here as the predicate and is taken formally. And it is not the custom for the article to accompany names used as predicates, since the article indicates a distinction. But if God were used here as the subject, it could stand for any of the persons, as the Son or the Holy Spirit; then, no doubt, the article would be used in the Greek.

60. Then he says, **he was in the beginning with God**.

This is the fourth clause and is introduced because of the preceding clause. For from the Evangelist's statement that **the Word was God**, two false interpretations could be held by those who misunderstand. One of these is by the pagans, who acknowledge many and different gods, and say that their wills are in opposition. For example, those who put out the fable of Jupiter fighting with Saturn; or as the Manicheans, who have two contrary principles of nature. The Lord said against this error: *hear O Israel, the Lord our God is one Lord* (Deut 6:4).

Since the Evangelist had said, **the Word was with God, and the Word was God**, they could adduce this in support of their error by understanding the God with whom the Word is to be one God, and the Word to be another, having another, or contrary, will to the former; and this is against the law of the Gospel.

And so to exclude this he says, **he was in the beginning with God**, as if to say, according to Hilary: I say that the Word is God, not as if he has a distinct divinity, but he is with God, that is, in the one same nature in which he is. Further, lest his statement, **and the Word was God**, be taken to mean that the Word has an opposed will, he added that **the Word was in the beginning with God**, namely, the Father; not as divided from him or opposed, but having an identity of nature with him and a harmony of will. This union comes about by the sharing of the divine nature in the three persons, and by the bond of the natural love of the Father and the Son.

61. The Arians were able to draw out another error from the above. They think that the Son is less than the Father because it says: **the Father is greater than I** (John 14:28). And they say the Father is greater than the Son both as to eternity and as to divinity of nature. And so to exclude this the Evangelist added: **he was in the beginning with God**.

For Arius admits the first clause, **in the beginning was the Word**, but he will not admit that **principium** should be taken for the Father, but rather for the beginning of creatures. So he says that the Word was in the beginning of creatures, and consequently is in no sense coeternal with the Father. But this is excluded, according to Chrysostom, by this clause, **he was in the beginning**, not of creatures, but **in the beginning with God**, i.e., whenever God existed. For

Numquam enim Pater solitarius fuit a Filio, sive Verbo, sed semper hoc, scilicet Verbum, apud **Deum erat**.

62. Item, Arius confitetur quod Verbum erat Deus, sed tamen minor Patre. Sed hoc excluditur per ea quae sequuntur.

Duo enim sunt propria magni Dei, quae Arius Deo Patri singulariter attribuebat, scilicet aeternitas et omnipotentia. In quocumque ergo ista duo inveniuntur, ille est magnus Deus, quo nullus est maior; sed haec duo Evangelista Verbo attribuit; ergo Verbum est magnus Deus, et non minor. Aeternitatem quidem dicit esse in Verbo per hoc quod dicit **hoc erat in principio apud Deum**; idest Verbum ab aeterno, non solum in principio creaturarum, ut Arius intellexit, erat, sed apud Deum, accipiens esse et divinitatem ab eo. Omnipotentiam vero attribuit Verbo per hoc quod subdit **omnia per ipsum facta sunt**.

63. Origenes vero hanc eamdem clausulam satis pulchre exponens, dicit ipsam non esse aliam a tribus primis; sed ipsam esse quemdam epilogum praemissorum.

Evangelista enim postquam insinuaverat veritatem esse Filii, transiturus ad eius insinuandum virtutem, recolligit, quasi in summa epilogando, in quarta clausula, quod in primis tribus praedixerat. Primo enim per hoc quod dicit **hoc**, intelligit tertiam clausulam; per hoc vero quod dicit **erat in principio**, recolligit primam; per hoc vero quod subdit **erat apud Deum**, recolligit secundam, ut sic non intelligas aliud Verbum, quod erat in principio et quod erat Deus; sed hoc Verbum, quod erat Deus, **erat in principio apud Deum**.

64. Si quis ergo recte consideret has quatuor propositiones, inveniet evidenter per eas destrui omnes haereticorum et philosophorum errores.

Quidam enim haeretici, sicut Ebion et Cerintus, dixerunt, Christum non praeextitisse Beatae Virgini, sed ab ea sumpsisse essendi et durationis principium, ponentes eum fuisse hominem purum, sed meruisse divinitatem per bona merita. Quod etiam Photinus et Paulus Samosatenus eos secuti dixerunt. Horum errorem Evangelista excludit, dicens **in principio erat Verbum**, idest ante omnia, et in Patre ab aeterno; ergo non sumpsit initium ex Virgine.

Sabellius vero, licet fateretur quod Deus qui carnem suscepit, ex Virgine non sumpsit initium, sed fuit ab aeterno, tamen dicebat quod non erat alia persona Patris, qui fuit ab aeterno, Filii, qui carnem assumpsit ex Virgine, sed idem erat Pater et Filius personaliter; Trinitatem personarum in divinis confundens. Contra hunc errorem dicit Evangelista **et Verbum erat apud Deum**, scilicet Filius apud Patrem, ut alius apud alium.

the Father was never alone without the Son or Word, but **he**, that is, the Word, was always **with God**.

62. Again, Arius admits that the Word was God, but nevertheless inferior to the Father. This is excluded by what follows.

For there are two attributes proper to the great God which Arius attributed solely to God the Father, that is, eternity and omnipotence. So in whomever these two attributes are found, he is the great God, than whom none is greater. But the Evangelist attributes these two to the Word. Therefore, the Word is the great God and not inferior. He says the Word is eternal when he states, **he was in the beginning with God**, i.e., the Word was with God from eternity, and not only in the beginning of creatures, as Arius held; but he was with God, receiving being and divinity from him. Further, he attributes omnipotence to the Word when he adds, **all things were made through him** (John 1:3).

63. Origen gives a rather beautiful explanation of this clause, **he was in the beginning with God**, when he says that it is not separate from the first three, but is in a certain sense their epilogue.

For the Evangelist, after he had indicated that truth was the Son's and was about to describe his power, in a way gathers together in a summary form, in this fourth clause, what he had said in the first three. For in saying **he**, he understands the third clause; by adding **was in the beginning**, he recalls the first clause; and by adding **was with God**, he recalls the second, so that we do not think that the Word which was in the beginning is different than the Word which was God; but this Word which was God **was in the beginning with God**.

64. If one considers these four propositions well, he will find that they clearly destroy all the errors of the heretics and of the philosophers.

For some heretics, as Ebion and Cerinthus, said that Christ did not exist before the Blessed Virgin, but took from her the beginning of his being and duration; for they held that he was a mere man, who had merited divinity by his good works. Photinus and Paul of Samosata, following them, said the same thing. But the Evangelist excludes their errors saying, **in the beginning was the Word**, i.e., before all things, and in the Father from eternity. Thus he did not derive his beginning from the Virgin.

Sabellius, on the other hand, although he admitted that the God who took flesh did not receive his beginning from the Virgin, but existed from eternity, still said that the person of the Father, who existed from eternity, was not distinct from the person of the Son, who took flesh from the Virgin. He maintained that the Father and Son were the same person; confusing the trinity of persons in the divine. The Evangelist says against this error, **and the Word was with God**, i.e., the Son was with the Father, as one person with another.

Eunomius vero posuit Filium omnino dissimilem esse Patri: et hoc consequenter Evangelista excludit, dicens *et Deus erat Verbum*.

Arius vero dicebat Filium Patre minorem; sed hoc excludit Evangelista cum dicit *hoc erat in principio apud Deum*, quod supra fuit expositum.

65. Per hoc etiam excluduntur errores philosophorum.

Quidam enim philosophorum antiqui, scilicet naturales, ponebant mundum non ex aliquo intellectu, neque per aliquam rationem, sed a casu fuisse; et ideo a principio rationem non posuerunt seu intellectum aliquam causam rerum, sed solam materiam fluitantem, utpote athomos, sicut Democritus posuit, et alia huiusmodi principia materialia, ut alii posuerunt. Contra hos est quod Evangelista dicit *in principio erat Verbum*, a quo res scilicet principium sumpserunt et non a casu.

Plato autem posuit rationes omnium rerum factarum subsistentes, separatas in propriis naturis, per quarum participationem res materiales essent: puta per rationem hominis separatam, quam dicebat per se hominem, haberet quod sint homines. Sic ergo ne hanc rationem, per quam omnia facta sunt, intelligas rationes separatas a Deo, ut Plato ponebat, addit Evangelista *et Verbum erat apud Deum*.

Alii etiam Platonici, ut Chrysostomus refert, ponebant Deum Patrem eminentissimum, et primum, sub quo ponebant mentem quamdam, in qua dicebant esse similitudines et ideas omnium rerum. Ne ergo sic intelligas, quod Verbum erat apud Patrem, quasi sub eo et minor eo, addit Evangelista *et Verbum erat Deus*.

Aristoteles vero posuit in Deo rationes omnium rerum, et quod idem est in Deo intellectus et intelligens et intellectum; tamen posuit mundum coaeternum sibi fuisse. Et contra hoc est quod Evangelista dicit *hoc*, scilicet *Verbum* solum, *erat in principio apud Deum*; ita quod ly hoc non excludit aliam personam, sed aliam naturam coaeternam.

66. Nota etiam in praedictis differentiam Ioannis ab aliis Evangelistis, quomodo scilicet dignius Evangelium suum incepit, quam alii. Ipsi enim annuntiaverunt Christum Filium Dei ex tempore natum; Matth. II, 1: *cum natus esset Iesus in Bethlehem*. Ioannes vero dicit eum ab aeterno fuisse, *in principio*, inquit, *erat Verbum*. Ipsi etiam dicunt eum subito inter homines apparuisse; Lc. II, 29: *nunc dimittis servum tuum, Domine, secundum verbum tuum in pace; quia viderunt oculi mei salutare tuum, quod parasti ante faciem omnium populorum, lumen ad revelationem gentium, et gloriam plebis tuae, Israel*. Ioannes vero dicit eum apud Patrem semper fuisse. *Et Verbum*, inquit, *erat apud Deum*. Alii vero

Eunomius declared that the Son is entirely unlike the Father. The Evangelist rejects this when he says, *and the Word was God*.

Finally, Arius said that the Son was less than the Father. The Evangelist excludes this by saying, *he was in the beginning with God*, as was explained above.

65. These words also exclude the errors of the philosophers.

Some of the ancient philosophers, namely, the natural philosophers, maintained that the world did not come from any intellect or through some purpose, but by chance. Consequently, they did not place at the beginning as the cause of things a reason or intellect, but only matter in flux; for example, atoms, as Democritus thought, or other material principles of this kind as different philosophers maintained. Against these the Evangelist says, *in the beginning was the Word*, from whom, and not from chance, things derive their beginning.

Plato, however, thought that the ideas of all the things that were made were subsistent, i.e., existing separately in their own natures; and material things exist by participating in these. For example, he thought men existed through the separated idea of man, which he called man *per se*. So lest you suppose, as did Plato, that this idea through which all things were made be ideas separated from God, the Evangelist adds, *and the Word was with God*.

Other Platonists, as Chrysostom relates, maintained that God the Father was most eminent and first, but under him they placed a certain mind in which there were the likenesses and ideas of all things. So lest you think that the Word was with the Father in such a way as to be under him and less than he, the Evangelist adds, *and the Word was God*.

Aristotle, however, thought that the ideas of all things are in God, and that in God, the intellect, the one understanding, and what is understood, are the same. Nevertheless, he thought that the world is coeternal with him. Against this the Evangelist says, *he*, the *Word* alone, *was in the beginning with God*, in such a way that he does not exclude another person, but only another coeternal nature.

66. Note the difference in what has been said between John and the other Evangelists: how he began his Gospel on a loftier plane than they. They announced Christ the Son of God born in time: *when Jesus was born in Bethlehem* (Matt 2:1); but John presents him existing from eternity: *in the beginning was the Word*. They show him suddenly appearing among men: *now you dismiss your servant, O Lord, in peace, according to your word; because my eyes have seen your salvation, which you have prepared in the sight of all people, a light to reveal you to the the nations and the glory of your people Israel* (Luke 2:29); but John says that he always existed with the Father: *and the Word was with God*. The others show him as a man: *they gave glory to God who had*

ipsum hominem; Matth. IX, v. 8: *glorificabant Deum, qui potestatem talem hominibus dedit.* Ioannes vero dicit ipsum esse Deum. **Et Verbum**, inquit, **erat Deus**. Alii dixerunt eum fuisse cum hominibus conversatum; Matth. XVII, 21: *conversantibus autem illis in Galilaea, dixit Iesus* etc.; sed Ioannes dicit eum apud Patrem semper fuisse. **Hoc**, inquit, **erat in principio apud Deum**.

67. Nota etiam quod Evangelista signanter recitat hoc verbum **erat**, ut ostendat Verbum Dei omnia tempora, scilicet praesens, praeteritum et futurum, excedere. Quasi dicat: erat ultra tempus praesens, praeteritum et futurum, secundum quod tangitur in Glossa.

given such authority to men (Matt 9:8); but John only says that he is God: **and the Word was God**. The others say he lives with men: *while living in Galilee, Jesus said to them* (Matt 17:21); but John says that he has always been with the Father: **he was in the beginning with God**.

67. Note also how the Evangelist designedly uses the word **was** to show that the Word of God transcends all times: present, past and future. It is as though he were saying: he was beyond time: present, past and future, as the Gloss says.

Lecture 2

1:3 Omnia per ipsum facta sunt. Et sine ipso factum est nihil. Quod factum est [n. 69]	**1:3** πάντα δι᾽ αὐτοῦ ἐγένετο, καὶ χωρὶς αὐτοῦ ἐγένετο οὐδὲ ἕν. ὃ γέγονεν	**1:3 All things were made through him: and without him was made nothing that was made.** [n. 69]
1:4 in ipso vita erat. Et vita erat lux hominum. [n. 89]	**1:4** ἐν αὐτῷ ζωὴ ἦν, καὶ ἡ ζωὴ ἦν τὸ φῶς τῶν ἀνθρώπων·	**1:4 In him was life, and the life was the light of men.** [n. 89]

---

68. Postquam Evangelista esse et naturam divini Verbi, quantum dici potest ab homine, insinuaverat, consequenter manifestat eius virtutem. Et

primo ostendit eius virtutem quantum ad omnia, quae in esse procedunt;

secundo specialiter quantum ad homines, ibi **erat vita lux hominum.**

Circa primum ponit tres clausulas, quas non distinguimus ad praesens, quia secundum diversas expositiones sanctorum sunt diversimode distinguendae.

69. Prima ergo clausula est **omnia per ipsum facta sunt**; quae inducitur ad ostendendum tria de Verbo. Et primo, secundum Chrysostomum, ad ostendendum aequalitatem Verbi ad Patrem.

Sicut enim dictum est supra, Evangelista excluserat errorem Arii, ostendens coaeternitatem Filii ad Patrem per hoc quod dixerat **hoc erat in principio apud Deum**, hic vero eumdem errorem excludit, ostendendo omnipotentiam Filii, dicens, **omnia per ipsum facta sunt.** Esse enim principium omnium factorum proprium est Dei magni omnipotentis, iuxta illud Ps. CXXXIV, 6: *omnia quaecumque Dominus voluit, fecit in caelo et in terra.* Verbum ergo per quod facta sunt omnia, est Deus magnus et coaequalis Patri.

70. Secundo, ad ostendendum coaeternitatem Verbi ad Patrem, secundum Hilarium.

Quia enim per hoc quod dixerat **in principio erat Verbum**, posset aliquis intelligere hoc dictum fuisse de principio creaturarum, id est fuisse aliquod tempus ante omnem creaturam, in quo Verbum non erat, ideo hoc excludens Evangelista dixit **omnia per ipsum facta sunt.** Si enim omnia sunt facta per Verbum ergo et ipsum tempus. Ex quo sic argumentatur: si omne tempus ab ipso factum est; ergo nullum tempus fuit ante ipsum; nec cum ipso; quia ante omnia erat; ergo sunt ab aeterno coaeterni.

71. Tertio, secundum Augustinum, ad ostendendam consubstantialitatem Verbi ad Patrem.

Si enim facta omnia sunt per Verbum, ergo ipsum Verbum non potest dici factum: quia si est factum, est factum per aliquod Verbum, quia **omnia per Verbum facta sunt.** Oportet ergo esse aliud Verbum, per quod

68. After the Evangelist has told of the existence and nature of the divine Word, so far as it can be told by man, he then shows the might of his power.

First, he shows his power with respect to all things that come into existence.

Second, with especial respect to man, at **and the life was the light of men.**

As to the first, he uses three clauses; and we will not distinguish these at present because they will be distinguished in different ways according to the different explanations given by the saints.

69. The first clause is **all things were made through him**; which is used to show three things concerning the Word. First, according to Chrysostom, to show the equality of the Word to the Father.

For as stated earlier, the error of Arius was rejected by the Evangelist when he showed the coeternity of the Son with the Father by saying, **he was in the beginning with God.** Here he excludes the same error when he shows the omnipotence of the Son, saying, **all things were made through him.** For to be the principle of all the things that are made is proper to the great omnipotent God, as it is said, *whatever the Lord wills he does, in heaven and on earth* (Ps 134:6). Thus the Word, through whom all things were made, is God, great and coequal to the Father.

70. Second, according to Hilary, this clause is used to show the coeternity of the Word with the Father.

For since someone might understand the earlier statement, **in the beginning was the Word**, as referring to the beginning of creatures, i.e., that before there were any creatures there was a time in which the Word did not exist, the Evangelist rejects this by saying, **all things were made through him.** For if all things were made through the Word, then time was also. From this we can form the following argument: if all time was made through him, there was no time before him or with him, because before all these, he was. Therefore the Son and the Father are eternally coeternal.

71. Third, according to Augustine, this clause is used to show the consubstantiality of the Word with the Father.

For if all things were made through the Word, the Word himself cannot be said to have been made; because, if made, he was made through some Word, since **all things were made through the Word.** Consequently, there would have

Verbum, de quo hic loquitur Evangelista, sit factum. Et illud Verbum dicimus unigenitum Dei, per quem facta sunt omnia, quia nec factum est, nec creatura est; et si non est creatura, necesse est dicere ipsum esse eiusdem substantiae cum Patre, cum omnis substantia praeter essentiam divinam facta sit. Substantia autem, quae creatura non est, Deus est. Verbum ergo, per quod omnia facta sunt, consubstantiale est Patri, cum nec factum, nec creatura sit.

72. Sic ergo habes Verbi aequalitatem ad Patrem, secundum Chrysostomum, coaeternitatem secundum Hilarium, et consubstantialitatem, secundum Augustinum per hoc quod dicit *omnia per ipsum facta sunt*.

73. Cavendi sunt autem hic tres errores.

Et primo error Valentini. Ipse enim intellexit per hoc quod dicitur *omnia per ipsum facta sunt*, quod Verbum dederit causam Creatori, quod mundum crearet, ut dicantur omnia sic per Verbum facta, quasi ex Verbo processerit quod Pater mundum creavit. Et hoc videtur ducere in positionem illorum, qui dicebant Deum mundum fecisse propter aliquam exteriorem causam; quod est contra illud Prov. XVI, 4: *universa propter semetipsum operatus est Dominus*.

Sed hoc est falsum, quia, sicut Origenes dicit, si Verbum fuisset causa Creatori praestans ei materiam ad faciendum, non dixisset *omnia per ipsum facta sunt*, sed, e converso, omnia facta sunt per Creatorem a Verbo.

74. Secundo vitandus est error Origenis, qui dicit Spiritum Sanctum, inter omnia, factum esse per Verbum, ex quo sequitur ipsum esse creaturam: et hoc posuit Origenes.

Hoc autem est haereticum et blasphemum, cum Spiritus Sanctus eiusdem sit gloriae et substantiae et dignitatis cum Patre et Filio, iuxta illud Matth. ult., 19: *docete omnes gentes, baptizantes eos in nomine Patris, et Filii, et Spiritus Sancti*; et iuxta illud I Io. V, v. 7: *tres sunt qui testimonium dant in caelo, Pater, Verbum et Spiritus Sanctus: et hi tres unum sunt*. Cum ergo dicit Evangelista *omnia per ipsum facta sunt*, non est intelligendum simpliciter *facta omnia*, sed in genere creaturarum et rerum factarum. Quasi dicat: omnia, quae facta sunt, per ipsum facta sunt. Alias, si simpliciter intelligatur, sequeretur Patrem et Spiritum Sanctum factos per ipsum: quod est blasphemum. Igitur nec Pater, nec aliquid substantiale Patri, per Verbum factum est.

75. Tertio vitandus est alius error ipsius Origenis.

Ipse enim sic omnia facta esse *per* Verbum dixit, sicut aliquid fit a maiori per minorem, quasi minor sit Filius, et ut organum Patris. Sed quod per hanc praepositionem

been another Word through whom was made the Word of whom the Evangelist is speaking. This Word, through whom all things are made, we call the only begotten Son of God, because he is neither made nor is he a creature. And if he is not a creature, it is necessary to say that he is of the same substance with the Father, since every substance other than the divine essence is made. But a substance that is not a creature is God. And so the Word, through whom all things were made, is consubstantial with the Father, since he is neither made, nor is he a creature.

72. And so in saying *all things were made through him*, you have, according to Chrysostom, the equality of the Word with the Father; the coeternity of the Word with the Father, according to Hilary; and the consubstantiality of the Word with the Father, according to Augustine.

73. Here we must guard against three errors.

First, the error of Valentine. He understood *all things were made through him* to mean that the Word proferred to the Creator the cause of his creating the world; so that all things were made through the Word as if the Father's creating the world came from the Word. This leads to the position of those who said that God created the world because of some exterior cause; and this is contrary to Proverbs, *the Lord made all things for himself* (Prov 16:4).

The reason this is an error is that, as Origen says, if the Word had been a cause to the Creator by offering him the material for making things, he would not have said, *all things were made through him*, but on the contrary, that all things were made through the Creator by the Word.

74. Second, we must avoid the error of Origen. He said that the Holy Spirit was included among all the things made through the Word; from which it follows that he is a creature. And this is what Origen thought.

This is heretical and blasphemous, since the Holy Spirit has the same glory and substance and dignity as the Father and the Son, according to what is said: *make disciples of all the nations, baptizing them in the name of the Father, and of the Son, and of the Holy Spirit* (Matt 28:19). And, *there are three who give testimony in heaven, the Father, the Word, and the Holy Spirit; and these three are one* (1 John 5:7). Thus when the Evangelist says, *all things were made through him*, one should not understand *all things* absolutely, but in the realm of creatures and of things made. As if to say: all things that were made, were made through him. Otherwise, if *all things* were taken absolutely, it would follow that the Father and the Holy Spirit were made through him; and this is blasphemous. Consequently, neither the Father nor anything substantial with the Father was made through the Word.

75. Third, we must avoid another of Origen's errors.

For he said that all things were made *through* the Word as something is made by a greater through a lesser, as if the Son were inferior to, and an instrument of, the Father.

'per' non significetur minoritas in obliquo, scilicet Filio, seu Verbo, patet ex pluribus Scripturae locis. Dicit enim Apostolus, 1 Cor. I, 9, loquens de Patre: *fidelis Deus, per quem vocati estis in societatem Filii eius*. Si ille, per quem fit aliquid, habet superiorem, ergo et Pater superiorem habebit; hoc autem est falsum; ergo per praepositionem *per* non significatur minoritas in Filio, cum dicuntur omnia facta per ipsum.

76. Ad maiorem autem evidentiam huius sciendum est, quod quando dicitur aliquid 'per' aliquem fieri, haec praepositio per denotat causalitatem in obliquo, respectu operationis aliquo modo, sed diversimode.

Cum enim operatio, secundum modum significandi, consideretur media inter operantem et operatum, potest considerari ipsa operatio dupliciter. Uno modo secundum quod exit ab operante, qui est causa ipsius actionis; alio modo secundum quod terminatur ad operatum. Quandoque ergo praepositio 'per' significat causam operationis, secundum quod exit ab operante; quandoque autem, secundum quod terminatur ad operatum.

Causam autem operationis, secundum quod exit ab operante, significat quando illud quod significatur per obliquum, est causa operanti quod operetur, vel efficiens, vel formalis. Formalis quidem, sicut ignis calefacit per calorem: est enim calor causa formalis calefactionis ignis. Causa vero movens, seu efficiens, ut secunda agentia operantur per prima, ut si dicam quod balivus operatur per regem, quia rex est causa efficiens balivo quod operetur. Et hoc modo intellexit Valentinus, omnia facta esse per Verbum, ac si Verbum esset causa conditori ut omnia faceret.

Causalitatem vero operationis, secundum quod terminatur ad operatum, importat haec praepositio 'per', quando illud, quod significatur per ipsam causalitatem, non est causa ipsa quod operetur, sed est causa operationis, secundum quod terminatur ad operatum. Sicut cum dico carpentarius facit scamnum per securim, quae non est causa carpentario quod operetur, sed ponimus esse causam quod scamnum fiat ab operante.

Sic ergo cum dicitur **omnia per ipsum facta sunt**; si ly **per** denotet efficientem causam, seu moventem Patrem ad operandum, dicendum est quod Pater nihil operatur per Filium, sed per seipsum omnia operatur, ut dictum est. Si vero ly **per** denotet causam formalem, sic cum Pater operetur per sapientiam suam, quae est sua essentia, operatur per suam sapientiam, sicut operatur per suam essentiam; et quia sapientia et virtus Patris attribuitur Filio, I Cor. I, 24, dicimus: *Christum Dei virtutem, et Dei sapientiam*, ideo appropriate dicimus quod

But it is clear from many places in Scripture that the preposition 'through' does not signify inferiority in the thing which is its grammatical object, i.e., in the Son or Word. For the Apostle says, speaking of the Father, *God is faithful, through whom you were called into the fellowship of his Son* (1 Cor 1:9). If he through whom something is done has a superior, then the Father has a superior. But this is false. Therefore, the preposition **through** does not signify any inferiority in the Son when all things are said to have been made through him.

76. To explain this point further, we should note that when something is said to be made through someone, the preposition 'through' denotes some sort of causality in its object with respect to an operation; but not always the same kind of causality.

For since an operation, according to our manner of signifying, is considered to be medial between the one acting and the thing produced, the operation itself can be regarded in two ways. In one way, as issuing from the one operating, who is the cause of the action itself; in another way, as terminated in the thing produced. Accordingly, the preposition 'through' sometimes signifies the cause of the operation insofar as it issues from the one operating: but sometimes as terminated in the thing which is produced.

It signifies the cause of the operation as issuing from the one operating when the object of the preposition is either the efficient or formal cause why the one operating is operating. For example, we have a formal cause when fire is heating through heat; for heat is the formal cause of the fire's heating. We have a movent or efficient cause in cases where secondary agents act through primary agents; as when I say that the bailiff acts through the king, because the king is the efficient cause of the bailiff's acting. This is the way Valentine understood that all things were made through the Word: as though the Word were the cause of the maker's production of all things.

The preposition 'through' implies the causality of the operation as terminated in the thing produced when what is signified through that causality is not the cause which operates, but the cause of the operation precisely as terminated in the thing produced. So when I say that the carpenter is making a bench by means of a hatchet, the hatchet is not the cause of the carpenter's operating; but we do say that it is the cause of the bench's being made by the one acting.

And so when it says that **all things were made through him**, if the **through** denotes the efficient or movent cause, causing the Father to act, then in this sense the Father does nothing by the Son, but he does all things by himself, as has been said. But if the **through** denotes a formal cause, as when the Father operates by his widsom, which is his essence, he operates by his wisdom as he operates by his essence. And because the wisdom and power of the Father are attributed to the Son, as when we say, *Christ, the power of God and the wisdom of God* (1 Cor 1:24), then by

Pater omnia operatur per Filium, idest per sapientiam suam. Et ideo dicit Augustinus quod hoc quod dicitur *ex quo omnia*, appropriatur Patri; *per quem omnia*, Filio; *in quo omnia*, Spiritui Sancto. Si vero ly **per** denotet causalitatem ex parte operati, tunc hoc quod dicimus *Patrem omnia operari per Filium* non est appropriatum Verbo, sed proprium eius, quia hoc quod est causa creaturarum, habet ab alio, scilicet a Patre, a quo habet esse.

Nec tamen propter hoc sequitur ipsum esse instrumentum Patris, licet omne quod movetur ab alio ad aliquid operandum, rationem instrumenti habeat. Cum autem dico aliquem operari per virtutem receptam ab alio, potest dupliciter intelligi. Uno modo quod eadem numero sit virtus et dantis, et accipientis: et hoc modo qui operatur per virtutem acceptam ab alio, non est minor, sed aequalis ei a quo accipit. Quia ergo Pater eamdem virtutem, quam habet, dat Filio, per quam Filius operatur, cum dicitur Pater operari per Filium, propter hoc Filius non est dicendum minor Patre, neque instrumentum eius. Sed hoc sequitur in illis qui non eamdem virtutem accipiunt ab aliquo, sed aliam et creatam.

Sic ergo patet quod nec Spiritus Sanctus, nec Filius, est causa Patri quod operetur, neque Patris minister seu instrumentum, ut deliravit Origenes.

77. Si autem recte considerentur verba praedicta **omnia per ipsum facta sunt**, evidenter apparet Evangelistam propriissime fuisse locutum.

Quicumque enim aliquid facit, oportet quod illud praeconcipiat in sua sapientia, quae est forma et ratio rei factae: sicut forma in mente artificis praeconcepta est ratio arcae faciendae. Sic ergo Deus nihil facit nisi per conceptum sui intellectus, qui est sapientia ab aeterno concepta, scilicet Dei Verbum, et Dei Filius: et ideo impossibile est quod aliquid faciat nisi per Filium. Unde Augustinus *de Trinitate* dicit quod Verbum est ars plena omnium rationum viventium. Et sic patet quod omnia quae Pater facit, facit per ipsum.

78. Notandum autem, secundum Chrysostomum, quod omnia quae Moyses per multa enumerat in productione rerum a Deo, dicens: *dixit Dominus, 'fiat lux,' et 'fiat firmamentum'* etc., haec omnia Evangelista excedens, uno verbo comprehendit, dicens **omnia per ipsum facta sunt**.

Cuius ratio est quia Moyses tradere volebat emanationem creaturarum a Deo, et ideo sigillatim enumerat; Ioannes vero ad altiorem festinans materiam, in hoc

appropriation we say that the Father does all things by the Son, i.e., by his wisdom. And so Augustine says that the phrase *from whom all things*, is appropriated to the Father; *through whom all things*, is appropriated to the Son; and *in whom all things*, is appropriated to the Holy Spirit. But if the **through** denotes causality from the standpoint of the thing produced, then the statement, *the Father does all things by the Son*, is not mere appropriation but proper to the Word, because the fact that he is a cause of creatures is had from someone else, namely the Father, from whom he has being.

However, it does not follow from this that the Word is the instrument of the Father, although whatever is moved by another for some operation, has the nature of an instrument. However, when I say that someone works through a power received from another, this can be understood in two ways. In one way, as meaning that the power both of the giver and of the receiver is numerically one and the same power; and in this way the one operating through a power received from another is not inferior but equal to the one from whom he receives it. Therefore, since it is the same power which the Father has and which he gives to the Son, and through which the Son works, when it is said that the Father works through the Son, one should not on that account say that the Son is inferior to the Father or is his instrument. This would be the case, rather, in those who receive from another not the same power, but another and created one.

And so it is plain that neither the Holy Spirit nor the Son are causes of the Father's working, and that neither is the minister or instrument of the Father, as Origen raved.

77. If we carefully consider the words, ***all things were made through him***, we can clearly see that the Evangelist spoke with the utmost exactitude.

For whoever makes something must preconceive it in his wisdom, which is the form and pattern of the thing made: as the form preconceived in the mind of an artisan is the pattern of the cabinet to be made. So, God makes nothing except through the conception of his intellect, which is an eternally conceived wisdom, that is, the Word of God, and the Son of God. Accordingly, it is impossible that he should make anything except through the Son. And so Augustine says in *The Trinity*, that the Word is the art full of the living patterns of all things. Thus it is clear that all things which the Father makes, he makes through him.

78. It should be remarked that, according to Chrysostom, all the things which Moses enumerates individually in God's production of things, saying, *and God said, 'let there be light'* (Gen 1:3), and *'let there be a firmament'* (Gen 1:6), and so forth, all these the Evangelist transcends and embraces in one phrase, saying, ***all things were made through him***.

The reason is that Moses wished to teach the emanation of creatures from God; hence he enumerated them one by one. But John, hastening toward loftier things, intends in

libro intendit nos inducere specialiter in cognitionem ipsius Creatoris.

79. Deinde dicit *et sine ipso factum est nihil*. Haec est secunda clausula quam quidam perverse intellexerunt, ut dicit Augustinus in Lib. *de Nat. Boni*. Nam, ex hoc modo loquendi quo Ioannes hic utitur, ponens hoc quod dicitur *nihil* in fine orationis, crediderunt ipsum nihil teneri affirmative, quasi nihil sit aliquid, quod sine Verbo factum sit; unde voluerunt quod haec clausula posita sit ab Evangelista ad excludendum aliquid quod a Verbo non sit factum. Unde dicunt quod postquam Evangelista dixerat *omnia per ipsum facta sunt*, consequenter adiungit *et sine ipso factum est nihil* quasi dicat: ita dico omnia per ipsum facta esse, quod tamen sine ipso factum est aliquid, scilicet ipsum *nihil*.

80. Ex hoc autem processit triplex haeresis, scilicet Valentini, qui, ut dicit Origenes, ponit multa principia, et ex illis principiis dicit procedere triginta saecula. Prima tamen principia quae ponit, sunt duo, scilicet Profundum, quod vocat Deum Patrem, et Silentium. Ex his duobus dicit processisse decem saecula. Ex Profundo autem, et Silentio dicit esse alia duo principia, scilicet Intellectum et Veritatem, ex quibus processerunt octo saecula. Ex Intellectu autem et Veritate dicit esse alia duo principia, scilicet Verbum et Vitam, ex quibus procedunt duodecim saecula, et sic sunt triginta. Ex Verbo autem et Vita, secundum aevum, processit homo Christus, et Ecclesia. Sic ergo Valentinus ponebat prolationem Verbi multa saecula praecessisse.

Et ideo dicit quod, quia Evangelista dixerat *omnia per ipsum facta sunt*, ne aliquis intelligeret illa saecula praecedentia esse perfecta per Verbum, consequenter adiunxit *et sine ipso factum est nihil*, idest omnia saecula praeexistentia et quae in eis fuerunt; quae ideo Ioannes vocat *nihil*, quia humanam rationem excedunt, nec possunt capi per intellectum.

81. Secundus error, ex hoc procedens, fuit Manichaei, qui ponebat duo contraria principia, unum scilicet rerum incorruptibilium, et aliud corruptibilium. Dicit ergo quod postquam Ioannes dixerat *omnia per ipsum facta sunt*, ne crederetur Verbum esse corruptibilium rerum causam, statim subiunxit *et sine ipso factum est nihil*, idest corruptioni subiecta, quae *nihil* esse dicuntur, quia eorum esse est continue transmutari in nihil.

82. Tertius error est eorum qui volunt quod per *nihil* intelligatur diabolus, iuxta illud Iob XVIII, 15: *habitent in tabernaculo eius socii eius, qui non est*. Dicunt ergo omnia esse facta per Verbum, praeter diabolum. Et ideo exponunt *sine ipso factum est nihil*, idest diabolus.

83. Sed omnes isti tres errores ex uno fonte procedentes, scilicet ex hoc quod ipsum *nihil* volunt affirmative accipi, excluduntur per hoc quod *nihil* non ponitur

this book to lead us specifically to a knowledge of the Creator himself.

79. Then he says, *and without him was made nothing*. This is the second clause which some have distorted, as Augustine says in his work, *The Nature of the Good*. Because of John's manner of speaking here, they believed that he was using *nothing* in an affirmative sense; as though nothing was something which was made without the Word. And so they claimed that this clause was added by the Evangelist in order to exclude something which was not made by the Word. They say that the Evangelist, having said that *all things were made through him*, added *and without him was made nothing*. It was as if to say: I say that all things were made through him in such a way that still something was made without him, that is, the *nothing*.

80. Three heresies came from this. First, that of Valentine. He affirmed, as Origen says, a multitude of principles, and taught that from them came thirty eras. The first principles he postulates are two: the Deep, which he calls God the Father, and Silence. And from these proceed ten eras. But from the Deep and from Silence, he says, there are two other principles, Mind and Truth; and from these issued eight eras. Then from Mind and Truth, there are two other principles, Word and Life; and from these issued twelve eras; thus making a total of thirty. Finally, from the Word and Life there proceeded in time, the man Christ and the Church. In this way Valentine affirmed many eras previous to the issuing forth of the Word.

And so he said that because the Evangelist had stated that *all things were made through him*, then, lest anyone think that those previous eras had been effected through the Word, he added, *and without him was made nothing*, i.e., all the preceding eras and all that had existed in them. All of these John calls *nothing*, because they transcend human reason and cannot be grasped by the intellect.

81. The second error to arise from this was that of Manichaeus, who affirmed two opposing principles: one is the source of incorruptible things, and the other of corruptible things. He said that after John had stated that *all things were made through him*, then, lest it be thought that the Word is the cause of corruptible things, he immediately added, *and without him was made nothing*, i.e., things subject to corruption, which are called *nothing* because their being consists in being continually transformed into nothing.

82. The third error is that of those who claim that by *nothing* we should understand the devil, about whom is said: *may the companions of him who is not dwell in his house* (Job 18:15). And so they say that all things except the devil were made through the Word. In this way they explain, *without him was made nothing*, that is, the devil.

83. All these three errors, arising as they do from the same source, namely, taking *nothing* in a positive sense, are excluded by the fact that *nothing* in not used here in an

hic affirmative, sed negative tantum. Ut sit sensus: ita facta sunt omnia per Verbum, quod nihil est participans esse, quod non sit factum per ipsum.

84. Sed instabit forsitan aliquis, dicens hanc clausulam superflue fuisse appositam, si intelligatur negative, eo quod Evangelista dicens, *omnia per ipsum facta sunt*, sufficienter videtur dixisse non esse aliquid quod non sit factum per Verbum.

Ad quod dicendum quod secundum multos introducta est haec particula multipliciter, ex multis de causis. Quarum una causa est, secundum Chrysostomum, ne aliquis legens in Veteri Testamento et inveniens solum visibilia enumerata a Moyse in creatione rerum, crederet illa tantum facta esse per Verbum.

Ideo Evangelista, dum dixisset *omnia per ipsum facta sunt*, quae scilicet enumerat Moyses, ideo consequenter adiunxit *sine ipso factum est nihil*; quasi dicat: nihil eorum quae sunt, sive visibile sive invisibile, est factum sine Verbo. Et hoc modo loquitur Apostolus, Col. I, 16, dicens omnia condita esse in Christo, sive visibilia, sive invisibilia: ubi Apostolus specialiter mentionem facit de invisibilibus, quia de eis Moyses aperte mentionem non fecerat, propter ruditatem illius populi, qui supra sensibilia elevari non poterat.

Introducitur etiam, secundum Chrysostomum, alio modo sic. Posset enim aliquis legens Evangelium, multa signa et miracula facta per Christum, sicut illud Matth. XI, 5: *caeci vident, claudi ambulant, leprosi mundantur* etc., credere per hoc quod dicit Ioannes *omnia per ipsum facta sunt*, debere intelligi omnia illa tantum quae in illis Evangeliis continentur, et nihil aliud factum per ipsum. Et ideo ne hoc suspicetur quis, consequenter Evangelista inducit *et sine ipso factum est nihil*; quasi dicat: non solum ea quae in Evangeliis continentur, sunt facta per ipsum, sed nihil eorum quae facta sunt, est factum sine ipso. Et sic, secundum Chrysostomum, haec particula introducitur ad ostendendum totalem causalitatem, et est quasi completiva praemissae.

85. Secundum Hilarium vero introducitur haec particula ad ostendendum quod Verbum habet virtutem operativam ab alio. Quia enim Evangelista dixerat *omnia per ipsum facta sunt*, posset intelligi Patrem excludi ab omni causalitate; ideo consequenter addit *et sine ipso factum est nihil*. Quasi dicat: sic per eum facta sunt omnia, ut tamen Pater cum eo omnia fecerit. Nam tantum valet *sine* eo, ac si dicatur non solus; ut sit sensus: non ipse solus est per quem facta sunt omnia, sed ipse est alius, sine quo factum est nihil. Quasi dicat *sine ipso*,

affirmative, but in a merely negative sense: the sense being that all things were made through the Word in such a way that there is nothing participating in existence that was not made through him.

84. Perhaps someone will object and say that it was superfluous to add this clause, if it is to be understood negatively, on the ground that the Evangelist, in stating that *all things were made through him*, seems to have already said adequately enough that there is not something that was not made through the Word.

The answer to this is that, according to many expositors, this clause was added in many ways for a number of reasons. One of these reasons is, according to Chrysostom, so that no one reading the Old Testament and finding only visible things listed by Moses in the creation of things, would think that these were the only things made through the Word.

And so, the Evangelist, after he had said, *all things were made through him*, namely, those that Moses listed, the Evangelist then added, *and without him was made nothing*, as though he were saying: none of the things which exist, whether visible or invisible, was made without the Word. Indeed, the Apostle also speaks in this way (Col 1:16), saying that all things, visible and invisible, were created in Christ; and here the Apostle makes specific mention of invisible things because Moses had made no express mention of them on account of the lack of erudition of that people, who could not be raised above the things of sense.

Chrysostom also gives another reason why this clause was added. For someone reading in the Gospel of the many signs and miracles worked by Christ, such as, *the blind see, the lame walk, lepers are cleansed* (Matt 11:5), might believe that in saying, *all things were made through him*, John meant that only the things mentioned in those Gospels, and nothing else, were made through him. So lest anyone suspect this, the Evangelist adds, *and without him was made nothing*. As if to say: not only all the things contained in the Gospels were made through him, but none of the things that were made, was made without him. And so, according to Chrysostom, this clause is added to bring out his total causality, and serves, as it were, to complete his previous statement.

85. According to Hilary, however, this clause is introduced to show that the Word has operative power from another. For since the Evangelist had said, *all things were made through him*, it might be supposed that the Father is excluded from all causality. For that reason he added, *and without him was made nothing*. As if to say: all things were made through him, but in such a way that the Father made all things with him. For *without him* is equivalent to saying, not alone, so that the meaning is: it is not he alone through whom all things were made, but he is the other one without

cum alio operante, scilicet Patre, *factum est nihil*; iuxta illud Prov. VIII, 30: *cum eo eram cuncta componens.*

86. In quadam autem homilia quae incipit, *vox spiritualis aquilae*, et attribuitur Origeni, invenitur alia expositio satis pulchra.

Dicitur enim ibi quod in Graeco est thoris, ubi in Latino habemus *sine*. Thoris autem idem est quod 'foris' vel 'extra'; quasi dicat ita *omnia per ipsum facta sunt* quod extra ipsum *factum est nihil*. Et ideo hoc dicit ut ostendat, per Verbum et in Verbo omnia conservari; iuxta illud Hebr. I, 3: *portans omnia verbo virtutis suae.*

Quaedam enim sunt quae non indigent operante, nisi quantum ad fieri, cum possint substinere postquam fuerunt facta, absque agentis influxu; sicut domus indiget quidem artifice quantum ad suum fieri, sed tamen persistit in suo esse absque artificis influentia. Ne ergo credat aliquis, omnia per Verbum sic facta esse quod sit causa eorum quantum ad fieri solum, et non quantum ad conservationem in esse, ideo consequenter Evangelista subiunxit *et sine ipso factum est nihil*. Hoc est: nihil factum est extra ipsum, quia ipse ambit omnia, conservans ea.

87. Exponitur autem haec particula secundum Augustinum et Origenem et plures alios sic ut per *nihil* intelligatur peccatum.

Quia ergo cum diceret *omnia per ipsum facta sunt*, posset intelligi malum et peccatum per ipsum fieri; ideo consequenter adiunxit *et nihil*, idest peccatum, *est factum sine ipso*. Nam sicut ars non est principium sed causa alicuius defectus in artificiatis, sed per se est causa perfectionis ipsorum et formae, ita et Verbum, quod est ars Patris, plena rationum viventium, non est causa alicuius mali vel inordinationis in rebus, et praecipue mali culpae, quod habet perfectam rationem mali; sed huius mali causa per se est voluntas creaturae, sive hominis sive angeli, libere declinans a fine, ad quem naturaliter ordinatur. Operans secundum artem, voluntarie errans, est causa defectuum incidentium in artificiatis, non per artem, sed per voluntatem. Unde in talibus ars non est principium seu causa defectuum, sed voluntas: et ideo malum est defectus voluntatis, et non artis alicuius: et ideo inquantum tale, nihil est.

88. Sic ergo ista particula additur ad ostendendum ipsius Verbi universalem causalitatem secundum Chrysostomum, societatem ad Patrem, secundum Hilarium et virtutem Verbi in conservando, secundum Origenem. Item puritatem causalitatis: quia sic est causa bonorum, quod non est causa peccati, secundum Augustinum et Origenem et plures alios.

89. Deinde dicit *quod factum est, in ipso vita erat*. Hic ponitur tertia particula, ubi cavendus est falsus

whom nothing was made. It is as if he said: *without him*, with another working, i.e., with the Father, *was made nothing*, as it says, *I was with him forming all things* (Prov 8:30).

86. In a certain homily attributed to Origen, and which begins, *the spiritual voice of the eagle*, we find another rather beautiful exposition.

It says there that the Greek has *thoris* where the Latin has *without*. Now *thoris* is the same as 'outside' or 'outside of.' It is as if he had said: *all things were made through him* in such a way that outside him *was made nothing*. And so he says this to show that all things are conserved through the Word and in the Word: *he sustains all things by his powerful word* (Heb 1:3).

Now there are certain things that do not need their producer except to bring them into existence, since after they have been produced they are able to subsist without any further activity on the part of the producer. For example, a house needs a builder if it is to come into existence, but it continues to exist without any further action on the part of the builder. So lest anyone suppose that all things were made through the Word in such a way that he is merely the cause of their production and not of their continuation in existence, the Evangelist added, *and without him was made nothing*, i.e., nothing was made outside of him, because he encompasses all things, preserving them.

87. This clause is also explained by Augustine and Origen and several others in such a way that *nothing* indicates sin.

Accordingly, because *all things were made through him* might be interpreted as including evil and sin, he added, *and without him was made nothing*, i.e., sin. For just as art is not the principle or cause of the defects in its products, but is through itself the cause of their perfection and form, so the Word, who is the art of the Father, full of living archetypes, is not the cause of any evil or disarrangement in things, particularly of the evil of sin, which carries the full notion of evil. The *per se* cause of this evil is the will of the creature, either a man or an angel, freely declining from the end to which it is ordained by its nature. One who can act in virtue of his art but purposely violates it, is the cause of the defects occurring in his works, not by reason of his art, but by reason of his will. So in such cases, his art is not the source or cause of the defects, but his will is. Consequently, evil is a defect of the will and not of any art. And so to the extent that it is such, it is nothing.

88. So then, this clause is added to show the universal causality of the Word, according to Chrysostom; his association with the Father, according to Hilary; the power of the Word in the preserving of things, according to Origen; and finally, the purity of his causality, because he is so the cause of good as not to be the cause of sin, according to Augustine, Origen, and a number of others.

89. Then he says, *what was made in him was life*; and this is the third clause. Here we must avoid the false

intellectus Manichaei, qui ex hoc verbo motus est ad dicendum quod omnia quae sunt, vivunt; puta lapis, lignum, et homo, et quicquid aliud est in mundo. Et punctabat sic: *quod factum est in ipso*, distingue, *erat vita*. Sed non erat vita nisi viveret; ergo quicquid factum est in ipso, vivit. Vult etiam quod *in ipso* idem sit ac si dicatur per ipsum, cum communiter in Scriptura in ipso, vel per ipsum accipiatur; sicut illud Col. I, 16: *in ipso, et per ipsum condita sunt omnia.*

Sed hunc intellectum ista expositio ostendit esse falsum.

90. Potest tamen sine errore multipliciter exponi. Nam in illa homilia *Vox spiritualis* exponitur sic: *quod factum est in ipso*, idest per ipsum, hoc vita erat non in seipso sed in sua causa. In omnibus enim causatis hoc commune est, quod effectus, sive per naturam sive per voluntatem producti, sunt in suis causis non secundum proprium esse, sed secundum virtutem propriae suae causae; sicut effectus inferiores sunt in sole ut in causa, non secundum eorum esse, sed secundum virtutem solis. Quia ergo causa omnium effectuum productorum a Deo, est vita quaedam et ars plena rationum viventium, ideo omne, *quod factum est in ipso*, idest per ipsum, *vita erat* in sua causa, scilicet in ipso Deo.

91. Augustinus autem aliter legit, sic punctando: *quod factum est*, distingue, *in ipso vita erat.*

Res enim dupliciter considerari possunt, secundum scilicet quod sunt in seipsis et secundum quod sunt in Verbo. Si considerentur secundum quod sunt in seipsis, sic non omnes res sunt vita nec etiam viventes, sed aliquae carent vita, aliquae vivunt. Sicut facta est terra, facta sunt etiam et metalla, quae nec vita sunt, nec vivunt; facta sunt animalia, facti sunt homines, quae secundum quod sunt in seipsis, non sunt vita, sed vivunt solum.

Si vero considerentur secundum quod sunt in Verbo, non solum sunt viventes, sed etiam vita. Nam rationes in sapientia Dei spiritualiter existentes, quibus res factae sunt ab ipso Verbo, sunt vita: sicut arca facta per artificem in se quidem nec vivit nec vita est, ratio vero arcae, quae praecessit in mente artificis, vivit quodammodo, inquantum habet esse intelligibile in mente artificis, non tamen est vita, quia per ipsum intelligere artificis non est in sua essentia, neque suum esse. In Deo autem suum intelligere est sua vita et sua essentia: et ideo quicquid est in Deo, non solum vivit sed est ipsa vita, quia quicquid est in Deo, est sua essentia. Unde creatura in Deo est creatrix essentia. Si ergo considerentur res secundum quod in Verbo sunt, vita sunt.

Hanc expositionem habes alibi.

interpretation of Manichaeus, who was led by this to maintain that everything that exists is alive: for example, stones, wood, men, and anything else in the world. He understood the clause this way: *what was made in him*, comma, *was life*. But it was not life unless alive. Therefore, whatever was made in him is alive. He also claimed that *in him* is the same as saying through him, since very often in Scripture *in him* and *through him* are interchangeable, as in *in him and through him all things were created* (Col 1:16).

However, our present explanation shows that this interpretation is false.

90. There are, nevertheless, a number of ways to explain it without error. In that homily, *The Spiritual Voice*, we find this explanation: *what was made in him*, i.e., through him, *was life*, not in each thing itself, but in its cause. For in the case of all things that are caused, it is always true that effects, whether produced by nature or by will, exist in their causes, not according to their own existence, but according to the power of their appropriate cause. Thus, lower effects are in the sun as in their cause, not according to their respective existences but according to the power of the sun. Therefore, since the cause of all effects produced by God is a certain life and an art full of living archetypes, for this reason *what was made in him*, i.e., through him, *was life*, in its cause, i.e., in God.

91. Augustine reads this another way, as: *what was made*, distinguished from *in him was life*.

For things can be considered in two ways: as they are in themselves, and as they are in the Word. If they are considered as they are in themselves, then it is not true that all things are life or even alive, but some lack life and some are alive. For example, the earth was made and metals were made, but none is life, none is living; animals and men were made, and these, considered in themselves, are not life, but merely living.

Yet considered as they are in the Word, they are not merely living, but also life. For the archetypes which exist spiritually in the wisdom of God, and through which things were made by the Word, are life, just as a chest made by an artisan is in itself neither alive nor life, yet the exemplar of the chest in the artisan's mind prior to the existence of the chest is in some sense living, insofar as it has an intellectual existence in the mind of the artisan. Nevertheless it is not life, because it is neither in his essence nor is it his existence through the act of understanding of the artisan. But in God, his act of understanding is his life and his essence. And so whatever is in God is not only living, but is life itself, because whatever is in God is his essence. Hence the creature in God is the creating essence. Thus, if things are considered as they are in the Word, they are life.

This is explained in another place.

92. Origenes vero super Ioannem legit hoc aliter, punctando sic: *quod factum est in ipso*, distingue, *vita erat*.

Ubi notandum est quod de Filio Dei dicitur aliquid, secundum se, sicut dicitur Deus omnipotens, et huiusmodi; aliquid vero dicitur de eo per comparationem ad nos, sicut Salvator et Redemptor; aliquid vero utroque modo, sicut sapientia et iustitia. In omnibus autem quae absolute et secundum se de Filio dicuntur, non dicitur quod sit factus, sicut non dicitur Filius factus Deus, neque omnipotens; sed in illis quae dicuntur in comparatione ad nos, seu utroque modo, potest addi adiunctio facti, ut dicatur secundum illud I Cor. I, 30: *qui factus est nobis a Deo sapientia, et iustificatio, et sanctificatio, et redemptio*. Et sic, licet semper fuerit in seipso sapientia et iustitia, tamen potest dici quod de novo factus est nobis iustitia et sapientia.

Secundum hoc ergo Origenes exponens dicit quod quamvis in seipso sit vita, tamen nobis factus est vita per hoc quod nos vivificavit, iuxta illud I Cor. XV, 22: *sicut in Adam omnes moriuntur, ita et in ipso omnes vivificabuntur*. Et ideo dicit quod *Verbum quod factum est* nobis vita, *in ipso vita erat*, ut quandoque nobis fieret vita; et ideo statim subdit *et vita erat lux hominum*.

93. Hilarius enim sic punctat *et sine ipso factum est nihil, quod factum est in ipso*, et postea dicatur *vita erat*. Quia ipse dicit in *II de Trin.* cum dicit Evangelista *et factum est nihil*, posset esse ambiguum an quaedam alia adhuc quae per ipsum facta sunt, fuerunt facta non per ipsum, non tamen sine ipso; sed in eis associavit facientem; et hanc clausulam esse additam ad correptionem praecedentis. Ne ergo hoc intelligeretur, ideo Evangelista cum dixisset *omnia per ipsum facta sunt*, subiungit *et sine ipso factum est nihil, quod tamen factum est in ipso*, idest per ipsum: et ratio huius est, quia *vita erat*.

Manifestum est enim quod hoc modo omnia dicuntur per Verbum facta, inquantum Verbum ex Patre procedens est Deus. Ponamus autem quod aliquis pater filium habeat, qui non sit perfecte habens operationes hominis, sed paulatim ad hoc perveniat, manifestum est quod multa faciet, non per ipsum Filium, licet non sine eo. Quia ergo Filius Dei eamdem vitam habuit ab aeterno, quam et Pater, secundum illud infra V, 26: *sicut Pater habet vitam in semetipso, sic dedit et Filio vitam habere in semetipso*, ideo non potest dici quod Deus Pater, etsi nihil fecerit sine Filio, tamen fecit aliqua non per ipsum, quia vita erat. In viventibus enim quae vitam participant, potest contingere quod vita imperfecta praecedat vitam perfectam; sed in per se vita, quae non participat vitam, sed est absolute et simpliciter vita, nullo modo potest imperfectio aliqua esse. Quia ergo Verbum est per se vita, numquam fuit in eo vita imperfecta, sed semper

92. Origen, commenting on John, gives another reading, thus: *what was made in him*; and then, *was life*.

Here we should note that some things are said of the Son of God as such; for example, that he is God, omnipotent, and the like. And some things are said of him in relation to ourselves; for example, we say he is savior and redeemer. Some things are said in both ways, such as wisdom and justice. Now in all things said absolutely and of the Son as such, it is not said that he was made, for example, we do not say that the Son was made God or omnipotent. But in things said in reference to us, or in both ways, the notion of being made can be used, as in, *God made him our wisdom, our justice, our sanctification and redemption* (1 Cor 1:30). And so, although he was always wisdom and justice in himself, yet it can be said that he was newly made justice and wisdom for us.

And so Origen, explaining it along these lines, says that although in himself the Son is life, yet he was made life for us by the fact that he gave us life, as is said, *just as in Adam all die, so in Christ all will come to life* (1 Cor 15:22). And so he says *the Word that was made* life for us *in himself was life*, so that after a time he could become life for us; and so he immediately adds, *and the life was the light of men*.

93. But Hilary interprets thus: *and without him was made nothing, that was made in him*, and later it says, *he was life*. For he says (*On the Trinity II*) that when the Evangelist says *without him was made nothing*, one might be perplexed and ask whether there are still other things made by him, that were not made through him, although not without him, but with respect to which he was associated with the maker; and this clause is added to correct the aforesaid error. Therefore lest this be so understood, when the Evangelist says, *all things were made through him*, he adds, *and without him was made nothing, that was made*, *in him*, that is, through him; and the reason for this is that *he was life*.

For it is plain that all things are said to have been made through the Word inasmuch as the Word, who proceeds from the Father, is God. But let us suppose that some father has a son who does not perfectly exercise the operations of a man, but reaches such a state gradually. In that case the father will do many things, not through the son, yet not without him. Since, therefore, the Son of God has from all eternity the same life that the Father has, *for as the Father has life in himself, so he has also given to the Son to have life in himself* (John 5:26), one cannot say that God the Father, although he made nothing without the Son, nevertheless made some things not through him, because he was life. For in living things which participate life, it can happen that imperfect life precedes perfect life; but in life *per se*, which does not participate life but is simply and absolutely life, there can be no imperfection at all. Accordingly, because the Word is life *per se*, there was never imperfect life

perfecta; et ideo ita *nihil factum est sine eo*, quod tamen non sit factum *in ipso*, idest per ipsum.

94. Chrysostomus autem aliud modum legendi habet, et punctat sic: *et sine ipso factum est nihil quod factum est*. Et ratio huius est, quia aliquis posset credere quod Spiritus Sanctus esset factus per Verbum.

Et ideo Evangelista hoc volens excludere dicit *quod factum est*, quia Spiritus Sanctus non est quid factum; et postea sequitur *in ipso vita erat*; quod introducitur propter duo. Unum est ut post productionem omnium rerum ostendatur indeficientia causalitatis ad res non solum productas, sed etiam producendas. Quasi dicat *in ipso vita erat*, qua scilicet non solum omnia producere potuit, sed etiam quae habet indeficientem fluxum et causalitatem absque mutationis dispendio ad res continue producendas, utpote fons vivus qui non minoratur ex fluxu continuo; aqua vero collecta et non viva, cum defluit, minoratur et deficit; unde dicitur in Ps. XXXV, 10: *apud te est fons vitae*. Secundum est ut ostendatur gubernatio rerum esse per Verbum. Quia enim *in ipso vita erat*, ostenditur quod non produxit res per necessitatem naturae, sed per voluntatem et intellectum, et quod res productas gubernat; Hebr. IV, 12: *vivus est sermo Dei* etc.

Et quia apud Graecos Chrysostomus est tantae auctoritatis in suis expositionibus, quod ubi ipse aliquid exposuit in Sacra Scriptura, nullam aliam expositionem admittant, ideo in omnibus libris Graecis invenitur sic punctatum, sicut punctat Chrysostomus, scilicet hoc modo: *sine ipso factum est nihil quod factum est*.

in him, but always perfect life. And so in such a way that *without him was made nothing* that was not also made *in him*, i.e., through him.

94. Chrysostom has a different reading and punctuation, thus: *and without him was made nothing that was made*. The reason for this is that someone might believe that the Holy Spirit was made through the Word.

So to exclude this, the Evangelist says, *that was made*, because the Holy Spirit is not something that is made. And afterward follows, *in him was life*, which is introduced for two reasons. First, to show that after the creation of all things his causality was indefectible not only with respect to the things already produced, but also with respect to things yet to be produced. As if to say: *in him was life*, by which he could not only produce all things, but which has an unfailing flow and a causality for producing things continually without undergoing any change, being a living fountain which is not diminished in spite of its continuous outflow; whereas collected water, that is not living water, is diminished when it flows out, and is used up. So it is said, *with you is the fountain of life* (Ps 35:10). The second reason is to show that things are governed by the: Word. For since *in him was life*, this shows that he produced things by his intellect and will, not by a necessity of his nature, and that he governs the things he made: *the Word of God is living* (Heb 4:12).

Chrysostom is held in such esteem by the Greeks in his explanations that they admit no other where he expounded anything in Holy Scripture. For this reason, this passage in all the Greek works is found to be punctuated exactly as Chrysostom did, namely, *and without him was made nothing that was made*.

Lecture 3

^{1:4} in ipso vita erat. Et vita erat lux hominum. [n. 95]

^{1:5} Et lux in tenebris lucet, et tenebrae eam non comprehenderunt. [n. 102]

^{1:4} ἐν αὐτῷ ζωὴ ἦν, καὶ ἡ ζωὴ ἦν τὸ φῶς τῶν ἀνθρώπων·

^{1:5} καὶ τὸ φῶς ἐν τῇ σκοτίᾳ φαίνει, καὶ ἡ σκοτία αὐτὸ οὐ κατέλαβεν.

^{1:4} In him was life, and the life was the light of men. [n. 95]

^{1:5} And the light shines in darkness, and the darkness did not comprehend it. [n. 102]

---

95. Evangelista supra insinuavit virtutem Verbi, secundum quam omnia produxit in esse; hic vero insinuat eius virtutem, secundum quam se habet ad homines, dicens, hoc Verbum esse lucem hominibus. Ubi

primo introducit nobis lucem quamdam, cum dicit *et vita erat lux hominum*;

secundo lucis irradiationem, cum dicit *et lux in tenebris lucet*;

tertio lucis participationem, cum dicit *et tenebrae eam non comprehenderunt*.

Potest autem totum dupliciter exponi. Uno modo secundum influxum cognitionis naturalis; alio modo secundum communicationem gratiae.

Dicit ergo quantum ad primum, quod *vita erat lux hominum*.

96. Ubi primo considerandum est quod, secundum Augustinum et plures alios, nomen 'lucis' magis proprie dicitur in spiritualibus quam in sensibilibus. Ambrosius tamen vult quod splendor metaphorice dicatur de Deo. Sed in hoc non est magna vis facienda: nam de quocumque nomen *lucis* dicatur ad manifestationem refertur, sive illa manifestatio sit in intelligibilibus, sive in sensibilibus. Si ergo comparentur manifestatio intelligibilis et sensibilis, secundum naturam prius invenitur lux in spiritualibus; sed quoad nos, qui nomina rebus imponimus ex earum proprietatibus nobis notis, prius invenitur in sensibilibus, quia prius impositum est a nobis hoc nomen ad significandum lucem sensibilem, quam intelligibilem; quamvis secundum virtutem prius et verius conveniat spiritualibus quam sensibilibus.

97. Ad evidentiam autem eius quod dicitur *et vita erat lux hominum*, sciendum est quod multipliciter est gradus vitae. Quaedam namque vivunt, sed absque luce, quia nullam cognitionem habent, sicut sunt plantae: unde vita earum non est lux. Quaedam vero vivunt et cognoscunt; sed tamen eorum cognitio, cum sit sensus tantum, non est nisi particularium et materialium, sicut est in brutis: et ideo haec et vitam habent et lucem quamdam, sed non lucem hominum qui vivunt et cognoscunt non solum ipsa vera, sed ipsius veritatis rationem, sicut sunt creaturae rationales, quibus non solum manifestatur hoc vel illud, sed ipsa veritas quae manifestabilis est et manifestativa omnium.

95. Above, the Evangelist described the power of the Word insofar as he brought all things into existence; here he describes his power as it is related to men, saying that this Word is a light to men. Where

first, he introduces a certain light to us, at *and the life was the light of men*;

second, the light's irradiation, at *and the light shines in darkness*;

third, participation in the light, at *and the darkness did not comprehend it*.

This whole section may be explained in two ways: first, according to the influx of natural knowledge; second, according to the communication of grace.

As to the first point he says, *and the life was the light of men*.

96. Here we should note first that, according to Augustine and many others, 'light' is more properly said of spiritual things than of sensible things. Ambrose, however, thinks that brightness is said metaphorically of God. But this is not a great issue, for in whatever way the name *light* is used, it implies a manifestation, whether that manifesting concerns intelligible or sensible things. If we compare sensible and intelligible manifestation, then, according to the nature of things, light is found first in spiritual things. But for us, who give names to things on the basis of their properties as known to us, light is discovered first in sensible things, because we first used this name to signify sensible light before intelligible light; although as to power, light belongs to spiritual things in a prior and truer way than to sensible things.

97. To clarify the statement, *and the life was the light of men*, we should remark that there are many grades of life. For some things live, but do so without light, because they have no knowledge; for example, plants. Hence their life is not light. Other things both live and know, but their knowledge, since it is on the sense level, is concerned only with individual and material things, as is the case with the brutes. So they have both life and a certain light. But they do not have the light of men, who live, and know, not only truths, but also the very nature of truth itself. Such are rational creatures, to whom not only this or that are made manifest, but truth itself, which can be manifested and is manifestive to all.

Et ideo Evangelista loquens de Verbo dicit non solum esse vitam, sed etiam esse *lucem*, ne intelligas vitam sine agnitione; *hominum* autem ne tantum cognitionem sensibilem suspiceris, qualis est in brutis.

98. Sed quare dixit *hominum*, cum etiam sit lux angelorum?

Ad hoc est duplex responsio. Chrysostomus enim dicit quod Evangelista intendebat in isto Evangelio tradere nobis cognitionem de Verbo, secundum quod ad salutem hominum ordinatur; et ideo magis refert secundum suam intentionem ad homines quam ad angelos. Origenes vero dicit quod participatio huius lucis pertinet ad homines, inquantum sunt rationalis naturae; et ideo Evangelista dicens *erat lux hominum*, voluit intelligi omnis rationalis naturae.

99. In hoc etiam ostenditur perfectio et dignitas huius vitae, quia est intellectualis seu rationalis.

Cum enim illa dicuntur viventia, quae se aliquo modo movent, illa dicuntur vitam habere perfectam, quae perfecte seipsa movent; movere autem seipsum perfecte et proprie, in inferioribus creaturis soli homini convenit. Nam etsi alia ex seipsis ab aliquo principio intrinseco moveantur, non tamen illud principium se habet ad apposita; et ideo ex necessitate moventur, et non libere. Mota igitur a tali principio magis aguntur quam agunt. Homo vero, cum sit dominus sui actus, libere se movet ad omnia quae vult; et ideo homo habet vitam perfectam, et similiter quaelibet intellectus natura.

Vita ergo Verbi, quae est lux hominum, est vita perfecta.

100. Attenditur etiam in praemissis verbis congruus ordo: nam in naturali rerum ordine primo invenitur esse, et hoc primo Evangelista insinuavit, dicens *in principio erat Verbum*, secundo vivere, et hoc est quod sequitur *in ipso vita erat*, tertio intelligere, et hoc consequenter adiunxit *vita erat lux hominum*.

Unde, secundum Origenem, convenienter vitae attribuit lucem, quia lux nonnisi viventi attribui potest.

101. Est tamen notandum quod lux ad viventem dupliciter comparari potest, vel ut obiectum, vel ut participata, ut patet in visu exteriori. Oculus enim lucem exteriorem cognoscit tamquam obiectum, sed oportet ad hoc quod eam videat, quod participet aliquam lucem interiorem, per quam aptetur et disponatur oculus ad lucem exteriorem videndam.

Sic ergo, quod hic dicit *et vita erat lux hominum*, dupliciter potest intelligi. Ut dicatur *lux hominum* per modum obiecti quasi a solis hominibus conspicabilis; quia ipsam sola rationalis creatura conspicere potest, cum ipsa sola divinae visionis sit capax (Iob XXXV, v. 11: *docet nos super iumenta terrae, et super volucres caeli erudit nos*); quia licet alia animalia cognoscant aliqua quae vera

And so the Evangelist, speaking of the Word, not only says that he is life but also *light*, lest anyone suppose he means life without knowledge. And he says that he is the *light of men*, lest anyone suppose he meant only sensible knowledge, such as exists in the brutes.

98. But since he is also the light of angels, why did he say, *of men*?

Two answers have been given to this. Chrysostom says that the Evangelist intended in this Gospel to give us a knowledge of the Word precisely as directed to the salvation of men and therefore refers, in keeping with his aim, more to men than to angels. Origen, however, says that participation in this light pertains to men insofar as they have a rational nature; accordingly, when the Evangelist says, *the light of men*, he wants us to understand every rational nature.

99. We also see from this the perfection and dignity of this life, because it is intellectual or rational.

For whereas all things that in some way move themselves are called living, only those that perfectly move themselves are said to have perfect life; and among lower creatures only man moves himself, properly speaking, and perfectly. For although other things are moved by themselves by some inner principle, that inner principle is nevertheless not open to opposite alternatives; hence they are not moved freely but from necessity. As a result, those things that are moved by such a principle are more truly made to act than act themselves. But man, since he is master of his act, moves himself freely to all that he wills. Consequently, man has perfect life, as does every intellectual nature.

And so the life of the Word, which is the light of men, is perfect life.

100. We find a fitting order in the above. For in the natural order of things, existence is first; and the Evangelist implies this in his first statement, *in the beginning was the Word* (John 1:1). Second, comes life; and this is mentioned next, *in him was life*. Third comes understanding; and that is mentioned next; *and the life was the light of men*.

And, according to Origen, he fittingly attributes light to life because light can be attributed only to the living.

101. We should note that light can be related in two ways to what is living: as an object and as something in which they participate, as is clear in external sight. For the eyes know external light as an object, but if they are to see it, they must participate in an inner light by which the eyes are adapted and disposed for seeing the external light.

And so his statement, *and the life was the light of men*, can be understood in two ways. First, that the *light of men* is taken as an object that man alone can look upon, because the rational creature alone can see it, since he alone is capable of the vision of God who *teaches us more than the beasts of the earth, and enlightens us more than the birds of the air* (Job 35:11); for although other animals may know

sunt, solus tamen homo ipsam rationem veritatis cognoscit. Potest etiam dici *lux hominum* participata. Numquam enim ipsum Verbum et ipsam lucem conspicere possemus nisi per participationem eius, quae in ipso homine est, quae est superior pars animae nostrae, scilicet lux intellectiva, de qua dicitur in Ps. IV, 7: *signatum est super nos lumen vultus tui*, idest Filii tui, qui est facies tua, qua manifestaris.

102. Introduxit supra Evangelista lucem quamdam; nunc vero agit de ipsius irradiatione cum dicit *lux in tenebris lucet*.

Quod quidem dupliciter exponi potest, secundum duplicem acceptionem 'tenebrarum.'

Primo vero accipiamus *tenebras* naturalem defectum, ac creatae mentis. Nam, ita se habet mens ad lucem istam, de qua hic loquitur Evangelista, sicut se habet aer ad lucem solis: quia, licet aer capax sit lucis solis, tamen, in se consideratus, tenebra est. Et secundum hoc sensus est: *lux*, idest vita illa, quae est *lux hominum*, *in tenebris lucet*, scilicet in animabus et mentibus creatis, irradiando semper omnes. Iob III, 23: *viro cui abscondita est lux*.

Sed *tenebrae eam non comprehenderunt*, idest includere non potuerunt. Illud enim dicitur comprehendi, cuius fines concluduntur et conspiciuntur. Quia, sicut dicit Augustinus, attingere Deum mente, magna beatitudo est: comprehendere vero, impossibile est. *Tenebrae* ergo *eam non comprehenderunt*. Iob XXXVI, 26: *ecce Deus magnus vincens scientiam nostram*; Ier. XXXII, 19: *magnus consilio et incomprehensibilis cogitatu*.

Et haec expositio habetur in illa homilia quae incipit *vox spiritualis aquilae*.

103. Alio modo potest exponi accipiendo *tenebras*, secundum Augustinum, pro naturali insipientia hominum, quae tenebra dicitur. Eccle. II, 13: *vidi quia tantum praecederet sapientia stultitiam, quantum differt lux a tenebris*.

Ex eo ergo aliquis insipiens est quod privatur lumine sapientiae divinae. Sicut ergo mentes sapientum participatione istius divinae lucis et sapientiae lucidae sunt, ita eius privatione tenebrae sunt. Quod ergo quidam tenebrosi sint, non est ex defectu istius lucis; quia, inquantum est de se, in tenebris lucet et omnes irradiat; sed ideo insipientes privati sunt ea luce, quia *tenebrae eam non comprehenderunt*, idest non apprehenderunt, ad ipsius participationem eorum insipientia pertingere non valentes, ut post elati non durantes. Iob XXXVI, 32: *immanibus*, idest superbis, *abscondit lucem*, idest lumen sapientiae, *et annuntiat de eo amico suo, quod possessio eius sit, et ad eam possit ascendere*; Baruch III, 23: *viam autem sapientiae nescierunt, neque commemorati sunt semitas eius*.

certain things that are true, nevertheless, man alone knows the nature itself of truth. The *light of men* can also be taken as a light in which we participate. For we would never be able to look upon the Word and light itself except through a participation in it; and this participation is in man and is the superior part of our soul, i.e., the intellectual light, about which it is said, *the light of your countenance, O Lord, is marked upon us* (Ps 4:7), i.e., of your Son, who is your face, by whom you are manifested.

102. Having introduced a certain light, the Evangelist now considers its irradiation, saying, *and the light shines in the darkness*.

This can be explained in two ways, according to the two meanings of 'darkness.'

First, we might take *darkness* as a natural defect, that of the created mind. For the mind is to that light of which the Evangelist speaks here as air is to the light of the sun; because, although air is receptive of the light of the sun, considered in itself it is a darkness. According to this the meaning is: *the light*, i.e., that life which is the *light of men*, *shines in the darkness*, i.e., in created souls and minds, by always shedding its light on all: *on a man from whom the light is hidden* (Job 3:23).

And the darkness did not comprehend it, that is, it was not able to enclose it. For to comprehend something, is to enclose and understand its boundaries. As Augustine says, to reach God with the mind is a great happiness; but to comprehend him is impossible. And so, the darkness did not comprehend it. *Behold, God is great, exceeding our knowledge* (Job 36:26); as Jeremiah says *great in counsel, incomprehensible in thought* (Jer 32:19).

This explanation is found in that homily which begins, *the spiritual voice of the eagle*.

103. We can explain this passage in another way by taking *darkness* as Augustine does, for the natural lack of wisdom in man, which is called a darkness. *And I saw that wisdom excells folly as much as light excells knowledge* (Eccl 2:13).

Someone is without wisdom, therefore, because he lacks the light of divine wisdom. Consequently, just as the minds of the wise are lucid by reason of a participation in that divine light and wisdom, so by the lack of it they are darkness. Now the fact that some are darkness is not due to a defect in that light, since on its part it shines in the darkness and radiates upon all. Rather, the foolish are without that light because *the darkness did not comprehend it*, i.e., they did not apprehend it, not being able to attain a participation in it due to their foolishness; after having been lifted up, they did not persevere. *From the savage*, i.e., from the proud, *he hides his light*, i.e., the light of wisdom, *and shows his friend that it belongs to him, and that he may approach it* (Job 36:32); *they did not know the way to wisdom, nor did they remember her paths* (Bar 3:23).

Licet autem aliquae mentes sint tenebrosae, idest sapida et lucida sapientia privatae, nulla tamen adeo tenebrosa est quin aliquid lucis divinae participet. Quia quidquid veritatis a quocumque cognoscitur, totum est ex participatione istius lucis, quae in tenebris lucet, quia omne verum, a quocumque dicatur, a Spiritu Sancto est. Et tamen **tenebrae**, idest homines tenebrosi, **eam non comprehenderunt**, secundum veritatem.

Sic ergo exponitur ista clausula, secundum Origenem et secundum Augustinum.

104. Alio modo ab illo loco **et vita erat lux hominum**, exponitur secundum fluxum gratiae, quia irradiamur per Christum; et continuatur sic ad praecedentia.

Supra egit Evangelista de creatione rerum per Verbum, hic vero tractat de restauratione rationalis creaturae facta per Christum dicens: **et vita**, Verbi, **erat lux hominum**, communiter, et non Iudaeorum tantum; quia Filius Dei carnem assumere venit in mundum, ut illuminaret gratia et veritate omnes homines. Io. c. XVIII, 37: **in hoc natus sum, et ad hoc veni, ut testimonium perhibeam veritati**. Item, infra IX, 5: **quamdiu in mundo sum, lux sum mundi**. Et ideo non dicit *lux Iudaeorum*, quia licet olim tantum in Iudaea notus esset, tamen postea toti mundo innotuit; Is. XLIX, v. 6: *dedit te in lucem gentibus, ut sis salus mundo usque ad extremum terrae*.

Congrue etiam coniungit lucem et vitam dicens **et vita erat lux hominum**, ut ostendat ista duo, lucem scilicet et vitam, nobis provenisse per Christum. Vitam quidem per participationem gratiae; infra: **gratia et veritas per Iesum Christum facta est**; lucem vero per cognitionem veritatis et sapientiae.

105. Hoc autem quod dicit **lux in tenebris lucet**, potest secundum hanc expositionem exponi tripliciter, secundum quod tripliciter possumus accipere 'tenebras.'

Uno modo pro poena: nam quaelibet tristitia et afflictio cordis tenebra quaedam dici potest, sicut quodlibet gaudium lux; Mich. ult., v. 8: *cum sedero in tenebris et in afflictionibus, Dominus lux mea est*, idest gaudium et consolatio.

Dicit ergo Origenes: secundum **hoc lux in tenebris lucet**, idest Christus in mundum veniens, et corpus passibile et absque peccato habens *in similitudinem carnis*, secundum quod dicitur Rom. VIII, 3. Lux in carne, quae scilicet caro Christi, secundum quod in se habet similitudinem carnis peccati, tenebra dicitur. Quasi dicat: lux, idest Verbum Dei circumvelatum tenebris carnis, luxit in mundo, secundum illud Ez. XXXII, 7: *solem nube tegam*.

106. Secundo, accipiendo per **tenebras** Daemones, iuxta illud Eph. ult., 12: *non est nobis colluctatio adversus*

Although some minds are darkness, i.e., they lack savory and lucid wisdom, nevertheless no man is in such darkness as to be completely devoid of divine light, because whatever truth is know by anyone is due to a participation in that light which shines in the darkness; for every truth, no matter by whom it is spoken, comes from the Holy Spirit. Yet the **darkness**, i.e., men in darkness, **did not comprehend it**, apprehend it in truth.

This is the way to explain this clause according to Origen and Augustine.

104. Starting from **and the life was the light of men**, we can explain this according to the influx of grace, since we are illuminated by Christ; and he thus continues to excell.

After he had considered the creation of things through the Word, the Evangelist considers here the restoration of the rational creature through Christ, saying, **and the life**, of the Word, was the **light of men**, i.e., of all men in general, and not only of the Jews. For the Son of God assumed flesh and came into the world to illumine all men with grace and truth. **For this I was born, and for this I came into the world, that I should give testimony to the truth** (John 18:37); **as long as I am in the world, I am the light of the world** (John 9:5). So he does not say, *the light of the Jews*, because although previously he had been known only in Judea, he later became known to the world. *I have given you as a light to the nations, that you might be my salvation to the ends of the earth* (Isa 49:6).

It was fitting to join light and life by saying, **and the life was the light of men**, in order to show that these two have come to us through Christ: life, through a participation in grace, **grace and truth came through Jesus Christ** (John 1:17); and light, through a knowledge of truth and wisdom.

105. According to this explanation, **the light shines in the darkness**, can be expounded in three ways, in the light of the three meanings of 'darkness.'

In one way, we can take **darkness** for punishment. For any sadness and suffering of heart can be called a darkness, just as any joy can be called a light. *When I sit in darkness and in suffering the Lord is my light*, i.e., my joy and consolation (Mic 7:8).

And so Origen says: in this explanation, **the light shines in the darkness**, is Christ coming into the world, having a body capable of suffering and without sin, but *in the likeness of sinful flesh* (Rom 8:3). The light is in the flesh, that is, the flesh of Christ, which is called a darkness insofar as it has a likeness to sinful flesh. As if to say: the light, i.e., the Word of God, veiled about by the darkness of the flesh, shines on the world; *I will cover the sun with a cloud* (Ezek 32:7).

106. Second, we can take **darkness** to mean the devils, as in *our struggle is not against flesh and blood; but against*

carnem et sanguinem tantum, sed adversus principes et potestates, adversus mundi rectores tenebrarum harum.

Secundum hoc dicit: *lux*, idest Filius Dei, *in tenebris lucet*, idest in mundum descendit, ubi tenebrae, idest Daemones, dominabantur. Infra XII, 31: *princeps huius mundi, eiicietur foras. Et tenebrae*, idest Daemones, *eam non comprehenderunt*, idest eum obscurare non potuerunt tentando, ut patet Matth. IV.

107. Tertio accipiendo *tenebras* errores sive ignorantias, quibus totus mundus ante adventum Christi plenus erat, secundum quod dicit apostolus: *eratis aliquando tenebrae.*

Dicit ergo quod *lux*, idest Verbum Dei incarnatum, *in tenebris lucet*, idest hominibus mundi, erroris et ignorantiae tenebris obscuratis. Lc. I, 79: *illuminare his qui in tenebris et in umbra mortis sedent*; et Is. IX, 2: *populus qui sedebat in tenebris, vidit lucem magnam. Et tenebrae eum non comprehenderunt*, idest non vicerunt. Quia quantumcumque homines peccatis obscurati, invidia excaecati, superbia tenebrosi, contra Christum pugnaverunt, ut patet ex Evangelio, exprobrando scilicet, iniurias et contumelias inferendo, et tandem occidendo, non tamen *eum comprehenderunt*; idest non vicerunt eum obscurando, quin eius claritas per totum mundum fulgeret. Sap. VII, 29: *luci comparata invenitur prior: illi enim succedit nox, sapientiam autem*, idest Filium Dei incarnatum, *non vincit malitia*, Iudaeorum scilicet et haereticorum; quia, ut dicitur Sap. X, 12, *certamen forte dedit illi, ut vinceret, et sciret quoniam omnium potentior est sapientia.*

principalities and powers, against the rulers of the world of this darkness (Eph 6:12).

Looked at this way he says, *the light*, i.e., the Son of God, *shines in the darkness*, i.e., has descended into the world where darkness, i.e., the devils, hold sway: *now shall the prince of this world be cast out* (John 12:31). *And the darkness*, i.e., the devils, *did not comprehend it*, i.e., were unable to obscure him by their temptations (Matt 4).

107. Third, we can take *darkness* for the error or ignorance which filled the whole world before the coming of Christ, *you were at one time darkness* (Eph 5:8).

And so he says that *the light*, i.e., the incarnate Word of God, *shines in the darkness*, i.e., upon the men of the world, who are blinded by the darkness or error and ignorance. *To enlighten those who sit in darkness and in the shadow of death* (Luke 1:79), *the people who were sitting in darkness saw a great light* (Isa 9:2). *And the darkness did not comprehend it*, i.e., did not overcome him. For in spite of the number of men darkened by sin, blinded by envy, shadowed over by pride, who have struggled against Christ, as is plain from the Gospel, by upbraiding him, heaping insults and calumnies upon him, and finally killing him, nevertheless they *did not comprehend it*, i.e., gain the victory of so obscuring him that his brightness would not shine throughout the whole world. Wisdom says, *compared to light, she takes precedence, for night supplants it, but wisdom*, that is, the incarnate Son of God, *is not overcome by wickedness* (Wis 7:30), that is, of the Jews and of heretics, because it says, *she gave him the prize for his stern struggle that he might know that wisdom is mightier than all else* (Wis 10:12).

Lecture 4

^{1:6} **Fuit homo missus a Deo, cui nomen erat Ioannes:** [n. 109]

^{1:7} **hic venit in testimonium, ut testimonium perhiberet de lumine, ut omnes crederent per illum.** [n. 115]

^{1:8} **Non erat ille lux, sed ut testimonium perhiberet de lumine.** [n. 118]

^{1:6} Ἐγένετο ἄνθρωπος, ἀπεσταλμένος παρὰ θεοῦ, ὄνομα αὐτῷ Ἰωάννης·

^{1:7} οὗτος ἦλθεν εἰς μαρτυρίαν ἵνα μαρτυρήσῃ περὶ τοῦ φωτός, ἵνα πάντες πιστεύσωσιν δι' αὐτοῦ.

^{1:8} οὐκ ἦν ἐκεῖνος τὸ φῶς, ἀλλ' ἵνα μαρτυρήσῃ περὶ τοῦ φωτός.

^{1:6} **There was a man sent from God, whose name was John.** [n. 109]

^{1:7} **He came as a witness, that he might bear witness to the light, so that through him all men might believe.** [n. 115]

^{1:8} **He was not the light, but that he might bear witness to the light.** [n. 118]

---

108. Supra Evangelista egit de Verbi divinitate; in parte vero ista incipit agere de Verbi incarnatione:

et circa hoc duo facit.

Primo agit de teste Verbi incarnati seu praecursore;

secundo de adventu Verbi, ibi *erat lux vera.*

Circa primum duo facit.

Primo describit praecursorem in testimonium venientem;

secundo ostendit eum ad salvandum insufficientem, ibi *non erat ille lux.*

Praecursorem autem describit quadrupliciter.

Primo a naturae conditione, cum dicit *fuit homo*;

secundo ab auctoritate, cum dicit *missus a Deo*;

tertio ab officii idoneitate, cum dicit *cui nomen erat Ioannes*;

quarto ab officii dignitate, ibi *hic venit.*

109. Considerandum autem est circa primum, quod statim cum Evangelista incipit de aliquo temporali, mutat modum loquendi. Cum enim supra loqueretur de aeternis, utebatur hoc verbo *erat*, quod est praeteriti imperfecti, ostendens per hoc, aeterna interminata esse; nunc vero, cum loquitur de temporalibus, utitur hoc verbo, *fuit*, ad ostendendum quod temporalia sic praeterierunt quod tamen terminantur.

110. Dicit ergo *fuit homo*; per quod in principio excludit perversam opinionem haereticorum, contra conditionem seu naturam Ioannis, qui, propter id quod Dominus, Matth. c. XI, 10, dicit de Ioanne: *hic est de quo scriptum est: ecce mitto angelum meum ante faciem meam*, et etiam Mc. I, 2 dicitur de ipso, opinati sunt quod Ioannes fuisset natura angelus. Quod excludens Evangelista dicit *fuit homo*, natura, non angelus. Eccle. c. VI, 10: *scitur quod sit homo, et quod non possit contra fortiorem se in iudicio contendere.*

108. Above, the Evangelist considered the divinity of the Word; here he begins to consider the incarnation of the Word.

And he does two things concerning this:

first, he treats of the witness to the incarnate Word, or the precursor;

second, of the coming of the Word, at **he was the true light** (John 1:9).

As to the first, he does two things:

first, he describes the precursor who comes to bear witness;

second, he shows that he was incapable of the work of our salvation, at **he was not the light.**

He describes the precursor in four ways.

First, according to his nature, **there was a man.**

Second, as to his authority, **sent from God.**

Third, as to his suitability for the office, **whose name was John.**

Fourth, as to the dignity of his office, **he came as a witness.**

109. We should note with respect to the first that, as soon as the Evangelist begins speaking of something temporal, he changes his manner of speech. When speaking above of eternal things, he used the word **was**, which is the past imperfect tense; and this indicates that eternal things are without end. But now, when he is speaking of temporal things, he uses **there was**; this indicates temporal things as having taken place in the past and coming to an end there.

110. And so he says, **there was a man.** This excludes at the very start the incorrect opinion of certain heretics who were in error on the condition or nature of John. They believed that John was an angel in nature, basing themselves on the words of the Lord, *I send my messenger before you, who will prepare your way* (Matt 11:10); and the same thing is found elsewhere (Mark 1:2). But the Evangelist rejects this, saying, **there was a man** by nature, not an angel. *The nature of man is known, and that he cannot contend in judgment with one who is stronger than himself* (Eccl 6:10).

Convenienter autem homo ad homines mittitur, per quem homines magis alliciuntur, utpote per sibi similem; unde dicitur Hebr. c. VII, 28: *lex enim homines constituit sacerdotes infirmitatem habentes.* Poterat enim Deus homines gubernare per angelos; sed maluit per homines, ut ipsorum exemplo magis instruerentur. Et ideo Ioannes homo fuit, et non angelus.

111. Ex auctoritate quidem describitur, cum dicit *missus a Deo.*

Equidem, licet Ioannes natura non fuerit angelus, fuit tamen officio, quia *missus a Deo.* Proprium enim angelorum officium est quod a Deo mittantur, et sint nuntii Dei; Hebr. I, 14: *omnes sunt administratorii spiritus in ministerium missi,* unde 'angelus' nuntius interpretatur. Possunt ergo homines, qui a Deo ad aliquid annuntiandum mittuntur, angeli dici, iuxta illud Aggaei I, 13: *dixit Aggaeus, nuntius Domini ex nuntiis Domini.*

Requiritur autem ad hoc quod aliquis testimonium de Deo perhibeat, quod sit a Deo missus; iuxta illud Rom. X, 15: *quomodo praedicabunt nisi mittantur?* Et quia cum a Deo mittuntur, non sua quaerunt, sed quae Iesu Christi II Cor. IV, 5: *non enim praedicamus nosmetipsos, sed Iesum Christum:* qui vero mittitur a seipso, non a Deo, sua quaerit, vel quae sunt hominis, non autem quae Christi, ideo hic dicitur *fuit homo missus a Deo*: ut intelligas quia non annuntiavit nisi divinum, non humanum.

112. Nota autem, quod tripliciter invenimus aliquos missos a Deo. Scilicet per internam inspirationem, sicut Is. XLVIII, 16: *et nunc misit me Dominus, et spiritus eius*; quasi dicat: per interiorem spiritus inspirationem sum a Deo missus. Item, per expressam et apertam iussionem sive corporalem, sive imaginariam. Et sic iterum missus est Isaias; unde dicit ibid. VI, 8: *audivi vocem Domini dicentis: quem mittam, et quis ibit nobis? Et dixi: ecce ego, mitte me.* Item, per praelati iniunctionem, qui gerit in hoc personam Dei; II Cor. II, 10: *nam et ego, si quid donavi propter vos in persona Christi.* Et inde est quod qui mittuntur a praelato, mittuntur a Deo, sicut missi fuerunt ab Apostolo Barnabas et Timotheus.

Cum autem dicitur hic *fuit homo missus a Deo,* intelligendum est per interiorem inspirationem; vel etiam forte per exteriorem iussionem a Deo eum missum fuisse. Infra: *qui misit me, ipse dixit: super quem videris spiritum descendentem et manentem super eum, hic est qui baptizat in Spiritu Sancto.*

113. Per hoc etiam quod dixit *fuit homo missus a Deo,* non est intelligendum, sicut quidam haeretici ponebant, credentes animas hominum ante corpus fuisse cum angelis ab initio creatas, et mitti animam cuiuscumque, quando nascitur, ad corpus; et quod Ioannes

Now it is fitting that a man be sent to men, for men are more easily drawn to a man, since he is like themselves. So it says, *the law appoints men, who have weakness, priests* (Heb 7:28). God could have governed men through angels, but he preferred men so that we could be more instructed by their example. And so John was a man, and not an angel.

111. John is described by his authority when it says, *sent from God.*

Indeed, although John was not an angel in nature, he was so by his office, because he was *sent from God.* For the distinctive office of angels is that they are sent by God and are messengers of God. *All are ministering spirits, sent to serve* (Heb 1:14). Hence it is that 'angel' means messenger. And so men who are sent by God to announce something can be called angels. *Haggai the messenger of the Lord* (Hag 1:13).

If someone is to bear witness to God, it is necessary that he be sent by God. *How can they preach unless they are sent?* (Rom 10:15). And since they are sent by God, they seek the things of Jesus Christ, not their own. *We do not preach ourselves, but Jesus Christ* (2 Cor 4:5). On the other hand, one who sends himself, and is not sent by God, seeks his own things or those of man, and not the things of Christ. And so he says here, *there was a man sent from God*, so that we would understand that John proclaimed something divine, not human.

112. Note that there are three ways in which we see men sent by God. First, by an inward inspiration. *And now the Lord God has sent me, and his spirit* (Isa 48:16). As if to say: I have been sent by God through an inward inspiration of the spirit. Second, by an expressed and clear command, perceived by the bodily senses or the imagination. Isaiah was also sent in this way; and so he says, *and I heard the voice of the Lord saying, 'whom shall I send, and who will go for us?' Then I said, 'here I am! Send me'* (Isa 6:8). Third, by the order of a prelate, who acts in the place of God in this matter. *I have pardoned in the person of Christ for your sake* (2 Cor 2:10). This is why those who are sent by a prelate are sent by God, as Barnabas and Timothy were sent by the Apostle.

When it is said here, *there was a man sent from God,* we should understand that he was sent by God through an inward inspiration, or perhaps even by an outward command. He who sent me to baptize with water had said to me: *he upon whom you shall see the Spirit descending, and remaining upon him, it is he who baptizes with the Holy Spirit* (John 1:33).

113. We should not understand, *there was a man sent from God,* as some heretics did, who believed that from the very beginning human souls were created without bodies along with the angels, and that one's soul is sent into the body when he is born, and that John was sent to life, i.e., his

sit missus ad vitam, idest eius anima ad corpus; sed quod fuit missus a Deo ad officium baptizandi et praedicandi.

114. Ex idoneitate vero commendatur, cum dicit **cui nomen erat Ioannes**.

Ad officium namque testimonii requiritur idoneitas: nam nisi testis sit idoneus, qualitercumque mittatur ab alio, non est sufficiens testimonium eius. Homo autem efficitur idoneus ex gratia Dei; I Cor. XV, 10: *gratia Dei sum id quod sum*; II Cor. III, 6: *qui idoneos nos fecit ministros Novi Testamenti*. Satis ergo congrue Evangelista idoneitatem praecursoris insinuat ex eius nomine, dicens **cui nomen erat Ioannes**, quod interpretatur *in quo est gratia*. Quod quidem nomen non fuit frustra sibi impositum, sed ex divina praeordinatione, et antequam nasceretur, ut patet Lc. I, 13: *et vocabis nomen eius Ioannem*, dixit angelus ad Zachariam. Unde potest dicere illud Is. XLIX, 1: *Dominus ab utero vocavit me*; et Eccl. VI, 10: *qui futurus est, iam vocatum est nomen eius*. Quod etiam ostendit Evangelista ex modo loquendi, cum dicit **erat**, quantum ad Dei praeordinationem.

115. Ex officii etiam dignitate describitur, cum dicit **hic venit in testimonium**; ubi

primo ponitur officium;

secundo ratio officii, ibi **ut testimonium perhiberet de lumine**.

116. Officium autem huius est testificandi; unde dicit **hic venit in testimonium**.

Ubi notandum est quod Deus et homines, et omnia quae facit, propter se operatur; Prov. XVI, 4: *universa propter semetipsum operatus est Dominus*; non quidem ut aliquid ei accrescat, quia bonorum nostrorum non eget, sed ut eius bonitas manifestetur in omnibus a se factis, inquantum *per ea quae facta sunt, intellecta conspiciuntur; sempiterna eius virtus, et divinitas*; Rom. I, 20. Fit ergo quaelibet creatura in testimonium Dei, inquantum quaelibet creatura est testimonium quoddam divinae bonitatis. Et quidem magnitudo creaturae testimonium quoddam est divinae virtutis et omnipotentiae; pulchritudo vero divinae sapientiae. Speciali vero modo ordinantur a Deo quidam homines; et non solum naturaliter inquantum sunt, sed etiam spiritualiter per sua bona opera Deo testimonium ferunt. Unde omnes sancti viri testes sunt Dei, inquantum propter eorum bona opera Deus gloriosus apud homines efficitur; Matth. V, 16: *sic luceat lux vestra coram hominibus, ut videant opera vestra bona, et glorificent Patrem vestrum qui in caelis est*. Sed tamen illi, qui participant non solum dona Dei in seipsis per gratiam Dei bene operando, sed etiam diffundunt ad alios dicendo, movendo et exhortando, specialius sunt testes Dei. Is. XLIII, 7: *omnem qui invocat nomen meum, in laudem meam creavi illum*.

Ioannes ergo venit in testimonium ad hoc, ut in alios diffunderet dona Dei, et annuntiaret laudem.

soul was sent to a body. Rather, we should understand that he was sent by God to baptize and preach.

114. John's fitness is given when he says, **whose name was John**.

One must be qualified for the office of bearing witness, because unless a witness is qualified, then no matter in what way he is sent by another, his testimony is not acceptable. Now a man becomes qualified by the grace of God. *By the grace of God I am what I am* (1 Cor 15:10); *who has made us fit ministers of a New Covenant* (2 Cor 3:6). So, the Evangelist appropriately implies the precursor's fitness from his name when he says, **whose name was John**, which is interpreted, *in whom is grace*. This name was not given to him meaninglessly, but by divine preordination and before he was born: *you will name him John* (Luke 1:13), as the angel said to Zechariah. Hence he can say: *the Lord called me from the womb* (Isa 49:1); *he who will be, his name is already called* (Eccl 6:10). The Evangelist also indicates this from his manner of speaking, when he says **was**, as to God's preordination.

115. Then he is described by the dignity of his office: **he came as a witness**.

First, his office is mentioned.

Second, the reason for his office, **that he might bear witness to the light**.

116. Now his office is to bear witness; hence he says, **he came as a witness**.

Here it should be remarked that God makes men, and everything else he makes for himself. *The Lord made all things for himself* (Prov 16:4). Not, indeed, to add anything to himself, since he has no need of our good, but so that his goodness might be made manifest in all of the things made by him, in that *his eternal power and divinity are clearly seen, being understood through the things that are made* (Rom 1:20). Thus, each creature is made as a witness to God in so far as each creature is a certain witness of the divine goodness. So, the vastness of creation is a witness to God's power and omnipotence; and its beauty is a witness to the divine wisdom. But certain men are ordained by God in a special way, so that they bear witness to God not only naturally by their existence, but also spiritually by their good works. Hence all holy men are witnesses to God inasmuch as God is glorified among men by their good works. *Let your light so shine before men, that they may see your good works, and glorify your Father who is in heaven* (Matt 5:16). But those who not only share in God's gifts in themselves by acting well through the grace of God, but also spread them to others by their teaching, influencing and encouraging others, are in a more special way witnesses to God. *Everyone who calls upon my name, I have created for my glory* (Isa 43:7).

And so John came as a witness in order to spread to others the gifts of God and to proclaim his praise.

117. Hoc autem officium Ioannis, scilicet testificandi, est valde magnum, quia nullus potest de aliquo testificari, nisi eo modo quo illud participat; infra III, 11: *quod scimus loquimur, et quod vidimus testamur*. Unde testimonium perhibere divinae veritati, indicium est cognitionis ipsius veritatis. Et inde est quod etiam Christus hoc officium habuit; infra XVIII, 37: *ad hoc veni, et in hoc natus sum, ut testimonium perhibeam veritati*. Sed aliter Christus, et aliter Ioannes. Christus enim ut ipsum lumen comprehendens, immo ipsum lumen existens; Ioannes vero, ut ipsum lumen participans tantum. Et ideo Christus perfecte testimonium perhibet, et perfecte manifestat veritatem, Ioannes vero et alii sancti inquantum ipsam veritatem divinam participant.

Est ergo magnum officium Ioannis et ex participatione divini luminis et ex similitudine ad Christum, qui hoc officio usus fuit. Is. LV, 4: *ecce testem populis dedi eum, ducem ac praeceptorem gentibus*.

118. Ratio autem huius officii ponitur, cum dicit *ut testimonium perhiberet de lumine*.

Ubi sciendum est, quod alicui rei testimonium perhibetur duplici de causa. Una causa potest esse ex parte rei, cui testimonium adhibetur, puta si est dubia, vel incerta; alia causa est ex parte audientium, si sunt duri et tardi corde ad credendum. Ioannes vero in testimonium quidem venit non propter ipsam rem, cui testimonium perhibebat, quia lumen erat. Unde dicit *ut testimonium perhiberet de lumine*, non de re obscura sed de re manifesta. Venit ergo in testimonium propter ipsos quibus testificabatur, *ut omnes crederent per eum*, scilicet Ioannem. Nam sicut lumen non solum in seipso et per se visibile est, sed etiam omnia alia per ipsum videri possunt, ita Verbum Dei non solum in se lumen est, sed etiam est omnia manifestans quae manifestantur. Cum enim unumquodque manifestatur per suam formam et cognoscatur, omnes autem formae sint per Verbum, quod est ars plena rationum viventium: est ergo lumen, non solum in se, sed omnia manifestans; Eph. V, 13: *omne quod manifestatur, lumen est*.

Congrue autem Evangelista Filium dicit *lumen*, quia venit *lumen ad revelationem gentium*, Lc. II, 32. Supra autem dixit Filium Dei Verbum, quo Pater dicit se, et omnem creaturam. Unde cum proprie sit lux hominum, et hic Evangelista de eo agat secundum quod venit ad salutem hominum procurandam, congrue intermittit hoc nomen *Verbum*, cum loquitur de Filio, et dicit illud *lumen*.

119. Sed si istud lumen sufficiens est per se omnia manifestare, non solum seipsum, quid ergo indigebat ut testificaretur? Non ergo necessaria sunt testimonia Ioannis et prophetarum de Christo.

Respondeo dicendum, quod haec obiectio est Manichaeorum, qui volunt destruere Vetus Testamentum.

117. This office of John, that of bearing witness, is very great, because no one can testify about something except in the manner in which he has shared in it. ***We speak what we know, and we testify what we have seen*** (John 3:11). Hence, to bear witness to divine truth indicates a knowledge of that truth. So Christ also had this office: ***for this I came into the world, that I should give testimony to the truth*** (John 18:37). But Christ testifies in one way and John in another. Christ bears witness as the light who comprehends all things, indeed, as the existing light itself. John bears witness only as participating in that light. And so Christ gives testimony in a perfect manner and perfectly manifests the truth, while John and other holy men give testimony in so far as they have a share of divine truth.

John's office, therefore, is great both because of his participation in the divine light and because of a likeness to Christ, who carried out this office. *I made him a witness to the peoples, a leader and a commander of the nations* (Isa 55:4).

118. The purpose of this office is given when he says, ***that he might bear witness to the light***.

Here we should understand that there are two reasons for bearing witness about something. One reason can be on the part of the thing with which the witness is concerned; for example, if there is some doubt or uncertainty about that thing. The other is on the part of those who hear it; if they are hard of heart and slow to believe. John came as a witness, not because of the thing about which he bore witness, for it was light. Hence he says, ***that he might bear witness to the light***, i.e., not to something obscure, but to something clear. He came, therefore, to bear witness on account of those to whom he testified, ***so that through him***, John, ***all men might believe***. For as light is not only visible in itself and of itself, but through it all else can be seen, so the Word of God is not only light in himself, but he makes known all things that are known. For since a thing is made known and understood through its form, and all forms exist through the Word, who is the art full of living forms, the Word is light not only in himself, but as making known all things; *all that appears is light* (Eph 5:13).

And so it was fitting for the Evangelist to call the Son *light*, because he came as *a revealing light to the gentiles* (Luke 2:32). Above, he called the Son of God the Word, by which the Father expresses himself and every creature. Now since he is, properly speaking, the light of men, and the Evangelist is considering him here as coming to accomplish the salvation of men, he fittingly interrupts the use of the name ***Word*** when speaking of the Son, and says, ***light***.

119. But if that light is adequate of itself to make known all things, and not only itself, what need does it have of any witness? The testimonies of John and the prophets concerning Christ were not necessary.

This was the objection of the Manichaeans, who wanted to destroy the Old Testament. Consequently, the saints gave

Unde a sanctis contra hos multiplex ratio assignatur, quare Christus testimonium prophetarum voluit habere.

Origenes quidem assignat tres rationes ad hoc. Primo quidem quod Deus vult aliquos testes habere, non quod ipse eorum testimonio indigeat, sed ut eos nobilitet quos constituit testes; sicut videmus etiam in ordine universi, quod Deus producit aliquos effectus per causas medias, non quia ipse impotens sit ad eos immediate producendos, sed quia ad nobilitandas ipsas causas medias eis causalitatis dignitatem communicare dignatur. Sic ergo, etsi Deus potuerit omnes homines illuminare per se et in cognitionem suam adducere, ut tamen debitus ordo servaretur in rebus, et ut aliquos homines nobilitaret, voluit divinam cognitionem ad homines per aliquos homines devenire. Is. XLIII, 10: *vere vos testes mei estis, dicit Dominus.*

Secunda ratio est, quia Christus illuxit mundo per miracula: quae quidem, quia in tempore facta erant, temporaliter transierunt, neque pervenerunt ad omnes. Verba vero prophetarum commendata Scripturae, poterant non solum ad praesentes, sed etiam ad posteros pervenire. Voluit ergo Dominus homines ad cognitionem Verbi venire per testimonia prophetarum, ut non solum praesentes, sed etiam futuri de ipso illuminarentur; et ideo signanter dicit **ut omnes crederent per illum**, non solum praesentes, sed etiam futuri.

Tertia ratio est, quia homines sunt diversae conditionis, et diversimode ad veritatis cognitionem perducti et dispositi. Quidam namque ad veritatis cognitionem magis perducuntur per signa et miracula; quidam vero magis per sapientiam; unde I Cor. I, 22: *Iudaei signa petunt, et Graeci sapientiam quaerunt.* Ut ergo Dominus omnibus ostenderet viam salutis, utramque viam pandere voluit, scilicet signorum et sapientiae, ut qui non perducerentur ad viam salutis per miracula in Veteri et Novo Testamento facta, saltem per viam sapientiae, ut in prophetis et aliis Sacrae Scripturae libris, ad veritatis cognitionem perveniant.

Quarta ratio est Chrysostomi, quia scilicet homines infirmi intellectus, veritatem et cognitionem Dei seipsa capere non possunt; unde voluit Deus eis condescendere et illuminare quosdam homines de divinis prae aliis, ut ab eis humano modo cognitionem de divinis acciperent, quorum cognitionem in seipsis attingere non valebant. Et ideo dicit **ut omnes crederent per illum**. Quasi dicat: venit in testimonium, non propter ipsum lumen, sed propter ipsos homines, ut scilicet **crederent per illum**.

Sic ergo patet idonea esse et congruentia testimonia prophetarum, et ideo recipienda utpote nobis necessaria ad veritatis cognitionem.

many reasons, against their opinion, why Christ wanted to have the testimony of the prophets.

Origen gives three reasons. The first is that God wanted to have certain witnesses, not because he needed their testimony, but to ennoble those whom he appointed witnesses. Thus we see in the order of the universe that God produces certain effects by means of intermediate causes, not because he himself is unable to produce them without these intermediaries, but he deigns to confer on them the dignity of causality because he wishes to ennoble these intermediate causes. Similarly, even though God could have enlightened all men by himself and led them to a knowledge of himself, yet to preserve due order in things and to ennoble certain men, he willed that divine knowledge reach men through certain other men. *'You are my witnesses,' says the Lord* (Isa 43:10).

A second reason is that Christ was a light to the world through his miracles. Yet, because they were performed in time, they passed away with time and did not reach everyone. But the words of the prophets, preserved in Scripture, could reach not only those present, but could also reach those to come after. Hence the Lord willed that men come to a knowledge of the Word through the testimony of the prophets, in order that not only those present, but also men yet to come, might be enlightened about him. So it says expressly, **so that through him all men might believe**, i.e., not only those present, but also future generations.

The third reason is that not all men are in the same condition, and all are not led or disposed to a knowledge of the truth in the same way. For some are brought to a knowledge of the truth by signs and miracles; others are brought more by wisdom. *The Jews require signs, and the Greeks seek wisdom* (1 Cor 1:22). And so the Lord, in order to show the path of salvation to all, willed both ways to be open. i.e., the way of signs and the way of wisdom, so that those who would not be brought to the path of salvation by the miracles of the Old and New Testaments, might be brought to a knowledge of the truth by the path of wisdom, as in the prophets and other books of Sacred Scripture.

A fourth reason, given by Chrysostom, is that certain men of weak understanding are unable to grasp the truth and knowledge of God by themselves. And so the Lord chose to come down to them and to enlighten certain men before others about divine matters, so that these others might obtain from them in a human way the knowledge of divine things they could not reach by themselves. And so he says, **so that through him all men might believe**. As if to say: he came as a witness, not for the sake of the light, but for the sake of men, **so that through him all men might believe**.

And so it is plain that the testimonies of the prophets are fitting and proper, and should be received as something needed by us for the knowledge of the truth.

120. Dicit autem *crederent* quia est duplex participatio divini luminis. Una scilicet perfecta, quae est in gloria, Ps. XXXV, v. 10: *in lumine tuo videbimus lumen*, alia est imperfecta, quae scilicet habetur per fidem, quia *venit in testimonium*. De istis duobus modis dicitur I Cor. XIII, 12: *videmus nunc per speculum in aenigmate; tunc autem facie ad faciem*; et ibidem dicitur: *nunc cognosco ex parte; tunc autem cognoscam sicut et cognitus sum*. Istorum autem modorum prior est modus participationis per fidem; quia per ipsam pervenitur ad speciem. Unde Is. VII, 9, secundum aliam litteram: *nisi credideritis, non intelligetis*; ubi nostra habet: *si non credideritis, non permanebitis*. II Cor. c. III, 18: *nos autem omnes revelata facie gloriam Domini speculantes, in eamdem imaginem*, scilicet quam perdidimus, *transformamur a claritate in claritatem*; Glossa: a claritate fidei, in claritatem speciei.

Dicit ergo *ut omnes crederent per illum*; non ut omnes viderent illum perfecte statim, sed ut primo per fidem credendo, et postea per speciem in patria perfruendo.

121. Dicit autem *per eum*, ut ostendat differentiam eius ad Christum. Christus enim venit, ut omnes crederent in eum; infra VII, v. 38: *qui credit in me, sicut dicit Scriptura, flumina de ventre eius fluent aquae vivae*. Ioannes *vero ut omnes crederent*, non quidem in eum, sed in Christum *per eum*.

Sed contra. Non omnes crediderunt per illum. Si ergo venit ut omnes crederent per illum, frustra venit.

Respondeo dicendum, quod quantum est ex parte Dei mittentis, et ex parte Ioannis venientis, sufficiens modus adhibitus est omnibus perveniendi ad finem; sed ex parte eorum qui *oculos suos statuerunt declinare in terra*, et noluerunt videre ipsum lumen, defectus fuit, quia non omnes crediderunt.

122. Licet autem Ioannes, de quo tot dicta sunt, et quod missus a Deo, magnus sit, nihilominus tamen eius adventus non est sufficiens hominibus ad salutem; quia salus hominis in hoc consistit, quod participet ipsam lucem. Unde, etsi Ioannes lux fuisset, suffecisset hominibus ad salutem eius adventus; sed ipse non erat lux; unde dicit *non erat ille lux*. Et ideo necessaria erat lux, quae sufficeret hominibus ad salutem.

Vel aliter. Ioannes venit ut testimonium perhiberet de lumine. Consuetum est autem testificantem esse maioris auctoritatis, quam ille cui perhibet testimonium. Ne ergo credatur Ioannem esse maioris auctoritatis, quam Christus, dicit Evangelista *non erat ille lux, sed ut testimonium perhiberet de lumine*. Testatur enim non quia maior, sed quia notior, etiamsi sit minor.

120. He says *believe*, because there are two ways of participating in the divine light. One is the perfect participation which is present in glory, *in your light, we shall see the light* (Ps 35:10). The other is imperfect and is acquired through faith, since *he came as a witness*. Of these two ways it is said, *now we see through a mirror, in an obscure manner, but then we shall see face to face . . . now I know in part, but then I shall know even as I am known* (1 Cor 13:12). Among these two ways, the first is the way of participation through faith, because through it we are brought to vision. So where our version has, *if you do not believe, you will not persist* (Isa 7:9), another version has, *if you do not believe, you will not understand*. All of us, gazing on the Lord's glory with unveiled faces, are being transformed from glory to glory into his very image, which we have lost (2 Cor 3:18). *From the glory of faith to the glory of vision*, as a Gloss says.

And so he says, *so that through him all men might believe*, not as though all would see him perfectly at once, but first they would believe through faith, and later enjoy him through vision in heaven.

121. He says *through him*, to show that John is different than Christ. For Christ came so that all might believe in him. *He who believes in me, as the Scripture says, out of his heart shall flow rivers of living water* (John 7:38). John, on the other hand, came *so that all men might believe*, not in him, but in Christ *through him*.

On the contrary, one may object that not all have believed. So if John came to that all might believe through him, he failed.

I answer that both on the part of God, who sent John, and of John, who came, the method used is adequate to bring all to the truth. But on the part of those *who have fixed their eyes on the ground* (Ps 16:11), and refused to see the light, there was a failure, because all did not believe.

122. Now although John, of whom so much has been said, even including that he was sent by God, is an eminent person, his coming is not sufficient to save men, because the salvation of man lies in participating in the light. If John had been the light, his coming would have sufficed to save men; but he was not the light. So he says, *he was not the light*. Consequently, a light was needed that would suffice to save men.

Or, we could look at it another way. John came to bear witness to the light. Now it is the custom that the one who testifies is of greater authority than the one for whom he bears witness. So, lest John be considered to have greater authority than Christ, the Evangelist says, *he was not the light, but that he might bear witness to the light*. For he bears witness not because he is greater, but because he is better known, even though he is not as great.

123. Sed quaeritur de hoc quod dicit **non erat ille lux**. Contra dicitur Eph. V, 8: *eratis aliquando tenebrae, nunc autem lux in Domino*; et Matth. V, 14: *vos estis lux mundi*. Sunt ergo Ioannes, et apostoli, et omnes boni, lux.

Respondeo. Quidam dicunt quod Ioannes non erat **lux** cum articulo, quia hoc est solius Dei proprium; sed si 'lux' ponatur sine articulo, erat Ioannes et omnes sancti facti lux. Quod est dictu: Filius Dei est lux per essentiam, Ioannes vero et omnes sancti per participationem. Et ideo quia Ioannes participabat verum lumen, congruenter testimonium perhibebat de lumine: ignis enim convenientius manifestatur per aliquod ignitum quam per aliquid aliud, et color per coloratum.

123. There is a difficulty about his saying, **he was not the light**. Conflicting with this is, *you were at one time darkness, but now you are light in the Lord* (Eph 5:8); and *you are the light of the world* (Matt 5:14). Therefore, John and the apostles and all good men are a light.

I answer that some say that John was not **the light**, because this belongs to God alone. But if 'light' is taken without the article, then John and all holy men were made lights. The meaning is this: the Son of God is light by his very essence; but John and all the saints are light by participation. So, because John participated in the true light, it was fitting that he bear witness to the light; for fire is better exhibited by something afire than by anything else, and color by something colored.

Lecture 5

1:9 Erat lux vera, quae illuminat omnem hominem venientem in hunc mundum. [n. 125]

1:10 In mundo erat. Et mundus per ipsum factus est, et mundus eum non cognovit. [n. 128]

1:9 Ἦν τὸ φῶς τὸ ἀληθινόν, ὃ φωτίζει πάντα ἄνθρωπον, ἐρχόμενον εἰς τὸν κόσμον.

1:10 ἐν τῷ κόσμῳ ἦν, καὶ ὁ κόσμος δι᾽ αὐτοῦ ἐγένετο, καὶ ὁ κόσμος αὐτὸν οὐκ ἔγνω.

1:9 He was the true light, which enlightens every man coming into this world. [n. 125]

1:10 He was in the world, and through him the world was made, and the world did not know him. [n. 128]

---

124. Superius egit Evangelista de praecursore, et teste Verbi incarnati; in parte vero ista agit de ipso Verbo incarnato: et circa hoc tria facit.

Primo ostendit adventus Verbi necessitatem;

secundo ex adventu Verbi collatam nobis utilitatem, ibi *in propria venit*;

tertio veniendi modum, ibi *et Verbum caro factum est* .

Necessitas autem adventus Verbi videtur esse defectus divinae cognitionis, quae in mundo erat. Unde hanc necessitatem sui adventus assignat, dicens, infra XVIII, 37: *in hoc natus sum, et ad hoc veni*. Ad insinuandum ergo hunc divinae cognitionis defectum, duo facit Evangelista.

Primo ostendit quod iste defectus non est ex parte Dei, neque ex defectu Verbi;

secundo ostendit quod est ex parte hominum, ibi *et mundus eum non cognovit*.

Quod autem non fuerit defectus ex parte Dei et Verbi, quin homines Deum cognoscerent et illuminarentur a Verbo, ostendit ex tribus.

Primo ex ipsius divinae lucis efficacia, quia *erat lux vera, quae illuminat omnem hominem venientem in hunc mundum*;

secundo ex ipsius divinae lucis praesentia, quia *in mundo erat*;

tertio ex eius evidentia, quia *mundus per ipsum factus est*.

Non fuit ergo defectus divinae cognitionis in mundo ex parte Verbi, quia efficax est. Unde

primo ostendit rationem huius efficaciae, quia *erat lux vera*;

secundo ipsam eius efficaciam, quia *illuminat omnem hominem venientem in hunc mundum*.

125. Est enim efficax divinum Verbum ad illuminandum, quia *erat lux vera*. Quomodo autem Verbum sit lux, et quomodo sit lux hominum, quia supra satis explanatum est, superfluum est ad praesens reiterare. Istud tamen ad praesens est dicendum, quomodo sit *lux vera*.

Notandum est ergo ad huiusmodi evidentiam, quod *verum* in Scriptura tribus opponitur. Aliquando enim

124. Above, the Evangelist considered the precursor and his witness to the incarnate Word; in the present section he considers the incarnate Word himself. As to this he does three things.

First, he shows why it was necessary for the Word to come.

Second, the benefit we received from the coming of the Word, at *he came unto his own* (John 1:11).

And third, the way he came, at *and the Word was made flesh* (John 1:14).

The necessity for the Word's coming is seen to be the lack of divine knowledge in the world. He points out this need for his coming when he says, *for this I was born, and for this I came into the world, that I should give testimony to the truth* (John 18:37). To indicate this lack of divine knowledge, the Evangelist does two things.

First, he shows that this lack does not pertain to God or the Word.

Second, that it does pertain to men, at *and the world did not know him*.

He shows in three ways that there was no defect in God or in the Word that prevented men from knowing God and from being enlightened by the Word.

First, from the efficacy of the divine light itself, because *he was the true light, which enlightens every man coming into this world*.

Second, from the presence of the divine light, because *he was in the world*.

Third, from the obviousness of the light, because *through him the world was made*.

So the lack of divine knowledge in the world was not due to the Word, because it is sufficient.

First, he shows the nature of this efficiency, that is, *he was the true light*.

Second, its very efficiency, *which enlightens every man*.

125. The divine Word is efficacious in enlightening because *he was the true light*. How the Word is light, and how he is the light of men need not be discussed again, because it was sufficiently explained above. What we must discuss at present is how he is the *true light*.

To explain this, we should note that in Scripture the *true* is contrasted with three things. Sometimes it is contrasted

dividitur contra falsum, sicut illud Eph. IV, 25: *deponentes mendacium, loquimini veritatem*. Aliquando autem dividitur contra figurale, sicut illud infra I, 17: **lex per Moysen data est; gratia et veritas per Iesum Christum facta est**, quia veritas figurarum legis facta est per Christum. Aliquando vero dividitur contra participans, sicut illud I Ioan. ult., 20: *ut simus in vero Filio eius*; qui scilicet non est Filius per participationem.

Fuit autem ante adventum Verbi in mundo quaedam lux, quam scilicet philosophi se habere iactabant; sed haec quidem falsa fuit, quia, ut dicitur Rom. I, 21: *evanuerunt in cogitationibus suis, et obscuratum est insipiens cor eorum; dicentes enim se esse sapientes, stulti facti sunt*; Ier. X, 14: *stultus factus est omnis homo a scientia sua*. Fuit etiam quaedam alia lux, quam gloriabantur se habere Iudaei ex doctrina legis; sed haec quidem lux erat lux figuralis; Hebr. X, 1: *umbram habens lex futurorum bonorum, non ipsam imaginem rerum*. Erat etiam in angelis et in sanctis hominibus lux quaedam, inquantum specialiori modo per gratiam Deum cognoscebant; sed haec lux participata erat; Iob XXV, 3: *super quem non resplendet lumen illius?* Quasi dicat: quicumque lucidi sunt, intantum lucent inquantum participant lumen illius, idest Dei. Sed Verbum Dei non erat lux falsa, non figuralis, non participata, sed lux vera, idest per essentiam suam. Et ideo dicit **erat lux vera**.

126. In quo quidem excluditur duplex error, scilicet Photini, qui Christum opinatus est ex Virgine initium sumpsisse. Et ideo ne aliquis hoc suspicari posset, Evangelista loquens de incarnatione Verbi, dicit **erat lux vera**, scilicet ab aeterno, non solum ante Virginem, sed ante omnem creaturam.

Excluditur etiam error Arii et Origenis dicentium Christum non fuisse verum Deum, sed per participationem tantum. Quod si verum esset, non esset lux vera, ut Evangelista dicit. Sicut enim dicitur I Io. I, 5: *Deus lux est*, non per participationem, sed **lux vera**. Si ergo Verbum erat lux vera, manifestum est illud esse Deum verum.

Patet ergo ratio efficaciae divini Verbi ad divinam cognitionem causandam.

127. Efficacia autem ipsius Verbi est, quia **illuminat omnem hominem venientem**.

Omne enim quod est per participationem, derivatur ab eo quod est per essentiam suam tale; ut omne ignitum est hoc per participationem ignis, qui est ignis per suam naturam. Quia ergo Verbum est lux vera per suam naturam, oportet quod omne lucens luceat per ipsum, inquantum ipsum participat. Ipse ergo **illuminat omnem hominem venientem in hunc mundum**.

128. Sciendum est autem ad horum intellectum, quod *mundus* in Scriptura accipitur tribus modis. Aliquando

with the false, as in *put an end to lying, and let everyone speak the truth* (Eph 4:25). Sometimes it is contrasted with what is figurative, as in **the law was given through Moses; grace and truth came through Jesus Christ** (John 1:17), because the truth of the figures contained in the law was fulfilled by Christ. Sometimes it is contrasted with what is something by participation, as in *that we may be in his true Son* (1 John 5:20), who is not his Son by participation.

Before the Word came there was in the world a certain light which the philosophers prided themselves on having; but this was a false light, because as is said, *they became stultified in their speculations, and their foolish hearts were darkened; claiming to be wise, they became fools* (Rom 1:21); *every man is made foolish by his knowledge* (Jer 10:14). There was another light from the teaching of the law which the Jews boasted of having; but this was a symbolic light, *the law has a shadow of the good things to come, not the image itself of them* (Heb 10:1). There was also a certain light in the angels and in holy men in so far as they knew God in a more special way by grace; but this was a participated light, *upon whom does his light not shine?* (Job 25:3), which is like saying: whoever shine, shine to the extent that they participate in his light, i.e., God's light. But the Word of God was not a false light, nor a symbolic light, nor a participated light, but the true light, i.e., light by his essence. Therefore he says, **he was the true light**.

126. This excludes two errors. First, that of Photinus, who believed that Christ derived his beginning from the Virgin. So, lest anyone suppose this, the Evangelist, speaking of the incarnation of the Word, says, **he was the true light**, i.e., eternally, not only before the Virgin, but before every creature.

This also excludes the error of Arius and Origen; they said that Christ was not true God, but God by participation. If this were so, he could not be the true light, as the Evangelist says here, and as in *God is light* (1 John 1:5), i.e., not by participation, but **the true light**. So if the Word was the true light, it is plain that he is true God.

Now it is clear how the divine Word is effective in causing divine knowledge.

127. The effectiveness or efficiency of the Word lies in the fact that he **enlightens every man coming into this world**.

For everything that is what it is by participation is derived from that which is such by its essence; just as everything afire is so by participation in fire, which is fire by its very essence. Then since the Word is the true light by his very essence, then everything that shines must do so through him, insofar as it participates in him. And so he **enlightens every man coming into this world**.

128. To understand this, we should know that *world* is taken in three ways in Scripture. Sometimes, from the

enim ratione suae creationis, sicut hic inferius ait Evangelista *mundus per ipsum factus est*. Aliquando autem ratione suae perfectionis, ad quam per Christum pertingit, sicut illud II Cor. V, 19: *Deus erat in Christo mundum reconcilians sibi*. Aliquando ratione suae perversitatis sicut illud I Io. V, 19: *totus mundus in maligno positus est*.

Illuminatio seu illuminari per Verbum, intelligitur dupliciter: scilicet de lumine naturalis cognitionis, de quo dicitur in Ps. IV, 7: *signatum est super nos lumen vultus tui, Domine*. Item de lumine gratiae, de quo dicitur Is. LX, 1: *illuminare, Ierusalem*.

129. His duabus distinctionibus suppositis, facile solvitur dubitatio quae ex istis oritur.

Cum enim dicit Evangelista *illuminat omnem hominem*, videtur subesse falsum, cum adhuc multi sint in mundo tenebrosi.

Si ergo nos, memores dictarum distinctionum, accipiamus *mundum* secundum quod ponitur ratione suae creationis; et *illuminare*, secundum quod accipitur pro lumine naturalis rationis, verbum Evangelistae nullam habet calumniam: quia homines omnes venientes in hunc mundum sensibilem illuminantur lumine naturalis cognitionis ex participatione huius verae lucis, a qua derivatur quicquid de lumine naturalis cognitionis participatur ab hominibus. Utitur autem Evangelista hoc modo loquendi, ut dicat *venientem in hunc mundum*, non quod homines vixissent aliquo temporis spatio extra mundum, et postea venirent in mundum, cum hoc sit contra sententiam Apostoli, Rom. IX, 11: *cum enim nondum nati essent, aut aliquid egissent boni, aut mali (ut secundum electionem propositum Dei manere), non ex operibus, sed ex vocante dictum est* etc. Unde cum non egissent aliquid antequam nati essent, manifestum est quod anima non est antequam corpori coniungatur.

Dicit ergo *venientem in hunc mundum*, ut ostendat quod homines illuminantur a Deo, secundum hoc scilicet quod veniunt in mundum, idest secundum intellectum qui est ab extrinseco. Homo enim ex duplici natura constituitur, corporali scilicet et intellectuali: et secundum corporalem quidem naturam, seu sensibilem, illuminatur homo lumine corporeo et sensibili; secundum animam vero et intellectualem naturam, illuminatur lumine intellectuali et spirituali. Cum ergo homo, secundum naturam corporalem non veniat in hunc mundum, sed sit ex mundo, sed secundum intellectualem naturam, quae est ab extrinseco, ut dictum est, sit a Deo per creationem, unde dicitur Eccle. XII, 7: *donec omnis caro in suam revertatur originem, et spiritus dirigatur ad Deum qui fecit illum*: ostendit Evangelista quod haec illuminatio est secundum illud quod est ab extrinseco, scilicet secundum intellectum, cum dicit *venientem in hunc mundum*.

point of view of its creation, as when the Evangelist says here, *through him the world was made*. Sometimes, from the point of view of its perfection, which it reaches through Christ, as in *God was, in Christ, reconciling the world to himself* (2 Cor 5:19). And sometimes it is taken from the point of view of its perversity, as in *the whole world lies under the power of the evil one* (1 John 5:19).

On the other hand, *enlightenment* or *being enlightened* by the Word is taken in two ways. First, in relation to the light of natural knowledge, as in *the light of your countenance, O Lord, is marked upon us* (Ps 4:7). Second, as the light of grace, *be enlightened, O Jerusalem* (Isa 60:1).

129. With these two sets of distinctions in mind, it is easy to solve a difficulty which arises here.

For when the Evangelist says, *enlightens every man*, this seems to be false, because there are still many in darkness in the world.

However, if we bear in mind these distinctions and take *world* from the standpoint of its creation, and *enlightens* as referring to the light of natural reason, the statement of the Evangelist is beyond reproach. For all men coming into this visible world are enlightened by the light of natural knowledge through participating in this true light, which is the source of all the light of natural knowledge participated in by men. When the Evangelist speaks of *man coming into this world*, he does not mean that men had lived for a certain time outside the world and then came into the world, since this is contrary to the teaching of the Apostle: *when the children were not yet born nor had they done anything good or evil (in order that, according to the proposed election of God flow), not out of works, but out of calling, as it has been said* (Rom 9:11). Therefore, since they had done nothing before they were born, it is plain that the soul does not exist prior to its union with the body.

He refers to *every man coming into this world*, to show that men are enlightened by God with respect to that according to which they came into the world, i.e., with respect to the intellect, which is something external. For man is constituted of a twofold nature, bodily and intellectual. According to his bodily or sensible nature, man is enlightened by a bodily and sensible light; but according to his soul and intellectual nature, he is enlightened by an intellectual and spiritual light. Now man does not come into this world according to his bodily nature, but under this aspect, he is from the world. His intellectual nature is derived from a source external to the world, as has been said, i.e., from God through creation; as in *until all flesh returns to its origin, and the spirit is directed to God, who made it* (Eccl 12:7). For these reasons, when the Evangelist speaks of *coming into this world*, he is showing that this enlightenment refers to what is from without, that is, the intellect.

130. Si vero accipiatur *illuminari* pro lumine gratiae, sic hoc quod dicitur, *illuminat omnem hominem* potest tripliciter exponi.

Uno modo, secundum Origenem in illa Hom. *Aquila grandis*, exponitur hoc modo, ut accipiamus **mundum** ratione suae perfectionis, ad quam perducitur homo reconciliatus per Christum. Et tunc dicitur *illuminat omnem hominem venientem*, per fidem, *in hunc mundum*, spiritualem, scilicet Ecclesiam illuminatam lumine gratiae.

Alio modo, secundum Chrysostomum, exponitur, accipiendo **mundum** ratione suae creationis, et talis est sensus: *illuminat*, scilicet Verbum, quantum de se est, quia ex parte sua nulli deest, imo *vult omnes salvos fieri, et ad agnitionem veritatis venire*, ut dicitur I Tim. II, 4, *omnem hominem venientem*, idest qui nascitur in hunc mundum sensibilem. Quod si aliquis non illuminatur, ex parte hominis est, avertentis se a lumine illuminante.

Tertio modo, secundum Augustinum, exponitur, ut ly 'omnem' sit distributio accommoda. Ut sit sensus *illuminat omnem hominem venientem in hunc mundum*, non simpliciter, sed *omnem hominem*, qui illuminatur, scilicet quia nullus illuminatur nisi a Verbo. Dicit ergo, secundum Augustinum, *venientem*, ut assignet rationem quare homo indiget illuminari; accipiendo tamen **mundum** ratione suae perversitatis et defectus. Quasi dicat: ideo indiget illuminari, quia venit in hunc mundum, perversitate et defectibus tenebrosum et ignorantia plenum. De mundo spirituali primi hominis; Lc. I, 79: *illuminare his, qui in tenebris et in umbra mortis sedent*.

131. Destruitur autem per verba praedicta error Manichaei ponentis, homines a principio contrario, idest diabolo, in mundo creatos fuisse: quia si homo fuisset creatura diaboli, veniens in mundum, non illuminaretur a Deo, sive a Verbo; quia *Christus venit in mundum, ut dissolvat opera diaboli*; I Io. III.

132. Sic ergo patet ex efficacia divini Verbi, quod defectus cognitionis in hominibus non est ex parte ipsius Verbi: quia ad omnes illuminandos efficax est, cum sit **lux vera quae illuminat omnem hominem venientem in hunc mundum**. Sed ne credas defectum ipsum esse ex remotione seu absentia verae lucis, hoc excludens Evangelista, subdit: *in mundo erat*.

Simile huic habetur Act. XVII, 27: *non longe est ab unoquoque nostrum*, scilicet Deus, *in ipso enim vivimus, et movemur, et sumus*. Quasi dicat Evangelista: Verbum divinum efficax est et praesens est ad illuminandum.

133. Notandum vero quod in mundo dicitur aliquid esse tripliciter. Uno modo per continentiam, sicut locatum in loco; infra c. XVII, 11: *hi in mundo sunt*. Alio modo, sicut pars in toto; nam pars mundi dicitur esse in

130. If we understand *enlightenment* with respect to the light of grace, then **he enlightens every man** may be explained in three ways.

The first way is by Origen in his homily, *The Great Eagle*, and is this. **World** is understood from the point of view of its perfection, which man attains by his reconciliation through Christ. And so we have, **he enlightens every man coming**, by faith, **into this world**, i.e., this spiritual world, that is, the Church, which has been enlightened by the light of grace.

Chrysostom explains it another way. He takes **world** under the aspect of creation. Then the sense is: **he enlightens**, i.e., the Word does, in so far as it depends on him, because he fails no one, but rather *wants all men to be saved, and to come to the knowledge of the truth* (1 Tim 2:4); **every man coming**, i.e., who is born into this sensible world. If anyone is not enlightened, it is due to himself, because he turns from the light that enlightens.

Augustine explains it a third way. For him, 'every' has a restricted application, so that the sense is: **he enlightens every man coming into this world**, not **every man** universally, but every man who is enlightened, since no one is enlightened except by the Word. According to Augustine, the Evangelist says, **coming into this world**, in order to give the reason why man needs to be enlightened, and he is taking **world** from the point of view of its perversity and defect. It is as though he were saying: man needs to be enlightened because he is coming into this world which is darkened by perversity and defects and is full of ignorance. This followed the spiritual world of the first man: *to enlighten those who sit in darkness and in the shadow of death* (Luke 1:79).

131. The above statement refutes the error of the Manichaeans, who think than men were created in the world from an opposing principle, i.e., the devil. For if man were a creature of the devil when coming into this world, he would not be enlightened by God or by the Word, for *Christ came into the world to destroy the works of the devil* (1 John 3:8).

132. So it is clear, from the efficacy of the divine Word, that the lack of knowledge in men is not due to the Word, because he is effective in enlightening all, being **the true light, which enlightens every man coming into this world**. But so you do not suppose this lack arose from the withdrawal or absence of the true light, the Evangelist rules this out adding, **he was in the world**.

A comparable statement is found in *he is not far from any one of us*, that is, God, *for in him we live, and move, and are* (Acts 17:28). It is as though the Evangelist were saying: The divine Word is effective and is at hand in order to enlighten us.

133. We should remark that something is said to be 'in the world' in three ways. In one way, by being contained, as a thing in place exists in a place: **these are in the world** (John 17:11). In another way, as a part in a whole; for a part

mundo, etiamsi non sit locata; sicut substantiae superna-turales, licet localiter non sint in mundo, tamen sunt ut partes Ps. CXLV, v. 6: *qui fecit caelum et terram, mare et omnia quae in eis sunt.*

Neutro autem istorum modorum lux vera in mun-do erat, quia nec localis est, nec pars universi: immo quodammodo (ut ita liceat loqui), totum universum est pars, bonitatem eius partialiter participans. Erat ergo in mundo tertio modo, sicut causa efficiens et conservans; Ier. XXIII, 24: *caelum et terram ego impleo.*

Sed tamen aliter est de Verbo agente et causante om-nia, et aliter de aliis agentibus. Nam alia agentia operan-tur ut extrinsecus existentia: cum enim non agant nisi movendo et alterando aliquo modo quantum ad ea quae sunt extrinseca rei, ut extrinseca operantur. Deus vero operatur in omnibus ut interius agens, quia agit creando. Creare autem est dare esse rei creatae. Cum ergo esse sit intimum cuilibet rei, Deus, qui operando dat esse, ope-ratur in rebus ut intimus agens. In mundo ergo erat ut dans esse mundo.

134. Consuetum est autem dici Deum esse in omni-bus per essentiam, praesentiam et potentiam.

Ad cuius intellectum sciendum est quod per poten-tiam dicitur esse aliquis in omnibus quae subduntur potentiae eius: sicut rex dicitur esse in toto regno sibi subiecto, per suam potentiam; non tamen ibi est per praesentiam, neque per essentiam. Per praesentiam di-citur esse in omnibus quae sunt in conspectu eius, sicut rex dicitur esse per praesentiam in domo sua. Per essen-tiam vero dicitur esse in illis rebus, in quibus est sua sub-stantia: sicut est rex in uno loco determinato.

Dicimus enim Deum esse ubique per potentiam, quia omnia eius potestati subduntur; Ps. CXXXVIII, 8: *si ascendero in caelum, tu illic es . . . si sumpsero pennas meas diluculo et habitavero in extremis maris: etenim il-luc manus tua deducet me et tenebit me dextera tua.* Per praesentiam vero, quia *omnia nuda et aperta sunt oculis eius,* quae sunt in mundo, ut habetur Hebr. IV, 13. Per essentiam autem, quia essentia sua intima est omnibus rebus: oportet enim de necessitate omne agens, inquan-tum agens, immediate coniungi suo effectui, cum mo-vens et motum oporteat simul esse. Deus autem actor est et conservator omnium secundum esse uniuscuiusque rei. Unde, cum esse rei sit intimum in qualibet re, ma-nifestum est quod Deus per essentiam suam, per quam omnia creat, sit in omnibus rebus.

135. Notandum autem quod Evangelista signanter utitur hoc verbo **erat** cum dicit **in mundo erat**, osten-dens ab initio creaturae semper ipsum fuisse in mundo, causans et conservans omnia: quia si ad momentum

of the world is said to be in the world even though it is not in a place. For example, supernatural substances, although not in the world as in a place, are nevertheless in it as parts: *God . . . who made heaven and earth, the sea, and all things that are in them* (Ps 145:6).

But the true light was not in the world in either of these ways, because that light is neither localized nor is it a part of the universe. Indeed, (if we can speak this way,) the entire universe is in a certain sense a part, since it participates in a partial way in his goodness. Accordingly, the true light was in the world in a third way, i.e., as an efficient and preserv-ing cause: *I fill heaven and earth* (Jer 23:24).

However, there is a difference between the way the Word acts and causes all things and the way in which other agents act. For other agents act as existing externally: since they do not act except by moving and altering a thing quali-tatively in some way with respect to its exterior, they work from without. But God acts in all things from within, be-cause he acts by creating. Now to create is to give being to the thing created. So, since existence is innermost in each thing, God, who by acting gives existence, acts in things from within. Hence God was in the world as one giving existence to the world.

134. It is customary to say that God is in all things by his essence, presence and power.

To understand what this means, we should know that someone is said to be by his power in all the things that are subject to his power; as a king is said to be in the entire kingdom subject to him, by his power. He is not there, how-ever, by presence or essence. Someone is said to be by pres-ence in all the things that are within his range of vision; as a king is said to be in his house by presence. And someone is said to be by essence in those things in which his substance is; as a king is in one determinate place.

Now we say that God is everywhere by his power, since all things are subject to his power: *if I ascend into heaven, you are there . . . if I take my wings early in the morning, and dwell in the furthest part of the sea, even there your hand will lead me, and your right hand will hold me* (Ps 138:8). He is also everywhere by his presence, because *all things are bare and open to his eyes* (Heb 4:13). He is present everywhere by his essence, because his essence is innermost in all things. For every agent, as acting, has to be immediately joined to its effect, because mover and moved must be together. Now God is the maker and preserver of all things with respect to the existence of each. Hence, since the existence of a thing is innermost in that thing, it is plain that God, by his es-sence, through which he creates all things, is in all things.

135. It should be noted that the Evangelist significant-ly uses the word **was**, when he says, **he was in the world**, showing that from the beginning of creation he was always in the world, causing and preserving all things; because if God for even a moment were to withhold his power from

subtraheret Deus virtutem suam a rebus conditis, omnia in nihilum redigerentur, et esse desinerent.

Unde Origenes satis ad hoc congruo exemplo utitur, dicens quod sicut se habet vox humana ad verbum humanum in mente conceptum, sic se habet creatura ad Verbum divinum: nam sicut vox nostra est effectus Verbi concepti in mente nostra, ita et creatura est effectus Verbi in divina mente concepti; *dixit enim et facta sunt.* Ps. CXLVIII, v. 5. Unde sicut videmus quod statim, deficiente verbo nostro, vox sensibilis deficit, ita si virtus Verbi divini subtraheretur a rebus, statim res omnes in ipso momento deficerent; et hoc quia est *portans omnia verbo virtutis suae*, Hebr. I, 3.

136. Sic ergo patet quod defectus divinae cognitionis non est in hominibus ex Verbi absentia, quia **in mundo erat**; non est etiam ex Verbi indivisibilitate seu occultatione, quia fecit opus, in quo similitudo evidenter relucet, scilicet mundum. Sap. XIII, 5: *a magnitudine speciei et creaturae cognoscibiliter poterit eorum creator videri*; et Rom. I, 20: *invisibilia Dei per ea quae facta sunt intellecta conspiciuntur.* Et ideo statim Evangelista subiungit **et mundus per ipsum factus est**, ut scilicet in ipso lux ipsa manifestaretur. Sicut in artificio manifestatur ars artificis, ita totus mundus nihil aliud est quam quaedam repraesentatio divinae sapientiae in mente Patris conceptae; Eccli. I, 10: *sparsit illam super omnia opera sua.*

Sic ergo patet quod defectus divinae cognitionis non est ex parte Verbi, quia efficax est, cum sit **lux vera**; praesens est, quia **in mundo erat**; evidens est, quia **mundus per ipsum factus est**.

137. Unde autem sit huius defectus, ostendit Evangelista consequenter, cum dicit **et mundus eum non cognovit**; quasi dicat, non est ex parte ipsius, sed ex parte mundi, qui **eum non cognovit**.

Dicit autem **eum** in singulari, quia supra Verbum dixerat non solum **lucem hominum**, sed **Deum**: unde cum dicit **eum**, intelligit Deum.

Ponitur autem hic **mundus** pro homine: angeli namque cognoverunt eum intelligendo; elementa cognoverunt eum obediendo; sed **mundus**, idest homo habitator mundi, **eum non cognovit**.

138. Et possumus hunc defectum cognitionis divinae referre vel ad naturam hominis, vel ad culpam.

Ad naturam quidem, quia licet omnia haec praedicta auxilia data sint homini, ut ducatur in cognitionem Dei, tamen ratio humana in se deficiens est ab hac cognitione; Iob XXXVI, v. 25: *unusquisque intuetur eum procul*; et iterum ibi: *ecce Deus magnus vincens scientiam nostram.* Sed si aliqui eum cognoverunt, hoc fuit non inquantum fuerunt in mundo, sed inquantum fuerunt

the things he established, all would return to nothing and cease to be.

Hence Origen uses an apt example to show this, when he says that as a human vocal sound is to a human word conceived in the mind, so is, the creature to the divine Word; for as our vocal sound is the effect of the word conceived in our mind, so the creature is the effect of the Word conceived in the divine mind. *For he spoke, and they were created* (Ps 148:5). Hence, just as we notice that as soon as our inner word vanishes, the sensible vocal sound also ceases, so, if the power of the divine Word were withdrawn from things, all of them would immediately cease to be at that moment. And this is because he is *sustaining all things by his powerful word* (Heb 1:3).

136. So it is plain that a lack of divine knowledge in minds is not due to the absence of the Word, because **he was in the world**; nor is it due to the invisibility or concealment of the Word, because he has produced a work in which his likeness is clearly reflected, that is, the world: *for from the greatness and beauty of creatures, their creator can be seen accordingly* (Wis 13:5), and *the invisible things of God are clearly seen, being understood through the things that are made* (Rom 1:20). And so the Evangelist at once adds, **and through him the world was made**, in order that that light might be manifested in it. For as a work of art manifests the art of the artisan, so the whole world is nothing else than a certain representation of the divine wisdom conceived within the mind of the Father, *he poured her out upon all his works* (Sir 1:10).

Now it is clear that the lack of divine knowledge is not due to the Word, because he is efficacious, being **the true light**; and he is at hand, since **he was in the world**; and he is knowable, since **through him the world was made**.

137. The Evangelist indicates the source of this lack when he says, **and the world did not know him**, as if to say: it is not due to him, but to the world, who **did not know him**.

He says **him** in the singular, because earlier he had called the Word not only the **light of men** (John 1:4), but also **God** (John 1:1); and so when he says **him**, he means God.

Again, he uses **world** for man. For the angels knew him by their understanding, and the elements by their obeying him; but **the world**, i.e., man, who lives in the world, **did not know him**.

138. We attribute this lack of divine knowledge either to the nature of man or to his guilt.

To his nature, indeed, because although all the aforesaid aids were given to man to lead him to the knowledge of God, human reason in itself lacks this knowledge. *Man beholds him from afar* (Job 36:25), and immediately after, *God is great beyond our knowledge.* But if some have known him, this was not insofar as they were in the world, but insofar as there were above the world; and the kind for whom the

supra mundum, et tales quibus dignus non erat mundus, quia *mundus eum non cognovit*. Et est quasi ratio quare ab hominibus Deus non cognoscitur. Et sic mundus accipitur pro inordinato mundi amore; quasi dicat *mundus eum non cognovit*. Unde si aliquid aeternum in mente perceperunt, hoc fuit inquantum non erant de hoc mundo.

Si vero referatur ad culpam hominis, tunc hoc quod dixit *mundus eum non cognovit*, est quasi ratio quare ab hominibus Deus non cognoscitur; et sic accipitur *mundus* pro inordinato mundi amatore. Quasi dicat *mundus eum non cognovit*, quia sunt mundi amatores. Amor enim mundi, ut dicit Augustinus, maxime retrahit a Dei cognitione; quia *amor mundi inimicum Dei constituit*, Iac. c. IV, 4. Qui autem non diligit Deum, non potest eum cognoscere; I Cor. II, 14: *animalis homo non percipit ea quae sunt spiritus Dei*.

139. Notandum autem quod ex hoc solvitur quaestio gentilium, qui vane quaerunt: si a paucis temporibus Filius Dei pro salute humana mundo innotuit, videtur quod ante tempus illud naturam humanam despiceret.

Quibus dicendum est quod non despexit, sed semper fuit in mundo, et quantum in se est, cognoscibilis est ab hominibus; sed quod aliqui eum non cognoverunt, fuit eorum culpa, quia mundi amatores erant.

140. Notandum etiam quod Evangelista loquitur de incarnatione Verbi, ut ostendat idem esse Verbum incarnatum, et quod *erat in principio apud Deum* et Deus.

Resumit quae de ipso supra dixerat. Ibi enim dixerat quod *Verbum erat lux hominum*; hic vero dicit quod *erat lux vera*. Ibi quod *omnia per ipsum facta sunt*; hic vero *et mundus per ipsum factus est*. Supra vero dixit, quod *sine ipso factum est nihil*, idest, secundum unam expositionem, omnia conservans; hic vero dicit *in mundo erat*, mundum et omnia creans et conservans. Ibi dixit: *et tenebrae eam non comprehenderunt*; hic vero *et mundus eum non cognovit*.

Et ideo totum hoc quod sequitur ab illo loco *erat lux vera*, videtur quaedam explicatio superiorum.

141. Possumus etiam ex praedictis accipere triplicem rationem, quare Deus voluit incarnari.

Una est perversitas humanae naturae, quae ex sui malitia iam obtenebrata erat vitiorum et ignorantiae obscuritate. Unde supra dixerat quod *tenebrae eam non comprehenderunt*. Venit ergo in carnem Deus, ut tenebrae possent apprehendere lucem, idest cognitionem eius pertingere. Is. IX, 2: *populus, qui ambulabat in tenebris, vidit lucem magnam.*

Secunda propter insufficientiam prophetici testimonii. Venerunt enim prophetae, venerat Ioannes; sed

world was not worthy, because *the world did not know him*. And this is a certain kind of reason why God is not known by man. And also as the world has an inordinate love of the world; thus it is said *the world did not know him*. Hence if they mentally perceived anything eternal, that was insofar as they were not of this world.

But if this lack is attributed to man's guilt, then the phrase, *the world did not know him*, is a kind of reason why God was not known by man; in this sense *world* is taken for inordinate lovers of the world. It is as though it said, *the world did not know him*, because they were lovers of the world. For the love of the world, as Augustine says, is what chiefly withdraws us from the knowledge of God, because *love of the world makes one an enemy to God* (Jas 4:4); *the sensual man does not perceive the things that pertain to the Spirit of God* (1 Cor 2:14).

139. From this we call answer the question of the gentiles who futilely ask this: if it is only recently that the Son of God is set before the world as the savior of men, does it not seem that before that time he scorned human nature?

We should say to them that he did not scorn the world but was always in the world, and on his part is knowable by men; but it was due to their own fault that some have not known him, because they were lovers of the world.

140. We should also note that the Evangelist speaks of the incarnation of the Word to show that the incarnate Word and that which *was in the beginning with God* (John 1:1), and God, are the same.

He repeats what he had said of him earlier. For above he had said he that the *Word was the light of men* (John 1:4); here he says he was *the true light*. Above, he said that *all things were made through him* (John 1:3); here he says that *through him the world was made*. Earlier he had said, *without him was made nothing* (John 1:3), that is, according to one explanation, he conserves all things; here he says, *he was in the world*, creating and conserving the world and all things. There he had said, *the darkness did not comprehend it* (John 1:5); here he says, *the world did not know him*.

And so, all he says after he was the *true light*, is an explanation of what he had said before.

141. We can gather three reasons from the above why God willed to become incarnate.

One is because of the perversity of human nature which, because of its own malice, had been darkened by vices and the obscurity of its own ignorance. And so he said before, *the darkness did not comprehend it* (John 1:5). Therefore, God came in the flesh so that the darkness might apprehend the light, i.e., obtain a knowledge of it. *The people who walked in darkness saw a great light* (Isa 9:2).

The second reason is that the testimony of the prophets was not enough. For the prophets came and John had

sufficienter illuminare non poterant, quia **non erat ille lux**. Unde necessarium erat ut post prophetarum vaticinia, post Ioannis adventum, lux ipsa veniret, et sui cognitionem mundo traderet; et hoc est quod Apostolus dicit, Hebr. I, 1: *multifarie, multisque modis olim Deus loquens patribus in prophetis, novissime locutus est nobis in Filio*; et II Petr. I, 19: *habetis propheticum sermonem, cui bene facitis attendentes, donec dies illucescat.*

Tertia propter creaturarum defectum. Nam creaturae insufficientes erant ad ducendum in cognitionem Creatoris; unde **mundus per ipsum factus est, et ipsum non cognovit**. Unde necessarium erat ut ipse Creator per carnem in mundum veniret, et per seipsum cognosceretur: et hoc est quod Apostolus dicit, I Cor. I, 21: *nam, quia in Dei sapientia mundus non cognovit per sapientiam Deum, placuit Deo per stultitiam praedicationis salvos facere credentes.*

come; but they were not able to give sufficient enlightenment, because **he was not the light** (John 1:8). And so, after the prophecies of the prophets and the coming of John, it was necessary that the light itself come and give the world a knowledge of itself. And this is what the Apostle says: *in past times, God spoke in many ways and degrees to our fathers through the prophets; in these days he has spoken to us in his Son* (Heb 1:1). *We have the prophetic message, to which you do well to give attention, until the day dawns* (2 Pet 1:19).

The third reason is because of the shortcomings of creatures. For creatures were not sufficient to lead to a knowledge of the Creator; hence he says, **through him the world was made, and the world did not know him**. Thus it was necessary that the Creator himself come into the world in the flesh, and be known through himself. And this is what the Apostle says: *since in the wisdom of God the world did not know God by its wisdom, it pleased God to save those who believe by the foolishness of our preaching* (1 Cor 1:21).

Lecture 6

1:11 In propria venit: et sui eum non receperunt; [n. 143]

1:12 quotquot autem receperunt eum, dedit eis potestatem filios Dei fieri, his qui credunt in nomine eius. [n. 146]

1:13 Qui non ex sanguinibus, neque ex voluntate carnis, neque ex voluntate viri, sed ex Deo nati sunt. [n. 160]

1:11 εἰς τὰ ἴδια ἦλθεν, καὶ οἱ ἴδιοι αὐτὸν οὐ παρέλαβον.

1:12 ὅσοι δὲ ἔλαβον αὐτόν, ἔδωκεν αὐτοῖς ἐξουσίαν τέκνα θεοῦ γενέσθαι, τοῖς πιστεύουσιν εἰς τὸ ὄνομα αὐτοῦ,

1:13 οἳ οὐκ ἐξ αἱμάτων οὐδὲ ἐκ θελήματος σαρκὸς οὐδὲ ἐκ θελήματος ἀνδρὸς ἀλλ' ἐκ θεοῦ ἐγεννήθησαν.

1:11 He came unto his own, and his own did not receive him. [n. 143]

1:12 But as many as received him, he gave them power to be made the sons of God, to those who believe in his name: [n. 146]

1:13 Who are born, not of blood, nor of the will of the flesh, nor of the will of man, but of God. [n. 160]

---

142. Assignata necessitate incarnationis Verbi, consequenter Evangelista manifestat utilitatem ex ipsa incarnatione ab hominibus consecutam. Et

primo insinuat lucis adventum, quia *in propria venit*;

secundo hominum occursum, ibi *et sui eum non receperunt*;

tertio fructum ex adventu lucis allatum, ibi *dedit eis potestatem filios Dei fieri*.

143. Ostendit ergo quod lux quae erat praesens in mundo et evidens seu manifesta per effectum, non tamen cognoscebatur a mundo. Et ideo *venit in propria*, ut cognosceretur.

Sed ne, cum dicit *venit*, intelligeres motum localem hoc modo, ut scilicet venerit quasi desinens esse ubi prius erat, et denuo incipiens esse, ubi prius non erat, dicit Evangelista *in propria*; idest in ea quae erant sua, quae ipse fecit; et venit ipse, ubi erat. Infra XVI, 28: *exivi a Patre, et veni in mundum. Venit*, inquam, *in propria*, idest in Iudaeam, secundum quosdam, quae quidem speciali modo sua erat; Ps. LXXV, 2: *notus in Iudaea Deus*; Is. V, 7: *vinea Domini exercituum, domus Israel est*. Sed melius est ut dicatur, *propria*, idest in mundum ab eo creatum; Ps. XX III, 1: *Domini est terra*.

144. Sed si prius erat in mundo, quomodo venit in mundum?

Respondeo, dicendum quod 'venire in aliquem locum' dicitur dupliciter, scilicet vel quod aliquis veniat ubi nullo modo prius fuerat, vel quod ubi aliquo modo prius fuerat, incipiat esse quodam novo modo. Sicut rex, qui prius erat in civitate aliqua sui regni per potentiam, ad illam postmodum veniens personaliter, dicitur venire ubi prius erat: venit enim per suam substantiam ubi prius erat solum per suam potentiam. Sic ergo Filius Dei venit in mundum, et tamen in mundo erat. Erat quidem per essentiam, potentiam et praesentiam, sed venit per

142. Having given the necessity for the incarnation of the Word, the Evangelist then shows the advantage men gained from that incarnation.

First, he shows the coming of the light, because *he came unto his own*;

second, its reception by men, at *and his own did not receive him*;

third, the fruit brought by the coming of the light, at *he gave them power to be made the sons of God*.

143. He shows that the light which was present in the world and evident, i.e., disclosed by its effect, was nevertheless not known by the world. Hence, *he came unto his own*, in order to be known.

The Evangelist says, *unto his own*, i.e., to things that were his own, which he had made. And he says this so that you do not think that when he says, *he came*, he means a local motion in the sense that he came as though ceasing to be where he previously was and newly beginning to be where he formerly had not been. He came where he already was. *I came forth from the Father, and have come into the world* (John 16:28). *He came*, I say, *unto his own*, i.e., to Judea, according to some, because it was in a special way his own. *In Judea God is known* (Ps 75:1); *the vineyard of the Lord of hosts is the house of Israel* (Isa 5:7). But it is better to say, *unto his own*, i.e., into the world created by him. *The earth is the Lord's* (Ps 23:1).

144. But if he was previously in the world, how could he come into the world?

I answer that 'coming to some place' is understood in two ways. First, that someone comes where he absolutely had not been before. Or, second, that someone begins to be in a new way where he was before. For example, a king, who up to a certain time was in a city of his kingdom by his power and later visits it in person, is said to have come where he previously was: for he comes by his substance where previously he was present only by his power. It was in this way that the Son of God came into the world and yet was in the world. For he was there, indeed, by his essence,

carnis assumptionem; erat invisibilis, venit ut esset visibilis.

145. Deinde cum dicit *et sui eum non receperunt*, sequitur hominum occursus, qui differenter se habuerunt ad venientem. Quia quidam eum receperunt, non sui; unde dicitur *et sui eum non receperunt*. *Sui* sunt homines, quia ab eo formati; Gen. II, 7: *formavit Deus hominem*; Ps. XCIX, 3: *scitote, quoniam Dominus ipse fecit nos*, quia ad eius imaginem facti: Gen. I, 26: *faciamus hominem*.

Sed melius est ut dicamus *sui*, idest Iudaei, *eum non receperunt*, per fidem credendo et honorando; infra V, 43: *ego veni in nomine Patris mei, et non recepistis me*; et infra VIII, 49: *ego honorifico Patrem meum, et vos inhonorastis me*. Sunt quidem Iudaei, sui, quia ab ipso in populum peculiarem electi; Deut. XXVI, 18: *elegit te Dominus in populum peculiarem*. Sui secundum carnem coniuncti; Rom. IX, 5: *ex quibus Christus secundum carnem*. Item sui, ab eo beneficiis promoti; Is. I, 2: *filios enutrivi, et exaltavi*. Sed licet *sui*, Iudaei *eum non receperunt*.

146. Non defuerunt tamen, qui eum receperunt; unde subdit *quotquot autem receperunt*. Utitur Evangelista hoc modo loquendi, dicens *quotquot*, ut ostendat ampliorem esse factam solutionem, quam fuerit promissio, quae facta fuit solum suis, scilicet Iudaeis; Is. XXXIII, 22: *Dominus legifer noster, Dominus rex noster; ipse salvabit nos*.

Sed solutio non solum fuit facta suis, sed *quotquot receperunt eum*, idest omnibus in eum credentibus; Rom. XV, 8: *dico autem Christum ministrum fuisse circumcisionis propter veritatem Dei, ad confirmandas promissiones patrum*, idest patribus factas. Gentes autem super misericordia, quia misericorditer sunt recepti.

147. Dicit *quotquot*, ut ostendat quod gratia Dei indifferenter datur omnibus recipientibus Christum; Act. X, 45: *ergo in nationes gratia Spiritus Sancti effusa est*. Et non solum liberis, sed etiam servis, non solum masculis, sed etiam feminis; Gal. III, 28: *in Christo Iesu non est masculus, nec femina, gentilis, vel Iudaeus, circumcisio et praeputium* etc.

148. Deinde cum dicit *dedit eis potestatem filios Dei fieri*, sequitur fructus eius adventus. Ubi

primo ponit fructus magnificentiam, quia *dedit eis potestatem*;

secundo ostendit quibus datur, quia *his qui credunt*;

tertio insinuat modum dandi, quia *non ex sanguinibus*.

149. Est ergo factus adventus Filii Dei magnus, quia homines fiunt per hoc Filii Dei; Gal. IV, 4: *misit Deus Filium suum factum ex muliere, ut adoptionem Filiorum*

power, and presence, but he came by assuming flesh. He was there invisibly, and he came in order to be visible.

145. Then when he says, *and his own did not receive him*, we have the reception given him by men, who reacted in different ways. For some did receive him, but these were not his own; hence he says, *his own did not receive him*. *His own* are men, because they were formed by him. *The Lord God formed man* (Gen 2:7); *know that the Lord is God: he made us* (Ps 99:3). And he made them to his own image, *let us make man to our image* (Gen 1:26).

But it is better to say, *his own*, i.e., the Jews, *did not receive him*, through faith by believing, and by showing honor to him. *I have come in the name of my Father, and you do not receive me* (John 5:43), and *I honor my Father, and you have dishonored me* (John 8:49). Now the Jews are his own because they were chosen by him to be his special people. *The Lord chose you to be his special people* (Deut 26:18). They are his own because they are related according to the flesh, *from whom is Christ, according to the flesh* (Rom 9:3). They are also his own because they are enriched by his kindness, *I have reared and brought up sons* (Isa 1:2). But although the Jews were *his own*, they *did not receive him*.

146. However, there were not lacking those who did receive him. Hence he adds, *but as many as received him*. The Evangelist uses this manner of speaking, saying, but *as many as*, to indicate that the deliverance would be more extensive than the promise, which had been made only to his own, i.e., to the Jews. *The Lord is our law giver, the Lord is our king; he will save us* (Isa 33:22).

But this deliverance was not only for his own, but for *as many as received him*, i.e., whoever believe in him. *For I say that Christ was a minister to the circumcised, for the sake of God's truth, to confirm the promises made to the fathers* (Rom 15:8). The gentiles, however, according to his mercy, are recieved because of mercy.

147. He says, *as many as*, to show that God's grace is given without distinction to all who receive Christ. *The grace of the Holy Spirit has been poured out upon the gentiles* (Acts 10:45). And not only to free men, but to slaves as well; not only to men, but to women also. *In Christ Jesus there is neither male nor female, Jew or Greek, the circumcised or uncircumcised* (Gal 3:28).

148. Then when he says, *he gave them power to be made the sons of God*, we have the fruit of his coming. Where

first, he mentions the grandeur of the fruit, for *he gave them power*;

second, he shows to whom it is given, *to those who believe*;

third, he indicates the way it is given, which is *not of blood*.

149. The fruit of the coming of the Son of God is great, because by it men are made sons of God. *God sent his Son made from a woman . . . so that we might receive our*

reciperemus. Et hoc congrue, ut qui sumus Filii Dei, per hoc quod assimilamur Filio, reformemur per Filium.

150. Dicit ergo ***dedit eis potestatem filios Dei fieri***.

Ad cuius evidentiam sciendum est, quod homines fiunt filii Dei per assimilationem ad Deum; et ideo secundum triplicem assimilationem hominum ad Deum homines sunt filii Dei.

Primo enim per gratiae infusionem: unde quicumque habet gratiam gratum facientem, efficitur filius Dei; Rom. VIII, 15: *non enim accepistis spiritum servitutis* etc.; Gal. IV, 6: *quoniam estis filii Dei, misit Deus spiritum Filii sui*.

Secundo assimilamur Deo per operum perfectionem, quia qui facit opera iustitiae, est filius; Matth. V, 44: *diligite inimicos vestros*.

Tertio assimilamur Deo per gloriae adeptionem, et quantum ad animam per lumen gloriae, I Io. III, 2: *cum apparuerit, similes ei erimus*, et quantum ad corpus, Phil. III, v. 21: *reformabit corpus humilitatis nostrae*. Unde de istis duobus dicitur Rom. VIII, 23: *adoptionem filiorum Dei expectantes*.

151. Si ergo accipiamus potestatem filios Dei fieri quantum ad operum perfectionem et gloriae adeptionem, nullam difficultatem habebit sermo, quia cum dicit ***dedit eis potestatem***, intelligitur de potestate gratiae, qua habita, potest homo facere opera perfectionis, et adipisci gloriam; quia, ut dicitur Rom. VI, 23, *gratia Dei vita aeterna*. Et secundum hunc modum dicitur ***dedit eis***, qui eum receperunt, ***potestatem***, idest infusionem gratiae, ***filios Dei fieri***, bene operando, et gloriam acquirendo.

152. Si vero intelligatur de gratiae infusione, tunc dubitationem habet hoc quod dicitur ***dedit eis potestatem***, quia non est in potestate nostra fieri filios Dei, cum non sit in potestate nostra gratiam habere.

Hoc ergo quod dicit ***dedit eis potestatem***, aut intelligitur de potestate naturae: et hoc non videtur esse verum, quia infusio gratiae est supra naturam nostram. Aut intelligitur de potestate gratiae: et tunc hoc ipsum est gratiam habere, quod habere ***potestatem filios Dei fieri***; et sic non dedit potestatem filios fieri Dei, sed filios Dei esse.

153. Ad quod dicendum quod in datione gratiae requiritur in homine adulto ad iustificationem suam consensus per motum liberi arbitrii: unde quia in potestate hominis est ut consentiat et non consentiat, ***dedit eis potestatem***.

Dedit autem hanc potestatem suscipiendi gratiam dupliciter: praeparando, et hominibus proponendo. Sicut enim qui facit librum, et proponit homini ad legendum, dicitur dare potestatem legendi; ita Christus, per

adoption as sons (Gal 4:5). And it was fitting that we, who are sons of God by the fact that we are made like the Son, should be reformed through the Son.

150. So he says, ***he gave them power to be made the sons of God***.

To understand this we should remark that men become sons of God by being made like God. Hence men are sons of God according to a threefold likeness to God.

First, by the infusion of grace; hence anyone having sanctifying grace is made a son of God. *You did not receive the spirit of slavery . . . but the spirit of adoption as sons* (Rom 8:15). *Because you are sons of God, God sent the Spirit of his Son into your hearts* (Gal 4:6).

Second, we are like God by the perfection of our actions, because one who acts justly is a son: *love your enemies . . . so that you may be the children of your Father* (Matt 5:44).

Third, we are made like God by the attainment of glory. The glory of the soul by the light of glory, *when he appears we shall be like him* (1 John 3:2); and the glory of the body, *he will reform our lowly body* (Phil 3:21). Of these two it is said, *we are waiting for our adoption as sons of God* (Rom 8:23).

151. If we take the power to become the sons of God as referring to the perfection of our actions and the attainment of glory, the statement offers no difficulty. For then when he says, ***he gave them power***, he is referring to the power of grace; and when a man possesses this, he can perform works of perfection and attain glory, since *the grace of God is eternal life* (Rom 6:23). According to this way we have, ***he gave them***, to those who received him, ***power***, i.e., the infusion of grace, ***to be made the sons of God***, by acting well and acquiring glory.

152. But if this statement refers to the infusion of grace, then his saying, ***he gave them power***, gives rise to a difficulty. And this is because it is not in our power to be made sons of God, since it is not in our power to possess grace.

We can understand, ***he gave them power***, as a power of nature; but this does not seem to be true since the infusion of grace is above our nature. Or we can understand it as the power of grace, and then to have grace is to have ***power to be made the sons of God***. And in this sense he did not give them power to become sons of God, but to be sons of God.

153. The answer to this is that when grace is given to an adult, his justification requires an act of consent by a movement of his free will. So, because it is in the power of men to consent and not to consent, ***he gave them power***.

However, he gives this power of accepting grace in two ways: by preparing it, and by offering it to him. For just as one who writes a book and offers it to a man to read is said to give the power to read it, so Christ, through whom grace

quem gratia facta est, ut dicitur infra, et *qui operatus est salutem in medio terrae*, ut dicitur in Ps. LXXIII, 12, *dedit* nobis *potestatem filios Dei fieri* per gratiae susceptionem.

154. Secundo, quia hoc non sufficit, cum etiam liberum arbitrium indigeat ad hoc quod moveatur ad gratiae susceptionem, auxilio gratiae divinae, non quidem habitualis, sed moventis, ideo dat potestatem movendo liberum arbitrium hominis, ut consentiat ad susceptionem gratiae, iuxta illud Thren. ult., v. 21: *converte nos, Domine, ad te*, movendo voluntatem nostram ad amorem tuum, *et convertemur*. Et hoc modo vocatur interior vocatio, de qua dicitur Rom. VIII, 30: *quos vocavit*, interius voluntatem instigando ad consentiendum gratiae, *hos iustificavit*, gratiam infundendo.

155. Quia vero per hanc gratiam habet homo hanc potestatem conservandi se in divina filiatione, potest et aliter dici: *dedit eis*, idest eum recipientibus, *potestatem filios Dei fieri*, idest gratiam, per quam potentes sunt in divina filiatione conservari; I Io. ult., 18: *omnis qui natus est ex Deo, non peccat, sed gratia Dei*, per quam regeneramur in filios Dei, *conservat eum*.

156. Sic ergo *dedit eis potestatem filios Dei fieri*, per gratiam gratum facientem, per operum perfectionem, per gloriae adeptionem, et haec praeparando, movendo et conservando gratiam.

157. Deinde cum dicit *his qui credunt in nomine eius*, ostenditur quibus conferatur fructus eius adventus. Et hoc quidem potest accipi dupliciter, vel ut sit expositivum superiorum, vel determinativum. Expositivum quidem, quia Evangelista dixerat *quotquot autem receperunt eum*; ut ergo ostendat quid est recipere eum, quasi exponendo, consequenter subiungit *his qui credunt in nomine eius*; quasi dicat: hoc est recipere eum, in eum credere, quia per fidem Christus habitat in cordibus nostris, iuxta illud Eph. III, 17: *habitare Christum per fidem in cordibus vestris*. Illi ergo *receperunt eum, qui credunt in nomine eius*.

158. Ut determinativum vero ponitur ab Origene in homilia quae incipit *Vox spiritualis*. Hoc modo multi recipiunt Christum, dicentes se esse Christianos, qui tamen non fiunt filii Dei, quia non vere credunt in nomine eius, falsa dogmata de Christo suggerendo, subtrahendo scilicet aliquid sibi de divinitate, vel de humanitate, iuxta illud I Io. c. IV, 3: *omnis spiritus qui solvit Christum, ex Deo non est*. Et ideo Evangelista quasi determinando dicit *dedit eis*, scilicet recipientibus eum per fidem, *potestatem filios Dei fieri*, illis tamen, *qui credunt in nomine eius*, idest qui nomen Christi integrum servant, ut nihil de divinitate, vel humanitate Christi diminuant.

was produced, as it is said below, and who *accomplished salvation on the earth* (Ps 73:12), *gave* us *power to become the sons of God* by offering grace.

154. Yet this is not sufficient since even free will, if it is to be moved to receive grace, needs the help of divine grace, not indeed habitual grace, but movent grace. For this reason, second, he gives power by moving the free will of man to consent to the reception of grace, as in *convert us to yourself, O Lord*, by moving our will to your love, *and we will be converted* (Lam 5:21). And in this sense we speak of an interior call, of which it is said, *those whom he called*, by inwardly moving the will to consent to grace, *he justified*, by infusing grace (Rom 8:3).

155. Since by this grace man has the power of maintaining himself in the divine sonship, one may read these words in another way. *He gave them*, i.e., those who receive him, *power to be made the sons of God*, i.e., the grace by which they are able to be maintained in the divine sonship. *Everyone who is born from God does not sin, but the grace of God, through which we are reborn as children of God, preserves him* (1 John 5:18).

156. Thus, *he gave them power to be made the sons of God*, through sanctifying grace, through the perfection of their actions, and through the attainment of glory; and he did this by preparing this grace, moving their wills, and preserving this grace.

157. Then when he says, *to those who believe in his name*, he shows those on whom the fruit of his coming is conferred. We can understand this in two ways: either as explaining what was said before, or as qualifying it. We can regard it as explaining as the Evangelist had said, *as many as received him*, and now to show what it is to receive him, he adds by way of explanation, *those who believe in his name*. It is as though he were saying: to receive him is to believe in him, because it is through faith that Christ dwells in your hearts, as in *that Christ may dwell in your hearts through faith* (Eph 3:17). Therefore, they *received him, who believe in his name*.

158. Origen regards this as a qualifying statement, in his homily, *The Spiritual Voice*. In this sense, many receive Christ, declaring that they are Christians, but they are not sons of God, because they do not truly believe in his name; for they propose false dogmas about Christ by taking away something from his divinity or humanity, as in *every spirit that denies Christ is not from God* (1 John 4:3). And so the Evangelist says, as though contracting his meaning, *he gave them*, i.e., those who receive him by faith, *power to be made the sons of God, to those*, however, *who believe in his name*, i.e., who keep the name of Christ whole, in such a way as not to lessen anything of the divinity or humanity of Christ.

159. Potest etiam hoc referri ad formationem fidei, ut dicatur *his* scilicet *dedit potestatem filios Dei fieri, qui credunt in nomine eius*, idest per fidem caritate formatam opera salutis faciunt. Illi enim qui habent solum fidem informem, non credunt in nomine eius, quia non operantur ad salutem.

Sed prima expositio, quae accipitur ut expositivum praemissorum, melior est.

160. Deinde cum dicit *qui non ex sanguinibus* etc., ostenditur qualiter conferatur hominibus tam magnificus fructus.

Quia enim dixerat quod fructus advenientis lucis est potestas fieri filios Dei hominibus data; filius autem dicitur aliquis ex eo quod nascitur: ne aestimes eos materiali generatione nasci, dicit *non ex sanguinibus*.

Et licet hoc nomen sanguis in Latino non habeat plurale, quia tamen in Graeco habet, ideo translator regulam grammaticae servare non curavit, ut veritatem perfecte doceret. Unde non dicit *ex sanguine*, secundum Latinos, sed *ex sanguinibus*; per quod intelligitur quicquid ex sanguine generatur, concurrens ut materia ad carnalem generationem. *Semen autem*, secundum Philosophum, *est ultimi superfluitas cibi sanguinei*. Unde sive *semen* viri, sive menstruum mulieris, intelligitur per sanguinem. Causa vero motiva ad actum carnalem est voluntas se commiscentium, scilicet maris et feminae, quia licet actus virtutis generativae secundum quod huiusmodi, non sit subiectus voluntati, praeambula tamen ad ipsum voluntati subiiciuntur; et ideo dicit *neque ex voluntate carnis*, pro persona mulieris, *neque ex voluntate viri*, ut ex causa efficiente *sed ex Deo nati sunt*; quasi dicat: non carnaliter, sed spiritualiter filii Dei fiunt.

Accipitur autem hic *caro*, secundum Augustinum, pro muliere, quia sicut caro obedit spiritui, sic mulier debet obedire viro; Gen. c. II, 23 dixit Adam de muliere: *hoc nunc os ex ossibus meis*. Et attendendum, secundum Augustinum, quod sicut dissipatur possessio domus, in qua principatur mulier et subiicitur vir, ita dissipatur homo, cum caro dominatur spiritui; propter quod dicit Apostolus, Rom. VIII, 12: *debitores sumus non carni, ut secundum carnem vivamus*. De modo autem dictae generationis carnalis dicitur Sap. VII, 1: *in ventre matris figuratus sum caro*.

161. Vel possumus dicere quod motivum ad carnalem generationem est duplex; unum scilicet ex parte appetitus intelligitur, quae est voluntas; aliud a parte sensitivi, quod est concupiscentia. Ad designandum ergo materialem causam, dixit *non ex sanguinibus*; sed ad designandum causam efficientem quantum ad concupiscentiam, dicit *neque ex voluntate carnis*; quamvis improprie voluntas dicatur concupiscentia carnis, quo tamen modo dicitur Gal. V, 17: *caro concupiscit adversus spiritum* etc. Ad designandum vero appetitum intellectivum dicit *non ex voluntate viri*. Sic ergo generatio

159. We can also refer this to formed faith, in the sense that to all, that is, *he gave power to be made the sons of God, to those who believe in his name*, i.e., those who do the works of salvation through a faith formed by charity. For those who have only an unformed faith do not believe in his name because they do not work unto salvation.

However, the first exposition, which is taken as explaining what preceded, is better.

160. Then when he says, *who are born, not of blood*, he shows the way in which so great a fruit is conferred on men.

For since he had said that the fruit of the light's coming is the power given to men to become the sons of God, then to forestall the supposition that they are born through a material generation he says, *not of blood*.

And although the word blood has no plural in Latin, but does in Greek, the translator ignored a rule of grammar in order to teach the truth more perfectly. So he does not say, *from blood*, in the Latin manner, but *from bloods*. This indicates whatever is generated from blood, serving as the matter in carnal generation. According to the Philosopher, *semen is a residue derived from useful nourishment in its final form*. So *blood* indicates either the seed of the male or the menses of the female. The cause moving to the carnal act is the will of those coming together, the man and the woman. For although the act of the generative power as such is not subject to the will, the preliminaries to it are subject to the will. So he says, *nor of the will of the flesh*, referring to the woman; *nor of the will of man*, as from an efficient cause; *but of God*. It is as though he were saying: they became sons of God, not carnally, but spiritually.

According to Augustine, *flesh* is taken here for the woman, because as the flesh obeys the spirit, so woman should obey man. Adam said of the woman, *this, at last, is bone of my bones* (Gen 2:23). And note, according to Augustine, that just as the possessions of a household are wasted away if the woman rules and the man is subject, so a man is wasted away when the flesh rules the spirit. For this reason the Apostle says, *we are not debtors to the flesh, so that we should live according to the flesh* (Rom 8:12). Concerning the manner of this carnal generation, we read, *in the womb of my mother I was molded into flesh* (Wis 7:1).

161. Or, we might say that the moving force to carnal generation is twofold: the intellectual appetite on the one hand, that is, the will; and on the other hand, the sense appetite, which is concupiscence. So, to indicate the material cause he says, *not of blood*. To indicate the efficient cause, in respect to concupiscence, he says, *nor of the will of the flesh*, even though the concupiscence of the flesh is improperly called a *will* in this sense: *the flesh lusts against the spirit* (Gal 5:17). Finally, to indicate the intellectual appetite he says, *nor of the will of man*. So, the generation of the sons of God is not carnal but spiritual, because they were

filiorum Dei non est carnalis, sed est spiritualis, quia *ex Deo nati sunt*. I Io. V, 4: *omne quod natum est ex Deo vincit mundum.*

162. Nota autem quod haec praepositio *de* semper denotat materialem causam, et efficientem, et etiam consubstantialem: dicimus enim quod faber facit cultellum de ferro, et pater generat filium suum de seipso, quia aliquid sui concurrit aliquo modo ad generationem. Haec vero praepositio 'a' semper denotat causam moventem. Haec vero praepositio 'ex' accipitur ut communis, quia importat causam materialem et efficientem, non tamen consubstantialem.

Unde quia solus Filius Dei, qui est Verbum, est de substantia Patris, imo cum Patre est una substantia, alii vero sancti, qui sunt Filii adoptivi, non sunt de eius substantia; ideo Evangelista utitur hac praepositione *ex*, dicens de aliis *ex Deo nati sunt*; de Filio vero naturali, quod de Patre est natus.

163. Notandum est etiam quod secundum ultimam expositionem carnalis generationis possumus accipere differentiam carnalis generationis ad spiritualem.

Quia enim illa est ex sanguinibus, ideo carnalis; ista vero, quia non est ex sanguinibus, ideo spiritualis; infra III, 6: *quod natum est ex carne, caro est, et quod natum est ex Spiritu, spiritus est*. Item, quia materialis generatio est ex voluntate carnis, idest ex concupiscentia, ideo est immunda, et generat filios peccatores; Eph. II, 3: *eramus natura filii irae*. Item, quia illa est *ex voluntate viri*, idest hominis, facit filios hominum; haec vero, quia est *ex Deo*, facit filios Dei.

164. Si vero hoc quod dicit *dedit eis potestatem*, voluit referre ad baptismum, propter quod in filios Dei regeneramur, possumus videre in hoc ordinem baptismi, ut scilicet primo requiratur fides, quod fit in cathecumenis, qui debent primo instrui de fide, ut scilicet credant in nomine eius, et deinde regenerentur per baptismum, non quidem ex sanguinibus carnaliter, sed ex Deo spiritualiter.

born *of God*. *Every one who is born from God conquers the world* (1 John 5:4).

162. Note, however, that this preposition *from*, always signifies a material cause as well as an efficient and even a consubstantial cause. Thus we say a blacksmith makes a knife from iron, and a father generates his son from himself, because something of his concurs somehow in begetting. But the preposition 'by' always signifies a moving cause. The preposition 'out of' is taken as something common, since it implies an efficient as well as a material cause, although not a consubstantial cause.

Consequently, since only the Son of God, who is the Word, is of the substance of the Father and indeed is one substance with the Father, while the saints, who are adopted sons, are not of his substance, the Evangelist uses the preposition *out of* saying of others that *they are born of God*, but of the natural Son, he says that he is born of the Father.

163. Note also that in the light of our last exposition of carnal generation, we can discern the difference between carnal and spiritual generation.

For since the former is from blood, it is carnal; but the latter, because it is not from blood, is spiritual. *That which is born of the flesh, is flesh; and that which is born of the Spirit, is spirit* (John 3:6). Again, because material generation is from the desires of the flesh, i.e., from concupiscence, it is unclean and begets children who are sinners: *we were by nature children of wrath* (Eph 2:3). Again, because the former is *of the will of man*, that is, from man, it makes children of men; but the latter, because it is *of God*, makes children of God.

164. But if he intends to refer his statement, *he gave them power*, to baptism, in virtue of which we are reborn as sons of God, we can detect in his words the order of baptism: that is, the first thing required is faith, as shown in the case of catechumens, who must first be instructed about the faith so that they may believe in his name; then through baptism they are reborn, not carnally from blood, but spiritually from God.

Lecture 7

1:14 Et Verbum caro factum est, et habitavit in nobis. Et vidimus gloriam eius, gloriam quasi unigeniti a Patre, plenum gratiae et veritatis. [n. 165]

1:14 Καὶ ὁ λόγος σὰρξ ἐγένετο καὶ ἐσκήνωσεν ἐν ἡμῖν, καὶ ἐθεασάμεθα τὴν δόξαν αὐτοῦ, δόξαν ὡς μονογενοῦς παρὰ πατρός, πλήρης χάριτος καὶ ἀληθείας.

1:14 And the Word was made flesh, and dwelt among us, and we saw his glory, the glory as it were of the only begotten of the Father, full of grace and truth. [n. 165]

---

165. Posita necessitate adventus Verbi in carnem et etiam utilitate, consequenter Evangelista modum veniendi manifestat dicens *et Verbum caro factum est*.

Et secundum hoc continuatur ad hoc quod dixerat: *in propria venit*; quasi dicat: Verbum Dei *in propria venit*. Sed ne credas ipsum venisse, locum mutando, ostendit modum quo venit, scilicet per incarnationem: eo enim modo venit, quo missus est Patre, a quo missus est, inquantum factus est caro. Gal. IV, 4: *misit Deus Filium suum, factum ex muliere* etc., ubi dicit Augustinus: *eo missum, quo factum*.

Secundum Chrysostomum autem continuatur ad illud *dedit eis potestatem* etc.; quasi dicat: si quaeris unde potuit dare hanc potestatem hominibus, ut Filii Dei fierent, respondet Evangelista *quia Verbum caro factum est*, dedit nobis quod possemus Filii Dei fieri. Gal. IV, 5: *misit Deus Filium suum, ut adoptionem Filiorum Dei reciperemus*.

Secundum vero Augustinum continuatur sic ad hoc quod dixerat *sed ex Deo nati sunt*: quasi enim dure videbatur, ut homines ex Deo nascerentur, ideo quasi in argumentum huius dicti, ut scilicet Verbum esse credatur, subdit Evangelista illud de quo minus videtur, scilicet quod *Verbum caro factum est*. Quasi dicat: ne mireris si homines ex Deo sunt nati, quia V*erbum caro factum est*, idest Deus factus est homo.

166. Notandum quod hoc quod dicitur V*erbum caro factum est*, quidam male intelligentes, sumpserunt occasionem erroris.

Quidam namque posuerunt Verbum ita carnem factum esse ac si ipsum vel aliquid eius sit in carnem conversum, sicut cum farina fit panis, et aer ignis. Et hic fuit Eutiches, qui posuit commixtionem naturarum in Christo, dicens in eo eamdem fuisse Dei et hominis naturam.

Sed huius opinionis falsitas manifeste apparet, quia, sicut est dictum supra, *Verbum erat Deus*. Deus autem immutabilis est, ut dicitur Mal. III, 6: *ego Deus, et non mutor*, unde nullo modo potest esse quod in aliam naturam convertatur. Est ergo dicendum contra Eutichem *Verbum caro factum est*: Verbum carnem assumpsit,

165. Having explained the necessity for the Word's coming in the flesh as well as the benefits this conferred, the Evangelist now shows the way he came, at **and the Word was made flesh**.

He thus resumes the thread with his earlier statement, **he came unto his own** (John 1:11). As if to say: the Word of God **came unto his own**. But lest anyone suppose that he came by changing his location, he shows the manner in which he came, that is, by an incarnation. For he came in the manner in which he was sent by the Father, by whom he was sent, i.e., he was made flesh. *God sent his Son made from a woman* (Gal 4:4). And Augustine says about this that *he was sent in the manner in which he was made*.

According to Chrysostom, however, he is here continuing the earlier statement, **he gave them power to be made the sons of God** (John 1:12). As if to say: if you wonder how he was able to give this power to men, i.e., that they become sons of God, the Evangelist answers: because **the Word was made flesh**, he made it possible for us to be made sons of God. *God sent his Son . . . so that we might receive our adoption as sons* (Gal 4:5).

But according to Augustine, he is continuing the earlier statement, **who are born . . . of God** (John 1:13). For since it seemed a hard saying that men be born from God, then, as though arguing in support of this and to produce belief in the existence of the Word, the Evangelist adds something which seems less seemly, namely, that **the Word was made flesh**. As if to say: do not wonder if men are born from God, because **the Word was made flesh**, i.e., God became man.

166. It should be noted that this statement, **the Word was made flesh**, has been misinterpreted by some and made the occasion of error.

For certain ones have presumed that the Word became flesh in the sense that he or something of him was turned into flesh, as when flour is made into bread, and air becomes fire. One of these was Eutyches, who postulated a mixture of natures in Christ, saying that in him the nature of God and of man was the same.

We can clearly see that this is false because, as was said above, **the Word was God** (John 1:1). Now God is immutable, as is said, *I am the Lord, and I do not change* (Mal 3:6). Hence in no way can it be said that he was turned into another nature. Therefore, one must say in opposition to Eutyches, **the Word was made flesh**, i.e., the Word assumed

non quod ipsum Verbum sit ipsa caro; sicut si dicamus: homo factus est albus, non quod ipse sit ipsa albedo, sed quod albedinem assumpsit.

167. Fuerunt etiam alii qui, licet crederent Verbum non in carnem mutatum sed quod eam assumpsit, tamen dixerunt ipsum assumpsisse carnem sine anima; nam si carnem animatam assumpsisset, dixisset Evangelista: ***Verbum caro*** cum anima ***factum est***. Et sic fuit error Arii, qui dixit quod in Christo non erat anima, sed Verbum Dei erat ibi loco animae.

Et huius positionis falsitas apparet, tum quia repugnat Sacrae Scripturae, quae in pluribus locis mentionem facit de anima Christi, sicut illud Matth. XXVI, 38: *tristis est anima mea usque ad mortem*; tum etiam quia quaedam passiones animae recitantur de Christo, quae in Verbo Dei nullo modo esse possunt, nec etiam in carne sola, sicut illud Matth. XXVI, 37: *coepit Iesus taedere, et maestus esse*; tum etiam quia Deus non potest esse forma alicuius corporis; nec etiam angelus corpori uniri potest per modum formae, cum secundum naturam a corpore sit separatus; anima autem unitur corpori sicut forma. Non igitur Verbum Dei corporis forma esse potest.

Praeterea, constat quod caro non sortitur speciem carnis, nisi per animam: quod patet, quia recedente anima a corpore hominis, seu bovis, caro hominis vel bovis, non dicitur caro nisi aequivoce. Si ergo Verbum non assumpsit carnem animatam, manifestum est quod non assumpsit carnem. Sed ***Verbum caro factum est***; ergo carnem animatam assumpsit.

168. Fuerunt autem alii, qui, ex hoc moti, dixerunt Verbum carnem quidem animatam assumpsisse, sed animam sensitivam tantum, non intellectivam, loco cuius in corpore Christi dixerunt Verbum esse. Et hic fuit error Apollinaris, qui quandoque Arium secutus est, tandem propter auctoritates praedictas coactus fuit ponere aliquam animam in Christo, quae posset harum passionum esse subiectum, ita tamen quod ratione et intellectu careret sed loco horum Verbum esset in homine Christo.

Sed hoc manifeste apparet esse falsum, quia repugnat auctoritati Sacrae Scripturae, in qua quaedam dicuntur de Christo, quae nec in divinitate, nec in anima sensitiva, nec in carne inveniri possunt: sicut illud quod admiratus est, ut dicitur Matth. VIII, 10; admiratio autem est passio animae rationalis et intellectivae, cum sit desiderium cognoscendi causam occultam effectus visi. Sic igitur, sicut tristitia cogit in Christo ponere partem animae sensitivam, contra Arium, ita admiratio cogit ponere in ipso partem animae intellectivam, contra Apollinarem.

Idem etiam apparet per rationem. Sicut enim non est caro sine anima, ita non est vera caro humana sine

flesh, but not in the sense that the Word himself is that flesh. It is as if we were to say: the man became white, not that he is that whiteness, but that he assumed whiteness.

167. There were others who, although they believed that the Word was not changed into flesh but assumed it, nevertheless said that he assumed flesh without a soul; for if he had assumed flesh with a soul, the Evangelist would have said, ***the Word was made flesh*** with a soul. This was the error of Arius, who said that there was no soul in Christ, but that the Word of God was there in place of a soul.

The falsity of this opinion is obvious, both because it is in conflict with Sacred Scripture, which often mentions the soul of Christ, as: *my soul is sad, even to the point of death* (Matt 26:38), and because certain affections of the soul are observed in Christ which can not possibly exist in the Word of God or in flesh alone: *he began to be sorrowful and troubled* (Matt 26:37). Also, God cannot be the form of a body. Nor can an angel be united to a body as its form, since an angel, according to its very nature, is separated from body, whereas a soul is united to a body as its form. Consequently, the Word of God cannot be the form of a body.

Furthermore, it is plain that flesh does not acquire the specific nature of flesh except through its soul. This is shown by the fact that when the soul has withdrawn from the body of a man or a cow, the flesh of the man or the cow is called flesh only in an equivocal sense. So if the Word did not assume flesh with a soul, it is obvious that he did not assume flesh. But ***the Word was made flesh***; therefore, he assumed flesh with a soul.

168. And there were others who, influenced by this, said that the Word did indeed assume flesh with a soul, but this soul was only a sensitive soul, not an intellectual one; the Word took the place of the intellectual soul in Christ's body. This was the error of Apollinaris. He followed Arius for a time, but later in the face of the authorities cited above, was forced to admit a soul in Christ which could be the subject of these emotions. But he said this soul lacked reason and intellect, and that in the man Christ their place was taken by the Word.

This too is obviously false, because it conflicts with the authority of Sacred Scripture in which certain things are said of Christ that cannot be found in his divinity, nor in a sensitive soul, nor in flesh alone; for example, that Christ marvelled, as in Matthew (Matt 8:10). For to marvel or wonder is a state which arises in a rational and intellectual soul when a desire arises to know the hidden cause of an observed effect. Therefore, just as sadness compels one to place a sensitive element in the soul of Christ, against Arius, so marvelling or amazement forces one to admit, against Apollinaris, an intellectual element in Christ.

The same conclusion can be reached by reason. For as there is no flesh without a soul, so there is no human flesh

anima humana, quae est anima intellectiva. Si ergo Verbum assumpsit carnem animatam anima sensitiva tantum, et non rationali, non assumpsit carnem humanam: et ita non poterit dici: *Deus factus est homo.*

Praeterea ad hoc Verbum humanam naturam assumpsit, ut eam repararet. Ergo id reparavit quod assumpsit. Si ergo non assumpsit animam rationalem, non reparasset eam: et sic nullus fructus proveniret nobis ex Verbi incarnatione, quod falsum est. **Verbum** ergo **caro factum est**, idest carnem animatam anima rationali assumpsit.

169. Sed forte dicis: si Verbum carnem sic animatam assumpsit, quare Evangelista de anima rationali mentionem non fecit, sed de carne solum dicens **Verbum caro factum est**?

Respondeo dicendum quod propter quatuor rationes Evangelista hoc fecit. Primo ad ostendendum veritatem incarnationis contra Manichaeos, qui dicebant Verbum non assumpsisse veram carnem, sed phantasticam tantum, cum non esset conveniens ut boni Dei Verbum assumeret carnem, quam ipsi dicebant diaboli creaturam. Et ideo Evangelista, ut hoc excluderet, fecit de carne specialiter mentionem; sicut et Christus, Lc. XXIV, 39, existimantibus discipulis eum esse phantasma, veritatem resurrectionis ostendit, dicens: *spiritus carnem et ossa non habet, sicut me videtis habere.*

Secundo ad demonstrandam Dei erga nos magnitudinem benignitatis. Constat enim quod anima rationalis magis conformis est Deo quam caro, et quidem magnum pietatis sacramentum fuisset si Verbum assumpsisset animam humanam, utpote sibi conformem, sed assumere etiam carnem elongatam a simplicitate suae naturae, fuit multo amplioris, immo inaestimabilis pietatis indicium; secundum quod Apostolus dicit I ad Tim. III, 16: *et manifeste magnum est pietatis sacramentum, quod manifestatum est in carne.* Et ideo ut hoc ostenderet Evangelista, solum de carne mentionem fecit.

Tertio ad demonstrandam veritatem et singularitatem unionis in Christo. Aliis enim hominibus sanctis unitur quidem Deus, quantum ad animam solum; unde dicitur Sap. VII, v. 27: *per nationes in animas sanctas se transfert, amicos Dei et prophetas constituens.* Sed quod Verbum Dei uniretur carni, hoc est singulare in Christo, secundum illud in Ps. CXL, 10: *singulariter sum ego donec transeam*; Iob XXVIII, 17: *non adaequabitur ei aurum.* Hanc ergo singularitatem unionis in Christo ostendere volens Evangelista, de carne solum mentionem fecit, dicens **Verbum caro factum est**.

Quarto ad insinuandam congruitatem humanae reparationis. Homo enim per carnem infirmabatur, et ideo Evangelista volens insinuare adventum Verbi congruum esse nostrae reparationi, mentionem de carne specialiter fecit, ut ostenderet quod caro infirma per

without a human soul, which is an intellectual soul. So if the Word assumed flesh which was animated with a merely sensitive soul to the exclusion of a rational soul, he did not assume human flesh; consequently, one could not say: *God became man.*

Besides, the Word assumed human nature in order to repair it. Therefore, he repaired what he assumed. But if he did not assume a rational soul, he would not have repaired it. Consequently, no fruit would have accrued to us from the incarnation of the Word; and this is false. Therefore, **the Word was made flesh**, i.e., assumed flesh which was animated by a rational soul.

169. But you may say: if the Word did assume flesh with such a soul, why did the Evangelist not mention rational soul, instead of only flesh, saying, **the Word was made flesh**?

I answer that the Evangelist had four reasons for doing this. First, to show the truth of the incarnation against the Manichaeans, who said that the Word did not assume true flesh, but only imaginary flesh, since it would not have been becoming for the Word of the good God to assume flesh, which they regarded as a creature of the devil. And so to exclude this the Evangelist made special mention of the flesh, just as Christ showed the truth of the resurrection to the disciples when they took him for a spirit, saying: *a spirit does not have flesh and bones, as you see that I have* (Luke 24:39).

Second, to show the greatness of God's kindness to us. For it is evident that the rational soul has a greater conformity to God than does flesh, and that it would have been a great sign of compassion if the Word had assumed a human soul, as being conformed to himself. But to assume flesh too, which is something far removed from the simplicity of his nature, was a sign of a much greater, indeed, of an incomprehensible compassion. As the Apostle says: *obviously great is the mystery of godliness which appeared in the flesh* (1 Tim 3:16). And so to indicate this, the Evangelist mentioned only flesh.

Third, to demonstrate the truth and uniqueness of the union in Christ. For God is indeed united to other holy men, but only with respect to their soul; so it is said: *she passes into holy souls, making them friends of God and prophets* (Wis 7:27). But that the Word of God is united to flesh is unique to Christ, according to the Psalmist: *I am alone until I pass* (Ps 140:10), and *gold cannot equal it* (Job 28:17). So the Evangelist, wishing to show the uniqueness of the union in Christ, mentioned only the flesh, saying, **the Word was made flesh**.

Fourth, to suggest its relevance to man's restoration For man was weak because of the flesh. And thus the Evangelist, wishing to suggest that the coming of the Word was suited to the task of our restoration, made special mention of the flesh in order to show that the weak flesh was repaired by

carnem Verbi reparata fuit; et hoc est quod Apostolus dicit, Rom. VIII, 3: *nam quod impossibile erat legi, in quo infirmabatur per carnem, Deus Filium suum mittens in similitudinem carnis peccati, et de peccato damnavit peccatum in carne.*

170. Sed quaeritur, quare Evangelista non dixit Verbum carnem assumpsit, sed potius **Verbum caro factum est**.

Respondeo dicendum, quod hoc ideo fecit, ut excluderet errorem Nestorii, qui dixit in Christo fuisse duas personas, et duos filios, et alium esse filium Virginis: unde non concedebat quod Beata Virgo esset mater Dei.

Sed secundum hoc Deus non esset factus homo; quia impossibile est quod duorum singularium, quae diversa sunt secundum suppositum, unum praedicetur de alio. Unde si alia est persona Verbi, seu suppositum, et alia persona hominis, seu suppositum in Christo, tunc non erit verum quod dicit Evangelista **Verbum caro factum est**. Ad hoc enim fit aliquid, ut sit; si ergo Verbum non esset homo, non posset dici quod Verbum sit factum homo. Et ideo signanter Evangelista dixit **factum est**, et non dixit assumpsit, ut ostendat quod unio Verbi ad carnem non est talis qualis est assumptio prophetarum, qui non assumebantur in unitatem suppositi, sed ad actum propheticum: sed est talis quod Deum vere faceret hominem, et hominem Deum, idest quod Deus esset homo.

171. Fuerunt et alii, qui non intelligentes modum incarnationis, posuerunt quidem assumptionem praedictam esse terminatam ad veritatem personae, confitentes in Deo unam personam Dei et hominis; sed tamen dicunt in ipso fuisse duas hypostases, sive duo supposita, unum naturae humanae creatum, et temporale, aliud divinae increatum, et aeternum. Et talis est prima opinio quae ponitur III Sent. dist. VI.

Sed secundum hanc opinionem non habet veritatem ista propositio: Deus factus est homo, et homo factus est Deus. Et ideo haec opinio damnata est tamquam haeretica in Quinto Concilio, ubi dicitur: *si quis in Domino Iesu Christo unam personam, et duas hypostases dixerit, anathema sit.* Et ideo Evangelista, ut omnem assumptionem excluderet, quae non terminatur ad unitatem personae, utitur hoc verbo **factum est.**

172. Si vero quaeris quomodo Verbum est homo, dicendum quod eo modo est homo quo quicumque alius est homo, scilicet habens humanam naturam. Non quod Verbum sit ipsa humana natura, sed est divinum suppositum unitum humanae naturae.

Hoc autem quod dicitur **Verbum caro factum est**, non aliquam mutationem in Verbo, sed solum in natura assumpta de novo in unitatem personae divinae dicit. **Et Verbum caro factum est**, per unionem ad carnem. Unio autem relatio quaedam est. Relationes autem de novo dictae de Deo in respectu ad creaturas, non important

the flesh of the Word. And this is what the Apostle says: *the law was powerless because it was weakened by the flesh. God, sending his Son in the likeness of sinful flesh and in reparation for sin, condemned sin in his flesh* (Rom 8:3).

170. A question arises as to why the Evangelist did not say that the Word assumed flesh, but rather that **the Word was made flesh**.

I answer that he did this to exclude the error of Nestorius. He said that in Christ there were two persons and two sons, the other being the son of the Virgin. Thus he did not admit that the Blessed Virgin was the mother of God.

But if this were so, it would mean that God did not become man, for one particular suppositum cannot be predicated of another. Accordingly, if the person or suppositum of the Word is different than the person or suppositum of the man, in Christ, then what the Evangelist says is not true, namely, **the Word was made flesh**. For a thing is made or becomes something in order to be it; if, then, the Word is not man, it could not be said that the Word became man. And so the Evangelist expressly said **was made**, and not assumed, to show that the union of the Word to flesh is not such as was the lifting up of the prophets, who were not taken up into a unity of person, but for the prophetic act. This union is such as would truly make God man and man God, i.e., that God would be man.

171. There were some, too, who, misunderstanding the manner of the incarnation, did indeed admit that the aforesaid assumption was terminated at a oneness of person, acknowledging in God one person of God and man. But they said that in him there were two hypostases, i.e., two supposita; one of a human nature, created and non-eternal, and the other of the divine nature, non-created and eternal. This is the first opinion presented in the *Sentences* (III, d6).

According to this opinion the proposition, that God was made man and man was made God, is not true. Consequently, this opinion was condemned as heretical by the Fifth Council, where it is said: *if anyone shall assert one person and two hypostases in the Lord Jesus Christ, let him be anathema.* And so the Evangelist, to exclude any assumption not terminated at a oneness of person, says, **was made**.

172. If you ask how the Word is man, it must be said that he is man in the way that anyone is, man, namely, as having human nature. Not that the Word is human nature itself, but he is a divine suppositum united to a human nature.

The statement, **the Word was made flesh**, does not indicate any change in the Word, but only in the nature newly assumed into the oneness of a divine person. **And the Word was made flesh** through a union to flesh. Now a union is a relation. And relations newly said of God with respect to

mutationem ex parte Dei, sed ex parte creaturae novo modo se habentis ad Deum.

173. Sequitur *et habitavit in nobis*; quod quidem dupliciter distinguitur a praemissis.

Primo ut dicatur quod supra Evangelista egit de Verbi incarnatione, dicens *Verbum caro factum est*; hic vero modum incarnationis insinuat, dicens *et habitavit in nobis*. Secundum enim Chrysostomum et Hilarium, per hoc quod Evangelista dicit *Verbum caro factum est*, posset aliquis intelligere quod sit conversum in carnem, et non sint in Christo duae naturae distinctae, sed una tantum natura ex humana et divina commixta; ideo Evangelista hoc excludens, subiunxit *et habitavit in nobis*, idest in nostra natura, ut tamen in sua maneret distinctum. Illud enim quod in aliquid convertitur, non manet ab eo in quod convertitur secundum naturam distinctum; quod autem ab aliquo non distinguitur, non inhabitat illud; quia habitare distinctionem inhabitantis et in quo habitat importat. Sed Verbum habitavit in nostra natura ergo naturaliter est ab ipsa distinctum. Et ideo inquantum humana natura a natura Verbi fuit in Christo distincta, dicitur habitaculum divinitatis et templum, iuxta illud infra II, 21: *hoc autem dicebat de templo corporis sui*.

174. Et quidem, quamvis a praedictis sanctis hoc sane dicatur, cavenda est tamen calumnia quam aliqui ex hoc incurrunt. Nam antiqui doctores et sancti, emergentes errores circa fidem ita persequebantur, ut interdum viderentur in errores labi contrarios; sicut Augustinus contra Manichaeos, qui destruebant libertatem arbitrii, taliter disputat, quod videtur in haeresim Pelagii incidisse.

Hoc igitur modo Evangelista Ioannes, ne per hoc quod dixerat *Verbum caro factum est*, intelligeretur in Christo confusio vel transmutatio naturarum, subiunxit *et habitavit in nobis*: ex quo Verbo Nestorius occasionem sumens erroris, dixit, Filium Dei sic esse unitum homini ut tamen Dei et hominis non esset una persona: voluit enim quod Verbum per solam inhabitationem per gratiam fuerit humanae naturae unitum. Ex hoc autem sequitur quod Filius Dei non sit homo.

175. Ad quorum evidentiam sciendum est quod in Christo duo considerare possumus, scilicet naturam et personam.

Secundum naturam autem attenditur in Christo distinctio, non secundum personam, quae una et eadem est in duabus naturis; quia humana natura in Christo fuit assumpta in unitatem personae. Inhabitatio ergo, quam ponunt sancti, referenda est ad naturam, ut dicatur quod *habitavit in nobis*, idest natura Verbi inhabitavit naturam nostram, non secundum hypostasim seu personam, quae est eadem utriusque naturae in Christo.

creatures do not imply a change on the side of God, but on the side of the creature relating in a new way to God.

173. Now follows, *and dwelt among us*. This is distinguished in two ways from what went before.

The first consists in stating that above the Evangelist dealt with the incarnation of the Word when he said, *the Word was made flesh*; but now he touches on the manner of the incarnation, saying, *and dwelt among us*. For according to Chrysostom and Hilary, by the Evangelist saying *the Word was made flesh*, someone might think that he was converted into flesh and that there are not two distinct natures in Christ, but only one nature compounded from the human and divine natures. And so the Evangelist, excluding this, added, *and dwelt among us*, i.e., in our nature. Furthermore, something which is not distinct from another does not dwell in it, because to dwell implies a distinction between the dweller and that in which it dwells. But the Word dwelt in our nature; therefore, he is distinct in nature from it. And so, inasmuch as human nature was distinct from the nature of the Word in Christ, the former is called the dwelling place and temple of the divinity: *but he spoke of the temple of his body* (John 2:21).

174. Now although what is said here by these holy men is orthodox, care must be taken to avoid the reproach which some receive for this. For the early doctors and saints were so intent upon refuting the emerging errors concerning the faith that they seemed meanwhile to fall into the opposite ones. For example, Augustine, speaking against the Manichaeans, who destroyed the freedom of the will, disputed in such terms that he seemed to have fallen into the heresy of Pelagius.

In this way, lest through saying *the Word was made flesh* it might be thought that there was a confusion or change of natures in Christ, John the Evangelist added, *and dwelt among us*. Nestorius misunderstood this phrase and said that the Son of God was united to man in such a way that there was not one person of God and of man. For he held that the Word was united to human nature only by an indwelling through grace. From this, however, it follows that the Son of God is not man.

175. To clarify this we should know that we can consider two things in Christ: his nature and person.

In Christ there is a distinction in nature, but not in person, which is one and the same in the two natures, since the human nature in Christ was assumed into a oneness of person. Therefore, the indwelling which the saints speak of must be referred to the nature, so as to say, he *dwelt among us*, i.e., the nature of the Word inhabited our nature; not according to the hypostasis or person, which is the same for both natures in Christ.

176. Quod autem blasphemat Nestorius, auctoritate Sacrae Scripturae evidenter refellitur.

Apostolus enim Phil. II, 6 unionem Dei et hominis exinanitionem vocat, dicens de Filio Dei: *qui cum in forma Dei esset, non rapinam arbitratus est se esse aequalem Deo; sed semetipsum exinanivit, formam servi accipiens.* Non autem dicitur Deus exinaniri ex eo quod creaturam rationalem per gratiam inhabitet, quia sic Pater et Spiritus Sanctus exinanirentur, cum et ipsi inhabitare hominem dicantur per gratiam; dicit enim Christus de se et de Patre loquens, infra XIV, 23: **ad eum veniemus et mansionem apud eum faciemus.** De spiritu autem sancto dicit Apostolus, I Cor. III, 16: *Spiritus Dei habitat in nobis.*

Praeterea, si Christus personaliter Deus non esset, praesumptuosissime dixisset: **ego et Pater unum sumus**; et **antequam Abraham fieret, ego sum. Ego** autem personam loquentis demonstrat; homo autem erat, qui loquebatur; unum cum Patre praeexistebat Abrahae.

177. Potest etiam aliter continuari, ut dicatur quod supra egit de Verbi incarnatione, nunc autem agit de Verbi incarnati conversatione, dicens **et habitavit in nobis**, idest inter nos apostolos conversatus est familiariter, secundum quod dicit Petrus, Act. I, 21: *in omni tempore quo intravit et exivit inter nos Dominus Iesus.* Baruch IV, 38: *post haec in terris visus est.*

178. Hoc autem Evangelista addidit propter duo. Primo ut ostendat mirabilem conformitatem Verbi ad homines, inter quos sic conversatus est, ut videretur quasi unus ex eis. Non solum enim in natura voluit assimilari hominibus, sed etiam in convictu et familiari conversatione absque peccato, cum eis voluit esse simul, ut sic homines suae conversationis dulcedine allectos traheret ad seipsum.

Secundo ut ostendat sui testimonii veritatem. Evangelista enim supra de Verbo magna quaedam dixerat et adhuc multa de eo mirabilia dicturus erat, et ideo ut eius testimonium credibilius fieret, accepit quasi in veritatis argumentum, se cum Christo conversatum fuisse, dicens **et habitavit in nobis.** Quasi dicat: bene possum testimonium perhibere de ipso quia cum ipso conversatus sum; I Io. c. I, 1: *quod fuit ab initio, quod audivimus, quod vidimus oculis nostris, quod perspeximus, et manus nostrae contrectaverunt de Verbo vitae* etc., et Act. X, 40: *dedit eum manifestum fieri, non omni populo, sed testibus praeordinatis a Deo* idest nobis qui manducavimus et bibimus cum illo.

176. The blasphemy of Nestorius is further refuted by the authority of Sacred Scripture.

For the Apostle calls the union of God and man an emptying, saying of the Son of God: *he, being in the form of God . . . emptied himself, taking the form of a servant* (Phil 2:6). Clearly, God is not said to empty himself insofar as he dwells in the rational creature by grace, because then the Father and the Holy Spirit would be emptying themselves, since they too are said to dwell in man through grace: for Christ, speaking of himself and of the Father says, **we will come to him, and will make our abode with him** (John 14:23); and of the Holy Spirit the Apostle says: *the Spirit of God dwells in us* (1 Cor 3:16).

Furthermore, if Christ was not God as to his person, he would have been most presumptuous to say: **I and the Father are one** (John 10:30), and **before Abraham was made, I am** (John 8:58). Now **I** refers to the person of the speaker. And the one who was speaking was a man, who, as one with the Father, existed before Abraham.

177. However, another connection with what went before is possible, by saying that above he dealt with the incarnation of the Word, but that now he is treating the manner of life of the incarnate Word, saying, he **dwelt among us**, i.e., he lived on familiar terms with us apostles. Peter alludes to this when he says, *during all the time that the Lord Jesus came and went among us* (Acts 1:21). *Afterwards, he was seen on earth* (Bar 3:38).

178. The Evangelist added this for two reasons. First, to show the marvelous likeness of the Word to men, among whom he lived in such a way as to seem one of them. For he not only willed to be like men in nature, but also in living with them on close terms without sin, in order to draw to himself men won over by the charm of his way of life.

Second, to show the truthfulness of the Evangelist's statements. For the Evangelist had already said many great things about the Word, and was yet to mention more wonderful things about him; and so that his testimony would be more credible he took as a proof of his truthfulness the fact that he had lived with Christ, saying, he **dwelt among us**. As if to say: I can well bear witness to him, because I lived on close terms with him. *We tell you . . . what we have heard, what we have seen with our eyes* (1 John 1:1); *God raised him up on the third day, and granted that he be seen, not by all the people, but by witnesses preordained by God*, that is, *to us who ate and drank with him* (Acts 10:40).

Lecture 8

1:14 Et Verbum caro factum est, et habitavit in nobis. Et vidimus gloriam eius, gloriam quasi unigeniti a Patre, plenum gratiae et veritatis. [n. 180]

1:14 Καὶ ὁ λόγος σὰρξ ἐγένετο καὶ ἐσκήνωσεν ἐν ἡμῖν, καὶ ἐθεασάμεθα τὴν δόξαν αὐτοῦ, δόξαν ὡς μονογενοῦς παρὰ πατρός, πλήρης χάριτος καὶ ἀληθείας.

1:14 And the Word was made flesh, and dwelt among us, and we saw his glory, the glory as it were of the only begotten of the Father, full of grace and truth. [n. 180]

---

179. Posita Verbi incarnatione, hic consequenter Evangelista insinuat Verbi incarnati evidentiam.

Et circa hoc duo facit.

Primo enim ostendit modum manifestationis Verbi incarnati;

secundo utrumque modum exponit, ibi *de plenitudine eius nos omnes accepimus.*

Innotuit autem apostolis Verbum incarnatum dupliciter. Primo quidem per visum acceperunt de eo notitiam; secundo per auditum ex testimonio Ioannis Baptistae.

Primo ergo manifestat quid de Verbo viderunt;

secundo quid a Ioanne audierunt, ibi *Ioannes testimonium perhibet de ipso.*

Dicit autem tria de Verbo.

Primo eius gloriae manifestationem; unde dicit *et vidimus gloriam eius;*

secundo eius gloriae singularitatem, cum subdit *quasi unigeniti;*

tertio huius gloriae determinationem, quia *plenum gratiae et veritatis.*

180. Hoc autem quod dicit *vidimus gloriam eius,* potest continuari ad praecedentia tripliciter.

Primo ut sit argumentum eius quod dixerat *Verbum caro factum est*: quasi dicat: ex hoc habeo et scio quod Verbum Dei est incarnatum, quia ego et alii apostoli vidimus gloriam eius. Infra III, 11: *quod scimus, loquimur: et quod vidimus, testamur.* Et I Io. c. I, 1: *quod fuit ab initio, quod audivimus, quod vidimus oculis nostris* etc.

181. Secundo continuatur, secundum Chrysostomum, ut sit expressivum multiplicis beneficii. Quasi dicat: non solum hoc beneficium collatum est nobis per incarnationem Verbi, scilicet quod efficiamur filii Dei, sed etiam quod videamus gloriam. Oculi enim debiles et infirmi lucem solis non possunt videre; sed tunc eam videre possunt, cum in nube vel in aliquo corpore opaco resplendet. Ante incarnationem enim Verbi mentes humanae erant invalidae ad videndum in seipsa lucem divinam, quae illuminat omnem rationalem naturam; et ideo ut a nobis facilius cerni contemplarique posset nube nostrae carnis se texit, iuxta illud Ex. XVI, 10:

179. Having set forth the incarnation of the Word, the Evangelist then begins to give the evidence for the incarnate Word.

He does two things about this.

First, he shows the ways in which the incarnate Word was made known.

Second, he clarifies each way, at *and of his fullness we have all received* (John 1:16).

Now the incarnate Word was made known to the apostles in two ways: first of all, they obtained knowledge of him by what they saw; second, by what they heard of the testimony of John the Baptist.

So first, he states what they saw about the Word;

second, what they heard from John, at *John bears witness to him* (John 1:15).

He states three things about the Word.

First, the manifestation of his glory; hence he says, *and we saw his glory.*

Second, the uniqueness of his glory, when he adds, *as it were of the only begotten.*

Third, the precise nature of this glory, because *full of grace and truth.*

180. *And we saw his glory,* can be connected in three ways with what went before.

First, it can be taken as an argument for his having said, *the Word was made flesh.* As if to say: I hold and know that the Word of God was incarnate because I and the other apostles have seen his glory. *We speak what we know, and we testify what we have seen* (John 3:11). *We tell you . . . what we have heard, what we have seen with our eyes* (1 John 1:1).

181. Second, according to Chrysostom, the connection is made by taking this statement as expressing many benefits. As if to say: the incarnation of the Word not only conferred on us the benefit of becoming sons of God, but also the good of seeing his glory. For dull and feeble eyes cannot see the light of the sun; but they can see it when it shines in a cloud or on some opaque body. Now before the incarnation of the Word, human minds were incapable of seeing the divine light in itself, the light which enlightens every rational nature. And so, in order that it might be more easily seen and contemplated by us, he covered it with the cloud of our flesh: *they looked towards the wilderness: and behold*

respexerunt ad solitudinem, et viderunt gloriam Domini in nube, idest Verbum Dei in carne.

182. Secundum Augustinum autem continuatur sic quod referatur ad beneficium gratiae.

Spirituales enim oculi hominum non solum naturaliter deficiebant a contemplatione divinae lucis, sed etiam ex defectu peccati, secundum illud Ps. LVII, 9: *supercecidit ignis*, scilicet concupiscentiae, *et non viderunt solem*, scilicet iustitiae. Ut ergo ipsa divina lux posset a nobis videri, sanavit oculos hominum, faciens de carne sua salutare collirium, ut sic oculos ex concupiscentia carnis corruptos Verbum collirio suae carnis curaret. Et inde est quod statim cum **Verbum factum est caro**, dixerunt **et vidimus gloriam eius**. Ad hoc significandum fecit Dominus lutum ex sputo, et linivit oculus caeci nati, infra IX, 6. Lutum quidem de terra est, sputum autem a capite derivatur. Ita in persona Christi, natura quidem humana assumpta de terra est; Verbum vero incarnatum a capite est, scilicet a Deo Patre. Hoc ergo lutum statim cum appositum fuit oculis hominum, **vidimus gloriam eius**.

183. Hanc autem Verbi gloriam Moyses videre optavit, dicens *ostende mihi gloriam tuam* (Ex. XXXIII, 18). Sed eam videre non meruit: immo dictum est ei a Domino: *posteriora mea videbis*, idest umbras et figuras. Apostoli vero ipsam claritatem viderunt; II Cor. III, 18: *nos autem revelata facie gloriam Dei speculantes in eamdem imaginem transformamur de claritate in claritatem*.

Moyses enim et alii prophetae Verbi gloriam manifestandam mundo in fine temporum speculabantur in aenigmatibus et figuris; unde dicit Apostolus, 1 Cor. XII: **haec dixit Isaias, quando vidit gloriam eius**. Apostoli autem ipsam Verbi claritatem per praesentiam corporalem viderunt. II Cor. III, v. 18: *nos autem revelata facie* etc.; et Lc. c. X, 23: *beati oculi qui vident quae vos videtis. Multi enim reges et prophetae voluerunt videre quae vos videtis et non viderunt*.

184. Consequenter cum dicit **gloriam quasi unigeniti**, ostendit gloriae eius singularitatem.

Cum enim de quibusdam hominibus inveniatur quod fuerunt gloriosi, sicut de Moyse legitur Ex. XXXIV, 29: *et facies eius facta est splendida*, vel *cornuta*, secundum aliam litteram, posset aliquis dicere quod ex hoc quod viderunt eum gloriosum, non debet dici quod Verbum Dei sit factum caro. Sed hoc Evangelista excludit, dicens **gloriam quasi unigeniti a Patre**. Quasi dicat: gloria eius non est sicut gloria angeli, vel Moysis, et Eliae, vel Elisei, vel cuiusque alterius, sed **quasi unigeniti**; quia, ut dicitur Hebr. III, 3: *ampliori gloria iste prae Moyse dignus est habitus*. Ps. LXXXVIII, 7: *quis similis Deo in filiis Dei?*

the glory of the Lord appeared in a cloud (Exod 16:10), i.e., the Word of God in the flesh.

182. According to Augustine, however, the connection refers to the gift of grace.

For the failure of the spiritual eyes of men to contemplate the divine light is due not only to their natural limitations but also to the defects incurred by sin: *fire*, that is, of concupiscence, *fell on them, and they did not see the sun*, of justice (Ps 57:9). Hence in order that the divine light might be seen by us, he healed our eyes, making an eye salve of his flesh, so that with the salve of his flesh the Word might heal our eyes, weakened by the concupiscence of the flesh. And this is why just after saying, **the Word was made flesh**, he says, **we saw his glory**. To indicate this the Lord made clay from his saliva and spread the clay upon the eyes of the man born blind (John 9:6). For clay is from the earth, but saliva comes from the head. Similarly, in the person of Christ, his human nature was assumed from the earth; but the incarnate Word is from the head, i.e., from God the Father. So, when this clay was spread on the eyes of men, **we saw his glory**.

183. This is the glory of the Word Moses longed to see, saying, *show me your glory* (Exod 32:18). But he did not deserve to see it; indeed, he was answered by the Lord: *you shall see my back* (Exod 33:23), i.e., shadows and figures. But the apostles saw his brightness: *all of us, gazing on the Lord's glory with unveiled faces, are being transformed from glory to glory into his very image* (2 Cor 3:18).

For Moses and the other prophets saw obscurely and in figures the glory of the Word that was to be manifested to the world at the end of their times, as the Apostle says (1 Cor 13:12). Thus, it is also said: **these things said Isaias, when he saw his glory, and spoke of him** (John 12:41). But the apostles saw the very brilliance of the Word through his bodily presence: *all of us, gazing on the Lord's glory*, and so forth (2 Cor 3:18); *blessed are the eyes which see what you see. For many kings and prophets desired to see what you see, and did not see it* (Luke 10:23).

184. Then when he says, **the glory as it were of the only begotten**, he shows the uniqueness of his glory.

For since it is written of certain men that they were in glory, as of Moses it says that *his face shone* (Exod 34:29), or was *horned*, according to another text, someone might say that from the fact that they saw him in glory, it should not be said that the Word of God was made flesh. But the Evangelist excludes this when he says, **the glory as it were of the only begotten of the Father**. As if to say: his glory is not like the glory of an angel, or of Moses, or Elijah, or Elisha, or anything like that but **the glory as it were of the only begotten**; for as it is said, *he was counted worthy of more glory than Moses* (Heb 3:3); *who among the sons of God is like God?* (Ps 88:7).

185. Hoc autem quod dicit *quasi* est expressivum veritatis, secundum Gregorium, et est modus, ut Chrysostomus dicit. Sicut si aliquis vidisset regem multiplici gloria incedentem, et interrogatus ab aliquo, qualiter regem vidisset, volens se expedire, illam multiplicem gloriam uno Verbo exprimeret, dicens quod ipse incedebat sicut rex, idest sicut regem decebat; ita hic Evangelista, quasi interrogaretur ab aliquo, qualis esset gloria Verbi quam viderat, non valens eam plene exprimere, dicit eam esse *quasi unigeniti a Patre*, idest talem qualem decebat unigenitum Dei.

186. Attenditur autem singularitas gloriae Verbi quantum ad quatuor. Primo quantum ad Patris testimonium, quod Filio reddidit. Quia Ioannes fuit unus de tribus qui viderant Christum transfiguratum in monte, et audierunt vocem Patris dicentis: *hic est Filius meus dilectus, in quo mihi bene complacui*; et de ista gloria dicitur II Petr. I, 17: *accepit a Deo Patre honorem et gloriam, voce delapsa ad eum huiuscemodi a magnifica gloria: 'hic est Filius meus dilectus.'*

Secundo quantum ad angelorum ministerium. Nam ante incarnationem Christi homines erant angelis subiecti; postmodum vero, Christo subiecti ministraverunt, Matth. IV, 11: *tunc accesserunt angeli et ministrabant ei.*

Tertio vero quantum ad naturae obsequium. Tota enim natura Christo obediens ei obsequebatur ad nutum, utpote ab ipso instituta, quia *omnia per ipsum facta sunt*: quod quidem nec angelis, nec alicui alii creaturae concessum est, nisi soli Verbo incarnato. Et hoc est quod dicitur Matth. VIII, 27: *qualis est iste, quia mare et venti obediunt ei?*

Quarto quantum ad docendi, seu operandi modum. Moyses enim et alii prophetae non propria auctoritate praecepta dabant et homines instruebant, sed Dei; unde dicebant: *haec dicit Dominus* etc.; et: *locutus est Dominus ad Moysen* etc. Christus vero loquitur tamquam Dominus et potestatem habens, idest propria virtute: unde dicebat, Matth. V, v. 22: *ego dico vobis* etc.; propter quod in fine sermonis eius in monte dicitur, quod erat docens quasi *potestatem habens* etc. Item, alii sancti operabantur miracula virtute non sua; Christus vero virtute propria; unde dicitur Mc. I, 27: *quaenam est haec nova doctrina, quia in potestate etiam spiritibus immundis imperat, et obediunt ei?* Sic ergo singularis est gloria Verbi.

187. Nota autem quod aliquando dicimus in Scriptura Christum unigenitum, sicut hic, et infra: *unigenitus, qui est in sinu Patris ipse enarravit.* Aliquando vero dicimus ipsum primogenitum; Hebr. I, 6: *et cum iterum introducit primogenitum in orbem terrae, dicit: 'et adorent eum omnes angeli Dei.'* Quod ideo est, quod sicut totius Sanctae Trinitatis proprium est esse Deum, ita Verbo

185. The word *as*, according to Gregory, is used to express the fact. But according to Chrysostom, it expresses the manner of the fact: as if someone were to see a king approaching in great glory and being asked by another to describe the king he saw, he could, if he wanted to be brief, express the grandeur of his glory in one word, and say that he approached as a king, i.e., as became a king. So too, here, the Evangelist, as though asked by someone to describe the glory of the Word which he had seen, and being unable to fully express it, said that it was *as it were of the only begotten of the Father*, i.e., such as became the only begotten of God.

186. It should be noted that he uniqueness of the glory of the Word is brought out in four ways. First, in the testimony which the Father gave of the Son. For John was one of the three who had seen Christ transfigured on the mountain and heard the voice of the Father saying: *this is my beloved Son, with whom I am well pleased* (Matt 17:5). Of this glory it is said, *he received honor and glory from God the Father: this voice coming down to him from excellent glory: 'this is my beloved Son'* (2 Pet 1:17).

Second, it is brought out by the service of the angels. For prior to the incarnation of Christ, men were subject to the angels. But after it, angels ministered, as subjects, to Christ. *Angels came and ministered to him* (Matt 4:11).

Third, it is brought out by the submission of nature. For all nature obeyed Christ and heeded his slightest command, as something established by him, because *all things were made through him* (John 1:3). This is something granted neither to angels nor to any creature, but to the incarnate Word alone. And this is what we read, *what kind of man is this, for the winds and the sea obey him?* (Matt 8:27)

Fourth, we see it in the way he taught and acted. For Moses and the other prophets gave commands to men and taught them not on their own authority, but on the authority of God. So they said: *the Lord says this*; and *the Lord spoke to Moses*. But Christ speaks as the Lord, and as one having power, i.e., by reason of his own power. Hence he says, *I say to you* (Matt 5:22). This is the reason why, at the end of the Sermon on the Mountain, it is said that he taught as one *having authority* (Matt 7:29). Furthermore, other holy men worked miracles, but not by their own power. But Christ worked them by his own power, hence it is said *what is this new doctrine? for with power he commands even the unclean spirits, and they obey him* (Mark 1:27). In these ways, then, the glory of the Word is unique.

187. Note that sometimes in Scripture we call Christ the only begotten, as here and elsewhere: *the only begotten Son, who is in the bosom of the Father, has made him known* (John 1:18). At other times we call him the firstborn: *when he brings the firstborn into the world, he says, 'let all the angels of God adore him'* (Heb 1:6). The reason for this is that just as it belongs to the whole Blessed Trinity to

Dei proprium est quod sit Deus genitus: et quandoque quidem nominamus Deum, secundum quod est in se, et sic ipse solus singulariter est Deus per essentiam suam. Unde hoc modo dicimus quod est tantum unus Deus, secundum illud Deut. VI, 4: *audi Israel, Dominus Deus tuus, unus est.* Quandoque nomen deitatis derivamus etiam ad alios, secundum quod aliqua similitudo divinitatis ad homines derivatur: et sic dicimus multos deos, secundum illud I Cor. VIII, 5: *siquidem sunt dii multi, et domini multi.*

Eodem modo ergo, si consideremus proprietatem Filii qua genitus est, quantum ad modum quo sibi ista filiatio attribuitur, scilicet per naturam, dicimus ipsum unigenitum Dei: quia cum ipse solus sit naturaliter genitus a Patre, unus tantum est genitus Dei. Si vero consideremus ipsum Filium, secundum quod per similitudinem ad ipsum filiatio derivatur ad alios, sic sunt multi Filii Dei per participationem. Et quia per eius similitudinem dicuntur Filii Dei, ideo ipse dicitur primogenitus omnium. Rom. VIII, 29: *quos praescivit conformes fieri imaginis Filii sui, ut sit ipse primogenitus in multis fratribus.*

Sic ergo Christus dicitur unigenitus Dei per naturam, primogenitus vero inquantum ab eius naturali filiatione per quamdam similitudinem et participationem filiatio ad multos derivatur.

188. Consequenter cum dicit **plenum gratiae et veritatis**, ipsam gloriam Verbi determinat, quasi dicat: talis est eius gloria quod plenus est gratia et divinitate.

Possunt autem haec verba exponi de Christo tripliciter.

Primo secundum unionem. Ad hoc enim alicui datur gratia, ut per ipsam uniatur Deo. Ille ergo gratia plenus est qui perfectissime Deo unitur. Et alii quidem coniunguntur Deo per participationem similitudinis naturalis, Gen. I, 26: *faciamus hominem ad imaginem et similitudinem nostram*, alii per fidem, Eph. III, 17: *habitare per fidem Christum* etc., alii per caritatem, quia, *qui manet in caritate, in Deo manet*, ut dicitur I Io. IV, v. 16. Sed omnes isti modi particulares sunt: quia neque per participationem naturalis similitudinis perfecte aliquis Deo coniungitur, neque videtur Deus per fidem sicuti est, neque per caritatem diligitur, quantum diligibilis est: quia enim ipse est infinitum bonum, ideo sua amabilitas est infinita, ad quam infinite amandam non potest pertingere alicuius creaturae amor; et ideo non potest esse plena coniunctio.

In Christo autem, in quo humana natura est unita divinitati in unitate suppositi, est invenire plenam et perfectam coniunctionem ad Deum, quia talis fuit illa unio, ut omnes actus tam divinae quam humanae naturae essent actus suppositi. Fuit ergo **plenus gratia**, inquantum non accepit a Deo aliquod donum gratuitum speciale, sed quod esset ipse Deus; Phil. II, 9: *dedit illi nomen,*

be God, so it belongs to the Word of God to be God Begotten. Sometimes, too, he is called God according to what he is in himself; and in this way he alone is uniquely God by his own essence. It is in this way that we say there is but one God: *hear, O Israel: the Lord your God is one* (Deut 6:4). At times, we even apply the name of deity to others, insofar as a certain likeness of the divinity is given to men; in this sense we speak of many gods: *indeed, there are many gods and many lords* (1 Cor 8:5).

Along these lines, if we consider what is proper to the Son as begotten, and consider the way in which this sonship is attributed to him, that is, through nature, we say that he is the only begotten of God: because, since he alone is naturally begotten by the Father, the begotten of the Father is one only. But if we consider the Son, insofar as sonship is conferred on others through a likeness to him, then there are many sons of God through participation. And because they are called sons of God by a likeness to him, he is called the first-born of all. *Those whom he foreknew, he predestined to become conformed to the image of his Son, so that he might be the first-born of many brothers* (Rom 8:29).

So, Christ is called the only begotten of God by nature; but he is called the first-born insofar as from his natural sonship, by means of a certain likeness and participation, a sonship is granted to many.

188. Then when he says, **full of grace and truth**, he determines the glory of the Word. As if to say: his glory is such that he is full of grace and divinity.

Now these words can be applied to Christ in three ways.

First, from the point of view of union. For grace is given to someone so that he might be united to God through it. So he who is most perfectly united to God is full of grace. Now some are joined to God by participating in a natural likeness: *let us make man to our image and likeness* (Gen 1:26). Some are joined by faith: *that Christ may dwell in your hearts through faith* (Eph 3:17). And others are united by charity, because *he who abides in love abides in God* (1 John 4:16). But all these ways are partial: because one is not perfectly united to God through the participation of a natural likeness; nor is God seen as he is by faith; nor is he loved to the extent that he is lovable by charity—for since he is the infinite Good, his lovableness is infinite, and the love of no creature is able to love this infinitely. And so these unions are not able to be full.

But in Christ, in whom human nature is united to the divinity in the unity of a *suppositum*, we find a full and perfect union with God. The reason for this is that this union was such that all the acts not only of his divine but also of his human nature were acts of the person. So he was **full of grace** insofar he did not receive any special gratuitous gift from God, but that he should be God himself. *He gave him,*

scilicet Deus Pater Filio, *quod est super omne nomen*; Rom. I, 4: *qui praedestinatus est Filius Dei in virtute.* Fuit etiam **plenus veritatis**, quia humana natura in Christo pervenit ad ipsam veritatem divinam, scilicet quod ille homo esset ipsa divina veritas: in aliis enim hominibus sunt multae veritates participatae, secundum quod ipsa veritas prima per multas similitudines in mentibus eorum relucet, sed Christus est ipsa veritas. Unde dicitur Col. II, 3 quod *in ipso sunt absconditi omnes thesauri sapientiae.*

189. Secundo possunt exponi secundum animae perfectionem, secundum quam dicitur **plenus gratiae et veritatis**, secundum quod in anima eius fuit plenitudo omnium gratiarum absque mensura aliqua; Io. III, 34: **non enim datus est Spiritus ad mensuram**, qui tamen mensurate datus est omnibus creaturis rationalibus, tam angelis, quam hominibus. Nam, secundum Augustinum, sicut in singulis membris corporis est unus sensus communis, scilicet sensus tactus, in capite vero sunt sensus omnes, ita in Christo, qui est caput omnis rationalis naturae, et specialiter sanctorum, qui ei uniuntur per fidem et caritatem, superabundanter omnes virtutes, et gratiae, et dona inveniuntur: in aliis vero sanctis participationes sunt donorum et gratiarum, quamvis commune donum omnium sanctorum sit caritas. De plenitudine gratiae Christi dicitur Is. XI, 1: *egredietur virga de radice Iesse et flos de radice eius ascendet, et requiescet super eum spiritus Domini: spiritus sapientiae et intellectus, spiritus consilii et fortitudinis, spiritus scientiae et pietatis, et replebit eum spiritus timoris Domini.*

Fuit etiam Christus **veritate plenus**, quia eius pretiosa et beata anima omnem veritatem, tam divinam quam humanam, ab instanti conceptionis cognovit; unde dicit ei Petrus: **tu omnia scis**, et in Ps. LXXXVIII, 25: *veritas mea,* idest cognitio omnis veritatis *et misericordia mea,* idest omnium gratiarum plenitudo *cum ipso.*

190. Tertio modo possunt exponi secundum capitis dignitatem, scilicet inquantum Christus est caput Ecclesiae. Et sic sibi competit gratiam communicare aliis, tam in mentibus hominum operando virtutem per gratiae infusionem, quam merendo per doctrinam et opera et passiones mortis superabundantem gratiam infinitis mundis, si essent. Inquantum igitur nobis largitus est perfectam iustitiam, quam non poteramus habere per legem, quae infirmabatur, quae nullum iustificare posset, neque ad perfectum adducere, intantum **gratia plenus** est, ut dicitur Rom. c. VIII, 3: *quod impossibile erat legi, in quo infirmabatur per carnem, Deus Filium suum mittens in similitudinem carnis peccati, de peccato damnavit peccatum in carne.*

Item fuit **veritate plenus**, inquantum figuras veteris legis et promissiones factas patribus adimplevit; Rom. XV, 8: *dico Christum Iesum ministrum*

i.e., God the Father gave to the Son, *a name which is above every name* (Phil 2:9). *He was foreordained to be the Son of God in power* (Rom 1:4). He was also **full of truth**, because the human nature in Christ attained to the divine truth itself, that is, that this man should be the divine truth itself. In other men we find many participated truths, insofar as the first truth gleams back into their minds through many likenesses; but Christ is truth itself. Thus it is said: *in whom all the treasures of wisdom are hidden* (Col 2:3).

189. Second, these words can be applied in relation to the perfection of his soul. Then he is said to be **full of grace and truth** inasmuch as in his soul there was the fullness of all graces without measure: **for God does not give the Spirit by measure** (John 3:34). Yet it was given in fractions to all rational creatures, both angels and men. For according to Augustine, just as there is one sense common to all the parts of the body, namely, the sense of touch, while all the senses are found in the head, so in Christ, who is the head of every rational creature, and in a special way of the saints who are united to him by faith and charity, all virtues and graces and gifts are found superabundantly; but in others, i.e., the saints, we find participations of the graces and gifts, although there is a gift common to all the saints, and that is charity. We read about this fullness of Christ's grace: *there shall come forth a shoot out of the root of Jesse, and a flower shall spring up out of his root. And the spirit of the Lord shall rest upon him: the spirit of wisdom and of understanding, the spirit of counsel and of fortitude, the spirit of knowledge and of piety* (Isa 11:1).

Further, Christ was also **full of truth** because his precious and blessed soul knew every truth, human and divine, from the instant of his conception. And so Peter said to him, **you know all things** (John 21:17). And it is also said: *my truth,* i.e., the knowledge of every truth, *and my mercy,* i.e., the fullness of all graces, *shall be with him* (Ps 88:25).

190. In a third way these words can be explained in relation to his dignity as head, i.e., inasmuch as Christ is the head of the Church. In this way it is his prerogative to communicate grace to others, both by producing virtue in the minds of men through the inpouring of grace and by meriting, through his teaching and works and the sufferings of his death, superabundant grace for an infinite number of worlds, if there were such. Therefore, he is **full of grace** insofar as he conferred perfect justice upon us. We could not acquire this perfect justice through the law, which was infirm and could make no one just or bring anyone to perfection. As we read: *the law was powerless because it was weakened by the flesh. God, sending his Son in the likeness of sinful flesh and in reparation for sin, condemned sin in his flesh* (Rom 8:3).

Again, he was **full of truth** insofar as he fulfilled the figures of the old law and the promises made to the fathers. *Christ was a minister to the circumcised to confirm the*

fuisse circumcisionis ad confirmandas promissiones patrum; II Cor. I, v. 20: *quotquot promissiones Dei sunt in illo est.*

Item dicitur **plenus gratia**, quia eius doctrina et conversatio gratiosissima fuit; Ps. XLIV, 3: *diffusa est gratia in labiis tuis.* Unde dicitur Lc. XXI, 3, quod *omnes mane ibant*, idest mane ire studebant. Sed **plenus veritate**, quia non docebat in aenigmatibus et figuris, nec palpabat vitia hominum, sed veritatem omnibus aperte sine ulla fraude praedicabat; infra XVI, 29: **ecce palam loqueris** etc.

promises made to the fathers (Rom 15:8); *all the promises of God are fulfilled in him* (2 Cor 1:20).

Further, he is said to be **full of grace** because his teaching and manner of life were most gracious. *Grace is poured out upon your lips* (Ps 44:3). And so it is said, *all the people came to him early in the morning*, i.e., in the morning they were eager to come (Luke 21:38). He was **full of truth**, because he did not teach in enigmas and figures, nor gloss over the vices of men, but preached the truth to all, openly and without deception. As it says below: **now you speak plainly** (John 16:29).

Lecture 9

1:15 Ioannes testimonium perhibet de ipso, et clamat dicens: hic erat, quem dixi: qui post me venturus est, ante me factus est, quia prior me erat. [n. 191]

1:15 Ἰωάννης μαρτυρεῖ περὶ αὐτοῦ καὶ κέκραγεν λέγων· οὗτος ἦν ὃν εἶπον· ὁ ὀπίσω μου ἐρχόμενος ἔμπροσθέν μου γέγονεν, ὅτι πρῶτός μου ἦν.

1:15 John bears witness to him, and cries out, saying: this was he of whom I spoke: he who will come after me, is preferred before me: because he was before me. [n. 191]

---

191. Posita evidentia Verbi, qua ipsis apostolis innotuit per visum, consequenter Evangelista ponit eius evidentiam, secundum quod aliis quam apostolis innotuit per auditum, per testimonium ipsius Ioannis etc.

Et circa hoc tria facit.
Primo enim testis introducitur;
secundo testificandi modus innuitur, ibi *et clamat*;

tertio testimonium ponitur, ibi *hic erat quem dixi* etc.

192. Dicit ergo: nos quidem *gloriam eius vidimus*, sicut *unigeniti a Patre*, sed hoc nobis non creditur, quia forte habemur suspecti: accedat illius testis, scilicet Ioannes Baptista, qui testimonium Christo perhibuit; est enim testis fidelis, qui non mentietur; Prov. XIV, 5: *testis fidelis non mentietur* etc. Infra V, 33: *vos misistis ad Ioannem, et testimonium perhibuit veritati*.

Hic enim Ioannes testimonium perhibet; quasi dicat, perseveranter suum officium implet, quia ipse venit in testimonium. Prov. c. XII, 19: *labium veritatis firmum erit in perpetuum*.

193. Deinde cum dicit *et clamat dicens*, ponitur modum testificandi, qui fit cum clamore. Et ideo dicit *clamat*, inquantum libere sine timore; Is. XL, 9: *exalta in fortitudine vocem tuam . . . ecce Deus noster*. Ardenter et ex magno fervore; quia, ut dicitur Eccli. XLVIII, 1, *verbum eius ut facula ardebat*; Is. VI, 3: *seraphim clamabant alter ad alterum*, per quod intimior ardor mentis exprimitur.

Per manifestationem etiam clamoris ostenditur, quod non sub figuris, neque occulte ad paucos sermo testificantis dirigitur; sed aperte et ostensive declaratur et denuntiatur veritas iam non paucis, sed multis; Is. LVIII, v. 1: *clama, ne cesses*.

194. Deinde cum dicit *hic erat quem dixi*, quid sit testificatus subiungit. Ubi duo facit.

Primo enim describit continuitatem sui testimonii;

secundo describit eum, cui testimonium perhibet, ibi *qui post me venturus est, ante me factus est*.

191. Having given the evidence by which the Word was made known to the apostles by sight, the Evangelist then presents the evidence by which the Word was made known to persons other than the apostles by their hearing the testimony of John.

He does three things about this.
First, the witness is presented.
Second, his manner of testifying is indicated: *and he cries out*.
Third, his testimony is given: *this was he of whom I spoke: he who will come after me, is preferred before me: because he was before me*.

192. So he says: *we* indeed *saw his glory, the glory as it were of the only begotten of the Father* (John 1:14). But we are not believed, perhaps because we are held in suspicion. So let his witness come forth, that is, John the Baptist, who bears witness to Christ. He is a faithful witness who will not lie: *a faithful witness will not lie* (Prov 14:5); *you sent to John, and he gave testimony to the truth* (John 5:33).

John gives his testimony here and fulfills his office with perseverance because he came as a witness. *Truthful lips endure forever* (Prov 12:19).

193. Then when he says, *and cries out, saying*, he describes the way he bore witness, that is, it was with a cry. So he says, *he cries out*, i.e., freely without fear. *Cry out in a loud voice . . . say to the cities of Judah: here is your God* (Isa 40:9). He cried out ardently and with great fervor, because it is said, *his word burned like a torch* (Sir 48:1); *seraphim cried one to another* (Isa 6:3), which is expressive of a more interior eagerness of spirit.

The use of a cry shows that the statements of the witness are not made to a few in figurative language or secretly, but that a truth is being declared openly and publicly, and told not to a few but to many. *Cry out, and do not stop* (Isa 58:1).

194. Then he adds his testimony: *this was he of whom I spoke*. And he does two things.

First, he shows that his testimony was continuous. Second,

he describes the person to whom he bore witness: *he who will come after me, is preferred before me: because he was before me*.

195. Fuit ergo testimonium Baptistae continuum, quia non semel tantum sed multoties, et etiam antequam Christus ad ipsum venisset, Ioannes testimonium ei perhibuit: et ideo dixit *hic erat quem dixi*, idest antequam vidissem eum corporaliter, testimonium ei perhibui. Lc. I, 76: *tu puer propheta Altissimi vocaberis*. Et hoc ideo quia praesentem et futurum ostendit.

Est etiam eius testimonium certum, quia non solum futurum esse praedixit, sed praesentem digito demonstravit, dicens *ecce Agnus Dei*. Ex quo insinuatur quod Christus corporaliter praesens erat Ioanni; nam solitus erat saepe ad Ioannem venire, antequam baptizatus fuisset.

196. Describit autem consequenter eum, cui testimonium perhibet, dicens *qui post me venturus est, ante me factus est*.

Ubi notandum est, quod Ioannes non statim praedicat discipulis Christum esse Filium Dei, sed paulatim eos ad altiora provehit: primo praeferens eum sibi, qui tamen tantae famae et auctoritatis erat ut crederetur esse Christus, vel aliquis de magnis prophetis.

Comparat autem Christum sibi
primo quantum ad ordinem praedicationis;
secundo quantum ad ordinem dignitatis;
tertio quantum ad ordinem durationis.

197. Quantum ad ordinem praedicationis, Ioannes praecessit Christum sicut famulum dominum, et sicut miles regem, et sicut Lucifer solem; Mal. III, 1: *ecce ego mitto angelum meum, et praeparabit viam ante faciem meam*. *Qui* igitur *post me venit*, scilicet in notitiam hominum praedicando.

Et notandum, quod ly *venit* est temporis praesentis, quia in Graeco ponitur participium praesentis temporis.

Praecessit autem Ioannes Christum duplici ratione.

Primo, secundum Chrysostomum, quia Ioannes erat consanguineus Christi secundum carnem; Lc. I, 36: *et ecce Elisabeth cognata tua* etc. Si ergo testimonium perhibuisset Christo postquam eum cognoverat, potuisset suum testimonium suspectum habere, et ideo Ioannes venit ad praedicandum, nondum habens familiaritatem cum Christo, ut eius testimonium efficacius esset. Unde dicebat infra: *ego nesciebam eum; sed ut manifestetur in Israel propterea veni ego, in aqua baptizans*.

Secundo quia in his quae de potentia procedunt ad actum, imperfectum naturaliter praecedit perfectum: unde dicitur I Cor. XV, 46: *non prius quod spirituale est, sed quod animale*. Et ideo perfectam Christi doctrinam debuit praecedere imperfectior doctrina Ioannis, quae quodam modo fuit media inter doctrinam legis et prophetarum, quae annuntiabat de longinquo Christum

195. The testimony of the Baptist was continuous because he bore witness to him not only once but many times, and even before Christ had come to him. And so he says, *this was he of whom I spoke*, i.e., before I saw him in the flesh I bore witness to him. *And you, child, shall be called the prophet of the Most High* (Luke 1:76). He pointed him out both as present and when about to come.

And his testimony is certain because he not only predicted that he would come, but pointed him out when he was present, saying, *behold the Lamb of God* (John 1:36). This implies that Christ was physically present to John; for he had often come to John before being baptized.

196. Then he describes the one to whom he bore witness, saying, *he who will come after me, is preferred before me*.

Here we should note that John does not at once preach to his disciples that Christ is the Son of God, but he draws them little by little to higher things: first, by preferring Christ to himself, even though John had such a great reputation and authority as to be considered the Christ or one of the great prophets.

Now he compares Christ to himself:
first, with regard to the order of their preaching;
second, as to the order of dignity; and
third, as to the time of their existence.

197. With respect to the order of their preaching, John preceded Christ as a servant precedes his master, and as a soldier his king, or as the morning star the sun: *see, I am sending my messenger, and he will prepare the way before me* (Mal 3:1). *He* therefore, *comes after me*, in being known to men, through my preaching.

Observe that *comes* is in the present tense, because in Greek the present participle is used.

Now John preceded Christ for two reasons.

First, according to Chrysostom, because John was a blood relation of Christ according to the flesh: *your relative, Elizabeth* (Luke 1:36). Therefore, had he borne witness to Christ after knowing him, his testimony might have been open to question; accordingly, John came preaching before he was acquainted with Christ, in order that his testimony might have more force. Hence he says, *and I did not know him, but that he may be made manifest in Israel, therefore I came baptizing with water* (John 1:31).

Second, John preceded Christ because in things that pass into act from potency, the imperfect is naturally prior to the perfect; hence it is said in: *the spiritual is not first, but the animal* (1 Cor 15:46). Accordingly, the perfect doctrine of Christ should have been preceded by the less perfect teaching of John, which was in a certain manner midway between the doctrine of the law and the prophets, which

futurum, et doctrinam Christi, quae manifesta erat, et Christum manifeste annuntiabat.

198. Comparat sibi quantum ad ordinem dignitatis, cum dicit *ante me factus est*: unde sciendum est, quod ex hoc Ariani sumpserunt occasionem erroris. Dicebant enim quod hoc quod dixit *post me venit*, intelligitur de Christo secundum carnem assumptam, sed hoc quod addit *ante me factus est*, non potest intelligi nisi de Verbo Dei, quod carni praeexistebat; et propterea Christum, inquantum est Verbum, factum esse, et non esse Patri coaeternum.

Sed, secundum Chrysostomum, haec expositio stulta est, quia si hoc esset verum, non dixisset Baptista *ante me factus est, quia prior me erat*, cum nullus ignoret, quod si prior eo erat, ante eum factus est; sed potius e converso dixisset: *prior me erat, quia factus est ante me*. Et ideo, secundum Chrysostomum, intelligendum est de prioritate dignitatis, idest mihi praelatus est, et antepositus. Quasi dicat: *quamvis Iesus post me ad praedicandum venerit, tamen factus est ante me, idest dignior, et superior auctoritate, et hominum reputatione*; Iob XXVIII, 17: *non adaequabitur ei aurum* etc. Vel *ante me factus est*, idest *coram me*, ut habetur in Glossa, et littera in Graeco hoc sonat. Quasi dicat *coram me*, idest in conspectu meo, quia mihi apparuit, et innotuit.

199. Item comparat eum sibi quantum ad ordinem durationis, dicens *quia prior me erat*. Quasi dicat: *ipse est ab aeterno Deus, ego ex tempore homo fragilis; et ideo, licet eum praedicando praecesserim, tamen rationabiliter praelatus est mihi in fama et opinione hominum, qui sua aeternitate praecedit omnia*. Hebr. ult., 8: *Iesus Christus heri et hodie, ipse et in saecula*; et infra VIII, 58: *antequam Abraham fieret, ego sum*.

Potest etiam exponi quod dictum est *ante me factus est* ut referatur ad ordinem temporis secundum carnem. Christus enim in instanti suae conceptionis fuit perfectus Deus et perfectus homo, habens rationalem animam perfectam virtutibus, et corpus omnibus lineamentis distinctum, non tamen secundum quantitatem perfectam; Ier. XXXI, 22: *mulier circumdabit virum*, scilicet perfectum. Constat autem quod Christus ante fuit conceptus quam Ioannes esset natus, et perfectus homo; et ideo dicit *ante me factus est* quia ipse prius fuit homo perfectus, quam natus fuisset ex utero.

announced the coming of Christ from afar, and the doctrine of Christ, which was clear and plainly made Christ known.

198. John compares him to himself with respect to dignity when he says, *he is preferred before me*. It should be noted that it is from this text that the Arians took occasion for their error. For they said that *he who comes after me*, is to be understood of Christ as to the flesh he assumed, but what follows, *is preferred before me*, can only be understood of the Word of God, who existed before the flesh; and for this reason Christ as the Word was made, and was not coeternal with the Father.

According to Chrysostom, however, this exposition is stupid, because if it were true, the Baptist would not have said, *he is preferred before me, because he was before me*, since no one is unaware that if he was before him, he was made before him. He rather would have said the opposite: *he was before me, because he was made before me*. And so, according to Chrysostom, these words should be taken as referring to Christ's dignity, that is, he was preferred to me and placed ahead of me. It is as though he said: *although Jesus came to preach after me, he was made more worthy than I both in eminence of authority and in the repute of men: gold will not be equal to it* (Job 28:17). Or alternatively: *he is preferred before me*, that is, *before my eyes*, as the Gloss says and as the Greek text reads. As if to say: *before my eyes*, i.e., in my sight, because he came into my view and was recognized.

199. He compares him to himself with respect to their duration, saying, *because he was before me*. As if to say: *he was God from all eternity, I am a frail man of time*. And therefore, even though I came to preach ahead of him, yet it was fitting that he rank before me in the reputation and opinion of men, because he preceded all things by his eternity: *Jesus Christ is the same yesterday, today, and forever* (Heb 13:8). *Before Abraham was made, I am* (John 8:58).

If we understand this passage as saying that *he is preferred before me*, it can be explained as referring to the order of time according to the flesh. For in the instant of his conception Christ was perfect God and perfect man, having a rational soul perfected by the virtues, and a body possessed of all its distinctive features, except that it lacked perfect size: *a woman shall enclose a man*, i.e., a perfect man (Jer 31:22). Now it is evident that Christ was conceived as a perfect man before John was born; consequently he says that *he is preferred before me*, because he was a perfect man before I came forth from the womb.

Lecture 10

1:16 Et de plenitudine eius nos omnes accepimus, et gratia pro gratia. [n. 200]

1:17 Quia lex per Moysen data est; gratia et veritas per Iesum Christum facta est. [n. 205]

1:16 ὅτι ἐκ τοῦ πληρώματος αὐτοῦ ἡμεῖς πάντες ἐλάβομεν καὶ χάριν ἀντὶ χάριτος·

1:17 ὅτι ὁ νόμος διὰ Μωϋσέως ἐδόθη, ἡ χάρις καὶ ἡ ἀλήθεια διὰ Ἰησοῦ Χριστοῦ ἐγένετο.

1:16 And of his fullness we have all received, indeed grace upon grace: [n. 200]

1:17 For the law was given through Moses; grace and truth came through Jesus Christ. [n. 205]

---

200. Sequitur *et de plenitudine eius nos omnes accepimus*.

Verba ista usque ad locum illum *et hoc est testimonium Ioannis*, dupliciter inseruntur. Nam, secundum Origenem, sunt verba prolata a Ioanne Baptista, et subduntur ab eo quasi in argumentum praemissorum; quasi dicat: vere *prior me erat*, quia *de plenitudine eius*, scilicet gratiarum, non solum ego, sed etiam *omnes*, prophetae et patres, *accepimus*, quia omnes gratiam quam habuerunt, habuerunt per fidem incarnati Verbi. Et secundum hoc, ab illo loco *Ioannes testimonium perhibet* etc., incepit texere exordium suae incarnationis.

Secundum Augustinum autem et Chrysostomum, sunt verba Ioannis Evangelistae ab hoc quod dicitur *Ioannes testimonium perhibet*; et tunc continuatur ad hoc quod dixerat *plenum gratiae et veritatis*, ut dicatur sic: supra Evangelista ostendit evidentiam Verbi, quae innotuit et per visum, et per auditum, hic vero utrumque explicat: et primo quomodo apostolis innotuit visu, quasi a Christo accipientibus; secundo quomodo Ioannes testificatus est de eo, ibi *et hoc est testimonium Ioannis*.

Circa primum duo facit.

Primo ostendit Christum esse fontalem originem omnis spiritualis gratiae;

secundo ostendit derivatam in nos gratiam per ipsum et ab ipso, ibi *et gratiam pro gratia*.

201. Dicit ergo primo: experimento patet, quod vidimus eum *plenum gratiae et veritatis*, quia *de plenitudine eius nos omnes accepimus*.

Est autem plenitudo sufficientiae, qua aliquis est sufficiens ad actus meritorios et excellentes faciendos, sicut in Stephano. Item est plenitudo redundantiae, qua Beata Virgo excellit omnibus sanctis, propter eminentiam, et abundantiam meritorum. Est etiam plenitudo efficientiae et effluentiae, quae soli homini Christo competit, quasi auctori gratiae. Sic enim Beata Virgo redundavit gratiam in nos, ut tamen auctrix gratiae nequaquam esset, sed ab anima eius gratia redundavit in carnem; nam per Spiritus Sancti gratiam, non solum mens Virginis fuit Deo per amorem perfecte unita, sed eius uterus a Spiritu Sancto est supernaturaliter impraegnatus. Et ideo

200. He follows with, *and of his fullness we have all received*.

These words and those that follow to *this is the testimony of John* (John 1:19), are taken in two ways. According to Origen, these are the words of John the Baptist and are added by him to support what he had said previously. It is as though he said: truly, *he was before me* (John 1:15), because *of his fullness*, i.e., of his grace, not only I but *we all*, including the prophets and patriarchs, *have received*, because all had the grace they possessed by faith in the incarnate Word. According to this explanation, John the Baptist began weaving the story of the incarnation at, *John bore witness to him* (John 1:15).

But according to Augustine and Chrysostom, the words from *John bore witness to him* (John 1:15), are those of John the Evangelist. And they are connected with the previous words, *full of grace and truth* (John 1:14), as though he were saying: above, the Evangelist gave the evidence for the Word which was learned through sight and by hearing, but here he explains each. First, how he was made known to the apostles through sight, which was tantamount to receiving the evidence from Christ. Second, how John bore witness to him, at *this is the testimony of John* (John 1:19).

As to the first he does two things.

First, he shows that Christ is the origin, as a fountain, of every spiritual grace.

Second, he shows that grace is dispensed to us through him and from him, at *grace upon grace*.

201. He says first of all: we know from our own experience that we have seen him *full of grace and truth* (John 1:14), because *of his fullness we have all received*.

Now one fullness is that of sufficiency, by which one is able to perform acts that are meritorious and excellent, as in the case of Stephen. Again, there is a fullness of superabundance, by which the Blessed Virgin excels all the saints because of the eminence and abundance of her merits. Further, there is a fullness of efficiency and overflow, which belongs only to the man Christ as the author of grace. For although the Blessed Virgin superabounds her grace into us, it is never as authoress of grace. But grace flowed over from her soul into her body: for through the grace of the Holy Spirit, not only was the mind of the Virgin perfectly united to God by love, but her womb was supernaturally

statim cum dixisset Gabriel, *ave gratia plena*, subiunxit de plenitudine ventris, dicens *Dominus tecum*.

Ut ergo Evangelista hanc singularem plenitudinem redundantiae et efficientiae de Christo ostenderet, dixit **de plenitudine eius omnes accepimus**, scilicet omnes apostoli, et patriarchae, et prophetae, et iusti, qui fuerunt, sunt et erunt, et etiam omnes angeli.

202. Nota, quod haec propositio 'de' aliquando quidem denotat efficientiam, seu originalem causam, sicut cum dicitur, radius est vel procedit de sole; et hoc modo denotat in Christo efficientiam gratiae, seu auctoritatem, quia plenitudo gratiae, quae est in Christo, est causa omnium gratiarum quae sunt in omnibus intellectualibus creaturis. Eccli. c. XXIV, 26: *venite ad me, omnes, qui concupiscitis me, et a generationibus meis*, quae scilicet de me procedunt, *adimplemini*, participatione sufficientis plenitudinis.

Aliquando autem haec praepositio 'de' denotat consubstantialitem, ut cum dicitur, Filius est de Patre; et secundum hoc plenitudo Christi est Spiritus Sanctus, qui procedit ab eo consubstantialis ei in natura, in virtute et maiestate. Quamvis enim dona habitualia alia sint in anima Christi quam ea quae sunt in nobis, tamen Spiritus Sanctus, qui est in ipso, unus et idem replet omnes sanctificandos. I Cor. XII, 11: *haec omnia operatur unus atque idem Spiritus*; Ioel. II, 28: *effundam de Spiritu meo super omnem carnem*; Rom. c. VIII, 9: *si quis Spiritum Christi non habet, hic non est eius*. Nam unitas Spiritus Sancti facit in Ecclesia unitatem; Sap. I, 7: *Spiritus Domini replevit orbem terrarum*.

Tertio modo haec praepositio 'de' denotat partialitatem, sicut cum dicimus, *accipe de hoc pane, vel vino*, idest partem accipe, et non totum; et hoc modo accipiendo, notat in accipientibus partem de plenitudine derivari. Ipse enim accepit omnia dona Spiritus Sancti sine mensura, secundum plenitudinem perfectam; sed nos de plenitudine eius partem aliquam participamus per ipsum; et hoc secundum mensuram, quam unicuique Deus divisit. Eph. IV, 7: *unicuique autem nostrum data est gratia, secundum mensuram donationis*.

203. Deinde cum dicit **et gratiam pro gratia** ostendit derivationem gratiarum in nos per Christum. Ubi duo facit.

Primo ostendit quod accepimus gratiam a Christo, eo auctore;

secundo accepimus ab eo sapientiam, ibi **Deum nemo vidit unquam**.

Circa primum duo facit.

Primo ostendit quod de plenitudine eius accepimus;

secundo necessitatem accipiendi ostendit, ibi **quia lex per Moysen data est** etc.

impregnated by the Holy Spirit. And so after Gabriel said, *hail, full of grace*, he refers at once to the fullness of her womb, adding, *the Lord is with you* (Luke 1:28).

And so the Evangelist, in order to show this unique fullness of efficiency and overflow in Christ, said, **of his fullness we have all received**, i.e., all the apostles and patriarchs and prophets and just men who have existed, do now exist, and will exist, and even all the angels.

202. Note that the preposition 'from' sometimes signifies efficiency, as in an originative cause, as when it is said that a ray is or proceeds from the sun. In this way it signifies the efficiency of grace in Christ, i.e., authorship, because the fullness of grace in Christ is the cause of all graces that are in intellectual creatures. *Come to me, all you who desire me, and be filled with my fruits* (Sir 24:26), that is to say, share in the fullness of those fruits which come from me.

But sometimes this preposition 'from' signifies consubstantiality, as when it is said that the Son is from the Father. In this usage, the fullness of Christ is the Holy Spirit, who proceeds from him, consubstantial with him in nature, in power and in majesty. For although the habitual gifts in the soul of Christ are other than those in us, nevertheless it is one and the same Holy Spirit who is in him and who fills all those to be sanctified. *One and the same Spirit produces all these* (1 Cor 12:11); *I will pour out my Spirit upon all flesh* (Joel 2:28); *if anyone does not have the Spirit of Christ, he does not belong to him* (Rom 8:9). For the unity of the Holy Spirit produces unity in the Church: *the Spirit of the Lord filled the whole world* (Wis 1:7).

In a third way, the preposition 'from' can signify a portion, as when we say *take from this bread or wine*, i.e., take a portion and not the whole. Taken in this way it signifies that those who take a part derive it from the fullness. For Christ received all the gifts of the Holy Spirit without measure, according to a perfect fullness; but we participate, through him, of some portion of his fullness; and this is according to the measure which God grants to each. *Grace has been given to each of us according to the degree to which Christ gives it* (Eph 4:7).

203. Then when he says, **grace upon grace**, he shows the distribution of graces into us through Christ. Here he does two things.

First, he shows that we receive grace from Christ, as its author.

Second, that we receive wisdom from him, at **no man has ever seen God** (John 1:18).

As to the first he does two things.

First, he shows that we have received of his fullness.

Second, our need to receive it: **for the law was given through Moses; grace and truth came through Jesus Christ**.

204. Dicit autem primo quod accepimus de plenitudine Christi hoc quod dico *et gratiam pro gratia*.

Sed per hoc quod ponitur, cogimur intelligere quod de plenitudine eius accepimus gratiam, et pro illa gratia accepimus aliam; et ideo videndum est quae sit prima gratia, pro qua secundam accepimus, et quae ipsa secunda.

Secundum Chrysostomum autem, prima gratia, quam totum genus humanum accepit, fuit gratia Veteris Testamenti accepta in lege, quae quidem magna fuit, iuxta illud Prov. IV, v. 2: *donum bonum tribuam vobis* etc. Magnum enim fuit quod hominibus idolatris data sunt praecepta a Deo, et unius veri Dei vera cognitio; Rom. III, 1: *quid amplius Iudaeo, aut quae utilitas circumcisionis? Multum quidem per omnem modum. Primum quidem quia credita sunt eis eloquia Dei*. Pro gratia ergo ista, quae prima fuit, secundam longe meliorem accepimus; Zach. IV, 7: *exequabit gratiam gratiae*.

Sed numquid non sufficiebat prima gratia?

Respondeo dicendum, quod non, quia per legem solum cognitio peccati datur, non ablatio. *Neminem enim ad perfectum adduxit lex*, Hebr. VII, 19. Et ideo erat necesse quod alia gratia peccata auferens, et reconcilians Deo, veniret.

205. Et ideo dicit *quia lex per Moysen data est; gratia et veritas per Iesum Christum facta est*. Ubi Evangelista praefert Christum legislatori Moysi, quem Baptista sibi praetulerat. Moyses autem reputabatur maximus prophetarum; Deut. ult., 10: *non surrexit ultra propheta in Israel sicut Moyses*.

Praefert autem eum Moysi, quantum ad excellentiam et dignitatem operum *quia per Moysen lex data est*; et horum duorum, tantum unum excellit alium, quantum figuratum excellit figuram et veritas ipsam umbram. *Umbram enim habuit lex futurorum bonorum* etc.; Hebr. X, 1. Item excellit quantum ad modum operandi: quia lex data est per Moysen, sicut per proponentem, non per facientem; quia, *solus Dominus est legifer noster*: Is. XXXIII, v. 22. *Gratia* autem, *et veritas facta est per Christum*, sicut per Dominum et auctorem veritatis et gratiae, ut supra expositum est.

206. Secundum Augustinum vero, prima est iustificans et praeveniens, quae non datur nobis ex operibus; Rom. XI, 6: *si autem gratia, iam non ex operibus*. Pro ista ergo gratia, scilicet imperfecta, accepimus aliam gratiam consummatam, scilicet aeternae vitae. Et quamvis aeterna vita aliquo modo meritis acquiratur, tamen quia principium merendi in omnibus est gratia praeveniens, ideo vita aeterna dicitur gratia; Rom. VI, 23: *gratia Dei vita aeterna*. Et, ut breviter concludatur, quicquid praevenienti gratiae de gratia additur, totum *gratia pro gratia* dicitur.

204. First, he says that we have received of the fullness of Christ what is described as *grace upon grace*.

In the light of what is said, we are forced to understand that of his fullness we have received grace, and that upon that grace we have received another. Accordingly, we must see what that first grace is upon which we have received a second one, and also what that second grace is.

According to Chrysostom, the first grace, which was received by the whole human race, was the grace of the Old Testament received in the law. And this was indeed a great grace: *I will give you a good gift* (Prov 4:2). For it was a great benefit for idolatrous men to receive precepts from God, and a true knowledge of the one true God. *What is the advantage of being a Jew, or the benefit of circumcision? It is great in every way. First indeed, because the words of God were entrusted to them* (Rom 3:1). Upon that grace, then, which was first, we have received a second far better. *He will follow grace with grace* (Zech 4:7).

But was not the first grace sufficient?

I answer that it was not, because the law gives only a knowledge of sin, but does not take it away. *The law brought nothing to perfection* (Heb 7:19). Hence it was necessary that another grace come that would take away sin and reconcile one with God.

205. And so he says, *for the law was given through Moses; grace and truth came through Jesus Christ*. Here the Evangelist ranks Christ above Moses the lawgiver, whom the Baptist ranked above himself. Now Moses was regarded as the greatest of the prophets: *there did not arise again in Israel a prophet like Moses* (Deut 34:10).

But he ranks Christ above Moses in excellence and in dignity of works, *for the law was given through Moses*; and between these two, the one excels the other as the reality excels the symbol and the truth the shadow: *the law had a shadow of the good things to come* (Heb 10:1). Further, Christ excels him in the way he works, because the law was given by Moses as by one proclaiming it, but not originating it; for *the Lord alone is our lawgiver* (Isa 33:22). But *grace and truth came through Jesus Christ*, as through the Lord and author of truth and grace, as was explained above.

206. According to Augustine, however, the first grace is justifying and prevenient grace, which is not given to us because of our works: *if it is by grace, it is not now by works* (Rom 11:6). Upon that grace, then, which is imperfect, we have received another grace which is perfect, i.e., the grace of eternal life. And although eternal life is in some way acquired by merits, nevertheless, because the principle of meriting in everyone is prevenient grace, eternal life is called a grace: *the grace of God is eternal life* (Rom 6:23). To be brief, whatever grace is added to prevenient grace, the whole is called *grace upon grace*.

Necessitas autem secundae gratiae est ex insufficientia legis, quae ostendebat quid faciendum et quid cavendum erat; sed ad implendum ea quae praecipiebat, non praebebat auxilium; immo per occasionem operabatur mortem quae tamen videbatur fuisse ad vitam; Apostolus, Rom. VII, 10, et II Cor. III, v. 9, dicit, legem ministram fuisse mortis: *nam si ministratio damnationis in gloria est, multo magis abundat ministerium iustitiae in gloria.* Item promittebat auxilium gratiae, sed non solvebat, quia *neminem ad perfectum adducit lex,* ut dicitur Hebr. VII, 19. Item per sacrificia et caeremonias veritatem novae gratiae figurabat, ipso suo ritu clamans eam figuram; et ideo necesse fuit quod Christus veniret, qui per mortem propriam alienas mortes perimeret, et conferret auxilium novae gratiae, ut faciliter et delectabiliter adimpleremus praecepta, et moreremur transgressioni et conversationi antiquae; Rom. VI, 6: *vetus homo noster simul crucifixus est* etc. Item ut manifestaretur veritas figurarum contentarum in lege, et ut promissiones factae patribus solverentur; II Cor. I. Vel aliter, **veritas per Christum facta est,** quantum ad sapientiam et veritatem occultam a saeculis, quam veniens in mundum aperte docuit, infra XVIII, v. 37: **in hoc natus sum, et ad hoc veni in mundum, ut testimonium perhibeam veritati.**

207. Sed si ipse Christus est veritas, ut infra XIV, 6 dicitur, quomodo per ipsum facta est veritas, cum nihil possit fieri a seipso?

Respondeo, dicendum est, quod ipse est per suam essentiam veritas increata; quae aeterna est, et non facta, sed a Patre est genita; sed per ipsum factae sunt omnes veritates creatae, quae sunt quaedam participationes et refulgentiae primae veritatis, quae in animabus sanctis relucent.

The need for this second grace arises from the insufficiency of the law, which showed what was to be done and what avoided; but it gave no help to fulfill what was commanded. Indeed, what seemed to have been directed to life was the occasion for producing death. Hence the Apostle says that the law was a minister of death: *if the ministry that condemned had glory, the ministry that justifies has much more glory* (2 Cor 3:9). Also, it promised the help of grace but did not fulfill, because *the law brought nothing to perfection* (Heb 7:19). Again, it prefigured the truth of the new grace by its sacrifices and ceremonies; indeed, its very rites proclaimed that it was a figure. Hence is was necessary that Christ come, who by his own death would destroy other deaths and grant the help of new grace, in order that we might both fulfill his precepts with ease and joy, and die to our sins and our old way of life: *our old self was crucified with him* (Rom 6:6), and in order that the truth of the figures contained in the law might be revealed and the promises made to the fathers be fulfilled (2 Cor 1). This can be explained in another way: **truth came through Jesus Christ,** as to the wisdom and truth which was hidden for centuries, and which he openly taught when he came into the world: **for this I was born, and for this I came into the world, that I should give testimony to the truth** (John 18:37).

207. But if Christ is the truth, as it says below *I am . . . the truth* (John 14:6), how did truth come to be made through him, because nothing can make itself?

I answer that by his essence he is the uncreated truth, which is eternal and not made, but is begotten of the Father; but all created truths were made through him, and these are certain participations and reflections of the first truth, which shines out in those souls who are holy.

Lecture 11

1:18 Deum nemo vidit unquam. Unigenitus Filius, qui est in sinu Patris, ipse enarravit. [n. 209]

1:18 Θεὸν οὐδεὶς ἑώρακεν πώποτε· μονογενὴς θεὸς ὁ ὢν εἰς τὸν κόλπον τοῦ πατρὸς ἐκεῖνος ἐξηγήσατο.

1:18 No man has ever seen God: the only begotten Son, who is in the bosom of the Father, has made him known. [n. 209]

---

208. Supra Evangelista ostendit quomodo gratiam apostoli acceperunt a Christo, eo faciente; hic ostendit quomodo acceperunt ab ipso eam docente.

Et circa hoc tria facit.

Primo ostendit huius doctrinae necessitatem, dicens *Deum nemo vidit unquam*;

secundo doctoris ad docendum eam facultatem, ibi *unigenitus qui est in sinu Patris*;

tertio ipsam doctrinam declarat, ibi *enarravit*.

209. Necessitas autem huius doctrinae erat defectus sapientiae in hominibus, quem quidem defectum Evangelista insinuabat per ignorantiam Dei, quae in hominibus abundant, dicens *Deum nemo vidit unquam*. Et hoc facit congrue: nam sapientia proprie in cognitione Dei, et divinorum consistit. Unde Augustinus dicit, quod sapientia est divinarum rerum cognitio, sicut et scientia humanarum.

210. Quod autem hic dicit Evangelista *Deum nemo vidit unquam* contrariari videtur pluribus auctoritatibus divinae Scripturae. Dicitur enim Is. VI, 1: *vidi Dominum sedentem super solium excelsum et elevatum*; II Reg. VI, 2, fere idem habetur: *nomen Domini sedentis super Cherubim* etc.; Matth. V, v. 8, dicit Dominus: *beati mundo corde, quoniam ipsi Deum videbunt*.

Sed si aliquis responderet ad hoc ultimum, dicens, verum esse quod in praeterito nullus vidit, sed in futuro videbit, sicut Dominus promittit, Apostolus hoc excludit, dicens I Tim. ult., 16: *lucem habitat inaccessibilem, quam nullus hominum vidit, sed nec videre potest*.

Sed quia Apostolus dicit: *nullus hominum vidit*, posset aliquis dicere, quod si non ab hominibus videri possit, saltem videtur ab angelis; praesertim cum Deus dicat Matth. XVIII, 10: *angeli eorum in caelis semper vident faciem Patris*.

Sed nec isto modo dici potest: quia, ut dicitur Matth. XXII, 30: *filii resurrectionis erunt sicut angeli Dei in caelo*. Si ergo angeli vident Deum in caelo, manifestum est etiam quod et filii resurrectionis eum vident; I Io. III, 2: *cum apparuerit, similes ei erimus, et videbimus eum sicut est*.

211. Quomodo ergo intelligendum est hoc quod dicit Evangelista *Deum nemo vidit unquam*?

Ad huius ergo intellectum sciendum est, quod Deus dicitur videri tripliciter. Uno quidem modo per subiectam creaturam, visui corporali propositam; sicut creditur

208. Above, the Evangelist showed how the apostles received grace from Christ as its author; here he shows how they received it from him as a teacher.

About this he does three things.

First, he shows the need for this teaching: *no man has ever seen God*.

Second, the competency of the teacher: *the only begotten Son, who is in the bosom of the Father*.

Third, the teaching itself: *has made him known*.

209. The need for this teaching arose from the lack of wisdom among men, which the Evangelist implies by alluding to the ignorance concerning God which prevailed among men, saying: *no man has ever seen God*. And he does this fittingly, for wisdom consists properly in the knowledge of God and of divine things. Hence Augustine says that wisdom is the knowledge of divine things, as science is the knowledge of human things.

210. But this statement of the Evangelist, *no man has ever seen God*, seems to contradict many passages of divine Scripture. For it is said: *I saw the Lord seated on a high and lofty throne* (Isa 6:1); and at *the name of the Lord of hosts is invoked, who sitteth over it upon the cherubims* (2 Sam 6:2). Again when the Lord says: *blessed are the pure in heart, for they shall see God* (Matt 5:8).

If someone were to answer this last statement by saying that it is true that in the past no one has seen God, but will see him in the future, as the Lord promises, the Apostle would exclude this, saying, *he dwells in unapproachable light, whom no man has seen or can see* (1 Tim 6:16).

Because the Apostle says, *no man has ever seen*, someone might say that if he cannot be seen by men, then at least he can be seen by angels; especially since God says, *their angels in heaven always see the face of my Father* (Matt 18:10).

But it cannot be taken in this way either, because it is said, *the sons of the resurrection will be like the angels of God in heaven* (Matt 22:30). If, therefore, the angels see God in heaven, then it is plain that the sons of the resurrection also see him: *when he appears we shall be like him, and we shall see him as he is* (1 John 3:2).

211. How then are we to understand what the Evangelist says: *no man has ever seen God*?

To understand it we must know that God is said to be seen in three ways. First, through a created substitute presented to the bodily sight; as Abraham is believed to have

Abraham vidisse Deum, quando tres vidit, et unum adoravit, Gen. XVIII; unum quidem adoravit, quia tres, quos prius homines reputaverat, et postmodum angelos credidit, recognovit mysterium Trinitatis. Alio modo per repraesentatam imaginationem; et sic Isaias vidit *Dominum sedentem super solium excelsum et elevatum.* Plures visiones huic similes in Scripturis reperiuntur. Alio vero modo videtur per aliquam speciem intelligibilem a sensibilibus abstractam, ab his qui per considerationem magnitudinis creaturarum, intellectu intuentur magnitudinem Creatoris, ut dicitur Sap. XIII, 5: *a magnitudine speciei et creaturae cognoscibiliter poterit Creator horum videri,* et Rom. I, 20: *invisibilia Dei a creatura mundi per ea quae facta sunt, intellecta conspiciuntur.* Alio modo per aliquod spirituale lumen a Deo infusum spiritualibus mentibus in contemplatione; et hoc modo vidit Iacob *Deum facie ad faciem,* Gen. XXXII, 30 quae visio, secundum Gregorium, facta est per altam contemplationem.

Sed per nullam istarum visionum, ad visionem divinae essentiae pervenitur: nulla enim species facta, sive qua informatur sensus exterior, sive qua informatur imaginatio, sive qua informatur intellectus, est repraesentativa divinae essentiae sicut est. Illud autem homo per essentiam cognoscit quod species quam habet in intellectu, repraesentat ut est: per nullam ergo speciem ad visionem divinae essentiae pervenitur.

Quod autem nulla creata species divinam essentiam repraesentet, patet: quia nullum finitum potest repraesentare infinitum ut est; omnis autem species creata est finita: ergo etc. Praeterea, Deus est suum esse; et ideo eius sapientia et bonitas, et quaecumque alia, idem sunt; per unum autem creatum non possent omnia ista repraesentari: ergo cognitio qua Deus per creaturas videtur, non est ipsius essentia, sed aenigmatica et specularis, et a remotis. Iob XXXVI, 25: *omnes homines vident eum,* aliquo dictorum modorum, *sed unusquisque intuetur procul,* quia per omnes illas cognitiones non scitur de Deo quid est, sed quid non est, vel an est. Unde dicit Dionysius libro *Mysticae theologiae,* quod perfectus modus quo Deus in vita praesenti cognoscitur, est per privationem omnium creaturarum, et intellectorum a nobis.

212. Fuerunt autem aliqui dicentes, quod divina essentia numquam videbitur ab aliquo intellectu creato, et quod nec ab angelis vel beatis videtur. Sed haec propositio ostenditur esse falsa et haeretica tripliciter. Primo quidem, quia contrariatur auctoritati divinae Scripturae; I Io. III, 2: *videbimus eum sicuti est;* et infra XVII, 3: **haec est vita aeterna ut cognoscant te solum Deum verum, et quem misisti Iesum Christum.** Secundo quia claritas Dei non est aliud quam eius substantia: non enim est lucens per participationem luminis, sed per seipsam. Tertio quia impossibile est quod aliquis perfectam beatitudinem consequatur, nisi in visione divinae essentiae:

seen God when he saw three and adored one (Gen 18:2). He adored one because he recognized the mystery of the Trinity in the three, whom he first thought to be men, and later believed to be angels. In a second way, through a representation in the imagination; and in this way Isaiah saw *the Lord seated on a high and lofty throne* (Isa 6:1). Many visions of this sort are recorded in the Scriptures. In a third way, he is seen through an intelligible species abstracted from material things; and in this way he is seen by those who, considering the greatness of creatures, see with their intellect the greatness of the Creator, as it is said: *from the greatness and beauty of creatures, their Creator can be seen accordingly* (Wis 13:5); *the invisible things of God are clearly seen, being understood through the things that are made* (Rom 1:20). In another way, God is seen through a certain spiritual light infused by God into spiritual minds during contemplation; and this is the way Jacob saw *God face to face* (Gen 32:30). According to Gregory, this vision came about through his lofty contemplation.

But the vision of the divine essence is not attained by any of the above visions: for no created species, whether it be that by which an external sense is informed, or by which the imagination is informed, or by which the intellect is informed, is representative of the divine essence as it is. Now man knows as to its essence only what the species he has in his intellect represents as it is. Therefore, the vision of the divine essence is not attained through any species.

The reason why no created species can represent the divine essence is plain: for nothing finite can represent the infinite as it is; but every created species is finite; therefore it cannot represent the infinite as it is. Further, God is his own existence and therefore his wisdom and greatness and anything else are the same. But all those cannot be represented through one created thing. Therefore, the knowledge by which God is seen through creatures is not a knowledge of his essence, but a knowledge that is dark and mirrored, and from afar. *Everyone sees him,* in one of the above ways, *from afar* (Job 36:25), because we do not know what God is by all these acts of knowing, but what he is not, or that he is. Hence Denis says, in his *Mystical Theology,* that the perfect way in which God is known in this present life is by taking away all creatures and every thing understood by us.

212. There have been some who said that the divine essence will never by seen by any created intellect, and that it is seen neither by the angels nor by the blessed. But this statement is shown to be false and heretical in three ways, First, because it is contrary to the authority of divine Scripture: *we shall see him as he is* (1 John 3:2); **this is eternal life, that they may know you, the only true God, and Jesus Christ, whom you have sent** (John 17:3). Second, because the brightness of God is the same as his substance; for he does not give forth light by participating in light, but through himself. And third, because it is impossible for anyone to attain perfect happiness except in the vision

quia naturale desiderium intellectus est scire et cognoscere causas omnium effectuum cognitorum ab eo; quod non potest impleri nisi scita et cognita prima universali omnium causa, quae non est composita ex effectu et causa, sicut causae secundae. Et ideo auferre possibilitatem visionis divinae essentiae ab hominibus, est auferre ipsam beatitudinem.

Necesse est ergo ad beatitudinem intellectus creati, ut divina essentia videatur, Matth. V, 8: *beati mundo corde, quoniam ipsi Deum videbunt.*

213. Quo ad visionem autem divinae essentiae, oportet tria attendere.

Primo, quia numquam videbitur oculo corporali, vel aliquo sensu, vel imaginatione, cum per sensus non percipiantur nisi sensata corporea; Deus autem incorporeus est; infra IV, v. 24: **Deus spiritus est.**

Secundo, quia intellectus humanus quamdiu corpori est coniunctus, Deum videre non potest, quia aggravatur a corruptibili corpore, ne possit ad summum contemplationis pertingere. Et inde est quod anima quanto magis est a passionibus libera, et purgata ab affectibus terrenorum, tanto amplius in contemplationem veritatis ascendit, et gustat quam suavis est Dominus. Summus gradus autem contemplationis est videre Deum per essentiam; et ideo quamdiu homo in corpore subiecto ex necessitate passionibus multis vivit, Deum non potest per essentiam videre. Ex. c. XXXIII, 20: *non videbit me homo et vivet.* Ad hoc ergo quod intellectus humanus divinam essentiam videat, necesse est ut totaliter deserat corpus; vel per mortem, sicut Apostolus dicit II Cor. V, 8: *audemus, et bonam voluntatem habemus magis peregrinari a corpore, et praesentes esse ad Dominum*; vel quod totaliter abstrahatur per raptum a corporis sensibus, sicut de Paulo legitur II Cor. c. XII, 3.

Tertio modo, quod nullus intellectus creatus quantumcumque abstractus, sive per mortem, vel a corpore separatus, videns divinam essentiam, ipsam nullo modo comprehendere potest. Et ideo communiter dicitur, quod, licet divina essentia tota videatur a beatis, cum sit simplicissima et partibus carens, tamen non videtur totaliter, quia hoc esset eam comprehendere. Hoc enim quod dico 'totaliter,' dicit modum quemdam. Quilibet autem modus Dei est divina essentia; unde qui non videt eum totaliter, non comprehendit eum. Comprehendere autem proprie dicitur aliquis aliquam rem cognoscendo, qui cognoscit rem illam quantum in se cognoscibilis est; alias, quamvis cognoscat eam, non tamen comprehendit. Sicut qui cognoscit hanc propositionem: *triangulus habet tres angulos aequales duobus rectis,* syllogismo dialectico, non cognoscit eam quantum cognoscibilis est, et ideo non cognoscit totaliter; sed qui cognoscit eam syllogismo demonstrativo, totaliter scit eam. Unumquodque enim tantum cognoscibile est, quantum habet de

of the divine essence. This is because the natural desire of the intellect is to understand and know the causes of all the effects that it knows; but this desire cannot be fulfilled unless it understands and knows the first universal cause of all things, which is a cause that is not composed of cause and effect, as second causes are. Therefore, to take away the possibility of the vision of the divine essence by man is to take away happiness itself.

Therefore, in order for the created intellect to be happy, it is necessary that the divine essence be seen. *Blessed are the pure in heart, for they shall see God* (Matt 5:8).

213. Three things should be noted about the vision of the divine essence.

First, because it will never be seen with a bodily eye, either by sense or by imagination, since only senible bodily things are perceived by the senses, and God is not bodily: **God is spirit** (John 4:24).

Second, that as long as the human intellect is in the body it cannot see God, because it is weighed down by the body so that it cannot attain the summit of contemplation. So it is that the more a soul is free of passions and is purged from affections for earthly things, the higher it rises in the contemplation of truth and tastes how sweet the Lord is. Now the highest degree of contemplation is to see God through his essence; and so as long as a man lives in a body which is necessarily subject to many passions, he cannot see God through his essence. *Man will not see me and live* (Exod 33:20). Therefore, if the human intellect is to see the divine essence it must wholly depart from the body: either by death, as the Apostle says, *we would prefer to be absent from the body and present with the Lord* (2 Cor 5:8); or by being wholly abstracted by rapture from the senses of the body, as is mentioned of Paul at *and I know such a man (whether in the body, or out of the body, I know not: God knows)* (2 Cor 12:3).

Third, no created intellect, however abstracted, either by death, or separated from the body, which does see the divine essence, can comprehend it in any way. And so it is commonly said that although the whole divine essence is seen by the blessed, since it is most simple and has no parts, yet it is not wholly seen, because this would be to comprehend it. For 'wholly' implies a certain mode. But any mode of God is the divine essence. Hence one who does not see him wholly does not comprehend him. For one is properly said to comprehend a thing through knowledge when he knows that thing to the extent that it is knowable in itself; otherwise, although he may know it, he does not comprehend it. For example, one who knows this proposition, that *a triangle has three angles equal to two right angles,* by a dialectical syllogism, does not know it as well as it is knowable in itself; thus he does not know it wholly. But one who knows this by a demonstrative syllogism does know it wholly. For each thing is knowable to the extent that it has being and truth; while one is a knower according to

ente et veritate; sed ipse cognoscens tantum cognoscit quantum habet de virtute cognoscitiva. Omnis autem substantia intellectualis creata est finita: ergo finite cognoscit. Cum ergo Deus sit infinitae virtutis et entitatis, et per consequens infinite cognoscibilis, a nullo intellectu creato cognosci potest quantum est cognoscibilis; et ideo omni intellectui creato remanet incomprehensibilis; Iob XXXVI, 26: *ecce Deus magnus vincens scientiam nostram.* Solus autem ipse comprehendendo contemplatur seipsum, quia tanta est eius virtus in cognoscendo quanta est eius entitas in essendo. Ier. XXXII, 18: *fortissime, magne, potens Dominus exercituum nomen tibi, magnus consilio, incomprehensibilis cogitatu.*

214. Sic ergo, secundum praemissa, intelligitur **Deum nemo vidit unquam**. Primo sic: **nemo**, idest nullus hominum, **vidit Deum**, idest essentiam divinam, oculo corporali et imaginario. Secundo **nemo**, in hac mortali vita vivens, **vidit** divinam essentiam in seipsa. Tertio **nemo**, homo vel angelus, **vidit Deum**, visione comprehensionis.

Quod autem de aliquibus dicitur, quod Deum viderunt oculo, seu viventes in corpore, intelligitur non per essentiam, sed per subiectam creaturam, ut dictum est.

Sic ergo necessarium erat quod reciperemus sapientiam, quia **Deum nemo vidit unquam**.

215. Huius autem sapientiae sufficiens doctor nobis proponitur ab Evangelista, cum subdit **unigenitus Filius qui est in sinu Patris**, in quo ostendit nobis doctoris ipsius facultatem per tria. Scilicet per naturalem similitudinem, et per singularem excellentiam, et per perfectissimam consubstantialitatem.

216. Per naturalem similitudinem, quia filius naturaliter similitudinem patris habet. Et inde est etiam quod intantum aliquis dicitur filius Dei, inquantum similitudinem Filii naturalis participat; et intantum cognoscit, inquantum de similitudine eius habet: quia cognitio fit per assimilationem. I Io. III, 2: *nunc Filii Dei sumus*, et sequitur: *cum apparuerit, similes ei erimus, et videbimus eum sicuti est.* Et ideo in hoc quod Evangelista dicit **Filius**, importatur similitudo, et aptitudo ad cognoscendum Deum.

217. Sed quia iste doctor specialius quam alii filii Deum cognoscit, ideo Evangelista hoc insinuat per excellentiam singularem, cum dicit **unigenitus**; quasi dicat: iste cognoscit Deum prae aliis filiis. Ideo dicitur **unigenitus**, quia est Filius naturalis, eamdem habens cum Patre naturam et cognitionem; Ps. II, 7: *Dominus dixit ad me: Filius meus es tu.*

218. Quamvis autem singulariter cognosceret, posset tamen sibi deesse facultas docendi, si non cognosceret totaliter; et ideo addit tertium, scilicet consubstantialitatem eius ad Patrem, cum dicit **in sinu Patris**: ut non

his amount of cognitive power. Now a created intellectual substance is finite; hence it knows in a finite way. And since God is infinite in power and being, and as a consequence is infinitely knowable, he cannot be known by any created intellect to the degree that he is knowable. And thus he remains incomprehensible to every created intellect. *Behold, God is great, exceeding our knowledge* (Job 36:26). He alone contemplates himself comprehensively, because his power to know is as great as his entity in being. *O most mighty, great, powerful, your name is Lord of hosts, great in counsel, incomprehensible in thought* (Jer 32:18).

214. Using the above explanations, we can understand, **no man has ever seen God**. First, **no man has ever seen God**, that is, the divine essence, with the eye of the body or of the imagination. Second, **no man**, living in this mortal life, **has ever seen** the divine essence in itself. Third, **no man**, man or angel, **has ever seen God** by a vision of comprehension.

So when it is said that certain ones have seen God with their eyes or while living in the body, he is not seen through his essence, but through a creature acting as a substitute, as was said.

And thus it was necessary for us to receive wisdom, because **no man has ever seen God**.

215. The Evangelist mentions the competent teacher of this wisdom when he adds, **the only begotten Son, who is in the bosom of the Father**. He shows the competence of this teacher in three ways: by a natural likeness, by a singular excellence, and by a most perfect consubstantiality.

216. By natural likeness, because a son is naturally like his father. Wherefore it also follows that one is called a son of God insofar as he shares in the likeness of his natural son; and one knows him insofar he has a likeness to him, since knowledge is attained through assimilation. Hence it is said: *now we are sons of God* (1 John 3:2), and he immediately adds, *when he comes, we will be like him, and we will see him as he is.* Therefore, when the Evangelist says **Son**, he implies a likeness as well as all aptitude for knowing God.

217. Because this teacher knows God in a more special way than other sons do, the Evangelist suggests this by his singular excellence, saying, **the only begotten**. As if to say: he knows God more than other sons do. Hence, because he is the natural Son, having the same nature and knowledge as the Father, he is called the **only begotten**. *The Lord said to me: 'you are my Son'* (Ps 2:7).

218. Although he may know in a unique way, he would be lacking the ability to teach if he were not to know wholly. Hence he adds a third point, namely, his consubstantiality to the Father, when he says, **who is in the bosom of the**

accipiatur *sinus* prout in hominibus veste praecinctis dici consuevit, sed pro Patris occulto. Illud enim in occulto gerimus, quod in sinu portamus. Occultum autem Patris est, quia superexcedit omnem virtutem, et cognitionem, cum divina essentia sit infinita. In illo ergo *sinu*, idest in occultissimo paternae naturae et essentiae, quae excedit omnem virtutem creaturae, est *unigenitus Filius*; et ideo consubstantialis est Patri.

Et quod Evangelista hic significavit per *sinum* hoc David expressit per uterum, dicens Ps. CIX, 3: *ex utero ante Luciferum*, idest ex intimo et occulto meae essentiae, incomprehensibili omni intellectui creato, *genui te*, et consubstantialem mihi, et eiusdem naturae et virtutis et potestatis et cognitionis; I Cor. II, v. 11: *quae sunt hominis, nemo novit nisi spiritus hominis . . . et quae sunt Dei, nemo novit nisi Spiritus Dei*. Comprehendit ergo divinam essentiam, quae sua est.

219. Anima autem Christi Deum cognoscendo non comprehendit, quia hoc non dicitur, nisi de unigenito, qui est in sinu Patris. Unde et Dominus dicit Matth. XI, 27: *nemo novit Patrem, nisi Filius, et cui voluerit Filius revelare*; ut utrumque intelligatur de notitia comprehensionis, de qua hic videtur loqui Evangelista. Nullus enim divinam comprehendit essentiam, nisi solus Deus Pater, et Filius, et Spiritus Sanctus.

Sic ergo patet facultas doctoris ad docendum.

220. Notandum etiam, quod per hoc quod dicit *qui est in sinu Patris*, excluditur error quorumdam, dicentium, Patrem invisibilem esse, Filium vero visibilem, et non visum fuisse in Veteri Testamento. Nam, ex hoc quod est in abscondito Patris, manifestum est quod naturaliter invisibilis est, sicut Pater. Et propter hoc dicebat de ipso Is. XLV, 15: *tu es vere Deus absconditus*. Et ideo in Scriptura divina fit mentio de incomprehensibilitate Filii; Matth. XI, 27: *nemo novit Filium nisi Pater, neque Patrem quis novit nisi Filius*; Prov. XXX, 4: *quod nomen Filii eius, si nosti?*

221. Consequenter Evangelista modum tradendi ipsam doctrinam insinuat, cum dicit *ipse enarravit*. Olim enim unigenitus Filius manifestavit Dei cognitionem per prophetas, qui eum intantum annuntiaverunt inquantum aeterni Verbi fuerunt participes. Unde dicebant: *factum est Verbum Domini* etc. Sed nunc *ipse unigenitus*, Filius, *enarravit* fidelibus. Is. LII, 6: *ego ipse qui loquebar, ecce adsum*; Hebr. I, 1: *multifariam, multisque modis olim Deus loquens patribus in prophetis, novissime diebus istis locutus est nobis in Filio*.

Et haec doctrina ideo omnibus aliis doctrinis supereminet dignitate, auctoritate et utilitate, quia ab unigenito Filio, qui est prima sapientia, immediate est tradita.

Father. *Bosom* is not to be taken here as referring to men in their garments but it indicates the secret things of the Father. For what we carry in our bosom we do in secret. The secret things of the Father refer to his unsurpassed power and knowledge, since the divine essence is infinite. Therefore, in that *bosom*, i.e., in the most secret things of the paternal nature and essence, which transcends all the power of the creature, is *the only begotten Son*; and so he is consubstantial with the Father.

What the Evangelist signifies by *bosom*, David expressed by 'womb,' saying: *from the womb, before the daystar*, i.e., from the inmost secret things of my essence, incomprehensible to every created intellect, *I begot you* (Ps 109:3), consubstantial with me, and of the same nature and power, and virtue and knowledge. *What man knows the things of a man except the spirit of the man that is in him? So also, no one knows the things of God except the Spirit of God* (1 Cor 2:11). Therefore, he comprehends the divine essence, which is his own.

219. But the soul of Christ, which knows God, does not comprehend him, because this is attributed only to the only begotten Son who is in the bosom of the Father. So the Lord also says: *no one knows the Father except the Son, and any to whom the Son wishes to reveal him* (Matt 11:27); we should understand this as referring to the knowledge of comprehension, about which the Evangelist seems to be speaking here. For no one comprehends the divine essence except the Father, the Son, and the Holy Spirit.

And so we have shown the competence of the teacher.

220. We should note that the phrase, *who is in the bosom of the Father*, rejects the error of those who say that the Father is invisible, but the Son is visible, though he was not seen in the Old Testament. For from the fact that he is among the hidden things of the Father, it is plain that he is naturally invisible, as is the Father. So it is said of him: *truly, you are a hidden God* (Isa 45:15). And so Scripture mentions the incomprehensibility of the Son: *no one knows the Son except the Father, and no one knows the Father except the Son* (Matt 11:27); *what is the name of his son, if you know?* (Prov 30:4).

221. Then the Evangelist indicates the way in which this teaching is handed down, saying that it is the only begotten Son who *has made him known*. For in the past, the only begotten Son revealed knowledge of God through the prophets, who made him known to the extent that they shared in the eternal Word. Hence they said things like, *the Word of the Lord came to me*. But now *the only begotten Son has made him known* to the faithful: *it is I who spoke; here I am* (Isa 52:6); *God, who in many and varied ways, spoke to the fathers in past times through the prophets, has spoken to us in these days in his Son* (Heb 1:1).

And this teaching surpasses all other teachings in dignity, authority and usefulness, because it was handed on immediately by the only begotten Son, who is the first

Hebr. II, 3: *quae cum initium accepisset enarrari per Dominum, ab eis qui audierunt, in nos confirmata est.*

222. Sed quid narravit nisi unum Deum? Hoc ipsum et Moyses enarravit, Deut. VI, 4: *audi, Israel: Dominus Deus tuus, Dominus unus est.* Quid ergo amplius Moyse? Multum per omnem modum, quia mysterium Trinitatis, et multa alia, quae nec Moyses, nec aliquis prophetarum narravit.

wisdom. *It was first announced by the Lord, and confirmed to us by those who heard him* (Heb 2:3).

222. But what did he make known except the one God? And even Moses did this: *hear, O Israel: the Lord your God is one* (Deut 6:4). What did this add to Moses? It added the mystery of the Trinity, and many other things that neither Moses nor any of the prophets made known.

Lecture 12

1:19 Et hoc est testimonium Ioannis, quando miserunt Iudaei ab Ierosolymis sacerdotes et levitas ad eum, ut interrogarent eum: tu quis es? [n. 224]

1:20 Et confessus est, et non negavit, et confessus est, quia non sum ego Christus. [n. 225]

1:21 Et interrogaverunt eum: quid ergo? Elias es tu? Et dixit, non sum. Propheta es tu? Et respondit: non. [n. 228]

1:22 Dixerunt ergo ei: quis es? ut responsum demus his qui miserunt nos. Quid dicis de teipso? [n. 234]

1:23 Ait: ego vox clamantis in deserto: dirigite viam Domini, sicut dicit Isaias propheta. [n. 236]

1:19 Καὶ αὕτη ἐστὶν ἡ μαρτυρία τοῦ Ἰωάννου, ὅτε ἀπέστειλαν [πρὸς αὐτὸν] οἱ Ἰουδαῖοι ἐξ Ἱεροσολύμων ἱερεῖς καὶ Λευίτας ἵνα ἐρωτήσωσιν αὐτόν· σὺ τίς εἶ;

1:20 καὶ ὡμολόγησεν καὶ οὐκ ἠρνήσατο, καὶ ὡμολόγησεν ὅτι ἐγὼ οὐκ εἰμὶ ὁ χριστός.

1:21 καὶ ἠρώτησαν αὐτόν· τί οὖν; σὺ Ἡλίας εἶ; καὶ λέγει· οὐκ εἰμί. ὁ προφήτης εἶ σύ; καὶ ἀπεκρίθη· οὔ.

1:22 εἶπαν οὖν αὐτῷ· τίς εἶ; ἵνα ἀπόκρισιν δῶμεν τοῖς πέμψασιν ἡμᾶς· τί λέγεις περὶ σεαυτοῦ;

1:23 ἔφη· ἐγὼ φωνὴ βοῶντος ἐν τῇ ἐρήμῳ· εὐθύνατε τὴν ὁδὸν κυρίου, καθὼς εἶπεν Ἡσαΐας ὁ προφήτης.

1:19 And this is the testimony of John, when the Jews sent priests and Levites from Jerusalem to him, to ask him: who are you? [n. 224]

1:20 And he declared openly, and did not deny, and stated clearly: I am not the Christ. [n. 225]

1:21 And they asked him: who then? Are you Elijah? And he said: I am not. Are you the prophet? And he responded: no. [n. 228]

1:22 Therefore they said to him: who are you, that we may give an answer to those who sent us? What do you say about yourself? [n. 234]

1:23 He said: I am a voice of one crying out in the wilderness: make straight the way of the Lord, as the prophet Isaiah says. [n. 236]

---

223. Supra ostendit Evangelista quomodo Christus innotuit testimonio Ioannis ipsis apostolis; hic plenius explicat ipsum testimonium. Et

primo ponit testimonium Ioannis ad turbas;

secundo vero testimonium quod perhibuit de Christo discipulis suis, ibi *altera die iterum stabat*.

Si autem bene considerentur quae dicta sunt, duplex testimonium Ioannis ad Christum invenitur. Unum quod tulit Christo in eius praesentia, aliud in eius absentia: nisi enim in eius praesentia testimonium Ioannes tulisset, non dixisset *hic erat*, et nisi in eius absentia, non diceret *quem dixi vobis*.

Primo ergo Evangelista explicat testimonium Ioannis quod tulit de Christo in eius absentia;

secundo quod tulit in eius praesentia, ibi *altera die vidit*.

Differunt autem haec duo testimonia, quia primum tulit interrogatus, alterum spontaneus; et ideo in primo testimonio non solum ponitur testimonium quod tulit, sed etiam ipsa interrogatio.

Primo autem fuit interrogatus de persona;

secundo de officio, ibi *et qui missi fuerant*.

Ostenditur ergo

primo quomodo Ioannes confessus est se non esse quod non erat;

223. Above, the Evangelist showed how Christ was made known to the apostles through the testimony of John; here he develops this testimony more fully.

First, he presents John's testimony to the people.

Second, the testimony he gave of Christ to his own disciples, at *on the following day, John was standing there again* (John 1:35).

If we carefully consider what was said, we discover a twofold testimony of John to Christ: one which he gave to Christ in his presence, the other in his absence. For he would not have said, *this was he* (John 1:15), unless he had given testimony in Christ's presence; and he would not have said, *of whom I spoke*, unless he gave testimony to him in his absence.

So first, the Evangelist develops the testimony John gave to Christ in his absence;

second, that he gave in his presence, at *the next day, John saw* (John 1:29).

Now these two testimonies differ, because the first was given when he was questioned; the other was spontaneous. So in the first instance, we are given not only his testimony, but also the questions.

First, he was asked about himself;

second, about his office, at *and they who had been sent* (John 1:24).

We are shown therefore:

first we are shown how John stated that he was not what he really was not;

secundo quomodo non negavit se esse quod erat, ibi **dixerunt ergo ei: quis es?**

224. Circa primum ponuntur tres interrogationes est tres responsiones, sicut patet in littera.

In prima autem interrogatione est magna Iudaeorum reverentia ad Ioannem, qui mittunt ad eum, eius testimonium inquirentes. Ubi magnitudo reverentiae ex quatuor colligitur. Primo ex mittentium dignitate: non enim Galilaei miserunt, sed illi qui praecipui fuerunt in populo Israel, scilicet Iudaei, qui sunt de tribu Iuda, habitantes iuxta Ierusalem; I Paral. V, de Iuda elegit Dominus principes populi; infra IV, 22: **salus ex Iudaei est**.

Secundo ex loci praeeminentia, quia ab Ierusalem, quae est civitas sacerdotalis, et divino cultui mancipata; infra IV, 20: **vos dicitis, quia Ierosolymis est locus ubi adorare oportet**. Is. XIX, 21: *et colent eum in hostiis et in muneribus*.

Tertio ex nuntiorum auctoritate, qui solemnes erant, et sanctiores in populo, quia sacerdotes et Levitae; Is. LXI, 6: *vos sacerdotes Domini vocabimini*.

Quarto ex hoc quod miserunt ut Ioannes de se testimonium perhiberet, quasi tantam fidem habentes dictis suis, ut crederent Ioanni de seipso etiam testimonium perhibenti. Unde dicitur **ut interrogarent eum, tu quis es?** Quod Christo non faciebant; immo dicebant ei, Io. VIII, 13: **tu testimonium perhibes de teipso** etc.

225. Consequenter cum dicit **et confessus est, et non negavit**, ponitur Ioannis responsio.

Ideo autem Evangelista ingeminat hoc quod dicit **et confessus est**, ut ostendat humilitatem Ioannis: quia licet esset tantae auctoritatis apud Iudaeos ut eum crederent Christum, non tamen honorem sibi non debitum usurpabat; immo **confessus est, quia non sum ego Christus**.

226. Sed quid est hoc quod dicit **confessus est, et non negavit?** Videtur autem quod negavit, quia dicit se non esse Christum.

Sed dicendum est, quod ideo non negavit veritatem, quia dixit se non esse Christum: alias negasset veritatem. Iob XXXI, 26: *si vidi solem cum fulgeret, et lunam incedentem clare; et laetatum est cor meum in abscondito et osculatus sum manum meam ore meo: quae est iniquitas maxima, et negatio contra Deum altissimum*. Non negavit ergo veritatem quia quantumcumque haberetur magnus, non est elatus in superbiam, usurpans sibi honorem alienum. **Et confessus est, quia, non sum ego Christus**: quia vere non erat. Supra: **non erat ille lux** etc.

227. Sed cum hi qui missi erant non quaererent an esset Christus, sed quis esset; quare Ioannes respondit **non sum ego Christus?**

second, that he did not deny what he was, at **therefore they said to him: who are you?** (John 1:22).

224. As to the first, there are three questions and three answers, as is plain from the text.

In the first question there is great respect for John shown by the Jews. They had sent certain ones to him to ask about his testimony. The greatness of their respect is gathered from four facts. First, from the dignity of those who sent the questioners; for they were not sent by Galileans, but by those who were first in rank among the people of Israel, namely, Judeans, of the tribe of Judah, who lived about Jerusalem. It was from Judah that God chose the princes of the people: **salvation is of the Jews** (John 4:22).

Second, from the preeminence of the place, that is, from Jerusalem, which is the city of the priesthood, the city dedicated to divine worship: **you say that Jerusalem is the place where it is fitting for men to worship** (John 4:20); *they will worship him with sacrifices and offerings* (Isa 19:21).

Third, from the authority of the messengers, who were religious and from among the holier of the people, namely, priests and Levites; *you will be called the priests of the Lord* (Isa 61:6).

Fourth, from the fact that they sent them so that John might bear witness to himself, indicating that they put such trust in his words as to believe John even when giving testimony about himself. Hence he says **to ask him, who are you?** They did not do this to Christ; in fact they said to him: **you give testimony about yourself, but your testimony is not true** (John 8:13).

225. Then when he says, **and he declared openly, and did not deny**, John's answer is given.

The Evangelist twice mentioned that John **stated clearly** to show his humility; for although he was held in such high esteem among the Jews that they believed he might be the Christ, he, on his part, usurped no honor what was not due him; indeed, he **stated clearly: I am not the Christ**.

226. What of the statement, **he declared openly, and did not deny?** For it seems that he did deny, because he said that he was not the Christ.

It must be answered that he did not deny the truth, for he said he was not the Christ; otherwise he would have denied the truth. *If I have looked at the sun when it shone, or the moon moving in splendor and my heart has been secretly enticed, and my mouth has kissed my hand; this also would be a very great iniquity, and a denial of the most high God* (Job 31:28). Thus he did not deny the truth, because however great he might have been considered, he did not become proud, usurping for himself the honor of another. He stated clearly, **I am not the Christ**; because in truth he was not. **He was not the light** (John 1:8).

227. Why did John answer, **I am not the Christ**, since those who had been sent did not ask if he was the Christ, but who he himself was?

Sed dicendum, quod magis respondet ad mentem quaerentium, quam ad quaestionem; et hoc potest accipi dupliciter. Secundum Origenem enim intelligendum est, quod sacerdotes et Levitae bona intentione venerant ad ipsum. Cognoverant enim ex Scripturis, et praecipue ex prophetia Danielis, quia iam venerat tempus adventus Christi. Unde videntes sanctitatem Ioannis, suspicabantur eum esse Christum: unde miserunt ad Ioannem, quasi scire volentes per hoc quod dicunt ei **tu quis es?** An ipse se Christum fateretur. Et ideo eorum respondit menti **non sum ego Christus**.

Chrysostomus vero dicit, quod isti fraudulenter interrogabant. Nam Ioannes cognatus erat sacerdotum, utpote principis sacerdotum filius, erat etiam sanctus; et tamen testimonium perhibebat Christo, cuius genus humile videbatur. Unde et dicebant: *nonne iste est fabri filius?* Et ignotus erat eis. Et ideo cupientes magis habere magistrum Ioannem quam Christum, mittunt ad eum volentes eum per blanditias allicere, et inducere ut sibi honorem hunc attribuens, confiteatur se esse Christum. Quam quidem malitiam videns Ioannes, dicit **non sum ego Christus**.

228. Secunda interrogatio ponitur consequenter, cum dicitur **et interrogaverunt eum: quid ergo? Elias es tu?**

Sciendum est autem, quod a populo Iudaeorum sicut expectabatur Dominus venturus, ita expectabatur Elias Christum praecessurus; Mal. ult., 5: *mittam vobis Eliam* etc. Et ideo videntes, qui missi erant quod Ioannes non confitebatur se esse Christum, instant quod saltem confiteatur si est Elias. Et hoc est quod dicunt **quid ergo? Elias es tu?**

229. Quidam autem haeretici dicunt, quod anima de corpore transmittitur in corpus. Et hoc dogma tunc temporis erat in auctoritate apud Iudaeos, unde credebant quod propter similitudinem operum Ioannis ad Eliam, anima Eliae esset in corpore Ioannis. Et dicunt quod quaerebant isti a Ioanne, an esset Elias; idest, an anima Eliae esset in Ioanne; et adducunt pro eis, quod dicit Dominus, Matth. XI, 14, de Ioanne: *si vultis scire, ipse est Elias.*

Sed tamen contrariatur eis responsio Ioannis dicentis **non sum** Elias.

Ad quod ipsi respondent, quod Ioannes ex ignorantia respondit, nesciens, an anima sua esset anima Eliae. Sed contra hoc dicit Origenes, quod valde irrationabile videtur, quod Ioannes tamquam propheta a Spiritu illuminatus, et de Dei unigenito tanta narrans, ignoraret de seipso, an numquam eius anima fuerit in Elia.

230. Non hac ergo intentione quaerebant **Elias es tu?** Sed quia habentes ex Scripturis, IV Reg. II, 11 quod Elias

I answer that John directed his answer more to the mind of the questioners than to their question. And we can understand this in two ways. According to Origen, the priests and Levites came to John with a good intention. For they knew from the Scriptures, and particularly from the prophecy of Daniel, that the time for the coming of the Christ had arrived. So, seeing John's holiness, they suspected that he might be the Christ. So they sent to John, wishing to learn by their question, **who are you?** whether John would admit that he was the Christ. And so he directs his answer to their thoughts: **I am not the Christ**.

Chrysostom, however, says that they questioned him as a stratagem. For John was related to priests, being the son of a chief priest, and he was holy. Yet, he bore witness to Christ, whose family seemed lowly; for that reason they even said, *is not this the son of the carpenter?* (Matt 13:55; Mark 6:3). And they did not know him. So, preferring to have John as their master, not Christ, they sent to him, intending to entice him by flattery and persuade him to take this honor for himself, and to state that he was the Christ. But John, seeing their evil intent, said, **I am not the Christ**.

228. The second question is stated when they ask him, **who then? Are you Elijah?**

Here we should note that just as the Jews awaited the Lord who was to come, so to they waited for Elijah, who would precede the Messiah: *I will send you Elijah, the prophet* (Mal 4:5). And so those who were sent, seeing that John did not say that he was the Messiah, pressed him that at least he state if he were Elijah. And this is what they ask: **who then? Are you Elijah?**

229. There are certain heretics who say that souls migrate from one body to another. And this belief was current among the Jews of that time. For this reason they believed that the soul of Elijah was in John's body, because of the similarity of John's actions to those of Elijah. And they say that these messengers asked John whether he was Elijah, i.e., whether the soul of Elijah was in John. They support this with Christ's statement, *he is Elijah who is to come* (Matt 11:14).

But John's answer conflicts with their opinion, as he says, **I am not** Elijah.

They counter this by saying that John answered in ignorance, not knowing whether his soul was the soul of Elijah. But Origen says in answer to this that it seems most unreasonable that John, a prophet enlightened by the Spirit, and telling such things about the only begotten Son of God, should be ignorant of himself, and not know whether his soul had been in Elijah.

230. So this was not the reason John was asked, **are you Elijah?** Rather it was because they took it from Scripture (2 Kings 2:11) that Elijah did not die, but had been carried

non fuit mortuus, sed vivus raptus est per turbinem in caelum, credebant eum subito inter eos apparuisse.

Sed contra hoc est quod Ioannes ex notis parentibus natus erat, et nativitas eius omnibus nota erat. Unde dicitur Lc. I, 63, quod *mirati sunt universi, et ponebant in corde suo, dicentes: quis putas puer iste erit?* Ad quod potest dici, quod non est incredibile quod ita aestimarent de Ioanne, sicut dictum est. Quia et simile habetur Matth. XIV, 1 quod Herodes credebat de Christo quod esset Ioannes, quem ipse decollaverat, et tamen diu antequam Ioannes decollatus esset, Christus praedicaverat, et notus fuerat. Et ideo, ex simili amentia et crassitudine, Iudaei quaerebant a Ioanne an ipse esset Elias.

231. Sed quid est hoc quod dicit Ioannes **non sum**, scilicet Elias cum Christus dixerit, Matth. XI, 14, *ipse est Elias*?

Hanc autem quaestionem solvit angelus, Lc. I, 17: *ipse praecedet ante eum in spiritu et virtute Eliae*, in suis scilicet operibus. Non fuit ergo Elias in persona, sed in spiritu, et virtute: quia scilicet similitudinem Eliae in suis operibus ostendebat.

232. Potest autem attendi similitudo quantum ad tria. Primo quantum ad officium: quia sicut Elias secundum domini adventum praeveniet, ita iste praecessit primum etc. Unde et angelus dixit: *ipse praecedet ante ipsum* etc.

Secundo quantum ad vivendi modum: quia Elias in desertis morabatur, parco utebatur cibo et duris vestibus operiebatur, ut dicitur III Reg. XIX, 3 ss. et IV Reg. I, 8. Et Ioannes in desertis erat, cibus eius locustae et mel silvestre, et zona eius de pilis camelorum.

Tertio quantum ad zelum: quia maximi zeli fuit; unde dicebat III Reg. XIX, 10: *zelo zelatus sum pro domino.* Sic et Ioannes zelo veritatis mortuus est, ut patet Matth. XIV, v. 6 ss.

233. Consequenter cum dicit **propheta es tu?** Ponitur tertia quaestio.

Ubi primo quaeritur. Cum dicatur Lc. I, v. 76: *tu puer propheta Altissimi vocaberis* etc. quid est quod Ioannes interrogatus si esset propheta, respondit se non esse prophetam?

Ad quod tripliciter respondetur. Uno modo quod Ioannes non est propheta simpliciter, sed plusquam propheta. Alii namque prophetae solum futura praedicebant a remotis; Hab. II, 3: *si moram fecerit, expecta illum*; Ioannes vero Christum praesentem annuntiavit, quasi digito ostendens; infra: **ecce Agnus Dei**. Et ideo, Matth. XI, 9, Dominus dicit eum esse plus quam prophetam.

Item alio modo, secundum Origenem, quia Iudaei ex malo intellectu tres excellentes personas futuras credebant circa adventum Christi, scilicet ipsum Christum, Eliam et quemdam alium maximum prophetam, de quo

alive by a whirlwind into heaven. Accordingly, they believed that he had suddenly appeared among them.

But against this opinion is the fact that John was born from parents who were known, and his birth had been known to everyone. So it all said, *what do you think this child will be?* (Luke 1:66). One might say to this that it is not incredible that they should regard John in the manner described. For a similar situation in found in Matthew: for Herod thought that Christ was John, whom he had beheaded, even though Christ had been preaching and was known for some time before John had been beheaded (Matt 14:1). And so from a similar stupidity and madness the Jews asked John whether he was Elijah.

231. Why does John say, **I am not** Elijah, while Christ said, *he is Elijah* (Matt 11:14).

The angel gives us the answer: *he will go before him in the spirit and power of Elijah* (Luke 1:17), i.e., in his works. Thus he was not Elijah in person, but in spirit and power, i.e., because he showed a similarity to Elijah in his works.

232. But this similarity can be noticed in three things. First, as to his office: for just as Elijah will appear before the second coming of the Lord, so did this man precede his first coming. Which is why the angel also said: *he shall go before him in the spirit and power of Elijah* (Luke 1:17).

Second, as to his manner of living: for Elijah dwelt in the desert, took scanty food and clothed himself in rough garments, just as it says in Kings (1 Kgs 19:3 ff; 2 Kgs 1:8). And John was in the desert, his food of locusts and wild honey, and his tunic of camel hair.

Third, as to his zeal: for it was the greatest zeal; which is why it was said: *with zeal I have been zealous for the Lord* (1 Kgs 19:10). And this is how John died, for zeal of the truth, as is evident from Mathew (Matt 14:6 ff).

233. Afterward, when it says, **are you the prophet?** a third question is asked.

So first it must be considered. Since it says: *you shall be called the prophet of the Most High* (Luke 1:76), when John is asked if he is a prophet, why does he answer that he is not a prophet?

This can be answered three ways. In one way, that John is not simply a prophet, but even more than a prophet. For while other prophets only predicted far distant future things, as in Habakkuk: *if it make any delay, wait for it* (Hab 2:3); but John announced the present Christ, as though pointing his finger: **behold the Lamb of God** (John 1:36). And thus, in Matthew, the Lord says he is more than a prophet (Matt 11:9).

Or again, in another way, according to Origen, because the Jews, by a bad understanding, believed in three preeminent future persons surrounding the coming of the Christ, which were the Christ himself, Elijah, and some other great

Deut. XVIII, 15: *prophetam suscitabit nobis Dominus* etc. Et licet hic maximus propheta, secundum veritatem, non sit alius quam Christus, tamen secundum Iudaeos alius est a Christo; et ideo non quaerunt simpliciter utrum sit propheta, sed an sit ille propheta maximus. Quod quidem ex ordine quaestionis apparet. Nam primo, quaerunt an sit Christus; secundo, an sit Elias; tertio, an sit propheta ille. Et ideo in Graeco ponitur hic articulus, ut dicatur **ly propheta**, quasi anthonomastice dictum.

Tertio modo quia Pharisaei movebantur contra Ioannem, quod sibi baptizandi officium praeter ordinem legis et traditionem eorum assumpsisset. De tribus autem habetur in Veteri Testamento quibus competere poterat baptizare, scilicet de Christo; Ez. XXXVI, 25, ex persona Christi dicitur: *effundam super vos aquam mundam* etc. Item de Elia, de quo dicitur IV Reg. II, 8, quod divisit aquas Iordanis, et transiens raptus est. Item de Eliseo, qui Naaman Syrum lavari fecit septies in Iordane, ut lavaretur a lepra: ut dicitur IV Reg. c. V, 9. Videntes ergo Iudaei Ioannem baptizare, credebant eum aliquem istorum esse, scilicet Christum, vel Eliam, vel Eliseum; et ideo cum dicunt hic **propheta es tu?** Interrogant an sit Eliseus. Et dicitur singulariter propheta, propter multa miracula quae fecerat; unde et ipse dicit IV Reg. V, 8: *sciat prophetam esse in Israel*. Et secundum hoc respondet **non sum**, scilicet Eliseus.

234. Consequenter cum dicit **dixerunt ergo ei, quis es?** Ostendit quomodo confessus est se esse quod erat, et

primo ponitur interrogatio nuntiorum;
secundo responsio, ibi **ego vox clamantis in deserto**.

235. Dixerunt ergo: **quis es tu ut responsum demus his qui miserunt nos?** Quasi dicant: ad hoc missi sumus, ut sciamus quis es; ideo dicas nobis **quid dicis de te ipso?**

Sed attende Ioannis devotionem: iam implevit quod apostolus dicit, Gal. II, 20, *vivo ego, iam non ego, vivit vero in me Christus*. Et ideo non respondet: ego sum filius Zachariae, vel talis, et talis; sed solum illud in quo Christum sequebatur.

236. Unde dicit: **ego vox clamantis in deserto**.

Dicit autem se vocem esse, quia vox origine posterior est Verbo, sed notitia prior. Nam Verbum in corde conceptum, per vocem prolatam cognoscimus, cum sit signum eius. Deus autem pater praecursorem misit Ioannem in tempore factum, ut Verbum suum ab aeterno conceptum annuntiaretur; et ideo congrue dicit **ego vox**.

prophet, about whom Deuteronomy says: *the Lord will raise up for you a prophet* (Deut 18:15). And given that this is the greatest prophet, according to the truth it is no other than the Christ; however, according to the Jews it is someone other than the Christ. And so they do not ask simply whether he is a prophet, but whether he is the greatest prophet. Which indeed appears from the order of the question. For first, they ask whether he is the Christ; second, whether he is Elijah; third, whether he is that prophet. And thus in the Greek this article is used, so as to indicate **the prophet**, as though speaking antonomastically.

In the third way, because the Pharisees were being moved against John, because he had assumed the office of the one baptizing outside the order of their law and tradition. But the Old Testament speaks about three who are qualified to baptize, namely, the Christ, as in Ezekial it is said by the person of the Christ: *I will pour upon you clean water* (Ezek 36:25). Also, Elijah, of whom it is said that he divided the waters of the Jordan, and crossing over it, he was taken up (2 Kgs 2:8). Or again, Elisha, who made Naaman the Syrian wash seven times in the Jordan, so that he would be cleansed of his leprosy, as it said (2 Kgs 5:9). Therefore, when the Jews saw John baptize, they believed him to be one of those, that is, the Christ, Elijah, or Elisha. And so when they say here **are you the prophet?** they are asking if he is Elisha. And prophet is said in the singular because of the many miracles that he had done; which is why it also says in Kings: *let him know that there is a prophet in Israel* (2 Kgs 5:8). And according to this he answers, **I am not**, that is, not Elisha.

234. Afterward when it says, **and they asked him: who then?** it shows how he confessed himself to be what he was, and

first the questioning of the messengers is set forth;
second, the answer, at **I am a voice of one crying out in the wilderness**.

235. Therefore they said: **who are you that we may give an answer to those who sent us?** As though saying, we were sent for this, to know who you are; will you then say to us **what do you say about yourself?**

But note the devotion of John: for he fulfilled what the Apostle says in Galatians, *I live, now not I, but Christ lives in me* (Gal 2:20). And so he does not respond, I am the son of Zechariah, or so and so; but only how he was following Christ.

236. Which is why he says: **I am a voice of one crying out in the wilderness**.

But he calls himself a voice, because a voice in its origin comes after a word, but in its perception it comes before. For a word that was conceived in the heart, we come to know when it is brought forth by a voice, for that is its sign. But God the Father sent John as a forerunner created in time, so that his Word, conceived from all eternity, might be announced; and thus he fittingly says, **I am a voice**.

237. Quod autem addit *clamantis*, potest intelligi dupliciter, ut scilicet sit vel Ioannis in deserto clamantis et praedicantis, vel Christi clamantis in ipso, secundum illud II Cor. ult., 3: *an experimentum eius quaeritis qui in me loquitur Christus?*

Clamat autem propter quatuor. Primo namque clamor manifestationem importat; et ideo ut ostendat quod Christus in Ioanne et in se manifeste loquebatur, clamat; infra VII, 37: *in novissimo die magno festivitatis stabat Iesus, et clamabat dicens: si quis sitit, veniat ad me et bibat.* In prophetis autem non clamavit, quia prophetiae in aenigmate et figuris datae sunt; unde in Ps. XVII, 12 dicitur: *tenebrosa aqua in nubibus aeris.* Secundo quia clamor fit ad distantes; Iudaei autem elongati erant a Deo, ideo necesse erat quod clamaret. Ps. LXXXVII, 19: *elongasti a me amicum et proximum.* Tertio clamat, quia surdi erant. Is. XLII, 19: *quis surdus, nisi servus meus?* Quarto clamat, quia cum indignatione loquitur, quia ipsi iram Dei meruerunt. Ps. II, 5: *loquetur ad eos in ira sua* etc.

238. Sed attende quod clamat *in deserto*, quia, Lc. III, 2, *factum est verbum domini super Ioannem Zachariae filium in deserto.* Et potest esse huiusmodi ratio et litteralis et mystica.

Litteralis quidem, ut in deserto manens, immunis esset ab omni peccato, ut sic dignior esset Christo testimonium ferre, et ex vita sua testimonium suum credibilius esset hominibus.

Mystica autem causa duplex est. Nam per desertum gentilitas designatur, iuxta illud Is. c. LIV, 1: *multi filii desertae, magis quam eius quae habet virum.* Ut ergo ostenderet quod doctrina Dei de cetero non debet esse in Ierusalem tantum, sed in gentibus, clamavit in deserto. Matth. XXI, 43: *auferetur a nobis regnum Dei, et dabitur genti facienti fructus eius.* Item, per desertum intelligitur Iudaea, quae iam deserta erat; Matth. c. XXIII, 38: *ecce relinquetur vobis domus vestra deserta.* Clamavit ergo *in deserto*, idest in Iudaea, ut per hoc daretur intelligi, quod populus cui praedicabat, iam desertus erat a Deo; Ps. LXII, 3: *in terra deserta et invia et inaquosa sic in sancto apparui tibi.*

239. Sed quid clamat? *Dirigite viam domini*: quia ad hoc missus fuit; Lc. I, 76: *tu puer propheta Altissimi vocaberis, praeibis enim ante faciem Domini parare vias eius.*

Via autem ad recipiendum Deum parata et recta, est via iustitiae, secundum illud Is. c. XXVI, 7: *semita iusti recta est* etc. Tunc enim semita iusti est recta quando homo totus subiicitur Deo, ut scilicet intellectus per fidem, voluntas per amorem, operatio per obedientiam

237. But the fact that he adds, *crying out*, can be understood in two ways. Either it could be referring to John in the desert crying out and preaching, or to Christ crying out in him: *do you seek a proof that the one who speaks in me is Christ?* (2 Cor 13:3)

But he cries out on account of four things. First, inasmuch as shouting conveys a revelation; and thus in order to show that Christ was speaking in John and in himself, he shouted: *and on the last and great day of the festivity, Jesus stood and cried out, saying: if any man thirst, let him come to me and drink* (John 7:37). But among the prophets, he did not cry out, because prophecies were given in riddles and figures; which is why it is said: *dark water was in the clouds of the air* (Ps 18:11). Second, because crying out happens toward those who are far away. The Jews had been estranged from God, so that it was necessary for him to shout; *you have borne away from me friend and neighbor* (Ps 88:18). Third, he shouts, because they were deaf; *who is deaf, but my servant?* (Isa 42:19). Fourth, he cries out, because he speaks with indignation, because they deserved the wrath of God; *he spoke to them in his anger* (Ps 2:5).

238. But note that he cries out *in the wilderness*, because, as Luke says, *the word of God was made unto John, the son of Zechariah, in the wilderness* (Luke 3:2). And the account of this can be both literal and mystical.

Literally, that he was remaining in the wilderness, in order to be preserved from all sin, so that he might be worthier to bear Christ witness, and his witness might be more convincing to men by his life.

But the mystical reason is twofold. For by the wilderness the gentiles are signified, according to this passage: *many are the children of the deserted woman, more than of her who has a husband* (Isa 54:1). Therefore, so that he might show that the teaching of God concerning the rest should not be in Jerusalem alone, but also among the gentiles, he cried out in the wilderness. In Matthew, it says, *the kingdom of God shall be taken from you and shall be given to a nation yielding the fruits of it* (Matt 21:43). Again, by wilderness is understood Judea, which was then a desert; *behold, your house shall be left to you deserted* (Matt 23:38). Therefore he cried out *in the wilderness*, that is, in Judea, so that by that it might be understood that the people to whom he preached, were already deserted by God; *in a desert land where there is no way and no water, so I have come before you in the sanctuary* (Ps 63:1).

239. But what does he cry out? *Make straight the way of the Lord*: for he was sent for this, see Luke: *you, child, shall be called the prophet of the Most High, for you will go before the face of the Lord to prepare his ways* (Luke 1:76).

But the way that is prepared and right for receiving the Lord, is the way of justice, as it says in Isaiah: *the path of the just man is right* (Isa 26:7). For the path of the just man is right when a man is completely subjected to God, namely so that his intellect is subjected to God by faith, his will by

Deo subdantur. Et hoc, *sicut dicit Isaias propheta*; idest, sicut praedixit. Quasi dicat: ego sum ille in quo ista complentur.

love, and his working by obedience. And this, *as the prophet Isaiah says*, that is, as he predicted. As though he were saying: I am the one in whom these things are fulfilled.

Lecture 13

1:24 Et qui missi fuerant, erant ex Pharisaeis: [n. 241]

1:25 et interrogaverunt eum, et dixerunt ei: quid ergo baptizas, si tu non es Christus, neque Elias, neque propheta? [n. 241]

1:26 Respondit eis Ioannes, dicens: ego baptizo in aqua: medius autem vestrum stetit, quem vos nescitis: [n. 244]

1:27 ipse est, qui post me venturus est, qui ante me factus est: cuius ego non sum dignus, ut solvam eius corrigiam calceamenti. [n. 247]

1:28 Haec in Bethania facta sunt trans Iordanem, ubi erat Ioannes baptizans. [n. 251]

1:24 Καὶ ἀπεσταλμένοι ἦσαν ἐκ τῶν Φαρισαίων.

1:25 καὶ ἠρώτησαν αὐτὸν καὶ εἶπαν αὐτῷ· τί οὖν βαπτίζεις εἰ σὺ οὐκ εἶ ὁ χριστὸς οὐδὲ Ἠλίας οὐδὲ ὁ προφήτης;

1:26 ἀπεκρίθη αὐτοῖς ὁ Ἰωάννης λέγων· ἐγὼ βαπτίζω ἐν ὕδατι· μέσος ὑμῶν ἔστηκεν ὃν ὑμεῖς οὐκ οἴδατε,

1:27 ὁ ὀπίσω μου ἐρχόμενος, οὗ οὐκ εἰμὶ [ἐγὼ] ἄξιος ἵνα λύσω αὐτοῦ τὸν ἱμάντα τοῦ ὑποδήματος.

1:28 ταῦτα ἐν Βηθανίᾳ ἐγένετο πέραν τοῦ Ἰορδάνου, ὅπου ἦν ὁ Ἰωάννης βαπτίζων.

1:24 And they who had been sent, were of the Pharisees. [n. 241]

1:25 And they asked him, and said to him: why then do you baptize, if you are not the Christ, nor Elijah, nor the prophet? [n. 241]

1:26 John answered them, saying: I baptize with water; but there is one who stands in your midst, whom you do not know. [n. 244]

1:27 The same is he who will come after me, who ranks ahead of me: the strap of whose sandal I am not worthy to unfasten. [n. 247]

1:28 These things were done in Bethany, beyond the Jordan, where John was baptizing. [n. 251]

---

240. Supra Ioannes interrogatus perhibuit testimonium Christo de seipso quantum ad personam; hic vero quantum ad officium.

Et circa hoc ponuntur quatuor.

Primo interrogantes;

secundo interrogatio, ibi *et interrogaverunt eum*;

tertio responsio, in qua testimonium perhibuit, ibi *respondit eis Ioannes* etc.

Quarto locus ubi haec facta sunt, ibi *haec in Bethania facta sunt* .

241. Interrogantes autem sunt Pharisaei. Unde dicit *et qui missi fuerant, erant ex Pharisaeis*. Et quidem, secundum Origenem, quod dicitur ex hoc loco, ad aliud testimonium pertinet: et isti qui missi sunt ex Pharisaeis, non sunt iidem cum sacerdotibus et Levitis, qui missi sunt a Iudaeorum universitate, sed alii specialiter missi a Pharisaeis. Et secundum hoc dicitur: *et qui missi sunt*, non a Iudaeis scilicet, sicut fuerunt sacerdotes et Levitae, sed alii *erant ex Pharisaeis*. Et ideo dicit quod, quia sacerdotes et Levitae disciplinati erant et reverentes, humiliter et cum reverentia Ioannem interrogant de eius dignitate, utrum scilicet Christus esset, an Elias, an propheta; isti vero, qui ex Pharisaeis erant, secundum nomen suum divisi et importuni, contumeliosas voces praetendunt Baptistae, unde dixerunt ei: *quid ergo baptizatis, si tu non es Christus, neque Elias, neque propheta?*

Secundum alios vero, Gregorium scilicet, Chrysostomum et Augustinum, isti qui ex Pharisaeis, sunt illi iidem qui missi fuerant a Iudaeis sacerdotes et Levitae. Quaedam enim secta erat inter Iudaeos, qui propter

240. Above, we saw John bear witness to Christ as he was being questioned on matters concerning himself; here, on matters concerning his office.

Four things are set forth:

first, those who question him;

second, their questions: *and they asked him*;

third, his answer, in which he bore witness: *John answered them, saying*;

and fourth, the place where all this happened: *these things were done in Bethany*.

241. His interrogators were Pharisees. Hence he says, *and they who had been sent, were of the Pharisees*. According to Origen, what is being said from this point on describes a different testimony given by John; and further, those who were sent from the Pharisees are not the same as those priests and Levites sent by the generality of the Jews, but others who were specifically sent by the Pharisees. And according to this it says: *and they who had been sent*, not by the Jews, as the priests and Levites had been, but were others, *were of the Pharisees*. So he says about this that because the priests and Levites were educated and respectful, they ask John humbly and respectfully whether he is the Messiah, or Elijah, or the Prophet. But these others, who were from the Pharisees, according to their name are divisive and importunate, and used disdainful language. Thus they asked him, *why then do you baptize, if you are not the Christ, nor Elijah, nor the prophet?*

But according to others, such as Gregory, Chrysostom, and Augustine, these Pharisees are the same priests and Levites who had been sent by the Jews. For there was among the Jews a certain sect which was separated from

exteriorem cultum divisi erant ab aliis: unde et Pharisaei, idest divisi vocabantur; in qua quidem erant aliqui de sacerdotibus et Levitis, et aliqui de populo. Ut ergo nuntii maioris auctoritatis essent, miserunt sacerdotes et Levitas, qui erant ex Pharisaeis, ut eis nec sacerdotalis ordinis dignitas, nec religioni deesset auctoritas.

242. Ideo autem Evangelista addit hoc quod dicitur *et qui missi fuerant, erant ex Pharisaeis*, ut primo quidem rationem quaestionis baptismi Ioannis, pro qua missi non fuerant, assignet; quasi dicat: missi fuerant, ut interrogarent a Ioanne quis esset. Sed quod quaerunt *quid ergo baptizas?* Fecerunt, quia erant ex Pharisaeis, quibus eorum religio ausum praebebat.

Secundo, ut dicit Gregorius, ut ostendat qua intentione quaesierunt a Ioanne *tu quis es?* Pharisaei enim inter omnes alios insidiose, et calumniose se habebant ad Christum. Unde ipsi dixerunt ei, Matth. XII, 24: *in Beelzebub principe daemoniorum daemonia eiicit.* Ipsi etiam inierunt cum Herodianis consilium, *ut caperent Iesum in sermone.* Matth. XXII, 15. Et ideo per hoc quod dicit *qui missi fuerant, erant ex Pharisaeis*, ostendit, quod calumniose se habebant, et ex invidia eum interrogaverunt.

243. Interrogatio autem est de officio baptizandi, unde dicitur et interrogaverunt eum, et dixerunt ei: *quid ergo baptizas?* etc.

Unde notandum est, quod non quaerunt ut sciant, sed ut impediant. Quia enim videbant multitudinem populi ad Ioannem currere, propter novum ritum baptizandi, et extraneum a ritu Pharisaeorum et legis, invidebant Ioanni, et conabantur pro posse impedire baptismum eius; et ideo, se continere non valentes, suam manifestant invidiam, et dicunt *quid ergo baptizas, si tu non es Christus, neque Elias, neque propheta?* Quasi dicant: non debes baptizare, ex quo negas te esse aliquem illorum trium in quibus praefiguratus est baptismus, ut dictum est supra. Scilicet, *si tu non es Christus*, qui habiturus est fontem in ablutionem peccati; et si *non es Elias, sive propheta*, idest Eliseus, qui sicco vestigio Iordanem transiverunt, ut dicitur IV Reg. II, 8, quomodo audes baptizare?

Similes isti sunt invidi, animarum profectum impedientes, *qui dicunt videntibus: nolite videre* etc.: Is. XXX, 10.

244. Responsio autem est vera: unde dicit respondit eis Ioannes, *dicens: ego baptizo in aqua.* Quasi dicat: non debetis mirari, si ego, qui non sum Christus, nec Elias, nec propheta, baptizo: quia baptismus meus non est completivus, sed imperfectus.

Nam ad perfectionem baptismi exigitur lotio corporis et animae; et corpus quidem secundum naturam lavatur aqua, anima vero non nisi spiritu. Unde *ego baptizo in aqua*, idest, corpore lavo corpus; veniet autem

the others by reason of its external cult; and for this reason its members were called Pharisees, i.e., divided. In this sect there were some priests and Levites, and some of the people. And so, in order that the delegates might possess a greater authority, they sent priests and Levites, who were Pharisees, thus furnishing them with the dignity of a priestly caste and with religious authority.

242. The Evangelist adds, *and they who had been sent, were of the Pharisees*, to disclose, first, the specific reason of their question about John's baptizing, which was not why they were sent. It is as though he were saying that they were sent to ask John who he was. But they asked, *why do you baptize?* The did this because they were from the Pharisees, whose religion was being challenged.

Second, as Gregory says, in order to show with what intention they asked John, *who are you?* (John 1:19) For the Pharisees, more than all the others, showed themselves crafty and insulting to Christ. Thus they said of him: *he casts out devils by Beelzebub, the prince of devils* (Matt 12:24). Further, they consulted with the Herodians on *how to trap Jesus in his speech* (Matt 22:15). And so in saying that *they who had been sent, were of the Pharisees*, he shows that they were disrespectful and were questioning him out of envy.

243. Their questions concerned his office of baptizing. Hence he says that they asked him, *why then do you baptize?*

Here we should note that they are asking not to learn, but to obstruct. For since they saw many people coming to John because of the new rite of baptism, foreign both to the rite of the Pharisees and of the law, they became envious of John and tried all they could to hinder his baptism. But being unable to contain themselves any longer, they reveal their envy and say, *why then do you baptize, if you are not the Christ, nor Elijah, nor the prophet?* As if to say: you should not baptize, since you deny that you are any of those three persons in whom baptism was prefigured, as was said above. In other words, *if you are not the Christ*, who will possess the fountain by which sins are washed away, *nor Elijah, nor the prophet*, i.e., Elisha, who made a dry passageway through the Jordan (2 Kgs 2:8), how do you dare baptize?

They are like envious persons who hinder the progress of souls, *who say to the seers: see no visions* (Isa 30:10).

244. His answer is true: and so he says that John answered, *I baptize with water*. As if to say: you should not be disturbed, if I, who am not the Messiah, nor Elijah, nor the Prophet, baptize; because my baptism is not completive but imperfect.

For the perfection of baptism requires the washing of the body and of the soul; and the body, by its nature, is indeed washed by water, but the soul is washed by the Spirit alone. So, *I baptize with water*, i.e., I wash the body with

alius, qui perfecte baptizabit, scilicet in aqua et Spiritu Sancto; Deus et homo, qui et corpus aqua et spiritum spiritu lavabit, ita quod sanctificatio spiritus derivabitur ad corpus. Act. I, 5: *Ioannes quidem baptizavit aqua, vos autem baptizabimini Spiritu Sancto non post multos hos dies.*

245. Testimonium autem perhibet de Christo, cum dicit *medius autem vestrum stetit* etc., et

primo per comparationem ad Iudaeos;

secundo per comparationem ad seipsum, ibi *ipse est qui post me venturus est.*

246. Ad Iudaeos autem comparat eum, dicens *medius autem vestrum stetit*; quasi dicat: ego imperfectum opus feci; sed est alius qui perficiet opus meum, qui *medius vestrum stetit.*

Quod quidem exponitur multipliciter. Uno siquidem modo, secundum Gregorium, Chrysostomum et Augustinum, ut referatur ad communem Christi conversationem inter homines, quia, secundum naturam humanam, aliis hominibus similis apparuit; Phil. II, 6: *qui cum in forma Dei esset, non rapinam arbitratus est esse se aequalem Deo; sed semetipsum exinanivit formam servi accipiens, in similitudinem hominum factus, et habitu inventus ut homo.* Et secundum hoc dicit *medius vestrum stetit*, idest multoties conversatus est quasi unus ex vobis; Lc. XXII, v. 27: *ego in medio vestrum sum. Quem vos nescitis*, idest, hoc quod Deus factus est homo, capere non potestis. Item, *nescitis* quam magnus sit secundum naturam divinam, quae in eo latebat; Iob XXXVI, 26: *ecce Dominus magnus vincens scientiam vestram.* Et ideo, ut Augustinus dicit, *accensa est lucerna*, scilicet Ioannes, *ut inveniatur Christus.* Ps. CXXXI, 17: *paravi lucernam Christo meo.*

Alio modo exponitur, secundum Origenem, et hoc dupliciter. Primo ut referatur ad Christi divinitatem; et secundum hoc *medius vestrum*, idest in medio omnium rerum, *stetit*, scilicet Christus: quia ipse secundum quod Verbum a principio creaturae implevit universam creaturam. Ier. XXIII, 24: *caelum et terram ego impleo.* **Quem tamen vos nescitis**, quia, ut dicitur supra, *in mundo erat . . . et mundus eum non cognovit.* Alio modo ut referatur ad causalitatem humanae sapientiae, et dicatur *medius vestrum stetit*; idest, in intellectu omnium relucet: quia quicquid lucis et sapientiae est in hominibus, provenit eis ex participatione Verbi. Et dicit *in medio*, quia in medio hominis corporaliter est cor, cui attribuitur quaedam sapientia et intellectus: unde, licet intellectus non habeat organum corporale, tamen quia cor est principale organum, consuevit accipi pro intellectu; unde in medio stare dicitur secundum hanc similitudinem, inquantum *illuminat omnem hominem venientem in hunc mundum.*

something bodily; but another will come who will baptize perfectly, namely, with water and with the Holy Spirit; God and man, who will wash the body with water and the spirit with the Spirit, in such a way that the sanctification of the spirit will be distributed throughout the body. *For John indeed baptized with water but you will be baptized with the Holy Spirit not many days from now* (Acts 1:5).

245. Then he bears witness to Christ: **but there is one who stands in your midst, whom you do not know**.

First, in relation to the Jews.

Second, in relation to himself, at **the same is he who will come after me, who ranks ahead of me**.

246. He relates him to the Jews when he says, **but there is one who stands in your midst**. As if to say: I have done an incomplete work, but there is another who will complete my work, and he **stands in your midst**.

This is explained in a number of ways. First, according to Gregory, Chrysostom and Augustine, it refers to the ordinary way Christ lived among men, because according to his human nature he appeared to be like other men: *he, being in the form of God, did not account equality with God something to be grasped, rather he emptied himself, taking the form of a servant* (Phil 2:6). And according to this he says, **there is one who stands in your midst**, i.e., in many ways he lived as one of you: *I am in your midst* (Luke 22:27), *whom you do not recognize*, i.e., you cannot grasp the fact that God was made man. Likewise, *you do not recognize* how great he is according to the divine nature which is concealed in him: *God is great, and exceeds our knowledge* (Job 36:26). And so, as Augustine says, *the lantern was lighted*, namely, John, *so that Christ might be found. I have prepared a lamp for my anointed* (Ps 131:17).

It is explained differently by Origen; and in two ways. First, as referring to the divinity of Christ: and according to this, **there is one who stands**, namely, Christ, **in your midst**, that is, in the midst of all things; because he, as Word, has filled all from the beginning of creation: *I fill heaven and earth* (Jer 23:24). **Whom you do not know**, because *he was in the world . . . and the world did not know him* (John 1:10). It is explained another way as referring to his causality of human wisdom. **But there is one who stands in your midst**, i.e., he shines in everyone's understanding; because whatever light and whatever wisdom exists in men has come to them from participating in the Word. And he says, **in your midst**, because in the midst of man's body lies the heart, to which is attributed a certain wisdom and understanding; hence, although the intellect has no bodily organ, yet because the heart is our chief organ, it is the custom to take it for the intellect. So he is said to stand among men because of this likeness, insofar as he **enlightens every man**

Quem tamen *vos nescitis*; quia, ut dicitur supra, *lux in tenebris lucet, et tenebrae eam non comprehenderunt.*

Quarto modo exponitur ut referatur ad propheticam Christi praenuntiationem, ut sic respondeatur principaliter Pharisaeis, qui continue Scripturas Veteris Testamenti, in quibus praenuntiabatur Christus, inquirebant, et tamen eum non cognoscebant. Et secundum hoc dicitur *medius vestrum stetit*; idest, in Sacra Scriptura, quam vos semper revolvitis; infra V, 39: *scrutamini Scripturas. Quem tamen vos nescitis*, quia cor vestrum induratum est propter infidelitatem et oculi vestri excaecati sunt, ut non agnoscatis praesentem, quem creditis futurum.

247. Comparat autem Christum ad se Ioannes, cum dicit *ipse est qui post me venturus est*. Ubi

primo ponit excellentiam Christi ad seipsum;

secundo vero excellentiae immensitatem ostendit, ibi *cuius non sum dignus ut solvam corrigiam calceamenti.*

248. Excellentiam autem Christi ad seipsum ostendit et quantum ad ordinem praedicationis, et quantum ad ordinem dignitatis. Quantum quidem ad ordinem praedicationis, Ioannes primo innotuit. Et ideo dicit *ipse est qui post me venit*, ad praedicandum, baptizandum et moriendum; quia, ut dicitur Lc. I, 76, *praeibis ante faciem Domini, parare vias eius.* Sed Ioannes quidem praecessit Christum, sicut imperfectum perfectum, et sicut dispositio formam; sicut dicitur I Cor. c. XV, 46: *non prius quod spirituale, sed quod animale.* Nam tota vita Ioannis fuit quoddam praeparatorium ad Christum; unde dixit supra *ego vox clamantis in deserto.* Sed Christus praecessit Ioannem et nos omnes, sicut perfectum imperfectum, et sicut exemplar exemplatum. Matth. XVI, 24: *si quis vult venire post me, abneget semetipsum, et tollat crucem suam, et sequatur me*; I Pet. c. II, 21: *Christus passus est pro nobis, vobis relinquens exemplum.*

Quantum vero ad ordinem dignitatis, cum dicit *qui ante me factus est*, idest, mihi praelatus est, et dignitate praepositus; quia, ut dicit infra III, 30, *me oportet minui, illum autem crescere.*

249. Immensitatem autem excellentiae assignat cum dicit *cuius ego non sum dignus ut solvam eius corrigiam calceamenti.* Quasi dicat: non intelligatis ipsum mihi in dignitate praepositum sicut unus homo praefertur alteri, sed tam excellenter, quod nihil sum in comparatione ad ipsum. Et hoc patet, quia *non sum dignus ut solvam corrigiam calceamenti eius*: quod est minimum obsequium quod hominibus fieri potest.

Ex quo patet quod Ioannes multum accesserat ad Dei cognitionem, inquantum ex consideratione infinitae magnitudinis Dei se totaliter vilipendebat, et nihil se esse dicebat. Sicut Abraham, cum Deum cognovisset,

coming into this world (John 1:9). *Whom you do not know*, because *the light shines in the darkness, and the darkness did not comprehend it* (John 1:5).

In a fourth way, it is explained as referring to the prophetic foretelling of the Messiah. In this sense the answer is directed chiefly to the Pharisees, who continually searched the writings of the Old Testament in which the Messiah was foretold; and yet they did not recognize him. And according to this it says, *there is one who stands in your midst* i.e., in the Sacred Scriptures which you are always considering: *search the Scriptures* (John 5:39); *whom you do not know*, because your heart is hardened by unbelief, and your eyes blinded, so that you do not recognize as present the person you believe is to come.

247. Then John compares Christ to himself: *the same is he who will come after me.*

First, he states the superiority of Christ as compared to himself.

Second, he shows the greatness of this superiority: *the strap of whose sandal I am not worthy to unfasten.*

248. He shows the superiority of Christ in comparison to himself both in preaching and in dignity. Now, as to the order of preaching, John was the first to become known. Thus he says, *the same is he who will come after me*, to preach, to baptize and to die, because, as was said: *you will go before the face of the Lord to prepare his way* (Luke 1:76). John preceded Christ as the imperfect the perfect, and as the disposition the form; for as is said, *the spiritual is not first, but the animal* (1 Cor 15:46). For the entire life of John was a preparation for Christ; so he said above, **I am a voice of one crying out in the wilderness** (John 1:23). But Christ preceded John and all of us as the perfect precedes the imperfect and the exemplar precedes the copy: *if any one wishes to come after me, let him deny himself, and take up his cross, and follow me* (Matt 16:24); *Christ suffered for us, leaving you an example* (1 Pet 2:21).

Then he compares Christ to himself as to dignity, saying, *who ranks ahead of me*, i.e., he has been placed above me and is above me in dignity, because as he says, *he must increase, but I must decrease* (John 3:30).

249. He touches on the greatness of his superiority when he says, *the strap of whose sandal I am not worthy to unfasten*. As if to say: you must not suppose that he ranks ahead of me in dignity in the way that one man is placed ahead of another, rather he is ranked so far above me that I am nothing in comparison to him. And this is clear from the fact that it is he *the strap of whose sandal I am not worthy to unfasten*, which is the least service that can be done for men.

It is clear from this that John had made great progress in the knowledge of God, so far that from the consideration of God's infinite greatness, he completely lowered himself and said that he himself was nothing. So did Abraham, when

dicebat, Gen. XVIII, 27: *loquar ad Dominum meum, cum sim pulvis et cinis.* Sic Iob c. XLII, 5, cum Dominum vidisset, dixit: *nunc oculus meus videt te; idcirco ipse me reprehendo, et ago poenitentiam in favilla et cinere.* Sic Is. XL, 17, postquam vidit gloriam Dei dixit: *omnes gentes quasi non sint, sic sunt coram eo.* Et haec quidem expositio est litteralis.

250. Exponitur autem et mystice. Uno modo secundum Gregorium, ut per calceamentum, quod fit de pellibus mortuorum animalium, intelligatur humana natura mortalis, quam Christus assumpsit; Ps. LIX, 10: *in Idumaea extendam calceamentum meum* etc. Corrigia autem calceamenti eius, est ipsa unio divinitatis et humanitatis, quam nec Ioannes, nec aliquis, potest solvere nec potuit plene investigare, cum talis esset quod hominem faceret Deum, et Deum hominem. Et ideo dicit **cuius non sum dignus ut solvam corrigiam calceamenti**; idest, ut explicem mysterium incarnationis etc. Intelligendum est plene et perfecte: nam quoquo modo et Ioannes et alii praedicatores, licet imperfecte, solvunt corrigiam calceamenti.

Alio modo exponitur, quia in veteri lege praeceptum erat, Deut. XXV, 5–10 quod quando aliquis moriebatur sine liberis, frater defuncti uxorem defuncti recipere tenebatur, et ex ea semen fratri suo suscitare; quod si nollet eam in uxorem recipere, tunc aliquis propinquus defuncti eam recipere volens, debebat eum discalceare in signum huius cessionis, et illam in uxorem recipere, et domus eius debebat vocari domus discalceati. Secundum hoc ergo dicit **cuius non sum dignus corrigiam calceamenti solvere**; idest, non sum dignus habere sponsam, quae sibi debetur, Ecclesiam. Quasi dicat: non sum dignus ut vocer sponsus Ecclesiae, quae consecratur Christo in baptismo Spiritus; ego autem baptizo in aqua tantum. Infra III, 29: **qui habet sponsam, sponsus est** etc.

251. Locus autem, ubi praedicta facta sunt, subditur consequenter, cum dicit **haec in Bethania facta sunt trans Iordanem**.

Sed circa hoc primo consurgit quaestio. Cum Bethania sit in Monte Oliveti quod est iuxta Ierusalem, sicut dicitur Io. XI, 1 et Matth. XXVI, 6 quomodo dicit quod facta sunt trans Iordanem, qui multum distabat ab Ierusalem?

Sed dicendum, secundum Origenem et Chrysostomum, quod non debet dici Bethania, sed Bethabora, quae est quaedam villa ultra Iordanem: et hoc quod dicit 'Bethania', corruptum est vitio scriptorum. Sed quia tam libri Graeci quam Latini habent Bethania, ideo dicendum est aliter, quod est duplex Bethania: una quae est prope Ierusalem in latere Montis Oliveti, alia trans Iordanem, ubi erat Ioannes baptizans.

he recognized God, and it is said, *I will speak to my Lord, although I am but dust and ashes* (Gen 18:27). Thus did Job say, when he had seen the Lord: *now I see you, and so I reprove myself, and do penance in dust and ashes* (Job 42:5). Isaiah also said, after he had seen the glory of God, *before him all the nations are as if they are not* (Isa 40:17). And this is the literal explanation.

250. This is also explained mystically. Gregory explains it so that the sandal, made from the hides of dead animals, indicates our mortal human nature, which Christ assumed: *I will stretch out my sandal to Edom* (Ps 59:10). The strap of Christ's sandal is the union of his divinity and humanity, which neither John nor anyone can unfasten or fully investigate, since it is this which made God man and made man God. And so he says, **the strap of whose sandal I am not worthy to unfasten**, i.e., to explain the mystery of the incarnation perfectly and fully. For John and other preachers unfasten the strap of Christ's sandal in some way, although imperfectly.

It is explained in another way by recalling that it was ordered in the old law that when a man died without children, his brother was obligated to marry the wife of the dead man and raise up children from her as his brother's. And if he refused to marry her, then a close relative of the dead man, if willing to marry her, was to remove the sandals of the dead man as a sign of this willingness and marry her; and his home was then to be called the home of the man whose sandals were removed (Deut 25:5). And so according to this he says, **the strap of whose sandal I am not worthy to unfasten**, i.e., I am not worthy to have the bride, that is, the Church, to which Christ has a right. As if to say: I am not worthy to be called the bridegroom of the Church, which is consecrated to Christ in the baptism of the Spirit; but I baptize only in water. Thus it is said: **he who has the bride is the bridegroom** (John 3:29).

251. The place where these events happened is mentioned when he says, **these things were done in Bethany, beyond the Jordan**.

A question arises on this: since Bethany is on the Mount of Olives, which is near Jerusalem (John 11:1; Matt 26:6), how can he say that these things happened beyond the Jordan, which is quite far from Jerusalem?

Origen and Chrysostom answer that it should be called Bethabora, not Bethany, which is a village on the far side of the Jordan; and that the reading 'Bethany' is due to a copyist's error. However, since both the Greek and Latin versions have Bethany, one should rather say that there are two places called Bethany: one is near Jerusalem on the side of the Mount of Olives, and the other is on the far side of the Jordan where John was baptizing.

252. Quod autem mentionem facit de loco, habet rationem litteralem et mysticam. Litteralem quidem secundum Chrysostomum, quia Ioannes scribebat Evangelium istud viventibus forte aliquibus qui et tempus quo ista facta sunt, et locum viderunt, et ideo quasi ad maiorem certitudinem illos testes facit illorum quae viderant.

Mysticam vero, quia haec loca conveniunt baptismo. Nam, si dicatur Bethania, quae domus obedientiae interpretatur, significat quod necesse est per obedientiam fidei ad baptismum pervenire; Rom. I, 5: *ad obediendum fidei in omnibus gentibus*. Si vero dicatur Bethabora, quae interpretatur domus praeparationis, significat quod per baptismum praeparatur homo ad vitam aeternam.

Nec vacat mysterio quod trans Iordanem sit. *Iordanis* enim interpretatur 'descensus eorum;' et, secundum Origenem, significat Christum, qui descendit de caelis, ut dicit ipse: *descendit de caelo, ut facerem voluntatem patris mei*. Unde dicitur Eccli. XXIV, 41: *ego quasi fluvius Dorix*. Per ipsum autem omnes ingredientes in hunc mundum, mundari convenit, secundum illud Apoc. I, 5: *lavit nos a peccatis nostris in sanguine suo*.

Convenienter etiam Iordanis baptismum significat. Ipse enim confinium est inter illos qui acceperunt sortes hereditatis a Moyse ex una parte Iordanis, et illos qui acceperunt a Iosue ex alia; et ita baptismus quasi quoddam confinium est inter Iudaeos et gentiles, qui proficiscuntur illuc, ut se lavent ad Christum venientes, ut opprobrium peccati deponant. Sicut enim filios Israel terram promissionis intrantes oportuit transire Iordanem, ita et per baptismum oportet patriam caelestem intrare. Dicit autem, *trans Iordanem* ut insinuet quod etiam transgressoribus et peccatoribus baptismum poenitentiae praedicabat Ioannes; unde et Dominus, Matth. c. IX, 13: *non veni vocare iustos, sed peccatores*.

252. The fact that he mentions the place has both a literal and a mystical reason. The literal reason, according to Chrysostom, is that John wrote this Gospel for certain ones, perhaps still alive, who would recall the time and who saw the place where these things happened. And so, to lead us to a greater certitude, he makes them witnesses of the things they had seen.

The mystical reason is that these places are appropriate for baptism. For in saying Bethany, which is interpreted as house of obedience, he indicates that one must come to be baptized through obedience to the faith. *To bring all the nations to have obedience to the faith* (Rom 1:5). But if the name of the place is Bethabora, which is interpreted as house of preparation, it signifies that a man is prepared for eternal life through baptism.

There is also a mystery in the fact that this happened on the far side of the Jordan. For *Jordan* is interpreted as the 'descent of them;' and according to Origen it signifies Christ, who descended from heaven, as he himself says, *I came down from heaven, not to do my own will, but the will of him who sent me* (John 6:38). From whence it is said: *I am like a river of the Dorix* (Sir 24:41). Through him however, everyone coming into this world are made clean, according: *he who has washed us from our sins in his own blood* (Rev 1:5).

Further, the river Jordan aptly signifies baptism. For it is the border line between those who received their inheritance from Moses on one side of the Jordan, and those who received it from Josue on the other side. Thus baptism is a kind of border between Jews and gentiles, who journey to this place to wash themselves by coming to Christ so that they might put off the debasement of sin. For just as the Jews had to cross the Jordan to enter the promised land, so one must pass through baptism to enter into the heavenly land. And he says, *beyond the Jordan*, to show that John preached the baptism of repentance even to those who trangressed the law and sinners; and so the Lord also says, *I did not come to call the righteous, but sinners* (Matt 9:13).

Lecture 14

1:29 Altera die vidit Ioannes Iesum venientem ad se, et ait: ecce Agnus Dei, ecce qui tollit peccata mundi. [n. 254]

1:30 Hic est de quo dixi: post me venit vir, qui ante me factus est, quia prior me erat. [n. 260]

1:31 Et ego nesciebam eum. Sed ut manifestetur in Israel, propterea veni ego in aqua baptizans. [n. 263]

1:32 Et testimonium perhibuit Ioannes, dicens: quia vidi Spiritum descendentem quasi columbam de caelo, et mansit super eum. [n. 267]

1:33 Et ego nesciebam eum; sed qui misit me baptizare in aqua, ille mihi dixit: super quem videris Spiritum descendentem, et manentem super eum, hic est qui baptizat in Spiritu Sancto. [n. 274]

1:34 Et ego vidi, et testimonium perhibui, quia hic est Filius Dei. [n. 278]

1:29 Τῇ ἐπαύριον βλέπει τὸν Ἰησοῦν ἐρχόμενον πρὸς αὐτὸν καὶ λέγει· ἴδε ὁ ἀμνὸς τοῦ θεοῦ ὁ αἴρων τὴν ἁμαρτίαν τοῦ κόσμου.

1:30 οὗτός ἐστιν ὑπὲρ οὗ ἐγὼ εἶπον· ὀπίσω μου ἔρχεται ἀνὴρ ὃς ἔμπροσθέν μου γέγονεν, ὅτι πρῶτός μου ἦν.

1:31 κἀγὼ οὐκ ᾔδειν αὐτόν, ἀλλ' ἵνα φανερωθῇ τῷ Ἰσραὴλ διὰ τοῦτο ἦλθον ἐγὼ ἐν ὕδατι βαπτίζων.

1:32 Καὶ ἐμαρτύρησεν Ἰωάννης λέγων ὅτι τεθέαμαι τὸ πνεῦμα καταβαῖνον ὡς περιστερὰν ἐξ οὐρανοῦ καὶ ἔμεινεν ἐπ' αὐτόν.

1:33 κἀγὼ οὐκ ᾔδειν αὐτόν, ἀλλ' ὁ πέμψας με βαπτίζειν ἐν ὕδατι ἐκεῖνός μοι εἶπεν· ἐφ' ὃν ἂν ἴδῃς τὸ πνεῦμα καταβαῖνον καὶ μένον ἐπ' αὐτόν, οὗτός ἐστιν ὁ βαπτίζων ἐν πνεύματι ἁγίῳ.

1:34 κἀγὼ ἑώρακα καὶ μεμαρτύρηκα ὅτι οὗτός ἐστιν ὁ υἱὸς τοῦ θεοῦ.

1:29 The next day, John saw Jesus coming to him, and he said: behold the Lamb of God, behold him who takes away the sin of the world. [n. 254]

1:30 This is he, of whom I said: after me there comes a man who ranks ahead of me: because he existed before me. [n. 260]

1:31 And I did not know him, but that he may be made manifest in Israel, therefore I came baptizing with water. [n. 263]

1:32 And John gave testimony, saying: I saw the Spirit coming down, as a dove from heaven, and he rested upon him. [n. 267]

1:33 And I did not know him; but he who sent me to baptize with water, said to me: he upon whom you shall see the Spirit descending, and remaining upon him, it is he who baptizes with the Holy Spirit. [n. 274]

1:34 And I have seen, and I have given testimony, that this is the Son of God. [n. 278]

---

253. Supra Ioannes perhibuit testimonium Christo interrogatus; hic vero perhibet aliud testimonium Christo spontaneus. Et

primo quidem fert ipsum testimonium; secundo testimonium latum confirmat, ibi *et testimonium perhibuit Ioannes*.

Circa primum autem

primo quidem describuntur circumstantiae testimonii;

secundo ponitur ipsum testimonium, ibi *ecce Agnus Dei*;

tertio excluditur suspicio testis, ibi *et ego nesciebam eum*.

254. Describuntur autem circumstantiae. Una quidem ex parte temporis. Unde dicit *altera die*: in quo quidem commendatur Ioannis constantia, quia non uno die, non semel tantum, sed pluribus diebus et multoties Christo testimonium perhibebat. Ps. CXLIV, 2: *per singulos dies benedicam tibi*. Commendatur etiam eius profectus: quia non debet nobis succedere una dies sicut alia; sed quae succedit debet esse altera, idest melior; iuxta illud Ps. LXXXIII, 8: *ibunt de virtute in virtutem*.

253. Above, John had given testimony to Christ when he was questioned. Here, he gives a voluntary testimony.

First, he gives the testimony; second, he confirms it, at *and John gave testimony*.

As to the first:

first, the circumstances of the testimony are given; and

second, the testimony itself is given, at *behold the Lamb of God*;

third, suspicion is removed from the witness, at *and I did not know him*.

254. The circumstances are first described as to the time. Hence he says, *the next day*. This gives credit to John for his steadfastness, because he bore witness to Christ not for just one day or once, but on many days and frequently: *every day I will bless you* (Ps 144:2). His progress, too, is cited, because one day should not be just like the day before, but the succeeding day should be different, i.e., better: *they will go from strength to strength* (Ps 83:8).

Alia circumstantia ponitur ex parte modi testificandi, quia **vidit Ioannes Iesum**: in quo insinuatur certitudo. Nam testimonium de visu certissimum est.

Alia vero circumstantia ponitur ex parte eius cui testimonium perhibetur. Unde dicit **Iesum ad se venientem**, scilicet de Galilaea, ut dicitur Matth. III, 13: *venit Iesus a Galilaea*. Nec tamen intelligendum est de adventu quo venit ad baptismum, de quo ibi loquitur Matthaeus, sed de alio adventu quo iam baptizatus, et circa Iordanem aliquamdiu commoratus, venit ad Ioannem, alias non dixisset: **super quem videris Spiritum descendentem et manentem super eum, hic est qui baptizat in Spiritu Sancto. Et ego vidi** etc. Iam ergo viderat eum, et Spiritum super eum descendentem quasi columbam etc., ut infra dicit.

255. Huius autem Christi ad Ioannem adventus post baptismum una causa fuit ut testimonium Ioannis certificaretur. Dixerat enim Ioannes de Christo: **ipse est qui post me venturus est**: nam aliquis posset errare in cognitione venturi, cum adesset; venit ad Ioannem, ab eo digito ostendendus, dicente Ioanne **ecce Agnus Dei** etc.

Alia ratio ut excluderet errorem. Posset enim aliquis credere quod Christus prima vice, cum venit ad baptismum, venerit ad Ioannem sicut a peccatis purgandus. Christus ergo, ut hoc excluderet, venit etiam ad eum post baptismum. Unde signanter dicit Ioannes **ecce qui tollit**. Peccatum nullum fecit, sed venit peccatum tollere. Venit etiam ut praeberet humilitatis exemplum: quia, ut dicitur Eccli. III, 20, *quanto maior es, humilia te in omnibus*.

Et advertendum, quod sicut Christo iam concepto, quando Virgo mater ascendit in montana cum festinatione, Elisabeth matrem Ioannis visere, Ioannes in utero matris existens, nec loqui valens, reverentiam Christo et tripudium faciens, exultavit in utero; ita et nunc, Christo ex humilitate ad eum venientem testimonium et reverentiam praebet, et in vocem prorumpit, dicens **ecce Agnus Dei** etc.

256. Ubi testimonium Ioannis ponitur: in quo quidem ostendit virtutem Christi, et dignitatem eius, ibi **hic est de quo dixi**.

Virtutem quidem ostendit dupliciter.

Primo proponendo figuram;

secundo exponendo eam, ibi **ecce qui tollit peccata mundi**.

257. Circa primum sciendum est, quod, sicut dicit Origenes, in veteri lege consueverunt quinque animalia offerri in templo: tria de terrestribus, scilicet vitulus, capra et ovis, sed ovium quidem aries, ovis et agnus; de volatilibus vero duo, turtur scilicet, et columba: quae quidem omnia praefigurativa fuerunt veri sacrificii, quod

Another circumstance mentioned is his manner of testifying, because **John saw Jesus**. This shows his certitude, for testimony based on sight is most certain.

The last circumstance he mentions is about the one to whom he bore witness. Hence he says that he saw **Jesus coming to him**, i.e., from Galilee, as it says, *Jesus came from Galilee* (Matt 3:13). We should not understand this as referring to the time when he came to be baptized, of which Matthew is here speaking, but of another time, i.e., a time when he came to John after he had already been baptized and was staying near the Jordan. Otherwise, he would not have said, **he upon whom you shall see the Spirit descending, and remaining upon him, it is he who baptizes with the Holy Spirit. And I have seen**. Therefore, he had already seen him and the Spirit come down as a dove upon him.

255. One reason why Christ now came to John was to confirm the testimony of John. For John had spoken of Christ as **the same is he who will come after me** (John 1:27). But since Christ was now present, some might not understand who it was that was to come. So Christ came to John to be pointed out by him, with John saying, **behold the Lamb of God** (John 1:36).

Another reason Christ came was to correct an error. For some might believe that the first time Christ came, i.e., to be baptized, he came to John to be cleansed from his sins. So, in order to preclude this, Christ came to him even after his baptism. Accordingly, John clearly says, **behold him who takes away**. He committed no sin, but came to take away sin. He also came to give us an example of humility, because as it is said, *the greater you are the more humble you should be in all matters* (Sir 3:20).

Note that after the conception of Christ, when his mother, the Virgin, went in haste to the mountainous country to visit John's mother, Elizabeth, that John, still in his mother's womb and unable to speak, leaped in her womb as though performing a religious dance out of reverence for Christ. And as then, so even now; for when Christ comes to John out of humility, John offers his testimony and reverence and breaks out saying, **behold the Lamb of God**.

256. With these words John gives his testimony showing the power of Christ. Then Christ's dignity is shown, at **this is he, of whom I said**.

He shows the power of Christ in two ways:

first, by means of a symbol;

second, by explaining it, at **behold him who takes away the sins of the world**.

257. As to the first, we should note, as Origen says, that it was customary in the old law for five animals to be offered in the temple: three from the earth, namely, the heifer, goat and sheep, although the sheep might be a ram, a sheep or a lamb; and two birds, namely, the turtle-dove and the dove. All of these were prefigurements of the true sacrifice,

est Christus, qui *semetipsum obtulit oblationem Deo*, ut dicitur Eph. V, 2.

Quare ergo Baptista Christo testimonium perhibens, agnum specialiter nominavit? Huius ratio est, quia sicut dicitur Num. XXVIII, v. 3 s., licet alia fierent sacrificia in templo ceteris temporibus, unum tamen erat quotidianum, in quo iugiter unus agnus mane, et alius vespere offerebatur; nec hoc mutabatur unquam, sed tamquam principale observabatur, alia vero ex adiuncto. Et ideo per agnum, qui erat principale sacrificium, significatur Christus, qui est principale sacrificium. Nam licet omnes sancti, qui pro fide Christi passi sunt, prosint ad salutem fidelium, hoc tamen non habent nisi inquantum super oblationem Agni, quasi oblatio adiuncta principali sacrificio, immolantur. Offertur quidem mane et vespere, quia per Christum patet aditus ad intelligibilia divinorum contemplanda et fruenda, quod pertinet ad cognitionem matutinam; et instruimur quomodo utamur terrenis absque inquinamento, quod pertinet ad vespertinam. Et ideo dicit: *ecce Agnus Dei*, etc., idest per agnum significatus.

Dicit autem *Dei*, quia in Christo sunt duae naturae, humana scilicet et divina. Et quod hoc sacrificium esset virtuosum ad purgandum et sanctificandum a peccatis, habet ex virtute divinitatis, inquantum scilicet *Deus erat in Christo mundum reconcilians sibi*, II Cor. V, v. 19.

Vel dicitur *Agnus Dei*, quasi oblatus a Deo, scilicet ab ipso Christo, qui est Deus; sicut dicitur oblatio hominis, quam homo offert. Vel dicitur *Agnus Dei*, scilicet Patris: quia ipse providit homini oblationem ad offerendum pro peccatis sufficientem, quod homo per se habere non potest. Unde Gen. c. XXII, 7, cum Isaac quaereret ab Abraham: *ubi est victima holocausti?* Respondit: *Deus providebit sibi victimam holocausti*. Rom. VIII, v. 32: *proprio Filio suo non pepercit Deus; sed pro nobis omnibus tradidit illum*.

258. Dicitur autem Christus agnus primo propter puritatem; Ex. XII, 5: *erit agnus anniculus* etc.; I Petr. I, 18: *non corruptibilibus auro vel argento redempti estis*. Secundo propter mansuetudinem; Is. LIII, 7: *quasi agnus coram tondente se obmutuit*. Tertio propter fructum, Prov. XXVII, 26: *agni sunt tibi ad vestimentum tuum*. Et hoc quantum ad indumentum, iuxta illud Rom. XIII, v. 14: *induimini Dominum Iesum Christum*. Et quantum ad cibum, infra VI, 52: **caro mea est pro mundi vita**. Et ideo dicebat Isaias, c. XVI, 1: *emitte agnum, Domine, dominatorem terrae*.

259. Consequenter propositam figuram exponit cum dicit **qui tollit peccata mundi**, idest aufert; quod in lege nec per agnum, nec per alia sacrificia auferri poterat, quia, ut dicitur Hebr. X, 6: *impossibile est per sanguinem taurorum et hircorum auferri peccata*.

which is Christ, who *gave himself for us as an offering to God* (Eph 5:2).

Why then did the Baptist, when giving witness to Christ, specifically call him a Lamb? The reason for this is that, although there were other sacrifices in the temple at other times, yet each day there was a time in which a lamb was offered every morning, and another was offered in the evening (Num 28:3). This never varied, but was regarded as the principal offering, and the other offerings were in the form of additions. And so the lamb, which was the principal sacrifice, signified Christ, who is the principal sacrifice. For although all the saints who suffered for the faith of Christ contribute something to the salvation of the faithful, they do this only inasmuch its they are immolated upon the oblation of the Lamb, they being, as it were, in oblation added to the principal sacrifice. The lamb is offered in the morning and in the evening because it is through Christ that the way is opened to the contemplation and enjoyment of the intelligible things of God, and this pertains to morning knowledge; and we are instructed how to use earthly things without staining ourselves, and this pertains to the evening. And so he says, **behold the Lamb of God**, i.e., the one signified by the lamb.

He says, **of God**, because there are two natures in Christ, a human nature and a divine nature. And it is due to the power of the divinity that this sacrifice has the power to cleanse and sanctify us from our sins, inasmuch as *God was, in Christ, reconciling the world to himself* (2 Cor 5:19).

Or, he is called **the Lamb of God**, because offered by God, i.e., by Christ himself, who is God; just as we call what a man offers the offering of the man. Or, he is called **the Lamb of God**, that is, of the Father, because the Father provided man with an oblation to offer that satisfied for sins, which man could not have through himself. So when Isaac asked Abraham, *where is the victim for the holocaust?* he answered, *God himself will provide a victim for the holocaust* (Gen 22:7); *God did not spare his own Son, but delivered him up for all of us* (Rom 8:32).

258. Christ is called a lamb, first, because of his purity: *your lamb will be without blemish* (Exod 12:5); *you were not redeemed by perishable gold or silver* (1 Pet 1:18). Second, because of his gentleness: *like a lamb before the shearer, he will not open his mouth* (Isa 53:7). Third, because of his fruit; both with respect to what we put on: *lambs will be your clothing* (Prov 27:26), *put on the Lord Jesus Christ* (Rom 13:14); and with respect to food: **my flesh for the life of the world** (John 6:52). And it is said: *send forth, O Lord, the lamb, the ruler of the earth* (Isa 16:1).

259. Then when he says, **who takes away the sins of the world**, he explains the symbol he used. In the law, sin could not be taken away either by a lamb or by any other sacrifice, because as is said in, *it is impossible that sins be taken away by the blood of bulls and goats* (Heb 10:4).

Sanguis iste **tollit**, idest aufert, **peccata mundi**. Oseae ult., 3: *omnem aufert iniquitatem*. Vel **tollit**, idest in se accipit, **peccata** totius **mundi**; quia, ut dicitur I Petr. II, v. 24, *qui peccata nostra pertulit in corpore suo*. Is. LIII, 4: *dolores nostros ipse tulit, et languores nostros ipse portavit*.

Dicit autem, secundum Glossam, *peccatum*, et non **peccata**, ut ostendat in universali, quod abstulit totum genus peccati; I Io. II, 2: *ipse est propitiatio pro peccatis nostris*. Vel quia pro uno peccato, scilicet originali, mortuus; Rom. V, 12: *per unum hominem peccatum intravit in mundum* etc.

260. Supra perhibuit Baptista testimonium Christo quantum ad eius virtutem; hic vero perhibet testimonium quantum ad eius dignitatem, comparans eum sibi tripliciter. Et

primo quantum ad officium et ordinem praedicationis; unde dicit **hic**, scilicet Agnus, digito eum demonstrans, **est ille de quo dixi**, scilicet in eius absentia, **post me venit vir**, ad praedicandum et baptizandum, qui post me venit nascendo. Dicitur autem vir Christus ratione perfectae aetatis: quia quando incepit docere post baptismum, iam erat in aetate perfecta; Lc. III, 23: *Iesus erat incipiens quasi annorum triginta*. Item, ratione perfectionis omnium virtutum quae in eo fuerunt; Is. IV, 1: *apprehendent septem mulieres*, idest virtutes, *virum unum*, scilicet Christum perfectum. Zach. VI, 12: *ecce vir, Oriens nomen eius*: quia ipse est origo omnium virtutum in aliis. Item, ratione desponsationis; quia ipse sponsus est Ecclesiae; Oseae II, 16: *vocabis me virum* etc.; II Cor. XI, 2: *despondi vos uni viro*.

261. Secundo quantum ad ordinem dignitatis, cum dicit **qui ante me factus est**. Quasi dicat: licet post me venerit ad praedicandum, tamen **ante me** idest praelatus mihi factus est dignitate. Cant. II, 8: *ecce iste venit saliens in montibus, transiliens colles*. Collis unus fuit Ioannes Baptista, quem Christus transivit: quia, ut dicitur infra III, 30: **me oportet minui, illum autem crescere**.

262. Tertio quantum ad ordinem durationis, cum dicit **quia prior me erat**. Quasi dicat: non mirum si praefertur mihi dignitate, quia, etsi posterior sit tempore, est tamen prior aeternitate **quia prior me erat**.

Ex hoc autem duplex error destruitur. Error Arii: quia non dicit prior me factus est ut sit creatura, sed **prior me erat**, ab aeterno ante omnem creaturam; Prov. VIII, 25: *ante omnes colles generavit me Dominus*. Item error Pauli Samosateni: quia dixit **prior me erat**, ut ostendat, quod non ex Maria sumpserat exordium. Nam, si essendi principium sumpsisset ex Virgine, non extitisset utique

This blood **takes away**, i.e., removes, **the sins of the world**; *take away all iniquity* (Hos 14:3); or, **takes away**, i.e., he takes upon himself the **sins** of the whole **world**, as is said, *he bore our sins in his own body* (1 Pet 2:24); *it was our infirmities that he bore, our sufferings that he endured* (Isa 53:4).

However, according to a Gloss, he says *sin*, and not **sins**, in order to show in a universal way that he has taken away every kind of sin: *he is the offering for our sins* (1 John 2:2); or because he died for one sin, that is, original sin: *sin entered into this world through one man* (Rom 5:12).

260. Above, the Baptist bore witness to the power of Christ; now he bears witness to his dignity, comparing Christ to himself in three respects.

First, with respect to their office and order of preaching. So he says, **this is he**, that is the Lamb, pointing him out with his finger, **of whom I said**, i.e., in his absence, **after me there comes a man**, to preach and baptize, who in birth came after me. Christ is called a man by reason of his perfect age, because when he began to teach, after his baptism, he had already reached a perfect age: *Jesus was now about thirty years of age* (Luke 3:23). He is also called a man because of the perfection of all the virtues that were in him: *seven women, i.e., the virtues, will take hold of one man*, the perfect Christ (Isa 4:1); *look, a man! His name is the Orient* (Zech 6:12), because he is the origin of all the virtues found in others. He is also called a man because of his espousal, since he is the spouse of the Church: *you will call me 'my husband'* (Hos 2:16); *I espoused you to one husband* (2 Cor 11:2).

261. Second, he compares himself to Christ with respect to dignity when he says, **who ranks ahead of me**. As if to say: Although he comes to preach after me, yet he **ranks ahead of me** in dignity. *See, he comes, leaping upon the mountains, skipping over the hills* (Song 2:8). One such hill was John the Baptist, who was passed over by Christ, as is said, **he must increase, but I must decrease** (John 3:30).

262. Third, he compares himself to Christ with respect to duration, saying, **because he existed before me**. As if to say: it is not strange if he ranks ahead of me in dignity; because although he is after me in time, he is before me in eternity, **because he existed before me**.

This statement refutes a twofold error. First, that of Arius, for John does not say that he was made before me, as though he were a creature, but **he existed before me**, from eternity, before every creature: *the Lord brought me forth before all the hills* (Prov 8:25). The second error refuted is that of Paul of Samosata: for John said, **he existed before me**, in order to show that he did not take his beginning

prior praecursore, qui Christum in sex mensibus secundum generationem praecedebat humanam.

263. Consequenter cum dicit **et ego nesciebam eum**, excludit falsam suspicionem a suo testimonio.

Posset enim aliquis dicere, Ioannem testimonium perhibuisse Christo propter affectionem specialis familiaritatis quam ad ipsum habebat; et ideo hoc excludens Ioannes, dicit **ego nesciebam eum**: nam Ioannes in deserto a pueritia sua conversatus est. Licet autem miracula multa facta sint in nativitate Christi, puta de Magis et de stella, et huiusmodi, tamen non erant nota Ioanni: tum quia infans erat secundum aetatem, tum quia ad desertum secedens, Christi familiaritatem non habuit. Medio vero tempore a nativitate usque ad baptismum, nullum miraculum Christus operatus est; sed conformis conversatione aliis erat, et sua virtus ignota omnibus existebat.

264. Quod autem medio tempore non fuerit miracula operatus usque ad triginta annos, patet per hoc quod dicitur infra II, 11: **hoc fecit initium signorum Iesus** etc. Ex quo apparet falsitas libri _de Infantia Salvatoris_. Ideo autem non fecit miracula medio tempore, ut non putaretur mysterium circumcisionis et incarnationis phantasma esse, si non se habuisset aetate sicut alii infantes. Et ideo demonstrationem scientiae et virtutis suae in aliud distulit tempus, in quo alii homines scientia et virtute vigere consueverunt. Iuxta quod dicitur Lc. II, 52: _puer autem proficiebat gratia et sapientia_; non quod ipse virtutem et sapientiam ante non habitam susciperet, cum in eis fuerit ab instanti suae conceptionis perfectus, sed quia virtus eius et sapientia magis innotescebat hominibus. Is. c. XLV, 15: _vere tu es Deus absconditus_.

265. Ideo ergo Ioannes nesciebat eum, quia nulla signa adhuc de eo viderat, neque aliis per signa innotuerat. Unde subdit **sed ut manifestetur in Israel, propterea ego veni in aqua baptizans**. Quasi dicat: totum ministerium meum est ad manifestationem. Supra, **non erat ille lux, sed ut testimonium perhiberet de lumine**.

266. Dicit autem **veni in aquam baptizans**, ad differentiam baptismi Christi. Quia Christus non in aqua solum baptizavit, sed in spiritu, conferens gratiam; unde et baptismus Ioannis fuit significativum tantum, non effectivum.

Manifestavit autem baptismus Ioannis Christum tripliciter. Primo scilicet per Ioannis praedicationem. Licet enim Ioannes etiam sine baptismo potuisset praedicando parare viam Domino, et inducere turbas ad Christum, tamen propter novitatem officii plures ad eum concurrebant quam si sine baptismo praedicatio facta esset. Secundo profuit baptismus Ioannis propter Christi humilitatem, quam demonstravit, baptizari volens a Ioanne; Matth. III, 13: _venit Christus ad Ioannem ut baptizaretur_

from Mary. For if he had taken the beginning of his existence from the Virgin, he would not have existed before the precursor, who, in the order of human generation, preceded Christ by six months.

263. Next, he precludes an erroneous conjecture from his testimony, at **and I did not know him**.

For someone might say that John bore witness to Christ because of the affection of an especial friendship which he had for him. And so, excluding this, John says, **and I did not know him**; for John had lived in the desert from boyhood. And although many miracles happened during the birth of Christ, such as the Magi and the star and others, they were not known to John: both because he was an infant at the time, and because, after withdrawing to the desert, he had no association with Christ. In the interim between his birth and baptism, Christ did not perform any miracles, but led a life similar to any other person, and his power remained unknown to all.

264. It is clear that he worked no miracles in the interim until he was thirty years old from what is said: **Jesus did this beginning of miracles in Cana of Galilee** (John 2:11). This shows the error of the book, _The Infancy of the Savior_. The reason he performed no miracles during this period was that if his life had not been like that of other infants, the mystery of the circumcision and incarnation might have been regarded as pure fancy. Accordingly, he postponed showing his knowledge and power to another time, corresponding to the age when other men reach the fullness of their knowledge and power. About this we read, _and Jesus increased in grace and wisdom_ (Luke 2:52); not that he acquired a power and wisdom that he previously lacked, for in this respect he was perfect from the instant of his conception, but because his power and wisdom were becoming known to men: _indeed, you are a hidden God_ (Isa 45:15).

265. The reason why John did not know him was that he had so far seen no signs, and no one else had known Christ through signs. Hence he adds: **but that me may be made manifest in Israel, therefore I came baptizing with water**. As if to say: my entire ministry is to reveal: **he was not the light, but that he might bear witness to the light** (John 1:8).

266. He says, **I came baptizing with water**, to distinguish his baptism from that of Christ. For Christ baptized not just in water, but in the Spirit, conferring grace; and so the baptism of John was merely a sign, and not causative.

John's baptism made Christ known in three ways. First, by the preaching of John. For although John could have prepared the way for the Lord and led the people to Christ without baptizing, yet because of the novelty of the service many more came to him than would have come if his preaching were done without baptism. Second, John's baptism was useful because of Christ's humility, which he showed by willing to be baptized by John: _Christ came to John, to be baptized by him_ (Matt 3:13). This example of

ab eo. In quo quidem exemplum humilitatis praebuit, ut scilicet nullus, quantumcumque magnus, dedignetur a quocumque ad hoc ordinato, sacramenta suscipere. Tertio, quia Christo baptizato a Ioanne, affuit virtus Patris in voce, et Spiritus Sanctus in columba, per quam virtus Christi et dignitas magis manifestata fuit. Lc. III, 22: *et vox Patris intonuit: hic est Filius meus dilectus.*

267. Consequenter cum dicit *et testimonium perhibuit Ioannes* ipse magna quae testatus est de Christo quod totius orbis terrarum solus peccata tolleret, confirmat auctoritate Dei.

Et circa hoc tria facit.

Primo proponit visionem;

secundo praebet de intellectu visionis instructionem, ibi *et ego nesciebam eum*;

tertio suam ex ipsa visione conceptionem ostendit, ibi *et ego vidi, et testimonium perhibui.*

268. Visionem quidem proponit cum dicit *vidi Spiritum descendentem quasi columbam de caelo.* Quod quidem quando factum fuerit, Ioannes Evangelista non refert; sed Matthaeus et Lucas dicunt hoc factum fuisse quando Christus baptizatus est a Ioanne.

Et quidem congruebat quod Spiritus Sanctus adesset baptizato et baptismo. Baptizato namque congruebat, quia sicut Filius existens a Patre, manifestat Patrem infra XVII, 6: *Pater, manifestavi nomen tuum* etc., ita et Spiritus Sanctus a Filio existens, Filium manifestat. Infra XVI, 14: *ille me clarificabit, quia de meo accipiet* etc. Baptismo autem congruit, quia baptisma Christi est inchoativum et consecrativum nostri baptismatis. Nostrum autem baptisma consecratur per invocationem Sanctae Trinitatis; Matth. ult., 19: *baptizantes eos in nomine Patris, et Filii, et Spiritus Sancti* etc. Quod ergo nos invocamus in baptismo nostro, affuit baptismo Christi, scilicet Pater in voce, Spiritus Sanctus in columba, Filius in humana natura.

269. Dicit autem *descendentem*, quia cum descensus duos terminos habeat, scilicet principium sursum et terminum deorsum, quantum ad utrumque convenit baptismo.

Est enim duplex spiritus, unus mundi et alius Dei. Et spiritus quidem mundi est amor mundi, qui non est desursum, sed ab inferiori ascendit in hominem, et eum descendere facit; Spiritus autem Dei, scilicet Dei amor, desursum descendit ad hominem, et eum ascendere facit. I Cor. II, 12: *nos autem non spiritum huius mundi accepimus, sed Spiritum Dei.* Quia ergo ille Spiritus de supernis est, ideo dicit *descendentem.*

Similiter etiam, quia impossibile est creaturam recipere Dei bonitatem in tanta plenitudine, secundum quod convenit Deo, ideo bonitatis ipsius ad nos derivatio, est quasi quidam descensus; Iac. I, 17: *omne datum*

humility he gives us here is that no one, however great, should disdain to receive the sacraments from any person ordained for this purpose. Third, because it was during Christ's baptisin by John that the power of the Father was present in the voice, and the Holy Spirit was present in the dove, by which the powerand dignity of Christ were all the more shown: *and the voice of the Father was heard: this is my beloved Son* (Luke 3:22).

267. Then when he says, *and John gave testimony*, he confirms by the authority of God the great things he testified to about Christ, that Christ alone would take away the sins of the whole world.

As to this he does three things.

First, he presents a vision.

Second, he tells us the meaning of the vision, at *and I did not know him*.

Third, he shows what he learned from this vision, at *and I have seen, and I have given testimony.*

268. He presents the vision when he says, *I saw the Spirit coming down, as a dove from heaven.* When this actually happened John the Evangelist does not tell us, but Matthew and Luke say that it took place when Christ was being baptized by John.

And it was indeed fitting for the Holy Spirit to be present at this baptism and to the person being baptized. It was appropriate for the one baptized, for as the Son, existing by the Father, manifests the Father: *Father, I have manifested your name* (John 17:6), so the Holy Spirit, existing by the Son, manifests the Son, *he will glorify me, because he will receive from of mine* (John 16:14). It was appropriate for this baptism because the baptism of Christ begins and consecrates our baptism. Now our baptism is consecrated by invoking the whole Trinity: *baptizing them in the name of the Father, and of the Son, and of the Holy Spirit* (Matt 28:19). Thus, the ones we invoke in our baptism were present at the baptism of Christ: the Father in the voice, the Holy Spirit in the dove, and the Son in his human nature.

269. He says, *coming down*, because descent, since it has two termini, the start, which is from above, and the end, which is below, suits baptism in both respects.

For there is a twofold spirit: one of the world and the other of God. The spirit of the world is the love of the world, which is not from above; rather, it comes up to man from below and makes him descend. But the Spirit of God, i.e., the love of God, comes down to man from above and makes him ascend: *we have not received the spirit of this world, but the Spirit of God* (1 Cor 2:12). And so, because that Spirit is from above, he says, *coming down.*

Similarly, because it is impossible for the creature to receive God's goodness in the fullness in which it is present in God, the communication of this goodness to us is in a

optimum, et omne donum perfectum desursum est, descendens a Patre luminum.

270. Sed quia Spiritus Sanctus in sua natura videri non potest, ut dicitur infra III, 8: ***spiritus ubi vult spirat, et nescis unde veniat, aut quo vadat,*** spiritus etiam non est descendere, sed ascendere. Ez. VIII, 3: *elevavit me spiritus* etc. Ideo consequenter Evangelista modum visionis et descensus exponit, dicens, hic non fuisse in spiritu, idest natura sed in specie columbae, in qua apparuit: unde dicit ***quasi columbam.***

Et hoc quidem congrue, ut scilicet Filius Dei per carnem visibilis factus, manifestaretur per Spiritum Sanctum visibili specie columbae. Quae quidem columba non est assumpta a Spiritu Sancto in unitatem personae, sicut humana natura assumpta est a Filio Dei. Cuius ratio est, quia Filius apparuit non solum ut manifestator, sed ut salvator. Et ideo, secundum quod dicit Leo Papa, oportuit quod esset Deus et homo: Deus quidem, ut afferret remedium; homo vero, ut praeberet exemplum. Spiritus vero sanctus apparuit solum ad manifestandum, ad quod sufficiebat speciem corporalem assumere solum ad significationem quamdam.

271. Utrum autem columba illa fuerit verum animal, et utrum praeexistens apparitioni: sciendum, quod rationabiliter dicitur illa fuisse vera columba. Venit enim Spiritus Sanctus ad manifestandum Christum, qui cum sit veritas, non nisi per veritatem manifestandus erat.

Quantum vero ad secundum, dicendum, quod non praeextitit apparitioni; sed tunc virtute divina absque commixtione maris et feminae formata fuit, sicut et corpus Christi virtute Spiritus Sancti conceptum, non ex virili semine. Et tamen fuit vera columba, quia, ut Augustinus dicit in libro *de Agone Christiano, omnipotenti Deo, qui universam creaturam ex nihilo fabricavit, non erat difficile verum corpus columbae sine aliarum columbarum ministerio figurare, sicut non fuit difficile verum corpus in utero B. Virginis sine naturali semine fabricare.* Cyprianus in libro *de Unitate Ecclesiae: idcirco et in columba dicitur Spiritus Sanctus apparuisse, quia columba simplex animal et innocens est, non felle amarum, non morsibus ferum, non unguium laceratione violentum: hospitia humana diligere, unius domus consortium nosse, cum generat simul filios edere, cum conveniat volantibus invicem cohaerere, communi conversatione vitam suam degere, oris osculo concordiam pacis agnoscere, legem circa omnia unanimitatis implere.*

272. Quare autem potius in columba, quam in alia specie apparuit, multipliciter ratio assignatur. Primo quidem propter columbae simplicitatem. Nam columba simplex est; Matth. X, 16: *estote prudentes sicut serpentes, et simplices sicut columbae.* Spiritus autem Sanctus, quia facit respicere unum, scilicet Deum, simplices facit; et ideo in specie columbae apparet. Et quidem, secundum

way a certain coming down: *every perfect gift is from above, coming down from the Father of lights* (Jas 1:17).

270. Because the Holy Spirit cannot be seen in his own nature, as is said, ***the wind blows where it wills, and you hear its sound, but you do not know where it comes from or where it goes*** (John 3:8), and because a spirit does not come down but goes up, *the spirit lifted me up* (Ezek 8:3). Therefore, the Evangelist, in describing the manner of the vision and of the coming down, says that the Holy Spirit did not appear in the spirit, i.e., in his nature, but in the form of a dove, saying, that he came ***as a dove.***

It was appropriate that the Son of God, who was made visible through flesh, should be made known by the Holy Spirit in the visible form of a dove. However, the Holy Spirit did not assume the dove into a unity of person, as the Son of God assumed human nature. The reason for this is that the Son did not appear as a manifester but as a savior. And so, according to Pope Leo, it was appropriate that he be God and man: God, in order to provide a remedy; and man, in order to offer an example. But the Holy Spirit appeared only to make known, and for this it was sufficient merely to assume a visible form which was suitable for this purpose.

271. As to whether this dove was a real animal and whether it existed prior to its appearance, it seems reasonable to say that it was a real dove. For the Holy Spirit came to manifest Christ, who, being the truth, ought to have been manifested only by the truth.

As to the other part of the question, it would seem that the dove did not exist prior to its appearance, but was formed at the time by the divine power, without any parental union, as the body of Christ was conceived by the power of the Holy Spirit, and not from a man's seed. Yet it was a real dove, for as Augustine says in his work, *The Christian Combat: it was not difficult for the omnipotent God, who produced the entire universe of creatures from nothing, to form a real body for the dove without the aid of other doves, just as it was not difficult to form the true body of Christ in the womb of the Blessed Virgin without natural semen.* Cyprian, in his *The Unity of the Church,* says: *it is said that the Holy Spirit appeared in the form of a dove because the dove is a simple harmless animal, not bitter with gall, not savage with its bites, not fierce with rending talons; it loves the dwellings of men, is able to live together in one nest, together it raises its young, they remain together when they fly, spend their life in mutual association, signify the concord of peace with the kiss of their bill, and fulfill the law of harmony in all things.*

272. Many reasons are given why the Holy Spirit appeared as a dove rather than in some other form. First, because of its simplicity, for the dove is simple: *be wise as serpents, and simple as doves* (Matt 10:16). And the Holy Spirit, because he inclines souls to gaze on one thing, that is, God, makes them simple; and so he appeared in the form of a dove. Further, according to Augustine, the Holy Spirit also

Augustinum, apparuit etiam super discipulos congregatos per ignem, quia quidam sunt simplices, sed tepidi; quidam autem ferventes, sed malitiosi. Ut ergo Spiritu sanctificati dolo careant, Spiritus in columbae specie demonstratur; et ne simplicitas frigiditate tepescat, demonstratur in igne.

Secundo, propter caritatis unitatem. Nam columba amore multum fervet; Cant. VI, 8: *una est columba mea*. Ut ergo ostendat Ecclesiae unitatem, in specie columbae Spiritus Sanctus apparet. Nec te moveat quod discipulis dispartitae linguae apparuerunt, quando sedit supra singulos eorum Spiritus Sanctus, qui et dispartitus apparet, secundum diversa donorum officia, et tamen unit per caritatem; et sic propter primum apparuit in dispartitis linguis, ut dicitur I Cor. XII, 4: *divisiones gratiarum sunt*, in columbae specie propter secundum.

Tertio, propter gemitum. Columba enim habet gemitum pro cantu; sic Spiritus Sanctus *postulat pro nobis gemitibus inenarrabilibus*, ut dicitur Rom. VIII, 26, et Nahum II, 7: *ancillae eius mirabantur*.

Quarto, propter fecunditatem. Columba enim animal fecundissimum est, idcirco ad designandum fecunditatem gratiae spiritualis in Ecclesia, in specie columbae Spiritus Sanctus apparuit. Hic est quod Levit. V, 7 Dominus pullos columbarum offerre praecepit.

Quinto, propter columbae cautelam. Sedet enim super rivos aquarum, in quibus respiciens, falconem volitantem conspicit, et sibi ab eo cavet; Cant. V, 12: *oculi tui sicut columbae* etc. Unde, quia in baptismo est nostra tutela et defensio, congrue in specie columbae Spiritus Sanctus apparuit.

Respondet igitur figurae Veteris Testamenti. Sicut etenim columba deferens ramum virentis olivae, ostendit signum clementiae Dei his qui residui fuerant ex aquis diluvii; ita et in baptismo veniens Spiritus Sanctus in columbae specie, ostendit signum divinae clementiae, quae baptizatis et peccata remittit, et gratiam confert.

273. Dicit autem **manentem super eum**, quia in mansione quies designatur.

Et quod Spiritus Sanctus in aliquo non quiescat, duplici de causa contingit. Una est ex peccato. Omnes enim alii homines, praeter Christum, vel saucientur vulnere peccati mortalis, per quod effugatur Spiritus Sanctus, vel obfuscantur macula veniali, per quam aliqua operatio Spiritus Sancti impeditur. In Christo autem neque mortale, nec veniale, nec originale peccatum fuit: unde nec in eo fuit Spiritus Sanctus inquietatus; sed **super eum mansit**, idest quievit.

Alia causa: quia quantum ad gratias gratis datas, non semper adest aliis sanctis potestas operandi. Sicut non semper adest sanctis potestas operandi miracula,

appeared in the form of fire over the heads of the assembled apostles. This was done because some are simple, but lukewarm; while others are fervent but guileful. And so in order that those sanctified by the Spirit may have no guile, the Spirit is shown in the form of a dove; and in order that their simplicity may not grow tepid, the Spirit is shown in fire.

A dove was used, second, because of the unity of charity; for the dove is much aglow with love: *one is my dove* (Song 6:9). So, in order to show the unity of the Church, the Holy Spirit appears in the form of a dove. Nor should it disturb you that when the Holy Spirit rested on each of the disciples, there appeared separate tongues of fire; for although the Spirit appears to be different according to the different functions of his gifts, he nevertheless unites us through charity. And so, because of the first he appeared in separate tongues of fire, as is said, *there are different kinds of gifts* (1 Cor 12:4); but he appears in the form of a dove because of the second.

A dove was used, third, because of its groaning, for the dove has a groaning chant; so also the Holy Spirit *pleads for us with indescribable groanings* (Rom 8:26); *her maidens, groaning like doves* (Neh 2:7).

Fourth, because of the doves fertility, for the dove is a very prolific animal. And so in order to signify the fecundity of spiritual grace in the Church, the Holy Spirit appeared in the form of a dove. This is why the Lord commanded an offering of two doves (Lev 5:7).

A dove was used, fifth, because of its cautiousness. For it rests upon watery brooks, and gazing into them can see the hawk flying overhead and so save itself: *his eyes are like doves beside brooks of water* (Song 5:12). And so, because our refuge and defense is found in baptism, the Holy Spirit appropriately appeared in the form of a dove.

The dove also corresponds to a figure in the Old Testament. For as the dove bearing the green olive branch was a sign of God's mercy to those who survived the waters of the deluge, so too in baptism, the Holy Spirit, coming in the form of a dove, is a sign of the divine mercy which takes away the sins of those baptized and confers grace.

273. He says that the Holy Spirit was **remaining upon him**.

If the Holy Spirit does not rest on someone, it is due to two causes. One is sin. For all men except Christ are either suffering from the wound of mortal sin, which banishes the Holy Spirit, or are darkened with the stain of venial sin, which hinders some of the works of the Holy Spirit. But in Christ there was neither mortal nor venial sin; so, the Holy Spirit in him was never disquieted, but was **remaining upon him**.

The other reason concerns charismatic graces, for the other saints do not always possess their power. For example, the power to work miracles is not always present in the

nec prophetis spiritus prophetiae. Christus vero semper habuit potestatem ad omnem operationem virtutum et gratiarum: et ideo ad hoc designandum, ***super eum mansit***.

Unde hoc proprium signum fuit agnoscendi Christum, ut dicitur in Glossa Is. XI, 2: *requiescet super eum Spiritus Domini*. Quod intelligendum est de Christo, inquantum est homo, secundum quod est minor Patre et Spiritu Sancto.

274. Consequenter cum dicit ***et ego nesciebam eum***, instruit de intellectu visionis praedictae.

Quidam enim haeretici, scilicet Ebionitae, dicebant, Christum a principio nativitatis suae, neque Christum fuisse, nec Filium Dei, sed ex tunc Filius Dei et Christus esse incepit quando in baptismo oleo Spiritus Sancti unctus fuit. Sed hoc falsum, quia in ipsa hora nativitatis angelus dixit pastoribus, Lc. II, 11: *natus est vobis hodie salvator, qui est Christus Dominus in civitate David*. Ne ergo aliquis crederet Spiritum Sanctum in baptismo supra Christum descendisse, quasi de novo Christus indigeret Spiritu ad sui sanctificationem, ideo causam sui descensus Baptista ostendit, dicens quod non descendit propter sui necessitatem, sed propter nos, ut scilicet gratia eius nobis manifestaretur. Et ideo dicit ***ego nesciebam eum. Sed ut manifestaretur in Israel, propterea veni ego in aqua baptizans***.

275. Sed hic oritur quaestio. Dicit enim ***qui misit me baptizare*** etc., si dicatur quod Pater misit eum, verum est; similiter si dicatur quod Filius, manifestius, cum dicatur quod et Pater et Filius misit eum, quia Ioannes non est de illis de quibus dicit Ierem. c. XXIII, 21: *non mittebam eos, et ipsi currebant*. Quomodo ergo dicit ***ego nesciebam eum***, si Filius misit eum?

Si dicatur, quod licet cognosceret eum secundum divinitatem, non tamen cognoscebat eum secundum humanitatem, nisi postquam vidit Spiritum descendentem super eum, contra: Spiritum enim Sanctus descendit super Christum quando baptizatus est. Ioannes autem cognovit Christum antequam baptizaretur, alias non dixisset *ego debeo a te baptizari, et tu venis ad me?*

Est ergo dicendum, quod tripliciter potest ad hanc quaestionem responderi. Uno modo, secundum Chrysostomum, ut referatur ad cognitionem familiaritatis, ut sit sensus ***ego nesciebam eum***, scilicet familiariter. Et si obiiciatur, quod dicit Ioannes *ego a te debeo baptizari* etc., dicitur quod ista duo sunt ad diversa tempora referenda, ut hoc quod dicit ***ego nesciebam eum***, referatur ad tempus diu ante baptismum, in quo nondum Christo familiaris erat; hoc vero quod dicit *ego a te debeo baptizari*, referatur ad tempus illud in quo baptizatus est Christus, quando iam propter frequentem visitationem

saints, nor is the spirit of prophecy always in the prophets. But Christ always possessed the power to accomplish any work of the virtues and the graces. So to indicate this, he says, ***remaining upon him***.

Hence this was the characteristic sign for recognizing Christ, as the Gloss says. *The Spirit of the Lord will rest on him* (Isa 11:2), which we should understand of Christ as man, according to which he is less than the Father and the Holy Spirit.

274. Then when he says, ***I did not know him***, he teaches us how this vision should be understood.

For certain heretics, as the Ebionites, said that Christ was neither the Christ nor the Son of God from the time he was born, but only began to be the Son of God and the Christ when he was anointed with the oil of the Holy Spirit at his baptism. But this is false, because at the very hour of his birth the angel said to the shepherds: *this day a savior has been born for you in the city of David, Christ the Lord* (Luke 2:11). Therefore, so that we do not believe that the Holy Spirit descended upon Christ in his baptism as though Christ needed to receive the Spirit anew for his sanctification, the Baptist gives the reason for the Spirit's coming down. He says that the Spirit descended not for the benefit of Christ, but for our benefit, that is, so that the grace of Christ might be made known to us. And so he says, ***and I did not know him, but that he may be made manifest in Israel, therefore I came baptizing with water***.

275. There is a problem here. For he says, ***he who sent me to baptize***. If he is saying that the Father sent him, it is true. Also, if he is saying that the Son sent him, it is even more clear, since it is said that both the Father and the Son sent him, because John is not one of those referred to at *I did not send the prophets, yet they ran* (Jer 23:21). But if the Son did send him, how can he then say, ***I did not know him***?

If it is said that although he knew Christ according to his divinity, yet he did not know him according to his humanity until after he saw the Spirit coming down upon him, one might counter that the Holy Spirit descended upon Christ when he was being baptized, and John had already known Christ before he was baptized, otherwise he would not have said: *I ought to be baptized by you, and you come to me?* (Matt 3:14).

So we must say that this problem can be resolved in three ways. In one way, according to Chrysostom, so that the meaning is to know familiarly; the sense being that *I did not know him*, i.e., in a familiar way. And if the objection is raised that John says, *I ought to be baptized by you* (Matt 3:14), it can be answered that two different times are being discussed: so that ***I did not know him***, refers to a time long before baptism, when he was not yet familiar with Christ: but when he says, *I ought to be baptized by you*, he is referring to the time when Christ was being baptized, when he was now familiar with Christ because of his frequent

eius, Christus familiaris erat. Alio modo, secundum Hieronymum, dicendum quod erat Christus Filius Dei et salvator mundi, et hoc quidem sciebat Ioannes; sed nesciebat eum per baptismum mundi salvatorem: et ideo hoc quod nescivit addidit, scilicet quod *hic est qui baptizat in Spiritu Sancto*. Sed melius dicendum est, secundum Augustinum, quod aliquid scivit et aliquid nescivit, et hoc quod nescivit addidit, scilicet quod potestatem baptizandi, quam potuit fidelibus suis communicare, sibi soli retinuit. Et hoc est quod dicit *qui misit me baptizare in aqua . . . hic est*, singulariter scilicet, et solus, *qui baptizat in Spiritu Sancto*, et nullus alius: quia hanc potestatem sibi soli retinuit.

276. Notandum autem, quod triplex potestas Christi attenditur in baptismo. Una est efficientiae, qua mundat interius animam a macula peccati; quam quidem potestatem habet Christus inquantum est Deus, non autem inquantum homo; et haec potestas nulli alii potest communicari.

Alia potestas est ministerii, quam quidem communicavit fidelibus; Matth. ult., 19: *baptizantes eos in nomine Patris, et Filii, et Spiritus Sancti*. Et ideo sacerdotes, ut ministri, potestatem habent baptizandi; Christus autem, inquantum homo, minister dicitur, ut Apostolus dicit sed tamen caput est omnium ministrorum Ecclesiae.

Et quantum ad hoc habet singulariter potestatem excellentiae in sacramentis: quae quidem excellentiae apparet in quatuor. Primo in sacramentorum institutione: quia nullus homo purus, nec etiam tota Ecclesia, posset sacramenta instituere, vel sacramenta mutare, aut a sacramentis absolvere. Nam sacramenta invisibilem gratiam conferunt ex eorum institutione; conferre autem gratiam solius Dei est: et ideo solus qui est verus Deus potest sacramenta instituere. Secundum est quantum ad meriti Christi efficaciam: nam ex merito passionis Christi sacramenta virtutem habent; Rom. VI, 3: *quicumque baptizati sumus in Christo Iesu, in morte ipsius baptizati sumus*. Tertium est quia Christus potest conferre effectum baptismi sine sacramento: quod solius Christi est. Quarto quia aliquo tempore baptismus conferebatur ad invocationem nominis Christi; sed modo non ita fit. Quae quidem quatuor nulli hominum communicavit; licet aliquid eorum communicare potuisset, puta quod in nomine Petri, vel alicuius alterius, conferretur baptismus, et forte aliquod aliorum. Sed hoc ideo non fuit factum ne fieret schisma in Ecclesia, si baptizati spem suam ponerent in illis in quorum nominationem baptizarentur.

Et ideo didicit Ioannes per hoc quod Spiritus Sanctus descendit super eum, quod Christus solus est qui sua virtute interius baptizat.

277. Et forte posset dici, quod cum dixit *ego a te debeo baptizari* etc. cognovit eum per internam revelationem;

visits. In another way, according to Jerome, it could be said that Christ was the Son of God and the savior of the world, and that John did in fact know this; but it was not through the baptism that he knew that he was the savior of the world. And so to remedy this ignorance he adds, *it is he who baptizes with the Holy Spirit*. But it is better to say with Augustine that John knew certain things and was ignorant of others. Explaining what he did not know, he adds that the power of baptizing, which Christ could have shared with his faithful followers, would be reserved for himself alone. And this is what he says, *he who sent me to baptize with water . . . it is he*, exclusively and solely, *who baptizes with the Holy Spirit*, i.e., he and no one else, because this power he reserved for himself alone.

276. We should note that a threefold power of Christ is found in baptism. One is the power of efficiency, by which he interiorly cleanses the soul from the stain of sin. Christ has this power as God, but not as man, and it cannot be communicated to any other.

Another is the power of ministry, which he does share with the faithful: *baptizing them in the name of the Father, and of the Son, and of the Holy Spirit* (Matt 28:19). Therefore priests have the power to baptize as ministers. Christ too, as man, is called a minister, as the Apostle says. But he is also the head of all the ministers of the Church.

Because of this he alone has the power of excellence in the sacraments. And this excellence shows itself in four things. First, in the institution of the sacraments, because no mere man or even the entire Church could institute sacraments, or change the sacraments, or dispense with the sacraments. For by their institution the sacraments give invisible grace, which only God can give. Therefore, only one who is true God can institute sacraments. The second lies in the efficacy of Christ's merits, for the sacraments have their power from the merit of Christ's passion: *all of us who have been baptized into Christ Jesus, have been baptized into his death* (Rom 6:3). The third is that Christ can confer the effect of baptism withmit the sacrament; and this is peculiar to Christ. Fourth, because at one time baptism was conferred in the name of Christ, although this is no longer done. Now he did not communicate these four things to anyone; although he could have communicated some of them, for example, that baptism be conferred in the name of Peter or of someone else, and perhaps one of the remaining three. But this was not done lest schisms arise in the Church by men putting their trust in those in whose name they were baptized.

And so John, in stating that the Holy Spirit came down upon Christ, teaches that it is Christ alone who baptizes interiorly by his own power.

277. One might also say that when John said, *I ought to be baptized by you* (Matt 3:14), he recognized Christ

sed cum vidit Spiritum Sanctum descendentem super eum, cognovit eum per exterioris signi manifestationem. Et ideo utrumque modum cognitionis tangit. Primum, cum dicit *qui me misit baptizare, ille mihi dixit*, idest interius revelavit. Secundum, quando addidit *super quem videris Spiritum descendentem . . . hic est qui baptizat*.

278. Consequenter ostendit quid Baptista ex hac visione intellexit, scilicet quod Christus esset Filius Dei; et hoc est quod dicit *et ego vidi*, scilicet Spiritum descendentem super eum, et *testimonium perhibuit, quia hic*, scilicet Christus, *est Filius Dei*, scilicet verus et naturalis.

Filii enim adoptivi Patris fuerunt ad similitudinem Filii Dei naturalis; Rom. VIII, 29: *quos praescivit conformes fieri imaginis Filii sui*. Ille ergo debet Filios Dei facere qui baptizat in Spiritu Sancto, per quem Filii adoptantur; Rom. VIII, 15: *non enim accepistis spiritum servitutis . . . sed spiritum adoptionis* etc. Quia ergo iste, scilicet Christus, est qui baptizat in Spiritu Sancto, ideo recte concludit Baptista, quod est Filius Dei verus et purus. I Io. ult., 20: *ut simus in vero Filio eius* etc.

279. Sed si alii viderunt Spiritum Sanctum descendentem super eum, quare non crediderunt?

Respondeo, quia non erant dispositi ad hoc, vel forte quia soli Baptistae visio illa demonstrata est.

through an interior revelation, but that when he saw the Holy Spirit coming down upon him, he knew him through an exterior sign. And so he mentions both of these ways of knowing. The first when he says, *he who sent me to baptize with water, said to me*, i.e., revealed something in an interior way. The second when he adds, *he upon whom you shall see the Spirit descending . . . it is he who baptizes with the Holy Spirit*.

278. Then he shows what the Baptist understood from this vision, that is, that Christ is the Son of God. And this is what he says, *And I have seen* the Spirit coming down on him, *and I have given testimony that this*, that is, Christ, *is the Son of God*, that is, the true and natural Son.

For there were adopted sons of the Father who had a likeness to the natural Son of God: *conformed to the image of his Son* (Rom 8:29). So he who baptizes in the Holy Spirit, through whom we are adopted as sons, ought to fashion sons of God. *You did not receive the spirit of slavery ... but the spirit of adoption* (Rom 8:15). Therefore, because Christ is the one who baptizes in the Holy Spirit, the Baptist correctly concludes that he is the true and pure Son of God: *that we may be in his true Son* (1 John 5:20).

279. But if there were others who saw the Holy Spirit coming down upon Christ, why did they not also believe?

I answer that they had not been so disposed for this. Or perhaps, this vision was seen only by the Baptist.

Lecture 15

1:35 Altera die iterum stabat Ioannes et ex discipulis eius duo: [n. 281]

1:36 et respiciens Iesum ambulantem, dixit: ecce Agnus Dei. [n. 282]

1:37 Et audierunt eum duo discipuli loquentem, et secuti sunt Iesum. [n. 285]

1:38 Conversus autem Iesus, et videns eos sequentes se, dicit eis: quid quaeritis? Qui dixerunt ei: Rabbi (quod dicitur interpretatum Magister), ubi habitas? [n. 286]

1:39 Dicit eis: venite, et videte. Venerunt, et viderunt ubi maneret, et apud eum manserunt die illo; hora autem erat quasi decima. [n. 292]

1:40 Erat autem Andreas frater Simonis Petri, unus ex duobus qui audierant a Ioanne, et secuti fuerant eum. [n. 298]

1:41 Invenit hic primum fratrem suum Simonem, et dicit ei: invenimus Messiam (quod est interpretatum Christus), [n. 300]

1:42 et adduxit eum ad Iesum. Intuitus autem eum Iesus dixit: tu es Simon filius Ioanna: tu vocaberis Cephas, quod interpretatur Petrus. [n. 302]

1:35 Τῇ ἐπαύριον πάλιν εἱστήκει ὁ Ἰωάννης καὶ ἐκ τῶν μαθητῶν αὐτοῦ δύο

1:36 καὶ ἐμβλέψας τῷ Ἰησοῦ περιπατοῦντι λέγει· ἴδε ὁ ἀμνὸς τοῦ θεοῦ.

1:37 καὶ ἤκουσαν οἱ δύο μαθηταὶ αὐτοῦ λαλοῦντος καὶ ἠκολούθησαν τῷ Ἰησοῦ.

1:38 στραφεὶς δὲ ὁ Ἰησοῦς καὶ θεασάμενος αὐτοὺς ἀκολουθοῦντας λέγει αὐτοῖς· τί ζητεῖτε; οἱ δὲ εἶπαν αὐτῷ· ῥαββί, ὃ λέγεται μεθερμηνευόμενον διδάσκαλε, ποῦ μένεις;

1:39 λέγει αὐτοῖς· ἔρχεσθε καὶ ὄψεσθε. ἦλθαν οὖν καὶ εἶδαν ποῦ μένει καὶ παρ᾽ αὐτῷ ἔμειναν τὴν ἡμέραν ἐκείνην· ὥρα ἦν ὡς δεκάτη.

1:40 Ἦν Ἀνδρέας ὁ ἀδελφὸς Σίμωνος Πέτρου εἷς ἐκ τῶν δύο τῶν ἀκουσάντων παρὰ Ἰωάννου καὶ ἀκολουθησάντων αὐτῷ·

1:41 εὑρίσκει οὗτος πρῶτον τὸν ἀδελφὸν τὸν ἴδιον Σίμωνα καὶ λέγει αὐτῷ· εὑρήκαμεν τὸν Μεσσίαν, ὅ ἐστιν μεθερμηνευόμενον χριστός.

1:42 ἤγαγεν αὐτὸν πρὸς τὸν Ἰησοῦν. ἐμβλέψας αὐτῷ ὁ Ἰησοῦς εἶπεν· σὺ εἶ Σίμων ὁ υἱὸς Ἰωάννου, σὺ κληθήσῃ Κηφᾶς, ὃ ἑρμηνεύεται Πέτρος.

1:35 On the following day, John was standing there again with two of his disciples. [n. 281]

1:36 And seeing Jesus walking by, he said: behold the Lamb of God. [n. 282]

1:37 And the two disciples heard him speaking, and they followed Jesus. [n. 285]

1:38 And Jesus turned, and seeing them following him, said to them: what are you looking for? They said to him: Rabbi (which means Master), where do you live? [n. 286]

1:39 He said to them: come and see. They came, and saw where he lived, and they stayed with him that day: it was about the tenth hour. [n. 292]

1:40 And Andrew, the brother of Simon Peter, was one of the two who had heard of John, and followed him. [n. 298]

1:41 He first found his brother Simon and said to him: we have found the Messiah (which is interpreted as Christ). [n. 300]

1:42 And he brought him to Jesus. And Jesus looking upon him said: you are Simon the son of John: you will be called Cephas, which is interpreted Peter. [n. 302]

---

280. Supra Evangelista posuit testimonia Baptistae ad turbas; hic consequenter ponit eius testimonia ad discipulos Ioannis. Et

primo ponitur testimonium;

secundo ostenditur testimonii fructus, ibi *et audierunt eum duo discipuli loquentem* etc.

Circa primum tria facit.

Primo describitur testis;

secundo assignatur modus testificandi;

tertio ponitur eius testimonium.

281. Sed testis describitur, cum dicit *altera die iterum stabat Ioannes, et ex discipulis eius duo*.

In hoc autem quod dicit *stabat*, tria notantur circa Ioannem. Scilicet doctrinae ipsius modus, qui differens fuit a modo doctrinae Christi, et discipulorum

280. Above, the Evangelist presented the Baptist's testimony to the people; here he presents his testimony to John's disciples.

First, his testimony is given;

second, the fruit of this testimony, at *and the two disciples heard him speaking*.

As to the first he does three things:

first, the one giving the testimony is described;

second, his way of testifying is given; and

third, his testimony itself.

281. The witness is described when he says, *on the following day, John was standing there again with two of his disciples*.

In saying *standing*, three things are noted about John. First, his manner of teaching, which was different from that of Christ and his disciples. For Christ went about teaching;

eius. Christus enim circumeundo docebat; unde dicitur, Matth. IV, 23, quod *circuibat Iesus totam Galilaeam* etc. Similiter et apostoli discurrendo per mundum, docebant; Mc. ult., 15: *euntes in mundum universum, praedicate Evangelium omni creaturae.* Sed Ioannes stando docebat; unde dicitur **stabat Ioannes**, scilicet in uno loco trans Iordanem, et instruebat de Christo omnes ad eum venientes.

Ratio autem quare Christus et eius discipuli discurrendo docebant, est quia praedicatio Christi facta erat credibilis per miracula, et ideo circuibant diversa loca, ut miracula et virtutes Christi innotescerent. Praedicatio vero Ioannis non est confirmata miraculis, unde dicitur infra X, 41: **Ioannes signum fecit nullum**: sed merito et sanctitate vitae. Et ideo stabat in loco uno, ut diversi ad eum confluerent, et per eius sanctitatem ducerentur ad Christum. Similiter etiam si Ioannes sine miraculis discurrisset ad praenuntiandum Christum, eius testimonium incredibilius redderetur, cum videretur importune, et quasi ingerendo se hoc facere.

Secundo notatur Ioannis constantia in veritate, quia Ioannes non fuit arundo vento agitata, sed firmus in fide, secundum illud I Cor. X, 12: *qui se existimat stare videat ne cadat.* Hab. II, 1: *super custodiam meam stabo.*

Tertio allegorice notatur, quod stare allegorice idem est quod deficere; IV Reg. IV, 6: *stetitque oleum*, idest defecit. Stabat ergo Ioannes veniente Christo, quia cum venit veritas, defecit figura. Ioannes stat, quia lex transit.

282. Modus autem testificandi ponitur certus, quia cum aspectu. Unde dicit **et respiciens Iesum ambulantem**. Ubi sciendum est, quod prophetae perhibuerunt testimonium Christo, Act. X, 43: *huic omnes prophetae testimonium perhibent.* Similiter et apostoli per mundum discurrentes, Act. I, 8: *eritis mihi testes in Ierusalem, et in omni Iudaea* etc. Sed tamen non per visum, neque de praesente, sed de absente. Prophetae quidem ut de futuro, apostoli vero ut de praeterito. Sed Ioannes, Christo sibi praesente et a se viso, testimonium perhibuit: et ideo dicit *et respiciens*, oculis corporis, et mentis, iuxta illud Ps. LXXXIII, 10: *respice in faciem Christi tui*; Is. LII, 8: *oculo ad oculum videbunt.*

Sed dicit **ambulantem**, ut designet incarnationis mysterium, per quod Dei Verbum mutabilem naturam assumpsit; infra XVI, 28: **exivi a Patre, et veni in mundum**.

283. Consequenter ponitur testimonium, cum dicit **ecce Agnus Dei**, quod non solum est demonstrativum, sed admirativum virtutis ipsius; Is. IX, 6: *vocabitur nomen eius admirabilis.*

hence it is said: *Jesus traveled over all Galilee* (Matt 4:23). The apostles also traveled the world teaching: *go to the whole world, and preach the good news to every creature* (Mark 16:15). But John taught in one place; hence he says, **John was standing**, that is, in one place, on the far side of the Jordan. And John spoke of Christ to all who came to him.

The reason why Christ and his disciples taught going about is that the preaching of Christ was made credible by miracles, and so they went to various places in order that the miracles and powers of Christ might be made known. But the preaching of John was not confirmed by miracles, so that is is written, **John indeed did no sign** (John 10:41), but by the merit and sanctity of his life. And so he was standing in one place so that various people might stream to him and be led to Christ by his holiness. Furthermore, if John had gone from place to place to announce Christ without performing any miracles, his testimony would have been quite unbelievable, since it would seem to be inopportune and he would seem to be forcing himself upon the people.

Second, John's perseverence in the truth is noted, because John was not a reed shaken by the wind, but was firm in the faith; *let him who thinks that he stands, take heed so he will not fall* (1 Cor 10:12); *I will stand my watch* (Heb 2:1).

Third, and allegorically, it is noted that to stand is, in an allegorical sense, the same as to fail or cease: *the oil stood,* i.e., failed (2 Kgs 4:6). So when Christ came John was standing, because when the truth comes the figure ceases. John stands because the law passes away.

282. The manner of his testifying is presented as being certain, because it is according to sight. So he says, **and seeing Jesus walking by**. Here it should be remarked that the prophets bore witness to Christ: *all the prophets bear witness to him* (Acts 10:43). So did the apostles as they traveled the world: *you will be my witnesses in Jerusalem and in all of Judea and Samaria, and to the remotest parts of the world* (Acts 1:8). However, their testimony was not about a person then visible or present, but on one who was absent. In the case of the prophets about one who was to come; in the case of the apostles, about one who was now gone. But John bore witness when Christ was present and seen by him; and so he says, seeing Jesus, with the eyes of his body and of his mind: *look on the face of your Christ* (Ps 83:10); *they will see eye to eye* (Isa 52:8).

He says, **walking by**, to point out the mystery of the incarnation, in which the Word of God assumed a changeable nature: **I came forth from the Father, and have come into the world** (John 16:28).

283. Then he gives John's testimony in saying, **behold the Lamb of God**. He says this not just to point out the power of Christ, but also in admiration of it: *his name will be called wonderful* (Isa 9:6).

Et vere admirabilis virtutis est iste Agnus, qui occisus, leonem interfecit: illum, inquam, leonem de quo dicitur I Petr. ult., 8: *adversarius vester diabolus, tamquam leo rugiens, circuit quaerens quem devoret.* Et ideo ipse Agnus leo vocari meruit victor et gloriosus; Apoc. V, 5: *ecce vicit leo de tribu Iuda.*

Breviter autem testimonium profert, dicens **ecce Agnus Dei**, tum quia discipuli quibus hoc testimonium perhibebat, ex his quae audierant a Ioanne, iam satis instructi erant de Christo; tum etiam quia per hoc satis intelligitur tota intentio Ioannis, quae ad hoc solum erat ut eos ad Christum duceret.

Nec dicit: *ite ad eum*, ne videantur discipuli gratiam praestare Christo, si eum sequerentur; sed commendat Christi gratiam, ut quasi in beneficium sibi computent, si Christum sequuntur. Et ideo dicit **ecce Agnus Dei**; idest, ecce in quo est gratia, et virtus purgativa peccatorum: agnus enim offerebatur pro peccatis, ut dictum est.

284. Consequenter ponitur fructus testimonii, cum dicit **et audierunt eum duo discipuli loquentem**, et

primo ponitur fructus proveniens ex testimonio Ioannis et discipulorum eius;

secundo vero ponitur fructus proveniens ex praedicatione Christi, ibi **in crastinum autem voluit exire in Galilaeam**.

Circa primum primo ponitur fructus proveniens ex testimonio Ioannis;

secundo fructus proveniens ex praedicatione unius discipulorum eius, ibi **erat autem Andreas frater Simonis Petri** etc.

Circa primum duo facit.

Primo ponitur inchoatio huius fructus ex testimonio Ioannis facta.

Secundo ponitur consummatio facta per Christum, ibi **conversus autem Iesus** etc.

285. Dicit ergo primo **et audierunt eum**, scilicet Ioannem, **duo discipuli**, qui erant cum eo, **loquentem (ecce Agnus Dei) et secuti sunt Iesum**, ad litteram: euntes cum eo.

Ubi quatuor, secundum Chrysostomum, considerari possunt. Primo quia hoc quod Ioannes loquitur et Christus tacet, et verbo Ioannis discipuli congregantur ad Christum, competit mysterio: Christus enim est sponsus Ecclesiae, Ioannes vero amicus et paranymphus sponsi. Officium autem paranymphi est sponsam tradere sponso, et loquendo, pacta tradere; sponsi autem est quasi prae verecundia tacere, et de sponsa iam habita pro velle disponere. Sic ergo discipuli traduntur a Ioanne Christo quasi desponsati per fidem. Ioannes loquitur, Christus tacet; sed tamen susceptos diligenter instruxit.

Secundo vero quod cum Ioannes dignitatem Christi commendans dixit **ante me factus est**, et quoniam **non**

And this Lamb did possess truly wonderful power, because being slain, it killed the lion—that lion, I say, of which it says: *your enemy, the devil, goes about like a roaring lion, seeking whom he can devour* (1 Pet 5:8). And so this Lamb, victorius and glorious, deserved to be called a lion: *behold! The Lion of the tribe of Judah has conquered* (Rev 5:5).

The testimony he bears is brief, saying, **behold the Lamb of God**. It is brief both because the disciples before whom he testified had already been sufficiently instructed about Christ from the things they had heard from John, and also because this is sufficient for John's intention, whose only aim was to lead them to Christ.

Yet he does not say, *go to him*, so that the disciples would not seem to be doing Christ a favor by following him. But he does praise the grace of Christ so that they would regard it as of benefit to themselves if they followed Christ. And so he says, **behold the Lamb of God**, i.e., here is the One in whom is found the grace and the power which cleanses from sin; for the lamb was offered for sins, as we have said.

284. The fruit of his testimony is given when he says, **and the two disciples heard him speaking**.

First, the fruit resulting from the testimony of John and his disciples is given.

Second, the fruit resulting from the preaching of Christ, at **on the following day, Jesus wanted to go to Galilee** (John 1:43).

In relation to the first: first, the fruit arising from John's testimony is given;

second, the fruit coming from the preaching of one of his disciples, at **Andrew, the brother of Simon Peter**.

With respect to the first he does two things.

First, he shows the very beginning of the fruit coming from John's testimony.

Second, its consummation as accomplished by Christ, at **and Jesus turned**.

285. He says first, **the two disciples**, who were with John, **heard him**, namely, John, **speak (behold the Lamb of God) and they followed Jesus**, literally: going with him.

First, the fact that it is John who speaks while Christ is silent, and that disciples gather to Christ through the words of John, both point out a mystery. For Christ is the groom of the Church, and John, the friend and groomsman of the groom. Now the function of the groomsman is to present the bride to the groom, and verbally make known the agreements; the role of the groom is to be silent, from modesty, and to make arrangements for his new bride as he wills. Thus, the disciples are presented by John to Christ and espoused in faith. John speaks, Christ is silent; yet after Christ accepts them, he carefully instructs them.

We can note, second, that no one was converted when John praised the dignity of Christ, saying, he **ranks ahead**

sum dignus solvere corrigiam calceamenti eius, nullus conversus est; sed quando humilia de Christo, et incarnationis mysterio locutus est, tunc secuti sunt eum discipuli: quia humilia, et quae pro nobis passus est Christus, magis movent nos; et ideo dicitur Cant. I, 2: *oleum effusum nomen tuum*, idest misericordia, qua salutem omnium procurasti; et ideo statim sequitur *adolescentulae dilexerunt te nimis*.

Tertio, quia verbum praedicationis est sicut semen cadens in diversas terras: in una quidem fructificat, in alia non. Ita et Ioannes cum praedicat, non omnes discipulos convertit ad Christum, sed duos tantum, scilicet qui bene dispositi erant; alii vero e contrario invidia moventur ad Christum: unde et quaestionem ei movent, ut dicitur Matth. IX, 14.

Quartum est quod discipuli Ioannis audito eius testimonio de Christo, non statim ingesserunt se ad loquendum cum eo ex abrupto, sed quasi studiosi cum quadam verecundia singulariter loqui cum eo, et in secreto loco studuerunt. Eccle. VIII, 6: *omni negotio tempus est, et opportunitas*.

286. Consequenter ponitur consummatio fructus, cum dicit *conversus autem Iesus*. Quod enim Ioannes inchoavit, consummatur per Christum, quia *neminem ad perfectum adduxit lex*, ut habetur Hebr. VII, 19.

Et circa hoc Christus duo facit:

primo enim examinavit discipulos sequentes;

secundo eos instruxit, ibi *dicit eis: venite, et videte*.

Circa primum primo ponitur Christi examinantis interrogatio;

secundo discipulorum examinatorum responsio, ibi *qui dixerunt ei: Rabbi, ubi habitas?*

287. Dicit ergo *conversus autem Iesus, et videns eos sequentes se, dixit eis*. Et quidem per litteralem sensum intelligendum est quod Christus eos praeibat, et hi duo discipuli eum sequentes, faciem eius minime videbant: et ideo Christus ut daret eis fiduciam, convertit se ad eos. In quo datur nobis intelligi, quod omnibus, qui Christum sequi incipiunt puro corde, dat fiduciam vel spem misericordiae; Sap. VI, 14: *praeoccupat eos qui se concupiscunt*.

Convertit autem se Iesus ad nos, ut videatur a nobis: hoc erit in illa beata visione, quando ostendet nobis faciem suam, ut dicitur in Ps. LXXIX, 4: *ostende nobis faciem tuam, et salvi erimus*. Quamdiu enim in mundo isto sumus, videmus posteriora eius, quia per effectus in eius cognitionem venimus; unde dicitur Ex. XXXIII, 23: *posteriora mea videbis*. Item convertit se ut opem suae misericordiae nobis impendat. Hoc petebat Ps. LXXXIX, 13: *convertere, Domine, aliquantulum* etc. Quamdiu enim

of me, and *the strap of whose sandal I am not worthy to unfasten* (John 1:27). But the disciples followed Christ when John revealed Christ's humility and about the mystery of the incarnation; and this is because we are more moved by Christ's humility and the sufferings he endured for us. So it is said: *your name is like oil poured out*, i.e., mercy, by which you have obtained salvation for all; and the text immediately follows with, *young maidens have greatly loved you* (Song 1:2).

We can note, third, that the words of a preacher are like seed falling on different kinds of ground: on one they bear fruit, and on another they do not. So too, John, when he preaches, does not convert all his disciples to Christ, but only two, those who were well disposed. The others are envious of Christ, and they even question him (Matt 9:14).

Fourth, we may note that John's disciples, after hearing his witness to Christ, did not at once thrust themselves forward to speak with him hastily; rather, seriously and with a certain modesty, they tried to speak to Christ alone and in a private place: *there is a time and fitness for everything* (Eccl 8:6).

286. Thus the consummation of this fruit is now set forth, at *and Jesus turned*, for what John began is completed by Christ, since *the law brought nothing to perfection* (Heb 7:19).

And Christ does two things.

First, he questions the disciples who were following him.

Second, he teaches them, at *he said to them: come and see*.

As to the first we have: first, the question of Christ is given;

second, the answer of the disciples, at *they said to him: Rabbi . . . where do you live?*

287. He says, *Jesus turned, and seeing them following him, said to them*. According to the literal sense we should understand that Christ was walking in front of them, and these two disciples, following him, did not see his face at all; and so Christ turns to them to give them confidence. In which it is given to us to understand that Christ gives confidence or the hope of mercy to all who begin to follow him with a pure heart: *she goes to meet those who desire her* (Wis 6:14).

Now Jesus turns to us in order that we may see him; this will happen in that blessed vision when he will show us his face, as is said: *Show us your face, and we will be saved* (Ps 79:4). For as long as we are in this world we see his back, because it is through his effects that we acquire a knowledge of him; so it is said, *you will see my back* (Exod 33:23). Again, he turns to give us the riches of his mercy. This is requested: *turn to us, O Lord* (Ps 89:13). For as long as Christ withholds the help of his mercy he seems to be turned away

Christus opem suae miserationis non impendit, videtur a nobis aversus. Conversus est ergo Iesus ad discipulos Ioannis eum sequentes, ut faciem suam eis ostenderet, et gratiam eis infunderet.

288. Examinat autem eos specialiter de intentione. Sequentium namque Christum non eadem intentio est: quidam enim eum sequuntur propter bona temporalia; alii vero propter bona spiritualia. Et ideo quid isti intendant, Dominus quaerit, dicens **quid quaeritis?** Non quidem ut discat, sed ut rectam intentionem aperientes, magis familiares faciat, et ostendat eos auditione dignos.

289. Notandum autem, quod hoc est primum verbum quod Christus in isto Evangelio loquitur. Et congrue, quia primum quod quaerit Deus ab homine, est recta intentio. Et secundum Origenem, post sex verba quae Ioannes dixerat, Christus septimum locutus est. Primum namque Ioannes Baptista locutus est, quando testimonium perhibens de Christo, clamabat dicens **hic est de quo dixi.** Aliud quando dixit **non sum dignus solvere corrigiam calceamenti eius.** Tertium quando dixit **ego baptizo in aqua, medius autem vestrum stetit quem vos nescitis.** Quartum **ecce Agnus Dei.** Quintum **vidi Spiritum descendentem quasi columbam** etc. Sextum, cum hic dicit **ecce Agnus Dei.** Et Christus septimum loquitur, ut intelligas mystice, quod quies, quae designatur per septimum diem, nobis est futura per Christum, et quod in ipso est plenitudo septiformis gratiae Spiritus Sancti.

290. Consequenter respondent discipuli **qui dixerunt ei** etc. Et quidem interrogati de uno, duo respondent.

Primo quidem quare Christum sequuntur, scilicet ut addiscant, unde et Magistrum eum vocant **Rabbi (quod dicitur interpretatum Magister)** quasi dicerent: quaerimus, ut nos doceas. Iam enim praecognoscebant quod dicitur Matth. XXIII, 10, *unus est magister vester Christus.*

Secundo vero quod sequendo quaerunt, scilicet **ubi habitas?** Et quidem litteraliter dici potest quod in veritate domum Christi quaerebant. Propter enim mira et magna, quae a Ioanne de eo audierant, nolebant eum perfunctorie interrogare, nec semel tantum, sed frequenter et seriose; et ideo domum eius scire volebant, ut frequenter ad eum accederent, iuxta consilium sapientis, Eccli. VI, 36: *si videris sensatum, evigila ad illum*, et Prov. c. VIII, 34: *beatus qui audit me, et vigilat ad fores meas quotidie.*

Allegorice autem in caelis est habitaculum Dei, secundum illud Ps. CXXII, 1: *ad te levavi oculos meos qui habitas in caelis.* Quaerunt ergo ubi Christus habitet,

from us. And so Jesus turned to the disciples of John who were following him in order to show them his face and to pour his grace upon them.

288. Christ examines them specifically about their intention. For all who follow Christ do not have the same intention: some follow him for the sake of temporal goods, and others for spiritual goods. And so the Lord asks their intention, saying, **what are you looking for?** He does not do this in order to learn their intention, but so that, after they showed a proper intention, he might make them more intimate friends and show that they are worthy to hear him.

289. It may be remarked that these are the first words which Christ speaks in this Gospel. And this is appropriate, because the first thing that God asks of a man is a proper intention. And, according to Origen, after the six words that John had spoken, Christ spoke the seventh. The first words spoken by John were when, bearing witness to Christ, he cried out, saying, **this is he, of whom I said** (John 1:30). The second is when he said, **the strap of whose sandal I am not worthy to unfasten** (John 1:27). The third is, **I baptize with water. But there is one who stands in your midst, whom you do not know** (John 1:26). The fourth is, **behold the Lamb of God** (John 1:29). The fifth, **I saw the Spirit coming down, as a dove from heaven, and he rested upon him** (John 1:32). The sixth, when he says here, **behold the Lamb of God.** But it is Christ who speaks the seventh words so that we may understand, in a mystical sense, that rest, which is signified by the seventh day, will come to us through Christ, and that in him is found the fullness of the seven gifts of the Holy Spirit.

290. The disciples answer at: **they said to him: Rabbi.** And although there was one question, they gave two answers.

First, why they are following Christ, namely, to learn; thus they call him Teacher, **Rabbi (which means Master).** As if to say: we ask you to teach us. For they already knew what is stated: *you have one teacher, the Christ* (Matt 23:10).

The second answer is what they want in following him, that is, **where do you live?** And literally, it can be said that in truth they were looking for the home of Christ. For because of the great and wonderful things they had heard about him from John, they were not satisfied with questioning him only once and in a superficial way, but wanted to do so frequently and seriously. And so they wanted to know where his home was so that they might visit him often, according to the advice of the wise man: *if you see a man of understanding, go to him early* (Sir 6:36), and *happy is the man who hears me, who watches daily at my gates* (Prov 8:34).

In the allegorical sense, God's home is in heaven: *I have lifted up my eyes to you, who live in heaven* (Ps 122:1). So they asked where Christ was living because our purpose in

quia ad hoc debemus Christum sequi ut per eum ducamur ad caelos, idest ad gloriam caelestem.

Moraliter autem interrogant **ubi habitas?** Quasi vellent scire, quales debent esse homines qui digni sunt quod Christus habitet in eis; de quo habitaculo dicitur Eph. II, 22: *aedificamini in habitaculum Dei*, et Cant. I, v. 6: *indica mihi, quem diligit anima mea, ubi pascas, ubi cubes in meridie.*

291. Consequenter cum dicit **venite, et videte**, ponitur instructio discipulorum a Christo, et

primo describitur ipsa instructio discipulorum a Christo;

secundo commendatur discipulorum obedientia **venerunt, et viderunt**;

tertio determinatur tempus **quia hora erat quasi decima.**

292. Dicit ergo primo **venite, et videte**, scilicet ubi habitem.

Sed hic est quaestio. Cum Dominus dicat, Matth. VIII, 20, *Filius hominis non habet ubi caput suum reclinet*, quare dicit **venite, et videte** ubi habito?

Respondeo dicendum, secundum Chrysostomum, quod per hoc quod dixit Dominus: *Filius hominis non habet ubi caput suum reclinet*, demonstravit quod non habuit proprium habitaculum, non quod in domo alicuius alterius non maneret. Et ad hanc videndum istos invitabat, dicens **venite, et videte.**

Mystice autem dicit **venite, et videte** quia habitatio Dei, sive gloriae, sive gratiae, agnosci non potest nisi per experientiam: nam verbis explicari non potest; Apoc. II, 17: *in calculo nomen novum* etc. Et ideo dicit **venite, et videte. Venite**, credendo et operando, **et videte**, experiendo et intelligendo.

293. Notandum autem, quod quatuor modis pervenitur ad hanc cognitionem. Primo per bonorum operum actionem: unde dicit **venite.** Ps. XLI, 3: *quando veniam, et apparebo ante faciem Domini.* Secundo per mentis quietem, seu vacationem; Ps. XLV, 11: *vacate, et videte.* Tertio per divinae dulcedinis gustationem; Ps. XXXIII, 9: *gustate, et videte, quoniam suavis est Dominus.* Quarto per operationem devotionis; Thren. III, v. 41: *levemus corda nostra cum manibus orando* etc. Et ideo dicit Dominus Lc. XXIV, v. 39: *palpate, et videte* etc.

294. Consequenter ponitur discipulorum obedientia, quia statim sequitur **venerunt, et viderunt**, quia veniendo viderunt, et videntes non deseruerunt, unde dicitur **et manserunt ibi die illo** quia, ut dicitur infra c. VI, 45, **omnis qui audit a Patre, et didicit, venit ad me.** Qui enim recedunt a Christo, non viderunt eum adhuc, sicut videre oportet. Isti autem qui perfecte credendo, eum

following him should be that Christ leads us to heaven, i.e., to heavenly glory.

Finally, in the moral sense, they ask, **where do you live?** as though desiring to learn what qualities men should possess in order to be worthy to have Christ dwell in them. Concerning this dwelling it is said: *you are being built into a dwelling place for God* (Eph 2:22). And it is also said: *show me, you whom my soul loves, where you graze your flock, where you rest at midday* (Song 1:6).

291. Then when he says, **come and see**, Christ's instruction of the disciples is given.

First we have the instruction of the disciples by Christ;

second, their obedience is cited: **they came, and saw**; and

third, the time is given: **it was about the tenth hour.**

292. First he says, **come and see**, that is, where I live.

There is a difficulty here: for since the Lord says, *the Son of man does not have any place to lay his head* (Matt 8:20), why does he tell them to **come and see** where he lives?

I answer, according to Chrysostom, that when the Lord says, *the Son of man does not have any place to lay his head*, he showed that he had no home of his own, but not that he did not remain in someone else's home. And such was the home he invited them to see, saying, **come and see.**

In the mystical sense, he says, **come and see**, because the dwelling of God, whether it is of glory, or grace, cannot be known except by experience: for it cannot be explained in words: *I will give him a white stone upon which is written a new name, which no one knows but he who receives it* (Rev 2:17). And so he says, **come and see. Come**, by believing and working; **and see**, by experiencing and understanding.

293. It should be noted that we can attain to this knowledge in four ways. First, by doing good works; so he says, **come**: *when shall I come and appear before the face of God* (Ps 41:3). Second, by the rest or stillness of the mind: *be still and see* (Ps 45:10). Third, by tasting the divine sweetness: *taste and see that the Lord is sweet* (Ps 33:9). Fourth, by acts of devotion: *let us lift up our hearts and hands in prayer* (Lam 3:41). And so the Lord says: *it is I myself. Feel and see* (Luke 24:39).

294. Next the obedience of the disciples is mentioned; for immediately **they came and saw**, because by coming they saw him, and seeing they did not leave him. Thus it says, **and they stayed with him that day**, for **every one who has heard of the Father and has learned, comes to me** (John 6:45). For those who leave Christ have not yet seen him as they should. But those who have seen him by

viderunt, *manserunt ibi die illo*; audientes et videntes beatum diem, beatam noctem duxerunt; III Reg. X, 8: *beati viri tui, et beati servi tui, qui stant coram te semper.* Et ideo, ut dicit Augustinus, *aedificemus et nosmetipsi in corde nostro, et faciamus domum quo veniat ille, et doceat nos.*

Et dicit *die illo*, quia nox esse non potest ubi est lumen Christi, ubi est sol iustitiae.

295. Tempus autem determinatur consequenter, cum dicit *hora autem erat quasi decima.* Quod quidem Evangelista determinat, ut, secundum litteram, insinuet commendationem Christi, et discipulorum. Hora enim decima est in occasu diei: ex quo et Christus commendatur, qui tam studiosus erat ad docendum, quod nec propter temporis tarditatem eos docere distulit, sed in hora decima docuit eos; Eccle. XI, 6: *mane semina semen tuum, et vespere ne cesset manus tua.*

296. Similiter etiam commendatur et discipulorum temperantia. Quia etiam hora decima qua consueverunt homines comedisse et esse minus sobrii ad perceptionem sapientiae, ipsi et sobrii et apti erant ad sapientiam audiendam, nec propter cibum, aut vinum impediebantur. Nec mirum, quia discipuli eius fuerant, scilicet Ioannis, cuius potus erat aqua, esca autem locusta et mel silvestre.

297. Secundum autem Augustinum, per horam decimam lex signatur, quae in decem praeceptis data est. Erat ergo hora decima quando isti venerunt, et manserunt cum Christo, et ab eo erudiuntur, ut impleretur lex per Christum quae a Iudaeis impleri non poterat. Et ideo etiam in ipsa hora vocatus est Rabbi, idest Magister.

298. Consequenter cum dicit *erat autem Andreas frater Simonis Petri* etc. ponitur fructus quem fecit discipulus Ioannis conversus ad Christum. Et super hoc

primo describitur discipulus;

secundo fructus ab ipso inchoatus, ibi *invenit hic primum fratrem suum Simonem*;

tertio ponitur consummatio fructus facta per Christum, ibi *intuitus autem eum Iesus dixit*.

299. Describitur autem discipulus primo a nomine, cum dicit *erat autem Andreas*, idest *virilis*. Ps. XXX, 25: *viriliter agite, et confortetur cor vestrum.* Exprimit autem nomen, ut ostendatur eius privilegium: tum quia prior conversus est ad fidem Christi perfecte, tum etiam quia Christum praedicavit: unde sicut Stephanus fuit primus martyr post Christum, ita et Andreas fuit primus Christianus.

Secundo describitur a cognatione, quia *frater Simonis Petri*: quia iunior erat. Et hoc quidem est ad commendationem suam, ut qui aetate posterior, fide efficiatur primus.

perfectly believing **stayed with him that day**; hearing and seeing that blessed day, they spent a blessed night: *happy are your men, and happy are your servants, who always stand before you* (1 Kgs 8:10). And as Augustine says: *let us also build a dwelling in our heart and fashion a home where he may come and teach us.*

And he says, **that day**, because there can be no night where the light of Christ is present, where there is the Sun of justice.

295. The time is given when he says, **it was about the tenth hour**. The Evangelist mentions this in order that, considering the literal sense, he might give credit to Christ and the disciples. For the tenth hour is near the end of the day. And this praises Christ who was so eager to teach that not even the lateness of the hour induced him to postpone teaching them; but he taught them at the tenth hour. *In the morning sow your seed, and in the evening do not let your hands be idle* (Eccl 11:6).

296. The moderation of the disciples is also praised, because even at the tenth hour, when men usually have eaten and are less self-possessed for receiving wisdom, they were both self-possessed and prepared to hear wisdom and were not hindered because of food or wine. But this is not unexpected, for they had been disciples of John, whose drink was water and whose food was the locust and wild honey.

297. According to Augustine, however, the tenth hour signifies the law, which was given in ten precepts. And so the disciples came to Christ at the tenth hour and remained with him to be taught so that the law might be fulfilled by Christ, since it could not be fulfilled by the Jews. And so at that hour he is called Rabbi, that is, Teacher.

298. Then at **and Andrew, the brother of Simon Peter**, he sets forth the fruit produced by the disciple of John who was converted to Christ.

First, the disciple is described;

second, the fruit begun by him, at **he first found his brother Simon**;

third, the consummation of this fruit by Christ, at **and Jesus looking upon him said**.

299. The disciple is described first by name when he says, **Andrew**, i.e., *manly. Act manfully, and let your heart be strong* (Ps 30:25). He mentions his name in order to show his privilege: for he was the first to be perfectly converted to Christ, but also he proclaimed Christ. So, as Stephen was the first martyr after Christ, so Andrew was the first Christian.

He is described, second, by his relationship, that is, as **the brother of Simon Peter**, for he was the younger. And this is mentioned to commend him, for although younger in age, he became first in faith.

Tertio a disciplina, quia **unus ex duobus qui audierant a Ioanne.** Et huius quidem nomen describitur ad ostendendum Andreae privilegium quod insignis fuerit. Alterius enim nomen tacetur: aut quia ille alius fuit Ioannes Evangelista, cuius consuetudo est in suo Evangelio cum de eo agitur, nomen suum non exprimere propter humilitatem; aut, secundum Chrysostomum, non fuit aliquis insignis, nec fecit aliquid magnum: unde non fuisset utilitas nomen eius ponere. Sic enim et Lucas, cap. X, nomina septuaginta duorum discipulorum, quos Dominus binos misit ante faciem suam, non posuit, quia non erant solemnes personae et insignes, sicut apostoli fuerunt. Aut, secundum Alcuinum, ille discipulus fuit Philippus: et hoc patet, quia statim postquam Evangelista prosecutus est de Andrea, prosequitur de Philippo, dicens: **in crastinum autem voluit exire in Galilaeam, et invenit Philippum** etc.

Quarto commendatur a devotionis studio: unde dicitur **et secuti fuerant eum,** idest Iesum. Iob XXIII, 11: *vestigia eius secutus est pes meus.*

300. Fructus autem inchoatus per Andream ponitur, cum dicit **invenit hic primum Simonem fratrem suum.** Et primo insinuat apud quem fructum fecit, scilicet apud fratrem suum, ut commendet suae conversionis perfectionem: sicut enim Petrus dicit in *itinerario Clementis,* evidens signum perfectae conversionis alicuius est, cum conversus, quanto aliquis sibi est magis coniunctus, tanto magis satagit eum convertere ad Christum. Et ideo Andreas perfecte conversus non detinuit apud seipsum inventum thesaurum, sed festinat et currit cito ad fratrem, traditurus ei bona quae suscepit.

Et ideo dicit **invenit hic,** scilicet Andreas, **primum,** idest primo adverbialiter, **fratrem suum Simonem,** quem quaerebat, ut sicut erat sanguine, ita faceret eum germanum fide. Prov. XVIII, 19: *frater qui adiuvatur a fratre quasi civitas firma;* Apoc. ult., 17: *qui audit, dicat, veni.*

301. Secundo ponit verba quae dicit Andreas **invenimus Messiam (quod interpretatur Christus)**; ubi, secundum Chrysostomum, tacite respondet cuidam quaestioni. Scilicet, si quis eum interrogaret de quo instructi fuissent a Christo, in promptu est responsio, scilicet quod per testimonia Scripturae instruxit eum intantum quod cognosceret eum esse Christum. Et ideo dicit **invenimus.** Per quod etiam innuit quod diu cum desiderio eum quaesierat; Prov. III, 13: *beatus homo qui invenit sapientiam.* **Messia** Hebraice, quod Graece interpretatum est *Christus,* idest *unctus* Latine: quia specialiter unctus est oleo invisibili, idest Spiritus Sancti. Ideo signanter nomine isto manifestat eum: unde in Ps. XLIV, 8 dicitur: *unxit te Deus tuus oleo laetitiae prae consortibus,* idest prae omnibus sanctis: nam omnes sancti isto oleo unguntur; sed iste singulariter unctus est, et singulariter

He is described, third, by his discipleship, because he was **one of the two who had heard of John.** His name is mentioned in order to show that Andrew's privilege was remarkable. For the name of the other disciple is not mentioned: either because it was John the Evangelist himself, who through humility followed the practice in his Gospel of not mentioning his own name when he was involved in some event; or, according to Chrysostom, because the other one was not a notable person, nor had he done anything great, and so there was no need to mention his name. Luke does the same in his Gospel (Luke 10:1), where he does not mention the names of the seventy-two disciples sent out by the Lord, because they were not the outstanding and important persons that the apostles were. Or, according to Alcuin, this other disciple was Philip: for the Evangelist, after discussing Andrew, begins at once with Philip, saying: **on the following day, Jesus wanted to go to Galilee, and he found Philip** (John 1:43).

He is commended, fourth, for the zeal of his devotion: hence he says that Andrew **followed him,** i.e., Jesus: *my foot has followed in his steps* (Job 23:11).

300. The fruit begun by Andrew is mentioned when he says, **he first found his brother Simon.** He first mentions the one for whom he bore fruit, that is, his brother, in order to mark the perfection of his conversion. For as Peter says, in the *Itinerary of Clement,* the evident sign of a perfect conversion of anyone is that, once converted, the closer one is to him the more he tries to convert him to Christ. And so Andrew, being now perfectly converted, does not keep the treasure he found to himself, but hurries and quickly runs to his brother to share with him the good things he has received.

And so he says the **he first found,** that is, Andrew, **his brother Simon,** so that related in blood he might make him related in faith: *a brother that is helped by his brother is like a strong city* (Prov 18:19); *let him who hears say, come* (Rev 22:17).

301. Second, he mentions the words spoken by Andrew, **we have found the Messiah (which is interpreted as Christ).** Here, according to Chrysostom, he is tacitly responding to a certain question: namely, that if someone were to ask what they had been instructed about by Christ, they would have the ready answer that through the testimony of the Scriptures he had instructed them in such a way that they knew he was the Christ. And so he says, **we have found the Messiah.** He implies by this that he had previously sought him by desire for a long time: *happy is the man who finds wisdom* (Prov 3:13). **Messiah,** which is Hebrew, is translated as *Christos* in Greek, and in Latin as *anointed,* because he was anointed in a special way with invisible oil, which is the Holy Spirit. So Andrew explicitly designates him by this title: *your God has anointed you with the oil of gladness above your fellows,* i.e., above all the saints. For all the saints are anointed with that oil, but Christ was singularly

sanctus. Ideo secundum Chrysostomum, non dicit 'Messiam' simpliciter, sed cum adiectione articuli.

302. Tertio ponit fructum quem fecit, quia *adduxit eum ad Iesum*, scilicet Petrum. In quo Petri obedientia commendatur: confestim enim occurrit, in hoc non tardans. Et Andreae devotionem considera: quia duxit eum ad Iesum, non ad se (sciebat enim se infirmum), et ideo eum ad Christum adducit, ut ipse eum instruat; instruens simul per hoc, quod hic debet esse praedicatorum conatus et studium, ut fructus praedicationis et studium non sibi vindicent, seu ad utilitatem et honorem proprium convertant, sed ut adducant ad Iesum, idest ad eius gloriam et honorem referant. II Cor. IV, 5: *non enim praedicamus nosmetipsos, sed Iesum Christum.*

303. Consummatio autem huius fructus ponitur cum dicit *intuitus autem eum Iesus dixit*, etc. Ubi Christus, ad fidem divinitatis eum elevare volens, incipit quae divinitatis sunt opera facere, occulta praedicans.

Et primo quidem quantum ad occulta praesentiae; unde *intuitus eum*, idest, statim cum vidit eum virtute divinitatis, consideravit, et dixit ei nomen suum: unde dicit *tu es Simon*. Nec mirum, quia, ut dicitur I Reg. XVI, v. 7, *homines vident ea quae apparent, Deus autem intuetur cor.*

Congruit autem hoc nomen mysterio. Nam *Simon* interpretatur obediens; ut insinuet quod obedientia necessaria est ei qui conversus est ad Christum per fidem. Act. V, 32: *dat Spiritum Sanctum obedientibus sibi.*

304. Secundo vero quantum ad occulta praeterita. Unde dicit *filius Ioanna*, quia hoc nomine vocatus est pater suus, vel, secundum Matthaeum, filius Iona, cum dicit *Simon Bariona.*

Et utrumque congruit mysterio. *Ioanna* enim interpretatur gratia, ut insinuet quod homines per gratiam veniunt ad fidem Christi; Eph. II, 5: *gratia salvati estis* etc. *Iona* vero interpretatur columba, ut insinuet quod per Spiritum Sanctum, qui datus est nobis, firmamur in amore Dei, ut dicitur Rom. V, 5: *caritas Dei diffusa est in cordibus nostris.*

305. Tertio vero quantum ad occulta futura; unde dicit *tu vocaberis Cephas, quod interpretatur Petrus*, et in Graeco caput.

Et congruit mysterio, ut ille qui debet esse aliorum caput et Christi vicarius, firmitati inhaereret. Matth. XVI, 18: *tu es Petrus, et super hanc petram aedificabo Ecclesiam meam.*

306. Sed hic est quaestio litteralis. Et primo quare Christus imposuit ei in principio suae conversionis nomen, et non voluit quod a principio nativitatis suae hoc nomine vocaretur?

Ad hoc respondetur dupliciter. Secundum Chrysostomum, primo quidem quia nomina divinitus

anointed and is singularly holy. So, as Chrysostom says, he does not simply call him 'Messiah,' but **the Messiah**.

302. Third, he mentions the fruit he produced, because **he brought him**, that is, Peter, **to Jesus**. This gives recognition to Peter's obedience, for he came at once, without delay. And consider the devotion of Andrew: for he brought him to Jesus and not to himself (for he knew that he himself was weak); and so he leads him to Christ to be instructed by him. This shows us that the efforts and the aim of preachers should not be to win for themselves the fruits of their preaching, i.e., to turn them to their own private benefit and honor, but to bring them to Jesus, i.e., to refer them to his glory and honor: *what we preach is not ourselves, but Jesus Christ* (2 Cor 4:5).

303. The consummation of this fruit is given when he says, **and Jesus looking upon him said: you are Simon**. Here Christ, wishing to raise him up to faith in his divinity, begins to perform works of divinity, making know things that are hidden.

First of all, things which are hidden in the present: thus, **looking upon him**, i.e, as soon as Jesus saw him, he considered him by the power of his divinity and called him by name, saying, **you are Simon**. This is not surprising, for as it is said: *man sees the appearances, but the Lord sees the heart* (1 Sam 16:7).

This name is appropriate for the mystery. For **Simon** means obedient, to indicate that obedience is necessary for one who has been converted to Christ through faith: *he gives the Holy Spirit to all who obey him* (Acts 5:32).

304. Second, he reveals things hidden in the past. Hence he says, **son of John**, because that was the name of Simon's father; or he says, son of Jonah (Matt 16:17), when he says *Simon Bar-Jonah.*

And each name is appropriate to this mystery. For **John** means grace, to indicate that it is through grace that men come to the faith of Christ: *you are saved by his grace* (Eph 2:5). And *Jonah* means dove, to indicate that it is by the Holy Spirit, who has been given to us, that we are made strong in our love for God: *the love of God is poured out into our hearts by the Holy Spirit* (Rom 5:5).

305. Third, he reveals things hidden in the future. So he says, **you will be called Cephas, which is interpreted Peter**, and in Greek, *head.*

And this is appropriate to this mystery, which is that he who was to be the head of the others and the vicar of Christ should remain firm. As it is said: *you are Peter, and upon this rock I will build my church* (Matt 16:18).

306. There is a question here about the literal meaning. First, why did Christ give Simon a name at the beginning of his conversion, rather than will that he have this name from the time of his birth?

Two different answers have been given for this. The first, according to Chrysostom, is that divinely given names

imposita aliquam eminentiam gratiae spiritualis designant. Quando autem Deus confert specialem gratiam alicui, ab ipsa nativitate nomen gratiam illam significans imponitur; sicut patet de Ioanne Baptista, qui ante a Deo est nominatus quam natus, quia fuit sanctificatus in utero matris. Aliquando autem aliter confertur eminentia gratiae specialis tempore procedenti; et talia nomina divinitus imponuntur non a principio nativitatis, sed in ipso processu temporis; sicut patet de Abraham et Sara, quibus nomina mutata sunt quando promissionem multiplicandi germinis acceperunt. Eodem modo et Petrus nominatur divinitus quando ad fidem Christi, et gratiam apostolatus vocatur, et specialiter quia constitutus est Princeps apostolorum totius Ecclesiae; quod in aliis apostolis non est factum.

Secundum Augustinum autem, quia si a principio fuisset nominatus Cephas, non apparuisset mysterium. Et ideo voluit Dominus quod tunc nomen haberet, ut mutatione nominis, Ecclesiae mysterium appareret, quae in confessione fidei eius fundata erat. 'Petrus' enim a petra dicitur; petra autem erat Christus. In *Petri* ergo nomine figurata est Ecclesia, quae supra firmam petram immobilem, idest Christum, aedificata est.

307. Secunda quaestio est utrum hic fuerit impositum hoc nomen Simoni, an in Matthaeo cum dicitur *tu es Petrus.*

Et ad hoc respondet Augustinus dicens, quod istud nomen hoc loco fuit Simoni impositum; sed quod dicit ei Dominus in Matth. *tu es Petrus* etc. non est nominis impositio, sed impositi nominis commemoratio, ut quasi utatur illo nomine tamquam iam imposito.

Alii autem dicunt, quod hoc nomen fuit impositum Simoni quando Dominus dixit ei *tu es Petrus, et super hanc petram aedificabo Ecclesiam meam.* Hic vero non imponit ei hoc nomen, sed praesignat quod sit ei postmodum imponendum.

308. Tertia quaestio est de vocatione Petri et Andreae: quia hic dicitur, quod fuerunt vocati iuxta Iordanem, quia fuerunt discipuli Ioannis; et Matth. IV, 18 dicitur, quod Christus vocavit eos iuxta mare Galilaeae.

Et ad hoc dicendum, quod triplex fuit vocatio apostolorum. Prima fuit ad cognitionem, seu familiaritatem, et fidem; et de hac dicitur hic. Secunda fuit in officii praesignatione, de qua habetur Lc. V, 10: *ex hoc eris homines capiens.* Tertia fuit ad apostolatum, de qua dicitur Matth. IV, 18 s., quae fuit perfecta, quia postea non redierunt ad propria.

indicate a certain eminence in spiritual grace. Now when God confers a special grace upon anyone, the name indicating that grace is given at one's birth: as in the case of John the Baptist, who was named before he was born, because he had been sanctified in his mother's womb. But sometimes a special grace is given during the course of one's life: then such names are divinely given at that time and not at birth: as in the case of Abraham and Sarah, whose names were changed when they received the promise that their posterity would multiply. Likewise, Peter is named in a divine way when he is called to the faith of Christ and to the grace of apostleship, and particularly because he was appointed Prince of the apostles of the entire Church—which was not done with the other apostles.

But, according to Augustine, if he had been called Cephas from birth, this mystery would not have been apparent. And so the Lord willed that he should have one name at birth, so that by changing his name the mystery of the Church, which was built on his confession of faith, would be apparent. Now 'Peter' is derived from rock. But the rock was Christ. Thus, the name **Peter** signifies the Church, which was built upon that solid and immovable rock which is Christ.

307. The second question is whether this name was given to Peter at this time, or at *you are Peter* (Matt 16:18).

Augustine answers that this name was given to Simon at this time; and at the event reported by Matthew: *you are Peter* (Matt 16:18) the Lord is not giving this name but reminding him of the name that was given, so that Christ is using this name as already given.

But others think that this name was given when the Lord said, *you are Peter, and upon this rock I will build my church* (Matt 16:18); and in this passage in the Gospel of John, Christ is not giving this name, but foretelling what will be given later.

308. The third question is about the calling of Peter and Andrew: for here it says that they were called near the Jordan, because they were John's disciples; but it is said that Christ called them by the Sea of Galilee (Matt 4:18).

The answer to this is that there was a triple calling of the apostles. The first was a call to knowledge or friendship and faith; and this is the one recorded here. The second consisted in the prediction of their office: *from now on you will be catching men* (Luke 5:10). The third call was to their apostleship (Matt 4:18). This was the perfect call because after this they were not to return to their own pursuits.

Lecture 16

1:43 In crastinum voluit exire in Galilaeam; et invenit Philippum, et dicit ei Iesus: sequere me. [n. 310]

1:44 Erat autem Philippus a Bethsaida, civitate Andreae et Petri. [n. 313]

1:45 Invenit Philippus Nathanaelem, et dixit ei: quem scripsit Moyses in lege et Prophetis, invenimus Iesum filium Ioseph a Nazareth. [n. 316]

1:46 Et dixit ei Nathanael: a Nazareth potest aliquid boni esse? Dixit ei Philippus: veni, et vide. [n. 318]

1:47 Vidit Iesus Nathanaelem venientem ad se, et dixit de eo: ecce vere Israelita, in quo dolus non est. [n. 320]

1:48 Dixit ei Nathanael: unde me nosti? Respondit Iesus, et dixit ei: priusquam te Philippus vocaret, cum esses sub ficu, vidi te. [n. 324]

1:49 Respondit ei Nathanael, et ait: Rabbi, tu es Filius Dei, tu es Rex Israel. [n. 327]

1:50 Respondit Iesus, et dixit ei: quia dixi tibi, vidi te sub ficu, credis: maius his videbis. [n. 329]

1:51 Et dixit ei: amen, amen dico vobis, videbitis caelum apertum, et angelos Dei ascendentes et descendentes super Filium hominis. [n. 329]

1:43 Τῇ ἐπαύριον ἠθέλησεν ἐξελθεῖν εἰς τὴν Γαλιλαίαν καὶ εὑρίσκει Φίλιππον. καὶ λέγει αὐτῷ ὁ Ἰησοῦς· ἀκολούθει μοι.

1:44 ἦν δὲ ὁ Φίλιππος ἀπὸ Βηθσαϊδά, ἐκ τῆς πόλεως Ἀνδρέου καὶ Πέτρου.

1:45 εὑρίσκει Φίλιππος τὸν Ναθαναὴλ καὶ λέγει αὐτῷ· ὃν ἔγραψεν Μωϋσῆς ἐν τῷ νόμῳ καὶ οἱ προφῆται εὑρήκαμεν, Ἰησοῦν υἱὸν τοῦ Ἰωσὴφ τὸν ἀπὸ Ναζαρέτ.

1:46 καὶ εἶπεν αὐτῷ Ναθαναήλ· ἐκ Ναζαρὲτ δύναταί τι ἀγαθὸν εἶναι; λέγει αὐτῷ [ὁ] Φίλιππος· ἔρχου καὶ ἴδε.

1:47 εἶδεν ὁ Ἰησοῦς τὸν Ναθαναὴλ ἐρχόμενον πρὸς αὐτὸν καὶ λέγει περὶ αὐτοῦ· ἴδε ἀληθῶς Ἰσραηλίτης ἐν ᾧ δόλος οὐκ ἔστιν.

1:48 λέγει αὐτῷ Ναθαναήλ· πόθεν με γινώσκεις; ἀπεκρίθη Ἰησοῦς καὶ εἶπεν αὐτῷ· πρὸ τοῦ σε Φίλιππον φωνῆσαι ὄντα ὑπὸ τὴν συκῆν εἶδόν σε.

1:49 ἀπεκρίθη αὐτῷ Ναθαναήλ· ῥαββί, σὺ εἶ ὁ υἱὸς τοῦ θεοῦ, σὺ βασιλεὺς εἶ τοῦ Ἰσραήλ.

1:50 ἀπεκρίθη Ἰησοῦς καὶ εἶπεν αὐτῷ· ὅτι εἶπόν σοι ὅτι εἶδόν σε ὑποκάτω τῆς συκῆς, πιστεύεις; μείζω τούτων ὄψῃ.

1:51 καὶ λέγει αὐτῷ· ἀμὴν ἀμὴν λέγω ὑμῖν, ὄψεσθε τὸν οὐρανὸν ἀνεῳγότα καὶ τοὺς ἀγγέλους τοῦ θεοῦ ἀναβαίνοντας καὶ καταβαίνοντας ἐπὶ τὸν υἱὸν τοῦ ἀνθρώπου.

1:43 On the following day, Jesus wanted to go to Galilee, and he found Philip. And Jesus said to him: follow me. [n. 310]

1:44 Now Philip was from Bethsaida, the city of Andrew and Peter. [n. 313]

1:45 Philip found Nathanael and said to him: we have found him of whom Moses in the law and the prophets wrote, Jesus the son of Joseph from Nazareth. [n. 316]

1:46 And Nathanael said to him: can anything good come from Nazareth? Philip said to him: come and see. [n. 318]

1:47 Jesus saw Nathanael coming to him, and he said to him: behold a true Israelite, in whom there is no guile. [n. 320]

1:48 Nathanael said to him: how do you know me? Jesus answered and said to him: before Philip called you, when you were under the fig tree, I saw you. [n. 324]

1:49 Nathanael answered him and said: Rabbi, you are the Son of God, you are the King of Israel. [n. 327]

1:50 Jesus answered and said to him: because I said to you, I saw you under the fig tree, you believe: you will see greater things than these. [n. 329]

1:51 And he said to him: amen, amen I say to you, you will see the heavens opened, and the angels of God ascending and descending on the Son of man. [n. 329]

---

309. Posito fructu qui provenit ex praedicatione Ioannis, et eius discipuli, consequenter Evangelista manifestat fructum qui provenit ex praedicatione Christi, et

primo agit de conversione unius discipuli ad praedicationem Christi;

secundo de conversione aliorum ad praedicationem discipuli ad Christum conversi, ibi **invenit Philippus Nathanaelem** etc.

Circa primum tria facit.

Primo ponitur discipuli vocandi occasio;

secundo subditur ipsius discipuli vocatio;

309. After having shown the fruit produced by John's preaching and that of his disciples, the Evangelist now shows the fruit obtained from the preaching of Christ.

First, he deals with the conversion of one disciple as the result of Christ's preaching.

Second, the conversion of others due to the preaching of the disciple just converted to Christ, at **Philip found Nathanael**.

As to the first he does three things:

first, the occasion when the disciple is called is given;

second, his calling is described;

tertio describitur vocati discipuli conditio, ibi *erat autem Philippus a Bethsaida*.

310. Occasio quidem vocationis fuit exitus Iesu a Iudaea. Et ideo dicitur *in crastinum* autem *voluit exire*, scilicet Iesus a Iudaea, *in Galilaeam, et invenit Philippum*.

Ratio autem exitus Iesu in Galilaeam assignatur triplex: duae videlicet litterales, quarum una est quia postquam baptizatus fuerat a Ioanne, volens honorem deferre Baptistae, exivit in Galilaeam, a Iudaea recedens, ne sua praesentia offuscaret, et minueret Ioannis magisterium, dum adhuc statum haberet: docens nos honore invicem praevenire, ut dicitur Rom. XII, 10.

Secunda ratio est quia in Galilaea non sunt insignes personae, infra VII, 52: *a Galilaea propheta non surgit* etc. et ideo voluit exire illuc Iesus, et eligere inde principes orbis terrae, qui sunt prophetis maiores, ut per hoc suam virtutem ostendat. Ps. CVI, 35: *posuit desertum in stagna aquarum*.

Tertia ratio est mystica: quia *Galilaea* interpretatur *transmigratio*. Voluit ergo exire a Iudaea in Galilaeam ut insinuaret quod *in crastinum*, idest in die gratiae, scilicet Evangelii, exiret a Iudaea in Galilaeam, idest ad gentes salvandas; infra VII, 35: *numquid hic iturus est in dispersionem gentium?*

311. Vocatio ergo discipuli est ad sequendum; et ideo dicit invenit Philippum, et dicit ei: *sequere me*.

Et nota, quod aliquando homo invenit Deum, sed quasi ignotum; Prov. VIII, 35: *qui invenerit me, inveniet vitam, et hauriet salutem a Domino*. Aliquando Deus invenit hominem, sed ut eum manifestet, et magnificet; Ps. LXXXVIII, 21: *inveni David servum meum*. Et sic Christus invenit Philippum, ut eum ad fidem et gratiam vocet: et ideo statim dicit *sequere me*.

312. Quaestio est quare Iesus a principio non vocavit discipulos.

Ad quod respondet Chrysostomus, quod noluit a principio aliquem vocare, antequam aliquis spontaneus ei adhaereret per praedicationem Ioannis: quia homines magis exemplo trahuntur quam verbis Ex. XXVI, *cortina trahit cortinam*.

313. Quaeritur etiam quare Philippus statim ad unum verbum secutus est Christum, cum Andreas eum secutus fuerit audiens a Ioanne de Christo, Petrus autem ab Andrea.

Ad hoc est triplex responsio. Una, quia Philippus iam instructus erat a Ioanne; quia, secundum unam expositionem supra positam, ille alius, qui cum Andrea secutus est Christum, erat Philippus. Alia ratio est quia vox Christi virtutem quamdam habebat ut non solum exterius, sed etiam interius cor moveret; Ier. XXIII, 29: *verba mea sunt quasi ignis*. Non enim vox Christi solum

third, his situation, at *now Philip was from Bethsaida*.

310. The occasion of his calling was the departure of Jesus from Judea. So he says, *on the following day, Jesus wanted to go to Galilee, and he found Philip*.

There are three reasons why Jesus left for Galilee, two of which are literal. One of these is that after being baptized by John and desiring to shed honor on the Baptist, he left Judea for Galilee so that his presence would not obscure and lessen John's teaching authority, while he still retained that state; and this teaches us to show honor to one another (Rom 12:10).

The second reason is that there are no distinguished persons in Galilee: *out of Galilee, a prophet does not rise* (John 7:52). And so, to show the greatness of his power, Christ wished to go there and choose there the princes of the earth, who are greater than the prophets: *he has turned the desert into pools of water* (Ps 106:35).

The third reason is mystical: for *Galilee* means *passage*. So Christ desired to go from Judea into Galilee in order to indicate that on *on the following day*, i.e., on the day of grace, that is, the day of the Good News, he would pass from Judea into Galilee, i.e., to save the gentiles: *will he go to the dispersed among the gentiles and teach the gentiles?* (John 7:35).

311. A disciple's vocation is to follow: hence he says that after Christ found Philip he said, *follow me*.

Note that sometimes man finds God, but without knowing it, as it were: *he who finds me will find life, and will have salvation from the Lord* (Prov 8:35). And at other times God finds the man, in order to bestow honor and greatness upon him: *I have found David, my servant* (Ps 88:21). Christ found Philip in this way, that is, to call him to the faith and to grace. And so he says at once, *follow me*.

312. There is a question here: why did not Jesus call his disciples at the very beginning?

Chrysostom answers that he did not wish to call anyone before someone clung to him spontaneously because of John's preaching, for men are drawn by example more than by words, for *the curtain draws the curtain* (Exod 26).

313. One might also ask why Philip followed Christ immediately after only a word, while Andrew followed Christ after hearing about him from John, and Peter after hearing from Andrew.

Three answers can be given. One is that Philip had already been instructed by John: for according to one of the explanations given above, Philip was that other disciple who followed Christ along with Andrew. Another is that Christ's voice had power not only to act on one's hearing from without, but also on the heart from within: *my words are like fire* (Jer 23:29). For the voice of Christ was spoken

exterioribus dicebatur, sed fidelium interiora ad eius inflammabat amorem. Tertio, quia forte Philippus iam de Christo fuerat instructus ab Andrea et Petro, quia ex eadem villa erant; quod Evangelista videtur innuere per hoc quod subdit **erat autem Philippus a Bethsaida civitate Andreae et Petri.**

314. In quo discipuli vocati conditio exprimitur: quia erant a Bethsaida.

Et sic congruit mysterio. **Bethsaida** enim *domus venatorum* interpretatur: ut ostendat quales tunc animo erant Philippus, Petrus et Andreas, et quod de domo venatorum, congrue venatores ad capiendas animas ad vitam vocaret. Ier. XVI, 16: *mittam meos venatores* etc.

315. Consequenter ponitur fructus discipuli ad Christum conversi, et

primo ponitur inchoatio fructus facta a discipulo;

secundo consummatio facta per Christum, ibi **vidit Iesus Nathanaelem.**

Circa primum tria facit.

Primo ponitur Annuntiatio Philippi;

secundo responsio Nathanaelis, ibi **et dixit Nathanael**;

tertio consequens admonitio Philippi, ibi **dicit ei Philippus.**

316. Circa primum attende, quod sicut Andreas perfecte conversus studuit adducere fratrem suum ad Christum, ita et Philippus fratrem suum Nathanaelem. Et ideo dicit **invenit Philippus Nathanaelem**, quem forte quaerebat, sicut Andreas Petrum quaesierat: quod fuit signum perfectae conversionis. **Et dixit ei.** Nathanael interpretatur *donum Dei*; et quod aliquis ad Christum convertatur, ex dono Dei est. Annuntiat autem ei omnes prophetias et legem complementum habere, et desideria sanctorum patrum non esse frustrata, sed esse verificata, et quod eorum desideriis erat promissum a Deo, iam adimpletum esse. **Quem scripsit Moyses in lege et prophetis, invenimus Iesum**; per quod datur intelligi quod Nathanael erat satis peritus in lege, et quod etiam Philippus iam instructus de Christo, voluit Nathanaelem ex sibi notis, scilicet ex lege et prophetis, inducere ad Christum, et ideo dicit **quem scripsit Moyses** etc. Moyses enim de Christo scripsit; infra V, 46: **si crederetis Moysi, crederetis forsitan et mihi: de me enim ille scripsit.** Similiter prophetae de Christo scripserunt; Act. c. X, 43: *huic omnes prophetae testimonium perhibent.*

317. Etiam attende, quod tria dicit de Christo Philippus, legi et prophetis consona. Primo quidem nomen; unde dixit **invenimus Iesum.** Et hoc consonat prophetis: Is. XIX, v. 20: *mittam eis salvatorem* etc.; Hab. ult., v. 18: *exultabo in Deo Iesu meo.*

Secundo vero genus, unde duxit originem humanam cum dicit **filium Ioseph**, scilicet qui erat de domo

not only to the exterior, but it enkindled the interior of the faithful to love him. The third answer is that Philip. had perhaps already been instructed about Christ by Andrew and Peter, since they were from the same town. In fact, this is what the Evangelist seems to imply by adding, **now Philip was from Bethsaida, the city of Andrew and Peter.**

314. This gives us the situation of the disciples he called: for they were from Bethsaida.

And this is appropriate to this mystery. For **Bethsaida** means *house of hunters*, to show the attitude of Philip, Peter and Andrew at that time, and because it was fitting to call, from the house of hunters, hunters who were to capture souls for life: *I will send my hunters* (Jer 16:16).

315. Now the fruit produced by the disciple who was converted to Christ is given.

First, the beginning of the fruit, coming from this disciple.

Second, its consummation by Christ, at **Jesus saw Nathanael.**

As to the first, he does three things:

first, the statement of Philip is given;

second, Nathanael's response, at **Nathanael said**;

and third, Philip's ensuing advice, at **Philip said to him.**

316. As to the first, note that just as Andrew, after having been perfectly converted, was eager to lead his brother to Christ, so too Philip with regard to his brother, Nathanael. And so he says that **Philip found Nathanael**, whom he probably looked for as Andrew did for Peter; and this was a sign of a perfect conversion. **And said to him.** The word **Nathanael** means *gift of God*; and it is God's gift if anyone is converted to Christ. He tells him that all the prophecies and the law have been fulfilled, and that the desires of their holy forefathers are not in vain, but have been guaranteed, and that what God has promised was now accomplished. **we have found him of whom Moses in the law and the prophets wrote, Jesus.** We understand by this that Nathanael was fairly learned in the law, and that Philip, now having learned about Christ, wished to lead Nathanael to Christ through the things he himself knew, that is, from the law and the prophets. So he says, **him of whom Moses in the law and the prophets wrote.** For Moses wrote of Christ: **if you believed Moses, you would perhaps believe me also , for he wrote of me** (John 5:46). The prophets too wrote of Christ: *all the prophets bear witness to him* (Acts 10:43).

317. Note that Philip says three things about Christ that are in agreement with the law and the prophets. First, the name: for he says, **we have found . . . Jesus.** And this agrees with the prophets: *I will send them a savior* (Isa 19:20); *I will rejoice in God, my Jesus* (Heb 3:18).

Second, the family from which Christ took his human origin, when he says, **son of Joseph**, i.e., who was of

David et familia. Et quamvis ex eo Christus originem non duxerit, tamen ex virgine duxit, quae erat de eadem progenie cum Ioseph. Vocat autem *filium Ioseph*, quia eius filius aestimabatur esse, cui scilicet desponsata erat mater eius. Unde dicitur Lc. c. III, 23: *ut putabatur filius Ioseph*. Nec mirum, si Philippus vocabat eum filium Ioseph, cum et mater eius divinae incarnationis conscia, ipsum eius filium diceret; Lc. II, 48, *pater tuus, et ego dolentes quaerebamus te*. Et si quidem aliquis filius alicuius vocatur, quia nutritur ab ipso, Ioseph multo amplius pater Iesu dici poterat, licet secundum carnem pater non esset: quia et eum nutriverat, et sponsus matris Virginis erat. Dicitur autem hic a Philippo non tamquam de commixtione Ioseph et virginis natus esset, sed quia sciebat Christum de generatione David nasciturum, de cuius domo et familia erat Ioseph, cui desponsata erat Maria. Et hoc etiam consonat prophetis: Ierem. XXIII, 5: *suscitabo David germen iustum* etc.

Tertio commemorat patriam, dicens *a Nazareth*: non quia in ea natus esset, immo in Bethlehem, sed quia in ea erat nutritus. Quia enim nativitas eius multis erat incognita, locus autem ubi nutritus erat, cognitus erat multis, ideo Philippus Bethlehem tacuit, et posuit Nazareth. Et hoc quidem consonat dictis prophetarum; nam, Is. XI, 1: *egredietur virga de radice Iesse, et flos*, sive Nazaraeus, secundum aliam litteram, *de radice eius ascendet*.

318. Consequenter cum dicit *et dixit ei Nathanael* etc. ponitur responsio Nathanaelis: quod quidem potest legi et assertive et interrogative; et utroque modo eiusmodi responsio congruit verbis Philippi.

Si enim, secundum quod Augustinus vult, legatur assertive, est sensus: *a Nazareth potest aliquid boni esse*. Idest, a civitate, tanti nominis, potest esse quod aliquid summae gratiae nobis oriatur, seu aliquis doctor eximius, qui florem virtutum et munditiam sanctitatis nobis praedicet. *Nazareth* enim *flos* interpretatur. Ex quo datur intelligi quod Nathanael doctissimus in lege, scrutatus Scripturas, praenoscebat quod de Nazareth expectandus esset salvator, quod non facile alii Scribae et Pharisaei noverant; et ideo, cum Philippus diceret *invenimus Iesum a Nazareth*, erectus in spem, respondit: *vere a Nazareth potest esse* etc.

Si vero legatur, secundum Chrysostomum, interrogative, tunc est sensus: *a Nazareth potest aliquid boni esse?* Quasi dicat: omnia alia quae dicis credibilia videntur esse, quia et nomen et genus prophetis consonat, sed hoc quod dicis *a Nazareth*, non videtur possibile. Nathanael enim habuerat per Scripturas, quod a Bethlehem oportet Christum venire, secundum illud Matth. II, 6: *et tu, Bethlehem terra Iuda, nequaquam minima es in*

the house and family of David. And although Jesus did not derive his origin from him, yet he did derive it from the Virgin, who was of the same line as Joseph. He calls him the *son of Joseph*, because Jesus was considered to be the son of the one to whom his mother was married. So it is said: *the son of Joseph (as was supposed)* (Luke 3:23). Nor is it strange that Philip called him the son of Joseph, since his own mother, who was aware of his divine incarnation, called him his son: *your father and I have been looking for you in sorrow* (Luke 2:48). Indeed, if one is called the son of another because he is nurtured by him, Joseph is all the more able to be called the father of Jesus, even though he was not so according to the flesh: for he not only supported him, but was the husband of his virgin mother. However, Philip calls him the son of Joseph, not as though he was born from the union of Joseph and the Virgin, because he knew that Christ would be born from the line of David; and this was the house and family of Joseph, to whom Mary was married. And this also is in agreement with the prophets: *I will raise up a just branch for David* (Jer 23:5).

Third, he mentions his native land, saying, *from Nazareth*; not because he had been born there, but because he was brought up there; but he had been born in Bethlehem. Philip omits to mention Bethlehem but not Nazareth because, while the birth of Christ was not known to many, the place where he was brought up was. And this also agrees with the prophets: *a shoot will arise from the root of Jesse, and a flower* (or Nazarene, according to another version) *will rise up from his roots* (Isa 11:1).

318. Then when he says, *Nathanael replied*, the answer of Nathanael is given. His answer can be interpreted as an assertion or as a question; and in either way it is suitable to Philip's affirmation.

If it is taken as an assertion, as Augustine does, the meaning is: *some good can come from Nazareth*. In other words, from a city with that name it is possible that there come forth to us some very excellent grace or some outstanding teacher to preach to us about the flower of the virtues and the purity of sanctity; for *Nazareth* means *flower*. We can understand from this that Nathanael, being quite learned in the law and a student of the Scriptures, knew that the savior was expected to come from Nazareth—something that was not so clear even to the Scribes and Pharisees. And so when Philip said, *we have found . . . Jesus . . . from Nazareth*, his hopes were lifted and he answered: *indeed, some good can come from Nazareth*.

But if we take his answer as a question, as Chrysostom does, then the sense is: *can anything good come from Nazareth?* As if to say: everything else you say seems credible, because his name and his lineage are consistent with the prophecies, but your statement that he is *from Nazareth* does not seem possible. For Nathanael understood from the Scriptures that the Christ was to come from Bethlehem, according to: *and you, Bethlehem, land of Judah, are not the*

principibus Iuda: ex te enim exiet dux qui regat populum meum Israel. Et ideo, non inveniens convenire enunciationem Philippi cum prophetica praedicatione, prudenter et mansuete de veritate dicti interrogat *a Nazareth potest aliquid boni esse?*

319. Consequenter ponitur admonitio Philippi: *dixit ei Philippus: veni et vide*; quae quidem admonitio utrique responsioni Nathanaelis convenit. Assertive quidem, ut dicatur: tu dicis quod a Nazareth potest aliquid boni esse, sed ego dico, quod illud bonum quod tibi annuntio, tantum et tam magnificum est quod ego exprimere non valeo; et ideo *veni, et vide*. Interrogative autem legitur sic. Tu admirando dicis: *a Nazareth potest aliquid boni esse?* Reputans hoc esse impossibile secundum Scripturas; sed si experiri volueris quae ego expertus sum, intelliges vera esse quae dico; et ideo *veni, et vide*.

Trahit quidem Philippus Nathanaelem ad Christum, eius interrogationibus non fractus, qui scit de reliquo eum non contradicturum, si verba et doctrinam Christi gustaverit: et in hoc Philippus Christum secutus est, qui superius interrogantibus eum de habitaculo, respondit: *venite, et videte.* Ps. XXXIII, 6: *accedite ad eum, et illuminamini.*

320. Consequenter cum dicit *vidit Iesus Nathanaelem*, ponitur consummatio fructus per Christum.

Sciendum autem, quod aliqui dupliciter convertuntur ad Christum: quidam per miracula visa, et experta in se, sive in aliis; quidam vero per spirationes internas, et per prophetiam et praenoscentiam occultorum futurorum. Sed efficacior est modus per prophetias et praenoscentiam futurorum converti, quam per miracula. Ipsi enim Daemones, et aliqui homines eorum auxilio, aliqua mira praetendere possunt: sed futura praedicere solius divinae virtutis opus est; Is. XLI, 23: *ventura quoque annuntiate, et dicemus quod dii estis*; I Cor. c. XIV, 22: *prophetiae datae sunt fidelibus.* Et inde est quod Dominus non per miracula, sed per praenuntiationem occultorum Nathanaelem ad fidem trahit; et ideo dicit de eo *ecce vere Israelita, in quo dolus non est.*

321. Ubi tria occulta ei insinuat, scilicet occulta praesentia, quae sunt in corde, praeterita facta, et futura caelestia: quae quidem tria scire, divinum est, non humanum opus.

Occulta quidem praesentia insinuat ei, cum dicit *ecce vere Israelita, in quo dolus non est*: ubi quidem

primo ponitur Christi praenuntiatio;

secundo vero Nathanaelis inquisitio, ibi *unde me nosti?*

322. Dicit ergo circa primum *vidit Iesus Nathanaelem venientem ad se*, quasi dicat: antequam ad ipsum perveniret, dixit de eo: *ecce vere Israelita* etc. Dixit

least among the princes of Judah: for out of you a ruler will come forth, who will rule my people Israel* (Matt 2:6). And so, not finding Philip's statement in agreement with the prophecy, he prudently and moderately inquires about its truth, *can anything good come from Nazareth?*

319. Then Philip's advice is given: *Philip said to him: come and see.* And this advice suits either interpretation of Nathanael's answer. To the assertive interpretation it is as though he says: You say that something good can come from Nazareth, but I say that the good I state to you is of such a nature and so marvelous that I am unable to express it in words, so *come and see.* To the interpretation that makes it a question, it is as though he says: You wonder and say: *can anything good come from Nazareth?*, thinking that this is impossible according to the Scriptures. But if you are willing to experience what I experienced, you will understand that what I say is true, so *come and see.*

Then, not discouraged by his questions, Philip brings Nathanael to Christ. He knew that he would no longer argue with him if he tasted the words and teaching of Christ. And in this, Philip was imitating Christ who earlier answered those who had asked about the place where he lived: *come and see* . Come to him, and be enlightened (Ps 33:6).

320. Then when he says, *Jesus saw Nathanael*, the consummation of this fruit by Christ is described.

We should note that there are two ways in which men are converted to Christ: some by miracles they have seen and things experienced in themselves or in others; others are converted through internal insights, through prophecy and the foreknowledge of what is hidden in the future. The second way is more efficacious than the first: for devils and certain men who receive their help can simulate marvels; but to predict the future can only be done by divine power. *Tell us what is to come, and we will say that you are gods* (Isa 41:23); *prophecies are for those who believe* (1 Cor 14:22). And so our Lord draws Nathanael to the faith not by miracles but by making known things which are hidden. And so he says of him, *behold a true Israelite, in whom there is no guile.*

321. Christ mentions three hidden matters: things hidden in the present, in the heart; past facts; and future heavenly matters. To know these three things is not a human but a divine achievement.

He mentions things hidden in the present when he says, *behold a true Israelite, in whom there is no guile.* Here we have,

first, the prior revelation of Christ;

second, Nathanael's question, *how do you know me?*

322. First he says, *when Jesus saw Nathanael coming to him.* As if to say: before Nathanael reached him, Jesus said, *behold a true Israelite.* He said this about him before he

autem hoc de eo antequam ad ipsum perveniret, quia si dixisset hoc postquam ad Iesum pervenisset, potuisset credere Nathanael quod hoc Iesus audivisset a Philippo.

Dixit autem **ecce vere Israelita, in quo dolus non est**: *Israel* autem duas interpretationes habet. Uno enim modo interpretatur rectissimus; Is. XLIV, 2: *noli timere, serve meus rectissime, quem elegi*, ubi dicit Glossa, quod Israel interpretatur rectissimus. Alio modo Israel interpretatur *vir videns Deum*. Et secundum utrumque, Nathanael est vere Israelita: quia enim ille dicitur rectus in quo non est dolus, ideo dicitur **vere Israelita, in quo dolus non est**; quasi dicat: vere repraesentas genus tuum, quia tu es rectus et sine dolo. Quia vero per munditiam et simplicitatem homo Deum videt, ideo dixit **vere Israelita**; idest, tu es vir vere videns Deum, quia tu es simplex et sine dolo.

Dixit autem **in quo dolus non est**, ne credatur quod malitiose dixerit: **a Nazareth potest aliquid boni esse?** Quasi interrogans.

323. Augustinus autem aliter exponit. Manifestum est enim quod omnes sub peccato nascuntur. Illi ergo dicuntur dolosi qui peccatum habentes in corde, exterius fingunt se iustos; qui vero peccator est, et se peccatorem confitetur, non est dolosus. Dixit ergo **ecce vere Israelita, in quo dolus non est**, non quod peccatum non haberet, non quod illi medicus necessarius non esset, quia nemo sic natus est ut nullo medico indigeat; sed in eo confessionem peccati laudavit.

324. Consequenter cum dicit **unde me nosti?** ponitur Nathanaelis inquisitio.

Admirans enim Nathanael virtutem Dei in occultorum manifestatione, quia hoc solius Dei est: Ier. XVII, 9, *pravum est cor hominis, et inscrutabile, et quis cognoscet illud? Ego Dominus scrutans cor et probans renes*; et I Reg. XVI, 7, *homines vident ea quae parent, Deus autem intuetur cor*, ideo quaerit **unde me nosti?** In quo commendatur Nathanaelis humilitas: quia licet laudaretur, non est elatus; sed laudem propriam suspectam habuit: contra quod dicitur Is. III, 12: *popule meus, qui beatum te dicunt, ipsi te decipiunt.*

325. Praeterita vero absentia insinuat, cum dicit **priusquam te Philippus vocaret, cum esses sub ficu, vidi te**, ubi

primo ponitur denuntiatio Christi;

secundo confessio Nathanaelis, ibi **respondit et Nathanael, et ait: Rabbi, tu es Filius Dei.**

326. Circa primum sciendum est, quod Nathanael posset habere duplicem suspicionem de Christo: unam quod dixisset Christus praemissa, volens ei blandiri et ad amicitiam suam trahere; aliam quod ea quae dixit supra, ab alio cognovisset. Ut ergo suspicionem auferat, et ad altiora erigat, illa occulta manifestat quae nullus nisi divinitus scire potuisset, ea videlicet quae statim circa

came to him, because had he said it after he came, Nathanael might have believed that Jesus had heard it from Philip.

Christ said, **behold a true Israelite, in whom there is no guile**. Now *Israel* has two meanings. One of these, as the Gloss says, is *most righteous.—do not fear, my most righteous servant, whom I have chosen* (Isa 44:2). Its second meaning is *the man who sees God*. And according to each meaning Nathanael is a true Israelite. For since one in whom there is no guile is called righteous, Nathanael is said to be a **true Israelite, in whom there is no guile**. As if to say: you truly represent your race because you are righteous and without guile. Further, because man sees God through cleanness of heart and simplicity, Christ said, **a true Israelite**, i.e., you are a man who truly sees God because you are simple and without guile.

Further, he said, **in whom there is no guile**, so that we do not think that it was with malice that Nathanael asked: **can anything good come from Nazareth?**

323. Augustine has a different explanation of this passage. It is clear that all are born under sin. Now those who have sin in their hearts but outwardly pretend to be just are called guileful. But a sinner who admits that he is a sinner is not guileful. So Christ said, **behold a true Israelite, in whom there is no guile**, not because Nathanael was without sin, or because he had no need of a physician, for no one is born in such a way as not to need a physician; but he was praised by Christ because he admitted his sins.

324. Then when he says, **how do you know me?**, we have Nathanael's question.

For Nathanael, in wonder at the divine power in this revelation of what is hidden, because this can only be from God—*the heart is depraved and inscrutable, and who is able to know it? I the Lord search the heart and probe the loins* (Jer 17:9); *man sees the appearances, but the Lord sees the heart* (1 Sam 16:7)—asks, **how do you know me?** Here we can recognize Nathanael's humility, because, although he had been praised, he did not become elated, but held this praise of himself suspect. *My people, who call you blessed, they are deceiving you* (Isa 3:12).

325. Then he touches on matters in the past, saying, **before Philip called you, when you were under the fig tree, I saw you**.

First we have the statement of Christ;

second, the confession of Nathanael: **Nathanael answered him and said: Rabbi, you are the Son of God.**

326. As to the first, we should note that Nathanael might have had two misgivings about Christ. One, that Christ said this in order to win his friendship by flattery; the other, that Christ had learned what he knew from others. So, to remove Nathanael's suspicions and raise him to higher things, Christ reveals certain hidden matters that no one could know except in a divine way, that is, things that

ipsum Nathanaelem contigerant: et hoc est quod dicit *priusquam te Philippus vocaret, cum esses sub ficu, vidi te*. Ad litteram enim, sub arbore fici fuerat Nathanael, cum a Philippo vocaretur: quod Christus virtute divinitatis coniecerat, quia, ut dicitur Eccli. XXIII, v. 28, *oculi Domini multo lucidiores super solem*.

Mystice autem per ficum designatur peccatum: tum quia invenimus arborem fici maledictam folia sola habentem, et non fructum, Matth. XXI, 19 quod factum est in figuram peccati; tum quia Adam et Eva cum peccassent, de foliis ficus perizomata fecerunt. Dicit ergo *cum esses sub ficu*, idest, sub umbra peccati antequam ad gratiam vocatus esses, *ego vidi te*, scilicet oculo misericordiae: nam ipsa Dei praedestinatio oculo pietatis respicit praedestinatos sub peccatis viventes; Eph. I, 4: *elegit nos ante mundi constitutionem* etc. Et de isto oculo loquitur hic. *Vidi te*, praedestinando scilicet ab aeterno.

Vel, secundum Gregorium, *cum esses sub ficu*, idest sub umbra legis, *vidi te*. Hebr. X, v. 1: *umbram habens lex futurorum bonorum* etc.

327. Statim autem Nathanael ad hoc conversus, et virtutem divinitatis in Christo cognoscens, in vocem confessionis et laudem prorumpit, dicens *Rabbi, tu es Filius Dei*. Ubi tria considerat de Christo, scilicet plenitudinem scientiae, cum dicit *Rabbi*, quod interpretatur Magister; ac si dicat, perfectus es in scientia. Iam praesentiebat quod dicitur Matth. XXIII, 10: *magister vester unus est, Christus*.

Secundo excellentiam singularis gratiae, cum dicit *tu es Filius Dei*. Nam quod homo sit filius Dei per adoptionem, non est nisi gratiae; et etiam esse filium Dei per unionem, quod est proprium homini Christo, per gratiam est: quia non ex aliquibus praecedentibus meritis, sed per gratiam unionis homo ille est Filius Dei.

Tertio vero immensitatem potentiae, cum dicit *tu es Rex Israel*, idest expectatus ab Israel in regem et defensorem; Dan. VII, 14: *potestas eius, potestas aeterna* etc.

328. Sed circa hoc insurgit quaestio, secundum Chrysostomum. Cum Petrus, qui post multa miracula, post magnam doctrinam confessus fuit quod hic confitetur Nathanael de Christo, *tu es Filius Dei*, meruit beatificari, dicente Domino: *beatus es, Simon Bariona* etc., cur et Nathanael, qui simile dixerat ante visa miracula et perceptam doctrinam, beatificatus non fuit?

Et ad hoc respondet Chrysostomus, quod huius causa est, quia licet eadem verba Nathanael et Petrus protulerint, non tamen fuit eadem intentio utriusque. Petrus quidem confessus fuit, Christum esse Filium Dei verum per naturam, ut scilicet sic esset homo quod tamen esset verus Deus; hic autem confessus est esse Filium Dei

related only to Nathanael. He refers to these when he says, **before Philip called you, when you were under the fig tree, I saw you**. In the literal sense, this means that Nathanael was under a fig tree when he was called by Philip—which Christ knew by divine power, for *the eyes of the Lord are far brighter than the sun* (Sir 23:28).

In the mystical sense, the fig tree signifies sin: both because we find a fig tree, bearing only leaves but no fruit, being cursed, as a symbol of sin (Matt 11:19); and because Adam and Eve, after they had sinned, made clothes from fig leaves. So he says here, **when you were under the fig tree**, i.e., under the shadow of sin, before you were called to grace, *I saw you*, with the eye of mercy; for God's predestination looks upon the predestined, who are living under sin, with an eye of pity, for *he chose us before the foundation of the world* (Eph 1:4). And he speaks of this eye here: *I saw you*, by predestining you from eternity.

Or, the meaning is, according to Gregory: **when you were under the fig tree**, i.e., under the shadow of the law, *I say you*. *The law has only a shadow of the good things to come* (Heb 10:1).

327. Hearing this, Nathanael is immediately converted, and, seeing the power of the divinity in Christ, breaks out in words of conversion and praise, saying, **Rabbi, you are the Son of God**. Here he considers three things about Christ. First, the fullness of his knowledge, when he says, **Rabbi**, which is translated as Teacher. As if to say: you are perfect in knowledge. For he had already realized what is said: *you have one teacher, the Christ* (Matt 23:10).

Second, the excellence of his singular grace, when he says, **you are the Son of God**. For it is due to grace alone that one becomes a son of God by adoption. And it is also through grace that one is a son of God through union; and this is exclusive to the man Christ, because that man is the Son of God not due to any preceding merit, but through the grace of union.

Third, he considers the greatness of his power when he says, **you are the King of Israel**, i.e., awaited by Israel as its king and defender: *his power is everlasting* (Dan 7:14).

328. A question comes up at this point, according to Chrysostom. For since Peter, who after many miracles and much teaching, confessed what Nathanael confesses here about Christ, that is, you are **the Son of God**, merited a blessing, as the Lord said: *blessed are you, Simon Bar-Jona* (Matt 16:17), why not the same for Nathanael, who said the same thing before seeing any miracles or receiving any teaching?

Chrysostom answers that the reason for this is that even though Nathanael and Peter spoke the same words, the meaning of the two was not the same. For Peter acknowledged that Christ was the true Son of God by nature, i.e., he was man, and yet truly God; but Nathanael acknowledged that Christ was the Son of God by means of adoption, in the

per adoptionem, secundum illud Ps. LXXXI, 6: *ego dixi: dii estis, et Filii Excelsi omnes.* Et hoc patet per verba sequentia. Si enim intellexisset eum esse Filium Dei per naturam, non dixisset, **tu es Rex Israel** solum, sed totius mundi. Hoc etiam patet, quia ad fidem Petri Christus nihil addidit, quasi perfectam existentem, sed Ecclesiam dixit se fabricaturum esse in confessione illius. Sed Nathanaelem, quasi maiori parte suae confessionis deficiente, elevat ad maiora, scilicet ad cognitionem divinitatis suae.

329. Unde dixit **maius his videbis**.

Ubi notatur tertium, scilicet insinuatio futurorum, quasi dicat: quia dixi tibi praeterita, credis me esse Filium Dei per adoptionem et Regem Israel tantum, sed ducam te ad maiorem cognitionem, ut scilicet credas me Filium Dei naturalem et Regem omnium saeculorum. Et ideo sequitur **amen, amen dico vobis, videbitis caelum apertum, et angelos Dei ascendentes et descendentes super Filium hominis**, ubi, secundum Chrysostomum, vult probare Dominus quod sit verus Dei Filius, et Deus. angelorum enim est proprium ministrare, et subiici, Ps. CII: *benedicite Domino, omnes angeli eius, ministri eius, qui facitis voluntatem eius.* Cum ergo videbitis quod angeli administrabunt mihi, certum erit vobis quod sum verus Filius Dei. Hebr. c. I, 6: *cum introducit primogenitum in orbem terrae, dicit: et adorent eum omnes angeli Dei.*

330. Sed quando viderunt hoc apostoli?

Viderunt, inquam, in passione, quando angelus affuit illi, confortans eum, Lc. XXII, 43. Item in resurrectione, quando apostoli invenerunt duos angelos stantes supra sepulcrum. Similiter in ascensione, quando dixerunt apostolis, Act. I, 11: *viri Galilaei, quid admiramini aspicientes in caelum? Hic Iesus qui assumptus est a vobis in caelum, sic veniet quemadmodum vidistis eum euntem in caelum.*

331. Et quia de praeteritis ei vera iam dixerat, magis ei credibile fuit quod praenuntiat de futuro, cum dicit **videbitis**. Evidens enim argumentum est vera dicere de futuris qui de occultis praeteritis manifestaverat veritatem. Dicit autem **super Filium hominis angelos ascendentes et descendentes**, quia secundum carnem mortalem paulo minoratus est ab angelis: et intantum angeli ascendunt et descendunt super eum; sed secundum quod est Filius Dei, ipse super angelos est, ut dictum est.

332. Secundum Augustinum autem, pulchre in verbis praedictis suam divinitatem manifestat. Legitur enim Gen. XXVIII, 12 quod *Iacob vidit scalam, et angelos ascendentes et descendentes.* Et Iacob intelligens quid vidit, surgens unxit lapidem oleo, et deinde dixit: *vere Dominus est in loco isto.* Lapis iste Christus est, quem reprobaverunt aedificantes; et est unctus oleo invisibili

sense of, *I said: you are gods, and all of you the sons of the Most High* (Ps 81:6). This is clear from what Nathanael said next, for if he had understood that Christ was the Son of God by nature, he would not have said, *you are the King of Israel*, but of the whole world. It is also clear from the fact that Christ added nothing to the faith of Peter, since it was perfect, but stated that he would build the Church on that profession. But he raises Nathanael to greater things, since the greater part of his profession was deficient; to greater things, i.e., to a knowledge of his divinity.

329. And so he said, *you will see greater things than these*.

Here we have, third, an allusion to the future. As if to say: Because I have revealed the past to you, you believe that I am the Son of God only by adoption, and the King of Israel; but I will bring you to greater knowledge, so that you may believe that I am the natural Son of God, and the King of all ages. And accordingly he says, *amen, amen, I say to you, you will see the heavens opened and the angels of God ascending and descending on the Son of man*. By this, according to Chrysostom, the Lord wishes to prove that he is the true Son of God, and God. For the peculiar task of angels is to minister and be subject: *bless the Lord, all of you, his angels, his ministers, who do his will* (Ps 102:20). So when you see angels minister to me, you will be certain that I am the true Son of God. *When he leads his first-begotten into the world, he says: let all the angels of God adore him* (Heb 1:6).

330. When did the apostles see this?

They saw it, I say, during the passion, when an angel stood by to comfort Christ (Luke 22:43); again, at the resurrection, when the apostles found two angels who were standing over the tomb. Again, at the ascension, when the angels said to the apostles: *men of Galilee, why are you standing here looking up to heaven? This Jesus, who has been taken from you into heaven, will come in the same way as you have seen him going into heaven* (Acts 1:11).

331. Because Christ spoke the truth about the past, it was easier for Nathanael to believe what he foretells about the future, saying, *you will see*. For one who has revealed the truth about things hidden in the past, has an evident argument that what he is saying about the future is true. He says, *the angels of God ascending and descending on the Son of man*, because, in his mortal flesh, he was a little less than the angels; and from this point of view, angels ascend and descend upon him. But insofar as he is the Son of God, he is above the angels, as was said.

332. According to Augustine, Christ is here revealing his divinity in a beautiful way. For it is recorded that Jacob dreamed of a ladder, standing on the ground, with *the angels of God ascending and descending on it* (Gen 28:16). Then Jacob arose and poured oil on a stone and said, *truly, the Lord is in this place* (Gen 28:16). Now that stone is Christ, whom the builders rejected; and the invisible oil of

Spiritus Sancti; sed erigitur in titulum, quia futurus erat Ecclesiae fundamentum, ut dicitur I ad Cor. c. III, 11: *fundamentum aliud nemo potest ponere praeter id quod positum est.* angeli autem ascendunt et descendunt, inquantum ei adsunt obsequendo et ministrando. Dixit ergo: **amen, amen dico vobis, videbitis caelum apertum** etc., quasi dicat: quia vere Israelita es, attende ad id quod Israel vidit, ut scilicet credas me illum esse qui est significatus per unctum lapidem a Iacob: nam tu etiam videbis super ipsum angelos ascendentes et descendentes.

333. Vel angeli sunt praedicatores, secundum Augustinum, praedicantes Christum; Is. XVIII, 2: *ite veloces angeli ad gentem convulsam et dilaceratam*; qui quidem ascendunt per contemplationem, sicut Paulus ascenderat usque ad tertium caelum, ut dicitur II Cor. c. XII, 2, et descendunt per proximorum eruditionem **super Filium hominis**, idest ad honorem Christi: quia, ut dicitur II Cor. IV, v. 5: *non enim praedicamus nos ipsos, sed Iesum Christum dominum nostrum.* Sed ut ascendant et descendant, apertum est caelum, quia oportet quod gratia caelestis detur praedicatoribus, ut ascendant et descendant. Ps. LXVII, 9: *caeli distillaverunt* etc.; Apoc. IV, v. 1: *postea vidi caelum apertum* etc.

334. Ratio autem quare Nathanael non eligitur in apostolum post tantam fidei confessionem, ista est, quia Christus noluit quod mundi conversio ad fidem ascriberetur humanae sapientiae, sed solum potentiae Dei. Et ideo non voluit Nathanaelem in lege peritissimum, in apostolum eligere; sed simplices et indoctos elegit; ut dicitur I Cor. I, 26: *non multi sapientes . . . sed quae stulta sunt mundi elegit Deus.*

the Holy Spirit was poured on him. He is set up as a pillar, because he was to be the foundation of the Church: *no one can lay another foundation except that which has been laid* (1 Cor 3:11). The angels are ascending and descending inasmuch as they are ministering and serving before him. So he said, **amen, amen, I say to you, you will see the heavens opened**, as if to say: because you are truly an Israelite, give heed to what Israel saw, so that you many believe that I am the one signified by the stone anointed by Jacob, for you also will see angels ascending and descending upon him.

333. Or, the angels are preachers, proclaiming Christ according to Augustine: *go, swift angels, to a nation rent and torn to pieces* (Isa 18:2). They ascend through contemplation, just as Paul had ascended even to the third heaven (2 Cor 12:2); and they descend by instructing their neighbor, **on the Son of man**, i.e., for the honor of Christ, because *what we preach is not ourselves, but Jesus Christ our Lord* (2 Cor 4:5). In order that they might ascend and descend, the heavens were opened, because heavenly graces must be given to preachers if they are to ascend and descend. *The heavens broke at the presence of God* (Ps 67:9); *I saw the heavens open* (Rev 4:1).

334. Now the reason why Nathanael was not chosen to be an apostle after such a profession of faith is that Christ did not want the conversion of the world to the faith to be attributed to human wisdom, but solely to the power of God. And so he did not choose Nathanael as an apostle, since he was very learned in the law; he rather chose simple and uneducated men. *Not many of you are learned*, and *God chose the simple of the world* (1 Cor 1:26).

CHAPTER 2

Lecture 1

2:1 Et die tertia nuptiae factae sunt in Cana Galilaeae. Et erat mater Iesu ibi. [n. 336]

2:2 Vocatus est autem Iesus, et discipuli eius ad nuptias. [n. 341]

2:3 Et deficiente vino, dixit mater Iesu ad eum: vinum non habent. [n. 344]

2:4 Dixit ei Iesus: quid mihi et tibi est, mulier? Nondum venit hora mea. [n. 348]

2:5 Dixit mater eius ministris: quodcumque dixerit vobis, facite. [n. 354]

2:6 Erant autem ibi lapideae hydriae sex positae secundum purificationem Iudaeorum, capientes singulae metretas binas, vel ternas. [n. 356]

2:7 Dixit eis Iesus: implete hydrias aqua. Et impleverunt eas usque ad summum. [n. 358]

2:8 Et dixit eis Iesus: haurite nunc, et ferte architriclino. Et tulerunt. [n. 360]

2:9 Ut autem gustavit architriclinus aquam vinum factam, et non sciebat unde esset (ministri autem sciebant, qui hauserant aquam), vocat sponsum architriclinus; [n. 362]

2:10 et dicit ei: omnis homo primum bonum vinum ponit, et cum inebriati fuerint, tunc id quod deterius est; tu autem servasti bonum vinum usque adhuc. [n. 362]

2:11 Hoc fecit initium signorum Iesus in Cana Galilaeae; et manifestavit gloriam suam; et crediderunt in eum discipuli eius. [n. 364]

2:1 Καὶ τῇ ἡμέρᾳ τῇ τρίτῃ γάμος ἐγένετο ἐν Κανὰ τῆς Γαλιλαίας, καὶ ἦν ἡ μήτηρ τοῦ Ἰησοῦ ἐκεῖ·

2:2 ἐκλήθη δὲ καὶ ὁ Ἰησοῦς καὶ οἱ μαθηταὶ αὐτοῦ εἰς τὸν γάμον.

2:3 καὶ ὑστερήσαντος οἴνου λέγει ἡ μήτηρ τοῦ Ἰησοῦ πρὸς αὐτόν· οἶνον οὐκ ἔχουσιν.

2:4 [καὶ] λέγει αὐτῇ ὁ Ἰησοῦς· τί ἐμοὶ καὶ σοί, γύναι; οὔπω ἥκει ἡ ὥρα μου.

2:5 λέγει ἡ μήτηρ αὐτοῦ τοῖς διακόνοις· ὅ τι ἂν λέγῃ ὑμῖν ποιήσατε.

2:6 ἦσαν δὲ ἐκεῖ λίθιναι ὑδρίαι ἓξ κατὰ τὸν καθαρισμὸν τῶν Ἰουδαίων κείμεναι, χωροῦσαι ἀνὰ μετρητὰς δύο ἢ τρεῖς.

2:7 λέγει αὐτοῖς ὁ Ἰησοῦς· γεμίσατε τὰς ὑδρίας ὕδατος. καὶ ἐγέμισαν αὐτὰς ἕως ἄνω.

2:8 καὶ λέγει αὐτοῖς· ἀντλήσατε νῦν καὶ φέρετε τῷ ἀρχιτρικλίνῳ· οἱ δὲ ἤνεγκαν.

2:9 ὡς δὲ ἐγεύσατο ὁ ἀρχιτρίκλινος τὸ ὕδωρ οἶνον γεγενημένον καὶ οὐκ ᾔδει πόθεν ἐστίν, οἱ δὲ διάκονοι ᾔδεισαν οἱ ἠντληκότες τὸ ὕδωρ, φωνεῖ τὸν νυμφίον ὁ ἀρχιτρίκλινος

2:10 καὶ λέγει αὐτῷ· πᾶς ἄνθρωπος πρῶτον τὸν καλὸν οἶνον τίθησιν καὶ ὅταν μεθυσθῶσιν τὸν ἐλάσσω· σὺ τετήρηκας τὸν καλὸν οἶνον ἕως ἄρτι.

2:11 Ταύτην ἐποίησεν ἀρχὴν τῶν σημείων ὁ Ἰησοῦς ἐν Κανὰ τῆς Γαλιλαίας καὶ ἐφανέρωσεν τὴν δόξαν αὐτοῦ, καὶ ἐπίστευσαν εἰς αὐτὸν οἱ μαθηταὶ αὐτοῦ.

2:1 And on the third day, there was a marriage in Cana of Galilee, and the mother of Jesus was there. [n. 336]

2:2 And Jesus also was invited, and his disciples, to the marriage. [n. 341]

2:3 And when the wine ran out, the mother of Jesus said to him: they have no wine. [n. 344]

2:4 And Jesus said to her: woman, what is that to me and to you? My hour has not yet come. [n. 348]

2:5 His mother said to the waiters: do whatever he tells you. [n. 354]

2:6 Now there were six stone waterpots nearby, according to the purification of the Jews, containing two or three measures apiece. [n. 356]

2:7 Jesus said to them: fill the waterpots with water. And they filled them all the way to the brim. [n. 358]

2:8 And Jesus said to them: draw out now, and carry to the head waiter. And they carried it. [n. 360]

2:9 And when the head waiter had tasted the water made wine and did not know where it was from (but the waiters, who had drawn the water, knew), the head waiter called the bridegroom, [n. 362]

2:10 and he said to him: every man at first sets forth the good wine, and when men have drunk well, then that which is worse. But you have kept the good wine until now. [n. 362]

2:11 Jesus did this beginning of miracles in Cana of Galilee and manifested his glory, and his disciples believed in him. [n. 364]

---

335. Supra Evangelista ostendit dignitatem Verbi incarnati, et evidentiam eius multipliciter; hic consequenter

335. Above, the Evangelist showed the dignity of the incarnate Word and gave various evidence for it. Now he

incipit determinare de effectibus et operibus quibus manifestata est mundo divinitas Verbi incarnati, et

primo narrat ea quae Christus fecit in mundo vivendo, ad manifestationem suae divinitatis;

secundo quomodo Christus suam divinitatem monstravit moriendo; et hoc a XII cap. et ultra.

Circa primum duo facit:

primo enim ostendit Christi divinitatem quantum ad dominium quod habuit supra naturam;

secundo quantum ad effectus gratiae, et hoc in III cap. ibi *erat homo ex Pharisaeis Nicodemus nomine* etc.

Dominium autem Christi super naturam proponitur nobis per hoc quod naturam mutavit: quae quidem mutatio facta est a Christo in signum

primo discipulis ad confirmandum;

secundo vero turbis ad credendum, ibi *post hoc descendit Capharnaum*.

Mutatio autem naturae ad confirmandos discipulos in nuptiis facta est, in quibus convertit aquam in vinum; et hoc est quod dicit *nuptiae factae sunt in Cana Galilaeae*: ubi

primo describuntur nuptiae;

secundo illi qui nuptiis interfuerunt, ibi *erat autem mater Iesu*;

tertio describitur ipsum miraculum patratum, ibi *et deficiente vino* etc.

336. Describit autem nuptias primo quidem quantum ad tempus; unde dicit *et die tertia nuptiae factae sunt*, scilicet postquam praedicta de vocatione discipulorum fecerat. Postquam enim manifestatus fuerat testimonio Ioannis, voluit etiam seipsum manifestare.

Secundo vero, quantum ad locum; unde dicit *in Cana Galilaeae*. Galilaea namque provincia est, Cana viculus quidam in ipsa provincia.

337. Quantum autem ad litteram pertinet, sciendum est, quod circa tempus praedicationis Christi est duplex opinio. Quidam namque dicunt, quod a baptismate Christi usque ad passionem eius, fuerint duo anni et dimidius. Et secundum hos, hoc quod hic legitur de nuptiis, eodem anno factum est quo Christus baptizatus est. Sed his contrariatur sententia et consuetudo Ecclesiae: nam in festo Epiphaniae trium miraculorum commemoratio fit, scilicet adorationis magorum, quae fuit primo anno nativitatis Dominicae; et baptismi Christi, quo baptizatus est eodem die, revolutis triginta annis; et de nuptiis, quae sunt factae eodem die, revoluto anno. Ex quo sequitur quod ad minus unus annus elapsus fuit a baptismo usque ad nuptias.

In quo quidem anno nil aliud legitur Dominus fecisse nisi quod dicitur Matth. IV de ieiunio in deserto, et de tentatione a diabolo, et ea quae hic Ioannes refert

begins to relate the effects and actions by which the divinity of the incarnate Word was made known to the world.

First, he tells the things Christ did, while living in the world, that show his divinity.

Second, he tells how Christ showed his divinity while dying; and this from chapter twelve on.

As to the first he does two things.

First, he shows the divinity of Christ in relation to the power he had over nature.

Second, in relation to the effects of grace, and this from chapter three on, at *and there was a man of the Pharisees, named Nicodemus* (John 3:1).

Christ's power over nature is pointed out to us by the fact that he changed a nature. And this change was accomplished by Christ as a sign:

first, to his disciples, to strengthen them;

second, to the people, to lead them to believe, at *after this he went down to Capernaum* (John 2:12).

This transformation of a nature, in order to strengthen the disciples, was accomplished at a marriage, when he turned water into wine, at *there was a marriage in Cana of Galilee*.

First, the marriage is described.

Second, those present, at *and the mother of Jesus was there*.

Third, the miracle performed by Christ, at *and when the wine ran out*.

336. In describing the marriage, the time is first mentioned. Hence he says *and on the third day, there was a marriage in Cana of Galilee*, i.e., after the calling of the disciples mentioned earlier. For, after being made known by the testimony of John, Christ also wanted to make himself known.

Second, the place is mentioned; hence he says, *in Cana of Galilee*. Galilee is a province, and Cana a small village located in that province.

337. As far as the literal meaning is concerned, we should note that there are two opinions about the time of Christ's preaching. Some say that there were two and a half years from Christ's baptism until his death. According to them, the events at this wedding took place in the same year that Christ was baptized. However, both the teaching and practice of the Church are opposed to this. For three miracles are commemorated on the feast of the Epiphany: the adoration of the Magi, which took place in the first year of the Lord's birth; second, the baptism of Christ, which implies that he was baptized on the same day thirty years later; third, this marriage, which took place on the same day one year later. It follows from this that at least one year elapsed between his baptism and this marriage.

In that year the only things recorded to have been done by the Lord are found in the sixth chapter of Matthew: the fasting in the desert, and the temptation by the devil;

de testimonio Baptistae et conversione discipulorum. A nuptiis autem coepit publice praedicare et miracula facere usque ad passionem, ita quod duobus annis cum dimidio publice praedicavit.

338. Mystice autem per nuptias intelligitur coniunctio Christi et Ecclesiae, quia, ut dicit Apostolus Eph. V, 32, *sacramentum hoc magnum est, dico autem in Christo et in Ecclesia.*

Et illud quidem matrimonium initiatum fuit in utero Virginali, quando Deus Pater Filio humanam naturam univit in unitate personae, unde huius coniunctionis thalamus fuit uterus Virginalis; Ps. XVIII, 6: *in sole posuit tabernaculum suum.* De istis nuptiis dicitur Matth. XXII, 2: *simile est regnum caelorum homini regi, qui fecit nuptias Filio suo,* tunc scilicet quando Deus Pater humanam naturam Verbo suo copulavit in utero virginali. Publicatum autem fuit, quando Ecclesia sibi per fidem coniuncta est; Oseae II, 20: *sponsabo te mihi in fide* etc. De istis nuptiis dicitur Apoc. XIX, 9: *beati qui ad caenam nuptiarum agni vocati sunt.* Consummatum autem erit, quando sponsa, idest Ecclesia, introducetur in thalamum sponsi, in caelestem scilicet gloriam.

Nec vacat a mysterio quod die tertio nuptiae factae sunt. Primus namque dies est tempus legis naturae; secundus tempus legis scriptae; tertius vero dies tempus gratiae, in quo Dominus incarnatus nuptias celebravit; Oseae VI, 3: *vivificabit nos post duos dies: in die tertia suscitabit nos.*

Locus autem congruit mysterio: **Cana** enim interpretatur *zelus*; **Galilaea** vero *transmigratio.* In zelo ergo transmigrationis hae nuptiae celebrantur, ut denuntiet eos maxime Christi coniunctione dignos existere qui zelo piae devotionis ferventes transmigrant de statu culpae ad gratiam Ecclesiae, Eccli. XXIV, 26: *transite ad me, omnes qui concupiscitis me* etc., et de morte ad vitam, idest de statu mortalitatis et miseriae, ad statum immortalitatis et gloriae; Apoc. XXI, 5: *ecce nova facio omnia.*

339. Consequenter cum dicit **erat autem mater Iesu ibi,** describuntur personae invitatae: ubi agitur de tribus, scilicet de matre, de Iesu, et de discipulis.

340. De matre quidem, cum dicit **et erat mater Iesu ibi.** Quae quidem praemittitur, ut ostendatur quod Iesus adhuc ignotus erat, et non vocatus ad nuptias sicut insignis persona, sed ex quadam familiaritate, tamquam notus, et unus aliorum: sicut enim vocaverunt matrem, ita et filium.

Vel forte prius invitatur mater, quia ambigebant de Iesu, an invitatus venturus esset ad nuptias propter summam religiositatem, quam videbant in eo, et quia non viderunt eum se immiscuisse conviviis. Et ideo puto quod primo consuluerunt matrem, an Iesus esset vocandus. Et

and what John tells us in this Gospel of the testimony by the Baptist and the conversion of the disciples. After this wedding, Christ began to preach publicly and to perform miracles up to the time of his passion, so that he preached publicly for two and a half years.

338. In the mystical sense, marriage signifies the union of Christ with his Church, because as the Apostle says: *this is a great mystery: I am speaking of Christ and his Church* (Eph 5:32).

And this marriage was begun in the womb of the Virgin, when God the Father united a human nature to his Son in a unity of person. So, the chamber of this union was the womb of the Virgin: *he established a chamber for the sun* (Ps 18:6). Of this marriage it is said: *the kingdom of heaven is like a king who married his son* (Matt 22:2), that is, when God the Father joined a human nature to his Word in the womb of the Virgin. It was made public when the Church was joined to him by faith: *I will bind you to myself in faith* (Hos 2:20). We read of this marriage: *blessed are they who are called to the marriage supper of the Lamb* (Rev 19:9). It will be consummated when the bride, i.e., the Church, is led into the resting place of the groom, i.e., into the glory of heaven.

The fact that this marriage took place on the third day is not without it own mystery. For the first day is the time of the law of nature; the second day is the time of the written law. But the third day is the time of grace, when the incarnate Lord celebrated the marriage: *he will revive us after two days: on the third day he will raise us up* (Hos 6:3).

The place too is appropriate. For **Cana** means *zeal* and **Galilee** means *passage.* So this marriage was celebrated in the zeal of a passage, to suggest that those persons are most worthy of union with Christ who, burning with the zeal of a conscientious devotion, pass over from the state of guilt to the grace of the Church. *Pass over to me, all who desire me* (Sir 24:26). And they pass from death to life, i.e., from the state of mortality and misery to the state of immortality and glory: *I make all things new* (Rev 21:5).

339. Then the persons invited are described: **the mother of Jesus was there.** Mention is made of three: the mother of Jesus, Jesus himself, and the disciples.

340. The mother of Jesus is mentioned when he says, **the mother of Jesus was there.** She is mentioned first to indicate that Jesus was still unknown and not invited to the wedding as a famous person, but merely as one acquaintance among others; for as they invited the mother, so also her son.

Or, perhaps his mother is invited first because they were uncertain whether Jesus would come to a wedding if invited, because of the unusual piety they noticed in him and because they had not seen him at other social gatherings. So I think that they first asked his mother whether Jesus

ideo signanter dixit Evangelista primo matrem adesse iam in nuptiis, et Iesum postmodum fuisse vocatum.

341. Et hoc est quod sequitur *vocatus est Iesus*. Voluit autem Christus nuptiis interesse primo quidem ut daret nobis humilitatis exemplum: neque enim ad dignitatem suam respiciebat, sed *quomodo dignatus est formam servi accipere, ita non dedignatus est ad nuptias venire servorum*, ut dicit Chrysostomus. Et ideo Augustinus: *erubescat homo esse superbus, quoniam factus est humilis Deus*. Nam inter cetera humilia quae fecit Filius Virginis, venit ad nuptias, qui eas, cum esset apud Patrem, instituit in Paradiso. Et de hoc exemplo dicitur, Matth. XI, v. 29: *discite a me quia mitis sum et humilis corde*.

Secundo vero, ut errorem quorumdam excluderet, qui nuptias damnant, quia, ut dicit Beda *si thoro immaculato, et nuptiis debita castitate celebratis, culpa inesset, nequaquam Dominus ad has venire voluisset*. Quia ergo ad nuptias venit, insinuat quod sit damnabilis eorum perfidia qui nuptiis detrahunt. I Cor. VII, 36: *non peccat mulier, si nubat*.

342. De discipulis vero agitur, cum dicit *et discipuli eius*.

343. Mystice autem in nuptiis spiritualibus est mater Iesu, Virgo scilicet Beata, sicut nuptiarum consiliatrix, quia per eius intercessionem coniungitur Christo per gratiam; Eccli. XXIV, 25: *in me omnis spes vitae et virtutis*. Christus autem, sicut verus animae sponsus, ut dicitur infra III, 29: *qui habet sponsam, sponsus est*. Discipuli vero ut paranymphi, quasi coniungentes Ecclesiam Christo, de quo uno dicebatur II Cor. XI, 2: *despondi vos uni viro virginem castam exhibere Christo*.

344. Et quia in istis nuptiis materialibus aliquid de miraculo pertinet ad matrem, aliquid ad Christum et aliquid ad discipulos, ideo consequenter cum dicit *et deficiente vino* etc. ostendit quid pertineat ad matrem, quid ad Christum et quid ad discipulos.

Ad matrem quidem pertinet miraculi procuratio;

ad Christum autem miraculi consummatio, et hoc ibi *erant ibi lapideae hydriae sex* etc.;

ad discipulos vero miraculi contestatio, ibi *hoc fecit initium signorum Iesus*.

Gessit ergo, quantum ad primum, mater Christi, mediatricis personam; et ideo duo facit:

primo enim interpellat ad Filium;

secundo erudit ministros, ibi *et dicit mater eius ministris* etc.

Circa primum quidem duo ponuntur.

Primo matris interpellatio;

secundo Filii responsio, ibi *dixit ei Iesus: quid mihi et tibi est, mulier?*

should be invited. That is why the Evangelist expressly said first that his mother was at the wedding, and that later Jesus was invited.

341. And this is what comes next: *and Jesus also was invited*. Christ decided to attend this wedding, first of all, to give us an example of humility. For he did not look to his own dignity, but *just as he condescended to accept the form of a servant, so he did not hesitate to come to the marriage of servants*, as Chrysostom says. And as Augustine says: *let man blush to be proud, for God became humble*. For among his other acts of humility, the Son of the Virgin came to a marriage, which he had already instituted in paradise when he was with his Father. Of this example it is said: *learn from me, for I am gentle and humble of heart* (Matt 11:29).

He came, second, to reject the error of those who condemn marriage, for as Bede says: *if there were sin in a holy marriage bed and in a marriage carried out with due purity, the Lord would not have come to the marriage*. But because he did come, he implies that the baseness of those who denounce marriage deserves to be condemned. *If she marries, it is not a sin* (1 Cor 7:36).

342. The disciples are mentioned when he says, *and his disciples*.

343. In its mystical meaning, the mother of Jesus, the Blessed Virgin, is present in spiritual marriages as the one who arranges the marriage, because it is through her intercession that one is joined to Christ through grace: *in me is every hope of life and of strength* (Sir 24:25). Christ is present as the true groom of the soul, as is said: *he who has the bride is the bridegroom* (John 3:29). The disciples are the groomsmen uniting the Church to Christ, the one of whom it is said: *I betrothed you to one husband, to present you as a chaste virgin to Christ* (2 Cor 11:2).

344. At this physical marriage some role in the miracle belongs to the mother of Christ, some to Christ, and some to the disciples. When he says, *and when the wine ran out*, he indicates the part of each.

The role of Christ's mother was to superintend the miracle;

the role of Christ to perform it, at *there were six stone waterpots nearby*;

and the disciples were to bear witness to it, at *Jesus did this beginning of miracles*.

As to the first, Christ's mother assumed the role of a mediatrix. Hence she does two things.

First, she intercedes with her Son.

In the second place, she instructs the servants, at *his mother said to the waiters*.

As to the first, two things are mentioned.

First, his mother's intercession;

second, the answer of her Son, at *and Jesus said to her: woman, what is that to me and to you?*

345. In matre autem interpellante, primo quidem nota pietatem et misericordiam. Ad misericordiam enim pertinet ut quis defectum alterius reputet quasi suum: misericors enim dicitur, quasi miserum habens cor super miseria alterius; II Cor. XI, 29: *quis infirmatur, et ego non infirmor?* Quia ergo Virgo Beata misericordia plena erat, defectus aliorum sublevare volebat; et ideo dicit *deficiente vino, dicit mater Iesu ad eum*.

Secundo reverentiam eius ad Christum: ex reverentia enim quam ad Deum habemus, sufficit nobis ei tantum defectus nostros exponere, secundum illud Ps. XXXVII, 10: *Domine, ante te omne desiderium meum*. Qualiter autem nobis Deus subveniat, non est nostrum inquirere; quia, sicut dicitur Rom. VIII, v. 26, *nam quid oremus, sicut oportet, nescimus*. Et ideo mater eius defectum aliorum simpliciter exposuit, dicens *vinum non habent*.

Tertio, Virginis sollicitudinem et diligentiam: quia usque ad extremam necessitatem non distulit, sed *deficiente vino*, idest dum esset in deficiendo, iuxta illud quod dicitur in Ps. IX, 10 de Deo: *adiutor in opportunitatibus, in tribulatione*.

346. Sed quaerit Chrysostomus: quare ante non incitavit Christum ad miracula? Nam de virtute eius erat instructa per angelum, et confirmata per multa quae viderat circa ipsum fieri, quae omnia conservabat, conferens in corde suo, ut dicitur Lc. II, 51.

Cuius ratio est, quia antea ut unus aliorum conversabatur: unde quia non viderat tempus opportunum, hoc facere distulit. Nunc vero post Ioannis contestationem et post discipulorum conversionem, confidenter Christum ad miracula facienda provocat, gerens in hoc figuram synagogae, quae est mater Christi: nam familiare est Iudaeis miracula requirere; I Cor. I, 22: *Iudaei signa petunt*.

347. Dicit ergo ei *vinum non habent*.

Ubi sciendum est, quod ante incarnationem Christi, triplex vinum deficiebat, scilicet iustitiae, sapientiae et caritatis, seu gratiae. Vinum enim mordicat, et quantum ad hoc iustitia dicitur vinum. Lc. X, 34, Samaritanus vinum et oleum apposuit vulneribus sauciati, idest cum dulcedine misericordiae severitatem iustitiae; Ps. LIX, 5: *potasti nos vino compunctionis*. Vinum etiam laetificat cor, iuxta illud Ps. CIII, 15, *vinum laetificat cor hominis*, et quantum ad hoc dicitur vinum sapientia, cuius meditatio maxime laetificat; Sap. VIII, 16: *non habet amaritudinem convictus illius*. Vinum similiter inebriat, Cant. V, v. 1: *bibite, amici, et inebriamini, carissimi*, et secundum hoc caritas dicitur vinum, Cant. c. V, 1, *bibi vinum meum cum lacte meo*. Et dicitur caritas etiam vinum ratione fervoris; Zach. IX, 17: *vinum germinans virgines*.

345. In Mary's intercession, note first her kindness and mercy. For it is a quality of mercy to regard another's distress as one's own, because to be merciful is to have a heart distressed at the distress of another: *who is weak, and I am not weak?* (2 Cor 11:29). And so because the Blessed Virgin was full of mercy, she desired to relieve the distress of others. So he says, *and when the wine ran out, the mother of Jesus said to him*.

Note, second, her reverence for Christ: for because of the reverence we have for God it is sufficient for us merely to express our needs: *Lord, all my desires are known by you* (Ps 37:10). But it is not our business to wonder about the way in which God will help us, for as it is said: *we do not know what we should pray for as we ought* (Rom 8:26). And so his mother merely told him of their need, saying, *they have no wine*.

Third, note the Virgin's concern and care. For she did not wait until they were in extreme need, but *when the wine ran out*, that is, immediately. This is similar to what is said of God: *a helper in times of trouble* (Ps 9:10).

346. Chrysostom asks: why did Mary never encourage Christ to perform any miracles before this time? For she had been told of his power by the angel, whose work had been confirmed by the many things she had seen happening in his regard, all of which she remembered, thinking them over in her heart (Luke 2:51).

The reason is that before this time he lived like any other person. So, because the time was not appropriate, she put off asking him. But now, after John's witness to him and after the conversion of his disciples, she trustingly prompted Christ to perform miracles. In this she was true to the symbol of the synagogue, which is the mother of Christ: for it was customary for the Jews to require miracles: *the Jews require signs* (1 Cor 1:22).

347. She says to him, *they have no wine*.

Here we should note that before the incarnation of Christ three wines were running out: the wine of justice, of wisdom, and of charity or grace. Wine stings, and in this respect it is a symbol of justice. The Samaritan poured wine and oil into the wounds of the injured man, that is, he mingled the severity of justice with the sweetness of mercy. *You have made us drink the wine of sorrow* (Ps 59:5). But wine also delights the heart, *wine cheers the heart of man* (Ps 103:15). And in this respect wine is a symbol of wisdom, the meditation of which is enjoyable in the highest degree: *her companionship has no bitterness* (Wis 8:16). Further, wine intoxicates: *drink, friends, and be intoxicated, my dearly beloved* (Song 5:1). And in this respect wine is a symbol of charity: *I have drunk my wine with my milk* (Song 5:1). It is also a symbol of charity because of charity's fervor: *wine makes the virgins flourish* (Zech 9:17).

Et quidem iustitiae vinum deficiebat in veteri lege; in qua iustitia imperfecta erat. Sed Christus eam perfecit; Matth. V, 20: *nisi abundaverit iustitia vestra plusquam Scribarum et Pharisaeorum, non intrabitis in regnum caelorum*. Deficiebat etiam vinum sapientiae, quae erat occulta et figuralis, quia, ut dicitur I Cor. X, 11, *omnia in figura contingebant illis*. Sed Christus eam manifestavit; Matth. c. VII, 29: *erat enim docens eos, sicut potestatem habens*. Sed et vinum caritatis deficiebat ibi: quia acceperant spiritum servitutis tantum in timore. Sed Christus aquam timoris convertit in vinum caritatis, quando dedit *spiritum adoptionis filiorum, in quo clamamus, Abba Pater*, ut dicitur Rom. VIII, 15, et quando *caritas Dei diffusa est in cordibus nostris*, ut dicitur Rom. V, 5.

348. Consequenter cum dicit **dixit ei Iesus** etc. ponitur responsio Christi: ex qua quidem responsione triplicis haeresis occasio sumpta est.

349. Manichaei namque dicunt Christum non habuisse verum corpus, sed phantasticum. Valentinus asserit Christum attulisse corpus caeleste, dicens quod, quantum ad corpus, Christus nihil pertinet ad Virginem. Et huius erroris fulcimentum sumit per hoc quod dicit ei Iesus. **Quid mihi et tibi est, mulier?** Quasi dicat: nihil a te suscepi.

Sed hoc est contra auctoritatem Sacrae Scripturae: dicit enim Apostolus, Gal. IV, 4: *misit Deus Filium suum, factum ex muliere*: non enim posset dici ex ea factus, nisi ex ea aliquid sumpsisset. Arguit praeterea contra eos Augustinus, dicens: *quomodo scis, quod Dominus dixit quid mihi et tibi? Respondes, quia Ioannes Evangelista hoc narrat. Sed ipse etiam Evangelista dicit de Virgine quod erat mater eius. Si ergo credis Evangelistae in eo quod narrat Iesum dixisse matri: quid mihi et tibi est, mulier? Credas etiam in hoc ei quod dicit: et erat mater Iesu ibi*.

350. Ebion autem dicens ex virili semine Christum conceptum, et Elvidius, qui dicit quod Virgo post partum non permansit virgo, sumpserunt erroris fulcimentum ex hoc quod dicit **mulier**, quod videtur corruptionem importare.

Sed hoc est falsum, quia 'mulier' in Sacra Scriptura quandoque importat solum sexum femineum, secundum illud Gal. IV, 4: *factum ex muliere* etc. Et hoc patet etiam per hoc quod Adam ad Deum loquens de Eva, dixit: *mulier quam dedisti mihi sociam, dedit mihi de ligno, et comedi*, Gen. III, 12. Constat enim tunc Evam adhuc virginem fuisse, cum adhuc esset in Paradiso, ubi non cognoverat eam. Unde hoc quod hic dicitur **mulier**, non importat corruptionem, sed determinat sexum.

351. Sumpserunt etiam Priscillianistae erroris occasionem ex hoc quod dixit **nondum venit hora mea**, dicentes, omnia ex fato accidere, et facta hominum certis

The wine of justice was indeed running out in the old law, in which justice was imperfect. But Christ brought it to perfection: *unless your justice is greater than that of the scribes and of the Pharisees, you will not enter into the kingdom of heaven* (Matt 5:20). The wine of wisdom was also running out, for it was hidden and symbolic, as it says: *all these things happened to them in symbol* (1 Cor 10:11). But Christ plainly brought wisdom to light: *he was teaching them as one having authority* (Matt 7:29). The wine of charity was also running out, because they had received a spirit of serving only in fear. But Christ converted the water of fear into the wine of charity when he gave *the spirit of adoption as sons, by which we cry: 'Abba, Father'* (Rom 8:15), and when *the charity of God was poured out into our hearts* (Rom 5:5).

348. Then when he says, **Jesus said to her: woman** the answer of Christ is given. This answer has been the occasion for three heresies.

349. The Manicheans claim that Christ had only an imaginary body, not a real one. Valentinus maintained that Christ assumed a celestial body and that, as far as his body was concerned, Christ was not related to the Virgin at all. The source of this error was that he understood, **woman, what is that to me and to you**? as if it meant: I have received nothing from you.

But this is contrary to the authority of Sacred Scripture. For the Apostle says: *God sent his Son, made from a woman* (Gal 4:4). Now Christ could not be said to have been made from her, unless he had taken something from her. Further, Augustine argues against them: *how do you know that our Lord said, what does that have to do with me and you? You reply that it is because John says so. But he also says that the Virgin was the mother of Christ. So, if you believe the Evangelist when he states that Jesus said this to his mother, you should also believe him when he says, and the mother of Jesus was there*.

350. Then there was Ebion who said that Christ was conceived from a man's seed, and Elvidius, who said that the Virgin did not remain a virgin after childbirth. They were deceived by the fact that he said, **woman**, which seems to imply the loss of virginity.

But this is false, for in Sacred Scripture the word 'woman' sometimes refers merely to the female sex, as it does in *made from a woman* (Gal 4:4). This is obvious also by the fact that Adam, speaking to God about Eve, said: *the woman whom you gave me as a companion, gave me fruit from the tree, and I ate it* (Gen 3:12); for Eve was still a virgin in Paradise, where Adam had not known her. Hence the fact that the mother of Christ is here called **woman** in this Gospel does not imply a loss of virginity, but refers to her sex.

351. The Priscillianists, however, erred by misunderstanding the words of Christ, **my hour has not yet come**. They claimed that all things happen by fate, and that the actions of men, including those of Christ, are subject to

horis esse subiecta, et etiam Christi: unde propter hoc dixit *nondum venit hora mea*.

Sed hoc est falsum de quolibet homine. Cum enim homo liberam electionem habeat, libera autem electio competat ei ex hoc quod rationem et voluntatem habet, quae quidem sunt immaterialia: manifestum est quod homo quantum ad electionem nulli corpori subiicitur, sed potius dominatur. Immaterialia enim nobiliora sunt materialibus, et ideo dicit Philosophus, quod sapiens dominatur astris. Praeterea, hoc multo minus locum habet in Christo, qui est Dominus et conditor siderum. Unde per hoc quod dixit *nondum venit hora mea*, intelligitur hora passionis, sibi, non ex necessitate, sed secundum divinam providentiam determinata. Contra eos etiam est quod dicitur Eccli. XXXIII, 7: *quare dies diem superat?* Respondet: *a Domini scientia separati sunt*; idest, divina providentia distincti sunt adinvicem, non a casu.

352. His ergo exclusis, investigemus huius Dominicae responsionis causam. *Quid mihi et tibi est, mulier?*

Et quidem, secundum Augustinum, in ipso sunt duae naturae, divina scilicet et humana; et quamvis idem Christus fit in utraque natura, ea tamen quae conveniunt ei secundum humanam naturam, distincta sunt ab his quae conveniunt ei secundum divinam. Miracula autem facere competit ei secundum divinam naturam, quam accepit a Patre; pati vero secundum humanam, quam accepit a matre. Et ideo matri exigenti miraculum, respondit dicens *quid mihi et tibi est, mulier?* Ac si dicat: illud quod in me facit miracula, non accepi a te, sed illud unde patior; idest secundum quod competit mihi pati, scilicet humanam naturam, a te accepi; et ideo tunc te cognoscam, cum ipsa infirmitas pendebit in cruce. Et ideo subdit *nondum venit hora mea*; quasi dicat: cum venerit hora passionis, ibi te matrem recognoscam. Unde et in cruce pendens matrem discipulo commendavit.

353. Secundum Chrysostomum vero, aliter exponitur.

Dicitur enim quod Beata Virgo fervens zelo honoris Filii, voluit quod statim antequam opportunum esset, Christus miracula faceret; et ideo Christus, matre haud dubio sapientior, eam repressit. Noluit enim prius facere miraculum, quam sciretur defectus: quia ex hoc fuisset minus notum et minus credibile, et ideo dicit *quid mihi et tibi est, mulier?* Quasi dicat. Quid me molestas? *Nondum venit hora mea*; idest, nondum cognitus sum his qui adsunt. Sed neque defectum vini sentiunt; sine primo hoc sentire, quia cum necessitatem cognoverint, maius reputabunt beneficium quod recipient.

predetermined times. And that is why, according to them, Christ said, *my hour has not yet come*.

But this is false for any man. For since man has free choice, and this is because he has reason and will, both of which are spiritual, then obviously, as far as choice is concerned, man, so far from being subject to bodies, is really their master. For spiritual things are superior to material things, so much so that the Philosopher says that the wise man is master of the stars. Further, their heresy is even less true of Christ, who is the Lord and Creator of the stars. Thus when he says, *my hour has not yet come*, he is referring to the time of his passion, which was fixed for him, not by necessity, according to divine providence. What is said is also contrary to their opinion: *why is one day better than another?* (Sir 33:7). The answer is: *they have been differentiated by the knowledge of the Lord*, i.e., they were differentiated from one another not by chance, but by God's providence.

352. Since we have eliminated the above opinions, let us look for the reason why our Lord answered, *woman, what is that to me and to you?*

For Augustine, Christ has two natures, the divine and the human. And although the same Christ exists in each, nevertheless things appropriate to him according to his human nature are distinct from what is appropriate to him according to his divine nature. Now to perform miracles is appropriate to him according to his divine nature, which he received from the Father; while to suffer is according to his human nature, which he received from his mother. So when his mother requests this miracle, he answers, *woman, what is that to me and to you?* as if saying: I did not receive from you that in me which enables me to perform miracles, but that which enables me to suffer, which is to say: that which makes it appropriate for me to suffer, i.e., I have received a human nature from you. And so I will recognize you when this weakness hangs on the cross. And so he continues with, *my hour has not yet come*. As if to say: I will recognize you as my mother when the time of my passion arrives. And so it was that on the cross he entrusted his mother to the disciple.

353. Chrysostom explains this differently.

He says that the Blessed Virgin, burning with zeal for the honor of her Son, wanted Christ to perform miracles at once, before it was opportune; but that Christ, being much wiser than his mother, restrained her. For he was unwilling to perform the miracle before the need for it was known; otherwise, it would have been less appreciated and less credible. And so he says, *woman, what is that to me and to you?* As if to say: why bother me? *My hour has not yet come*, i.e., I am not yet known to those present. Nor do they know that the wine ran out; and they must first know this, because when they know their need they will have a greater appreciation of the benefit they will receive.

354. Quamvis autem mater repulsa sit, tamen de Filii misericordia non diffidit; ideo consequenter monet ministros, dicens ***quodcumque dixerit vobis, facite***, in quo quidem consistit totius iustitiae perfectio. Perfecta namque iustitia est Christo in omnibus obedire; Ex. XXIX, 35: *omnia quae praecepit nobis Dominus faciemus.*

Hoc autem verbum ***omnia quaecumque dixerit vobis facite***, non convenit dici nisi de solo Deo, homo enim aliquando potest errare. Unde in talibus quae sunt contra Deum, hominibus obedire non tenemur; Act. V, 29: *oportet obedire Deo magis quam hominibus.* Deo autem, qui non errat nec falli potest, in omnibus obedire debemus.

355. Consequenter cum dicit ***erant autem ibi lapideae hydriae***, ponitur consummatio miraculi per Christum: circa quod

primo describuntur vasa in quibus miraculum patratum est;

secundo designatur materia miraculi, ibi ***dixit eis Iesus: implete hydrias aqua***;

tertio insinuatur miraculi demonstratio et approbatio, ibi ***dixit eis Iesus: haurite nunc***.

356. Vasa autem in quibus miraculum patratum est, ponuntur sex; et est quod dicit ***erant autem ibi lapideae hydriae sex***.

Ubi sciendum est, quod sicut Mc. VII, 2 ss., dicitur, Iudaei observabant multas ablutiones corporales, et baptismata calicum et vasorum: unde quia erant in Palaestina, in qua est defectus aquarum, habebant vasa in quibus servabatur aqua purissima, qua se, et vasa crebro lavarent. Et ideo dicit, quod ***erant ibi sex lapideae hydriae***, idest vasa ad conservandum aquam, ab hydros, quod est aqua, ***posita secundum purificationem Iudaeorum***, idest ad usum purificationis, ***capientes singulae metretas***, idest mensuras, ***binas, vel ternas***: 'metros' enim Graece, 'mensura' Latine dicitur. Et, ut dicit Chrysostomus, vasa ista deferuntur ad tollendam miraculi suspicionem: tum propter eorum puritatem, ne posset aliquis suspicari quod aqua saporem vini sumpsisset ex faecibus vini prius in eis repositi, nam vasa illa erant ***secundum purificationem***, et ideo purissima oportebat ea esse; tum etiam propter vasorum quantitatem, ut evidenter pateat quod aqua tot vasorum in vinum mutari non potuisset, nisi virtute divina.

357. Mystice vero per sex hydrias significantur sex aetates Veteris Testamenti, in quibus erant corda hominum receptiva Scripturarum Dei parata, et proposita in exemplum vivendi, ut dicit Glossa.

Hoc vero quod dicit ***metretas***, secundum Augustinum, refertur ad Trinitatem personarum. Et dicuntur binae, vel ternae, quia quandoque in Sacra Scriptura tres personae distinctim ponuntur, secundum illud Matth.

354. Now although his mother was refused, she did not lose hope in her Son's mercy. So she instructs the servants, saying ***do whatever he tells you***, in which, indeed, consists the perfection of all justice. For perfect justice consists in obeying Christ in all things: *we will do all that the Lord commanded us* (Exod 29:35).

However, the phrase ***do whatever he tells you***, is not fittingly said except of God alone, for man is able to err at times. Hence in matters that are against God, we are not held to obey men: *we ought to obey God rather than men* (Acts 5:29). We ought to obey God, who does not err and cannot be deceived, in all things.

355. Now Christ's completion of the miracle is set forth, at ***now there were six stone waterpots nearby***.

First, the vessels in which the miracle was performed are described.

Second, the matter of the miracle is stated, at ***Jesus said to them: fill the waterpots with water***.

Third, we have how the miracle was made known and approved, at ***and Jesus said to them: draw out now***.

356. The miracle was performed in six vessels: ***now there were six stone waterpots nearby***.

Here we should note, that as mentioned, the Jews observed many bodily washings and the cleansing of their cups and dishes (Mark 7:2). So, because they were in Palestine where there was a shortage of water, they had vessels in which they kept the purest water to be used for washing themselves and their utensils. Hence he says, ***there were six stone waterpots nearby***, i.e., vessels for holding water, ***according to the purification of the Jews***, i.e., to use for purification, ***containing two or three measures apiece***, that is, two or three measures; for the Greek 'metrete' is the same as the Latin 'mensura.' These jars were standing there, as Chrysostom says, in order to eliminate any suspicion about the miracle: both on account of their cleanliness, lest anyone suspect that the water had acquired the taste of wine from the dregs of wine previously stored in them, for these jars were standing there for ***according to the purification***, and so had to be very pure; and also on account of the capacity of the jars, so that it would be abundantly clear that the water in such jars could be changed into wine only by divine power (John 2:6).

357. In the mystical sense, the six water jars signify the six eras of the Old Testament during which the hearts of men were prepared and made receptive of God's Scriptures, and put forward as an example for our lives.

The term ***measures***, according to Augustine, refers to the Trinity of persons. And they are described as two or three because at times in Scripture three persons in the Trinity are distinctly mentioned: *baptizing them in the*

ult., 19: *baptizantes eos in nomine Patris, et Filii, et Spiritus Sancti*, quandoque vero duo tantum, scilicet Pater et Filius, in quibus intelligitur persona Spiritus Sancti, qui est connexio amborum, secundum illud infra XIV, 23: *si quis sermonem meum servabit, Pater meus diliget eum, et ad eum veniemus.* Vel binas propter duas conditiones hominum, Iudaeorum scilicet, et gentilium, ex quibus propagata est Ecclesia. Vel ternas propter tres Filios Noe, ex quibus propagatum est humanum genus post diluvium.

358. Consequenter cum dicit **dixit eis Iesus: implete hydrias aqua**, agitur de miraculi materia.

Sed circa hoc insurgit quaestio quare non ex nihilo, sed ex materia praeiacente hoc miraculum factum est: ad quod triplex ratio assignatur. Una est secundum Chrysostomum, et litteralis, quia ex nihilo aliquid facere, maius est et mirabilius, quam facere aliquid ex subiecta materia; sed non est ita evidens et credibile multis. Et ideo volens magis credibile esse quod fiebat, ex aqua fecit vinum, capacitati hominum condescendens.

Alia ratio est, ad confutandum perversa dogmata. Quidam namque sunt (ut Marcionistae et Manichaei) qui dixerunt alium esse conditorem mundi, quam Deum, et omnia visibilia ab illo, idest diabolo, condita esse. Et ideo Dominus plura miracula etiam ex substantiis creatis, et visibilibus fecit, ut ostendat ipsas substantias bonas esse, et a Deo creatas.

Tertia ratio est mystica. Ideo enim noluit ex nihilo vinum facere, sed ex aqua vinum fecit, ut ostenderet se non omnino novam doctrinam condere et veterem reprobare, sed adimplere; ut dicitur Matth. V, 17: *non veni solvere legem, sed adimplere*: dum quod figurabat vetus lex, et promittebat, Christus exhibuit, et aperuit; Lc. ult., 45: *aperuit illis sensum ut intelligerent Scripturas.*

Voluit autem per ministros hydrias impleri aqua, ut eos, eius quod fiebat, testes haberet: unde infra dicitur: **ministri autem sciebant** etc.

359. Consequenter cum dicit **et dixit eis Iesus** etc. ponitur miraculi publicatio. Statim enim quod hydriae impletae sunt, aqua in vinum conversa est; et ideo statim Dominus miraculum publicat, dicens **haurite nunc, et ferte architriclino**, ubi

primo ponitur mandatum Christi examinatorem eligentis;

secundo sententiam architriclini degustantis, ibi **ut autem gustavit architriclinus** etc.

360. **Dixit** ergo **eis**, scilicet ministris, **haurite nunc**, scilicet vinum de hydriis, **et ferte architriclino**.

Ubi sciendum est, quod triclinium est locum ubi sunt tres ordines mensarum, et dicitur triclinium a triplici

name of the Father, and of the Son, and of the Holy Spirit (Matt 28:19), and at other times only two, the Father and the Son, in whom the Holy Spirit, who is the union of the two, is implied: **if anyone loves me, he will keep my word, and my Father will love him, and we will come to him** (John 14:23). Or they are described as two on account of the two states of mankind from which the Church arose, that is, Jews and gentiles. Or three on account of the three sons of Noah, from whom the human race arose after the deluge.

358. Then when he says **Jesus said to them: fill the waterpots with water**, he gives the material of the miracle.

Here we might ask why this miracle was performed with already existing material, and not from nothing. There are three reasons for this. The first reason is literal, and is given by Chrysostom: to make something from nothing is much greater and more marvelous than to make something from material already existing; but it is not so evident and believable to many. And so, wishing to make what he did more believable, Christ made wine from water, thus condescending to man's capacity.

Another reason was to refute wrong dogmas. For there are some (as the Marcionists and Manicheans) who said that the founder of the world was someone other than God, and that all visible things were established by such a one, that is, the devil. And so the Lord performed many miracles using created and visible substances in order to show that these substances are good and were created by God.

The third reason is mystical. Christ made the wine from water, and not from nothing, in order to show that he was not laying down an entirely new doctrine and rejecting the old, but was fulfilling the old: *I have not come to destroy the law, but to fulfill it* (Matt 5:17). In other words, what was prefigured and promised in the old law, was disclosed and revealed by Christ: *then he opened their minds so they could understand the Scriptures* (Luke 24:45).

Finally, he had the servants fill the jars with water so that he might have witnesses to what he did; so it is said, **but the waiters, who had drawn the water, knew**.

359. Then, the miracle is made known, at **and Jesus said to them**. For as soon as the jars were filled, the water was turned into wine. So the Lord reveals the miracle at once, saying: **draw out now, and carry to the head waiter**.

Here, we first have the command of Christ selecting who is to test the wine;

second, the judgment of the head waiter who tasted it: **and when the headwaiter had tasted the water made wine**.

360. Then **Jesus said to them**, i.e., to the waiters, **draw out**, that is, the wine, from the jars, **and carry to the head waiter**.

Here we should note that a 'triclinium' is a place where there are three rows of tables, and it is called a 'triclinium'

ordine lectorum: 'cline' enim in Graeco lectum significat. Nam antiqui in lectis accumbentes consueverant comedere, ut maximus Valerius narrat. Et ideo dicunt in Scripturis accumbere et recumbere. Architriclinus ergo dicitur primus et princeps inter convivas.

Vel aliter, secundum Chrysostomum, architriclinus erat qui erat ordinator et dispensator totius convivii. Quia vero sollicitus nondum aliquid gustaverat, voluit Dominus quod ipse iudicaret de eo quod factum erat, et non convivae, ne aliquis posset miraculo detrahere, dicens eos ebrios esse, et eorum sensus per comestionem corruptos, ita quod non possent discernere, an vinum esset, vel aqua. Sed, secundum Augustinum, architriclinus erat maior inter discumbentes, ut dictum est; et ideo, ut eius sententia acceptabilior fieret, voluit in eo quod factum erat habere sententiam praesidentis.

361. Mystice autem, qui hauriunt aquam sunt praedicatores; Is. XII, 3: *haurietis aquas in gaudio de fontibus Salvatoris*. Architriclinus autem est aliquis legisperitus, puta Nicodemus, Gamaliel et Paulus. Dum ergo talibus verbum Evangelii committitur, quod latebat in littera legis, quasi vinum de aqua factum architriclino propinatur: qui hoc degustans approbat fidem Christi.

362. Consequenter cum dicit **ut autem gustavit architriclinus**, ponitur examinantis iudicium: ubi primo inquirit veritatem facti; secundo profert sententiam, dicens **omnis homo primum bonum vinum ponit**.

Dicit ergo **ut autem gustavit architriclinus aquam vinum factam, et non sciebat unde esset**, quia ignorabat aquam vinum factam miraculo per Christum, **ministri autem sciebant** cuius ratio est, quia **hauserant aquam; vocat sponsum architriclinus**, ut veritatem inquirat, et de vino sententiam proferat; unde subdit **omnis homo primum bonum vinum ponit** etc.

Ubi, secundum Chrysostomum, hoc considerandum est in miraculis Christi, quod omnia perfectissima fuerunt; unde et socrui Petri perfectissimam sanitatem restituit, ut statim surgens ministraret, ut dicitur Mc. I, 30 et Mt. c. IX, 6. Paralyticum etiam ita perfecte sanitati restituit quod statim surgens, et sublato lecto iret in domum suam, ut dicitur infra V, 9. Hoc etiam in isto miraculo apparet: quia non qualecumque vinum de aqua fecit, sed optimum quo poterat esse. Et ideo dicit architriclinus **omnis homo primum bonum vinum ponit, et cum inebriati fuerint, tunc id quod deterius est**, quia minus bibunt, et quia vinum bonum in quantitate sumptum, cum quantitate cibi magis gravat; quasi dicat: unde est tale vinum, quod tu servasti usque adhuc? Contra consuetudinem scilicet faciens.

from its three rows of dining couches: for 'cline' in Greek means couch. For the ancients were accustomed to eat reclining on couches, as Maximus Valerius recounts. This is the reason why the Scriptures speak of lying next to and lying down. Thus the architriclinus was the first and chief among those dining.

Or, according to Chrysostom, the headwaiter was the one in charge of the whole banquet. And because he had been busy and had not tasted anything, the Lord wanted him, and not the guests, to be the judge of what had been done, so some could not detract from the miracle by saying the guests were drunk and, their senses dulled, could not tell wine from water. For Augustine, he was the chief guest, as was inentioned; and Christ wanted to have the opinion of this person in high position so it would be more acceptable.

361. In the mystical sense, those who pour out the water are preachers: *with joy you will draw water from the springs of the Savior* (Isa 12:3). And the architriclinus is someone skilled in the law, as Nicodenius, Gamaliel or Paul. So, when the word of the Gospel, which was hidden under the letter of the law, is entrusted to such persons, it is as though wine made from water is poured out for the architriclinus, who, when he tastes it, gives his assent to the faith of Christ.

362. Then the judgment of the one examining the wine is given, **and when the head waiter had tasted**. First, he inquires into the truth of the fact; second, he gives his opinion, at **every man at first sets forth the good wine**.

He says, **and when the head waiter had tasted the water made wine and did not know where it was from**, because he did not know that the water had miraculously been made wine by Christ, **but the waiters knew**, the reason being that they **had drawn the water**, **the head waiter called the bridegroom**, in order to learn the truth and give his opinion of the wine. Hence he adds: **every man at first sets forth the good wine**.

Here we should consider, according to Chrysostom, that everything is most perfect in the miracles of Christ. Thus, he restored most complete health to Peter's mother-in-law, so that she arose at once and waited on them (Mark 1:30 and Matt 7:14). Again, he restored the paralytic to health so perfectly that he also arose immediately, took up his mat, and went home, as we read (John 5:9). And this is also evident in this miracle, because Christ did not make mediocre wine from the water, but the very best possible. And so the head waiter says, **every man at first sets forth the good wine, and when men have drunk well, then that which is worse**, because they drink less, and because good wine consumed in quantity along with a quantity of food causes greater discomfort. It is as though he were saying: Where did this very good wine come from which, contrary to custom, you saved until now? Against this counsel an argument is made.

363. Competit autem mysterio. Nam aliquis dicitur mystice primo bonum vinum ponere, qui alios decipere intendens, errorem quem intendit non proponit primo, sed quae alliciant auditores, ut postquam inebriati et allecti fuerint ad consensum suae intentionis, perfidiam manifestet; et de isto vino dicitur Prov. XXIII, 31: *ingreditur blande, et in novissimo mordebit sicut coluber.* Dicitur autem aliquis primo bonum vinum ponere, qui a principio suae conversionis sancte et spiritualiter vivere incipiens, tandem in vitam carnalem degenerat; Gal. III, 3: *sic stulti facti estis, ut cum Spiritu coeperitis, nunc carne consummemini?* Christus vero non primo vinum bonum ponit: quia a principio amara et dura proponit; Mt. VII, 14: *arcta est via quae ducit ad vitam.* Sed quanto plus homo in eius fide et doctrina procedit, tanto plus dulcoratur, et maiorem suavitatem sentit; Prov. IV, 11: *ducam te per semitam aequitatis, quam cum ingressus fueris non arctabuntur gressus tui.* Item in mundo isto amaritudines et tribulationes patiuntur omnes qui pie volunt vivere in Christo; infra XVI, 20: **amen, amen dico vobis, quia plorabitis et flebitis vos** etc. Sed in futuro delectationes et gaudia suscipient; unde et sequitur: *tristitia vestra vertetur in gaudium.* Rom. VIII, 18: *existimo quod non sunt condignae passiones huius temporis ad futuram gloriam quae revelabitur in nobis.*

364. Consequenter cum dicit **hoc fecit initium signorum Iesus**, ponitur miraculi contestatio per discipulos facta. Ex quo habetur quod falsa est historia *de Infantia Salvatoris*, in qua recitantur multa miracula facta a Christo adhuc puero existente; si enim hoc verum esset, non utique Evangelista diceret **hoc fecit initium signorum Iesus**. Et ratio quare non in pueritia miracula fecit, assignata est supra, ne ea scilicet homines phantastica reputarent: ergo hac de causa hoc miraculum, scilicet de aqua vinum, fecit in Cana Galilaeae Iesus, quod est initium signorum, quae fecit Iesus postea. **Et manifestavit gloriam suam**, idest potentiam qua gloriosus est; Ps. c. XXIII, 10: *Dominus virtutum ipse est Rex gloriae.*

365. *Et crediderunt in eum discipuli eius.*

Sed quomodo crediderunt? Iam enim discipuli erant, et ante crediderant.

Sed dicendum est, quod aliquid dicitur esse aliquando non secundum quod nunc est, sed secundum quod futurum est; sicut dicitur quod Paulus apostolus natus est Tharso Ciliciae: non quod ibi sit natus apostolus, sed quod futurus apostolus, ibi natus fuit; ita dicitur hic **et crediderunt in eum discipuli eius**, scilicet qui erant discipuli eius.

Vel dicendum, quod ante crediderunt ei sicut bono viro, iusta et recta praedicanti; sed modo crediderunt in eum tamquam in Deum etc.

363. This is appropriate to a mystery. For in the mystical sense, he serves good wine first who, with an intent to deceive others, does not first mention the error he intends, but other things that entice his hearers, so that he can disclose his evil plans after they have been intoxicated and enticed to consent. We read of such wine: *it goes down pleasantly, but finally it will bite like a serpent* (Prov 23:31). Again, he serves good wine first who begins to live in a saintly and spiritual manner at the start of his conversion, but later sinks into a carnal life: *are you so foolish as, having begun in the Spirit, to end in the flesh?* (Gal 3:3). Christ, however, does not serve the good wine first, for at the outset he proposes things that are bitter and hard: *narrow is the way that leads to life* (Matt 7:14). Yet the more progress a person makes in his faith and teaching, the more pleasant it becomes and he becomes aware of a greater sweetness: *I will lead you by the path of justice, and when you walk you will not be hindered* (Prov 4:11). Likewise, all those who desire to live conscientiously in Christ stiffer bitterness and troubles in this world: **amen, amen I say to you, that you will lament and weep** (John 16:20). But later they will experience delights and joys. So he goes on: *but your sorrow will be turned into joy. I consider that the sufferings of this present time are not worthy to be compared with the glory to come, which will be revealed in us* (Rom 8:18).

364. Then when he says, **Jesus did this beginning of miracles in Cana of Galilee**, he gives testimony of the miracleb through the disciples. We can see from this the falsity of the *History of the Infancy of the Savior*, which recounts many miracles worked by Christ as a boy. For if these accounts were true, the Evangelist would not have said, **Jesus did this beginning of miracles in Cana of Galilee**. We have already given the reason why Christ worked no miracles during his childhood, that is, lest men regard them as illusions. It was for the reason given above, then, that Jesus performed this miracle of turning water into wine at Cana of Galilee; **and manifested his glory**. And Jesus revealed his glory, i.e., the power by which he is glorious: *the Lord of hosts, he is the King of glory* (Ps 23:10).

365. *And his disciples believed in him*.

But how did they believe? For they already were his disciples and had believed before this.

I answer that sometimes a thing is described not according to what it is at the time, but according to what it will be. For example, we say that the apostle Paul was born at Tarsus, in Cilicia; not that an actual apostle was born there, but a future one was. Similarly, it says here that **his disciples believed in him**, i.e., those who would be his disciples.

Or, one might answer that previously they had believed in him as a good man, preaching what was right and just; but now they believed in him as God.

Lecture 2

2:12 Post hoc descendit Capharnaum ipse, et mater eius, et fratres eius, et discipuli eius; et ibi manserunt non multis diebus. [n. 367]

2:13 Et prope erat Pascha Iudaeorum. Et ascendit Iesus Ierosolymam. [n. 374]

2:14 Et invenit in templo vendentes oves, et boves, et columbas, et nummularios sedentes. [n. 380]

2:15 Et cum fecisset quasi flagellum de funiculis, omnes eiecit de templo, oves quoque et boves, et nummulariorum effudit aes, et mensas subvertit. [n. 384]

2:16 Et his qui columbas vendebant, dixit: auferte ista hinc, et nolite facere domum Patris mei domum negotiationis. [n. 387]

2:17 Recordati sunt vero discipuli eius, quia scriptum est: zelus domus tuae comedit me. [n. 392]

2:12 Μετὰ τοῦτο κατέβη εἰς Καφαρναοὺμ αὐτὸς καὶ ἡ μήτηρ αὐτοῦ καὶ οἱ ἀδελφοὶ [αὐτοῦ] καὶ οἱ μαθηταὶ αὐτοῦ καὶ ἐκεῖ ἔμειναν οὐ πολλὰς ἡμέρας.

2:13 Καὶ ἐγγὺς ἦν τὸ πάσχα τῶν Ἰουδαίων, καὶ ἀνέβη εἰς Ἱεροσόλυμα ὁ Ἰησοῦς.

2:14 Καὶ εὗρεν ἐν τῷ ἱερῷ τοὺς πωλοῦντας βόας καὶ πρόβατα καὶ περιστερὰς καὶ τοὺς κερματιστὰς καθημένους,

2:15 καὶ ποιήσας φραγέλλιον ἐκ σχοινίων πάντας ἐξέβαλεν ἐκ τοῦ ἱεροῦ τά τε πρόβατα καὶ τοὺς βόας, καὶ τῶν κολλυβιστῶν ἐξέχεεν τὸ κέρμα καὶ τὰς τραπέζας ἀνέτρεψεν,

2:16 καὶ τοῖς τὰς περιστερὰς πωλοῦσιν εἶπεν· ἄρατε ταῦτα ἐντεῦθεν, μὴ ποιεῖτε τὸν οἶκον τοῦ πατρός μου οἶκον ἐμπορίου.

2:17 ἐμνήσθησαν οἱ μαθηταὶ αὐτοῦ ὅτι γεγραμμένον ἐστίν· ὁ ζῆλος τοῦ οἴκου σου καταφάγεταί με.

2:12 After this he went down to Capernaum, he and his mother, and his brethren, and his disciples: and they did not remain there many days. [n. 367]

2:13 And the Passover of the Jews was at hand, and Jesus went up to Jerusalem. [n. 374]

2:14 And he found in the temple merchants selling oxen and sheep and doves, and moneychangers sitting. [n. 380]

2:15 And when he had made a whip of little cords, he drove them all out of the temple, the sheep and the oxen also, and he poured out the money of the changers, and overturned the tables. [n. 384]

2:16 And to those who sold doves he said: take these things from here and do not make the house of my Father a marketplace. [n. 387]

2:17 And his disciples remembered that it was written: zeal for your house consumes me. [n. 392]

---

366. Supra Evangelista posuit signum quod fecit Christus pertinens ad virtutem immutativam naturae, ad discipulorum confirmationem; hic consequenter agit de signo resurrectionis ad eamdem virtutem pertinente, quod proposuit Christus ad turbarum conversionem.

Circa hoc ergo miraculum duo facit Evangelista.

Primo ponit miraculi proponendi occasionem;

secundo ipsius miraculi praenuntiationem, ibi *responderunt ergo Iudaei* etc.

Circa primum duo facit.

Primo describit locum;

secundo narrat factum, quod fuit occasio miraculi proponendi, ibi *et invenit in templo vendentes oves et boves*.

Locus autem in quo hoc fuit, est Ierosolyma: et ideo Evangelista gradatim ostendit quo ordine Ierusalem Dominus venerit.

Primo ergo ostendit quomodo in Capharnaum descendit;

secundo vero quomodo Ierosolymam ascendit, ibi *et prope erat Pascha*.

Circa primum tria facit.

Primo assignat locum quo descendit;

366. Above, the Evangelist presented the sign Christ worked in order to confirm his disciples; and this sign pertained to his power to change nature. Now he deals with the sign of his resurrection; a sign pertaining to the same power, but proposed by Christ to convert the people.

The Evangelist does two things as to this miracle.

First, he mentions its occasion.

Second, the prediction of the miracle, at *the Jews, therefore, answered* (John 2:18).

As to the first he does two things.

First, he describes the place.

Second, he tells of the incident which was the occasion for proposing this miracle, at *and he found in the temple merchants selling oxen and sheep*.

Now the place where this happened was Jerusalem. And so the Evangelist recounts step by step how the Lord had come to Jerusalem.

First, then, he shows how he went down to Capernaum.

Second, how he then went up to Jerusalem, at *and the Passover of the Jews was at hand*.

As to the first he does three things.

First, he mentions the place to which he went down.

secundo, describit societatem quam habuit;

tertio innuit moram quam protraxit.

367. Locus quidem quo descendit est Capharnaum; et ideo dicit *post hoc*, scilicet miraculum de vino, *descendit Capharnaum.*

Videtur, quantum ad historiam pertinet, huic dicto contrariari quod dicitur Matth. IV, v. 12 s., scilicet quod Dominus descenderit Capharnaum post incarcerationem Ioannis. Hoc autem quod hic refert Evangelista, totum factum est ante incarcerationem Ioannis.

Respondeo dicendum, quod ad huius quaestionis intelligentiam sciendum est, quod sicut ex *Ecclesiastica historia* habetur, reliqui evangelistae, scilicet Matthaeus, Marcus et Lucas narrationem evangelicam inceperunt ab eo tempore quo Ioannes fuit inclusus in carcere. Unde statim Matth. IV, 12, post baptismum, et ieiunium, et tentationem eius, texere incepit suam narrationem ante incarcerationem Ioannis, dicens: *cum audivisset Iesus quod traditus esset Ioannes* etc., et similiter Marcus; unde dicit: *postquam autem traditus est Ioannes, venit Iesus in Galilaeam* etc. Ioannes vero Evangelista qui supervixit aliis, cum trium evangelistarum ad ipsum notitia pervenisset, dictorum fidem et veritatem probavit; tamen, quia vidit aliqua deesse, illa scilicet quae primo praedicationis suae tempore, ante Ioannis incarcerationem, Dominus gesserat, ideo ad preces fidelium ipse Evangelium suum altius inchoans, ea quae praeterierant, priora, ante traditionem Ioannis, Domini gesta conscripsit, scilicet a primo anno quo baptizatus est; ut in eius Evangelii serie apparet. Secundum hoc ergo evangelistae non dissonant; sed quia Dominus bis Capharnaum descendit, semel ante incarcerationem Ioannis, de quo agitur hic, et semel post incarcerationem eius, de quo agitur Matth. IV, 13 et Lc. IV, 31.

368. *Capharnaum* autem interpretatur *villa pulcherrima*, et significat mundum istum, qui habet decorem ex ordine et dispositione divinae sapientiae; Ps. XLIX, 11: *pulchritudo agri mecum est.* Descendit ergo Dominus in Capharnaum, idest mundum istum, cum matre, et fratribus, et discipulis. Nam in caelis Dominus Patrem habet sine matre, in terris matrem sine Patre; et ideo signanter matrem solum nominat. In caelis etiam fratres non habet; sed est ipse *unigenitus, qui est in sinu Patris*: supra I, 18. In terris vero est *primogenitus in multis fratribus*, ut dicitur Rom. VIII, v. 29. In terris habet discipulos quos doceat mysteria divinitatis, quae ante hominibus ignota fuerant, quia, ut dicitur Hebr. I, 2, *novissime diebus istis locutus est nobis in Filio* etc.

Vel *Capharnaum* interpretatur *ager consolationis*: per quod signatur omnis homo qui fructum bonum facit; Gen. XXVII, 27: *ecce odor filii mei sicut odor agri pleni.* Et talis homo dicitur ager consolationis, quia Dominus consolatur, et gaudet de profectu eius; Is. LXII, 5:

Second, he describes his company.

Third, he mentions the length of his stay.

367. The place to which Christ went down was Capernaum; and so he says, *after this*, i.e., the miracle of the wine, *he went down to Capernaum.*

Now as far as the historical truth is concerned, this seems to conflict with Matthew's account that the Lord went down to Capernaum after John had been thrown into prison (Matt 4:12), while the entire series of events the Evangelist refers to here took place before John's imprisonment.

I answer that in order to settle this question we should bear in mind what is learned from the *Ecclesiastical History*, that is, that the other evangelists, Matthew, Mark and Luke, began their account of the public life of Christ from the time that John was thrown into prison. Thus Matthew, after describing the baptism, fast and temptation of Christ, began at once to weave his story after John's imprisonment, saying: *when Jesus heard that John had been arrested* (Matt 4:12). And Mark says the same: *after John had been arrested, Jesus came into Galilee* (Mark 1:14). John, who outlived the other three evangelists, approved the accuracy and truth of their accounts when they came to his notice. Yet he saw that certain things had been left unsaid, namely, things which the Lord had done in the very first days of his preaching before John's imprisonment. And so, at the request of the faithful, John, after he began his own Gospel in a loftier manner, recorded events that took place during the first year in which Christ was baptized before John's imprisonment, as is plain from the order of the events in his Gospel. According to this, then, the evangelists are not in disagreement. Rather, the Lord went down to Capernaum twice: once before John's imprisonment, which is the one dealt with here, and once after his imprisonment (Matt 4:13 and Luke 4:31).

368. Now *Capernaum* means *very pretty village*, and signifies this world, which has its beauty from the order and disposition of divine wisdom: *the beauty of the land is mine* (Ps 49:2). So the Lord went down to Capernaum, i.e., this world, with his mother and brethren and disciples. For in heaven the Lord has a Father without a mother; and on earth a mother without a father. Thus, he significantly mentions only his mother. In heaven he does not have brothers either, but is *the only begotten Son, who is in the bosom of the Father* (John 1:18). But on earth he is *the firstborn of many brothers* (Rom 8:29). And on earth he has disciples, to whom he can teach the mysteries of the divinity, which were not known to men before: *in these days he has spoken to us in his Son* (Heb 1:1).

Or, *Capernaum* means *the field of consolation*; and this signifies every man who bears good fruit: *the odor of my son is like the odor of a fruitful field* (Gen 27:27). Such a person is called a field of consolation because the Lord is consoled and rejoices in his achievement: *God will rejoice*

gaudebit Dominus super te etc., quia de eius bono angeli gaudent; Lc. XV, v. 10: *gaudium est angelis Dei super uno peccatore poenitentiam agente.*

369. Dicit *ipse, et mater.*

Societas eius fuit primo matris; unde dicit *et mater eius,* quia enim ad nuptias venerat, et fuerat miraculi procuratrix, reducebat eam Dominus Nazareth, quae erat villa in Galilaea, in qua Capharnaum metropolis erat.

370. Secundo fuit fratrum; unde dicit *et fratres eius* etc.

Ubi cavendi sunt duo errores, scilicet Elvidii dicentis, quod Beata Virgo post Christum alios filios habuit, et hos dicit fratres Domini, quod est haereticum: quia fides nostra tenet, quod mater Christi sicut fuit virgo ante partum, ita et in partu, et post partum virgo permansit.

Item error quorumdam dicentium, Ioseph ex alia coniuge filios genuisse, et hos vocari fratres Domini, quod Ecclesia non tenet. Et ideo Hieronymus eos improbat: nam Dominus in cruce pendens virginem matrem virgini discipulo custodiendam dimisit. Cum ergo Ioseph fuerit specialis custos Virginis et etiam salvatoris in pueritia, credibile est eum virginem fuisse.

Et ideo sane intelligentes, fratres Domini dicimus consanguineos virginis matris, in quocumque gradu, vel etiam Ioseph, qui putabatur pater; et hoc quidem secundum consuetudinem Scripturae, quae communiter consanguineos fratres appellat. Unde Gen. XIII, v. 8: *ne quaeso sit iurgium inter me et te: fratres enim sumus,* dicit Abraham ad Lot; cum tamen esset nepos eius.

Et attende, quod separatim nominat fratres et discipulos: quia non omnes consanguinei Christi, eius discipuli erant. Unde infra VII, 5 dicitur: **nondum credebant in eum fratres eius.**

371. Tertio socii eius fuerunt discipuli sui: unde dicit *et discipuli eius.*

Sed ex hoc insurgit quaestio, qui fuerint eius discipuli. Videtur enim, secundum Matthaeum, quod primi qui conversi sunt ad Christum, fuerint Petrus et Andreas, Ioannes et Iacobus; sed hi vocati sunt a Christo post incarcerationem Ioannis, ut patet Matth. IV, v. 18 ss. non videtur ergo quod descenderint cum Christo in Capharnaum, ut hic habetur, cum hoc fuerit ante Ioannis incarcerationem.

Sed ad hoc duplex est responsio. Una, secundum Augustinum, *de Consensu evangelistarum,* quod Matthaeus non servat ordinem historiae, sed illud quod praetermiserat recapitulans, ea narrat post Ioannis incarcerationem quae ante facta fuerant. Unde sine ulla temporis consequentis differentia dixit: *ambulans Iesus iuxta mare Galilaeae, vidit duos fratres* etc., non addens post hoc vel

over you (Isa 62:5), and because the angels rejoice over his good: *there is joy in the angels of God over one repentant sinner* (Luke 15:10).

369. It says **he and his mother.**

His companions were, first of all, his mother. So he says, **and his mother,** for because she had come to the wedding and had brought about the miracle, the Lord accompanied her back to the village of Nazareth. Nazareth was a village in Galilee, whose chief town was Capernaum.

370. Second, his companions were his brethren; and so he says, **and his brethren.**

We must avoid two errors here. First, that of Elvidius, who said that the Blessed Virgin had other sons after Christ; and he called these the brothers of the Lord. This is heretical, because our faith maintains that just as the mother of Christ was a virgin before giving birth, so in giving birth and after giving birth, she remained a virgin.

We must also avoid the error of those who say that Joseph fathered sons with another wife, and that these are called the brothers of the Lord; for the Church does not admit this. Jerome refutes this opinion: for on the cross the Lord entrusted his virgin mother to the care of his virgin disciple. Therefore, since Joseph was the special guardian of the Virgin, and of the Savior too, in his childhood, one may believe that he was a virgin.

Consequently, it is a reasonable interpretation to say that the brothers of the Lord were those related to his virgin mother in some degree of consanguinity, or even to Joseph, who was the reputed father. And this conforms to the custom of Scripture which generally refers to relatives as brothers. Thus we read: *let us not quarrel, for we are brothers* (Gen 13:8), as Abram said to Lot, who was his nephew.

And note that he distinguishes between relatives and disciples, because not all of Christ's relatives were his disciples; hence we read: **for neither did his brethren believe in him** (John 7:5).

371. Third, his disciples were his companions; hence he says, and **and his disciples.**

Bur from this there arises the question of who were his disciples. For it seems, according to Matthew, that the first ones to be converted to Christ were Peter and Andrew, John and James; but they were called after John's imprisonment, as is clear from Matthew (Matt 4:18). Thus it does not seem that they went down to Capernaum with Christ, as it says here, since this was before John's imprisonment.

There are two answers to this. One is from Augustine, in his *De Consensu Evangelistarum,* namely, that Matthew does not follow the historical order, but in summarizing what he omitted, relates events that occurred before John's imprisonment as though they happened after. So, without any suggestion of a time lapse he says, *as Jesus was walking by the sea of Galilee, he saw two brothers* (Matt 4:18),

in diebus illis. Alia est, secundum eumdem, quod discipuli Domini, in Evangelio dicuntur non solum illi duodecim quos eligit Dominus, et apostolos nominavit, ut habetur Lc. VI, 13, sed etiam omnes qui in eum credentes, eius magisterio ad regnum caelorum erudiebantur. Potuit ergo esse quod quamvis illi duodecim nondum eum secuti fuissent, nihilominus tamen aliqui alii qui sibi adhaeserunt, hic eius discipuli nominentur. Sed prima responsio melior est.

372. Moram autem contraxit ibi parvam; unde dicit *et ibi manserunt non multis diebus*.

Huius ratio est, quia cives Capharnaum non se exhibuerunt devotos ad suscipiendum doctrinam Christi, quia erant valde corrupti; unde et Matth. XI, 23 Dominus eos obiurgat, quod nec ad virtutes in eis factas, nec ad doctrinam Christi poenitentiam egerunt, dicens: *et tu, Capharnaum, numquid ad caelum exaltaberis? Usque in Infernum descendes: quia si in Sodomis factae fuissent virtutes quae factae sunt in te, forte mansissent usque in hanc diem*. Et tamen quamquam mali essent, descendit illuc, ut deduceret matrem ad cuius consolationem et honorem ibidem aliquamdiu moratur.

373. Mystice autem signatur per hoc quod aliqui multis sermonibus Christi immorari non possunt, sed pauca ad eorum illuminationem de multis sufficiunt, propter intellectus eorum imbecillitatem. Unde apud tales Christus paucis documentis immoratur ut Origenes dixit; secundum illud infra XVI, v. 12: *multa habeo vobis dicere; sed non potestis portare modo*.

374. Consequenter cum dicit *et prope erat Pascha*, manifestat locum quo ascendit.

Et circa hoc duo facit.

Primo innuit occasionem ascensus;

secundo ponit ascensum, ibi *et ascendit Iesus*.

375. Occasio autem ascensus fuit Pascha Iudaeorum. Ex. XXIII, 17 praecipitur quod ter in anno omne masculinum praesentetur coram Domino, et inter illos terminos unus erat Pascha Iudaeorum. Quia ergo Dominus venit ut doceret omnes humilitatis et perfectionis exemplum, voluit legem, quamdiu statum habuit, observare: non enim venit legem solvere, sed adimplere, ut ipse dicit Matth. V, v. 17. Ex quo, quia Pascha Iudaeorum imminebat, Ierusalem ascendit.

Nos ergo ad eius exemplum deberemus sollicite divina praecepta servare. Si enim ipse Dei Filius decreta legis a se datae implebat, celebrans solemnitates; quanto studio bonorum operum deberemus nos eas et praevenire, et celebrare?

376. Notandum est, quod in Evangelio Ioannis in tribus locis fit mentio de Pascha, scilicet hic, et infra VI, 4, ubi fecit miraculum de panibus, ubi dicitur: *erat autem proximum Pascha, dies festus Iudaeorum*; et infra c. XIII, 1, ubi dicitur: *ante diem festum Paschae*.

without adding after this or at that time. The other answer, also by Augustine, is that in the Gospel not only the twelve whom the Lord chose and named apostles are called disciples of the Lord (Luke 6:13), but also all who believed in him and were instructed for the kingdom of heaven by his teaching. Therefore, it is possible that although those twelve did not yet follow him, others who adhered to him are called disciples here. But the first answer is better.

372. His stay there was short; hence he says, ***and they did not remain there many days***.

The reason for this was that the citizens of Capernaum were not eager to accept the teachings of Christ, being very corrupt, so that the Lord rebukes them for not doing penance in spite of the miracles done there and of Christ's teaching: *and you Capernaum, will you be lifted up to heaven? You will go down to hell. For if the mighty works that were done in you had been performed in Sodom, it would have stood until this day* (Matt 11:23). But although they were evil, he went there to accompany his mother, and to stay there for a few days for her consolation and honor.

373. As for its mystical sense, this signifies that some cannot remain long with the many words spoken by Christ; a few of these words are enough for them, to enlighten them, because of the weakness of their understanding. Hence as Origen said, Christ reveals few things to such persons, according to *I have yet many things to say to you: but you cannot bear them now* (John 16:12).

374. Then when he says, ***and the Passover of the Jews was at hand***, he mentions the place to which he went up.

And concerning this he does two things.

First, the occasion is given.

Second, the going up, at ***and Jesus went up***.

375. Now the occasion for his going up was the Jewish Passover. For it is commanded that every male be presented to the Lord three times a year (Exod 13:17); and one of these times was the Jewish Passover. So, since the Lord came to teach everyone by his example of humility and perfection, he wished to observe the law as long as it was in force. For he did not come to destroy the law, but to fulfill it (Matt 5:17). And so, because the Passover of the Jews was at hand, he went up to Jerusalem.

So we, after his example, should carefully observe the divine precepts. For if the Son of God fulfilled the decrees of a law he himself had given, and celebrated the great feasts, with what zeal for good works ought we both to prepare for them and observe them?

376. It should be noted that in John's Gospel mention is made of the Passover in three passages: here, and when he worked the miracle of the loaves, where it is said: ***now the Pasch, the festival day of the Jews, was near at hand*** (John 6:4), and again, where it says: ***before the festival***

Unde secundum hoc Evangelium, habemus quod post miraculum de vino Christus praedicavit duobus annis, et quantum est a diebus baptismi usque ad Pascha; nam hoc quod fecit hic, fuit prope Pascha, ut hic dicitur, et postea, revoluto anno, prope aliud Pascha fecit miraculum de panibus, et tunc Ioannes fuit decollatus. Unde Ioannes circa Pascha decollatus fuit; quia, ut dicitur Matth. c. XIV, 13, statim post decollationem Ioannis, Christus secessit in desertum, et ibi fecit miraculum de panibus: quod quidem miraculum fuit factum prope Pascha, ut dicitur infra VI. Sed tamen festum huius decollationis celebratur eo die quo caput eius inventum est. Postea, in alio Paschate, passus est Christus.

Secundum opinionem ergo illorum qui dicunt, quod miraculum factum in nuptiis, et ea quae hic dicuntur, eodem anno gesta sunt quo baptizatus est Christus, a baptismo Christi usque ad eius passionem fuerunt duo anni et dimidius: et ideo, secundum eos, Evangelista dicit *prope erat Pascha Iudaeorum*, ut ostendat quod ante paucos dies fuerat baptizatus.

Sed Ecclesia tenet contrarium. Credimus enim quod eodem die quo Dominus baptizatus est, revoluto anno, factum fuerit miraculum de vino; et postea revoluto anno, prope Pascha, Ioannes fuerit decollatus; et quod ab isto Paschate circa quod Ioannes fuit decollatus, fuerit unus annus usque ad Pascha in quo Christus passus est. Unde oportet aliud Pascha a baptismo Christi usque ad miraculum de vino intermedium esse, de quo nullus Evangelista facit mentionem: et sic, secundum quod Ecclesia tenet, Christus tribus annis et dimidio praedicavit.

377. Ait autem *Iudaeorum*, non quod alterius nationis homines Pascha celebrarent, sed duplici de causa. Una quia quando aliqui festum aliquod sancte et pure celebrant, dicitur illud Domino celebrare; cum vero nec pure, nec sancte celebrant, non Domino, sed sibi solemnizant; Is. I, 14: *Kalendas vestras, et festivitates vestras odivit anima mea*; quasi dicat: quia vobis, et non mihi celebratis, non placent mihi; Zach. VII, 5: *cum ieiunaretis, numquid ieiunium ieiunastis mihi?* Quasi dicat, non, sed vobis. Quia ergo isti Iudaei depravati erant, et eorum Pascha indebite celebrabant, ideo Evangelista non dicit: prope erat Pascha Domini, sed *Iudaeorum*.

Vel hoc dicit ad differentiam nostri Paschae: nam Pascha Iudaeorum erat figurale, utpote immolatione agni figuralis celebratum; sed nostrum Pascha verum est, in quo recolimus veram passionem Agni immaculati; I Corint. V, 7: *Pascha nostrum immolatus est Christus*.

378. Ascensus fuit in Ierusalem; et ideo dicit *et ascendit Iesus Ierosolymam*.

day of the Pasch (John 13:1). So, according to this Gospel, we understand that after the miracle of the wine Christ preached for two years plus the interval between his baptism and this Passover. For what he did here occurred near the Passover, as it says here, and then a year later, near the time of another Passover, he performed the miracle of the loaves, and in the same year John was beheaded. Thus John was beheaded near the time of the Passover, because we read that immediately after John was beheaded Christ withdrew to the desert, where he worked the miracle of the loaves (Matt 14:13); and this miracle took place near Passover time (John 6:4). Nevertheless, the feast of this beheading of John is celebrated on the day his head was found. It was later, during another Passover, that Christ suffered.

So, according to the opinion of those who say that the miracle worked at the wedding and the events being discussed here occurred in the same year in which Christ was baptized, there was an interval of two and one half years between Christ's baptism and his passion. So, according to them, the Evangelist says, *and the Passover of the Jews was at hand*, in order to show that Christ had been baptized just a few days before.

But the Church holds the opposite. For we believe that Christ worked the miracle of the wine on the first anniversary of the day of his baptism; then a year later, near Passover time, John was beheaded; and then there was another year between the Passover near which John was beheaded and the Passover during which Christ suffered. So between the baptism of Christ and the miracle of the wine there had to be another Passover which the Evangelist does not mention. And so, according to what the Church holds, Christ preached for three and one half years.

377. He says, *the Passover of the Jews*, not as though the people of other nations celebrated a Passover, but for two reasons. One, because when people celebrate a feast in a holy and pure way, it is said that they celebrate it for the Lord; but when they celebrate it in neither of those ways, they do not celebrate it for the Lord, but for themselves: *my soul hates your new moons and your feasts* (Isa 1:14). It is as though he said: Those who celebrate for themselves and not for me, do not please me: *when you fasted, did you fast for me?* (Zech 7:5). As if to say: you did not do it for me, but for yourselves. And so because these Jews were corrupt and celebrated their Passover in an unbecoming manner, the Evangelist does not say: the Passover of the Lord, but *the Passover of the Jews*.

Or, he says this to differentiate it from our Passover. For the Passover of the Jews was symbolic, being celebrated by the immolation of a lamb which was a symbol. But our Passover is true, in which we recall the true passion of the immaculate Lamb: *Christ, our Passover, has been sacrificed* (1 Cor 5:7).

378. The journey was to Jerusalem, and so he says, *and Jesus went up to Jerusalem*.

Ubi nota, secundum ordinem historiae, Iesum bis circa festum Paschae Ierosolymam ascendisse, et expulisse de templo ementes et vendentes. Semel quidem ante incarcerationem Ioannis, quod hic Evangelista commemorat, alia vice, imminente Paschate, et tempore passionis, quod narrat Matthaeus. Nam frequenter Dominus similia facta operatus est, sicut patet de duplici illuminatione caecorum: una Matth. IX, 28, et alia Mc. c. X, 46 ss. Et similiter bis eiecit ementes et vendentes de templo.

379. Mystice autem *ascendit Ierosolymam*, quae interpretatur *visio pacis*, et significat aeternam beatitudinem: in quam ascendit, et suos transduxit.

Sed non vacat a mysterio, quod in Capharnaum descendit, et postmodum Ierosolymam ascendit. Nisi enim descendisset primum, non competisset ei ascendere: quia, ut dicitur Eph. IV, 10, *qui descendit, ipse est et qui ascendit*. Non facit autem mentionem de discipulis in ascensu ad Ierosolymam: quia discipulorum ascensus est ex ascensu Christi; infra III, 13: *nemo ascendit in caelum nisi qui descendit de caelo, Filius hominis*.

380. Consequenter cum dicit *et invenit in templo vendentes oves et boves* etc. narrat Evangelista factum quod movit Christum ad signum resurrectionis proponendum.

Et circa hoc tria facit.

Primo manifestat Iudaeorum vitium;

secundo innuit Christi remedium, ibi *et cum fecisset quasi flagellum* etc.;

tertio subdit prophetiae oraculum, ibi *recordati vero sunt discipuli* etc.

381. Circa primum sciendum, quod diabolus insidiatur his quae Dei sunt, et ea nititur corrumpere. Inter cetera autem quibus sancta corrumpit, praecipuum est vitium avaritiae; unde dicitur Is. LVI, 11: *pastores eius nescierunt intelligentiam, omnes in viam suam declinaverunt: unusquisque ad avaritiam suam a summo usque ad novissimum*. Quod quidem ab antiquis temporibus diabolus fecit. Nam sacerdotes Veteris Testamenti, qui instituti erant ut divinis vacarent, avaritiae studebant. Praeceptum autem erat a Deo in lege, quod in certis solemnitatibus Domino immolarent aliqua animalia; ad quod quidem praeceptum implendum de prope venientes ad templum, secum animalia ducebant, illi autem qui a remotis veniebant, non valebant animalia ducere de domibus suis. Quia ergo oblationes huiusmodi cedebant in utilitatem sacerdotum, ne deessent animalia de remotis venientibus ad offerendum, providerunt ipsi sacerdotes ut animalia in templo venderentur; et ideo faciebant ea in templo, idest in atrio templi, exponi ad

Note here that according to the historical order, Jesus went up to Jerusalem near the time of the Passover and expelled the merchants from the temple on two occasions. The first, before John's imprisonment, is the one the Evangelist mentions here; the other is mentioned elsewhere as occurring when the Passover and the hour of his passion were at hand (Matt 21:13). For the Lord frequently repeated works that were similar. For example, the two cases of giving sight to the blind (Matt 9:28 and Mark 10:46). In like manner he twice cast merchants from the temple.

379. In the mystical sense, *Jesus went up to Jerusalem*, which is translated as *the vision of peace*, and signifies eternal happiness. It is to here that Jesus ascended, and he took his own with him.

There is no lack of mystery in the fact that he went down to Capernaum and later went up to Jerusalem. For if he did not first go down, he would not have been suited to go up, because, as it is said: *he who descended is the same as he who ascended* (Eph 4:10). Further, no mention is made of the disciples in the ascent to Jerusalem because the ascent of the disciples comes from the ascent of Christ: *and no man has ascended into heaven, except he who descended from heaven, the Son of man, who is in heaven* (John 3:13).

380. Then when he says, *and he found in the temple merchants selling oxen and sheep and doves, and money changers sitting*, the Evangelist sets down what moved Christ to propose the sign of the resurrection.

He does three things with this.

First, he exposes the faulty behavior of the Jews.

Second, he discloses Christ's remedy: *and when he had made a whip of little cords*.

Third, he gives the announcement of the prophecy, at *and his disciples remembered that it was written*.

381. With respect to the first, we should note that the devil plots against the things of God and strives to destroy them. Now among the means by which he destroys holy things, the chief is avarice; hence it is said: *the shepherds have no understanding. All have turned aside to their own way; everyone after his own gain, from the first one to the last* (Isa 56:11). And the devil has done this from the earliest times. For the priests of the Old Testament, who had been established to care for divine matters, gave free rein to avarice. God commanded, in the law, that animals should be sacrificed to the Lord on certain feasts. And in order to fulfill this command, those who lived nearby brought the animals with them. But those who came a long distance were unable to bring animals from their own homes. And so because offerings of this kind resulted in profit for the priests, and so animals to offer would not be lacking to those who came from a distance, the priests themselves saw to it that animals were sold in the temple. And so they had them shown for sale in the temple, i.e., in the atrium of the

vendendum. Et hoc est quod dicit *et invenit Dominus in templo vendentes oves, et boves, et columbas* etc.

Ubi primo facit mentionem de duobus animalibus terrestribus, quae secundum legem Domino offerri poterant, scilicet de bove et ove. Tertium vero animal terrestre, quod offerebatur capra scilicet, annumeratur cum *ove*: similiter etiam turtura numeratur cum *columba*.

382. Et quia contingebat aliquando aliquos ad templum venire, qui nec animalia secum ducebant, nec pecuniam, unde emere non valebant; ideo sacerdotes aliam avaritiae artem adinvenerant, ut scilicet in templo constituerent nummularios et campsores, qui praedictis non habentibus pecuniam mutuarent. Et licet usuram inde non reciperent, quia hoc erat in lege prohibitum, loco tamen eius quaedam collibia, idest parva munuscula et vilia recipiebant. Et haec ipsa in utilitatem sacerdotum cedebant; et hoc est quod dicit *et nummularios sedentes* scilicet in templo, paratos ad pecuniam mutuandam.

383. Sed hoc quidem mystice tripliciter intelligi potest. Primo enim per vendentes et ementes significantur illi qui Ecclesiasticas res vendunt, vel emunt: nam bona Ecclesiastica spiritualia, et eis annexa, significantur per oves, et boves, et columbas. Ipsa consecrata quidem, et confirmata sunt ex doctrinis apostolorum et doctorum, qui significantur per boves; Prov. XIV, 4: *ubi plurimae sunt segetes, ibi manifesta fortitudo bovis.* Item ex sanguine martyrum, qui significantur per oves. Unde in persona eorum dicitur in Ps. XLIII, et Rom. VIII, 36: *aestimati sumus ut oves occisionis.* Item dona Spiritus Sancti, quae significantur per columbas: quia, ut dicitur supra I, 32, Spiritus Sanctus in specie columbae apparuit. Omnia ergo haec vendunt, scilicet doctrinam apostolorum, sanguinem martyrum et dona Spiritus Sancti, quicumque bona ecclesiastica spiritualia, et eis annexa vendere praesumunt.

Secundo, contingit aliquos praelatos, seu Ecclesiarum praepositos, etsi non manifeste per simoniam, occulte tamen per negligentiam boves, et oves, et columbas vendere, tunc scilicet quando tantum inhiant temporalibus lucris, et occupantur in eis, et negligunt spiritualem salutem subditorum: nam per hoc vendunt oves, et boves, et columbas, idest tria genera hominum eis subditorum. Scilicet praedicatores et operatores, qui significantur per boves; Is. XXXII, 20: *beati qui seminatis super omnes aquas, immittentes pedem bovis et asini.* Quia praelati debent ordinare boves, idest doctores et sapientes cum asinis, idest rudibus et simplicibus. Vendunt etiam activos, et ministeriis vacantes, qui significantur per oves, infra X, 27: *oves meae vocem meam audiunt* etc.; II Reg. ult., 17: *isti, qui oves sunt, quid fecerunt?*

temple. And this is what he says: in the temple precincts he came upon merchants selling oxen, sheep and doves: *and he found in the temple merchants selling oxen and sheep and doves, and the moneychangers sitting.*

Mention is first made of two land animals, which according to the law could be offered to the Lord: the ox and the sheep. The third land animal offered, the goat, is implied when he says *sheep*, similarly, the turtle-dove is included when he says *doves*.

382. It sometimes happened that some came to the temple not only without animals, but also without money to buy them. And so the priests found another avenue for their avarice; they set up money-changers who would lend money to those who came without it. And although they would not accept a usurious gain, because this was forbidden in the law, nevertheless in place of this they accepted certain offerings i.e., trifles and small gifts. So this also was turned to the profit of the priests. And this is what he says, *moneychangers sitting*, i.e., in the temple, ready to lend money.

383. This can be understood mystically in three ways. First of all, the merchants signify those who sell or buy the things of the Church: for the oxen, sheep and doves signify the spiritual goods of the Church and the things connected with them. These goods have been consecrated and authenticated by the teachings of the apostles and doctors, signified by the oxen: *when there is an abundant harvest the strength of the ox is evident* (Prov 14:4); and by the blood of the martyrs, who are signified by the sheep: so it is said for them: *we are regarded as sheep for the slaughter* (Rom 8:36): and by the gifts of the Holy Spirit, signified by the doves, for as stated above, the Holy Spirit appeared in the form of a dove. Therefore, those who presume to sell the spiritual goods of the Church and the goods connected with them are selling the teachings of the apostles, the blood of the martyrs, and the gifts of the Holy Spirit.

Second, it happens that certain prelates or heads of churches sell these oxen, sheep and doves, not overtly by simony, but covertly by negligence; that is, when they are so eager for and occupied with temporal gain that they neglect the spiritual welfare of their subjects. And this is the way they sell the oxen, sheep and doves, i.e., the three classes of people subject to them. First of all, they sell the preachers and laborers, who are signified by the oxen: *happy are you who sow beside all the streams, letting the ox and the donkey range free* (Isa 32:20). Because prelates ought to arrange the oxen, i.e., teachers and wise men, with the donkeys, i.e., the simple and uneducated. They also sell those in the active life, and those occupied with ministering, signified by the sheep: *my sheep hear my voice* (John 10:27); and as is said: *but these, who are the sheep, what have they done?*

Vendunt et contemplantes, qui significantur per columbas; Ps. LIV, 7: *quis dabit mihi pennas sicut columbae et volabo?*

Tertio per templum Dei potest intelligi spiritualis anima, ut dicitur I Cor. III, 17: *templum Dei sanctum est, quod estis vos.* Tunc ergo homo vendit in templo oves, et boves, et columbas, quando in anima bestiales motus retinet, pro quibus homo vendit se diabolo. Nam per boves, qui agriculturae deserviunt, significantur terrena desideria; per ovem, quae est animal stultum, significatur hominis stoliditas; per columbas vero hominis instabilitas: quae quidem Deus de cordibus hominum expellit.

384. Et ideo statim ponitur Domini remedium, cum dicit *et cum fecisset quasi flagellum de funiculis, omnes eiecit de templo*: ubi Dominus apposuit remedium et operis, et verbi, ut doceret eos qui curam habent Ecclesiae, subditos facto et verbo debere corrigere.

Et ideo circa hoc duo facit.

Primo ponitur remedium quod adhibuit facto;

secundo remedium quod adhibuit verbo, ibi *et his qui vendebant columbas dixit* etc.

385. Circa primum tria facit. Primo eiecit homines; secundo oves et boves; tertio effudit pecuniam.

Eiecit quidem homines flagello, et hoc est quod dicit *et cum fecisset quasi flagellum de funiculis*, quod quidem non potuit fieri nisi virtute divina; nam, et Origenes dicit, quod divina potestas Iesu poterat cum volebat accensam iracundiam hominum suffocare, sicut sedare mentium turbines; Ps. XXXII, v. 10: *Dominus dissipat cogitationes hominum.* Facit autem flagellum de funiculis, quia, ut dicit Augustinus, de peccatis nostris sumit materiam, unde nos puniat: ipsa enim protelatio peccatorum, secundum quod peccata peccatis adduntur, funiculi dicuntur; Prov. V, v. 22: *funibus peccatorum suorum constringitur*; Is. V, 18: *vae qui trahitis iniquitatem in funiculis* etc. Sicut ergo eiecit de templo negotiatores, ita nummulariorum aes effudit, et mensas subvertit.

386. Attende, quod si ista, quae videbantur aliquo modo licita, quasi ad cultum Dei ordinata, de templo eiecit, quanto magis si invenisset aliqua illicita? Ideo autem eos eiecit, quia sacerdotes in hoc non intendebant honorem Dei, sed utilitatem propriam. Unde dicitur Ez. XLIV, 8: *posuistis custodes observationum mearum in sanctuario meo vobismetipsis.* Ostendit autem Dominus zelum ad ea quae sunt legis, ut ex hoc ipso confutaret pontifices et sacerdotes, qui erant ei de lege calumniam illaturi.

(2 Sam 24:17). They also sell the contemplatives, signified by the doves: *who will give me wings like a dove, and I will fly?* (Ps 54:7)

Third, by the temple of God we can understand the spiritual soul, as it says: *the temple of God is holy, and that is what you are* (1 Cor 3:17). Thus a man sells oxen, sheep and doves in the temple when he harbors bestial movements in his soul, for which he sells himself to the devil. For oxen, which are used for cultivating the earth, signify earthly desires; sheep, which are stupid animals, signify man's obstinacy; and the doves signify man's instability. It is God who drives these things out of men's hearts.

384. The Lord's remedy is at once set forth, at *and when he had made a whip of little cords, he drove them all out of the temple.* Here the Lord's remedy consisted in action and in words, in order to instruct those who have charge of the Church that they must correct their subjects in deed and in word.

And he does two things with respect to this.

First, he gives the remedy Christ applied by his action.

Second, the remedy he applied by word, at *and to those who sold doves he said.*

385. As to the first he does three things. First, he drives the men out. Second, the oxen and sheep. Third, he sweeps away the money.

He drives the men out with a whip; and this is what he says, when he had made a kind of whip from cords: *he drove them all out of the temple.* This is something that could be done only by divine power. For as Origen says, the divine power of Jesus was as able, when he willed, to quench the swelling anger of men as to still the storms of minds: *the Lord brings to naught the thoughts of men* (Ps 32:10). He makes the whip from cords because, as Augustine says, it is from our own sins that he forms the matter with which he punishes us: for a series of sins, in which sins are added to sins, is called a cord: *he is bound fast by the cords of his own sins* (Prov 5:22); *woe to you who haul wickedness with cords* (Isa 5:18). Then, just as he drove the merchants from the temple, so he swept away the gold of the money-changers and knocked over their tables.

386. And mark well that if he expelled from the temple things that seemed somehow licit, in the sense that they were ordained to the worship of God, how much more if he comes upon unlawful things? The reason he cast them out was because in this matter the priests did not intend God's glory, but their own profit. Hence it is said: *it is for yourselves that you placed guardians of my service in my sanctuary* (Ezek 44:8). Further, our Lord showed zeal for the things of the law so that he might by this answer the chief priests and the priests who were later to bring a charge against him concerning the law.

Per hoc etiam quod huiusmodi eiecit de templo, dedit intelligere quod appropinquabat tempus quo sacrificia legis cessare debebant, et verus Dei cultus ad gentes transferri; Matth. c. XXI, 43: *auferetur a vobis regnum* etc. Similiter etiam ut ostenderet eorum damnationem qui spiritualia vendunt; Act. VIII, 20: *pecunia tua tecum sit in perditione.*

387. Consequenter cum dicit *et his qui columbas vendebant, dixit* etc., ponit remedium quod adhibuit verbo.

Ubi notandum est, quod simoniaci primo quidem fugandi sunt de Ecclesia. Sed quia adhuc dum vivunt, per liberum arbitrium possunt se convertere, et adiuti a Deo ad statum gratiae redire, non sunt desperandi. Si vero non convertuntur, tunc quidem non fugantur, sed ligantur ab illis, quibus dicitur, Matth. XXII, 13: *ligatis manibus et pedibus eius, mittite eum in tenebras exteriores.*

Et ideo Dominus hoc attendens,
primo quidem admonet;
secundo rationem admonitionis inducit, ibi *et nolite facere* etc.

388. Monet quidem venditores columbarum eos increpando, quia per eos signantur illi qui vendunt dona Spiritus Sancti, scilicet simoniaci.

389. Rationem huius inducit, cum dicit: *et nolite facere domum Patris mei, domum negotiationis.* Is. I, 16: *auferte malum cogitationum vestrarum ab oculis meis.*

Attende autem, quod Matth. XXI, 13 dicit: *nolite facere domum meam speluncam latronum,* hic vero dicit: *domum negotiationis,* quod Dominus ideo fecit ut, sicut bonus medicus, primo a levioribus incipiens, postea dura proponeret. Hoc enim quod hic factum dicitur, primo factum fuit: unde in ipso principio, non latrones, sed negotiatores eos vocat. Sed quia ex eorum duritia adhuc a tali negotiatione non cessabant, ideo Dominus alia vice eos expellens de quo agitur in Mc. c. IX, 15 ss. durius eos increpat, vocans latrocinium quod primo vocaverat negotiationem.

Dicit autem *domum Patris mei,* ad excludendum errorem Manichaei, qui dicebat, quod Deus Veteris Testamenti non fuerat Pater Christi, sed Deus Novi. Sed si hoc verum esset, cum templum fuisset domus Veteris Testamenti, non utique Christus dixisset templum domum Patris sui.

390. Sed quare non sunt turbati Iudaei de hoc quod hic vocat Deum Patrem suum, sicut dicitur infra V, 18, quod *propter hoc eum persequerentur?*

Ad quod dicendum est, quod Deus est Pater aliquorum per adoptionem, puta iustorum, et hoc non erat novum apud Iudaeos; Ier. III, 19: *Patrem vocabis me, et post me ingredi non cessabis.* Sed per naturam solius Christi

Again, by casting things of this kind out of the temple, he let it be understood that the time was coming in which the sacrifices of the law were due to cease, and the true worship of God transferred to the gentiles: *the kingdom of God will be taken away from you* (Matt 21:43). Also, this shows us the condemnation of those who sell spiritual things: *may your money perish together with you* (Acts 8:20).

387. Then when he says, *to those who sold doves he said,* he records the treatment which the Lord applied by word.

Here it should be noted that those who engage in simony should, of course, first be expelled from the Church. But because as long as they are alive, they can change themselves by free will and by the help of God return to the state of grace, they should not be given up as hopeless. If, however, they are not converted, then they are not merely to be expelled, but handed over to those to whom it is said: *bind him hand and foot, and cast him into outer darkness* (Matt 22:13).

And so the Lord, attending to this,
first warns them,
second, he gives the reason for his warning, at *and do not make the house of my Father a marketplace.*

388. He warns those selling the doves by reproaching them, for they signify those who sell the gifts of the Holy Spirit, i.e., those who engage in simony.

389. He gives his reason for this when he says, *and do not make the house of my Father a marketplace. Take away your evil from my sight* (Isa 1:10).

Note what is said: *do not make my house a den of thieves* (Matt 21:13), while here he says, *a marketplace.* Now the Lord does this because, as a good physician, he begins first with the gentler things; later on, he would propose harsher things. Now the action recorded here was the first of the two; hence in the beginning he does not call them thieves but merchants. But because they did not stop such business out of obstinacy, the Lord, when driving them out the second time (Mark 11:15), rebukes them more severely, calling robbery what he had first called business.

He says, *the house of my Father,* to exclude the error of Manicheus, who said that while the God of the New Testament was the Father of Christ, the God of the Old Testament was not. But if this were true, then since the temple was the house of the Old Testament, Christ would not have referred to the temple as my Father's house.

390. Why were the Jews not disturbed here when he called God his Father? for as is said, this is why *the Jews sought the more to kill him* (John 5:18).

I answer that God is the Father of certain men through adoption; for example, he is the Father of the just in this way. This was not a new idea for the Jews: *you will call me Father, and you will not cease to walk after me* (Jer 3:19).

est, Ps. II, 7: *Dominus dixit ad me: Filius meus es tu*, scilicet verus et naturalis; et hoc inauditum erat apud eos. Et ideo quia Christus se verum Dei Filium dicebat, Iudaei persequebantur ipsum; infra V, 18: **propter hoc persequebantur Iudaei Christum, quia non solum solvebat Sabbatum; sed et Patrem suum dicebat Deum, aequalem se Deo faciens.** Cum autem hic Deum vocat Patrem, dicebant de eo quod esset per adoptionem.

391. Quod autem domus Dei non debeat fieri domus negotiationis, habetur Zach. c. ult., 21: *non erit ultra mercator in domo Domini exercituum in die illo.* Et in Ps. LXX, v. 16 secundum aliam litteram: *quoniam non cognovi negotiationem, introibo in potentias Domini.*

392. Consequenter cum dicit **recordati sunt vero discipuli eius** etc. ponit prophetiae oraculum, quod quidem scriptum est in Ps. LXVIII, 10: **zelus domus tuae comedit me.**

Ubi sciendum, quod zelus proprie dicit quamdam intensionem amoris, qua intense diligens, nihil sustinet quod amori suo repugnet. Et inde est quod viri diligentes intense uxores, nec in eis sustinentes aliorum consortium, utpote amori eorum contrarium, zelotypi dicuntur. Ille igitur proprie zelum Dei habet qui nihil patienter sustinere potest contra honorem Dei, quem maxime diligit; III Reg. c. XIX, 10: *zelo zelatus sum pro Domino exercituum* etc. Nos autem debemus diligere donum Domini, secundum illud Ps. XXV, 8: *Domine, dilexi decorem domus tuae.* Et intantum debemus diligere quod zelus eius nos comedat: dum si quid contrarium fieri videbimus, studeamus etiam quantumcumque cari nostri sint qui hoc facient, removere, nec timeamus propter hoc aliqua mala perpeti. Unde dicitur in Glossa: *bonus zelus est fervor animi, quo quis mortis abiecto timore, pro defensione veritatis accenditur. Eo comeditur, qui quaelibet prava quae viderit, corrigere satagit; et si nequit, tolerat, et gemit.*

However, by nature he is the Father of Christ alone: *the Lord said to me: 'you are my Son'* (Ps 2:7), i.e., the true and natural Son. It is this that was unheard of among the Jews. And so the Jews persecuted him because he called himself the true Son of God: **therefore, the Jews sought the more to kill him, because he did not only break the Sabbath, but also said that God was his Father, making himself equal to God** (John 5:18). But when he called God his Father on this occasion, they said it was by adoption.

391. That the house of God shall not be made a marketplace is taken from: *on that day there will no longer be any merchants in the house of the Lord of hosts* (Zech 14:21); and from the Psalm, where one version has the reading: *because I was not part of the marketplace, I will enter into the strength of the Lord* (Ps 70:16).

392. Then when he says, **and his disciples remembered**, he sets down a prophecy: **zeal for your house consumes me** (Ps 69:9).

Here we should remark that zeal, properly speaking, signifies an intensity of love, whereby the one who loves intensely does not tolerate anything which is repugnant to his love. So it is that men who love their wives intensely and cannot endure their being in the company of other men, as this conflicts with their own love, are called *zelotypes.* Thus, properly speaking, one is said to have zeal for God who cannot patiently endure anything contrary to the honor of God, whoin he loves above all else: *I have been very zealous for the Lord God of hosts* (1 Kgs 19:10). Now we should love the house of the Lord: *O Lord, I have loved the beauty of your house* (Ps 25:8). Indeed, we should love it so much that our zeal consumes us, so that if we notice anything amiss being done, we should try to eliminate it, no matter how dear to us are those who are doing it; nor should we fear any evils that we might have to endure as a result. So the Gloss says: *good zeal is a fervor of spirit, by which, scorning the fear of death, one is on fire for the defense of the truth. He is consumed by it who takes steps to correct any perversity he sees; and if he cannot, he tolerates it with sadness.*

Lecture 3

^{2:18} Responderunt ergo Iudaei, et dixerunt ei: quod signum ostendis nobis, quia haec facis? [n. 394]

^{2:19} Respondit Iesus, et dixit eis: solvite templum hoc, et in tribus diebus excitabo illud. [n. 397]

^{2:20} Dixerunt ergo Iudaei: quadraginta et sex annis aedificatum est templum hoc, et tu in tribus diebus excitabis illud? [n. 406]

^{2:21} Ille autem dicebat de templo corporis sui. [n. 412]

^{2:22} Cum ergo resurrexisset a mortuis, recordati sunt discipuli eius, quia hoc dicebat: et crediderunt Scripturae et sermoni, quem dixit Iesus. [n. 414]

^{2:23} Cum autem esset Ierosolymis in Pascha in die festo, multi crediderunt in nomine eius, videntes signa quae faciebat. [n. 417]

^{2:24} Ipse autem Iesus non credebat semetipsum eis: eo quod ipse nosset omnes, [n. 420]

^{2:25} et quia opus ei non erat, ut quis testimonium perhiberet de homine: ipse enim sciebat quid esset in homine. [n. 421]

^{2:18} Ἀπεκρίθησαν οὖν οἱ Ἰουδαῖοι καὶ εἶπαν αὐτῷ· τί σημεῖον δεικνύεις ἡμῖν ὅτι ταῦτα ποιεῖς;

^{2:19} ἀπεκρίθη Ἰησοῦς καὶ εἶπεν αὐτοῖς· λύσατε τὸν ναὸν τοῦτον καὶ ἐν τρισὶν ἡμέραις ἐγερῶ αὐτόν.

^{2:20} εἶπαν οὖν οἱ Ἰουδαῖοι· τεσσεράκοντα καὶ ἓξ ἔτεσιν οἰκοδομήθη ὁ ναὸς οὗτος, καὶ σὺ ἐν τρισὶν ἡμέραις ἐγερεῖς αὐτόν;

^{2:21} ἐκεῖνος δὲ ἔλεγεν περὶ τοῦ ναοῦ τοῦ σώματος αὐτοῦ.

^{2:22} ὅτε οὖν ἠγέρθη ἐκ νεκρῶν, ἐμνήσθησαν οἱ μαθηταὶ αὐτοῦ ὅτι τοῦτο ἔλεγεν, καὶ ἐπίστευσαν τῇ γραφῇ καὶ τῷ λόγῳ ὃν εἶπεν ὁ Ἰησοῦς.

^{2:23} Ὡς δὲ ἦν ἐν τοῖς Ἱεροσολύμοις ἐν τῷ πάσχα ἐν τῇ ἑορτῇ, πολλοὶ ἐπίστευσαν εἰς τὸ ὄνομα αὐτοῦ θεωροῦντες αὐτοῦ τὰ σημεῖα ἃ ἐποίει·

^{2:24} αὐτὸς δὲ Ἰησοῦς οὐκ ἐπίστευεν αὐτὸν αὐτοῖς διὰ τὸ αὐτὸν γινώσκειν πάντας

^{2:25} καὶ ὅτι οὐ χρείαν εἶχεν ἵνα τις μαρτυρήσῃ περὶ τοῦ ἀνθρώπου· αὐτὸς γὰρ ἐγίνωσκεν τί ἦν ἐν τῷ ἀνθρώπῳ.

^{2:18} The Jews, therefore, answered and said to him: what sign can you show us, because you do these things? [n. 394]

^{2:19} Jesus answered and said to them: destroy this temple, and in three days I will raise it up. [n. 397]

^{2:20} The Jews then said: this temple was built in forty-six years, and you will raise it up in three days? [n. 406]

^{2:21} But he spoke of the temple of his body. [n. 412]

^{2:22} When, therefore, he had risen from the dead, his disciples remembered that he had said this, and they believed the Scripture and the word that Jesus had said. [n. 414]

^{2:23} Now when he was at Jerusalem during the Passover, upon the festival day, many believed in his name, seeing the signs that he did. [n. 417]

^{2:24} But Jesus did not trust himself to them, for he knew all men, [n. 420]

^{2:25} and because he did not need anyone to give testimony of man: for he knew what was in man. [n. 421]

393. Posita occasione signi exhibendi, hic consequenter Evangelista manifestat signum exhibendum: et

primo ponit signum quod exhibetur;

secundo ponit fructum factorum signorum, qui sequitur, ibi *cum autem esset Ierosolymis* etc.

Circa primum tria facit.

Primo ponitur signi postulatio;

secundo signi exhibitio, ibi *respondit Iesus, et dixit eis: solvite templum hoc* etc.;

tertio signi exhibiti intellectus, seu conceptio, ibi *dixerunt ergo ei: quadraginta et sex annis aedificatum est templum hoc* etc.

394. Signum autem postulatur a Iudaeis; et hoc est quod dixit *responderunt ergo Iudaei, et dixerunt ei: quod signum ostendis nobis, quia haec facis?*

395. Ubi sciendum est, quod in eiectione negotiatorum de templo per Iesum, duo considerari poterant in Christo: rectitudo et zelus, quae pertinent ad virtutem;

393. Having set forth the occasion for showing the sign, the Evangelist then states the sign which would be given.

First, he gives the sign.

Second, he mentions the fruit of the signs Christ performed, at *when he was at Jerusalem during the Passover*.

As to the first he does three things.

First, the request for the sign is given.

Second, the sign itself, at *Jesus answered and said to them: destroy this temple*.

Third, the way the sign was understood, at *the Jews then said: this temple was built in forty-six years*.

394. The Jews ask for a sign; and this is what the Evangelist says: *the Jews, therefore, answered and said to him: what sign can you show us, because you do these things?*

395. Here we should note that when Jesus drove the merchants out of the temple, two things could be considered in Christ: his rectitude and zeal, which pertain to

et potestas, seu auctoritas. Sed de virtute et zelo Christi, quibus praedicta fecerat, non oportebat peti signum a Christo; cum unicuique liceat operari secundum virtutem. De auctoritate tamen eius, qua eos de templo expellit, signum ab eo quaeri poterat; cum hoc non cuilibet liceret facere, sed auctoritatem habenti.

Praetermisso igitur Iudaei zelo et virtute, signum petunt de eius auctoritate; et ideo dicunt **quod signum ostendis nobis, quia haec facis?** Idest, quare cum tanta potestate et auctoritate nos expellis? Non videtur hoc esse tui officii. Simile dicunt, Matth. XXI, 23: *in qua potestate haec facis?* etc.

396. Signum autem quaerunt: quia familiare erat Iudaeis, signum quaerere, utpote per ea ad legem vocati; Deut. ult., 10. *Non surrexit ultra propheta in Israel sicut Moyses, quem nosset Dominus facie ad faciem, in omnibus signis atque portentis.* Et, I Cor. c. I, 22, *Iudaei signa quaerunt.* Ideo David in persona Iudaeorum conqueritur, dicens, Ps. LXXIII, 9: *signa nostra non vidimus.*

Quaerebant autem signum, non ut crederent, sed quasi desperantes, quod signum ostendere non posset, et sic eum reprimerent et impedirent. Quia ergo prave quaerebant, non dedit eis signum apertum, sed occultum in figura, scilicet signum de resurrectione.

397. Unde dicit **respondit Iesus, et dixit eis** etc. in quo ponitur signi postulati exhibitio.

Ideo autem dat eis signum resurrectionis futurum, quia in hoc maxime virtus divinitatis eius ostenditur. Non enim puri hominis est ut se excitaret a mortuis; sed solum Christus, qui fuit inter mortuos liber, hoc virtute suae divinitatis fecit. Simile etiam signum ostendit eis. Matth. XII, 39: *generatio prava, et adultera signum quaerit; sed signum non dabitur ei nisi signum Ionae prophetae.* Et licet utrobique dederit signum occultum et figurale; illud tamen manifestius, istud vero obscurius fuit.

398. Notandum autem, quod ante incarnationem dedit Deus signum futurae incarnationis, Is. VII, 14: *ipse Dominus dabit vobis signum: ecce virgo concipiet, et pariet filium* etc.; similiter et ante resurrectionem dedit signum de resurrectione futura: quia istis duobus maxime virtus divinitatis commendatur in Christo. Nihil enim mirabilius fieri potuit quam quod Deus factus est homo, et quod humanitas in Christo, post eius resurrectionem, immortalitatis divinae particeps effecta est; Rom. VI, 9: *Christus resurgens ex mortuis, iam non moritur . . . quod enim vivit, vivit Deo,* idest ad similitudinem Dei.

399. Sed attendenda sunt verba signi dati. Nam Christus corpus suum templum dicit: cuius ratio est, quia

virtue; and his power or authority. It was not appropriate to require a sign from Christ concerning the virtue and zeal with which he did the above action, since everyone may lawfully act according to virtue. But he could be required to give a sign concerning his authority for driving them out of the temple, since it is not lawful for anyone to do this unless he has the authority.

And so the Jews, not questioning his zeal and virtue, ask for a sign of his authority; and so they say, **what sign can you show us, because you do these things?** i.e., why do you drive us out with such power and authority, for this does not seem to be your office? They say the same thing elsewhere: *by what authority are you doing these things?* (Matt 21:23).

396. The reason they ask for a sign is that it was the usual thing for Jews to require a sign, seeing that they were called to the law by signs: *there did not arise again in Israel a prophet like Moses, whom, the Lord knew face to face, with all his signs and wonders* (Deut 34:10), and *the Jews require signs* (1 Cor 1:22). Hence David complains for the Jews saying: *we have not seen our signs* (Ps 73:9).

However, they asked him for a sign not in order to believe, but in the hope that he would not be able to provide the sign, and then they could obstruct and restrain him. And so, because they asked in an evil manner, he did not give them an evident sign, but a sign clothed in a symbol, a sign concerning the resurrection.

397. Hence it says, **Jesus answered and said to them: destroy this temple, and in three days I will raise it up**, and he gives the sign for which they asked.

He gives them the sign of his future resurrection because this shows most strikingly the power of his divinity. For it is not within the power of mere man to raise himself from the dead. Christ alone, who was free among the dead, did this by the power of his divinity. He shows them a similar sign: *an evil and adulterous generation asks for a sign. And a sign will not be given it, except the sign of Jonah the prophet* (Matt 12:30). And although he gave a hidden and symbolic sign on both occasions, the first was stated more clearly, and the second more obscurely.

398. We should note that before the incarnation, God gave a sign of the incarnation to come: *the Lord himself will give you a sign. A virgin will conceive, and give birth to a son* (Isa 7:14). And in like manner, before the resurrection he gave a sign of the resurrection to come. And he did this because it is especially by these two events that the power of the divinity in Christ is evidenced. For nothing more marvelous could be done than that God become man and that Christ's humanity should become a partaker of divine immortality after his resurrection: *Christ, rising from the dead, will not die again . . . his life is life with God* (Rom 6:9), i.e., in a likeness to God.

399. We should note the words Christ used in giving this sign. For Christ calls his body a temple, because a

templum dicitur in quo Deus inhabitat etc. secundum illud Ps. X, 5: *Dominus in templo sancto suo.* Et inde est quod anima sancta, quam Deus inhabitat, dicitur templum Dei; I Cor. III, 17: *templum Dei sanctum est, quod estis vos.* Quia ergo in corpore Christi divinitas inhabitat, ideo corpus Christi est templum Dei, non solum secundum animam, sed etiam secundum corpus; Col. II, 9: *in quo inhabitat omnis plenitudo divinitatis corporaliter.*

Et in nobis quidem habitat Deus secundum gratiam, scilicet secundum actum intellectus et voluntatis, qui non est actus corporis, sed animae tantum; sed in Christo habitat secundum unionem in persona: quae quidem unio non solum ipsam animam, sed et corpus includit; et ideo ipsum corpus Christi est templum Dei.

400. Ex hoc autem Nestorius, sui erroris occasionem sumens, dicit Verbum Dei unitum humanae naturae secundum inhabitationem tantum; ex quo sequitur quod alia sit persona Dei, alia hominis in Christo.

Et ideo dicendum est, quod inhabitatio Dei in Christo refertur ad naturam, quia alia est divina natura, alia humana in Christo; sed non ad personam, quae est eadem in Christo Dei et hominis, scilicet persona Verbi, ut dictum est supra.

401. Hoc igitur supposito, circa hoc signum Dominus duo facit.

Primo quidem praenuntiat suam mortem futuram; secundo vero resurrectionem.

402. Mortem quidem praenuntiat cum dicit **solvite templum hoc.** Christus enim mortuus fuit, et ab aliis occisus, Matth. XVII, v. 22: *et occident eum,* eo tamen volente: quia, ut dicitur Is. LIII, 7, *oblatus est quia ipse voluit.* Et ideo dicit **solvite templum hoc,** idest corpus meum.

Et non dicit, solvetur, ne intelligas eum seipsum occidisse; sed dicit **solvite,** quod non est imperantis, sed praenuntiantis, et permittentis. Praenuntiantis quidem, ut sit sensus **solvite templum hoc,** idest, solvetis; permittentis vero, ut sit sensus **solvite templum hoc,** idest, facite de corpore meo quod vultis, illud vobis expono, sicut dicit Iudae, infra XIII, 27: **quod facis, fac citius:** non quidem imperans ei, sed eum eius arbitrio derelinquens.

Dicit autem **solvite,** quia mors Christi est solutio corporis eius, aliter tamen quam aliorum hominum. Nam corpora aliorum hominum solvuntur per mortem usque ad incinerationem carnis, et pulverationem: qualis quidem solutio non fuit in Christo; quia, ut dicitur in Ps. XV, 10, *non dabis Sanctum tuum videre corruptionem.* Fuit ibi tamen solutio per mortem, quia anima separata est a corpore, ut forma a materia, et quia sanguis separatus est a corpore, et quia corpus eius perforatum est clavis et lancea.

temple is something in which God dwells, according to *the Lord is in his holy temple* (Ps 10:5). And so a holy soul, in which God dwells, is also called a temple of God: *the temple of God is holy, and that is what you are* (1 Cor 3:17). Therefore, because the divinity dwells in the body of Christ, the body of Christ is the temple of God, not only according to the soul but also according to the body: *in him all the fullness of the divinity dwells bodily* (Col 2:9).

God dwells in us by grace, i.e., according to an act of the intellect and will, which is not an act of the body, but of the soul alone. But he dwells in Christ according to a union in the person; and this union includes not only the soul, but the body as well. And so the very body of Christ is God's temple.

400. But Nestorius, using this text in support of his error, claims that the Word of God was joined to human nature only by an indwelling, from which it follows that the person of God is distinct from that of man in Christ.

Therefore it is important to insist that God's indwelling in Christ refers to the nature, since in Christ human nature is distinct from the divine, and not to the person, which in the case of Christ is the same for both God and man, that is, the person of the Word, as was said above.

401. Therefore, granting this, the Lord does two things with respect to this sign.

First, he foretells his future death.

Second, his resurrection.

402. Christ foretells his own death when he says, **destroy this temple**. For Christ died and was killed by others: *and they will kill him* (Matt 17:22), yet with him willing it: because as is said: *he was offered because it was his own will* (Isa 53:7). And so he says, **destroy this temple**, i.e., my body.

He does not say, that it will be destroyed, lest you suppose he killed himself. He says, **destroy**, which is not a command but a prediction and a permission. A prediction, so that the sense is, **destroy this temple**, i.e., you will destroy. And a permission, so that the sense is, **destroy this temple**, i.e., do with my body what you will, I submit it to you. As he said to Judas: **that which you do, do quickly** (John 13:27), not as commanding him, but as abandoning himself to his decision.

He says **destroy**, because the death of Christ is the dissolution of his body, but in a way different from that of other men. For the bodies of other men are destroyed by death even to the point of the body's returning to dust and ashes. But such a dissolution did not take place in Christ, for is it is said: *you will not allow your Holy One to see corruption* (Ps 15:10). Nevertheless, death did bring a dissolution to Christ, because his soul was separated from his body as a form from matter, and because his blood was separated from his body, and because his body was pierced with nails and a lance.

403. Resurrectionem autem praenuntiat cum dicit *et in tribus diebus excitabo illud*, scilicet corpus; idest a mortuis suscitabo.

Non autem dicit *excitabitur*, nec *excitabis illud Pater*, sed *ego excitabo*: ut ostendat se propria virtute a mortuis resurgere. Nec tamen negamus quin Pater eum a mortuis suscitaverit, quia, ut dicitur Rom. c. VIII, 11, *qui suscitavit Iesum a mortuis*. Et in Ps. XL, 11: *tu autem, Domine, miserere mei, et resuscita me*. Sic ergo Deus Pater Christum suscitavit a mortuis, et Christus propria virtute resurrexit; Ps. III, 6: *ego dormivi, et soporatus sum, et exurrexi, quia Dominus suscepit me*. Nec est in hoc contrarietas, quia eadem est virtus utriusque: unde *quaecumque Pater facit, haec similiter, et Filius facit*: infra V, 19. Nam si Pater eum suscitavit, et Filius; II Cor. ult., 4: *nam si crucifixus est ex infirmitate, sed vivit ex virtute Dei*.

404. Dicit autem *et in tribus diebus* et non post tres dies, quia non diebus tribus completis in monumento permansit; sed, sicut Augustinus dicit, est synecdochica locutio, in qua ponitur pars pro toto.

Origenes autem huius locutionis mysticam rationem assignat, dicens: corpus Christi verum est templum Dei, quod quidem corpus figurat corpus mysticum, idest Ecclesiam; I Cor. XII, 27: *vos estis corpus Christi, et membra de membro*. Et sicut in corpore Christi habitat divinitas per gratiam unionis, ita et in Ecclesia per gratiam adoptionis. Et quamvis corpus istud mystice dissolvi videatur adversitatibus tribulationum, quibus affligitur, tamen suscitatur *in tribus diebus*, scilicet in die legis naturae, et in die legis scriptae, et in die legis gratiae; quia, etsi in his diebus, quantum ad aliquos corpus dissolvatur, quantum ad aliquos tamen vivit. Et ideo dicit *in tribus diebus*, quia huius resurrectio spiritualis in tribus diebus perficitur. Sed post tres dies perfecte resuscitabimus, non solum quantum ad primam resurrectionem, sed etiam quantum ad secundam; Apoc. XX, v. 6: *beatus qui habet partem in resurrectione secunda*.

405. Consequenter cum dicit *dixerunt ergo Iudaei* etc. ponitur signi exhibiti intellectus, et

primo quidem ponitur intellectus falsus, conceptus a Iudaeis;

secundo vero intellectus verus, conceptus ab apostolis, ibi *ille autem dicebat de templo corporis sui*.

406. Falsus autem intellectus Iudaeorum erat quia credebant quod Christus diceret hoc de templo materiali, in quo tunc erat; et ideo secundum hunc intellectum, respondent de templo materiali, et dicunt *quadraginta et sex annis aedificatum est templum hoc*, scilicet materiale, in quo sumus, *et in tribus diebus excitabis illud?*

403. He foretells his resurrection when he says, and *in three days I will raise it up*, that is, his body; i.e., I will raise it from the dead.

He does not say that *I will be raised up*, or *the Father will raise it up*, but *I will raise it up*, to show that he would rise from the dead by his own power. Yet we do not deny that the Father raised him from the dead, because as it is said: *who raised Jesus from the dead* (Rom 8:11); and *O Lord, have pity on me, and raise me up* (Ps 40:10). And so God the Father raised Christ from the dead, and Christ arose by his own power: *I have slept and have taken my rest, and I have risen, because the Lord has taken me* (Ps 3:6). There is no contradiction in this, because the power of both is the same; hence *whatever the Father does, these the Son also does in like manner* (John 5:19). For if the Father raised him up, so too did the Son: *although he was crucified through weakness, he lives through the power of God* (2 Cor 13:4).

404. He says, and *in three days*, and not after three days, because he did not remain in the tomb for three complete days; but, as Augustine says, he is employing synecdoche, in which a part is taken for the whole.

Origen, however, assigns a mystical reason for this expression, and says: the true body of Christ is the temple of God, and this body symbolizes the mystical body, i.e., the Church: *you are the body of Christ and members of member* (1 Cor 12:27). And as the divinity dwells in the body of Christ through the grace of union, so too he dwells in the Church through the grace of adoption. Although that body may seem to be destroyed mystically by the adversities of persecutions with which it is afflicted, nevertheless it is raised up *in three days*, namely, in the day of the law of nature, the day of the written law, and the day of the law of grace; because in those days a part of that body was destroyed, while another still lived. And so he says, *in three days*, because the spiritual resurrection of this body is accomplished in three days. But after those three days we will be perfectly risen, not only as to the first resurrection, but also as to the second: *happy are they who share in the second resurrection* (Rev 20:6).

405. Then when he says, *the Jews then said*: *this temple was built in forty-six years*, we have the interpretation of the sign he gave.

First, the false interpretation of the Jews.

Second, its true understanding by the apostles, at *but he spoke of the temple of his body*.

406. The interpretation of the Jews was false, because they believed that Christ was saying this of the material temple in which he then was; consequently, they answer according to this interpretation and say: *this temple was built in forty-six years*, i.e., this material temple in which we are standing, *and you will raise it up in three days?*

407. Sed contra hoc est obiectio litteralis. Nam templum in Ierusalem per Salomonem fuit aedificatum, et ut habetur III Reg. c. VI, 1 s. a Salomone fuit consummatum septem annis, quid est ergo quod hic dicit **quadraginta et sex annis aedificatum est templum hoc?**

Respondeo. Dicendum, secundum quosdam, quod hoc non est intelligendum de prima aedificatione templi, quae completa est a Salomone septem annis: nam templum quod Salomon aedificaverat, destructum fuit a Nabuchodonosor, sed intelligendum est de reaedificatione facta sub Zorobabel, postquam reversi fuerunt a captivitate, sicut legitur in libro Esdrae quae quidem multis impugnantibus undique inimicis, intantum impedita et dilata fuit, quod non potuit consummari templum usque ad quadragesimum sextum annum.

408. Vel dicendum, secundum Origenem, quod intelligitur de templo Salomonis: quod quidem dicitur aedificatum quadraginta et sex annorum tempore, ut numeretur tempus ab eo die quo David mentionem fecit de aedificatione templi, consulens super hoc Nathan prophetam, ut habetur II Reg. VII, 2 s., usque ad consummationem perfectam per Salomonem: nam ex illo die David incepit praeparare materiam et necessaria ad aedificationem templi. Et si diligenter dictum tempus consideretur, ascendit ad numerum quadraginta sex annorum.

409. Quamvis autem Iudaei intentionem suam referrent ad templum materiale, tamen, secundum Augustinum, potest referri ad templum corporis Christi: quia, sicut ipse dicit in *Lib. LXXXIII quaest.*, conceptio et formatio humani corporis perficitur quadraginta quinque diebus hoc modo. Primis enim sex diebus corporis humani conceptio, quasi lactis habet similitudinem; novem vero diebus sequentibus convertitur in sanguinem; duodecim inde diebus solidatur in carnem; sed decem et octo reliquis diebus formatur usque ad perfecta lineamenta omnium membrorum. Isto ergo numero sex, novem, duodecim et octodecim in unum coacto, exurgit numerus quadraginta et quinque, cui addito uno propter sacramentum unitatis, sunt quadraginta sex.

410. Sed ex hoc insurgit quaestio: quia huius processus formationis non videtur habere locum in corpore Christi, quia in ipso instanti conceptionis formatum fuit et animatum.

Sed dicendum, quod licet in corporis Christi formatione sit aliquid singulare, quia in ipso instanti corpus Christi fuit perfectum quantum ad omnia lineamenta membrorum, non tamen quantum ad debitam corporis quantitatem; et ideo in utero Virginis tamdiu permansit quousque ad quantitatem debitam perveniret. Accipiamus autem dictum numerum suprapositum, scilicet senarium, qui primus erat et quadraginta sex, qui erat ultimus; et ducamus unum in alterum: ex eis surgunt ducenta septuaginta sex. Dividendo ergo tot dies in

407. There is a literal objection against this. For the temple in Jerusalem was built by Solomon, and it is recorded that it was completed by Solomon in seven years (2 Chr 6:1). How then can it be said that **this temple was built in forty-six years**?

I answer that it is said according to some, that this is not to be understood of the very first temple, which was completed by Solomon in seven years: for that temple built by Solomon was destroyed by Nebuchadnezzar. But it is to be understood of the temple rebuilt under Zerubbabel, after they returned from captivity (Ezra 5:2). However, this rebuilding was so hindered and delayed by the frequent attacks of their enemies on all sides, that the temple was not finished until forty-six years had passed.

408. Or it could be said, according to Origen, that they were speaking of Solomon's temple: and it did take forty-six years to build if the time be reckoned from the day when David first spoke of building a temple, discussing it with Nathan the prophet (2 Sam 7:2), until its final completion under Solomon. For from that first day onward David began preparing the material and the things necessary for building the temple. Accordingly, if the time in question is carefully calculated, it will come up to the number forty-six years.

409. But although the Jews referred their interpretation to the material temple, nevertheless, according to Augustine, it can be referred to the temple of Christ's body. As he says in *The Book of Eighty-three Questions*, the conception and formation of the human body is completed in forty-five days in the following manner. During the first six days, the conception of a human body has a likeness to milk; during the next nine days it is converted into blood; then in the next twelve days, it is hardened into flesh; then the remaining eighteen days, it is formed into a perfect outlining of all the members. But if we add six, nine, twelve and eighteen, there arises the number forty-five; and if we add one for the sacrament of unity, we get forty-six.

410. However a question arises about this: because this process of formation does not seem to have taken place in Christ, who was formed and animated at the very instant of conception.

But one may answer that although in the formation of Christ's body there was something unique, in that Christ's body was perfect at that instant as to the outlining of its members, it was not perfect as to the quantity due the body; and so he remained in the Virgin's womb until he attained the due quantity. However, let us take the above numbers and select six, which was the first, and forty-six, which was the last, and let us multiply one by the other. The result is two hundred seventy-six. Now if we assemble these days into months, allotting thirty days to a month,

menses, dando cuilibet mensi triginta dies sunt novem menses et sex dies. Recte ergo quadraginta et sex annis templum dicitur aedificatum esse, quod significabat corpus Christi, ut insinuet, quod tot anni fuerunt in fabricatione templi quod fuerunt dies in perfectione corporis Christi: nam ab octavo Kal. Aprilis in quo Christus fuit conceptus, et (ut creditur) passus, usque ad octavum Kal. Ianuarii sunt tot dies, scilicet ducenti septuaginta sex, quod numerus surgit ex senario ducto in quadraginta et sex.

411. Ex hoc etiam numero Augustinus (ut patet per Glossam) aliud intelligit mystice. Dicit enim, quod ex litteris nominis Adam multiplicatis, secundum numerum quem more Graecorum ipsae litterae important, surgit numerus quadraginta et sex. Nam a in Graeco secundum numerum importat unum, cum sit prima littera in alphabeto; d vero secundum ordinem importat quatuor. Addito ergo uno quod importat a, et quadraginta quod importat m, habemus quadraginta et sex. In quo significatur quod corpus Christi assumptum est de corpore Adam.

Item secundum Graecos ex primis litteris acceptis ex nominibus quatuor partium mundi componitur hoc nomen Adam: scilicet anatole, quod est oriens; disis quod est occidens; Arctos, quod est Septemtrio; mensembria, quod est meridies: in quo significatur quod Christus ex Adam carnem assumpsit, ut congreget electos suos a quatuor partibus mundi; Matth. XXIV, 31: *congregabit electos suos a quatuor ventis.*

412. Consequenter cum dicit *ille autem dicebat de templo corporis sui*, ponitur intellectus signi verus, conceptus a discipulis, et

primo ponitur ipsorum intellectus;

secundo vero unde apostoli hoc conceperunt, ibi *cum ergo surrexit* etc.

413. Dicit ergo: Iudaei hoc dixerunt ignorantes, sed Christus non sic intelligebat, immo intelligebat de templo corporis sui; et hoc est quod dicit *ille autem dicebat de templo corporis sui*. Qua autem ratione corpus Christi dicatur templum, dictum est supra.

Et ex hoc Apollinaris occasionem erroris sumens, dixit, quod caro Christi esset materia inanimata, quia templum est res inanimata. Sed in hoc decipitur: quia cum dicitur quod corpus Christi est templum, est metaphorica locutio, in qua quidem locutione non attenditur similitudo quantum ad omnia, sed quantum ad aliquid, scilicet quantum ad inhabitationem, quod quidem refertur ad naturam, ut dictum est supra. Praeterea hoc manifeste apparet per auctoritatem Sacrae Scripturae, cum dicit ipse Christus: *potestatem habeo ponendi animam meam.*

414. Unde autem apostoli hunc verum intellectum conceperunt, ostendit consequenter Evangelista, cum

we get nine months and six days. Thus it was correct to say that it took forty-six years to build the temple, which signifies the body of Christ; the suggestion being that there were as many years in building the temple as there were days in perfecting the body of Christ. For from March twenty-five, when Christ was conceived, and (as is believed) when he suffered, to December twenty-five, there are this number of days, namely, two hundred seventy-six, a number that is the result of multiplying forty-six by six.

411. Augustine (as is plain from the Gloss) has another mystical interpretation of this number. For he says that if one adds the letters in the name Adam, using for each the number it represented for the Greeks, the result is forty-six. For in Greek, A represents the number one, since it is the first letter of the alphabet. And according to this order, D is four. Adding to the sum of these another one for the second A and forty for the letter M, we have forty-six. This signifies that the body of Christ was derived from the body of Adam.

Again, according to the Greeks, the name Adam is composed of the first letters of the names of the four directions of the world: namely, Anathole, which is the east; Disis, which is the west; Arctos, which is the north; and Mensembria, the south. This signifies that Christ derived his flesh from Adam in order to gather his elect from the four parts of the world: *he will gather his elect from the four winds* (Matt 24:31).

412. Then, the true interpretation of this sign as understood by the apostles is given, at *but he spoke of the temple of his body.*

First, the way they understood it is given.

Second, the time when they understood it, at *when, therefore, he had risen from the dead.*

413. He says therefore: the Jews said this out of ignorance. But Christ did not understand it in their way; in fact, he meant the temple of his body, and this is what he says: *but he spoke of the temple of his body.* We have already explained why the body of Christ could be called a temple.

Apollinaris misunderstood this and said that the body of Christ was inanimate matter because the temple was inanimate. He was mistaken in this for when it is said that the body of Christ is a temple, one is speaking metaphorically. And in this way of speaking a likeness does not exist in all respects, but only in some respect, namely, as to indwelling, which is referred to the nature, as was explained. Further, this is evident from the authority of Sacred Scripuire, when Christ himself said: *I have the power to lay it down* (John 10:18).

414. The time when the apostles acquired this true understanding is then shown by the Evangelist when he says,

subdit *cum ergo surrexisset a mortuis, recordati sunt discipuli eius* etc. Nam ante resurrectionem difficile erat hoc intelligere: primo quia per hoc ostendebatur quod in corpore Christi erat vera divinitas, alias non potuisset dici templum; et hoc tunc temporis intelligere, humanam capacitatem excedebat. Secundo quia in hoc facit mentionem de passione et resurrectione, cum dicit *excitabo illud*, quod nullus discipulorum adhuc audierat. Unde quando Christus resurrectionem et passionem suam expressit apostolis, Petrus hoc audiens, scandalizatus est, dicens: *absit a te, Domine* (Matth. XVI, 22). Sed post resurrectionem, quando iam plene cognoverant Christum esse Deum, per ea quae circa passionem et resurrectionem ostenderat, et quando sacramentum resurrectionis ipsius didicerant *tunc recordati sunt discipuli eius quia hoc dicebat* de corpore suo, et tunc *crediderunt Scripturae*, scilicet prophetarum; Oseae VI, 3: *vivificabit nos post duos dies, et tertia die suscitabit nos*; Ionae II, 1: *erat Ionas in ventre ceti tribus diebus et tribus noctibus*. Et inde est quod in ipsa die resurrectionis aperuit illis sensum ut intelligerent Scripturas. *Et sermoni eius, quem dixit Iesus*, huic scilicet, *solvite templum hoc, et in tribus diebus excitabo illud*.

415. Analogice autem per hoc datur nobis intelligi, secundum Origenem, quod in ultima resurrectione naturae, erimus Christi discipuli, quando in magna resurrectione totum corpus Iesu, idest Ecclesia eius, certificabitur de his quae nunc per fidem aenigmatice cognoscimus; et tunc recipiemus fidei complementum, videndo per speciem quod nunc per speculum intuemur.

416. Consequenter cum dicit *cum autem esset Ierosolymis*, ponit fructum consecutum ex signis, scilicet conversionem aliquorum credentium:

et circa hoc tria facit.

Primo proponit ipsos credentes, propter miracula;

secundo ostendit quomodo Christus se habuit ad eos, ibi *ipse autem Iesus non credebat semetipsum eis*;

tertio rationem assignat ad hoc, ibi *eo quod ipse nosset omnes*.

417. Fructus autem qui provenit ex signis Iesu magnus est, quia multi crediderunt, et conversi sunt ad eum; et hoc est quod dicit *cum autem esset Ierosolymis in Pascha, in die festo, multi crediderunt in nomine eius*, idest in eum, *videntes signa quae faciebat*.

418. Nota autem, quod dupliciter aliqui crediderunt. Quidam namque propter miracula visa, quidam vero propter occultorum revelationem et prophetiam. Sed commendabiliores sunt qui propter doctrinam credunt, quia sunt magis spirituales, quam qui propter signa, qui sunt grossiores et magis sensibiles. Isti autem qui conversi sunt, sensibiles ostenduntur per hoc quod non propter doctrinam, sicut discipuli, sed *videntes signa quae*

when, therefore, he had risen from the dead, his disciples remembered that he had said this. First, because this statement asserted that the true divinity was in the body of Christ; otherwise it could not be called a temple. And to understand this at that time was above human ability. Second, because in this statement mention is made of the passion and resurrection, when he says, *I will raise it up*; and this is something none of the disciples had heard mentioned before. Consequently, when Christ spoke of his resurrection and passion to the apostles, Peter was scandalized when he heard it, saying, *God forbid, Lord* (Matt 16:22). But after the resurrection, when they now clearly understood that Christ was God, through what he had shown in regard to his passion and resurrection, and when they had learned of the mystery of his resurrection, *his disciples remembered that he had said this* of his body, and they then *believed the Scripture*, i.e., the prophets: *he will revive us after two days; on the third day he will raise us up* (Hos 6:3), and *Jonah was in the belly of the fish three days and three nights* (Jonah 2:1). So it is that on the very day of the resurrection he opened their understanding so that they might understand the Scriptures and the statement Jesus had made, namely, *destroy this temple, and in three days I will raise it up*.

415. In the anagogical sense, according to Origen, we understand by this that in the final resurrection of nature we will be disciples of Christ, when in the great resurrection the entire body of Jesus, that is, his Church, will be made certain of the things we now hold through faith in a dark manner. Then we shall receive the fulfillment of faith, seeing in actual fact what we now observe through a mirror.

416. Then at *when he was at Jerusalem*, he sets forth the fruit which resulted from the signs, namely, the conversion of certain believers.

Concerning this he does three things.

First, he mentions those who believed on account of the miracles.

Second, he shows the attitude of Christ to them, at *but Jesus did not trust himself to them*.

Third, he gives the reason for this, at *for he knew all men*.

417. The fruit which developed from the signs of Jesus was abundant, because many believed and were converted to him; and this is what he says, *now when he was at Jerusalem during the Passover, upon the festival day, many believed in his name*, i.e., in him, *seeing the signs that he did*.

418. Note that they believed in two ways: some on account of the miracles they saw, and some on account of the revelation and prophecy of hidden things. Now those who believe on account of doctrine are more commendable, because they are more spiritual than those who believe on account of signs, which are grosser and on the level of sense. Those who were converted are shown to be more on the level of sense by the fact that they did not believe on

faciebat, crediderunt in nomine eius. I Cor. XIV, v. 22: *prophetiae datae sunt fidelibus* etc.

419. Sed quaeritur hic quaenam signa viderunt facta a Iesu, cum nullum legamus eum tunc signum fecisse in Ierusalem.

Ad hoc potest dupliciter responderi, secundum Origenem. Uno modo quod multa signa facta sint a Iesu ibi tunc temporis, quae hic non habentur; nam Evangelistae scienter multa praetermiserunt de miraculis Christi, cum tot fecerit quod non possent de facili scribi; infra ult., 25: *multa quidem alia signa fecit Iesus: quae si scribantur per singula, nec ipsum arbitror mundum capere posse eos qui scribendi sunt libros*. Et hoc signanter Evangelista ostendit cum dicit *videntes signa quae faciebat*, quae iam praetermissa sunt, quia non fuit intentio Evangelistarum omnia signa Iesu conscribere, sed tot quot necessaria erant ad Ecclesiam fidelium instruendam.

Alio modo, quia inter miracula potest maximum signum reputari, quod cum flagello facto ex funibus, hominum multitudinem Iesus de templo solus eiecerit.

420. Qualiter autem ad credentes se habuit, ostendit dicens *ipse autem Iesus non credebat semetipsum eis*, scilicet qui crediderant in eum.

Sed quid est hoc quod homines credunt Deo, et ipse Iesus non credebat se eis? Numquid potuissent eum occidere, ipso nolente? Sed dicet aliquis, quod ideo non credebat se eis, quia sciebat eos ficte credere. Sed si hoc verum esset, non utique diceret Evangelista, quod multi crediderant in nomine eius, et tamen non credebat se eis. Et ratio est, secundum Chrysostomum, quia isti crediderunt in eum, sed imperfecte, quia nondum poterant attingere ad perfecta mysteria Christi, *et ideo non credebat se eis*, idest, secreta sua mysteria eis nondum revelabat: nam et ipsis apostolis multa non revelavit; infra XVI, 12: *multa habeo vobis dicere; sed non potestis portare modo*; I Cor. III, 1: *non potui vobis loqui quasi spiritualibus, sed quasi carnalibus*. Et ideo notanter Evangelista, ut ostendat eos imperfecte credere, non dicit, quod credebant in eum, quia nondum credebant eius divinitatem; sed dicit *in nomine eius*: illud quod de eo, nomine tenus dicebatur, scilicet quod iustus, vel huiusmodi.

Vel, secundum Augustinum, isti gerunt in Ecclesia typum catechumenorum, qui etsi credant in nomine Christi, Iesus tamen non credit se illis, quia Ecclesia non dat eis corpus Christi: quod quidem corpus, sicut nullus sacerdos conficere potest nisi in sacerdotem consecratus, ita nullus sumere debet nisi baptizatus.

account of the doctrine, as the disciples did, but *seeing the signs that he did, believed in his name*: prophecies are for those who believe (1 Cor 14:22).

419. One might ask which signs worked by Jesus they saw, for we do not read of any sign worked by him in Jerusalem at that time.

According to Origen, there are two answers to this. First, Jesus did work many miracles there at that time, which are not recorded here; for the Evangelist purposely omitted many of Christ's miracles, since he worked so many that they could not easily be recorded: *but there are also many other things which Jesus did; which, if every one of them was written, the world itself, I think, would not be able to contain the books that should be written* (John 21:25). And the Evangelist expressly shows this when he says, *seeing the signs that he did*, without mentioning them, because it was not the intention of the Evangelist to record all the signs of Jesus, but as many as were needed to instruct the Church of the faithful.

The second answer is that among the miracles the greatest could be the sign in which Jesus by himself drove from the temple a crowd of men with a whip of small cords (John 2:15).

420. The attitude of Jesus to those who believed in him is shown when he says, *but Jesus did not trust himself to them*, i.e., those who had believed in him.

What is this, men entrust themselves to God, and Jesus himself does not entrust himself to them? Could they kill him against his will? Some will say that he did not trust himself to them because he knew that their belief was not genuine. But if this were true, the Evangelist would surely not have said that many believed in his name, and yet he did not trust himself to them. According to Chrysostom, the reason is that they did believe in him, but imperfectly, because they were not yet able to attain to the profound mysteries of Christ, and so *Jesus did not trust himself to them*, i.e., he did not yet reveal his secret mysteries to them; for there were many things he would not reveal even to the apostles: *I have yet many things to say to you: but you cannot bear them now* (John 16:12), and *I could not speak to you as spiritual persons, but as sensual* (1 Cor 3:1). And so it is significant that in order to show that they believed imperfectly, the Evangelist does not say that they believed in him, because they did not yet believe in his divinity, but he says, *in his name*, i.e., they believed what was said about him, nominally, i.e., that he was just, or something of that sort.

Or, according to Augustine, these people represent the catechumens in the Church, who, although they believe in the name of Christ, Jesus does not trust himself to them, because the Church does not give them the body of Christ. For just as no priest except one ordained in the priesthood can consecrate that body, so no one but a baptized person may receive it.

421. Ratio autem huius quod non credebat se eis, ostenditur ex perfecta Christi cognitione; unde dicit *eo quod ipse nosset omnes*.

Licet autem homo ignorans debeat de quolibet praesumere bonum; tamen postquam veritas innotescit de aliquibus, debet se homo habere ad eos secundum eorum conditionem. Et quia Christum nihil latebat eorum quae sunt in homine, cum sciret eos imperfecte credere, non credebat se eis.

422. Describitur autem cognitio Christi universalis, quia non solum familiares, sed etiam alios extraneos cognoscebat, et ideo dicit *eo quod ipse nosset omnes*, et hoc per potentiam divinitatis; Eccli. XXIII, 28: *oculi Domini multo plus lucidiores sunt super solem*. Nam homo, etsi cognoscat alios, non tamen certam cognitionem de eis potest habere, quia non videt nisi ea quae apparent; et ideo opus est ei testimonio aliorum. Christus autem certissime cognoscit, quia intuetur cor: et ideo *non erat ei opus ut quis testimonium perhiberet de homine*; immo ipse testis est, Iob XVI, 20: *ecce in caelo est testis meus*.

Perfecta, quia non solum quantum ad exteriora, sed etiam quantum ad interiora sua cognitio se extendit; et ideo dicit *ipse enim sciebat quid esset in homine*, idest occulta cordis. Prov. XV, 11: *Infernus, et perditio coram Domino*.

421. The reason Jesus did not trust himself to them arises from his perfect knowledge; hence he says, *for he knew all men*.

For although one must ordinarily presume good of everyone, yet after the truth about certain people is known, one should act according to their condition. Now because nothing in man was unknown to Christ and since he knew that they believed imperfectly, he did not trust himself to them.

422. The universal knowledge of Christ is then described: for he knew not only those who were on close terms with him, but strangers too. And therefore he says, *for he knew all men*; and this by the power of his divinity: *the eyes of the Lord are far brighter than the sun* (Sir 23:28). Now a man, although he may know other people, cannot have a sure knowledge of them, because he sees only what appears; consequently, he must rely on the testimony of others. But Christ knows with the greatest certainty, because he beholds the heart; and so *he did not need anyone to give testimony of man*. In fact, he is the one who gives testimony: *look, my witness is in heaven* (Job 16:20).

His knowledge was perfect, because it extended not only to what was exterior, but even to the interior; thus he says, he was well aware of what was in man's heart, i.e., the secrets of the heart: *hell and destruction are open to the Lord: how much more the hearts of the children of men* (Prov 15:11).

Chapter 3

Lecture 1

3:1 Erat autem homo ex Pharisaeis, Nicodemus nomine, princeps Iudaeorum. [n. 424]

3:2 Hic venit ad Iesum nocte, et dixit ei: Rabbi, scimus quia a Deo venisti magister: nemo enim potest haec signa facere quae tu facis, nisi fuerit Deus cum eo. [n. 427]

3:3 Respondit Iesus, et dixit ei: amen, amen dico tibi, nisi quis natus fuerit denuo, non potest videre regnum Dei. [n. 430]

3:4 Dicit ad eum Nicodemus: quomodo potest homo nasci, cum sit senex? Numquid potest in ventrem matris suae iterato introire, et renasci? [n. 436]

3:5 Respondit Iesus: amen, amen dico tibi, nisi quis renatus fuerit ex aqua et Spiritu Sancto, non potest introire in regnum Dei. [n. 441]

3:6 Quod natum est ex carne, caro est; et quod natum est ex Spiritu, spiritus est. [n.

3:1 Ἦν δὲ ἄνθρωπος ἐκ τῶν Φαρισαίων, Νικόδημος ὄνομα αὐτῷ, ἄρχων τῶν Ἰουδαίων·

3:2 οὗτος ἦλθεν πρὸς αὐτὸν νυκτὸς καὶ εἶπεν αὐτῷ· ῥαββί, οἴδαμεν ὅτι ἀπὸ θεοῦ ἐλήλυθας διδάσκαλος· οὐδεὶς γὰρ δύναται ταῦτα τὰ σημεῖα ποιεῖν ἃ σὺ ποιεῖς, ἐὰν μὴ ᾖ ὁ θεὸς μετ᾽ αὐτοῦ.

3:3 ἀπεκρίθη Ἰησοῦς καὶ εἶπεν αὐτῷ· ἀμὴν ἀμὴν λέγω σοι, ἐὰν μή τις γεννηθῇ ἄνωθεν, οὐ δύναται ἰδεῖν τὴν βασιλείαν τοῦ θεοῦ.

3:4 λέγει πρὸς αὐτὸν [ὁ] Νικόδημος· πῶς δύναται ἄνθρωπος γεννηθῆναι γέρων ὤν; μὴ δύναται εἰς τὴν κοιλίαν τῆς μητρὸς αὐτοῦ δεύτερον εἰσελθεῖν καὶ γεννηθῆναι;

3:5 ἀπεκρίθη Ἰησοῦς· ἀμὴν ἀμὴν λέγω σοι, ἐὰν μή τις γεννηθῇ ἐξ ὕδατος καὶ πνεύματος, οὐ δύναται εἰσελθεῖν εἰς τὴν βασιλείαν τοῦ θεοῦ.

3:6 τὸ γεγεννημένον ἐκ τῆς σαρκὸς σάρξ ἐστιν, καὶ τὸ γεγεννημένον ἐκ τοῦ πνεύματος πνεῦμά ἐστιν.

3:1 And there was a man of the Pharisees, named Nicodemus, a member of the Sanhedrin. [n. 424]

3:2 This man came to Jesus at night and said to him: Rabbi, we know that you are a teacher come from God; for no man can do these signs which you do, unless God is with him. [n. 427]

3:3 Jesus answered and said to him: amen, amen I say to you, unless a man is born again, he cannot see the kingdom of God. [n. 430]

3:4 Nicodemus said to him: how can a man be born when he is old? Can he enter a second time into his mother's womb and be born again? [n. 436]

3:5 Jesus answered: amen, amen I say to you, unless a man is born again of water and the Holy Spirit, he cannot enter into the kingdom of God. [n. 441]

3:6 That which is born of the flesh, is flesh; and that which is born of the Spirit, is spirit. [n. 447]

---

423. Supra ostendit Evangelista virtutem Christi quantum ad mutationem naturae; hic vero ostendit eam quantum ad reformationem gratiae, de qua principaliter intendit. Reformatio autem gratiae fit per spiritualem generationem, et per beneficiorum regeneratis collationem.

Primo ergo tractat de spirituali generatione;

secundo de beneficiorum spiritualium regeneratis divinitus collatione; et hoc in V cap. ibi **post haec erat dies festus Iudaeorum** etc.

Circa primum duo facit.

Primo agit de spirituali regeneratione quantum ad Iudaeos;

secundo de propagatione fructuum huius regenerationis etiam quantum ad externas nationes. Et hoc in IV cap. ibi **ut ergo cognovit Iesus, quia audierunt Pharisaei** etc.

423. Above, the Evangelist showed Christ's power in relation to changes affecting nature; here he shows it in relation to our reformation by grace, which is his principal subject. Reformation by grace comes about through spiritual generation and by the conferring of benefits on those regenerated.

First, then, he treats of spiritual generation.

Second, of the spiritual benefits divinely conferred on the regenerated, at **after these things was a festival day of the Jews** (John 5:1)

As to the first he does two things.

First, he treats of spiritual regeneration in relation to the Jews.

Second, of the spreading of the fruits of this regeneration even to foreign peoples, at **when Jesus therefore understood that the Pharisees had heard** (John 4:1).

Circa primum duo facit.

Primo manifestat spiritualem regenerationem verbis;

secundo implet eam factis, ibi *post haec venit Iesus, et discipuli eius in terram Iudaeam* etc.

Circa primum tria facit.

Primo ostendit spiritualis regenerationis necessitatem;

secundo eius qualitatem, ibi *dicit ad eum Nicodemus: quomodo potest homo nasci, cum sit senex?*

Tertio eius modum et rationem, ibi *respondit ad eum Nicodemus, et dixit ei: quomodo possunt haec fieri?*

Circa primum duo facit.

Primo ostendit demonstrandae necessitatis occasionem;

secundo necessitatem huius regenerationis, ibi *respondit Iesus, et dixit ei: amen, amen dico tibi* etc.

Occasio autem huius necessitatis inducitur ex Nicodemo; et ideo dicit *erat autem homo ex Pharisaeis, Nicodemus nomine* etc. Quem describit ex persona, ex tempore, et ex confessione ipsius.

424. Ex persona quidem describitur quantum ad tria. Scilicet quantum ad religionem, quia Pharisaeus; unde dicit *erat homo ex Pharisaeis*. Duplex namque secta erat apud Iudaeos, scilicet Pharisaeorum et Sadducaeorum. Sed Pharisaei magis conveniebant nobiscum in opinionibus, quia credebant resurrectionem et dicebant esse creaturas aliquas spirituales. Sadducaei vero magis discordabant, quia nec resurrectionem futuram, nec spiritum esse credebant. Et dicebantur isti Pharisaei, quasi ab aliis divisi. Et quia opinio eorum probabilior erat, et magis propinqua veritati, ideo Nicodemus facilius conversus est ad Christum. Act. XXVI, 5: *secundum certissimam sectam religionis nostrae* etc.

425. Item quantum ad nomen, cum dicit *Nicodemus nomine*: quod interpretatur victor, seu victoria populi, per quem significantur illi qui ex Iudaeis ad Christum conversi, fide vicerunt mundum. I Io. ult., 4: *haec est victoria, quae vincit mundum, fides nostra.*

426. Item tertio, quantum ad dignitatem; unde dicit *princeps Iudaeorum*. A principio namque licet Dominus non elegerit sapientes, potentes, aut nobiles, ne virtus fidei sapientiae et potentiae humanae attribueretur ut dicitur I Cor. I, 26: *non multi sapientes, secundum carnem, non multi potentes, non multi nobiles, sed quae stulta sunt mundi eligit Deus,* voluit tamen aliquos sapientes et potentes a principio ad se convertere, ne si doctrina sua solum ab ignobilibus et insipientibus reciperetur, haberetur contemptui, et ne credentium multitudo potius attribueretur rusticitati, et insipientiae conversorum, quam virtuti fidei. Nihilominus tamen voluit istos nobiles et potentes non multos esse ad eum conversos, ne ut

Concerning the first he does two things.

First, he explains spiritual regeneration with words.

Second, he completes it with deeds, at *after these things Jesus and his disciples came into Judean territory* (John 3:22).

As to the first he does three things.

First, he shows the need for a spiritual regeneration.

Second, its quality, at *Nicodemus said to him: how can a man be born when he is old?*

Third, its mode and nature, at *Nicodemus answered and said to him: how can these things be done?* (John 3:9).

As to the first he does two things.

First, he mentions the occasion for showing this need.

Second, the need itself for this regeneration, at *Jesus answered, and said to him: amen, amen I say to you, unless a man be born again*.

The occasion was presented by Nicodemus; hence he says, *and there was a man of the Pharisees named Nicodemus*. And he describes him as to his person, from the time, and from his statements.

424. He describes his person in three ways. First, as to his religion, because he was a Pharisee, hence he says, *there was a man of the Pharisees*. For there were two sects among the Jews: the Pharisees and the Sadducees. The Pharisees were closer to us in their beliefs, for they believed in the resurrection, and admitted the existence of spiritual creatures. The Sadducees, on the other hand, disagree more with us, for they believed neither in the resurrection to come nor in the existence of spirits. The former were called Pharisees, as being separated from the others. And because their opinion was the more credible and nearer to the truth, it was easier for Nicodemus to be converted to Christ. *I lived as a Pharisee, according to the strictest sect of our religion* (Acts 26:5).

425. As to his name he says, *named Nicodemus*, which means *victor*, or *the victory of the people*. This signifies those who overcame the world through faith by being converted to Christ from Judaism. *This is the victory that overcomes the world, our faith* (1 John 5:4).

426. Third, as to his rank he says, *a member of the Sanhedrin*. For although our Lord did not choose the wise or powerful or those of high birth at the beginning, lest the power of the faith be attributed to human widsom and power—*not many of you are learned in the worldly sense, not many powerful, not many of high birth. But God chose the simple ones of the world* (1 Cor 1:26)—still he willed to convert some of the wise and powerful to himself at the very beginning. And he did this so that his doctrine would not be held in contempt, as being accepted exclusively by the lowly and uneducated, and so that the number of believers would not be attributed to the rusticity and ignorance of the converts rather than to the power of the faith.

dictum est humanae potentiae, aut sapientiae ascriberetur. Et ideo dicitur Io. XII, 42, quod *aliqui ex principibus crediderunt in eum*: inter quos fuit iste Nicodemus; Ps. XLVI, 10: *principes populorum congregati sunt.*

427. Ex tempore vero describit eum, cum dicit *hic venit ad Iesum nocte* etc.

Circa quod sciendum est, quod qualitas temporis consuevit in Scriptura describi circa aliquos, ad insinuandam cognitionem mentis, seu conditionem actionis eorum. Describitur autem hic tempus istud obscurum, unde dicit *venit nocte*. Nox enim obscura est, et competebat qualitati affectus Nicodemi, qui non cum securitate et libera propalatione, sed cum timore ad Iesum veniebat; nam erat de illis principibus, de quibus dicitur Io. XII, 42 quod *crediderunt in eum; sed propter Pharisaeos non confitebantur, ut de synagoga non eiicerentur.* Non enim perfecte diligebant; unde subditur: *dilexerunt enim magis gloriam hominum quam gloriam Dei.*

Competit etiam nox eius ignorantiae, et imperfectae cognitioni, quam iste habebat de Christo; Rom. XIII, 12: *nox praecessit* etc.; Ps. LXXXI, 5: *nescierunt, neque intellexerunt, in tenebris ambulant.*

428. Ex confessione vero describitur, cum subdit *et dixit ei: Rabbi, scimus quia a Deo venisti magister.* Ubi confitetur Christi officium in docendo, cum dicit *Rabbi,* etc. et eius potestatem in agendo, ibi *nemo enim potest haec signa facere quae tu facis, nisi fuerit Deus cum eo.* Et quidem in utroque verum dicit, licet parum confessus est.

Verum enim est quod vocat eum *Rabbi,* idest magister, quia, ut dicitur infra XIII, 13: *vos vocatis me Magister, et Domine, et bene dicitis, sum etenim.* Legerat enim Nicodemus quod scriptum est Ioel II, 23: *filii Sion, exultate, et laetamini in Domino Deo vestro, quia dedit vobis doctorem iustitiae.*

Sed parum dicit, quia dicit eum a Deo venisse magistrum sed tacet eum Deum esse. Nam venire a Deo magister, commune est omnibus bonis praelatis, Ier. III, 15, *et dabo vobis pastores iuxta cor meum; et pascent vos scientia, et doctrina*; unde hoc non est singulare Christo: quamquam aliter doceant homines, aliter Christus. Alii enim magistri docent tantum exterius, sed Christus etiam interius, quia, ut dicitur supra I, 9, *erat lux vera, quae illuminat omnem hominem*: et ideo ipse solus dat sapientiam; Lc. XXI, 15: *ego dabo vobis os et sapientiam.* Et hoc nullus purus homo dicere potest.

429. Potestatem vero confitetur ex signis visis, quasi dicat: credo quod *a Deo venisti magister,* quia *nemo potest haec signa facere.* Et verum dicit, quia signa quae

However, he did not will that a large number of those converted to him be powerful and of high birth, lest, as has been said, it should be ascribed to human power and wisdom. And so it says, *many of the chief men also believed in him* (John 12:42), among whom was this Nicodemus. *The rulers of the people have come together* (Ps 46:10).

427. Then he describes him as to the time, saying, *this man came to Jesus at night*.

In regard to this, it might be noted that in Scripture the quality of the time is mentioned as to certain persons in order to indicate their knowledge or the condition of their actions. Here an obscure time is mentioned, when it says he *came at night*. For the night is obscure and suited to the state of mind of Nicodemus, who did not come to Jesus free of care and anxiety, but in fear; for he was one of those of whom it is said that they *believed in him; but because of the Pharisees they did not confess him, that they might not be cast out of the synagogue* (John 12:42). For their love was not perfect; so it continues, *for they loved the glory of men more than the glory of God* (John 12:43).

Further, night was appropriate to his ignorance and the imperfect understanding he had of Christ: *the night has passed, and day is at hand. So let us cast off the works of darkness* (Rom 13:12); *they have not known or understood; they are walking in darkness* (Ps 81:5).

428. Then he is described from his statements, when he says that Nicodemus said to Jesus: *Rabbi, we know that you are a teacher come from God*. Here he affirms Christ's office as teacher when he says, *Rabbi*, and his power of acting, saying, *for no man can do these signs which you do, unless God is with him*. And in both remarks he says what is true, but he does not affirm enough.

He is right in calling Jesus *Rabbi*, i.e., Teacher, because, *you call me Master, and Lord; and you say well, for so I am* (John 13:13). For Nicodemus had read what was written: *children of Zion, rejoice, and be joyful in the Lord your God, because he has given you a teacher of justice* (Joel 2:23).

But he says too little, because he says that Jesus came as a teacher from God, but is silent on whether he is God. For to come as a teacher from God is common to all good prelates: *I will give you shepherds after my own heart, and they will feed you with knowledge and doctrine* (Jer 3:15). Therefore, this is not unique to Christ even though Christ taught in a manner unlike other men. For some teachers teach only from without, but Christ also instructs within, because *he was the true light, which enlightens every man* (John 1:9); thus he alone gives wisdom: *I will give you an eloquence and a wisdom* (Luke 21:15), and this is something that no mere man can say.

429. He affirms his power because of the signs he saw. As if to say: I believe that *you are a teacher come from God, for no man can do these signs which you do*. And he

Christus fecit, non possunt fieri nisi divinitus, et quia Deus cum eo erat; infra VIII, v. 29: *qui me misit, mecum est*. Sed parum dicit, quia credebat quod Christus non propria potestate signa faceret, quasi indigens extranea virtute, ac si Deus non esset cum eo per unitatem essentiae, sed per infusionem gratiae solum. Quod quidem falsum est, quia non extranea virtute, sed propria, signa faciebat: nam eadem est potestas Dei et Christi. Simile est quod dicit mulier Eliae, III Reg. XVII, 24: *in hoc facto cognovi quoniam vir Dei es tu*.

430. Consequenter cum dicit *respondit Iesus, et dixit ei* etc. ponit necessitatem spiritualis regenerationis provenientem ex ignorantia Nicodemi. Et ideo dicit *amen, amen*.

Ubi notandum est, quod haec dictio *amen* est Hebraea, qua frequenter Christus usus est: unde ob eius reverentiam nullus translator, tam Graecorum quam Latinorum, transferre voluit. Et quandoque quidem significat idem quod verum, aut idem quod vere; quandoque vero idem quod fiat. Unde in Ps. LXXI, LXXXVIII et CVI, ubi nos habemus, *fiat*, in Hebraeo est *amen, amen*.

Sed hanc dictionem solus Ioannes Evangelista ingeminat inter Evangelistas. Cuius ratio est, quia alii Evangelistae ea principaliter tradunt quae ad humanitatem Christi pertinent: ad quae, cum facilius credibilia sint, minor assertio necessaria erat; Ioannes vero ea quae ad divinitatem Christi pertinent, principaliter tractat, quae, cum occulta sint, et a cognitione hominum remota, maiori assertione indigebant.

431. Deinde attendendum est, quod haec responsio Christi videtur omnino inconsona propositis a Nicodemo, nisi diligenter consideretur. Quomodo namque convenire videtur quod dixit Nicodemus *Rabbi, scimus quia a Deo venisti*, cum hoc quod respondit Dominus *nisi quis renatus fuerit denuo, non potest videre regnum Dei*?

Sed notandum, sicut iam dictum est, quod Nicodemus imperfectam opinionem habens de Christo, confitebatur eum magistrum et haec signa facere tamquam hominem purum. Vult ergo ei Dominus ostendere, quomodo ad altiorem cognitionem de ipso posset pervenire. Et quidem poterat de hoc Dominus disputare; sed quia hoc fuisset versum in contentionem, cuius contrarium de eo scriptum est Is. XLII, 2: *non contendet*, ideo cum mansuetudine voluit eum ad veram cognitionem perducere, quasi diceret: non mirum si me purum hominem credis, quia illa secreta divinitatis non potest aliquis scire, nisi adeptus fuerit spiritualem regenerationem. Et hoc est quod dicit *nisi quis natus fuerit denuo, non potest videre regnum Dei*.

432. Ubi sciendum, quod cum visio sit actus vitae, secundum diversas vitas, diversae sunt visiones. Nam

is speaking the truth, because the signs which Christ did cannot be worked except by God, and because God was with him: *he who sent me is with me* (John 8:29). But he says too little, because he believed that Christ did not perform these signs through his own power, but as relying on the power of another; as though God were not with him by a unity of essence but merely by an infusion of grace. But this is false, because Christ performed these signs not by an exterior power but by his own; for the power of God and of Christ is one and the same. It is similar to what the woman says to Elijah: *because of this I know that you are a man of God* (1 Kgs 17:24).

430. Then when he says that *Jesus answered, amen, amen, I say to you*, he sets down the necessity for spiritual regeneration, because of the ignorance of Nicodemus. And so he says, *amen, amen*.

Here we should note that this word *amen*, is a Hebrew word frequently employed by Christ; hence out of reverence for him no Greek or Latin translator wanted to translate it. Sometimes it means the same as true or truly; and sometimes the same as so be it. Thus we have, in the Psalms *so be it* and the Hebrew has *amen, amen* (Ps 71:19, 88:53 and 106).

But John is the only Evangelist who duplicates or makes a twin use of this word. The reason for this is that the other Evangelists are concerned mainly with matters pertaining to the humanity of Christ, which, since they are easier to believe, need less reinforcement; but John deals chiefly with things pertaining to the divinity of Christ, and these, since they are hidden and remote from men's knowledge and experience, require greater formal declaration.

431. Next we should point out that at first glance this answer of Christ seems to be entirely foreign to Nicodemus' statement. For what connection is there between Nicodemus' statement, *Rabbi, we know that you are a teacher come from God*, and the Lord's reply, *unless a man is born again, he cannot see the kingdom of God*?

But we should note, as has already been stated, that Nicodemus, having an imperfect opinion about Christ, affirmed that he was a teacher and performed these signs as a mere man. And so the Lord wishes to show Nicodemus how he might arrive at a deeper understanding of him. And as a matter of fact, the Lord might have done so with an argument, but because this might have resulted in a quarrel—the opposite of which was prophesied about him: *he will not quarrel* (Isa 42:2)—he wished to lead him to a true understanding with gentleness. As if to say: it is not strange that you regard me as a mere man, because one cannot know these secrets of the divinity unless he has achieved a spiritual regeneration. And this is what he says: *unless a man is born again, he cannot see the kingdom of God*.

432. Here we should point out that since vision is an act of life, then according to the diverse kinds of life there will

est quaedam vita carnalis, qua communiter omnia alia vivunt, et haec habet carnalem visionem, seu cognitionem. Est et vita spiritualis, qua homo conformatur Deo et spiritibus sanctis, et haec habet spiritualem visionem. Secundum carnalem quidem spiritualia videri non possunt; I Cor. c. II, 14: *animalis homo non percipit ea quae sunt Spiritus Dei*, sed percipiuntur visione spirituali; unde ibidem subditur *quae Dei sunt, nemo novit nisi Spiritus Dei*. Spiritus autem est qui regenerat; unde apostolus Rom. VIII, v. 15: *non accepistis spiritum servitutis iterum in timore; sed accepistis spiritum adoptionis*. Et hunc quidem spiritum per regenerationem spiritualem accipimus. Ad Tit. III, 5: *salvos nos fecit per lavacrum regenerationis Spiritus Sancti*.

Si ergo visio spiritualis non est nisi per Spiritum Sanctum, et Spiritus Sanctus infunditur nobis per lavacrum regenerationis spiritualis: ergo non possumus videre regnum Dei, nisi per lavacrum regenerationis, et ideo dicit **nisi quis renatus fuerit ex aqua et Spiritu Sancto, non potest introire in regnum Dei**. Quasi dicat: non est mirum si non vides regnum Dei, quia nullus illud videre potest nisi accipiat Spiritum Sanctum, per quem renascitur in filium Dei.

433. Ad regnum autem non solum pertinet regale solium, sed etiam quae sunt ad regni gubernationem, scilicet regia dignitas, beneficia gratiarum et via iustitiae, qua solidatur regnum, et ideo dicit **non potest videre regnum Dei**, idest gloriam et dignitatem Dei, idest mysteria salutis aeternae, quae per fidei iustitiam inspiciuntur; Rom. XIV, 17: *regnum Dei non est esca et potus*.

In veteri autem lege fuit quaedam regeneratio spiritualis, sed imperfecta et figuralis; I Cor. X, 2: *omnes in Moyse baptizati sunt, in nube et in mari*; idest, in figura baptismum acceperunt. Et ideo mysteria regni Dei videbant quidem, sed figuraliter tantum; Hebr. c. XI, 13: *a longe aspicientes*. In nova vero lege est manifesta regeneratio spiritualis, sed tamen est imperfecta, quia renovamur interius tantum per gratiam, sed non exterius per incorruptionem; II Cor. IV, 16: *licet is qui foris est noster homo corrumpatur, tamen is qui intus est renovatur de die in diem*. Et ideo videmus regnum Dei et mysteria salutis aeternae, sed imperfecte, quia, ut dicitur I Cor. XIII, 12, *videmus nunc per speculum in aenigmate* etc. In patria vero est perfecta regeneratio, quia renovabuntur interius et exterius. Et ideo regnum Dei perfectissime videbimus; unde I Cor. XIII, 12: *tunc autem videbimus facie ad faciem*; et I Io. III, 2: *cum apparuerit, similes ei erimus, quia videbimus eum sicuti est*.

434. Patet ergo quod sicut visionem corporalem non habet quis nisi natus, ita nec spiritualem habere potest nisi renatus. Et secundum triplicem regenerationem est triplex modus visionis.

be diversity of vision. For there is a sentient life which some living things share in common, and this life has a sentient vision or knowledge. And there is also a spiritual life, by which man is made like God and other Holy Spirits; and this life enjoys a spiritual vision. Now spiritual things cannot be seen by the sentient: *the sensual man does not perceive those things that pertain to the Spirit of God* (1 Cor 2:14), but they are perceived by the spiritual vision: *no one knows the things of God but the Spirit of God* (1 Cor 2:11). So the apostle says: *you did not receive the spirit of slavery, putting you in fear again, but the spirit of adoption* (Rom 8:15). And we receive this spirit through a spiritual regenaration: *he saved us by the cleansing of regeneration in the Holy Spirit* (Titus 3:5).

Therefore, if spiritual vision comes only through the Holy Spirit, and if the Holy Spirit is given through a cleansing of spiritual regeneration, then it is only by a cleansing of regeneration that we can see the kingdom of God. Thus he says, **unless a man is born again of water and the Holy Spirit, he cannot enter the kingdom of God**. As if to say: it is not surprising if you do not see the kingdom of God, because no one can see it unless he receives the Holy Spirit, through whom one is reborn a son of God.

433. It is not only the royal throne that pertains to a kingdom, but also the things needed for governing the kingdom, such as the royal dignity, royal favors, and the way of justice by which the kingdom is consolidated. Hence he says, **he cannot see the kingdom of God**, i.e., the glory and dignity of God, i.e., the mysteries of eternal salvation which are seen through the justice of faith: *the kingdom of God is not food and drink* (Rom 14:17).

Now in the old law there was a spiritual regeneration; but it was imperfect and symbolic: *all were baptized into Moses, in the cloud and in the sea* (1 Cor 10:2), i.e., they received baptism in symbol. Accordingly, they did see the mysteries of the kingdom of God, but only symbolically: *seeing from afar* (Heb 11:13). But in the new law there is an evident spiritual regeneration, although imperfect, because we are renewed only inwardly by grace, but not outwardly by incorruption: *although our outward nature is wasting away, yet our inward nature is being renewed day by day* (2 Cor 4:16). And so we do see the kingdom of God and the mysteries of eternal salvation, but imperfectly, for as it says, *now we see in a mirror, in an obscure manner* (1 Cor 13:12). But there is perfect regeneration in heaven, because we will be renewed both inwardly and outwardly. And therefore we shall see the kingdom of God in a most perfect way: *but then we will see face to face* (1 Cor 13:12); and *when he appears we will be like him, because we will see him as he is* (1 John 3:2).

434. It is clear, therefore, that just as one does not have bodily vision unless he is born, so one cannot have spiritual vision unless he is reborn. And according to the threefold regeneration, there is a threefold kind of vision.

435. Nota autem, quod in Graeco non habetur *de-nuo*, sed *anothe*, idest desuper, quod Hieronymus trans-tulit *denuo*, ut scilicet importet additionem. Et sic Hiero-nymus intellexit dicens **nisi renatus fuerit denuo**; quasi dicat: nisi renatus iterato per fraternalem generationem.

Chrysostomus autem dicit, nasci desuper, esse pro-prium Filii Dei, quia ipse solus natus est desuper; infra (hoc cap.) **qui desursum venit, super omnes est**. Et dici-tur Christus nasci desuper quantum ad tempus (ut ita liceat loqui) quia ab aeterno genitus; Ps. CIX, v. 3: *ante Luciferum genui te*. Et quantum ad generationis princi-pium, quia a Patre caelesti; infra VI, 38: **descendi, non ut faciam voluntatem meam, sed eius qui misit me**. Quia ergo nostra regeneratio est ad similitudinem Filii Dei, secundum illud Rom. VIII, v. 29: *quos praescivit confor-mes fieri imaginis Filii sui*, ideo, quia illa generatio su-perna est, et nostra generatio desuper est, quantum ad tempus, per aeternam praedestinationem, Eph. I, 4: *ele-git nos in ipso ante mundi constitutionem*, et quantum ad donum Dei, infra VI, 44: **nemo potest venire ad me, nisi Pater qui misit me, traxerit eum**. Eph. II, 5: *gratia Dei salvati estis* etc.

436. Consequenter cum dicit **dicit ad eum Nicode-mus** etc., ponit modum, et rationem huius spiritualis re-generationis: et circa hoc

primo ponitur dubitatio Nicodemi;

secundo responsio Christi **respondit Iesus: amen, amen dico tibi** etc.

437. Circa primum sciendum est, quod, sicut dici-tur I Cor. II, 14, *animalis homo non percipit ea quae sunt spiritus Dei*, et ideo, quia Nicodemus carnalis adhuc et animalis erat, non potuit quae dicebantur, nisi carnaliter intelligere. Et ideo ea quae Dominus dixerat de regene-ratione spirituali, ipse de regeneratione carnali intellige-bat. Et hoc est quod dicit **quomodo potest homo nasci, cum sit senex?**

Ubi, secundum Chrysostomum, sciendum est, quod Nicodemus voluit obiicere contra verba salvatoris. Sed tamen obiectio eius derisibilis est, quia Christus loquitur de regeneratione spirituali, hic autem obiicit de carnali. Similiter omnes rationes inductae ad impugnandum ea quae sunt fidei, derisibiles sunt, quia non sunt secundum intentionem Sacrae Scripturae.

438. Obiicit autem Nicodemus contra verba Domini dupliciter, secundum quod dupliciter videbatur dictum Domini impossibile, scilicet quod homo denuo renasca-tur. Uno modo scilicet propter irreversibilitatem huma-nae vitae: nam a senectute non potest homo redire ad pueritiam. Unde dicitur Iob XVI, v. 23: *semitam*, scilicet vitam praesentem, *per quam non revertar, ambulo*. Et se-cundum hoc dicit **quomodo potest homo nasci, cum sit**

435. Note that the Greek reading is not **again**, but *an-other*, i.e., from above, which Jerome translated as **again**, in order to suggest addition. And this is the way Jerome understood the saying, **unless one is born again**. It is as if he were saying: unless one is reborn once more through a supernatural generation.

Chrysostom, however, says that to be born from above is peculiar to the Son of God, because he alone is born from above: **he who came from above is above all** (John 3:31). And Christ is said to be born from above both as to time (if we may speak thus), because he was begotten from eter-nity: *before the daystar I begot you* (Ps 109:3), and as to the principle of his generation, because he proceeds from the heavenly Father: **I came down from heaven, not to do my own will, but the will of him who sent me** (John 6:38). Therefore, because our regeneration is in the likeness of the Son of God, according to: *those whom he foreknew he predestined to become conformed to the image of his Son* (Rom 8:29), and because that generation is from above, our generation also is from above, as to the time, because of our eternal predestination, *he chose us in him before the founda-tion of the world* (Eph 1:4), and as to its being a gift of God, **no man can come to me, unless the Father, who has sent me, draws him** (John 6:44); and *you have been saved by the grace of God* (Eph 2:5).

436. Then when he says, **Nicodemus said to him**: **how can a man be born when he is old?** he gives the manner of and the reason for this spiritual regeneration.

First, the doubt of Nicodemus is set forth.

Second, Christ's response, at **Jesus answered: amen, amen I say to you**.

437. As to the first we should note that: *the sensual man does not perceive those things that pertain to the Spirit of God* (1 Cor 2:14). And so because Nicodemus was yet car-nal and sensual, he was unable to grasp, except in a carnal manner, the things that were said to him. Consequently, what the Lord said, to him about spiritual regeneration, he understood of carnal generation. And this is what he says: **how can a man be born when he is old?**

We should note here, according to Chrysostom, that Ni-codemus wanted to object to what was said by the Savior. But his objection is foolish, because Christ was speaking of spiritual regeneration, and he is objecting in terms of carnal regeneration. In like manner, all the reasons brought forth to attack the things of faith are foolish, since they are not according to the meaning of Sacred Scripture.

438. Nicodemus objected to the Lord's statement that a man must be born again according to the two ways in which this seemed impossible. In one way, on account of the irreversibility of human life; for a man cannot return to infancy from old age. Hence we read, *I am walking on a path*, namely, this present life, *by which I will not return* (Job 16:23). And it is from this point of view that he says, **how can a man be born when he is old?** As if to say: shall

senex? Quasi dicat: numquid iterum efficietur puer ut renascatur? Iob VII, 10: *non revertetur ultra in domum suam, neque cognoscet eum amplius locus eius.*

Secundo ex modo carnalis generationis: nam homo in principio cum generatur est in parva quantitate, ita ut possit eum uterus maternus capere; postmodum vero, cum iam natus est, ad continua crementa paulatim perducitur, ita ut non possit in materno utero contineri. Et ideo dicit **numquid potest in ventrem matris suae iterato introire, et renasci?** Quasi dicat, non, quia non capit eum venter.

439. Sed haec locum non habent in generatione spirituali, quia homo, quantumcumque per peccatum spiritualiter inveteratus, secundum illud Ps. XXXI, 3: *quoniam tacui, inveteraverunt omnia ossa mea*, potest per auxilium gratiae divinae ad novitatem venire, secundum illud Ps. CII, 5: *renovabitur ut aquilae iuventus tua.* Potest, et quantumcumque magnus, in uterum spiritualem, scilicet Ecclesiae, per sacramentum baptismi introire. Quis autem sit uterus spiritualis, manifestum est; alias numquam diceretur: *ex utero ante Luciferum genui te.*

Nihilominus tamen aliqualem similitudinem habet quod dicitur; nam, sicut homo semel carnaliter natus, non potest iterum nasci, ita et semel per baptismum spiritualiter natus, non potest iterum nasci, quia non debet iterum baptizari; Eph. IV, 5: *unus Dominus, una fides, unum baptisma.*

440. Consequenter cum dicit **respondit Iesus** etc., ponitur responsio Christi.

Et circa hoc tria facit.

Primo solvit rationes Nicodemi, ostendendo qualitatem regenerationis;

secundo manifestat solutionem per rationem, ibi **quod natum est ex carne, caro est** etc.;

tertio per exemplum, ibi **non mireris** etc.

441. Solvit ergo obiectiones, ostendens quod regeneratio de qua loquitur, est spiritualis, et non carnalis. Et hoc est quod dicit **amen, amen dico tibi, nisi quis renatus fuerit ex aqua et Spiritu Sancto, non potest introire in regnum Dei**, quasi dicat: tu intelligis de generatione carnali, sed ego loquor de spirituali.

Sed attende quod supra dixerat **non potest videre regnum Dei**, hic vero dicit **non potest introire in regnum Dei**, quod idem est. Nam quae regni Dei sunt, nullus videt, nisi regnum Dei intret; et tantum videt quantum intrat. Apoc. II, 17: *in calculo nomen novum scriptum, quod nemo scit nisi qui accipit.*

442. Quod autem spiritualis regeneratio ex Spiritu fiat, rationem habet. Nam oportet generatum generari ad similitudinem generantis; nos autem regeneramur in

he become a child once more so that he can be reborn? *He will not return again to his home, and his place will not know him any more* (Job 7:10).

In the second way, regeneration seemed impossible because of the mode of carnal generation. For in the beginning, when a man is generated, he is small in size, so that his mother's womb can contain him; but later, after he is born, he continues to grow and reaches such a size that he cannot be contained within his mother's womb. And so Nicodemus says, **can he enter a second time into his mother's womb and be born again**? As if to say: he cannot, because the womb cannot contain him.

439. But this does not apply to spiritual generation. For no matter how spiritually old a man might become through sin: *because I kept silent, all my bones grew old* (Ps 31:3), he can, with the help of divine grace, become new: *your youth will be renewed like the eagle's* (Ps 102:5). And no matter how enormous he is, he can enter the spiritual womb of the Church by the sacrament of baptism. And it is clear what that spiritual womb is; otherwise it would never have been said: *from the womb, before the daystar, I begot you* (Ps 109:3).

Yet there is a sense in which his objection applies. For just as a man, once he is born according to nature, cannot be reborn, so once he is born in a spiritual way through baptism, he cannot be reborn, because he cannot be baptized again: *one Lord, one faith, one baptism* (Eph 4:5).

440. Following this, when it says **Jesus answered**, the response of Christ is given.

Concerning this he does three things.

First, he answers the arguments of Nicodemus by showing the nature of regeneration.

Second, he explains this answer with a reason, at **that which is born of the flesh, is flesh.**

Third, he explains it with an example, at **do not wonder that I said to you, you ought to be born again** (John 3:7).

441. He answers the objections by showing that he is speaking of a spiritual regeneration, not a carnal one. And this is what he says: **unless a man is born again of water and the Holy Spirit, he cannot enter into the kingdom of God**. As if to say: you are thinking of a carnal generation, but I am speaking of a spiritual generation.

Note that above he had said, **he cannot see the kingdom of God**, while here he says, **he cannot enter into the kingdom of God**, which is the same thing. For no one can see the things of the kingdom of God unless he enters it; and to the extent that he enters, he sees. *I will give him a white stone upon which is written a new name, which no one knows but he who receives it* (Rev 5:5).

442. Now there is a reason why spiritual generation comes from the Spirit. It is necessary that the one generated be generated in the likeness of the one generating; but we

filios Dei, ad similitudinem veri filii: oportet ergo quod regeneratio spiritualis fiat per id per quod assimilamur vero Filio; quod quidem est per hoc quod Spiritum eius habemus. Rom. VIII, 9: *si quis Spiritum Christi non habet, hic non est eius*; I Io. IV, 13: *in hoc cognoscimus, quoniam in eo manemus, et ipse in nobis, quia de Spiritu suo dedit nobis* etc. Oportet ergo quod spiritualis regeneratio per Spiritum Sanctum fiat. Rom. VIII, 15: *non accepistis spiritum servitutis iterum in timore, sed spiritum adoptionis Filiorum*; infra VI, 63: **Spiritus est qui vivificat** etc.

443. Et etiam huic regenerationi necessaria aqua propter tria. Primo quidem propter humanae naturae conditionem. Homo enim ex anima et corpore constat, et si in eius regeneratione esset Spiritus tantum, solum quod spirituale est hominis, ostenderetur regenerari. Ut ergo regeneretur etiam caro, oportet quod sicut est ibi Spiritus, per quem regeneratur anima, ita sit ibi aliquid corporale, per quod regeneretur corpus; et hoc est aqua.

Secundo propter humanam cognitionem: nam, sicut Dionysius dicit, divina sapientia ita omnia ordinat ut unicuique provideat secundum modum suae conditionis. Homo autem est naturaliter cognoscitivus; oportet ergo eo modo dona spiritualia hominibus conferri, ut ea cognoscant; I Cor. II, 12: *ut sciamus quae a Deo donata sunt nobis*. Naturalis autem modus huius cognitionis est ut spiritualia per sensibilia cognoscat, cum omnis nostra cognitio a sensu incipiat. Oportuit ergo ad hoc quod intelligamus id quod spirituale est in hac regeneratione, quod esset in ea aliquid sensibile et materiale, scilicet aqua: per quod intelligamus quod sicut aqua lavat et purgat corporaliter exterius, ita et per baptismum homo lavatur et purgatur interius spiritualiter.

Tertio propter causae congruitatem: nam causa nostrae regenerationis est Verbum incarnatum. Supra I, 12: **dedit eis potestatem filios Dei fieri**. Congruit ergo quod in sacramentis, quae efficaciam habent ex virtute Verbi incarnati, sit aliquid correspondens Verbo, et aliquid correspondens carni, seu corpori. Et hoc est spiritualiter aqua in sacramento baptismi, ut scilicet per eam configuremur morti Christi, dum submergimur in ea, quando baptizamur, sicut Christus tribus diebus fuit in ventre terrae; Rom. VI, 4: *consepulti enim sumus cum illo per baptismum*.

Hoc etiam mysterium in prima rerum productione signatum est, Gen. I, quando Spiritus Domini ferebatur super aquas. Sed per tactum mundissimae carnis Christi maior virtus collata est aquis: quia in principio producebant aquae reptile animae viventis; sed ex quo Christus baptizatus est in Iordane, animas spirituales aqua reddit.

are regenerated as sons of God, in the likeness of his Son. Therefore, it is necessary that our spiritual regeneration come about through that by which we are made like the true Son. and this conies about by our having his Spirit: *if any one does not have the Spirit of Christ, he is not his* (Rom 8:9); *by this we know that we abide in him, and he in us: because he has given us of his Spirit* (1 John 4:13). Thus spiritual regeneration must come from the Holy Spirit. *You did not receive the spirit of slavery, putting you in fear again, but the spirit of adoption* (Rom 8:15); **it is the Spirit that gives life** (John 6:64).

443. Water, too, is necessary for this regeneration, and for three reasons. First, because of the condition of human nature. For man consists of soul and body, and if the Spirit alone were involved in his regeneration, this would indicate that only the spiritual part of man is regenerated. Hence in order that the flesh also be regenerated, it is necessary that, in addition to the Spirit through whom the soul is regenerated, something bodily be involved, through which the body is regenerated; and this is water.

Second, water is necessary for the sake of human knowledge. For, as Dionysius says, divine wisdom so disposes all things that it provides for each thing according to its nature. Now it is natural for man to know; and so it is fitting that spiritual things be conferred on men in such a way that he may know them: *so that we may know what God has given us* (1 Cor 2:12). But the natural manner of this knowledge is that man know spiritual things by means of sensible things, since all our knowledge begins in sense knowledge. Therefore, in order that we might understand what is spiritual in our regeneration, it was fitting that there be in it something sensible and material, that is, water, through which we understand that just as water washes and cleanses the exterior in a bodily way, so through baptism a man is washed and cleansed inwardly in a spiritual way.

Third, water was necessary so that there might be a correspondence of causes. For the cause of our regeneration is the incarnate Word: **he gave them power to be made the sons of God** (John 1:12). Therefore it was fitting that in the sacraments, which have their efficacy from the power of the incarnate Word, there be something corresponding to the Word, and something corresponding to the flesh, or body. And spiritually speaking, this is water when the sacrament is baptism, so that through it we may be conformed to the death of Christ, since we are submerged in it during baptism as Christ was in the womb of the earth for three days: *we are buried with him by baptism* (Rom 6:4).

Further, this mystery was suggested in the first production of things, when the Spirit of God hovered over the waters (Gen 1:2). But a greater power was conferred on water by contact with the most pure flesh of Christ; because in the beginning water brought forth crawling creatures with living souls, but since Christ was baptized in the Jordan, water has yielded spiritual souls.

444. Per hoc autem quod hic dicit *nisi quis renatus fuerit ex aqua et Spiritu Sancto*, manifeste apparet Spiritum Sanctum esse Deum. Supra enim I, 13, dicit: *non ex sanguinibus, neque ex voluntate carnis, neque ex voluntate viri, sed ex Deo nati sunt*. Ex quo sic formatur ratio. Ille ex quo spiritualiter renascuntur homines, est Deus; sed homines renascuntur spiritualiter per Spiritum Sanctum, ut hic dicitur: ergo Spiritus Sanctus est Deus.

445. Sed hic est duplex quaestio. Prima est. Si nullus intrat regnum Dei, nisi renascatur aqua, antiqui autem patres non sunt renati aqua, quia non baptizabantur: ergo non intraverunt regnum Dei.

Alia est, quia cum sit triplex baptismus, scilicet fluminis, flaminis et sanguinis, et multi fuerint baptizati ultimis duobus, quos dicimus intrasse regnum Dei statim (cum tamen non fuerint renati aqua) non videtur esse verum quod hic dicitur *nisi quis renatus fuerit ex aqua et Spiritu Sancto*.

Responsio. Dicendum est quantum ad primum, quia regeneratio ex aqua et Spiritu Sancto fit dupliciter, scilicet in veritate et figura. Antiqui autem patres, licet non fuerint regenerati regeneratione vera, fuerunt tamen regenerati regeneratione figurali, quia semper habuerunt aliquod signum sensibile, in quo vera regeneratio praefigurabatur; et secundum hoc renati intraverunt regnum Dei, soluto pretio.

Quantum ad secundum dicendum, quod illi qui renascuntur baptismo sanguinis et flaminis, licet non habeant regenerationem in actu, habent tamen in voto: alias enim neque baptismus sanguinis aliquid valeret; nec esse posset baptismus Spiritus. Sic ergo ad hoc quod homo intret regnum Dei, oportet quod adsit baptismus aquae in re, sicut est in omnibus baptizatis; vel in voto, sicut est in martyribus et catechumenis, qui morte praeveniuntur antequam votum impleant; vel in figura, sicut in antiquis patribus.

446. Ex hoc quod dicitur *nisi quis renatus fuerit ex aqua et Spiritu Sancto*, Pelagiani errantes dixerunt, quod pueri baptizantur, non quidem ut mundentur a peccatis quae nondum habent, sed ut possint intrare regnum Dei.

Sed hoc est falsum: quia, secundum quod Augustinus dicit in Lib. *de baptismo parvulorum*, inconveniens est quod imago Dei, scilicet homo, subtrahatur a regno Dei, nisi propter aliquod impedimentum; quod esse non potest, nisi peccatum. Oportet ergo quod in pueris qui subtrahuntur a regno, sit aliquod peccatum scilicet originale.

444. It is clear that the Holy Spirit is God, since he says, *unless a man is born again of water and the Holy Spirit*. For he says: *who are born not of blood, nor of the will of the flesh, nor of the will of man, but of God* (John 1:13). From this we can form the following argument: he from whom men are spiritually reborn is God; but men are spiritually reborn through the Holy Spirit, as it is stated here; therefore, the Holy Spirit is God.

445. Two questions arise here. First, if no one enters the kingdom of God unless he is born again of water, and if the fathers of old were not born again of water, for they were not baptized, then they have not entered the kingdom of God.

The other is since baptism is of three kinds, that is, of water, of desire, and of blood, and many have been baptized in the latter two ways, who we say have entered the kingdom of God immediately, (even though they were not born again of water), it does not seem to be true to say that *unless a man is born again of water and the Holy Spirit*, he cannot enter the kingdom of God.

The answer to the first is that rebirth or regeneration from water and the Holy Spirit takes place in two ways: in truth and in symbol. Now the fathers of old, although they were not reborn with a true rebirth, were nevertheless reborn with a symbolic rebirth, because they always had a sense perceptible sign in which true rebirth was prefigured. So according to this, thus reborn, they did enter the kingdom of God, after the ransom was paid.

The answer to the second is that those who are reborn by a baptism of blood and desire, although they do not have regeneration in deed, they do have it in desire. Otherwise neither would the baptism of blood mean anything nor could there be a baptism of the Spirit. Consequently, in order that man may enter the kingdom of heaven, it is necessary that there be a baptism of water in deed, as in the case of all baptized persons, or in desire, as in the case of the martyrs and catechumens, who are prevented by death from fulfilling their desire, or in symbol, as in the case of the fathers of old.

446. It might be remarked that it was from this statement, *unless a man is born again of water and the Holy Spirit*, that the Pelagians derived their error that children are baptized not in order to be cleansed from sin, since they have none, but in order to be able to enter the kingdom of God.

But this is false, because as Augustine says in his book, *The Baptism of Children*, it is not fitting for an image of God, namely, man, to be excluded from the kingdom of God except for some obstacle, which can be nothing but sin. Therefore, there must be some sin, namely, original sin, in children who are excluded from the kingdom.

447. Consequenter cum dicit *quod natum est ex carne, caro est* etc. probat per rationem, quod oportet nasci ex aqua et Spiritu Sancto: et est ratio sua talis. Nullus potest pervenire ad regnum, nisi spiritualis efficiatur; sed aliquis non efficitur spiritualis nisi per Spiritum Sanctum: ergo nullus potest intrare regnum Dei nisi renatus ex Spiritu Sancto.

Dicit ergo *quod natum est ex carne, caro est*; idest, nativitas secundum carnem, facit nasci in vitam carnalem, I Cor. XV, 47: *primus homo de terra terrenus*, et *quod natum est ex Spiritu*, idest ex virtute Spiritus Sancti, *spiritus est*, idest spiritualis.

448. Nota autem, quod haec praepositio 'ex' quandoque designat causam materialem; sicut cum dico, cultellus est ex ferro; quandoque causam efficientem; sicut domus est ex aedificatore. Et secundum hoc, quod dicitur *quod natum est ex carne*, potest intelligi dupliciter, effective et materialiter. Effective quidem, quia virtus quae est in carne, est effectiva generationis; materialiter vero, quia aliquod carnale in animalibus est materia generati. Sed ex spiritu non dicitur aliquid nasci materialiter, cum spiritus immutabilis sit, materia vero sit subiectum transmutationis, sed dicitur effective.

Secundum hoc ergo, possumus accipere triplicem generationem. Unam quae est ex carne materialiter et effective, quae est communis omnibus qui carnalem statum habent. Alia est secundum Spiritum effective, secundum quam regeneramur in Filios Dei per gratiam Spiritus Sancti, et efficimur spirituales. Tertia est media, scilicet quae est ex carne materialiter solum, et ex Spiritu Sancto effective. Et haec est singularis et propria Christi: quia materialiter est habens carnem ex carne matris natus, et effective est ex Spiritu Sancto; Matth. I, 20: *quod enim in ea natum est, de Spiritu Sancto est*. Et ideo natus est sanctus; Lc. I, 35: *Spiritus Sanctus superveniet in te, et virtus Altissimi obumbrabit tibi: ideoque quod nascetur ex te sanctum, vocabitur Filius Dei.*

447. Then when he says, *that which is born of flesh, is flesh*, he proves by reason that it is necessary to be born of water and the Holy Spirit. And the reasoning is this: no one can reach the kingdom unless he is made spiritual; but no one is made spiritual except by the Holy Spirit; therefore, no one can enter the kingdom of God unless he is born again of the Holy Spirit.

So he says, *that which is born of flesh*, *is flesh*, i.e., birth according to the flesh makes one be born into the life of the flesh: *the first man was from the earth, earthly* (1 Cor 15:47); and *that which is born of the Spirit*, i.e., from the power of the Holy Spirit, *is spirit*, i.e., spiritual.

448. Note, however, that this preposition 'of' sometimes designates a material cause, as when I say that a knife is made of iron; sometimes it designates an efficient cause, as when I say that the house was built of a carpenter. Accordingly, the phrase, *that which is born of flesh, is flesh*, can be understood according to either efficient or material causality. As efficient cause, indeed, because a power existing in flesh is productive of generation; and as material cause, because some carnal element in animals makes up the animal generated. But nothing is said to be made out of spirit in a material sense, since spirit is unchangeable, whereas matter is the subject of change; but it is said in the sense of efficient causality.

According to this, we can discern a threefold generation. One is materially and effectively from the flesh, and is common to all who exist according to the flesh. Another is according to the Spirit effectively, and according to it we are reborn as sons of God through the grace of the Holy Spirit, and are made spiritual. The third is midway, that is, only materially from the flesh but effectively from the Holy Spirit. And this is true in the singular case of Christ: because he was born deriving his flesh materially from the flesh of his mother, but effectively from the Holy Spirit: *what she has conceived is of the Holy Spirit* (Matt 1:20). Therefore, he was born holy: *the Holy Spirit will come upon you, and the power of the Most High will overshadow you. And so the Holy One who will be born from you, will be called the Son of God* (Luke 1:35).

Lecture 2

3:7 Non mireris, quia dixi tibi: oportet vos nasci denuo. [n. 449]

3:8 Spiritus ubi vult spirat, et vocem eius audis; sed nescis unde veniat, aut quo vadat: sic est omnis qui natus est ex Spiritu. [n. 449]

3:9 Respondit Nicodemus, et dixit ei: quomodo possunt haec fieri? [n. 458]

3:10 Respondit Iesus, et dixit ei: tu es magister in Israel, et haec ignoras? [n. 459]

3:11 Amen, amen dico tibi, quia quod scimus loquimur, et quod vidimus testamur; et testimonium nostrum non accipitis. [n. 462]

3:12 Si terrena dixi vobis, et non creditis: quomodo si dixero vobis caelestia, credetis? [n. 463]

3:13 Et nemo ascendit in caelum nisi qui descendit de caelo, Filius hominis, qui est in caelo. [n. 467]

3:14 Et sicut Moyses exaltavit serpentem in deserto, ita exaltari oportet Filium hominis: [n. 473]

3:15 ut omnis qui credit in ipsum, non pereat, sed habeat vitam aeternam. [n. 475]

3:7 μὴ θαυμάσῃς ὅτι εἶπόν σοι· δεῖ ὑμᾶς γεννηθῆναι ἄνωθεν.

3:8 τὸ πνεῦμα ὅπου θέλει πνεῖ καὶ τὴν φωνὴν αὐτοῦ ἀκούεις, ἀλλ᾽ οὐκ οἶδας πόθεν ἔρχεται καὶ ποῦ ὑπάγει· οὕτως ἐστὶν πᾶς ὁ γεγεννημένος ἐκ τοῦ πνεύματος.

3:9 ἀπεκρίθη Νικόδημος καὶ εἶπεν αὐτῷ· πῶς δύναται ταῦτα γενέσθαι;

3:10 ἀπεκρίθη Ἰησοῦς καὶ εἶπεν αὐτῷ· σὺ εἶ ὁ διδάσκαλος τοῦ Ἰσραὴλ καὶ ταῦτα οὐ γινώσκεις;

3:11 ἀμὴν ἀμὴν λέγω σοι ὅτι ὃ οἴδαμεν λαλοῦμεν καὶ ὃ ἑωράκαμεν μαρτυροῦμεν, καὶ τὴν μαρτυρίαν ἡμῶν οὐ λαμβάνετε.

3:12 εἰ τὰ ἐπίγεια εἶπον ὑμῖν καὶ οὐ πιστεύετε, πῶς ἐὰν εἴπω ὑμῖν τὰ ἐπουράνια πιστεύσετε;

3:13 καὶ οὐδεὶς ἀναβέβηκεν εἰς τὸν οὐρανὸν εἰ μὴ ὁ ἐκ τοῦ οὐρανοῦ καταβάς, ὁ υἱὸς τοῦ ἀνθρώπου.

3:14 Καὶ καθὼς Μωϋσῆς ὕψωσεν τὸν ὄφιν ἐν τῇ ἐρήμῳ, οὕτως ὑψωθῆναι δεῖ τὸν υἱὸν τοῦ ἀνθρώπου,

3:15 ἵνα πᾶς ὁ πιστεύων ἐν αὐτῷ ἔχῃ ζωὴν αἰώνιον.

3:7 Do not wonder that I said to you, you ought to be born again. [n. 449]

3:8 The wind blows where it wills; and you hear its sound, but you do not know where it comes from or where it goes: so it is with every man who is born of the Spirit. [n. 449]

3:9 Nicodemus answered and said to him: how can these things be done? [n. 458]

3:10 Jesus answered and said to him: you are a teacher in Israel, and you do not know these things? [n. 459]

3:11 Amen, amen I say to you, that we speak what we know, and we testify what we have seen, and you do not receive our testimony. [n. 462]

3:12 If I have spoken to you of earthly things, and you do not believe, how will you believe if I speak to you of heavenly things? [n. 463]

3:13 And no man has ascended into heaven, except he who descended from heaven, the Son of man, who is in heaven. [n. 467]

3:14 Just as Moses lifted up the serpent in the desert, so must the Son of man be lifted up: [n. 473]

3:15 so that whoever believes in him may not perish but have eternal life. [n. 475]

---

449. Supra posuit Dominus rationem ad instruendam spiritualem generationem; hic ponit exemplum. Datur autem intelligi, quod Nicodemus, audito *quod natum est ex Spiritu, spiritus est,* turbationem quamdam dubietatis incurrit; et ideo Dominus dicit ei *non mireris, quia dixi tibi: oportet vos nasci denuo.*

Ubi sciendum est, quod duplex est admiratio. Una devotionis, secundum quod aliquis magnalia Dei considerans, cognoscit ea sibi incomprehensibilia esse: unde relinquitur admirationi locus, secundum illud Ps. XCII, 4: *mirabilis in altis Dominus*; et alibi CXVIII, v. 129: *mirabilia testimonia tua.* Et ad hanc homines sunt inducendi, non prohibendi. Alia est infidelitatis, dum quis ea quae dicuntur non credens, miratur. Unde dicitur Matth. c. XIII, 57 quod *mirabantur in doctrina Christi*: et sequitur, quod *scandalizabantur in eo.* Et ab hac

449. Above, in his instruction on spiritual generation, the Lord presented a reason; here he gives an example. For we are led to see that Nicodemus was troubled when he heard that *that which is born of the Spirit, is spirit* (John 3:6). And so the Lord says to him, *do not wonder that I said to you, you ought to be born again.*

Here we should note that there are two kinds of surprise or astonishment. One is the astonishment of devotion in the sense that someone, considering the great things of God, sees that they are incomprehensible to him; and so he is full of astonishment: *the Lord on high is wonderful* (Ps 92:4), *your testimonies are wonderful* (Ps 118:129). Men are to be encouraged, not discouraged, to this kind of astonishment The other is the astonishment of disbelief, when someone does not believe what is said. So it is said: *they were astonished,* and further on adds that *they did not*

admiratione Dominus Nicodemum removet, inducens exemplum, cum dicit *spiritus ubi vult spirat*.

Quod quidem, eadem servata sententia, dupliciter quantum ad litteram exponi potest.

450. Uno enim modo, secundum Chrysostomum, accipitur pro vento, sicut in Ps. c. CXLVIII, 8: *spiritus procellarum, quae faciunt verbum eius*. Et secundum hoc quatuor dicit de vento. Primo venti potestatem, cum dicit *spiritus ubi vult spirat*; idest, ventus quo *vult* flat. Et si dicas, quod ventus non habet voluntatem; dicendum, quod voluntas sumitur pro appetitu naturali, qui nihil est aliud quam naturalis inclinatio, de qua dicitur Iob XXVIII, 25: *qui creavit ventis pondus*.

Secundo ponitur venti indicium, cum dicit *et vocem eius audis*; et sumitur *vox* pro sono quem facit ventus ex percussione ad aliquod corpus; de quo dicitur in Ps. LXXVI, 19: *vox tonitrui tui in rota*.

Tertio ponit venti originem, quae occulta est; unde dicit *et nescis unde veniat*, idest ubi oriatur; Ps. CXXXIV, 7: *qui producit ventos de thesauris suis*.

Quarto ponit venti finem, qui similiter occultus est; unde dicit *aut quo vadat*; supple, nescis, idest ubi persistat. Et hanc quidem similitudinem inducit ad propositum, cum dicit *sic est omnis qui natus est ex Spiritu*; quasi dicat: si ventus, qui est corporeus, habet occultam originem, nec potest sciri eius processus; quomodo miraris, si tu non potes scire processum regenerationis spiritualis?

451. Sed contra hanc expositionem obiicit Augustinus dicens, quod Dominus non intellexit de vento, cum dixit *spiritus ubi vult spirat* etc. nam de quolibet vento scimus, unde veniat, aut quo vadat: nam Auster venit a meridie, et vadit ad Aquilonem; Boreas vero e converso ab Aquilone ad meridiem vadit. Quomodo ergo de spiritu corporeo dicit Dominus *nescis unde veniat, aut quo vadat*?

Sed ad hoc responderi potest, quod principium venti potest sciri dupliciter. Uno modo in generali; et hoc modo scitur unde veniat, idest a qua parte mundi, sicut scitur, quod Auster venit a meridie; et quo vadat, quia ad Aquilonem. Alio modo in speciali; et hoc modo nescitur unde veniat, idest in qua plaga determinate incipiat: aut quo vadat, idest ubi determinate cesset. Et cum Chrysostomo ad hanc expositionem conveniunt omnes fere Graeci doctores.

452. Alio modo exponitur de Spiritu Sancto; et secundum hoc quatuor ponit de Spiritu Sancto. Primo quidem eius potestatem, cum dicit *Spiritus ubi vult spirat*: quia pro libero potestatis arbitrio inspirat ubi vult, et quando vult, corda illustrando; I Cor. XII, 11: *haec omnia operatur unus atque idem Spiritus, dividens singulis*

accept him (Matt 13:54). It is from this kind of astonishment that the Lord diverts Nicodemus when he proposes an example and says: *the wind blows where it wills*.

In the literal sense, the same words can he explained in two ways.

450. In the first way, according to Chrysostom, *wind* is actually taken for the wind: *the winds of the storm that fulfill his word* (Ps 148:8). According to this interpretation, he says four things about the wind. First, the power of the wind, when he says, *the wind blows where it wills*. And if you say that the wind has no will, one may answer that *will* is taken for a natural appetite, which is nothing more than a natural inclination, about which it is said: *he created the weight of the wind* (Job 28:25).

Second, he tells the evidence for the wind, when he says, *and you hear its sound*, where *sound* refers to the sound the wind makes when it strikes a body. Of this we read: *the sound of your thunder was in the whirlwind* (Ps 76:19).

Third, he mentions the origin of the wind, which is unknown; so he says, *but you do not know where it comes from*, i.e., from where it starts: *he brings forth the winds out of his storehouse* (Ps 134:7).

Fourth, he mentions the wind's destination, which is also unknown; so he says, *or where it goes*, i.e., where it remains. And he applies this similarity to the subject under discussion, saying, *so it is with every man who is born of the Spirit*. As if to say: if the wind, which is corporeal, has an origin which is hidden and a course that is unknown, why are you surprised if you cannot understand the course of spiritual regeneration?

451. Augustine objects to this explanation and says that the Lord was not speaking here about the wind when he said, *the wind blows where it wills*, for we know where each of the winds comes from and where it goes. For auster comes from the south and goes to the north; boreas comes from the north and goes to the south. Why, then, does the Lord say of this wind, *but you do not know where it comes from or where it goes*?

One may answer that there are two ways in which the source of the wind might be unknown. In one way, in general: and in this way it is possible to know where it comes from, i.e., from which direction of the world, for example, that Auster comes from the south, and where it goes, that is, to the north. In another way, in particular: and in this sense it is not known where the wind comes from, i.e., at which precise place it originated, or where it goes, i.e., exactly where it stops. And almost all the Greek doctors agree with this exposition of Chrysostom.

452. In another way, *wind* is taken for the Holy Spirit. And according to this, he mentions four things about the Holy Spirit. First, his power, saying, *the wind blows where it wills*, because it is by the free use of his power that he breathes where he wills and when he wills, by instructing hearts: *one and the same Spirit does all these things,*

prout vult. Ex quo confutatur error Macedonii ponentis Spiritum Sanctum esse ministrum Patris et Filii. Non enim spiraret ubi ipse vellet, sed ubi ei mandaretur.

453. Secundo vero ponit Spiritus Sancti indicium, cum dicit **et vocem eius audis**; Ps. XCIV, 8: *hodie si vocem eius audieritis, nolite obdurare corda vestra.*

Sed contra hoc obiicit Chrysostomus dicens, quod non potest intelligi de Spiritu Sancto. Dominus enim loquebatur Nicodemo, qui adhuc infidelis erat, cui non competebat audire vocem Spiritus Sancti.

Sed dicendum, secundum Augustinum, quod Spiritus Sancti est duplex vox. Una, qua loquitur intus in corde hominis; et hanc audiunt solum fideles et sancti: de qua dicitur in Ps. c. LXXXIV, 9: *audiam quid loquatur in me Dominus Deus.* Alia est, qua Spiritus Sanctus loquitur in Scripturis, vel per praedicatores, secundum quod dicitur Matth. X, 20: *non enim vos estis qui loquimini, sed Spiritus Sanctus qui loquitur in vobis.* Et hanc audiunt etiam infideles et peccatores.

454. Tertio ponit Spiritus Sancti originem, quae occulta est, unde dicit **et nescis unde veniat**, licet vocem eius audias: et hoc ideo quia venit a Patre et Filio; infra XV, 26: **cum autem venerit Paraclitus, quem ego mittam vobis a Patre spiritum veritatis, qui a Patre procedit.** Pater autem, et Filius lucem habitant inaccessibilem, *quam nemo hominum vidit, sed nec videre potest*: ut dicitur I Tim. ult. 16.

455. Quarto ponit Spiritus Sancti finem, qui quidem occultus est, et ideo dicit **aut quo vadat**, supple: nescis, quia perducit ad occultum finem, scilicet ad beatitudinem aeternam. Unde dicitur *pignus hereditatis*, Eph. I, v. 14 et I Cor. II, 9: *oculus non vidit nec auris audivit, nec in cor hominis ascendit, quae praeparavit Deus iis qui diligunt illum.* Vel **nescis unde veniat**, idest quomodo hominem introeat, **aut quo vadat**, idest ad quam perfectionem illum adducat; Iob IX, 11: *si venerit ad me, non videbo eum.*

456. Sic est omnis qui natus est ex Spiritu; idest, sicut Spiritus Sanctus.

Nec mirum: nam sicut supra dixerat, **quod natum est ex Spiritu, spiritus est**: quia in viro spirituali sunt proprietates Spiritus Sancti, sicut in carbone succenso sunt proprietates ignis.

Sunt autem in eo qui natus est ex Spiritu Sancto praedictae quatuor proprietates Spiritus. Primo namque habet libertatem; II Cor. c. III, 17: *ubi Spiritus Domini, ibi libertas*, quia Spiritus Domini ducit ad id quod rectum est, Ps. CXLII, 10: *Spiritus tuus bonus deducet me in terram rectam*, et liberat a servitute peccati et legis, Rom. VIII, 2: *lex Spiritus vitae in Christo liberavit me* etc.

distributing to each as he wills (1 Cor 12:11). This refutes the error of Macedonius who thought that the Holy Spirit was the minister of the Father and the Son. But then he would not be breathing where he willed, but where he was commanded.

453. Second, he mentions the evidence for the Holy Spirit, when he says, **and you hear its sound**; *today, if you hear his voice, do not harden your hearts* (Ps 94:8).

Chrysostom objects to this and says that this cannot pertain to the Holy Spirit. For the Lord was speaking to Nicodemus, who was still an unbeliever, and thus not fit to hear the voice of the Holy Spirit.

We may answer to this, with Augustine, that there is a twofold voice of the Holy Spirit. One is that by which he speaks inwardly in man's heart; and only believers and the saints hear this voice: *I will hear what the Lord God says within me* (Ps 84:9). The other voice is that by which the Holy Spirit speaks in the Scriptures or through those who preach: *for it is not you who speak, but the Holy Splirit who is speaking through you* (Matt 10:20). And this voice is heard by unbelievers and sinners.

454. Third, he refers to the origin of the Holy Spirit, which is hidden; thus he says, but **you do not know where it comes from**, although you may hear its voice. And this is because the Holy Spirit comes from the Father and the Son: **when the Paraclete comes whom I will send you from the Father, the Spirit of truth, who proceeds from the Father** (John 15:26). But the Father and the Son *dwell in inaccessible light, whom no man has seen or is able to see* (1 Tim 6:16).

455. Fourth, he gives the destination of the Holy Spirit, which is also hidden; and so he says, **you do not know . . . where it goes**, because the Spirit leads one to a hidden end, that is, eternal happiness. Thus it is said that the Holy Spirit is *the pledge of our inheritance* (Eph 1:14). And again, *the eye has not seen, nor has the ear heard, nor has the heart of man conceived, what God has prepared for those who love him* (1 Cor 2:9). Or, **you do not know where it comes from**, i.e., how the Spirit enters into a person, **or where it goes**, i.e., to what perfection he may lead him: *if he comes toward me, I will not see him* (Job 9:11).

456. So it is with every man who is born of the Spirit, i.e., they are like the Holy Spirit.

And no wonder: for as he had said before, **that which is born of the Spirit, is spirit** (John 3:6), because the qualities of the Holy Spirit are present in the spiritual man, just as the qualities of fire are present in burning coal.

Therefore, the above four qualities of the Holy Spirit are found in one who has been born of the Holy Spirit. First of all, he has freedom: *where the Spirit of the Lord is, there is freedom* (2 Cor 3:17), for the Holy Spirit leads us to what is right: *your good Spirit will lead me to the right path* (Ps 142:10); and he frees us from the slavery of sin and of the law: *the law of the Spirit, of life in Christ, has set me free* (Rom 8:2).

Secundo vero eius indicium sumis per vocem verborum suorum, quam dum audis, cognoscis eius spiritualitatem; Matth. XII, 34: *ex abundantia cordis os loquitur.*

Tertio vero habet originem occultam, et finem, quia nullus potest spiritualem iudicare I Cor. II, 15: *spiritualis omnia iudicat, et ipse a nemine iudicatur.*

Vel **nescis unde veniat**, principium spiritualis nativitatis eius, quod est gratia baptismalis **aut quo vadat**, idest quo dignus efficitur, idest vita aeterna, quae tibi adhuc occulta est.

457. Hic ponitur causa et ratio spiritualis regenerationis: et

primo ponitur interrogatio Nicodemi;

secundo responsio Domini **respondit Iesus, et dixit ei** etc.

458. Apparet autem ex primo, quod Nicodemus adhuc rudis, et adhuc Iudaeus sensibilis existens, mysteria Christi, et per ea exempla, et per rationes proposita intelligere non poterat; et ideo dicit **quomodo possunt haec fieri?**

Dupliciter namque aliqui inquirunt. Quidam namque ex diffidentia; sicut Zacharias, Lc. I, v. 18: *unde hoc sciam? Ego enim sum senex, et uxor mea processit in diebus suis*: et ideo punitus fuit; Is. XL, 23: *qui dat scrutatores eius quasi non sint.* Aliqui vero ex studio addiscendi, sicut Virgo Beata, cum dixit angelo, Lc. I, 34: *quomodo fiet istud, quoniam virum non cognosco?* Et tales instruuntur. Quia ergo iste quaesivit ex studio addiscendi, ideo meruit instrui.

459. Et hoc est quod sequitur **respondit Iesus** etc. ubi

primo Dominus arguit eius tarditatem;

secundo respondet ad quaestionem ipsius, ibi **et nemo ascendit in caelum.**

460. Tarditatem eius arguit ex tribus: primo ex conditione personae eius cui loquitur, cum dicit **tu es magister**: ubi non reprehendit eum Dominus ut insultaret ei, sed quia confidebat adhuc de magisterio suo, praesumens de sua scientia, voluit eum humiliando efficere habitaculum Spiritus Sancti; Is. ult., 2: *ad quem respiciam, nisi ad pauperculum, et contritum spiritu?* Et dicit **tu es magister**: quia si aliquis simplex non potest profunda capere, tolerabile est; sed hoc in magistro valde est reprehensibile, et ideo dicit ei **tu es magister**, idest litterae quae occidit, I Cor. III; **in Israel, et haec**, scilicet spiritualia **ignoras?** Hebr. V, 12: *etenim cum deberitis esse magistri propter tempus, rursus indigetis ut vos doceamini.*

Second, we get an indication of him through the sound of his words; and when we hear them we know his spirituality, for *it is out of the abundance of the heart that the mouth speaks* (Matt 12:34).

Third, he has an origin and an end that are hidden, because no one can judge one who is spiritual: *the spiritual man judges all things, and he himself is judged by no one* (1 Cor 2:15).

Or, **you do not know where it comes from**, the source of his spiritual birth, which is baptismal grace; **or where it goes**, i.e., of what he is made worthy, that is, of eternal life, which remains concealed from us.

457. Then the cause and reason for spiritual regeneration are set forth.

First, a question is asked by Nicodemus;

second, the Lord's answer is given, at **Jesus answered and said to him**.

458. It is apparent from the first that Nicodemus, as yet dull, and remaining a Jew on the level of sense, was unable to understand the mysteries of Christ in spite of the examples and explanations that were given. And so he says, **how can these things be done?**

There are two reasons why one may question about something. Some question because of disbelief, as did Zechariah, saying: *how will I know this? For I am an old man, and my wife is advanced in age* (Luke 1:18); *he confounds those who search into mysteries* (Isa 40:23). Others, on the other hand, question because of a desire to know, as the Blessed Virgin did when she said to the angel: *how shall this be, since I do not know man?* (Luke 1:34). It is the latter who are instructed. And so, because Nicodemus asked from a desire to learn, he deserved to be instructed.

459. And this is what follows: **Jesus answered, and said to him: you are a teacher in Israel**.

First the Lord chides him for his slowness.

Second, he answers his question, at **and no man has ascended into heaven**.

460. He chides him for his slowness, basing himself on three things. First, the condition of the person to whom he is speaking, when he says, **you are a teacher in Israel**. And here the Lord did not chide him to insult him. Rather, because Nicodemus, presuming on his own knowledge, was still relying on his status as a teacher, the Lord wished to make him a temple of the Holy Spirit by humbling him: *for whom will I have regard? For he who is humble and of contrite spirit* (Isa 66:2). And he says, **you are a teacher**, because it is tolerable if a simple person cannot grasp profound truths, but in a teacher, it deserves rebuke. And so he says, **you are a teacher**, i.e., of the letter that kills (2 Cor 3:6), **and you do not know these things?** i.e., spiritual things. *For although you ought to be teachers by now, you yourselves need to be taught again* (Heb 5:12).

461. Si dicas, quod Dominus iuste argueret Nicodemus, si dixisset ei aliquid de veteri lege, et ipse non intellexisset; sed dixit ei de nova lege.

Dicendum, quod ea quae Dominus dicit de spirituali generatione, continentur in lege veteri, sed sub figura, secundum quod habetur I Cor. X, 2: *omnes in Moyse baptizati sunt in nube et in mari.* Et prophetae etiam hoc dixerunt; Ez. XXXVI, 25: *effundam super vos aquam mundam, et mundabimini ab omnibus inquinamentis vestris.*

462. Secundo vero arguit eius tarditatem ex conditione dicentis. Quod enim non acquiescatur dictis alicuius hominis rudis, tolerari potest; sed repugnare dictis hominis sapientis, et magnae auctoritatis, reprehensibile est; et ideo dicit **amen, amen dico tibi, quia quod scimus loquimur, et quod vidimus testamur.** Requiritur enim ad idoneitatem testis ut perhibeat testimonium de auditu, vel visu; I Io. I, 3: *quod vidimus, et audivimus.* Et ideo Dominus utrumque dicit **quod scimus loquimur, et quod vidimus testamur.** Scit autem Dominus, secundum quod homo, omnia; infra ult., 17: **Domine, tu omnia nosti**; II Mac. VI, 30: *Domine, qui habes sanctam scientiam, manifeste tu scis.* Sed et videt omnia cognitione divinitatis; infra VIII, v. 38: **ego quae vidi apud Patrem meum, haec facio.**

Dicit autem pluraliter **scimus** et **vidimus**, ut insinuet mysterium Trinitatis. Ideo **Pater in me manens, ipse facit opera**: infra XIV, 10. Vel **quod scimus**, ego et alii spirituales effecti: quia, dicitur Matth. XI, 26: *nemo novit Patrem nisi Filius, et cui voluerit Filius revelare.* Et tamen **testimonium**, ita probatum, ita firmum, **non accipitis.** Infra eodem **et testimonium eius nemo accipit.**

463. Tertio arguit eius tarditatem ex conditione eorum quae dicuntur. Quod enim aliqua difficilia non capiantur ab aliquo, non est mirum; sed quod facilia quis non capiat, reprehensibilis est. Et ideo dicit **si terrena dixi vobis, et non creditis; quomodo si dixero vobis caelestia, credetis?** Quasi dicat: si haec quae sunt levia, non capis; quomodo capere poteris processum Spiritus Sancti? Sap. c. IX, 16: *quae in terris sunt, difficile invenimus, et quae in caelis sunt quis investigabit?*

464. Sed contra. Non invenitur ex praemissis quod Dominus dixerit Nicodemo aliqua terrena.

Et dicendum, secundum Chrysostomum hic, quod dicit Dominus **si terrena dixi vobis** etc. Intelligitur de exemplo venti. Ventus enim cum sit generabilis et corruptibilis, numeratur inter res terrenas. Vel potest dici, secundum eumdem, quod spiritualis generatio, quae est in baptismo, caelestis quidem est quantum ad principium, quod sanctificat et regenerat, sed terrena quantum

461. You might say that the Lord would have rebuked Nicodemus justly if he had spoken to him about matters of the old law and he did not understand them; but he spoke to him about the new law.

I answer that the things which the Lord says of spiritual generation are contained in the old law, although under a figure, as is said: *all were baptized into Moses, in the cloud and in the sea* (1 Cor 10:2). And the prophets also said this: *I will pour clean water upon you, and you will be cleansed from all your uncleanness* (Ezek 36:25).

462. Second, he rebukes him for his slowness on account of the character of the person who is speaking. For it is tolerable if one does not acquiesce to the statements of an ignorant person; but it is reprehensible to reject the statements of a man who is wise and who possesses great authority. And so he says, **amen, amen I say to you, that we speak what we know, and we testify what we have seen.** For a qualified witness must base his testimony on hearing or sight: *what we have seen and heard* (1 John 1:3). And so the Lord mentions both: **we speak what we know, and we testify what we have seen.** Indeed, the Lord as man knows all things: **Lord, you know all things** (John 21:17); *the Lord, whose knowledge is holy, knows clearly* (2 Macc 6:30). Further, he sees all things by his divine knowledge: **I speak that which I have seen with my Father** (John 8:38).

He speaks in the plural, **we know** and **we have seen,** in order to suggest the mystery of the Trinity: **the Father who abides in me, he does the works** (John 14:10). Or, **we know,** i.e., I and others who have been made spiritual, because *no one knows the Father but the Son, and he to whom the Son wishes to reveal him* (Matt 11:27). But you **do not receive our testimony,** so approved, so solid. **And no man receives his testimony** (John 3:32).

463. Third, he rebukes him for his slowness because of the quality of the things under discussion. For it is not unusual when someone does not grasp difficult matters, but it is inexcusable not to grasp easy things. So he says, **if I have spoken of earthly things, and you do not believe, how will you believe if I speak to you of heavenly things?** As if to say: if you do not grasp these easy things, how will you be able to understand the progress of the Holy Spirit? *What is on earth we find difficult, and who will search out the things in heaven* (Wis 9:10).

464. But one might object that the above does not show that the Lord spoke of earthly things to Nicodemus.

I answer, according to Chrysostom, that the Lord's statement, **if I have spoken to you of earthly things,** refers to the example of the wind. For the wind, being something which is generable and corruptible, is regarded as an earthly thing. Or one might say, again according to Chrysostom, that the spiritual generation which is given in baptism is heavenly as to its source, which sanctifies and regenerates; but it is

ad subiectum: quod enim regeneratur, scilicet homo, terrenus est.

Vel dicendum, secundum Augustinum, quod intelligendum est de eo quod supra dixerat: *solvite templum hoc* etc. quod ideo terrenum est, quia hoc dixit de templo corporis sui, quod de terra acceperat. *Si terrena dixi vobis, et non creditis; quomodo si caelestia, credetis?* Quasi dicat: si non creditis generationem spiritualem temporalem, quomodo credetis aeternam Filii generationem? Vel si non creditis quae dico de potestate corporis mei, quomodo credetis de potestate divinitatis meae, et de potestate Spiritus Sancti?

465. *Respondit Iesus*, etc. Hic respondet quaestioni: et

primo ponit causas spiritualis regenerationis;

secundo manifestat quod dicit, ibi *sic enim Deus dilexit mundum ut Filium suum unigenitum daret*.

Causa autem spiritualis regenerationis est duplex, scilicet mysterium incarnationis Christi et passionis eius: et ideo

primo agit de incarnatione;

secundo de passione, ibi *et sicut Moyses exaltavit serpentem* etc.

466. Est autem considerandum primo, quomodo ista responsio Christi quaestioni Nicodemi satisfaciat. Dixerat enim supra Dominus, de Spiritu loquens, quod *nescis unde veniat, aut quo vadat*: per quod dabatur intelligi, quod spiritualis regeneratio haberet occultum principium et occultum finem. Occulta autem nobis sunt quae in caelis sunt, secundum illud Sap. IX, 16: *quae in caelis sunt, quis investigabit?* Quaestio ergo Nicodemi *quomodo possunt haec fieri?* Sic debet intelligi: quomodo possit aliquid de occulto caelorum venire aut ad occultum caelorum ire? Unde antequam quaestioni satisfaceret, hunc intellectum quaestionis explicavit, dicens *quomodo si dixero vobis caelestia, credetis?* Et statim incipit ostendere, cuius sit in caelum ascendere proprium: quia omnis qui de caelo descendit, secundum illud Eph. IV, 10: *qui descendit ipse est et qui ascendit.* Hoc enim et in rebus naturalibus invenitur quod unumquodque corpus tendit in locum, secundum suam originem vel naturam. Unde hoc modo potest fieri ut aliquis per Spiritum vadat ad locum quem carnales nesciunt, ascendendo in caelum, si hoc fiat per virtutem eius qui descendit de caelo: quia ad hoc descendit, ut ascendens, nobis viam aperiret; Mich. II, v. 13: *ascendit pandens iter ante eos.*

467. Sed quia dicit *qui descendit de caelo Filius hominis*: quidam errandi sumpserunt occasionem. Cum enim Filius hominis designet humanam naturam, quae componitur ex anima et corpore, per hoc quod dicit

earthly as to its subject, for the one regenerated, man, is of the earth.

Or one might answer, according to Augustine, that we must understand this in reference to what Christ said earlier: *destroy this temple* (John 2:19), which is earthly, because he said this about the temple of his body, which he had taken from the earth. *If I have spoken to you of earthly things, and you do not believe, how will you believe if I speak to you of heavenly things?* As if to say: if you do not believe in a spiritual generation occurring in time, how will you believe in the eternal generation of the Son? Or, if you do not believe what I tell you about the power of my body, how will you believe what I tell you about the power of my divinity and about the power of the Holy Spirit?

465. *Jesus replied and said to him: you are a teacher.* Here he answers the question.

First, he lays down the causes of spiritual regeneration.

Second, he explains what he says, *for God so loved the world that he gave his only begotten Son* (John 3:16).

Now there are two causes of spiritual regeneration, namely, the mystery of the incarnation of Christ, and his passion.

So first, he treats of the incarnation;

second, of the passion, at *just as Moses lifted up the serpent.*

466. Here we should consider, first of all, how this answer of Christ is an adequate reply to the question of Nicodemus. For above, when the Lord was speaking of the Spirit, he said: *but you do not know where it comes from or where it goes.* We understand by this that spiritual regeneration has a hidden source and a hidden end. Now the things in heaven are hidden from us: *who will search out the things in heaven?* (Wis 9:16). Therefore, the sense of Nicodemus' question, *how can these things be done?* is this: how can something come from the secret things of heaven or go to the secret things of heaven? So before answering, the Lord expressed this interpretation of the question, saying, *how will you believe if I speak to you of heavenly things?* And immediately he begins to show whose prerogative it is to ascend into heaven, namely, anyone who came down from heaven: *he who descended is he who ascended* (Eph 4:10). This is verified even in natural things, namely, that each body tends to a place according to its origin or nature. And so in this way it can come about that someone, through the Spirit, may go to a place which carnal persons do not know, i.e., by ascending into heaven, if this is done through the power of one who descended from heaven: because he descended in order that, in ascending, he might open a way for us: *he ascends, opening the way before them* (Mic 2:13).

467. Some have fallen into error because of his saying, *he who descended from heaven, the Son of man.* For since Son of man designates human nature, which is composed of soul and body, then because he says that the Son descended

quod Filius descendit de caelo, Valentinus accipere voluit, quod etiam corpus de caelo detulisset, et transisset per Virginem, nihil ex ea accipiens, sicut aqua per fistulam: ergo non de terrena substantia, nec sumptum de Virgine: quod est contra Apostolum, Rom. I, 3: *qui factus est ei ex semine David secundum carnem.*

Origenes vero dixit, quod descendit de caelo secundum animam, quam dicit ab initio fuisse creatam cum angelis, et verbo unitam, et postmodum de caelo descendisse assumendo carnem de Virgine. Sed et hoc repugnat Catholicae fidei, quae animas dicit ante corpora non extitisse.

468. Non ergo intelligendum est quod Filius hominis secundum humanam naturam de caelo descenderit, sed secundum divinam. Cum enim in Christo sit unum suppositum, vel hypostasis, vel persona duarum naturarum, divinae scilicet, et humanae; ex quacumque earum hoc suppositum nominetur, possunt ei attribui et divina et humana. Possumus enim dicere, quod Filius hominis creavit stellas, et quod Filius Dei crucifixus est. Sed Filius Dei crucifixus est, non secundum divinam naturam, sed secundum humanam; Filius autem hominis creavit stellas secundum divinam naturam. Ita in his quae de Christo dicuntur, non est attendenda distinctio quantum ad id de quo dicuntur, quia indifferenter et divina et humana dicuntur de Deo et homine; sed est attendenda distinctio quantum ad id secundum quod dicuntur, quia divina dicuntur de Christo secundum divinam naturam, humana vero secundum humanam. Descendere ergo de caelis dicitur de Filio hominis, non secundum humanam naturam, sed secundum divinam, secundum quam convenit ei ante incarnationem de caelo fuisse, secundum illud Ps. CXIII, 16: *caelum caeli Domino.*

469. Dicitur autem descendisse, non motu locali, quia sic non remaneret in caelo: nihil enim localiter motum manet unde descendit. Et ideo ad excludendum motum localem, subdit *qui est in caelo*; quasi dicat: sic descendit de caelo, quod tamen est in caelo. Descendit enim de caelo, non quidem desinens esse sursum, sed assumens naturam quae est deorsum: quae, quia non includitur, vel comprehenditur, corpore eius existente in terra, ipse secundum divinitatem erat in caelis, et ubique. Et ideo ad designandum, quod hoc modo dicitur descendisse, quia assumpsit naturam, dixit quod *descendit Filius hominis*; idest, inquantum factus est Filius hominis.

470. Vel potest dici etiam, quod quantum ad corpus descendit de caelo, ut Hilarius dicit: non quod materia corporis Christi descenderit de caelo, sed quod virtus formativa eius de caelo fuit.

from heaven, Valentinus wanted to maintain that he even took his body from heaven and thus passed through the Virgin without receiving anything from her, as water passes through a pipe; so that his body was neither of an earthly substance nor taken from the Virgin. But this is contrary to the statement of the Apostle: *who was made from the seed of David according to the flesh* (Rom 1:3).

On the other hand, Origen said that he descended from heaven as to his soul, which, he says, had been created along with the angels from the very beginning, and that later this soul descended from heaven and took flesh from the Virgin. But this also conflicts with the Catholic faith, which teaches that souls do not exist before their bodies.

468. Therefore, we should not understand that the Son of man descended from heaven according to his human nature, but only according to his divine nature. For since in Christ there is one suppositum, or hypostasis, or person of the two natures, the divine and human natures, then no matter from which of these two natures this suppositum is named, divine and human things can be attributed to him. For we can say that the Son of man created the stars and that the Son of God was crucified. But the Son of God was crucified, not according to his divine nature, but according to his human nature; and the Son of man created the stars according to his divine nature. And so in things that are said of Christ, the distinction is not to be taken with respect to that about which they are said, because divine and human things are said of God and man indifferently; but a distinction must be made with respect to that according to which they are said, because divine things are said of Christ according to his divine nature, but human things according to his human nature. Thus, to descend from heaven is said of the Son of man, not according to his human nature, but according to his divine nature, according to which it was appropriate to him to have been from heaven before the incarnation, as is said, *heaven belongs to the Lord* (Ps 113:16).

469. He is said to have come down, but not by local motion, because then he would not have remained in heaven; for nothing which moves locally remains in the place from which it comes down. And so to exclude local motion, he adds, *who is in heaven*. As if to say: he descended from heaven in such a way as yet to be in heaven. For he came down from heaven without ceasing to be above, yet assuming a nature which is from below. And because he is not enclosed or held fast by his body which exists on earth, he was, according to his divinity, in heaven and everywhere. And therefore to indicate that he is said to have come down in this way, because he assumed a nature, he said, the *Son of man descended*, i.e., insofar as he became Son of man.

470. Or it can be said, as Hilary does, that he came down from heaven as to his body: not that the material of Christ's body came down from heaven, but that the power which formed it was from heaven.

471. Sed quid est quod dicit **nemo ascendit in caelum, nisi Filius hominis, qui est in caelo**? Nonne Paulus, et Petrus, et alii sancti ascenderunt, secundum illud II Cor. c. V, 1: *domum habemus, non manufactam in caelis* etc.

Respondeo dicendum, quod nemo ascendit in caelum nisi Christus et membra sua, idest iusti fideles: propterea Filius Dei de caelis descendit, ut nos faciendo membra sua ad ascensum caelorum praepararet; nunc quidem in spe, tandem vero in re; Eph. II, 6: *qui resuscitavit nos, et consedere nos fecit in caelestibus in Christo Iesu.*

472. Hic ponit mysterium passionis, cuius virtute baptismus efficaciam habet; Rom. c. VI, 3: *quicumque baptizati sumus in Christo Iesu, in morte ipsius baptizati sumus.*

Et circa hoc tria facit:

primo namque proponit passionis figuram;

secundo passionis modum;

tertio passionis fructum.

473. Figuram quidem assumit de veteri lege, ut reducat ad intellectum Nicodemum; unde dicit **sicut Moyses exaltavit serpentem in deserto** etc. quod quidem habetur Num. XXI, 5 quoniam Dominus, populo Iudaeorum dicenti: *nauseat anima nostra super hoc cibo levissimo,* in ultionem misit serpentes, et postea concurrente populo ad Moysen, et ipso clamante ad Dominum, mandavit Dominus in remedium fieri serpentem aeneum, qui quidem fuit et in remedium contra illos serpentes, et in figuram passionis Dominicae. Unde et dicitur: *in signum posuit eum.* Proprium autem serpentis est habere venenum; sed serpens aeneus venenum non habuit, sed figura fuit serpentis venenosi. Sic et Christus non habuit peccatum, quod est venenum: quia *cum consummatum fuerit, generat mortem,* ut dicitur Iac. c. I, 15, sed habuit similitudinem peccati, Rom. c. VIII, 3: *misit Deus Filium suum in similitudinem carnis peccati.* Ideo Christus habuit effectum serpentis contra motum concupiscentiarum ignitarum.

474. Modum autem passionis ostendit, cum dicit **sic exaltari oportet Filium hominis**: quod intelligitur de exaltatione crucis. Unde infra XII, 34 cum diceret: **oportet exaltari Filium hominis** etc. sequitur: **hoc dicebat significans qua morte clarificaturus esset Deum.** Voluit autem mori exaltatus, primo ut purgaret caelestia: iam enim per sanctitatem suae conversationis purgaverat terra, restabat per mortem purgare aerea. Col. I, 20: *pacificans per sanguinem suum quae in caelis et quae in terris.* Secundo ut triumpharet de Daemonibus, qui in aere bellum praeparant; Eph. c. II, 2: *secundum principem potestatis aeris* etc. Tertio ut corda nostra ad se traheret; infra XII, 32: **ego si exaltatus fuero a terra, omnia traham ad me ipsum.** Quarto quia in morte crucis fuit

471. But why does he say, **and no man has ascended into heaven, except he who descended from heaven, the Son of man, who is in heaven**? For have not Paul and Peter and the other saints gone up: *we have a house in the heavens* (2 Cor 5:1).

I answer that no one goes up into heaven except Christ and his members, i.e., those believers who are just. Accordingly, the Son of God came down from heaven in order that, by making us his members, he might prepare us to ascend into heaven: now, indeed, in hope, but later in reality. *He has raised us up, and has given us a place in heaven in Christ Jesus* (Eph 2:6).

472. Here he mentions the mystery of the passion, in virtue of which baptism has its efficacy: *we who have been baptized into Christ Jesus, have been baptized into his death* (Rom 6:3).

And with regard to this he does three things.

First, he gives a symbol for the passion.

Second, the manner of the passion.

Third, the fruit of the passion.

473. He takes the symbol from the old law, in order to adapt to the understanding of Nicodemus; so he says, **just as Moses lifted up the serpent in the desert, so must the Son of man be lifted up**. This refers to when the Lord, faced with the Jewish people saying, *we are sick of this useless food,* sent serpents to punish them (Num 21:5); and when the people came to Moses and he interceded with the Lord, the Lord commanded that for a remedy they make a serpent of bronze; and this was to serve both as a remedy against those serpents and as a symbol of the Lord's passion. Hence it says that this bronze serpent *was lifted up as a sign* (Num 21:9). Now it is characteristic of serpents that they are poisonous, but not so the serpent of bronze, although it was a symbol of a poisonous serpent. So, too, Christ did not have sin, which is also a poison: *sin, when it is fully developed, brings forth death* (Jas 1:15); but he had the likeness of sin: *God sent his own Son, in the likeness of sinful flesh* (Rom 8:3). And thus Christ had the effect of the serpent against the insurgence of inflamed concupiscences.

474. He shows the manner of the passion when he says, **so must the Son of man be lifted up**; and this refers to the lifting up of the cross. So when it says below, **the Son of man must be lifted up**, it also has, **he said this signifying what death he should die** (John 12:33–34). He willed to die lifted up, first of all, to cleanse the heavens: for since he had cleansed the things on earth by the sanctity of his life, the things of the air were left to be cleansed by his death: *through him he should reconcile all things to himself, whether on earth or in the heavens, making peace through his blood* (Col 1:20). Second, to triumph over the demons who prepare for war in the air: *the prince of the power of the air* (Eph 2:2). Third, he wished to die lifted up to draw our hearts to himself: **I, if I am lifted up from the earth, will**

exaltatus, inquantum ibi de inimicis triumphavit: unde mors non vocatur, sed exaltatio; Ps. 109: *de torrente in via bibet, propterea exaltabit caput* etc. Quinto quia crux fuit causa exaltationis eius; Phil. II, 8: *factus est obediens Patri usque ad mortem, mortem autem crucis: propter quod et Deus exaltavit illum.*

475. Fructus autem passionis Christi est vita aeterna; unde dicit **ut omnis qui credit in ipsum**, bene operando, **non pereat, sed habeat vitam aeternam**. Et respondet hic fructus fructui figuralis serpentis. Quicumque enim respiciebant serpentem aeneum, liberabantur a veneno, et praeservabantur vitae. Ille autem respicit Filium hominis exaltatum qui credit Christo crucifixo; et sic liberatur a veneno et a peccato, infra XI, 26: **qui credit in me, non morietur in aeternum**: et praeservatur ad vitam aeternam; infra XX, 31: **haec scripta sunt ut credatis, et ut credentes vitam habeatis in nomine eius.**

draw all things to myself (John 12:32). And fourth, because in the death of the cross he was lifted up in the sense that there he triumphed over his enemies; so it is not called a death, but a lifting up: *he will drink from the stream on the way, therefore he will lift up his head* (Ps 109:7). Fifth, he willed to die lifted up because the cross was the reason for his being lifted up, i.e., exalted: *he became obedient to the Father even to death, the death of the cross; on account of which God has exalted him* (Phil 2:8).

475. Now the fruit of Christ's passion is eternal life; hence he says, **so that whoever believes in him**, by good works, **may not perish but have eternal life**. And this fruit corresponds to the fruit of the symbolic serpent. For whoever looked upon the serpent of bronze was freed from poison and his life was preserved. But he who looks upon the lifted up Son of man, and believes in the crucified Christ, he is freed from poison and sin: **all who live and believe in me will never die** (John 11:26), and are preserved for eternal life. **These are written, so that you may believe . . . and so that believing, you may have life in his name** (John 20:31).

Lecture 3

3:16 Sic enim Deus dilexit mundum ut Filium suum unigenitum daret: Ut omnis qui credit in eum, non pereat, sed habeat vitam aeternam. [n. 477]

3:17 Non enim misit Deus Filium suum in mundum, ut iudicet mundum, sed ut salvetur mundus per ipsum. [n. 482]

3:18 Qui credit in eum, non iudicatur. Qui autem non credit, iam iudicatus est: quia non credit in nomine unigeniti Filii Dei. [n. 485]

3:19 Hoc est autem iudicium: quia lux venit in mundum, et dilexerunt homines magis tenebras, quam lucem: erant enim eorum mala opera. [n. 491]

3:20 Omnis enim qui male agit, odit lucem, et non venit ad lucem, ut non arguantur opera eius. [n. 493]

3:21 Qui autem facit veritatem, venit ad lucem, ut manifestentur opera eius, quia in Deo sunt facta. [n. 495]

3:16 οὕτως γὰρ ἠγάπησεν ὁ θεὸς τὸν κόσμον, ὥστε τὸν υἱὸν τὸν μονογενῆ ἔδωκεν, ἵνα πᾶς ὁ πιστεύων εἰς αὐτὸν μὴ ἀπόληται ἀλλ' ἔχῃ ζωὴν αἰώνιον.

3:17 οὐ γὰρ ἀπέστειλεν ὁ θεὸς τὸν υἱὸν εἰς τὸν κόσμον ἵνα κρίνῃ τὸν κόσμον, ἀλλ' ἵνα σωθῇ ὁ κόσμος δι' αὐτοῦ.

3:18 ὁ πιστεύων εἰς αὐτὸν οὐ κρίνεται· ὁ δὲ μὴ πιστεύων ἤδη κέκριται, ὅτι μὴ πεπίστευκεν εἰς τὸ ὄνομα τοῦ μονογενοῦς υἱοῦ τοῦ θεοῦ.

3:19 αὕτη δέ ἐστιν ἡ κρίσις ὅτι τὸ φῶς ἐλήλυθεν εἰς τὸν κόσμον καὶ ἠγάπησαν οἱ ἄνθρωποι μᾶλλον τὸ σκότος ἢ τὸ φῶς· ἦν γὰρ αὐτῶν πονηρὰ τὰ ἔργα.

3:20 πᾶς γὰρ ὁ φαῦλα πράσσων μισεῖ τὸ φῶς καὶ οὐκ ἔρχεται πρὸς τὸ φῶς, ἵνα μὴ ἐλεγχθῇ τὰ ἔργα αὐτοῦ·

3:21 ὁ δὲ ποιῶν τὴν ἀλήθειαν ἔρχεται πρὸς τὸ φῶς, ἵνα φανερωθῇ αὐτοῦ τὰ ἔργα ὅτι ἐν θεῷ ἐστιν εἰργασμένα.

3:16 For God so loved the world that he gave his only begotten Son; so that whoever believes in him should not perish but have eternal life. [n. 477]

3:17 For God did not send his Son into the world to judge the world, but that the world might be saved through him. [n. 482]

3:18 He who believes in him is not judged; but whoever does not believe is already judged, because he does not believe in the name of the only begotten Son of God. [n. 485]

3:19 And this is the judgment: that the light has come into the world, and men loved darkness more than the light: for their works were evil. [n. 491]

3:20 For everyone who does evil hates the light and does not come to the light, so that his works may not be reproved. [n. 493]

3:21 But he who practices truth comes to the light, so that his works may be made manifest, because they are done in God. [n. 495]

---

476. Supra Dominus assignavit causam spiritualis regenerationis quantum ad descensum Filii, et exaltationem Filii hominis, et posuit fructum, scilicet vitam aeternam, qui quidem fructus incredibilis videbatur hominibus habentibus necessitatem moriendi: et ideo Dominus hoc manifestat, et

primo probat magnitudinem fructus ex magnitudine divini amoris;

secundo excludit quamdam responsionem, ibi **non enim misit Deus Filium suum in mundum, ut iudicet mundum**.

477. Notandum est autem, quod omnium bonorum nostrorum causa est Dominus et divinus amor. Amare enim proprie est velle alicui bonum. Cum ergo voluntas Dei sit causa rerum, ex hoc provenit nobis bonum, quia Deus amat nos. Et quidem amor Dei est causa boni naturae; Sap. XI, 25: *diligis omnia quae sunt* etc. Item est causa boni gratiae; Ier. XXXI, 3: *in caritate perpetua dilexi te, ideo attraxi te*, scilicet per gratiam. Sed quod sit etiam dator boni gloriae, procedit ex magna caritate.

476. Above, the Lord assigned as the cause of spiritual regeneration the coming down of the Son and the lifting up of the Son of man; and he set forth its fruit, which is eternal life. But this fruit seemed unbelievable to men laboring under the necessity of dying. And so now the Lord explains this.

First, he proves the greatness of the fruit from the greatness of God's love.

Second, he rejects a certain reply, at **for God did not send his Son into the world to judge the world**.

477. Here we should note that the cause of all our good is the Lord and divine love. For to love is, properly speaking, to will good to someone. Therefore, since the will of God is the cause of things, good comes to us because God loves us. And God's love is the cause of the good of nature: *you love everything which exists* (Wis 11:25). It is also the cause of the good which is grace: *I have loved you with an everlasting love, and so I have drawn you* i.e., through grace (Jer 31:3). But it is because of his great love that he gives us the good of glory.

Et ideo ostendit hic, hanc Dei caritatem esse maximam ex quatuor. Primo namque ex persona amantis, quia Deus est qui diligit, et immense; et ideo dicit **sic Deus dilexit**; Deut. XXXIII, 3: *dilexit populos: omnes sancti in manu illius sunt*. Secundo ex conditione amati, quia homo est qui diligitur, mundanus scilicet, corporeus, idest in peccatis existens; Rom. V, 10: *commendat Deus suam caritatem in nobis: quoniam cum adhuc inimici essemus, reconciliati sumus Deo per mortem Filii eius*. Et ideo dicit **mundum**. Tertio ex magnitudine munerum: nam dilectio ostenditur per donum, quia, ut dicit Gregorius probatio dilectionis, exhibitio operis est. Deus autem maximum donum nobis dedit, quia Filium suum unigenitum; et ideo dicit *ut Filium suum unigenitum daret*; Rom. VIII, 32: *proprio Filio suo non pepercit, sed pro nobis omnibus tradidit illum*.

Et dicit **suum**, idest Filium naturalem, ibi consubstantialem, non adoptivum: de quibus in Ps. LXXXI, 6: *ego dixi, dii estis*. Et per hoc patet falsitas Arii: quia si Filius Dei esset creatura, ut ipse dicebat, non posset in eo ostendi immensitas divini amoris, per susceptionem infinitae bonitatis, quam nulla creatura recipere potest. Dicit etiam **unigenitum**, ut ostendat Deum non divisum amorem habere ad plures filios, sed totum in Filio, quem dedit ad comprobandum immensitatem sui amoris; infra V, 20: **Pater diligit Filium, et omnia demonstrat ei**. Quarto ex fructus magnitudine, quia per eum habemus vitam aeternam, unde dicit **ut omnis qui credit in eum, non pereat, sed habeat vitam aeternam**: quam acquisivit nobis per mortem crucis.

478. Sed numquid ad hoc dedit eum ut moreretur in cruce? Dedit quidem eum ad mortem crucis, inquantum dedit voluntatem patiendi in ea: et hoc dupliciter. Primo quia inquantum Filius Dei, ab aeterno habuit voluntatem assumendi carnem, et patiendi pro nobis, et hanc voluntatem habuit a Patre. Secundo vero quia animae Christi inspirata est a Deo voluntas patiendi.

479. Nota autem, quod Dominus supra loquens de descensu qui competit Christo secundum divinitatem, nominavit eum Filium Dei; et hoc est ratione unius suppositi in duabus naturis, sicut supra dictum est. Et ideo divina possunt praedicari de supposito humanae naturae, et humana de supposito divinae, non tamen secundum eamdem naturam; sed divina secundum divinam naturam, et humana secundum humanam. Specialis autem causa quare hic nominavit eum Filium Dei est quia ipse proposuit donum istud in signum divini amoris, per quem provenit nobis fructus vitae aeternae. Tali ergo nomine nominandus erat, cui competeret indicare virtutem factivam vitae aeternae, quae non est in Christo inquantum Filius hominis, sed inquantum Filius Dei; Io.

So he shows us here, from four standpoints, that this love of God is the greatest. First, from the person of the one loving, because it is God who loves, and immeasurably. So he says, **for God so loved**; *he has loved the people; all the holy ones are in his hand* (Deut 33:3). Second, from the condition of the one who is loved, because it is man, a bodily creature of the world, i.e., existing in sin: *God shows his love for us, because while we were still his enemies, we were reconciled to God by the death of his Son* (Rom 5:8). Thus he says, **the world**. Third, from the greatness of his gifts, for love is shown by a gift; as Gregory says: *the proof of love is given by action*. But God has given us the greatest of gifts, his only begotten Son, and so he says, that he gave his only begotten Son. *God did not spare his own Son, but delivered him up for all of us* (Rom 8:32).

He says **his Son**, i.e., his natural Son, consubstantial, not an adopted son, i.e., not those sons of which the Psalmist says: *I said: you are gods* (Ps 81:6). This shows that the opinion of Arius is false: for if the Son of God were a creature, as he said, the immensity of God's love through the taking on of infinite goodness, which no creature can receive, could not have been revealed in him. He further says **only begotten**, to show that God does not have a love divided among many sons, but all of it is for that Son whom he gave to prove the immensity of his love: **for the Father loves the Son and shows him all things that he himself does** (John 5:20). Fourth, from the greatness of its fruit, because through him we have eternal life. Hence he says, **so that whoever believes in him should not perish but have eternal life**, which he obtained for us through the death of the cross.

478. But did God give his Son with the intention that he should die on the cross? He did indeed give him for the death of the cross inasmuch as he gave him the will to suffer on it. And he did this in two ways. First, because as the Son of God he willed from eternity to assume flesh and to suffer for us; and this will he had from the Father. Second, because the will to suffer was infused into the soul of Christ by God.

479. Note that above, when the Lord was speaking about the coming down which belongs to Christ according to his divinity, he called him the Son of God; and this because of the one suppositum of the two natures, as was explained above. And so divine things can be said about the suppositum of the human nature, and human things can be said about the suppositum of the divine nature, but not with reference to the same nature. Rather, divine things are said with reference to the divine nature, and human things with reference to the human nature. Now the specific reason why he here calls him the Son of God is that he set forth that gift as a sign of the divine love, through which the fruit of eternal life comes to us. And so, he should have been called by that name which indicates the power that produces eternal life; and this power is not in Christ as Son

ult., 20: *hic est verus Deus, et vita aeterna*; supra I, 4: *in ipso vita erat*.

480. Sed nota, quod dicit **non pereat**. Perire namque dicitur aliquid quod impeditur ne perveniat ad finem ad quem ordinatur. Homo autem ordinatur ad finem, qui est vita aeterna; et quamdiu peccat, avertit se ab ipso fine. Et licet dum vivit omnino non pereat, ita quod non possit restaurari, tamen quando moritur in peccato, tunc perit omnino; Ps. I, 6: *inter impiorum peribit*.

In hoc autem quod dicit **habeat vitam aeternam**, indicatur divini amoris immensitas: nam dando vitam aeternam, dat seipsum. Nam vita aeterna nihil aliud est quam frui Deo. Dare autem seipsum, magni amoris est indicium; Eph. II, 5: *Deus autem, qui dives est in misericordia, convivificavit nos in Christo*, idest fecit nos habere vitam aeternam.

481. Hic excludit Dominus obiectionem quae posset fieri. In veteri enim lege promittebatur quod Dominus esset venturus ad iudicandum; Is. III, 14: *Dominus ad iudicium veniet* etc. Unde posset aliquis dicere, quod non venerat Filius Dei, ut det vitam aeternam, sed ut iudicet mundum: et ideo hoc excludens Dominus,

primo ostendit se non venisse ad iudicandum;

secundo probat, ibi **qui credit in eum, non iudicatur**.

482. Dicit ergo: non enim venit Filius Dei ad iudicandum, quia **non misit Deus Filium suum**, scilicet quantum ad primum adventum, **ut iudicet mundum, sed ut salvetur mundus**. Simile habetur infra XII, 47: **non enim veni ut iudicem mundum, sed ut salvificem mundum**.

Salus autem hominis est ut perveniat ad Deum; Ps. LXI, 8: *in Deo salutare meum*. Pervenire autem ad Deum est consequi vitam aeternam: unde idem est salvari quod habere vitam aeternam. Nec debent homines esse pigri, et abutentes Dei misericordia, propter hoc quod dicit **non veni ut iudicem mundum** licentiam sibi indulgere peccandi, quia etsi in primo adventu non venerit ad iudicandum, sed ad dimittendum; in secundo tamen veniet ad iudicandum, sed non ad dimittendum, ut Chrysostomus dicit. Ps. LXXIV, 3: *cum accepero tempus, ego iustitias iudicabo*.

483. Contra est, quod dicitur infra IX v. 39: *in iudicium ego veni*.

Sed dicendum est, quod duplex est iudicium. Unum est discretionis; et ad hoc venit Filius Dei in primo adventu: quia eo veniente homines discreti sunt, quidam per caecitatem, quidam per lumen gratiae. Aliud est condemnationis; et in hoc quantum de se non venit.

484. Hic probat quae dixerat, quasi per locum a divisione, hoc modo. Quicumque iudicabitur, aut erit fidelis,

of man but as Son of God: *this is the true God and eternal life* (1 John 5:20); **in him was life** (John 1:4).

480. Note also that he says, **should not perish**. Someone is said to be perishing when he is hindered from arriving at the end to which he is ordained. But the end to which man is ordained is eternal life, and as long as he sins, he turns himself from that end. And although while he is living he cannot entirely perish in the sense that he cannot be restored, yet when he dies in sin, then he entirely perishes: *the way of the wicked will perish* (Ps 1:7).

He indicates the immensity of God's love in saying, **have eternal life**: for by giving eternal life, he gives himself. For eternal life is nothing else than enjoying God. But to give oneself is a sign of great love: *but God, who is rich in mercy, has brought us to life in Christ* (Eph 2:5), i.e., he gave us eternal life.

481. Here the Lord excludes an objection that might be made. For in the old law it was promised that the Lord would come to judge: *the Lord will come to judge* (Isa 3:14). So someone might say that the Son of God had not come to give eternal life but in order to judge the world. The Lord rejects this.

First, he shows that he has not come to judge.

Second, he proves it, at **he who believes in him is not judged**.

482. So he says: the Son of God has not come to judge, because **God did not send his Son**, referring to his first coming, **into the world to judge the world, but that the world might be saved through him**. The same thing is is said later: **I came not to judge the world, but to save the world** (John 12:47).

Now man's salvation is to attain to God: *my salvation is in God* (Ps 61:8). And to attain to God is to obtain eternal life; hence to be saved is the same as to have eternal life. However, because the Lord says, **I came not to judge the world** (John 12:47), men should not be lazy or abuse God's mercy, or give themselves over to sin, because although in his first coming he did not come to judge but to forgive, yet in his second coming, as Chrysostom says, he will come to judge but not to forgive. *At the appointed time I will judge with rigor* (Ps 74:3).

483. However, this seems to conflict with what is said: **for judgment I came into the world** (John 9:39).

I answer that there are two kinds of judgment. One is the judgment of distinction, and the Son has come for this in his first coming; because with his coming men are distinguished, some by blindness and some by the light of grace. The other is the judgment of condemnation; and he did not come for this as such.

484. Now he proves what he had said, as though by a process of elimination, in the following way: whoever will

aut infidelis; sed non veni ad iudicandum infideles, quia iam iudicati sunt: ergo a principio **non misit Deus Filium suum, ut iudicet mundum**.

Primo ergo ostendit, quod fideles non iudicantur; secundo quod nec infideles, ibi **qui autem non credit, iam iudicatus est**.

485. Dicit ergo: **non veni ut iudicem mundum**: quia non venit ad iudicandum fideles, quia **qui credit in eum, non iudicatur**, scilicet iudicio condemnationis, quo nullus credens in eum fide formata iudicatur; infra c. V, 24: **in iudicium non venit, sed transit a morte in vitam**: sed iudicabitur iudicio praemiationis et approbationis, de quo dicit Apostolus I Cor. IV, 4: *qui autem iudicat me, Dominus est*.

486. Sed numquid multi fideles peccatores non damnabuntur?

Respondeo dicendum, quod quidam haeretici dixerunt, quod nullus fidelis, quantumcumque peccator, damnabitur; sed salvabitur merito fundamenti, scilicet fidei, licet aliquam poenam patiatur. Et erroris sui fundamentum sumunt ex hoc quod dicit Apostolus I Cor. c. III, 11: *fundamentum aliud nemo potest ponere*; et infra: *si cuiusquam opus arserit, ipse tamen salvus erit, quasi per ignem*.

Sed hoc manifeste est contra Apostolum ad Gal. V, 19: *manifesta sunt opera carnis, quae sunt fornicatio, immunditia, impudicitia* etc. *Qui talia agunt, regnum Dei non possidebunt*.

Dicendum est ergo, quod fundamentum non est fides informis, sed formata, quae per caritatem operatur. Et ideo signanter non dicit Dominus qui credit ei, sed **qui credit in eum**; idest, qui credendo in eum, per caritatem tendit, **non iudicatur**; et hoc, quia non peccat mortaliter, per quod tollitur fundamentum. Vel, secundum Chrysostomum, omnis qui male agit, non credit; ad Tit. I, 16: *confitentur se nosse Deum, factis autem negant*; sed qui bene agit, Iac. II, 18: *ostende mihi ex operibus fidem tuam*: et talis non iudicatur et non condemnatur propter infidelitatem.

487. Hic ostendit quod infideles non iudicantur. Et primo ponit suam sententiam; secundo manifestat eam, ibi **hoc autem est iudicium** etc.

488. Sciendum est autem circa primum, secundum Augustinum, quod non dicit Christus: qui non credit, iudicatur; sed dicit **non iudicatur**: quod potest tripliciter exponi. Secundum Augustinum enim qui non credit non iudicatur, quia iam iudicatus est, non in re, sed in Dei praescientia; idest, iam praecognitus est apud Deum

be judged will be either a believer or an unbeliever. But I have not come to judge unbelievers, because they are already judged. Therefore, from the outset, **for God did not send his Son into the world to judge the world**.

So first he shows that believers are not judged.

Second, that unbelievers are not judged, at **whoever does not believe is already judged**.

485. He says therefore: **I came not to judge the world** (John 12:47): because he did not come to judge believers, for **he who believes in him is not judged**, with the judgment of condemnation, with which no one who believes in him with faith informed by love is judged: **he will not come into judgment but passes from death to life** (John 5:24). But he is judged with the judgment of reward and approval, of which the Apostle says: *it is the Lord who judges me* (1 Cor 4:4).

486. But will there be many believing sinners who will not be damned?

I reply that some heretics have said that no believer, however great a sinner he may be, will be damned, but he will be saved by reason of his foundation of salvation, namely, his faith, although he may be allowed to suffer some punishment. They take as the basis of their error the statement of the Apostle: *no one can lay a foundation other that the one that has been laid, that is, Jesus Christ* (1 Cor 3:11); and further on: *if a man's building burns . . . he himself will be saved as one fleeing through fire* (1 Cor 3:15).

But this view is clearly contrary to what the Apostle says: *it is obvious what proceeds from the flesh: lewd conduct, impurity, licentiousness . . . those who do such things will not inherit the kingdom of God* (Gal 5:1).

Therefore we must say that the foundation of salvation is not faith unformed, but formed, which operates through charity. Significantly therefore the Lord did not say: he who believes in him, but **whoever believes in him**, that is, whoever by believing tends toward him through love, **is not judged**, because he does not sin mortally, through which the foundation is removed. Or one could say, following Chrysostom, that everyone who acts sinfully does not believe: *they profess to know God, but they deny him by their actions* (Titus 1:16); but he who acts worthily: *show me your faith by your works* (Jas 2:18); such a one who is not judged and not condemned for unbelief.

487. Here he shows that unbelievers are not judged.

First he makes the statement;

second, he explains it at: **and this is the judgment**.

488. Concerning the first we should note, according to Augustine, that Christ does not say, that he that doth not believe is judged, but rather **is not judged**. This can be explained in three ways. For, according to Augustine, whoever does not believe is not judged, because he is already judged, not in fact, but in God's foreknowledge, that is, it is

condemnandus; II Tim. c. II, 19: *novit Dominus qui sunt eius.*

Alio modo, secundum Chrysostomum, **qui non credit iam iudicatus est**; idest, hoc ipsum quod non credit, est sibi ad condemnationem: non credere enim, est non adhaerere lumini, quod est esse in tenebris; et haec est magna condemnatio; Sap. XVII, 17: *una catena tenebrarum omnes erant colligati*; Tob. V, 12: *quale gaudium mihi erit qui in tenebris sedeo, et lumen caeli non video?*

Tertio modo secundum eumdem, **qui non credit**, non iudicatur, idest, iam condemnatus est; idest, iam manifestam causam condemnationis habet. Et simile est ac si diceretur de aliquo qui manifestam causam mortis habet, ante etiam quam feratur sententia mortis contra eum, quia iam mortuus est.

Unde Gregorius dicit quod in iudicio duplex est ordo. Quidam etenim iudicabuntur iudicio discussionis, illi videlicet qui habent aliquid condemnationi repugnans, scilicet bonum fidei, scilicet fideles peccatores. Sed infideles, quorum damnatio est manifesta, absque discussione damnantur; et de istis dicitur **qui non credit, iam iudicatus est**; Ps. I, 5: *non resurgent impii in iudicio*, scilicet discussionis.

489. Sciendum est autem, quod iudicari idem est quod condemnari; condemnari autem est a salute excidere, ad quam una sola via pervenitur, scilicet per nomen Filii Dei; Act. IV, 12: *non est aliud nomen datum sub caelo, in quo oporteat nos salvos fieri.* Et in Ps. LIII, 3: *Deus in nomine tuo salvum me fac.* Qui ergo non credunt in Filium Dei, excidunt a salute, et manifesta est in eis causa damnationis.

490. Hic manifestat Dominus suam sententiam, scilicet quod causa condemnationis manifesta est in infidelibus: et

primo ponit manifestans signum;

secundo ostendit signi convenientiam, ibi **omnis enim qui male agit, odit lucem.**

491. In signo autem proposito tria facit: primo enim proponit Dei beneficium; secundo perversitatem mentis infidelium; tertio perversitatis causam.

Dicit ergo: manifeste apparet quod **qui non credit, iam iudicatus est**, quod apparet ex Dei beneficio: quia **lux venit in mundum**. Homines enim erant in tenebris ignorantiae, quas quidem tenebras Deus destruxit, mittens lucem in mundum, ut homines cognoscerent veritatem; infra VIII, 12: **ego sum lux mundi: qui sequitur me non ambulat in tenebris, sed habebit lumen vitae**; Lc. I, 78: *visitavit nos oriens ex alto. Illuminare his qui in tenebris et in umbra mortis sedent.* Sed ista venit in mundum, scilicet lux, quia homo ad eam accedere non poterat: nam *lucem habitat inaccessibilem, quam nemo hominum vidit, sed nec videre potest*: I Tim. VI, 16.

already known to God that he will be condemned: *the Lord knows who are his* (2 Tim 2:19).

In another way: according to Chrysostom, whoever does not believe is already judged, that is, the very fact that **whoever does not believe is already judged**: for not to believe is not to adhere to the light—which is to live in darkness, and this is a momentous condemnation: *all were bound with one chain of darkness* (Wis 17:17). *What kind of joy can I have, I who sit in darkness and do not see the light of heaven?* (Tob 5:12).

In a third way: also according to Chrysostom, **whoever does not believe**, that is, being already condemned, he displays the obvious reason for his condemnation. This is like saying that a person who is proven guilty of death is already dead, even before the sentence of death has been passed on him, because he is as good as dead.

Hence Gregory says that in passing judgments there is a twofold order. Some will be sentenced by a trial; such are the ones who have something not deserving of condemnation, namely, the good of faith, that is, sinners who believe. But unbelievers, Whose reason for condemnation is manifest, are sentenced without trial; and of these it is said, **whoever does not believe is already judged**. *In judgment the wicked will not stand* (Ps 1:6), that is, stand in trial.

489. It should be noted that to be judged is the same as to be condemned; and to be condemned is to be shut out from salvation, to which only one road leads, that is, the name of the Son of God: *there is no other name under heaven given to men, by which we are saved* (Acts 4:12); *O God, save me by your name* (Ps 53:3). Therefore, those who do not believe in the Son of God are cut off from salvation, and the cause of their damnation is evident.

490. Here the Lord explains his statement that unbelievers have an evident cause for their condemnation.

First, he sets forth the sign which shows this.

Second, the fittingness of this sign: **for everyone who does evil hates the light**.

491. In the sign he sets forth he does three things. First, he mentions the gift of God. Second, the perversity of mind in unbelievers. Third, the cause of this perversity.

So he says: it is abundantly clear that **whoever does not believe is already judged**, which is apparent from the kindness of God, because **the light has come into the world**. For men were in the darkness of ignorance, and God destroyed this darkness, sending a light into the world in order that men might know the truth: **I am the light of the world: he who follows me does not walk in darkness but will have the light of life** (John 8:12); *to enlighten those who sit in darkness and in the shadow of death* (Luke 1:78). Now the light came into the world because men could not come to it: for *he dwells in inaccessible light, whom no man has seen or is able to see* (1 Tim 6:16).

Apparet etiam ex perversitate mentis infidelium, qui **dilexerunt magis tenebras quam lucem**, idest, magis voluerunt esse in tenebris ignorantiae quam instrui per Christum; Iob c. XXIV, 13: *ipsi fuerunt rebelles lumini*: Is. c. V, 20: *vae qui ponunt lucem tenebras* etc.

Cuius quidem perversitatis causa est quia **erant eorum mala opera**: quae a luce dissonant et tenebras quaerunt; Rom. XIII, 12: *abiiciamus opera tenebrarum*, idest peccata, quae tenebras quaerunt; I Thess. ult., 7: *qui dormiunt, nocte dormiunt*; Iob XXIV, 15: *oculus adulteri observat caliginem*. Ex hoc autem aliquis non credit luci, quod ei repugnat, discedendo.

492. Sed numquid omnes infideles habent mala opera? Videtur quod non: nam multi gentiles secundum virtutem operati sunt; puta Cato, et alii plures.

Sed dicendum, secundum Chrysostomum, quod aliud est bene operari ex virtute, aliud ex aptitudine et dispositione naturali. Nam aliqui ex dispositione naturali bene operantur, quia ex eorum dispositione non inclinantur ad contrarium. Et hoc modo etiam infideles potuerunt bene operari: sicut quod aliquis caste vixit, quia non impugnabatur a concupiscentia, et sic de aliis. Illi autem ex virtute bene operantur, qui, etsi inclinantur ad vitium contrarium, tamen ex rectitudine rationis, et bonitate voluntatis a virtute non declinant et hoc est proprium fidelium.

Vel dicendum, quod licet infideles bona facerent, non tamen faciebant propter amorem virtutis, sed propter inanem gloriam. Nec etiam omnia bene operabantur, quia Deo cultum debitum non reddebant.

493. Consequenter dicit **omnis enim qui male agit, odit lucem**, ostendit propositi signi convenientiam: et

primo quidem quantum ad malos;

secundo quantum ad bonos, ibi **qui autem facit veritatem venit ad lucem**.

494. Dicit ergo: ideo non dilexerunt lucem, quia **erant eorum mala opera**. Et hoc patet, quia **omnis qui male agit, odit lucem**. Non autem dicit egit sed **agit**: quia si quis male egit, tamen poenitens, et videns se male fecisse, dolet, non odit lucem, sed ad lucem venit. Sed **omnis qui male agit**, idest in malo perseverat, non dolet, nec ad lucem venit, sed eam odit: non inquantum veritatis quidem est manifestativa, sed inquantum per eam peccatum hominis manifestatur.

Diligit enim malus homo cognoscere lucem et veritatem; sed odit per eam manifestari; Iob XXIV, 17: *si subito apparuerit aurora, arbitrantur umbram mortis*. Et ideo **non venit ad lucem**. Et hoc **ut non arguantur opera eius**: nullus enim homo, qui non vult malum deserere, vult reprehendi; sed fugit, et odit; Amos V, 10: *odio habuerunt*

It is also clear from the perversity of mind in unbelievers who **loved darkness more than the light**, i.e., they preferred to remain in the darkness of ignorance rather than be instructed by Christ: *they have rebelled against the light* (Job 24:13); *woe to you who substitute darkness for light, and light for darkness* (Isa 5:20).

And the cause of this perversity is that **their works were evil**: and such works do not conform to the light but seek the darkness: *let us cast off the works of darkness* (Rom 13:12), i.e., sins, which seek the darkness; *those who sleep, sleep at night* (1 Thess 5:7); *the eye of the adulterer watches for the darkness* (Job 24:15). Now it is by withdrawing from the light, which is unpleasant to him, that one does not believe the light.

492. But do all unbelievers produce evil works? It seems not: for many gentiles have acted with virtue; for example, Cato, and many others.

I answer, with Chrysostom, that is it one thing to work by reason of virtue, and another by reason of a natural aptitude or disposition. For some act well because of their natural disposition, because their temperament is not inclined in a contrary way. And even unbelievers can act well in this way. For example, one may live chastely because he is not assailed by concupiscence; and the same for the other virtues. But those who act well by reason of virtue do not depart from virute, in spite of inclinations to the contrary vice, because of the rightness of their reason and the goodness of their will; and this is proper to believers.

Or, one might answer that although unbelievers may have done good things, they do not do them for love of virute but out of vainglory. Further, they did not do all things well; for they failed to render to God the worship due him.

493. Then when he says, **for everyone who does evil hates the light**, he shows the appropriateness of the sign he used.

First, with respect to those who are evil.

Second, with respect to the good, at **but he who practices truth comes to the light**.

494. So he says: they did not love the light because **their works were evil**. And this is plain because **for everyone who does evil hates the light**. He does not say: did, but rather **does**: because if someone has acted in an evil way, but has repented and is sorry, seeing that he has done wrong, such a person does not hate the light but comes to the light. But **everyone who does evil**, i.e., persists in evil, is not sorry, nor does he come to the light, but he hates it; not because it reveals truth, but because it reveals a person's sins.

For an evil person still wants to know the light and the truth; but he hates to be unmasked by it. *If the dawn suddenly appears, they regard it as the shadow of death* (Job 24:17). And so **he does not come to the light**; and this **so that his works may not be reproved**. For no one who is unwilling to desert evil wants to be rebuked; this is fled

corripientem in porta; Prov. XV, 12: *non amat pestilens eum qui se corripit.*

495. Hic ostendit idem quantum ad bonos facientes veritatem, idest bona opera. Veritas enim non solum in cogitatione et dictis consistit, sed et in factis. **Venit ad lucem**.

Sed numquid aliquis ante Christum fecit ita? Videtur quod non. Ille enim facit veritatem, qui non peccat; sed *ante Christum omnes peccaverunt*: ut dicitur Rom. III, 23.

Respondeo dicendum, secundum Augustinum, quod ille facit veritatem in seipso, cui displicet malum quod fecit; et relictis tenebris, observat se a peccatis, et de praeteritis poenitens **venit ad lucem**, ad hoc ut specialiter **manifestentur opera eius**.

496. Sed contra est, quod nullus debet publicare bona quae facit: unde Pharisaei de hoc a Domino reprehenduntur.

Dicendum est, quod licitum est velle manifestare opera sua coram Deo, ut approbentur, secundum quod dicitur II Cor. X, 18: *non enim qui seipsum commendat, ille probatus est, sed quem Deus commendat.* Et Iob XVI, 20: *ecce in caelo est testis meus.* Velle etiam manifestari in sua conscientia ut gaudeat; secundum quod dicitur II Cor. I, 12: *gloria nostra haec est, testimonium conscientiae nostrae.* Velle autem manifestari hominibus ad laudem, vel gloriam propriam, reprehensibile est. Nihilominus tamen sancti viri bona quae faciunt, manifestari desiderant hominibus propter honorem Dei et propter utilitatem fidei; Matth. V, 16: *sic luceat lux vestra coram hominibus ut videant opera vestra bona, et glorificent Patrem vestrum qui in caelis est.* Sed veniunt **ad lucem, ut manifestentur opera eorum, quoniam in Deo sunt facta**, idest secundum mandatum Dei, vel per gratiam Dei. Quicquid enim boni facimus, sive vitando peccatum, seu poenitendo de commissis, sive bona operando, totum est a Deo, iuxta illud Is. XXVI, 12: *omnia opera nostra operatus es in nobis.*

from and hated. *They hate the one who rebukes at the city gate* (Amos 5:10); *a corrupt man does not love the one who rebukes him* (Prov 15:12).

495. Now he shows the same things with respect to the good, who practice the truth, i.e., perform good works. For truth is found not only in thought and words, but also in deeds. Everyone of these **comes to the light**.

But did anyone practice the truth before Christ? It seems not, for to practice the truth is not to sin; and *before Christ all have sinned* (Rom 3:23).

I answer, according to Augustine, that he practices the truth in himself who is displeased at the evil he has done; and after leaving the darkness, keeps himself from sin, and repenting of the past, **comes to the light**, with the special intention **so that his works may be made manifest**.

496. But this conflicts with the teaching that no one should make public the good he has done; and this was a reason why the Lord rebuked the Pharisees.

I answer that it is lawful to want one's works to be seen by God so that they may be approved: *it is not the one who commends himself who is approved, but the one whom God commends* (2 Cor 10:18); *my witness is in heaven* (Job 16:20). It is also lawful to want them to be seen by one's own conscience, so that one may rejoice: *our glory is this: the testimony of our conscience* (2 Cor 1:12). But it is reprehensible to want them to be seen by men in order to be praised or for one's own glory. Yet, holy persons desire that their good works be known to men for the sake of God's glory and for the good of the faith: *let your light so shine before men that they may see your good works, and glorify your Father in heaven* (Matt 5:16). Such a person **comes to the light, so that his works may be made manifest, because they are done in God**, that is, according to God's commandment or through the grace of God. For whatever good we do, whether it be avoiding sin, repenting of what has been done, or doing good works, it is all from God: *you have accomplished all our works* (Isa 26:12).

Lecture 4

³:²² Post haec venit Iesus et discipuli eius in terram Iudaeam: et illic morabatur cum eis, et baptizabat. [n. 498]

³:²³ Erat autem et Ioannes baptizans in Aennon iuxta Salim, quia aquae multae erant illic; et veniebant, et baptizabantur. [n. 500]

³:²⁴ Nondum enim missus fuerat Ioannes in carcerem. [n. 504]

³:²⁵ Facta est autem quaestio ex discipulis Ioannis cum Iudaeis de purificatione. [n. 507]

³:²⁶ Et venerunt ad Ioannem, et dixerunt ei: Rabbi, qui erat tecum trans Iordanem, cui tu testimonium perhibuisti, ecce hic baptizat, et omnes veniunt ad eum. [n. 508]

³:²² Μετὰ ταῦτα ἦλθεν ὁ Ἰησοῦς καὶ οἱ μαθηταὶ αὐτοῦ εἰς τὴν Ἰουδαίαν γῆν καὶ ἐκεῖ διέτριβεν μετ᾽ αὐτῶν καὶ ἐβάπτιζεν.

³:²³ Ἦν δὲ καὶ ὁ Ἰωάννης βαπτίζων ἐν Αἰνὼν ἐγγὺς τοῦ Σαλείμ, ὅτι ὕδατα πολλὰ ἦν ἐκεῖ, καὶ παρεγίνοντο καὶ ἐβαπτίζοντο·

³:²⁴ οὔπω γὰρ ἦν βεβλημένος εἰς τὴν φυλακὴν ὁ Ἰωάννης.

³:²⁵ Ἐγένετο οὖν ζήτησις ἐκ τῶν μαθητῶν Ἰωάννου μετὰ Ἰουδαίου περὶ καθαρισμοῦ.

³:²⁶ καὶ ἦλθον πρὸς τὸν Ἰωάννην καὶ εἶπαν αὐτῷ· ῥαββί, ὃς ἦν μετὰ σοῦ πέραν τοῦ Ἰορδάνου, ᾧ σὺ μεμαρτύρηκας, ἴδε οὗτος βαπτίζει καὶ πάντες ἔρχονται πρὸς αὐτόν.

³:²² After these things Jesus and his disciples came into Judean territory: and he stayed with them there and was baptizing. [n. 498]

³:²³ And John also was baptizing in Aenon near Salim, where there was much water; and they came and were baptized. [n. 500]

³:²⁴ For John was not yet cast into prison. [n. 504]

³:²⁵ And there arose a question between some of John's disciples and the Jews concerning purification. [n. 507]

³:²⁶ And they came to John and said to him: Rabbi, he who was with you beyond the Jordan, to whom you gave testimony, behold he baptizes, and all men come to him. [n. 508]

---

497. Supra Dominus tradidit doctrinam de spirituali regeneratione per verba; hic vero doctrinam illam implet per opera, baptizando. Et

primo inducitur duplex baptismus;

secundo movetur quaestio de comparatione eorum, ibi *facta est ergo quaestio* etc.

Circa primum duo facit.

Primo inducitur baptismus Christi;

secundo baptismus Ioannis, ibi *erat autem Ioannes baptizans* etc.

498. Dicit ergo primo: *post haec*, scilicet quae de doctrina spiritualis regenerationis praemissa sunt, *venit Iesus, et discipuli eius in terram Iudaeam.*

Sed hic est quaestio litteralis: nam supra dixerat Evangelista, quod Dominus de Galilaea venerat in Ierusalem, quae est Iudea terra, ubi instruxerat Nicodemum. Quomodo ergo post instructionem Nicodemi, venit in Iudaeam, cum iam esset ibi?

Ad quod est duplex responsio: nam secundum Bedam, Christus post verba Nicodemi, ivit in Galilaeam, et ibi aliquandiu moratus rediit in Iudaeam: et ideo cum dicitur *post haec venit Iesus*, non est intelligendum quod immediate venerit in Iudaeam post verba Nicodemi.

Alio modo, secundum Chrysostomum, intelligendum est quod post haec immediate venerit in terram Iudaeam. Christus enim volebat praedicare ubi multitudo conveniebat, ut multi converterentur; Ps. XXXIX, 10: *annuntiavi iustitiam tuam in Ecclesia*

497. Above, the Lord gave us his teaching on spiritual regeneration in words, here he completes his teaching through action, by baptizing.

First, two kinds of baptism are mentioned.

Second, a question about their relationship is raised, at *and there arose a question*.

As to the first, two things are done.

Mention is first made of the baptism of Christ.

Second, of the baptism of John, at *and John also was baptizing*.

498. He says first, *after these things*, i.e., the teaching on spiritual regeneration, *Jesus and his disciples came into Judean territory*.

There is a question here about the literal meaning. For above, the Evangelist had said that the Lord had come from Galilee to Jerusalem, which is in Judean territory, where he taught Nicodemus. So how, after teaching Nicodemus, can he come into Judea, since he was already there?

Two answers are given to this. According to Bede, after his discussion with Nicodemus, Christ went to Galilee, and after remaining there for a time, returned to Judea. And so *after these things Jesus and his disciples came into Judean territory*, should not be understood to mean that he came into Judea immediately after his talk with Nicodemus.

Another explanation, given by Chrysostom, is that he did come into the territory of Judea immediately after this discussion: for Christ wanted to preach where the people gathered, so that many might be converted: *I have declared your justice in the great assembly* (Ps 39:10); *I have spoken*

magna. Et infra c. XVIII, 20: *ego palam locutus sum* etc. Duo autem loca erant in Iudaea, ad quae confluebat multitudo Iudaeorum, scilicet Ierusalem, ad quam ibant ad festa, et Iordanis, ad quem concurrebant propter praedicationem et baptismum Ioannis. Et ideo Dominus ista duo loca frequentans, statim completis diebus festis in Ierusalem, quae est in una parte Iudaeae, venit in aliam partem Iudaeae, ubi Ioannes baptizabat, scilicet in Iordanem.

499. Moraliter autem *Iudaea* interpretatur *confessio,* ad quam venit Iesus, quia Christus confitentes sua peccata, vel divinam laudem, visitat; Ps. CXIII, 2: *facta est Iudaea sanctificatio eius.* Et illic moratur, quia tales non transitorie visitat; infra XIV, 23: **ad eum veniemus et mansionem apud eum faciemus.** Et illic baptizat, idest purgat a peccatis: quia nisi quis peccata sua confiteatur, remissionem non consequitur; Prov. XXVIII, 13: *qui abscondi scelera sua, non dirigetur.*

500. Deinde cum dicit **erat autem et Ioannes baptizans in Aennon**, introducit Evangelista baptisma Ioannis:

et circa hoc quatuor facit.

Primo enim ponit personam baptizantis;

secundo locum baptismi;

tertio fructum;

quarto tempus.

501. Persona baptizans est Ioannes; et ideo dicit **erat autem Ioannes baptizans**.

Sed hic est quaestio: quia cum baptisma Ioannis ordinaretur ad baptismum Christi, videtur quod, veniente baptismate Christi, Ioannes cessare debuerit a baptizando, sicut veniente veritate, cessat figura.

Ad hoc est triplex responsio. Una, quantum ad personam Christi: nam Ioannes baptizavit ut Christus baptizaretur ab eo. Nec oportebat quod solus Christus ab eo baptizaretur, ne baptismus Ioannis ex huius singularitate, melior Christi baptismate videretur: et ideo expediens fuit ut alii ante Christum baptizarentur a Ioanne, quia antequam Christi doctrina publicata esset, necessarium erat homines praeparari ad Christum baptismo Ioannis. Unde secundum hoc, ita se habet baptismus Ioannis ad baptismum Christi sicut catechismus, in quo baptizandi instruuntur de fide et praeparantur ad baptismum, se habet ad verum baptisma. Necessarium etiam fuit ut postquam Christus baptizatus fuerat a Ioanne, alii baptizarentur ab eo, ne Ioannis baptisma reprobandum videretur; sicut etiam non statim veniente veritate cessavit usus legalium, sed, secundum Augustinum, licuit Iudaeis determinato tempore legalia servare.

Alio modo quantum ad personam Ioannis: nam si Ioannes statim cum Christus baptizare coepit, destitisset a baptismo, potuisset credi, quod hoc fecisset ex invidia, vel ira. Et quia, ut dicitur Rom. XII, 17: *providere*

openly to the world (John 18:20). Now there were two places in Judea where the Jewish people gathered: Jerusalem, where they went for their feasts, and the Jordan, where they gathered on account of John's preaching and his baptism. And so the Lord used to visit both places; and after the feast days were over in Jerusalem, which is in one part of Judea, he went to another part, to the Jordan, where John was baptizing.

499. As for the moral sense, *Judea* means *confession,* to which Jesus came, for Christ visits those who confess their sins or speak in praise of God: *Judea became his sanctuary* (Ps 113:2). He stayed there, because he did not make a merely temporary visit: **we will come to him, and will make our abode with him** (John 14:23). And there he baptizes, i.e., cleanses from sin; because unless one confesses his sins he does not obtain forgiveness: *he who hides his sins will not prosper* (Prov 28:13).

500. Then when he says, **and John also was baptizing in Aenon**, the Evangelist presents the baptism of John.

And in regard to this he does four things.

First, he presents the person who is baptizing.

Second, the place of the baptism.

Third, its fruit.

Fourth, the time.

501. John is the person who is baptizing; so he says, **John also was baptizing**.

There is a question about this: since John's baptism was ordained to the baptism of Christ, it seems that John should have stopped baptizing when Christ started to baptize, just as the symbol does not continue when the truth comes.

Three reasons are given for this. The first is in relation to Christ, for John baptized in order that Christ might be baptized by him. But it was not fitting that John baptize just Christ; otherwise, on this point alone, it might seem that John's baptism was superior to Christ's. Accordingly, it was expedient that John baptize others before Christ, because before Christ's teaching was to be made public it was necessary that men be prepared for Christ by John's baptism. In this way, the baptism of John is related to the baptism of Christ as the catechesis or religious instruction given to prospects to teach and prepare them for baptism is related to the true baptism. It was likewise important that John baptize others after he had baptized Christ, so that John's baptism would not seem to be worthless. For the same reason, the practice of the ceremonies of the old law was not abolished as soon as the truth came, but as Augustine says, the Jews could lawfully observe them for a time.

The second reason relates to John. For if John had stopped baptizing at once after Christ began baptizing, it might have been thought that he stopped out of envy or anger. And because, as the Apostle says, *we ought to look*

debemus bona non solum coram Deo, sed etiam coram omnibus hominibus: ideo Ioannes non statim cessavit.

Alio modo quantum ad discipulos Ioannis, qui iam incipiebant se zelotypos habere ad Christum, et ad discipulos eius, quia baptizabant. Unde si statim Ioannes totaliter baptizare cessasset, dimisisset discipulos suos in maiori zelo et controversia contra Christum et discipulos eius. Iam enim etiam Ioanne baptizante, ipsi aegre ferebant baptismum Christi: quod patet ex sequentibus. Et ideo non statim cessavit; I Cor. VIII, 9: *videte ne forte haec licentia vestra offendiculum fiat infirmis*.

502. Locus autem baptismi erat *in Aennon iuxta Salim: quia aquae multae erant ibi*. Salim alio nomine dicitur Salem quae est villa, unde Melchisedech rex fuit. Et dicitur hic Salim, quia apud Iudaeos, lector pro voluntate uti potest vocalibus litteris in medio dictionum: unde, sive dicatur Salim, sive Salem, non refert apud Iudaeos. Hoc autem quod addit *quia aquae multae erant ibi* ponit ad exponendum hoc nomen loci, scilicet *Aennon*, quod idem est quod *aqua*.

503. Fructus autem baptismi est remissio peccatorum; et ideo dicit *et veniebant et baptizabantur*, idest mundabantur: quia, ut dicitur Matth. III, 5, Lc. III, 7 multitudo magna ibat ad Ioannem.

504. Tempus ponitur ibi *nondum enim missus fuerat Ioannes in carcerem*: quod ideo dicit, ut det intelligere quod ipse incepit narrationem de factis Christi ante alios Evangelistas. Alii namque inceperunt narrare opera Christi solum a tempore incarcerationis Ioannis. Unde dicitur Matth. IV, 12: *cum audisset Iesus, quia Ioannes traditus esset, secessit in Galilaeam*. Et ideo, quia omnia facta Christi ante Ioannis incarcerationem praeterierant, Ioannes, qui ultimo Evangelium scripsit, defectum hunc supplevit; et hoc insinuat, cum dicit *nondum enim missus fuerat Ioannes in carcerem*.

505. Sed nota, quod dispensatione divina factum est ut Ioannes, Christo baptizante, non diu baptizaret et praedicaret, ne ex hoc fieret schisma in populo; quamquam hoc ei aliquo tempore permissum fuerit, ne reprobandus videretur, ut supra dictum est. Sic etiam dispensatione factum est ut post praedicationem fidei, et conversionem fidelium, templum totaliter destrueretur, ut videlicet tota devotio, et spes fidelium traheretur ad Christum.

506. Deinde cum dicit *facta est autem quaestio* etc., inducitur quaestio baptismatum: et

primo proponitur ipsa quaestio;

secundo relatio quaestionis ad Ioannem, ibi *et venerunt ad Ioannem*;

---

after what is good, not only before God, but also before all men (Rom 12:17), this is the reason why John did not stop at once.

The third reason relates to John's disciples, who were already beginning to act like zealots toward Christ and his disciples, because they were baptizing. So if John had entirely stopped from baptizing, it would have provoked his disciples to an even greater zeal and opposition to Christ and his disciples. For even while John continued baptizing, they were hostile to Christ's baptism, as later events showed. And so John did not stop at once: *take care that your freedom does not become a hindrance to those who are weak* (1 Cor 8:9).

502. The place of his baptism was at **Aenon near Salim, where there was much water**. Another name for Salim is Salem, which is the village from which the king Melchizedek came. It is called Salim here because among the Jews a reader may use any vowel he chooses in the middle of his words; hence it made no difference to the Jews whether it was pronounced Salim or Salem. He added, **where there was much water**, to explain the name of this place, i.e., **Aenon**, which is the same as *water*.

503. The fruit of his baptism is the remission of sins; thus he says, **and they came and were baptized**, i.e., cleansed: for great crowds came to John (Matt 3:5 and Luke 3:7).

504. The time is indicated when he says, **for John was not yet cast into prison**. He says this so that we may know that he began his narrative of Christ's life before the other Evangelists. For the others began their account only from the time of John's imprisonment. So it is said: *when Jesus heard that John had been arrested, he withdrew into Galilee* (Matt 4:12). And so, because they had passed over the things that Christ did before John's imprisonment, John, who was the last to write a Gospel, supplied these omissions. He suggests this when he says: **for John was not yet cast into prison**.

505. Note that by divine arrangement it came about that when Christ began to baptize, John did not continue his own baptizing and preaching for very long, in order not to create disunion among the people. But he was granted a little time so that it would not seem that he deserved to be repudiated, as was mentioned before. Again, by God's arrangement, it came about that after the faith had been preached and the faithful converted, the temple was utterly destroyed, in order that all the devotion and hope of the faithful could be directed to Christ.

506. Then when he says, **there arose a question**, he brings in the issue of the two baptisms.

First, the issue is mentioned.

Second, it is brought to John's attention, at **and they came to John**.

tertio ponitur quaestionis determinatio, ibi ***respondit Ioannes, et dixit eis***.

507. Quia ergo duo baptizabant, ut dictum est, scilicet Christus et Ioannes, discipuli ipsius Ioannis pro magistro suo zelantes, occasionem dissidii sumpserunt. Et hoc est quod dicit ***facta est quaestio***, idest controversia, ***ex discipulis Ioannis***, ipsis scilicet primo moventibus hanc quaestionem, ***cum Iudaeis***: quos reprehendebant discipuli Ioannis, eo quod ad Christum magis currerent propter miracula quae faciebat, quam ad Ioannem, qui miraculum nullum faciebat.

Et quaestio ista facta est ***de purificatione***, idest de baptismo. Causam autem unde invidebant discipuli Ioannis, et controversiam movebant, sumpserunt ex eo quod Ioannes illos quos baptizabat, mittebat ad Christum; Christus vero quos baptizabat non mittebat ad Ioannem. Ex quo videbatur, et forte Iudaei dicebant, Christum maiorem esse Ioanne: et ideo isti nondum spirituales, de baptismo contendunt cum Iudaeis; I Cor. III, 3: *cum enim sit inter vos zelus et contentio, nonne carnales estis?*

508. Sed motam quaestionem referunt ad Ioannem; et ideo dicit ***et venerunt ad Ioannem***. Et si attenditur diligenter, conati sunt commovere Ioannem contra Christum. Similes isti sunt bilinguibus et susurronibus; Eccli. c. XXVIII, 15: *susurro et bilinguis maledictus multos enim turbabit pacem habentes.*

Proponunt autem quatuor, quae commotionem in animo Ioannis contra Christum causarent. Primo enim commemorant humilitatem status Christi praeteriti; secundo beneficium a Ioanne impensum; tertio officium assumptum a Christo; quarto detrimentum quod provenit Ioanni ex Christi officio.

509. Humilitatem autem status commemorant, cum dicunt ***qui erat tecum***, quasi unus de discipulis; non autem tu cum illo, sicut cum magistro: nam si alicui maiori honor exhibeatur, non est tanta causa invidiae; sed tunc quis invidet, quando minori se magis honor exhibetur; Eccle. X, 7: *vidi servos in equis sedentes, et principes ambulantes super terram quasi servos*; Iob XIX, 16: *servum meum vocavi, et non respondit*. Quia plus turbatur dominus aliquid de rebellione servi et subditi, quam alicuius alterius.

510. Secundo commemorantes beneficium impensum a Ioanne, non dicunt quem tu baptizasti, quia in hoc confessi fuissent magnificentiam Christi, quae in baptismo demonstrata est, et descensum Spiritus Sancti super eum in specie columbae, et vocem Patris sibi factam; sed dicunt ***cui tu testimonium perhibuisti***; idest, quem tu clarum et circumspectum fecisti, talia tibi rependere audet, quod multum concitat exacerbationem; Ps. XL, 10: *qui edebat panes meos, magnificavit super me supplantationem*. Sed quia quaerentes propriam gloriam,

Third, the issue is resolved, at ***John answered and said*** (John 3:27).

507. Therefore because there were two baptizing, as it is said, namely Christ and John, the disciples of John, zealous for their teacher, started a controversy over this. And this is what he says, ***there arose a question***, i.e., a dispute, ***between some of John's disciples***, who were the first to raise the issue, ***and the Jews***, whom the disciples of John had rebuked for preferring Christ, because of the miracles he did, to John, who did not do any miracles.

The issue was ***concerning purification***, i.e., baptizing. The cause of their envy and the reason why they started the controversy was the fact that John sent those he baptized to Christ, but Christ did not send those he baptized to John. It seemed from this, and perhaps the Jews even said so, that Christ was greater than John. Thus, the disciples of John, having not yet become spiritual, quarreled with the Jews over the baptisms. *While there is envy and fighting among you, are you not carnal?* (1 Cor 3:3).

508. They referred this issue to John; hence he says, ***they came to John***. If we examine this closely, we see that they were trying to incite John against Christ. Indeed, they are like the gossip and the double-tongued: *those who gossip and are double-tongued are accursed, for they disturb many who are at peace* (Sir 28:15).

So they bring up four things calculated to set John against Christ. First, they recall the previous unimportant status of Christ. Second, the good John did for him. Third, the role which Christ took on. Fourth, the loss to John because of Christ's new role.

509. They recall Christ's unimportance when they say, ***he who was with you***, as one of your disciples; and not the one you were with as your teacher. For there is no good reason for envy if honor is shown to one who is greater; rather, envy is aroused when honor is given to an inferior: *I have seen slaves on horses, and princes walking like slaves* (Eccl 10:7); *I called my servant, and he did not answer me* (Job 19:16). For a master is more disturbed at the rebellion of a servant and a subject than of anyone else.

510. Second, they remind John of the good he did Christ. Thus they do not say, the one whom you baptized, because they would then be admitting the greatness of Christ which was shown during his baptism when the Holy Spirit came upon him in the form of a dove and in the voice of the Father speaking to him. So they say, ***to whom you gave testimony***, i.e., we are very angry that the one you made famous and admired dares to repay you in this way: *the one who ate my bread has lifted his heel against me* (Ps 40:10). They said this because those who seek their own glory and personal

et intendentes lucrum proprium in suo officio, dolent si alius officium illud assumat.

511. Ideo, tertio, isti addunt etiam, quod Christus Ioannis officium sibi assumpsit, cum dicunt: *ecce hic baptizat*; idest, officium tuum exercet: quod multum concitat ad turbationem. Nam communiter videmus hic, homines eiusdem artis insidiose et invide se habere ad invicem. Figulus figulo invidet, non autem fabro. Sic etiam doctores proprium honorem quaerentes, dolent si alius veritatem docet; contra quos dicit Gregorius: *mens pii pastoris optat ut veritatem, quam solus docere non sufficit, alii doceant.* Sic et Moyses, Num. XI, 29: *quis det ut omnis hic populus prophetet?*

512. Sed non solum sufficiebat istis concitare Ioannem; sed quod magis movet, referunt, scilicet detrimentum quod Ioanni ex assumpto officio a Christo provenire videbatur; quod quarto exponunt, cum dicunt *et omnes veniunt ad eum*, qui scilicet ad te venire solebant: quia te dimisso et contempto, omnes ad baptismum eius currunt. Quod autem ante consueverant ire ad Ioannem, patet ex testimonio Matth. XI, 7: *quid existis in desertum videre?* etc. Tali invidia movebantur Pharisaei contra Christum; unde dicebant, infra XII, 19: *ecce totus mundus post eum vadit.* Sed ex his Ioannes non fuit motus contra Christum: non enim erat arundo vento agitata, ut dicitur Matt. XI, 7. Et hoc patet ex responsione Ioannis, quae sequitur in determinatione quaestionis sibi delatae.

profit from their office become dejected if their office is taken over by someone else.

511. And so third, they even add that Christ took over John's office for himself, when they say, *behold he baptizes*, i.e., he is exercising your office; and this also distrubed them very much. For we generally see that men of the same craft are envious and underhanded with respect to one another; a potter envies another potter, but does not envy a carpenter. So, even teachers, who are seeking their own honor, become sad if another teaches the truth. In opposition to them, Gregory says: *the mind of a holy pastor wishes that others teach the truth which he cannot teach all by himself.* So also Moses: *would that all the people might prophesy* (Num 11:29).

512. Yet they were not satisfied with merely disturbing John, rather they report something that should really excite him, that is, the loss that John seemed to be having because of the office Christ took over. They give this when they say: *and all men come to him*, i.e., the ones who used to come to you. In other words, they have rejected and disowned you, and now are all going to his baptism. It is clear from testimony of Mathew that before this counsel, they used to go to John, (Matt 11:7): *what did you go out to the desert to see?* By such envy the Pharisees were moved against Christ; and they said that *the whole world is gone after him* (John 12:19). But John was not moved against Christ by this: he was not a reed shaken by the wind, as Mathew says (Matt 11:7). Which follows from his response to the question submitted to him.

Lecture 5

3:27 Respondit Ioannes, et dixit: non potest homo accipere quicquam, nisi fuerit ei datum de caelo. [n. 515]

3:28 Ipsi vos mihi testimonium perhibetis, quod dixerim: Non sum ego Christus, sed quia missus sum ante illum. [n. 516]

3:29 Qui habet sponsi, sponsus est. Amicus autem sponsi, quia stat et audit eum, gaudio gaudet propter vocem sponsi. In hoc ergo gaudium meum impletum est. [n. 517]

3:30 Illum oportet crescere, me autem minui. [n. 522]

3:31 Qui desursum venit, super omnes est. Qui est de terra, de terra est, et de terra loquitur. Qui de caelo venit, super omnes est. [n. 525]

3:32 Et quod vidit, et audivit, hoc testatur. Et testimonium eius nemo accipit. [n. 534]

3:27 ἀπεκρίθη Ἰωάννης καὶ εἶπεν· οὐ δύναται ἄνθρωπος λαμβάνειν οὐδὲ ἓν ἐὰν μὴ ᾖ δεδομένον αὐτῷ ἐκ τοῦ οὐρανοῦ.

3:28 αὐτοὶ ὑμεῖς μοι μαρτυρεῖτε ὅτι εἶπον [ὅτι] οὐκ εἰμὶ ἐγὼ ὁ χριστός, ἀλλ᾽ ὅτι ἀπεσταλμένος εἰμὶ ἔμπροσθεν ἐκείνου.

3:29 ὁ ἔχων τὴν νύμφην νυμφίος ἐστίν· ὁ δὲ φίλος τοῦ νυμφίου ὁ ἑστηκὼς καὶ ἀκούων αὐτοῦ χαρᾷ χαίρει διὰ τὴν φωνὴν τοῦ νυμφίου. αὕτη οὖν ἡ χαρὰ ἡ ἐμὴ πεπλήρωται.

3:30 ἐκεῖνον δεῖ αὐξάνειν, ἐμὲ δὲ ἐλαττοῦσθαι.

3:31 Ὁ ἄνωθεν ἐρχόμενος ἐπάνω πάντων ἐστίν· ὁ ὢν ἐκ τῆς γῆς ἐκ τῆς γῆς ἐστιν καὶ ἐκ τῆς γῆς λαλεῖ. ὁ ἐκ τοῦ οὐρανοῦ ἐρχόμενος [ἐπάνω πάντων ἐστίν]·

3:32 ὃ ἑώρακεν καὶ ἤκουσεν τοῦτο μαρτυρεῖ, καὶ τὴν μαρτυρίαν αὐτοῦ οὐδεὶς λαμβάνει.

3:27 John answered and said: a man cannot receive anything, unless it is given to him from heaven. [n. 515]

3:28 You yourselves bear witness to me, that I said, I am not the Christ, but that I am sent before him. [n. 516]

3:29 He who has the bride is the bridegroom: but the friend of the bridegroom, who stands and hears him, rejoices with joy because of the bridegroom's voice. Therefore my joy is fulfilled. [n. 517]

3:30 He must increase, but I must decrease. [n. 522]

3:31 He who came from above is above all. He who is of the earth is earthly, and he speaks of the earth. He who comes from heaven is above all. [n. 525]

3:32 And he testifies to what he has seen and heard: and no man receives his testimony. [n. 534]

---

513. Hic ponitur responsio Ioannis super quaestione sibi delata a discipulis quae quidem quaestio duo continebat, scilicet querimoniam de officio assumpto: unde dicebant *ecce hic baptizat*, et de Christi profectu in fama et opinione hominum: unde dicebant *et omnes veniunt ad eum*. Et ideo Ioannes dirigit responsionem suam ad haec duo: et

primo respondet ad querimoniam de officio assumpto;

secundo vero ad querimoniam de profectu Christi, ibi *illum oportet crescere, me autem minui*.

Circa primum tria facit.

Primo ostendit officiorum Christi et sui originem;

secundo ipsorum distinctionem, ibi *ipsi vos mihi testimonium perhibetis*;

tertio ostendit habitudinem Christi et suam ad dicta officia, ibi *qui habet sponsam, sponsus est*.

514. Circa primum autem nota quod discipuli Ioannis licet malitiose Ioanni quaestionem proponant, et ex hoc sint reprehensione digni, Ioannes tamen non eos vehementer increpat; et hoc propter imperfectionem: timebat enim ne commoti ex reprehensione, recederent ab eo, et iungentes se Pharisaeis, Christo publice

513. Here we have John's answer to the question presented to him by his disciples. Their question contained two points: a complaint about the office Christ took on, and so they said, *behold he baptizes* (John 3:26); and about Christ's increasing fame and reputation among the people, and so they said, *and all men come to him* (John 3:26). Accordingly, John directs his answer to these two complaints.

First he answers the complaint about the office Christ took on.

Second, the complaint about Christ's increasing reputation, at *he must increase, but I must decrease*.

As to the first he does two things.

First, he shows the source of Christ's office and of his own.

Second, their difference, at *you yourselves bear witness to me*.

Third, how Christ and he are related to these offices, at *he who has the bride is the bridegroom*.

514. As to the first, note that although John's disciples broach their question maliciously, and so deserve to be rebuked, John nevertheless does not sharply reprove them; and this because of their imperfection. For he feared that they might be provoked by a rebuke, leave him, and, joining forces with the Pharisees, publicly harass Christ. In acting

insidiarentur; implens in hoc quod de Domino dicitur, Is. XLII, 3: *calamum quassatum non confringet* etc. Similiter advertendum, quod a principio suae responsionis non ardua et praeclara de Christo asserit, sed humilia et plana propter ipsorum invidiam. Cum enim excellentia sit alterius invidiae provocativa, si Ioannes statim Christi excellentiam eis proposuisset, illorum invidiae fomentum praestitisset.

515. Et ideo humilia proponens, dicit ***non potest homo a se accipere quicquam***: intendens in hoc eis terrorem incutere; quasi dicat: hoc quod omnes ad eum currunt, non est nisi a Deo, quia ***non potest homo accipere quicquam***, scilicet perfectionis et boni, ***nisi fuerit ei datum de caelo***, et ideo si vos contradicitis, contradicitis Deo; Actor. V, 38: *si ex hominibus est consilium hoc, aut opus istud, dissolvetur.* Et sic exponit Chrysostomus, referens hoc ad Christum.

Augustinus autem refert ad ipsum Ioannem, et melius. ***Non potest homo accipere quicquam, nisi fuerit ei datum de caelo***; quasi dicat: vos zelatis pro me, et vultis quod ego maior sim quam Christus; sed hoc non est mihi datum, nec ego volo mihi usurpare; secundum illud Hebr. V, 4: *nemo assumit sibi honorem* etc. Sic ergo patet officiorum origo.

516. Sequitur officiorum distinctio, cum dicit ***ipsi vos mihi testimonium perhibetis***; quasi dicat: ex testimonio meo, quod sibi perhibui, potestis scire officium mihi commissum a Christo: nam ***ipsi vos mihi testimonium perhibetis***, idest perhibere potestis, ***quod dixerim: non sum ego Christus***; supra I, 20: *confessus est et non negavit.* Sed hoc dixi, ***quia missus sum ante illum***, sicut praeco ante iudicem. Sic ergo ex testimonio meo scire potestis officium meum, quod est praecedere Christum, et praeparare sibi viam; supra I, 6: ***fuit homo missus a Deo, cui nomen erat Ioannes***. Sed officium Christi est iudicare et praeesse.

Et si bene attenditur, Ioannes more providi respondentis, proponentes ex verbis eorum arguit, secundum illud Lc. XIX, 22: *ex ore tuo te iudico.*

517. Qualiter autem Ioannes se habet ad officium suum, ostendit cum subdit ***qui habet sponsam, sponsus est***: et

primo ponit quamdam similitudinem;

secundo adaptat eam ad propositum, ibi ***in hoc autem gaudium meum impletum est***.

Circa primum duo facit.

Primo ponit similitudinem quantum ad id quod pertinet ad Christum;

secundo quantum ad id quod pertinet ad seipsum, ibi ***amicus autem sponsi*** etc.

518. Circa primum notandum est, quod in rebus humanis disponere, et dominari, et habere sibi sponsam,

this way he was putting into practice what is said of the Lord: *the bruised reed he will not break* (Isa 42:3). Again, we should also note that he begins his answer not by telling them what is great and wonderful about Christ, but what is common and obvious; and he did this on account of their envy. For since the excellence of a person provokes others to envy, if John had stressed Christ's excellence at once, he would have fed the fire of their envy.

515. Thus he states something unpretentious, and says, ***a man cannot receive anything, unless it is given to him from heaven***; and he said this to them in order to inspire them with reverence. As if to say: if all men are going to him, it is God's doing, because ***a man cannot receive anything***, in the order of perfection and goodness, ***unless it is given to him from heaven***. Therefore, if you oppose him, you oppose God. *If this plan or work is from men, it will fail* (Acts 5:38). This is the way Chrysostom explains it, applying these words to Christ.

Augustine, on the other hand, does much better when he refers them to John. ***A man cannot receive anything, unless it is given to him from heaven***; as if to say: you are zealous on my behalf and you want me to be greater than Christ; but that has not been given to me, and I do not wish to usurp it: *no one takes this honor on himself* (Heb 5:4). This is the origin of their offices.

516. Then follows the difference of their offices, when he says, ***you yourselves bear witness to me***. As if to say: from the testimony which I bore to him, you can know the office committed to me by Christ: for ***you yourselves bear witness to me***, i.e., you can testify, to the fact ***that I said: I am not the Christ***—he declared openly and did not deny (John 1:20). But this I said, ***that I am sent before him***, as a herald before a judge. And so from my own testimony you can know my office, which is to go before Christ and prepare the way for him: ***there was a man sent from God, whose name was John*** (John 1:6). But the office of Christ is to judge and to preside.

If we look at this closely we can see that John, like a skillful disputant, answers them with their own arguments: *I judge you out of your own mouth* (Luke 19:22).

517. He shows how John is related to his own office when he says: ***he who has the bride is the bridegroom***.

First, he gives a simile.

Second, he applies it to his own situation, at ***therefore, my joy is fulfilled***.

With respect to the first he does two things.

First, he gives a simile which applies to Christ; and

second, to himself, at ***but the friend of the bridegroom***.

518. As to the first, we should note that on the human level it is the bridegroom who regulates, governs and has

pertinet ad sponsum tantum; et ideo dicit *qui habet sponsam*, idest ad quem pertinet habere sponsam, *sponsus est*. Iste autem sponsus est Christus; Ps. XVIII, 6: *tamquam sponsus procedens de thalamo suo*. Sponsa sua est Ecclesia, quae coniungitur ei per fidem; Oseae II, 20: *sponsabo te mihi in fide*. Et in huius figuram dixit Sephora ad Moysen, Ex. IV, 25: *sponsus sanguinum tu mihi es*. Et de istis nuptiis dicitur Apoc. XIX, 7: *venerunt nuptiae agni*. Sic ergo, quia Christus sponsus est, etiam ad eum pertinet habere sponsam, scilicet Ecclesiam; sed ad me non pertinet nisi gaudere quod sponsam habet.

519. Unde dicit *amicus autem sponsi . . . gaudio gaudet*. Et licet supra dixerit quod non erat dignus solvere corrigiam calceamentorum Iesu, hic tamen vocat se eius amicum, ut insinuet caritatis suae fidelitatem ad Christum. Nam servus ad ea quae domini sui sunt, non movetur affectu caritatis, sed spiritu servitutis; amicus vero ex amore, quae amici sunt procurat, et fideliter. Unde servus fidelis est sicut amicus domini sui; Eccli. XXXIII, 31: *si est tibi servus fidelis, sit tibi quasi anima tua*. Et ex hoc patet fidelitas servi, quando gaudet de bonis domini, et quando non sibi, sed domino suo bona procurat. Sic ergo, quia Ioannes sponsam sibi creditam, non sibi, sed sponso reservavit, servus fidelis fuit, et amicus sponsi. Et ideo ad hoc insinuandum, se amicum sponsi dicit.

Simile debent facere homines amici veritatis, ut sponsam eis ad custodiendum commissam non ad propriam utilitatem et gloriam convertant, sed ad honorem et gloriam sponsi honorifice praeservent: alias non essent amici sponsi, sed potius adulteri. Unde Gregorius dicit, quod adulterinae cogitationis puer reus est, si placere oculis sponsae desiderat, per quem sponsus dona transmittit. Quod non faciebat Apostolus II Cor. c. XI, 2: *despondi enim vos uni viro virginem castam exhibere Christo*. Simile et Ioannes faciebat, quia sponsam, scilicet populum fidelem, non sibi retinuit, sed ad sponsum, scilicet Christum, duxit.

520. Sic ergo insinuat caritatis suae fidelitatem per hoc quod dicit *amicus sponsi*.

Item permanentiam, cum dicit *stat*, firmus in amicitia et fidelitate, non elevans se supra se; Hab. II, 58: *super custodiam meam stabo*; I Cor. XV, 58: *estote stabiles et immobiles*; Eccli. VI, 11: *amicus, si permaneat fixus, erit tibi quasi coaequalis*.

Item attentionem, cum dicit *et audit eum*; idest, attente considerat modum quo sponsus sponsae coniungitur. In quo, secundum Chrysostomum, explicat modum istorum sponsalium; nam per fidem celebrantur: *fides autem est ex auditu*, Rom. X, 17. Vel *audit*, idest reverenter obedit, disponendo de sponsa secundum imperium

the bride. Hence he says, *he who has the bride is the bridegroom*. Now the groom is Christ: *like a bridegroom coming out of his bridal chamber* (Ps 18:6). His bride is the Church, which is joined to him by faith: *I will espouse you to myself in faith* (Hos 2:20). In keeping with this figure, Zipporah said to Moses: *you are a spouse of blood to me* (Exod 4:25). We read of the marriage: *the marriage of the Lamb has come* (Rev 19:7). So, because Christ is the groom, he has the bride, that is, the Church; but my part is only to rejoice in the fact that he has the bride.

519. Consequently he says, *but the friend of the bridegroom, who stands and hears him, rejoices with joy*. Although John had said earlier that he was not worthy to unfasten the strap of Jesus' sandal, he here calls himself the friend of Jesus in order to bring out the fidelity of his love for Christ. For a servant does not act in the spirit of love in regard to the things that pertain to his master, but in a spirit of servitude; a friend however, seeks his friend's interests out of love and faithfulness. Hence a faithful servant is like a friend to his master: *if you have a faithful servant, treat him like yourself* (Sir 33:31). Indeed, it is proof of a servant's faithfulness when he rejoices in the prosperity of his master, and when he obtains, not his own, but his own master's good. And so because John did not keep the bride entrusted to his care for himself, but for the bridegroom, we can see that he was a faithful servant and a friend of the bridegroom. It is to suggest this that he calls himself the bridegroom's friend.

Those who are friends of the truth should act in the same way, not turning the bride entrusted to their care to their own advantage and glory, but treating her honorably for the honor and glory of the groom; otherwise they would not be friends of the groom but adulterers. This is why Gregory says that a servant who is sent by the groom with gifts for the bride is guilty of adulterous thoughts if he himself desires to please the bride. This is not what the Apostle did: *I espoused you to one husband in order to present you to Christ as a chaste virgin* (2 Cor 11:2). And John did the same, because he did not keep the bride, i.e., the faithful, for himself, but brought them to the groom, that is, to Christ.

520. And so by saying, *the bridegroom's friend*, he suggests the faithfulness of his love.

Further, he suggests his constancy when he says, *stands*, firm in friendship and faithfulness, not extolling himself above what he really is: *I will stand my watch* (Heb 2:1); *Be steadfast and unchanging* (1 Cor 15:58); *a faithful friend, if he is constant, is like another self* (Sir 6:11).

He suggests his attention when he says, *and hears him*, i.e., attentively considers the way in which the groom is united to the bride. For according to Chrysostom, these words explain the manner of this marriage, for it is accomplished through faith, and *faith comes through hearing* (Rom 10:17). Or, he *hears* him, i.e., reverently obeys him,

sponsi; Is. l, 4: *audiam eum quasi magistrum*: quod est contra malos praelatos, qui non secundum Christi mandatum disponunt Ecclesiam.

Item insinuat spiritualem iucunditatem, cum dicit *et gaudio gaudet propter vocem sponsi*; scilicet, cum sponsus sponsam suam alloquitur. Et dicit *gaudio gaudet*, ut ostendat veritatem et perfectionem sui gaudii. Qui enim non gaudet de bono, non vero gaudio gaudet. Et ideo, si ego dolerem ex hoc quod Christus, qui est verus sponsus, sponsae, idest Ecclesiae, praedicat, non essem amicus sponsi: sed ego non doleo.

521. Immo *in hoc gaudium meum impletum est*, scilicet quod video quod diu desideravi, sponsum videlicet sponsam alloquentem. Vel *in hoc gaudium meum impletum est*, idest, ad perfectam et debitam mensuram pervenit, quando sponsa iam coniungitur sponso: quia iam habeo gratiam meam, et officium meum perfeci; Habac. III, 18: *ego autem in Domino gaudebo, et exultabo in Deo Iesu meo.*

522. Consequenter cum dicit *illum oportet crescere, me autem minui* solvit quaestionem quantum ad querimoniam de profectu gratiae Christi. Et

primo ponit huius profectus convenientiam;

secundo rationem assignat, ibi *qui de sursum est, super omnes est*.

523. Dicit ergo: vos dicitis, quod omnes currunt ad eum, idest ad Christum; et sic proficit in honore et fama populi: sed ego dico, quod hoc non est inconveniens, quia *illum oportet crescere*, non in se, sed quantum ad alios, inquantum eius virtus magis ac magis innotescit; sed *me oportet minui*, in reverentia et fama quoad populum: nam honor et reverentia non debetur mihi sicut principali, sed Christo. Et ideo ipso veniente, cessat exhibitio reverentiae quantum ad me; sed crescit quantum ad Christum: sicut veniente principe, cessat officium legati; I Cor. XIII, 10: *cum venerit quod perfectum est, evacuabitur quod ex parte est*. Et sicut in caelo Lucifer praecedit solem ad illuminandum, quo veniente, cessat eius lux; ita Ioannes praecessit Christum: unde Lucifero comparatur; Iob XXXVIII, 32: *numquid produces Luciferum?*

Significatur hoc etiam in nativitate Ioannis, et in morte eius. In nativitate quidem, quia natus est Ioannes eo tempore quo dies decrescere incipiunt; Christus vero quando dies crescere incipiunt, scilicet octavo Kalendas Ianuarii. Quantum ad mortem vero, quia Ioannes mortuus minoratus per capitis abscissionem, Christus vero sublimatus per crucis exaltationem.

524. Moraliter autem hoc debet esse in unoquoque nostrum. *Oportet illum*, idest Christum, in te *crescere*, ut scilicet in cognitione et amore eius proficias: quia inquantum magis eum potes cognoscendo et amando

by caring for the bride according to the commands of the groom: *I will listen to him as my master* (Isa 50:4). This is in opposition to those evil prelates who do not follow Christ's command in governing the Church.

Likewise, he hints at his spiritual joy when he says, *rejoices with joy because of the bridegroom's voice*. And he says, *rejoices with joy*, to show the truth and perfection of his joy. For one whose rejoicing is not over the good, does not rejoice with true joy. And so, if it made me sad that Christ, who is the true groom, preaches to the bride, i.e., the Church, I would not be a friend of the groom; but I am not sad.

521. Hence *therefore, my joy is fulfilled*, namely, in seeing what I have so long desired, that is, the groom speaking clearly to his bride. Or, *therefore, my joy is fulfilled*, that is, brought to its perfect and due measure, when the bride is united to the groom, because I now have my grace and I have completed my work: *I will rejoice in the Lord, and I will take joy in God, my Jesus* (Heb 3:18).

522. Then when he says, *he must increase, but I must decrease*, he answers their question as to their complaint about the increasing esteem given to Christ.

First, he notes that such an increase is fitting.

Second, he gives the reason for it, at *he who came from above is above all*.

523. So he says: you say that all the people are flocking to him, i.e., to Christ, and therefore that he is growing in honor and esteem among the people. But I say that this is not unbecoming, because *he must increase*, not in himself, but in relation to others, in the sense that his power becomes more and more known. And *I must decrease*, in the reverence and esteem of the people: for esteem and reverence are not due to me as if I were a principal; but they are due to Christ. And therefore since he has come, the signs of honor cease in my regard, but increase in regard to Christ, just as with the coming of the prince, the office of the ambassador ceases: *when the perfect comes, what is imperfect will pass away* (1 Cor 13:10). And just as in the heavens the morning star appears and gives light before the sun, when the sun comes its light ceases; thus John went before Christ and is compared to the morning star: *can you bring out the morning star?* (Job 38:32).

This is also signified in John's birth and in his death. In his birth, because John was born at a time when the days were beginning to be shorter; Christ, however, was born when the days were beginning to grow longer, on the twenty-fifth of December. As pertains to his death, it is signified because John dies shortened by decapitation; but Christ died raised up by the lifting up of the cross.

524. In the moral sense, this should take place in each one of us. *He*, that is, Christ, *must increase* in you, i.e., you should grow in the knowledge and love of Christ, because the more you are able to grasp him by knowledge and love,

percipere, tanto magis Christus crescit in te; sicut qui magis proficit in videndo unam et eamdem lucem, reputat lucem magis crescere.

Et ex hoc oportet homines sic proficientes minui in sua reputatione: quia quanto plus cognoscit quis de altitudine divina, tanto minorem reputat parvitatem humanam; unde Prov. XXX, 1, dicitur: *visio quam locutus est vir, cum quo est Deus;* et sequitur: *stultissimus sum virorum, et sapientia hominum non est mecum.* Et Iob ult., 5: *auditu auris audivi te, nunc autem oculus meus videt te: idcirco ipse me reprehendo, et ago paenitentiam in favilla et cinere.*

525. Consequenter cum dicit **qui desursum venit, super omnes est**, assignat rationem dictorum: et hoc dupliciter.

Primo ex origine;

secundo ex doctrina, ibi **qui de terra est, de terra loquitur**.

526. Circa primum sciendum est, quod in rebus unumquodque, ad hoc quod sit perfectum, oportet venire ad terminum sibi debitum ex sua origine: sicut si aliquis ex rege oritur, oportet eum tamdiu crescere quousque fiat rex. Christus autem habet originem excellentissimam et aeternam; et ideo oportet illum crescere per manifestationem suae virtutis, quantum ad alios, quousque innotescat, eum super omnes esse; et ideo dicit **qui desursum est**, scilicet Christus secundum divinitatem. Supra (hoc cap.): **nemo ascendit in caelum, nisi qui descendit de caelo**; infra c. VIII, 23: **vos de deorsum estis, ego autem de superius sum**.

527. Vel desursum venit secundum humanam naturam, idest de altitudine humanae naturae, assumendo eam in altitudine sua secundum quod fuit in quolibet statu.

Consideratur enim secundum triplicem statum. Primus enim status humanae naturae est ante peccatum; et de hoc assumpsit puritatem, assumendo carnem non inquinatam contagio culpae originalis; Ex. XII, 5: *erit agnus anniculus absque macula.* Secundus status est post peccatum: et de hoc assumpsit passibilitatem et mortem, assumendo similitudinem carnis peccati, quantum ad poenam, non ipsum peccatum quantum ad culpam; secundum illud Rom. VIII, 3: *misit Deus Filium suum in similitudinem carnis peccati.* Tertius est status resurrectionis et gloriae; et de hoc assumpsit impossibilitatem peccandi, et fruitionem animae.

528. Sed cavendus est hic error quorumdam dicentium in Adam remansisse aliquod materialiter non inquinatum macula originali, et traductum in posteros, puta usque ad Beatam Virginem; et de hoc corpus Christi fuisse formatum. Quod quidem haereticum est: quia quicquid in Adam materialiter fuit, macula originalis peccati inquinatum est. Materia vero, de qua formatum

the more Christ increases in you; just as the more one improves in seeing one and the same light, the more that light seems to increase.

And from this it is necessary that as men advance, their self-esteem decreases; because the more one knows of the divine greatness, the less he thinks of his human smallness, wherefore it is said: *the revelation spoken by the man close to God* (Prov 30:1); and then there follows: *I am the most foolish of men, and the wisdom of men is not in me. I have heard you, but now I see you, and so I reprove myself, and do penance in dust and ashes* (Job 42:5).

525. Then when he says, **he who came from above is above all**, he gives the reason for what he has just said. And he does this in two ways.

First, on the basis of Christ's origin.

And second, by considering Christ's teaching, at **he who is of the earth is earthly, and he speaks of the earth**.

526. Regarding the first, we should note that in order for a thing to be perfect, it must reach the goal fixed for it by its origin; for example, if one is born from a king, he should continue to progress until he becomes a king. Now Christ has an origin that is most excellent and eternal; therefore he must increase by the manifestation of his power, in relation to others, until it is recognized that he is above all things. Thus he says, **he who came from above**, that is, Christ, according to his divinity. **No man has ascended into heaven, except he who descended from heaven** (John 3:13); **you are from below, and I am from above** (John 8:23).

527. Or, he came from above, as to his human nature, i.e., from the highest condition of human nature, by assuming it according to what was predominant in it in each of its states.

For it is considered according to three states. First, is the state of human nature before sin; and from this state he took his purity by assuming a flesh unmarked by the stain of original sin: *a lamb without blemish* (Exod 12:5). The second state is after sin; and from this he took his capability to suffer and die by assuming the likeness of sinful flesh as regards its punishment, it was not however, sinful as regards guilt: *God sent his own Son in the likeness of sinful flesh* (Rom 8:3). The third state is that of resurrection and glory; and from this he took the impossibility of sinning and joy of soul.

528. Here we must be on guard against the error of those who say that there was left in Adam something materially unmarked by the original stain, and this was passed on to his descendants; for example, to the Blessed Virgin, and that Christ's body was formed from this. This is heretical, because whatever existed in Adam in a material way was marked by the stain of original sin. Further, the matter

est corpus Christi, depurata fuit virtute Spiritus Sancti, Beatam Virginem sanctificantis.

529. Iste, inquam, *qui desursum venit* secundum divinitatem et secundum humanam naturam, *super omnes est*, et per eminentiam gradus, secundum illud Ps. CXII, 4: *excelsus super omnes gentes Dominus*, et per auctoritatem et potestatem; Eph. I, 22: *ipsum dedit caput super omnem Ecclesiam*.

530. Hic ostendit rationem quantum ad doctrinam. Et

primo ostendit modum doctrinae Christi, et eius altitudinem;

secundo diversitatem recipientium vel non recipientium ipsam doctrinam, ibi *et testimonium eius nemo accipit* etc.

Circa primum duo facit.

Primo proponit conditionem doctrinae Ioannis;

secundo conditionem doctrinae Christi; ibi *qui de caelo venit, super omnes est*.

531. Circa primum sciendum est quod homo per loquelam suam maxime cognoscitur, Matth. XXVI, 73: *loquela tua manifestum te facit*; et ibid. XII, 34: *ex abundantia cordis os loquitur*. Et inde est quod conditio doctrinae attenditur secundum conditionem suae originis.

Sic ergo ad cognoscendum conditionem doctrinae Ioannis, consideremus primo conditionem suae originis; unde dicit *qui est de terra*, scilicet Ioannes, non solum materialiter, sed etiam active: quia corpus eius virtute creata formatum fuit; Iob IV, 19: *qui habitant domos luteas, et terrenum habent fundamentum*.

Secundo consideremus eius conditionem quae terrena est: unde dicit *de terra est*, idest terrenus.

Et ideo tertio doctrina eius est, describitur; unde dicit *de terra loquitur*, idest de terrenis; Is. XXIX, 4: *de terra loqueris, et de humo audietur eloquium tuum*.

532. Sed quomodo de terra loquitur qui fuit Spiritu Sancto repletus adhuc ex utero matris suae?

Respondeo, secundum Chrysostomum, dicendum, quod Ioannes de terra se loqui dicit in comparatione ad Christi doctrinam; quasi dicat: ea quae loquitur, parva et humilia sunt, qualia decens est suscipere terrestrem naturam, in comparatione ad illum, *in quo sunt omnes thesauri sapientiae et scientiae Dei absconditi*, ut dicitur Col. II, 3. Is. LV, v. 9: *sicut exaltantur caeli a terra, ita exaltatae sunt viae meae a viis vestris*.

Vel dicendum, secundum Augustinum, et melius, quod considerandum est in quolibet homine quid habeat ex se, et quid ex alio. Ioannes autem, et quilibet homo purus ex se habet quod sit de terra. Et ideo quantum ad ipsum pertinet, non habet quod loquatur nisi de

---

from which the body of Christ was formed was purified by the power of the Holy Spirit when he sanctified the Blessed Virgin.

529. He, who as it is said *came from above*, according to his divinity as well as his human nature, *is above all*, both by eminence of rank: *the Lord is high above all nations* (Ps 112:4), and by his authority and power: *he has made him the head of the Church* (Eph 1:22).

530. Now he gives the reason as regards the the teaching of Christ.

First, he describes the doctrine of Christ and its grandeur.

Second, the difference in those who receive or reject this doctrine, at *and no man receives his testimony*.

He does two things with respect to the first.

First, he describes John's doctrine.

Second, he describes the doctrine of Christ, at *he who came from above is above all*.

531. As to the first we should note that a man is known mainly by what he says: *your accent gives you away* (Matt 26:73); *out of the abundance of the heart the mouth speaks* (Matt 12:34). This is why the quality of a teaching or doctrine is considered according to the quality of its origin.

Accordingly, in order to understand the quality of John's doctrine, we should first consider his origin. So he says, *he who is of the earth*, that is John, not only as to the matter from. which he was made, but also in his efficient cause: because the body of John was formed by a created power: *they dwell in houses of clay, and have a foundation of earth* (Job 4:19).

Second, we should consider the quality of John himself, which is earthly; and so he says, *is of the earth*.

Third, his teaching is described: *he speaks of the earth*. *Thou shalt speak out of the earth, and they speech shall be heard out of the ground* (Isa 29:4).

532. But since John was full of the Holy Spirit while still in his mother's womb, how can he be said to speak of earthly things?

I answer that, according to Chrysostom, John says he speaks of earthly things by comparison with the teaching of Christ. As if to say: the things I speak of are slight and inferior as becomes one of an earthly nature, in comparison to him *in whom are hidden all the treasures of wisdom and knowledge* (Col 2:3); *as the heavens are high above the earth, so my ways are high above your ways* (Isa 55:9).

Or we could say according to Augustine, and this is a better explanation, that we can consider what any person has of himself and what he has received from another. Now John and every mere human of himself is of the earth. Therefore, from this standpoint, he has nothing to speak

terra; et si aliqua divina loquitur, hoc habet ex divina illuminatione; Eccli. XXXIV, 6: *cor tuum quasi phantasias patitur, nisi ab Omnipotente fuerit emissa visitatio.* Unde et Apostolus dicit, I Cor. XV, 10: *non autem ego, sed gratia Dei mecum*; Matth. X, 20: *non enim vos estis qui loquimini, sed Spiritus patris vestri qui loquitur in vobis.* Sic ergo, quantum ad Ioannem pertinet, **de terra est, et de terra loquitur.** Si quid autem divinum in eo fuit, non recipientis, sed illuminantis est.

533. Hic proponit conditionem doctrinae Christi; et circa hoc tria facit.

Primo enim ostendit conditionem originis quae caelestis est; unde dicit **qui de caelo venit, super omnes est.** Licet enim corpus Christi materialiter de terra fuerit, active tamen de caelo venit, inquantum virtute divina corpus eius formatum fuit. Venit etiam de caelo, quia persona aeterna et increata Filii de caelo venit per carnis assumptionem. Supra eodem: **nemo ascendit in caelum, nisi qui descendit de caelo Filius hominis, qui est in caelo.**

Secundo ostendit dignitatem suae conditionis, quae altissima est; unde dicit **super omnes est**: et hoc expositum est supra.

Tertio concludit dignitatem doctrinae suae, quae certissima est, quia quod vidit et audivit, hoc testatur. Christus enim, inquantum est Deus, est ipsa veritas; sed inquantum homo, est testis veritatis; infra XVIII, 37: **in hoc natus sum, et ad hoc veni, ut testimonium perhibeam veritati.** Ideo testimonium perhibet de seipso; infra VII, 13: **testimonium perhibes de teipso.** Sed testatur certa, quia quae audivit apud Patrem; infra VIII, 26: **ego quae audivi a Patre meo, haec loquor in mundo**; I Io. I, 3: *quod vidimus et audivimus.*

534. Sed nota, quod aliter habetur cognitio rei per visum, et aliter per auditum; nam per visum habetur cognitio rei per ipsam rem visam; sed per auditum non cognoscitur res per ipsam vocem auditam, sed per intellectum loquentis. Quia ergo Dominus habet scientiam acceptam a Patre, ideo dicitur **quod vidit**, inquantum procedit de essentia Patris, **et audivit**, inquantum procedit ut Verbum intellectus Paterni. Sed quia in rebus intelligentibus aliud est eorum esse, et aliud eorum intelligere; ideo aliter accipitur ab eis cognitio per visum, et aliter per auditum. Sed in Deo Patre idem est esse et intelligere; ideo in Filio idem est videre et audire. Similiter etiam quia in vidente non est ipsa essentia rei in se, sed similitudo eius, similiter et in audiente non est ipsa conceptio loquentis, sed signum ipsius; ideo videns non est ipsa essentia rei in se, nec audiens est ipsum Verbum. In Filio autem est ipsa essentia Patris accepta per

of except earthly things. And if he does speak of divine things, it is due to a divine enlightenment: *your heart has visions, but unless they come from the Almighty, ignore them* (Sir 34:6). So the Apostle says, *it is not I, but the grace of God which is with me* (1 Cor 15:10); *for it is not you who speak, but the Holy Spirit who is speaking through you* (Matt 10:20). Accordingly, as regards John, **he is earthly and speaks of the earth.** And if there was anything divine in him, it did not come from him, as he was the recipient, but from the one enlightening him.

533. Now he describes the doctrine of Christ. And he does three things.

First, he shows its origin, which is heavenly; hence he says, **he who came from above is above all.** For although the body of Christ was of the earth as regards the matter of which it was made, yet it came from heaven as to its efficient cause, inasmuch as his body was formed by divine power. It also came from heaven because the eternal and uncreated person of the Son came from heaven by assuming a body. **And no man has ascended into heaven, except he who descended from heaven, the Son of man, who is in heaven** (John 3:13).

Second, he shows the dignity of Christ, which is very great; so he says, **is above all.** This was explained above.

Third, he infers the dignity of Christ's doctrine, which is most certain, because he testifies to what he sees and to what he hears. For Christ, as God, is truth itself; but as man, he is its witness: **for this I was born, and for this I came into the world, that I should give testimony to the truth** (John 18:37). Therefore, he gives testimony to himself: **you give testimony about yourself** (John 8:13). And he testifies to what is certain, because his testimony is about what he has heard with the Father: **the things that I have heard from him are the same that I speak to the world** (John 8:26); *what we have seen and heard* (1 John 1:3).

534. Note that in one way, knowledge of a thing is acquired through sight and in another way through hearing. For by sight, knowledge of a thing is acquired by the thing itself being seen; but by hearing, a thing is not known through its own voice being heard, but by means of the understanding of the one speaking. And so, because the Lord has knowledge which he has received from the Father, he says, **what he has seen**, insofar as he proceeds from the essence of the Father; and **heard**, insofar as he proceeds as the Word of the Father's intellect. Now because among intellectual beings, their act of being is other than their act of understanding, their knowledge through sight is other than their knowledge through hearing. But in God the Father, the act of being and the act of understanding are the same. Thus in the Son, to see and hear are the same. Moreover, since even in one who sees there is not the essence of the thing seen in itself but only its similitude, as also in the hearer there is not the actual thought of the speaker but

generationem, et est ipsum Verbum; et ideo in ipso idem est videre et audire.

Et hoc sic concludit Ioannes, quod ex quo doctrina Christi altior et certior est quam mea, ideo magis audiendus est Christus quam ego.

only an indication of it, so the one who sees is not the essence of the thing in itself, nor is the listener the very word expressed. In the Son, however, the very essence of the Father is received by generation, and he himself is the Word; and so in him to see and to hear are the same.

And so John concludes that since the doctrine of Christ has more grandeur and is more certain than his, one must listen to Christ rather than to him.

Lecture 6

3:32 Et quod vidit, et audivit, hoc testatur. Et testimonium eius nemo accipit. [n. 536]

3:33 Qui autem acceperit eius testimonium, signavit, quia Deus verax est. [n. 538]

3:34 Quem enim misit Deus, verba Dei loquitur. Non enim ad mensuram dat Deus Spiritum. [n. 540]

3:35 Pater diligit Filium, et omnia dedit in manu eius. [n. 545]

3:36 Qui credit in Filium, habet vitam aeternam. Qui autem incredulus est Filio, non videbit vitam; sed ira Dei manet super eum. [n. 546]

3:32 ὃ ἑώρακεν καὶ ἤκουσεν τοῦτο μαρτυρεῖ, καὶ τὴν μαρτυρίαν αὐτοῦ οὐδεὶς λαμβάνει.

3:33 ὁ λαβὼν αὐτοῦ τὴν μαρτυρίαν ἐσφράγισεν ὅτι ὁ θεὸς ἀληθής ἐστιν.

3:34 ὃν γὰρ ἀπέστειλεν ὁ θεὸς τὰ ῥήματα τοῦ θεοῦ λαλεῖ, οὐ γὰρ ἐκ μέτρου δίδωσιν τὸ πνεῦμα.

3:35 ὁ πατὴρ ἀγαπᾷ τὸν υἱὸν καὶ πάντα δέδωκεν ἐν τῇ χειρὶ αὐτοῦ.

3:36 ὁ πιστεύων εἰς τὸν υἱὸν ἔχει ζωὴν αἰώνιον· ὁ δὲ ἀπειθῶν τῷ υἱῷ οὐκ ὄψεται ζωήν, ἀλλ᾽ ἡ ὀργὴ τοῦ θεοῦ μένει ἐπ᾽ αὐτόν.

3:32 And he testifies to what he has seen and heard: and no man receives his testimony. [n. 536]

3:33 He who has received his testimony has given a sign that God is true. [n. 538]

3:34 For he whom God has sent speaks the words of God: for God does not give the Spirit by measure. [n. 540]

3:35 The Father loves the Son, and he has given all things into his hand. [n. 545]

3:36 He who believes in the Son has eternal life; but he who does not believe in the Son shall not see life; but the wrath of God rests on him. [n. 546]

---

535. Supra Ioannes Baptista commendavit Christi doctrinam; hic vero agit de diversitate recipientium: unde tractat de fide adhibenda ipsi doctrinae, et circa hoc tria facit.

Primo ostendit raritatem credentium;

secundo credendi debitum, ibi *qui autem acceperit eius testimonium* etc.;

tertio fidei praemium, ibi *qui credit in Filium, habet vitam aeternam*.

536. Dicit ergo: dico quod Christus certam scientiam habet, et vera loquitur. Tamen licet pauci testimonium eius accipiant, non propter hoc doctrinae ipsius derogatur, quia hoc non est ex parte eius, sed ex parte eorum qui non recipiunt, scilicet discipulorum Ioannis, qui nondum credebant, et Pharisaeorum, qui ipsius doctrinae detrahebant. Et ideo dicit *et testimonium eius nemo accipit*.

537. Hoc autem quod dicit *nemo*, potest dupliciter exponi. Uno modo, *nemo*, idest pauci, et si aliqui accipiant. Et quod aliqui accipiant, ostendit subdens: *qui autem accepit eius testimonium* etc. Hoc modo loquendi usus est Evangelista cum dixit, supra I, 11: *in propria venit, et sui eum non receperunt*: quia pauci eum receperunt. Alio modo, quia accipere eius testimonium est credere in Deum; sed nullus potest credere ex seipso, sed ex Deo; Eph. II, 8: *gratia salvatis estis*. Et ideo dicit *nemo accipit*, scilicet ex se, nisi donetur sibi a Deo.

Vel aliter. Consuetum est in Scriptura divina populo loqui de duobus. Quia quamdiu sumus in hoc mundo, mali sunt permixti bonis; et ideo Scriptura aliquando

535. Above, John the Baptist commended the teaching of Christ; here, however, he considers the difference in those who receive it. Thus, he treats of the faith that must be given to this teaching. And he does three things.

First, he shows the scarcity of those who believe.

Second, the obligation to believe, at *he who has received his testimony*.

Lastly, the reward for belief, at *he who believes in the Son has eternal life*.

536. He says therefore: I say that Christ has certain knowledge and that he speaks the truth. Yet although few accept his testimony, that is no reflection on his teaching, because it is not the fault of the teaching but of those who do not accept it: namely, the disciples of John, who did not yet believe, and the Pharisees, who slandered his teaching. Thus he says, *and no man receives his testimony*.

537. *No man* can be explained in two ways. In the first way, *no man* implies a few; and so some did accept his testimony. He shows that some did accept it when he adds, *and he who has received his testimony*. The Evangelist used this way of speaking before when he said: *he came unto his own, and his own did not receive him* (John 1:11): because a few did receive him. In another way, to accept his testimony is understood as to believe in God. But no one can believe of himself, but only due to God: *you are saved by grace* (Eph 2:8). And so he says, *no man receives*, i.e., of himself, but it is given to him by God.

This can be explained in another way by realizing that Scripture refers to people in two ways. As long as we are in this world the wicked are mingled with the good; and so

loquitur *de populo*, referendo intentionem suam ad malos, aliquando ad bonos. Et hic modus loquendi habetur Ier. XXVI: nam primo dicit: omnis populus et sacerdotes quaerebant occidere Ieremiam: referens intentionem suam ad malos: et postea statim dicit, quod omnis populus quaerebat eum liberare, loquens de bonis. Eodem modo et Ioannes Baptista habens oculos suos ad sinistram, idest ad malos, dicit **et testimonium eius nemo accipit**: et ex alia referens ad dexteram, idest ad bonos, dicit **qui autem acceperit eius testimonium** etc.

538. Qui autem acceperit eius testimonium, ubi ostendit debitum fidei, quod est supponere se veritati divinae.

Et circa hoc quatuor facit.

Primo proponit divinam veritatem;

secundo subdit divinae veritatis denuntiationem, ibi **quem enim misit Deus, verba Dei loquitur**;

tertio insinuat denuntiandi facultatem, ibi **non enim ad mensuram dat Deus Spiritum**;

quarto assignat facultatis rationem, ibi **Pater diligit Filium** etc.

539. Debitum autem fidei est ut homo veritati divinae se supponat; et ideo dicit quod si pauci testimonium eius accipiunt, tamen aliqui accipiunt; unde dicit **qui autem acceperit eius testimonium**; idest quicumque sit ille, **signavit** idest signum quoddam in corde suo ponere debet seu posuit, quod ipse Christus est Deus. Et **est verax**, quia ipse dicebat se esse Deum: quod si non esset, non esset verax, cum tamen scriptum sit, Rom. III, 4: *est autem Deus verax* etc. De isto signaculo dici tur Cant. VIII, 6: *pone me ut signaculum super cor tuum*. Et II Tim. II, 19: *firmum fundamentum Dei stat, habens signaculum* etc.

Vel, secundum Chrysostomum, **signavit**, idest monstravit, **quia Deus**, scilicet Pater, **verax est**; quia scilicet misit Filium suum, quem promisit mittendum. Quod ideo dicit Evangelista ut ostendat eos qui non credunt Christo, veritatem Patris negare.

540. Et ideo statim subdit divinae veritatis commendationem, dicens **quem enim misit Deus, verba Dei loquitur**; quasi dicat: hoc signavit, quod Christus, cuius testimonium accipit, **quem Deus misit, verba Dei loquitur**: et ideo qui credit ei, credit Patri, infra VIII, 26: **ego quae audivi a Patre loquor in mundo**. Unde non loquebatur nisi Patrem, et verba Patris; quia missus erat a Patre, et quia ipse est Verbum Patris: unde etiam se loqui Patrem dicit.

Vel si hoc quod dicit, **quod Deus verax est**, referatur ad Christum, datur intelligi distinctio personarum: cum enim Pater sit Deus verax, et Christus est verax Deus;

Scripture sometimes speaks of *the people*, or *they*, meaning those who are good; while at other times, the same words can refer to the wicked. We can see this: for first it says that all the people and the priests sought to kill Jeremiah (Jer 26), and this referred to those who were evil; then at once it says that all the people sought to free him, and this referred to those who were good. In the same way, John the Baptist says, looking to the left, i.e., toward those who are evil, and **no man receives his testimony**; and later, referring to those on the right, i.e., to the good, he says, **but he who has received his testimony**.

538. He who has received his testimony. Here he speaks of the obligation to believe, i.e., to submit oneself to divine truth.

As to this he does four things.

First, he presents the divine truth.

Second, he speaks of the proclamation of the divine truth, at **for he whom God has sent speaks the words of God**.

Third, of the ability to proclaim it, at **for God does not give the Spirit by measure**.

Fourth, he gives the reason for this ability, at **the Father loves the Son**.

539. Man's obligation to the faith is to submit himself to divine truth, and so he says that if few accept his testimony that means that some do. Hence he says, **he who has received his testimony**, i.e., whoever he may be, **has given a sign**, i.e., he ought to affix a certain sign or has in fact placed a seal in his own heart, that Christ is God. And he **is true**, because he said that he is God. If he were not, he would not be true, but it is written: *God is true* (Rom 3:4). Concerning this seal it is said: *set me as a seal on your heart* (Song 8:6), and *the foundation of God stands firm, bearing a seal* (2 Tim 2:19).

Or, following Chrysostom, **he has given a sign**, i.e., he has shown **that God**, that is, the Father, **is true**, because he sent his Son whom he promised to send. The Evangelist says this to show that those who do not believe Christ deny the truthfulness of the Father.

540. Then immediately he adds a commendation of divine truth, saying, **for he whom God has sent speaks the words of God**. As if to say: this is a sign, namely, that Christ, whose testimony he accepts, **he whom God has sent speaks the words of God**; and therefore he who believes in him believes the Father: **the things that I have heard from him are the same that I speak to the world** (John 8:26). So he spoke of nothing but the Father and the words of the Father, because he has been sent by the Father, and because he himself is the Word of the Father. Hence, he says that he even bespeaks the Father.

Or, if the statement **God is true** refers to Christ, we understand the distinction of persons; for since the Father is true God, and Christ is true God, it follows that the true

sequitur, quod verus Deus misit Deum verum, distinctum ab eo in persona, non in natura.

541. Denuntiandi autem facultas subest Christo maxima, quia non ad mensuram recipit spiritum; et ideo dicit *non enim ad mensuram dat Deus Spiritum*.

Posses enim dicere, quod licet miserit eum Deus, tamen non omnia a Deo loquitur, sed aliqua: nam et prophetae aliquando quidem locuti sunt ex spiritu suo, aliquando vero ex Spiritu Dei. Sicut II Reg. VII, 3 legitur de Natham propheta, quod ex spiritu suo loquens, consulit David, quod aedificaret templum; quod quidem postmodum ex spiritu et nutu divino retractavit. Sed hoc ostendit Baptista locum non habere in Christo; quia prophetae quidem accipiunt Spiritum Dei mensurate, scilicet quantum ad aliquid non quantum ad omnia, et ideo non quantum ad omnia verba Dei loquuntur; Christus autem, qui absque mensura et quantum ad omnia Spiritum recepit, ideo quantum ad omnia verba Dei loquitur.

542. Sed quomodo Spiritus Sanctus datur ad mensuram, cum sit immensus, secundum Athanasium in suo symbolo: *immensus Pater, immensus Filius, immensus Spiritus Sanctus?*

Responsio. Dicendum, quod Spiritus Sanctus datur ad mensuram, non quantum ad essentiam suam et virtutem eius, secundum quod est infinitus; sed quantum ad dona, quae dantur mensurate. Ephes. IV, 7: *unicuique nostrum data est gratia secundum mensuram.*

543. Notandum autem, quod hoc quod dicitur hic de Christo, quod non ad mensuram dedit ei Deus Pater Spiritum, potest dupliciter intelligi. Uno modo intelligitur de Christo secundum quod Deus; alio modo secundum quod homo. Ad hoc enim datur alicui aliquid ut habeat illud: habere autem Spiritum Sanctum, convenit Christo et inquantum Deus et inquantum homo; et sic secundum utrumque habet Spiritum Sanctum. Sed inquantum homo, habet Spiritum Sanctum ut sanctificantem; Is. LXI, 1: *Spiritus Domini super me, eo quod unxerit me,* scilicet hominem; inquantum vero Deus habet Spiritum Sanctum ut manifestantem tantum, secundum quod ab eo procedit. Io. XVI, 14: *ille clarificabit,* idest manifestabit, *quia de meo accipiet.*

Sic ergo utroque modo, scilicet inquantum Deus et inquantum homo, Christus habet Spiritum Sanctum non ad mensuram. Nam Christo, inquantum Deus, dicitur Deus Pater dare Spiritum Sanctum, non ad mensuram, quia dat ei virtutem et potestatem spirandi Spiritum Sanctum, qui, cum sit infinitus, in infinitum dat ei Pater: quem quidem Pater dat ei sicut ipse habet, ut scilicet sicut ab eo procedit, ita et Filio. Et hoc dedit ei per aeternam generationem. Similiter et Christus, inquantum homo, non ad mensuram habuit spiritum; nam hominibus datur Spiritus Sanctus ad mensuram, quia gratia eius *ad mensuram* eis datur; sed Christus inquantum homo

God sent the true God, who is distinct from him in person, but not in nature.

541. The ability to proclaim divine truth is present in Christ in the highest degree, because he does not receive the Spirit in a partial way; and so he says, *for God does not give the Spirit by measure*.

You might say that although God sent Christ, yet not all that Christ says is from God, but only some of the things; for even the prophets spoke at times from their own spirit, and at other times from the Spirit of God. For example, we read that the prophet Nathan (2 Sam 7:3), speaking out of his own spirit, advised David to build a temple, but that later, under the influence of the Spirit of God, he retracted this. However, the Baptist shows that such is not the case with Christ. For the prophets receive the Spirit of God only fractionally, i.e., in reference to some things, but not as to all things. Consequently, not all they say are the words of God. But Christ, who received the Spirit fully and in regards to all things, speaks the words of God as to all things.

542. But how can the Holy Spirit be given according to measure since he is immense or infinite, according to the Creed of Athanasius: *immense is the Father, immense the Son, immense the Holy Spirit?*

I answer that it is said that the Holy Spirit is given according to measure, not in respect to his essence or power, according to which he is infinite, but as to his gifts, which are given according to measure: *grace has been given to each of us according to degree* (Eph 4:7).

543. We should note that we can understand in two ways what is said here, namely, that God the Father did not give the Spirit to Christ in a partial way. We can understand it as applying to Christ as God, and, in another way, as applying to Christ as man. Something is given to someone in order that he may have it: and it is appropriate to Christ to have the Spirit, both as God and as man. And so he has the Holy Spirit with respect to both. As man, Christ has the Holy Spirit as Sanctifier: *the Spirit of the Lord is upon me, because the Lord has anointed me* (Isa 6 1:1), namely, as man. But as God, he has the Holy Spirit only as manifesting himself, inasmuch as the Spirit proceeds from him: *he will glorify me,* that is, make me known, *because he will receive of me* (John 16:14).

Therefore, both as God and as man, Christ has the Holy Spirit beyond measure. For God the Father is said to give the Holy Spirit without measure to Christ as God, because he gives to Christ the power and might to bring forth the Holy Spirit, who, since he is infinite, was infinitely given to him by the Father: for the Father gives it just as he himself has it, so that the Holy Spirit proceeds from him as much as from the Son. And he gave him this by an everlasting generation. Similarly, Christ as man has the Holy Spirit without measure, for the Holy Spirit is given to different men in differing degrees, because grace is given to each *by measure*. But Christ as man did not receive a certain amount

non ad mensuram recepit gratiam: et ideo non ad mensuram recepit Spiritum Sanctum.

544. Sed notandum, quod in Christo est triplex gratia, scilicet unionis, singularis personae, quae est habitualis, et capitis, quae est influentiae; et quamlibet istarum recepit Christus non ad mensuram.

Nam gratia unionis, quae non est habitualis, sed quoddam gratuitum donum, datur Christo, ut scilicet in humana natura sit verus Filius Dei non per participationem, sed per naturam, inquantum scilicet humana natura Christi unita Filio Dei in persona sit: quae quidem unio gratia dicitur, quia nullis praecedentibus meritis hoc habuit. Natura autem divina infinita est: unde ex ipsa unione accepit donum infinitum. Sic ergo non ad mensuram recepit Spiritum Sanctum, idest donum et gratiam unionis, quae Spiritui Sancto attribuitur inquantum gratuita.

Gratia autem habitualis dicitur, secundum quod anima Christi plena fuit gratia et sapientia, secundum quod dicitur supra I, 14: *vidimus eum quasi unigenitum a Patre, plenum gratiae* etc. De qua quidem gratia dubium esse potest, an recepit eam non ad mensuram. Cum enim huiusmodi gratia sit donum creatum, confiteri oportet quod habeat essentiam finitam: quod quidem quantum ad essentiam, secundum quod quid creatum est, ipsa gratia habitualis finita fuit. Sed tamen Christus dicitur eam recepisse non ad mensuram, triplici ratione.

Primo quidem ex parte recipientis. Manifestum est enim uniuscuiusque naturae capacitatem esse finitam: quia, etsi infinitum bonum recipere possit cognoscendo, et amando, et fruendo, tamen ipsum recipit fruendo finite. Est autem cuiuslibet creaturae, secundum suam speciem et naturam, determinata capacitatis mensura; quae tamen divinae potestati non praeiudicat quin posset aliam creaturam facere maioris capacitatis; sed iam non esset eiusdem naturae secundum speciem; sicut si ternario addatur unitas, erit alia species numeri. Quando igitur alicui naturae non datur de bonitate divina, quanta est capacitas naturalis speciei suae, videtur ei secundum aliquam mensuram donatum; quando vero tota naturalis capacitas impletur, non videtur ei secundum mensuram donatum; quia etsi sit mensura ex parte recipientis, non est tamen mensura ex parte dantis, qui totum paratus est dare: sicut aliquis vas ad fluvium deferens, absque mensura invenit ibi aquam paratam, quamvis ipse cum mensura accipiat, propter vasis determinatam quantitatem. Sic igitur gratia Christi habitualis, finita quidem est secundum essentiam, sed infinite, et non secundum mensuram dicitur dari, quia tantum ei datur quantum natura creata capere potest.

Secundo vero ex parte doni recepti. Nam omnis forma, seu actus secundum rationem suam consideratus,

of grace; and so he did not receive the Holy Spirit in any limited degree.

544. It should be noted, however, that there are three kinds of grace in Christ: the grace of union, the grace of a singular person, which is habitual, and capital grace, which is animating. And Christ received each of these graces without measure.

The grace of union, which is not habitual grace, but a certain gratuitous gift, is given to Christ in order that in his human nature he be the true Son of God, not by participation, but by nature, insofar as the human nature of Christ is united to the Son of God in person. This union is called a grace because he had it without any preceding merits. Now the divine nature is infinite; hence from that union he received an infinite gift. Thus it was not by degree or measure that he received the Holy Spirit, i.e., the gift and grace of union which, as gratuitous, is attributed to the Holy Spirit.

His grace is termed habitual insofar as the soul of Christ was full of grace and wisdom: *the only begotten of the Father, full of grace and truth* (John 1:14). We might wonder if Christ did receive this grace without measure. For since such grace is a created gift, we must admit that it has a finite essence. Therefore, as far as its essence is concerned, since it is something created, this habitual grace was finite. Yet Christ is not said to have received this in a limited degree for three reasons.

First, because of the one who is receiving the grace. For it is plain that each thing's nature has a finite capacity, because even though one might receive an infinite good by knowing, loving and enjoying it, nevertheless one receives it by enjoying it in a finite way. Further, each creature has, according to its species and nature, a finite amount of capacity. But this does not make it impossible for the divine power to make another creature possessing a greater capacity; but then such a creature would not be of a nature which is specifically the same, just as when one is added to three, there is another species of number. Therefore, when some nature is not given as much of the divine goodness as its natural capacity is able to contain, then it is seen to be given to it by measure; but when its total natural capacity is filled, it is not given to it by measure, because even though there is a measure on the part of the one receiving, there is none on the part of the one giving, who is prepared to give all. Thus, if someone takes a pail to a river, he sees water present without measure, although he takes the water by measure on account of the limited dimensions of the pail. Thus, the habitual grace of Christ is indeed finite according to its essence, but it is said to be given in an infinite way and not by measure or partially, because as much was given to him as created nature was able to hold.

Second, Christ did not receive habitual grace in a limited way by considering the gift which is received. For every

non est finitus eo modo quo, finitur per subiectum in quo recipitur; sed nihil prohibet illum secundum suam essentiam finitum esse, inquantum esse suum est in aliquo receptum. Illud enim secundum essentiam suam infinitum est, quod habet totam plenitudinem essendi: quod quidem soli Deo convenit, qui est summum esse. Si autem ponatur aliqua forma spiritualis esse non in subiecto existens, puta albedo, vel color, non quidem haberet essentiam infinitam, quia essentia eius esset determinata ad genus, vel speciem; nihilominus tamen totam plenitudinem illius speciei possideret: unde secundum rationem speciei, absque termino, vel mensura esset, habens quicquid ad illam speciem pertinere potest. Si autem in aliquo subiecto recipiatur albedo, vel color, non habet semper totum quicquid pertinet ad rationem formae huius de necessitate et semper, sed solum quando sic habetur sicut perfecte haberi potest; ita scilicet quod modus habendi adaequet rei habitae potestatem. Sic igitur gratia Christi habitualis, finita quidem fuit secundum essentiam; sed tamen dicitur absque termino et mensuram fuisse, quia quicquid ad rationem gratiae poterat pertinere, totum Christus accepit. Alii autem non totum accipiunt; sed unus sic, et alius sic. *Divisiones enim gratiarum sunt*: I Cor. XII, 4.

Tertio autem ex parte causae. In causa enim quodammodo habetur effectus. Cuicumque ergo adest causa infinitae virtutis ad influendum, dicitur habere illud quod influitur, absque mensura, et aliquo modo infinite. Puta, si quis haberet fontem, qui aquam infinitam posset effluere, infinite diceretur et absque mensura aquam habere. Sic anima Christi, infinitam et absque mensuram gratiam habet, ex hoc ipso quod habet Verbum sibi unitum, quod est totius emanationis creaturarum infinitum et indeficiens principium.

Patet autem ex his quae dicta sunt, quod gratia ipsius Christi, quae dicitur capitis, secundum quod Christus est caput Ecclesiae, est infinita quantum ad influentiam. Ex hoc enim quod habuit unde effunderet absque mensura Spiritus dona, accepit virtutem effundendi ipsa absque mensura, ut scilicet gratia Christi non solum sufficiat ad salutem hominum aliquorum, sed hominum totius mundi, secundum illud I Io. II, 2: *ipse est propitiatio pro peccatis nostris, et non pro nostris tantum, sed etiam totius mundi*, ac etiam plurium mundorum, si essent.

545. Habet etiam Christus denuntiandi veritatem divinam opportunam facultatem, quia omnia sunt in potestate eius; unde dicit **Pater diligit Filium, et omnia dedit in manu eius**: quod quidem potest referri ad Christum secundum quod homo, et secundum quod Deus; sed aliter et aliter.

form or act, considered in its very nature, is not finite in the way in which it is made finite by the subject in which it is received. Nevertheless, there is nothing to prevent it from being finite in its essence, insofar as its existence is received in some subject. For that is infinite according to its essence which has the entire fullness of being: and this is true of God alone, who is the supreme being. But if we consider some spiritual form as not existing in a subject, for example, whiteness or color, it would not be infinite in essence, because its essence would be confined to some genus or species; nevertheless it would still possess the entire fullness of that species. Thus, considering the nature of the species, it would be without limit or measure, since it would have everything that can pertain to that species. But if whiteness or color should be received into some subject, it does not always have everything that pertains necessarily and always to the nature of this form, but only when the subject has it as perfectly as it is capable of being possessed, i.e., when the way the subject possesses it is equivalent to the power of the thing possessed. Thus, Christ's habitual grace was finite according to its essence; yet it is said to have been in him without a limit or measure because he received everything that could pertain to the nature of grace. Others, however, do not receive all this, but one receives in one way, and another in another way: *there are different graces* (1 Cor 12:4).

The third reason for saying that the habitual grace of Christ was not received in a limited way is based on its cause. For an effect is in some way present in its cause. Therefore, if someone has an infinite power to produce something, he is said to have what can be produced without measure and, in a way, infinitely. For example, if someone has a fountain which could produce an infinite amount of water, he would be said to have water in an infinite way and without measure. Thus, the soul of Christ has infinite grace and grace without measure from the fact that he has united to himself the Word, which is the infinite and unfailing source of the entire emanation of all created things.

From what has been said, it is clear that the grace of Christ which is called capital grace, insofar as he is head of the Church, is infinite in its influence. For from the fact that he possessed that from which the gifts of the Spirit could flow out without measure, he received the power to pour them out without measure, so that the grace of Christ is sufficient not merely for the salvation of some men, but for all the people of the entire world: *he is the offering for our sins; and not for ours only, but also for those of the entire world* (1 John 2:2), and even for many worlds, if they exsited.

545. Christ also had the ability appropriate for declaring divine truth, because all things are in his power; hence he says, **the Father loves the Son, and he has given all things into his hand**. This can refer to Christ both as man and as God, but in different ways.

Si enim referatur ad Christum, secundum naturam divinam, tunc *diligit* non designat principium, sed signum: non enim possumus dicere quod Pater omnia Filio dat, quia diligit eum, propter duo. Primo, diligere est actus voluntatis; dare autem naturam Filio, est generare ipsum. Si ergo Pater daret voluntate naturam Filio, voluntas Patris esset principium generationis Filii; et sic sequeretur quod Pater generaret Filium voluntate, et non natura: quod est haeresis Ariana.

Secundo autem, quia dilectio Patris ad Filium est Spiritus Sanctus. Si ergo dilectio Patris ad Filium esset ratio quare dedit omnia Pater in manu Filii, sequeretur quod Spiritus Sanctus esset principium generationis Filii; quod est inconveniens. Dicendum est ergo, quod ly *diligit* importat signum tantum, ut dicatur, quod dilectio perfecta, qua *Pater diligit Filium*, est signum quod Pater *dedit omnia in manu eius*, quae scilicet Pater habet. Matth. XI, 27: *omnia mihi tradita sunt a Patre meo.* Infra XIII, 3: *sciens quia omnia dedit ei Pater in manus.*

Si referatur autem ad Christum, secundum quod homo, sic ly *diligit* dicit rationem principii, ut dicatur Pater omnia in manu Filii tradidisse, scilicet quae in caelis et quae in terris sunt, secundum illud Matth. ult., 18: *data est mihi omnis potestas in caelo et in terra.* Hebr. I, 2: *quem constituit heredem universorum.* Et huius traditionis ratio est, quia diligit eum; unde dicit *Pater diligit Filium*: dilectio enim Patris ratio est creandi quamlibet creaturam. Sap. XI, 25: *diligis omnia quae sunt, et nihil odisti eorum quae fecisti.* De dilectione autem Filii habetur Lc. c. III, et Matth. III, 17: *hic est Filius meus dilectus, in quo complacui mihi.* Et Coloss. I, v. 13: *transtulit nos in regnum Filii dilectionis suae*, idest Filii sui dilecti.

546. Consequenter cum dicit *qui credit in Filium, habet vitam aeternam*, ostendit fructum fidei: et

    primo ponit fidei praemium;

    secundo infidelitatis supplicium, ibi *qui autem incredulus est* etc.

547. Sed praemium fidei est inaestimabile, quia vita aeterna; et ideo dicit *qui credit in Filium habet vitam aeternam.* Et hoc ex praemissis ostenditur. Si Pater omnia dedit Filio, scilicet quae habet, et ipse habet vitam aeternam: ergo et Filio dedit ut sit vita aeterna. Infra V, 26: *sicut Pater habet vitam in semetipso, sic dedit et Filio habere vitam in semetipso*: quod quidem competit Christo inquantum est verus et naturalis Dei Filius. I Io. ult., v. 20: *ut sitis in vero Filio eius Christo: hic est verus Deus, et vita aeterna.* Qui credit in eum habet illud in quod tendit, scilicet ipsum Filium in quem credit; sed ipse est vita aeterna: ergo qui credit in eum, habet vitam

If it refers to Christ according to his divine nature, then *loves* does not indicate a principle but a sign: for we cannot say that the Father gives all things to the Son because he loves him. There are two reasons for this. First, because to love is an act of the will; but to give a nature to the Son is to generate him. Therefore, if the Father gave a nature to the Son by his will, the will of the Father would be the principle of the generation of the Son; and then it would follow that the Father generated the Son by will, and not by nature; and this is the Arian heresy.

Second, because the love of the Father for the Son is the Holy Spirit. So, if the love of the Father for the Son were the reason why the Father put everything into his hands, it would follow that the Holy Spirit would be the principle of the generation of the Son; and this is not acceptable. Therefore, we should say that *love* implies only a sign. As if to say: The perfect love with which **the Father loves the Son**, is a sign that the Father **has given all things into his hand**, i.e., everything which the Father has: *all things have been given to me by my Father* (Matt 11:27); **Jesus, knowing that the Father had given him all things into his hands** (John 13:3).

But if *loves* refers to Christ as man, then it implies the notion of a principle, so that the Father is said to have put everything into the hands of the Son, everything, that is, that is in heaven and on earth: *all authority has been given to me, in heaven and on earth* (Matt 28:18); *he has appointed him the heir of all things* (Heb 1:2). And the reason why the Father gives to the Son is because he loves the Son; hence he says, **the Father loves the Son**, for the Father's love is the reason for creating each creature: *you love everything which exists, and hate nothing which you have made* (Wis 11:25). Concerning his love for the Son we read: *this is my beloved Son, in whom I am well pleased* (Matt 3:17); *he has brought us into the kingdom of the Son of his love*, that is, i.e., of his beloved Son (Col 1:13).

546. Then when he says, **he who believes in the Son has eternal life** he shows the fruit of faith.

First, he sets forth the reward for faith.

Second, the penalty for unbelief, at **he who does not believe in the Son**.

547. The reward for faith is beyond our comprehension, because it is eternal life. Hence he says, **he who believes in the Son has eternal life**. And this is shown from what has already been said. For if the Father has given everything he has to the Son, and the Father has eternal life, then he has given to the Son to be eternal life: **for as the Father has life in himself, so he has also given to the Son to have life in himself** (John 5:26): and this belongs to Christ insofar as he is the true and natural Son of God. *That you may be in his true Son, Christ. This is the true God and eternal life* (1 John 5:20). Whoever believes in the Son has that toward which he tends, that is, the Son, in whom he believes. But

aeternam. Infra X, 17: *oves meae vocem meam audiunt . . . et ego vitam aeternam do eis*.

548. Supplicium autem infidelitatis est intolerabile et quantum ad poenam damni, et quantum ad poenam sensus.

Quantum quidem ad poenam damni, quia privatur vita; unde dicit *qui autem incredulus est Filio, non videbit vitam*. Non autem dicit non habebit sed *non videbit*: quia vita aeterna in visione verae vitae consistit. Infra XVII, 3: *haec est vita aeterna, ut cognoscant te solum Deum verum, et quem misisti Iesum Christum*: quam quidem visionem et cognitionem increduli non habebunt; Iob XX, v. 17: *non videat rivulos lactis* etc., idest dulcedinem vitae aeternae. Dicit autem *non videbit*, quia videre vitam ipsam, est proprium praemium fidei formatae.

Quantum vero ad poenam sensus, quia graviter punitur; unde dicit *sed ira Dei manet super eum*. Ira enim in Scripturis pro afflictione qua Deus malos punit, accipitur; unde cum dicit *ira Dei* Patris *manet super eum*, idem est ac si dicat: sentient poenam a Deo Patre. Et licet Pater *omne iudicium dederit Filio*, ut dicitur infra V, 22 tamen Baptista refert hoc ad Patrem, intendens per hoc Iudaeos reducere ad credendum Filio. Et de isto iudicio dicitur Hebr. X, 31: *horrendum est incidere in manus Dei viventis*. Dicit autem *manet super eum*, quia ista poena numquam ab incredulis desistet; et quia omnes qui nascuntur in ista vita mortali, habent secum iram Dei, quam accepit primus Adam. Eph. II, 3: *eramus natura*, idest per nativitatem, *Filii irae*. Ab hac autem ira non liberamur nisi per fidem Christi; et ideo qui non credunt in Christum Filium Dei, manet in eis ira Dei.

the Son is eternal life; therefore, whoever believes in him has eternal life: *my sheep hear my voice . . . and I give them eternal life* (John 10:27–28).

548. The penalty for unbelief is unendurable, both as to the punishment of loss and as to the punishment of sense.

As to the punishment of loss, because it deprives one of life; hence *he who does not believe in the Son shall not see life*. He does not say, will not have, but *shall not see*, because eternal life consists in the vision of the true life: *this is eternal life: that they may know you, the only true God, and Jesus Christ, whom you have sent* (John 17:3): and unbelievers will not have this vision and this knowledge: *let him not see the brooks of honey* (Job 20:19), that is, the sweetness of eternal life. And he says, *will not see*, because to see life itself is the proper reward for faith united with love.

As to the punishment of sense, because one is being severely punished; he says: *the wrath of God rests on him*. For in the Scriptures wrath indicates the pain with which God punishes the evil. So when he says, *the wrath of God*, the Father, *rests on him*, it is the same as saying: they will feel punishment from God the Father. Although the Father *has given all judgment to the Son* (John 5:22), the Baptist refers this to the Father in order to lead the Jews to believe in the Son. Concerning this judgment it is said: *it is a terrible thing to fall into the hands of the living God* (Heb 10:31). He says, *rests on him*, because this punishment will never be absent from the unbelieving, and because all who are born into this mortal life have God's anger with them, which was first received by Adam: *we were by nature*, that is, through birth, *children of anger* (Eph 2:3). And we are freed from this anger only by faith in Christ; and so those who do not believe in Christ, the Son of God, remain in the wrath of God.

CHAPTER 4

Lecture 1

4:1 Ut ergo cognovit Iesus quia audierunt Pharisaei quod Iesus plures discipulos facit, et baptizat quam Ioannes: [n. 550]

4:2 quamquam Iesus non baptizaret, sed discipuli eius: [n. 554]

4:3 reliquit Iudaeam. Et abiit iterum in Galilaeam. [n. 556]

4:4 Oportebat autem eum transire per Samariam. [n. 558]

4:5 Venit ergo in civitatem Samariae, quae dicitur Sichar, iuxta praedium quod dedit Iacob filio suo Ioseph. [n. 560]

4:6 Erat autem ibi fons Iacob. Iesus autem fatigatus ex itinere, sedebat sic supra fontem. Hora autem erat quasi sexta. [n. 561]

4:7 Venit mulier de Samaria haurire aquam. Dixit ei Iesus: da mihi bibere. [n. 566]

4:8 Discipuli enim eius abierant in civitatem, ut cibos emerent. [n. 570]

4:9 Dixit ergo ei mulier illa Samaritana: quomodo tu, Iudaeus cum sis, bibere a me poscis, quae sum mulier Samaritana? Non enim coutuntur Iudaei Samaritanis. [n. 572]

4:1 Ὡς οὖν ἔγνω ὁ Ἰησοῦς ὅτι ἤκουσαν οἱ Φαρισαῖοι ὅτι Ἰησοῦς πλείονας μαθητὰς ποιεῖ καὶ βαπτίζει ἢ Ἰωάννης

4:2 — καίτοιγε Ἰησοῦς αὐτὸς οὐκ ἐβάπτιζεν ἀλλ᾽ οἱ μαθηταὶ αὐτοῦ —

4:3 ἀφῆκεν τὴν Ἰουδαίαν καὶ ἀπῆλθεν πάλιν εἰς τὴν Γαλιλαίαν.

4:4 Ἔδει δὲ αὐτὸν διέρχεσθαι διὰ τῆς Σαμαρείας.

4:5 ἔρχεται οὖν εἰς πόλιν τῆς Σαμαρείας λεγομένην Συχὰρ πλησίον τοῦ χωρίου ὃ ἔδωκεν Ἰακὼβ [τῷ] Ἰωσὴφ τῷ υἱῷ αὐτοῦ·

4:6 ἦν δὲ ἐκεῖ πηγὴ τοῦ Ἰακώβ. ὁ οὖν Ἰησοῦς κεκοπιακὼς ἐκ τῆς ὁδοιπορίας ἐκαθέζετο οὕτως ἐπὶ τῇ πηγῇ· ὥρα ἦν ὡς ἕκτη.

4:7 ἔρχεται γυνὴ ἐκ τῆς Σαμαρείας ἀντλῆσαι ὕδωρ. λέγει αὐτῇ ὁ Ἰησοῦς· δός μοι πεῖν·

4:8 οἱ γὰρ μαθηταὶ αὐτοῦ ἀπεληλύθεισαν εἰς τὴν πόλιν ἵνα τροφὰς ἀγοράσωσιν.

4:9 λέγει οὖν αὐτῷ ἡ γυνὴ ἡ Σαμαρῖτις· πῶς σὺ Ἰουδαῖος ὢν παρ᾽ ἐμοῦ πεῖν αἰτεῖς γυναικὸς Σαμαρίτιδος οὔσης; οὐ γὰρ συγχρῶνται Ἰουδαῖοι Σαμαρίταις.

4:1 When Jesus therefore understood that the Pharisees had heard that he makes more disciples and baptizes more than John, [n. 550]

4:2 although Jesus himself did not baptize, but his disciples did, [n. 554]

4:3 he left Judea and went again into Galilee. [n. 556]

4:4 And he had to pass through Samaria. [n. 558]

4:5 He came therefore to a city of Samaria, which is called Sychar, near the land that Jacob gave to his son Joseph. [n. 560]

4:6 Now Jacob's well was there. Jesus therefore, being wearied from his journey, sat on the well. It was about the sixth hour. [n. 561]

4:7 There came a woman of Samaria to draw water. Jesus said to her: give me a drink. [n. 566]

4:8 For his disciples were gone into the city to buy food. [n. 570]

4:9 Then the Samaritan woman said to him: how can you, being a Jew, ask me for a drink, who am a Samaritan woman? For the Jews do not communicate with the Samaritans. [n. 572]

---

549. Posita doctrina Christi de spirituali regeneratione, et quod Christus gratiam spiritualis regenerationis Iudaeis communicaverat, hic consequenter ostendit quomodo ipsa gratia etiam ad gentes derivata est per Christum. Salutaris autem gratia Christi derivata est dupliciter in gentibus: per doctrinam et per miracula. Marc. ult., 20: *illi autem profecti praedicaverunt ubique*, ecce doctrina, *Domino cooperante, sequentibus signis*, ecce miracula.

Primo ergo ostendit futuram gentium conversionem per doctrinam;

secundo futuram gentium conversionem per miracula, ibi *post duos autem dies exiit inde*.

549. Having set forth the teaching of Christ on spiritual regeneration, and that Christ had given this grace of spiritual regeneration to the Jews, he now shows how Christ gave this grace to the gentiles. Now the salutary grace of Christ had been dispensed in two ways to the gentiles: through teaching and through miracles. *Going forth, they preached everywhere*: this is the teaching; *the Lord cooperated with them, and confirmed the word with signs*. These are the miracles (Mark 16:20).

First, he shows the future conversion of the gentiles through teaching.

Second, their future conversion through miracles, at *now after two days, he departed from there* (John 4:43).

Circa primum duo facit.

Primo praemittit quaedam praeambula ad doctrinam;

secundo proponit doctrinam, et eius effectum, ibi *respondit Iesus, et dixit ei: si scires donum Dei* etc.

Quantum ad primum tria praeambula praemittit.

Primum ex parte ipsius docentis;

secundum ex parte eius de quo doctrina erat, ibi *erat autem ibi fons Iacob*;

tertium ex parte personae audientis, ibi *venit mulier de Samaria*, etc.

Ex parte autem docentis, praeambulum est eius accessus ad locum doctrinae; et ideo dicit *ut ergo cognovit Iesus*, etc.

Ubi tria facit.

Primo innuit terminum a quo recedit, quia a Iudaea;

secundo terminum ad quem accedit, in Galilaeam;

tertio insinuat medium per quod transit, quia per Samariam.

Quantum ad primum ponit

primo causam recessus de loco in quo erat;

secundo exponit quaedam dicta in causa assignata, ibi *quamquam Iesus non baptizaret* etc.;

tertio describit recessum Christi a Iudaea, ibi *reliquit Iudaeam*, etc.

550. Dicit ergo *ut cognovit Iesus quod audierunt Pharisaei* etc., volens ostendere Evangelista, quod postquam Baptista repressit discipulorum suorum invidiam, Christus declinavit Pharisaeorum malitiam.

551. Sed cum dicatur Eccli. XXIII, 29: *Domino Deo nostro nota sunt omnia antequam fiant*; et Hebr. IV, 13: *omnia nuda et aperta sunt oculis eius*, quaerendum videtur quomodo Iesus dicitur aliquid de novo cognoscere.

Ad quod dicendum est, quod Iesus virtute divinitatis suae ab aeterno cognovit omnia praeterita, praesentia et futura, ut praedictae auctoritates ostendunt; sed inquantum homo aliqua de novo cognovit, scientia experimentali; et de hac dicitur hic *ut cognovit Iesus*, postquam fuit ei nuntiatum, *quia audierunt Pharisaei* etc. Et hanc cognitionem Christus de novo accipere voluit dispensative, ad ostendendum veritatem humanae naturae, sicut et multa alia humanae naturae propria voluit facere et pati.

552. Sed quid est hoc quod dicit *quia audierunt Pharisaei, quod Christus plures discipulos facit et baptizat quam Ioannes*, cum ad eos non pertineat? Nam ipsi Ioannem persecuti sunt, nec ei credebant: quia, ut dicitur Matth. XXI, 26, cum Dominus quaereret baptismum Ioannis unde esset, dicebant intra se: *si dixerimus*

As to the first, he does two things.

First, he sets down certain matters preliminary to the teaching.

Second, he presents the teaching and its effect, at *Jesus answered and said to her: if you knew the gift of God* (John 4:10).

As to the first, he sets down three preliminary facts.

First, what relates to the one teaching.

Second, something about the matter taught, at *now Jacob's well was there*.

Third, something about who received the instruction, at *there came a woman of Samaria*.

As to the person teaching, the preliminary remark is about his journey to the place where he taught; thus he says, *when Jesus therefore understood*.

Here he does three things.

First, he gives the place which he left, that is, from Judea.

Second, the place where he was going, to Galilee.

Third, the place through which he passed, Samaria.

As to the first, he does three things.

First, he gives the reason for his leaving Judea.

Second, he explains certain facts included in this reason, at *although Jesus himself did not baptize, but his disciples did*.

Third, he describes Christ's departure from Judea, at *he left Judea*.

550. The Evangelist says, *when Jesus therefore understood that the Pharisees had heard that he makes more disciples and baptizes more than John*, because he wished to show that after the Baptist had calmed the envy of his disciples, Jesus avoided the ill will of the Pharisees.

551. Since we read: *all things were known to the Lord God before they were created* (Sir 23:29), and *all things are naked and open to his eyes* (Heb 4:13), it seems that we should ask why Jesus is said to acquire new knowledge.

We must answer that Jesus, in virtue of his divinity, knew from eternity all things, past, present and to come, as the scriptural passages cited above indicate. Nevertheless, as man, he did begin to know certain things through experiential knowledge. And it is this experiential knowledge that is indicated when it says here, *when Jesus therefore understood*, after the news was brought to him, *that the Pharisees had heard*. And Christ willed to acquire this knowledge anew as a concession, to show the reality of his human nature, just as he willed to do and endure many other things characteristic of human nature.

552. Why does he say: *the Pharisees had heard that he makes more disciples and baptizes more than John*, when this would seem to be of no concern to them? For they persecuted John and did not believe in him, for when the Lord questioned them about the source of John's baptism, they said: *if we say from heaven, he will say to us, why then did*

de caelo, dicet nobis: quare ergo non credidistis? Non ergo crediderant Ioanni.

Sed ad hoc est duplex responsio. Una: quod ipsi discipuli Ioannis, qui supra quaestionem concitaverant contra Christum, erant Pharisaei, vel Pharisaeis confoederati, unde, Matth. IX, 11 et 14 dicitur quod Pharisaei simul cum discipulis Ioannis proposuerunt quaestiones contra discipulos Christi. Et secundum hoc concludit Evangelista *ut ergo cognovit Iesus quia audierunt* etc.: idest postquam intellexit quaestionem et commotionem discipulorum Ioannis, qui erant Pharisaei, vel Pharisaeis confoederati, super baptismo suo et discipulorum eius, *reliquit Iudaeam.*

Vel dicendum, quod Pharisaei propter invidiam turbati sunt de praedicatione Ioannis, unde suaserunt Herodi ut caperet eum. Et hoc patet Matth. XVII, 12, ubi cum Christus loqueretur de Ioanne, dicit: *Elias iam venit, et fecerunt in eum quaecumque voluerunt:* et postea subdit: *sic et Filius hominis passurus est ab eis,* ubi Glossa dicit quod Pharisaei incitaverunt Herodem ad incarcerationem Ioannis et mortem. Videtur ergo probabile quod similiter moverentur contra Christum, ex hoc quod praedicabat. Et hoc est quod dicitur *audierunt,* scilicet ad persequendum *Pharisaei* invidi et persecutores Christi *quia Iesus plures discipulos facit et baptizat quam Ioannes.*

553. De isto auditu dicitur Iob XXVIII, v. 22: *perditio et mors dixerunt: auribus nostris audivimus facta eius.* Sed boni audiunt ad obediendum. Ps. CXXXI, 6: *ecce audivimus eum in Ephrata:* et postea sequitur: *adorabimus in loco ubi steterunt pedes eius.*

Audierunt, inquam, duo: scilicet quod plures discipulos faceret quam Ioannes, quod quidem iustum erat et rationabile, quia, ut dicitur supra III, 30, Christum *oportet crescere,* et Ioannem minui. Aliud quod baptizabat; et hoc merito, quia ipse mundat. Ps. l, v. 4: *lava me, Domine, ab iniustitia mea.* Et alibi, Ps. VII, 7: *exurge, Domine* (scilicet baptizando), *in praecepto quod mandasti* (scilicet de baptismo), *et synagoga populorum* (per baptismum congregatorum) *circumdabit te.*

554. Consequenter cum dicit *quamquam Iesus non baptizaret* etc., exponit quod supra dixerat de baptismo Christi *quod audierunt Pharisaei* etc.

Sed Augustinus dicit, hic apparere inconveniens: nam supra dixerat *et baptizat,* hic vero quasi corrigens id, utpote falsum, dicit *quamquam Iesus non baptizaret.*

Et ad hoc est duplex responsio. Una Chrysostomi: quod hoc quod Evangelista dicit, verum est, quod Christus non baptizavit aliquem; illud autem quod supra dictum est, scilicet baptizat, intelligendum est secundum

you not believe him? (Matt 21:25). Thus they did not believe in John.

There are two answers to this. One is that those disciples of John who had spoken against Christ were either Pharisees or allies of the Pharisees. For we see, that the Pharisees along with the disciples of John raised questions against the disciples of Christ (Matt 9:11 and 14). And so according to this explanation, then, the Evangelist says that *when Jesus therefore learned that the Pharisees had heard,* that is, after he learned that John's disciples, who were Pharisees or allied with the Pharisees, had raised questions and had been disturbed about his baptism and that of his disciples, *he left Judea.*

Or, we might say that the Pharisees were disturbed at John's preaching due to their envy, and for this reason they persuaded Herod to arrest him. This is plain where Christ, speaking of John, says, *Elijah has already come . . . and they did with him whatever they wanted,* and then he adds, *so also will the Son of man suffer from them* (Matt 17:12). The Gloss comments on this that it was the Pharisees who incited Herod to arrest John and put him to death. Thus it seems probable that they felt the same way toward Christ because of what he was preaching. And this is what it says, that is, the envious *Pharisees* and persecutors of Christ *had heard,* with the intention of persecuting him, *that Jesus makes more disciples and baptizes more than John.*

553. This kind of hearing is described: *death and destruction have said: we have heard of his deeds* (Job 28:22). The good, on the other hand, hear in order to obey: *we have heard him in Ephrathah* (Ps 131:6), followed by, *we will adore at his footstool.*

The Pharisees heard two things. First, that Christ made more disciples than John. This was right and reasonable, for as we read, *he must increase, but I must descrease* (John 3:30). The second thing was that Christ baptized; and rightly so, because he cleanses: *wash me from my injustice* (Ps 50:4), and again: *rise up, O Lord,* by baptizing, *in the command you have given,* concerning baptism, *and a congregation of people,* united through baptism, *will surrond you* (Ps 7:7).

554. Then when he says, *although Jesus himself did not baptize,* he explains what he has just said about Christ's baptizing: *when Jesus therefore understood that the Pharisees had heard that he makes more disciples and baptizes more than John.*

Augustine says that there is an apparent inconsistency here: for he had stated that Jesus *baptizes,* whereas now he says, as though correcting himself, *Jesus himself did not baptize.*

There are two ways to understand this. This first way is that of Chrysostom. What the Evangelist now says is true, i.e., that Christ did not baptize. When he said above that Jesus was baptizing, this was the report received by the

famam currentem ad Pharisaeos, quod Christus baptizaret, quod aliqui venientes ad ipsos Pharisaeos dicerent: vos invidebatis Ioanni quod discipulos habebat et baptizabat; sed ecce quod hic, scilicet Iesus, plures discipulos facit quam Ioannes, et baptizat. Quare ergo sustinetis eum? Et ideo non dicit Evangelista ex se, quod baptizat, sed quod audierunt Pharisaei. Et ideo falsum rumorem populi Evangelista corrigere volens, dicit: verum est quod audierunt Pharisaei, quod Christus baptizat, sed est falsum; unde subdit quamquam Iesus non baptizaret, sed discipuli eius. Ideo autem, secundum Chrysostomum, Christus non baptizavit, quia in omni baptismate, quo Ioannes et discipuli baptizaverunt per totum tempus ante Christi passionem, non dabatur Spiritus Sanctus; sed ad hoc erat ut assuescerent homines ad baptismum Christi, et congregarentur ad praedicationem, ut ipse dicit. Inconveniens autem esset quod Christus baptizaret, si non daretur in illo baptismo Spiritus Sanctus, quod non dabatur ante Christi passionem: quia, ut dicitur infra VII, 39, **nondum erat Spiritus datus, quia nondum Iesus erat glorificatus.**

Sed, secundum Augustinum, dicendum est, et verius, quod discipuli baptizabant baptismo Christi, aqua scilicet et Spiritu, qui in ipso baptismo dabatur: et etiam ipse Christus baptizabat, et non baptizabat. Baptizabat quidem quia ipse mundabat interius; sed non baptizabat, quia ipse non tingebat aqua exterius; nam discipuli praebebant ministerium per ablutionem corporis, Christus vero praebebat Spiritum interius mundantem. Unde ipse proprie baptizabat. Supra I, 33: **supra quem videris Spiritum descendentem, et manentem super eum, hic est qui baptizat.**

Ad hoc ergo quod Chrysostomus dicit, quod nondum erat Spiritus datus etc., dicendum, quod non erat datus visibilibus signis, sicut post resurrectionem Christi datus est discipulis; sed tamen datus est, et dabatur, per internam sanctificationem, credentibus.

Per hoc autem quod Christus non semper baptizavit, dat nobis exemplum quod maiores Ecclesiarum praelati in his quae per alios fieri possunt, non occupentur, sed ea minoribus facienda relinquant. I Cor. I, 17: *non enim misit me Christus baptizare, sed evangelizare.*

555. Si autem quaeritur an discipuli Christi baptizati fuerint; dicendum, secundum Augustinum ad Stelentium, quod baptizati fuerunt baptismo Ioannis, quia aliqui ex discipulis Christi fuerant discipuli Ioannis: sive quod magis credibile est baptismo Christi; neque enim ministerio baptizandi defuisse creditur, ut haberet baptizatos servos, per quos ceteros baptizaret. Et hoc intelligendum est per hoc quod dicitur Io. XIII, 10: **qui lotus**

Pharisees. For certain people came to the Pharisees and said: you are envious of John because he has disciples and is baptizing. But Jesus is making more disciples than John and is also baptizing. Why do you put up with him? So the Evangelist is not himself saying that Jesus was baptizing, but only that the Pharisees heard that he was. It is with the intention of correcting this false rumor that the Evangelist says: It is true that the Pharisees heard that Christ was baptizing, but this is not true. So he adds: although Jesus did not himself baptize, but his disciples did. And so for Chrysostom, Christ did not baptize, because the Holy Spirit was not given at any time before the passion of Christ in the baptism of John and his disciples. The purpose of John's baptism was to accustom men to the baptism of Christ and to gather people in order to instruct them, as he says. Moreover, it would not have been fitting for Christ to baptize if the Holy Spirit were not given in his baptism; but the Spirit was not given until after the passion of Christ: *for the Spirit was not yet given, because Jesus was not yet glorified* (John 7:39).

According to Augustine, however, one should say, and this is the preferable, way, that the disciples did baptize with the baptism of Christ, that is, in water and the Spirit, and the Spirit was given in this baptism, and also that Christ did and did not baptize. Christ did baptize because he performed the interior cleansing; but he did not baptize because he did not wash them externally with the water. It was the office of the disciples to wash the body, while Christ gave the Spirit which cleansed within. So in the proper sense Christ did baptize, according to: *he upon whom you shall see the Spirit descending, and remaining upon him, it is he who baptizes with the Holy Spirit* (John 1:33).

With respect to the opinion of Chrysostorn that the Holy Spirit was not yet given and so on, we might say that the Spirit was not yet given in visible signs, as he was given to the disciples after the resurrection; nevertheless, the Spirit had been given and was being given to believers through an interior sanctification.

The fact that Christ was not always baptizing gives an example to us that the major prelates of the churches should not occupy themselves with things that can be performed by others, but should allow them to be done by those of lesser rank: *Christ did not send me to baptize, but to preach the Gospel* (1 Cor 1:17).

555. If someone should ask whether Christ's disciples had been baptized, it could be said, as Augustine answered Stelentius, that they had been baptized with the baptism of John, because some of Christ's disciples had been disciples of John. Or, which is more likely, they were baptized with the baptism of Christ, in order that Christ might have baptized servants through whom he would baptize others. This is the meaning of what is said: *he who has washed,*

est non indiget nisi ut pedes lavet. Et postea sequitur: *et ideo vos mundi estis, sed non omnes*.

556. Consequenter Christi recessum ponit, dicens *reliquit Iudaeam*: et hoc triplici de causa. Una ut subtraheret se invidiae Pharisaeorum, qui ex his quae audierant de Christo, turbabantur, et persecutionem parabant; dans nobis exemplum, ut per mansuetudinem malis cedamus ad tempus. Eccli. VIII, v. 4: *nec strues ligna in ignem illius*. Alia de causa ut ostenderet non esse peccatum persecutores fugere. Matth. X, 23: *si vos persecuti fuerint in una civitate, fugite in aliam*. Tertia causa est, quia nondum venerat tempus suae passionis. Infra II, 4: *tempus meum nondum advenit* etc. Est autem et alia causa, propter mysterium: nam per huiusmodi recessum significavit quod discipuli propter persecutionem relicturi erant Iudaeos, et ituri ad gentes.

557. Consequenter cum dicit *et abiit iterum in Galilaeam*, ostendit locum ad quem accessit. Dicit autem, *iterum*, quia supra II, v. 12 fecerat mentionem de quodam alio descensu Christi in Galilaeam, quo *post miraculum nuptiarum descendit Capharnaum*. Quia ergo alii tres Evangelistae non faciunt mentionem de illo descensu primo, ideo Evangelista, ut det intelligere quod alii Evangelistae omnia quae dixerunt usque ad istud capitulum, dimiserunt, et ex hoc loco ipse historiam eis contemporaneam texere incepit, dicit *iterum*,

per *Galilaeam* enim, secundum unam interpretationem, intelligitur gentilitas, ad quam Christus a Iudaeis vadit: interpretatur enim *Galilaea transmigratio*. Secundum aliam interpretationem, per *Galilaeam* intelligitur caelestis gloria, nam *Galilaea revelatio interpretatur*.

558. Consequenter cum dicit *oportebat autem eum transire per Samariam*, describit medium per quod transit: et

primo in generali;

secundo in speciali, ibi *venit ergo in civitatem Samariae, quae dicitur Sichar*.

559. Medium autem quod transit abiens in Galilaeam, est Samaria; et ideo dicit *oportebat eum transire per Samariam*. Dicit autem *oportebat*, ne videatur contrarius suae doctrinae: nam Matth. X, 5, praecepit discipulis, dicens: *in viam gentium ne abieritis*. Quia ergo Samaria terra gentium erat, ideo ostendit quod non ex proposito, sed ex necessitate illuc ivit. Dicit *oportebat*: et ratio huius necessitatis erat, quia Samaria erat sita media inter Iudaeam et Galilaeam.

De ista Samaria sciendum est, quod Amri rex Israel, montem a quodam Somer emit, ut habetur III Reg. XVI, 23 ss., civitatemque quam in montis vertice construxerat, a vendentis nomine Samariam nuncupavit; hac deinde reges Israelitarum pro regia usi sunt, et tota regio ab hac civitate Samaria vocabatur. Unde hoc quod dicitur hic *oportebat eum transire per Samariam*,

needs not but to wash his feet, and then follows, *and you are clean, but not all* (John 13:10).

556. He then mentions Christ's going away, *he left Judea*. He left for three reasons. First, to get away from the envy of the Pharisees, who were disturbed because of what they had heard about Christ, and were preparing to harass him. By this he gives us the example that we should, with gentleness, yield ground to evil for a time: *do not pile wood on his fire* (Sir 8:4). Another reason was to show us that it is not sinful to flee from persecution: *if they persecute you in one town, flee to another* (Matt 10:23). The third reason was that the time of his passion had not yet come: *my hour has not yet come* (John 2:4). And there is an additional reason, a mystical one: he indicated by his leaving that because of persecution the disciples were destined to abandon the Jews and go to the gentiles.

557. Then when he says, *and went again into Galilee*, he shows where he was going. He says, *again*, because he had mentioned another time when Christ went to Galilee: *after this he went down to Capernaum* (John 2:12). Since the other three evangelists did not mention this first trip, the Evangelist says *again* to let us know that the other evangelists had mentioned none of the matters he mentions up to this point, and that he is now beginning to give his account contemporaneous with theirs.

According to one interpretation, *Galilee* is understood to signify the gentile world, to which Christ passed from the Jews; for *Galilee* means *passage*. According to another interpretation, *Galilee* signifies the glory of heaven, for *Galilee* also means *revelation*.

558. Then, at *and he had to pass through Samaria*, he describes the intermediate place through which Christ passed;

first in a general way,

then specifically, at *he came therefore to a city of Samaria, which is called Sychar*.

559. Halfway through his journey to Galilee, Christ passes through Samaria; hence he says, *and he had to pass through Samaria*. He says, *had to pass*, lest he seem to be acting contrary to his own teaching, for Christ says: *do not go on the roads of the gentiles* (Matt 10:5). Now since Samaria was gentile territory, he shows that he went there of necessity and not by choice. Thus he says, *and he had to*, the reason for this necessity being that Samaria was between Judea and Galilee.

It was Amri, the king of Israel, who bought the hill of Samaria from a certain Somer (1 Kgs 16:24); and it was there he built the city which he called Samaria, after the name of the person from whom he bought the land. After that, the kings of Israel used it as their royal city, and the entire region surrounding this city was called Samaria. When

non est intelligendum per civitatem illam transitum esse facturum, sed per regionem.

560. Et ideo speciale medium describens, subdit *venit ergo in civitatem Samariae*, idest regionis Samariae, *quae dicitur Sichar*. Sichar enim idem est quod Sichem, secundum aliud nomen: de qua civitate habetur Gen. XXXIII, 16 ss., quod Iacob iuxta eam tetendit tentoria sua, et propter raptum Dinae filiae suae a filio regis Sichem, duo filii Iacob indignati, occiderunt homines civitatis illius; et sic cessit in possessionem Iacob, et habitavit ibi fodiens in ea puteos. Postmodum vero circa mortem suam, dedit eam Ioseph filio suo, secundum quod legitur Gen. XLVIII, 22: *do tibi partem unam extra fratres tuos*. Et hoc est quod dicit *iuxta praedium*, idest agrum, *quod dedit Iacob filio suo*.

Ideo autem haec omnia diligenter Evangelista narrat, ut ostendat quod omnia quae contigerunt circa patriarchas, fuerunt ducentia ad Christum; et quod Christus signatus est per eos, et ab eis secundum carnem descendit.

561. Consequenter cum dicit *erat autem ibi fons Iacob*, ponit praeambulum doctrinae ex parte rei de qua doctrina tradenda erat. Et hoc congruenter: nam doctrina futura erat de aqua et fonte spirituali, et ideo fit hic mentio de fonte materiali, ex quo sumitur occasio disputandi de fonte spirituali qui est Christus. Ps. XXXV, 10: *apud te est fons vitae*, scilicet Spiritus Sanctus, qui est spiritus vitae. Item fons est baptismus, de quo dicitur Zach. XIII, 1: *erit fons patens domui Iacob in ablutionem peccatoris et menstruatae*.

Circa hoc tria facit.

Primo describit ipsum fontem;

secundo sessionem Christi super eum; et

tertio sessionis tempus designat.

562. Fontem quidem describit cum dicit *erat autem ibi fons Iacob*.

Sed contra. Inferius dicitur *puteus altus est*: non ergo erat fons. Sed dicendum, secundum Augustinum, quod fons erat, et puteus. Omnis enim puteus fons est, sed non convertitur, nam ubi aqua de terra scaturit, fons est: et si quidem aqua in superficie terrae scaturit, fons tantum dicitur; si vero in alto et in profundo scaturit, ita puteus vocatur ut nomen fontis non amittat. Dicitur autem fons Iacob, quia ipse puteum illum foderat in terra illa propter defectum aquae, ut dicitur Gen. XXXIV.

563. Sessio autem Christi innuitur cum subdit *Iesus autem fatigatus ex itinere, sedebat sic supra fontem*. Ostendit infirmitatem, quamquam esset virtutis immensae, non propter defectum virtutis, sed ut ostenderet veritatem naturae assumptae. Nam, secundum Augustinum, Iesus fortis est, quia (supra I, 1) *in principio erat Word* (John 1:1); but he is weak, for *the Word was made*

we read here that *and he had to pass through Samaria*, we should understand the region rather than the city.

560. Describing it in more detail, he adds, *and he came therefore to a city of Samaria*, i.e., of the region of Samaria, *which is called Sychar*. This Sychar is the same as Shechem, according to another name, by which city, it is said that Jacob camped, and here and that two of his sons, enraged at the rape of Dinah, Jacob's daughter, by the son of the king of Shechem, killed all the males in that city (Gen 33:18). And so Jacob took possession of the city, and he lived there and dug many wells. Later, as he lay dying, he gave the land to his son Joseph: *I am giving you a portion more than your brothers* (Gen 48:22). And this is what he says: *near the land that Jacob gave to his son Joseph*.

The Evangelist is so careful to record all these matters in order to show us that all the things which happened to the patriarchs were leading up to Christ, and that they pointed to Christ, and that he descended from them according to the flesh.

561. Then when he says, *now Jacob's well was there*, the Evangelist gives the material setting for the spiritual doctrine about to be taught. And this was most fitting: for the doctrine about to be taught was about water and a spiritual font, and so he mentions the material well, thus giving rise to a discussion of the spiritual font, which is Christ: *for with you is the fountain of life* (Ps 35:10), namely, the Holy Spirit, who is the spirit of life. Likewise, the well symbolizes baptism: *on that day a fountain will be open to the house of David, to cleanse the sinner and the unclean* (Zech 13:1).

He does three things here.

First, he describes the well.

Second, Christ's rest at the well.

Third, the time.

562. He describes the water source saying, *Jacob's well was there*.

Here one might object that further on he says *the well is deep* (John 4:11); thus it did not gush water like a fountain. I answer, as does Augustine, that it was both a well and gushed water like a fountain. For every well is a fountain, although the converse is not true. For when water gushes from the earth we have a fountain; and if this happens just on the surface, the source is only a fountain. But if the water gushes both on the surface and below, we have a well; although it is also still called a fountain. It is called Jacob's well because he had dug this well there due to a shortage of water (Gen 34).

563. *Jesus therefore, being wearied from his journey, sat on the well*. Jesus reveals his weakness, even though his power was unlimited, not because of a lack of power, but to show us the reality of the nature he assumed. According to Augustine, Jesus is strong, for *in the beginning was the Word* (John 1:1); but he is weak, for *the Word was made*

Verbum, sed infirmus est, quia *Verbum caro factum est*. Christus ergo volens ostendere veritatem humanae naturae, permittebat eam agere et pati quae sunt propria homini: volens etiam ostendere in se veritatem divinae naturae, faciebat et operabatur propria Dei. Unde quando retrahebat influxum virtutis divinae a corpore, esuriebat et fatigabatur; quando vero ipsam virtutem divinam corpori exhibebat, sine cibo non esuriebat, et in laboribus non fatigabatur. Matth. IV, 2: *ieiunavit quadraginta diebus et quadraginta noctibus, et postea esuriit.*

564. Ex hoc autem quod Iesus fatigatus est ex itinere, datur nobis exemplum non refugiendi laborem propter salutem aliorum. Ps. LXXXVII, 16: *pauper sum ego, et in laboribus a iuventute mea.* Similiter etiam datur exemplum paupertatis, quia *sedebat sic*, idest super nudam terram.

Mystice autem sessio humilitatem passionis Christi significat. Ps. CXXXVIII, 2: *tu cognovisti sessionem meam* (idest passionem) *et resurrectionem meam.* Item significat auctoritatem docendi, quia loquitur tamquam potestatem habens: unde dicitur Matth. V, 1 s., quod *sedens docebat eos.*

565. Tempus autem determinatur, cum subdit **hora autem erat quasi sexta**. Et ratio huius determinationis assignatur litteralis et mystica.

Litteralis quidem, ut ostendat causam fatigationis: nam in calore, et sexta hora diei, homines magis fatigantur ex labore. Item ut ostendat causam sessionis: libenter enim homines in aestu et calore diei, iuxta aquas quiescunt.

Mystica autem causa assignatur triplex. Una, quia Christus in sexta aetate saeculi in mundum venit, carnem assumens. Alia, quia sexto die homo factus est, et in sexto mense conceptus est Christus. Tertia, quia in sexta hora sol in alto existit, et non restat nisi ut declinet. Sol autem, quantum ad hoc pertinet, temporalem prosperitatem significat, secundum illud Iob XXXI, 26: *si vidi solem cum fulgeret* etc. Tunc ergo Christus venit quando prosperitas mundi in alto erat, idest, in cordibus hominum per amorem florebat; sed per eum amor a cordibus hominum declinare debebat.

566. Consequenter cum dicit **venit mulier de Samaria**, ponitur praeambulum ex parte audientis: et circa hoc duo facit.

Primo ponitur persona cui exhibetur doctrina;

secundo innuitur praeparatio eius ad doctrinam, ibi **dixit ergo ei mulier illa Samaritana**.

567. Persona autem, cui exhibetur doctrina, est mulier Samaritana; unde dicit **venit mulier de Samaria haurire aquam**. Mulier ista significat Ecclesiam gentium nondum iustificatam, quae idolatria detinebatur, sed tamen per Christum iustificandam. Venit autem

flesh (John 1:14). And so Christ, wishing to show the truth of his human nature, allowed it to do and to endure things proper to men; and to show the truth of his divine nature, he worked and performed things proper to God. Hence when he checked the inflow of divine power to his body, he became hungry and tired; but when he let his divine power influence his body, he did not become hungry in spite of a lack of food, and he did not become tired in his labors. *He had fasted forty days and forty nights, and was hungry* (Matt 4:2).

564. From this, that Jesus is tired from the journey, an example is given to us not to shrink from our work for the salvation of others: *I am poor, and have labored since my youth* (Ps 87:16). Similarly, an example of poverty is given, because Jesus **sat on** the bare earth.

In its mystical meaning, this sitting of Christ's indicates the abasement of his passion: *you know when I sit down* (i.e., the passion), *and when I rise* (Ps 138:2). Also, it indicates the authority of his teaching, for he speaks as one having power; thus we read that Christ, *sitting down, taught them* (Matt 5:1).

565. He indicates the time, saying, **it was about the sixth hour**. There are both literal and mystical reasons for fixing the time.

The literal reason was to show the cause of his fatigue: for men are more weary from work in the heat and at the sixth hour. Again, it shows why Christ was resting: for men gladly rest near the water in the boiling heat of the day.

There are three mystical reasons for mentioning the time. First, because Christ assumed flesh and came into the world in the sixth age of the world. Another is that man was made on the sixth day, and Christ was conceived in the sixth month. Third, at the sixth hour the sun is at its highest, and there is nothing left for it but to decline. In this context, the *sun* signifies temporal prosperity, as suggested: *if I had looked at the sun when it shone* (Job 31:26). Therefore Christ came when the prosperity of the world was at its highest, that is, it flourished through love in the hearts of men; but because of him natural love was bound to decline.

566. Next, at **there came a woman of Samaria**, we have a preliminary remark concerning the one who listens to Christ.

Concerning which he does two things.

First, we are introduced to the person who is taught.

Second, we are given her preparation for his teaching, at **then the Samaritan woman said to him**.

567. The teaching is given to a Samaritan woman; so he says, **there came a woman of Samaria to draw water**. This woman signifies the Church, not yet justified, of the gentiles. It was then involved in idolatry, but was destined to be justified by Christ. She came from foreigners, i.e.,

ab alienigenis, scilicet a Samaritanis, qui alienigenae fuerant, licet vicinas terras incolerent: quia Ecclesia de gentibus, aliena a genere Iudaeorum, ventura erat ad Christum; Matth. VIII, 11: *multi venient ab Oriente et Occidente, et recumbent cum Abraham Isaac et Iacob in regno caelorum.*

568. Haec autem mulier praeparatur ad doctrinam per Christum, cum dicit *da mihi bibere*. Et

primo dat ei occasionem quaerendi;

secundo Evangelista interponit quaerendi opportunitatem, ibi *discipuli autem eius abierant*.

569. Occasio autem et praeparatio mulieris fuit petitio Christi; unde dicit *da mihi bibere*. Petit namque potum, et quia sitiebat aquam propter aestum diei, et quia sitiebat salutem hominis propter amorem eius; unde in cruce pendens dixit: *sitio.*

570. Opportunitatem autem quaerendi a muliere habuit Christus, quia non erant ibi discipuli eius, a quibus quaereret aquam; et ideo dicit Evangelista *discipuli enim eius abierant in civitatem.*

Ubi tria de Christo nota: scilicet eius humilitatem, in eo quod solus relinquebatur; dabat enim in hoc exemplum discipulis suis omnem superbiam conculcare.

Sed quaereret fortasse aliquis, quae necessitas fuerat assuescere discipulos ad humilitatem, quia piscatores et humiles extiterant, et tabernaculorum factores. Sed advertere debent, qui talia dicunt, quod repente piscatores huiusmodi facti sunt reverentiores omnibus regibus, facundiores philosophis et rhetoribus, et familiares Domini orbis terrarum: et tales sic repente promoti consueverunt superbire, utpote inexpertes ad tantum honorem.

Secundo nota Christi parsimoniam: nam ita parum curabat de cibis quod nihil comestibile secum ferebat.

Tertio etiam nota, quod dimiserunt eum solum in cruce; Is. LXIII, 3: *torcular calcavi solus, et de gentibus non est vir mecum.*

571. Praeparavit Dominus mulierem ad recipiendum spiritualem doctrinam, dando ei occasionem quaerendi;

hic consequenter ponitur quaestio;

secundo assignatur ratio quaestionis, ibi *non enim coutuntur Iudaei Samaritanis.*

572. Sciendum est autem, quod Dominus petierat a muliere potum, intendens magis de spirituali quam de corporali potu; mulier vero, potum spiritualem nondum capiens, intendebat solum de corporali; et ideo respondet *quomodo tu, Iudaeus cum sis, bibere a me poscis, quae sum mulier Samaritana?* Christus Iudaeus erat; quia et de Iuda promissus, Gen. XLIX, 10: *non auferetur sceptrum de Iuda, et dux de femore eius, donec veniat qui mittendus est,* et de Iuda natus; Hebr. VII, 14: *manifestum*

from the Samaritans, who were foreigners, even though they lived in the neighboring territory: because the Church of the gentiles, foreign to the Jewish race, would come to Christ: *many will come from the East and the West, and will sit down with Abraham, and Isaac, and Jacob, in the kingdom of heaven* (Matt 8:11).

568. Christ prepares this woman for his teaching when he says, *give me a drink.*

First, we have the occasion for his asking her.

Second, the Evangelist suggests why it was opportune to make this request, at *for his disciples were gone into the city.*

569. The occasion and the preparation of the woman was the request of Christ; thus he says, *give me a drink.* He asks for a drink both because he was thirsty for water on account of the heat of the day, and because he thirsted for the salvation of man on account of his love. Accordingly, while hanging on the cross he cried out: *I thirst* (John 19:28).

570. Christ had the opportunity to ask this of the woman because his disciples, whom he would have asked for the water, were not there, thus the Evangelist says, *his disciples were gone into the city.*

Here we might notice three things about Christ. First, his humility, because he was left alone. This is an example to his disciples that they should suppress all pride.

Someone might ask what need there was to train the disciples in humility, seeing that they had been but lowly fishermen and tentmakers. Those who say such things should remember that these very fishermen were suddenly made more deserving of respect than any king, more eloquent than philosophers and orators, and were the intimate companions of the Lord of creation. Persons of this kind, when they are suddenly promoted, ordinarily become proud, not being accustomed to such great honor.

Second, note Christ's temperance: for he was so little concerned about food that he did not bring anything to eat.

Third, note that he was also left alone on the cross: *I have trodden the wine press alone, and no one of the people was with me* (Isa 63:3).

571. Our Lord prepared the woman to receive his spiritual teaching by giving her an occasion to question him.

First, her question is given.

Second, her reason for asking it, at *for the Jews do not communicate with the Samaritans.*

572. Here we should point out that our Lord, when asking the woman for a drink, had in mind more a spiritual drink than a merely physical one. But the woman, not yet understanding about such a spiritual drink, had in mind only a physical drink. So she responds: *how can you, being a Jew, ask me for a drink, who am a Samaritan woman?* For Christ was a Jew, because it was promised that he would be from Judah: *the scepter will not be taken away from Judah . . . until he who is to be sent comes* (Gen 49:10); and

est quod ex Iuda ortus sit Dominus noster. Cognoscebat autem mulier Christum esse Iudaeum ex habitu: nam, sicut dicitur Num. XV, 37 ss., Dominus praecepit quod Iudaei portarent fimbrias hyacinthinas in quatuor angulis vestium suarum, ut per eas discernerentur ab aliis populis.

573. Consequenter assignatur ratio quaestionis, sive ab Evangelista, secundum Glossam, sive a muliere, secundum Chrysostomum, cum dicit **non enim coutuntur Iudaei Samaritanis**.

Sciendum est autem circa hoc quod sicut dicitur IV Reg. XVIII, propter peccata populi Israel, scilicet decem tribuum, qui colebant idola, ducti sunt in captivitatem a rege Assyriorum in Babylonem, et ne Samaria absque habitatoribus remaneret, fecit ibi gentes ex diversis locis ductas habitare. Et cum ibi essent, volens Dominus ostendere quod non propter imbecillitatem suae virtutis, sed propter Iudaeorum malitiam tradidit eos, immisit ipsis gentibus leones, et saevas bestias, quae eos laedebant. Quae ubi nuntiata sunt regi Assyriorum, habito ex consilio, quod hoc ideo eis contingeret quia non servabant legitima Dei terrae, misit ad eos sacerdotem quemdam ex Iudaeis, traditurum eis Dei legem, secundum legem Moysi. Unde et isti licet non essent ex populo Iudaeorum, servabant tamen legem Moysi; sed cum Deo vero colebant idola, nec prophetis attendebant, et vocabant se Samaritanos a civitate Samariae quae erat sita in monte Somer: III Reg. c. XVI, 24. Revertentibus ergo Iudaeis ex captivitate in Ierusalem, semper infesti fuerunt et contrarii; et, sicut dicitur in Esdra, impediebant eos aedificare templum et civitatem. Et licet Iudaei vitarent omnes alias nationes, specialiter tamen vitabant istos, nec in aliquo coutebantur eis; et hoc est quod dicit **non enim coutuntur Iudaei Samaritanis**. Non dicit quod Samaritani non coutantur Iudaeis, quia libenter voluissent adiungi et couti Iudaeis; sed Iudaei eos repellebant, secundum illud Deut. VII, 2: *non inibis cum eis foedus* etc.

574. Sed si non erat fas Iudaeis couti Samaritanis, quare Deus petebat a Samaritana potum?

Ad quod, secundum quod dicit Chrysostomus, posset aliquis respondere, quod Dominus sciebat eam non sibi tradituram potum, ideo petivit. Sed hoc non sufficit: quia petens quod non licet, a peccato non est immunis, quantum in se est, quin scandalizet, etsi non detur ei quod ipse petit. Et ideo dicendum est, quod, sicut dicitur Matth. XII, v. 8, *Filius hominis est Dominus etiam sabbati.* Unde tamquam Dominus legis poterat uti et non uti lege et observantiis et legalibus, secundum quod sibi expediens videbatur. Et quia imminebat tempus quo gentes vocarentur ad fidem, ipsis gentibus coutebatur.

he was born from Judah: *it is evident that our Lord came from Judah* (Heb 7:14). The woman knew that Christ was Jewish from the way he dressed: for the Lord commanded the Jews to wear tassels on the corners of their garments, and put a violet cord on each tassel, so that they could be distinguished from other people (Num 15:37).

573. Then the reason for this question is given: either by the Evangelist, as the Gloss says, or by the woman herself, as Chrysostom says; **for the Jews do not communicate with the Samaritans**.

Apropos of this, we should note that, it was on account of their sins that the people of Israel, i.e., of the ten tribes, who were worshipping idols, were captured by the king of the Assyrians, and led as captives into Babylonia (2 Kgs 18). Then, so that Samaria would not remain unpopulated, the king gathered people from various nations and forced them to live there. While they were there, the Lord sent lions and other wild beasts to trouble them; he did this to show that he let the Jews be captured because of their sins, and not because of any lack in his own power. When news of their trouble reached the Assyrian king and he was informed that this was happening because these people were not observing the rites of the God of that territory, he sent them a priest of the Jews who would teach them God's law as found in the law of Moses. This is why, although these people were not Jewish, they came to observe the Mosaic law. However, along with their worship of the true God, they also worshipped idols, paid no attention to the prophets, and referred to themselves as Samaritans, from the city of Samaria which was built on a hill called Somer (1 Kgs 16:24). After the Jews returned to Jerusalem from their captivity, the Samaritans were a constant source of trouble, and as we read in Ezra, interfered with their building of the temple and the city. Although the Jews did not mix with other people, they especially avoided these Samaritans and would have nothing to do with them. And this is what we read: **for the Jews do not communicate with the Samaritans**. He does not say that the Samaritans do not associate with Jews, for they would have gladly done so and have cooperated with them. But the Jews rebuffed them in keeping with what is said: *do not make agreements with them* (Deut 7:2).

574. If it was not lawful for the Jews to associate with Samaritans, why did God ask a Samaritan woman for a drink?

One might answer, as Chrysostom does, that the Lord asked her because he knew that she would not give him the drink. But this is not an adequate answer, because one who asks what is not lawful is not free from sin—not to mention the scandal—even though what he asks for is not given to him. So we should say, *the Son of man is Lord even of the sabbath* (Matt 12:8). Thus, as Lord of the law, he was able to use or not use the law and its observances and legalities as it seemed suitable to him. And because the time was near when the nations would be called to the faith, he associated with those nations.

Lecture 2

4:10 Respondit Iesus, et dixit ei: si scires donum Dei, et quis est qui dicit tibi, da mihi bibere; tu forsitan petisses ab eo, et dedisset tibi aquam vivam. [n. 575]

4:10 ἀπεκρίθη Ἰησοῦς καὶ εἶπεν αὐτῇ· εἰ ᾔδεις τὴν δωρεὰν τοῦ θεοῦ καὶ τίς ἐστιν ὁ λέγων σοι· δός μοι πεῖν, σὺ ἂν ᾔτησας αὐτὸν καὶ ἔδωκεν ἄν σοι ὕδωρ ζῶν.

4:10 Jesus answered and said to her: if you knew the gift of God, and who it is who says to you, give me a drink, you perhaps would have asked of him, and he would have given you living water. [n. 575]

4:11 Dixit ei mulier: Domine, neque in quo haurias, habes, et puteus altus est. Unde ergo habes aquam vivam? [n. 580]

4:11 λέγει αὐτῷ [ἡ γυνή]· κύριε, οὔτε ἄντλημα ἔχεις καὶ τὸ φρέαρ ἐστὶν βαθύ· πόθεν οὖν ἔχεις τὸ ὕδωρ τὸ ζῶν;

4:11 The woman said to him: Lord, you have nothing with which to draw, and the well is deep; from where do you have living water? [n. 580]

4:12 Numquid tu maior es patre nostro Iacob, qui dedit nobis puteum, et ipse ex eo bibit, et filii eius, et pecora eius? [n. 583]

4:12 μὴ σὺ μείζων εἶ τοῦ πατρὸς ἡμῶν Ἰακώβ, ὃς ἔδωκεν ἡμῖν τὸ φρέαρ καὶ αὐτὸς ἐξ αὐτοῦ ἔπιεν καὶ οἱ υἱοὶ αὐτοῦ καὶ τὰ θρέμματα αὐτοῦ;

4:12 Are you greater than our father Jacob, who gave us the well, and drank from it himself, and his children, and his cattle? [n. 583]

4:13 Respondit Iesus, et dixit ei: omnis qui biberit ex aqua hac, sitiet iterum; qui autem biberit ex aqua quam ego dabo ei, non sitiet in aeternum. [n. 584]

4:13 ἀπεκρίθη Ἰησοῦς καὶ εἶπεν αὐτῇ· πᾶς ὁ πίνων ἐκ τοῦ ὕδατος τούτου διψήσει πάλιν·

4:13 Jesus answered and said to her: whoever drinks of this water will thirst again, but he who will drink of the water that I give to him will not thirst again: [n. 584]

4:14 Sed aqua quam ego dabo ei, fiet in eo fons aquae salientis in vitam aeternam. [n. 587]

4:14 ὃς δ᾽ ἂν πίῃ ἐκ τοῦ ὕδατος οὗ ἐγὼ δώσω αὐτῷ, οὐ μὴ διψήσει εἰς τὸν αἰῶνα, ἀλλὰ τὸ ὕδωρ ὃ δώσω αὐτῷ γενήσεται ἐν αὐτῷ πηγὴ ὕδατος ἁλλομένου εἰς ζωὴν αἰώνιον.

4:14 but the water that I will give to him will become in him a fountain of water, springing up into eternal life. [n. 587]

4:15 Dixit ad eum mulier: Domine, da mihi hanc aquam, ut non sitiam, neque veniam huc haurire. [n. 588]

4:15 λέγει πρὸς αὐτὸν ἡ γυνή· κύριε, δός μοι τοῦτο τὸ ὕδωρ, ἵνα μὴ διψῶ μηδὲ διέρχωμαι ἐνθάδε ἀντλεῖν.

4:15 The woman said to him: Lord, give me this water, so that I may not thirst, nor come here to draw. [n. 588]

4:16 Dixit ei Iesus: vade, voca virum tuum, et veni huc. [n. 590]

4:16 λέγει αὐτῇ· ὕπαγε φώνησον τὸν ἄνδρα σου καὶ ἐλθὲ ἐνθάδε.

4:16 Jesus said to her: go, call your husband and then come back here. [n. 590]

4:17 Respondit mulier, et dixit: non habeo virum. Dixit ei Iesus: bene dixisti, quia; non habeo virum: [n. 591]

4:17 ἀπεκρίθη ἡ γυνὴ καὶ εἶπεν αὐτῷ· οὐκ ἔχω ἄνδρα. λέγει αὐτῇ ὁ Ἰησοῦς· καλῶς εἶπας ὅτι ἄνδρα οὐκ ἔχω·

4:17 The woman answered and said: I have no husband. Jesus said to her: you have said well, I have no husband: [n. 591]

4:18 quinque enim viros habuisti, et nunc quem habes, non est tuus vir: hoc vere dixisti. [n. 593]

4:18 πέντε γὰρ ἄνδρας ἔσχες καὶ νῦν ὃν ἔχεις οὐκ ἔστιν σου ἀνήρ· τοῦτο ἀληθὲς εἴρηκας.

4:18 for you have had five husbands, and he whom you have now is not your husband: this you have said truly. [n. 593]

4:19 Dixit ei mulier: Domine, video quia propheta es tu. [n. 596]

4:19 λέγει αὐτῷ ἡ γυνή· κύριε, θεωρῶ ὅτι προφήτης εἶ σύ.

4:19 The woman said to him: Lord, I perceive that you are a prophet. [n. 596]

4:20 Patres nostri in monte hoc adoraverunt: et vos dicitis, quia Ierosolymis est locus ubi adorare oportet. [n. 597]

4:20 οἱ πατέρες ἡμῶν ἐν τῷ ὄρει τούτῳ προσεκύνησαν· καὶ ὑμεῖς λέγετε ὅτι ἐν Ἱεροσολύμοις ἐστὶν ὁ τόπος ὅπου προσκυνεῖν δεῖ.

4:20 Our fathers worshipped on this mountain, and you say that Jerusalem is the place where it is fitting for men to worship. [n. 597]

4:21 Dixit et Iesus: mulier, crede mihi, quia venit hora, quando neque in monte hoc, neque in Ierosolymis adorabitis Patrem. [n. 599]

4:22 Vos adoratis quod nescitis; nos adoramus quod scimus: quia salus ex Iudaeis est. [n. 602]

4:23 Sed venit hora, et nunc est, quando veri adoratores adorabunt Patrem in spiritu et veritate. Nam et Pater tales quaerit, qui adorent eum. [n. 607]

4:24 Spiritus est Deus, et eos qui adorant eum, in spiritu et veritate oportet adorare. [n. 611]

4:25 Dixit ei mulier: scio quia Messias venit, qui dicitur Christus. Cum ergo venerit, ille annuntiabit nobis omnia. [n. 616]

4:26 Dixit ei Iesus: Ego sum qui loquor tecum. [n. 619]

4:21 λέγει αὐτῇ ὁ Ἰησοῦς· πίστευέ μοι, γύναι, ὅτι ἔρχεται ὥρα ὅτε οὔτε ἐν τῷ ὄρει τούτῳ οὔτε ἐν Ἱεροσολύμοις προσκυνήσετε τῷ πατρί.

4:22 ὑμεῖς προσκυνεῖτε ὃ οὐκ οἴδατε· ἡμεῖς προσκυνοῦμεν ὃ οἴδαμεν, ὅτι ἡ σωτηρία ἐκ τῶν Ἰουδαίων ἐστίν.

4:23 ἀλλὰ ἔρχεται ὥρα καὶ νῦν ἐστιν, ὅτε οἱ ἀληθινοὶ προσκυνηταὶ προσκυνήσουσιν τῷ πατρὶ ἐν πνεύματι καὶ ἀληθείᾳ· καὶ γὰρ ὁ πατὴρ τοιούτους ζητεῖ τοὺς προσκυνοῦντας αὐτόν.

4:24 πνεῦμα ὁ θεός, καὶ τοὺς προσκυνοῦντας αὐτὸν ἐν πνεύματι καὶ ἀληθείᾳ δεῖ προσκυνεῖν.

4:25 λέγει αὐτῷ ἡ γυνή· οἶδα ὅτι Μεσσίας ἔρχεται ὁ λεγόμενος χριστός· ὅταν ἔλθῃ ἐκεῖνος, ἀναγγελεῖ ἡμῖν ἅπαντα.

4:26 λέγει αὐτῇ ὁ Ἰησοῦς· ἐγώ εἰμι, ὁ λαλῶν σοι.

4:21 Jesus said to her: woman, believe me, that the hour is coming, when you shall adore the Father neither on this mountain nor in Jerusalem. [n. 599]

4:22 You adore that which you do not know: we adore that which we do know; for salvation is of the Jews. [n. 602]

4:23 But the hour is coming, and now is, when the true adorers shall worship the Father in spirit and in truth. For the Father also seeks such to adore him. [n. 607]

4:24 God is spirit, and they who adore him ought to worship him in spirit and in truth. [n. 611]

4:25 The woman said to him: I know that the Messiah is coming, who is called the Christ. Therefore, when he has come, he will tell us all things. [n. 616]

4:26 Jesus said to her: I am he, who is speaking with you. [n. 619]

---

575. Consequenter cum dicit *respondit Iesus et dixit ei* etc., narrat Evangelista ipsam doctrinam spiritualem. Et

primo ponitur ipsa doctrina;

secundo effectus doctrinae, ibi *et continuo venerunt discipuli eius.*

Circa primum duo facit.

Primo ponit summarie totam doctrinam;

secundo explicat eam per partes, ibi *dixit ei mulier: Domine, neque in quo haurias habes, et puteus altus est.*

576. Dixit ergo: tu miraris quod ego Iudaeus potum petii a te Samaritana; sed non debes mirari, quia ad hoc veni ut etiam gentibus potum darem. Et ideo dixit *si scires donum Dei, et quis est qui dicit tibi, da mihi bibere, tu forsitan petisses ab eo.*

577. Et, ut incipiamus ab ultimo, requirendum est quid intelligatur per aquam. Et dicendum, quod per aquam intelligitur gratia Spiritus Sancti: quae quidem quandoque dicitur ignis, quandoque aqua, ut ostendatur quod nec hoc, nec illud dicitur secundum substantiae proprietatem, sed secundum similitudinem actionis. Nam ignis dicitur, quia elevat cor per fervorem et calorem, Rom. XII, 11: *Spiritu ferventes* etc. et quia

575. Now, at *Jesus answered and said to her*, the Evangelist gives us Christ's spiritual teaching.

First, he gives the teaching itself.

Second, the effect it had, at *and immediately his disciples came* (John 4:27).

As to the first, he does two things.

First, a summary of the entire instruction is given.

Second, he unfolds it part by part, at *the woman said to him: Lord, you have nothing with which to draw, and the well is deep.*

576. He said therefore: you are amazed that I, a Jew, should ask you, a Samaritan woman, for water; but you should not be amazed, because I have come to give drink, even to the gentiles. Thus he says: *if you knew the gift of God, and who it is who says to you, give me a drink, you perhaps would have asked of him.*

577. We may begin with what is last, and we should know first what is to be understood by water. And we should say that water signifies the grace of the Holy Spirit. Sometimes this grace is called fire, and at other times water, to show that it is neither one of these in its nature, but like them in the way it acts. It is called fire because it lifts up our hearts by its ardor and heat: *ardent in Spirit* (Rom 12:11), and because it burns up sins: *its light is fire and flame*

consumit peccata; Cant. VIII: *lampades eius, lampades ignis atque flammarum.* Aqua vero dicitur propter purgationem; Ez. XXXVI, 25: *effundam super vos aquam mundam, et mundabimini ab omnibus inquinamentis vestris.* Et propter refrigerationem ab aestibus tentationum; Eccli. c. III, 33: *ignem ardentem extinguit aqua.* Et propter satietatem contra sitim terrenorum, et quorumcumque temporalium; Is. LV, 1: *omnes sitientes, venite ad aquas.*

Est autem duplex aqua: scilicet viva et non viva. Non viva quidem est quae non continuatur suo principio unde scaturit; sed collecta de pluvia, seu aliunde, in lacunas et cisternas a suo principio separata servatur. Viva autem aqua est quae suo principio continuatur, et effluit. Secundum hoc ergo gratia Spiritus Sancti recte dicitur aqua viva, quia ita ipsa gratia Spiritus Sancti datur homini quod tamen ipse fons gratiae datur, scilicet Spiritus Sanctus. Immo per ipsum datur gratia; Rom. V, 5: *caritas Dei diffusa est in cordibus nostris per Spiritum Sanctum, qui datus est nobis.* Nam ipse Spiritus Sanctus est fons indeficiens, a quo omnia dona gratiarum effluunt; I Cor. XIII, 11: *haec omnia operatur unus atque idem Spiritus* etc. Et inde est quod si aliquis donum Spiritus Sancti habeat, et non Spiritum, aqua non continuatur suo principio, et ideo est mortua, et non viva; Iac. II, v. 20: *fides sine operibus mortua est.* Sic ergo patet quid per aquam intelligatur.

578. Sed consequenter ostenditur, quod ad habendum aquam vivam, idest gratiam, in adultis per desiderium pervenitur, idest per petitionem; Ps. IX, 17: *desiderium pauperum exaudivit Dominus,* quia absque petitione et desiderio non datur alicui gratia. Unde dicimus quod in iustificatione impii requiritur liberum arbitrium ad detestandum peccata et ad desiderandum gratiam, secundum illud Matth. VII, 7: *petite, et accipietis.* Intantum enim requiritur desiderium, quod etiam ipse Filius ad petendum inducitur; Ps. II, 8: *postula a me, et dabo tibi.* Unde nec aliquis contradicens gratiae eam recipit, nisi prius reducatur ad desiderium gratiae, sicut patet in Paulo, qui antequam gratiam reciperet, reductus est ad desiderium gratiae, dicens, Act. IX, 6, *Domine, quid me vis facere?* Et inde est quod signanter dicitur *tu forsitan petisses ab eo.* Et dicit **forsitan**, propter liberum arbitrium, quo homo aliquando desiderat et petit gratiam, aliquando non.

579. Sed ad petendum gratiam incitatur desiderium hominis ex duobus, scilicet ex cognitione desiderandi boni, et ex cognitione datoris: et ideo duo cognoscenda proponit. Primo scilicet ipsum donum; unde dicit **si scires donum Dei**, quod est omne bonum desiderabile, quod est a Spiritu Sancto; Sap. c. VIII, 21: *scio quod non possum esse continens, nisi Deus det.* Et hoc donum Dei est etc. Secundo proponit ipsum datorem; unde dicit **et quis est qui dicit tibi** etc., scilicet, si scires eum qui dare

(Song 8:6). Grace is called water because it cleanses: *I will pour clean water upon you, and you will be cleansed from all your uncleanness* (Ezek 36:25), and because it brings a refreshing relief from the heat of temptations: *water quenches a flaming fire* (Sir 3:33), and also because it satisfies our desires, in contrast to our thirst for earthly things and all temporal things whatever: *come to the waters, all you who thirst* (Isa 55:1).

Now water is of two kinds: living and non-living. Non-living water is water which is not connected or united with the source from which it springs, but is collected from the rain or in other ways into ponds and cisterns, and there it stands, separated from its source. But living water is connected with its source and flows from it. So according to this understanding, the grace of the Holy Spirit is correctly called living water, because the grace of the Holy Spirit is given to man in such a way that the source itself of the grace is also given, that is, the Holy Spirit. Indeed, grace is given by the Holy Spirit: *the love of God is poured out into our hearts by the Holy Spirit, who has been given to us* (Rom 5:5). For the Holy Spirit is the unfailing fountain from whom all gifts of grace flow *one and the same Spirit does all these things* (1 Cor 13:11). And so, if anyone has a gift of the Holy Spirit without having the Spirit, the water is not united with its source, and so is not living but dead: *faith without works is dead* (Jas 2:20).

578. Thus it is evident what is understood by water. Then we are shown that in the case of adults, living water, i.e., grace, is obtained by desiring it, i.e., by asking, *the Lord has heard the desire of the poor* (Ps 9:17), for grace is not given to anyone without their asking and desiring it. Thus we say that in the justification of a sinner an act of free will is necessary to detest sin and to desire grace: *ask and you will receive* (Matt 7:7). In fact, desire is so important that even the Son himself is told to ask: *ask me, and I will give to you* (Ps 2:8). Therefore, no one who resists grace receives it, unless he first desires it; this is clear is the case of Paul who, before he received grace, desired it, saying: *Lord, what do you want me to do?* (Acts 9:6). Thus it is significant that he says, you perhaps would have asked him. He says **perhaps** on account of free will, with which a person sometimes desires and asks for grace, and sometimes does not.

579. There are two things which lead a person to desire and ask for grace: a knowledge of the good to be desired and a knowledge of the giver. So, Christ offers these two to her. First of all, a knowledge of the gift itself; hence he says, **if you knew the gift of God**, which is every desirable good which comes from the Holy Spirit: *I know that I cannot control myself unless God grants it to me* (Wis 8:21). And this is a gift of God, and so forth. Second, he mentions the giver; and he says, and realized **who it is who says to you**,

potest, qui sum ego; infra XV, 26: *cum venerit Paraclitus, quem ego mittam vobis a Patre . . . ille testimonium perhibebit de me*; Ps. LXVII, 19: *dedit dona hominibus.*

Sic ergo haec doctrina est de tribus: scilicet de dono aquae vivae, de petitione ipsius doni et de datore eius.

580. Et ideo cum dicit **dixit ei mulier** etc., de ipsa doctrina tractat explicite quantum ad haec tria: et

primo quantum ad donum;

secundo quantum ad petitionem, ibi **dicit ei mulier: Domine, ut video, propheta es tu**;

tertio quantum ad datorem, ibi **dicit ei mulier: scio quia Messias venit** etc.

Circa primum duo facit.

Primo explicat donum, ostendendo eius virtutem;

secundo agit de perfectione ipsius doni, ibi **dicit ei mulier: Domine, da mihi hanc aquam** etc.

Circa primum duo facit.

Primo ponitur inquisitio mulieris;

secundo responsio Christi, ibi **respondit Iesus, et dixit ei: omnis qui biberit ex aqua hac, sitiet iterum.**

581. Circa primum sciendum est, quod mulier ista Samaritana, verba quae Dominus spiritualiter intelligebat, carnaliter accipiebat, quia erat animalis. I Cor. II, 14: *animalis homo non percipit ea quae sunt Spiritus Dei.* Et ideo verba quae Dominus dicebat, quasi inconvenientia et impossibilia, argumento quodam utens, infringere conabatur, hoc modo: tu promittis mihi aquam vivam, aut ergo de isto puteo, aut de alio; sed non de isto, quia **nec in quo haurias habes, et puteus altus est**; de alio autem non videtur credibile quod dare possis, quia non **maior es patre nostro Iacob, qui dedit nobis puteum.**

582. Primo ergo prosequens primum, videamus hoc quod dicit **Domine, neque in quo haurias habes**, idest hauritorio cares, quo aquam de puteo extrahere possis, et **puteus altus est**, scilicet ut absque hauritorio manu non possis attingere.

Per altitudinem, seu profunditatem putei, intelligitur Sacrae Scripturae profunditas, et sapientiae divinae; Eccle. VII, 25: *alta profunditas et quis*, etc.; hauritorium autem quo aqua sapientiae salutaris hauritur, est oratio; Iac. I, 5: *si quis indiget sapientia, postulet a Deo.*

583. Secundum ostendit, cum dicit **numquid tu es maior patre nostro Iacob, qui dedit nobis puteum?** etc.; quasi dicat: numquid meliorem aquam habes ad dandum nobis quam Iacob? Dicit autem patrem suum Iacob, non quod Samaritani de generatione sint Iacob, ut ex supradictis apparet, sed quia legem Moysi habebant, et quia intraverunt terram semini Iacob repromissam.

i.e., if you knew the one who can give it, namely, that it is I: **when the Paraclete comes whom I will send you from the Father, the Spirit of truth . . . he will give testimony of me** (John 15:26); *you have given gifts to men* (Ps 67:19).

Accordingly, this teaching concerns three things: the gift of living water, asking for this gift, and the giver himself.

580. When he says, **the woman said to him**, he treats these three things explicitly.

First, the gift;

second, asking for the gift, at **Lord, I perceive that you are a prophet**; and

third, the giver, at **the woman said to him: I know that the Messiah is coming**.

He does two things about the first.

First, he explains the gift by showing its power.

Second, he considers the perfection of the gift, **the woman said to him: Lord, give me this water**.

About the first he does two things.

First, he gives the woman's request.

Second, Christ's answer, at **Jesus answered and said to her: whoever drinks of this water will thirst again**.

581. We should note, with respect to the first, that this Samaritan woman, because she was sensual, understood in a worldly sense what the Lord understood in a spiritual sense: *the sensual man does not perceive those things that pertain to the Spirit of God* (1 Cor 2:14). Consequently, she tried to reject what our Lord said as unreasonable and impossible with the following argument: you promise me living water; and it must come either from this well or from another one. But it cannot come from this well because **you have nothing with which to draw, and the well is deep; from where do you have living water?**; and it does not seem probable that you can get if from some other well, because you are not **greater than our father Jacob, who gave us the well.**

582. Let us first examine what she says, **you have nothing with which to draw**, i.e., no pail to use to draw water from the well, and **the well is deep**, so you cannot reach the water by hand without a bucket.

Through the depth or vastness of the well is signified the depth of Sacred Scripture and of divine wisdom: *it has great depth. Who can find it out?* (Eccl 7:25). The bucket with which the water of saving wisdom is drawn out is prayer: *if any of you lack wisdom, ask God* (Jas 1:5).

583. The second point is given at, **are you greater than our father Jacob, who gave us the well?** As if to say: have you better water to give us than Jacob? She calls Jacob her father not because the Samaritans were descendants of the Jews, as is clear from what was said before, but because the Samaritans had the Mosaic law, and because they occupied the land promised to the descendants of Jacob.

Commendat autem mulier ista puteum istum ex tribus. Primo ex auctoritate dantis; unde dicit **patre nostro Iacob, qui dedit nobis puteum**. Secundo ex suavitate aquae, et dicit, quod **ipse** Iacob **ex eo bibit, et filii eius**: nisi enim fuisset suavis, non ipsi bibissent, sed pecoribus eam tradidissent. Tertio ex ubertate, cum dicit **et pecora eius**: quia enim erat suavis, nisi fuisset uberrima, non dedissent eam pecoribus. Sic et Sacra Scriptura magna est auctoritate, quia a Spiritu Sancto est data; delectabilis est suavitate, Ps. c. CXVIII, 103: *quam dulcia sunt faucibus meis eloquia tua.* Iterum fecunda est ubertate, quia non solum sapientibus, sed etiam insipientibus communicatur.

584. Consequenter cum dicit **respondit Iesus** etc. ponitur responsio Domini, ubi explicat virtutem suae doctrinae: et

primo quantum ad hoc quod dixerat eam esse aquam;

secundo quantum ad hoc quod dixerat eam esse aquam vivam, ibi **sed aqua quam ego dabo ei, fiet in eo fons aquae salientis in vitam aeternam**.

585. Ostendit autem, quod doctrina sua sit optima aqua, ex hoc quod habet aquae effectum, scilicet quod auferat sitim multo amplius quam aqua ista corporalis; ostendens se in hoc esse maiorem quam Iacob. Et ideo dicit **respondit Iesus, et dixit ei**, quasi dicat: tu dicis, quod Iacob dedit vobis puteum, sed ego dabo aquam meliorem, quia **omnis qui biberit ex hac aqua**, scilicet corporali vel carnalis cupiditatis et concupiscentiae, licet ad horam sedetur appetitus, tamen **sitiet iterum**, quia insatiabilis est delectationis appetitus; Prov. XXIII, 35: *quando evigilabo, et rursus vina reperiam?* Sed **qui biberit ex hac aqua**, scilicet spirituali, **quam ego dabo ei, non sitiet in aeternum**; Is. penult., 13: *servi mei bibent, et vos sitietis.*

586. Sed contra. Eccli. XXIV, 29, dicitur: *qui bibunt me, adhuc sitient.* Quomodo ergo non sitiet in aeternum qui biberit ex hac aqua, scilicet divina sapientia, cum ipsa sapientia dicat: *qui bibunt me, adhuc sitient?*

Sed dicendum, quod utrumque verum est: quia qui bibit ex aqua quam Christus dat et sitit adhuc et non sitit; sed qui bibit ex aqua corporali, sitiet iterum: et hoc propter duo. Primo, quia aqua materialis et carnalis non est perpetua, nec causam perpetuam habet, sed deficientem: unde et effectus oportet quod cesset; Sap. V, 9: *transierunt haec omnia quasi umbra* etc. Aqua vero spiritualis causam perpetuam habet, scilicet Spiritum Sanctum, qui est fons vitae, numquam deficiens: et ideo qui ex ea bibit, non sitiet in aeternum; sicut qui haberet in ventre fontem aquae vivae, non sitiret unquam.

Alia ratio est, quia differentia est inter rem spiritualem et temporalem. Licet enim utraque generet sitim, tamen aliter et aliter: quia res temporalis habita, causat

The woman praised this well on three counts. First, on the authority of the one who gave it; so she says: **our father Jacob, who gave us the well**. Second, on account of the freshness of its water, saying: Jacob **drank from it himself, and his children**: for they would not drink it if it were not fresh, but only give it to their cattle. Third, she praises its abundance, saying, **and his cattle**: for since the water was fresh, they would not have given it to their flocks unless it were also abundant. So, too, Sacred Scripture has great authority: for it was given by the Holy Spirit. It is delightfully fresh: *how sweet are your words to my palate* (Ps 118:103). Finally, it is exceedingly abundant, for it is given not only to the wise, but also to the unwise.

584. Then when he says, **Jesus answered and said to her: whoever drinks of this water**, he sets down the Lord's response, in which he explains the power of his doctrine.

First, with respect to the fact that he had called it water.

Second, with respect to the fact that he called it living water, at **but the water that I will give to him will become in him a fountain of water, springing up into eternal life**.

585. He shows that his doctrine is the best water because it has the effect of water, that is, it takes away thirst much more than does that natural water. He shows by this that he is greater than Jacob. So he says, **Jesus answered and said to her**, as if to say you say that Jacob gave you a well; but I will give you better water, because **whoever drinks of this water**, that is, natural water, or the water of sensual desire and concupiscence, although it may satisfy his appetite for a while, **will thirst again**, because the desire for pleasure is insatiable: *when will I wake up and find wine again?* (Prov 23:35). But **he who will drink of this water**, that is, spiritual water, **that I give to him will not thirst again**. *My servants will drink, and you will be thirsty* (Isa 65:13).

586. Since we read that *those who drink me will still thirst* (Sir 24:29), how is it possible that we will never be thirsty if we drink this water of divine wisdom, since this wisdom itself says we will still thirst: *those who drink me will still thirst?* (Sir 24:29).

I answer that both are true: because he who drinks the water that Christ gives still thirsts and does not thirst. But whoever drinks natural water will become thirsty again for two reasons. First, because material and natural water is not eternal, and it does not have an eternal cause, but an impermanent one; therefore its effects must also cease: *all these things have passed away like a shadow* (Wis 5:9). But spiritual water has an eternal cause, that is, the Holy Spirit, who is the unfailing fountain of life. Accordingly, he who drinks of this will never thirst; just as someone who had within himself a fountain of living water would never thirst.

The other reason is that there is a difference between a spiritual and a temporal thing. For although each produces a thirst, they do so in different ways. When a temporal

quidem sitim non sui ipsius, sed alterius rei; spiritualis vero tollit sitim alterius rei, et causat sui ipsius sitim. Cuius ratio est, quia res temporalis antequam habeatur, aestimatur magni pretii et sufficiens; sed postquam habetur, quia nec tanta, nec sufficiens ad quietandum desiderium invenitur, ideo non satiat desiderium, quin ad aliud habendum moveatur. Res vero spiritualis non cognoscitur, nisi cum habetur Apoc. II, 17: *nemo novit nisi qui accipit*. Et ideo non habita, non movet desiderium; sed cum habetur et cognoscitur, tunc delectat affectum et movet desiderium, non quidem ad aliud habendum, sed quia imperfecte percipitur propter recipientis imperfectionem, movet ut ipsa perfecte habeatur.

Et de hac siti dicitur in Ps. XLI, 2: *sitivit anima mea ad Deum fontem vivum*. Sed haec sitis in mundo isto usquequaque non tollitur, quia bona spiritualia in vita ista percipere non possumus; et ideo qui biberit ex hac aqua, adhuc quidem sitiet eius perfectionem; sed non sitiet in aeternum, quasi ipsa aqua deficiat; quia, ut dicitur in Ps. XXXV, 9: *inebriabuntur ab ubertate domus tuae*. In vita autem gloriae, ubi beati perfecte bibunt aquam divinae gratiae, non sitient in aeternum; Matth. c. V, 6: *beati qui esuriunt et sitiunt iustitiam*, scilicet in mundo isto, *quia saturabuntur* in vita gloriae.

587. Consequenter cum dicit **sed aqua quam ego dabo ei, fiet in eo fons aquae salientis in vitam aeternam**, ostendit doctrinam suam esse aquam vivam ex motu ipsius aquae; unde dicit, quod est fons decurrens, Ps. XIV, 5: *fluminis impetus laetificat civitatem Dei*.

Sed alius est cursus aquae materialis, scilicet deorsum, alius istius spiritualis, quia ducit sursum; et ideo dicit: dico, quod talis est aqua materialis quod non tollit sitim, sed aqua quam ego do, non solum sitim aufert, sed est viva quia est coniuncta fonti; unde dicit quod **fiet in eo fons**: fons, inquam perducens per bona opera ad vitam aeternam. Ideo dicit **aquae salientis**, idest salire facientis, **in vitam aeternam**, ubi non est sitis, infra c. VII, 38: **qui credit in me, flumina**, scilicet bonorum desideriorum, **de ventre eius fluent aquae vivae**; Ps. XXXV, 10: *apud te est fons vitae*.

588. Consequenter cum dicit **dixit ad eum mulier**, agitur de petitione doni: et

primo ponitur modus percipiendi ipsum donum;

secundo convincitur mulier, ibi **dixit ei Iesus: bene dixisti** etc.

Modus percipiendi, ut dictum est, est per orationem et petitionem: et ideo

primo ponitur petitio mulieris;

thing is possessed it causes us to be thirsty, not for the thing itself, but for something else; while a spiritual thing when possessed takes away the thirst for other things, and causes us to thirst for it. The reason for this is that before temporal things are possessed, they are thought to be of great price and to be satisfying; but after they are possessed, they are found to be neither so great as thought nor sufficient to satisfy our desires, and so our desires are not satisfied but move on to something else. On the other hand, a spiritual thing is not known unless it is possessed: *no one knows but he who receives it* (Rev 2:17). So, when it is not possessed, it does not produce a desire; but once it is possessed and known, then it brings pleasure and produces desire, but not to possess something else. Yet, because it is imperfectly known on account of the deficiency of the one receiving it, it produces a desire in us to possess it perfectly.

We read of this thirst: *my soul thirsted for God, the living fountain* (Ps 41:2). This thirst is not completely taken away in this world because in this life we cannot understand spiritual things; consequently, one who drinks this water will still thirst for its completion. But he will not always be thirsty, as though the water will run out, for we read (Ps 35:9): *they will be intoxicated from the richness of your house*. In the life of glory, where the blessed drink perfectly the water of divine grace, they will never be thirsty again: *blessed are they who hunger and thirst for what is right*, that is, in this world, *for they will be satisfied*, in the life of glory (Matt 5:6).

587. Then when he says, **but the water that I will give to him will become in him a fountain of water, springing up into eternal life**, he shows from the movement of the water that his doctrine is living water; thus he says that it is a leaping fountain: *the streams of the river bring joy to the city of God* (Ps 45:4).

The course of material water is downward, and this is different from the course of spiritual water, which is upward. Thus he says: I say that material water is such that it does not slake your thirst; but the water that I give not only quenches your thirst, but it is a living water because it is united with its source. Hence he says that it **will become in him a fountain**: a fountain leading, through good works, **into eternal life**. So he says, **springing up**, that is, making us leap up, **into eternal life**, where there is no thirst: **he who believes in me, as the Scripture says, out of his heart shall flow rivers of living water** (John 7:38); *with you is the fountain of life* (Ps 35:10).

588. Then when he says, **the woman said to him**, he states her request for the gift.

First, her understanding of the gift is noted.

Second, the woman is found guilty, at **you have said well**: **I have no husband**.

As was said, the way to obtain this gift is by prayer and request.

And so first, we have the woman's request.

secundo responsio Christi, ibi *dixit ei Iesus, vade* etc.

589. Quantum ad primum notandum, quod mulier ista in exordio collationis mutuae, Christum non vocavit Dominum, sed simpliciter Iudaeum, dicens: *quomodo tu, Iudaeus cum sis, bibere a me poscis?* Hic vero statim cum audit eum fore sibi utilem, et aquam dare posse, Dominum eum vocat; unde *dixit ad eum mulier: Domine, da mihi hanc aquam*. Quia enim hoc carnaliter intelligebat, et duplici corporali necessitate tenebatur, scilicet sitis et laboris, veniendo ad puteum et portando, ideo aquam petens, haec duo allegat, dicens quo ad primum, *ut non sitiam*; et quo ad secundum, *neque veniam huc haurire*. Naturaliter enim homo laborem refugit; Ps. LXXII, 5: *in labore hominum non sunt*.

590. *Dixit ei Iesus: vade*, etc. Hic ponitur responsio Domini. Sed sciendum est, quod Dominus respondebat spiritualiter, sed mulier intellexit carnaliter: et ideo potest hoc dupliciter exponi. Uno modo secundum Chrysostomum, qui dicit, quod Dominus volebat dare aquam spiritualis doctrinae non sibi soli, sed specialiter viro suo; quia, ut dicitur I Cor. c. XI, 3, *caput mulieris vir*, et ideo voluit ut praecepta Dei ad mulieres per virum devenirent, I Cor. XIV, 35, dicitur quod *si mulier aliquid addiscere vult, domi virum interroget*. Et ideo dicit *vade, voca virum tuum, et veni huc*; et tunc cum eo et per eum dabo tibi.

Alio modo, secundum Augustinum, exponitur mystice. Nam sicut de aqua Dominus figurative loquebatur, ita de viro. Vir autem iste, secundum Augustinum, est intellectus: nam voluntas parit et concipit a vi apprehensiva movente eam: unde voluntas est sicut mulier; ratio vero movens voluntatem est vir eius. Quia ergo mulier, idest voluntas, prompta erat ad recipiendum, sed non movebatur ab intellectu et ratione, ut specialiter hoc intelligeret sed adhuc sub sensu detinebatur, ideo Dominus dixit ei *vade*, tu sensualis, *voca virum tuum*, idest, rationabilem intellectum advoca, quo spiritualiter et intelligibiliter intelligas quod modo carnaliter sapis; *et veni huc*, intelligendo ducta ratione.

591. *Respondit mulier*, etc. Hic convincitur a Christo mulier. Et

primo ponitur eius responsio;

secundo contestatio qua convincitur a Christo, ibi *bene dixisti*.

592. Circa primum sciendum est, quod mulier turpitudinem suam occultare volens, et Christum sicut purum hominem credens, licet verum responderit Christo, tamen ficte et occulte dedecus suum tacebat; quia, secundum quod dicitur Eccli. IX, 10: *mulier fornicaria quasi stercus in via conculcabitur*. Et ideo *respondit et*

Second, Christ's answer, at *Jesus said to her: go, call your husband*.

589. We should note with respect to the first that at the beginning of this conversation the woman did not refer to Christ as *Lord*, but simply as a Jew, for she said: *how is it that you, being a Jew, ask me for a drink, who am a Samaritan woman?* (John 4:9). But now as soon as she hears that he can be of use to her and give her water, she calls him Lord: *the woman said to him: Lord, give me this water*. For she was thinking of natural water, and was subject to the two natural necessities of thirst and labor, that is, of going to the well and of carrying the water. So she mentions these two things when asking for the water: saying in reference to the first, *so that I may not thirst*; and in reference to the second, *nor come here to draw*, for man naturally shrinks from labor: *they do not labor as other men* (Ps 72:5).

590. Then, at *Jesus said to her: go, call your husband*, the answer of Jesus is given. Here we should note that our Lord answered her in a spiritual way, but she understood in a sensual way. Accordingly, this can be explained in two ways. One way is that of Chrysostom, who says that our Lord intended to give the water of spiritual instruction not only to her, but especially to her husband, for as is said, *man is the head of woman* (1 Cor 11:3), so that Christ wanted God's precepts to reach women through men, and *if the wife wishes to learn anything, let her ask her husband at home* (1 Cor 14:35). So he says, *go, call your husband and then come back here*; and then I will give it to you with him and through him.

Augustine explains it another way, mystically. For as Christ spoke symbolically of water, he did the same of her husband. Her husband, according to Augustine, is the intellect: for the will brings forth and conceives because of the cognitive power that moves it; thus the will is like a woman, while the reason, which moves the will, is like her husband. Here the woman, i.e., the will, was ready to receive, but was not moved by the intellect and reason to a correct understanding, but was still detained on the level of sense. For this reason the Lord said to her, *go*, you who are still sensual, *call your husband*, call in the reasoning intellect so you can understand in a spiritual and intellectual way what you now perceive in a sensual way; and then *come back here*, by understanding under the guidance of reason.

591. Here, at *the woman answered and said: I have no husband*, the woman is found guilty by Christ.

First, her answer is set down.

Second, the encounter in which she is found guilty by Christ, at *you have said well*.

592. As to the first, we should note that the woman, desiring to hide her wrongdoing, and regarding Christ as only a mere man, did answer Christ truthfully, although she keep silent about her sin, for as we read, *a fornicating woman will be walked on like dung in the road* (Sir 9:10). *The woman answered and said: I have no husband*. This was true; for

dixit: *virum non habeo*. Et verum erat: quia licet ante plures habuerit, scilicet quinque, nunc vero non legitimum habebat virum, sed cuidam adhaeserat; et ideo convincitur a Domino.

593. Unde dicit *dixit ei Iesus: bene dixisti, quia non habeo virum*, scilicet legitimum; *quinque enim viros habuisti*, ante ipsum, et nunc quem habes, idest hoc modo uteris ut viro, *non est tuus vir*; hoc vere dixisti: quia virum non habes. Ideo autem dixit ei Dominus ea quae ab ea non didicerat, et occulta sibi videbantur, ut mulierem ad spiritualem intelligentiam reducat et credat, in Christo aliquid divinum esse.

594. Mystice autem quinque viri sunt quinque libri Moysi, quia Samaritani, ut dictum est, eos recipiebant; et ideo dicit *quinque enim viros habuisti; et nunc quem habes*, idest quem audis, scilicet Christum, *non est tuus vir*, quia non credis.

Sed, ut dicit Augustinus, haec expositio non est bona, quia mulier ista dimissis quinque viris, venit ad hunc quem habebat, sed isti qui veniunt ad Christum, non dimiserunt quinque libros Moysi. Et ideo aliter dicendum, quod *quinque viros habuisti*, idest quinque sensus, quibus usque modo utebaris; sed hunc *quem habes*, scilicet rationem errantem, qua spiritualiter dicta adhuc carnaliter intelligis, *non est tuus vir*, legitimus, sed adulter; et ideo tolle istum adulterum errorem, qui te corrumpit et *voca virum tuum*, idest intellectum, ut intelligas me.

595. Hic agitur de petitione qua donum acquiritur, quae est oratio. Et

primo ponitur quaestio mulieris de oratione;

secundo responsio Christi, ibi *dixit ei Iesus: mulier, crede mihi*.

Circa primum duo facit mulier.

Primo confitetur idoneitatem Christi ad respondendum quaestioni;

secundo quaestionem proponit, ibi *patres nostri in monte hoc adoraverunt*, etc.

596. Mulier autem ista auditis quae Christus de occultis ei manifestaverat, quem usque modo purum hominem credidit, nunc prophetam confitetur, idoneum ad satisfaciendum de dubiis. Hoc est proprium prophetarum, ut absentia et incognita annuntient; I Reg. IX, 9: *qui olim dicebatur videns, nunc dicitur propheta*. Et ideo dicit *Domine, ut video, propheta es tu*; quasi dicat: in hoc quod occulta mihi dicis, ostenderis propheta. In quo, secundum Augustinum, patet quod coepit ad eam venire vir, sed non plene venit: quia dominum prophetam putabat: licet enim propheta esset, Matth. XIII, 57: *non est propheta sine honore nisi in patria sua*: tamen erat plusquam propheta, quia prophetas ipse constituit;

although she previously had a number of husbands, five of them, she did not now have a lawful husband, but was just living with a man; and it is for this that the Lord judges her.

593. Then the Evangelist reports that *Jesus said to her: you have said well, I have no husband, for you have had five husbands, and he whom you have now is not your husband: this you have said truly*. What you said is true, because you do not have a husband. The reason our Lord spoke to her about these things he had not learned from her and which were her secrets, was to bring her to a spiritual understanding so that she might believe there was something divine about Christ.

594. In the mystical sense, her five husbands are the five books of Moses: for, as was said, the Samaritans accepted these. And so Christ says, *you have had five husbands*, and then follows *and he whom you have now*, i.e., he to whom you are now listening, i.e., Christ, *is not your husband*, for you have not believed.

This explanation, as Augustine says, is not very good. For this woman, having left the other five, came to her present husband, but those who come to Christ do not put aside the five books of Moses. We should rather say, *you have had five husbands*, i.e., the five senses, which you have used up to this time; but the man *you have now*, i.e., an erring reason, with which you still understand spiritual things in a sensual way, *is not your husband*, but an adulterer who is corrupting you. *Call your husband*, i.e., your intellect, so that you may really understand me.

595. Now the Evangelist treats of the request by which the gift is obtained, which is prayer.

First there is the woman's inquiry about prayer.

Second, Christ's answer, at *Jesus said to her: woman, believe me*.

Concerning the first the woman does two things.

First, she admits that Christ is qualified to answer her question.

Second, she asks the question, at *our fathers worshipped on this mountain*.

596. And so this woman, hearing what Christ had told her about things that were secret, admits that the one who up to now she believed was a mere man, is a prophet, and capable of settling her doubts. For it is characteristic of prophets to reveal what is not present, and hidden: *he who is now called a prophet was formerly called a seer* (1 Sam 9:9). And so she says, *Lord, I perceive that you are a prophet*. As if to say: you show that you are a prophet by revealing hidden things to me. It is clear from this, as Augustine says, that her husband was beginning to return to her. But he did not return completely because she regarded Christ as a prophet: for although he was a prophet—*a prophet is not without honor except in his own country* (Matt 13:57)—he

Sap. VII, 27: *in animas sanctas per nationes se transfert, amicos Dei et prophetas constituit.*

597. Consequenter ponit quaestionem de oratione, dicens *patres nostri in monte hoc adoraverunt; et vos dicitis quia Ierosolymis est locus ubi adorare oportet.* In quo admiranda est mulieris diligentia, quia mulieres, utpote curiosae et infructuosae, et non solum infructuosae, sed et otiosae, I Tim. V, non de mundanis, non de futuris eum interrogabat, sed de his quae Dei sunt; secundum illud Matth. VI, 33: *primum quaerite regnum Dei.* Et movet primo quaestionem de his quae in terra illa homines movere consueverant, scilicet de loco orationis, de quo quaestio vertebatur inter Iudaeos et Samaritanos; et hoc est quod dicit *patres nostri in monte hoc adoraverunt, et vos dicitis* etc.

Circa quod sciendum est, quod Samaritani (secundum legis mandata) Deum colentes, fecerunt templum, in quo eum adorarent, non euntes in Ierusalem propter Iudaeos eis infestos: quod quidem templum fecerunt in Monte Garizim, Iudaei vero in Monte Sion. Unde quaestio vertebatur inter eos quis istorum montium esset convenientior locus orationi; et utrique adducebant rationes pro parte sua: Samaritani quidem dicebant magis in Monte Garizim esse adorandum, quia antiqui patres adoraverunt ibi Dominum; et ideo dicit *patres nostri in monte hoc adoraverunt.*

598. Sed quomodo dicit mulier *patres nostri*, cum Samaritani non essent ex semine Israel?

Ad hoc est responsio, secundum Chrysostomum, quod aliquid dicunt Abraham in Monte illo filium obtulisse; alii autem in monte Sion, ut habetur Gen. XXII. Vel potest dici, quod *patres nostri* intelligantur Iacob et filii eius, qui, ut habetur Gen. XXXIII, et dictum est supra, habitavit in Sichem, quae est sita iuxta Montem Garizim, et forte ibi adoraverunt in Monte Dominum. Vel potest dici quod filii Israel adoraverunt in monte hoc, quando Moyses praecepit ut ascenderent in montem Garizim ad benedicendum servantibus mandata Domini, ut dicitur Deut. VI.

Et vocat istos patres suos, vel propter legem datam filiis Israel, quam servabant Samaritani, vel propter terram eorum quam inhabitabant, ut dictum est supra. Iudaei autem dicunt orandum esse in Ierusalem auctoritate Domini qui praecepit Deut. XII, 13: *cave ne offeras holocausta tua in omni loco quem videris, sed in loco quem elegerit Dominus Deus tuus*: qui quidem orationis locus primo fuit in Silo, postea vero auctoritate Salomonis et Nathan prophetae, arca Dei portata est de Silo in Ierusalem, et ibi factum est templum, secundum illud Ps. LXXVII, 60: *repulit tabernaculum Silo.* Et postea sequitur: *sed elegit tribum Iuda, montem Sion, quem dilexit.* Sic ergo Samaritani adducebant pro se auctoritatem

was more than a prophet, because he produces prophets: *wisdom produces friends of God and prophets* (Wis 7:27).

597. Then she asks her question about prayer, saying: *our fathers worshipped on this mountain, and you say that Jerusalem is the place where it is fitting for men to worship.* Here we should admire the woman's diligence and attention: for women are considered curious and unproductive, and not only unproductive, but also lovers of ease (1 Tim 5), whereas she did not ask Christ about worldly affairs, or about the future, but about the things of God, in keeping with the advice, *seek first the kingdom of God* (Matt 6:33). She first asks a question about a matter frequently discussed in her country, that is, about the place to pray; this was the subject of argument between Jews and Samaritans. She says, *our fathers worshipped on this mountain, but you say that Jerusalem is the place where it is fitting for men to worship.*

We should mention that the Samaritans, worshiping God according to the precepts of the law, built a temple in which to adore him; and they did not go to Jerusalem where the Jews interfered with them. They built their temple on Mount Gerizim, while the Jews built their temple on Mount Zion. The question they debated was which of these places was the more fitting place of prayer; and each presented reasons for its own side. The Samaritans said that Mount Gerizim was more fitting, because their ancestors worshiped the Lord there. So she says, *our fathers worshipped on this mountain.*

598. How can this woman say, *our fathers*, since the Samaritans were not descended from Israel?

The answer, according to Chrysostom, is that some claim that Abraham offered his son on that mountain; but others claim that is was on Mount Zion (Gen 22). Or, we could say that *our fathers* means Jacob and his sons, who as it is said, lived in Shechem, which is near Mount Gerizim, and who probably worshiped the Lord there on that mountain (Gen 33). Or it could be said that the children of Israel worshiped on this mountain when Moses ordered them to ascend Mount Gerizim that he might bless those who observed God's precepts (Deut 6).

And she calls them her ancestors either because the Samaritains observed the law given to the children of Israel, or because the Samaritans were now living in the land of Israel, as said before. The Jews said that the place to worship was in Jerusalem, by command of the Lord, who, had said: *take care not to offer your holocausts in every place, but offer them in the place the Lord will choose* (Deut 12:13). At first, this place of prayer was in Shiloh, and then after, on the authority of Solomon and the prophet Nathan, the arc was taken from Shiloh to Jerusalem, and it was there the temple was built: so we read: *he left the tabernacle in Shiloh*, and a few verses later, *but he chose the tribe of Judah, Mount Zion, which he loved* (Ps 77:60). Thus the Samaritans appealed to

patrum; Iudaei vero auctoritatem prophetarum, quos Samaritani non recipiebant.

Hanc ergo quaestionem mulier proponit: nec est mirandum a quo docta fuerit, quia communiter contingit ut in terris in quibus diversa sunt dogmata, etiam simplices in eis sint instructi. Unde, quia Samaritani fuerant in continuo iurgio cum Iudaeis, ideo mulieres et simplices in materia ista edocti erant.

599. Consequenter cum dicit **dixit ei Iesus** etc., ponitur responsio Christi. Et

primo distinguit trinam orationem;

secundo comparat eas adinvicem, ibi **vos adoratis quod nescitis**.

600. Circa primum reddit primo mulierem attentam, utpote grandia locuturus, dicens **crede mihi**, et fidem adhibe, quia ubique opus est fide. Hebr. XI, 6: *accedentem ad Deum oportet credere*; Is. VII, 9: *nisi credideritis, non intelligetis*.

Secundo proponit trinam adorationem, quarum duae iam erant, alia vero expectabatur futura. Duarum autem quae erant, una erat Samaritanorum, qua orabant in Monte Garizim; et hanc exprimit dicens **venit hora quando neque in monte hoc**, scilicet Garizim, **adorabitis**. Alia est Iudaeorum qua orabant in Monte Sion, scilicet in Ierusalem; et hanc exprimit dicens **neque in Ierusalem**. Tertia est futura, quae expectatur, quae est alia ab istis; et hanc insinuat excipiendo utramque adorationem: nam si veniat hora quando adorabunt, non tamen in Monte Garizim neque in Ierusalem, manifestum est quod erit tertia adoratio Christi, evacuans utrorumque adorationem. Nam si aliquis vellet duos populos in unum coniungere, oportet in utroque removeri illud in quo abinvicem dissiderent, et aliquid eis commune in quo conveniant, concedere. Christus ergo, volens coniungere Iudaeos et gentiles, removit a Iudaeis caeremonias, et a gentibus idolatriam, quae duo erant sicut paries unus in quo uterque abinvicem dissidebant, et fecit ex utroque populo unum populum secundum illud Eph. c. II, 14: *ipse est pax nostra, qui fecit utraque unum*. Sic ergo cessavit caeremonialis cultus et idolatriam gentium, et sic introductus est verus Dei cultus a Christo.

601. Mystice autem, secundum Origenem, per tres adorationes intelliguntur divinae sapientiae tres participationes.

Quidam namque participant eam obnubilantes tenebris erroris, et isti adorant in monte: quia omnis error ex superbia causatur; Ier. LI, 25: *ecce ego ad te mons pestifer*. Quidam vero participant ipsam divinam sapientiam sine errore, sed imperfecte, quia in speculo et aenigmate; et isti adorant in Ierusalem, quae significat praesentem Ecclesiam; Ps. CXLVI, 2: *aedificans Ierusalem Dominus* etc.

the authority of the patriarchs, and the Jews appealed to the authority of the prophets, whom the Samaritans did not accept.

This is the issue the woman raises. It is not surprising that she was taught about this, for it often happens in places where there are differences in beliefs that even the simple people are instructed about them. Because the Samaritans were continually arguing with the Jews over this, it came to the knowledge of the women and ordinary people.

599. Christ's answer is now set down, at **Jesus said to her: woman, believe me**.

First he distinguishes three types of prayer.

Second, he compares them to each other, at **you adore that which you do not know**.

600. As to the first, he first of all gains the woman's attention, to indicate that he was about to say something important, saying, **believe me**, and have faith, for faith is always necessary: *to come to God, one must believe* (Heb 11:6); *if you do not believe, you will not understand* (Isa 7:9).

Second, he mentions the three kinds of worship: two of these were already being practiced, and the third was to come. Of the two that were current, one was practiced by the Samaritans, who worshiped on Mount Gerizim; he refers to this when he says, **the hour is coming, when you shall adore the Father neither on this mountain**, of Gerizim. The other way was that of the Jews, who prayed on Mount Zion; and he refers to this when he says, **nor in Jerusalem**. The third type of worship was to come, and it was different from the other two. Christ alludes to this by excluding the other two: for if the hour is coming when they will no longer worship on Mount Gerizim or in Jerusalem, then clearly the third type to which Christ refers will be a worship that does away with the other two. For if someone wishes to unite two people, it is necessary to eliminate that over which they disagree, and give them something in common on which they will agree. And so Christ, wishing to unite the Jews and gentiles, eliminated the observances of the Jews and the idolatry of the gentiles; for these two were like a wall separating the peoples. And he made the two people one: *he is our peace, he who has made the two of us one* (Eph 2:14). Thus the ritual observances and the idolatry of the gentiles were abolished, and the true worship of God established by Christ.

601. As for the mystical sense, and according to Origen, the three types of worship are three kinds of participation in divine wisdom.

Some participate in it under a dark cloud of error, and these adore on the mountain: for every error springs from pride: *I am against you, destroying mountain* (Jer 51:25). Others participate in divine wisdom without error, but in an imperfect way, because they see in a mirror and in an obscure way; and these worship in Jerusalem, which signifies the present Church: *the Lord is building Jerusalem* (Ps 146:2). But the blessed and the saints participate in

Beati vero et sancti participant illam sine errore perfecte, quia vident Deum sicuti est, ut dicitur I Io. III.

Et ideo dicit *venit hora*, idest expectabitur, quando neque in erroribus, neque per speculum et in aenigmate participabitis divinam sapientiam, sed sicuti est.

602. Consequenter cum dicit *vos adoratis quod nescitis*, comparat praedictas adorationes ad invicem: et

primo comparat secundam ad primam;

secundo tertiam ad primam et secundam, ibi *sed venit hora*.

Circa primum tria facit.

Primo ostendit defectum primae adorationis;

secundo veritatem secundae;

tertio rationem utriusque assignat.

603. Quantum ad primum dicit *vos adoratis quod nescitis*.

Sed videtur alicui quod Dominus explicare debuisset veritatem quaestionis, et rationem mulieris exsolvere. Sed Dominus de hoc non curat, quia utraque adoratio cessare debebat.

Quantum autem ad hoc quod dicit *vos adoratis*, sciendum est, quod Philosophus dicit, aliter est cognitio in rebus compositis, et aliter in simplicibus. Nam composita quidem possunt quantum ad aliquid cognosci, ita ut quantum ad aliquid in eis remaneant incognita: unde potest de his haberi falsa cognitio. Sicut si aliquis habens veram cognitionem de animali quantum ad eius substantiam, tamen potest errare circa cognitionem accidentis, utrum scilicet sit album vel nigrum; et differentiae, utrum scilicet sit alatum vel quadrupes. In simplicibus autem nullo modo potest esse falsa cognitio: quia aut perfecte cognoscuntur, inquantum scitur eorum quidditas; aut nullo modo cognoscuntur, si non possit ad eam attingi. Cum ergo Deus sit omnino simplex, non potest de eo haberi falsa cognitio per hoc quod aliquid de eo sciatur et aliquid nesciatur, sed per hoc quod non attingitur. Unde quicumque credit Deum esse aliquid quod non est, puta corpus, vel aliquid huiusmodi, non adorat Deum, quia nescit eum, sed aliquid aliud.

Samaritani autem falsam opinionem habebant de Deo dupliciter. Primo, quia aestimabant eum esse corporeum, unde et credebant ipsum in uno loco corporeo tantum determinate ibidem adorari oportere. Deinde, quia non credebant eum esse super omnia, sed aequalem aliquibus creaturis: unde simul cum eo et idola adorabant, quasi sibi aequalia. Et ideo nesciebant eum, quia non attingebat ad veram cognitionem eius. Et ideo dicit Dominus *vos adoratis quod nescitis*; idest, non adoratis Deum, quia nescitis ipsum, sed phantasiam vestram,

divine wisdom without error in a perfect way, for they see God as he is (1 John 3:2).

And so Christ says, *the hour is coming*, i.e., is waited for, when you will participate in divine wisdom neither in error nor in a mirror in an obscure way, but as it is.

602. Then, at *you adore that which you do not know*, he compares the different kinds of worship to each other.

First, he compares the second to the first,

Second, the third to the first and second, at *but the hour is coming*.

As to the first he does three things.

First, he shows the shortcomings of the first type of worship.

Second, the truth of the second.

Third, the reason for each statement.

603. As to the first he says, *you adore that which you do not know*.

Some might think that the Lord should have explained the truth of the matter and solve the woman's problem. But the Lord does not bother to do so because each of these kinds of worship was due to end.

As to his saying, *you adore*, and so on, it should be pointed out that, as the Philosopher says, knowledge of complex things is different than knowledge of simple things. For something can be known about complex things in such a way that something else about them remains unknown; thus there can be false knowledge about them. For example, if someone has true knowledge of an animal as to its substance, he might be in error touching the knowledge of one of its accidents, such as whether it is black or white; or of a difference, such as whether it has wings or is four-footed. But there cannot be false knowledge of simple things: because they are either perfectly known inasmuch as their quiddity is known; or they are not known at all, if one cannot attain to a knowledge of them. Therefore, since God is absolutely simple, there cannot be false knowledge of him in the sense that something might be known about him and something remain unknown, but only in the sense that knowledge of him is not attained. Accordingly, anyone who believes that God is something that he is not, for example, a body, or something like that, does not adore God but something else, because he does not know him, but something else.

Now the Samaritans had a false idea of God in two ways. First of all, because they thought he was corporeal, so that they believed that he should be adored in only one definite corporeal place. Further, because they did not believe that he transcended all things, but was equal to certain creatures, they adored along with him certain idols, as if they were equal to him. Consequently, they did not know him, because they did not attain to a true knowledge of him. So the Lord says, *you adore that which you do not know*, i.e., you do not adore God because you do not know him, but

qua aliquid apprehenditis ut Deum; Eph. IV, 17: *sicut et gentes ambulant in vanitate sensus sui* etc.

604. Quantum vero ad secundum, scilicet quantum ad diversitatem adorationis Iudaeorum, dicit **nos adoramus quod scimus**. Et connumerat se Iudaeis, quia et Iudaeus erat secundum gentem, et etiam mulier opinabatur eum et prophetam et Iudaeum esse. **Nos adoramus quod scimus**: quia Iudaei per legem et prophetas veram cognitionem seu aestimationem de Deo habebant, in hoc quod non credebant ipsum esse corporeum, nec in uno loco determinato esse, quasi eius maiestas a loco capi possit; III Reg. VIII, 27: *si enim caeli caelorum te capere non possunt, quanto magis domus haec quam aedificavi?* Nec etiam idola colebant; et ideo in Ps. LXXV, v. 2 dicitur: *notus in Iudaea Deus*.

605. Rationem autem huius assignat cum dicit **quia salus ex Iudaeis est**; quasi dicat: ideo vera notitia de Deo habebatur solum a Iudaeis, quia futurum erat quod salus ex Iudaeis proveniret; et sicut principium sanitatis debet esse sanum, ita principium salutis, quae habetur per Dei veram cognitionem et verum cultum, oportet veram cognitionem de Deo habere: et ideo, quia ex eis principium salutis et causa, scilicet Christus, provenire debebat, secundum illud Gen. c. XXII, 18: *in semine tuo benedicentur omnes gentes*, oportet Deum notum esse in Iudaea.

606. Provenit autem ex Iudaeis salus tripliciter. Primo quantum ad doctrinam veritatis, quia omnes gentes erant in erroribus; Iudaei autem in veritate permanebant; Rom. c. III, 2: *quid amplius est Iudaeo? Quia tradita sunt eis eloquia Dei*.

Secundo quantum ad spiritualia dicta: nam prophetia, et alia dona Spiritus Sancti, prius eis data fuerunt, et ex eis devenerunt ad alios; Rom. XI, 17: *tu*, scilicet gentiles, *cum esses oleaster, insertus es in illis*, scilicet Iudaei; Rom. XV, 27: *nam si spiritualium eorum*, scilicet Iudaeorum, *participes facti sunt gentiles, debent et in carnalibus ministrare illis*.

Tertio quantum ad ipsum salutis auctorem, quia ex eis processit secundum carnem; Rom. c. IX, 5: *ex quibus Christus est secundum carnem*.

607. Consequenter cum dicit **sed venit hora** etc. comparat aliam adorationem duabus primis: et

primo ponit eminentiam eius ad alias;

secundo praeeminentiae convenientiam, ibi **nam et pater tales quaerit**.

608. Sed attendendum est circa primum, secundum Origenem, quod supra loquens de tertia adoratione, cum dixit **venit hora quando non in monte hoc neque in Ierosolymis adorabitis Patrem**, non addidit Dominus, et nunc est; hic vero de ipsa loquens, dicit **venit hora, et nunc est**: quia tunc locutus est de adoratione in Patria, secundum quam perfectam Dei cognitionem

only an imaginary being you think is God, *as the gentiles do, with their foolish ideas* (Eph 4:17).

604. As to the second, i.e., the truth of the worship of the Jews, he says, **we adore that which we do know**. He includes himself among the Jews, because he was a Jew by race, and because the woman thought he was a prophet and a Jew. **We adore that which we do know**, because through the law and the prophets the Jews acquired a true knowledge or opinion of God, in that they did not believe that he was corporeal nor in one definite place, as though his greatness could be enclosed in a place: *if the heavens, and the heavens of the heavens cannot contain you, how much less this house that I have built?* (1 Kgs 8:27). And neither did they worship idols: *God is known in Judah* (Ps 75:2).

605. He gives the reason for this when he says, **for salvation is of the Jews**. As if to say: the true knowledge of God was possessed exclusively by the Jews, for it had been determined that salvation would come from them. And as the source of health should itself be healthy, so the source of salvation, which is acquired by the true knowledge and the true worship of God, should possess the true knowledge of God. Thus, since the source of salvation and its cause, i.e., Christ, was to come from them, according to the promise: *all the nations will be blessed in your descendents* (Gen 22:18), it was fitting that God be known in Judah.

606. Salvation comes from the Jews in three ways. First in their teaching of the truth, for all other peoples were in error, while the Jews held fast to the truth: *what advantage do Jews have? First, they were entrusted with the words of God* (Rom 3:2).

Second, in their spiritual gifts: for prophecy and the other gifts of the Spirit were given to them first, and from them they reached others: *you*, i.e., the gentiles, *a wild olive branch, are ingrafted on them*, i.e., on the Jews (Rom 11:17); *if the gentiles have become sharers in their*, namely the Jews', *spiritual goods, they ought to help the Jews as to earthly goods* (Rom 15:27).

Third, since the very author of salvation is from the Jews according to the flesh, since *Christ came from then in the flesh* (Rom 9:5).

607. Now, at **but the hour is coming**, he compares the third kind of worship to the first two.

First, he mentions its superiority to the others.

Second, how appropriate this kind of worship is, at **for the Father also seeks such to adore him**.

608. As to the first point, we should note, as Origen says, that when speaking above of the third kind of worship, the Lord said, **the hour is coming, when you shall adore the Father neither on this mountain nor in Jerusalem**; but he did not then add: *and is now here*. But now, in speaking of it, he does say, **the hour is coming, and now is**. The reason is because the first time he was speaking of the worship found

participabimus, quae nondum viventibus in hac carne mortali venit; hic vero loquitur de ea quae est in vita ista, quae iam venit per Christum.

609. Et ideo dicit *venit hora, et nunc est, quando veri adoratores adorabunt Patrem in spiritu et veritate.* Quod potest legi primo quidem, secundum Chrysostomum, ut per hoc totum ostendatur eminentia istius adorationis ad adorationem Iudaeorum, ut sit sensus: sicut adoratio Iudaeorum praeeminet adorationi Samaritanorum, ita adoratio Christianorum praeeminet ei quae est Iudaeorum; et hoc in duobus. Primo, quia illa est secundum carnales caeremonias, Hebr. IX, 10: *in iustitiis carnis usque ad tempus correctionis impositis,* haec vero est secundum spiritum.

Secundo vero, quia illa est secundum figuras: nam Deo illae victimae, secundum quod sunt res quaedam, non placebant; unde in Ps. XLIX, 13, dicitur: *numquid manducabo carnes taurorum, aut sanguinem hircorum potabo?* Et alibi, Ps. l, 18: *sacrificium dedissem utique: holocaustis non delectaberis,* inquantum scilicet sunt res quaedam; sed delectabatur in eis inquantum erant figura verae victimae, et veri sacrificii; Hebr. X, 1: *umbram habet lex futurorum bonorum, non rerum ipsam imaginem* etc. Haec autem adoratio est in veritate, quia ipsa secundum se Deo placet. Supra I, 17: *gratia et veritas per Iesum Christum facta est.*

Et ideo quantum ad primum dicit, quod *veri adoratores adorabunt in spiritu,* non in caeremoniis carnalibus; quantum ad secundum dicit *in veritate,* non in figura .

610. Secundo potest legi quod Dominus per haec duo quae dicit, scilicet *in spiritu et veritate,* vult ostendere differentiam huius adorationis, non tantum ad illam Iudaeorum, verum etiam ad eam quae erat Samaritanorum. Ad illam quidem Iudaeorum, per hoc quod dicitur *et veritate:* nam illa, ut dictum est, cum errore erat, quia adorabant quod nesciebant, ista vero est cum vera Dei cognitione.

611. Tertio modo legitur ut per hoc quod dicit *in spiritu et veritate,* ostendatur conditio verae adorationis.

Ad hoc enim quod adoratio vera sit, duo requiruntur. Unum quod sit spiritualis: unde dicit *in spiritu,* idest in fervore spiritus; I Cor. XIV, 15: *orabo spiritu, orabo et mente;* Eph. V, 19: *psallentes in cordibus vestris Deo.* Aliud, quod sit in veritate. Primo quidem fidei, quia nullus fervor spiritualis desiderii est ad merendum idoneus, nisi adsit veritas fidei; Iac. I, 6: *postulet autem in fide nihil haesitans.* Secundo vero *in veritate,* idest sine fictione et simulatione: contra quod dicitur Matth. VI, 5: *amant in angulis orare, ut videantur ab hominibus.* Sic ergo ad ipsam orationem requiritur fervor caritatis quantum ad primum, et veritas fidei quantum ad secundum, et rectitudo intentionis quantum ad tertium.

in heaven, when we will participate in the perfect knowledge of God, which is not possessed by those still living in this mortal life. But now he is speaking of the worship of this life, and which has now come through Christ.

609. So he says, **but the hour is coming, and now is, when the true adorers shall worship the Father in spirit and in truth**. We can understand this, as Chrysostom does, as showing the superiority of this worship to that of the Jews. So that the sense is: just as the worship of the Jews is superior to that of the Samaritans, so the worship of the Christians is superior to that of the Jews. It is superior in two respects. First, because the worship of the Jews is in bodily rites: *rites for the body, imposed only until the time they are reformed* (Heb 9:10); while the worship of the Christians is in spirit.

Second, because the worship of the Jews is in symbols: for the Lord was not pleascd with their sacrificial victims insofar as they were things; so we read, *shall I eat the flesh of bulls, or drink the blood of goats?* (Ps 49:13). and again, *you would not be pleased with a holocaust* (Ps 50:18), that is, as a particular thing; but such a sacrificial victim would be pleasing to the Lord as a symbol of the true victim and of the true sacrifice: *the law has only a shadow of the good things to come* (Heb 10:1). But the worship of the Christians is in truth, because it is pleasing to God in itself: **grace and truth came through Jesus Christ** (John 1:17).

And thus, as to the first, he says that **true adorers shall worship in spirit**, not in bodily rites,; as to the second he says **and in truth**, not in symbols.

610. This passage can in interpreted in a second way, by saying that when our Lord says, **in spirit and in truth**, he wants to show the difference between the third kind of worship and not just that of the Jews, but also that of the Samaritans. In this case, **in truth**, refers to the Jews: for the Samaritans, as was said, were in error, because they worshiped what they did not understand. But the Jews worshiped with a true knowledge of God.

611. **In spirit and in truth** can be understood in a third way, as indicating the characteristics of true worship.

For two things are necessary for a true worship: one is that the worship be spiritual; so he says, **in spirit**, i.e., with fervor of spirit: *I will pray with spirit, and I will pray with my mind* (1 Cor 14:15); *singing to the Lord in your hearts* (Eph 5:19). Second, the worship should be in truth.First, in the truth of faith, because no fervent spiritual desire is meritorious unless united to the truth of faith, *ask with faith, without any doubting* (Jas 1:6). Second, **in truth**, i.e., without pretense or hypocrisy; against such attitudes we read: *they like to pray at street corners, so people can see them* (Matt 6:5). This prayer, then, requires three things: first, the fervor of love; second, the truth of faith; and third, a correct intention.

Sed dicit *Patrem*, quia adoratio legis non erat Patris, sed Domini. Nos adoramus ut filii per amorem, illi vero adorabant ut servi per timorem.

612. Sic ergo hoc quod dicit *veri*, opponitur contra tria, secundum dictas expositiones. Primo contra falsum adorationis ritum Samaritanorum; Eph. IV, 25: *deponentes mendacium, loquimini veritatem.* Secundo contra vanum et transitorium quod erat in caeremoniis carnalibus; Ps. IV, 3: *ut quid diligitis vanitatem, et quaeritis mendacium?* Tertio contra figurale; supra I, 17: *gratia et veritas per Iesum Christum facta est.*

613. Consequenter, cum dicit *nam et Pater tales quaerit*, ostendit convenientiam tertiae adorationis ex duobus.

Primo ex voluntate et acceptione eius qui adoratur;

secundo ex ipsius natura, ibi *spiritus est Deus*.

614. Circa primum sciendum est quod ad hoc quod homo mereatur quod petit accipere, ea debet petere quae non sint contra voluntatem dantis, et eo modo quo acceptum est danti; et ideo cum oramus Deum, esse debemus quales Deus quaerit: Deus autem tales quaerit qui scilicet eum adorent in spiritu et veritate, et in fervore caritatis, et veritate fidei; Deut. X, 12: *et nunc, Israel, quid Dominus Deus tuus petit a te, nisi ut timeas Dominum Deum tuum, et ambules in viis eius, et diligas eum, ac servias Domino Deo tuo in toto corde tuo, ut bene sit tibi?* Mich. c. VI, 8: *indicabo tibi, o homo, quid sit bonum, et quid Deus requirat a te: utique facere iudicium, et diligere misericordiam, et sollicitum ambulare cum Deo tuo.*

615. Hoc autem ostendit ex natura ipsius, dicens *spiritus est Deus*: nam, sicut dicitur Eccli. XIII, 19: *omne animal diligit sibi simile*, ergo Deus intantum diligit nos, inquantum ei assimilamur; sed non assimilamur ei secundum carnalia, quia est incorporeus, sed secundum spiritualia, quia *Deus spiritus est*; Eph. IV, 23: *renovamini spiritu mentis vestrae.*

Hoc autem quod dicit *spiritus est Deus*, denotat in Deo incorporeitatem; Lc. ult., 39: *spiritus carnem et ossa non habet.* Item vivificationem, quia tota vita nostra est a Deo, ut a principio effectivo. Est etiam Deus veritas; infra XIV, 6: *ego sum via, veritas et vita*: et ideo in spiritu et veritate oportet adorare eum.

616. Consequenter cum dicit *dixit ei mulier* etc. agitur hic de datore doni: quod respondet ei quod Dominus dixerat *si scires donum Dei, et quis est qui dicit tibi, da mihi bibere, petisses utique.* Et

primo ponitur confessio mulieris;

secundo doctrina Christi, ibi *ego sum qui loquor tecum.*

Circa primum duo facit:

He says, **the Father**, because under the law, worship was not given to the Father, but to the Lord. We worship in love, as sons; whereas they worshiped in fear, as slaves.

612. He says **true adorers**, in opposition to three things mentioned in the above interpretations. First, in opposition to the false worship of the Samaritans: *put aside what is not true, and speak the truth* (Eph 4:25). Second, in opposition to the fruitless and transitory character of bodily rites: *why do you love what is without profit, and seek after lies* (Ps 4:3). Third, it is opposed to what is symbolic: **grace and truth came through Jesus Christ** (John 1:17).

613. Then when he says, **for the Father also seeks such to adore him**, he shows that this third kind of worship is appropriate for two reasons.

First, because the one worshiped wills and accepts this worship.

Second, because of the nature of the one worshiped, at **God is spirit**.

614. Concerning the first, we should note that for a man to merit receiving what he asks, he should ask for things which are not in opposition to the will of the giver, and also ask for them in a way which is acceptable to the giver. And so when we pray to God, we ought to be such as God seeks. But God seeks those who will worship him in spirit and in truth, in the fervor of love and in the truth of faith: *and now, Israel, what does the Lord your God want from you, but that you fear the Lord your God, and walk in his ways, and love him, and serve the Lord your God with all your heart?* (Deut 10:12); *I will show you, man, what is good, and what the Lord requires of you: to do what is right, and to love mercy, and to walk attentively with your God* (Mic 6:8).

615. Then he shows that the third type of worship is appropriate from the very nature of God, saying, **God is spirit**. As is said, *every animal loves its like* (Sir 13:19); and so God loves us insofar as we are like him. But we are not like him by our body, because he is incorporeal, but in what is spiritual in us, for **God is spirit**: *be renewed in the spirit, of your mind* (Eph 4:23).

In saying, **God is spirit**, he means that God is incorporeal: *a spirit does not have flesh and bones* (Luke 24:39); and also that he is a life-giver, because our entire life is from God, as its creative source. God is also truth: **I am the way, and the truth, and the life** (John 14:6). Therefore, we should worship him in spirit and in truth.

616. When he says, **the woman said to him**, he mentions the one who gives the gift; and this corresponds to what our Lord said before, **if you knew the gift of God, and who it is who says to you, give me a drink, you perhaps would have asked of him**.

First, we have the woman's profession.

Second, the teaching of Christ, at **I am he, who is speaking with you**.

As to the first, he does two things.

primo enim profitetur mulier fidem Christi venturi;

secundo perfectionem doctrinae eius, ibi **cum ergo venerit, ille annuntiabit nobis omnia**.

617. Sciendum est ergo, quod mulier eorum quae dicta sunt altitudine fatigata, obstupuit, ea capere non valens. Dicit **scio quia Messias venit, qui dicitur Christus**; quasi dicat: ista verba non capio; sed veniet tempus quando veniet Messias, et tunc sciemus omnia ista: **Messias** enim Hebraice, *unctus* Latine, Graece **Christus** est. Sciebat autem mulier ista Messiam venturum, edocta per libros Moysi, ubi Christi adventus praenuntiatus est; Gen. penult., 10: *non auferetur sceptrum de Iuda, et dux de femore eius, donec veniat qui mittendus est.* Sicut autem Augustinus dicit, haec est prima locutio mulieris in qua nominat Christum: ut det intelligere, quod post quinque sensus corporeos, iam inciperet redire ad virum legitimum.

618. Hic autem Messias cum venerit, perfectam doctrinam proponet, cum dicit **cum ergo venerit, ille annuntiabit nobis**. Et hoc praedixerat Moyses; Deut. XVIII, 18: *prophetam suscitabo eis de medio fratrum suorum, similem eis; et ponam verba mea in ore eius, loqueturque ad eos omnia quae praecepero illi.*

Et quia iam advocaverat mulier ista virum suum, intellectum scilicet et rationem, ideo Dominus aquam doctrinae spiritualis ei propinat, optime manifestando se ei.

619. Et ideo dicitur **dixit ei Iesus: ego sum qui loquor tecum**, scilicet Christus; Sap. VI, 14: *praeoccupat eos qui se concupiscunt, ut illis se prior ostendat*; infra XIV, v. 21: **ego diligam eum, et manifestabo ei meipsum**.

Non autem Deus manifestavit se mulieri a principio: quia forte credidisset, et visum fuisset sibi ex vanitate loqui. Nunc autem paulatim in cognitione Christi eam reducens, opportune revelavit se ipsum; Prov. XXV, 11: *mala aurea in lectis argenteis, qui loquitur verbum in tempore suo.* Et quidem interrogatur a Pharisaeis, utrum esset Christus, infra X, 24: **si tu es Christus, dic nobis palam**, et tamen eis non se manifeste revelavit, quia non ad discendum quaerebant, sed ad tentandum. Haec vero simplici mente loquebatur.

First, the woman professes her faith in the Christ to come.

Second, in the fullness of his teaching, at **therefore, when he has come, he will tell us all things**.

617. The woman, wearied by the profound nature of what Christ was saying, was confused and unable to understand all this. She says: **I know that the Messiah is coming, who is called the Christ**. As if to say: I do not understand what you are saying, but a time will come when the Messiah will arrive, and then we will understand all these things. For **Messiah** in Hebrew means the same as *anointed one* in Latin, and **Christ** in Greek. She knew that the Messiah was coming because she had been taught by the books of Moses, which foretell the coming of Christ: *the scepter will not be taken away from Judah . . . until he who is to be sent comes* (Gen 49:10). As Augustine says, this is the first time the woman mentions the name *Christ*: and we see by this that she is now beginning to return to her lawful husband.

618. When this Messiah comes, he will give us a complete teaching. Hence she says, **when he has come, he will tell us all things**. This was foretold by Moses: *I will raise up a prophet for them, from among their own brothers, like them; and I will put my words in his mouth, and he will tell them all I command him* (Deut 18:18).

Because this woman had now called her husband, i.e., intellect and reason, the Lord now offers her the water of spiritual teaching by revealing himself to her in a most excellent way.

619. And so Jesus says: **I am he, who is speaking with you**, i.e., I am the Christ: *wisdom goes to meet those who desire her, so she may first reveal herself to them* (Wis 6:14), and: **I will love him, and will manifest myself to him** (John 14:21).

Our Lord did not reveal himself to this woman at once because it might have seemed to her that he was speaking out of vainglory. But now, having brought her step by step to a knowledge of himself, Christ revealed himself at the appropriate time: *words appropriately spoken are like apples of gold on beds of silver* (Prov 25:11). In contrast, when he was asked by the Pharisees whether he was the Christ, **if you are the Christ, tell us plainly** (John 10:24), he did not reveal himself to them clearly, because they did not ask to learn but to test him. But this woman is speaking in all simplicity.

Lecture 3

4:27 Et continuo venerunt discipuli eius, et mirabantur, quia cum muliere loquebatur. Nemo tamen dixit: quid quaeris, aut quid loqueris cum ea? [n. 621]

4:28 Reliquit ergo hydriam suam mulier, et abiit in civitatem. Et dicit illis hominibus: [n. 624]

4:29 venite, et videte hominem, qui dixit mihi omnia quaecumque feci. Numquid ipse est Christus? [n. 626]

4:30 Exierunt ergo de civitate, et veniebant ad eum. [n. 630]

4:31 Interea rogabant eum discipuli, dicentes: Rabbi, manduca. [n. 632]

4:32 Ille autem dixit eis: ebo cibum habeo manducare, quem vos nescitis. [n. 634]

4:33 Dicebant ergo discipuli ad invicem: numquid aliquis attulit ei manducare? [n. 634]

4:27 Καὶ ἐπὶ τούτῳ ἦλθαν οἱ μαθηταὶ αὐτοῦ καὶ ἐθαύμαζον ὅτι μετὰ γυναικὸς ἐλάλει· οὐδεὶς μέντοι εἶπεν· τί ζητεῖς ἢ τί λαλεῖς μετ᾽ αὐτῆς;

4:28 ἀφῆκεν οὖν τὴν ὑδρίαν αὐτῆς ἡ γυνὴ καὶ ἀπῆλθεν εἰς τὴν πόλιν καὶ λέγει τοῖς ἀνθρώποις·

4:29 δεῦτε ἴδετε ἄνθρωπον ὃς εἶπέν μοι πάντα ὅσα ἐποίησα, μήτι οὗτός ἐστιν ὁ χριστός;

4:30 ἐξῆλθον ἐκ τῆς πόλεως καὶ ἤρχοντο πρὸς αὐτόν.

4:31 Ἐν τῷ μεταξὺ ἠρώτων αὐτὸν οἱ μαθηταὶ λέγοντες· ῥαββί, φάγε.

4:32 ὁ δὲ εἶπεν αὐτοῖς· ἐγὼ βρῶσιν ἔχω φαγεῖν ἣν ὑμεῖς οὐκ οἴδατε.

4:33 ἔλεγον οὖν οἱ μαθηταὶ πρὸς ἀλλήλους· μή τις ἤνεγκεν αὐτῷ φαγεῖν;

4:27 And immediately his disciples came, and they wondered that he talked with the woman. Yet no man said: what do you seek? or, why do you talk with her? [n. 621]

4:28 The woman therefore left her waterpot and went into the city, and said to the men there: [n. 624]

4:29 come, and see a man who has told me all things whatsoever that I have done: is it possible that he is the Christ? [n. 626]

4:30 Therefore they went out of the city and came to him. [n. 630]

4:31 In the meantime, the disciples pleaded with him, saying: Rabbi, eat. [n. 632]

4:32 But he said to them: I have food to eat, which you do not know. [n. 634]

4:33 The disciples therefore said to one another: has anyone brought him something to eat? [n. 634]

---

620. Posita doctrina de aqua spirituali, hic agit de effectu ipsius doctrinae, et

primo proponit ipsum effectum;

secundo ipsum effectum manifestat, ibi *interea rogabant eum discipuli eius.*

Effectus autem huius doctrinae est fructus proveniens ex parte fidelium, et ideo

primo ponitur fructus proveniens ex parte discipulorum admirantium;

secundo fructus proveniens ex parte mulieris virtutem Christi annuntiantis ibi *reliquit ergo hydriam suam mulier.*

621. Tria autem ponuntur quantum ad discipulos: scilicet eorum reditus ad Christum; unde dicit *et continuo venerunt discipuli eius.* Et, ut dicit Chrysostomus, satis opportune, postquam se Christus mulieri manifestavit, discipuli occurrerunt, ut ostendatur, omnia tempora, divina providentia dispensari; Sap. VI, 8: *unumquodque fecit Deus, quia pusillum et magnum; et aequaliter est ei cura de omnibus . . . et in omni providentia occurret illis*; Eccle. VIII, 6: *omni negotio tempus est et opportunitas.*

622. Secundo ponitur eorum admiratio de Christo; unde dicit *et mirabantur, quia cum muliere loquebatur.*

620. After presenting the teaching on spiritual water, the Evangelist now deals with the effect of this teaching.

First, he sets down the effect itself.

Second, he elaborates on it, at *in the meantime, the disciples pleaded with him.*

The effect of this teaching is its fruit for those who believe.

And first we have its fruit which relates to the disciples, who were surprised at Christ's conduct.

Second, its fruit in relation to the woman, who proclaimed Christ's power, at *the woman therefore left her waterpot.*

621. We are told three things about the disciples. First, their return to Christ: he says, *and immediately his disciples came*, returning at this point. As Chrysostom reminds us, it was very convenient that the disciples returned after Christ had revealed himself to the woman, since this shows us that all events are regulated by divine providence: *he made the small and the great, and takes care for all alike* (Wis 6:8); *there is a time and fitness for everything* (Eccl 8:6).

622. Second, we see their surprise at what Christ was doing; he says, *they wondered that he talked with the*

Mirabantur quidem bonum; sed non suspicabantur malum, ut Augustinus dicit.

Mirabantur autem duo. Primo quidem superabundantem Christi mansuetudinem et humilitatem: quia Dominus orbis terrarum dignatus est cum inope muliere loqui, et diu, dans in hoc nobis exemplum humilitatis; Eccli. IV, 7: *congregationi pauperum affabilem te facito*.

Secundo quia cum Samaritana et alienigena loquebatur, nescientes mysterium, quod mulier typum Ecclesiae gentium gereret, quam quaerebat qui venit *quaerere et salvum facere quod perierat*: Lc. XIX, 10.

623. Tertio ponitur eorum reverentia ad Christum, quae ostenditur ex taciturnitate eorum. In hoc enim ostendimus reverentiam ad Deum quando facta eius discutere non audemus; Prov. XXV, 2: *gloria Dei est celare verbum, et gloria regum investigare sermonem*. Et ideo dicit, quod licet mirarentur, **nemo tamen dixit**: **quid quaeris, aut quid loqueris cum ea?** Eccli. XXXII, 9: *audi tacens, et pro reverentia accedet tibi bona gratia*.

Sed tamen sic eruditi erant discipuli ordinem servare, ex reverentia et timore filiali ad Christum, ut aliquando quidem confidenter eum interrogent de his quae ad eos pertinebant, scilicet quando Christus aliqua proponebat ad eos pertinentia, quae eorum capacitatem transcendebant; Eccli. XXXII, 10: *adolescens, vix loquere in causa tua*. Aliquando vero eum non interrogent, in his scilicet quae ad eos non pertinebant, sicut hic.

624. Consequenter cum dicit **reliquit ergo hydriam suam mulier, et abiit in civitatem**, ponitur fructus proveniens ex parte mulieris, officium apostolorum annuntiando assumentis: et ponuntur tria, quae colligi possunt ex dictis et factis eius: scilicet devotionis affectus;

secundo praedicationis modus, ibi **dicit illis hominibus: venite, et videte hominem, qui dixit mihi omnia quaecumque feci**;

tertio praedicationis effectus, ibi **et exierunt de civitate, et veniebant ad eum**.

625. Affectus autem mulieris apparet ex duobus. Primo ex hoc quod prae magnitudine devotionis, illud pro quo specialiter venerat ad fontem, quasi oblita, dereliquit aquam et hydriam: unde dicit, quod **reliquit mulier hydriam suam, et abiit in civitatem**, annuntiare scilicet magnalia de Christo, non curans de corporeo commodo propter utilitatem aliorum. In quo sequitur apostolorum exemplum, qui, ut dicitur Matth. IV, 20: *relictis retibus, secuti sunt Dominum*. Per hydriam autem intelligitur cupiditas saeculi, per quam de profundo tenebrarum, cuius imaginem puteus gerit, idest de terrena conversatione, homines hauriunt voluptates. Qui ergo cupiditates

woman. They were amazed at what was good; and as Augustine says, they did not suspect any evil.

They were amazed at two things. First, at the extraordinary gentleness and humility of Christ: for the Lord of the world stooped to speak with a poor woman, and for a long time, giving us an example of humility: *be friendly to the poor* (Sir 4:7).

Second, they were amazed that he was speaking with a Samaritan and a foreigner, for they did not know the mystery by which this woman was a symbol of the Church of the gentiles; and Christ sought the gentiles, for he came *to seek and to save what was lost* (Luke 19:10).

623. Third, we see the disciples' reverence for Christ, shown by their silence. For we show our reverence for God when we do not presume to discuss his affairs: *it is to the glory of God to conceal things; and to the glory of kings to search things out* (Prov 25:2). So the Evangelist says that although his disciples were surprised, **yet no man said**: **what do you seek? or, why do you talk with her?** *Hear in silence, and for they reverence good grace shall come to thee.* (Sir 32:9).

Yet the disciples had been so trained to observe order, because of their reverence and filial fear toward Christ, that now and then they would question him about matters that concerned themselves, i.e., when Christ said things relating to them, but which were beyond their understanding: *young men, speak if you have to* (Sir 32:10). At other times they did not question him; in those matters that were not their business, as here.

624. Then, at **the woman therefore left her waterpot and went into the city**, we have the fruit which relates to the woman; by what she said to her people, she was taking on the role of an apostle. From what she says and does, we can learn three things. First, her affective devotion;

second, her way of preaching, at **come, and see a man who has told me all things whatsoever that I have done**;

third the effect her preaching had, at **therefore they went out of the city and came to him**.

625. Her affection is revealed in two ways. First, because her devotion was so great that she forgot why she had come to the well, and left without the water and her water jar. So he says, **the woman therefore left her waterpot and went into the city**, to announce all the wonders Christ had done; and she was not now concerned for her own bodily comfort but for the welfare of others. In this respect she was like the apostles, who *leaving their nets, followed the Lord* (Matt 4:20). The water jar is a symbol of worldly desires, by which men draw out pleasures from the depths of darkness—symbolized by the well—i.e., from a worldly manner of life. Accordingly, those who abandon worldly desires

saeculi propter Deum derelinquunt, hydriam derelinquunt; II Tim. II, 4: *nemo militans Deo, implicat se negotiis saecularibus.*

Secundo vero apparet ex multitudine eorum quibus annuntiat: quia non uni tantum, nec duobus vel tribus, sed toti civitati, unde **abiit in civitatem**: in quo significatur apostolorum officium, quibus committit Dominus, Matth. ult., 19: *euntes docete omnes gentes*, infra c. XV, 16: **posui vos ut eatis, et fructum afferatis.**

626. Praedicationis autem modus innuitur cum dicit **et dicit illis hominibus** etc., ubi primo invitat ad Christi visionem cum dicit **venite, et videte hominem.** Audierat enim mulier ista a Christo, quod ego sum Christus; sed non statim dixit quod venirent ad Christum, seu crederent, ne daret occasionem blasphemandi; et ideo a principio dixit ea de Christo quae credibilia erant et in propatulo, scilicet quod esset homo; Phil. II, 7: *in similitudinem hominum factus.* Nec dixit credite, sed **venite, et videte**; quia manifeste noverat, quod si gustarent de illo fonte, eum videndo, eadem paterentur quae et ipsa; Ps. c. LXV, 16: *venite, et narrabo quanta fecit animae meae.* Nihilominus tamen in hoc veri praedicatoris imitatur exemplum, non ad se homines, sed ad Christum vocando; II Cor. IV, v. 5: *non enim praedicamus nosmetipsos, sed Christum.*

627. Secundo ponit divinitatis Christi indicium, cum dicit **qui dixit mihi omnia quaecumque feci**, scilicet quot viros habuerat. Hoc enim est divinitatis officium et indicium quod occulta et secreta cordium manifestet. Et licet illa quae fecerat, ad confusionem suam pertinerent, nihilominus tamen non est verecundata referre: nam, ut Chrysostomus dicit, *anima cum ignita fuerit igne divino, ad nihil eorum quae sunt in terra de reliquo respicit, neque ad gloriam, nec ad verecundiam; sed ad illam solam, quae detinet eam, flammam.*

628. Tertio autem concludit Christi maiestatem, dicens **numquid ipse est Christus?** Non est ausa asserendo ostendere quod esset Christus, ne videretur alios velle docere; et ipsi ex hoc irati exire ad eum nollent. Neque tamen totaliter hoc siluit; sed sub quaestione, quasi hoc eorum iudicio committens, proposuit dicens **numquid non ipse est Christus?** Hic enim facilior modus est suadendi.

629. Per hanc autem mulierem, quae infimae conditionis est, signatur apostolorum praedicantium modus: quia, ut dicitur I Cor. c. I, 26: *non multi sapientes, non multi potentes secundum carnem . . . sed quae stulta sunt mundi elegit Deus, ut confundat sapientes.* Unde Prov. IX, 3, ipsi apostoli ancillae dicuntur: *misit*, inquit sapientia divina, scilicet Filius Dei, *ancillas suas*, scilicet apostolos, *vocare ad arcem.*

630. Fructus autem praedicationis ponitur ibi **et exierunt de civitate** ad quam iverat mulier, et veniebant ad ipsum, scilicet Christum: in quo datur intelligi,

for the sake of God leave their water jars: *no soldier of God becomes entangled in the business of this world* (2 Tim 2:4).

Second, we see her affection from the great number of those to whom she brings the news: not to just one or two, but to the entire town; we read that she **went into the city.** This signifies the duty Christ gave to the apostles: *go, teach all nations* (Matt 28:19); and **I have appointed you, that you should go, and should bear fruit** (John 15:16).

626. Next we see her manner of preaching, at **and said to the men there.** She first invites them to see Christ, saying, **come, and see a man.** Although she had heard Christ say that he was the Christ, she did not at once tell the people that they should come to the Christ, or believe, so as not to give them a reason for scoffing. So at first she mentions things that were believable and evident about Christ, as that he was a man: *made in the likeness of men* (Phil 2:7). Neither did she say: believe, but **come, and see**; for she was convinced that if they were to taste from that well by seeing him, they would be affected in the same way she was: *come, and I will tell you the great things he has done for me* (Ps 65:16). In this she is imitating the example of a true preacher, not calling men to himself, but to Christ: *what we preach is not ourselves, but Jesus Christ* (2 Cor 4:5).

627. Second, she mentions a clue to Christ's divinity, saying, **who has told me all things whatsoever that I have done**, that is, how many husbands she had had. For it is the function and sign of the divinity to disclose hidden things and the secrets of hearts. Although the things she had done would cause her shame, she is still not ashamed to mention them; for as Chrysostom says: *when the soul is on fire with the divine fire, it no longer pays attention to earthly things, neither to glory nor to shame, but only to that flame that holds it fast.*

628. Third, she infers the greatness of Christ, saying, **is it possible that he is the Christ?** She did not dare to say that he was the Christ, lest she seem to be trying to teach them; they could have become angry at this and refuse to go with her. Yet she was not entirely silent on this point, but submitting it to their judgment, set it forth in the form of a question, saying, **is it possible that he is the Christ?** For this is an easier way to persuade someone.

629. This woman, who is of humblest condition, signifies the manner of the preching of the apostles, because as it is said: *not many of you are learned in the worldly sense, not many powerful . . . but God chose the simple ones of the world to embarrass the wise* (1 Cor 1:26). Thus the apostles are called handmaids: *she*, divine wisdom, i.e., the Son of God, *sent out her handmaids*, the apostles, *to summon to the tower* (Prov 9:3).

630. The fruit of her preaching is given when he says, **therefore they went out of the city**, to where she had returned, to meet him, Christ. We see by this that if we desire

quod si ad Christum ire volumus, oportet nos exire de civitate; idest, amorem carnalis cupiditatis deponere; Hebr. XIII, 13: *exeamus ad eum extra castra, improperium eius portantes.*

631. Consequenter cum dicit **interea rogabant eum discipuli** etc., manifestatur effectus spiritualis doctrinae: et

primo per doctrinam Christi ad discipulos;

secundo per effectum operis in alios, ibi **ex civitate autem illa multi crediderunt.**

Circa primum duo facit.

Primo ponitur occasio manifestationis huius fructus;

secundo ponitur ipsa manifestatio **ille autem dixit eis: ego cibum habeo manducare quem vos nescitis.**

632. Occasio autem manifestationis sumitur ex instantia discipulorum ad hoc ut Christus manducaret; et ideo dicit **interea**, idest, inter mulieris verba et locutionem Christi cum ea, et inter tempus adventus Samaritanorum, **rogabant eum**, scilicet Christum, **discipuli eius, dicentes: Rabbi, manduca**; arbitrantes hoc tempus fore aptum ad prandium, antequam multitudo eorum concurreret. Non enim coram aliquo advena sibi escas propinabant: unde dicitur Mc. VI, 31, quod tanta multitudo confluebat ad eum, quod non habebat tempus manducandi.

633. Hunc autem fructum manifestat, data sibi occasione dicens **ille autem dixit eis** etc.: ubi

primo ponit fructum figurata locutione;

secundo innuitur tarditas discipulorum ad intelligendum, ibi **dicebant ergo discipuli eius**;

tertio exponit Dominus quae dixerat, ibi **dixit eis Iesus: meus cibus est ut faciam voluntatem eius qui misit me.**

634. Fructus autem spiritualis doctrinae proponitur sub figura cibi et refectionis; et ideo dicit **ego cibum habeo manducare.** Et sciendum quod sicut refectio corporalis non est perfecta nisi cibo iungatur potus, et e converso; ita etiam ad spiritualem refectionem utrumque haberi debet; Eccli. XV, 3: *cibavit illum Dominus pane vitae et intellectus,* ecce cibus, *et aqua sapientiae salutaris,* ecce potus, *potavit illum.* Ideo congrue post poculi negotium, quo Samaritana potata fuerat, conveniens erat et de cibo disceptare: et sicut per aquam intelligitur sapientia salutaris, ita per cibum intelligitur operatio bona.

Cibus autem iste quem Christus manducare habebat, est salus hominum, quam quaerebat: ostendens per hoc quod dicit se cibum habere manducare, quantum desiderium habet salutis nostrae. Sicut enim nobis cum esurimus, concupiscibile est manducare, ita et ei salvare nos; Prov. VIII, 31: *deliciae meae sunt esse cum*

to come to Christ, we must set out from the town, i.e., leave behind our carnal desires: *let us go out to him outside the camp, bearing the abuse he took* (Heb 13:13).

631. Now, at **in the meantime, the disciples pleaded with him**, the effect of this spiritual teaching is elaborated.

First, by what Christ said to his disciples;

second, by the effect of all this on the Samaritans, at **now many of the Samaritans of that city believed in him** (John 4:39).

Concerning the first he does two things.

First, we have the situation in which Christ speaks to his disciples;

second, what he said, at **but he said to them: I have food to eat, which you do not know.**

632. The occasion of this manifestation arose from the insistence of the apostles that Christ eat. He says, **meanwhile**, i.e., between the time that Christ and the woman spoke and the Samaritans came, **his disciples pleaded with him**, that is, with Christ, **saying: Rabbi, eat**: for they thought that then was a good time to eat, before the crowds came from the town. For the disciples did not usually offer Christ food in the presence of strangers: so we read that so many people came to him that he did not even have time to eat (Mark 6:31).

633. After presenting the situation, he gives its fruit, at **but he said to them: I have food to eat, which you do not know.**

First, it is given in figurative language.

Second, we see the disciples are slow in understanding this, at **the disciples therefore said.**

Third, the Lord explains what he meant, at **Jesus said to them: my food is to do the will of him who sent me** (John 4:34).

634. The fruit of his spiritual teaching is proposed under the symbols of food and nourishment, so the Lord says, **I have food to eat.** We should note that just as bodily nourishment is incomplete unless there is both food and drink, so also both should be found in spiritual nourishment: *the Lord fed him with the bread of life and understanding*, this is the food, *and gave him a drink of the water of saving wisdom*, and this is the drink (Sir 15:3). So it was appropriate for Christ to speak of food after having given drink to the Samaritan woman. And just as water is a symbol for saving wisdom, so food is a symbol of good works.

The food that Christ had to eat is the salvation of men; this was what he desired. When he says that he has food to eat, he shows how great a desire he has for our salvation. For just as we desire to eat when we are hungry, so he desires to save us: *my delight is to be with the children of men* (Prov 8:31). So he says, **I have food to eat**, i.e., the

filiis hominum. Et ideo dicit *cibum*, idest conversionem gentium, *habeo manducare quem vos nescitis*: quia non poterant adhuc praecognoscere conversionem gentium.

635. Vel aliter, secundum Origenem, contingit sicut de cibo corporali, ita et de spirituali; non enim eadem quantitas omnibus sufficit, sed uni quidem maior quantitas necessaria est, alteri minor; et uni quidem sanum est quod alteri nocet. Eodem modo in spirituali refectione: non enim eadem qualitas, seu quantitas doctrinae spiritualis adhibenda est singulis, sed secundum dispositionis congruitatem et capacitatem hominum. Nam, secundum Apostolum: *nuper geniti infantes rationabile lac appetunt*. Perfectorum autem est solidus cibus: unde Origenes dicit, quod ille qui est altioris doctrinae, et aliis in spiritualibus praeest, potest hoc verbum dicere infirmis et debilioris intellectus existentibus. Et sic Apostolus loquitur, I Cor. III, 1: *tamquam parvulis in Christo, lac vobis potum dedi, non escam*. Et hoc multo amplius veridicus Iesus dicere potest *cibum habeo manducare*; infra XVI, 12: *multa habeo vobis dicere quae non potestis portare modo*.

636. Tarditas autem intellectus discipulorum innuitur ex hoc quod ea quae dixit Dominus de cibo spirituali, intelligebant de corporali: adhuc enim et ipsi sine intellectu erant, secundum illud Matth. XV, 16.

Et ideo dicebant discipuli ad invicem etc. Non est ergo mirum, si mulier illa Samaritana spiritualem aquam non intelligebat; ecce enim quod discipuli Iudaei spiritualem non intelligunt escam.

In hoc autem quod dicunt adinvicem *numquid aliquis attulit ei?* Consuetudinem Christi debemus attendere, quia cibos ab aliis oblatos solebat accipere: non quod bonis nostris indigeret, quia *bonorum nostrorum non indiget*, ut dicitur in Ps. XV, 2, nec esca hominum, quia dat escam omni carni.

637. Sed quare quaerebat, et ab aliis accipiebat?

Propter duo. Primo ut dantes et afferentes, meritum consequerentur; secundo, ut daret Christus exemplum, quod vacantes spiritualibus non erubescant paupertatem, nec grave putent ab aliis nutriri. Proprium est enim doctoribus alios habere procuratores ciborum, ut ipsi de nullo curantes, verbi ministrationem sollicite procurent, ut dicit Chrysostomus. Et hoc idem habetur in Glossa. I Tim. c. V, 17: *qui bene praesunt presbyteri, duplici honore digni habeantur, maxime qui laborant in verbo et doctrina*.

conversion of the nations, *which you do not know*; for they had no way of knowing beforehand about this conversion of the nations.

635. Origen explains this in a different way, it follows from the connection between spiritual food and bodily food. The same amount of bodily food is not enough for everyone; some need more, others less. Again, what is good for one is harmful to another. The same thing happens in spiritual nourishment: for the same kind and amount should not be given to everyone, but adjusted to what is appropriate to the disposition and capacity of each. *Like newborn babes, desire spiritual milk* (1 Pet 2:2). Solid food is for the perfect; thus Origen says that the man who understands the loftier doctrine, and who has charge of others in spiritual matters, can teach this doctrine to those who are weaker and have less understanding. Accordingly, the Apostle says: *being little ones in Christ, I gave you milk, not solid food* (1 Cor 3:2). And Jesus could say this with much more truth: I have food to eat; and *I have yet many things to say to you: but you cannot bear them now* (John 16:12).

636. The slowness of the disciples to understand these matters is implied by the fact that what our Lord said about spiritual food, they understood as referring to bodily food. For even they were still without understanding (Matt 15:16).

The disciples therefore said to one another: has anyone brought him something to eat? It is not surprising that this Samaritan woman did not understand about spiritual water, for even the Jewish disciples did not understand about spiritual food.

In their saying to each other, *has anyone brought him something to eat?* we should note that it was customary for Christ to accept food from others; but not because he needs our goods: *he does not need our goods* (Ps 15:2), nor our food, because it is he who gives food to every living thing.

637. Then why did he desire and accept goods from others?

For two reasons. First, so that those who give him these things might acquire merit. Second, in order to give us the example that those engrossed in spiritual matters should not be ashamed of their poverty, nor regard it burdensome to be supported by others. For it is fitting that teachers have others provide their food so that, being free from such concerns, they may carefully pay attention to the ministry of the word, as Chrysostom says, and as we find in the Gloss. *Let the elders who rule well be regarded as worthy of a double compensation; especially those concerned with preaching and teaching* (1 Tim 5:17).

Lecture 4

4:34 Dicit eis Iesus: meus cibus est, ut faciam voluntatem eius qui misit me, ut perficiam opus eius. [n. 639]

4:35 Nonne vos dicitis, quod adhuc quatuor menses sunt, et messis venit? Ecce dico vobis: levate oculos vestros, et videte regiones, quia albae sunt iam ad messem. [n. 645]

4:36 Et qui metit, mercedem accipit, et congregat fructum in vitam aeternam: ut et qui seminat, simul gaudeat, et qui metit. [n. 651]

4:37 In hoc enim est verbum verum, quia alius est qui seminat, et alius qui metit. [n. 652]

4:38 Ego misi vos metere quod vos non laborastis. Alii laboraverunt, et vos in labores eorum introistis. [n. 654]

4:34 λέγει αὐτοῖς ὁ Ἰησοῦς· ἐμὸν βρῶμά ἐστιν ἵνα ποιήσω τὸ θέλημα τοῦ πέμψαντός με καὶ τελειώσω αὐτοῦ τὸ ἔργον.

4:35 οὐχ ὑμεῖς λέγετε ὅτι ἔτι τετράμηνός ἐστιν καὶ ὁ θερισμὸς ἔρχεται; ἰδοὺ λέγω ὑμῖν, ἐπάρατε τοὺς ὀφθαλμοὺς ὑμῶν καὶ θεάσασθε τὰς χώρας ὅτι λευκαί εἰσιν πρὸς θερισμόν. ἤδη

4:36 ὁ θερίζων μισθὸν λαμβάνει καὶ συνάγει καρπὸν εἰς ζωὴν αἰώνιον, ἵνα ὁ σπείρων ὁμοῦ χαίρῃ καὶ ὁ θερίζων.

4:37 ἐν γὰρ τούτῳ ὁ λόγος ἐστὶν ἀληθινὸς ὅτι ἄλλος ἐστὶν ὁ σπείρων καὶ ἄλλος ὁ θερίζων.

4:38 ἐγὼ ἀπέστειλα ὑμᾶς θερίζειν ὃ οὐχ ὑμεῖς κεκοπιάκατε· ἄλλοι κεκοπιάκασιν καὶ ὑμεῖς εἰς τὸν κόπον αὐτῶν εἰσεληλύθατε.

4:34 Jesus said to them: my food is to do the will of him who sent me, so that I may accomplish his work. [n. 639]

4:35 Do you not say, there are yet four months and then the harvest comes? Behold, I say to you: lift up your eyes, and see the fields, which are already white for harvest. [n. 645]

4:36 And he who reaps receives wages and gathers fruit unto life everlasting: so that both he who sows, and he who reaps, may rejoice together. [n. 651]

4:37 For in this the saying is true: that it is one man who sows, and it is another who reaps. [n. 652]

4:38 I have sent you to reap that in which you did not labor: others have done the work, and you have entered into their labors. [n. 654]

---

638. Posita tarditate intellectus discipulorum circa figuratam locutionem, hic consequenter Dominus explanat eam, et

primo ponit explanationem figuratae locutionis;

secundo adhibet similitudinem, ibi ***nonne vos dicitis, quia adhuc quatuor menses sunt, et messis venit?***

639. Circa primum sciendum est, quod sicut Christus supra explanavit mulieri, quod figuraliter ei proposuit de aqua, sic et apostolis explanat quod figuraliter eis de cibo proposuit, sed aliter et aliter: nam apostolis tamquam capacioribus absque verborum involutione expositionem statim proponit; mulierem autem, utpote minus capacem, per multa verba ad veritatis cognitionem perducit.

640. Hoc autem quod dicit ***meus cibus est ut faciam voluntatem eius qui misit me, ut perficiam eius opus***, satis rationabilem habet causam. Cum enim cibus corporalis sustentet hominem, et perficiat ipsum, ille est spiritualis cibus animae, et creaturae rationalis, quo sustentatur et perficitur. Hoc autem est ut coniungatur suo fini et ut sequatur regulam superiorem; quod David intelligens dicebat, Ps. LXXII, 27: *mihi autem adhaerere Deo bonum est*. Et ideo Christus secundum quod homo, convenienter suum cibum esse dicit, ut Dei faciat voluntatem, et ut perficiat opus eius.

638. Since the disciples were slow to understand the Lord's figure of speech, the Lord now explains it.

First, we have its explanation;

second, its application, at ***do you not say, there are yet four months and then the harvest comes?***

639. As to the first, we should note that just as Christ explained to the Samaritan woman what he had told her in figurative language about water, so he explains to his apostles what he told them in figurative language about food. But he does not do so in the same way in both cases. Since the apostles were able to understand these matters more easily, he explains to them at once and in few words; but to the Samaritan woman, since she could not understand as well, our Lord leads her to the truth with a longer explanation.

640. There is a perfectly reasonable cause for Christ to say, ***my food is to do the will of him who sent me, so that I may accomplish his work***. For as bodily food sustains a man and brings him to perfection, the spiritual food of the soul and of the rational creature is that by which he is sustained and perfected; and this consists in being joined to his end and following a higher rule. David, understanding this, said: *for me, to adhere to God is good* (Ps 72:28). Accordingly, Christ, as man, fittingly says that his food is to do the will of God and to accomplish his work.

641. Et haec quidem duo possunt intelligi ut unum: ita tamen quod secundum sit expositio primi. Vel possunt intelligi ut aliud et aliud.

Si autem intelligantur ut unum, tunc est sensus: *meus cibus est*, idest, in hoc est firmitas et sustentatio mea, *ut faciam voluntatem eius qui misit me*, secundum illud Ps. XXXIX, 9: *facere voluntatem tuam, Deus meus, volui, et legem tuam in medio cordis mei*; infra VI, 38: *descendi de caelo, non ut faciam voluntatem meam, sed voluntatem eius qui misit me*. Sed quia facere voluntatem alicuius intelligitur dupliciter: uno modo ut faciat eum velle, alio modo ut opere compleat illud quod scit eum velle; ideo Dominus exponens quid sit facere voluntatem eius qui misit eum, dicit hoc scilicet esse *ut perficiam opus eius*, idest, ut compleam opera quae scio eum velle; infra IX, 4: *me oportet operari opera eius qui misit me donec dies est*.

Si autem intelligatur ut aliud et aliud; sic sciendum est, quod Christus duo fecit in mundo isto. Primo docuit veritatem, invitando, et vocando ad fidem: et in hoc complevit voluntatem Patris; infra VI, 40: *haec est voluntas Patris qui misit me, ut omnis qui videt Filium et credit in eum, habeat vitam aeternam*. Secundo consummavit ipsam veritatem, aperiendo per passionem suam in nobis ianuam vitae, dando potestatem perveniendi ad consummatam veritatem; infra XVII, 4: *opus consummavi quod dedisti ut faciam*. Sic ergo dicit *meus cibus est ut faciam voluntatem eius qui misit me*, vocabo homines ad fidem, *ut perficiam opus eius*, perducendo eos ad perfectum.

642. Vel, secundum Origenem, omnis homo qui bene operatur, ad duo debet dirigere suam intentionem, scilicet ad honorem Dei, et ad utilitatem proximi: quia, sicut dicitur I Tim. I, 5: *finis praecepti est caritas*: quae continet amorem Dei et proximi. Et sic quando aliquid facimus propter Deum, finis praecepti est Deus; quando vero propter utilitatem proximi, finis praecepti est proximus.

Secundum hoc ergo dicit Christus *meus cibus est ut faciam voluntatem Dei*, idest ut intentionem meam dirigam et regulem in his quae sunt ad honorem Dei, *ut perficiam opus eius*, idest, ea faciam quae sunt ad utilitatem et perfectionem hominis.

643. Sed contra, Dei perfecta sunt opera: non ergo convenienter dicitur opera perfici Dei.

Respondeo dicendum, quod inter ceteras creaturas inferiores homo est speciale opus Dei, quia ad imaginem et similitudinem suam fecit illum Gen. I, 26. Et hoc opus in principio quidem perfectum fuit, quia Deus fecit hominem rectum, ut dicitur Eccle. VII, 30. Postmodum vero per peccatum hanc perfectionem amisit, et a rectitudine recessit. Et ideo ut hoc opus Domini perfectum

641. These two expressions can be understood as meaning the same thing, in the sense that the second is explaining the first. Or, they can be understood in different ways.

If we understand them as meaning the same, the sense is this: *my food is*, i.e., in this is my strength and nourishment, *to do the will of him who sent me*; according to, *my God, I desired to do your will, and your law is in my heart* (Ps 39:9), and, *I came down from heaven, not to do my own will, but the will of him who sent me* (John 6:38). But because to do the will of another can be understood in two ways—one, by making him will it, and second, by fulfilling what I know he wills—therefore, explaining what it means to do the will of him who sent him, the Lord says, *so that I may accomplish his work*, that is, that I might complete the work I know he wants: *I must do the works of him who sent me while it is day* (John 9:4).

If these two expressions are understood as different, then we should point out that Christ did two things in this world. First, he taught the truth, in inviting and calling us to the faith; and by this he fulfilled the will of the Father: *this is the will of my Father who sent me: that everyone who sees the Son and believes in him may have eternal life* (John 6:40). Second, he accomplished the truth by opening in us, by his passion, the gate of life, and by giving us the power to arrive at complete truth: *I have finished the work that you gave me to do* (John 17:4). Thus he is saying: *my food is to do the will of him who sent me*, by calling men to the faith, *so that I may accomplish his work*, by leading them to what is perfect.

642. Another interpretation, given by Origen, is that every man who does good works should direct his intention to two things: the honor of God and the good of his neighbor: for as it is said: *the end of the commandment is love* (1 Tim 1:5), and this love embraces both God and our neighbor. And so, when we do something for God's sake, the end of the commandment is God; but when it is for our neighbor's good, the end of the commandment is our neighbor.

With this in mind, Christ is saying, *my food is to do the will of him who sent me*, God, i.e., to direct and regulate my intention to those matters that concern the honor of God, *so that I may accomplish his work*, i.e., to do things for the benefit and perfection of man.

643. On the other hand, since the works of God are perfect, it does not seem proper to speak of accomplishing or completing them.

I answer that among lower creatures, man is the special work of God, who made him to his own image and likeness (Gen 1:26). And in the beginning God made this a perfect work, because as we read: *God made man upright* (Eccl 7:30). But later, man lost this perfection by sin, and abandoned what was right. And so, this work of the Lord needed to be repaired in order to become right again; and

esset, reparari indigebat: quod quidem perfectum est per Christum, quia dicitur Rom. V, 19: *sicut enim per unius hominis inobedientiam peccatores constituti sunt multi, ita per unius obedientiam iusti constituentur multi.* Sic Christus dicit **ut perficiam opus eius**, idest ut hominem ad perfectum deducam.

644. Consequenter cum dicit **nonne vos dicitis quod adhuc quatuor menses sunt, et messis venit**? etc. ponit similitudinem.

Sed attende, quod Christus a muliere potum petivit, dicens: **da mihi bibere**, et ideo occasione huius petitionis introduxit similitudinem de aqua. Hic vero discipuli inducunt Dominum ad manducandum: unde et occasione huius introducit Dominus similitudinem de cibo spirituali, quia idem intelligitur per cibum et potum. Sic ergo sunt quidam a quibus Deus petit potum sicut a muliere; quidam vero Deo offerunt potum. Sed cibum nullus Deo offert nisi prius petierit ab eo Deus: tunc enim Deo cibum spiritualem offerimus quando ab eo poscimus salutem nostram, cum scilicet petimus: *fiat voluntas tua sicut in caelo et in terra.* Salutem ex nobis ipsis consequi non possumus nisi praeventi a gratia praeveniente, secundum illud Thren. ult., 21: *converte nos, Domine, ad te, et convertemur.* Ipse ergo prius petit qui per praevenientem gratiam nos petere facit.

In hac autem similitudine
primo agit de messe;
secundo de messoribus, ibi **et qui metit, mercedem accipit.**
Circa primum duo facit.
Primo ponit similitudinem de messe corporali;

secundo de messe spirituali, ibi **ecce dico vobis: levate oculos vestros**, etc.

645. Per hoc autem quod dicit **nonne vos dicitis, quod adhuc quatuor menses sunt, et messis venit?** datur intelligi quod Christus statim post captionem Ioannis de Iudaea recessit, sicut dicitur Matth. IV, 12, et transivit per Samariam; et quod hoc fuit in hieme: et Ioannes similiter captus. Unde quia ibi tempestivius messes perficiuntur, quatuor menses erant ab illo tempore usque ad messem. Dicit ergo **nonne vos dicitis**, loquendo de messe corporali, **quod adhuc quatuor menses sunt**, qui extant futuri, **et messis venit?** Idest, tempus collectionis messium. **Sed ecce dico vobis**, de spirituali messe loquens, **levate oculos vestros, et videte regiones, quae albae sunt iam ad messem.**

646. Ubi sciendum est, quod tempus messium dicitur tempus collectionis fructuum: et ideo omnis collectio fructuum comparatur tempori messium. Tempus autem collectionis fructuum duplex est. Nihil enim

this was accomplished by Christ, for *just as by the disobedience of one man, many were made sinners, so by the obedience of one man, many will be made just* (Rom 5:19). Thus Christ says, **so that I may accomplish his work**, i.e., to bring man back to what is perfect.

644. Then when he says, **do you not say, these are yet four months, and then the harvest comes? Behold, I say to you: lift up your eyes and see the fields, which are already white for harvest**, he makes use of a simile.

Note that when Christ asked the Samaritan woman for a drink, **give me a drink** (John 4:7), he made use of a simile concerning water. But here, the the disciples are urging the Lord to eat, and now he makes use of a simile concerning spiritual food. There are some persons whom God asks for a drink, as this Samaritan woman; and there are some who offer a drink to God. But no one offers food to God unless God first asks him for it: for we offer spiritual food to God when we ask him for our salvation, that is, when we ask, *your will be done on earth as it is in heaven* (Matt 6:10). We cannot obtain salvation of ourselves, unless we are premoved by *prevenient grace*, according to the statement: *make us come back to you, O Lord, and we will come back* (Lam 5:21). The Lord himself, therefore, first asks for that which makes us ask through prevenient grace.

In this simile, we have
first, the harvest.
Second, those who reap the harvest, at **and he who reaps receives wages**.
He does two things concerning the first.
First, he states the simile concerning the natural harvest;
second, concerning the spiritual harvest, at **behold, I say to you: lift up your eyes, and see the fields, which are already white for harvest**.

645. From what he says, **do you not say, there are four months and then the harvest comes?** we can see that, as stated, Christ left Judea and traveled through Samaria right after John was arrested, and that all this happened during the winter (Matt 4:12). So, because the harvests ripen there more according to the season, there were four months froin that time till the harvest. Thus he says, **do you not say**, how the natural harvest, **there are yet four months and then the harvest comes?** i.e., the time for gathering up the harvest. **Behold, I say to you**, speaking of the spiritual harvest, **lift up your eyes, and see the fields, which are already white for harvest**.

646. Here we should point out that harvest time is the time when the fruit is gathered; and so whenever fruit is gathered can be regarded as a harvest time. Now fruit is gathered at two times: for both in temporal and in spiritual

prohibet in temporalibus et in spiritualibus, quin illud quod est fructus respectu praecedentium, sit etiam semen respectu sequentium: nam bona opera sunt fructus spiritualis doctrinae, sicut fides, et huiusmodi; quae tamen sunt semina vitae aeternae, quia per ea ad vitam aeternam pervenitur. Eccli. XXIV, 23 dicit sapientia: *flores mei*, respectu fructus sequentis, *sunt fructus honoris et honestatis*, respectu praecedentium.

Secundum hoc ergo una est collectio messis spiritualis respectu fructuum aeternorum, scilicet congregatio fidelium in vitam aeternam: de qua dicitur Matth. XIII, 39: *messis est consummatio saeculi*. Et de ista non agitur hic. Alia est in praesenti. Et hoc potest intelligi dupliciter. Uno modo collectio fructuum, scilicet fidelium in Ecclesia congregandorum conversio; alio modo ipsa cognitio veritatis, qua aliquis fructum veritatis in anima sua congregat: et de utraque secundum diversas expositiones hic agitur.

647. De prima, secundum Augustinum et Chrysostomum, hoc modo: **vos dicitis**, quoniam adhuc non est tempus corporalis messis; sed non sic est de messe spirituali, **immo ecce dico vobis: levate oculos vestros**, scilicet mentis per considerationem, vel oculos etiam corporis, **et videte regiones, quoniam albae sunt iam ad messem**: quia scilicet tota regio plena erat Samaritanis ad Christum exeuntibus.

Hoc autem quod dicit **albae sunt**, metaphoricum est: cum enim segetes dealbatae sunt, signum est quod sunt preparatae ad messem. Nihil aliud per hoc significare voluit quam quod homines ad salutem et susceptionem verbi parati erant ei. Unde dicit **videte regiones**, quia non solum Iudaei, sed etiam gentiles parati sunt ad fidem. Matth. c. IX, 37: *messis quidem multa, operarii autem pauci*. Et sicut messes dealbantur propter praesentiam solis aestivo tempore magis ferventis, ita et homines per adventum solis iustitiae, scilicet Christi, et praedicationem atque virtutem suam, praeparabantur ad salutem. Et de isto sole dicitur Mal. IV, 2: *vobis timentibus nomen meum orietur sol iustitiae*. Et inde est quod tempus adventus eius dicitur tempus plenitudinis; Gal. IV, 4: *cum ergo venit plenitudo temporis, misit Deus Filium suum*.

648. De secunda autem collectione messis, idest veritatis in anima, exponit Origenes, qui dicit, quod tot fructus veritatis colligit in messe, quot quis veritates cognoscit. Et vult, quod totum hoc quod dicitur **nonne vos dicitis quoniam adhuc quatuor menses sunt et messis venit? Et ecce dico vobis: levate oculos vestros, et videte regiones, quia albae sunt iam ad messem**, intelligatur parabolice dictum. Et secundum hoc duo facit Dominus in verbis istis. Primo ponit falsam opinionem quorumdam; secundo excludit eam, ibi **ego dico vobis**.

matters there is nothing to prevent what is fruit in relation to an earlier state from being seed in relation to something later. For example, good works are the fruit of spiritual instruction, as is faith and other such things; but these in turn are seeds of eternal life, because eternal life is acquired through them. So it is said: *my blossoms*, in relation to the fruit to follow, *bear the fruit of of honor and riches*, in relation to what preceded (Sir 24:23).

With this in mind, there is a certain gathering of a spiritual harvest; and this concerns an eternal fruit, i.e., the gathering of the faithful into eternal life, of which we read: *the harvest is the end of the world* (Matt 13:39). We are not here concerned with this harvest. Another spiritual harvest is gathered in the present; and this is understood in two ways. In the first, the gathering of the fruit is the converting of the faithful to be assembled in the Church; in the second, the gathering is the very knowing of the truth, by which a person gathers the fruit of truth into his soul. And we are concerned with these two gatherings of the harvest, depending on the different expositions.

647. Augustine and Chrysostom understand the gathering of the harvest in the first way, as follows. **You say** that it is not yet the time for the natural harvest; but this is not true of the spiritual harvest. Indeed, **behold, lift up your eyes**, i.e., the eyes of your mind, by thinking, or even your physical eyes, **look at the fields, which are already white for the harvest**: because the entire countryside was full of Samaritans coming to Christ.

The statement that the fields **are already white** is metaphorical: for when sown fields are white, it is a sign that they are ready for harvest. And so he only means to say by this that the people were ready for salvation and to hear the word. He says, **see the fields**, because not only the Jews, but the gentiles as well, were ready for the faith: *the harvest is great, but the workers are few* (Matt 9:37). And just as harvests are made white by the presence of the burning heat of the summer sun, so by the coming of the Sun of justice, i.e., Christ, and his preaching and power, men are made ready for salvation. It is said: *the sun of justice will rise on you who fear my name* (Mal 4:2). Thus it is that the time of Christ's coming is called the time of plenitude or fullness: *when the fullness of time had come, God sent his Son* (Gal 4:4).

648. Origen deals with the second gathering of the harvest, i.e., the gathering of truth in the soul. He says that one gathers as much of the fruit of truth in the harvest as the truths he knows. And he says that everything said here, **do you not say, there are yet four months and then the harvest comes? Behold, I say to you: lift up your eyes, and see the fields, which are already white for harvest**, this should be understood as being spoken figureatively. And according to these two the Lord does two things. First he poses a false opinion concerning this; second he excludes it at **I say to you**.

Opinio namque quorumdam erat quod nulla veritas alicuius rei haberi possit ab homine et ex hoc derivata est haeresis Academicorum dicentium nihil pro certo sciri posse in vita ista; iuxta quod dicitur Eccle. VII, v. 24: *cuncta tentavi in sapientia. Dixi: sapiens efficiar. Illa autem recessit a me multo magis quam fuerat.* Hanc ergo opinionem tangit Dominus, dicens **nonne vos dicitis, quoniam adhuc quatuor menses sunt, et messis venit?** Idest, tota vita praesens, in qua homo quatuor elementis deservit, finiri oportet ut post eam collectio veritatis habeatur in alia vita.

Sed hanc opinionem consequenter excludit cum dicit: non est ita; sed *ecce dico vobis: levate oculos vestros.* Hoc enim in Sacra Scriptura dici consuevit quandocumque aliquod subtile et altum considerandum praecipitur, Is. XL, 26: *levate in excelsum oculos vestros, et videte quis creavit haec.* Nam oculi quando non sunt elevati a terrenis, vel a concupiscentia carnali, non sunt idonei ad cognitionem spiritualis fructus: nam quandoque deprimuntur ad terrena, retracti a consideratione divinorum, secundum illud Ps. XVI, 11: *oculos suos statuerunt declinare in terram,* quandoque excaecantur per concupiscentiam, Dan. XIII, 9: *et declinaverunt oculos suos, ut non viderent caelum, neque recordarentur iudiciorum Dei.*

649. Dicit ergo *levate oculos vestros, et videte regiones, quoniam albae sunt iam ad messem,* idest, ita dispositae, quod ex eis veritas sciri potest: nam per *regiones* specialiter intelliguntur omnia ex quibus veritas accipi potest. Et hae specialiter sunt Scripturae. Infra V, 39: *scrutamini Scripturas . . . quia ipsae testimonium perhibent de me.*

Et hae regiones erant quidem in Veteri Testamento; sed non erant albae ad messem, quia homines non poterant ex eis spiritualem fructum accipere quousque Christus venit, qui eas dealbavit, aperiendo eorum intellectum; Lc. ult., 45: *aperuit illis sensum, ut intelligerent Scripturas.* Item creaturae sunt messes, ex quibus colligitur fructus veritatis; ad Rom. I, 20: *invisibilia Dei per ea quae facta sunt, intellecta conspiciuntur.* Sed tamen gentiles qui earum cognitioni insistebant, erroris potius quam veritatis fructus ex eis colligebant: quia, ut ibidem dicitur, *servierunt creaturae potius quam Creatori.* Et ideo nondum albae erant; sed Christo veniente, albae factae sunt ad messem.

650. Consequenter cum dicit *et qui metit, mercedem accipit,* agit de messoribus: et circa hoc

primo ponit messorum praemium;

secundo inducit proverbium, ibi *in hoc enim est verbum verum;*

tertio exponit, idest adaptat ipsum, ibi *ego misi vos metere.*

Some thought that man could not acquire any truth about anything. This opinion gave rise to the heresy of the Academicians, who maintained that nothing can be known as certain in this life; about which we read: *I tested all things by wisdom. I said: 'I will acquire wisdom,' and it became further from me* (Eccl 7:24). Our Lord mentions this opinion when he says, **do you not say, there are yet four months and then the harvest comes?** i.e., this whole present life, in which man serves under the four elements, must end, so that after it truth may be gathered in another life.

Our Lord rejects this opinion when he says: this is not true, **behold, I say to you: lift up your eyes.** Sacred Scripture usually uses this expression when something subtle and profound is being presented; as, *lift up your eyes on high, and see who has created these things* (Isa 40:26). For when our eyes are not lifted away from earthly things or from the desires of the flesh, they are not fit to know spiritual fruit. For when they are lowered to the earth, they are prevented from considering divine things: *they have fixed their eyes on the earth* (Ps 16:11); sometimes they are blinded by concupiscence: *they have averted their eyes so as not to look at heaven or remember the judgments of God* (Dan 13:9).

649. So he says, **lift up your eyes and see the fields, for they are already white for the harvest,** i.e., they are such that the truth can be learned from them: for by the **fields** we specifically understand all those things from which truth can be acquired, especially the Scriptures: **search the Scriptures . . . they give testimony about me** (John 5:39).

Indeed, these fields existed in the Old Testament, but they were not white for the harvest because men were not able to pick spiritual fruit from them until Christ came, who made them white by opening their understanding: *he opened their minds so they could understand the Scriptures* (Luke 24:45). Again, creatures are harvests from which the fruit of truth is gathered: *the invisible things of God are clearly known by the things that have been made* (Rom 1:20). None the less, the gentiles who pursued a knowledge of these things gathered the fruits of error rather than of truth from them, because as we read, *they served the creature rather than the Creator* (Rom 1:25). So the harvests were not yet white; but they were made white for the harvest when Christ came.

650. Next, when he says, **he who reaps receives wages,** he deals with the reapers.

First, he gives their reward.

Second, he mentions a proverb, at **for in this the saying is true.**

And third, he explains it, i.e., applies it, at **I have sent you to reap.**

651. Quantum ad primum notandum est quod Dominus exponens supra quod de aqua dixerat spirituali, proposuit conditionem, per quam aqua spiritualis differt a corporali: quia scilicet qui biberit ex aqua corporali sitiet iterum qui vero biberit ex aqua spirituali non sitiet in aeternum. Eodem modo etiam hic exponens quod dicit de messe, proponit quod dissimile est inter messem corporalem et spiritualem; unde tria proponit.

Unum quidem secundum quod attenditur similitudo utriusque messis, scilicet quod qui metit tam in corporali messe quam in spirituali, mercedem accipit. Ille autem metit spiritualiter, qui congregat fideles in Ecclesia, vel qui colligit fructus veritatis in anima sua. Et uterque mercedem accipit, secundum illud I Cor. III, 8: *unusquisque propriam mercedem accipiet secundum suum laborem.*

Duo alia proponit, secundum quae attenditur dissimilitudo. Primo quidem, quia fructus messoris, qui metit messem corporalem, pertinet ad vitam corporalem; sed fructus eius qui metit messem spiritualem, pertinet ad vitam aeternam. Et ideo dicit *et congregat*, ille scilicet *qui metit* spiritualiter, *fructum in vitam aeternam*, scilicet fideles qui ad vitam aeternam pervenerint; Rom. VI, 22: *habetis fructum vestrum in sanctificationem, finem vero vitam aeternam.* Vel ipsam cognitionem et expositionem veritatis per quam homo acquirit vitam aeternam. Eccli. XXIV, v. 31: *qui elucidant me, vitam aeternam habebunt.*

Secundo vero attenditur dissimilitudo: quia in messe corporali ad miseriam reputatur quod unus seminet et alius metat, unde qui seminat tristatur de hoc quod alius metit; sed in semine spirituali aliter est, quia *qui seminat simul gaudet, et qui metit.*

Et quidem, secundum Chrysostomum et Augustinum, seminantes semen spirituale sunt patres Veteris Testamenti et prophetae: nam, ut dicitur Lc. VIII, 11, *semen est verbum Dei* quod Moyses et prophetae seminaverunt in Iudaea; sed apostoli messuerunt, quia ipsi quod intendebant, scilicet homines adducere ad Christum, efficere non potuerunt, quod tamen apostoli fecerunt. Et ideo utrique simul gaudent, scilicet apostoli et prophetae, in una mansione gloriae, de conversione fidelium; Is. LI, 3: *gaudium et laetitia invenietur in ea, gratiarum actio et vox laudis.*

Et per hoc confutatur haeresis Manichaeorum damnantium patres Veteris Testamenti; cum tamen, ut hic Dominus dicit, simul gaudebunt cum apostolis.

Secundum Origenem vero, seminantes in qualibet facultate dicuntur illi qui quaelibet illius facultatis principia tradunt; metentes vero qui ex illis procedunt ulterius: et hoc multo magis in ista, quae est omnium scientiarum scientia. Prophetae seminantes sunt, quia multa de divinis tradiderunt; messores vero sunt apostoli, qui

651. Concerning the first, we should note that when the Lord was explaining earlier about spiritual water, he mentioned the way in which spiritual water differs from natural water: a person who drinks natural water will become thirsty again, but one who drinks spiritual water will never be thirsty again. Here, too, in explaining about the harvest, he points out the difference between a natural and a spiritual harvest. Three things are mentioned.

First, the way in which the two harvests are similar: namely, in that the person who reaps either harvest receives a wage. But the one who reaps spiritually is the one who gathers the faithful into the Church, or who gathers the fruit of truth into his soul. Each of these will receive a wage, according to: *each one will receive his own wage according to his work* (1 Cor 3:8).

The two other points he mentions concern the ways the two harvests are unlike each other. First, the fruit gathered from a natural harvest concerns the life of the body; but the fruit gathered by one who reaps a spiritual harvest concerns eternal life. So he says, *he who reaps*, i.e., he who reaps spiritually, *gathers fruit unto life everlasting*, that is, the faithful, who will obtain eternal life: *your fruit is sanctification, your end is eternal life* (Rom 6:22). Or, this fruit is the very knowing and explaining of the truth by which man acquires eternal life: *those who explain me will have eternal life* (Sir 24:31).

Second, the two harvests are unlike because in a natural harvest it is considered a misfortune that one should sow and another reap; hence he who sows is saddened when another reaps. But it is not this way when the seed is spiritual, *so that both he who sows, and he who reaps, may rejoice together*.

According to Chrysostom and Augustine, the ones who sow spiritual seed are the fathers and prophets of the Old Testament, for *the seed is the word of God* (Luke 8:11), which Moses and the prophets sowed in the land of Judah. But the apostles were the reapers, because the former were not able to accomplish what they wanted to do, i.e., to bring men to Christ; this was done by the apostles. And so both the apostles and the prophets rejoice together, in one mansion of glory, over the conversion of the faithful: *joy and gladness will be found there, thanksgiving and the voice of praise* (Isa 51:3).

This refutes the heresy of the Manicheans who condemn the fathers of the Old Testament; for as the Lord says here, they will rejoice with the apostles.

According to Origen, however, the sowers in any faculty are those who confer the very first principles of that faculty; but the reapers are those who proceed from these principles to further truths. And this is all the more true of the science of all the sciences. The prophets are sowers, because they handed down many things concerning divine matters;

ea quae non manifestaverunt prophetae hominibus, praedicando et docendo revelaverunt. Eph. III, 5: *quod aliis generationibus non est agnitum . . . sicut nunc revelatum est sanctis apostolis eius.*

652. Consequenter cum dicit *in hoc enim est verbum verum* etc., inducitur proverbium; quasi dicat, quod *in hoc*, idest in isto facto, *verum est verbum*, idest impletur vulgare proverbium, quod erat apud Iudaeos, scilicet unus seminat et alius metit. Quod proverbium derivari videtur ex eo quod dicitur Lev. XXVI, 16: *seretis frustra segetem, quae ab hostibus devorabitur.* Ex quo consueverunt Iudaei, quando aliquis in re aliqua laborabat, et alius inde gaudebat, huiusmodi proverbium proferre. Hoc est ergo quod Dominus dicit: in hoc quod prophetae seminaverunt et laboraverunt, et vos metitis et gaudetis, impletur proverbium.

Vel aliter. *In hoc verbum verum est*, scilicet quod ego dico, *quod alius est qui seminat, et alius qui metit*; quia vos metetis fructus ex laboribus prophetarum. Sed prophetae quidem et apostoli alii sunt, non in fide: quia et illi et isti fidem habuerunt, Rom. c. III, 21: *nunc autem sine lege iustitia Dei manifestata est, testificata a lege et prophetis*, sunt tamen alii in conversatione: quia prophetae vivebant sub caeremoniis legalibus, a quibus Christiani et apostoli liberi sunt. Gal. c. IV, 3: *et cum essemus parvuli, sub elementis huius mundi eramus servientes. At ubi venit plenitudo temporis, misit Deus Filium suum factum ex muliere, factum sub lege, ut eos qui sub lege erant redimeret, ut adoptionem Filiorum reciperemus.*

Et licet disparis temporis labores habuerint apostoli et prophetae, tamen gaudio pariter perfruentur, et mercedem accipient *in vitam aeternam: ut simul gaudeat qui seminat et qui metit*. Et hoc praefiguratum fuit in transfiguratione Christi, ubi omnes gloriam suam habuerunt, et patres Veteris Testamenti, scilicet Moyses et Elias, et patres Novi Testamenti, scilicet Petrus, Ioannes et Iacobus: dans per hoc intelligere, quod in illa futura gloria simul gaudent novi et Veteris Testamenti iusti.

653. Consequenter cum dicit *ego misi vos metere quod non laborastis*, adaptat proverbium ad propositum, et

primo dicit apostolos esse messores;

secundo ostendit esse laboratores, ibi *alii laboraverunt, et vos in labores eorum introitis.*

654. Quantum ad primum dicit: dico quod *alius est qui metit*, quia vos estis messores, *alius est qui seminat*, quia *ego misi vos metere quod non laboratis*. Non autem dicit *mittam* sed *misi*, quia bis misit eos: semel ante passionem suam ad Iudaeos, cum dixit eis: *in viam gentium ne abieritis . . . sed ite potius ad oves quae perierunt*

but the apostles are the reapers, because in preaching and teaching they revealed many things which the prophets did not make known: *which was not made known to the sons of men in other generations as it has now been revealed to his holy apostles* (Eph 3:5).

652. Then when he says, *for in this the saying is true: that it is one man who sows, and it is another who reaps*. As if to say: *for in this*, i.e., in this fact, *the saying is true*, i.e., the proverb in current use among the Jews is fulfilled: One man sows, another reaps. This proverb seems to have grown out of the statement, *you will sow your seed in vain for it will be devoured by your enemies* (Lev 26:16). As a result, the Jews used this proverb when one person labored on something, but another received the pleasure from it. This then is what our Lord says: the proverb is verified here because it was the prophets who sowed and labored, while you are the ones to reap and rejoice.

Another interpretation would be this. *For in this the saying is true*, i.e., what I am saying to you, *that it is one man who sows, and it is another who reaps*, because you will reap the fruits of the labor of the prophets. Now the prophets and the apostles are different, but not in faith, for they both had faith: *but now the justice of God has been manifested outside the law; the law and the prophets bore witness to it* (Rom 3:21). They are different in their manner of life, for the prophets lived under the ceremonies of the law, from which the apostles and Christians have been freed: *when we were children, we were slaves under the elements of this world. But when the fullness of time came, God sent his Son, made of a woman, made under the law, to redeem those who were under the law, so that we could receive adoption as sons* (Gal 4:3).

And although the apostles and prophets labor at different times, nevertheless they will rejoice equally and receive wages *unto life everlasting: so that both he who sows, and he who reaps, may rejoice together*. This was prefigured in the transfiguration of Christ, where all had their own glory, both the fathers of the Old Testament, that is, Moses and Elijah, and the fathers of the New Testament, that is, Peter, John and James. We see from this that the just of the New and of the Old Testaments will rejoice together in the glory to come.

653. Then, at *I have sent you to reap that in which you did not labor*, he applies the proverb.

First, he calls the apostles reapers.

Second, he says they are laborers, at *others have done the work, and you have entered into their labors*.

654. He says concerning the first: I say that *it is one who reaps*, because you are reapers, *and another who sows*, for *I have sent you to reap that in which you did not labor*. He does not say, *I will send you*, but *I have sent you*. He says this because he sent them twice. One time was before his passion, when he sent them to the Jews, saying: *do not go*

domus Israel, ut dicitur Matth. X, 5. Et quantum ad hanc missionem, missi fuerunt metere quod non laboraverunt, scilicet ipsos Iudaeos convertere, in quibus prophetae laboraverunt.

Misit autem eos post resurrectionem ad gentes, dicens eis, Mc. ult., 15: *euntes in mundum universum, praedicate Evangelium omni creaturae.* In hac missione missi sunt de novo seminare; unde Apostolus, Rom. XV, v. 20 et 21: *sic autem praedicavi Evangelium, ubi non nominatus est Christus, ne super alienum fundamentum aedificarem; sed sicut scriptum est: quibus non est annuntiatum de eo, videbunt, et qui non audierunt, intelligent.* Et ideo dicit **misi**, habens respectum ad primam missionem.

Sic ergo Apostoli sunt messores, sed alii, scilicet prophetae, sunt seminatores.

655. Unde dicit **alii laboraverunt**, seminando primordia doctrinae Christi, **et vos in labores eorum introitis**, ad colligendum fructus. Sap. III, 15: *bonorum laborum gloriosus est fructus.* Laboraverunt, inquam, prophetae, ut adducerent homines ad Christum. Infra V, 46: **si crederetis Moysi, crederetis forsitan et mihi: de me enim ille scripsit. Si autem illius litteris non creditis, quomodo verbis meis credetis?** Sed non ipsi fructum messuerunt. Unde secundum hoc dicebat Is. c. XLIX, 4: *in vacuum laboravi, et sine causa: vane fortitudinem meam consumpsi.*

on the roads of the gentiles . . . but go rather to the lost sheep of the house of Israel (Matt 10:5). In this case, they were sent to reap that on which they did not work, that is, to convert the Jews, among whom the prophets worked.

After the resurrection, Christ sent them to the gentiles, saying: *go to the whole world, and preach the good news to every creature* (Mark 16:15). This time they were sent to sow for the first time; for as the Apostle says: *I have preached the good news, but not where Christ was already known, so as not to build on another's foundation. But as it is written: they to whom he was not proclaimed will see, and they who have not heard will understand.* (Rom 15:20). And so Christ says, **I have sent you**, referring to the first time they were sent.

This is the way, then, the apostles are reapers, and others, the prophets, are the sowers.

655. Accordingly, he says, **others have done the work**, by sowing the beginnings of the doctrine of Christ, **and you have entered into their labors**, to collect the fruit: *the fruit of good labors is glorious* (Wis 3:15). The prophets labored, I say, to bring men to Christ: **if you believed Moses, you would perhaps believe me also, for he wrote of me. But if you do not believe his writings, how will you believe my words?** (John 5:46–47). But the prophets did not reap the fruit; so Isaiah said with this in mind: *I have labored for nothing and without reason; in vain I have exhausted my strength* (Isa 49:4).

Lecture 5

4:39 Ex civitate autem illa multi crediderunt in eum Samaritanorum, propter verbum mulieris testimonium perhibentis: quia dixit mihi omnia quaecumque feci. [n. 657]

4:40 Cum venissent ergo ad illum Samaritani, rogaverunt eum, ut ibi maneret. Et mansit ibi duos dies. [n. 658]

4:41 Et multo plures crediderunt in eum propter sermonem eius: [n. 661]

4:42 et mulieri dicebant: quia non propter tuam loquelam credimus: ipsi enim audivimus, et scimus quia hic est vere Salvator mundi. [n. 662]

4:39 Ἐκ δὲ τῆς πόλεως ἐκείνης πολλοὶ ἐπίστευσαν εἰς αὐτὸν τῶν Σαμαριτῶν διὰ τὸν λόγον τῆς γυναικὸς μαρτυρούσης ὅτι εἶπέν μοι πάντα ἃ ἐποίησα.

4:40 ὡς οὖν ἦλθον πρὸς αὐτὸν οἱ Σαμαρῖται, ἠρώτων αὐτὸν μεῖναι παρ᾽ αὐτοῖς· καὶ ἔμεινεν ἐκεῖ δύο ἡμέρας.

4:41 καὶ πολλῷ πλείους ἐπίστευσαν διὰ τὸν λόγον αὐτοῦ,

4:42 τῇ τε γυναικὶ ἔλεγον ὅτι οὐκέτι διὰ τὴν σὴν λαλιὰν πιστεύομεν, αὐτοὶ γὰρ ἀκηκόαμεν καὶ οἴδαμεν ὅτι οὗτός ἐστιν ἀληθῶς ὁ σωτὴρ τοῦ κόσμου.

4:39 Now many of the Samaritans of that city believed in him, because of the word of the woman giving testimony: that he told me all things whatsoever that I have done. [n. 657]

4:40 So when the Samaritans came to him, they begged him to stay there. And he remained there two days. [n. 658]

4:41 And many more believed in him because of his own word. [n. 661]

4:42 And they said to the woman: now we believe, not just because of your story: for we ourselves have heard him and know that this indeed is the savior of the world. [n. 662]

---

656. Supra Dominus praenuntiavit apostolis fructum qui Samaritanis provenerat ex praedicatione mulieris; hic autem Evangelista agit de isto fructu, et

primo ponitur fructus proveniens ex praedicatione mulieris;

secundo insinuatur augmentatio ipsius fructus facta per Christum, ibi *et multo plures crediderunt in eum propter sermonem eius*.

Fructus autem ex praedicatione mulieris proveniens ostenditur quantum ad tria.

657. Primo quantum ad fidem, quia, in Christum crediderunt; unde dicit *ex civitate autem illa*, ad quam scilicet abierat mulier, *multi* homines *crediderunt in eum Samaritanorum*, et hoc *propter verbum mulieris*, a qua Christus aquam petierat, *testimonium perhibentis*, hoc scilicet *quia dixit mihi omnia quaecumque feci*: quod quidem testimonium satis inducens erat ad credendum Christo. Cum enim quae Christus dixerat pertinerent ad defectuum suorum manifestationem, nisi ipsa commota fuisset ad credendum, talia non referret: et ideo statim ad auditum verborum suorum crediderunt. In quo significatur quod fides est ex auditu.

658. Secundo ostenditur fructus quantum ad eorum accessum ad Christum: nam ex fide sequitur desiderium rei creditae. Et ideo postquam crediderunt, accedunt ad Christum, ut perficiantur per eum; unde dicit **cum venissent ad illum Samaritani**. Ps. XXXIII, 6: *accedite ad eum, et illuminamini*. Matth. XI, v. 28: *venite ad me, omnes qui laboratis et onerati estis, et ego reficiam vos*.

659. Tertio quantum ad desiderium: nam credenti non solum est necessarium venire ad Christum, sed

656. Above, the Lord foretold to the apostles the fruit to be produced among the Samaritans by the woman's witness. Now the Evangelist deals with this fruit.

First, the fruit of the woman's witness is given.

Second, there is an argument given concerning the growth of this fruit produced by Christ, at *and many more believed in him because of his own word*.

The fruit which is produced from the woman's witness is shown in three ways.

657. First, by the faith of the Samaritans, for they believed in Christ. Thus he says, *many of the Samaritans of that city*, to which the woman had returned, *believed in him*, and this, *because of the word of the woman*, from whom Christ asked for a drink of water, who said, *he told me all things whatsoever that I have done*, for this testimony was sufficient inducement to believe Christ. For since what Christ had said pertained to the manifestation of her failures, she would not have mentioned them unless she had been brought to believe. And so the Samaritans believed as soon as they heard her. This indicates that faith comes by hearing.

658. Second, the fruit of her witness is shown in their coming to Christ: for faith gives rise to a desire for the thing believed. Accordingly, after they believed, they came to Christ, to be perfected by him. So he says, **so when the Samaritans came to him**. Come to him, and be enlightened (Ps 33:6); come to me, all you who labor and are burdened, and I will refresh you (Matt 11:28).

659. Third, the fruit of her witness is shown in their desire: for a believer must not only come to Christ, but desire

quod habeat eum secum; unde dicit quod *rogaverunt eum ut ibi maneret. Et mansit ibi duos dies*.

Manet autem Dominus nobiscum per caritatem. Infra XIV, 23: *si quis diligit me, sermonem meum servabit*; et paulo post: *et mansionem apud eum faciemus*. Sed manet duos dies, quia duo sunt praecepta caritatis, scilicet dilectionis Dei et proximi, in quibus *lex pendet et prophetae*, ut dicitur Matth. c. XXII, 40. Tertia autem dies est dies gloriae: Oseae, VI, 3: *vivificabit nos post duos dies, in die tertia suscitabit nos*. Et in hac die non mansit ibi, quia Samaritani non erant adhuc capaces gloriae.

660. Consequenter cum dicit *et multo plures crediderunt in eum propter sermonem eius*, ponit Evangelista quod fructus proveniens ex praedicatione mulieris, augmentatus est ex praesentia Christi; et hoc tripliciter.

Primo ex multitudine credentium;

secundo ex modo credendi;

tertio ex veritate fidei.

661. Ex multitudine credentium augmentatus est, quia propter mulierem multi crediderunt in eum; sed *multo plures crediderunt propter sermonem eius*, scilicet Christi. In quo signatur, quod licet multi crediderint per prophetas, tamen multo plures conversi sunt ad fidem veniente Christo, secundum illud Ps. VII, 8: *exurge, Domine, in praecepto quod mandasti, et synagoga populorum circumdabit te*.

662. Secundo augmentatus est fructus ex modo credendi; unde dicunt mulieri *quia iam non propter tuam loquelam credimus*.

Sed notandum, quod tria sunt necessaria ad perfectionem fidei, quae hic per ordinem ponuntur. Primo ut sit recta; secundo ut sit prompta; tertio ut sit certa.

Recta quidem est fides, cum veritati non propter aliquod aliud, sed ei propter seipsam obeditur; et quantum ad hoc dicit, quod *mulieri dicebant*, quod iam *credimus* veritati, *non propter tuam loquelam*, sed propter ipsam veritatem.

Inducunt autem nos ad fidem Christi tria. Primo quidem ratio naturalis. Ad Rom. I, 20: *invisibilia Dei a creatura mundi per ea quae facta sunt, intellecta conspiciuntur*. Secundo testimonia legis et prophetarum. Rom. III, v. 21: *nunc autem iustitia Dei sine lege manifestata est, testificata a lege et prophetis*. Tertio praedicatio apostolorum et aliorum. Rom. X, 14: *quomodo credent sine praedicante?* Sed quando per hoc homo manuductus credit, tunc potest dicere, quod propter nullum istorum credit: nec propter rationem naturalem, nec propter testimonia legis, nec propter praedicationem aliorum, sed propter ipsam veritatem tantum; Gen. XV, 6: *credidit Abraham Deo, et reputatum est ei ad iustitiam*.

that Christ remain with him. So he says, *they begged him to stay there. And he remained there two days*.

The Lord remains with us through charity: *if anyone loves me, he will keep my word* (John 14:23), and further on he adds, *and we will make our abode with him*. The Lord remains for two days because there are two precepts of charity: the love of God and the love of our neighbor, *on these two commandments all the law and the prophets depend* (Matt 22:40). But the third day is the day of glory: *he will revive us after two days; on the third day he will raise us up* (Hos 6:3). Christ did not remain there for that day because the Samaritans were not yet capable of glory.

660. Then, at *and many more believed in him because of his own word*, the Evangelist says that the fruit resulting from the witness of the woman was increased by the presence of Christ; and this in three ways.

First, in the number of those who believed.

Second, in their reason for believing.

Third, in the truth they believed.

661. The fruit was increased as to the number of those who believed because while many believed in Christ on account of the woman, *many more believed in him because of his own word*, i.e., Christ's own words. This signifies that although many believed because of the prophets, many more were converted to the faith after Christ came: *rise up, O Lord, in the command you have given, and a congregation of people will surround you* (Ps 7:7).

662. Second, this fruit was increased because of the way in which they believed: for they say to the woman: *now we believe, not just because of your story*.

Here we should note that three things are necessary for the perfection of faith; and they are given here in order. First, faith should be right; second, it should be prompt; and third, it should be certain.

Now faith is right when it obeys the truth not for some alien reason, but for the truth itself; and as to this he says that *they said to the woman*, *now we believe*, the truth, *not just because of your story*, but because of the truth itself.

Three things lead us to believe in Christ. First of all, natural reason: *since the creation of the world the invisible things of God are clearly known by the things that have been made* (Rom 1:20). Second, the testimony of the law and the prophets: *but now justification from God has been manifested outside the law; the law and the prophets bore witness to it* (Rom 3:21). Third, the preaching of the apostles and others: *how will they believe without someone to preach to them?* (Rom 10:14). Yet when a person, having been thus instructed, believes, he can then say that it is not for any of these reasons that he believes: i.e., neither on account of natural reason, nor the testimony of the law, nor the preaching of others, but solely on account of the truth itself: *Abram believed God, who regarded this as his justification* (Gen 15:6).

Prompta quidem est fides, si cito credit: et hoc erat in istis, quia ad solum auditum conversi erant ad Deum; unde dicunt **ipsi enim audivimus, et tamen credimus ei, et scimus quia hic est vere Salvator mundi**, absque hoc quod miracula videremus, sicut Iudaei viderunt. Et licet credere cito hominibus pertineat ad levitatem, secundum illud Eccli. c. XIX, 4: *qui facile credit, levis est corde*, tamen credere cito Deo, magis laus est, secundum illud Ps. XVII, 45: *in auditu auris obedivit mihi.*

Debet fides esse certa, quia qui dubitat in fide, infidelis est; Iac. I, 6: *postulet autem in fide nihil haesitans.* Et ideo istorum fides certa erat, unde dicunt **et scimus**. Aliquando enim ipsum credere dicitur scire, sicut hic patet: quia scientia et fides conveniunt in certitudine. Nam sicut scientia est certa, ita et fides: immo multo magis, quia certitudo scientiae innititur rationi humanae, quae falli potest, certitudo vero fidei innititur rationi divinae, cui contrariari non potest. Differunt tamen in modo: quia fides habet certitudinem ex lumine infuso divinitus, scientia vero ex lumine naturali. Nam sicut certitudo scientiae habetur per prima principia naturaliter cognita, ita et principia fidei cognoscuntur ex lumine infuso divinitus; Eph. II, 8: *gratia salvati estis per fidem; et hoc non ex vobis, Dei enim donum est.*

663. Tertio augmentatus est fructus ex veritate credendi; et ideo dicit **quia hic est vere Salvator mundi**: ubi confitentur Christum salvatorem singularem, verum et universalem.

Singularem quidem, cum discretum eum ab aliis dicunt **hic est**, qui scilicet singulariter salvare venit. Is. XLV, 15: *vere tu es Deus absconditus, Deus Israel salvator.* Actor. IV, v. 12: *non est aliud nomen sub caelo datum hominibus, in quo oporteat salvos fieri.*

Verum autem, cum dicit **vere**: nam cum, secundum Dionysium, salus sit liberatio a malis et conservatio in bonis, est duplex salus: quaedam vera, quaedam non vera. Vera quidem salus, cum liberamur a veris malis, et conservamur in veris bonis. In veteri autem testamento licet missi fuerint aliqui salvatores, non tamen vere salvabant: quia liberabant a malis temporalibus, quae non sunt vera mala, nec vera bona, quia sunt transitoria. Sed Christus est vere salvator, qui liberat a veris malis, scilicet peccatis; Matth. I, 21: *ipse enim salvum faciet populum suum a peccatis eorum.* Et praeservat in veris bonis, idest spiritualibus.

Universalem vero, quia non particularem, scilicet Iudaeorum tantum, sed **mundi**. Supra c. III, 17: **non enim misit Deus Filium suum ut iudicet mundum, sed ut salvetur mundus per ipsum.**

Faith is prompt if it believes quickly; and this was verified in these Samaritans because they were converted to God by merely hearing him; so they say: **for we ourselves have heard him and know that this indeed is the savior of the world**, without seeing miracles, as the Jews saw. And although to believe men quickly is an indication of thoughtlessness: *he who believes easily is frivolous* (Sir 19:4), yet to believe God quickly is more praisworthy: *when they heard me, they obeyed me* (Ps 17:45).

Faith should be certain, because one who doubts in the faith is an unbeliever: *ask with faith, without any doubting* (Jas 1:6). And so their faith was certain; thus they say, **and we know**. Sometimes, one who believes is said to know, as here, because knowledge and faith agree in that both are certain. For just as knowledge is certain, so is faith; indeed, much more so, because the certainty of knowledge rests on human reason, which can be decieved, while the certainty of faith rests on divine reason, which cannot be contradicted. However they differ in mode: because faith possesses its certainty due to a divinely infused light, while knowledge possesses its certainty due to a natural light. For as the certitude of knowledge rests on first principles naturally known, so the principles of faith are known from a light divinely infused: *you are saved by grace, through faith; and this is not due to yourselves, for it is the gift of God* (Eph 2:8).

663. Third, the fruit was increased in the truth believed; so they say, **this indeed is the savior of the world**. Here they are affirming that Christ is the unique, true and universal savior.

He is the unique savior for they assert that he is different from others when they say, **this indeed**, i.e., here he alone is who has come to save: *truly, you are a hidden God, the God of Israel, the savior* (Isa 45:15); *there is no other name under heaven given to men, by which we are saved* (Acts 4:12).

They affirm that Christ is the true savior when they say, **indeed**. For since salvation, as Dionysius says, is deliverance from evil and preservation in good, there are two kinds of salvation: one is true, and the other is not true. Salvation is true when we are freed from true evils and preserved in true goods. In the Old Testament, however, although certain saviors had been sent, they did not truly bring salvation, for they set men free from temporal evils, which are not truly evils, nor true goods, because they do not last. But Christ is truly the savior, because he frees men from true evils, that is, sins: *he will save his people from their sins* (Matt 1:21), and he preserves them in true goods, that is, spiritual goods.

They affirm that he is the universal savior because he is not just for some, i.e., for the Jews alone, but is **the savior of the world. For God did not send his Son into the world to judge the world, but that the world might be saved through him** (John 3:17).

Lecture 6

4:43 Post duos autem dies exiit inde, et abiit in Galilaeam. [n. 665]

4:44 Ipse enim Iesus testimonium perhibuit, quia propheta in sua patria honorem non habet. [n. 666]

4:45 Cum ergo venisset in Galilaeam, exceperunt eum Galilaei, cum omnia vidissent quae fecerat Ierosolymis in die festo: et ipsi enim venerant ad diem festum. [n. 670]

4:46 Venit ergo iterum in Cana Galilaeae, ubi fecit aquam vinum. Et erat quidam regulus, cuius filius infirmabatur Capharnaum. [n. 673]

4:43 Μετὰ δὲ τὰς δύο ἡμέρας ἐξῆλθεν ἐκεῖθεν εἰς τὴν Γαλιλαίαν·

4:44 αὐτὸς γὰρ Ἰησοῦς ἐμαρτύρησεν ὅτι προφήτης ἐν τῇ ἰδίᾳ πατρίδι τιμὴν οὐκ ἔχει.

4:45 ὅτε οὖν ἦλθεν εἰς τὴν Γαλιλαίαν, ἐδέξαντο αὐτὸν οἱ Γαλιλαῖοι πάντα ἑωρακότες ὅσα ἐποίησεν ἐν Ἱεροσολύμοις ἐν τῇ ἑορτῇ, καὶ αὐτοὶ γὰρ ἦλθον εἰς τὴν ἑορτήν.

4:46 Ἦλθεν οὖν πάλιν εἰς τὴν Κανὰ τῆς Γαλιλαίας, ὅπου ἐποίησεν τὸ ὕδωρ οἶνον. Καὶ ἦν τις βασιλικὸς οὗ ὁ υἱὸς ἠσθένει ἐν Καφαρναούμ.

4:43 Now after two days, he departed from there and went into Galilee. [n. 665]

4:44 For Jesus himself gave testimony that a prophet has no honor in his own country. [n. 666]

4:45 And when he had come into Galilee, the Galileans received him, having seen all the things he had done at Jerusalem on the festival day; for they also went to the festival day. [n. 670]

4:46 Therefore he came again into Cana of Galilee, where he made the water wine. And there was a certain ruler, whose son was sick at Capernaum. [n. 673]

---

664. Posita conversione gentium per viam doctrinae hic ponitur ipsorum conversio per viam miraculi: unde et quoddam miraculum a Christo perpetratum Evangelista inducit, circa quod

primo ponitur locus;

secundo describitur miraculum, ibi *et erat quidam regulus* etc.;

tertio ponitur miraculi effectus, ibi *cognovit ergo pater* etc.

Circa primum duo facit.

Primo designat generalem locum miraculi, scilicet patriam;

secundo specialem, ibi *venit ergo iterum in Cana Galilaeae*.

Circa primum duo facit.

Primo designat generalem locum miraculi;

secundo insinuat quomodo Christus fuit ibi receptus, ibi *cum ergo venisset in Galilaeam*.

Circa primum duo facit.

Primo designat locum generalem;

secundo rationem assignat, ibi *ipse enim Iesus testimonium perhibuit*, etc.

665. Dicit ergo primo: dico quod mansit Iesus apud Samaritanos per duos dies, et *post duos dies exiit inde*, id est de Samaria, *et abiit in Galilaeam*, ubi nutritus fuerat: per quod significatur quod in fine saeculi, confirmatis gentibus in fide et veritate, revertetur ad Iudaeos convertendos, secundum illud Rom. XI, 25: *donec omnis plenitudo gentium intraret, et sic omnis Israel salvus fieret.*

664. Having described the conversion of the gentiles due to teaching, their conversion due to miracles is now given. The Evangelist mentions a miracle performed by Christ:

first, giving the place;

second, describing the miracle, at *and there was a certain ruler, whose son was sick at Capernaum*, and

third, its effect, at *the father therefore knew that it was at the same hour* (John 4:53).

He does two things about the first.

First, he gives the general location of the miracle, that is, Christ's own homeland.

Second, the specific place, at *therefore he came again into Cana of Galilee*.

With respect to the first he does two things.

First, he mentions the general place.

Second, he tells how Christ was received there, at *and when he had come into Galilee*.

Concerning the first he does two things.

First, he indicates the general place.

Second, he gives a certain reason, at *for Jesus himself gave testimony*.

665. He says first of all: I say that Jesus remained with these Samaritans for two days, and *after two days, he departed from there*, i.e., Samaria, *and went to Galilee*, where he had been raised. This signifies that at the end of the world, when the gentiles have been confirmed in the faith and in the truth, a return will be made to convert the Jews, according to: *until the full number of the gentiles enters, and so all Israel will be saved* (Rom 11:25).

666. Et rationem assignat, dicens *ipse enim Iesus testimonium perhibuit, quia propheta in sua patria honorem non habet*.

Hic oritur dubitatio: una quidem de sententia litterae; alia vero de eius continuatione.

De sententia quidem litterae dubitatur, quia non videtur verum esse quod hic dicitur, scilicet quod propheta in patria sua honorem non habet: nam aliqui prophetae honorati leguntur in terra sua.

Sed, secundum Chrysostomum, respondetur ad hoc, quia Dominus hic loquitur prout in pluribus accidit. Unde licet in aliquo singulari habeat instantiam, non tamen propter hoc debet reputari falsum, nam in naturalibus et in moralibus, regula eorum quae ut in pluribus verificatur, est vera; et si in aliquo particulari aliter sit, non reputatur falsa. Istud autem quod Dominus dicit, in pluribus prophetarum verum erat, quia in Veteri Testamento vix invenitur aliquis prophetarum, qui a suis contribulibus persecutionem passus non fuerit, secundum illud Actor. VII, 52: *quem prophetarum non sunt persecuti patres vestri?* Et Matth. XXIII, 37: *Ierusalem, Ierusalem quae occidis prophetas, et lapidas eos qui ad te missi sunt.*

Hoc etiam verbum Domini verificatur non solum in prophetis apud Iudaeos, sed etiam, ut Origenes dicit, in pluribus apud gentiles, quia a suis civibus sunt habiti contemptui, et ad mortem deducti: nam consueta conversatio cum hominibus, et nimia familiaritas, reverentiam minuit, et contemptum parit. Et ideo quos familiares magis habemus, minus revereri consuevimus, et quos familiares habere non possumus, magis reputamus. Cuius contrarium contingit de Deo: nam quanto aliquis Deo per amorem et contemplationem familiarior efficitur, tanto eum excellentiorem reputans, magis revereretur, et seipsum minorem reputat: Iob XLII, 5: *auditu auris audivi te, nunc autem oculus meus videt te: idcirco ipse me reprehendo, et ago poenitentiam in favilla et cinere.* Et huius ratio est, quia in homine, cum sit infirmae et fragilis naturae, quando cum alio diu conversatur, cognoscit in eo aliqua infirma, et ex hoc diminuitur reverentia eius ad eum. Sed cum Deus sit immense perfectus, quanto plus homo in cognitione eius proficit, tanto magis perfectionis eius excellentiam admiratur, et ex hoc eum magis reveretur.

667. Sed numquid Christus propheta fuit? Videtur quod non, quia prophetia importat aenigmaticam cognitionem. Num. XII, 6: *si quis fuerit inter vos propheta Domini, in visione apparebo ei.* Christus autem non habuit aenigmaticam cognitionem.

Quod autem propheta fuerit, patet per illud quod dicitur Deut. XVIII, 15: *prophetam suscitabit Dominus de fratribus tuis et de gente tua sicut me; ipsum audies*: quod exponitur de Christo.

666. Then he gives a certain reason, saying: *Jesus himself gave testimony that a prophet has no honor in his own country*.

There are two questions here: one is about the literal meaning; and the other about the continuity of this passage with the first.

The problem about the literal meaning is that it does not seem to be true, as stated here, that a prophet has no honor in his own country: for we read that other prophets were honored in their own land.

Chrysostom answers this by saying that the Lord is speaking here about the majority of cases. So, although there might be an exception in some individual cases, however, what is said here should not be considered false: for in matters concerning nature and morals, that rule is true which is verified in most cases; and if a few cases are otherwise, the rule is not considered to be false. Now what the Lord says was true with respect to most of the prophets, because in the Old Testament it is hard to find any prophet who did not suffer persecution from his own people: *which of the prophets did your fathers not persecute?* (Acts 7:52); *Jerusalem, Jerusalem, you kill the prophets and stone those who are sent to you* (Matt 23:37).

Further, this statement of our Lord holds true not only in the case of the prophets among the Jews, but also, as Origen says, with many among the gentiles, because they were held in contempt by their fellow citizens and put to death: for living with men in the usual way, and too much familiarity, lessen respect and breed contempt. So it is that those with whom we are more familiar we come to reverence less, and those with whom we cannot become acquainted we regard more highly. However, the opposite happens with God: for the more intimate we become with God through love and contemplation, realizing how superior he is, the more we respect him and the less do we esteem ourselves. *I have heard you, but now I see you, and so I reprove myself, and do penance in dust and ashes* (Job 42:5). The reason for this is that man's nature is weak and fragile; and when one lives with another for a long time, he notices certain weaknesses in him, and this results in a loss of respect for him. But since God is infinitely perfect, the more a person knows him the more he admires his superior perfection, and as a result the more he respects him.

667. But was Christ a prophet? At first glance it seems not, because prophecy involves an obscure knowledge: *if there is a prophet of the Lord among you, I will appear to him in a vision* (Num 12:6). Christ's knowledge, however, was not obscure.

Yet he was a prophet, as is clear from, *the Lord your God will raise up a prophet for you, from your nation and your brothers; he will be like me. You will listen to him* (Deut 18:15). This text is referred to Christ.

Respondeo dicendum, quod propheta duplex habet officium: scilicet visionis, I Reg. IX, 9: *qui nunc vocatur propheta, olim dicebatur videns*, item Annuntiationis, et quantum ad hoc Christus propheta fuit, quia veritatem de Deo annuntiavit; infra XVIII, 37: **ad hoc natus sum, et ad hoc veni in mundum, ut testimonium perhibeam veritati**. Sed quantum ad primum, sciendum est, quod Christus fuit simul viator et comprehensor. Viator quidem, quantum ad humanae naturae passibilitatem, et ad omnia quae ad eam pertinent; comprehensor vero quantum ad unionem divinitatis, secundum quam Deo perfectissime fruebatur.

Sed in visione prophetiae duo sunt. Scilicet lumen intellectuale mentis; et quantum ad hoc non habuit rationem prophetiae: quia non habuit lumen defectivum, sed comprehensoris. Item est ibi visio imaginaria; et quantum ad hoc habuit similitudinem cum prophetis, secundum quod viator fuit, et poterat diversa formare imaginatione sua.

668. De continuatione dubitatur: non enim videtur Evangelista recte continuare hoc quod dicit **post duos autem dies abiit Iesus in Galilaeam**, cum hoc quod dicitur: **ipse enim testimonium perhibuit** etc. Videtur enim quod non abiit in Galilaeam, quia **ipse Iesus testimonium perhibuit**. Si enim sine honore erat ibi, videtur ratio esse quod non iret illuc.

Ad hoc, uno modo respondet Augustinus dicens, hoc Evangelistam dixisse respondendo quaestioni quae posset fieri: quare ibat illuc, cum in Galilaea diu moratus fuisset, et non fuerunt ad eum conversi Galilaei; et Samaritani in duobus diebus conversi sunt? Quasi dicat: licet conversi non fuerint nihilominus tamen ipse illuc abiit **quia ipse testimonium perhibuit, quod propheta in sua patria honorem non habet**.

Alio modo respondet Chrysostomus sic: **post duos dies exiit inde, et abiit**, non in Capharnaum, quae erat patria sua propter continuam commorationem, Bethlehem autem propter originem, Nazareth vero propter educationem. Non ergo abiit in Capharnaum; unde Matth. XI, 23, hoc exprobrat eis, dicens: *et tu, Capharnaum, numquid usque in caelum exaltaberis? Usque in Infernum descendes*. Sed in Cana Galilaeae. Et rationem assignat hic, quia male se habebant ad eum. Et hoc est, quod dicit **ipse enim Iesus testimonium perhibuit, quod propheta in sua patria honorem non habet**.

669. Sed numquid Christus quaerebat gloriam ab hominibus? Videtur quod non, quia infra VIII, 50, dicit: **ego non quaero gloriam meam**.

Respondeo dicendum, quod solus Deus est qui sine vitio gloriam suam quaerit. Homo autem ab hominibus

I answer that a prophet has a twofold function. First, that of seeing: *he who is now called a prophet was formerly called a seer* (I Sam 9:9). Second, he makes known, announces; Christ was a prophet in this sense for he made known the truth about God: **for this I was born, and for this I came into the world, that I should give testimony to the truth** (John 18:37). As for the seeing function of a prophet, we should note that Christ was at once both a wayfarer and a blessed. He was a wayfarer in the sufferings of his human nature and in all the things that relate to this. He was a blessed in his union with the divinity, by which he enjoyed God in the most perfect way.

There are two things in the vision or seeing of a prophet. First, the intellectual light of his mind; and as regards this Christ was not a prophet, because his light was not at all deficient; his light was that of the blessed. Second, an imaginary vision is also involved; and with respect to this Christ did have a likeness to the prophets insofar as he was a wayfarer and was able to form various images with his imagination.

668. Second, there is the problem about continuity. For the Evangelist does not seem to be right in connecting the fact that **now after two days, he departed from there and went into Galilee**, with the statement of Jesus that **a prophet has no honor in his own country**. It would seem that the Evangelist should have said that Christ did not go into Galilee, for if he was not honored there, that would be a reason for not going there: **for Jesus himself gave testimony that a prophet has no honor in his own country**.

Augustine answers this by suggesting that the Evangelist said this to answer a question that could have been raised, namely: why did Christ return to Galilee since he had lived there for a long time, and the Galileans were still not converted to him; while the Samaritans were converted in two days? It is the same as saying: even though the Galileans had not been converted, still Jesus went there, **for Jesus himself gave testimony that a prophet has no honor in his own country**.

Chrysostom explains this in a different way: **after two days, he departed from there**, not for Capernaum, which was his homeland because of his continuous residence there, nor for Bethlehem, where he was born, nor for Nazareth, where he was educated. Thus he did not go to Capernaum; hence he upbraids them, saying: *and you, Capernaum, will you be exalted to heaven? You will descend even to hell* (Matt 11:23). He went rather to Cana in Galilee. And he gives the reason here: because they were ill-disposed toward him. This is what he says: **for Jesus himself gave testimony that a prophet has no honor in his own country**.

669. Was Christ seeking glory from men? It seems not, for he says: **I do not seek my own glory** (John 8:50).

I answer that it is only God who seeks his own glory without sin. A man should not seek his own glory from

quaerere non debet gloriam suam, sed gloriam Dei. Christus autem quaerebat inquantum Deus convenienter gloriam suam, et inquantum homo gloriam Dei in seipso.

670. Consequenter cum dicit **cum ergo venisset in Galilaeam** etc., ostendit quod honorifice fuerit Christus a Galilaeis receptus magis quam ante, cum dicit **cum ergo venisset in Galilaeam** Iesus, **exceperunt eum Galilaei** honorifice. Et huius ratio est, quia **viderunt omnia quae fecerat Ierosolymis in die festo: et ipsi enim venerant ad diem festum**, secundum quod mandabatur in lege.

Sed contra hoc est quia supra non legimus Christum aliquod miraculum Ierosolymis fecisse.

Respondeo dicendum, secundum Origenem, quod Iudaei maximum miraculum reputaverunt hoc quod Christus cum tanta auctoritate expulit ementes et vendentes de templo. Vel dicendum, quod forte fecit ibi plura miracula quae non scripta sunt, secundum illud infra ult., 25: **multa quidem et alia signa fecit Iesus . . . quae non sunt scripta in libro hoc**.

671. Mystice autem per hoc datur nobis exemplum, quod si volumus in nobis recipere Christum Iesum, oportet nos ascendere in Ierusalem in die festo; idest, captare quietem mentis, et videre singula quae peragit ibi Iesus. Is. XXXIII, 20: **respice Sion civitatem solemnitatis nostrae**; Ps. CXLII, 5: **meditatus sum in omnibus operibus tuis**.

672. Attende autem, quod secundum quod homines inferiores erant in ordine dignitatis, meliores erant quo ad Deum. Iudaei autem digniores erant quam Galilaei; infra c. VII, 52: **scrutamini Scripturas, et vide, quia propheta a Galilaea non surrexit**. Galilaei vero digniores erant quam Samaritani; supra eodem: **non coutuntur Iudaei Samaritanis**. Sed e converso Samaritani meliores erant quam Galilaei, quia plures ex eis crediderunt in Christum in duobus diebus et sine miraculo, quam de Galilaeis in multis diebus, et etiam cum miraculo vini: non enim crediderunt in eum nisi eius discipuli. Iudaei vero peiores erant ipsis Galilaeis; quia nullus ex eis crediderat, nisi forte Nicodemus.

673. Consequenter dicit **venit ergo iterum in Cana Galilaeae**: quod, secundum Chrysostomum, ponitur ut conclusio praemissorum; quasi dicat: quia non honorabatur in Capharnaum, ideo noluit ire illuc, ubi dehonorabatur. Sed in Cana Galilaeae ire debebat: nam primo erat invitatus ad nuptias, modo autem venit iterum non invitatus. Ideo autem de duplici adventu in Cana mentionem facit, ut ostendat eorum duritiam: nam in primo miraculo, scilicet de vino, soli discipuli eius crediderunt

men, but rather the glory of God. Christ, however, as God, fittingly sought his own glory, and as man, he sought the glory of God in himself.

670. Then he shows that Christ was received by the Galileans more respectfully than before, saying, **and when he had come into Galilee, the Galileans received him** honorably. The reason behind this was that they had **seen all the things he had done at Jerusalem on the festival day; for they also went to the festival day**, as the law commanded.

This seems to conflict with the fact that we did not read above of any miracles being performed by Christ at Jerusalem.

I answer, with the opinion of Origen, that the Jews thought it a great miracle that Christ drove the traders from the temple with such authority (John 2:14). Or, we could say that Christ performed many miracles which were not written down, according to, **many other signs as well did Jesus do . . . which are not written in this book** (John 20:30).

671. In its mystical sense, this gives us an example that if we wish to receive Jesus Christ within ourselves, we should go up to Jerusalem on a festive day, that is, we should seek tranquility of mind, and examine everything which Jesus does there: **look upon Zion, the city of our festive days** (Isa 33:20); **I have meditated on all Your works** (Ps 142:5).

672. Note that as men were lesser in dignity, they were better with respect to God. The Judeans were superior in dignity to the Galileans: **search the Scriptures and see that, out of Galilee, a prophet does not rise** (John 7:52); and the Galileans were superior in dignity to the Samaritans: **the Jews do not communicate with the Samaritans** (John 4:9). On the other hand, the Samaritans were better than the Galileans because more of them believed in Christ in two days without any miracles than the Galileans did in a long period of time and even with the miracle of the wine: for none of them believed in him except his disciples. Finally, the Judeans were worse than the Galileans, because none of them believed in Jesus, except perhaps Nicodemus.

673. Then he says, **he came again into Cana of Galilee**. According to Chrysostom, this is given as a conclusion from what went before; it is as though he were saying: Christ did not go to Capernaum because he was not held in honor there. But he was under an obligation to go to Cana in Galilee: for on the first occasion he had been invited to the wedding, and now he goes again without being invited. The two trips to Cana are mentioned by the Evangelist to show their hardness of heart: for at the first miracle of the

in eum; in secundo vero solus regulus, et domus eius tota. Sed Samaritani ad solum verbum crediderunt.

674. Mystice autem per duplicem adventum in Cana, signatur duplex effectus verbi Dei in mentem. Primo enim laetificat: quia, ut dicitur Matth. XIII, 20: *cum gaudio suscipiunt verbum.* Et hoc signatur in miraculo vini, quod *laetificat cor hominis,* ut dicitur in Ps. CIII. Secundo sanat; Sap. XVI, 12: *neque herba, neque malagma sanavit eos, sed sermo tuus, Domine, qui sanat omnia.* Et hoc significatur in cura infirmi.

Item per hoc significatur duplex adventus Filii Dei. Scilicet primus, qui fuit mansuetudinis ad laetificandum; Is. XII, 6: *exulta et lauda, habitatio Sion, quia magnus in medio tui Sanctus Israel.* Unde et angelus ad pastores ait, Lc. II, 10: *annuntio vobis gaudium magnum, quia natus est vobis hodie salvator.* Et hoc signatur per vinum. Secundus adventus eius in mundum erit maiestatis, quando veniet tollere infirmitates et poenalitates nostras, et configurare nos corpori claritatis suae; et hoc signatur in cura infirmi.

wine, only his disciples believed in Christ; and at the second miracle, only the official and his household believed. On the other hand, the Samaritans believed on Christ's words alone.

674. In the mystical sense, the two visits to Cana signify the effect of God's words on our minds. First of all they cause delight, because they who hear the word *receive the word with joy* (Matt 13:20). This is signified in the miracle of the wine, which *gladdens the heart of man* (Ps 103:15). Second, the word of God heals: *it was neither a herb nor a poultice that healed them, but your word, O Lord, which heals all things* (Wis 16:12). And this is signified by the curing of the sick son.

Further, these two visits to Cana indicate the two comings of the Son of God. The first coming was in all gentleness to bring joy: *rejoice and give praise, people of Zion, for he is great who is in your midst, the Holy One of Israel* (Isa 12:6). So the angel said to the shepherds: *I bring you good news of great joy . . . this day a savior has been born to you* (Luke 2:10). This is signified by the wine. His second coming into the world will be in majesty, when he will come to take away our weaknesses and our punishments, and to make us like his radiant body. And this is signified in the cure of the sick son.

Lecture 7

4:46 Venit ergo iterum in Cana Galilaeae, ubi fecit aquam vinum. Et erat quidam regulus, cuius filius infirmabatur Capharnaum. [n. 676]

4:47 Hic cum audisset, quia Iesus adveniret a Iudaea in Galilaeam, abiit ad eum; et rogabat eum ut descenderet, et sanaret filium eius: incipiebat enim mori. [n. 679]

4:48 Dixit ergo Iesus ad eum: nisi signa et prodigia videritis, non creditis. [n. 683]

4:49 Dicit ad eum regulus: Domine, descende priusquam moriatur filius meus. [n. 686]

4:50 Dicit ei Iesus: vade, filius tuus vivit. Credidit homo sermoni quem dixit ei Iesus, et ibat. [n. 687]

4:51 Iam autem eo descendente, servi occurrerunt ei, et nuntiaverunt dicentes, quia filius eius viveret. [n. 692]

4:52 Interrogabat ergo horam ab eis in qua melius habuerat. Et dixerunt ei, quia heri hora septima reliquit eum febris. [n. 694]

4:53 Cognovit ergo pater quod illa hora erat in qua dixit ei Iesus, filius tuus vivit; et credidit ipse, et domus eius tota. [n. 697]

4:54 Hoc iterum secundum signum fecit Iesus, cum venisset a Iudaea in Galilaeam. [n. 698]

4:46 ῏Ηλθεν οὖν πάλιν εἰς τὴν Κανὰ τῆς Γαλιλαίας, ὅπου ἐποίησεν τὸ ὕδωρ οἶνον. Καὶ ἦν τις βασιλικὸς οὗ ὁ υἱὸς ἠσθένει ἐν Καφαρναούμ.

4:47 οὗτος ἀκούσας ὅτι Ἰησοῦς ἥκει ἐκ τῆς Ἰουδαίας εἰς τὴν Γαλιλαίαν ἀπῆλθεν πρὸς αὐτὸν καὶ ἠρώτα ἵνα καταβῇ καὶ ἰάσηται αὐτοῦ τὸν υἱόν, ἤμελλεν γὰρ ἀποθνήσκειν.

4:48 εἶπεν οὖν ὁ Ἰησοῦς πρὸς αὐτόν· ἐὰν μὴ σημεῖα καὶ τέρατα ἴδητε, οὐ μὴ πιστεύσητε.

4:49 λέγει πρὸς αὐτὸν ὁ βασιλικός· κύριε, κατάβηθι πρὶν ἀποθανεῖν τὸ παιδίον μου.

4:50 λέγει αὐτῷ ὁ Ἰησοῦς· πορεύου, ὁ υἱός σου ζῇ. ἐπίστευσεν ὁ ἄνθρωπος τῷ λόγῳ ὃν εἶπεν αὐτῷ ὁ Ἰησοῦς καὶ ἐπορεύετο.

4:51 ἤδη δὲ αὐτοῦ καταβαίνοντος οἱ δοῦλοι αὐτοῦ ὑπήντησαν αὐτῷ λέγοντες ὅτι ὁ παῖς αὐτοῦ ζῇ.

4:52 ἐπύθετο οὖν τὴν ὥραν παρ' αὐτῶν ἐν ᾗ κομψότερον ἔσχεν· εἶπαν οὖν αὐτῷ ὅτι ἐχθὲς ὥραν ἑβδόμην ἀφῆκεν αὐτὸν ὁ πυρετός.

4:53 ἔγνω οὖν ὁ πατὴρ ὅτι [ἐν] ἐκείνῃ τῇ ὥρᾳ ἐν ᾗ εἶπεν αὐτῷ ὁ Ἰησοῦς· ὁ υἱός σου ζῇ, καὶ ἐπίστευσεν αὐτὸς καὶ ἡ οἰκία αὐτοῦ ὅλη.

4:54 Τοῦτο [δὲ] πάλιν δεύτερον σημεῖον ἐποίησεν ὁ Ἰησοῦς ἐλθὼν ἐκ τῆς Ἰουδαίας εἰς τὴν Γαλιλαίαν.

4:46 Therefore he came again into Cana of Galilee, where he made the water wine. And there was a certain ruler, whose son was sick at Capharnaum. [n. 676]

4:47 When he had heard that Jesus came from Judea into Galilee, he went to him, and begged him to come down and heal his son; for he was at the point of death. [n. 679]

4:48 Jesus therefore said to him: unless you see signs and wonders, you do not believe. [n. 683]

4:49 The ruler said to him: Lord, come down before my son dies. [n. 686]

4:50 Jesus said to him: go, your son lives. The man believed the word that Jesus said to him and went his way. [n. 687]

4:51 And as he was going down, his servants ran to meet him; and they brought word, saying that his son lived. [n. 692]

4:52 Therefore he asked of them the hour in which he grew better. And they said to him: yesterday, at the seventh hour, the fever left him. [n. 694]

4:53 The father therefore knew that it was at the same hour that Jesus said to him, your son lives; and he himself believed, and his whole household. [n. 697]

4:54 This is again the second miracle that Jesus did when he came out of Judea into Galilee. [n. 698]

---

675. Posito loco miraculi, consequenter agitur de ipso miraculo; et ponuntur tria, scilicet persona infirmans, persona interpellans et persona sanans.

Persona infirmans est filius reguli, persona interpellans est pater eius, sed persona sanans est Christus.

676. Circa personam infirmam primo ponitur eius conditio, quia *filius* reguli; secundo locus infirmitatis, quia *Capharnaum*; tertio conditio morbi, quia *febris*.

675. Having told us the place of this miracle, the Evangelist now describes the miracle itself: telling us of the person who was ill; the one who interceded for him; and the one who healed him.

The one who was ill was the son of the official; his father interceded for him; and it was Christ who was to heal him.

676. About the person who was ill, he first tells us of his status, the *son* of an official; second, where he was, at *Capernaum*; third, his illness, a *fever*.

Quantum ad primum dicit *erat quidam regulus, cuius filius infirmabatur*. Dicitur autem regulus multipliciter. Uno modo qui praeest parvo regno; et hoc modo non accipitur hic: quia tunc temporis nullus erat rex in Iudaea; infra XIX, 15: *non habemus regem nisi Caesarem*. Alio modo, secundum Chrysostomum, aliquis de stirpe regia: nec hoc modo accipitur. Sed tertio modo regulus dicitur aliquis officialis regis; et isto modo accipitur hic regulus.

Unde, secundum quod Chrysostomus dicit, quidam eumdem ipsum aestimant centurionem, de quo habetur Matth. VIII, 5. Sed hoc non est verum: nam quantum ad quatuor differunt. Primo quidem quantum ad genus infirmitatis: nam ille centurionis erat paralyticus, unde dicebat *puer meus iacet paralyticus in domo*. Filius autem reguli erat febricitans; unde dicit: *heri hora septima reliquit eum febris*. Secundo quantum ad personam infirmatam, quia ille erat servus: unde dicit *puer meus*, iste vero erat filius: unde dicit *cuius filius*. Tertio quantum ad petitionem: nam centurio Christum volentem ad domum suam ire, rogabat remanere, dicens: *Domine, non sum dignus ut intres sub tectum meum, sed tantum dic verbo, et sanabitur puer meus*. Regulus vero eum rogabat descendere in domum suam, dicens: *Domine, descende prius quam moriatur*. Quarto quantum ad locum: quia illud fuit in Capharnaum; istud vero in Cana Galilaeae. Ergo iste regulus non est idem quod centurio; sed erat quidam de familia Herodis Tetrarchae, sive nuntius, sive officialis Imperatoris.

677. Allegorice autem regulus iste, Abraham, vel aliquis ex patribus Veteris Testamenti dicitur, ex eo quod adhaeret magno regi per fidem, scilicet Christo; de quo dicitur in Ps. II, 6: *ego autem constitutus sum rex ab eo*. Huic autem Abraham adhaesit, secundum illud infra VIII, 56: *Abraham pater vester exultavit ut videret diem meum*. Filius eius est populus Iudaeorum, infra VIII, 33: *semen Abrahae sumus, et nemini servivimus unquam*, qui infirmatur pravis voluptatibus et dogmatibus, sed in Capharnaum, idest in abundantia, quae fuit Iudaeis causa recedendi a Deo; secundum illud Deut. XXXII, 15: *incrassatus est dilectus, et recalcitravit*; et sequitur: *dereliquit Deum factorem suum, et recessit a Deo salutari suo*.

678. Moraliter vero in regno animae rex est ipsa ratio, secundum illud Prov. XX, 8: *rex qui sedet in solio suo*.

Quare dicitur rex? Quia totum corpus hominis per eam regitur, et affectus hominis ab ea dirigitur et informatur, nec non et aliae vires animae eam sequuntur. Sed quandoque dicitur regulus, quando scilicet diminuitur in cognitione, qua obscurata, sequitur inordinatas passiones, et non resistit eis, secundum illud Eph. IV, 17: *ambulant in vanitate sensus sui, tenebris obscuratum habentes intellectum*. Et ideo filius eius, idest affectus,

He says about the first, *there was a certain ruler, whose son was sick*. Now one can be called an official for a variety of reasons. For example, if one is in charge of a small territory. This is not its meaning here for at this time there was no king in Judea: *we have no king but Caesar* (John 19:15). One is also called an official, as Chrysostom says, because he is from a royal family; and this is also not its meaning here. In a third way, an official is some officer of a king or ruler; and this is its meaning here.

Some think, as Chrysostom reports, that this official is the same as the centurion mentioned in Matthew (Matt 8:5). This is not so, for they differ in four ways. First, because the illness was not the same in each. The centurion was concerned with a paralytic, *my servant is lying paralyzed at home* (Matt 8:6); while this official's son is suffering from a fever, *yesterday, at the seventh hour, the fever left him*. Second, those who are sick are not the same. In the first case, it was a servant, *my servant*; but now we have a son, as it says, *whose son*. Third, what is requested is different. For when Christ wanted to go to the home of the centurion, the centurion discouraged him, and said: *Lord, I am not worthy to have you come under my roof; but only say the word and my servant will be healed* (Matt 8:8). But this official asked Christ to come to his house, *Lord, come down before my son dies*. Fourth, the places are different. For the first healing took place at Capernaum, while this one is at Cana in Galilee. So this official is not the same as the centurion, but was from the household of Herod the Tetrarch, or some kind of a herald, or an official of the Emperor.

677. In its allegorical sense, this official is Abraham or one of the fathers of the Old Testament, in so far as he adheres by faith to the king, that is, to Christ, about which we read, *I was made king by him over Zion* (Ps 2:6). Abraham adhered to him, for as is said: *your father Abraham rejoiced that he might see my day* (John 8:56). The son of this official is the Jewish people: *we are the seed of Abraham, and we have never been slaves to anyone* (John 8:33). But they are sick from evil pleasures and incorrect doctrines. They are sick at Capernaum, i.e., in the abundance of goods which caused them to leave their God, according to, *the beloved grew fat and rebellious . . . he deserted the God who made him, and left God his savior* (Deut 32:15).

678. In the moral sense, in the kingdom of the soul, the king is reason itself: *the king, who sits on his throne of judgment* (Prov 20:8).

But why is reason called the king? Because man's entire body is ruled by it: his affections are directed and informed by it, and the other powers of the soul follow it. But sometimes it is called an official, that is, when its knowledge is obscured, with the result that it follows inordinate passions and does not resist them: *they live with their foolish ideas, their understanding obscured by darkness* (Eph 4:17). Consequently, the son of this official, i.e., the affections, are sick,

infirmatur, idest deviat a bono, et declinat ad malum. Si enim ratio fuisset rex, idest fortis, filius eius non infirmaretur; sed quia regulus est, ideo filius eius infirmatur. Et hoc Capharnaum; quia abundantia temporalium est causa spiritualis infirmitatis; Ez. XVI, 49: *haec fuit iniquitas sororis tuae Sodomae, abundantia, saturitas panis, et otium ipsius et filiarum eius.*

679. Consequenter cum dicit **hic cum audisset** etc., ponitur persona interpellans, et

primo ponitur motivum ad interpellandum;

secundo ipsa interpellatio; et

tertio necessitas interpellandi.

680. Motivum ad interpellandum fuit adventus Christi; unde dicit **hic**, scilicet regulus, **cum audisset quod Iesus adveniret a Iudaea in Galilaeam, abiit ad eum**. Nam quamdiu adventus Christi differebatur, spes hominum invalidior erat de sanatione a peccatis; sed cum auditur adventus Christi appropinquare, spes sanitatis confortatur in nobis; et tunc imus ad eum: nam ad hoc ipse venit in mundum, ut peccatores salvos faceret; Lc. XIX, 10: *venit Filius hominis quaerere et salvum facere quod perierat.*

Sed, sicut dicit Eccli. XVIII, 23, ante orationem animam parare debemus, quod fit occurrendo Deo per desiderium: et hoc fecit iste; unde dicitur quod **abiit ad eum**. Amos c. IV, 12: *praeparare in occursum Dei tui Israel.*

681. Petitio autem fit de sanatione filii sui; unde dicit **rogabat eum ut descenderet**, scilicet per misericordiam; Is. LXIV, 1: *utinam dirumperes caelos, et descenderes; et sanaret filium eius.* Sic et nos debemus rogare ut sanemur a peccatis, secundum illud Ps. XL, v. 5: *sana animam meam, quia peccavi tibi.* Nam nullus per se potest ad statum iustitiae redire, nisi a Deo sanetur, secundum illud Iob VI, 13: *non est auxilium mihi ex me.* Sic et patres Veteris Testamenti rogabant pro populo Israel. Unde de uno eorum dicitur II Mac. ult. 14: *hic est fratrum amator, quia multum orat pro sancta civitate et pro populo Israel, Ieremias propheta Dei.*

682. Sed necessitas interpellandi est urgens, **incipiebat enim mori**.

Quando enim homo tentatur, incipit infirmari; sed quando tentatio praevalet ita ut inclinet ad consensum, est prope mortem, sed quando iam consentit, incipit mori. Cum ergo consummat peccatum, moritur, quia, ut dicitur Iac. I, 15: *peccatum cum consummatum fuerit, generat mortem.* De qua dicitur in Ps. c. XXXIII, 22: *mors peccatorum pessima*, quia hic incipit, et in futuro absque fine terminatur.

683. Consequenter cum dicit: **dixit ergo Iesus ad eum**, agitur de petitione sanitatis, quae fit per Christum, et

primo ponitur reprehensio Domini;

that is, they deviate from good and decline to what is evil. If reason were the king, that is, strong, its son would not be sick; but being only an official, its son is sick. This happens at Capernaum because a great many temporal goods are the cause of spiritual sickness: *this was the crime of your sister Sodom: richness, satiety in food, and idleness* (Ezek 16:49).

679. Now we see the person making his request, at **when he had heard that Jesus came from Judea into Galilee**.

First, we have the incentive for making his request.

Second, the request itself.

Third, the need for the request.

680. The incentive for making the request was the arrival of Christ. So he says, **when he**, i.e., the ruler, **had heard that Jesus came from Judea into Galilee, he went to him**. For as long as the coming of Christ was delayed, men's hope of being healed from their sins was that much fainter; but when it is reported that his coming is near, our hope of being healed rises, and then we go to him. For he came into this world to save sinners: *the Son of man came to seek and to save what was lost* (Luke 19:22).

Further, we should prepare our soul by prayer (Sir 18:23), and we do this by going to God through our desires. And this is what the official did, as we read, **he went to him**. Thus it is said *be prepared to meet your God, O Israel* (Amos 4:12).

681. The request of the official was that Christ heal his son. So the Evangelist says that **he begged him to come down**, out of compassion: *O that you would rend the heavens, and come down* (Isa 64:1), **and heal his son**. We, too, ought to ask to be healed from our sins: *heal my soul, for I have sinned against you* (Ps 40:5). For no one of himself can return to the state of justice; rather, he has to be healed by God: *I cannot help myself* (Job 6:13). The fathers of the Old Testament interceded for the people of Israel in the same way; for as we read of one: *he loves his brothers, because he prays much for the holy city and for the people of Israel, Jeremiah, the prophet of God* (2 Macc 15:14).

682. The need for this request was urgent, for the son **was at the point of death**.

When a person is tempted, he is beginning to become sick; and as the temptation grows stronger and takes the upper hand, inclining him to consent, he is near death. But when he has consented, he is at the point of death and beginning to die. Finally, when he completes his sin, he dies; for as we read: *sin, when it is completed, brings forth death* (Jas 1:15). It is said: *the death of sinners is the worst* (Ps 33:22), because it begins here and continues into the future without end.

683. Now he deals with the request for Christ to heal the son of the official, at **Jesus therefore said to him**.

First, our Lord's criticism is given.

secundo petitio reguli;

tertio impetratio petitionis.

684. Reprehendit autem eum Dominus de infidelitate; unde dicit ad eum *nisi signa et prodigia videritis, non creditis*.

Sed hoc habet quaestionem. Primo quidem videtur inconvenienter dictum de regulo *nisi signa et prodigia videritis, non creditis*: nisi enim eum salvatorem credidisset, non petivisset ab eo sanitatem.

Ad quod dicendum est, quod regulus iste adhuc non credebat perfecte: erat enim in eo duplex defectus fidei. Unus, quia licet crederet Christum esse verum hominem, non tamen credebat eum habere virtutem divinam; alias credidisset eum absentem posse sanare, cum Deus ubique sit praesens, secundum illud Ier. XXIII, 24: *caelum et terram ego impleo*. Et sic non rogasset eum quod descenderet in domum suam, sed quod mandaret tantum.

Secundus defectus fuit, quia, secundum Chrysostomum, dubitabat utrum Christus sanare posset filium suum: nam si pro certo hoc credidisset, non expectasset adventum Christi ad terram suam, sed ipse potius ivisset in Iudaeam. Sed modo quasi desperatus de salute filii, nolens negligere quidquid circa hoc facere posset, abiit ad eum more parentum, qui desperantes de salute filiorum, etiam imperitos medicos consulunt.

685. Secundo vero, quia non videtur reprehendendus de hoc quod signa quaerebat: nam fides per signa probatur.

Et ad hoc dicendum est quod aliter trahuntur ad fidem Christi infideles; et aliter fideles. Infideles non possunt trahi nec adduci auctoritate Sacrae Scripturae, quia ei non credunt; nec per rationem naturalem quia fides est supra rationem; et ideo ducendi sunt per miracula; I Cor. XIV, 22: *signa data sunt infidelibus, non fidelibus*. Fideles autem ducendi sunt et dirigendi in fidem auctoritate Scripturae, cui acquiescere tenentur. In hoc ergo regulus redarguitur: quia cum esset nutritus inter Iudaeos, et de lege instructus, non per Scripturae auctoritatem, sed per signa credere volebat. Et ideo Dominus eum reprehendens dicit *nisi signa et prodigia*, idest miracula quae sunt aliquando signa, inquantum sunt demonstrativa Dominicae veritatis: prodigia vero, vel quia certissime indicent, ut sic dicatur prodigium, quasi porrodicium; vel quia aliquid futurum protendit, ut sic dicatur prodigium, quasi procul ostendens aliquem effectum futurum.

686. Consequenter ponitur instantia reguli: non enim ad reprehensionem Domini desistit, sed cum

Second, the official's request.

Third, the granting of the request.

684. Our Lord criticizes him for his lack of faith, saying, *unless you see signs and wonders, you do not believe*.

This raises a question, for it does not seem right to say this to this official, for unless he had believed that Christ was the savior, he would not have asked him to heal his son: *unless you see signs and wonders, you do not believe*.

The answer to this is that this official did not yet believe perfectly; indeed, there were two defects in his faith. The first was that although he believed that Christ was a true man, he did not believe that he had divine power; otherwise he would have believed that Christ could heal one even while absent, since God is everywhere: *I fill heaven and earth* (Jer 23:24). And so he would not have asked Christ to come down to his house, but simply give his command.

The second defect in his faith, according to Chrysostom, was that he was not sure that Christ could heal his son: for had he been sure, he would not have waited for Christ to return to his homeland, but would have gone to Judea himself. But now, despairing of his son's health, and not wishing to overlook any possibility, he went to Christ like those parents who in their despair for the health of their children consult even unskilled doctors.

685. In the second place, it does not seem that he should have been criticized for looking for signs, for faith is proved by signs.

The answer to this is that unbelievers are drawn to Christ in one way, and believers in another way. For unbelievers cannot be drawn to Christ or convinced by the authority of Sacred Scripture, because they do not believe it; neither can they be drawn by natural reason, because faith is above reason. Consequently, they must be led by miracles: *signs are given to unbelievers, not to believers* (1 Cor 14:22). Believers, on the other hand, should be led and directed to faith by the authority of Scripture, to which they are bound to assent. This is why the official is criticized: although he had been brought up among the Jews and instructed in the law, he wanted to believe through signs, and not by the authority of the Scripture. So the Lord reproaches him, saying, *unless you see signs and wonders*, i.e., miracles, which sometimes are signs insofar as they bear witness to divine truth. Or wonders either because they indicate with utmost certitude, so that a prodigy is taken to be a portent or some sure indication; or because they portend something in the future, as if something were called a wonder as if showing at a great distance some future effect.

686. Now we see the official's persistence, for he does not give up after the Lord's criticism, but insists, saying,

instantia dicit ad eum **Domine, descende priusquam moriatur filius meus**; Lc. XVIII, 1: *oportet semper orare, et non deficere*.

Ostenditur in hoc profectus fidei eius quantum ad aliquid, quia scilicet vocat eum **Dominum**: licet non totaliter in fide profecerit, adhuc enim corporalem praesentiam Christi ad salutem filii sui necessariam credens, rogabat eum ut descenderet.

687. Sed quia oratio perseverans impetrat, ideo quod petit, conceditur ei a Domino; unde **dicit ei Iesus: vade, filius tuus vivit**. Ubi

primo ponitur Annuntiatio sanitatis per Christum, qui eam fecit;

secundo ponuntur personae, quae eam factam viderunt, ibi **iam autem eo descendente** etc.

Circa primum duo ponuntur: mandatum Domini et obedientia reguli, ibi **credidit homo sermoni quem dixit ei Iesus**.

688. Circa primum Dominus duo facit. Primo quidem praecipit; secundo vero annuntiat.

Praecipit autem ut vadat: unde dicit **vade**; idest dispone te praeparando ad gratiam per motum liberi arbitrii in Deum; Is. XLV, 22: *convertimini ad me, et salvi eritis*. Et per motum liberi arbitrii in peccatum. Nam in iustificatione impii quatuor exiguntur, specialiter in adultis; scilicet infusio gratiae et remissio culpae, motus liberi arbitrii in Deum, qui est fides, et in peccatum, qui est contritio.

Annuntiat autem salutem filii, quam petierat, dicens **filius tuus vivit**.

689. Sed quaeritur cur Christus rogatus a regulo ut descenderet in domum suam, corporaliter ire recusat, ad servum vero centurionis corporaliter ire pollicetur?

Huius autem duplex ratio assignatur. Una secundum Gregorium, ut in hoc superbiam nostram retundat, qui magnis hominibus nos ad serviendum offerimus, parvis autem servire recusamus: cum ipse, qui est Dominus omnium, ad servum centurionis se iturum obtulit, ire vero ad filium reguli recusavit; Eccli. c. IV, 7: *congregationi pauperum affabilem te facito*.

Alia ratio, secundum Chrysostomum, quia centurio iam confirmatus erat in fide Christi, credens quod etiam absens salvare posset; et ideo ad fidem et devotionem eius ostendendam Dominus ire promisit. Iste vero adhuc imperfectus erat, nondum noverat manifeste quod absens curare poterat: et ideo non accedit, ut eum imperfectionem suam cognoscere faciat.

690. Obedientia reguli ponitur quantum ad duo. Primo quia annuntianti credidit; unde dicit **credidit homo sermoni quem dixit Iesus**, scilicet, **filius tuus vivit**. Secundo vero, quia mandato obedivit; unde dicit **et ibat**,

Lord, come down before my son dies: *we should pray always, and not lose heart* (Luke 18:1).

This shows an improvement in his faith in one respect, that is, in that he calls him **Lord**. But there is not a total improvement, for he still thought that Christ had to be physically present to heal his son; so he asked Christ to come.

687. His request is granted by the Lord, for persevering prayer is answered: **Jesus said to him: go, your son lives**. Here we have

first, the statement by Christ, who cured the boy, that the boy was cured.

Second, we are told of the persons who witnessed the cure, at **and as he was going down**, **his servants ran to meet him**.

Two things are mentioned concerning the first: the command of the Lord and the obedience of the official, at **the man believed the word that Jesus said to him**.

688. As to the first, the Lord does two things. First, he orders; second, he affirms.

He orders the official to go: hence he says, **go**, i.e., prepare to receive grace by a movement of your free will toward God: *turn to me, and you will be saved* (Isa 45:22); and by a movement of your free will against sin. For four things are required for the justification of an adult sinner: the infusion of grace, the remission of guilt, a movement of the free will toward God, which is faith, and a movement of the free will against sin, which is contrition.

Then the Lord says that his son is healed, which was the request of the official: **your son lives**.

689. One may ask why Christ refused to go down to the home of this official as asked, while he promised to go see the servant of the centurion.

There are two reasons for this. One, according to Gregory, is to blunt our pride; the pride of we who offer our services to great men, but refuse to help the insignificant: since the Lord of all offered to go to the servant of the centurion, but refused to go to the son of an official: *be well-disposed to the poor* (Sir 4:7).

The other reason, as Chrysostom says, was that the centurion was already confirmed in the faith of Christ, and believed that he could heal even while not present; and so our Lord promised to go to show approval of his faith and devotion. But this official was still imperfect, and did not yet clearly know that Christ could heal even while absent. And so our Lord does not go, in order that he may realize his imperfection.

690. The obedience of this official is pointed out in two ways. First, because he believed what Christ said; so he says, **the man believed the word that Jesus said**, that is, **your son lives**. Second, because he did obey the order of Christ; so he

proficiendo in fide, licet adhuc neque integre neque sane, ut Origenes dicit. In quo signatur, quod ex fide iustificari oportet; Rom. V, 1: *iustificati ex fide, pacem habeamus ad Deum nostrum Iesum Christum.*

Oportet nos proficiendo ire: quia qui stat, exponit se periculo ut vitam gratiae conservare non possit; in via enim Dei non proficere, deficere est.

691. Annuntiatio autem sanitatis facta per servos ponitur consequenter, cum dicit *iam autem eo descendente, servi occurrerunt ei* etc. Et

primo ponitur denuntiatio salutis;

secundo fit inquisitio de tempore sanationis, ibi *interrogabat autem horam ab eis.*

692. Dicit ergo *iam autem eo descendente*, a Cana Galilaeae in domum suam, *servi occurrerunt ei*: ex quo patet quod regulus iste dives erat, habens multos servos; *et annuntiaverunt, dicentes, quia filius tuus vivit*: et hoc ideo quia credebant Christum personaliter accedere, cuius praesentia iam curato filio superflua videbatur.

693. Mystice autem servi reguli, scilicet rationis, sunt opera hominis, quia homo est dominus suorum actuum, et affectus sensitivae partis, quia obediunt rationi imperanti et dirigenti. Isti autem servi annuntiant quidem quod filius reguli, scilicet rationis, vivit, quando relucent in homine bona opera, et vires inferiores magis obediunt rationi, secundum illud Eccli. XIX, 27: *amictus corporis, et risus dentium, et ingressus hominis annuntiant de illo.*

694. Sed quia regulus neque integre neque sane adhuc credebat, adhuc volebat scire utrum casu an praecepto Christi filius curatus esset: et ideo tempus curationis inquirit. Et hoc est quod dicitur *interrogabat ergo horam ab eis*, scilicet servis, *in qua melius habuerat*, scilicet filius suus; et invenit quod illa hora curatus fuit statim quando Dominus dixit ei *vade, filius tuus vivit*. Nec mirum, quia ipse Christus est Verbum, quo factum est caelum et terra, secundum Ps. CXLVIII, 5: *ipse dixit, et facta sunt; ipse mandavit, et creata sunt*; Eccli. X, 5: *facile est in conspectu Domini* etc.

695. Et ideo *dixerunt ei*, scilicet servi, *quod heri hora septima reliquit eum febris.*

Mystice autem per horam septimam, in qua puer a febre dimittitur, significantur septem dona Spiritus Sancti, per quem fit remissio peccatorum, secundum illud Io. XX, c. 22: *accipe Spiritum Sanctum; quorum remiseritis peccata, remittuntur eis.* Per quem etiam vita spiritualis causatur in anima; infra VI, 64: *Spiritus est qui vivificat*. Etiam per horam septimam signatur tempus quieti conveniens, nam Dominus septimo die requievit ab omni opere quod patrarat: in quo significatur quod vita spiritualis hominis in quiete spirituali consistit, secundum illud Is. c. XXX, 15: *si quieveritis, salvi eritis*. De

says, *and went his way*, progressing in faith, although not yet fully or soundly, as Origen says. This signifies that we must be justified by faith: *justified by faith, let us have peace with God, through our Lord Jesus Christ* (Rom 5:1).

We also must go and start out by making progress: because he who stands still runs the risk of being unable to preserve the life of grace. For, along the road to God, if we do not go forward we fall back.

691. Next we see the servants bringing news of the healing, at *and as he was going down, his servants ran to meet him*.

First, the news of the healing is given.

Second, there is an inquiry about the time of the healing, at *he asked of them the hour*.

692. He says, *while he was going down*, from Cana of Galilee to his own home, *his servants ran to meet him*, which shows that this official was wealthy and had many servants, *they brought word, saying that his son lived*: and they did this because they thought that Christ was coming, and his presence was no longer necessary as the boy was already cured.

693. In the mystical sense, the servants of the official, i.e., of reason, are a man's works, because man is master of his own acts and of the affections of his sense powers, for they obey the command and direction of reason. Now these servants announce that the son of the official, that is, of reason, lives, when a man's good works shine out, and his lower powers obey reason, according to: *a man's dress, and laughter, and his walk, show what he is* (Sir 19:27).

694. Because this official did not yet believe either fully or soundly, he still wanted to know whether his son had been cured by chance or by the command of Christ. Accordingly, he asks about the time of the cure: *he asked of them*, namely, the servants, *the hour in which he grew better* namely, his son. And he found that his son was cured at exactly the same hour that our Lord said, *go, your son lives*. And no wonder, because Christ is the Word, through whom heaven and earth were made: *he spoke and they were made; he commanded and they were created* (Ps 148:5).

695. *And they*, namely, his servants, *said to him: yesterday, at the seventh hour, the fever left him*.

In the mystical sense, the seventh hour, when the boy is cured of his fever, signifies the seven gifts of the Holy Spirit, through whom sins are forgiven, according to: *receive the Holy Spirit; whose sins you will forgive, are forgiven them* (John 20:22–23), and through whom spiritual life is produced in the soul: *it is the Spirit that gives life* (John 6:64). Again, the seventh hour signifies the appropriate time for rest, for the Lord rested from all his work on the seventh day. This indicates that the spiritual life of man consists in spiritual rest or quiet, according to: *if you remain at rest, you will be saved* (Isa 30:15). But of the evil we read: *the*

malis dicit Is. LVII, 20: *cor impii quasi mare fervens, quod quiescere non potest.*

696. Consequenter cum dicit **cognovit ergo pater** etc., ponitur effectus miraculi: et

primo ponitur miraculi fructus;

secundo ipsum miraculum altero miraculo continuatur, ibi **hoc iterum secundum signum fecit Iesus.**

697. Dixit ergo **cognovit ergo pater**, comparans horam nuntiantium servorum, horae Christi praenuntiantis quia **illa hora erat in qua dixit ei Iesus: vade: filius tuus vivit.** Ex hoc conversus est ad Christum, cognoscens miraculum eius virtute factum: **credidit ipse, et domus eius tota**, scilicet servi et ministri, quia secundum conditionem dominorum, sive bonam sive malam, servi disponuntur, secundum illud Eccli. X, 2: *secundum iudicem populi, sic et ministri eius*; Gen. XVIII, v. 19: *scio enim quod praecepturus sit filiis suis.*

Patet autem ex hoc quod fides istius semper profecit: nam a principio quando interpellavit pro filio infirmo, debilis erat; postea plus firmitatis habere coepit, quando vocavit eum **Dominum**; deinde quando credidit homo sermoni, et ibat, magis perfecta erat; tamen non integre, quia adhuc dubitavit. Hic, cognita manifeste Dei virtute in Christo, perficitur in eius fide, quia, ut dicitur Prov. IV, v. 18: *iustorum semita quasi lux splendens procedit, et crescit usque ad perfectum diem.*

698. Continuatur autem miraculum istud praecedenti miraculo, cum dicitur **hoc iterum secundum signum fecit Iesus**: quod potest dupliciter intelligi. Uno modo quod in isto eodem adventu de Iudaea in Galilaeam fecerit Dominus duo miracula, quorum primo non scripto, istud ponitur secundum. Alio modo quod Iesus duo signa fecit in Galilaea diversis temporibus. Unum scilicet de vino, et istud secundum quod fecit circa filium reguli, veniens iterum a Iudaea in Galilaeam.

Ostenditur autem per hoc quod Galilaei peiores erant Samaritanis, qui nullum signum a Domino expectantes, verbo tantum eius crediderunt multi ex eis; sed ad istud miraculum non credidit Christo nisi regulus et domus eius tota: nam Iudaei propter eorum duritiam paulatim convertebantur ad fidem, secundum illud Mich. VII, 1: *factus sum sicut qui colligit in autumno racemos vindemiae; non est botrus ad comedendum; praecoquas ficus desideravit anima mea.*

heart of the wicked is like the raging sea, which cannot rest (Isa 57:20).

696. Next, we are given the effect of this miracle, at **the father therefore knew**.

First, its fruit is mentioned.

Second, this miracle is linked with another one, at **this is again the second miracle that Jesus did**.

697. He says, **the father therefore knew**, by comparing the hour mentioned by the servants with the hour of Christ's affirmation, **that it was at that same hour that Jesus said to him, your son lives**. Because of this he was converted to Christ, realizing that it was by his power that the miracle was accomplished: **he himself believed, and his whole household**, that is, his servants and his aides, because the attitude of servants depends on the condition, whether good or wicked, of their masters: *as the judge of the people is himself, so also are his ministers* (Sir 10:2); and we read: *I know that he will direct his sons* (Gen 18:19).

This also shows that the faith of the official was constantly growing: for at the beginning, when he pleaded for his sick son, it was weak; then it began to grow more firm, when he called Jesus **Lord** then when he believed what the Lord said and started for home, it was more perfect, but not completely so, because he still doubted. But here, clearly realizing God's power in Christ, his faith is made perfect, for as it is said: *the way of the just goes forward like a shining light, increasing to the full light of day* (Prov 4:18).

698. Finally, this miracle is linked with the previous one, **this is again the second miracle that Jesus did**. We can understand this in two ways. In one way, that our Lord performed two miracles during this one trip from Judea to Galilee; but the first of these was not recorded, only the second. In the other way, we could say that Jesus worked two signs in Galilee at different times: the one of the wine, and this second one about the son of this official after he returned again to Galilee from Judea.

We also see from this that the Galileans were worse than the Samaritans. For the Samaritans expected no sign from the Lord, and many believed in his word alone; but as a result of this miracle, only this official and his whole household believed: for the Jews were converted to the faith little by little on account of their hardness, according to: *I have become as one who harvests in the summer time, like a gleaner at the vintage: not one cluster to eat, not one of the early figs I desire* (Mic 7:1).

Chapter 5

Lecture 1

5:1 Post haec erat dies festus Iudaeorum, et ascendit Iesus Ierosolymam. [n. 700]

5:2 Est autem Ierosolymis Probatica Piscina, quae cognominatur hebraice Bethsaida, quinque porticus habens. [n. 701]

5:3 In his iacebat multitudo magna languentium, caecorum, claudorum, aridorum, expectantium aquae motum. [n. 705]

5:4 Angelus autem Domini descendebat secundum tempus in piscinam, et movebatur aqua: et qui prior descendisset in piscinam post motionem aquae, sanus fiebat a quacumque detinebatur infirmitate. [n. 707]

5:5 Erat autem quidam homo ibi triginta et octo annos habens in infirmitate sua. [n. 710]

5:6 Hunc cum vidisset Iesus iacentem, et cognovisset, quia iam multum tempus haberet, dixit ei: vis sanus fieri? [n. 713]

5:7 Respondit ei languidus: Domine, hominem non habeo, ut cum turbata fuerit aqua, mittat me in piscinam: dum venio enim ego, alius ante me descendit. [n. 714]

5:8 Dixit ei Iesus: surge, tolle grabatum tuum, et ambula. [n. 716]

5:9 Et statim sanus factus est homo ille, et sustulit grabatum suum, et ambulabat. Erat autem Sabbatum in die illo. [n. 719]

5:1 Μετὰ ταῦτα ἦν ἑορτὴ τῶν Ἰουδαίων καὶ ἀνέβη Ἰησοῦς εἰς Ἱεροσόλυμα.

5:2 Ἔστιν δὲ ἐν τοῖς Ἱεροσολύμοις ἐπὶ τῇ προβατικῇ κολυμβήθρα ἡ ἐπιλεγομένη Ἑβραϊστὶ Βηθζαθὰ πέντε στοὰς ἔχουσα.

5:3 ἐν ταύταις κατέκειτο πλῆθος τῶν ἀσθενούντων, τυφλῶν, χωλῶν, ξηρῶν.

5:4 [αγγελος γαρ κατα καιρον κατεβαινεν εν τη κολυμβηθρα και εταρασσε το υδωρ ο ουν πρωτος εμβας μετα την ταραχην του υδατος υγιης εγινετο ω δηποτε κατειχετο νοσηματι]

5:5 ἦν δέ τις ἄνθρωπος ἐκεῖ τριάκοντα [καὶ] ὀκτὼ ἔτη ἔχων ἐν τῇ ἀσθενείᾳ αὐτοῦ·

5:6 τοῦτον ἰδὼν ὁ Ἰησοῦς κατακείμενον καὶ γνοὺς ὅτι πολὺν ἤδη χρόνον ἔχει, λέγει αὐτῷ· θέλεις ὑγιὴς γενέσθαι;

5:7 ἀπεκρίθη αὐτῷ ὁ ἀσθενῶν· κύριε, ἄνθρωπον οὐκ ἔχω ἵνα ὅταν ταραχθῇ τὸ ὕδωρ βάλῃ με εἰς τὴν κολυμβήθραν· ἐν ᾧ δὲ ἔρχομαι ἐγώ, ἄλλος πρὸ ἐμοῦ καταβαίνει.

5:8 λέγει αὐτῷ ὁ Ἰησοῦς· ἔγειρε ἆρον τὸν κράβαττόν σου καὶ περιπάτει.

5:9 καὶ εὐθέως ἐγένετο ὑγιὴς ὁ ἄνθρωπος καὶ ἦρεν τὸν κράβαττον αὐτοῦ καὶ περιεπάτει. Ἦν δὲ σάββατον ἐν ἐκείνῃ τῇ ἡμέρᾳ.

5:1 After these things there was a festival day of the Jews, and Jesus went up to Jerusalem. [n. 700]

5:2 Now there is a pond at Jerusalem, called the Sheep Pool, which in Hebrew is named Bethsaida, having five porches. [n. 701]

5:3 In these lay a great multitude of the sick, the blind, the lame and the withered, waiting for the moving of the water. [n. 705]

5:4 And an angel of the Lord descended at certain times into the pond, and the water was moved. And whoever descended first into the pond after the motion of the water was made well from whatever infirmity he lay under. [n. 707]

5:5 And there was a certain man there, having been under his infirmity thirty-eight years. [n. 710]

5:6 When Jesus had seen him lying there and knew that he had been there a long time, he said to him: do you wish to be made well? [n. 713]

5:7 The infirm man answered him: Lord, I have no man who, when the water is troubled, might put me into the pond. For while I am coming, another goes down before me. [n. 714]

5:8 Jesus said to him: arise, take up your bed and walk. [n. 716]

5:9 And immediately the man was made well, and he took up his bed and walked. And it was the Sabbath that day. [n. 719]

---

699. Supra Dominus egit de regeneratione spirituali; hic agit consequenter de beneficiis quae regeneratis spiritualiter conferuntur a Deo. Sed his qui carnaliter generantur tria conferuntur a parentibus carnalibus: scilicet vita, nutrimentum et doctrina sive disciplina; et haec tria a Christo etiam regenerati spiritualiter percipiunt.

699. Above, our Lord dealt with spiritual rebirth; here he deals with the benefits God gives to those who are spiritually reborn. Now we see that parents give three things to those who are physically born from them: life, nourishment, and instruction or discipline. And those who are spiritually

Primo quidem spiritualem vitam; secundo vero spirituale nutrimentum; tertio spiritualem doctrinam.

Secundum hoc ergo de tribus hic agitur.

Primo de collatione spiritualis vitae;

secundo de collatione spiritualis cibi; et hoc infra VI, ibi *post haec abiit Iesus* etc.;

tertio de spirituali doctrina, infra VII *post haec ambulabat Iesus*.

Circa primum tria facit.

Primo proponit signum visibile, in quo manifestatur virtus Christi factiva et reparativa vitae, secundum consuetudinem huius Evangelii, in quo semper doctrinae Christi adiungitur aliquod visibile factum, pertinens ad illud de quo est doctrina, ut sic ex visibilibus invisibilia innotescant.

Secundo ponitur occasio doctrinae proponendae, ibi *erat autem Sabbatum* etc.

Tertio ponitur ipsa doctrina, ibi *respondit itaque Iesus: amen, amen dico vobis* etc.

Circa primum tria facit.

Primo describitur locus miraculi perpetrati;

secundo infirmitas, ibi *erat autem ibi homo* etc.;

tertio restitutio sanitatis, ibi *dixit ei Iesus: surge, tolle grabatum tuum, et ambula*.

700. Locus autem miraculi describitur dupliciter, scilicet generalis et specialis.

Generalis locus est Ierosolyma; et ideo dicit: *post haec*, idest post miraculum in Galilaea factum, *erat dies festus Iudaeorum*; scilicet Pentecostes, secundum Chrysostomum: nam supra fit mentio de festo Paschae, quando ierat in Ierusalem. Nunc ergo in sequenti festo Pentecostes, *ascendit Iesus Ierosolymam*, iterato: nam, sicut legitur Ex. XXIII, 17, mandatum erat a Domino, ut omne masculinum generis Iudaeorum tribus vicibus in anno, scilicet in die festo Paschae, Pentecostes, Scenopegiae, in templo praesentaretur.

Et in istis festis Dominus in Ierusalem ascendit propter duo: scilicet ne videretur legi fore contrarius, sicut ipse dixerat, Matth. c. V, 17: *non veni legem solvere, sed adimplere*: et ut multitudinem populi illuc concurrentis in diebus festis ad Deum per signa et doctrinam trahat, secundum illud Ps. CVIII, v. 30: *in medio multorum laudabo eum*: et alibi *annuntiabo iustitiam tuam in Ecclesia magna*. Unde et ipse dicit, infra XVIII, 20: *ego palam locutus sum mundo*.

701. Locus autem specialis miraculi fuit probatica piscina; et ideo dicit: *est Ierosolymis Probatica Piscina*

reborn receive these three from Christ: first spiritual life; second spiritual nourishment and third spiritual teaching.

And so these three things are considered here:

first, the giving of spiritual life;

second, the giving of spiritual food, at *after these things, Jesus went over the sea of Galilee, which is that of Tiberias* (John 6:1); and

third, spiritual teaching, at *after these things, Jesus walked in Galilee* (John 7:1).

About the first he does three things.

First, he sets forth a visible sign in which he shows Christ's power to produce and to restore life. This is the usual practice in this Gospel: to always join to the teaching of Christ some appropriate visible action, so that what is invisible can be made known through the visible.

Second, the occasion for this teaching is given, at *and it was the Sabbath that day*.

Third, the teaching itself is given, at *then Jesus answered and said to them: amen, amen I say unto you, the Son cannot do anything of himself* (John 5:18–19).

As to the first he does three things.

First, the place of the miracle is given.

Second, the illness involved, at *and there was a certain man there, having been under his infirmity thirty-eight years*.

Third, the restoration of the sick person to health, at *Jesus said to him: arise, take up your bed and walk*.

700. The place of this miracle is described in two ways: in general and in particular.

The general place is Jerusalem; so he says, *after this*, i.e., after the miracle performed in Galilee, *there was a festival day of the Jews*, that is Pentecost, according to Chrysostom. For above, when Christ went to Jerusalem, it was the Passover that was mentioned; and now, on the following festival of Pentecost, *Jesus went up to Jerusalem* again. For as we read, the Lord commanded that all Jewish males be presented in the temple three times a year: on the festival days of the Passover, Pentecost, and the Dedication (Exod 23:17).

There were two reasons why our Lord went up to Jerusalem for these festivals. First, so that he would not seem to oppose the law, for he said himself: *I have not come to destroy the law, but to complete it* (Matt 5:17); and in order to draw the many people gathered there on the feast days to God by his signs and teaching: *I will praise him in the midst of the people* (Ps 108:30); and again, *I have declared your justice in the great assembly* (Ps 39:10). So Christ himself says: *I have spoken openly to the world* (John 18:20).

701. The specific place of the miracle was the pool called the Sheep Pool; so he says, *now there is a pond at*

etc., quae quidem describitur ex quatuor, scilicet ex nomine, ex dispositione, ex inhabitatione, et ex virtute.

702. Ex nomine quidem cum dicit **Probatica Piscina**: probaton enim Graece ovis dicitur. **Probatica** ergo **Piscina**, quasi oviaria, vel pecuaria dicitur, ex eo quod sacerdotes cadavera bestiarum, et praecipue ovium, quae ut plurimum in sacrificiis offerebantur, ibi abluebant: et ideo Hebraice cognominabatur Bethsaida, idest 'domus ovium.' Erat enim prope templum ex aquis pluvialibus collecta.

703. Mystice autem, secundum Chrysostomum, haec piscina baptismum praefigurabat: nam Dominus volens gratiam baptismalem in diversis praefigurare, primo quidem dedit aquam expurgantem corporis sordes, quae erant ex tactu immundorum secundum legem, de qua habetur Num. XIX. Secundo dedit virtutem huic piscinae quae repraesentat expressius quam aqua illa virtutem baptismi, non solum ab immunditiis carnis sanando, sed etiam ab infirmitatibus corporis salvando: nam quanto figurae fuerunt propinquiores veritati, tanto expressiores erant.

Signabat ergo virtutem baptismi: quia sicut aqua illa per hoc quod lavabat corpora, habebat virtutem ex angelo, non natura propria, infirmitatem sanandi, ita aqua baptismi habet virtutem sanandi et abluendi animam a peccatis; Apoc. I, 5: *dilexit nos, et lavit nos a peccatis nostris*. Et inde est quod passio Christi per sacrificia veteris legis praefigurata, in baptismo repraesentatur; Rom. VI, 3: *quicumque baptizati estis in Christo Iesu, in morte ipsius baptizati estis* etc.

Secundum Augustinum vero, aqua illius piscinae significabat statum populi Iudaeorum, secundum illud Apoc. XVII, 15: *aquae multae, populi multi*. Nam populus gentium non erat inclusus sub limite divinae legis, sed unusquisque ambulabat secundum vanitatem cordis sui, secundum illud Eph. IV, 17. Populus vero Iudaeorum conclusus erat sub cultu unius Dei, secundum illud Gal. III, 23: *conclusi in eam fidem quae revelanda erat*. Et ideo iste populus significabatur per aquam in piscina conclusam. Et dicitur **Probatica**, quia ipsi erant speciales oves Dei, secundum illud Ps. XCIV, 7: *nos autem populus eius, et oves pascuae eius*.

704. Ex dispositione autem describitur, quia erat **quinque porticus habens**, scilicet per circuitum, ut multi sacerdotes absque impedimento commode starent ad lavandum cadavera bestiarum.

Per hos quinque porticus mystice significantur, secundum Chrysostomum, quinque vulnera corporis Christi, de quibus dicitur infra XX, 27: **mitte manum tuam in latus meum, et noli esse incredulus, sed fidelis**. Secundum Augustinum vero, quinque libri Moysi.

Jerusalem, called the Sheep Pool. This is described here in four ways: by its name, its structure, from its occupants, and from its power.

702. First, it is described from its name when he says, **the Sheep Pool**, for *probaton* is Greek for sheep. It was called the **Sheep Pool** for it was there that the priests washed the sacrificial animals; especially the sheep, who were used more than the other animals. And so in Hebrew it was called Bethsaida, that is, 'the house of sheep.' This pool was located near the temple, and formed from collected rain water.

703. In its mystical sense, this pool, according to Chrysostom, has prefigured Baptism. For the Lord, wishing to prefigure the grace of baptsim in different ways, first of all chose water: for this washes the body from the uncleanness which came from contact with what was legally unclean (Num 19). Second, he gave this pool a power that expresses even more vividly than water the power of Baptism: for it not only cleansed the body from its uncleanness, but also healed it from its illness; for symbols are more expressive, the closer they approach the reality.

Thus it signified the power of Baptism: for as this water when applied to the body had the power, not by its own nature, but from an angel, to heal its illness, so the water of Baptism has the power to heal and cleanse the soul from sins: *he loved us, and washed us from our sins* (Rev 1:5). This is the reason why the passion of Christ, prefigured by the sacrifices of the old law, is represented in Baptism: *all of us who have been baptized into Christ Jesus, have been baptized into his death* (Rom 6:3).

According to Augustine, the water in this pool signified the condition of the Jewish people, according to: *the waters are the peoples* (Rev 17:15). The gentiles were not confined within the limits of the divine law, but each of them lived according to the vanity of his heart (Eph 4:17). But the Jews were confined under the worship of the one God: *we were kept under the law, confined, until the faith was revealed* (Gal 3:23). So this water, confined to the pool, signified the Jewish people. And it was called the **Sheep Pool**, for the Jews were the special sheep of God: *we are his people, his sheep* (Ps 94:7).

704. The pool is described in its structure as **having five porches**, i.e., round about, so that a number of the priests could stand and wash the bodies of the animals without inconvenience.

In the mystical sense these five porticoes, according to Chrysostom, signify the five wounds in the body of Christ; about which we read: **bring your hand here, and put it in my side, and do not be faithless, but believing** (John 20:27). But according to Augustine, these five porticoes signify the five books of Moses.

705. Ex inhabitatione autem describitur, quia *in his*, scilicet porticus, *iacebat multitudo magna languentium, caecorum, claudorum, aridorum* etc. Cuius litteralis ratio est propter concursum omnium infirmorum ad virtutem aquae: quae quia continue non sanabat, nec multos simul, oportebat quod multi illic expectantes morarentur.

Per hoc autem mystice significatur, secundum Augustinum, quod lex non poterat peccata sanare, secundum illud Hebr. X, 4: *impossibile est per sanguinem hircorum aut taurorum peccata purgari*. Sed ostendebat ea tantum, secundum illud Rom. III, 20: *per legem enim cognitio peccati*.

706. Et ideo iacebant in ea infirmi diversis infirmitatibus, curari non valentes. Quae quidem describuntur quantum ad quatuor. Primo quidem quantum ad situm, quia iacebant prostrati, scilicet per peccata inhaerendo terrenis: qui enim iacet, ex toto inhaeret terrae; Matth. IX, 36: *misertus est eorum, quia erant vexati et iacentes, quasi oves non habentes pastorem*. Iusti autem non iacent, sed recti ad caelestia stant; Ps. XIX, 9: *ipsi*, scilicet peccatores, *obligati sunt, et ceciderunt; nos autem*, scilicet iusti *surreximus, et erecti sumus*.

Secundo quantum ad numerum quia multi, unde dicit: *multitudo magna*; Eccle. I, 15: *perversi difficile corriguntur, et stultorum infinitus est numerus*. Et Matth. VII, 13: *lata est via quae ducit ad perditionem, et multi incedunt per eam*.

Tertio quantum ad dispositionem seu habitum infirmorum. Et ponit quatuor quae homo per peccatum incurrit. Primo enim homo ex hoc quod subiicitur passionibus peccatorum ei praedominantibus, efficitur languidus: et quantum ad hoc dicit *languentium*. Unde et a Tullio passiones animae, puta irae et concupiscentiae, et huiusmodi, quaedam aegritudines animae dicuntur. Unde Ps. VI, 3, dicebat: *miserere mei, Domine quoniam infirmus sum*. Secundo vero ex dominio passionum et victoria in homine excaecatur ratio per consensum: et quantum ad hoc dicit *caecorum*, scilicet per peccata, secundum illud Sap. II, v. 21: *excaecavit eos malitia eorum*; Ps. LVII, v. 9: *supercecidit ignis*, scilicet irae et concupiscentiae, *et non viderunt solem*. Tertio, homo languens et caecus efficitur instabilis in suis operibus, et est quasi *claudus*; unde dicitur Prov. XI, 18: *impius facit opus instabile*. Et quantum ad hoc dicit *claudorum*; III Reg. XVIII, 21: *usquequo claudicatis in duas partes?* Quarto homo sic languidus, caecus intellectu, claudus in effectu, efficitur aridus in affectu, inquantum exsiccatur in eo omnis pinguedo devotionis, quam petebat Psalmus LXII, 6, dicens: *sicut adipe et pinguedine repleatur anima mea*. Et quantum ad hoc dicit *aridorum*; Ps. XXI, 16: *aruit tamquam testa virtus mea*.

705. The pool is also described from its occupants, for *in these*, porticoes, *lay a great multitude of the sick, the blind, the lame and the withered, waiting for the motion of the water*. The literal explanation of this is that since all the afflicted persons gathered because of the curative power of the water, which did not always cure nor cure many at the same time, it was inevitable that there be many remaining waiting to be cured.

The mystical meaning of this, for Augustine, was that the law was incapable of healing sins: *it is impossible that sins be taken away by the blood of bulls and goats* (Heb 10:4). The law merely shed light on them, for *the knowledge of sin comes from the law* (Rom 3:20).

706. And so, subject to various illnesses, these people lay there, unable to be cured. They are described in four ways. First, by their posture: for there they lay, i.e., clinging to earthly things by their sins; for one who is lying down is in direct contact with the earth: *he had compassion on them, for they were suffering, and lying like sheep without a shepherd* (Matt 9:36). But the just do not lie down, but stand upright, toward the things of heaven: *they*, i.e., sinners, *are bound, and have fallen down; but we*, the just, *have stood and are erect* (Ps 19:9).

Second, they are described as to their number, for there was a *great multitude*: *the evil are hard to correct, and the number of fools is infinite* (Eccl 1:15); and: *the road that leads to destruction is wide, and many go this way* (Matt 7:13).

Third, these sick people are described as to their condition. And he mentions four things which a person brings on himself through sin. First, a person who is ruled by sinful passions is made listless or feeble: and so he says, *the sick*. So it is that Cicero calls certain passions of the soul, such as anger and concupiscence and the like, illnesses of the soul. And the Psalm says: *have mercy on me, O Lord, for I am weak* (Ps 6:3). Second, due to the rule and victory of a man's passions, his reason is blinded by consent; and he says as to this, *the blind*, that is, through sins. *Their own evil blinded them* (Wis 2:21); and: *fire*, that is the fire of anger and concupiscence, *fell on them, and they did not see the sun* (Ps 57:9). Third, a person who is feeble and blind is inconstant in his works and is, in a way, *the lame*. So we read: *the work of the wicked is unsteady* (Prov 11:18). With respect to this the Evangelist says, *the lame*. *How long will you be lame?* (1 Kgs 18:21). Fourth, a man who is thus feeble, blind in understanding, and lame in his exterior actions, becomes dry in his affections, in the sense that all the fatness of devotion withers within him. This devotion is sought by the Psalm: *may my soul be filled with fat and marrow* (Ps 62:6). With respect to this the Evangelist says, *the withered*. *My strength is dried up like baked clay* (Ps 21:16).

Sed sunt aliqui sic affecti languore peccati, qui non expectant aquae motum, in peccatis suis requiescentes, secundum illud Sap. XIV, 22: *in magno viventes inscientiae bello, tot et tanta mala pacem appellant.* De quibus dicitur Prov. II, 14: *laetantur cum male fecerint, et exultant in rebus pessimis.* Cuius ratio est, quia non abhorrent peccata; nec peccant ex ignorantia, seu infirmitate, sed ex certa malitia. Isti autem, utpote non ex malitia peccantes, non quiescebant in peccatis sed per desiderium expectabant aquae motum. Unde dicit *et expectantium*; Iob XIV, 14: *cunctis diebus quibus nunc milito, expecto donec veniat immutatio mea.* Sic et illi qui erant in Veteri Testamento expectabant Christum, secundum illud Gen., penult., 18: *salutare tuum expectabo, Domine.*

707. Ex virtute vero describitur piscina, quia sanat ab omni infirmitate corporali, virtute angeli descendentis; et ideo dicit *angelus autem Domini secundum tempus descendebat in piscinam.*

Et quidem virtus piscinae in aliquo concordat cum baptismo, et in aliquo differt.

Concordat quidem in duobus. Primo quidem in occultatione virtutis: nam virtus aquae huius piscinae non erat ex natura sua, alias semper sanasset, sed ex aliqua virtute occulta, scilicet ex angelo; unde dicitur, quod *angelus Domini secundum tempus descendebat in piscinam.* Et similiter aqua baptismi, ex eo quod aqua non habet virtutem purgativam animarum, sed ex occulta virtute Spiritus Sancti, secundum illud supra III, 5: *nisi quis renatus fuerit ex aqua et Spiritu Sancto, non potest introire in regnum Dei.* Secundo concordat in effectu, quia sicut aqua baptismi sanat, ita et ista piscina sanabat: et ideo dicit, quod *qui prior descendisset, sanus fiebat.* Ideo autem virtutem sanandi corpora aquae istius piscinae Deus contulit, ut homines abluendo, per salutem corporalem assuescerent quaerere spiritualem.

Differt autem quantum ad tria. Primo quantum ad id cuius virtute hoc fiebat: quia aqua piscinae conferebat sanitatem virtute angeli; aqua vero baptismi virtute increata, non solum Spiritus Sancti, sed etiam Trinitatis. Unde etiam Matth. III, 16 s. super dominum baptizatum tota Trinitas affuit: Pater in voce, Filius in persona, Spiritus Sanctus in columbae specie. Et inde est quod in nostro baptismo fit invocatio Trinitatis. Secundo differt quantum ad efficaciam: quia aqua piscinae non habuit virtutem sanativam continue, sed *secundum tempus*, idest determinato tempore; aqua vero baptismi continuam abluendi virtutem habet, secundum illud Zach. XIII, 1: *erit fons patens domui Iacob, et habitantibus Ierusalem, in ablutionem peccatoris et menstruatae.* Tertio quantum ad multitudinem sanandorum: quia ad motum aquae illius piscinae, sanabatur tantum unus; sed ad motum aquae baptismi sanantur omnes. Nec mirum, quia virtus

But there are some so afflicted by the lassitude of sin, who do not wait for the motion of the water, wallowing in their sins: *they live in a great strife of ignorance, and they call so many and great evils peace* (Wis 14:22). We read of such people: *they are glad when they do evil, and rejoice in the worst of things* (Prov 2:14). The reason for this is that they do not hate their sins: they do not sin from ignorance or weakness, but from malice. But others, who do not sin from malice, do not wallow in their sins, but wait by desire for the motion of the water. So he says, *waiting. Every day of my service I wait for my relief to come* (Job 14:14). This is the way those in the Old Testament waited for Christ: *I will wait for your salvation, O Lord* (Gen 49:18).

707. Finally, the power of the pool is described, for it healed all physical illnesses in virtue of an angel who came to it; so he says, *and an angel of the Lord descended at certain times into the pond.*

In certain ways, the power of this pool is like that of Baptism, and in other ways it differs.

It is like it, first, in the fact that its power was unperceived: for the power of the water in this pool did not come from its very nature, otherwise it would have healed at all times; its power was unseen, being from an angel. So he says, *and an angel of the Lord descended at certain times into the pond.* The water of Baptism is like this in that precisely as water it does not have the power to cleanse souls, but this comes from the unseen power of the Holy Spirit, according to: *unless a man is born again of water and the Holy Spirit, he cannot enter the kingdom of God* (John 3:5). It is like it, in a second way, in its effect: for as the water of Baptism heals, so also the water of that pool healed. So he says, *and whoever descended first into the pond after the motion of the water was made well.* Further, God gave to that water the power to heal so that men by washing might learn through their bodily health to seek their spiritual health.

Yet the water of this pool differs from the water of Baptism in three ways. First, in the source of its power: for the water in the pool produced health because of an angel, but the water of Baptism produces its effect by the uncreated power not only of the Holy Spirit, but of the entire Trinity. Thus the entire Trinity was present at the baptism of Christ: the Father in the voice, the Son in person, and the Holy Spirit in the form of a dove. This is why we invoke the Trinity in our baptism. Second, this water differs in its power: for the water in the pool did not have a continuous power to cure, but only *at certain times*; while the water of Baptism has a permanent power to cleanse, according to: *on that day a fountain will be open to the house of David, and to the inhabitants of Jerusalem, to cleanse the sinner and the unclean* (Zech 13:1). Third, this water differs as regards the number of people healed: for only one person was cured when the water of this pool was moved; but all are healed when the

illius aquae, cum sit creata, finita est, et finitum habet effectum; in hac vero aqua virtus est infinita ad infinitas animas, si essent, abluendas; Ez. XXXVI, 25: *effundam super vos aquam mundam, et mundabimini ab omnibus inquinamentis vestris.*

708. Secundum vero Augustinum, per angelum istum intelligitur Christus, secundum illud Is. IX, 6, secundum aliam litteram: *vocabitur magni consilii angelus.* Sicut ille angelus **secundum tempus** descendebat in piscinam, ita et Christus secundum determinatum tempus a Patre descendit in mundum; Is. XIV, v. 1: *prope est ut veniat tempus eius, et dies eius non elongabuntur;* Gal. IV, 4: *at ubi venit plenitudo temporis, misit Deus Filium suum, factum ex muliere, factum sub lege.*

Item sicut ille angelus non videbatur nisi motu aquae, ita etiam Christus secundum divinitatem non cognoscebatur: quia *si cognovissent, numquam Dominum gloriae crucifixissent*: I Cor. II, 8. Nam Is. XLV, 15, dicitur: *vere tu es Deus absconditus.* Et ideo videbatur aqua turbata sed a quo turbaretur non videbatur, quia infirmitatem Christi videntes, divinitatem eius non cognoscebant. Et sicut ille qui descendebat in piscinam sanus fiebat; ita et qui humiliter credit in Deum, eius passione sanatur; Rom. III, 24: *iustificati per fidem per redemptionem quae est in Christo, quem proposuit Deus propitiatorem per fidem in sanguine ipsius.*

Sanabatur autem unus tantum, quia nullus sanari potest nisi in Ecclesiastica unitate; Eph. IV, 5: *unus Deus, una fides, unum baptisma.* Vae ergo illis qui oderunt unitatem, et partes sibi faciunt in hominibus.

709. Consequenter cum dicit, **erat autem quidam homo ibi triginta et octo annos in infirmitate habens**, ponit infirmitatem, et

primo ponitur diuturna infirmitas;

secundo ostenditur causa diuturnae infirmitatis, ibi **hunc cum vidisset ergo Iesus** etc.

710. Infirmitas diuturna erat, quia **homo erat habens triginta octo annos in infirmitate sua**. Quod satis pulchre introducitur: homo qui curari non poterat a piscina, curandus tamen a Christo; quia quos lex sanare non poterat, Christus perfecte sanat, secundum illud Rom. VIII, 3: *nam quod impossibile erat legi in quo infirmabatur per carnem, mittens Deus Filium suum in similitudinem carnis peccati, de peccato damnavit peccatum in carne, ut iustificatio legis impleretur in nobis.* Eccli. XXXVI, 6: *innova signa, et immuta mirabilia.*

711. Congruit autem iste numerus infirmitati, ad languorem pertinens magis quam ad sanitatem: nam, secundum Augustinum, quadragenarius numerus consecratur ad designandam perfectionem iustitiae, quae in observatione legis consistit. Lex autem in decem praeceptis data est, et praedicanda erat in quatuor partibus mundi, vel implenda per quatuor Evangelia, secundum

water of Baptism is moved. And no wonder: for the power of the water in the pool, since it is created, is finite and has a finite effect; but in the water of Baptism there is an infinite power capable of cleansing an infinite number of souls, if there were such: *I will pour clean water upon you, and you will be cleansed from all your uncleanness* (Ezek 36:25).

708. According to Augustine, however, the angel signifies Christ, according to this reading: *he will be called great counsel* (Isa 9:6). Just as the angel descended **at certain times** into the pool, so Christ descended into the world at a time fixed by the Father: *her time is near at hand, and her days shall not be prolonged* (Isa 14:1); *when the fullness of time had come God sent his Son, made from a woman, made under the law* (Gal 4:4).

Again, just as the angel was not seen except by the motion of the water, so Christ was not known as to his divinity, for *if they had known, they would never have crucified the Lord of glory* (1 Cor 2:8). For it is said: *truly, you are a hidden God* (Isa 45:15). And so the motion of the water was seen, but not the one who set it in motion, because, seeing the weakness of Christ, the people did not know of his divinity. And just as the one who went into the pool was healed, so a person who humbly believes in God is healed by his passion: *justified by faith, through the redemption which is in Christ, whoin God put forward as an expiation* (Rom 3:24).

Only one was healed, because no one can be healed except in the oneness or unity of the Church: *one Lord, one faith, one baptism* (Eph 4:5). Therefore, woe to those who hate unity, and divide men into sects.

709. Then, at **and there was a certain man there, having been under his infirmity thiry-eight years**, the Evangelist mentions the disability of a man who lay by the pool.

First, we are told how long he was disabled; and

second, why it was so long, at **when Jesus had seen him lying there and knew that he had been there a long time**.

710. He was disabled for a long time, for **and there was a certain man there, having been under his infirmity thirty-eight years**. This episode is very aptly mentioned: the man who could not be cured by the pool was to be cured by Christ, because those whom the law could not heal, Christ heals perfectly, according to: *God did what the law, weakened by the flesh, could not do: by sending his own Son in the likeness of sinful flesh, and as a sin-offering, he condemned sin in his flesh* (Rom 8:3), and: *perform new signs and wonders* (Sir 36:6).

711. The number thirty-eight is well-suited to his infirmity, for we see it associated with sickness rather than with health. For, as Augustine says, the number forty signifies the perfection of justice, which consists in observing the law. But the law was given in ten precepts, and was to be preached to the four corners of the world, or be completed by the four Gospels, according to: *the end of the law is Christ*

illud Rom. X, v. 4: *finis legis Christus.* Quia ergo denarius per quatuor multiplicatus pervenit ad quadragenarium, recte perfecta iustitia designatur: subtractis ergo duobus a quadragenario numero efficiuntur triginta octo. Haec autem duo sunt duo praecepta caritatis, quibus impletur omnis perfecta iustitia. Et ideo homo iste languebat, quia de quadraginta, duo minus habebat, idest imperfectam iustitiam: quia, ut dicitur Matth. XXII, 40: *in his duobus pendent lex et prophetae.*

712. Consequenter cum dicit **hunc cum vidisset Iesus**, exquiritur causa diuturnae infirmitatis. Et

primo ponitur interrogatio Domini;

secundo responsio languidi, ibi **respondit ei languidus**.

713. Dixit ergo: **hunc**, scilicet hominem, **cum vidisset Iesus iacentem**, non solum oculo corporis, sed etiam miserationis, qualiter videri petebat David dicens: *respice in me, Domine, et miserere mei.* **Et cognovisset quia multum tempus haberet**, in infirmitate; quod est contra cor Christi, et infirmi, secundum illud Eccli. X, v. 11: *languor prolixior gravat medicum.* **Dixit ei: vis sanus fieri?** Non quasi ignorans, nam satis constare poterat quod sanus fieri volebat, sed ut excitet desiderium infirmi, et ut ostendat patientiam, qui tot annis expectavit eripi ab aegritudine, non desistens, et ex hoc cognoscatur dignior ad sanandum; Ps. XXX, 25: *viriliter agite, et confortetur cor vestrum, omnes qui speratis in Deo.*

Excitat autem desiderium: quia stabilius tenetur quod cum desiderio percipitur et facilius acquiritur nobis; Matth. VII: *pulsate*, per desiderium, *et aperietur vobis.*

Sed notandum, quod Dominus a ceteris fidem requirit; Matth. IX, 28: *creditis quod possum hoc facere vobis?* Sed in isto nihil tale facit: quia illi quidem audierant aliqua de miraculis Iesu, iste autem nondum: et ideo fidem ab eo non requirit, nisi post factum miraculum.

714. Responsio languidi ponitur cum dicit: **Domine, hominem non habeo**. Et duo insinuat, quae causa erant diuturnae infirmitatis: scilicet paupertatem et debilitatem. Quia enim pauper erat, non poterat habere hominem qui mitteret eum in piscinam; unde dicit **Domine, hominem non habeo** etc. Et forte, secundum Chrysostomum, opinabatur sibi Christum utilem fore ad mittendum eum in aquam.

Quia vero debilis erat, et festinanter ire non poterat, praeveniebatur ab alio; unde dicit **dum venio enim ego, alius ante me descendit**. Et sic poterat dicere cum Iob VI, 13: *ecce non est auxilium mihi in me.* Per hoc

(Rom 10:4). So since ten times four is forty, this appropriately signifies perfect justice. Now if two is subtracted from forty, we get thirty-eight. These two are the two precepts of charity, by which all perfect justice is fulfilled. And so this man was sick because he had forty minus two, that is, his justice was imperfect, for *on these two commandments all the law and the prophets depend* (Matt 22:40).

712. Now, at **when Jesus had seen him lying there**, the reason for the length of the man's illness is considered.

First, we have the Lord's query;

second, the sick man's answer, **the infirm man answered him**.

713. John says, **when Jesus had seen him**, the man, **lying there**. Jesus saw him not only with his physical eyes, but also with the eyes of his mercy; this is the way David begged to be seen, saying: *look at me, O Lord, and have mercy on me* (Ps 85:16). And Jesus **knew that he had been there a long time** in infirmity—which was repugnant to the heart of Christ as well as to the sick man: *a long illness is a burden to the physician* (Sir 10:11)—**said to him: do you wish to be made well?** He did not say this because he did not know the answer, for it was quite evident that the man wanted to be healed, he said it to arouse the sick man's desire, and to show his patience in waiting so many years to be cured of his sickness. and in not giving up. We see from this that he was all the worthier to be cured: *act bravely, and let your heart be strengthened, all you who hope in the Lord* (Ps 30:25).

Jesus incites the man's desires because we keep more securely what we perceive with desire and more easily acquire. *Knock*, by your desire, *and it will be opened to you* (Matt 7:7).

Note that in other situations the Lord requires faith: *do you believe that I can do this for you?* (Matt 9:28); but here he does not make any such demand. The reason is that the others had heard of the miracles of Jesus, of which this man knew nothing. And so Jesus does not ask faith from him until after the miracle has been performed.

714. Then, at **Lord, I have no man**, the answer of the sick man is given. Two reasons are given for the length of his illness: his poverty and his weakness. As he was poor, he could not afford a man to plunge him into the pool; so he says, **Lord, I have no man who, when the water is troubled, might put me into the pond. For while I am coming, another goes down before me**. Perhaps he thought, as Chrysostom says, that Christ might even help to put him into the water.

Someone else always reached the pool before him because he was weak and not able to move fast; so he says, *for while I am coming, another goes down before me*. He could say with Job: *I cannot help myself* (Job 6:13). This signifies

significatur quod non erat aliquis homo purus qui humanum genus salvare posset, quia omnes peccaverunt, et egerunt gratia Dei, quousque veniret Christus Deus et homo, quem sanaretur.

715. Consequenter cum dicit **surge, tolle grabatum tuum**, ponitur restitutio sanitatis, seu perpetratio miraculi. Et

primo ponitur mandatum Domini;

secundo obedientia hominis, ibi **et statim sanus factus est homo** etc.

716. Praecipit autem Dominus naturae, et voluntati hominis; haec enim duo sub potestate eius sunt. Naturae praecipit, cum dicit **surge**: non enim hoc voluntati praecipitur, quia hoc non erat in eius potestate, sed naturae, quam Dominus praecipiendo immutavit, dando ei virtutem qua surgere posset.

Voluntati vero duo praecipit, scilicet **tolle grabatum tuum, et ambula**. Et quidem, quantum ad litteram, haec duo praecepit, ut ostendat perfectam sanitatem homini restitutam. In omnibus enim miraculis, secundum optimum illius naturae, Dominus perfectum opus fecit; Deut. XXXII, 4, dicitur: *Dei perfecta sunt opera*. Iste autem in duobus defecerat: scilicet in viribus propriis, se sustinere non valens, unde Dominus eum iacentem invenit; et in subsidio aliorum, unde dicebat **hominem non habeo**. Ut ergo perfecta sanitas innotesceret, ei qui se sustinere non valebat, praecipit ut lectum suum tollat; et ei qui ambulare non poterat, praecepit ut ambulet.

717. Nihilominus tamen haec tria in iustificatione Dominus praecipit. Primo quod surgat recedendo a peccato; Eph. V, 14: *surge qui dormis, et exurge a mortuis*. Secundo praecipitur **tolle grabatum**, satisfaciendo de commissis. Per grabatum enim, in quo homo requiescit, significatur peccatum. Tollit ergo homo grabatum suum, quando fert onus poenitentiae sibi pro peccato impositum; Mich. c. VII, 9: *iram Domini portabo, quoniam peccavi ei*. Tertio ut ambulet proficiendo in bono, secundum illud Ps. LXXXIII, 8: *ibunt de virtute in virtutem*.

718. Secundum Augustinum, duo deficiebant isti languido, scilicet praecepta geminae caritatis: et ideo voluntati, quae caritate perficitur, duo mandat, scilicet tollere grabatum, et ambulare. Primum pertinet ad dilectionem proximi, quae prior est ordine faciendi; secundum ad dilectionem Dei, quae prior est ordine praecipiendi.

Dicit ergo quantum ad primum **tolle grabatum tuum**, quasi dicat: quando infirmus es, proximus tuus sustinet te, et patienter fovet ut grabatus infirmum; Rom. XV, 1: *debemus nos firmiores, imbecillitates infirmorum sustinere, et non nobis ipsis placere*. Quando ergo sanus factus es, **tolle grabatum tuum**, idest, sustine et

that no mere man could save the human race, for all had sinned and needed the grace of God. Mankind had to wait for the coming of Christ, God and man, by whom it would be healed.

715. Now, at **arise, take up your bed**, we see the man restored to health, i.e., the working of the miracle.

First, the Lord's command is given;

second, the man's obedience, at **and immediately the man was made well, and he took up his bed and walked**.

716. The Lord commanded both the nature of the man and his will, for both are under the Lord's power. He commanded his nature when he said, **arise**. This command was not directed to the man's will, for this was not within the power of his will. But it was within the power of his nature, to which the Lord gave the power to stand by his command.

He gave two commands to the man's will: **take up your bed and walk**. The literal meaning for this is that these two things were commanded in order to show that the man had been restored to perfect health. For in all his miracles the Lord produced a perfect work, according to what was best in the nature of each case: *the works of God are perfect* (Deut 32:4). Now this man was lacking two things: first, his own energy, since he could not stand up by himself, thus our Lord found him lying by the pool. Second, he lacked the help of others; so he said, **I have no man**. So our Lord, in order that this man might recognize his perfect health, ordered him who could not help himself to pick up his mat, and him who could not walk to walk.

717. These are the three things which the Lord commands in the justification of a sinner. First, he should stand up, by leaving his sinful ways: *rise up, you who sleep, and arise from the dead* (Eph 5:14). Second, he is commanded to **take up your bed**, by making satisfaction for the sins he has committed. For the mat on which a man rests signifies his sins. And so a man takes up his mat when he begins to do the penance given to him for his sins. *I will bear the anger of God, because I have sinned against him* (Mic 7:9). Third, he is commanded to walk, by advancing in what is good, according to: *they will go from strength to strength* (Ps 83:8).

718. According to Augustine, this sick man was lacking two things: the two precepts of charity. And so our Lord gives two commands to his will, which is perfected by charity: to take up his mat, and to walk. The first concerns the love of neighbor, which is first in the order of doing; the second concerns the love of God, which is first in the order of precept.

Christ says, with respect to the first, **take up your bed**. As if to say: when you are weak, your neighbor bears with you and, like a mat, patiently supports you: *we who are stronger ought to bear with the infirmities of the weak, and not seek to please ourselves* (Rom 15:1). Thus, after you have been cured, **take up your bed**, i.e., bear and support your

supporta proximum tuum, qui te infirmum portabat; Gal. VI, 2: *alter alterius onera portate*.

Quantum vero ad secundum, dicit *ambula*, appropinquando ad Deum. Unde in Ps. LXXXIII, v. 8, dicitur: *ibunt de virtute in virtutem*; et sequitur: *videbitur Deus deorum in Sion*; infra XII, 35: *ambulate dum lucem habetis*.

719. Consequenter cum dicit *et statim sanus factus est homo ille*, ponitur obedientia: et primo vere quia *statim factus est homo sanus*. Nec mirum, quia ipse est Verbum per quod caelum et terra facta sunt; Ps. CXLVIII, 5: *dixit, et facta sunt*. Et alibi: *Verbo Domini caeli firmati sunt*. Secundo voluntas: et primo, quia *sustulit grabatum suum*; secundo, quia *ambulabat*; Ex. XXIV, 7: *omnia quaecumque praecepit Dominus faciemus, et erimus obedientes*.

neighbor, who carried you when you were weak: *carry each other's burdens* (Gal 6:2).

About the second he says, **walk**, by drawing near God; so we read: *they will go from strength to strength*, and it then says: *the God of gods shall be seen in Zion* (Ps 83:8); **walk while you have the light** (John 12:35).

719. Next we see the man's obedience: **and immediately the man was made well**. First, the obedience of his nature, because, **and immediately the man was made well**. And no wonder, because Christ is the Word through whom heaven and earth were made: *he commanded and they were created* (Ps 148:5); *by the Word of the Lord the heavens were made* (Ps 32:6). Second, we see the obedience of the man's will: first, because he **picked up his bed**, and second, because he **walked**. *We will do everything that the Lord commands, and obey him* (Exod 24:7).

Lecture 2

5:9 Et statim sanus factus est homo ille, et sustulit grabatum suum, et ambulabat. Erat autem Sabbatum in die illo. [n. 721]

5:10 Dicebant ergo Iudaei illi qui sanatus fuerat: Sabbatum est, non licet tibi tollere grabatum tuum. [n. 723]

5:11 Respondit eis: qui me sanum fecit, ille mihi dixit: tolle grabatum tuum, et ambula. [n. 724]

5:12 Interrogaverunt ergo eum: quis est ille homo, qui dixit tibi: tolle grabatum tuum, et ambula? [n. 726]

5:13 Is autem, qui sanus fuerat effectus, nesciebat quis esset: Iesus enim declinavit a turba constituta in loco. [n. 727]

5:14 Postea invenit eum Iesus in templo, et dixit illi: ecce sanus factus es: iam noli peccare, ne deterius tibi aliquid contingat. [n. 730]

5:15 Abiit ille homo et annuntiavit Iudaeis, quia Iesus esset qui fecit eum sanum. [n. 735]

5:16 Propterea persequebantur Iudaei Iesum, quia haec faciebat in Sabbato. [n. 736]

5:17 Iesus autem respondit eis: Pater meus usque modo operatur, et ego operor. [n. 738]

5:18 Propterea ergo magis quaerebant eum Iudaei interficere: quia non solum solvebat Sabbatum, sed et patrem suum dicebat Deum, aequalem se faciens Deo. Respondit itaque Iesus, et dixit eis: [n. 741]

5:9 καὶ εὐθέως ἐγένετο ὑγιὴς ὁ ἄνθρωπος καὶ ἦρεν τὸν κράβαττον αὐτοῦ καὶ περιεπάτει. Ἦν δὲ σάββατον ἐν ἐκείνῃ τῇ ἡμέρᾳ.

5:10 ἔλεγον οὖν οἱ Ἰουδαῖοι τῷ τεθεραπευμένῳ· σάββατόν ἐστιν, καὶ οὐκ ἔξεστίν σοι ἆραι τὸν κράβαττόν σου.

5:11 ὁ δὲ ἀπεκρίθη αὐτοῖς· ὁ ποιήσας με ὑγιῆ ἐκεῖνός μοι εἶπεν· ἆρον τὸν κράβαττόν σου καὶ περιπάτει.

5:12 ἠρώτησαν αὐτόν· τίς ἐστιν ὁ ἄνθρωπος ὁ εἰπών σοι· ἆρον καὶ περιπάτει;

5:13 ὁ δὲ ἰαθεὶς οὐκ ᾔδει τίς ἐστιν, ὁ γὰρ Ἰησοῦς ἐξένευσεν ὄχλου ὄντος ἐν τῷ τόπῳ.

5:14 μετὰ ταῦτα εὑρίσκει αὐτὸν ὁ Ἰησοῦς ἐν τῷ ἱερῷ καὶ εἶπεν αὐτῷ· ἴδε ὑγιὴς γέγονας, μηκέτι ἁμάρτανε, ἵνα μὴ χεῖρόν σοί τι γένηται.

5:15 ἀπῆλθεν ὁ ἄνθρωπος καὶ ἀνήγγειλεν τοῖς Ἰουδαίοις ὅτι Ἰησοῦς ἐστιν ὁ ποιήσας αὐτὸν ὑγιῆ.

5:16 καὶ διὰ τοῦτο ἐδίωκον οἱ Ἰουδαῖοι τὸν Ἰησοῦν, ὅτι ταῦτα ἐποίει ἐν σαββάτῳ.

5:17 Ὁ δὲ [Ἰησοῦς] ἀπεκρίνατο αὐτοῖς· ὁ πατήρ μου ἕως ἄρτι ἐργάζεται κἀγὼ ἐργάζομαι·

5:18 διὰ τοῦτο οὖν μᾶλλον ἐζήτουν αὐτὸν οἱ Ἰουδαῖοι ἀποκτεῖναι, ὅτι οὐ μόνον ἔλυεν τὸ σάββατον, ἀλλὰ καὶ πατέρα ἴδιον ἔλεγεν τὸν θεὸν ἴσον ἑαυτὸν ποιῶν τῷ θεῷ.

5:9 And immediately the man was made well, and he took up his bed and walked. And it was the Sabbath that day. [n. 721]

5:10 The Jews therefore said to him who was healed: it is the Sabbath; it is not lawful for you to take up your bed. [n. 723]

5:11 He answered them: he who made me well said to me, take up your bed and walk. [n. 724]

5:12 They asked him therefore: who is that man who said to you, take up your bed and walk? [n. 726]

5:13 But he who was healed did not know who it was; for Jesus went aside from the multitude that was in the place. [n. 727]

5:14 Afterwards, Jesus found him in the temple and said to him: behold, you are made well: sin no more, lest some worse thing happen to you. [n. 730]

5:15 The man went his way and told the Jews that it was Jesus who had made him well. [n. 735]

5:16 Therefore the Jews persecuted Jesus, because he did these things on the Sabbath. [n. 736]

5:17 But Jesus answered them: my Father works until now, and I also work. [n. 738]

5:18 Therefore the Jews sought the more to kill him, because he did not only break the Sabbath, but also said that God was his Father, making himself equal to God. Then Jesus answered and said to them: [n. 741]

---

720. Posito miraculo visibili, per quod ostenditur virtus Christi ad reparandam vitam spiritualem, hic ponitur occasio doctrinae Christi; quae quidem occasio sumitur ex persecutione Iudaeorum contra Christum mota. Cuius quidem persecutionis duplex causa fuit ex parte Iudaeorum invidentium Christo.

Prima quidem operatio pietatis;

720. Having seen a visible miracle which shows the power of Christ to restore spiritual life, we now see an opportunity given to him to teach. This opportunity was the persecution launched against him by the Jews. These Jews, who were envious of Christ, persecuted him for two reasons:

first, the above act of his mercy;

secunda vero doctrina veritatis, ibi *Iesus autem respondit eis: pater meus usque modo operatur* etc.

Circa primum tria facit.

Primo praemittitur occasio persecutionis;

secundo ponitur calumnia illata contra curatum, ibi *dicebant ergo Iudaei illi qui sanatus fuerat* etc.;

tertio ponitur calumnia illata contra Christum, ibi *interrogaverunt eum: quis est ille homo?* etc.

721. Occasio autem persecutionis inductae contra Christum sumitur ex eo quod in Sabbato curavit; et ideo dicit Evangelista *erat autem Sabbatum in die illo*, quando miraculum fecit Iesus, quando grabatum tollere iussit.

Assignatur autem triplex ratio quare Dominus in Sabbato operari incepit. Una ab Ambrosio *super Lucam*, Christus enim ad hoc venit, ut opus creationis, scilicet hominem, deformatum repararet. Inde autem incipere debebat, ubi actor in creationis opus consummato creaverat: hoc autem fuit in die Sabbati, ut dicitur Gen. I; et ideo, ut Christus ostenderet se reparatorem totius creaturae, incepit in Sabbato. Alia ratio est, quia dies Sabbati celebratur a Iudaeis in memoriam primae creationis. Christus autem venit, ut quasi novam creaturam faceret, secundum illud Gal. ult., 15: *in Christo Iesu neque circumcisio, neque praeputium aliquid valet; sed nova creatura*, et nova creatio per gratiam, quae fit per Spiritum Sanctum, secundum illud Ps. CIII, 30: *emittes Spiritum tuum, et creabuntur, et renovabis faciem terrae*. Volens ergo Christus ostendere, per eum recreationem fieri, in Sabbato operatur; Iac. I, 18: *ut simus initium aliquod creaturae*. Tertia ratio est, ut ostenderet se facturum quod lex facere non poterat; Rom. VIII, 3: *nam quod impossibile erat legi, in quo infirmabatur per carnem, misit Deus Filium suum in similitudinem carnis peccati*. Et infra *ut iustificatio legis impleretur in nobis*.

Iudaei autem nihil operabantur in Sabbato, in figura quod quaedam quae erant Sabbati, consummanda erant, quae per legem fieri non poterant. Et hoc patet in quatuor, quae Deus erga diem Sabbati ordinavit. Nam diem Sabbati sanctificavit, diem Sabbati benedixit, in eo opera sua consummavit, et in eo requievit. Quae quidem lex facere non potuit, nam sanctificare non poterat. Unde Ps. XI, 1, dicebat: *salvum me fac, Domine, quoniam defecit sanctus*. Neque etiam benedicere; quinimmo *qui sunt ex operibus legis, sub maledicto sunt*, ut dicitur Gal. III, 10. Nec consummare et perficere: quia *neminem ad perfectum adduxit lex*: Hebr. VII, 19. Nec etiam perfectam quietem praestare: quia, ut dicitur Hebr. IV, 8: *nam si eis Iesus requiem praestitisset, numquam de alia loqueretur*.

second, his teaching of the truth, at *but Jesus answered them: my Father works until now, and I also work*.

As to the first, the Evangelist does three things.

First, he gives the occasion for their persecution.

Second, the false accusation against the man who was just cured, at *the Jews therefore said to him who was healed*.

And third, their attempt to belittle Christ, at *they asked him therefore: who is that man?*

721. Their opportunity to persecute Christ was the fact that he cured the man on the Sabbath; accordingly, the Evangelist says, *and it was the Sabbath that day*, when Christ performed the miracle of commanding the man to pick up his mat.

Three reasons are given why our Lord began to work on the Sabbath. The first is given by Ambrose, in his commentary, *On Luke*. He says that Christ came to renovate the work of creation, that is, man, who had become deformed. And so he should have begun where the Creator had left off the work of creation, that is, on a Sabbath (Gen 1). Thus Christ began to work on the Sabbath to show that he was the renovator of the whole creature. Another reason was that the Sabbath day was celebrated by the Jews in memory of the first creation. But Christ came to make, in a way, a new creature: *in Christ Jesus, neither circumcision nor the lack of circumcision is a benefit; what counts is a new creation* (Gal 6:15), i.e., through grace, which comes through the Holy Spirit: *you will send forth your Spirit, and they will be created; and you will renew the face of the earth* (Ps 103:30). And so Christ worked on the Sabbath to show that a new creation, a re-creation, was taking place through him: *that we might be the first fruits of his creatures* (Jas 1:18). The third reason was to show that he was about to do what the law could not do: *God did what the law, weakened by the flesh, could not do: by sending his own Son in the likeness of sinful flesh, he condemned sin in his flesh, in order that the requirements of the law might be accomplished in us* (Rom 8:3).

The Jews, however, did not do any work on the Sabbath, as a symbol that there were certain things pertaining to the Sabbath which were to be accomplished, but which the law could not do. This is clear in the four things which God ordained for the Sabbath: for he sanctified the Sabbath day, blessed it, completed his work on it, and then rested. These things the law was not able to do. It could not sanctify; so we read: *save me, O Lord, for there are no holy people left* (Ps 11:1). Nor could it bless; rather, *those who rely on the works of the law are under a curse* (Gal 3:10). Neither could it, complete and perfect, because *the law brought nothing to perfection* (Heb 7:19). Nor could it bring perfect rest: *if Joshua had given them rest, God would not be speaking after of another day* (Heb 4:8).

Haec ergo quae lex facere non potuit, Christus fecit: ipsum enim populum sanctificavit per passionem. Heb. XIII, 12: *Iesus ut per suum sanguinem sanctificaret populum, extra portam passus est.* Ipse benedixit per gratiae infusionem; Ephes. I, 3: *benedictus Deus Pater Domini nostri Iesu Christi, qui benedixit nos in omni benedictione spirituali in caelestibus in Christo.* Ipse consummavit per perfectae iustitiae instructionem; Matth. V, v. 48: *estote perfecti, sicut et Pater caelestis perfectus est.* Ipse introduxit in veram requiem; Hebr. IV, 3: *nos qui credimus, ingrediemur in requiem, quemadmodum dixit: sicut iuravi in ira mea, si introibunt in requiem meam.* Ipsi ergo competit in die Sabbati operari, qui, quae ad Sabbatum pertinent, perficere potest, a quibus lex impotens quiescebat.

722. Consequenter ponit calumniam illatam contra curatum, cum dicit: *dicebant ergo Iudaei illi qui sanatus fuerat* etc. Et

primo ponitur calumniae contra curatum illatio;

secundo subditur curati excusatio, ibi *respondit eis: qui me sanum fecit* etc.

723. Calumniam autem inferunt contra istum de hoc quod in Sabbato grabatum portat, sed non de curatione; unde dicunt *Sabbatum est, non licet tibi tollere grabatum tuum.* Cuius ratio multiplex potest assignari.

Una, quia Iudaei frequenter Christo de curatione in die Sabbati calumniam inferentes, confutati erant a Christo, per hoc quod ipsi etiam iumenta de puteo in die Sabbati eruebant et salvabant, ut habetur Lc. XIV, 15. Et ideo de curatione tamquam de re utili et necessaria tacent; de portatione vero lecti, quae non necessaria videbatur, calumniantur; quasi dicant: si sanitas non erat differenda, quid erat necessarium lectum portare, seu portari praecipere?

Alia ratio est, quia Dominus dixerat, contra eos concludens, quod licet Sabbato benefacere. Et ideo, quia curari non est benefacere sed bene pati, curatum potius quam curantem calumniantur.

Tertia ratio est, quia hoc in lege videtur prohibitum esse Iudaeis, ne aliquid in die Sabbati operentur; specialiter tamen portatio onerum in die Sabbati prohibetur. Ier. XVII, 21: *ne portetis onera in die Sabbati.* Et ideo specialiter calumniati sunt portationem in die Sabbati, utpote dicto prophetae contrariam.

Sed hoc tamen mandatum prophetae mysticum est: nam per onera non portanda intendebat eos inducere ut in die Sabbati requiescerent ab oneribus peccatorum; de quibus dicitur in Ps. XXXVII, 5: *iniquitates meae sicut onus grave gravatae sunt super me.* Unde, quia iam erat tempus solvendi figuras occultas, mandat Christus isti

Therefore, these things, which the law could not do, Christ did. For he sanctified the people by his passion: *Jesus, in order to sanctify the people with his own blood, suffered outside the gate* (Heb 13:12). He blessed them by an inpouring of grace: *blessed be God, the Father of our Lord Jesus Christ, who has blessed us with every spiritual blessing of heaven, in Christ* (Eph 1:3). He brought the people to perfection by instructing them in the ways of perfect justice: *be perfect, as your heavenly Father is perfect* (Matt 5:48). He also led them to true rest: *we who have believed shall enter into rest; as he said: I have sworn in my wrath; if they shall enter ino my rest* (Heb 4:3). Therefore, it is proper for him to work on the Sabbath, who is able to make perfect those things that pertain to the Sabbath, from which an impotent law rested.

722. Then, at *the Jews therefore said to him who was healed*, the Evangelist gives the accusation brought against the man who was healed.

First, we have the accusation; and

second, the explanation given by the man who was healed, at *he answered them: he who made me well*.

723. The man was accused for carrying his mat on the Sabbath, and not for being healed; so they say: *it is the Sabbath; it is not lawful for you to take up your bed*. There are several reasons for this.

One is that the Jews, although frequently charging Christ with healing on the Sabbath, had been embarrassed by him on the ground that they themselves used to pull their cattle from ditches on the Sabbath in order to save them (Luke 14:15). For this reason the Jews did not mention his healing, as it was useful and necessary; but they charged him with carrying his mat, which did not seem to be necessary. As if to say: although your cure need not have been postponed, there was no need for you to carry your mat, or for the order to carry it.

Another reason was that the Lord had shown, contrary to their opinion, that it was lawful to do good on the Sabbath. And so, because being healed is not the same as doing good, but being done a good, they attack the one healed rather than the one healing.

The third reason was that the Jews thought that they were forbidden by the law to do any work on the Sabbath; and it was the carrying of burdens that was especially forbidden on the Sabbath: *do not carry a burden on the Sabbath* (Jer 17:21). Accordingly, they made a special point of being against the carrying of anything on the Sabbath, as being opposed to the teaching of the prophet.

But this command of the prophet was mystical: for when he forbade them to carry burdens, he wanted to encourage them to rest from the burdens of their sins on the Sabbath. Of these sins it is said: *my iniquities are a heavy burden and have weighed me down* (Ps 37:5). Therefore, since the time had come to explain the meaning of obscure

grabatum tollere, idest proximum in infirmitate sustentare, secundum illud Gal. VI, 2: *alter alterius onera portate, et sic adimplebitis legem Christi.*

724. Consequenter ponitur excusatio curati, cum subditur *respondit eis: qui me sanum fecit, ille mihi dixit.* Et quidem prudenter se excusat: numquam enim adeo bene probatur doctrina esse divinitus, sicut per ostensionem miraculorum, quae nonnisi divinitus fieri possunt. Mc. ult., 20: *illi autem profecti praedicaverunt ubique, Domino cooperante, et sermonem confirmante, sequentibus signis.* Et ideo iste, auctorem sanitatis suae calumniantibus, obiiciebat dicens **qui me sanum fecit, ille mihi dixit**; quasi dicat: vos dicitis prohibitum esse ne onus portetur in Sabbato, et hoc auctoritate divina; sed mihi eadem auctoritate est impositum ut tollam grabatum: nam **ille, qui me salvum fecit**, et per sanitatem restitutam se divinam virtutem habere ostendit, **mihi dixit: tolle grabatum tuum, et ambula.** Et ideo mandatis eius qui tantae est virtutis, et qui mihi tale beneficium contulit, merito teneor obedire. Ps. CXVIII, 93: *in aeternum non obliviscar iustificationes tuas, quia in ipsis vivificasti me.*

725. Consequenter dicit *interrogaverunt ergo eum.* Quia curatum hominem calumniari non poterant, Christi curationem calumniari nituntur: per hunc enim se excusaverat homo ille. Et quia eum determinate quis esset, non indicaverat, maligne interrogabant ab eo quis esset. Et ideo circa hoc

primo agitur de Christi inquisitione;

secundo de eius inventione, ibi *postea invenit eum Iesus*;

tertio de eius persecutione, ibi *propterea persequebantur Iudaei Iesum.*

726. Circa primum tria ponuntur: scilicet Iudaeorum inquisitio, curati ignorantia et ignorantiae causa.

Quantum ad primum dicitur: *interrogabant ergo eum Iudaei*, scilicet non bona intentione, ut proficiant, sed maligno animo, ut persequantur et perdant. Infra VIII, 21: *quaeretis me, et in peccato vestro moriemini.* Et hanc eorum malitiam eorum verba manifestant. Cum enim Dominus et sanari languidum, et grabatum tolli iusserit, primum divinae virtutis ostensivum et irrefragabile signum subticent; aliud quod contra legem videtur, replicant, dicentes **quis est ille homo qui dixit tibi: tolle grabatum tuum et ambula?** Eccli. XI, 33: *bona in mala pervertens, insidiatur, et in electis imponit*, scilicet imponere nititur *maculam.*

727. Quantum ad secundum dicit **qui autem sanus factus fuerat, nesciebat qui esset.** Sanus iste significat fideles per gratiam Christi sanatos. Ephes. II, 8: *gratia salvati estis.* Qui quidem nesciunt Christum quis est, sed effectum tantum eius cognoscunt. II Cor. c. V, 6:

symbols, Christ commanded him to take up his mat, i.e, to help his neighbors in their weaknesses: *bear one another's burdens, and so you will fulfill the law of Christ* (Gal 6:2).

724. Then, at **he answered them: he who made me well said to me**, we see the man who was healed defending himself. His defense is wisely taken: for a doctrine is never so well proved to be divinely inspired as by miracles which can be accomplished only by divine power: *going out, they preached everywhere, and the Lord worked with them and confirmed the word by the signs that followed* (Mark 16:20). Thus he argued with those who were defaming the one who healed him, saying: **he who made me well said to me.** As if to say: you say that I am forbidden to carry a burden on the Sabbath, and this on divine authority; but I was commanded by the same authority to pick up my mat. For, **he who made me well**, and by restoring my health showed that he had divine power, said to me, **take up your bed and walk.** Therefore, I was duty bound to obey the commands of one who has such power and who had done me such a favor. *I will never forget your precepts because you have brought me to life by them* (Ps 118:93).

725. Then he says, **they asked him therefore**, since they could not very well charge the man who was cured, they try to belittle Christ's cure, for this man defended himself through Christ. But since he did not indicate precisely who he was, they maliciously ask him who it was. With respect to this,

first, the search for Christ is set down.

Second, his discovery, at **afterwards, Jesus found him.**

And third, his persecution, at **therefore the Jews persecuted Jesus.**

726. Three things are mentioned about the first: the Jews' interrogation; the ignorance of the man who was cured, and the cause of that ignorance.

As to the first, we read: **they asked him therefore**, not with the good intention of making progress, but for the evil purpose of persecuting and destroying Christ: **you will seek me, and you will die in your sin** (John 8:21), Their very words show their malice: for while our Lord had commanded the man who was sick to become healed and to pick up his mat, they ignored the first, which is an undeniable sign of divine power, and harped on the second, which seemed to be against the law, saying, **who is that man who said to you, take up your bed and walk?** He lies in wait, and turns good into evil, and he will put blame, i.e., attempt to put blame, *on the elect* (Sir 11:33).

727. As to the second, the Evangelist says, **but he who was healed did not know who it was.** This cured man signifies those who believe and have been healed by the grace of Christ: *you are saved by grace* (Eph 2:8). Indeed, they do not know who Christ is, but they know only his effects: *while we*

quamdiu sumus in corpore, peregrinamur a Domino: per fidem enim ambulamus, et non per speciem. Sed tunc cognoscemus Christum quis est, *quando videbimus eum sicuti est*: I Io. III, 2.

728. Huius autem ignorantiae causam assignat quantum ad tria, cum dicit **Iesus autem declinavit a turba constituta in loco**. Quod quidem causam habet litteralem et mysticam.

Litteralem quidem quantum ad duo. Primo ut daret nobis exemplum occultandi opera nostra bona et non quaerendi in eis hominum favorem, secundum illud Matth. VI, 1: *attendite ne iustitiam vestram faciatis coram hominibus*. Secundo ut declinemus et fugiamus oculos invidorum ab omnibus operibus nostris, ne ex hoc eorum invidia crescat; Eccli. VIII, 14: *ne contra faciem stes contumeliosi, ne sedeat quasi insidiator ori tuo.*

Mysticam vero quantum ad duo. Primo, ut det intelligere quod Christus non de facili invenitur in hominum multitudine et in turbine curarum temporalium, sed in spirituali secreto. Osee II, 14: *ducam eam in solitudinem, et ibi loquar ad cor eius.* Nam *verba sapientium audiuntur in silentio*, ut dicitur Eccle. IX, 17. Secundo, ut insinuet quod Christus debebat declinare a Iudaeis ad gentes; Is. VIII, 17: *abscondit faciem suam parumper a Iacob*, idest subtraxit veritatis suae notitiam a populo Iudaeorum.

729. Consequenter agitur de inventione Christi, cum dicit **postea invenit eum Iesus in templo**. Et

primo dicit quod invenitur;

secundo insinuat quod inventus docet;

tertio quod post doctrinam manifestatur.

730. Quantum ad inventionem duo ponit, scilicet modum inveniendi, et locum.

Modus quidem est mirabilis, quia non invenitur nisi inveniat, unde dicit **postea**, scilicet quae dicta sunt, **invenit eum Iesus**: nam homo sua virtute Christum invenire non potest, nisi ei se Christus praesentet. Unde etiam Ps. CXVIII, 176 dicebat: *require servum tuum.* Sap. VI, 14: *praeoccupat eos qui se concupiscunt.*

Locus autem in quo invenitur Christus est venerabilis, quia **in templo**, secundum illud Ps. X, 5: *Dominus in templo sancto suo.* Nam et mater eius in templo eum invenit, Lc. II, 46 et hoc quia in his quae Patris sui sunt, oportebat eum esse. In quo datur nobis intelligi quod curatus iste non ad vanitatem, sed ad religionis studium conversus, templum frequentans, in ipso Christum cognoscit: quia si ad conditoris cognitionem venire volumus, fugienda est turba pravorum affectuum, et declinanda sunt malorum conventicula, et fugiendum est ad templum cordis nostri, quod Deus invisere et habitare dignatur.

are in the body, we are absent from the Lord: for we walk by faith, and not by sight (2 Cor 5:6). We will know who Christ is when *we shall see him as he is* (1 John 3:2).

728. Next, the Evangelist gives the reason for the man's ignorance, saying, for **Jesus went aside from the multitude that was in the place**. There are both literal and mystical reasons why Christ left.

Of the two literal reasons, the first is to give us the example of concealing our good deeds and of not using them to seek the applause of men: *take care not to perform your good actions in the sight of men, in order to be seen by them* (Matt 6:1). The second literal reason is to show us that, in all ouractions, we should leave and avoid those who are envious, so as not to feed and increase their envy: *do not be provoked by one who speaks evil of you, so he will not trap you by your own words* (Sir 8:14).

There are also two mystical reasons why Christ slipped away. First, it teaches us that Christ is not easy to find in the midst of men, or in the whirlwind of temporal cares; rather, he is found in spiritual seclusion: *I will lead her into the wilderness, and there I will speak to her heart* (Hos 2:14); and: *the words of the wise are heard in silence* (Eccl 9:17). Second, this suggests to us that Christ was to leave the Jews for the gentiles: *he hid his face for a while from the house of Jacob* (Isa 8:17), i.e., he withdrew the knowledge of his truth from the Jewish people.

729. Then, at **afterwards, Jesus found him in the temple**, the Evangelist tells us how Jesus was found.

First, he says that he was found.

Second, that after having been found, he taught.

Third, that after having taught, his identity was reported to the Jews.

730. The Evangelist tells us both where and the way in which Christ was found.

The way in which he was found was remarkable, for Christ is not found unless he first finds; hence he says, **afterwards**, after the above events, **Jesus found him**. For we cannot find Jesus by our own power unless Christ first presents himself to us; so we read: *seek your servant* (Ps 118:176); and, *she goes to meet those who desire her* (Wis 6:14).

The place Christ was found was holy, **in the temple**, according to: *the Lord is in his holy temple* (Ps 10:5). For his mother had also found him in the temple (Luke 2:46); and he was there for he had to be concerned with his Father's affairs. We see from this that this man was not cured in vain, but having been converted to a religious way of life, he visited the temple and found Christ: because if we desire to come to a knowledge of the Creator, we must run from the tumult of sinful affections, leave the company of evil men, and flee to the temple of our heart, where God condescends to visit and live.

731. Consequenter inventus docet; unde *et dixit illi: ecce sanus factus es, iam noli peccare.* Ubi

primo commemorat impensum beneficium;

secundo proponit sanum consilium;

tertio ostendit imminens periculum.

732. Sed beneficium est admirabile, quia subita restitutio sanitatis. Unde dicitur *ecce iam sanus factus es.* Et ideo semper oportet in memoria teneri, secundum illud Is. LXIII, v. 7: *miserationum Domini recordabor.*

733. Consilium vero utile, quia *iam amplius noli peccare*; Eccli. XXI, 1: *fili, peccasti, ne adiicias iterum.*

Quare Dominus isti paralytico et aliis quibusdam ab eo curatis mentionem facit de peccatis, et non aliis? Ideo scilicet ut ostendat per hoc, infirmitates aliquibus, ex peccatis prioribus provenire, secundum illud I Cor. XI, v. 30: *ideo multi imbecilles et infirmi, et dormiunt multi.* Per quod etiam se esse Deum ostendit, peccata et occulta cordium manifestans. Prov. XV, 11: *Infernus et perditio coram illo: quanto magis corda filiorum hominum?* Istis ergo solis mentionem de peccatis facit et non aliis ab eo curatis, quia non omnes infirmitates propter peccata priora proveniunt; sed quaedam ex naturali dispositione, quaedam propter probationem, sicut in Iob. Vel de istis tantum mentionem fecit, quia magis praeparati erant ad correctionem. Prov. c. IX, 8: *noli arguere derisorem, ne oderit te: argue sapientem, et diliget te.* Vel in istis, omnibus aliis hoc mandavit.

734. Periculum autem imminens erat terribile, unde dicit *ne deterius tibi aliquid contingat.* Quod quidem dupliciter intelligi potest, secundum duo quae in isto praecesserunt. Primo enim punitus fuit per prolixum morbum; secundo consecutus fuit magnum beneficium. Et ideo ad utrumque referri potest quod dicitur.

Ad primum quidem: quia cum aliquis pro peccato punitur et ex ipsa poena a peccato non retrahitur, iustum est ut gravius puniatur. Et ideo dicit *noli amplius peccare*, quia si peccaveris *deterius tibi continget.* Ier. c. II, 30: *frustra percussi filios vestros: disciplinam non receperunt.*

Ad secundum vero: quia qui post beneficia recepta ad peccata prolabitur, gravioris supplicii reus efficitur propter ingratitudinem, secundum illud II Pet. II, 20: *melius erat eis viam veritatis non agnoscere, quam post agnitionem retrorsum converti.* Similiter etiam quia postquam homo ad peccatum semel redierit, facilius peccat; secundum illud Mt. XII, v. 45: *fiunt novissima hominis illius peiora prioribus.* Ier. II, 20: *a saeculo fregisti iugum, rupisti vinculum, dixisti: non serviam.*

735. Consequenter ponitur inventi manifestatio, cum subditur *abiit ille homo et annuntiavit* etc. Et secundum quosdam posset intelligi, ut Chrysostomus dicit, quod ex malitia manifestasset eum; sed hoc non videtur probabile, scilicet quod post tantum beneficium

731. After Christ was found, he began to teach, at *and said to him: behold, you are made well: sin no more.*

First, Christ reminded the man of the gift he was given.

Second, he offered him sound advice.

And third, he pointed out an imminent danger.

732. The gift was remarkable, for it was a sudden restoration to health; so he says, *behold, you are made well.* Therefore, you should always keep this in mind, according to: *I will remember the tender mercies of the Lord* (Isa 63:7).

733. His advice, too, was useful, that is, *sin no more. My son, you have sinned. Do not sin again* (Sir 21:1).

Why did our Lord mention sin to this paralytic and to certain others that he cured, and not to the rest? He did this to show that illness comes to certain people as a result of their previous sins, according to: *for this reason many of you are weak and sick, and many have died* (1 Cor 11:30). In this way he even showed himself to be God, pointing out sins and the hidden secrets of the heart: *hell and destruction are open to the Lord; how much more the hearts of the children of men* (Prov 15:11). And so Christ mentioned sin only to some he cured and not to all, for not all infirmities are due to previous sins: some come from one's natural disposition, and some are permitted as a trial, as with Job. Or, Christ might have brought up sin to some because they were better prepared for his correction: *do not rebuke one who mocks, lest he hate you; rebuke a wise man, and he will love you* (Prov 9:8). Or, we could say, in telling some not to sin, he intended his words for all the others.

734. The imminent danger was great, so he says, *lest some worse thing happen to you.* This can be understood in two ways, according to the two events that preceded. For this man was first punished with a troublesome infirmity, and then received a marvelous favor. Accordingly, Christ's statement can refer to each.

To the first, for when anyone is punished for his sin, and the punishment does not check him from sinning, it is just for him to be punished more severely. So Christ says, *sin no more*, because if you do sin, *lest some worse thing happen to you. I have struck your children in vain* (Jer 2:30).

It can refer to the second, for one who falls into sin after receiving favors deserves a more severe punishment because of his ingratitude, as we see: *it would be better for them not to know the way of truth, than to turn back after knowing it* (2 Pet 2:20). Also, because after a man has once returned to sin, he sins more easily: *the last state of that man becomes worse than the first* (Matt 12:45); and: *you broke your yoke a long time ago, and snapped off your chains, and said: I will not serve* (Jer 2:20).

735. Then when he says, *the man went his way and told the Jews that it was Jesus who had made him well.* Some think, as Chrysostom reports, that this man identified Jesus out of malice. But this does not seem probable: that he would be so ungrateful after receiving such a favor. *He told*

ita ingratus esset. **Nuntiavit** ergo **Iudaeis, quia Iesus esset qui fecit eum sanum**, ut manifestaret Christi virtutem ad sanandum. Ps. LXV, 16: *venite, et narrabo . . . quanta fecit Dominus animae meae.* Et hoc patet, quia illi interrogaverunt eum, quis iusserit grabatum tollere. Iste autem annuntiavit eis quod **Iesus fecit eum sanum**.

736. Consequenter cum dicit **propterea persequebantur Iudaei Iesum**, ponitur persecutio contra Christum, quae est propter quoddam opus pietatis in Sabbato exhibitum; unde dicit **propterea persequebantur Iudaei Iesum**, quia haec faciebat in Sabbato. Ps. CXVIII, 161: *principes persecuti sunt me gratis.*

737. Consequenter cum dicit **Iesus autem respondit eis** etc., ponitur secunda causa persecutionis, quae sumitur ex doctrina. Et

primo ponitur doctrina veritatis;

secundo persecutio Iudaicae pravitatis, ibi **propterea ergo magis quaerebant eum Iudaei interficere**.

738. Doctrinam autem veritatis proponit Dominus, excusando se de solutione Sabbati.

Sed notandum est, quod Dominus de huius solutione aliquando quidem excusavit se, aliquando discipulos suos. Et discipulos quidem, quia homines puri erant, excusavit per similitudinem hominum, scilicet per exemplum sacerdotum, qui operabantur in templo in die Sabbati, et Sabbatum non solvebant. Et David, qui sub Achimelech sacerdote in die Sabbati a facie Saulis fugiens, panes propositionis accepit de templo, ut habetur I Reg. XXI, v. 1 ss. Se vero, quia homo erat et Deus, aliquando per similitudinem hominum excusavit a solutione Sabbati. Lc. XIV, 5: *quis vestrum, si ceciderit bos aut asinus suus in puteum, non continuo extrahet eum in die Sabbati?*

Aliquando vero, et praecipue in hoc loco, excusat se per similitudinem Dei, dicens **Pater meus usque modo operatur, et ego operor**; quasi dicat: nolite putare quod in Sabbato ita requieverit Pater meus, ut ex illo non operetur; sed sicut ipse et nunc sine labore operatur, ita et ego operor. In quo excludit falsum intellectum Iudaeorum, qui volentes conformari Deo, nihil in die Sabbati operantur, ac si Deus ipso die omnino destiterit operari. Et quidem licet in Sabbato requieverit a novis creaturis condendis, nihilominus tamen semper et continue usque modo operatur, creaturas in esse conservando. Unde et signanter verbo *requietionis* Moyses est usus post opera Dei, a quibus condendis requievit, ut signaret spiritualem requiem, quam Deus exemplo quietis suae fidelibus postea qui bona fecerint opera, arcana significatione pollicebatur. Unde dici potest, illud mandatum in umbra futuri fuisse praeceptum.

the Jews that it was Jesus who had made him well, in order to make it clear that Christ had the power to heal: *come . . . and I will tell you what great things the Lord has done for me* (Ps 65:16). This is obvious, for they had asked him who commanded him to pick up his mat, but he told them that **it was Jesus who had made him well**.

736. Next, at **therefore the Jews persecuted Jesus**, we have the persecution of Christ, begun because he performed a work of mercy on the Sabbath. Thus the Evangelist says, **therefore the Jews persecuted Jesus**, because he performed such works on the Sabbath. *Princes have persecuted me without cause* (Ps 118:161).

737. Then, at **but Jesus answered them: my Father works until now, and I also work**, the second reason for his persecution is given: what he taught.

First, we are given the truth he taught; and

second, the perversity of his persecutors, at **therefore the Jews sought the more to kill him**.

738. Our Lord taught the truth while justifying his breaking of the Sabbath.

Here we should note that our Lord justified both himself and his disciples from breaking the Sabbath. He justified his disciples, since they were men, by comparing them to other men: as the priests who, although they worked in the temple on the Sabbath, did not break the Sabbath; and to David, who, while Ahimelech was priest, took the consecrated bread from the temple oil the Sabbath when he was running from Saul (1 Sam 21:1). Our Lord, who was both God and man, sometimes justified himself in breaking the Sabbath by comparing himself to men: *which of you, if his donkey or ox falls into a pit, will not take him out on the Sabbath?* (Luke 14:5).

And sometimes he justified himself by comparing himself to God, and particularly in this place by saying: **my Father works until now, and I also work**. As if to say: do not think that my Father rested on the Sabbath in such a way that from that time he does not work; rather, just as he is working even now without laboring, so I also am working. By saying this, Christ eliminated the misunderstanding of the Jews: for in their desire to imitate God, they did not do any work on the Sabbath, as if God entirely ceased from work on that day. In fact, although God rested on the Sabbath from producing new creatures, he is working always and continuously even till now, conserving creatures in existence. Hence it is significant that Moses used the word *rest*, after recounting the works of God from which he rested: for this signifies, in its hidden meaning, the spiritual rest which God, by the example of his own rest, promised to the faithful, after they have done their own good works. So we may say that this command was a foreshadowing of something that lay in the future.

739. Signanter autem dicit *usque nunc operatur*; non autem operatus est, ut designet continuationem divini operis. Nam possent imaginari Deum esse causam mundi, sicut artifex est causa domus, quantum ad fieri tantum: ut sicut domus manet, etiam cessante operatione artificis, ita et mundus subsistere posset, influxu divino cessante. Sed, secundum Augustinum, Deus ita est causa omnium creaturarum quod sit etiam causa subsistendi; quia si eius potentia ad momentum cessaret, simul et illarum cessarent species omnes, quas natura continet: sicut si dicerem, quod aer tamdiu illuminatur quamdiu lumen solis manet in ipso. Cuius quidem ratio est, quia ea quae causam habent, quantum ad fieri solum, cessante causa subsistere possunt; ea vero quae non solum fieri, sed etiam subsistentiae causam habent, continua conservatione causae indigent.

740. Excludit etiam per hoc quod dicit *Pater meus usque modo operatur*, opinionem quorumdam dicentium, quod Deus mediantibus secundis causis res producit; quod est contra illud Is. XXVI, 12: *omnia opera nostra operatus es in nobis, Domine*. Sicut ergo *Pater meus*, in principio instituendo naturam, *usque modo operatur*, eadem operatione ipsam continendo et conservando, *et ego operor*, quia sum Patris Verbum, per quod omnia operatur; Gen. I, 3: *dixit Deus: fiat lux*. Unde sicut primam institutionem rerum per Verbum operatus est, ita et ipsarum conservationem. Et sic si ipse *usque modo operatur, et ego operor*, quia sum Verbum Patris, per quod omnia fiunt et conservantur.

741. Consequenter cum dicit *propterea ergo magis quaerebant eum Iudaei interficere*, ponitur persecutio ex doctrina proveniens: quia propter ipsam doctrinam *Iudaei magis*, idest avidiori animo, ferventiori zelo, *quaerebant eum interficere*.

Duo enim crimina in lege morte punita fuerunt: scilicet crimen solutionis Sabbati, unde ille qui collegit ligna in Sabbato lapidatus est, Num. XV, 32, et crimen blasphemiae, unde dicitur Lev. XXIV, 14: *educ blasphemum extra castra . . . et lapidet eum omnis multitudo filiorum Israel*. Blasphemiam autem isti reputabant quod homo diceret se esse Deum; infra X, 33: *de bono opere non lapidamus te, sed de blasphemia, quia homo cum sis, facis teipsum Deum*. Et haec duo crimina imponebant Christo: unum scilicet quia solvebat Sabbatum, aliud quia dicebat se aequalem Deo.

Unde dicit, quod ideo *quaerebant eum occidere, quia non solum solvebat Sabbatum, sed etiam Patrem suum dicebat Deum*. Sed quia etiam alii iusti Deum Patrem suum dicunt: Ier. III, 19: *Patrem vocabis me*, ideo non solum dicunt quod *Patrem suum dicebat Deum*, sed addunt quod pertinet ad blasphemiam *aequalem*

739. He expressly says, *works until now*, and not: has worked, to indicate that God's work is continuous. For they might have thought that God is the cause of the world as a craftsman is the cause of a house, i.e., the craftsman is responsible only for the making or coming into existence of the house: in other words, just as the house continues in existence even when the craftsman has ceased working, so the world would exist if God's influence ceased. But according to Augustine, God is the cause of all creatures in such a way as to be the cause of their existing: for it his power were to cease even for a moment, all things in nature would at once cease to be, just as we may say that the air is illuminated only as long as the light of the sun remains in it. The reason for this is that things which depend on a cause only for their coming into existence, are able to exist when that cause ceases; but things that depend on a cause not only for their coming into existence but also to exist, need that cause for their continuous conservation in existence.

740. Further, in saying, *my Father works until now*, he rejects the opinion of those who say that God creates through the instrumentality of secondary causes. This opinion conflicts with what is said: *O Lord, you have accomplished all our works for us* (Isa 26:12). Therefore, just as *my Father*, who in the beginning created nature, *works until now*, by preserving and conserving his creation by the same activity, *I also work*, because I am the Word of the Father, through whom he accomplishes all things: *God said: let there be light* (Gen 1:3). Thus, just as he accomplished the first production of things through the Word, so also their conservation. Consequently, if he *works until now*, then *I also work*, because I am the Word of the Father, through whom all things are made and conserved.

741. Then, at *therefore the Jews sought the more to kill him*, the Evangelist mentions the persecution of Christ, which resulted from his teaching: for it was because of his teaching that *the Jews sought the more*, i.e., with greater eagerness and a higher pitch of zeal, *to kill him*.

For in the law two crimes were punished by death: the crime of breaking the Sabbath—thus anyone who gathered wood on the Sabbath was stoned (Num 15:32); and the crime of blasphemy; so we read: *bring the blasphemer outside the camp . . . and let all the children of Israel stone him* (Lev 24:14). Now they thought it was blasphemy for a man to claim that he was God: *we do not stone you for a good work but for blasphemy; and because you, being a man, make yourself God* (John 10:33). It was these two crimes they imputed to Christ: the first because he broke the Sabbath; the second because he said he was equal to God.

So the Evangelist says *therefore the Jews sought the more to kill him, because he did not only break the Sabbath, but also said that God was his Father*. Because other just men had also called God their Father, as in *you will call me 'Father'* (Jer 3:19), they do not just say that *he said that God was his Father*, but added what made it blasphemy,

se faciens Deo, quod ex hoc colligunt quod dixit: **Pater meus operatur, et ego operor**.

Deum Patrem suum dicit, ut det intelligere quod Pater eius est per naturam, aliorum autem per adoptionem: secundum quem modum loquitur infra XX, 17: **vado ad Patrem meum**, scilicet per naturam, **et Patrem vestrum**, scilicet per gratiam.

Item ad similitudinem eius se operari dicit, solvens per hoc calumniam Iudaeorum de solutione Sabbati: quae non esset conveniens excusatio, nisi aequalis auctoritatis esset in operando cum Deo. Et ideo dicunt quod facit se aequalem Deo.

742. Et quidem magna est Arianorum caecitas, qui in verbis Domini non possunt intelligere quod Iudaei intelligunt, dicentes Christum Deo Patre minorem esse. Sed Ariani dicunt, quod Christus non fecit se aequalem Deo, sed Iudaei hoc suspicabantur.

Sed per ea quae dicta sunt in ipso textu, aliter etiam manifestum est. Nam Evangelista dicit quod Iudaei persequebantur Christum, quia solvebat Sabbatum, et quia dicebat Patrem suum Deum, et quia faciebat se aequalem Deo. Aut ergo Christus est mendax, aut est aequalis Deo. Sed si est aequalis Deo, ergo Christus Deus est per naturam.

743. Dicit autem Evangelista **se aequalem faciens Deo**, non quod ipse aequalem se Deo faceret, quia per aeternam generationem aequalis erat Deo; sed secundum intentionem Iudaeorum loquens, qui non credentes Christum esse Filium Dei per naturam, intellexerunt ex verbis eius quod se diceret Dei Filium, quasi volens se aequalem Deo facere, cum tamen hoc eum esse non crederent; infra c. X, 33: **tu homo cum sis, facis teipsum Deum**; idest, dicis te esse Deum: quod interpretatur ac si tu ipse facias teipsum Deum.

making himself equal to God, which they understood from his statement: **my Father works even until now, and I also work**.

He said that God was his Father so that we might understand that God is his Father by nature, and the Father of others by adoption. He referred to both of these when he said: **I ascend to my Father**, by nature, **and to your Father**, by grace (John 20:17). Again, he said that as the Father works, so he works.

This answers the accusation of the Jews about his breaking the Sabbath: for this would not be a valid excuse unless he had equal authority with God in working. It was for this reason they said he made himself equal to God.

742. How great then is the blindness of the Arians when they say that Christ is less than God the Father: for they cannot understand in our Lord's words what the Jews were able to understand. For the Arians say that Christ did not make himself equal to God, while the Jews saw this.

There is another way to settle this, from the very things mentioned in the text. For the Evangelist says that the Jews persecuted Christ because he broke the Sabbath, because he said God is his Father, and because he made himself equal to God. But Christ is either a liar or equal to God. But if he is equal to God, Christ is God by nature.

743. Finally, the Evangelist says, **making himself equal to God**, not as though he was making himself become equal to God, because he was equal to God through an eternal generation. Rather, the Evangelist is speaking according to the understanding of the Jews who, not believing that Christ was the Son of God by nature, understood him to say that he was the Son of God in the sense of wishing to make himself equal to God; but they could not believe he was such: **and because you, being a man, make yourself God** (John 10:33), i.e., you say that you are God, understanding this as you wish to make yourself God.

Lecture 3

5:18 Propterea ergo magis quaerebant eum Iudaei interficere: quia non solum solvebat Sabbatum, sed et patrem suum dicebat Deum, aequalem se faciens Deo. Respondit itaque Iesus, et dixit eis: [n. 744]

5:19 amen, amen dico vobis, non potest Filius a se facere quidquam, nisi quod viderit Patrem facientem. Quaecumque enim ille fecerit, haec et Filius similiter facit. [n. 745]

5:20 Pater enim diligit Filium: et omnia demonstrat ei, quae ipse facit. Et maiora his demonstrabit ei opera, ut vos miremini. [n. 753]

5:18 διὰ τοῦτο οὖν μᾶλλον ἐζήτουν αὐτὸν οἱ Ἰουδαῖοι ἀποκτεῖναι, ὅτι οὐ μόνον ἔλυεν τὸ σάββατον, ἀλλὰ καὶ πατέρα ἴδιον ἔλεγεν τὸν θεὸν ἴσον ἑαυτὸν ποιῶν τῷ θεῷ.

5:19 Ἀπεκρίνατο οὖν ὁ Ἰησοῦς καὶ ἔλεγεν αὐτοῖς· ἀμὴν ἀμὴν λέγω ὑμῖν, οὐ δύναται ὁ υἱὸς ποιεῖν ἀφ᾽ ἑαυτοῦ οὐδὲν ἐὰν μή τι βλέπῃ τὸν πατέρα ποιοῦντα· ἃ γὰρ ἂν ἐκεῖνος ποιῇ, ταῦτα καὶ ὁ υἱὸς ὁμοίως ποιεῖ.

5:20 ὁ γὰρ πατὴρ φιλεῖ τὸν υἱὸν καὶ πάντα δείκνυσιν αὐτῷ ἃ αὐτὸς ποιεῖ, καὶ μείζονα τούτων δείξει αὐτῷ ἔργα, ἵνα ὑμεῖς θαυμάζητε.

5:18 Therefore the Jews sought the more to kill him, because he did not only break the Sabbath, but also said that God was his Father, making himself equal to God. Then Jesus answered and said to them: [n. 744]

5:19 amen, amen, I say unto you, the Son cannot do anything of himself, but only what he sees the Father doing: for whatever he does, these the Son also does in like manner. [n. 745]

5:20 For the Father loves the Son and shows him all things that he himself does: and greater works than these will he show him, so that you may wonder. [n. 753]

---

744. Hic tradit doctrinam de potestate vivificativa. Et

primo ponitur ipsa doctrina;

secundo confirmatio eius, ibi *si ego testimonium perhibeo de meipso, testimonium meum non est verum*.

Circa primum duo facit.

Primo proponit doctrinam eius de potestate vivificativa in communi;

secundo in speciali, ibi *et maiora his demonstrabit ei opera*.

Circa primum tria facit.

Primo insinuat potestatis suae originem;

secundo ipsius potestatis magnitudinem, ibi *quaecumque enim ille fecerit, haec et Filius similiter facit*.

Tertio assignat utriusque rationem, ibi *Pater enim diligit Filium*.

745. Considerandum autem circa primum, quod Ariani ex his verbis quae hic Dominus dicit **non potest Filius a se facere quidquam** etc., errorem suum confirmare nituntur, scilicet quod Filius minor sit Patre, quia, secundum quod Evangelista dixit, Iudaei persequebantur Christum, quia faciebat se aequalem Deo. Quod videns Dominus, Iudaeos ex hoc moveri, volens hoc excludere, ut Ariani dicunt, talia verba subiunxit, ut se aequalem Patri non esse monstraret, dicens: **amen, amen dico vobis, non potest Filius a se facere quidquam, nisi quod viderit Patrem facientem**; quasi dicat: non intelligatis me per hoc quod dixi *Pater meus operatur, et ego operor*, sic operari quasi ego sim ei aequalis, quia nihil possum facere a meipso. Quia ergo **Filius non potest facere quidquam, nisi quod viderit Patrem facientem**, utique minor est Patre, ut ipsi dicunt.

744. Here we have Christ's teaching on his life-giving power.

First, his teaching is presented.

Second, it is confirmed, at *if I bear witness about myself, my witness is not true* (John 5:31).

Two things are done with the first.

First, Christ's teaching on his life-giving power in general is given.

Second, it is presented in particular, at *and greater works than these will he show him*.

As to the first, three things are done.

First, the origin of this power is mentioned.

Second, the greatness of this power, at *for whatever he does, these the Son also does in like manner*.

Third, the reason for each is given, at *for the Father loves the Son*.

745. We should point out, with respect to the first, that the Arians use what Christ said here, **the Son cannot do anything of himself**, to support their error that the Son is less than the Father, because as the Evangelist said, the Jews persecuted Christ for making himself equal to God. But the Arians say that when our Lord saw that this disturbed the Jews, he tried to correct this by stating that he was not equal to the Father, saying, **amen, amen, I say to you, the Son cannot do anything of himself, but only what he sees the Father doing**. As if to say: do not interpret what I said, *my Father works even until now, and so do I*, as meaning that I work as though I am equal to the Father, for I cannot do anything of myself. Therefore, they say, because **the Son cannot do anything of himself, but only what he see the Father doing**, he is less than the Father.

Sed hic intellectus falsus est et erroneus: quia si Filius non esset aequalis Patri, tunc non esset Filius idem cum Patre, quod est contra illud, infra X, 30: *ego et Pater unum sumus*. Nam aequalitas attenditur secundum magnitudinem, quae in divinis est ipsa essentia. Unde si esset Patri inaequalis, differret ab eo secundum essentiam.

746. Ad verum autem huius intellectum, sciendum est, quod in his quae in Filio minorationem importare videntur, posset dici ab aliquibus haec de Christo dicta esse secundum naturam assumptam, sicut dicitur infra XIV, v. 28: *Pater maior me est*. Unde secundum hoc vellent dicere, quod hoc quod Dominus dicit **non potest Filius a se facere quidquam**, intelligendum est de Filio secundum naturam assumptam. Quod quidem stare non potest, quia secundum hoc oportet dicere quod omnia quae Filius Dei fecit in natura assumpta, Pater ante eum fecisset; puta quod siccis pedibus super mare ambulasset, sicut Christus ambulavit, alias non diceretur *nisi quod viderit Patrem facientem*.

Sed si dicatur, quod quaecumque Christus in carne fecit, etiam Deus Pater fecit, inquantum in eo Pater operatur, secundum illud, infra XIV, 10: *Pater autem in me manens ipse facit opera*; ut sit sensus: *non potest Filius a se facere quidquam, nisi quod viderit Patrem facientem*, in seipso, scilicet Filio. Sed nec hoc stare potest, quia secundum hoc ea quae sequuntur, non possent ei adaptari, scilicet *quaecumque ille fecerit, haec et Filius similiter facit*. Numquam enim secundum naturam assumptam Filius creavit mundum, sicut Pater creavit. Non ergo ad naturam assumptam referendum est quod dicitur.

747. Secundum Augustinum autem, alius modus est intelligendi ea quae videntur in Filio minorationem importare, licet non important: ut scilicet referantur ad originem Filii a Patre. Quia licet Filius sit aequalis Patri per omnia, tamen hoc ipsum habet a Patre per aeternam generationem; sed Pater a nullo habet, cum sit ingenitus.

Unde secundum hoc continuatur sic. Quid scandalizati estis, quia Patrem meum dixi Deum, et quia aequalem me feci Deo? *Amen, amen dico vobis, non potest Filius a seipso facere quidquam*; quasi dicat: ita sum aequalis Patri, ut ab illo sim, non ille a me; et quidquid ego habeo ut faciam, est mihi a Patre.

748. Secundum hunc ergo modum in his verbis fit mentio de potestate Filii, per hoc verbum *potest*, et de eius operatione per hoc verbum *facere*. Et ideo utrumque potest hic intelligi: ut scilicet ostendatur primo derivatio potestatis Filii a Patre; secundo vero ut ostendatur conformitas operationis Filii ad operationem Patris.

But this interpretation is false and erroneous. For if the Son were not equal to the Father, then the Son would not be the same as the Father; and this is contrary to: *I and the Father are one* (John 10:30). For equality is considered with respect to greatness, which in divine realities is the essence itself. Hence, if the Son were not equal to the Father, he would be different from him in essence.

746. To get the true meaning of Christ's statement, we should know that in those matters which seem to imply inferiority in the Son, it could be said, as some do, that they apply to Christ according to the nature he assumed; as when he said: *the Father is greater than I* (John 14:28). According to this, they would say that our Lord's statement, *the Son cannot do anything of himself*, should be understood of the Son in his assumed nature. However, this does not stand up, because then one would be forced to say that whatever the Son of God did in his assumed nature, the Father had done before him. For example, that the Father had walked upon the water as Christ did: otherwise, he would not have said, *but only what he sees the Father doing*.

And if we say that whatever Christ did in his flesh, God the Father also did in so far as the Father works in him: *the Father who abides in me, he does the works* (John 14:10), then Christ would be saying that *the Son cannot do anything of himself, but only what he sees the Father doing* in him, i.e., in the Son. But this cannot stand either, because Christ's next statement, *for whatever he does, these the Son also does in like manner*, could not, in this interpretation, be applied to him, i.e., to Christ. For the Son, in his assumed nature, never created the world, as the Father did. Consequently, what we read here must not be understood as pertaining to Christ's assumed nature.

747. According to Augustine, however, there is another way of understanding statements which seem to, but do not, imply inferriority in the Son: namely, by referring them to the origin of the Son coming or begotten from the Father. For although the Son is equal to the Father in all things, he receives all these things from the Father in an eternal begetting. But the Father gets these from no one, for he is unbegotten.

According to this explanation, the continuity of thought is the following: why are you offended because I said that God is my Father, and because I made myself equal to God? *Amen, amen, I say to you, the Son cannot do anything of himself*. As if to say: I am equal to the Father, but in such a way as to be from him, and not he from me; and whatever I may do, is in me from the Father.

748. According to this interpretation, mention is made of the power of the Son when he says, *can*, and of his activity when he says, *do*. Both can be understood here, so that, first of all, the derivation of the Son's power from the Father is shown, and second, the conformity of the Son's activity to that of the Father.

749. Quantum ad primum, exponit Hilarius hoc modo. Supra Dominus dixit se esse aequalem Patri. Sed aliqui haeretici propter auctoritates Scripturae, quae dicunt unitatem et aequalitatem Filii ad Patrem, attribuunt Filio quod sit ingenitus, sicut Sabelliani, dicentes Filium esse idem cum Patre in persona.

Ne ergo hoc intelligas, dicit: **non potest Filius a se facere quidquam**, nam potentia Filii idem est quod natura eius. Ab eo ergo Filius habet posse a quo habet esse; esse autem habet a Patre, infra XVI, 28: **exivi a Patre, et veni in mundum**: a quo etiam habet naturam, quia Deus est de Deo, ergo ab eo habet posse.

Sic ergo hoc quod dicit: **non potest Filius facere quidquam, nisi quod Patrem viderit facientem**, tantum valet ac si dicatur: Filius, sicut non habet esse nisi a Patre, ita nec posse facere aliquid nisi a Patre. In naturalibus enim ab eodem aliquid accipit posse operari a quo recipit esse, sicut ignis ab eo recipit quod possit ascendere sursum a quo recipit formam et esse. Nec tamen per hoc quod dicit **non potest Filius a se facere quidquam**, importatur inaequalitas: quia hoc pertinet ad relationem; quaestio autem aequalitatis et inaequalitatis pertinet ad quantitatem.

750. Per hoc autem quod dicit **nisi quod viderit Patrem facientem**, posset alicui falsus intellectus subintrare, ut crederet Filium hoc modo facere, quia vidit Patrem facientem; scilicet, quod Pater primo fecit, hoc viso, Filius postea inceperit facere; ad modum duorum fabrorum, magistri scilicet et discipuli, qui arcam facit secundum modum quem viderit magistrum facere. Quod quidem non est verum de Verbo; nam supra dicitur: **omnia per ipsum facta sunt**. Ergo Pater non fecit aliquid, ita quod Filius videret fieri, et addisceret.

Sed hoc dictum est ut designetur communicatio Paternitatis Filio per generationem, quae convenienter designatur hoc verbo **viderit**, quia per visum et auditum in nos ab alio scientia transfunditur. Nam per visum quidem scientiam a rebus accipimus, per auditum vero a sermonibus. Filius autem non est aliud quam sapientia, secundum illud Eccli. XXIV, 5: **ego ex ore altissimi prodii primogenita ante omnem creaturam**. Et sic derivatio Filii a Patre nihil aliud est quam derivatio divinae sapientiae. Quia ergo visio designat derivationem cognitionis et sapientiae ab alio, recte per visionem generatio Filii a Patre designatur, ut sic nihil aliud sit Filium videre Patrem facientem, quam procedere intelligibili processione a Patre operante.

749. As to the first, Hilary explains it this way: shortly above our Lord said that he is equal to the Father. Some heretics, basing themselves on certain scriptural texts which assert the unity and equality of the Son to the Father, claim that the Son is unbegotten. For example, the Sabellians, who say that the Son is identical in person with the Father.

Therefore, so you do not understand this teaching in this way, he says, **the Son cannot do anything of himself**, for the Son's power is identical with his nature. Therefore the Son has his power from the same source as he has his being; but he has his being from the Father: **I came forth from the Father, and I have come into the world** (John 16:28). He also has his nature from the Father, because he is God from God; therefore, it is from him that the Son has his power.

So his statement, **the Son cannot do anything of himself, but only what he sees the Father doing**, is the same as saying: the Son, just as he does not have his being except from the Father, so he cannot do anything except from the Father. For in natural things, a thing receives its power to act from the very thing from which it receives its being: for example, fire receives its power to ascend from the very thing from which it receives its form and being. Further, in saying, **the Son cannot do anything of himself**, no inequality is implied, because this refers to a relation; while equality and inequality refer to quantity.

750. Someone might misunderstand his saying, **but only what he sees the Father doing**, and take it to mean that the Son works or acts in the way he sees the Father acting, i.e., that the Father acts first, and when the Son sees this, then the Son begins to act. It would be like two carpenters, a master and his apprentice, with the apprentice making a cabinet in the way he saw the master do. But this is not true for the Word, for it was said: **all things were made through him** (John 1:3). Therefore, the Father did not make something in such a way that the Son saw him doing it and so learned from it.

But this is said so that the communication of paternity to the Son might be designated through terms of generation, which is fittingly described by the verb **sees**, because knowledge is conveyed to us by another through seeing and hearing. For we receive our knowledge from things through seeing and we receive knowledge through hearing from words. Now the Son is not other than wisdom, as we read: *I came forth out of the mouth of the Most High, the first-born before all creatures* (Sir 24:5). Accordingly, the derivation of the Son from the Father is nothing other than the derivation of divine wisdom. And so, because the act of seeing indicates the derivation of knowledge and wisdom from another, it is proper for the generation of the Son from the Father to be indicated by an act of seeing; so that for the Son to see the Father doing something is nothing other than to proceed by an intellectual procession from the acting Father.

Potest autem et de huiusmodi, secundum Hilarium, alia ratio assignari; scilicet, ut per hoc quod dicit *viderit*, excludatur omnis imperfectio a generatione Filii vel Verbi; nam in generatione materiali illud quod generatur, paulatim per incrementa temporum ab imperfecto ad perfectum perducitur: non enim iam perfectum est aliquid quando generari incipit. Sed hoc in generatione aeterna locum non habet, cum sit generatio perfecti a perfecto. Et ideo dicit *nisi quod viderit Filius Patrem facientem*. Cum enim videre sit actus perfecti, manifestum est quod Filius statim perfectus genitus est, tamquam statim videns, et non per incrementa temporum ad perfectum perducitur.

751. Quantum vero ad secundum exponit Chrysostomus, scilicet ad ostendendum conformitatem Patris ad Filium, quantum ad operationem, hoc modo. Dico quod licet mihi operari in Sabbato, quia et Pater meus continue operatur, cui non possum operari contrarium; et hoc quia *non potest Filius a se facere quidquam* etc. Tunc enim quis aliquid a se facit, cum in faciendo non se conformat alteri. Quicumque autem est ab alio, si discordat ab eo, peccat; infra VII, 18: *qui a semetipso loquitur, gloriam propriam quaerit*. Quicumque ergo existens ab alio, a semetipso operatur, peccat; Filius autem est a Patre: ergo si operatur a semetipso, peccat; quod est impossibile. Per hoc ergo quod dicit Dominus, *Filius non potest a se facere quidquam* etc., nihil aliud insinuat, quam quod Filius non potest peccare. Quasi dicat: iniuste persequimini me de solutione Sabbati, quia non possum peccare, quia non operor contraria Patri meo.

Utramque autem expositionem, scilicet Hilarii et Chrysostomi, facit Augustinus, licet in diversis locis.

752. Consequenter cum dicit *quaecumque enim ille fecerit, haec et Filius similiter facit*, ponitur magnitudo potestatis Christi et excludit in his tria circa potestatem suam: scilicet particularitatem, diversitatem et imperfectionem.

Particularitatem: quia, cum sint diversa agentia in mundo, et agens primum universale virtutem habeat super omnia agentia, alia vero agentia, quae sunt ab ipso, tanto particularis virtutis sint, quanto sunt inferiora in ordine causalitatis, posset autem ex hoc aliquis credere, quod cum Filius non sit a se, habeat potestatem particularem respectu aliquorum existentium, et non universalem respectu omnium, sicut habet Pater. Et ideo hoc excludens dicit *quaecumque enim ille*, idest Pater, *fecerit*, idest ad omnia ad quae se extendit potestas Patris, extendit se etiam potestas Filii. Supra I, 3: *omnia per ipsum facta sunt*.

Diversitatem vero, quia aliquando unum, ab alio existens, potest quidem facere quaecumque ille a quo est facit, nihilominus tamen illa quae facit, non sunt eadem cum illis quae ille a quo est facit. Sicut si unus ignis

Another possible explanation of this is given by Hilary. For him, the word *sees* eliminates all imperfection from the generation of the Son or Word. For in physical generation, what is generated changes little by little in the course of time from what is imperfect to what is perfect, for such a thing is not perfect when it is first generated. But this is not so in eternal generation, since this is the generation of what is perfect from what is perfect. And so he says, *but only what he sees the Father doing*. For since the act of seeing is the act of a perfect thing, it is plain that the Son was begotten as perfect at once, as seeing at once, and not as coming to perfection over a course of time.

751. Apropos of the second point, Chrysostom explains it as showing the conformity of the Father to the Son in operation. So that the sense is: I say that it is lawful for me to work on the Sabbath, because my Father, too, continues to work, and I cannot do anything opposed to him: and this is because *the Son cannot do anything of himself*. For one does something of himself when he does not conform himself to another in his actions. But whoever is from another sins, if he is opposed to him: *he who speaks of himself seeks his own glory* (John 7:18). Therefore, whoever exists from another, but acts of himself, sins. Now the Son is from the Father; thus, if he acts of himself, he sins; and this is impossible. So by saying, *the Son cannot do anything of himself*, he means nothing more than that the Son cannot sin. As if to say: you are persecuting me unjustly for breaking the Sabbath, because I cannot sin, since I do not act in a way opposed to my Father.

Augustine makes use of both of these explanations, that of Hilary and the one given by Chrysostom, but in different places.

752. Then when he says, *for whatever he does, these the Son also does in like manner*, he affirms the greatness of Christ's power. He excludes three things in the power of Christ: limitation, difference, and imperfection.

First, limitation is excluded. Since there are diverse agents in the world, and the first universal agent has power over all other agents, but the other agents, which are from him, have a limited power in proportion to their rank in the order of causality, some might think that since the Son is not of himself, that he must have a power limited to certain existents, rather than a universal power over all, as the Father has. And so to exclude this he says, *whatever he*, namely, the Father, *does*, i.e., to all the things to which the Father's power extends, the Son's power also extends: *all things were made through him* (John 1:3).

Second, difference is excluded. For sometimes a thing that exists from another is able to do whatever that from which it exists does. And yet the things the former does are not the same as those done by that from which it is.

existens ab alio, potest facere quicumque alius facit, puta comburere, sed tamen alia comburit iste, alia ille, licet eadem sit combustio utriusque secundum speciem. Ne ergo intelligas sic operationem Filii diversam esse ab operatione Patris, dicit **haec** idest non diversa, sed eadem.

Imperfectionem vero, quia quandoque contingit aliquod unum et idem ex duobus agentibus fieri, sed ab uno quidem sicut a principali et perfecto, ab alio vero sicut ab instrumento et imperfecto; sed non similiter, quia aliter agit principale agens, et aliter instrumentum, quia instrumentum imperfecte agit, utpote in virtute alterius. Ne ergo sic intelligas Filium facere quaecumque facit Pater, addit **similiter**, idest, potestate qua Pater facit, facit et Filius; quia eadem virtus et eadem perfectio est in Patre et Filio; Prov. VIII, 30: *cum eo eram cuncta componens.*

753. Consequenter cum dicit **Pater enim diligit Filium**, assignat rationem utriusque, scilicet originis et magnitudinis potestatis Filii; quae quidem ratio assignatur ex dilectione Patris, qui diligit Filium; unde dicit: **Pater enim diligit Filium**.

Sed ad sciendum quomodo dilectio Patris ad Filium sit ratio originis, seu communicationis potestatis Filii, attendendum est, quod dupliciter aliquid diligitur. Cum enim bonum solum sit amabile, aliquod bonum potest se dupliciter ad amorem habere, scilicet vel ut causa amoris, vel ut ab amore causatum. In nobis autem bonum causat amorem; nam causa amoris nostri ad aliquem est bonitas eius. Non enim ideo bonus est, quia nos eum diligimus; sed ideo diligimus eum, quia bonus est: unde in nobis amor causatur a bono. Sed in Deo aliter est, quia ipse amor Dei est causa bonitatis in rebus dilectis: quia enim Deus diligit nos, ideo boni sumus, nam amare nihil est aliud quam velle bonum alicui. Cum ergo voluntas Dei sit causa rerum, quia *omnia quaecumque voluit, Dominus, fecit*, ut dicit Ps. CXIII, 3, manifestum est quod amor Dei, causa est bonitatis in rebus. Unde Dionysius dicit, VI cap. *de Divinis nominibus*, quod divinus amor non permisit eum sine germine esse. Ergo si consideremus originem Filii, videamus utrum amor quo Pater diligit Filium, sit principium originis vel procedat ab ea.

Amor autem in divinis dupliciter accipitur; scilicet essentialiter, secundum quod Pater diligit et Filius et Spiritus Sanctus; et notionaliter, seu personaliter, secundum quod Spiritus Sanctus procedit ut amor. Sed neutro horum modorum amor dictus, potest esse principium originis Filii. Nam secundum quod accipitur essentialiter, sic importat actum voluntatis. Si ergo esset principium

For example, if one fire which exists from another can do whatever that other does, i.e., cause combustion, the act of causing combustion would be specifically the same in each, even though one fire ignites certain things and the other fire ignites different things. And so that you do not think that the Son's activity is different from the activity of the Father in this way, he says, whatever the Father does, **these the Son also does**, i.e., not different things, but the very same.

Third, imperfection is excluded. Sometimes one and the same thing comes from two agents: from one as the principal and perfect agent, and from the other as an instrumental and imperfect agent. But it does not come in the same way, because the principal agent acts in a different way from the instrumental agent: for the instrumental agent acts imperfectly, and in virtue of the other. And so that no one thinks that this is the way the Son does whatever the Father does, he says that whatever the Father does, the Son does **in like manner** i.e., with the same power by which the Father acts, the Son also acts; because the same power and the same perfection are in the Father and the Son: *I was with him, forming all things* (Prov 8:30).

753. Then when he says, **for the Father loves the Son**, he gives the reason for each, i.e., for the origin of the Son's power and for its greatness. This reason is the love of the Father, who loves the Son. Thus he says, **for the Father loves the Son**.

In order to understand how the Father's love for the Son is the reason for the origin or communication of the Son's power, we should point out that a thing is loved in two ways. For since the good alone is loveable, a good can be related to love in two ways: as the cause of love, or as caused by love. Now in us, the good causes love: for the cause of our loving something is its goodness, the goodness in it. Therefore, it is not good because we love it, but rather we love it because it is good. Accordingly, in us, love is caused by what is good. But it is different with God, because God's love itself is the cause of the goodness in the things that are loved. For it is because God loves us that we are good, since to love is nothing else than to will a good to someone. Thus, since God's will is the cause of things, for *whatever he willed he made* (Ps 113:3), it is clear that God's love is the cause of the goodness in things. Hence Denis says in *The Divine Names* (c. 4) that the divine love did not allow itself to be without issue. So, if we wish to consider the origin of the Son, let us see whether the love with which the Father loves the Son, is the principle of his origin, so that he proceeds from it.

In divine realities, love is taken in two ways: essentially, so far as the Father and the Son and the Holy Spirit love; and notionally or personally, so far as the Holy Spirit proceeds as Love. But in neither of these ways of taking love can it be the principle of origin of the Son. For if is is taken essentially, it implies an act of the will; and if that were the sense in which it is the principle of origin of the Son, it would

originis Filii, sequeretur quod Pater genuisset Filium voluntate, non natura: quod est erroneum. Similiter etiam nec amor notionaliter sumptus, qua pertinet ad Spiritum Sanctum, quia tunc sequeretur quod Spiritus Sanctus esset principium Filii: quod est erroneum; immo nullus haereticus hoc dixit. Licet enim amor notionaliter sumptus sit principium omnium donorum quae nobis donantur a Deo, non tamen est principium Filii, sed potius ipse a Patre Filioque procedit.

Sic ergo dicendum, quod ratio ista non sumitur ex dilectione ut ex principio, sed ut ex signo. Cum enim similitudo sit causa dilectionis (omne enim animal diligit simile sibi): ubi invenitur perfecta similitudo Dei, ibi invenitur etiam perfecta dilectio Dei. Perfecta autem similitudo Patris in Filio est secundum illud Coloss. I, 15: *qui est Imago invisibilis Dei*; Hebr. I, 3: *qui cum sit splendor, gloria et figura substantiae eius*. Perfecte ergo Filius a Patre diligitur: et ideo quia perfecte diligit eum, signum est quod Pater omnia ostenderit ei et communicaverit ei suam potestatem et naturam. Et de huius dilectione dicitur supra II, 35: **Pater diligit Filium, et omnia dedit in manu eius**. Et Matth. III, 17: *hic est Filius meus dilectus*.

754. Circa hoc autem quod sequitur **et omnia demonstrat ei quae ipse facit**, sciendum est, quod dupliciter potest aliquis alicui sua opera demonstrare. Vel quantum ad visum, sicut artifex ea quae facit demonstrat discipulo; vel quantum ad auditum, sicut quando verbo instruit eum.

Quocumque ergo istorum modorum accipiatur **demonstrat**, sequi potest duplex inconveniens: quod tamen non est in ista demonstratione, qua Pater demonstrat Filio. Si enim Pater dicatur demonstrare Filio quantum ad visum, primo quidem sequitur in istis inferioribus quod prius operetur aliquid quod alteri demonstrat; deinde quod seorsum ab eo cui demonstrat. Sed Pater non demonstrat Filio ea quae prius facit, quia ipse Filius dicit Prov. VIII, 22: *Dominus possedit me in initio viarum suarum, antequam quidquam faceret*. Neque etiam ea quae seorsum a Filio facit: quia Pater omnia operatur per Filium; supra I, 3: **omnia per ipsum facta sunt**.

Si autem accipiatur demonstratio quantum ad auditum, duo videntur sequi: nam qui verbo docet, primo demonstrat ignoranti; deinde Verbum est inter demonstrantem et cui fit demonstratio. Sed neutro modo Pater demonstrat Filio: non enim sicut ignoranti, cum Filius sit sapientia Patris, I Cor. I, 24: *Christum Dei virtutem et Dei sapientiam*; nec aliquo alio verbo medio, quia ipse Filius est Verbum Patris, supra I: **Verbum erat apud Deum**.

follow that the Father generated the Son, not by nature, but by will—and this is false. Again, love is not understood notionally, as pertaining to the Holy Spirit. For it would then follow that the Holy Spirit would be the principle of the Son—which is also false. Indeed, no heretic ever went so far as to say this. For although love, notionally taken, is the principle of all the gifts given to us by God, it is nevertheless not the principle of the Son; rather it proceeds from the Father and the Son.

Consequently, we must say that this explanation is not taken from love as from a principle but as from a sign. For since likeness is a cause of love (for every animal loves its like), wherever a perfect likeness of God is found, there also is found a perfect love of God. But the perfect likeness of the Father is in the Son, as is said: *he is the Image of the invisible God* (Col 1:15); and *he is the brightness of the Father's glory, and the image of his substance* (Heb 1:3). Therefore, the Son is loved perfectly by the Father, and because the Father perfectly loves the Son, this is a sign that the Father has shown him everything and has communicated to him his very own power and nature. And it is of this love that we read: **the Father loves the Son, and he has given all things into his hand** (John 3:35); and, *this is my beloved Son* (Matt 3:17).

754. With respect to what follows, **and shows him all things that he himself does**, we should point out that someone can show another his works in two ways: either by sight, as an artisan shows his apprentice the things he has made, or by hearing, as when he verbally instructs him.

In whatever of these ways **shows** is understood, there can follow something which is not appropriate, that is, something that is not present when the Father shows things to the Son. For if we say the Father shows things to the Son by sight, then it follows, as with humans, that the Father first does something which he then shows to the Son; and that he does this by himself, without the Son. But the Father does not show the Son things which he did before, for the Son himself says: *the Lord possessed me at the beginning of his ways, before he made anything* (Prov 8:22). Nor does the Father show the Son things he has done without the Son, for the Father does all things through the Son: **all things were made through him** (John 1:3).

If **shows** is understood as a kind of hearing, two things seem to follow. For the one who teaches by word first points out something to the one who is ignorant; again, the word is something intermediate between the one showing and the one being shown. But it is in neither of these ways that the Father shows things to the Son: for he does not do so to one who is ignorant, since the Son is the Wisdom of the Father: *Christ is the power of God, and the wisdom of God* (1 Cor 1:24); nor does the Father use some intermediate word, because the Son himself is the Word of the Father: **the Word was with God** (John 1:1).

Dicitur ergo Pater omnia quae facit demonstrare Filio, inquantum communicat ei notitiam omnium suorum operum: sic enim magister dicitur demonstrare discipulo, inquantum dat ei notitiam eorum quae facit. Unde, secundum Augustinum, demonstrare Patrem Filio, nihil aliud est quam Patrem generare Filium. Et Filium videre quae Pater facit, nihil aliud est quam Filium esse et naturam a Patre recipere.

Potest tamen dici demonstratio illa similis visuali, inquantum ipse Filius est splendor visionis Paternae, ut dicitur Hebr. I, 3: nam Pater videns se et intelligens, concipit Filium, qui est conceptus huius visionis. Potest etiam esse similis ei quae fit per auditum, inquantum Filius procedit a Patre ut Verbum. Ut si dicatur quod Pater omnia demonstrat Filio, inquantum producit ipsum ut splendorem, et conceptum suae sapientiae, et Verbum. Hoc ergo quod dicit *demonstrat*, refertur ad illud quod supra dixit: ***non potest Filius a se facere quidquam, nisi quod viderit Patrem facientem***. Hoc vero quod dicit *omnia*, refertur ad illud quod dixit: ***quaecumque enim ille fecerit, haec similiter et Filius facit***.

Therefore, it is said that the Father shows all that he does to the Son, inasmuch as he gives the Son a knowledge of all of his works. For it is in this way that a master is said to show something to his disciple, inasmuch as he gives him a knowledge of the things he makes. Hence, according to Augustine, for the Father to show anything to the Son is nothing more than for the Father to beget or generate the Son. And for the Son to see what the Father does is nothing more than for the Son to receive his being and nature from the Father.

Nevertheless, this showing can be considered similar to seeing insofar as the Son is the brightness of the paternal vision, as we read: for the Father, seeing and understanding himself, conceives the Son, who is the concept of this vision (Heb 1:3). Again, it can be considered similar to hearing insofar as the Son proceeds from the Father as the Word. As if to say: the Father shows him everything, insofar he he generates him as the brightness and concept of his own wisdom, and as the Word. Thus the words, ***the Father shows***, refer to what was said before: ***the Son cannot do anything of himself, but only what he sees the Father doing***. And the words, ***all things***, refer to, ***for whatever he does, the Son also does in like manner***.

Lecture 4

5:20 Pater enim diligit Filium: et omnia demonstrat ei, quae ipse facit. Et maiora his demonstrabit ei opera, ut vos miremini. [n. 756]

5:21 Sicut enim Pater suscitat mortuos, et vivificat, sic et Filius quos vult, vivificat. [n. 761]

5:22 Neque enim Pater iudicat quemquam; sed omne iudicium dedit Filio: [n. 762]

5:23 ut omnes honorificent Filium, sicut honorificant Patrem. Qui non honorificat Filium, non honorificat Patrem, qui misit illum. [n. 764]

5:24 Amen, amen dico vobis, quia qui verbum meum audit, et credit ei qui misit me, habet vitam aeternam; et in iudicium non venit, sed transit a morte in vitam. [n. 772]

5:25 Amen, amen dico vobis, quia venit hora, et nunc est, quando mortui audient vocem Filii Dei: et qui audierint, vivent. [n. 778]

5:20 ὁ γὰρ πατὴρ φιλεῖ τὸν υἱὸν καὶ πάντα δείκνυσιν αὐτῷ ἃ αὐτὸς ποιεῖ, καὶ μείζονα τούτων δείξει αὐτῷ ἔργα, ἵνα ὑμεῖς θαυμάζητε.

5:21 ὥσπερ γὰρ ὁ πατὴρ ἐγείρει τοὺς νεκροὺς καὶ ζῳοποιεῖ, οὕτως καὶ ὁ υἱὸς οὓς θέλει ζῳοποιεῖ.

5:22 οὐδὲ γὰρ ὁ πατὴρ κρίνει οὐδένα, ἀλλὰ τὴν κρίσιν πᾶσαν δέδωκεν τῷ υἱῷ,

5:23 ἵνα πάντες τιμῶσι τὸν υἱὸν καθὼς τιμῶσι τὸν πατέρα. ὁ μὴ τιμῶν τὸν υἱὸν οὐ τιμᾷ τὸν πατέρα τὸν πέμψαντα αὐτόν.

5:24 Ἀμὴν ἀμὴν λέγω ὑμῖν ὅτι ὁ τὸν λόγον μου ἀκούων καὶ πιστεύων τῷ πέμψαντί με ἔχει ζωὴν αἰώνιον καὶ εἰς κρίσιν οὐκ ἔρχεται, ἀλλὰ μεταβέβηκεν ἐκ τοῦ θανάτου εἰς τὴν ζωήν.

5:25 ἀμὴν ἀμὴν λέγω ὑμῖν ὅτι ἔρχεται ὥρα καὶ νῦν ἐστιν ὅτε οἱ νεκροὶ ἀκούσουσιν τῆς φωνῆς τοῦ υἱοῦ τοῦ θεοῦ καὶ οἱ ἀκούσαντες ζήσουσιν.

5:20 For the Father loves the Son and shows him all things that he himself does: and greater works than these will he show him, so that you may wonder. [n. 756]

5:21 For as the Father raises up the dead and gives life, so the Son also gives life to whom he wills. [n. 761]

5:22 For neither does the Father judge any man, but he has given all judgment to the Son, [n. 762]

5:23 so that all men may honor the Son, as they honor the Father. He who does not honor the Son, does not honor the Father, who has sent him. [n. 764]

5:24 Amen, amen I say to you: he who hears my word, and believes him who sent me, has eternal life; and he will not come into judgment but passes from death to life. [n. 772]

5:25 Amen, amen I say to you, that the hour is coming, and now is, when the dead will hear the voice of the Son of God, and they who hear will live. [n. 778]

---

755. Ostensa potestate Filii in communi, hic consequenter ostendit eam in speciali, et

primo Dominus manifestat suam potestatem vivificativam;

secundo manifestat quaedam praedicta,

quae videbantur obscura, ibi *sicut enim pater habet vitam in semetipso, sic dedit Filio vitam habere in semetipso*.

Circa primum duo facit.

Primo ostendit Filium habere potestatem vivificativam;

secundo docet modum percipiendi vitam a Filio, ibi *amen, amen dico vobis, quia qui verbum meum audit* etc.

Circa primum tria facit.

Primo proponit potestatem vivificativam Filii;

secundo dicti rationem assignat, ibi *neque enim pater iudicat quemquam*;

tertio ostendit effectum exinde provenientem, ibi *ut omnes honorificent Filium* etc.

Et circa primum duo facit.

755. Having pointed out the power of the Son in general, he now shows it in more detail.

First, the Lord discloses his life-giving power.

Second, he manifests what was said before

which appeared to be obscure at *for as the Father has life in himself, so he has also given to the Son to have life in himself* (John 5:26).

As to the first he does two things.

First, he shows that the Son has life-giving power.

Second, he teaches how life is received from the Son, at *amen, amen I say to you: he who hears my word*.

Concerning the first he does three things.

First, he presents the life-giving power of the Son.

Second, he gives a reason for what he says, at *for neither does the Father judge any man*.

Third, he shows the effect of this, at *so that all men may honor the Son, as they honor the Father*.

With respect to the first he does two things.

Primo proponit potestatem vivificativam in communi;

secundo exprimit eam, ibi *sicut enim Pater* etc.

756. Quantum ad primum dicit *maiora his demonstrabit*; quasi dicat: miramini et turbamini de potestate Filii in sanatione languidi; sed adhuc Pater *maiora his demonstrabit opera*, scilicet in suscitatione mortuorum, *ut vos miremini*.

757. Sed ex his verbis insurgit dubitatio quantum ad duo: primo quidem quantum ad hoc quod dicit *demonstrabit*: nam hoc quod supra dictum est, quod Pater omnia demonstrat Filio, refertur ad aeternam generationem: quomodo ergo hic dicit *demonstrabit*, cum Filius sit ei coaeternus, et in aeternitate non sit accipere futurum?

Secundo vero quantum ad hoc quod dicit *ut vos miremini*. Si enim ideo demonstraturus est ut Iudaei mirentur, tunc Filio demonstraturus est simul et istis, alias non mirarentur, nisi viderent; cum tamen Filius ab aeterno omnia viderit apud Patrem.

758. Et ideo dicendum est, quod hoc exponitur tripliciter. Uno modo, secundum Augustinum, ut referatur haec demonstratio fienda discipulis.

Consuetus enim modus loquendi est Christi, ut aliquando attribuat sibi fieri quod fit membris suis, secundum illud Matth. XXV, v. 40: *quod uni ex minimis meis fecistis, mihi fecistis*. Et tunc est sensus: vos vidistis Filium magna facientem in curatione languidi, et miramini; sed adhuc *maiora his Pater demonstrabit ei*, in membris, scilicet discipulis; infra XIV, 12: *et maiora horum faciet*. Dicit ergo *ut vos miremini*: quia ex miraculis discipulorum Iudaei intantum mirati sunt quod maxima multitudo eorum conversa est ad fidem, sicut habetur Act. I.

759. Alio modo, secundum Augustinum, sic, ut scilicet referatur ad Christum secundum naturam assumptam.

In Christo enim est et natura divina et natura humana; et secundum utramque habet a Patre potestatem vivificativam; sed aliter et aliter, quia secundum divinitatem habet potestatem vivificandi animas, sed secundum naturam assumptam vivificat corpora unde Augustinus: *Verbum vivificat animas, sed Verbum caro factum vivificat corpora*. Nam resurrectio Christi, et mysteria quae Christus implevit in carne, sunt causa futurae resurrectionis corporum; Eph. II, 5: *convivificavit nos in Christo*; I Cor. XV, 12: *si autem Christus praedicatur quod resurrexit a mortuis, quomodo quidam dicunt in vobis, quoniam resurrectio mortuorum non est?* Sed primum habet ab aeterno, et hoc ostendit cum supra dixit: *et omnia demonstrat ei quae ipse facit*; quae quidem omnia demonstrat carni; sed alia ex tempore, et quantum ad hoc dicit: *et*

First, he sets forth this life-giving power in general.

Second, he expands on it, at *for as the Father raises up the dead*.

756. He says, to the first, *and greater works than these will he show him*. As if to say: you are astonished and affected by the power of the Son in his healing of the sick man, but the Father: *and greater works than these will he show him*, as in raising the dead, *so that you may wonder*.

757. This passage gives rise to two difficulties. First, about his saying, *will he show*. For the earlier statement that the Father shows everything to the Son (John 5:20), refers to his eternal generation. How, then, can he say here, *will he show*, if the Son is coeternal with him and eternity does not allow of a future?

The second difficulty is over, *so that you may wonder*. For if he intends to show something to amaze the Jews, then he will be showing it to the Son at the same time as to them; for they could not be amazed unless they saw it. And yet the Son saw all things from eternity with the Father.

758. We must say that this is explained in three ways. The first way is given by Augustine, and in it this future showing is referred to the disciples.

For it is Christ's custom that now and then he says that what happens to his members happens to himself: *as long as you did it to one of the least of my brethren, you did it to me* (Matt 25:40). And then the meaning is this: you saw the Son do something great in healing the sick man, and you were amazed; *and greater works than these will he show him*, in his members, that is, the disciples: *greater than these he will do* (John 14:12). He then says, such *so that you may wonder*, for the miracles of the disciples so amazed the Jews that a great many of them were converted to the faith, as we see in the Acts.

759. The second explanation, also by Augustine, refers this showing to Christ according to his assumed nature.

For in Christ there is both a divine nature and a human nature, and in each he has life-giving power from the Father, although not in the same way. According to his divinity he has the power to give life to souls; but according to his assumed nature, he gives life to bodies. Hence Augustine says: *the Word gives life to souls; but the Word made flesh gives life to bodies*. For the resurrection of Christ and the mysteries which Christ fulfilled in his flesh are the cause of the future resurrection of bodies: *God, who is rich in mercy, has brought us to life in Christ* (Eph 2:5); *if it is preached that Christ rose from the dead, how can some of you say that there is no resurrection of the dead?* (1 Cor 15:12). The first life-giving power he has from eternity; and he indicated this when he said: *the Father shows him all things that he himself does* (John 5:20), all of which he shows to his flesh.

maiora his demonstrabit ei, idest demonstratur potestas eius in hoc quod maiora faciet, suscitando mortuos: quosdam quidem hic, sicut Lazarum, puellam et unicum matris; omnes tandem in die iudicii.

760. Tertio modo ut referatur ad Christum secundum naturam divinam, secundum illum modum quo in Scriptura dici consuetum est, tunc aliquid fieri quando innotescit; sicut illud Matth. ult., 18: *data est mihi omnis potestas in caelo et in terra.* Cum enim Christus ab aeterno habuerit potestatem plenissimam, quia *quaecumque* Pater facit, *similiter et Filius facit*, dicit tamen, post resurrectionem domini potestatem datam esse: non quia tunc tantum eam recepit, sed quia per resurrectionis gloriam tunc maxime innotuit.

Secundum hoc ergo dicit sibi potestatem dari, secundum quod eam exequitur in opere, ut dicatur: *et maiora demonstrabit ei opera*; idest, sibi data per executionem ostendet: et hoc vobis mirantibus, quando scilicet qui vobis videtur ut homo tantum, apparebit virtutis divinae et Deus. Est autem verbum demonstrationis accipiendum ut verbum visionis, secundum quod supra expositum est.

761. Consequenter cum dicit *sicut enim Pater suscitat mortuos . . . sic et Filius*, explicat in speciali potestatem vivificativam Filii, ostendens quae sunt illa maiora quae Pater Filio demonstrabit.

Ubi sciendum est quod divina virtus in Veteri Testamento ex hoc praecipue commendatur quod Deus est auctor vitae; I Reg. II, 6: *Dominus mortificat, et vivificat.* Et Deut. c. XXXII, 39: *ego occidam, et ego vivere faciam.* Quam quidem virtutem sicut habet Pater, sic habet et Filius, et ideo dicit *sicut Pater suscitat mortuos et vivificat, sic et Filius quos vult vivificat*; quasi dicat: haec sunt maiora quae Pater Filio demonstrabit, scilicet ut mortuos vivificet. Plane maiora sunt ista valde: quia plus est ut resurgat mortuus, quam ut convalescat aegrotus. Sic ergo *Filius quos vult vivificat*, et primam vitam viventibus dando, et mortuos suscitando. Nec tamen putemus alios a Patre suscitari et alios a Filio, sed eosdem quos Pater suscitat et vivificat, Filius suscitat et vivificat: quia Pater, sicut omnia operatur per Filium, qui est virtus eius, ita et omnes vivificat per Filium, qui est vita, ut dicit infra XIV, 6: *ego sum via, veritas et vita.* Non tamen per Filium suscitat et vivificat mortuos sicut per instrumentum, quia secundum hoc Filius non esset constitutus in suae potestatis arbitrio. Et ideo ut hoc excludat, dicit: *Filius quos vult vivificat*; idest, in suae potestatis arbitrio est vivificare quod vult. Nam non aliud vult Filius quam Pater: sicut enim est illis una substantia, sic est illis una

The other life-giving power he has in time, and concerning this he says: *greater works than these will he show him*, i.e., his power will be shown by the fact that he will do greater works, by raising the dead. He will raise some of the dead here: as Lazarus, the young girl, and the mother's only son; and finally he will raise all on the day of judgment.

760. A third explanation refers this showing to Christ in his divine nature, according to the custom of Scripture in saying that a thing is beginning to take place when it is beginning to be known. For example: *all power has been given to me, in heaven and on earth* (Matt 28:18); for although Christ had the complete fullness of power from eternity, because *whatever he*, the Father, *does, these the Son also does in like manner* (John 5:19), he still speaks of this power as being given to him after the resurrection, not because he was then receiving it for the first time, but because it was through the glory of the resurrection that it became most known.

In this interpretation, then, he says that power is given to him insofar as he exercises it in some work. As if to say: *greater works than these will he show him*, i.e., he will show by his works what has been given to him. And this will come about when you are amazed, i.e., when the one who seems to you to be a mere man is revealed to be a person of divine power and as God. We could also take the word show as referring to an act of seeing, as was explained above.

761. Now he explains in more detail the life-giving power of the Son by indicating those greater works which the Father will show the Son, at *for as the Father raises up the dead . . . so the Son also*.

Here we should point out that in the Old Testament the divine power is particularly emphasized by the fact that God is the author of life: *the Lord kills, and brings to life* (1 Sam 2:6); *I will kill, and bring to life again* (Deut 32:39). Now just as the Father has this power, so also does the Son; hence he says, *for as the Father raises up the dead and gives life, so the Son also gives life to whom he wills*. As if to say: these are those greater works that the Father will show the Son, that is, he will give life to the dead. Such works are obviously greater, for it is greater to raise the dead than for a sick man to become well. Thus *the Son also gives life to whom he wills*, i.e., by giving initial life to the living, and by raising the dead. We should not think that some are raised up by the Father and others by the Son. Rather, the same ones who are raised and vivified by the Father, are raised and vivified by the Son also: because just as the Father does all things through the Son, who is his power, so he also gives life to all through the Son, who is life: *I am the way, and the truth, and the life* (John 14:6). The Father does not raise up and give life through the Son as through an instrument, because then the Son would not have freedom of power. And so to exclude this he says, *the Son also gives life to whom he wills*, i.e., it lies in the freedom of his

voluntas; unde Matth.: c. XX, 15, dicit: *an non licet mihi quod volo facere?*

762. Consequenter cum dicit *neque enim Pater iudicat quemquam,* assignat rationem dicti, manifestans suam potestatem.

Sed attendendum est, quod ex hoc loco usque ad finem sunt duae expositiones: una est Augustini, alia Hilarii et Chrysostomi.

Secundum Augustinum quidem exponitur sic. Dixerat Dominus supra, quod sicut Pater suscitat mortuos ita et Filius. Sed ne intelligeres illam mortuorum resuscitationem tantum qua aliquos ad hanc vitam resuscitavit ad miraculi ostensionem et non illam qua resuscitat ad vitam aeternam, ideo ducit eos ad altiorem considerationem alterius, scilicet resurrectionis quae erit in futuro iudicio. Unde et specialiter de iudicio mentionem facit, dicens *neque enim Pater iudicat quemquam.*

Potest et aliter, secundum eumdem, sub eodem sensu continuari, ut secundum hoc quod dixit *sicut Pater resuscitat mortuos, sic et Filius* etc., referatur ad resurrectionem animarum, quam facit Filius inquantum est Verbum; hoc vero quod dicit *neque enim Pater iudicat quemquam,* referatur ad resurrectionem corporum, quam facit inquantum Verbum caro factum est. Resurrectio enim animarum fit per personam Patris et Filii; unde et simul nominat Patrem et Filium, dicens *sicut Pater suscitat . . . sic et Filius.* Resurrectio vero corporum per dispensationem humanitatis Patri non coaeternam: et ideo soli Filio iudicium attribuit.

763. Sed attende mirabilem varietatem verborum: nam primo proponitur nobis Pater operans et Filius vacans, scilicet cum dicitur: *non potest Filius a se facere quidquam, nisi quod viderit Patrem facientem*; hic vero e converso proponitur Filius operans, et Pater vacans: *neque enim Pater iudicat quemquam; sed omne iudicium dedit Filio* etc. In quo datur intelligi, quod alio modo loquitur hic et alio modo ibi. Nam ibi loquitur de operatione quae est Patris et Filii, unde dicit quod *a se non facit quidquam, nisi quod viderit Patrem facientem*; hic vero loquitur de operatione qua Filius secundum quod homo iudicat et non Pater: unde dicit quod *omne iudicium dedit Filio.* Nam Pater in iudicio non apparebit; quia secundum iustitiam Deus in propria natura iudicandis omnibus apparere non potest: quia cum visio divina sit beatitudo nostra, si mali Deum in propria natura viderent, iam essent beati. Apparebit ergo solus Filius, qui solus habet naturam assumptam. Ipse ergo solus iudicat, qui solus omnibus apparebit; sed tamen auctoritate Patris; Act. X, 42: *hic est qui constitutus est*

power to grant life to whom he wills. For the Son does not will anything different than the Father wills: for just as they are one substance, so they have one will; hence it is said: *is it not lawful for me to do as I will?* (Matt 20:15).

762. Then when he says, *for neither does the Father judge any man,* he gives the reason for what was said above, and indicates his own power.

It should be remarked that there are two expositions for the present passages: one is given by Augustine, and the other by Hilary and Chrysostom.

Augustine's explanation is this. The Lord had said that just as the Father raises the dead, so also does the Son. But so that we do not think that this refers only to those miracles the Son performs in raising the dead to this life, and not to the Son's raising to eternal life, he leads them to the deeper consideration of the resurrection to occur at the future judgment. Thus he refers explicitly to the judgment, saying, *for neither does the Father judge any man.*

Another explanation by Augustine, in which the same meaning is maintained, is that the earlier statement, *as the Father raises the dead and grants life, so the Son also,* should be referred to the resurrection of souls, which the Son causes inasmuch as he is the Word; but the text, *for neither does the Father judge any man,* should be referred to the resurrection of bodies, which the Son causes inasmuch as he is the Word made flesh. For the resurrection of souls is accomplished through the person of the Father and of the Son; and for this reason he mentions the Father and Son together, saying, *as the Father raises the dead . . . so the Son also.* But the resurrection of bodies is accomplished through the humanity of the Son, not his coeternity with the Father. Consequently, he attributes judgment solely to the Son.

763. Note the wonderful variety of expressions. The Father is first presented as acting and the Son as resting, when it says: *the Son cannot do anything of himself, but only what he sees the Father doing* (John 5:19); but here, on the contrary, the Son is presented as acting and the Father as resting: *neither does the Father judge any man, but he has given all judgment to the Son.* We can see from this that he is speaking from different points of view at different times. At first, he was speaking of an action which belongs to the Father and the Son; thus he says that *the Son cannot do anything of himself, but only what he sees the Father doing* (John 5:19); but here he is speaking of an action by which the Son, as man, judges, and the Father does not: thus he says that the Father *has given all judgment to the Son.* For the Father will not appear at the judgment because, in accord with what is just, God cannot appear in his divine nature before all who are to be judged: for since our happiness consists in the vision of God, if the wicked were to see God in his own nature, they would be enjoying happiness. Therefore, only the Son will appear, who alone

a Deo iudex vivorum et mortuorum. Et in Ps. LXXI, 1: *Deus, iudicium tuum regi da*.

764. Consequenter cum dicit **ut omnes honorificent Filium**, ponit effectum qui provenit ex potestate Filii, et

primo ponit fructum consequentiae;

secundo excludit contradictionem, ibi **qui non honorificat Filium, non honorificat patrem qui misit illum**.

765. Dicit ergo: ideo Pater omne iudicium dedit Filio, secundum humanam naturam, quia in incarnatione se Filius exinanivit formam servi accipiens, in qua inhonoratus est ab hominibus, secundum illud infra VIII, 49: **ego honorifico Patrem meum, et vos inhonorastis me**. Ideo ergo in ipsa natura assumpta datum est ei iudicium, **ut omnes honorificent Filium, sicut honorificant Patrem**. *Tunc enim videbunt Filium hominis venientem cum potestate magna et maiestate*: Lc. XXI, 27. Et Apoc. VII, 11: *ceciderunt in facies suas, et adoraverunt, dicentes: benedictio, et claritas, et sapientia, et gratiarum actio, honor, virtus et fortitudo Deo nostro*.

766. Sed posset aliquis dicere: volo honorificare Patrem, et non curare de Filio. Sed hoc non potest esse, quia **qui non honorificat Filium, non honorificat Patrem qui misit illum**.

Aliud enim est honorare Deum ratione qua Deus est, aliud honorare Patrem. Nam bene potest aliquis honorare Deum inquantum Creator, omnipotens et incommutabilis, absque hoc quod honoret et Filium. Sed honorare Deum ut Patrem nullus potest quin honorificet Filium: nam Pater dici non potest si Filium non habet. Sed si inhonoras Filium dividendo eius virtutem, inhonoras et Patrem: ibi enim tollis virtutem Patri, ubi minorem das Filio.

767. Vel aliter, secundum eumdem: Christo debetur duplex honor: scilicet secundum divinitatem, secundum quam debetur ei honor aequalis Patri; et quantum ad hoc dicit **ut omnes honorificent Filium, sicut honorificant Patrem**: alius debetur ei secundum humanitatem, sed non aequalis Patri; et de isto dicit **qui non honorificat Filium, non honorificat Patrem qui misit illum**. Unde ibi signanter dicitur **sicut**; hic autem non dicit *sicut*, sed simpliciter dicit Filium esse honorandum; Lc. X, 16: *qui vos spernit, me spernit; qui autem me spernit, spernit eum qui misit me*.

768. Secundum autem Hilarium et Chrysostomum, exponitur magis ad litteram, quamvis parum mutetur, hoc modo.

has an assumed nature. Therefore, he alone will judge who alone will appear to all. Yet he will judge with the authority of the Father: *he is the one appointed by God to be the judge of the living and of the dead* (Acts 10:42); and we read: *O Lord, give your judgment to the king* (Ps 71:1).

764. Then when he says, **so that all men may honor the Son**, he gives the effect which results from the power of the Son.

First, he gives the effect.

Second, he excludes an objection, at **he who does not honor the Son, does not honor the Father, who has sent him**.

765. He says that the Father has given all judgment to the Son, according to his human nature, because in the incarnation the Son emptied himself, taking the form of a servant, under which form he was dishonored by men: **I honor my Father, and you have dishonored me** (John 8:49). Therefore, judgment was given to the Son in his assumed nature **so that all men may honor the Son, as they honor the Father**. For on that day *they will see the Son of man coming with great power and glory* (Luke 21:27); *they fell on their faces and worshipped, saying: blessing and glory, and wisdom and thanks, and honor, power and strength, to our God* (Rev 7:11).

766. Someone might say: I am willing to honor the Father, but do not care about the Son. This cannot be, because **he who does not honor the Son, does not honor the Father, who has sent him**.

For it is one thing to honor God precisely as God, and another to honor the Father. For someone may well honor God as the omnipotent and immutable Creator without honoring the Son. But no one can honor God as Father without honoring the Son; for he cannot be called Father if he does not have a Son. But if you dishonor the Son by diminishing his power, this also dishonors the Father; because where you give less to the Son, you are taking away from the power of the Father.

767. Another explanation, given by Augustine, is this. A twofold honor is due to Christ. One, according to his divinity, in regard to which he is owed an honor equal to that given the Father; and with respect to this he says, **so that all men may honor the Son, as they honor the Father**. Another honor is due the Son according to his humanity, but not one equal to that given the Father; and with respect to this he says, **he who does not honor the Son, does not honor the Father who sent him**. Thus in the first case he significantly used **as**; but now, the second time, he does not say *as*, but states absolutely that the Son should be honored: *he who rejects you, rejects me; and he who rejects me, rejects him who sent me* (Luke 10:16).

768. Hilary and Chrysostom give a more literal explanation, but it is only slightly different. They explain it this way.

Dominus supra dicit: *Filius quos vult vivificat*. Quicumque aliquid facit pro libero voluntatis arbitrio, agit ex proprio iudicio. Supra vero dictum est quod *omnia quaecumque facit Pater haec et Filius similiter facit*. Ergo Filius de omnibus habet liberum voluntatis arbitrium, quia ex proprio iudicio procedit. Et ideo statim facit mentionem de iudicio, dicens *neque Pater iudicat quemquam*, seorsum scilicet a Filio. Et hoc modo loquendi usus est Dominus infra XII, 47: *ego non iudico vos*, scilicet solum, *sed sermo quem locutus sum, ille iudicabit vos in novissimo*. Sed omne iudicium dedit Filio, sicut et dedit ei omnia. Sicut enim dedit ei vitam, et genuit eum viventem, ita dedit ei omne iudicium, idest genuit eum iudicem; infra ibid., 30: *sicut audio iudico*; idest, sicut habeo esse a Patre, ita et iudicium. Ratio huius est, quia Filius nihil aliud est, ut dictum est supra, quam conceptus Paternae sapientiae; unusquisque autem per conceptum suae sapientiae iudicat: unde sicut Pater omnia per Filium facit, ita et omnia per ipsum iudicat. Et fructus huius est *ut omnes honorificent Filium, sicut honorificant Patrem*; idest, exhibeant ei cultum latriae, sicut Patri.

Cetera vero non mutantur.

769. Sed attendenda est, secundum Hilarium, mirabilis connexio verborum, ut errores contra aeternam generationem confutentur.

Duae namque haereses contra ipsam generationem aeternam exortae fuerunt. Una Arii dicentis Filium minorem Patre; quod est contra aequalitatem et unitatem. Alia Sabellii dicentis non esse distinctionem personarum in divinis; quod est contra originem. Et ideo ubicumque facit mentionem de unitate et aequalitate, statim addit et distinctionem personarum secundum originem, et e converso. Unde, quia innuit originem personarum, dicens: *non potest Filius a seipso facere quidquam, nisi quod viderit Patrem facientem*, ne crederes inaequalitatem, statim subiungit: *quaecumque enim ille fecerit, haec et Filius similiter facit*. Et, e converso, cum innuit aequalitatem, dicens: *sicut Pater suscitat mortuos et vivificat, ita et Filius quos vult vivificat*, ne discredas originem et Filium genitum, subiungit: *neque enim Pater iudicat quemquam; sed omne iudicium dedit Filio*. Eodem modo cum insinuat aequalitatem personarum, dicens *ut omnes honorificent Filium, sicut honorificant Patrem*, statim subiungit de missione, in qua demonstratur origo, dicens *qui non honorificat Filium, non honorificat Patrem, qui misit illum*, non per separationem a seipso. Missionem audi, infra VIII, 29: *qui misit me, mecum est, et non reliquit me solum*.

Our Lord said above, *the Son also gives life to whom he wills*. Now whoever does anything according to the free decision of his will acts because of his own judgment. But it was stated above that *for whatever he does, these the Son also does in like manner* (John 5:19). Therefore, the Son enjoys a free decision of his own will in all things, since he acts because of his own judgment. Thus he immediately mentions judgment, saying that *neither does the Father judge any man*, i.e., without or apart from the Son. Our Lord used this way of speaking: *I do not judge him*, i.e., I alone, *but the word which I have spoken, the same will judge him on the last day* (John 12:47–48). But he has given all judgment to the Son, as he has given all things to him. For as he has given him life and begotten him as living, so he has given him all judgment, i.e., begotten him as judge: *as I hear, so I judge* (John 5:30), i.e., just as I have being from the Father, so also judgment. The reason for this is that the Son is nothing other than the conception of the paternal wisdom, as was said. But each one judges by the concept of his wisdom. Hence, just as the Father does all things through the Son, so he judges all things through him. And the fruit of this is *that all men may honor the Son, as they honor the Father*, i.e., that they may render to him the cult of *latria* as they do the Father.

The rest does not change.

769. Hilary calls our attention to the remarkable relationship of the passages so that the errors concerning eternal generation can be refuted.

Two heresies have arisen concerning this eternal generation. One was that of Arius, who said that the Son is less than the Father; and this is contrary to their equality and unity. The other was that of Sabellius, who said that that there is no distinction of persons in the divinity; and this is contrary to their origin. So, whenever he mentions the unity and equality, he immediately also adds their distinction as persons according to origin, and conversely. Thus, because he mentions the origin of the persons when he says, *the Son cannot do anything of himself, but only what he sees the Father doing* (John 5:19), then, so we do not think this involves inequality, he at once adds: *for whatever he does, these the Son also does in like manner* (John 5:19). Conversely, when he states their equality by saying: *for as the Father raises up the dead and gives life, so the Son also gives life to whom he wills*, then, so that we do not deny that the Son has an origin and is begotten, he adds, *for neither does the Father judge any man, but he has given all judgment to the Son*. Similarly, when he mentions the equality of the persons by saying: *that all men may honor the Son, as they honor the Father*, he immediately adds something about a mission, which indicates an origin, saying: *he who does not honor the Son, does not honor the Father, who has sent him*, but not in such a way that involves a separation. Christ mentions such mission in saying: *he who sent me is with me, and he has not left me alone* (John 8:29).

770. Supra ostendit Dominus se habere virtutem vivificativam; hic ostendit modum quo aliquis ab ipso vitam participare potest, et

primo ponit modum, quomodo aliquis per ipsum vitam participet;

secundo huiusmodi adimpletionem praenuntiat, ibi *amen, amen dico vobis, quia venit hora*.

771. Circa primum considerandum est, quod sunt quatuor gradus vitae. Unus quidem invenitur in plantis, quae nutriuntur, augentur et generantur et generant; alius in animalibus, quae tantum sentiunt; alius vero in his quae moventur, quae sunt animalia perfecta; ulterius vero est aliud genus vitae in his quae intelligunt. Tot ergo existentibus gradibus vitae, impossibile est vel vitam quae est in plantis, vel eam quae est in sensu, aut eam quae est ex motu, esse primam vitam. Nam prima vita debet esse per se vita, non participata. Nulla autem vita potest esse talis nisi sola vita intellectualis, aliae autem tres communes sunt corporali et spirituali creaturae; corpus autem quod vivit, non est ipsa vita; sed vitam participans: et ideo vita intellectualis est prima vita, quae est vita spiritualis, quae immediate percipitur a primo vitae principio, unde dicitur vita sapientiae. Et propter hoc in Scripturis vita attribuitur sapientiae. Prov. VIII, 35: *qui me invenerit, inveniet vitam, et hauriet salutem a Domino*. Sic ergo vitam a Christo, qui est Dei sapientia, participamus, inquantum anima nostra ab ipso sapientiam percipit.

Haec autem vita intellectualis perficitur in vera cognitione divinae sapientiae, quae est vita aeterna. Infra XVII, 3: *haec est vita aeterna, ut cognoscant te solum verum Deum, et quem misisti Iesum Christum*. Sed ad nullam sapientiam potest homo pervenire nisi per fidem: unde in scientiis nullus ad sapientiam pervenit, nisi prius fidem adhibeat dictis a magistro. Si ergo nos volumus ad illam vitam sapientiae pervenire, oportet nos per fidem credere ea quae ab illa nobis proponuntur. Ad Hebr. XI, 6: *oportet accedentem ad Deum credere quia est, et inquirentibus se remunerator sit*. Is. XXVIII, 16, secundum aliam litteram: *nisi credideritis, non intelligetis*.

772. Et ideo Dominus congrue modum perveniendi ad vitam ostendit esse per fidem, dicens *qui verbum meum audit, et credit ei qui misit me, habet vitam aeternam*. Et

primo ponit meritum fidei;

secundo subdit praemium eius, ibi *habet vitam aeternam*.

773. Circa meritum fidei primo ponit illud per quod fides introducitur; secundo illud cui fides innititur.

Introducitur quidem fides per verbum hominis; Rom. X, 17: *fides ex auditu, auditus autem per verbum Christi*. Innititur autem fides non verbo hominis sed ipsi

770. Above, our Lord showed that he had life-giving power; here he shows how someone can share in this life coming from him.

First, he tells how one can share in this life through him.

Second, he predicts its fulfillment, at *amen, amen I say unto you, that the hour is coming*.

771. With respect to the first, we should point out that there are four grades of life. One is found in plants, which take nourishment, grow, reproduce, and are reproduced. Another is in animals which only sense. Another in living things that move, that is, the perfect animals. Finally, there is another form of life which is present in those who understand. Now among those grades of life that exist, it is impossible that the foremost life be that found in plants, or in those with sensation, or even in those with motion. For the first and foremost life must be that which is 'per se,' not that which is participated. This can be none other than intellectual life, for the other three forms are common to a corporal and spiritual creature. Indeed, a body that lives is not life itself, but one participating in life. Hence intellectual life is the first and foremost life, which is the spiritual life, that is immediately received from the first principle of life, whence it is called the life of wisdom. For this reason in the Scriptures life is attributed to wisdom: *he who finds me finds life, and has salvation from the Lord* (Prov 8:35). Therefore we share life from Christ, who is the wisdom of God, insofar as our soul receives wisdom from him.

Now this intellectual life is made perfect by the true knowledge of divine wisdom, which is eternal life: *this is eternal life: that they may know you, the only true God, and Jesus Christ, whom you have sent* (John 17:3). But no one can arrive at any wisdom except by faith. Hence it is that in the sciences, no one acquires wisdom unless he first believes what is said by his teacher. Therefore, if we wish to acquire this life of wisdom, we must believe through faith the things that are proposed to us by it. *He who comes to God must believe that he is and rewards those who seek him* (Heb 11:6); and as we read in another version: *if you do not believe, you will not understand* (Isa 28:16).

772. Thus, our Lord fittingly shows that the way of obtaining life is through faith, saying, *he who hears my word, and believes him who sent him, has eternal life*.

First, he mentions the merit of faith.

Second, the reward of faith, *eternal life*.

773. Concerning the merit of faith, he first indicates how faith is brought to us; and second, the foundation of faith, that on which it rests.

Faith comes to us through the words of men: *faith comes through hearing, and hearing through the word of Christ* (Rom 10:17). But faith does not rest on man's word, but on

Deo; Gen. c. XV, 6: *credidit Abraham Deo, et reputatum est ei ad iustitiam*; Eccli. II, 8: *qui timetis Deum, credite illi*. Sic nos introducit per verbum hominis ad credendum, non ipsi homini qui loquitur, sed Deo cuius verba loquitur; I Thess. II, 13: *cum accepissetis a nobis verbum auditus Dei, accepistis illud non sicut verbum hominum, sed, sicut vere est, verbum Dei*. Et haec duo Dominus ponit. Primo illud per quod fides introducitur; unde dicit **qui verbum meum audit**, quod introducit ad fidem. Secundo illud cui innititur, cum dicit **et credit ei qui misit me**, non mihi, sed illi in cuius virtute loquor.

Quae quidem verba possunt competere Christo secundum quod homo inquantum per Verbum eius humanum homines conversi sunt ad fidem; et secundum quod Deus, inquantum Christus est Verbum Dei. Cum enim Christus sit Verbum Dei, manifestum est quod audientes Christum audiebant Verbum Dei et per consequens credebant Deo. Et hoc est quod dicit: **qui audit Verbum meum**, idest me Verbum Dei, **et credit ei**, idest Patri cuius sum Verbum.

774. Praemium autem fidei ponit cum subdit **habet vitam aeternam**. Et ponit tria quae nos habebimus in gloria, sed ordine retrogrado. Primo enim consequemur resurrectionem ex mortuis; secundo liberationem a futuro iudicio; tertio vitam aeternam: quia, ut dicitur Matth. XXV, 46 post iudicium ibunt iusti in vitam aeternam. Et haec tria ponit ad fidei praemium pertinere: et primo tertium tamquam magis desideratum.

775. Unde dicit **qui credit**, scilicet per fidem, **habet vitam aeternam**, quae consistit in plena Dei visione. Et dignum est ut qui credit propter Deum his quae non videt, perducatur ad plenam eorum visionem; infra c. XX, 31: **haec scripta sunt ut credatis . . . et ut credentes vitam habeatis in nomine eius**.

776. Secundo ponit secundum, cum dicit **et in iudicium non veniet**.

Sed contra hoc est quod Apostolus dicit II Cor. V, 10: *omnes nos astare oportet ante tribunal Christi*, etiam ipsos Apostolos: ergo qui credit, in iudicium veniet.

Sed dicendum, quod duplex est iudicium. Scilicet condemnationis, et in isto non veniet qui fide formata in Deum credunt: de quo dicebat Ps. CXLII, 2: *non intres in iudicium cum servo tuo, quia non iustificabitur in conspectu tuo omnis vivens*; supra III, 18: **qui credit non iudicatur**. Est etiam iudicium discretionis vel discussionis, et ad istud oportet nos omnes ante tribunal Christi exhibere, ut dicit Apostolus; et de isto dicitur in Ps. XLII: *iudica me, Deus, et discerne causam meam*.

God himself: *Abram believed God, who counted this as his justification* (Gen 15:6); *you who fear the Lord, believe in him* (Sir 2:8). Thus we are lead to believe through the words of men, not in the man himself who speaks, but in God, whose words he speaks: *when you heard the word we brought you as God's word, you did not receive it as the word of men, but, as what it really is, the word of God* (1 Thess 2:13). Our Lord mentions these two things. First, how faith is brought to us, when he says, **he who hears my word**, which leads to faith. Second, he mentions that on which faith rests, saying, **and believes him who sent me**, i.e., not in me, but in him in virtue of whom I speak.

This text can apply to Christ, as man, insofar as it is through Christ's human words that men were converted to the faith. And it can apply to Christ, as God, insofar as Christ is the Word of God. For since Christ is the Word of God, it is clear that those who heard Christ were hearing the Word of God, and as a consequence, were believing in God. And this is what he says: **he who hears my word**, i.e., me, the Word of God, **and believes him**, i.e., the Father, whose Word I am.

774. Then when he says, **has eternal life**, he mentions the reward of faith, and states three things we will possess in the state of glory; but they are mentioned in reverse order. First, there will be the resurrection from the dead. Second, we will have freedom from the future judgment. Third, we will enjoy everlasting life, for as we read, the just will enter into everlasting life (Matt 25:46). He mentions these three as belonging to the reward of faith; and the third was mentioned first since it is desired more than the others.

775. So he says, **he who believes**, i.e., through faith, **has eternal life**, which consists in the full vision of God. And it is fitting that one who believes on account of God certain things that he does not see, should be brought to the full vision of these things: **these things are written, so that you may believe . . . and so that believing, you may have life in his name** (John 20:31).

776. He mentions the second when he says, **and he will not come into judgment**.

But the Apostle says something which contradicts this: *we must all appear before the judgment seat of Christ* (2 Cor 5:10), even the apostles. Therefore, even one who does believe will encounter judgment.

I answer that there are two kinds of judgment. One is a judgment of condemnation, and no one encounters that judgment if he believes in God with formed faith. We read about this judgment: *do not enter into judgment with your servant, for no living man is just in your sight* (Ps 142:2); and it was said: **he who believes in him is not judged** (John 3:18). There is also a judgment of separation and examination; and, as the Apostle says, all must present themselves before the tribunal of Christ for this judgment. Of this judgment we read: *judge me, O God, and distinguish my cause from those people who are not holy* (Ps 42:1).

777. Tertio ponit praemium, cum dicit *sed transit a morte in vitam*, vel *transiet*, secundum aliam litteram. Quod quidem potest exponi dupliciter. Primo ut referatur ad resurrectionem animae et sic planus est sensus quasi dicat: non solum per fidem adipiscitur vitam aeternam et liberatur a iudicio, sed etiam remissionem peccatorum consequitur. Unde dicit *sed transit* de infidelitate ad fidem, de iniustitia ad iustitiam; I Io. III, 14: *nos scimus quoniam translati sumus de morte ad vitam.*

Secundo ut referatur ad resurrectionem corporum; et tunc est expositivum huius quod dicit *habet vitam aeternam*. Posset enim ex hoc aliquis credere quod qui credit in Deum, numquam moreretur, sed viveret in aeternum; quod esse non potest, quia omnes homines solvere oportet debitum primae praevaricationis, secundum illud Ps. LXXXVIII, 49: *quis est homo qui vivet, et non videbit mortem?* Et ideo non est intelligendum, eum qui credit sic habere vitam aeternam, quasi numquam moriturus; sed quia de hac vita transiet per mortem in vitam, idest per mortem corporis reparabitur in vitam aeternam. Vel *transiet* quantum ad causam: quia quando homo credit, iam habet meritum gloriosae resurrectionis; Is. XXVI, 19: *vivent mortui tui, interfecti tui resurgent.* Et tunc soluti a morte veteris hominis suscipiemus vitam novi hominis, scilicet Christi.

778. *Amen, amen dico vobis* etc. Quia possent aliqui dubitare utrum aliqui de morte ad vitam transirent, ideo Dominus praenuntiat huiusmodi adimpletionem dicens: dico quod *transiet de morte in vitam*, et hoc iam ante impletur. Et hoc est quod dicit: *amen, amen dico vobis, quia venit hora*, non fatali necessitate subiecta, sed a Deo praeordinata; I Io. II, 18: *novissima hora est.* Et ne credatur distare subiungit *et nunc est* (Rom. XIII, 11: *hora est iam nos de somno surgere*), hora scilicet nunc est, *quando mortui audient vocem Filii Dei, et qui audierint vivent.*

779. Quod potest dupliciter exponi. Uno modo ut referatur ad resurrectionem corporis et dicatur *venit hora, et nunc est* etc., quasi dicat: verum est quod omnes finaliter resurgent, sed etiam nunc est hora, quando aliqui, quos resuscitaturus erat Dominus, *audient vocem eius*. Sic audivit Lazarus quando dictum est ei, *veni foras*, ut dicitur infra XI, 43; sic audivit filia archisynagogi, ut dicitur Matth. IX, 18 et Filius viduae, ut habetur Lc. VII, 12. Et ideo, dicit signanter *et nunc est*, quia per me iam incipiunt mortui resuscitari.

Alio modo, secundum Augustinum, ut hoc quod dicit *nunc est*, referatur ad resurrectionem animae. Nam, sicut dictum est supra, duplex est resurrectio: scilicet corporum, quae erit; et hoc nondum est sed erit in iudicio futuro; alia est animarum, de morte infidelitatis ad

777. Third, he mentions a reward when he says, *but passes from death to life*, or *will pass*, as another version says. This statement can be explained in two ways. First, it can refer to the resurrection of the soul. In this case the obvious meaning is that he is saying: through faith we attain not only to eternal life and freedom from judgment, but also to the forgiveness of our sins as well. Hence he says, *but passes*, from unbelief to belief, from injustice to justice: *we know that we have passed from death to life* (1 John 3:14).

Second, this statement can be explained as referring to the resurrection of the body. Then it is an elaboration of the phrase, *has eternal life*. For some might think from what was said, that whoever believes in God will never die, but live forever. But this is impossible, because all men must pay the debt incurred by the. first sin, according to: *where is the man who lives, and will not see death?* (Ps 88:49). Consequently, we should not think that one who believes has eternal life in such a way as never to die; rather, he will pass from thi's life, through death, to life, i.e., through the death of the body he will be revived to eternal life. Or, *will pass*, might refer to the cause for when a person believes, he already has the merit for a glorious resurrection: *your dead will live, your slain will rise* (Isa 26:19). And then, once released from the death of the old man, we will receive the life of the new man, that is, Christ.

778. *Amen, amen, I say to you, the Son cannot do anything of himself, but only what he sees the Father doing* (John 5:19) since some might doubt if any would pass from death to life, our Lord predicts that this will happen, saying: I say that he *passes from death to life*; and I say it before it actually occurs. And this is what he states, saying: *amen, amen, I say to you, that the hour is coming*, not determined by a necessity of fate, but by God's decree: *it is the last hour* (1 John 2:18). And so that we do not think that it is far off, he adds, and is now here *it is now the time for us to rise from sleep* (Rom 13:11)—i.e., the hour is now here *when the dead will hear the voice of the Son of God, and they who hear will live.*

779. This can be explained in two ways. In one way as referring to the resurrection of the body, and so it is said that *the hour is coming, and now is*, as if he had said: it is true that eventually all will rise, but even now is the hour when some, whom the Lord was about to resuscitate, *will hear the voice* of the Son of God. This is the way Lazarus heard it when it was said to him, *come forth* (John 11:43); and in this way the daughter of the leader of the synagogue heard it (Matt 9:18); and the widow's son (Luke 7:12). Therefore, he says significantly, and *now is*, because through me the dead already are beginning to be raised.

Another explanation is given by Augustine, according to which *and now is* refers to the resurrection of the soul. For as was said above, resurrection is of two kinds: the resurrection of bodies, which will happen in the future; this does not take place now, but will occur at the future

vitam fidei, et iniustitiae ad iustitiam; et hoc iam **nunc est**. Et ideo dicit **venit hora, et nunc est, quando mortui**, scilicet infideles et peccatores, **audient vocem Filii Dei, et qui audierint vivent**, secundum veram fidem.

780. Sed duo mirabilia in his verbis implicari videntur. Unum, cum dicit mortuos audire; aliud cum subdit, eos per auditum reviviscere, quasi prior sit auditus quam vita, cum tamen auditus sit quidam actus vitae.

Sed si hoc referamus ad resurrectionem, verum est quod mortui audient, idest obedient voci Filii Dei. Vox enim expressiva est interioris conceptus. Tota autem natura ad nutum obedit voluntatis divinae; Rom. IV, 17: *vocat ea quae non sunt, tamquam ea quae sunt*. Secundum hoc ergo ligna, lapides et omnia, non solum ossa arida, sed et cineres corporum mortuorum **audient vocem Filii Dei**, inquantum ad nutum ei obedient. Et hoc non convenit Christo inquantum est Filius hominis sed inquantum est Filius Dei, quia Verbo Dei omnia obediunt. Et ideo signanter dicit **Filii Dei**; Matth. VIII, 27: *qualis est hic, quia mare et venti obediunt ei?*

Si vero referatur ad resurrectionem animarum, rationem habet quod dicitur: nam vox Filii Dei, qua interius per inspirationem vel exterius per praedicationem suam et aliorum, corda fidelium movet, habet vim vivificativam, infra VI, 64: **verba quae locutus sum vobis, spiritus et vita sunt**, et sic vivificat mortuos, dum iustificat impios.

Et quia auditus est via ad vitam vel naturae per obedientiam, ad reparationem scilicet naturae, vel auditus fidei ad reparationem vitae et iustitiae, ideo dicit **et qui audierint**, per obedientiam quantum ad resurrectionem corporum, vel per fidem quantum ad resurrectionem animarum, **vivent**, in corpore in aeterna vita et in iustitia in vita gratiae etc.

judgment. The other is the resurrection of souls from the death of unbelief to the life of faith, and from the life of injustice to that of justice; and this **now is**. Hence he says, **the hour is coming, and now is, when the dead**, i.e., unbelievers and sinners, **will hear the voice of the Son of God, and they who hear will live**, according to the true faith.

780. This passage seems to imply two strange occurrences. One, when he says that the dead will hear. The other, when he adds that it is through hearing that they will come to life again, as though hearing comes before life, whereas hearing is a certain function of life.

However, if we refer this to the resurrection, it is true that the dead will hear, i.e., obey the voice of the Son of God. For the voice expresses the interior concept. Now all nature obeys the slightest command of the divine will: *he calls into existence what does not exist* (Rom 4:17). According to this, then, wood, stones, all things, not just the dry bones but also the dust of dead bodies, **will hear the voice of the Son of God**, so far as they obey his slightest will. And this belongs to Christ, not insofar as he is the Son of man, but insofar as he is the Son of God, because all things obey the Word of God. And so he significantly says, **of the Son of God**; *what kind of man is this, for the sea and winds obey him?* (Matt 8:27).

If this statement is understood as referring to the resurrection of souls, then the reason for it is this: the voice of the Son of God has a life-giving power, that voice by which he moves the hearts of the faithful interiorly by inspiration, or exteriorly by his preaching and that of others: **the words that I have spoken to you are spirit and life** (John 6:64). And so he gives life to the dead when he justifies the wicked.

And since hearing is the way to life, either of nature through obedience, namely, by repairing nature, or the hearing of faith by repairing life and justice, he therefore says, **and they who hear**, by obedience as to the resurrection of the body, or by faith as to the resurrection of souls, **will live**, in the body in eternal life, and in justice in the life of grace.

Lecture 5

5:26 Sicut enim Pater habet vitam in semetipso, sic dedit et Filio habere vitam iri semetipso. [n. 782]

5:27 Et potestatem dedit ei iudicium facere: quia Filius hominis est. [n. 784]

5:28 Nolite mirari hoc: quia venit hora in qua omnes qui in monumentis sunt, audient vocem Filii Dei. [n. 787]

5:29 Et procedent qui bona facerunt, in resurrectionem vitae; qui vero mala egerunt, in resurrectionem iudicii. [n. 792]

5:30 Non possum ego a meipso facere quidquam, sed sicut audio, iudico. Et iudicium meum iustum est: quia non quaero voluntatem meam, sed voluntatem eius qui misit me. [n. 794]

5:26 ὥσπερ γὰρ ὁ πατὴρ ἔχει ζωὴν ἐν ἑαυτῷ, οὕτως καὶ τῷ υἱῷ ἔδωκεν ζωὴν ἔχειν ἐν ἑαυτῷ.

5:27 καὶ ἐξουσίαν ἔδωκεν αὐτῷ κρίσιν ποιεῖν, ὅτι υἱὸς ἀνθρώπου ἐστίν.

5:28 μὴ θαυμάζετε τοῦτο, ὅτι ἔρχεται ὥρα ἐν ᾗ πάντες οἱ ἐν τοῖς μνημείοις ἀκούσουσιν τῆς φωνῆς αὐτοῦ

5:29 καὶ ἐκπορεύσονται οἱ τὰ ἀγαθὰ ποιήσαντες εἰς ἀνάστασιν ζωῆς, οἱ δὲ τὰ φαῦλα πράξαντες εἰς ἀνάστασιν κρίσεως.

5:30 Οὐ δύναμαι ἐγὼ ποιεῖν ἀπ᾽ ἐμαυτοῦ οὐδέν· καθὼς ἀκούω κρίνω, καὶ ἡ κρίσις ἡ ἐμὴ δικαία ἐστίν, ὅτι οὐ ζητῶ τὸ θέλημα τὸ ἐμὸν ἀλλὰ τὸ θέλημα τοῦ πέμψαντός με.

5:26 For as the Father has life in himself, so he has also given to the Son to have life in himself. [n. 782]

5:27 And he has given him power to do judgment, because he is the Son of man. [n. 784]

5:28 Do not wonder at this; for the hour is coming in which all who are in the graves will hear the voice of the Son of God. [n. 787]

5:29 And they who have done good things shall come forth to the resurrection of life; but they who have done evil, to the resurrection of judgment. [n. 792]

5:30 I cannot do anything of myself; as I hear, so I judge: and my judgment is just, because I am not seeking my own will, but the will of him who sent me. [n. 794]

---

781. Supra ostendit Dominus se habere potestatem vivificativam et iudiciariam, et explicavit utramque per effectum, hic manifestat quomodo utraque potestas sibi competat, et

primo ostendit hoc de potestate vivificativa;

secundo de potestate iudiciaria, ibi **et potestatem dedit ei iudicium facere**.

782. Dicit ergo primo: dico quod sicut Pater suscitat mortuos ita et ego, et qui audit verbum meum, habet vitam aeternam: et hoc ideo habeo, quia **sicut Pater habet vitam in semetipso, sic et Filio dedit habere vitam in semetipso**.

Circa quod sciendum est, quod aliqui vivunt, sed non habent vitam in semetipsis sicut Paulus Gal. II, 20: *quod autem nunc vivo, in fide Filii Dei vivo*. Et iterum: *vivo ego, iam non ego, vivit vero in me Christus*. Vivebat ergo, sed non in semetipso, sed in alio per quem vivebat; sicut et corpus vivit, sed non habet vitam in semetipso, sed in anima per quam vivit. Illud ergo in semetipso vitam habet, quod habet vitam essentialem non participatam, idest quod ipsum est vita. In quolibet autem genere rerum, quod est per essentiam, est causa eorum quae sunt per participationem, sicut ignis est causa omnium ignitorum. Quod ergo est per essentiam vita, est causa et principium omnis vitae in viventibus. Et ideo ad hoc quod aliquod sit principium vitae requiritur quod sit per essentiam vita. Et ideo congrue manifestat Dominus se

781. Above, our Lord showed that he had the power to give life and to judge; and he explained each by its effect. Here he shows how each of these powers belongs to him.

First, he shows this with respect to his life-giving power.

Second, with respect to his power to judge, at **and he has given him power to do judgment**.

782. So he says, first: I say that as the Father raises the dead, so I do also; and anyone who hears my word has eternal life. And I possess this because, **as the Father has life in himself, so he has given to the Son to have life in himself**.

Apropos of this, we should note that some who live do not have life in themselves: as Paul, *I am living by faith in the Son of God* (Gal 2:20); and again in the same place: *it is not I who now live, but Christ lives in me*. Thus he lived, yet not in himself, but in another through whom he lived: as a body lives, although it does not have life in itself, but in a soul through which it lives. So that has life in itself which has an essential, non-participated life, i.e., that which is itself life. Now in every genus of things, that which is something through its essence is the cause of those things that are it by participation, as fire is the cause of all things afire. And so, that which is life through its essence, is the cause and principle of all life in living things. Accordingly, if something is to be a principle of life, it must be life through its essence. And so our Lord fittingly shows that he is the principle of

totius vitae principium, dicens se habere vitam in seme-tipso, idest per essentiam, cum dicit *sicut Pater habet vitam in semetipso*, idest sicut est vivens per essentiam, ita et Filius. Ideo sicut Pater est causa vitae, ita Filius suus.

Ostendit autem aequalitatem Filii ad Patrem, cum dicit *sicut Pater habet vitam in semetipso*; et distinctionem, cum dicit *dedit Filio*. Sunt enim aequales in vita Pater et Filius; sed distinguuntur, quia Pater dat, Filius accipit.

Nec est intelligendum, quod Filius a Patre dante accipiat vitam, quasi praeexistat eam non habens, sicut in istis inferioribus materia prima existens accipit formam, et subiectum subiicitur accidenti: quia nihil in Filio praeexistens est acceptioni vitae. Nam, sicut Hilarius dicit, *Filius nihil habet nisi natum*, idest quod per nativitatem accepit. Et cum sit ipsa vita, ideo intelligendum est *dedit Filio vitam*, idest, produxit Filium vitam. Sicut si dicatur: mens dat verbo vitam, non quasi verbum praeexistat et postea vitam recipiat, sed quia produxit verbum in eadem vita qua ipsa vivit.

783. Destruuntur autem per haec verba tres errores, secundum Hilarium. Primo Arianorum, qui dicentes Filium minorem Patre, coacti sunt per hoc quod supra dictum est *quaecumque Pater fecerit, haec et Filius facit*, dicere, quod Filius sit aequalis Patri in virtute; sed tamen adhuc negant eum esse aequalem sibi in natura. Sed ecce quod etiam in hoc confutantur, per hoc quod dicitur *sicut Pater habet vitam in semetipso, sic dedit et Filio vitam habere in semetipso*. Nam cum vita pertineat ad naturam, si Filius habet vitam in semetipso sicut et Pater, manifestum est quod tenet in se originis suae indivisibilem et aequalem cum Patre naturam.

Secundus error eorum, quantum ad hoc quod negabant Filii coaeternitatem ad Patrem, dicentes, Filium ex tempore incepisse: quod destruitur inquantum dicit *Filius vitam habet in semetipso*. Nam in omnibus viventibus quorum generatio est in tempore, semper est invenire aliquid quod aliquando fuit non vivens; sed in Filio quidquid est, est ipsa vita et ideo sic accepit ipsam vitam, quod vitam habet in semetipso, ut semper fuerit vivens.

Tertio per hoc quod dicit *dedit*, destruitur error Sabellii negantis distinctionem personarum. Si enim Pater vitam dedit Filio, manifestum est quod alius est Pater qui dedit, et alius Filius qui accepit.

784. Consequenter cum dicit *et potestatem dedit ei iudicium facere*, manifestat se habere iudiciariam potestatem, et

primo manifestat suam potestatem iudiciariam;

all life by saying that he has life in himself, i.e., through his essence, when he says: *as the Father has life in himself*, i.e., as he is living through his essence, so does the Son. Therefore, as the Father is the cause of life, so also is his Son.

Further, he shows the equality of the Son to the Father when he says, *for as the Father has life in himself*; and he shows their distinction when he says, *he has also given to the Son*. For the Father and the Son are equal in life; but they are distinct, because the Father gives, and the Son receives.

However, we should not understand this to mean that the Son receives life from the Father as if the Son first existed without having life, as in lower things a first matter, already existing, receives a form, and as a subject receives accidents: because in the Son there is nothing that exists prior to the reception of life. For as Hilary says: *the Son has nothing unless it is begotten*, i.e., nothing but what he receives through his birth. And since the Father is life itself, the meaning of, *he has also given to the Son to have life in himself*, is that the Father produced the Son as living. As if one were to say: the mind gives life to the word, not as though the word existed and then receives life, but because the mind produces the word in the same life by which it lives.

783. According to Hilary, this passage destroys three heresies. First, that of the Arians, who said that the Son is inferior to the Father. They were forced by what was stated earlier, that is, *for whatever he does, these the Son also does in like manner* (John 5:19), to say that the Son is equal to the Father in power; but they still denied that the Son is equal to the Father in nature. But now, this too is refuted by this statement, namely, *for as the Father has life in himself, so he has also given to the Son to have life in himself*. For since life pertains to the nature, if the Son has life in himself as does the Father, it is clear that he has in himself, by his very origin, a nature indivisible from and equal to that of the Father.

The second error is also Arian: their denial that the Son is coeternal with the Father, when they say that the Son began to exist in time. This is destroyed when he says, *the Son has life in himself*. For in all living things whose generation occurs in time, it is always possible to find something that at some time or other was not living. But in the Son, whatever is, is life itself. Consequently, he so received life itself that he has life in himself, so as always to have been living.

Third, by saying, *he has given*, he destroys the error of Sabellius, who denied the distinction of persons. For if the Father gave life to the Son, it is obvious that the Father, who gave it, is other than the Son, who received it.

784. Then, at *and he has given him power to do judgment*, he makes it clear that he has the power to judge.

First, he reveals his judiciary power.

secundo rationem dictorum assignat, ibi *non possum ego a me facere quidquam*.

Circa primum duo facit.

Primo ponit potestatis iudiciariae originem;

secundo ostendit iudicii aequitatem, ibi *et procedent qui bona fecerunt, in resurrectionem vitae*.

785. Circa primum notandum est, quod hoc quod dicit *potestatem dedit ei*, potest legi dupliciter. Uno modo secundum Chrysostomum, alio modo secundum Augustinum.

786. Si autem legatur secundum Chrysostomum, tunc haec pars dividitur in duas. Primo proponit iudiciariae potestatis derivationem; secundo excludit dubitationem, ibi *quia Filius hominis est*.

Sciendum est autem, quod haec littera sic punctatur secundum Chrysostomum: *potestatem dedit ei iudicium facere*, postea resumitur *quia Filius hominis est, nolite mirari hoc*. Et huius punctationis ratio est, quia Paulus Samosatenus, quidam antiquus haereticus, qui sicut et Photinus dicebat Christum purum hominem esse, et initium sumpsisse ex Virgine, punctabat sic: *potestatem dedit ei iudicium facere, quia Filius hominis est*, et postea resumitur: *nolite mirari hoc, quia venit hora* etc., quasi intelligens per hoc quod ideo necesse fuit dari potestatem iudiciariam Christo, *quia Filius hominis est*, idest purus homo, cui ex se non convenit iudicare homines. Et ideo oportet quod si iudicat alios, sibi detur potestas iudicandi.

Sed hoc, secundum Chrysostomum, non potest stare, quia nullam convenientiam habet quod dicitur. Si enim ideo suscepit potestatem iudiciariam, quia homo est, tunc pari ratione, cum cuilibet homini conveniat iudiciaria potestas per humanam naturam, non plus competet Christo quam aliis hominibus.

Non ergo sic legendum est; sed dicendum, quod quia est ineffabilis Dei Filius, propterea et iudex est. Et hoc est quod dicit: non solum dedit ei Pater quod vivificat; sed etiam *potestatem dedit ei*, per aeternam generationem, *iudicium facere*, sicut per eam dedit ei vitam habere in semetipso; Act. X, 42: *hic est qui constitutus est a Deo iudex vivorum et mortuorum*. Dubitationem excludit cum dicit *nolite mirari hoc*: et primo movet eam; secundo excludit, ibi, *quia venit hora* etc.

787. Dubitatio autem oriebatur in cordibus Iudaeorum, quia aestimantes Christum nihil plus esse quam purum hominem, ea vero, quae dicebantur de eo, erant supra hominem, et etiam supra angelum, mirabantur cum audirent. Et ideo dicit *nolite mirari hoc*, scilicet quod dixi, quod Filius vivificat mortuos et habet iudiciariam

Second, he gives a reason for what he has said, at *I cannot do anything of myself*.

As to the first he does two things.

First, he indicates the origin of his judiciary power.

Second, he shows that his judgment is just, at *and they who have done good things will come forth to the resurrection of life*.

785. With regard to the first, we should note that his statement, *he has given him the power*, can be understood in two ways. One way is that of Augustine; the other is that of Chrysostom.

786. If we understand it as Chrysostom does, then this section is divided into two parts. First, he reveals the origin of his judiciary power. Second, he settles a difficulty, at *because he is the Son of man*.

Chrysostom punctuates this section in the following way: *he gave him the power to do judgment*. And then a new sentence begins: *because he is the Son of man, do not wonder at this*. The reason for this punctuation is that Paul of Samosata, an early heretic, who like Photius said that Christ was only a man and took his origin from the Virgin, punctuated it as: *he gave him the power to do judgment because he is the Son of man*. And then he began a new sentence: *do not wonder at this, for the hour is coming*. It was as if he thought that it was necessary for judiciary power to be given to Christ *because he is the Son of man*, that is, a mere man, who, of himself, cannot judge men. And so, if Christ is to judge others, he must be given the power to judge.

But this, according to Chrysostom, cannot stand, because it is not at all in agreement with what is stated. For if it is because he is a man that he receives judiciary power, then for the same reason, since it would belong to every man to have judiciary power in virtue of his human nature, it would not belong to Christ any more than to other men.

So we should not understand it this way. Rather, we should say that because Christ is the ineffable Son of God, he is on that account also judge. And this is what he says: the Father not only give him the power to give life, but also *he has given him the power*, through eternal generation, *to do judgment*, just as he gave him, through eternal generation, to have life in himself: *he is the one appointed by God to be the judge of the living and of the dead* (Acts 10:42). He settles a difficulty when he says, *do not wonder at this*. First, he mentions the difficulty. Second, he clears it up, at *the hour is coming in which all who are in the graves will hear the voice of the Son of God*.

787. The difficulty arose in the hearts of the Jews and they were surprised because while they thought that Christ was no more than a man, he was saying things about himself that surpassed man and even the angels. So he says, *do not wonder at this*, that is, that I have said that the Son gives life to the dead and has the power to judge precisely

potestatem, propter hoc *quia Filius hominis est*. Et de hoc mirabantur, quia purum hominem aestimantes, videbant in eo facta divina; Matth. VIII, 27: *mirabantur omnes dicentes: qualis est hic, quia venti et mare obediunt ei?* Et subdit causam quare non mirentur, quia scilicet ipse idem qui est Filius hominis, est Filius Dei.

Et licet, secundum Chrysostomum, non exprimatur ista propositio, scilicet quod idem est Filius hominis qui est Filius Dei, ponit tamen Dominus illud ex quo propositio illa de necessitate sequitur: sicut videmus, quod syllogizantes in doctrinis frequenter non proponunt intentum principaliter, sed illud ex quo de necessitate sequitur. Et ideo Dominus non dicit quod ipse est Filius Dei, sed quod Filius hominis talis est quod ad vocem eius suscitantur omnes mortui: ex quo necessario sequitur quod sit Filius Dei, nam suscitare mortuos est opus proprium Dei. Et ideo dicit *nolite mirari, quia venit hora in qua omnes qui in monumentis sunt, audient vocem Filii Dei*. Sed non dicit et nunc est, ut supra dixit; neque quia ista *hora nunc non est*. Similiter hic dicit *omnes*, quod non dixerat supra: quia in prima resurrectione aliquos tantum resuscitavit, scilicet Lazarum, Filium viduae, et puellam; sed tunc in futura resurrectione, quae erit tempore iudicii, *omnes qui in monumentis sunt audient vocem Filii Dei*, et resurgent; Ezech. c. XXXVII, 12: *aperiam tumulos vestros, et educam vos de sepulcris vestris*.

788. Secundum autem Augustinum, loquitur sic punctando: *potestatem dedit ei iudicium facere, quia Filius hominis est*, et postea subditur *nolite mirari hoc*. Et secundum hoc dividitur in duas partes. In prima enim tangitur collatio iudiciariae potestatis facta Filio hominis; secundo manifestatur per maioris potestatis collationem, ibi *nolite mirari hoc*.

789. Circa primum sciendum est, secundum Augustinum, quod supra locutus est de resurrectione animarum, quae fit per Filium Dei; hic vero loquitur de resurrectione corporum, quae fit per Filium hominis. Et quia universalis resurrectio corporum futura est tempore iudicii, ideo hic praemittit de iudicio, dicens: *potestatem dedit ei*, scilicet Christo, *iudicium facere*, et hoc quia *Filius hominis est*, idest secundum humanam naturam. Unde et post resurrectionem dicit, Matth. ult., c. 18: *data est mihi omnis potestas in caelo et in terra*.

Est autem data iudiciaria potestas Christo secundum quod homo, propter tria. Primo ut ab omnibus videretur: necesse est enim iudicem a iudicandis videri. Iudicabuntur autem boni et mali, et boni quidem Christum videbunt secundum divinitatem et humanitatem; mali autem eum secundum divinitatem videre non poterunt, quia haec visio est beatitudo sanctorum, nec videtur nisi a mundis corde, ut dicitur Matth. V, 8: *beati mundo corde, quoniam ipsi Deum videbunt*. Et ideo ut videatur in

because he is the Son of man. They were surprised because, although they thought he was only a man, they saw that he accomplished divine effects: *what kind of man is this, for the sea and winds obey him?* (Matt 8:27). And he gives a reason why they should not be surprised, which is, because he who is the Son of man is the Son of God.

Although, as Chrysostom says, it is not said explicitly that the Son of man is the Son of God, our Lord lays down the premises from which this statement necessarily follows: just as we notice that those who use syllogisms in their teaching do not express their main conclusion, but only that from which it follows with necessity. So our Lord does not say that he is the Son of God, but that the Son of man is such that at his voice all the dead will rise. From this it necessarily follows that he is the Son of God: for it is a proper effect of God to raise the dead. Thus he says, *do not wonder at this, for the hour is coming when all who are in the graves will hear the voice of the Son of God*. But he does not say of this hour, as he said above, *and now is* (John 5:25). Again, here he says, *all*, which he did not say above: because at the first resurrection he raised only some, as Lazarus, the widow's son and the young girl; but at the future resurrection, at the time of judgment, *all who are in the graves will hear the voice of the Son of God*, and will rise. *I will open your graves, and lead you out of your tombs* (Ezek 37:12).

788. Augustine punctuates this passage in the following way. *And he gave him the power to do judgment, because he is the Son of man*. And then a new sentence follows: *do not wonder at this*. In this interpretation there are two parts. The first concerns the power to judge granted to the Son of man. In the second, the granting of an even greater power is made clear, at *do not wonder at this*.

789. As to the first we should note that, according to the mind of Augustine, he spoke above of the resurrection of souls, which is accomplished through the Son of God, but here he is speaking of the resurrection of bodies, which is accomplished through the Son of man. And because the general resurrection of bodies will take place at the time of judgment, he mentions the judgment first, in saying, *and he gave him*, i.e., Christ, *the power to do judgment*, and this, because *he is the Son of man*, i.e., according to his human nature. Thus it is also after the resurrection that he says: *all power has been given to me, in heaven and on earth* (Matt 28:18).

There are three reasons why judiciary power has been given to Christ as man. First, in order that he might be seen by all: for it is necessary that a judge be seen by all who are to be judged. Now both the good and the wicked will be judged. And the good will see Christ in his divinity and in his humanity; while the wicked will not be able to see him in his divinity, because this vision is the happiness of the saints and is seen only by the pure in heart: *happy are the pure in heart, for they will see God* (Matt 5:8). And so,

iudicio non solum a bonis, sed etiam a malis, iudicabit in forma humana; Apoc. I, 7: *videbit eum omnis oculus, et qui eum pupugerunt.* Secundo, quia per humilitatem passionis promeruit gloriam exaltationis. Unde sicut ille qui mortuus est, resurrexit, ita forma illa iudicabit quae iudicata est, et sedebit iudex in iudicio hominum qui stetit sub iudice homine; damnabit vere reos qui factus est falso reus, ut dicit Augustinus libro *de Verbis Domini.* Iob XXXVI, c. 17: *causa tua quasi impii iudicata est; sed iudicium causamque recipies.* Tertio ad insinuandum iudicis clementiam. Quod homo iudicetur a Deo, videtur valde terribile: *horrendum est enim incidere in manus Dei viventis,* ut dicitur Hebr. X, 31; sed quod homo iudicem habeat hominem, confidentiam praebet: et ideo ut iudicis experiaris clementiam, hominem habebis iudicem; Hebr. IV, 15: *non habemus pontificem qui non possit compati infirmitatibus nostris.*

Sic ergo **dedit potestatem** Christo, **iudicium facere, quia Filius hominis est.**

790. Sed hoc quidem **nolite mirari**, quia maiorem potestatem contulit ei, scilicet resuscitandi mortuos; unde dicit: **quia venit hora**, scilicet novissima, quae erit in fine mundi; Ez. VII, 7: *venit tempus, prope est dies occisionis; in qua omnes qui in monumentis sunt audient vocem Filii Dei.* Supra autem non dixit *omnes*, quia ibi loquebatur de resurrectione spirituali, secundum quam non omnes in primo adventu resurrexerunt; quia II Thess. III, 2, dicitur: *non enim omnium est fides.* Hic vero loquitur de resurrectione corporum secundum quam omnes resurgemus, I Cor. XV, 20 ss. sed addit **qui in monumentis sunt**, quod supra non dixerat: quia animae non sunt in monumentis, sed corpora, quorum tunc resurrectio erit. **Omnes** ergo **qui in monumentis sunt, audient vocem Filii Dei**. Vox ista erit sensibile signum Filii Dei, ad quam omnes suscitabuntur; I Thess. IV, 15: *Dominus veniet in iussu Archangeli, et in tuba Dei.* Et simile habetur I Cor. XV, 52, Matth. XXV, 6: *media nocte clamor factus est.* Quae quidem vox habebit virtutem ex divinitate Christi; Ps. LXVII, 34: *dabit voci suae vocem virtutis.*

791. Quia ergo Augustinus dicit, quod resurrectio corporum fit per Verbum carnem factum, resurrectio animarum per Verbum, ut dictum est supra; ideo quaerendum est quomodo hoc intelligatur. Aut enim subintelligitur de causa prima, aut de causa meritoria. Si quidem de causa prima, constat quod divinitas Christi est causa corporalis et spiritualis resurrectionis, idest corporum et animarum, secundum illud Deut. XXXII, 39: *ego occidam, et ego vivere faciam.* Si vero de causa meritoria, tunc humanitas Christi est causa utriusque resurrectionis:

in order that Christ can be seen at the judgment not only by the good, but also by the wicked, he will judge in human form: *every eye will see him, and all who pierced him* (Rev 1:7). Second, because by the self-abasement of his passion he merited the glory of an exaltation. Thus, just as he who died arose, so that form which was judged, will judge, and he who stood before a human judge will preside at the judgment of men. He who was falsely found guilty will condemn the truly guilty, as Augustine remarks in his work, *The Sayings of the Lord. Your cause has been judged as that of the wicked; but cause and judgment you will recover* (Job 36:17). Third, Christ as man was given judiciary power to suggest the compassion of the judge. For it is very terrifying for a man to be judged by God: *it is a terrible thing to fall into the hands of the living God* (Heb 10:31); but it produces confidence for a man to have another man as his judge. Accordingly, so you can experience the compassion of your judge, you will have a man as judge: *we do not have a high priest who cannot have compassion on our weakness* (Heb 4:15).

Thus, **he has given him**, Christ, **power to do judgment, because he is the Son of man**.

790. Do not wonder at this, for he has given him a greater power, that is, the power to raise the dead. Thus he says, **for the hour is coming**, that is, the last hour at the end of the world: *the time has come, the day of slaughter is near* (Ezek 7:7), when all those burried in tombs will hear the voice of the Son of God. Above he did not say *all*, because there he was speaking of the spiritual resurrection, in which all did not rise at his first coming, for we read: *all do not have faith* (2 Thess 3:2). But here he is speaking of the resurrection of the body, and all will rise in this way (1 Cor 15:20). He adds, **all who are in the graves**, which he had not mentioned above, because only bodies, not souls, are in tombs, and it is the resurrection of bodies that will then take place. **All** therefore **who are in the graves will hear the voice of the Son of God**. This voice will be a sense perceptible sign of the Son of God, at whose sound all will be raised: *the Lord will come with the cry of the archangel and with the trumpet of God* (1 Thess 4:15); we find the same in the epistle to the Corinthians (1 Cor 15:52); and: *there was a cry at midnight* (Matt 25:6). This voice will derive its power from the divinity of Christ: *he will make his voice a powerful voice* (Ps 67:34).

791. As we saw, Augustine says that the resurrection of the body will be accomplished through the Word made flesh, but the resurrection of the soul is accomplished through the Word. One may wonder how to understand this: whether we are talking about a first cause or a meritorious cause. If we are referring to a first cause, then it is clear that the divinity of Christ is the cause of the corporal and spiritual resurrection, i.e., of the resurrection of bodies and of souls, according to: *I will kill, and I will bring to life again* (Deut 32:39). But if we are referring to a meritorious cause,

quia per mysteria quae in carne Christi completa sunt, reparamur non solum quantum ad corpora ad vitam incorruptibilem, sed etiam quantum ad animas ad vitam spiritualem; Rom. IV, 25: *traditus est propter nostras iniquitates, et resurrexit propter iustificationem nostram.* Non ergo videtur verum quod dicit Augustinus.

Sed dicendum, quod Augustinus loquitur de causa exemplari et de causa qua illud quod vivificatur, conformatur vivificatori: nam omne illud quod per aliud vivit, conformatur ei per quod vivit. Resurrectio autem animarum non est per hoc quod animae conformantur humanitati Christi, sed Verbo, quia vita animae est per solum Verbum; et ideo dicit animarum resurrectionem fieri per Verbum. Resurrectio vero corporum erit per hoc quod corpora nostra conformabuntur corpori Christi per vitam gloriae, videlicet per claritatem corporum; secundum illud Phil. III, v. 21: *reformabit corpus humilitatis nostrae, configuratum corpori claritatis suae.* Et secundum hoc dicit resurrectionem corporum fieri per Verbum carnem factum.

792. Consequenter cum dicit *et procedent qui bona fecerunt, in resurrectionem vitae*, ostendit aequalitatem iudicii, quia boni praemiabuntur, unde dicit *procedent qui bona fecerunt, in resurrectione vitae*, idest ad hoc quod vivant in aeterna gloria, mali autem damnabuntur; unde dicit *qui vero mala egerunt, in resurrectionem iudicii*; idest, resurgent in condemnationem; Matth. XXV, 46: *ibunt hi in supplicium aeternum*, scilicet mali, *iusti autem in vitam aeternam*; Dan. XII, 2: *multi ex his qui in terrae pulvere dormierant, resurgent: quidam quidem ad vitam, alii autem ad opprobrium sempiternum, ut videant semper.*

793. Et nota, quod supra loquens de resurrectione animarum, dicit: *qui audierint vivent*, hic vero dicit quod *procedent*; et hoc propter malos, qui vadunt in condemnationem: nam vita eorum non est dicenda vita, sed potius mors aeterna.

Similiter etiam supra fecit mentionem de fide tantum, dicens: *qui verbum meum audit, et credit ei qui misit me, habet vitam aeternam, et in iudicium non venit*; hic ne credas solam fidem sine operibus ad salutem sufficere, facit mentionem de omnibus operibus, dicens *qui bona fecerunt, procedent in resurrectionem vitae*; quasi dicat: non qui credit tantum, sed qui cum fide bona operatur, *procedit in resurrectionem vitae*; Iac. II, 26: *fides sine operibus mortua est.*

794. Consequenter cum dicit *non possum ego a me ipso facere quidquam*, assignat rationem praemissorum. Duo autem praemiserat, scilicet originem potestatis, et aequitatem iudicii; et ideo utriusque causam assignat.

then it is the humanity of Christ which is the cause of both resurrections: because through the mysteries accomplished in the flesh of Christ we are restored not only to an incorruptible life in our bodies, but also to a spiritual life in our souls: *he was put to death on account of our sins, and he rose for our justification* (Rom 4:25). Accordingly, what Augustine says does not seem to be true.

I answer that Augustine is speaking of the exemplary cause and of that cause by which that which is brought to life is made conformable to that which brings it to life: for everything that lives through another is conformed to that through which it lives. Now the resurrection of souls does not consist in souls being conformed to the humanity of Christ, but to the Word, because the life of the soul is through the Word alone; and so he says that the resurrection of souls takes place through the Word. But the resurrection of the body will consist in our bodies being conformed to the body of Christ through the life of glory, that is, through the glory of our bodies, according to: *he will change our lowly body so it is like his glorious body* (Phil 3:21). And it is from this point of view that he says that the resurrection of the body will take place through the Word made flesh.

792. Then, at *and they who have done good things will come forth to the resurrection of life*, he shows the justness of his judgment: because the good will be rewarded, and so he says, *and they who have done good things will come forth to the resurrection of life*, i.e., to living in eternal glory; but the wicked will be damned, and so he says, *they who have done evil, to the resurrection of judgment*, i.e., they will rise for condemnation: *these*, the wicked, *will go into everlasting punishment; but the just will go to eternal life* (Matt 25:46); *many of those who sleep in the dust of the earth will awake: some to an everlasting life, and others to everlasting shame* (Dan 12:2).

793. Note than when he was speaking above of the resurrection of souls, he said, *they who hear will live* (John 5:25); but here he says, *will come forth*. He says this because of the wicked, who will be condemned: for their life should not be called a life, but rather an eternal death.

Again, above he mentioned only faith, saying, *he who hears my word, and believes him who sent me, has eternal life; and he will not come into judment* (John 5:24). But here he mentions works, so that we do not think that faith alone, without works, is sufficient for salvation, saying: *and they who have done good things will come forth to the resurrection of life*. As if to say: those will come forth to a resurrection of life who do not just believe, but who have accomplished good works along with their faith: *faith without works is dead* (Jas 2:26).

794. Then when he says, *I cannot do anything of myself*, he gives the reason for what he has just said. Now he had spoken of two things: the origin of his power, and the justness of his judgment. Consequently, he mentions the reason for each.

Primo de primo.

Secundo de secundo, ibi *et iudicium meum iustum est*.

795. Sciendum est autem circa primum, quod hoc quod dicit **non possum ego a meipso facere quidquam**, potest dupliciter legi, etiam secundum Augustinum.

Primo ut referatur ad Filium hominis hoc modo: tu dicis quod habes potestatem resuscitandi mortuos, quia Filius hominis est, sed numquid hoc est tibi inquantum tu es Filius hominis? Non, quia **non possum ego a meipso facere quidquam; sed sicut audio, iudico**. Non dicit, *sicut video*, secundum quod supra dixerat: **Filius non potest a se facere quidquam, nisi quod viderit Patrem facientem**, sed dicit **sicut audio**: nam audire idem est in hoc loco quod obedire. Obedire autem pertinet ad illum cui fit imperium. Imperare autem pertinet ad superiorem. Et ideo, quia Christus inquantum homo minor est Patre, dicit *sicut audio*; idest, secundum quod inspiratur a Deo in anima mea. De ipso auditu dicit Ps. LXXXIV, 9: *audiam quid loquatur in me Dominus Deus*. Supra autem, quia loquebatur de se secundum quod est Verbum Dei, dixit **viderit**.

796. Consequenter cum dicit **et iudicium meum iustum est**, manifestat aequitatem iudicii. Dixerat enim: **et procedent qui bona fecerunt in resurrectionem vitae**, sed posset aliquis dicere: numquid faciet gratiam aliquibus minus puniendo, et plus remunerando? Ideo respondet quod non, dicens: quia **iudicium meum verum est**. Cuius ratio est **quia non quaero voluntatem meam, sed voluntatem eius qui misit me**.

In Domino enim Iesu Christo sunt duae voluntates. Una divina quam habet eamdem cum Patre; alia humana, quae est sibi propria, sicut est proprium eius esse hominem. Voluntas humana fertur in bonum proprium; sed in Christo per rectitudinem rationis regebatur et regulabatur, ut semper in omnibus voluntati divinae conformaretur; et ideo dicit: non quaero implere **voluntatem meam** propriam, quae, quantum in se est, inclinatur ad bonum proprium, sed **voluntatem eius qui misit me**, Patris; Ps. XXXIX, 9: *ut facerem voluntatem tuam, Deus meus, volui*; Matth. XXVI, 39: *non quod ego volo, sed quod tu vis*.

Et si quidem diligenter attenditur, Dominus veram rationem assignat iusti iudicii, dicens **quia non quaero voluntatem meam**: non enim iudicium alicuius est iniustum, quando procedit ab eo secundum regulam legis; voluntas autem divina regula est, et lex voluntatis creatae: et ideo voluntas creata, et ratio quae regulatur secundum regulam divinae voluntatis, iusta est, et iudicium eius iustum.

797. Secundo vero exponitur ut referatur ad Filium Dei, et manet eadem divisio quae prius posita est. Dixit ergo Christus inquantum Verbum manifestans originem

First concerning the first.

second concerning the second, at **and my judgment is just**.

795. The first point, when he says, **I cannot do anything of myself**, can be understood in two ways, even according to Augustine.

First, as referring to the Son of man in this manner: You say that you have the power to raise the dead because you are the Son of man. But do you have this power precisely because you are the Son of man? No, because **I cannot do anything of myself; as I hear, so I judge**. He does not say, *as I see*, as he said above; **the Son cannot do anything of himself, but only what he sees the Father doing** (John 5:19). But he does say, **as I hear**: for in this context to hear is the same as to obey. Now to obey belongs to one who receives a command, while to command pertains to one who is superior. Accordingly, because Christ, as man, is inferior to the Father, he says, as I hear it, i.e., as infused into my soul by God. We read of this kind of hearing elsewhere: *I will hear what the Lord God says in me* (Ps 84:9). But above he said **sees** (John 5:19), because he was then speaking of himself as the Word of God.

796. Then when he says, **and my judgment is just**, he shows the justness of his judgment. For he had said: **and they who have done good will come forth to the resurrection of life**. But some might say: Will he be partial and uneven when he punishes and rewards? So he answers: no, saying: **my judgment is just**; and the reason is because **I am not seeking my own will, but the will of him who sent me**.

For there are two wills in our Lord Jesus Christ: one is a divine will, which is the same as the will of the Father; the other is a human will, which is proper to himself, just as it is proper to him to be a man. A human will is borne to its own good; but in Christ it was ruled and regulated by right reason, so that it would always be conformed in all things to the divine will. Accordingly he says: **I am not seeking my own will**, which as such is inclined to its own good, but **the will of him who sent me**, that is, of the Father: *I have desired to do your will, my God* (Ps 39:9); *not as I will, but as you will* (Matt 26:39).

If this is carefully considered, the Lord is assigning the true nature of a just judgment, saying: **because I am not seeking my own will**. For one's judgment is just when it is passed according to the norm of law. But the divine will is the norm and the law of the created will. And so, the created will, and the reason, which is regulated according to the norm of the divine will, is just, and its judgment is just.

797. Second, it is explained as referring to the Son of God; and then the aforesaid division still remains the same. Thus Christ, as the divine Word showing the origin

suae potestatis: *non possum ego a me facere quidquam*, eo modo sicut supra dixit: *non potest Filius a se facere quidquam*; nam suum facere, et suum posse, est suum esse; esse autem est ei ab alio, scilicet a Patre: et ideo, sicut non est a se, ita a se non potest facere quidquam; infra VIII, 28: *a meipso facio nihil*.

Hoc autem quod dicit *sed sicut audio, iudico*, eodem modo exponendum est sicut illud supra *nisi quod viderit Patrem facientem*.

Nos enim scientiam, seu cognitionem aliquam accipimus per visum et per auditum (isti enim duo sensus maxime serviunt disciplinae), sed quia in nobis alius est visus, alius auditus; ideo aliter accipimus scientiam per visum, quia inveniendo; aliter per auditum, quia addiscendo. In Filio vero Dei idem est auditus et visus; et ideo sive dicatur *audit*, sive *vidit*, idem significat secundum acceptionem scientiae. Et quia iudicium in qualibet natura intellectuali ex scientia procedit, signanter dicit *sicut audio, iudico*; idest, sicut cognitionem simul cum esse a Patre accepi, sic iudico; infra XV, 15: *omnia quae audivi a Patre meo, nota feci vobis*.

798. Manifestans vero iudicii aequitatem, dicit *et iudicium meum verum est*. Cuius ratio est, *quia non quaero voluntatem meam*.

Sed numquid non est eadem voluntas Patris et Filii?

Sed dicendum, quod eadem quidem voluntas est utriusque, sed tamen Pater non habet voluntatem ab alio, Filius vero habet ab alio, scilicet a Patre. Sic ergo Filius implet voluntatem suam ut alterius, idest ab alio habens; Pater vero ut suam, idest non habens ab alio: et ideo dicit *non quaero voluntatem meam*, quae sit mihi originaliter a me ipso, sed quae est mihi ab alio, scilicet a Patre.

of his power, says: *I cannot do anything of myself*, in the way he said above, *the Son cannot do anything of himself* (John 5:19). For his very doing and his power are his being; but being in him is from another, that is, from his Father. And so, just as he is not of himself, so of himself he cannot do anything: *I do nothing of myself* (John 8:28).

His statement, *as I hear, so I judge*, is explained as his previous statement, *but only what he sees the Father doing* (John 5:19).

For we acquire science or any knowledge through sight and hearing (for these two senses are those most used in learning). But because sight and hearing are different is us, we acquire knowledge in one way through sight, that is, by discovering things, and in a different way through hearing, that is, by being taught. But in the Son of God, sight and hearing are the same; thus, when he says either *sees* or *hears*, the meaning is the same so far as the acquisition of knowledge is concerned. And because judgment in any intelletual nature comes from knowledge, he says significantly, *as I hear, so I judge*, i.e., as I have acquired knowledge together with being from the Father, so I judge: *all I have heard from my Father I have made known to you* (John 15:15).

798. Showing the justness of his judgment he says: and *my judgment is just*: the reason being, *I am not seeking my own will*.

But do not the Father and the Son have the same will?

I answer that the Father and the Son do have the same will, but the Father does not have his will from another, whereas the Son does have his will from another, i.e., from the Father. Thus the Son accomplishes his own will as from another, i.e., as having it from another; but the Father accomplishes his will as his own, i.e., not having it from another. Thus he says: *I am not seeking my own will*, that is, such as would be mine if it originated from myself, but my will, as being from another, that is from the Father.

Lecture 6

5:31 Si ego testimonium perhibeo de meipso, testimonium meum non est verum. [n. 800]

5:32 Alius est qui testimonium perhibet de me: et scio quia verum est testimonium eius quod perhibet de me. [n. 801]

5:33 Vos misistis ad Ioannem: et testimonium perhibuit veritati. [n. 806]

5:34 Ego autem non ab homine testimonium accipio; Sed haec dico, ut vos salvi sitis. [n. 807]

5:35 Ille erat lucerna ardens et lucens. Vos autem voluistis ad horam exultare in luce eius. [n. 811]

5:36 Ego autem habeo testimonium maius Ioanne. Opera enim quae dedit mihi Pater ut perficiam ea, ipsa opera quae ego facio, testimonium perhibent de me, quia Pater misit me. [n. 814]

5:37 Et qui misit me Pater, ipse testimonium perhibuit de me: neque vocem eius unquam audistis, neque speciem eius vidistis: [n. 818]

5:38 et verbum eius non habetis in vobis manens, quia quem misit ille, huic vos non creditis. [n. 820]

5:39 Scrutamini Scripturas, quia vos putatis in ipsis vitam aeternam habere: et illae sunt, quae testimonium perhibent de me, [n. 822]

5:40 et non vultis venire ad me, ut vitam habeatis. [n. 824]

5:31 Ἐὰν ἐγὼ μαρτυρῶ περὶ ἐμαυτοῦ, ἡ μαρτυρία μου οὐκ ἔστιν ἀληθής·

5:32 ἄλλος ἐστὶν ὁ μαρτυρῶν περὶ ἐμοῦ, καὶ οἶδα ὅτι ἀληθής ἐστιν ἡ μαρτυρία ἣν μαρτυρεῖ περὶ ἐμοῦ.

5:33 ὑμεῖς ἀπεστάλκατε πρὸς Ἰωάννην, καὶ μεμαρτύρηκεν τῇ ἀληθείᾳ·

5:34 ἐγὼ δὲ οὐ παρὰ ἀνθρώπου τὴν μαρτυρίαν λαμβάνω, ἀλλὰ ταῦτα λέγω ἵνα ὑμεῖς σωθῆτε.

5:35 ἐκεῖνος ἦν ὁ λύχνος ὁ καιόμενος καὶ φαίνων, ὑμεῖς δὲ ἠθελήσατε ἀγαλλιαθῆναι πρὸς ὥραν ἐν τῷ φωτὶ αὐτοῦ.

5:36 Ἐγὼ δὲ ἔχω τὴν μαρτυρίαν μείζω τοῦ Ἰωάννου· τὰ γὰρ ἔργα ἃ δέδωκέν μοι ὁ πατὴρ ἵνα τελειώσω αὐτά, αὐτὰ τὰ ἔργα ἃ ποιῶ μαρτυρεῖ περὶ ἐμοῦ ὅτι ὁ πατήρ με ἀπέσταλκεν.

5:37 καὶ ὁ πέμψας με πατὴρ ἐκεῖνος μεμαρτύρηκεν περὶ ἐμοῦ. οὔτε φωνὴν αὐτοῦ πώποτε ἀκηκόατε οὔτε εἶδος αὐτοῦ ἑωράκατε,

5:38 καὶ τὸν λόγον αὐτοῦ οὐκ ἔχετε ἐν ὑμῖν μένοντα, ὅτι ὃν ἀπέστειλεν ἐκεῖνος, τούτῳ ὑμεῖς οὐ πιστεύετε.

5:39 ἐραυνᾶτε τὰς γραφάς, ὅτι ὑμεῖς δοκεῖτε ἐν αὐταῖς ζωὴν αἰώνιον ἔχειν· καὶ ἐκεῖναί εἰσιν αἱ μαρτυροῦσαι περὶ ἐμοῦ·

5:40 καὶ οὐ θέλετε ἐλθεῖν πρός με ἵνα ζωὴν ἔχητε.

5:31 If I bear witness about myself, my witness is not true. [n. 800]

5:32 There is another who bears witness to me, and I know what he holds about me is true testimony. [n. 801]

5:33 You sent to John, and he gave testimony to the truth. [n. 806]

5:34 I do not receive testimony from man, but I say these things so that you may be saved. [n. 807]

5:35 He was a burning and a shining light, and you were willing for a time to rejoice in his light. [n. 811]

5:36 But I have a greater testimony than that of John. For the works that the Father has given to me that I might perform them, the works themselves, which I do, give testimony about me, that the Father has sent me. [n. 814]

5:37 And the Father himself who has sent me has given testimony about me: neither have you ever heard his voice or seen his image. [n. 818]

5:38 And you do not have his word abiding in you: because he whom he has sent, you do not believe. [n. 820]

5:39 Search the Scriptures, for you think them to have eternal life, and they give testimony about me. [n. 822]

5:40 And you do not want to come to me so that you may have life. [n. 824]

---

799. Posita doctrina circa potestatem Filii vivificativam, hic consequenter confirmat eam, et

primo confirmat quae de excellentia potestatis suae dixerat, per multiplex testimonium;

secundo redarguit eorum tarditatem ad credendum, ibi *claritatem ab hominibus non accipio* etc.

Circa primum duo facit.

Primo ponit necessitatem inducendi testimonium;

799. Having given us the teaching on the life-giving power of the Son, he now confirms it.

First, he confirms, with several testimonies, what he had said about the excellence of his power.

In the second place, he reproves them because of their slowness to believe, at *I do not receive glory from men* (John 5:41).

He does two things about the first.

First, he states why there was a need to resort to such testimonies.

secundo inducit ipsa testimonia, ibi *alius est qui testimonium perhibet de me.*

800. Necessitas testimonii inducendi erat ex parte Iudaeorum qui ei non credebant; et propter hoc dicit *si ego testimonium perhibeo de meipso, testimonium meum non est verum.*

Sed admirationis praebet materiam quod dicitur. Nam sicut Dominus de se, infra XIV, v. 6 dicit, *ipse est veritas*: quomodo ergo testimonium eius non est verum? Si veritas est, cui credetur si veritati non creditur?

Et ideo dicendum, secundum Chrysostomum, quod Dominus hic de se loquitur secundum aliorum opinionem, ut sit sensus: *si ego testimonium perhibeo de meipso, testimonium meum non est verum*, quantum ad vestram reputationem, qui non accipitis illud quod de me dico, nisi per aliud testimonium confirmetur; infra VIII, 13: *tu de teipso testimonium dicis: testimonium tuum non est verum.*

801. Consequenter cum dicit *alius est qui testimonium perhibet de me*, inducit testimonia, et

primo testimonium humanum;

secundo testimonium divinum, ibi *ego autem habeo testimonium maius Ioanne.*

Circa primum duo facit.

Primo inducit testimonium Ioannis;

secundo rationem testimonii assignat, ibi *ego autem non ab homine testimonium accipio.*

Circa primum duo facit.

Primo inducit testimonium;

secundo commendat eius testimonium, ibi *scio quia verum est testimonium eius.*

802. Testem inducit dicens *alius est qui testimonium perhibet de me.* Iste alius, secundum Chrysostomum, est Ioannes Baptista, de quo dicitur supra I, 6: *fuit homo missus a Deo, cui nomen erat Ioannes: hic venit in testimonium ut testimonium perhiberet de lumine.*

803. Testificationem autem commendat cum dicit *et scio quia verum est testimonium eius.* Et hoc a duobus.

Primo a veritate;

secundo ab auctoritate: quia fuit ab eis requisitum, ibi *vos misistis ad Ioannem.*

804. A veritate quidem commendat eius testimonium, dicens *et scio*, idest pro certo experior, *quia verum est testimonium eius*, scilicet Ioannis, *quod perhibet de me.* Sic enim pater eius Zacharias prophetavit de eo, Lc. I, 76: *praeibis enim ante faciem Domini parare vias eius, ad dandam scientiam salutis plebi eius.*

Constat autem quod testimonium mendax non est salutiferum, sed mortiferum: quia mendacium est causa mortis; Sap. 2, 11: *os quod mentitur occidit animam.* Si ergo testimonium Ioannis est ad dandam scientiam salutis plebi eius, verum est testimonium eius.

Second, he invokes the testimonies, at *there is another who bears witness to me.*

800. The need to appeal to testimony arose because the Jews did not believe in him; for this reason he says: *if I bear witness about myself, my witness is not true.*

Some may find this statement puzzling: for if our Lord says of himself, *I am the truth* (John 14:6), how can his testimony not be valid? If he is the truth, in whom shall one believe if the truth itself is not believed in?

We may answer, according to Chrysostom, that our Lord is speaking here of himself from the point of view of the opinion of others, so that his meaning is: *if I bear witness about myself, my witness is not true*, so far as your outlook is concerned, because you do not accept what I say about myself unless it is confirmed by other testimony: *you give testimony about yourself, but your testimony is not true* (John 8:13).

801. Next, at *there is another who bears witness to me*, he presents these testimonies:

first, a human testimony;

second, a divine testimony, at *but I have a greater testimony than that of John.*

He does two things about the first.

First, he mentions the testimony of John;

second, he tells why this testimony was given, at *I do not receive testimony from man.*

With respect to the first he does two things.

First, he brings in the testimony;

second, he commends it, at *I know what he holds about me is true testimony.*

802. He brings on the witness when he says: *there is another who bears witness to me.* This is, in the opinion of Chrysostom, John the Baptist, of whom we read above: *there was a man sent from God, whose name was John. He came as a witness, that he might bear witness to the light* (John 1:6–7).

803. He commends John's testimony at *and I know what he holds about me is true testimony*, on two grounds:

first, because of its truth;

second, because of its authority, for the Jews had sought it: *you sent to John.*

804. He commends his testimony because of its truth, saying: *and I know*, from certain experience, *what he*, that is, John, *holds about me is true testimony*. His father, Zechariah, had prophesied this of him: *you will go before the face of the Lord to prepare his way, to give his people a knowledge of salvation* (Luke 1:76).

Now it is obvious that false testimony is not a testimony that saves, because lying is a cause of death: *a lying mouth kills the soul* (Wis 1:11). Therefore, if John's testimony was for the purpose of giving knowledge of salvation to his people, his testimony is true.

805. Sed secundum Glossam aliter: *si testimonium perhibeo de meipso, testimonium meum non est verum*. Supra Christus locutus est de se secundum quod Deus, hic vero loquitur secundum quod homo. Et est sensus: *si ego*, homo scilicet, *testimonium de me perhibeo*, scilicet absque Deo, idest quod Deus Pater non perhibeat; tunc sequitur quod *testimonium meum non est verum*: nam verbum humanum nisi a Deo fulciatur, nihil veritatis habet, secundum illud Rom. c. III, 4: *est autem Deus verax, omnis autem homo mendax*. Unde si intelligamus Christum ut hominem a deitate separatum et ei non conformem, et in essentia eius mendacium invenitur et in verbis; infra VIII, v. 14: *si ego testimonium perhibeo de me ipso, verum testimonium meum*; infra: *quia solus non sum; sed ego, et qui misit me Pater*. Et ideo quia non erat solus, sed cum Patre, verum est testimonium eius.

Unde ut ostendat testimonium eius veritatem non habere ex eius humanitate secundum se, sed inquantum est coniuncta divinitati et Verbo Dei, dicit *sed alius est qui testimonium perhibet de me*: non Ioannes, sed Pater, secundum istam expositionem: quia si testimonium Christi hominis de se non est verum et efficax, multo minus esset efficax testimonium Ioannis. Non ergo certificatur testimonio Ioannis, sed testimonio Patris: unde iste alius qui testimonium perhibet, intelligitur Pater. *Et scio quia verum est testimonium eius*, nam ipse veritas est; I Io. I, v. 5: *Deus lux est*, idest veritas, *et tenebrae*, mendacii, *in eo non sunt ullae*.

Sed prima expositio, quae Chrysostomi est, magis est litteralis.

806. Commendat etiam testimonium Ioannis ab auctoritate, quia fuit requisitum a Iudaeis, cum dicit *vos misistis ad Ioannem*; quasi diceret: scio quia verum est testimonium eius nec vos debetis illud repudiare, quia propter magnam auctoritatem qua erat apud vos Ioannes requisivistis ab eo testimonium de me; quod non fecissetis, si eum dignum fide non opinaremini. Supra I, 19: *miserunt Iudaei ab Ierosolymis sacerdotes et Levitas ad Ioannem*. Et Ioannes tunc *testimonium perhibuit*, non sibi, sed veritati, idest mihi. Sicut amicus veritatis veritati Christo testimonium perhibuit; supra I, 20: *confessus est, et non negavit: confessus est, quia non sum ego Christus*.

807. Consequenter cum dicit *ego autem non ab homine testimonium accipio*, assignat rationem testimonii Ioannis inducti, et

primo excludit rationem opinatam;

secundo asserit veram, ibi *sed hoc dico ut vos salvi sitis*.

808. Ratio autem inducti testimonii posset ab aliquo credi esse certificatio de Christo, propter eius insufficientiam; et ideo hanc excludit dicens *ego autem non ab homine testimonium accipio*.

805. The Gloss has a different explanation of this: *if I bear witness about myself, my witness is not true*. For above, Christ was referring to himself as God, but here he is referring to himself as a man. And the meaning is: *if I*, namely, a man, *bear witness to myself*, i.e., apart from God, that is, which God the Father does not certify, then it follows that *my witness is not true*, for human speech has no truth unless it is supported by God, according to: *God is true, but every man is a liar* (Rom 3:4). Thus, if we take Christ as a man separated from the Deity and not in conformity with it, we find a lie both in his essence and in his words: *although I give testimony about myself, my testimony is true* (John 8:14); *I am not alone, because the Father is with me* (John 16:32). And so, because he was not alone but with the Father, his testimony is true.

Accordingly, to show that his testimony is true, not in virtue of his humanity considered in itself, but in so far as it is united to his divinity and to the Word of God, he says, *there is another who bears witness to me*: not John, but the Father, according to this explanation. Because if the testimony of Christ as man is not of itself true and productive, much less is the testimony of John. Therefore, the testimony of Christ is not verified by the testimony of John, but by the testimony of the Father. So this someone else who testifies is understood to be the Father. *And I know what he holds about me is true testimony*: God is light, i.e., truth, *and in him there is no darkness*, i.e., lie (1 John 1:5).

The first explanation, which is that given by Chrysostom, is nearer to the letter of the text.

806. He also commends the testimony of John by reason of its authority, because it was sought after by the Jews, saying: *you sent to John*. As if to say: I know that his testimony is true and you should not reject it, because the great authority John enjoyed among you led you to seek his testimony about me; and you would not have done this if you did not think that he was worthy of belief: *the Jews sent priests and Levites from Jerusalem to him* (John 1:19). And on this occasion, *John bore witness*, not to himself, but to the truth, i.e., to me. As a friend of the truth, he bore testimony to the truth, which is Christ: *he declared openly, and did not deny, and stated clearly, I am not the Christ* (John 1:20).

807. Then, at *but I do not receive testimony from man*, he gives the reason why an appeal was made to the testimony of John.

First, he excludes a supposed reason.

Next, he presents the true reason, at *but I say these things so that you may be saved*.

808. Someone might think that John's testimony was brought in to assure them about Christ, on the ground that Christ's own testimony was not sufficient. He excludes this reason when he says, *I do not receive testimony from man*.

Ubi sciendum est, quod in scientiis aliquando probatur aliquid per minus notum secundum se, sed magis notum quoad nos; aliquando per aliquid magis notum secundum se et simpliciter. Sicut in hoc loco debebat quidem probari quod Christus esset Deus: et licet veritas Christi esset magis nota secundum se et simpliciter, nihilominus tamen probatur testimonio Ioannis, quod quantum ad Iudaeos magis notum erat. Et ideo Christus secundum se testimonio Ioannis non indigebat, et hoc est quod dicit *testimonium ab homine non accipio*.

809. Sed contra hoc videtur, quia Is. c. XLIII, 10: *vos testes mei, dicit Dominus*; Act. I, 8: *eritis mihi testes in omni Iudaea et Samaria, et usque ad ultimum terrae*. Quomodo ergo dicit hic *testimonium ab homine non accipio*?

Sed dicendum, quod hoc dupliciter potest intelligi. Uno modo ut sit sensus *non accipio ab homine testimonium*, quasi sim illo tantum contentus; sed habeo maius testimonium, scilicet divinum; I Cor. IV, 3: *mihi autem pro minimo est ut a vobis iudicer*; Ier. XVII, 16: *diem hominis*, idest claritatem humanam, *non desideravi: tu scis*. Alio modo *testimonium ab homine non accipio*, inquantum scilicet testificans est homo, sed inquantum est illustratus a Deo ad testificandum; supra I, 6: *fuit homo missus a Deo, cui nomen erat Ioannes*; I Thess. II, 6: *non quaerentes ab hominibus gloriam*; infra VIII, v. 50: *ego gloriam meam non quaero*. Sic ergo accipio testimonium Ioannis, non inquantum fuit homo, sed inquantum missus et illustratus a Deo ad testificandum. Tertio modo, et melius, *ego testimonium non accipio ab homine*, idest, testimonio humano; quantum ex me est, auctoritatem non accipio ab aliquo, sed a Deo, qui demonstrat me clarum.

810. Consequenter cum dicit *sed haec dico ut vos salvi sitis*, asserit rationem veram, quae erat ipsorum salus: et primo ponit rationem; secundo exponit eam.

Ratio vero inducti testimonii erat, ut Iudaei credentes Christo, testimonio Ioannis salvarentur; et ideo dicit: *non accipio testimonium* Ioannis propter me, *sed haec dico ut salvi sitis*; I Tim. II, 4: *vult omnes homines salvos fieri*; et ibid. I, 15: *Christus Iesus venit in hunc mundum peccatores salvos facere*.

811. Et exponit quod dicit *salvi sitis*: quia scilicet induco testimonium a vobis acceptatum.

Et ideo cum dicit *ille erat lucerna ardens et lucens*, ponit Ioannis acceptationem: et primo ponit quod Ioannes fuit testis secundum se acceptus; secundo quomodo fuit acceptatus apud eos, ibi *vos autem voluistis ad horam exultare in luce eius*.

Here we should note that sometimes in the sciences a thing is proved by something else which is more evident to us, but which is less evident in itself; and at other times a thing is proved by something else which is more evident in itself and absolutely. Now, in this case, the issue is to prove that Christ is God. And, although the truth of Christ is, in itself and absolutely, more evident, yet it is proved by the testimony of John, which was better known to the Jews. So Christ, of himself, did not have any need of John's testimony; and this is what he says: *I do not receive testimony from man*.

809. But this seems to conflict with: *you are my witnesses, said the Lord* (Isa 40:10); and with *you will be my witnesses in Jerusalem and in all of Judea and Samaria, and to the remotest part of the world* (Acts 1:8). So how can he say: *I do not receive testimony from man*?

This can be understood in two ways. In the first way, the sense is: *I do not receive testimony from man*, as relying on it alone; but I have stronger testimony, that is, divine testimony: *for me, it does not matter much if I am judged by you* (1 Cor 4:3); *you know that I have not desired the day of man*, i.e., human glory (Jer 17:16). Another interpretation is: *I do not receive testimony from man*, insofar as the one giving witness is a man, but insofar as he is enlightened by God in order to testify: *there was a man sent by God, whose name was John* (John 1:6); *we did not seek glory from men* (1 Thess 2:6); *I do not seek my own glory* (John 8:50). And so I receive the testimony of John not just as a man, but insofar as he was sent and enlightened by God in order to testify. A third explanation, and a better one, is: *I do not receive testimony from man*, i.e., human testimony. As far as I am concerned, I receive my authority from no one but God, who proves that I am great.

810. Next, at *but I say these things so that you may be saved*, he gives the real reason for appealing to John's testimony. First, he states the reason. Second, he explains it.

The reason for appealing to this testimony was so that the Jews might be saved by believing in Christ, and this because of John's testimony. Thus he says: *I do not receive testimony* from John for my sake, *but I say these things so that you may be saved*: he desires the salvation of all men (1 Tim 2:4). *Christ came into this world to save sinners* (1 Tim 1:15).

811. He explains his statement, *so that you may be saved*: that is, because I am appealing to testimony you have accepted.

And at *he was a burning and a shining light*, so he mentions that John was accepted by them: He was a lamp, blazing and burning brightly. First, he states that John was a witness accepted on his own merits. Second, he mentions to what degree he was accepted by them, at *and you were willing for a time to rejoice in his light*.

812. Quod autem Ioannes fuerit secundum se acceptus testis, ostendit per tria quae eum perficiebant. Primum pertinet ad conditionem naturae et hoc cum dicit *ille erat lucerna*; secundum pertinet ad perfectionem affectus, quia *ardens*; tertium ad perfectionem intellectus, quia *lucens*.

Erat ergo in natura perfectus, quia *lucerna*, idest, illustratus gratia, et illustratus luce Verbi Dei. Differt enim lucerna a luce: nam lux est quae per seipsam lucet; lucerna vero quae non per se lucet, sed per participationem lucet. Lux autem vera Christus est, ut dicitur supra I, 9: *erat lux vera quae illuminat omnem hominem*. Ioannes autem lux non erat, ut ibidem dicitur, sed lucerna, quia illustratus erat, *ut testimonium perhiberet de lumine*, ducendo ad Christum: de qua lucerna dicitur in Ps. CXXXI, 17: *paravi lucernam Christo meo*.

Sed erat in eo affectus ardens et fervens, unde dicit *ardens*. Nam aliqui sunt lucernae solum quantum ad officium, sed quantum ad affectum sunt extinctae: nam sicut lucerna lucere non potest nisi igne accendatur, ita lucerna spiritualis non lucet nisi prius ardeat et inflammetur igne caritatis. Et ideo ardor praemittitur illustrationi, quia per ardorem caritatis datur cognitio veritatis; infra XIV, 23: *si quis diligit me, sermonem meum servabit, et Pater meus diliget eum: et ad eum veniemus, et mansionem apud eum faciemus*; infra XV, 15: *vos autem dixi amicos, quia omnia quae audivi a Patre meo, nota feci vobis*. Eccli. II, 20: *qui timetis Deum, diligite illum, et illuminabuntur corda vestra*. Nam ignis duo habet: scilicet quod ardet et splendet.

Ardor autem ignis significat dilectionem propter tria. Primo quidem, quia ignis inter omnia corpora est magis activus: sic et ardor caritatis, intantum quod nihil eius impetum ferre potest, secundum illud II Cor. V, v. 14: *caritas Christi urget nos*. Secundo, quia sicut ignis per hoc quod est maxime sensitivus, facit multum aestuare, ita et caritas aestum causat quousque homo consequatur intentum; Cant. ult., 6: *lampades eius lampades ignis atque flammarum*. Tertio sicut ignis est sursum ductivus, ita et caritas, intantum quod coniungit nos Deo; I Io. IV, 16: *qui manet in caritate, in Deo manet, et Deus in eo*.

Erat etiam intellectus *lucens*. Primo quidem per veritatis cognitionem interius; Is. c. LVIII, 11: *implebit splendoribus* idest, splendere faciet. Secundo per praedicationem exterius; Phili II, 15: *inter quos lucetis tamquam luminaria in mundo, verbum vitae continentes*. Tertio per bonorum operum manifestationem; Matth. V, 16: *sic luceat lux vestra coram hominibus, ut videant opera vestra bona*.

812. Three things perfected John and show that he was a witness accepted in his own right. The first concerns the condition of his nature, and he refers to this when he says, *he was a light*. The second concerns the perfection of his love, because he was a *blazing* lamp. The third is related to the perfection of his understanding, because he was a lamp that was *burning* brightly.

John was perfect in his nature because he was a *light*, i.e., enriched by grace and illumined by the light of the Word of God. Now a lamp differs from a light: for a light radiates light of itself, but a lamp does not give light of itself, but by participating in the light. Now the true light is Christ: *he was the true light, which enlightens every man coming into this world* (John 1:9). John, however, was not a light, as we read in the same place, but a lamp, because he was enlightened *that he might bear witness to the light* (John 1:8), by leading men to Christ. We read of this lamp: *I have prepared a lamp for my anointed* (Ps 131:17).

Further, he was blazing and impassioned in his affections, so he says, *burning*. For some people are lamps only as to their office or rank, but they are snuffed out in their affections: for as a lamp cannot give light unless there is a fire burning within it, so a spiritual lamp does not give any light unless it is first set ablaze and burns with the fire of love. Therefore, to be ablaze comes first, and the giving of light depends on it, because knowledge of the truth is given due to the burning of love: *if any one love me, he will keep my word, and my Father will love him, and we will come to him, and will make our abode with him* (John 14:23); and *I have called you friends: because all I have heard from my Father, I have made known to you* (John 15:15); *you who fear the Lord, love him, and your hearts will be enlightened* (Sir 2:20). The two characteristics of fire are that it both burns and shines.

Its burning signifies love for three reasons. First, because fire is the most active of all bodies; so too is the warmth of charity, so much so that nothing can withstand its force: *the love of Christ spurs us on* (2 Cor 5:14). Second, because just as fire, because it is very volatile, causes great unrest, so also this love of charity makes a person restless until he achieves his objective: *its light is fire and flame* (Song 8:6). Third, just as fire is inclined to move upward, so too is charity; so much so that it joins us to God: *he who abides in love abides in God, and God in him* (1 John 4:16).

Finally, John had an intellect that was *burning* brightly. First, it was bright within, because of his knowledge of the truth: *the Lord will fill your soul with brightness*, i.e., he will make it shine (Isa 58:11). Second, it was bright without, because of his preaching: *you will shine in the world among them like stars, containing the word of life* (Phil 2:15). Third, it was bright because it manifested good works: *let your light so shine before men that they may see your good works* (Matt 5:16).

813. Quia ergo sic Ioannes acceptabilis erat secundum se, quia erat lucerna non extincta, sed ardens, non tenebrosa, sed lucens; dignus est quod et apud vos acceptaretur. Quod quidem ita fuit, quia *vos voluistis exultare ad horam in luce eius*. Et congrue exultationem luci adiungit: quia in illo homo exultat in quo maxime delectatur; nihil autem est in rebus corporalibus delectabilius luce, secundum illud Eccle. XI, 7: *delectabile est oculis videre solem*.

Dicit autem *voluistis exultare*, quiescendo et ponendo in eo finem, credendo eum Christum; sed tamen *ad horam*, quia in hoc fuistis instabiles: nam videntes Ioannem homines ad alium, non ad se, ducere, aversi estis ab eo. Unde dicitur Matth. XXI, 32 quod Iudaei non crediderunt in Ioannem. Sunt enim de illis de quibus dicitur Matth. XIII, quia *ad tempus credunt*.

814. Consequenter cum dicit *ego autem habeo testimonium maius Ioanne*, ponit testimonium divinum, et

primo inducit eius magnitudinem;

secundo prosequitur de ipso, ibi *opera quae dedit mihi Pater ut perficiam ea* etc.

815. Dicit ergo primo: dico quod ego quantum est ex me, non accipio ab homine testimonium, sed propter vos; nam *ego habeo testimonium maius Ioanne*, scilicet Dei, quod est maius testimonium quam Ioannis; I Io. ult., 9: *si testimonium hominum accipimus, testimonium Dei maius est*. Maius, inquam, propter maiorem auctoritatem, maiorem cognitionem, et infallibiliorem veritatem: nam Deus mentiri non potest. *Non est Deus ut homo, ut mentiatur*: Num. XXIII, 19.

816. Testimonium autem prosequitur cum dicit *opera enim quae dedit mihi Pater ut perficiam ea* etc. Tripliciter autem testificatus est Deus de Christo: scilicet per opera, per seipsum et per Scripturas, et ideo

primo ponit modum testificandi quantum ad opera miraculorum;

secundo modum testificandi per seipsum, ibi *et qui misit me Pater, ipse testimonium perhibuit*;

tertio per Scripturas, ibi *scrutamini Scripturas* etc.

817. Dicit ergo primo: *habeo aliud testimonium maius Ioanne*; et hoc quantum ad opera, quia *opera* miraculorum *quae dedit mihi Pater ut perficiam ea*.

Sciendum est enim, quod naturale est homini virtutem et naturas rerum ex earum actionibus cognoscere: et ideo convenienter Dominus per opera quae ipse facit, dicit se posse cognosci qualis sit. Cum ergo ipse propria virtute divina faceret, credendum erat in eo esse virtutem divinam; infra XV, 24: *si opera non fecissem in eis quae nemo alius fecit, peccatum non haberent*, scilicet infidelitatis. Et ideo ad sui cognitionem per opera sua

813. And so, because John was of himself so acceptable—for he was a lamp, not smothered out but blazing, not dark but burning brightly—he deserved to be accepted by you, as indeed he was, because *you were willing for a time to rejoice in his light*. He fittingly links their exulting or rejoicing with light; because a man rejoices most is that which most pleases him. And among physical things nothing is more pleasant than light, according to: *it is a delight for the eyes to see the sun* (Sir 11:7).

He says, *you were willing for a time to rejoice in his light*, i.e., you rested in John and put your end in him, thinking that he was the Messiah. But you did this only *for a time*, because you wavered on this; for when you saw that John was leading men to another, and not to himself, you turned away from him. Thus we read that the Jews did not believe in John (Matt 21:32). They belonged to that group referred to as believing *for a while* (Matt 13:21).

814. Then, at *but I have a greater testimony than that of John*, he presents the divine testimony.

First, he mentions its greatness;

and then he continues on to describe it, at *for the works that the Father has given to me*.

815. He says: I do not need proof from men for my sake, but for your sake, *but I have a greater testimony than that of John*, that is, the testimony of God, which is greater than the testimony of John: *if we receive the testimony of men, the testimony of God is greater* (1 John 5:9), it is greater, I say, because of its greater authority, greater knowledge, and infallible truth, for God cannot deceive: *God is not like man, a liar* (Num 23:19).

816. God bore witness to Christ at *for the works that the Father has given to me that I might perform them*, and this in three ways: by works, by himself, and by the Scriptures.

First, he mentions his witness as given by the working of miracles;

second, the way God gave witness by himself, at *and the Father himself who has sent me*;

third, the witness given through the Scriptures, at *search the Scriptures*.

817. He says first: *I have a greater testimony than that of John*, that is, my works, i.e., the working of miracles, *for the works that the Father has given to me that I might perform them*.

We should point out that it is natural for man to learn of the power and natures of things from their actions, and therefore our Lord fittingly says that the sort of person he is can be learned through the works he does. So, since he performed divine works by his own power, we should believe that he has divine power within him: *if I had not done among them the works that no other man has done, they would not have sin*, that is, the sin of unbelief (John 15:24).

ducit, dicens **opera quae dedit mihi**, in Verbo, **Pater**, per aeternam generationem dando mihi virtutem sibi aequalem. Vel **dedit mihi**, in conceptione, dando ut sim una persona Dei et hominis, **ut perficiam ea** idest, ut propria virtute faciam: quod dicit ad differentiam aliorum qui miracula faciunt non propria virtute, sed impetrando a Deo. Unde Petrus dicebat Act. III, 6: *in nomine Iesu Christi Nazareni surge*. Et ideo ipsi non perficiunt, sed Deus; Christus vero propria virtute ea perficiebat; infra XI, 43: *Lazare, veni foras*. Et ideo **opera quae ego facio, testimonium perhibent de me**; infra X, 38. **Si mihi non creditis, saltem operibus credite**.

Quod autem opera miraculorum sint testimonia Dei, dicitur Mc. ult., 20: *Domino cooperante, et sermonem confirmante sequentibus signis*.

818. Consequenter cum dicit **et qui misit me Pater, ipse testimonium perhibuit de me**, ponit secundum modum testificandi per ipsum Deum, et

primo ponit ipsum modum;

secundo ostendit eos huiusmodi non esse capaces, ibi **neque vocem eius unquam audistis** etc.

819. Dicit ergo: non solum opera quae dedit mihi Pater, testimonium perhibent de me, sed ipse **qui misit me, Pater, testimonium perhibuit de me**, in Iordane, quando fuit baptizatus, ut habetur Matth. IV, 5, et in monte, quando transfiguratus est, ut dicitur Matth. XVII, 5. Utrobique enim vox Patris audita est: *hic est Filius meus dilectus*. Et ideo credendum est ei, sicut vero et naturali Filio Dei; I Io. ult., 9: *hoc testimonium Dei, quod maius est, quia testificatus est de Filio suo*. Et sic, qui non credit eum esse Filium Dei, non credit Dei testimonio.

820. Sed posset aliquis dicere, quod Deus etiam aliis testimonium perhibuit per seipsum, sicut Moysi in monte, cum quo locutus est, cunctis audientibus; testimonium vero numquam audivimus, et ideo dicit Dominus, quod **neque vocem eius unquam audistis** etc.

Sed contra Deut. IV, 33, dicitur: *si factum est aliquando res huiuscemodi, ut audiret populus vocem Domini Dei loquentis de medio ignis, sicut tu audisti et vidisti*. Quid est ergo quod nunc dicit Christus **neque vocem eius unquam audistis**?

Respondeo, secundum Chrysostomum, quod Dominus eos in philosophica consideratione constituens, vult ostendere, quod Deus testificatur alicui dupliciter, scilicet sensibiliter et intelligibiliter.

Sensibiliter quidem, sicut per vocem sensibilem tantum; et hoc modo testificatus fuit Moysi in Monte Sinai; Deut. IV, 12: *vocem eius audistis, et formam penitus*

And so he leads them to a knowledge of himself by appealing to his works, saying, **the very works which have been given me**, in the Word, **Father** through an eternal generation, by giving me a power equal to his own. Or we could say, the very works which my Father has **given me**, in my conception, by making me one person who is both God and man, **that I might perform them**, i.e., by my own power. He says this to distinguish himself from those who do not perform miracles by their own power but have to obtain it as a favor from God; thus Peter says: *in the name of Jesus Christ of Nazareth: stand up* (Acts 3:6). Thus it was God, and not themselves, who accomplished these works; but Christ accomplished them by his own power: *Lazarus, come forth* (John 11:43). Accordingly, **the works themselves, which I do, give testimony about me**; as above: **even though you do not want to believe me, believe the works** (John 10:38).

We see that God bears witness by the working of miracles: *the Lord worked with them and confirmed the word by the signs that followed* (Mark 16:20).

818. Then, at **and the Father himself who has sent me has given testimony about me**, he presents the second way God bore witness to Christ, namely, by himself.

First, he mentions the way;

second, he shows that they were not able to receive this testimony, at **neither have you ever heard his voice or seen his image**.

819. He says: it is not only the works which my Father has given me to perform that bear witness to me, but **the Father himself who sent me has given testimony about me**: in the Jordan, when Christ was baptized (Matt 3:17); and on the mountain, when Christ was transfigured (Matt 17:5). For on both these occasions the voice of the Father was heard: *this is my beloved Son*. And so they should believe in Christ, as the true and natural Son of God: *this is the testimony of God: he has borne witness to his Son* (1 John 5:9). Consequently, anyone who does not believe that he is the Son of God, does not believe in the testimony of God.

820. Someone could say that God also gave testimony to others by himself: for example, to Moses, on the mountain, with whom God spoke while others were present. We, however, never heard his testimony, as the Lord says: **neither have you ever heard his voice**.

On the other hand, we read in (Deut 4:33): *did it ever happen before that the people heard the voice of God speaking from the midst of fire, as you heard, and have lived*? Then how can Christ say: **neither have you ever heard his voice**?

I reply, according to Chrysostom, that the Lord wishes to show those established in a philosophical frame of mind that God gives testimony to someone in two ways, namely, sensibly and intelligibly.

Sensibly, as by a sensible voice only; and in this way he gave witness to Moses on Mount Sinai: *you heard his voice, and saw no form at all* (Deut 4:12). Likewise, he gives

non vidistis. Item per sensibilem speciem, sicut apparuit Abrahae Gen. XXVI, et Is. VI, 1: *vidi Dominum sedentem supra solium excelsum et elevatum.* Sed tamen in istis visionibus nec vox corporalis nec figura Dei est sicut cuiusdam animalis, sed effective, inquantum a Deo formatur: nam cum Deus sit spiritus, neque vocem sensibilem de se emittit, nec figurari potest. Intelligibiliter autem testificatur inspirando in cordibus aliquorum quod credere debeant et tenere; Ps. LXXXIV, 9: *audiam quid loquatur in me Dominus Deus*; Osee II, v. 4: *ducam eam in solitudinem, et ibi loquar ad cor eius.*

Primo ergo testificationis capaces fuistis: nec mirum, quia non fuerunt Dei nisi effective, ut dictum est, voces illae et species. Sed non intelligibilis illius vocis. **Neque vocem eius unquam audistis** etc., idest participes eius non fuistis; infra VI, 45: **omnis qui audit a Patre et didicit, venit ad me.** Sed vos non venitis ad me; ergo **non audistis vocem eius, nec vidistis speciem eius**; idest non habuistis istud testimonium intelligibile, et ideo subdit **et verbum eius non habetis in vobis manens**; idest, non habetis verbum interius inspiratum. Et haec ratio est, **quia quem misit ille**, idest Pater, **huic vos non creditis.**

Verbum enim Dei ducit ad Christum: nam ipse Christus est naturale Dei Verbum. Omne autem verbum a Deo inspiratum, est quaedam participata similitudo illius. Cum ergo omnis similitudo participata ducat in suum principium, manifestum est quod omne verbum inspiratum a Deo ducit ad Christum. Et ideo, quia vos non ducimini ad me, non **habetis Verbum** Dei, inspiratum, **in vobis manens**; infra: qui non credit in Filium Dei, non habet vitam in se manentem. Et dicit **manens**, quia cum nullus sit quin aliquam veritatem habeat a Deo, illi tantum habent veritatem, et verbum in ipsis manens, quibus intantum cognitio proficit ut perducantur ad veri et naturalis Verbi cognitionem.

821. Vel per hoc quod dicit **neque vocem eius unquam audistis**, ostenditur triplex modus quo a Deo aliquid revelatur alicui. Quia vel per vocem sensibilem, et sic testificatus est Christo in Iordane et in monte, ut dictum est II Petri I, 16: *speculatores facti illius magnitudinis, voce lapsa de caelo a magnifica gloria.* Et hanc Iudaei non audierunt. Vel per visionem suae essentiae; et hanc revelat beatis. Et hanc speciem ipsi non viderunt, quia II Cor. V, 6: *quamdiu sumus in corpore, peregrinamur a Domino* etc. Vel per interius verbum inspirando; et hoc etiam ipsi non habebant.

testimony by a sensible form, as he appeared to Abraham (Gen 26), and to Isaiah: *I saw the Lord seated on a high and lofty throne* (Isa 6:1). However, in these visions, neither the audible voice nor the visible figure were like anything in the animal kingdom, except efficiently, in the sense that these were formed by God. For since God is a spirit, he neither emits audible sounds nor can he be portrayed as a figure. But he does bear testimony in an intelligible manner by inspiring in the hearts of certain persons what they ought to believe and to hold: *I will hear what the Lord God will speak within me* (Ps 84:9); *I will lead her into the wilderness and there I will speak to her heart* (Hos 2:14).

Now you were able to receive the testimony given in the first of these ways; and this is not surprising, because they were the words and image of God only efficiently, as was said. But they were not able to receive the testimony given in that intelligible voice; so he says: **neither have you ever heard his voice**, i.e., you were not among those who shared in it. *Everyone who has heard of the Father and has learned, comes to me* (John 6:45). But you do not come to me. Therefore, **neither have you ever heard his voice or seen his image**, i.e., you do not have his intelligible testimony. Hence he adds: and **you do not have his word abiding in you**, i.e., you do not have his word that is inwardly inspired. And the reason is, **because he whom he**, the Father, **has sent, you do not believe.**

For the word of God leads to Christ, since Christ himself is the natural Word of God. But every word inspired by God is a certain participated likeness of that Word. Therefore, since every participated likeness leads to its original, it is clear that every word inspired by God leads to Christ. And so, because you are not led to me, **and you do not have his word**, i.e., the inspired word of God, **abiding in you**; for he who does not believe in the Son of God does not have life abiding in him (John 3:36). He says **abiding**, because although there is no one who does not have some truth from God, they alone have the truth and the word abiding in them whose knowledge has progressed to the point where they have reached a knowledge of the true and natural Word.

821. Or we could say that, **neither have you ever heard his voice**, can be taken as showing the three ways in which God reveals things. This is done either by a sensible voice, as he bore witness to Christ in the Jordan and on the mountain: *we were eyewitnesses of his greatness. For he received honor and glory from God the Father, when a voice came from the heavens* (2 Pet 1:16). And the Jews did not hear this. Or, God reveals things through a vision of his essence, which he reveals to the blessed. And they did not see this, because *while we are in the body, we are absent from the Lord* (2 Cor 5:6). Third, it is accomplished by an interior word through an inspiration; and the Jews did not have this either.

822. Consequenter cum dicit *scrutamini Scripturas*, ponit tertium modum quo Deus testificatus est Christo per Scripturas, et

primo inducit Scripturarum testimonium;

secundo ostendit eos fructu huius testimonii non esse capaces, ibi *et non vultis venire ad me* etc.

823. Dicit ergo *scrutamini Scripturas*, quasi dicat: vos non habetis verbum Dei in cordibus vestris, sed in Scripturis; et ideo oportet vos illud alibi quaerere. Et ideo *scrutamini Scripturas*; scilicet Veteris Testamenti. Nam fides Christi in Veteri Testamento continebatur, sed non in superficie, quia in profundo obumbrata figura latebat; II Cor. III, 15: *usque in hodiernum diem ipsum velamen habentes*. Et ideo signanter dicit *scrutamini*, quasi in profundum quaeratis; Prov. II, 4: *si quaesieris eam quasi pecuniam, et sicut thesauros effoderis illam, tunc intelliges timorem Domini, et scientiam Dei invenies*; Ps. CXVIII, 69: *da mihi intellectum, et scrutabor mandata tua*.

Ratio autem scrutinii ex vestra opinione sumitur *quia putatis in eis*, scilicet Scripturis, *vitam aeternam habere*, ex hoc quod dicitur Ez. XVIII, 19: *qui fecerit iudicia mea, vita vivet*. Sed estis decepti; quia licet praecepta veteris legis vitalia sint, non tamen vitam habent in seipsis; sed intantum dicuntur vitalia inquantum ducunt ad me Christum; cum tamen vos utamini eis tamquam in se vitam habentibus: quod decepit vos. Nam *illae*, scilicet Scripturae, *sunt quae testimonium perhibent de me*; idest, intantum vitalia sunt inquantum ad meam cognitionem ducunt. Vel apertis prophetiis, sicut Is. VII, 14: *ecce virgo concipiet*, et iterum Deut. XVIII, v. 15: *prophetam suscitabit vobis Dominus Deus* etc. Unde dicitur Actor. X, 43: *huic omnes prophetae testimonium perhibent*. Vel operationibus prophetarum mysticis: unde dicitur Oseae XII, 10: *in manibus prophetarum assimilatus sum*. Vel in sacramentis et figuris; sicut est immolatio agni, et alia figuralia sacramenta legis; Hebr. X, 1: *umbram habens lex futurorum bonorum* etc. Et ideo, quia Scripturae Veteris Testamenti multipliciter testimonium perhibent de Christo, dicit Apostolus, Rom. I, 2: *quod ante promiserat per prophetas in Scripturis sanctis de Filio suo, qui factus est ei ex semine David secundum carnem*.

824. Sed fructum quem in Scripturis putatis habere, scilicet vitam aeternam, consequi non poteritis, quia testimoniis Scripturae de me non credentes, *non vultis venire ad me*; idest, non vultis credere mihi, in quem est fructus illarum Scripturarum, ut in me *vitam habeatis*, quam ego do credentibus in me; infra X, 28: *ego vitam aeternam do eis*; Eccli. IV, 12: *sapientia filiis suis vitam*

822. Then when he says, *search the Scriptures*, he gives the third way in which God bore witness to Christ, through the Scriptures.

First, he mentions the testimony of the Scriptures.

Second, he shows that they were not able to gather the fruit of this testimony, at *and you do not want to come to me so that you may have life*.

823. He says: *search the Scriptures*. As if to say: you do not have the word of God in your hearts, but in the Scriptures; therefore, you must seek for it elsewhere than in your hearts. Hence, *search the Scriptures*, that is, the Old Testament, for the faith of Christ was contained in the Old Testament, but not on the surface, for it lay hidden in its depths, under shadowy symbols: *even to this day, when Moses is read, a veil is over their hearts* (2 Cor 3:15). Thus he significantly says, *search*, probe into the depths: *if you search for her like money, and dig for her like a treasure, you will understand the fear of the Lord and will find the knowledge of God* (Prov 2:4); *give me understanding and I will search your commandments* (Ps 118:34).

The reason why you should search them I take from your own opinion, *for you think them to have eternal life*, since we read: *he who has kept my commands will live* (Ezek 18:19). But you are mistaken; because although the precepts of the old law are living, they do not contain life in themselves. They are said to be living only to the extent that they lead to me, the Christ. Yet you use them as though they contained life in themselves, and in this you are mistaken, for *they give testimony about me*, i.e., they are living to the extent that they lead to a knowledge of me. And they lead to a knowledge of me either by plain prophecies: *a virgin will conceive* (Isa 7:14); *the Lord your God will raise up a prophet for you* (Deut 18:15); *all the prophets bear witness to him* (Acts 10:43). The Scriptures also lead to a knowledge of Christ through the symbolic actions of the prophets; thus we read: *I have used resemblences in the ministry of the prophets* (Hos 12:10). Knowledge of Christ is also given in their sacraments and figures, as in the immolation of the lamb, and other symbolic sacraments of the law: *the law has only a shadow of the good things to come* (Heb 10:1). And so, because *the Scriptures of the Old Testament gave much testimony about Christ*, the Apostle says: *he promised the Good News before, through his prophets in the holy Scriptures; the Good News of his Son, a descendant of David in his human nature* (Rom 1:2).

824. The fruit which you think you have in the Scriptures, that is, eternal life, you will not be able to obtain, because in not believing the testimonies of the Scriptures about me, *and you do not want to not come to me*, i.e., you do not wish to believe in me, in whom the fruit of these Scriptures exists, in order that *you may have life* in me, the life which I give to those who believe in me: *I give them*

inspirat; Prov. VIII, 35: *qui me invenerit inveniet vitam, et hauriet salutem a Domino.*

eternal life (John 10:28); *wisdom infuses life into her children* (Sir 4:12); *he who finds me will find life, and will have salvation from the Lord* (Prov 8:35).

Lecture 7

5:41 **Claritatem ab hominibus non accipio,** [n. 826]

5:42 **sed cognovi vos, quia dilectionem Dei non habetis in vobis.** [n. 827]

5:43 **Ego veni in nomine Patris mei, et non accepistis me. Si alius venerit in nomine suo, illum accipietis.** [n. 829]

5:44 **Quomodo vos potestis credere, qui gloriam ab invicem accipitis, et gloriam quae a solo Deo est non quaeritis?** [n. 832]

5:45 **Nolite putare quia ego accusaturus sum vos apud Patrem: est qui accusat vos Moyses, in quo vos speratis.** [n. 833]

5:46 **Si enim crederetis Moysi, crederetis forsitan et mihi: de me enim ille scripsit.** [n. 836]

5:47 **Si autem illius litteris non creditis, quomodo verbis meis credetis?** [n. 837]

5:41 Δόξαν παρὰ ἀνθρώπων οὐ λαμβάνω,

5:42 ἀλλὰ ἔγνωκα ὑμᾶς ὅτι τὴν ἀγάπην τοῦ θεοῦ οὐκ ἔχετε ἐν ἑαυτοῖς.

5:43 ἐγὼ ἐλήλυθα ἐν τῷ ὀνόματι τοῦ πατρός μου, καὶ οὐ λαμβάνετέ με· ἐὰν ἄλλος ἔλθῃ ἐν τῷ ὀνόματι τῷ ἰδίῳ, ἐκεῖνον λήμψεσθε.

5:44 πῶς δύνασθε ὑμεῖς πιστεῦσαι δόξαν παρὰ ἀλλήλων λαμβάνοντες, καὶ τὴν δόξαν τὴν παρὰ τοῦ μόνου θεοῦ οὐ ζητεῖτε;

5:45 Μὴ δοκεῖτε ὅτι ἐγὼ κατηγορήσω ὑμῶν πρὸς τὸν πατέρα· ἔστιν ὁ κατηγορῶν ὑμῶν Μωϋσῆς, εἰς ὃν ὑμεῖς ἠλπίκατε.

5:46 εἰ γὰρ ἐπιστεύετε Μωϋσεῖ, ἐπιστεύετε ἂν ἐμοί· περὶ γὰρ ἐμοῦ ἐκεῖνος ἔγραψεν.

5:47 εἰ δὲ τοῖς ἐκείνου γράμμασιν οὐ πιστεύετε, πῶς τοῖς ἐμοῖς ῥήμασιν πιστεύσετε;

5:41 **I do not receive glory from men.** [n. 826]

5:42 **But I know you, that you do not have the love of God in you.** [n. 827]

5:43 **I have come in the name of my Father, and you do not receive me: if another shall come in his own name, you will receive him.** [n. 829]

5:44 **How are you able to believe, who receive glory from one another, and the glory that is from God alone, you do not seek?** [n. 832]

5:45 **Do not think that I will accuse you to the Father. There is one who accuses you, Moses, in whom you trust.** [n. 833]

5:46 **If you believed Moses, you would perhaps believe me also, for he wrote of me.** [n. 836]

5:47 **But if you do not believe his writings, how will you believe my words?** [n. 837]

---

825. Postquam Deus excellentiam suae potestatis confirmavit testimoniis hominum, Dei et Scripturarum, hic consequenter eorum tarditatem ad credendum redarguit.

Duplici autem occasione Iudaei persequebantur Christum: propter solutionem Sabbati, in quo videbatur contrarius legi; et quia dicebat se Dei Filium, in quo videbatur contrarius Deo. Unde propter reverentiam quam habebant ad Deum, et propter zelum quem habebant ad legem Moysi, persequebantur. Et ideo Dominus intendit ostendere quod non propter hoc eum persequebantur, sed propter contrarium. Unde

primo ostendit irreverentiam ipsorum ad Deum esse causam incredulitatis ipsorum;

secundo quod irreverentia, quam habebant ad Moysen, fuit causa incredulitatis ipsorum, ibi ***nolite putare quia ego accusaturus sum vos apud patrem***.

Circa primum duo facit.

Primo ponit irreverentiam ipsorum ad Deum;

secundo ostendit quod hoc sit causa incredulitatis ipsorum, ibi ***quomodo vos potestis credere, qui gloriam ab invicem accipitis?***

Circa primum duo facit.

Primo proponit eorum indevotionem ad Deum;

825. After God confirmed the greatness of his power by the testimonies of men, of God, and of the Scriptures, he here rebukes the Jews for being slow to believe.

Now the Jews persecuted Christ on two grounds: for breaking the Sabbath, by which he seemed to go against the law, and for saying that he is the Son of God, by which he seemed to go against God. Thus they persecuted him on account of their reverence for God and their zeal for the law. And so our Lord wishes to show that their persecution of him was really inspired not by these motives, but by contrary reasons.

He first shows that the cause of their unbelief was their lack of reverence for God.

Second, that another cause of their unbelief was their lack of reverence for Moses, at ***do not think that I will accuse you to the Father***.

As to the first he does two things.

First, he shows their irreverence for God.

Second, he shows that this is the cause of their unbelief, at ***how are you able to believe, who receive glory from one another?***

Concerning the first he does two things.

First, he mentions their lack of reverence for God.

secundo manifestat eam per signum, ibi *ego veni in nomine patris mei*.

Circa primum duo facit.

Primo excludit intentionem opinatam, quae ex verbis praemissis accipi posset;

secundo asserit veram, ibi *sed cognovi vos* etc.

826. Intentio opinata est, quod quia Dominus supra commemoraverat tot testimonia de seipso, scilicet Ioannis, Dei, et operum suorum, et Scripturarum, posset opinari a Iudaeis quod hoc fecerit quasi quaerens humanam gloriam. Contra hoc dicit *claritatem ab hominibus non accipio*; idest, laudem humanam non quaero. Non enim veni ut exemplum darem quaerendi gloriam hominum; I Thess. II, 6: *neque quaerentes ab hominibus gloriam: Deus testis est.* Vel *claritatem ab hominibus non accipio*, idest, claritate humana non indigeo, quia ab aeterno claritatem habeo apud Patrem; infra XVII, 5: *clarifica me Pater, claritate quam habui antequam mundus fieret.* Non enim veni clarificari ab hominibus, sed potius eos clarificare, cum a me omnis claritas procedat. Sap. c. VIII, 10: *habeo per hanc sapientiam claritatem.*

Dicitur autem Deus clarificari et gloriari ab hominibus, secundum illud Eccli. XLIII, v. 32: *glorificantes Deum quantumcumque potestis, praevalebit adhuc*, non ut ipse propter hoc gloriosior fiat, sed inquantum gloriosus apparet in nobis.

827. Non est ergo haec causa propositorum testimoniorum, sed alia est: quia *cognovi*, idest cognoscere feci, *quia non habetis dilectionem Dei in vobis*, quam habere vos fingitis, unde non propter Dei amorem me persequimini. Nam tunc propter Deum me persequeremini, si Deus et Scriptura non mihi testimonium perhiberent; sed ipse Deus mihi testatur et per opera, et per Scripturas, et per seipsum, ut dictum est; et ideo si Deum amaretis, oporteret ut sicut me abiicitis, ita ad me veniretis. Non ergo diligitis Deum.

Vel aliter *sed cognovi vos*, quasi dicat: non induxi huiusmodi testimonia, indigens vestra clarificatione; sed scio, et condoleo vobis errantibus, qui non diligitis Deum, et volo vos reducere ad viam veritatis; infra XV, 24: *nunc autem et viderunt, et oderunt et me et Patrem*; Ps. LXXIII, 23: *superbia eorum, qui te oderunt, ascendit semper.*

828. Sed sciendum, quod Deus in seipso a nullo potest haberi odio, nec secundum omnes effectus suos, cum omne bonum, quod est in rebus, sit a Deo, et impossibile sit quod aliquis habeat odium omnis boni, quin ad minus esse et vivere diligat. Sed tamen aliquem effectum Dei odio aliquis habet, inquantum suo appetitui

Second, he makes this obvious by a sign, at *I have come in the name of my Father*.

With respect to the first he does two things.

First, he rejects what they might have assumed to be his intention, from what he had said before.

Second, he presents his real intention, at *but I know you, that you do not have the love of God in you*.

826. The Jews might have assumed that Christ was seeking some kind of praise from men, since he had reminded them of so many witnesses to himself, as John, God, his own works, and the testimony of the Scriptures. Against this thought he says, *I do not receive glory from men*, i.e., I do not seek praise from men; for I have not come to be an example of one seeking human glory: *we did not seek glory from men* (1 Thess 2:6). Or, *I do not receive glory from men*, i.e., I do not need human praise, because from eternity I have glory with the Father: *glorify me, O Father, with yourself, with the glory which I had, before the world was made* (John 17:5). For I have not come to be glorified by men, but rather to glorify them, since all glory proceeds from me. *It is through this wisdom that I have glory* (Wis 7:25).

God is said to be praised and glorified by men—*glorify the Lord as much as you are able; he will still surpass even that* (Sir 43:30)—not that he might become by this more glorious, but so that he might appear glorious among us.

827. Thus Christ presented the various testimonies to himself not for the reason they thought, but for another one: *but I know you*, i.e., I have made known about you, *that you do not have the love of God in you*, although you pretend to have it. And so you are not persecuting me because of your love for God. You would be persecuting me for the love of God if God and the Scriptures did not bear witness to me; but God himself bears. witness to me by himself, his works and in the Scriptures, as has been said. Consequently, if you truly loved God, then so far from rejecting me, you would come to me. You, therefore, do not love God.

Another interpretation would be this: *but I know you, that you have not the love of God in you*. It is as though he were saying: I have not brought in these witnesses because I wanted your praise; but I know you do not love God and your waywardness makes me sad, and I want to lead you back to the way of truth: *now they have both seen and hated me and my Father* (John 15:24); *the pride of those who hate you continuously rises* (Ps 73:23).

828. Here we should point out that God cannot be hated in himself by anyone, nor can he be hated with respect to all his effects, since every good in things comes from God, and it is impossible for anyone to hate all good, for he will at least love existence and life. But someone may hate some effect of God, insofar as this is opposed to what he desires: for

contrariatur, ut poenam, vel aliquid huiusmodi. Et secundum hoc dicitur habere Deum odio.

829. Signum autem quod dilectionem Dei non habent, ponit cum dicit *ego veni in nomine patris mei, et non accepistis me*, et

primo ponit unum signum de praesenti;

secundo aliud de futuro, ibi *si alius venerit in nomine suo, illum accipietis*.

830. Signum de praesenti sumitur ex eius adventu; et ideo dicit *ego veni in nomine Patris mei*, quasi diceret: manifeste apparet quod dico, nam si aliquis diligit Dominum suum, manifestum est quod honorat et recipit eum qui venit ex parte sua, et honorem eius quaerit; sed *ego veni in nomine Patris mei*, manifestando nomen eius mundo; infra XVII, 6: *Pater, manifestavi nomen tuum hominibus quos dedisti mihi*, et vos non accepistis me, ergo non diligitis eum.

Dicitur autem Filius manifestare Patrem suum hominibus, quia licet Pater inquantum Deus, notus esset, secundum illud Ps. LXXV, v. 1: *notus in Iudaea Deus*, tamen inquantum est naturalis Pater Filii, non erat notus ante adventum Christi: et ideo Salomon quaerebat, Prov. XXX, 4: *quod nomen eius, et quod nomen Filii eius nosti?*

831. Signum de futuro sumitur ex adventu Antichristi. Possent autem Iudaei dicere: licet tu venias in nomine eius, ideo tamen non te recepimus, quia nullum volumus recipere nisi ipsum Deum Patrem. Sed contra hoc dicit Dominus, quod hoc non potest esse, quia vos recipietis alium, qui non veniet in nomine Patris, sed in nomine sui ipsius; et, quod plus est veniet *in nomine*, non Patris, sed *suo*: quia non quaeret gloriam Patris, sed suam propriam; nec Patri attribuet quae faciet, sed sibi, II Thess. II, 4: *qui adversatur et extollitur supra omne quod dicitur aut quod colitur Deus*. *Et illum accipietis*, unde ibidem subditur: *mittet Deus illis operationem erroris, ut credant mendacio*. Et hoc ideo, quia doctrinam veritatis non receperunt, ut salvi fierent; unde dicit Glossa: *quia Iudaei noluerunt accipere Christum, poena peccati huius congrue erit ut recipiant Antichristum: ut qui noluerunt credere veritati, credant mendacio*.

Sed secundum Augustinum, potest hoc intelligi de haereticis et falsis doctoribus, qui doctrinam ex corde suo proferunt, et non ex ore Dei; qui nomen suum laudant, et nomen Dei contemnunt: de quibus dicitur I Io. II, 18: *audistis quia Antichristus venit; et nunc Antichristi multi facti sunt*. Manifestum est ergo quod persecutio qua me persequimini, non est ex dilectione Dei,

example, he might hate punishment, and things of that sort. It is from this point of view that God is said to be hated.

829. Then, at *I have come in the name of my Father, and you do not receive me*, he gives a sign that they do not love God.

First, a present sign;

second, a future sign, at *if another shall come in his own name, you will receive him*.

830. The present sign concerns his own coming; so he says, *I have come in the name of my Father*. As if to say: what I say is obvious, for if one loves his Lord, it is clear that he will honor and receive one who comes from him, and seek to honor him. But *I have come in the name of my Father*, and I make his name known to the world: *I have manifested your name to the men whom you have given me* (John 17:6), and yet you do not accept me. Therefore, you do not love him.

The Son is said to make his Father known to men because, although the Father, as God, was known—*God is known in Judah* (Ps 75:1)—yet he was not known as the natural Father of the Son before Christ came. Thus Solomon asked: *what is his name? And what is the name of his son?* (Prov 30:4).

831. The future sign concerns the coming of the Antichrist. For the Jews could say: although you come in his name, we have not accepted you, because we will not accept anyone but God the Father. The Lord speaks against this, and says that it cannot be, because you will accept another, who will come, not in the Father's name, but in his own name; and what is more, he will come, not *in the name* of the Father, but *in his own name*, precisely because he will not seek the glory of the Father but his own. And whatever he does, he will attribute it, not to the Father, but to himself: *who opposes and is exalted above all that is called God, or is worshipped* (2 Thess 2:4). *You will receive him*; and so the Apostle continues in the same letter: *God will send them a misleading influence so that they might believe what is false* (2 Thess 2:11). And this, because they did not accept the true teaching, that they might be saved. So the Gloss says: *because the Jews were unwilling to accept Christ, the penalty for this sin will be, fittingly enough, that they will receive the Antichrist; with the result that those who were unwilling to believe the truth, will believe a lie.*

According to Augustine, however, we can understand this text as applying to heretics and false teachers: who spread a teaching that comes from their own hearts and not from the mouth of God, and who praise themselves and despise the name of God. Of such persons it is written: *you have heard that the Antichrist is coming; and now many antichrists have appeared* (1 John 2:18). So it is clear that your

sed ex odio et livore ad eum procedit: et ex hoc eorum incredulitas causabatur.

832. Et ideo concludit *quomodo vos potestis credere, qui gloriam ab invicem accipitis?* Idest gloriam humanam, et eam *quae a solo Deo est, non quaeritis?* Quae est vera gloria. Ideo autem credere non poterant in Christum, quia cum superba mens eorum gloriam et laudem appeteret, se super alios efferri reputabant in gloriam, et dedecus in Christum credere qui abiectus videbatur et pauper; et ideo ei credere non poterant. Sed ille in eum credere potest qui cor habens humile, solius Dei gloriam quaerit, et ei placere appetit. Et ideo, sicut infra XII, 42, dicitur: *multi ex principibus crediderunt in eum; sed propter Pharisaeos non confitebantur, ut de synagoga non eiicerentur.*

Ex quo apparet quod multum periculosa est inanis gloria. Unde dicit Tullius: *cavenda est homini gloria, quae aufert omnem libertatem, pro qua magnanimis viris omnis debet esse contentio.* Et ideo dicit Glossa: *magnum vitium est iactantia et humanae laudis ambitio, quae de se vult aestimari quae de se non habet.*

833. Consequenter cum dicit *nolite putare quia ego accusaturus sum vos,* ostendit quod non habent zelum ad Moysen, et

primo ostendit quomodo Moyses erat eis contrarius;

secundo rationem contrarietatis assignat, ibi *si enim crederetis Moysi, crederetis forsitan et mihi.*

Circa primum duo facit.

Primo removet opinatum zelum;

secundo asserit verum, ibi *est qui accusat vos Moyses.*

834. Quantum ad primum dicit *nolite putare quia ego accusaturus sum vos apud Patrem.*

Cuius quidem dicti est triplex ratio. Una, quod Filius Dei non venit in mundum ut condemnet mundum, sed ut salvet; et ideo dicit *nolite putare* quod venerim ad condemnandum, sed ad liberandum; supra III, v. 17: *non enim misit Deus Filium suum in mundum ut iudicet mundum,* idest ut condemnet mundum, *sed ut salvetur mundus per ipsum.* Et ideo sanguis Christi non clamat accusationem, sed remissionem, Hebr. XII, v. 24: *habemus sanguinem Christi melius clamantem quam Abel,* qui clamat accusando; Rom. VIII, 33: *quis accusabit adversus electos Dei? Christus est qui iustificat, quis est qui condemnet?*

Secundo modo *nolite putare quod ego accusaturus sum vos apud Patrem,* quia non ero accusator, sed iudex. Supra eodem: Pater *omne iudicium dedit Filio.*

Tertio modo *nolite putare quod ego,* tantum scilicet, *accusaturus sum vos apud Patrem* de hoc quod facitis

persecution of me does not spring from your love for God, but from your hatred and envy of him. And this was the reason why they did not believe.

832. He concludes: *how are you able to believe, who receive glory from one another,* i.e., human praise, *and the glory that is from God alone, you do not seek?* which is true glory. The reason they could not believe in Christ was that, since their proud minds were craving their own glory and praise, they considered themselves superior to others in glory, and regarded it as a disgrace to believe in Christ, who seemed common and poor. And this was why they could not believe in him. The one who can believe in Christ is the person of humble heart, who seeks the glory of God alone, and who strives to please him. And so we read: *many of the chief men also believed in him; but because of the Pharisees they did not confess him, that they might not be cast out of the synagogue* (John 12:42).

We can see from this just how dangerous vainglory is. For this reason Cicero says: *let a man beware of that glory that robs him of all freedom; that freedom for which a man of great spirit should risk everything.* And the Gloss says: *it is a great vice to boast and to strive for human praise: to desire that others think you have what you really do not have.*

833. Then, at *do not think that I will accuse you,* he shows that they do not have zeal for Moses.

First, how Moses was against them.

Second, he gives the reason for this opposition, at *if you believed Moses, you would perhaps believe me also.*

As to the first he does two things.

First, he rejects their false zeal;

second, he shows them true zeal, at *there is one who accuses you, Moses.*

834. As to the first he says: *do not think that I will accuse you to the Father.*

There are three reasons for his saying this. First, the Son of God did not come into the world to condemn the world, but to save it. So he says, *do not think* that I have come to condemn, I have come to free: *for God did not send his Son into the world to judge the world,* that is, to condemn the world, *but that the world might be saved through him* (John 3:17). And so the blood of Christ cries out, not to accuse, but to forgive: *we have the blood of Christ, crying out better than that of Abel* (Heb 12:24), whose blood cried out to accuse; *who will accuse God's elect? It is Christ who justifies. Who is it, then, who will condemn?* (Rom 8:33).

As to his second reason for saying this, he says: *do not think that I will accuse you to the Father,* because I will not be the one to accuse you, but to judge you: the Father *has given all judgment to the Son* (John 5:22).

The third reason is: *do not think that I,* i.e., I alone, *will accuse you to the Father* for what you are doing to me; for

mihi; sed etiam Moyses accusabit vos de hoc quod non creditis ei in his quae de me dixit.

835. Et ideo subdit *est qui accusat vos Moyses, in quo speratis*, quia creditis per praecepta eius salvari.

Accusat autem eos Moyses dupliciter. Materialiter, quia ex hoc quod praetergressi sunt mandata eius, sunt accusandi; Rom. II, 12: *quicumque in lege peccaverunt, per legem iudicabuntur.* Item accusat eos, quia Moyses et alii sancti potestatem habebunt in iudicio; Ps. XLIX, 6: *gladii ancipites in manibus eorum* etc.

836. Rationem contrarietatis ponit dicens *si enim crederetis Moysi, crederetis forsitan et mihi*, ut patet Deut. XVIII, 15: *prophetam suscitabit Deus de gente tua et de fratribus tuis sicut me: ipsum audies*, et in omnibus sacrificiis, quae erant figura Christi.

Et dicit *forsitan*, ad designandum voluntatem liberi arbitrii: non quod in Deo sit aliquod dubium.

837. Consequenter cum dicit *si autem illius litteris non creditis, quomodo verbis meis credetis?* ponit signum huius contrarietatis sumptum a maiori, negando per comparationem ad duo. Primo personae ad personam: licet enim Christus simpliciter maior esset Moyse, tamen in reputatione Iudaeorum Moyses erat maior, et ideo dicit si non creditis Moysi, nec mihi credetis.

Secundo per comparationem ad modum tradendi: quia Moyses praecepta dedit in scriptis, quae possunt diutius meditari, nec tradi oblivioni de facili; et ideo magis obligant ad credendum. Christus vero tradidit verbis; et quantum ad hoc dicit *si non creditis litteris illius*, quarum libros apud vos habetis, *quomodo creditis verbis meis?*

even Moses will accuse you for not believing him in the things he said of me.

835. Consequently he adds: *there is one who accuses you, Moses, in whom you trust*, because you believe you are saved through his precepts.

Moses accuses them in two ways. Materially, because they deserved to be accused for transgressing his commands: *those who have sinned under the law, will be judged by the law* (Rom 2:12). Again, Moses accuses them because he and the other saints will have authority in the judgment: *the two-edged swords will be in their hands* (Ps 149:6).

836. He presents the reason for this opposition when he says: *if you believed Moses, you would perhaps believe me also*, as is clear from *the Lord your God will raise up a prophet for you, from your nation and your brothers; he will be like me: you will listen to him* (Deut 18:15), and from all the sacrifices, which were a symbol of Christ.

He says, *perhaps*, to indicate that their will acts from a free judgment, and not to imply that there is any doubt on the part of God.

837. Then when he says, *but if you do not believe his writings, how will you believe my words?* he gives a sign of this opposition. He does this by comparing two things, and then denying of the lesser of them what is denied of the greater. First, there is a comparison between Moses and Christ: for although Christ, absolutely speaking, is greater than Moses, Moses was the greater in reputation among the Jews. Thus he says: if you do not believe Moses, you will not believe me either.

Second, he compares the way in which they presented their teaching: Moses gave his precepts in a written form; and so they can be studied for a long time, and are not easily forgotten. Hence they impose a stronger obligation to believe. But Christ presented his teachings in spoken words. Thus he says, *but if you do not believe his writings*, which you have preserved in your books, *how will you believe my words?*

CHAPTER 6

Lecture 1

6:1 Post haec abiit Iesus trans mare Galilaeae, quod est Tiberiadis. [n. 839]

6:2 Et sequebatur eum multitudo magna, quia videbant signa quae faciebat super his qui infirmabantur. [n. 842]

6:3 Subiit ergo in montem Iesus, et ibi sedebat cum discipulis suis. [n. 845]

6:4 Erat autem proximum Pascha, dies festus Iudaeorum. [n. 846]

6:5 Cum sublevasset ergo oculos Iesus, et vidisset quia multitudo maxima venit ad eum, dixit ad Philippum: unde ememus panes, ut manducent hi? [n. 847]

6:6 Hoc autem dicebat tentans eum: ipse enim sciebat quid esset facturus. [n. 850]

6:7 Respondit ei Philippus: ducentorum denariorum panes non sufficiunt eis ut unusquique modicum quid accipiat. [n. 851]

6:8 Dixit ei unus ex discipulis eius, Andreas frater Simonis Petri: [n. 853]

6:9 Est puer unus hic qui habet quinque panes hordeaceos, et duos pisces; sed haec quid sunt inter tantos? [n. 853]

6:10 Dixit ergo Iesus: facite homines discumbere. Erat autem foenum multum in loco. Discubuerunt ergo viri, numero quasi quinque milia. [n. 855]

6:11 Accepit ergo Iesus panes, et cum gratias egisset, distribuit discumbentibus: similiter et ex piscibus quantum volebant. [n. 859]

6:1 Μετὰ ταῦτα ἀπῆλθεν ὁ Ἰησοῦς πέραν τῆς θαλάσσης τῆς Γαλιλαίας τῆς Τιβεριάδος.

6:2 ἠκολούθει δὲ αὐτῷ ὄχλος πολύς, ὅτι ἐθεώρουν τὰ σημεῖα ἃ ἐποίει ἐπὶ τῶν ἀσθενούντων.

6:3 ἀνῆλθεν δὲ εἰς τὸ ὄρος Ἰησοῦς καὶ ἐκεῖ ἐκάθητο μετὰ τῶν μαθητῶν αὐτοῦ.

6:4 ἦν δὲ ἐγγὺς τὸ πάσχα, ἡ ἑορτὴ τῶν Ἰουδαίων.

6:5 Ἐπάρας οὖν τοὺς ὀφθαλμοὺς ὁ Ἰησοῦς καὶ θεασάμενος ὅτι πολὺς ὄχλος ἔρχεται πρὸς αὐτὸν λέγει πρὸς Φίλιππον· πόθεν ἀγοράσωμεν ἄρτους ἵνα φάγωσιν οὗτοι;

6:6 τοῦτο δὲ ἔλεγεν πειράζων αὐτόν· αὐτὸς γὰρ ᾔδει τί ἔμελλεν ποιεῖν.

6:7 ἀπεκρίθη αὐτῷ [ὁ] Φίλιππος· διακοσίων δηναρίων ἄρτοι οὐκ ἀρκοῦσιν αὐτοῖς ἵνα ἕκαστος βραχύ [τι] λάβῃ.

6:8 λέγει αὐτῷ εἷς ἐκ τῶν μαθητῶν αὐτοῦ, Ἀνδρέας ὁ ἀδελφὸς Σίμωνος Πέτρου·

6:9 ἔστιν παιδάριον ὧδε ὃς ἔχει πέντε ἄρτους κριθίνους καὶ δύο ὀψάρια· ἀλλὰ ταῦτα τί ἐστιν εἰς τοσούτους;

6:10 εἶπεν ὁ Ἰησοῦς· ποιήσατε τοὺς ἀνθρώπους ἀναπεσεῖν. ἦν δὲ χόρτος πολὺς ἐν τῷ τόπῳ. ἀνέπεσαν οὖν οἱ ἄνδρες τὸν ἀριθμὸν ὡς πεντακισχίλιοι.

6:11 ἔλαβεν οὖν τοὺς ἄρτους ὁ Ἰησοῦς καὶ εὐχαριστήσας διέδωκεν τοῖς ἀνακειμένοις ὁμοίως καὶ ἐκ τῶν ὀψαρίων ὅσον ἤθελον.

6:1 After these things, Jesus went over the sea of Galilee, which is that of Tiberias. [n. 839]

6:2 And a great multitude followed him, because they saw the miracles that he performed on those who were diseased. [n. 842]

6:3 Jesus therefore went up into a mountain, and he sat there with his disciples. [n. 845]

6:4 Now the Pasch, the festival day of the Jews, was near at hand. [n. 846]

6:5 When Jesus had lifted up his eyes, and saw that a very great multitude came to him, he said to Philip: where shall we buy bread, that they may eat? [n. 847]

6:6 And he said this testing him, for he himself knew what he would do. [n. 850]

6:7 Philip answered him: two hundred denarii worth of bread is not sufficient for them, that each one may take a little. [n. 851]

6:8 One of his disciples, Andrew, the brother of Simon Peter, said to him: [n. 853]

6:9 There is a boy here who has five barley loaves and two fishes, but what are these among so many? [n. 853]

6:10 Then Jesus said: make the men sit down. Now there was much grass in the place. The men therefore sat down, in number about five thousand. [n. 855]

6:11 Jesus took the loaves, and when he had given thanks, he distributed to those who were sitting: in like manner of the fishes, as much as they wanted. [n. 859]

6:12 Ut autem impleti sunt, dixit discipulis suis: colligite quae superaverunt fragmenta, ne pereant. [n. 863]

6:12 ὡς δὲ ἐνεπλήσθησαν, λέγει τοῖς μαθηταῖς αὐτοῦ· συναγάγετε τὰ περισσεύσαντα κλάσματα, ἵνα μή τι ἀπόληται.

6:12 And when they were filled, he said to his disciples: gather up the fragments that remain, lest they be lost. [n. 863]

6:13 Collegerunt ergo, et impleverunt duodecim cophinos fragmentorum ex quinque panibus hordeaceis, et duobus piscibus, quae superfuerunt his qui manducaverunt. [n. 865]

6:13 συνήγαγον οὖν καὶ ἐγέμισαν δώδεκα κοφίνους κλασμάτων ἐκ τῶν πέντε ἄρτων τῶν κριθίνων ἃ ἐπερίσσευσαν τοῖς βεβρωκόσιν.

6:13 They gathered up and filled twelve baskets with the fragments of the five barley loaves, which remained after they had eaten. [n. 865]

---

838. Posita doctrina de vita spirituali qua Christus regeneratos vivificat, consequenter Evangelista agit de spirituali nutrimento quo Christus vivificatos sustentat, et

primo ponit visibile miraculum, quod fecit Christus exhibendo nutrimentum corporale;

secundo agit de nutrimento spirituali, ibi *respondit eis Iesus, et dixit: amen, amen dico vobis, quaeritis me, non quia* etc.

Circa primum duo facit.

Primo ponit miraculum visibile de nutrimento corporali;

secundo ostendit effectum miraculi, ibi *illi ergo homines cum vidissent* etc.

Circa miraculum duo ponit:

scilicet eius circumstantias,

et eius patratione, ibi *et cum sublevasset oculos Iesus*.

Circa primum tria facit.

Primo describit multitudinem quam pavit;

secundo determinat locum ubi pavit, ibi *subiit ergo in montem Iesus*;

tertio tempus quando pavit, ibi *erat autem proximum Pascha* etc.

Circa primum tria facit.

Primo determinat locum quo multitudo eum sequitur;

secundo turbam sequentem;

tertio causam sequelae assignat.

839. Quo autem turba Dominum sequeretur, insinuat Evangelista cum dicit *post haec abiit Iesus trans mare Galilaeae*; idest, post mystica verba quae Dominus de sua potestate dixerat.

Mare autem istud Galilaeae frequenter in Scriptura et in diversis locis nominatur. Quia autem istud mare non est salsum, sed est quaedam congregatio aquarum ex influxu Iordanis, ideo a Luca dicitur stagnum, ut habetur Lc. V, 1; quia vero secundum proprietatem Hebraici idiomatis, omnes congregationes aquarum vocantur maria, secundum illud Gen. I, 10: *congregationesque aquarum appellavit maria*, ideo dicitur mare. Sed

838. The Evangelist has presented the teaching of Christ on the spiritual life, by which he gives life to those who are born again. He now tells us of the spiritual food by which Christ sustains those to whom he has given life.

First, he describes a visible miracle, in which Christ furnished bodily food.

Second, he considers spiritual food: *Jesus answered them and said: amen, amen I say to you, you seek me, not because you have seen miracles* (John 6:26).

He does two things about the first.

First, he describes the visible miracle about bodily nourishment.

Second, he shows the effect this miracle had: *now those men, when they had seen what a miracle Jesus had done* (John 6:14).

He tells us two things about this miracle.

First, its circumstances,

second, about its actual accomplishment: *when Jesus had lifted up his eyes*.

As to the first he does three things.

First he describes the crowd that Jesus fed,

second, the place; at: *Jesus therefore went up into a mountain*;

third, the time: *now the Pasch, the festival day of the Jews, was near at hand*.

As to the first he does three things.

First, he identifies the place where the crowd followed Jesus;

second, the people who followed him; and

third, he tells why they followed him.

839. The Evangelist describes the place to which the crowd followed our Lord when he says, *after these things, Jesus went over the Sea of Galilee*, i.e., after the mysterious words Jesus had spoken concerning his power.

This Sea of Galilee is mentioned frequently in various places in Scripture. Luke calls it a lake (Luke 5:1) because its water is not salty, but was formed from the waters flowing in from the Jordan. Yet it is still called a Sea, because in Hebrew all bodies of water are called seas: *God called the waters 'seas'* (Gen 1:10). It is also called Gennesaret because of the character of its location: for this water is tossed about a great deal, being buffeted by the winds that come

Genesareth cognominatur a natura loci: nam multum fluctuat ex reverberatione ventorum, qui ex ipsis aquae resolutionibus generantur: unde Genesareth in Graeco, idem est quod auram generans. Denominatur etiam Galilaeae a Galilaea provincia, in qua est. Tiberiadis vero a civitate sic dicta, quae erat ex una parte ipsius maris, ex opposito habens civitatem Capharnaum ex alia parte, quae prius vocabatur Zenereth, sed postea ab Herode tetrarcha instaurata in honorem Tiberii Caesaris, Tiberias appellata fuit.

840. Ratio autem litteralis quare Iesus abiit trans mare, assignatur a Chrysostomo, ut Christus cederet furori et turbationi Iudaeorum, quam conceperant contra Christum propter ea quae de se supra dixerat. Unde, ut ipse dicit, sicut iacula cum in durum aliquod incidunt gravius feriunt, quae autem non habuerint aliquod obvians, dissolvuntur cito immissa, et quiescunt; ita et cum audacibus hominibus impetuose et resistendo incesserimus, saeviunt magis; si autem eis cesserimus, facile mollimus eorum insaniam. Propterea Christus furorem Iudaeorum ex praemissis sermonibus natum, secedendo trans mare, mitigavit; dans nobis in hoc exemplum simile faciendi. Eccli. VIII, 14: *ne stes contra faciem contumeliosi.*

841. Mystice autem per mare, praesens saeculum turbidum designatur; Ps. CIII, v. 25: *hoc mare magnum et spatiosum manibus.*

Hoc mare transiit Dominus quando mare mortalitatis et poenalitatis assumpsit nascendo, calcavit moriendo et transiens resurgendo, in gloriam resurrectionis pervenit. De isto transitu dicitur infra XIII, 1: **sciens Iesus quia venit hora eius ut transeat ex hoc mundo ad Patrem.**

Eum transeuntem secutae sunt, credendo et imitando, turbae multae, ex utroque populo collectae; Is. LX, 5: *tunc mirabitur et dilatabitur cor tuum, quando conversa fuerit ad te multitudo maris;* Ps. VII, 7: *exsurge, Domine in praecepto quod mandasti, et synagoga populorum circumdabit te.*

842. Describitur ergo turba sequens copiosa, **quia sequebatur eum multitudo magna.**

843. Causa autem propter quam sequebatur, est operatio miraculorum; unde dicit **quia videbant signa quae faciebat super his qui infirmabantur.**

Sciendum est, quod quidam sequebantur eum propter doctrinam eius, qui scilicet melius erant dispositi; alii vero imperfectiores sequebantur eum propter admirationem signorum visibilium, grossioris mentis existentes. *Signa enim,* ut dicitur I Cor. XIV, 22, *non sunt data fidelibus, sed infidelibus.* Aliqui etiam propter devotionem et fidem eum sequebantur, scilicet illi quos corpore sanaverat: sic enim a Domino sanabantur

from the vapors rising from its surface. Thus in Greek the word Gennesaret means 'wind forming.' It is called the Sea of Galilee from the province of Galilee in which it is located. Again, it is called the Sea of Tiberias from the city of Tiberias: this city was situated on one side of the sea, facing Capernaum on the opposite side. The city of Tiberias was formerly called Chinnereth, but later, when it was rebuilt by Herod the Tetrarch, it was renamed as Tiberias in honor of Tiberius Caesar.

840. The literal reason why Jesus crossed the sea is given by Chrysostom: to give ground to the anger and agitation which the Jews felt against Christ because of the things he had said about them. As Chrysostom says: just as darts strike a hard object with great force if they meet it, but pass on and soon come to rest if nothing is in their way, so also the anger of defiant men increases when they are resisted, but if we yield a little, it is easy to keep their fury within bounds. So Christ, by going to the other side of the sea, was able to soften the anger of the Jews, caused by what he had said. He thus gives us an example to act in the same way: *do not be provoked by one who speaks evil of you* (Sir 8:14).

841. In the mystical sense, the sea signifies this present troubled world: *this great sea, stretching wide* (Ps 103:25).

Our Lord crossed over this sea when he assumed the sea of punishment and death by being born, trod it under foot by dying, and then crossing over it by his rising, arrived at the glory of his resurrection. We read of this crossing: **Jesus knowing that his hour was come, that he should pass out of this world to the Father** (John 13:1).

A great crowd, composed of both peoples, has followed him in this crossing, by believing in him and imitating him: *your heart will be full of wonder and joy, when the riches of the sea will be given to you* (Isa 60:5); *rise up, O Lord, you who demand that justice be done; and the people will gather round you* (Ps 7:7).

842. The crowd that followed him is described as large, **and a great multitude followed him.**

843. The reason why they followed him is because he was performing miracles, hence he says, **because they saw the miracles that he performed on those who were diseased.**

We should point out that some followed Christ because of his teachings, that is, those who were better disposed. But there were others, i.e., those who were less perfect and less perceptive, who followed him because they were attracted by visible miracles; *signs were given to unbelievers, not to believers* (1 Cor 14:22). Still others followed him out of devotion and faith, those, namely, whom he had cured of some bodily defect: for our Lord had so healed their body

in corpore ut etiam perfecte sanarentur in anima; Deut. XXXII, 4: *Dei perfecta sunt opera*. Et hoc patet, quia paralytico (supra VIII, 11), signanter dixit: ***vade, et amplius noli peccare***; et Matth. IX, 2: *fili, remittuntur tibi peccata*; quae magis ad sanitatem animae pertinent quam corporis.

844. Notandum autem quod cum Evangelista non fecerit mentionem, nisi de tribus miraculis, scilicet de nuptiis, de filio reguli, et paralytico, hic tamen indeterminate dicit ***signa quae faciebat***, ut det intelligere, quia Christus multa alia signa fecit, ut dicitur infra ult., 25, de quibus in hoc libro mentionem non facit. Intendebat enim specialiter ad manifestandum Christi doctrinam.

845. Consequenter determinat locum miraculi, qui est mons; unde dicit ***subiit ergo in montem***, idest latenter ascendit ***Iesus, et ibi sedebat cum discipulis suis***. Et quidem mons satis est congruus locus refectioni: per montem enim signatur perfectio iustitiae, secundum illud Ps. XXXV, 7: *iustitia tua sicut montes Dei*. Quia ergo haec terrena non satiant, immo ***qui biberit ex aqua hac sitiet iterum***, ut dicitur supra II, 13, spiritualia vero satiant; ideo Dominus ad altiora cum discipulis ascendit, ut ostendat in spiritualibus satietatem et perfectionem iustitiae inveniri: de quo monte dicitur in Ps. LXVII, 16: *mons Dei, mons pinguis*. Unde et ibi doctoris exercebat officium, sedens cum discipulis suis: ipse enim est qui docet omnem hominem scientiam.

846. Consequenter describitur tempus, cum dicit ***erat autem proximum Pascha***, quod quidem tempus congruit refectioni. ***Pascha*** enim interpretatur *transitus*: Ex. XII, 11: *est enim phase, idest transitus Domini*, ut det intelligere quod quisquis pane divini Verbi et corpore et sanguine Domini desiderat refici, debet transire de vitiis ad virtutes. I Cor. V, v. 7: *Pascha nostrum immolatus est Christus, itaque epulemur in azymis sinceritatis et veritatis*. Eccli. XXIV, 26, dicit divina sapientia: *transite ad me, omnes, qui concupiscitis me*.

Hoc autem est secundum Pascha, de quo Evangelista mentionem facit: ad quod quidem, iuxta legis praeceptum, quod habetur Ex. XXIII, 17, Dominus non ascendit in Ierusalem. Cuius ratio est, quia Christus Deus erat et homo: et inquantum homo suberat quidem legi; inquantum Deus supra legem erat. Ut ergo se hominem ostenderet, servabat aliquando legem; ut vero Deum, legem solvebat. Unde et per hoc quod non ivit, dedit intelligere quod paulatim et in brevi legalia cessarent.

847. Consequenter agit de patratione miraculi, cum dicit ***cum sublevasset ergo oculos Iesus, et vidisset*** etc., et

primo ostenditur necessitas patrandi miraculi;

---

that they were also completely healed in soul: *the works of God are perfect* (Deut 32:4). This is clear, because he expressly said to the paralytic, ***sin no more*** (John 5:14), and it is said, *son, your sins are forgiven* (Matt 9:2); and these remarks concern the health of the soul rather than that of the body.

844. We might remark that although the Evangelist had mentioned only three miracles, the one at the marriage reception, the son of the official, and the paralytic, he says here in a general way, ***the miracles he performed***. He does this to indicate that Christ worked many other miracles that are not mentioned in this book (John 21:25). For his main object was to present the teaching of Christ.

845. Then he gives the location of the miracle, on a mountain; hence he says: ***Jesus therefore went up into a mountain***, i.e., privately, ***and he sat there with his disciples***. Now a mountain is a place well suited for refreshment, for according to the Psalm a mountain signifies the perfection of justice: *your justice is like the mountains of God* (Ps 35:7). And so, because we cannot be satisfied by earthly things—indeed, ***whoever drinks this water will thirst again*** (John 4:13)—but spiritual things will satisfy us, our Lord leads his disciples to a higher place to show that full satisfaction and the perfection of justice are found in spiritual realities. We read of this mountain: *the mountain of God is a rich mountain* (Ps 67:16). Thus he also exercised his office of teacher there, sitting with his disciples; for he is the one who teaches every man.

846. The time is mentioned when he says, ***now the Pasch, the festival day of the Jews, was near at hand***. This time was also well suited for their refreshment, for ***Pasch*** means *passage*: *it is the Passover of the Lord, that is, his passage* (Exod 12:11). We understand from this that anyone who desires to be refreshed by the bread of the divine Word and by the body and blood of the Lord, must pass from vices to virtues: *our Passover, Christ, has been sacrificed, and so let us feast with the unleavened bread of sincerity and truth* (1 Cor 5:7). And again, divine wisdom says: *pass over to me, all who desire me* (Sir 24:26).

This is the second Passover the Evangelist has mentioned. However, our Lord did not go to Jerusalem this time, as the law commanded. The reason for this being that Christ was both God and man: as man he was subject to the law, but as God he was above the law. So, he observed the law on certain occasions to show that he was a man, but he also disregarded the law at other times to show that he was God. Further, by not going he indicated that the ceremonies of the law would end gradually and in a short time.

847. Then he considers the miracle itself, at ***when Jesus had lifted up his eyes, and saw that a very great multitude came to him***.

First, why it was needed.

secundo subditur ipsa patratio, ibi *dicit ergo Iesus: facite homines discumbere* etc.

Necessitas autem miraculi fiendi sumitur ex interrogatione Domini, et responsione discipulorum, et ideo

primo ponitur Domini interrogatio;

secundo discipulorum responsio, ibi *respondit ei Philippus* etc.

Circa primum tria facit.

Primo ponitur interrogandi occasio;

secundo subditur Christi interrogatio; et

tertio aperitur interrogantis intentio.

848. Occasio autem interrogandi fuit visio multitudinis ad Christum venientis. Et ideo dicit **cum sublevasset oculos Iesus**, existens in monte cum discipulis quasi perfectioribus, *et vidisset* etc. In quo duo circa Dominum sunt consideranda.

Unum, ut discamus Christi maturitatem oculos non erigentis huc atque illuc, sed pudice sedentis et attente cum discipulis suis: contra quod dicitur Prov. XXX, 13: *generatio cuius sublimes sunt oculi, et palpebrae eius in alta surrectae*; et Eccli. XIX, 26: *ex visu cognoscitur vir*.

Secundum, ut discamus, quod neque otiose sedebat cum discipulis suis; sed attente eos docens, et ad seipsum corda eorum convertens, discipulos quos docebat intuebatur; Lc. c. vi, 20: *Et ipse elevatis oculis in discipulos suos, dicebat* etc. Et ideo dicitur **cum sublevasset oculos Iesus** etc.

Mystice autem oculi Domini sunt dona spiritualia, quae cum electis suis misericorditer concedit, tunc in eos oculos suos sublevat, idest respectum pietatis impendit. Hoc petebat Ps. LXXXV, 16, dicens: *Respice in me, Domine, et miserere mei*.

849. Interrogatio vero est de refectione multitudinis; unde **dixit ad Philippum: unde ememus panes, ut manducent hi?** Unum supponit, et aliud quaerit. Supponit quidem penuriam, quia non habebant unde tantae multitudini cibum praeberent; quaerit autem modum inveniendi, cum dicit **unde ememus panes, ut manducent hi?**

Ubi notandum, quod omnis doctor necesse habet spiritualiter pascere turbam ad se venientem. Et quia nullus homo habet ex se unde pascat eam, ideo oportet quod aliunde emat labore, studio, assiduitate orationum; Is. LV, 1: *qui non habetis argentum, properate, et emite absque ulla commutatione vinum et lac*. Et iterum: *quare appenditis argentum vestrum*, idest eloquentiam, *et non in panibus*, idest, non in vera sapientia, quae reficit (Eccli. XV, 5: *cibavit illum pane vitae et intellectus, et laborem vestrum non in saturitate*) addiscendo ea quae non satiant, sed magis evacuant?

Second, its accomplishment, at **then Jesus said: make the men sit down**.

We can see the need for this miracle from our Lord's question to his disciple, and the disciple's answer.

First, our Lord's question is given; and

then the answer of his disciple, at **Philip answered him**.

He does three things about the first.

First, the occasion for the question is given;

second, we have the question itself;

third, we are told why Christ asked this question.

848. The occasion for Christ's question was his sight of the crowd coming to him. Hence he says, **when Jesus**, on the mountain with his disciples, i.e., with those who were more perfect, **had lifted up his eyes and saw that a very great multitude came to him, he said to Philip: where shall we buy bread that they may eat?** Here we should note two things about Christ.

First, his maturity: for he is not distracted by what does not concern him, but is appropriately concerned with his disciples. He is not like those spoken of: *a generation whose eyes are proud* (Prov 30:13). And: *a man's dress, and laughter, and his walk, show what he is* (Sir 19:27).

Second, we should note that Christ did not sit there with his disciples out of laziness; he was looking right at them, teaching them carefully and attracting their hearts to himself: *then he lifted his eyes to his disciples* (Luke 6:20). Thus we read: **when Jesus had lifted up his eyes**.

In the mystical sense, our Lord's eyes are his spiritual gifts; and he lifts his eyes on the elect, i.e., looks at them with compassion, when he mercifully grants these gifts to them: this is what the Psalm asks for: *look upon me, O Lord, and have mercy on me* (Ps 85:16).

849. Our Lord's question concerns the feeding of the crowd; **he said to Philip: where shall we buy bread that they may eat?** He assumes one thing and asks about another. He assumes their poverty, because they did not have food to offer this great crowd; and he asks how they might obtain it, saying, **where shall we buy bread that they may eat?**

Here we should note that every teacher is obliged to possess the means of feeding spiritually the people who come to him. And since no man possesses of himself the resources to feed them, he must acquire them elsewhere by his labor, study, and persistent prayer: *hurry, you who have no money, and acquire without cost wine and milk* (Isa 55:1). And there follows: *why do you spend your money*, i.e., your eloquence, *for what is not bread*, i.e., not the true wisdom which refreshes—*wisdom will feed him with the bread of life and understanding* (Sir 15:5)—*and why do you work for what does not satisfy you*, i.e., by learning things that drain you instead of filling you?

850. Intentio autem interrogantis aperitur cum dicit **hoc autem dicebat tentans eum** etc. Ubi Evangelista unam dubitationem excludens, ducit in aliam.

Potuisset enim dubitari quod Dominus Philippum quasi ignorans interrogasset; sed hoc excludit dicens **ipse enim sciebat quid esset facturus**. Sed cum tentare videatur etiam ignorantis esse, cum idem sit quod experimentum sumere, videtur quod Evangelista in aliam dubitationem inducat cum dicit **tentans eum**.

Sed dicendum, quod diversimode aliquis tentat aliquem, ut experimentum de eo sumat: aliter enim tentat homo, quia ut addiscat; aliter diabolus, quia ut decipiat; I Petr. V, v. 8: *adversarius vester diabolus tamquam leo rugiens, circuit quaerens quem devoret*. Deus vero et Christus tentat quidem non ut addiscat, quia ipse est qui scrutatur corda et renes; non ut decipiat, *quia ipse neminem tentat*, ut dicitur Iac. I, 13; sed tentat ut aliis experimentum de tentato tribuat. Sic tentavit Deus Abraham; Gen. XXII, 1: *tentavit Deus Abraham* etc., et sequitur: *nunc cognovi quod timeas Dominum*: idest, cognoscere feci quod timeas Dominum. Ita ex hoc Philippum tentat ut insinuaret aliis suam responsionem, inducens per hoc eos in certissimam futuri signi cognitionem.

851. Consequenter ponitur responsio discipulorum, cum dicit **respondit ei Philippus**, et

primo responsio Philippi;

secundo responsio Andreae, ibi **dicit ei unus ex discipulis eius** etc.

852. Sciendum est autem circa primum, quod Philippus inter alios magis tardus et rudis erat, et ideo inter alios frequentius Dominum interrogabat; infra XIV, 8: **Domine, ostende nobis Patrem, et sufficit nobis**. Sed in interrogatione istorum duorum, quantum ad litteram pertinet, Andreas melius dispositus erat quam Philippus, quia nullam intentionem et dispositionem habere videtur ad miraculum fiendum. Et ideo illum modum inducit quo omnes homines illos pascere possent, scilicet per pecuniam, dicens **ducentorum denariorum panes non sufficiunt eis**: quos nos non habemus, et ideo non possumus eis dare ad manducandum. In quo Christi paupertas insinuatur, qui nec ducentos denarios habebat.

853. Andreas vero videtur habere respectum ad miraculum fiendum. Fortassis enim in memoria habebat signum quod Eliseus de panibus hordeaceis fecerat, quando pavit de viginti panibus centum viros, ut legitur IV Reg. IV, 42 ss., et ideo dicit **est puer unus hic qui habet quinque panes hordeaceos**. Sed tamen opinatus est quod Christus non esset facturus maius miraculum quam Eliseus. Aestimabat enim quod de paucioribus panibus pauciora, et de pluribus plura miraculose fierent (quamvis ei qui subiecta materia non indiget, similiter facile sit de pluribus et de paucioribus pascere turbas), et

850. Our Lord's intention is given when he says, **and he said this testing him**. Here the Evangelist raises one difficulty in answering another.

For we could wonder, why our Lord asked Philip what to do, as though our Lord himself did not know. The Evangelist settles this when he says, **for he himself knew what he would do**. But it seems that the Evangelist raises another difficulty when he says, **testing him**. For to test is to try out; and this seems to imply ignorance.

I answer that one can test another in various ways in order to try him out. One man tests another in order to learn; the devil tests a man in order to ensnare him: *your enemy, the devil, as a roaring lion, goes about seeking whom he can devour* (1 Pet 5:8). But Christ and God does not test us in order to learn, because he sees into our hearts; nor in order to ensnare us: *God does not test anyone* (Jas 1:13). But he does test us that others might learn something from the one tested. This is the way God tested Abraham: *God tested Abraham* (Gen 22:1); and then it says: *now I know that you fear God*, i.e., I have made it known that you fear the Lord (Gen 22:12). He tests Philip in the same way: so that those who hear his answer might be very certain about the miracle to come.

851. Now we have the answer of the disciples, when he says **Philip answered him**.

First, the answer of Philip.

then that of Andrew, at **one of his disciples, Andrew, the brother of Simon Peter, said to him**.

852. With respect to the first, note that Philip was slower in learning than the others, and so he asks our Lord more questions: **Lord, show us the Father, and it is enough for us** (John 14:8). Here, according to the literal sense, Andrew is better disposed than Philip, for Philip does not seem to have any understanding or anticipation of the coming miracle. And so he suggests that money is the way by which they could feed all the people, saying: **two hundred denarii worth of bread is not sufficient for them, that each one may take a little**. And since we do not have that much, we cannot feed them. Here we see the poverty of Christ, for he did not even have two hundred denarii.

853. Andrew, however, seems to sense that a miracle is going to take place. Perhaps he recalled the miracle performed by Elisha with the barley loaves, when he fed a hundred men with twenty loaves (2 Kgs 4:42). And so he says, **there is a boy here who has five barley loaves**. Still, he did not suspect that Christ was going to perform a greater miracle than Elisha: for he thought that fewer loaves would be miraculously produced from fewer, and more from a larger number. But in truth, he who does not need any material to work with could feed a crowd as easily with few or many loaves. So Andrew continues: **but what are these among so**

ideo subdit *sed haec quid sunt inter tantos?* Quasi dicat: si etiam multiplicentur sicut Eliseus multiplicavit, non sufficit.

854. Mystice refectio spiritualis per sapientiam significatur. Una autem sapientia est quam docuit Christus, qui est vera sapientia; I Cor. I, 24: *Christum Dei virtutem et Dei sapientiam.* Sed ante adventum Christi duplex doctrina erat. Una humana quam habebant philosophi, alia legis scriptae.

De prima ergo mentionem facit Philippus et ideo utitur nomine emptionis, dicens *ducentorum denariorum panes non sufficiunt eis.* Nam sapientia humana per acquisitionem habetur. Centenarius numerus perfectionem importat. Unde ducenti duplicem perfectionem insinuant necessariam huic sapientiae; nam ad eius perfectionem duplici via pervenitur: scilicet per experimentum et per contemplationem. Dicit ergo *ducentorum denariorum panes non sufficiunt eis*, quia quidquid humana ratio potest experiri et cogitare de veritate, non sufficit ad perfectam satietatem sapientiae; Ier. IX, 23: *non glorietur sapiens in sapientia sua, et non glorietur fortis in fortitudine sua, et non glorietur dives in divitiis suis; sed in hoc glorietur qui gloriatur, scire et nosse me.* Nam nullius philosophi tanta fuit sapientia ut per eam homines ab errore revocari possent, quin potius multos ad errorem inducunt.

De secunda vero mentionem facit Andreas; et ideo noluit quod alii panes emerentur, sed de habitis turba reficeretur, scilicet de his quae lex continebat; unde melius dispositus erat quam Philippus; et ideo dicit *est puer unus hic qui habet quinque panes hordeaceos.* Puer iste potest dici Moyses propter imperfectionem status legis: Hebr. VII, 19: *neminem ad perfectum adduxit lex*: vel populus Iudaeorum, qui sub elementis mundi serviebat, ut dicitur Gal. IV, 3. Puer ergo iste quinque panes habet, idest doctrinam legis: vel quia in quinque libris Moysi contenta est, supra I, 17: *lex per Moysen data est*: vel quia data est hominibus vacantibus sensibilibus, quae per quinque sensus exprimuntur: qui sunt hordeacei: quia lex ipsa data erat ut in ea vitale alimentum corporalibus sacramentis obtegeretur: hordei enim medulla, tenacissima palea tegitur: vel quia populus Iudaeorum nondum expoliatus erat carnali desiderio, sed tamquam palea cordi eius inhaerebat: nam in Veteri Testamento exterius duritiam experiebantur, propter caeremoniales observantias; Actor. XV, 10: *hoc est onus quod nec nos, nec patres nostri portare potuerunt.* Et ipsi Iudaei corporalibus dediti, spiritualem sensum legis non capiebant; II ad Cor. III, 15: *velamen positum est supra corda ipsorum.*

Per pisces autem duos qui saporem suavem pani dabant, intelligitur doctrina Psalmorum et prophetarum:

many? As if to say: even if you increased them in the measure that Elisha did, it still would not be enough.

854. In the mystical sense, widsom is a symbol for spiritual refreshment. One kind of wisdom was taught by Christ, the true wisdom: *Christ is the power of God, and the wisdom of God* (1 Cor 1:24). Before Christ came, there were two other teachings or doctrines: one was the human teachings of the philosophers; the other was the teachings found in the written law.

Philip mentions the first of these when he speaks of buying: *two hundred denarii worth of bread is not sufficient for them*, for human wisdom must be acquired. Now the number one hundred implies perfection. Thus two hundred suggests the twofold perfection necessary for this wisdom: for there are two ways one arrives at the perfection of human wisdom, by experience and by contemplation. So he says, *two hundred denarii worth of bread is not sufficient for them*, because no matter what human reason can experience and contemplate of the truth, it is not enough to completely satisfy our desire for wisdom: *let not the wise man glory in his wisdom, nor the strong man in his strength, nor the rich man in his riches. But let him who glories glory in this: that he knows and understands me* (Jer 9:23). For the wisdom of no philosopher has been so great that it could keep men from error; rather, the philosophers have led many into error.

It is Andrew who mentions the second kind of teaching. He does not want to buy other bread, but to feed the crowd with the loaves of bread they had, that is, those contained in the law. And so he was better disposed than Philip. So he says: *there is a boy here who has five barley loaves.* This boy can symbolize Moses, because of the imperfection found in the state of the law: *the law brought nothing to perfection* (Heb 7:19); or the Jewish people, who were serving under the elements of this world (Gal 4:3). This boy had five loaves, that is, the teaching of the law: either because this teaching was contained in the five books of Moses, *the law was given through Moses* (John 1:17); or because it was given to men absorbed in sensible things, which are made known through the five senses. These loaves were of barley because the law was given in such a way that what was life-giving in it was concealed under physical signs: for the kernel in barley is covered with a very firm husk. Or, the loaves were of barley because the Jewish people had not yet been rubbed free of carnal desire, but it still covered their hearts like a husk: for in the Old Testament they outwardly experienced hardships because of their ceremonial observances: *a yoke, which neither our fathers nor we were able to bear* (Acts 15:10). Further, the Jews were engrossed in material things and did not understand the spiritual meaning of the law: *a veil is over their hearts* (2 Cor 3:15).

The two fishes, which gave a pleasant flavor to the bread, indicate the teachings of the Psalms and the prophets. Thus

et sic vetus lex non solum habebat panes, scilicet libros quinque Moysi; sed etiam duos pisces, scilicet prophetas et Psalmos. Unde et Scriptura Veteris Testamenti per haec tria dividitur, Lc. ult., 44: *quae scripta sunt in lege et prophetis et Psalmis de me*. Vel per duos pisces, secundum Augustinum, duae personae significantur: scilicet regia et sacerdotalis, quibus populus ille regebatur; quae tamen duae personae Christum praefigurabant, qui fuit verus rex et sacerdos. *Sed haec quid sunt inter tantos?* Quia per ea non potuit humanum genus ad cognitionem veritatis perfecte duci: licet enim Deus in Iudaea notus esset, gentes tamen eum ignorabant.

855. Consequenter cum dicitur *dixit ergo Iesus*, agitur de patratione miraculi, et

primo ponitur hominum dispositio;

secundo eorum refectio, ibi *accepit ergo Iesus panes* etc.;

tertio fragmentorum collectio, ibi *ut autem impleti sunt* etc.

Circa primum duo facit.

Primo ponitur mandatum de dispositione turbarum;

secundo opportunitas dispositionis; et

tertio numerus dispositorum.

856. Mandatum autem fuit Domini ad discipulos, ut disponerent turbam ad comedendum; unde dicit Iesus *facite homines discumbere*, idest sedere ad comedendum. Nam, sicut dictum est supra II, antiquitus homines lectis accumbentes prandebant, unde inolevit consuetudo, ut qui sedent ad manducandum, dicantur discumbere.

Per quod mystice significatur quies, quae necessaria est ad perfectionem sapientiae; Eccli. XXXVIII, 25: *qui minoratur actu, perficiet sapientiam*. Quae dispositio fit per discipulos, quia per eos ad nos cognitio veritatis derivata est; Ps. LXXI, 3: *suscipiant montes pacem populo*.

857. Opportunitas autem dispositionis captatur ex loco *erat autem foenum multum in loco*, quod, ad litteram, commodum est discumbentibus.

Mystice autem per foenum caro significatur, Is. XL, 6: *omnis caro foenum*, et secundum hoc potest ad duo referri. Competit doctrinae Veteris Testamenti, quae dabatur quiescenti in carnalibus, et populo carnaliter sapienti; Is. I, 19: *si volueritis et audieritis me, bona terrae comedetis*; Deut. XXXIII, 28: *oculus Iacob in terra frumenti, vini et olei*. Vel competit percipienti veram sapientiam, ad quam veniri non potest nisi calcatis carnalibus; Rom. XII, 2: *nolite conformari huic saeculo*.

858. Numerus autem erat magnus; unde dicit *discubuerunt ergo viri, numero quasi quinque millia*. Viros tantum Evangelista enumerat, legalem consuetudinem

the old law not only had five loaves, i.e., the five books of Moses, but also two fishes, that is, the Psalms and the prophets. So the Old Testament writings are divided into these three: *the things written about me in the law of Moses, and in the prophets and in the Psalms* (Luke 24:44). Or, according to Augustine, the two fishes signify the priests and kings who ruled the Jews; and they prefigured Christ, who was the true king and priest. *But what are these among so many?* for they could not bring man to a complete knowledge of the truth: for although God was known in Judea, the gentiles did not know him.

855. Next, at *then Jesus said*, the miracle is presented.

First, we see the people arranged;

second, the miracle itself, at *and Jesus took the loaves*; and

third, the gathering of the leftovers, at *and when they were filled he said to his disciples: gather up the fragments*.

He does two things about the first.

First, he shows Christ directing the disciples to have the people recline;

second, why this was appropriate; and

third, he tells us the number of people present.

856. Our Lord told his disciples to arrange the people so that they could eat; thus Jesus says, *make the men sit down*, i.e, to eat. For as mentioned before, in former times people took their meals lying on couches; consequently, it was the custom to say of those who sat down to eat that they were reclining.

In the mystical sense, this indicates that rest which is necessary for the perfection of wisdom: *he that is less in action, shall receive wisdom* (Sir 38:25). Again, the people are prepared by the disciples because it is through the disciples that the knowledge of the truth has come to us: *let the mountains receive peace for the people* (Ps 71:3).

857. The character of the place shows why it was convenient that they recline, *now there was much grass in the place*. This is the literal meaning.

In the mystical sense, grass indicates the flesh: *all flesh is grass* (Isa 40:6). In this sense it can refer to two things. First, to the teachings of the Old Testament, which were given to a people resting in things of the flesh and wise according to the flesh: *if you are willing, and listen to me, you will eat the good things of the land* (Isa 1:19); *the posterity of Jacob dwells in a land of grain, wine and oil* (Deut 33:28). Or, it can refer to one who perceives true wisdom, which cannot be attained without first abandoning the things of the flesh: *do not imitate this world* (Rom 12:2).

858. There was a great number of people; thus he says, *the men therefore sat down, in number about five thousand*. The Evangelist counted only the men, according to

sequens, in qua Moyses a viginti annis et supra, populum numeravit, nulla mentione de mulieribus facta, ut dicitur Num. I. Quod ideo Evangelista fecit, quia isti soli sunt capaces doctrinae perfectae; I Cor. II, 6: *sapientiam loquimur inter perfectos*; Hebr. V, 14: *perfectorum est solidus cibus*.

859. Consequenter cum dicit *accepit ergo Iesus panes*, agit de refectione, et primo insinuatur reficientis affectus; secundo materia refectionis; et tertio perfecta satietas.

In affectu autem Iesu reficientis primo quidem attenditur humilitas; secundo vero gratiarum actio.

860. Humilitas quidem, quia accepit panes, et distribuit. Et quidem Christus facturus miraculum poterat panibus ex nihilo creatis pascere turbas. Sed dispensatione panes praeexistentes multiplicavit ad refectionem turbarum. Primo quidem ut ostenderet sensibilia a diabolo non esse, sicut Manichaei errantes dicunt. Nam si hoc verum esset, Dominus non uteretur rebus sensibilibus ad opus divinae laudis, et praecipue cum *ipse venerit, ut dissolvat opera diaboli*, ut dicitur I Io. III, 8. Secundo ut ostendat falsum esse quod ipsi dicunt, scilicet doctrinam Veteris Testamenti non esse a Deo, sed a diabolo. Ut ergo ostenderet non esse doctrinam aliam Novi Testamenti quam quae praefigurabatur et continebatur in doctrina Veteris Testamenti, praeexistentes panes multiplicavit, innuens quod ipse est qui legem perfecit et implevit; Matth. V, 17: *non veni solvere legem*.

861. Gratiarum autem actio, quia gratias egit, ut ostendat se ab alio habere, scilicet a Patre, quidquid habet: in quo ostendit nobis exemplum simile faciendi. Specialiter tamen gratias egit, ut det nobis exemplum, cum comestionem incipimus, gratias debere agere Deo; I Tim. IV, 4: *nihil reiiciendum quod cum gratiarum actione percipitur*; Ps. XXI, 27: *edent pauperes, et saturabuntur, et laudabunt Dominum*. Item ut ostendat quod non propter se orabat, sed propter turbam, quae praesens erat, et oportebat ei suadere quod a Deo venerat. Et ideo cum coram multis miraculum facit, orat, ut ostendat se Deo non esse contrarium, sed secundum voluntatem eius operari.

Dicitur tamen in Marco, quod Christus per apostolos distribuit panes turbis. Sed hic dicitur quod ipse distribuit, quia ipse videtur fecisse quod per alios fecit. Sed utrumque, secundum mysterium, verum est, quia ipse solus interius reficit, et alii exterius et ut ministri reficiunt.

862. Materia autem refectionis fuit panis et piscis, de quibus satis dictum est supra.

Satietas vero refectionis perfecta fuit, quia *quantum volebant*. Solus enim Christus est qui pascit animam inanem, et animam esurientem replet bonis; Ps. XVI, 15:

the custom in the law, for as mentioned, Moses counted the people who were twenty years and older, without including the women (Num 1:3). The Evangelist does the same, because only men can be completely instructed: *we speak wisdom to those who are mature* (1 Cor 2:6); *solid food is for the mature* (Heb 5:14).

859. Then, at *and Jesus took the loaves*, the Evangelist presents the feeding of the crowd. First, we see the attitude of Christ; second, the food used; thirdly, that the people were satisfied.

As to the attitude of Jesus, both his humility and his giving of thanks are mentioned.

860. We see his humility because he took the bread and gave it to the people. Now although in this miracle Christ could have fed the people with bread created from nothing, he chose to do so by multiplying bread that already existed. He did this, first, to show that sensible things do not come from the devil, as the Manichean error maintains. For if this were so, our Lord would not have used sensible things to praise God, especially since *the Son of God appeared to destroy the works of the devil* (1 John 3:8). He did it, second, to show that they are also wrong in claiming that the teachings of the Old Testament are not from God but from the devil. Thus, to show that the doctrine of the New Testament is none other than that which was prefigured and contained in the teachings of the Old Testament, he multiplied bread that already existed, implying by this that he is the one who fulfills the law and brings it to perfection: *I have not come to destroy the law, but to fulfill it* (Matt 5:17).

861. We see that he gave thanks, when he had given thanks. He did this to show that whatever he had, he had from another, that is, from his Father. This is an example for us to do the same. More particularly, he gave thanks to teach us that we should thank God when we begin a meal: *nothing is to be rejected if it is received with thanksgiving* (1 Tim 4:4); *the poor will eat and be satisfied; and they will praise the Lord* (Ps 21:27). Again, he gave thanks to teach us that he was not praying for himself, but for the people who were there, for he had to convince them that he had come from God. Accordingly, he prays before he works this miracle before them, in order to show them that he is not acting against God, but according to God's will.

We read elsewhere that Christ had the apostles distribute the bread to the people (Mark 6:41). It says here that he distributed it because in a way he himself does what he does by means of others. In the mystical sense, both statements are true: for Christ alone refreshes from within, and others, as his ministers, refresh from without.

862. Their food was bread and fish, about which enough has been said above.

Finally, those who ate were completely satisfied, because they took *as much as they wanted*. For Christ is the only one who feeds an empty soul and fills a hungry soul

satiabor cum apparuerit gloria tua. Alii vero, quasi ex mensura habentes gratiam, miracula faciunt; Christus vero absoluta virtute, cum multa superabundantia omnia operabatur: unde dicitur quod *impleti sunt*.

863. Consequenter cum dicit *ut autem impleti sunt, dixit discipulis suis* etc., agitur de fragmentorum collectione, et

primo ponitur mandatum domini;

secundo executio discipulorum, ibi *collegerunt* etc.

864. Dicit ergo *ut autem impleti sunt, dixit discipulis suis: colligite quae superaverunt fragmenta*. Quod quidem Dominus non ad superfluam ostentationem fecit; sed ut ostenderet factum miraculum non esse phantasticum, per hoc quod collectae reliquiae diu servatae sunt, et aliis in cibum fuerunt.

Voluit etiam per hoc, miraculum illud firmius discipulorum cordibus inhaerere, quibus et fragmenta portanda praecepit; quoniam eos maxime erudire volebat qui orbis terrarum debebant esse magistri.

865. Sed discipuli fideliter exequuntur; unde sequitur *collegerunt ergo* etc.

Ubi notandum est, quod non quantaecumque reliquiae supersunt, neque ad casum, sed secundum certitudinem: quia neque plus neque minus, sed quantum voluit fecit superfluum esse. Cuius signum est quod cophinus cuiuslibet apostoli plenus fuit. Cophinus autem vas est rusticano officio deputatum. Duodecim ergo cophini significant duodecim apostolos et eorum imitatores, qui licet in praesenti sint contemptibiles, spiritualium tamen sacramentorum divitiis sunt interius referti: qui duodecim esse dicuntur, quia fides sanctae Trinitatis per eos praedicanda erat in quatuor partibus mundi.

with good things: *I will be satisfied when your glory appears* (Ps 16:15). Others perform miracles through having grace in a partial manner; Christ, on the other hand, does so with unlimited power, since he does all things superabundantly. Hence it says that *they were filled*.

863. Now we see the leftovers collected, at *and when they were filled, he said to his disciples: gather up the fragments that remain, lest they be lost*.

First, Christ gives the order;

second, his disciples obey, at *they gathered up and filled twelve baskets with the fragments*.

864. The Evangelist says that *and when they were filled, he said to his disciples: gather up the fragments that are left over*. This was not pretentious display on our Lord's part; he did it to show that the miracle he accomplished was not imaginary, since the collected leftovers kept for some time and provided food for others.

Again, he wanted to impress this miracle more firmly on the hearts of his disciples, whom he had carry the leftovers: for most of all he wanted to teach his disciples, who were destined to be the teachers of the entire world.

865. His disciples obeyed him faithfully; hence he says, *they gathered up and filled twelve baskets with the fragments of the five barley loaves, which remained after they had eaten*.

Here we should note that the amount of food that remained was not left to chance, but was according to plan: for as much as Christ willed was left over, no more and no less. This is shown by the fact that the basket of each apostle was filled. Now a basket is reserved for the work of peasants. Therefore, the twelve baskets signify the twelve apostles and those who imitate them, who, although they are looked down upon in this present life, are nevertheless filled with the riches of spiritual sacraments. There are twelve because they were to preach the faith of the Holy Trinity to the four parts of the world.

Lecture 2

6:14 Illi ergo homines cum vidissent quod Iesus fecerat signum, dicebant: quia hic vere propheta, qui venturus est in mundum. [n. 867]

6:15 Iesus ergo cum cognovisset quia venturi essent ut raperent eum, et facerent eum regem, fugit iterum in montem ipse solus. [n. 869]

6:16 Cum autem sero factum esset, descenderunt discipuli eius ad mare. [n. 874]

6:17 Et cum ascendissent navim, venerunt trans mare in Capharnaum: et tenebrae iam factae erant; et non venerat ad eos Iesus. [n. 875]

6:18 Mare autem, vento magno flante, exurgebat. [n. 878]

6:19 Cum remigassent ergo quasi stadia viginti quinque, aut triginta, vident Iesum ambulantem supra mare, et proximum navi fieri, et timuerunt. [n. 880]

6:20 Ille autem dixit eis: ego sum, nolite timere. [n. 881]

6:21 Voluerunt ergo accipere eum in navim: et statim navis fuit ad terram, in quam ibant. [n. 882]

6:14 Οἱ οὖν ἄνθρωποι ἰδόντες ὃ ἐποίησεν σημεῖον ἔλεγον ὅτι οὗτός ἐστιν ἀληθῶς ὁ προφήτης ὁ ἐρχόμενος εἰς τὸν κόσμον.

6:15 Ἰησοῦς οὖν γνοὺς ὅτι μέλλουσιν ἔρχεσθαι καὶ ἁρπάζειν αὐτὸν ἵνα ποιήσωσιν βασιλέα, ἀνεχώρησεν πάλιν εἰς τὸ ὄρος αὐτὸς μόνος.

6:16 Ὡς δὲ ὀψία ἐγένετο κατέβησαν οἱ μαθηταὶ αὐτοῦ ἐπὶ τὴν θάλασσαν

6:17 καὶ ἐμβάντες εἰς πλοῖον ἤρχοντο πέραν τῆς θαλάσσης εἰς Καφαρναούμ. καὶ σκοτία ἤδη ἐγεγόνει καὶ οὔπω ἐληλύθει πρὸς αὐτοὺς ὁ Ἰησοῦς,

6:18 ἥ τε θάλασσα ἀνέμου μεγάλου πνέοντος διεγείρετο.

6:19 ἐληλακότες οὖν ὡς σταδίους εἴκοσι πέντε ἢ τριάκοντα θεωροῦσιν τὸν Ἰησοῦν περιπατοῦντα ἐπὶ τῆς θαλάσσης καὶ ἐγγὺς τοῦ πλοίου γινόμενον, καὶ ἐφοβήθησαν.

6:20 ὁ δὲ λέγει αὐτοῖς· ἐγώ εἰμι· μὴ φοβεῖσθε.

6:21 ἤθελον οὖν λαβεῖν αὐτὸν εἰς τὸ πλοῖον, καὶ εὐθέως ἐγένετο τὸ πλοῖον ἐπὶ τῆς γῆς εἰς ἣν ὑπῆγον.

6:14 Now those men, when they had seen what a miracle Jesus had done, said: this is truly the prophet, who is to come into the world. [n. 867]

6:15 Jesus therefore, when he knew that they would come to seize him and make him king, fled again into the mountain himself alone. [n. 869]

6:16 And when evening came, his disciples went down to the sea. [n. 874]

6:17 And when they had gone up into the ship, they went across the sea to Capernaum; and it was now dark, and Jesus had not come to them. [n. 875]

6:18 And the sea arose by a great blowing wind. [n. 878]

6:19 When they had rowed therefore about twenty-five or thirty stadia, they saw Jesus walking upon the sea, drawing close to the ship, and they were afraid. [n. 880]

6:20 But he said to them: it is I; do not be afraid. [n. 881]

6:21 They wanted to take him into the ship, and presently the ship was at the land to which they were going. [n. 882]

---

866. Posito signo visibili de nutrimento corporali, hic ponitur effectus signi in turbis triplex.

Primo quantum ad fidei confessionem;

secundo quantum ad intentatam honoris exhibitionem, ibi *Iesus ergo cum cognovisset* etc.;

tertio quantum ad diligentem inquisitionem, ibi *ut autem sero factum est* etc.

867. Sciendum est circa primum, quod quasi ex ore Iudaeorum dictum est in Ps. LXXIII, 9: *signa nostra non vidimus, iam non est propheta.* Erat autem olim consuetudo ut prophetae multa signa facerent, unde, deficientibus signis, videbatur prophetia cessasse. Cum vero signa vident, redditam sibi prophetiam confitentur. Unde iam tantum de viso miraculo profecerant, quod Dominum prophetam dicebant. Dicitur ergo *illi homines*, qui satiati fuerant ex quinque panibus, *cum vidissent quod Iesus fecerat signum, dicebant, quia hic est vere propheta.*

866. Above, the Evangelist told us of the miracle of the loaves and fishes. Now he shows the threefold effect this miracle had on the people.

First, its effect on their faith;

second, on their plans to honor Jesus, at *Jesus therefore, when he knew;*

third, how it led them to search for Jesus, at *and when evening came, his disciples went down to the sea.*

867. With respect to the first, we should note that the Jews said in the Psalm: *we have not seen our signs; there is now no prophet* (Ps 73:9). For it was customary in earlier days for the prophets to work many signs; so, when these signs were absent, prophecy seemed to have ended. But when the Jews see such signs, they believe that prophecy is returning. Accordingly, the people were so impressed by this miracle they just saw that they called our Lord a prophet. Thus we read, *now those men,* who had been filled with the five loaves, *when they had seen what a miracle Jesus*

Sed tamen nondum ad perfectam fidem pervenerant, quia eum prophetam credebant qui etiam est Dominus prophetarum. Nec tamen ex toto falluntur, quia etiam ipse Dominus se prophetam nominat.

868. Sciendum est autem, quod propheta dicitur videns. I Reg. IX, 9: *qui nunc dicitur propheta, olim vocabatur videns*. Visio autem ad vim cognoscitivam pertinet. In Christo autem fuit triplex cognitio. Scilicet sensitiva: et secundum hanc habuit aliquam similitudinem cum prophetis, inquantum in imaginatione Christi formari poterant aliquae species sensibiles, quibus futura vel occulta praesentarentur, praecipue propter passibilitatem, quae sibi conveniebat propter statum viatoris. Item cognitio intellectiva: et quantum ad hanc non habet similitudinem cum prophetis; sed etiam est supra angelos, quia erat comprehensor excellentius quam aliqua creatura. Item cognitio divina: et quantum ad hanc fuit prophetarum et angelorum inspirator, cum omnis cognitio causetur per participationem Verbi divini.

Videntur tamen in Christo excellentiam prophetiae cognoscere in hoc quod dicitur **vere propheta**. Licet enim multi prophetae inter Iudaeos fuerint, unus tamen expectabatur, in eis praecipuus, secundum illud Deut. XVIII, v. 15: *prophetam suscitabit vobis Dominus*: et de hoc loquuntur; unde signanter dicit **qui venturus est in mundum**.

869. Deinde cum dicit **Iesus ergo cum cognovisset**, etc., ponitur secundus effectus quantum ad intentatam honoris exhibitionem, quam tamen Christus refugit. Et ideo

primo ponitur conatus plebis;
secundo fuga Christi.

870. Conatus quidem, cum dicitur **ut raperent eum, et facerent eum regem**. Illud enim rapi dicitur quod praeter voluntatem et opportunitatem accipitur. Verum autem erat quod dispositio Dei patris ab aeterno fuerat de regno Christi manifestando, sed manifestatio haec nondum opportuna erat secundum tempus; nam venerat tunc, sed non regnare, quomodo regnans est in eo quod dicimus Matth. VI, 10: *adveniat regnum tuum*, ubi regnabit etiam secundum illud quod homo factus est. Et ideo huic manifestationi aliud tempus est ordinatum, quando scilicet erit aperta claritas sanctorum eius, post iudicium ab eo factum. De ista manifestatione quaerebant discipuli, Act. I, 6: *Domine, si in tempore hoc restitues regnum Israel?*

Credentes ergo turbae eum regnaturum venisse, volebant eum facere regem. Cuius ratio est, quia homines frequenter talem in Dominum volunt qui eos in temporalibus pascat. Unde quia Christus paverat eos, eum regem facere voluerunt; Is. III, 6: *vestimentum tibi est: esto princeps noster*. Unde Chrysostomus dicit: *vide quanta*

had done, said: this is truly the prophet. However, they did not yet have perfect faith, for they believed that Jesus was only a prophet, while he was also the Lord of the prophets. Yet, they were not entirely wrong, because our Lord called himself a prophet.

868. Here we should remark that a prophet is called a seer: *he who is now called a prophet was formerly called a seer* (1 Sam 9:9). Further, seeing pertains to the cognitive power. Now in Christ there were three kinds of knowledge. First of all, there was sense knowledge. And in this respect he had some similarity to the prophets, insofar as sensible species could be formed in the imagination of Christ to present future or hidden events. This was especially due to his passibility, which was appropriate to his state as a wayfarer. Second, Christ had intellectual knowledge; and in this he was not like the prophets, but was even superior to all the angels: for he was a *comprehensor* in a more excellent way than any creature. Again, Christ had divine knowledge, and in this way he was the one who inspired the prophets and the angels, since all knowledge is caused by a participation in the divine Word.

Still, these people seemed to realize that Christ was a superior prophet, for they said: **this is truly the prophet**. For although there had been many prophets among the Jews, they were waiting for a particular one, according to: *the Lord your God will raise up a prophet for you* (Deut 18:15). This is the one they are speaking of here; thus it continues: **who is to come into the world**.

869. Next, at **Jesus therefore, when he knew that they would come to seize him and make him king**, we see the second effect of Christ's miracle: the honor the people planned for Christ, which he refused.

First, we have the attempt by the people;
second, Christ's flight from them.

870. The attempt of the people is mentioned when he says, **they would come to seize him and make him king**. A person or thing is seized if it is taken in a way that one does not will or is not opportune. Now it is true that God's plan from all eternity had been to establish the kingdom of Christ; but the time for this was not then opportune. Christ had come then, but not to reign in the way we ask for his reign when we say, *your kingdom come* (Matt 6:10); at that time he will reign even as man. Another time was reserved for this: after the judgment of Christ, when the saints will appear in glory. It was about this kingdom the disciples asked when they said: *Lord, will you restore the kingdom to Israel at this time?* (Acts 1:6).

So the people, thinking he had come to reign, wanted to make him their king. The reason for this is that men often want as their ruler someone who will provide them with temporal things. Thus, because our Lord had fed them, they were willing to make him their king: *you have a mantle, be our ruler* (Isa 3:6). Chrysostom says: *see the power of*

est gulae virtus. Non eis ultra cura est Sabbati transgressionis, nec ultra zelant pro Deo, sed omnia remota sunt, ventre repleto: sed et propheta iam erat apud eos, et regem eum inthronizare volebant.

871. Fuga autem Christi ponitur, cum dicit **fugit iterum in montem ipse solus.** Ubi datur intelligi, quod Dominus videns turbas, de monte descenderat, et circa inferiora loca paverat turbas: nisi enim de monte descendisset, non diceretur iterum fugere in montem.

Sed cum ipse sit vere rex, quare fugit? Ad quod triplex ratio assignatur. Una, quia derogasset dignitati eius, si regnum ab homine recepisset, qui sic rex erat ut eius participatione reges omnes essent; Prov. VIII, 15: *per me reges regnant.* Alia ratio, quia praeiudicasset suae doctrinae, si claritatem aut robur ab hominibus accepisset. Sic enim operabatur et docebat ut totum virtuti divinae ascriberetur, et non favori humano; supra V, 41: **claritatem ab hominibus non accipio.** Tertia ratio est, et erudiret nos mundanas dignitates contemnere; infra XIII, 15: **exemplum enim dedi vobis, ut quemadmodum ego feci vobis, ita et vos faciatis;** Eccli. VII, 4: *noli quaerere ab homine ducatum.* Sic ergo gloriam mundi recusavit, ut tamen poenam sponte subiret, secundum illud Hebr. XII, 2: *proposito sibi gaudio sustinuit crucem, confusione contempta.*

872. Sed huic videtur contrarium quod dicitur Mt. XIV, 23, scilicet quod *ascendit solus in montem orare.*

Sed, secundum Augustinum, haec non sunt contraria, quia causa fugiendi coniuncta est causae orandi. Tunc enim docet nos Dominus magnam causam esse orandi, cum imminet causa fugiendi.

Mystice autem tunc ascendit in montem quando turbae refectae paratae erant ei subiici, quia tunc ascendit in caelum quando populi parati erant se veritati fidei subiicere, secundum illud Ps. VII, 8: *synagoga populorum circumdabit te; et propter hanc in altum regredere;* idest, ut circumdet te synagoga populorum, regredere in altum.

Sed dictum est **fugit,** ut signaret quod non potuit intelligi altitudo eius: quod enim non intelligimus, dicimus a nobis fugere.

873. Hic agitur de tertio effectu, scilicet de diligenti inquisitione, et

primo quantum ad discipulos;

secundo vero quantum ad turbas, ibi **altera autem die** etc.

Circa primum duo facit.

Primo ponit studium discipulorum;

secundo explicat, ibi **et tenebrae iam factae erant** etc.

gluttony. They are no longer concerned about his breaking the Sabbath; they are no longer zealous for God. All these things are set in the background now that their bellies are full. *Now he is regarded as a prophet among them, and they want to set him on the royal throne as their king.*

871. We see Christ's flight when he says that **he fled again into the mountain himself alone.** We can see from this that when our Lord had first seen the crowd of people he came down from the mountain and fed them in the valley, for we would not read that he went again into the mountains if he had not come down from them.

Why did Christ flee from the people, since he really is a king? There are three reasons for this. First, because it would have detracted from his dignity to have accepted a kingdom from men: for he is so great a king that all other kings are kings by participating in his kingship: *it is by me that kings rule* (Prov 8:15). Another reason is that it would have been hanful to his teaching if he had accepted this dignity and support from men; for he had worked and taught in such a way that everything was attributed to divine power and not to the influence of men: **I do not receive glory from men** (John 5:41). The third reason was to teach us to despise the dignities of this world: **I have given you an example, that as I have done to you, so you do also** (John 13:15); *do not seek dignity from men* (Sir 7:4). And so, he refused the glory of this world, but still endured its punishment of his own will: *Jesus endured the cross, despising the shame, for the joy set before him* (Heb 12:2).

872. Matthew seems to conflict with this, for he says that *Jesus went up the mountain alone, to pray* (Matt 14:23).

However, in the opinion of Augustine, there is no conflict here, because he had reason both to flee and to pray. For our Lord is teaching us that when a reason for flight draws near, there is great reason to pray.

In the mystical sense, Christ went up into the mountain when the people he had fed were ready to subject themselves to him, because he went up into heaven when the people were ready to subject themselves to the truth of the faith, according to: *a congregation of people will surround you. Return above for their sakes,* i.e., return on high so a congregatation of people may surround you (Ps 7:8).

He says that Christ **fled,** to indicate that the people could not understand his grandeur: for if we do not understand something, we say that it flees or eludes us.

873. Now he considers the third effect of Christ's miracle, the search for Christ.

First, by his disciples;

second, by the people, at **the next day, the multitude that stood on the other side of the sea** (John 6:22).

As to the first, he does two things.

First, he tells of the eagerness of the disciples; and

second, enlarges upon this, at **and it was now dark.**

Circa primum duo facit.

Primo describit descensum discipulorum ad mare;

secundo transitum maris, ibi *et cum ascendissent navim*, etc.

874. Sciendum ergo circa primum, quod Christus ascendit montem nescientibus discipulis, unde expectaverunt usque ad vesperam, eum venturum esse putantes ad se. Facta autem vespera, non ultra sustinent eum non inquirere: tantus eos detinebat amor. Et ideo dicit *ut autem sero factum est, descenderunt discipuli eius ad mare, requirentes eum*.

Mystice autem per *sero*, Dominica passio, seu ascensio designatur: quamdiu enim Christus praesentia corporali cum discipulis fuit, nulla eos deprimebat turbatio, amaritudo nulla vexabat; Mt. IX, 15: *non possunt filii sponsi lugere quamdiu sponsus est cum illis*. Sed Christo recedente ab eis, descendunt *ad mare*, idest ad turbationes saeculi; Ps. CIII, 25: *hoc mare magnum*.

875. Sed quia amor quo igniti erant, non sinebat eos diutius Domini praesentia carere, ideo subdit eorum transitum, cum dicit *et cum ascendissent navim, venerunt trans mare in Capharnaum*.

876. Consequenter cum dicit *et tenebrae iam factae erant* etc., explicat quod summatim posuerat, et

primo de perventione ad mare;

secundo de transitu, ibi *mare autem, vento magno flante, exurgebat*.

877. Quantum ad primum dicit *tenebrae iam factae erant, et non venerat ad eos Iesus*: quod non sine causa Evangelista exprimit, ut per hoc ferventem eorum ostendat amorem. Non enim vespera nec nox eos detinuit.

Mysticae autem *tenebrae*, caritatis defectum designant; lux enim caritas est, secundum illud I Io. II, 10: *qui diligit fratrem suum, in lumine est*. Tenebrae ergo in nobis sunt quando non venit ad nos Iesus *lux vera*, ut dicitur supra I, in cuius praesentia omnes tenebrae propulsantur.

Subtraxit autem Christus se tamdiu discipulis, primo quidem ut sentirent quid esset eius absentia; quod quidem experti sunt in tempestate maris. Ier. II, 19: *scito, et vide quia malum et amarum est dereliquisse te Dominum*. Secundo ut diligentius quaererent; Cant. V, 17: *quo abiit dilectus tuus, o pulcherrima mulierum?. . . Et quaeremus eum tecum.*

878. Quantum ad transitum dicit *mare autem, vento magno flante, exurgebat*. Et

primo ponitur maris tempestas;

secundo Christi apparitio et tempus apparitionis, ibi *et cum remigassent* etc.;

tertio apparitionis effectus, ibi *et timuerunt* etc.

He does two things about the first.

First, he tells that they went down to the shore.

Second, he tells of their journey across the sea, at *and when they had gone up into the ship*.

874. Note, about the first, that Christ went up into the mountain without the knowledge of his disciples. So, they waited there until evening came, for they expected that he would come back to them. But their love was so great that when evening came they just had to go looking for him. Thus he says, *when evening came, his disciples went down to the sea*.

In the mystical sense, *evening* signifies our Lord's passion or his ascension. For as long as the disciples enjoyed Christ's physical presence, no trouble disturbed them and no bitterness vexed them: *can the friends of the groom mourn as long as the groom is with them?* (Matt 9:15). But when Christ was away, then they *went down to the sea*, to the troubles of this world: *this great sea, stretching wide* (Ps 103:25).

875. He adds that they crossed, saying, *and when they had gone up into the ship, they went across the sea to Capernaum*, for the love that burned within them could not endure our Lord's absence for very long.

876. Now, at *and it was now dark, and Jesus had not come to them*. he enlarges upon what he had already said in summary fashion.

First, on their going down to the sea;

second, on their crossing, at *and the sea arose*.

877. As to the first, he says, *it was now dark, and Jesus had not come to them*. The Evangelist does not tell us this without a reason, for it shows the intensity of their love, since not even night or evening could stop them.

In the mystical sense, the *dark* signifies the absence of love; for light is love, according to: *he who loves his brother dwells in the light* (1 John 2:10). Accordingly, there is darkness in us when Jesus, *the true light* (John 1:9) does not come to us, because his presence repels all darkness.

Jesus left his disciples alone for this length of time so that they might experience his absence; and they did indeed experience it during the storm at sea: *know and realize, that it is evil and bitter for you to have left the Lord* (Jer 2:19). He left them, in the second place, so that they might look for him more earnestly: *where has your beloved gone, most beautiful of women? We will search for him with you* (Song 5:17).

878. As for their crossing, at *and the sea arose*,

first we see the storm at sea; then Christ coming to them, and the time, at *when they had rowed twenty-five or thirty stadia*; and

third, the effect this had, at *and they were afraid*.

879. Tempestas autem in mari causabatur a flatu exorti venti; et ideo dicit *mare autem, vento magno flante, exurgebat*, in altum. Per ventum illum figuratur tentatio et persecutio quae futura est Ecclesiae propter defectum caritatis. Nam, sicut Augustinus dicit, unde caritas refrigescit, inde fluctus augentur, et turbatur navis. Nec tamen venti illi et tempestas et fluctus et tenebrae id agebant ut vel navis non promoveretur, vel soluta frangeretur, quia *qui perseveraverit usque in finem, hic salvus erit*, Mt. XXIV, 13; et ibid. c. VII, 27: *flaverunt venti, et irruerunt flumina et non cecidit domus*.

880. Apparitio autem Christi non fuit statim a principio tempestatis, sed post aliquod spatium; et ideo dicit *cum remigassent ergo quasi stadia vigintiquinque aut triginta, vident Iesum*. Et hoc ideo ut daretur intelligi, quia Dominus patitur nos ad tempus tribulari, ut virtus nostra probetur; finaliter tamen in necessitate non deserit, sed nobis proximus fit; I Cor. X, 13: *fidelis Deus, qui non patietur vos tentari supra id quod potestis; sed faciet etiam cum tentatione proventum, ut possitis sustinere.*

Secundum Augustinum vigintiquinque stadia, quae remigat, sunt quinque libri Moysi. Nam huiusmodi numerus est quadratus, de hoc numero quinque consurgens in multiplicatione sui in seipsum: quinquies enim quinque sunt vigintiquinque; numerus autem multiplicatus retinet significationem suae radicis: unde sicut per quinque signatur vetus lex, ita per vigintiquinque signatur perfectio Novi Testamenti. Per triginta autem signatur perfectio Novi Testamenti, quae deerat legi: nam si ipsa quinque multiplicentur per sex, qui est numerus perfectus, consurgit numerus terdenarius.

Ad eos ergo qui remigant vigintiquinque aut triginta stadia, idest qui implent legem, vel perfectionem evangelicam, venit Iesus, calcans omnes tumores mundi, altitudines saeculi praesentis. Ps. LXXXVIII, 10: *tu dominaris potestati maris, motum autem fluctuum eius tu mitigas.* Et tunc videbimus Christum proximum navi, quia divinum auxilium approximat. Ps. CXLIV, 18: *prope est Dominus omnibus timentibus eum.* Apparet ergo quod qui recte Christum quaerunt, eum habent praesentem. Isti autem ferventissime Christum desiderabant: quod patet ex temporis tenebrositate, ex maris tempestate et ex distantia portus, quibus non obstantibus ad eum ire conabantur. Et ideo Christus adfuit eis.

881. Effectus autem apparitionis ponitur cum dicit *et timuerunt. Ille autem dixit eis: ego sum, nolite timere*, et

primo ponitur effectus interior;

secundo exterior, ibi *et statim navis fuit ad terram.*

882. Effectus autem interior fuit timor; et ideo ponitur discipulorum timor conceptus ex subita Christi apparitione, cum dicit *et timuerunt*, bono timore, quia

879. The storm was caused by a rising wind; thus he says: *the sea arose by a great blowing wind*. This wind is a symbol for the trials and persecutions which would afflict the Church due to a lack of love. For as Augustine says, when love grows cold, the waves of the sea begin to swell and danger threatens the boat. Still, these winds and the storm, with its waves and darkness, did not stop the progress of the boat or so batter it that it broke apart: *he who perseveres to the end will be saved* (Matt 24:13); and again: *and the rains fell, and the floods came, and the house did not collapse* (Matt 7:25).

880. Christ did not appear to them when the storm first began, but only some time later; thus he says, *after they had rowed twenty-five or thirty stadia, they saw Jesus*. We see from this that our Lord allows us to be troubled for a while so our virtue may be tested; but he does not desert us in the end, but comes very close to us: *God is faithful, and will not allow you to be tested beyond your strength; but will make also with temptation issue, that you may be able to bear it* (1 Cor 10:13).

According to Augustine, the twenty-five stadia they rowed are the five books of Moses. For twenty-five is the square of five, since five times five is twenty-five. But a number that is multiplied in this way keeps the meaning of its root. Thus, just as five signifies the old law, so twenty-five signifies the perfection of the New Testament. Thirty, however, signifies that perfection of the New Testament which was lacking in the law: for thirty is the result of multiplying five by six, which is a perfect number.

So, Jesus comes to those who row twenty-five or thirty stadia, i.e., to those who fulfill the law or the perfection taught by the Gospel; and he comes treading under foot all the waves of pride and the dignities of this present world: *you rule the might of the sea and calm its waves* (Ps 88:10). And then we will see Christ near our boat, because divine help is close: *the Lord is near to all who fear him* (Ps 144:18). Thus it is clear that Christ is near to all those who seek him rightly. Now the Apostles loved Christ very keenly: this is obvious because they tried to go to him despite the darkness, the stormy sea, and the distance to shore. Consequently, Christ was with them.

881. Now we see the effect of Christ's appearance, at *and they were afraid. But he said to them: it is I; do not be afraid*.

First, the interior effect;

second, the exterior effect, at *and presently the ship was at the land*.

882. The interior effect of Christ's appearance was fear; and he mentions the fear of the disciples at the sudden appearance of Christ when he says, *and they were afraid*. This

causatum ex humilitate; Rom. XI, 20: *noli altum sapere, sed time*. Vel malo timore, quia, ut dicitur Mt. c. XIV, 26, *aestimabant eum phantasma esse*. Ps. XIII, 5: *trepidaverunt timore ubi non erat timor*. Quoniam timor praecipue carnalibus competit, quia spiritualia expavescunt.

Secundo ponitur Christi confortatio contra duplex periculum. Scilicet contra periculum fidei in intellectu, et quantum ad hoc dicit **ego sum**, quasi dubitationem omnem repellens; Lc. ult., 39: *videte manus meas et pedes meos, quia ego ipse sum*. Secundo contra periculum timoris in affectu; et quantum ad hoc dicit **nolite timere**; Ier. I, 8: *ne timeas a facie eorum*; Ps. XXVI, 1: *Dominus illuminatio mea et salus mea, quem timebo?*

Tertio ponitur discipulorum assecutio, quia **voluerunt eum accipere in navim**: quo significatur quod quando timor servilis excluditur a cordibus nostris, tunc recipimus Christum, amando et contemplando. Apoc. III, 20: *ego sto ad ostium et pulso: si quis aperuerit mihi, intrabo*.

883. Effectus autem exterior fuit quantum ad duo. Primo, quia sedata est tempestas; secundo, quia statim navis fuit ad terram, cum multum ab ea distaret: non enim fallacem, sed tranquillam praebuit eis navigationem; et volens maius miraculum operari, navem non ascendit.

Sic ergo triplex hic concurrit miraculum: scilicet ambulatio supra mare, subita tempestatis cessatio, et distantis navis ad portum deductio: ut discamus, quod fideles in quibus est Christus, tumorem mundi premunt, fluctus tribulationum calcant, et velociter ad terram viventium transeunt, secundum illud Ps. c. CXLII, 10: *spiritus tuus bonus deducet me in terram*.

884. Sed hic est multiplex quaestio.

Una est circa litteram, in qua videtur Matthaei contrarium dicere: nam, Mt. XIV, 22, dicitur quod discipuli venerunt ad mare de mandato domini; hic autem, quod descenderunt quaerentes eum. Alia quaestio est, quod Matthaeus ibidem dicit, quod discipuli mare transfretantes venerunt in terram Genesareth; hic autem dicitur, quod venerunt Capharnaum. Tertia quaestio est, quod Matthaeus dicit quod Christus intravit navem; hic autem, quod non.

Sed de his tribus breviter expediens se Chrysostomus dicit, istud non fuisse idem miraculum cum illo Matthaei. Nam, ut ipse dicit, Christus frequenter huiusmodi miraculum fecit ambulans supra mare, non tamen coram turbis, sed coram discipulis suis, ne turbae crederent eum non verum corpus habere.

Secundum Augustinum autem dicitur, et verius, idem miraculum fuisse quod hic Ioannes narrat, et ibi Matthaeus. Et ideo ad primam quaestionem respondens dicit, quod non refert quod dicit Matthaeus eos praecepto Christi ad mare descendisse. Potuit enim esse quod

was a good fear, because it was the effect of humility: *do not be proud; rather fear* (Rom 11:20); or it was an evil fear, because *they thought it was a ghost* (Mark 6:49); *they trembled with fear* (Ps 13:5): for fear is especially appropriate to the carnal, because they are afraid of spiritual things.

Second, we see Christ encouraging them against two dangers. First, they are encouraged against the danger to the faith in their intellect when he says, **it is I**, to eliminate their doubts: *look at my hands and my feet! It is really me* (Luke 24:39). Second, Christ encourages them against the danger of fear in their emotions, saying, **do not be afraid**: *do not be afraid when they are present* (Jer 1:8); *the Lord is my light and my salvation, whom shall I fear?* (Ps 26:1).

Third, we see the reaction of the disciples, for **they then wanted to take him into the ship**. This signifies that we receive Christ by love and contemplation after servile fear has been taken out of our hearts: *I stand at the door and knock. If any one opens it for me, I will enter* (Rev 3:20).

883. There were two exterior effects: the storm abated, and their boat suddenly landed, although it had just been at a distance from the shore, for our Lord gave them a calm journey, without danger. He himself did not enter the boat because he wished to accomplish a greater miracle.

So here we have three miracles: the walking on the sea, the quick calming of the storm, and the sudden arrival of the boat on the land although it had been far away. We learn from this that the faithful, in whom Christ is present, put down the swelling pride of this world, tread under their feet its waves of tribulation, and cross quickly to the land of the living: *your good spirit will lead me to land* (Ps 142:10).

884. There are a number of difficulties here.

The first concerns the literal sense: Matthew seems to conflict with our present account, for he says that the disciples were told by Christ to go the shore (Matt 14:22), while here it says the disciples went there to search for him. Another difficulty is that Matthew says that the disciples crossed over to Gennesaret, while we read here that they came to Capernaum (Matt 14:34). The third difficulty is that Matthew says that Christ got into the boat (Matt 14:32), but here he did not.

Chrysostom settles these difficulties quite briefly by saying that the two accounts do not deal with the same miracle. For, as he says, Christ frequently miraculously walked upon the sea in front of his disciples, but not for the people, lest they think he did not have a real body.

But, according to Augustine, and this is the better opinion, John and Matthew are describing the same miracle. Augustine answers the first difficulty by saying it makes no difference that Matthew says the disciples went down to the shore because our Lord told them to. For it is possible that

Dominus hoc eis mandasset, et ipsi descenderint credens Christum cum eis navigaturum: unde expectarent eum usque ad noctem. Et quia Christus non venit, tunc ipsi transierunt mare.

Ad secundam quaestionem est duplex responsio. Una est, quia Capharnaum et Genesareth ex eodem littore sunt, et vicinae. Et forte discipuli pervenerunt trans mare in confinio utriusque, ideo Matthaeus nominat unam, et Ioannes aliam. Vel potest dici, quod Matthaeus non dicit quod statim venerunt in Genesareth, et ideo forte primo venerunt Capharnaum, et postea in Genesareth etc.

our Lord did so, and they went believing that he would sail with them. And that is why they waited until night, and when Christ did not come, they crossed by themselves.

There are two answers to the second difficulty. One is that Capernaum and Gennesaret are neighboring towns on the same shore. And perhaps the disciples landed at a place near both, so that Matthew mentions one and John the other. Or, it might be said that Matthew does not say that they came to Gennesaret immediately, they could have come first to Capernaurn and then to Gennesaret.

Lecture 3

6:22 Altera die, turba quae stabat trans mare, vidit quia navicula alia non erat ibi, nisi una, et quia non introisset cum discipulis suis Iesus in navim, sed soli discipuli eius abiissent. [n. 886]

6:23 Aliae vero supervenerunt naves a Tiberiade iuxta locum ubi manducaverunt panem, gratias agentes Deo. [n. 887]

6:24 Cum ergo vidisset turba quia Iesus non esset ibi, neque discipuli eius, ascenderunt in naviculas, et venerunt Capharnaum, quaerentes Iesum. [n. 888]

6:25 Et cum invenissent eum trans mare, dixerunt ei: Rabbi, quando huc venisti? [n. 890]

6:26 Respondit eius Iesus, et dixit: amen, amen dico vobis: quaeritis me, non quia vidistis signa, sed quia manducastis ex panibus, et saturati estis. [n. 892]

6:27 Operamini non cibum qui perit, sed qui permanet in vitam aeternam, quem Filius hominis dabit vobis. Hunc enim Pater signavit Deus. [n. 894]

6:28 Dixerunt ergo ad eum: quid faciemus ut operemur opera Dei? [n. 899]

6:29 Respondit Iesus, et dixit eis: hoc est opus Dei, ut credatis in eum quem misit ille. [n. 901]

6:30 Dixerunt ergo ei: quod ergo tu facis signum ut videamus, et credamus tibi? Quid operaris? [n. 903]

6:31 Patres nostri manducaverunt manna in deserto, sicut scriptum est: panem de caelo dedit eis manducare. [n. 905]

6:22 Τῇ ἐπαύριον ὁ ὄχλος ὁ ἑστηκὼς πέραν τῆς θαλάσσης εἶδον ὅτι πλοιάριον ἄλλο οὐκ ἦν ἐκεῖ εἰ μὴ ἓν καὶ ὅτι οὐ συνεισῆλθεν τοῖς μαθηταῖς αὐτοῦ ὁ Ἰησοῦς εἰς τὸ πλοῖον ἀλλὰ μόνοι οἱ μαθηταὶ αὐτοῦ ἀπῆλθον·

6:23 ἄλλα ἦλθεν πλοιά[ρια] ἐκ Τιβεριάδος ἐγγὺς τοῦ τόπου ὅπου ἔφαγον τὸν ἄρτον εὐχαριστήσαντος τοῦ κυρίου.

6:24 ὅτε οὖν εἶδεν ὁ ὄχλος ὅτι Ἰησοῦς οὐκ ἔστιν ἐκεῖ οὐδὲ οἱ μαθηταὶ αὐτοῦ, ἐνέβησαν αὐτοὶ εἰς τὰ πλοιάρια καὶ ἦλθον εἰς Καφαρναοὺμ ζητοῦντες τὸν Ἰησοῦν.

6:25 καὶ εὑρόντες αὐτὸν πέραν τῆς θαλάσσης εἶπον αὐτῷ· ῥαββί, πότε ὧδε γέγονας;

6:26 Ἀπεκρίθη αὐτοῖς ὁ Ἰησοῦς καὶ εἶπεν· ἀμὴν ἀμὴν λέγω ὑμῖν, ζητεῖτέ με οὐχ ὅτι εἴδετε σημεῖα, ἀλλ᾽ ὅτι ἐφάγετε ἐκ τῶν ἄρτων καὶ ἐχορτάσθητε.

6:27 ἐργάζεσθε μὴ τὴν βρῶσιν τὴν ἀπολλυμένην ἀλλὰ τὴν βρῶσιν τὴν μένουσαν εἰς ζωὴν αἰώνιον, ἣν ὁ υἱὸς τοῦ ἀνθρώπου ὑμῖν δώσει· τοῦτον γὰρ ὁ πατὴρ ἐσφράγισεν ὁ θεός.

6:28 εἶπον οὖν πρὸς αὐτόν· τί ποιῶμεν ἵνα ἐργαζώμεθα τὰ ἔργα τοῦ θεοῦ;

6:29 ἀπεκρίθη [ὁ] Ἰησοῦς καὶ εἶπεν αὐτοῖς· τοῦτό ἐστιν τὸ ἔργον τοῦ θεοῦ, ἵνα πιστεύητε εἰς ὃν ἀπέστειλεν ἐκεῖνος.

6:30 Εἶπον οὖν αὐτῷ· τί οὖν ποιεῖς σὺ σημεῖον, ἵνα ἴδωμεν καὶ πιστεύσωμέν σοι; τί ἐργάζῃ;

6:31 οἱ πατέρες ἡμῶν τὸ μάννα ἔφαγον ἐν τῇ ἐρήμῳ, καθώς ἐστιν γεγραμμένον· ἄρτον ἐκ τοῦ οὐρανοῦ ἔδωκεν αὐτοῖς φαγεῖν.

6:22 The next day, the multitude that stood on the other side of the sea, saw that there was no other ship there but one, and that Jesus had not entered into the ship with his disciples, but that his disciples had gone away alone. [n. 886]

6:23 But other ships came in from Tiberias, near the place where they had eaten the bread, after giving thanks to God. [n. 887]

6:24 When therefore the multitude saw that Jesus was not there, nor his disciples, they ascended into the ships, and came to Capernaum, looking for Jesus. [n. 888]

6:25 And when they had found him on the other side of the sea, they said to him: Rabbi, when did you come here? [n. 890]

6:26 Jesus answered them and said: amen, amen I say to you, you seek me, not because you have seen miracles, but because you ate of the loaves and were filled. [n. 892]

6:27 Do not labor for the food that perishes, but for that which endures to eternal life, which the Son of man will give you. For God the Father has sealed him. [n. 894]

6:28 Therefore they said to him: what shall we do, that we may do the works of God? [n. 899]

6:29 Jesus answered, and said to them: this is the work of God, that you believe in him whom he has sent. [n. 901]

6:30 They therefore said to him: what sign do you show, that we may see and believe you? What work do you perform? [n. 903]

6:31 Our fathers ate manna in the desert, as it is written: he gave them bread from heaven to eat. [n. 905]

885. Postquam Evangelista posuit quomodo discipuli inquisierunt Christum hic consequenter agit de turbis eum quaerentibus, et

primo ponitur motivum ad inquirendum;

secundo inquirendi opportunitas, ibi *aliae vero supervenerunt naves* etc.;

tertio ponitur ipsa inquisitio, ibi *cum ergo vidisset turba* etc.

886. Movit autem ad inquirendum Christum turbas miraculum praecedens, scilicet quod absque vehiculo mare transierit. Quod quidem innotuit eis, eo quod de sero non erat in littore, quod erat iuxta locum ubi fecerat miraculum de panibus, ubi una navis tantum erat, quae quidem navis cum discipulis ad aliam partem transfretavit absque Christo. Unde cum de mane non invenissent Christum ex eadem parte ex qua fuerat praecedenti die, sed iam erat ex alia parte, nec habuisset aliquam aliam navem in qua transiret, suspicati sunt quod supra mare ambulans transivisset. Et hoc est quod dicit *altera die*, ab ea qua fecerat miraculum de panibus, *turba quae stabat trans mare*, ubi miraculum fecerat *vidit quod navicula alia non erat ibi nisi una*, quia in praecedenti die non fuerat nisi illa tantum, et vidit *quia non introisset cum discipulis suis Iesus in navim* etc.

Per hanc unam navem significatur Ecclesia, quae est una, unitate fidei et sacramentorum; Ephes. IV, 5: *una fides, unum baptisma.* Per hoc autem quod Iesus non est cum discipulis, significatur corporalis separatio Christi ab eis in ascensione; Mc. ult., 19: *Dominus quidem Iesus postquam locutus est eis, assumptus est in caelum.*

887. Opportunitas autem inquirendi datur ex adventu aliarum navium ab alia parte maris, cum quibus poterant transire ad quaerendum Christum; et ideo dicit *aliae vero naves supervenerunt*, ex alia parte, scilicet *a Tiberiade, iuxta locum ubi manducaverunt panes* etc.

Per istas alias naves quae supervenerunt, significantur conventicula haereticorum et eorum qui quae sua sunt, quaerunt, et non quae Iesu Christi; infra: *quaeritis me, quia manducastis ex panibus meis*; et quae sunt separatae vel fide quantum ad haereticos, vel caritate carentes quantum ad carnales, qui non sunt proprie in Ecclesia, sed tamen sunt iuxta eam, inquantum simulatam fidem praetendunt, et speciem sanctitatis habent; secundum illud II Tim. III, 5: *habentes quidem speciem pietatis, virtutem autem eius abnegantes.* Et II Cor. XI, 14: *non est mirum si ministri satanae transformant se.*

888. Sed inquisitio fuit studiosa; unde dicit *cum ergo vidisset turba* etc., et

primo ostendit quomodo inquirit turba Christum;

secundo quomodo inventum interrogat.

885. After having described how the disciples searched for Christ, the Evangelist now shows the people looking for him.

First, he states their motive;

second, the occasion, at *but other ships came in*; and

third, the search itself, at *when therefore the multitude saw that Jesus was not there.*

886. The crowd of people was looking for Christ because of the miracle mentioned above, that is, because he had crossed the sea without using any boat. They realized this because the other evening he had not been on the shore near where he had performed the miracle of the bread, and where there had been only one boat which had left for the opposite shore with the disciples, but without Christ. So that morning, when they could not find Christ on this side, since he was already on the other side although there was no other boat he could have used, they suspected that he had crossed by walking upon the sea. And this is what he says: *the next day*, following the one on which he had worked the miracle of the bread, *the multitude that stood on the other side of the sea*, where he had performed this miracle, *saw that there was no other ship there but one*, because the day before that was the only one there, and *that Jesus had not entered into the ship with his disciples, but that his disciples had gone away alone.*

This one ship signifies the Church, which is one by its unity of faith and sacraments: *one faith, one baptism* (Eph 4:5). Again, our Lord's absence from his disciples signifies his physical absence from them at the ascension: *after the Lord Jesus spoke to them, he was taken up into heaven* (Mark 16:19).

887. It was the arrival of other boats from the opposite side of the sea that gave the people the opportunity to look for Christ; they could cross on these and search for him. He says: *but other ships came in*, from the other side, that is, *from Tiberias, near the place where they had eaten the bread, after giving thanks to God.*

These other boats signify the various sects of heretics and of those who seek their own profit, and not the good of Jesus Christ: *you seek me . . . because you ate of the loaves and were filled.* These groups are either separated in faith, as are the heretics, or in the love of charity, as are the carnal, who are not properly in the Church, but next to it, insofar as they have a feigned faith and the appearance of holiness: *they have the appearance of devotion, but deny its power* (2 Tim 3:5); *do not be surprised if the ministers of satan disguise themselves* (2 Cor 11:14).

888. The people were eager to find Christ, at *when therefore the multitude saw that Jesus was not there.*

First, he shows how they looked for him;

second, how they questioned him after they found him.

889. Dicit ergo primo, quod *cum vidisset turba quod Iesus non erat ibi, nec discipuli eius, ascenderunt in naviculas*, quae venerant a Tiberiade, *quaerentes eum*: quod est laudabile; Is. LV, 6: *quaerite Dominum dum inveniri potest*; et Ps. LXVIII, 33: *quaerite Dominum, et vivet anima vestra*.

890. Sed inventum interrogant, unde dixit *et cum turbae invenissent eum*, scilicet Christum, *trans mare, dixerunt ei: Rabbi, quando huc venisti?*

Sed haec quaestio dupliciter potest intelligi. Uno modo ut quaerant tantum de tempore; et tunc, secundum Chrysostomum exprobranda est eorum ruditas, quia post tantum miraculum non quaerunt de modo transeundi, qualiter scilicet sine navi transisset; sed tantum de tempore transitus.

Vel potest dici, quod per hoc quod dicunt *quando*, non solum quaerunt de tempore, sed etiam de aliis circumstantiis quae concurrerunt ad transitum miraculosum.

891. Sed attende, quod supra post refectionem volebant eum facere regem; nunc vero eum praesentem habent, nec eum regem facere volunt. Cuius ratio est, quia ipsi volebant eum facere regem concitati a passione laetitiae causatae a refectione. Passiones autem huiusmodi cito transeunt, et ideo ea quae secundum ipsas passiones disponuntur, transitoria sunt: quae vero ratione disponuntur, magis permanent; Eccli. XXVII, 12: *homo sapiens in sapientia sua permanet sicut sol; stultus autem ut luna mutatur*; Prov. XI, 18: *impius facit opus instabile*.

892. Consequenter cum dicit *respondit ei Iesus* etc., agit Dominus de cibo spirituali; et

primo proponit veritatem de spirituali;

secundo contradictionem excludit, ibi *murmurabant ergo Iudaei de illo*.

Circa primum tria facit.

Primo proponit veritatem spiritualis cibi;

secundo insinuat eius originem, ibi *dixerunt ergo ei: quod ergo tu facis signum?* etc.;

tertio docet modum capiendi ipsum cibum, ibi *dixerunt ergo ad eum: Domine, semper da nobis panem hunc*.

Circa primum duo facit.

Primo ostendit cibum spiritualem, et eius virtutem;

secundo manifestat eum quis sit, ibi *dixerunt ergo ad eum: quid faciemus ut operemur opera Dei?*

Circa primum duo facit.

Primo arguit perversam eorum cupiditatem;

secundo hortatur ad veritatem, ibi *operamini* etc.

893. Dicit ergo *amen, amen dico vobis*, licet ostendatis vos quasi devotos, tamen *quaeritis me, non quia*

889. He says, *when therefore the multitude saw that Jesus was not there, nor his disciples, they ascended into the ships*, which had come from Tiberias, *looking for Jesus*; and this is praiseworthy: *search for the Lord while he can be found* (Isa 55:6); *seek the Lord, and your soul will have life* (Ps 68:33).

890. Once they found him, they questioned him. *And when they*, the people, *had found him*, Christ, *on the other side of the sea*, they asked him: *Rabbi, when did you come here?*

This can be understood in two ways. In the first way, they were asking about the time only. And then, Chrysostom says, they should be rebuked for their rudeness, because, after such a miracle, they did not ask how he crossed without a boat, but only when he did so.

Or, it can be said that by asking *when*, they wanted to know not just the time, but the other circumstances connected with this miraculous crossing.

891. Note that now, after they have found Christ, they do not wish do make him their king, while before, after he had fed them, they did. They wanted to make him their king then because they were emotionally excited with the joy of their meal; but such emotions quickly pass. So it is that things that we plan according to our emotions do not last; but matters that we arrange by our reason last longer: *a wise man continues on in his wisdom like the sun; a fool changes like the moon* (Sir 27:12); *the work of the wicked will not last* (Prov 11:18).

892. Then, at *Jesus answered them and said*, our Lord begins to mention a food that is spiritual.

First, he states a truth about this spiritual food.

In the second place, he clears up a misunderstanding, at *the Jews therefore murmured at him* (John 6:41).

As to the first he does three things.

First, he presents a truth about this spiritual food;

second, he mentions its origin, at *they said therefore to him: what sign do you show?* and

third, he tells them how this spiritual food is to be acquired, at *they therefore said to him: Lord, give us this bread always* (John 6:34).

He does two things about the first.

First, he explains this spiritual food and its power; in the second place, he tells what this food is, at *therefore they said to him: what shall we do, that we may do the works of God?*

As to the first, he does two things.

First, he rebukes them for their disordered desires;

in the second place, he urges them to accept the truth, at *do not labor for the food that perishes*.

893. He says, *amen, amen, I say to you*, that although you seem to be devout, *you seek me not because you have*

vidistis signa, sed quia manducastis ex panibus, et saturati estis; quasi dicat: propter carnem me quaeritis, non propter spiritum, quia scilicet ut iterum pascamini.

Et, sicut Augustinus dicit, locum istorum tenent qui quaerunt Iesum, non propter seipsum, sed ut aliqua commoda saecularia consequantur; sicut sunt illi qui negotia habentes, ad praelatos et clericos accedunt, non propter Christum, sed ut eorum intercessione promoveantur apud magnates; sicut sunt illi qui ad Ecclesias confugiunt, non propter Iesum, sed quia a potentioribus premuntur; sicut etiam sunt illi qui ad sacros ordines ad Dominum appropinquantes, non eisdem merita virtutum, sed subsidia vitae praesentis inquirunt, scilicet divitias et honores, ut Gregorius dicit XXIII *Moral.* Et hoc patet: nam facere signa, virtutis divinae est; sed manducare panem multiplicatum, est temporale. Quia ergo non veniunt ad Christum propter virtutem quam in eo vident, sed propter hoc quod ex panibus manducant, non Christo serviunt, sed suo ventri, ut dicitur Phil. III et Ps. XLVIII, v. 19: *confitebitur tibi cum benefeceris ei.*

894. Ad veritatem eos reducit proponendo eis spiritualem cibum, dicens **operamini non cibum qui perit, sed qui manet in vitam aeternam**, et

primo proponit eius virtutem;

secundo eius auctoritatem, ibi **quem Filius hominis dedit vobis**.

895. Virtus illius cibi consideratur in hoc quod non perit.

Unde sciendum est circa hoc, quod corporalia sunt quaedam similitudines spiritualium, utpote ab eis causata et derivata, et ideo imitantur ipsa spiritualia aliquo modo. Unde sicut corpus sustentatur cibo, ita illud quo sustentatur spiritus, dicitur eius cibus, quidquid sit illud. Illud autem quo sustentatur corpus, cum transeat in corporis naturam, corruptibile est; sed cibus quo sustentatur spiritus, est incorruptibilis, quia non mutatur in ipsum spiritum, sed potius e converso spiritus in cibum. Unde dictum est, Augustini: *cibus sum grandium: cresce, et manducabis me. Nec tu me mutabis in te, ut cibum carnis tuae, sed mutaberis in me*: ut dicitur Lib. confessionum.

Et ideo dicit Dominus **operamini**; idest, operando quaerite, seu operibus mereamini non cibum qui perit, scilicet corporalem; I Cor. c. VI, 13: *esca ventri, et venter escis, Deus autem et hunc et hanc destruet* quia non semper erit usus ciborum; **sed** illum cibum **operamini**, scilicet spiritualem, **qui manet in vitam aeternam**; qui quidem cibus est ipse Deus, inquantum est veritas contemplanda, et bonitas amanda, quibus reficitur spiritus; Prov. c. IX, 5: *comedite panem meum*; Eccli. XV, v. 3: *cibavit illum panem vitae et intellectus.* Item ipsa obedientia

seen miracles, but because you ate of the loaves and were filled. As if to say: you seek me, not for the sake of the spirit, but for the sake of the flesh, because you hope for more food.

As Augustine says, these people represent those who seek Jesus not for himself, but in order to gain certain worldly advantages: as those engaged in some business call on clerics and prelates, not for the sake of Christ, but so that through their intervention they might be advanced into the ranks of those who are important; and like those who hurry to the churches, not for Christ, but because they have been urged to do so by those who are more powerful; and like those who approach our Lord for sacred orders not because they desire the merits of the virtues, but because they are looking for the satisfactions of this present life, as wealth and praise, as Gregory says in his *Moralia*. This is obvious: for to perform miracles is a work of divine power, but to eat loaves of bread which have been multiplied is temporal. Accordingly, those who do not come to Christ because of the power they see in him, but because they eat his bread, are not serving Christ but their own stomachs (Phil 3:19); and again, *he will praise you when you are good to him* (Ps 48:19).

894. He leads them back to the truth by calling their attention to spiritual food, saying, **do not labor for the food that perishes, but for that which endures to eternal life**.

First, he mentions its power;

second, that it comes from him, **which the Son of man will give you**.

895. The power of this food is seen in the fact that it does not perish.

In this respect we should point out that material things are likenesses of spiritual things, since they are caused and produced by them; and consequently they resemble spiritual things in some way. Now just as the body is sustained by food, so that which sustains the spirit is called its food, whatever it might be. The food that sustains the body is perishable, since it is converted into the nature of the body; but the food that sustains the spirit is not perishable, because it is not converted into the spirit; rather, the spirit is converted into its food. Hence Augustine says in his *Confessions*: *I am the food of the great; grow and you will eat me. But you will not change me into yourself, as you do bodily food, but you will be changed into me*.

So our Lord says: **do not labor**, i.e., seek by your work, or merit by your works, for the food that perishes, i.e., bodily food: *food is for the stomach, and the stomach for food, but God will destroy both* (1 Cor 6:13), because we will not always need food; **but for that which**, that is, the spiritual food, **endures to eternal life**. This food is God himself, insofar as he is the truth which is to be contemplated and the Goodness which is to be loved, which nourish the spirit: *eat my bread* (Prov 9:5); *wisdom will feed him with the bread of life and understanding* (Sir 15:5). Again, this food is the

divinorum mandatorum; supra IV, 34: *meus cibus est ut faciam voluntatem eius qui misit me*. Item ipse etiam Christus. Infra eodem: *ego sum panis vitae*; item: *caro mea vere est cibus, et sanguis meus vere est potus*. Et hoc inquantum est coniuncta Verbo Dei, quod est cibus quo angeli vivunt. Similem autem differentiam assignavit supra c. IV, 13, de potu corporali et potu spirituali, cum dixit: *qui biberit ex aqua hac, sitiet iterum: qui autem biberit ex aqua quam ego dabo ei, non sitiet in aeternum*, quam hic assignat inter cibum corporalem et spiritualem. Cuius ratio est, quia corporalia sunt corruptibilia, spiritualia vero, et maxime Deus, sunt aeterna.

896. Sed sciendum est, secundum Augustinum in libro *de Operibus monachorum*, quod ex hoc verbo, scilicet *operamini non cibum qui perit*, quidam monachi erroris causam sumpserunt, dicentes, spirituales viros non debere aliquid corporaliter operari. Sed hic intellectus est falsus, quia Paulus, qui maxime spiritualis fuit, propriis manibus laboravit, ut habetur Ephes. IV, 28, ubi ipse dicit: *qui furabatur, iam non furetur; magis autem laboret manibus suis*. Ergo est verus intellectus, ut opus nostrum, idest principale studium et intentionem nostram dirigamus ad quaerendum cibum qui ducit ad vitam aeternam, scilicet bona spiritualia. Ad temporalia autem non debemus principaliter attendere, sed accessorie, idest solum ea procurare ratione corporis corruptibilis, quod sustentari oportet quamdiu in hac vita vivimus. Unde contra hoc signanter dicit Apostolus, II Thess. III, 10: *qui non laborat non manducet*; quasi diceret: qui dicunt quod nihil corporale est operandum, quia comestio est quid corporale, tales non debent comedere.

897. Consequenter cum dicit *quem Filius hominis dabit vobis*, ponit spirituali cibi datorem: et primo ponit auctorem huius cibi; secundo manifestat unde habeat auctoritatem cibandi.

Auctor autem et dator cibi spiritualis est Christus; et ideo dicit *quem*, scilicet cibum qui non perit, *Filius hominis dabit vobis*. Si dixisset Filius Dei, non fuisset visum mirum; sed hoc quod Filius hominis dat eum, magis elevat ad attentionem. Spiritualiter tamen ideo Filius hominis dat, quia natura humana infirma per peccatum fastidiebat spiritualem cibum, nec poterat ipsum in sua spiritualitate sumere: unde oportuit quod Filius Dei carnem sumeret, et per eam nos reficeret; Ps. XXII, 5: *parasti in conspectu meo mensam*.

898. Unde autem habeat auctoritatem dandi, subdit cum dicit *hunc enim Pater signavit Deus*; quasi dicat: quod Filius hominis dabit, hoc non habet nisi inquantum singularitate et eminentia plenitudinis gratiae praecellit omnes Filios hominum; unde dicit *hunc*, scilicet Filium hominis, *Pater signavit*: idest, signanter distinxit

obedience to the divine commands: *my food is to do the will of him who sent me* (John 4:34). Also, it is Christ himself: *I am the bread of life* (John 6:35); *for my flesh is meat indeed, and my blood is drink indeed* (John 6:56). And this is so insofar as the flesh of Christ is joined to the Word of God, which is the food by which the angels live. The difference between bodily and spiritual food which he gives here, is like the one he gave before between bodily and spiritual drink: *whoever drinks of this water will thirst again, but he who will drink of the water that I give to him will not thirst again* (John 4:13). The reason for this is that bodily things are perishable, while spiritual things, and especially God, are eternal.

896. We should note that according to Augustine, in his work, *On the Labor of Monks*, that certain monks misunderstood our Lord's saying, *do not labor for the food that perishes*, and claimed that spiritual men should not perform physical work. But this interpretation is false because Paul, who was most spiritual, worked with his hands: *let him who stole, steal no longer, rather let him work with his hands* (Eph 4:28). The correct interpretation, therefore, is that we should direct our work, i.e., our main interest and intention, to seeking the food that leads to eternal life, that is, spiritual goods. In regard to temporal goods, they should not be our principal aim but a subordinate one, that is, they are to be acquired only because of our mortal body, which has to be nourished as long as we are living this present life. So the Apostle speaks against this opinion, saying: *if any one will not work, neither let him eat* (2 Thess 3:10); as if to say: those who maintain that physical work is not to be done should not eat, since eating is physical.

897. Next, at *which the Son of man will give you*, he mentions the one who gives this spiritual food. First, we see the author of this food; second, the source of his authority to give us this food.

Christ is the author of this spiritual food, and the one who gives it to us. Thus he says, *which*, that is, the food that does not perish, *the Son of man will give you*. If he had said: the Son of God, it would not have been unexpected; but he captures their attention by saying that the Son of man gives this food. Yet the Son of man gives this food in a spiritual way, because human nature, weakened by sin, found spiritual food distasteful, and was not able to take it in its spirituality. Thus it was necessary for the Son of man to assume flesh and nourish us with it: *you have prepared a table before me* (Ps 22:5).

898. He adds the source of his authority to give us this food when he says, *for God the Father has sealed him*. As if to say: the Son of man will give us this food because he surpasses all the sons of men by his unique and preeminent fullness of grace. Thus he says, *him*, i.e., on the Son of man, *God the Father has sealed*, i.e., he has significantly

a ceteris; Ps. XLIV, 8: *unxit te Deus Deus tuus oleo laetitiae prae consortibus tuis.*

Vel, secundum Hilarium *signavit*, idest sigillavit. Quando autem sigillum in cera imprimitur, cera retinet totam figuram sigilli, sicut et Filius totam figuram Patris accepit. Est autem duplex receptio quam Filius recepit a Patre. Una aeterna; et de hac non intelligitur quod hic dicitur *signavit*, quia in sigillatione aliud est natura recipiens, et aliud imprimens. Sed hoc intelligitur de mysterio incarnationis, quia in natura humana Deus Pater impressit Verbum, qui *est splendor et figura substantiae eius*: ut dicitur Hebr. I, 3.

Vel secundum Chrysostomum *signavit*, idest, ad hoc specialiter eum Deus Pater instruit ut daret vitam aeternam mundo; infra X, 10: *ego veni ut vitam habeant* etc. Sic enim quando aliquis eligitur ad aliquod magnum officium peragendum, dicitur signari ad illud officium; Lc. X, 1: *post haec designavit Dominus et alios septuaginta discipulos* etc. Vel *signavit*, idest manifestavit per vocem in baptismo, et per opera, ut dictum est supra, V.

899. Consequenter cum dicit *dixerunt ergo ad eum: quid faciemus ut operemur opera Dei?* manifestat quid sit cibus spiritualis, et

primo ponitur quaestio Iudaeorum;

secundo subditur responsio Iesu Christi, ibi *respondit Iesus* etc.

900. Circa primum sciendum est, quod Iudaei instructi ex lege, credebant nihil aeternum esse nisi Deum. Unde, cum dixisset quod cibus spiritualis permaneat in vitam aeternam, intellexerunt cibum illum esse aliquid divinum. Et ideo quaerentes, non de cibo, sed de opere Dei mentionem faciunt, cum dicunt *quid faciemus ut operemur opera Dei?* In quo non longe erant a veritate, cum nihil aliud sit cibus spiritualis quam operari opera Dei; Lc. c. XVIII, 18: *quid faciendo vitam aeternam possidebo?*

901. Responsio Domini ponitur, cum dicit *hoc est opus Dei ut credatis in illum* etc.

Ubi considerandum est, quod Apostolus, Rom. IV, distinguit fidem ab operibus, dicens, quod Abraham non est iustificatus ex operibus, sed ex fide. Quid est ergo quod hic Dominus dicit, ipsam fidem, seu credere, esse opus Dei?

Sed ad hoc est duplex responsio. Una, quod Apostolus non distinguit fidem ab operibus simpliciter, sed ab exterioribus. Sunt enim quaedam opera exteriora, quae exercentur corporalibus membris, quae quia magis nota sunt, secundum communem usum opera dicuntur; alia vero sunt interiora, quae exercentur in ipsa anima, quae

distinguished him from others: *God, your God, has anointed you with the oil of gladness above your fellows* (Ps 44:8).

Hilary explains it this way. God *sealed*, i.e., impressed with a seal. For when a seal is impressed on wax, the wax retains the entire figure of the seal, just as the Son has received the entire figure of the Father. Now the Son receives from the Father in two ways. One of these ways is eternal, and *sealed* does not refer to this way, because when something is sealed the nature receiving the seal is not the same as the nature impressing the seal. Rather, these words should be understood as referring to the mystery of the incarnation, because God the Father has impressed his Word on human nature; this Word who is *the brightness of his glory, and the figure of his substance* (Heb 1:3).

Chrysostom explains it this way: **God the Father has sealed**, i.e., God the Father specifically chose Christ to give eternal life to the world: *I have come that they may have life* (John 10:10). For when someone is chosen to perform some great task, he is said to be sealed for that task: *after this, the Lord appointed seventy other disciples* (Luke 10:1). Or, it could be said that God the Father **has sealed**, i.e., Christ was made known by the Father, by his voice at Christ's baptism, and by his works, as we saw in the fifth chapter.

899. Next, at **therefore they said to him: what shall we do, that we may do the works of God?** we see the nature of spiritual food.

First, the Jews pose their question;

in the second place, we have the answer of Jesus Christ, at **Jesus answered, and said to them: this is the work of God**.

900. Concerning the first, we should note that the Jews, since they had been taught by the law, believed that only God was eternal. So when Christ said that his food would endure to eternal life, they understood that it would be a divine food. Thus when they question Christ, they do not mention this food, but rather the work of God, saying: **what shall we do, that we may do the works of God?** Indeed, they were not far from the truth, since spiritual food is nothing else than performing and accomplishing the works of God: *what shall I do to gain eternal life?* (Luke 18:18).

901. The Lord's answer is given when he says: **this is the work of God, that you believe in him whom he has sent**.

Here we should reflect that the Apostle distinguished faith from works, saying that Abraham was justified by his faith, not by his works (Rom 4:2). If this is so, why does our Lord say here that to have faith, i.e., to believe, is a work of God?

There are two answers to this. One is that the Apostle is not distinguishing faith from absolutely all works, but only from external works. External works, being performed by our body, are more noticeable, and so the word 'works' ordinarily refers to them. But there are other works, interior works, performed within the soul, and these are known

non sunt nota nisi sapientibus, et quae convertuntur ad cor. Alio modo dicitur, quod ipsum credere potest computari inter opera exteriora, non quod fides sit ipsa opera, sed eorum principium; unde et signanter dicit **ut credatis in illum**. Differt enim dicere credere Deum, sic enim designo obiectum; et credere Deo, quia sic designo testem; et credere in Deum, quia sic designo finem: ut sic Deus possit haberi ut obiectum fidei, ut testis, et ut finis; sed aliter et aliter. Quia obiectum fidei potest esse creatura, credo enim caelum esse creatum; similiter et creatura potest esse testis fidei, credo enim Paulo, seu cuicumque sanctorum; sed fidei finis non potest esse nisi Deus: nam mens nostra solum in Deum fertur sicut in finem. Finis autem cum habeat rationem boni, est obiectum amoris; et ideo credere in Deum ut in finem, est proprium fidei formatae per caritatem: quae quidem fides sic formata, est principium omnium bonorum operum; et intantum ipsum credere dicitur opus Dei.

902. Sed si fides est opus Dei, quomodo homines faciunt opera Dei?

Sed hoc solvitur per Is. XXVI, 12, cum dicit: *omnia opera nostra operatus est in nobis*. Nam hoc idem quod credimus, et quidquid operamur boni, est in nobis a Deo; Phil. II, v. 13: *ipse est qui operatur in nobis et velle, et perficere*. Et ideo signanter dicit, credere esse opus Dei, ut ostendat fidem esse donum Dei, ut dicitur Eph. II, 8.

903. Consequenter cum dicit **dixerunt ergo ei: quod ergo tu facis signum?** Agitur de origine cibi, et

primo ponitur quaestio Iudaeorum;

secundo responsio Christi, ibi **amen, amen dico vobis, non Moyses dedit vobis panem de caelo**.

Circa primum tria faciunt. Primo petunt signum; secundo determinant ipsum; tertio inducunt Scripturae testimonium.

904. Signum autem petunt proponendo quaestionem; unde **dixerunt illi: quod tu facis signum, ut videamus, et credamus tibi?**

Haec autem quaestio aliter inducitur ab Augustino, et aliter a Chrysostomo. Chrysostomus enim dicit, quod Dominus invitaverat eos ad fidem. Argumenta autem ad fidem inducentia sunt miracula; I Cor. XIV, 22: *signa data sunt infidelibus*. Et ideo ad hoc quaerunt signum quo credant: mos enim est Iudaeis signa petere; I Cor. I, 22: *quoniam Iudaei signa quaerunt*. Unde dicit **quod ergo signum tu facis?**

Sed hoc ridiculosum videtur, quod propter hoc quaerant aliqua miracula, quia statim fecerat aliqua multiplicando panes, et ambulando supra mare, quae in praesentia extiterant, quibus credere possent. Sed hoc ideo dicunt, ut provocent Dominum, et inducant ut semper eos pasceret. Quod patet, quia nullam mentionem faciunt de alio signo, nisi de eo quod factum est in eorum

only to the wise and those converted in heart. From another point of view, we can say that to believe can be regarded as included in our external works, not in the sense that it is an external work, but because it is the source of these works. Thus he significantly says: **that you believe in him**. Now it is one thing to say: I believe in God, for this indicates the object. It is another thing to say: I believe God, for this indicates the one who testifies. And it is still another thing to say: I believe in God, for this indicates the end. Thus God can be regarded as the object of faith, as the one who testifies, and as the end, but in different ways. For the object of faith can be a creature, as when I believe in the creation of the heavens. Again, a creature can be one who testifies, for I believe Paul or any of the saints. But only God can be the end of faith, for our mind is directed to God alone as its end. Now the end, since it has the character of a good, is the object of love. Thus, to believe in God as in an end is proper to faith living through the love of charity. Faith, living in this way, is the principle of all our good works; and in this sense to believe is said to be a work of God.

902. But if faith is a work of God, how do men do the works of God?

But this is made clear: *you have accomplished all our works for us* (Isa 26:12). For the fact that we believe, and any good we do, is from God: *it is God who is working in us, both to will and to accomplish* (Phil 2:13). Thus he explicitly says that to believe is a work of God in order to show us that faith is a gift of God (Eph 2:8).

903. Next, we see the origin of this food, at **they therefore said to him: what sign do you show?**

First, we have the question asked by the Jews;

second, the answer of Christ, at **amen, amen I say to you: Moses did not give you bread from heaven** (John 6:32).

Three things are done about the first: first, the Jews look for a sign; second, they decide what it should be; and third, they bring in what is narrated in Scripture.

904. They look for a sign by asking Christ: **what sign do you show, that we may see and believe you?**

This question is explained differently by Augustine and by Chrysostom. Chrysostom says that our Lord was leading them to the faith. But the evidence that leads one to the faith are miracles: *signs were given to unbelievers* (1 Cor 14:22). And so the Jews were looking for a sign in order to believe, for it is their custom to seek such signs: *for Jews demand signs* (1 Cor 14:22). So they say: **what sign do you show?**

But it seems foolish to ask for a miracle for this reason, for Christ had just performed some in their presence which could lead them to believe, as multiplying the bread and walking on the water. What they were asking was that our Lord always provide them with food. This is clear because the only sign they mention is the one given by Moses to their ancestors for forty years, and they ask in this way

parentibus per Moysen quadraginta annis, ut quasi per hoc petant quod semper eos pascat; unde dicunt *patres nostri manducaverunt manna in deserto*. Nec dicunt: Deus pavit patres nostros manna, ne videantur velle aequare eum Deo. Similiter non dicitur, Moyses pavit eos, ne videantur Moysen praeferre Christo, quasi in hoc eum allicere volentes, ut continue eos pascat. De cibo illo dicitur Ex. XVI, et in Ps. c. LXXVII, 25: *panem angelorum manducavit homo*.

905. Augustinus autem dicit, quod Dominus dixit se daturum eis cibum qui permanet in vitam aeternam; unde quasi videtur se Moysi praeferre. Iudaei autem Moysen reputabant maiorem Christo; unde dicebant, infra c. IX, 29: *nos scimus quia Moysi locutus est Deus; hunc autem nescimus unde sit*. Unde requirebant quod Christus faceret aliqua maiora quam Moyses fecerit; et ideo reducunt in memoriam ea quae Moyses fecit, dicentes: *patres nostri manducaverunt manna in deserto*; quasi dicerent: hoc quod dicis de te, maius est quam illud quod fecit Moyses: quia promittis cibum qui non perit; sed manna quod dabat Moyses si servabatur in alium diem, vermibus scaturiebat. Si ergo vis ut credamus tibi, facias aliquid maius Moyse: nam quod fecisti non est maius, quia satiasti quinque millia hominum, sed quinque panibus hordeaceis, et semel tantum; ille vero totum populum satiavit manna de caelo annis quadraginta, et hoc in deserto, sicut scriptum est in Ps. LXXVII, 24: *panem de caelo dedit eis manducare*.

that Christ always provide food for them. Thus they say: *our fathers ate manna in the desert*. They did not say that God provided their ancestors with the manna, so that they would not seem to be making Christ equal to God. Again, they did not say that Moses fed their ancestors, so they would not seem to be preferring Moses to Christ, trying in this way to influence our Lord. We read of this food: *man ate the bread of angels* (Ps 77:25).

905. According to Augustine, however, our Lord had said that he would give them food that would endure to eternal life. Thus, he seemed to put himself above Moses. The Jews, on the other hand, considered Moses greater than Christ; so they said: *we know that God spoke to Moses, but as for this man, we do not know from where he comes* (John 9:29). Accordingly, they required Christ to accomplish greater things than Moses; and so they recall what Moses did, saying: *our fathers ate manna in the desert*. As if to say: what you say about yourself is greater than what Moses did, for you are promising a food that does not perish, while the manna that Moses gave became wormy if saved for the next day. Therefore, if we are to believe you, do something greater than Moses did. Although you have fed five thousand men once with five barley loaves, this is not greater than what Moses did, for he fed all the people with manna from heaven for forty years, and in the desert too: *he gave them the bread of heaven* (Ps 77:24).

Lecture 4

6:32 Dixit ergo eis Iesus: amen, amen dico vobis, non Moyses dedit vobis panem de caelo; sed Pater meus dat vobis panem de caelo verum. [n. 907]

6:33 Panis enim verus est qui de caelo descendit, et dat vitam mundo. [n. 910]

6:34 Dixerunt ergo ad eum: Domine, semper da nobis panem hunc. [n. 911]

6:35 Dixit autem eis Iesus: ego sum panis vitae. Qui venit ad me, non esuriet, et qui credit in me, non sitiet in aeternum. [n. 913]

6:36 Sed dixi vobis, quia et vidistis me, et non credidistis. [n. 916]

6:37 Omne quod dat mihi Pater, ad me veniet. Et eum qui venit ad me, non eiiciam foras. [n. 917]

6:38 Quia descendi de caelo, non ut faciam voluntatem meam, sed voluntatem eius qui misit me. [n. 922]

6:39 Haec est enim voluntas eius qui misit me Patris, ut omne quod dedit mihi, non perdam ex eo, sed resuscitem illud in novissimo die. [n. 924]

6:40 Haec est autem voluntas Patris mei, qui misit me, ut omnis qui videt Filium, et credit in eum, habeat vitam aeternam. Et ego resuscitabo eum in novissimo die. [n. 927]

6:32 εἶπεν οὖν αὐτοῖς ὁ Ἰησοῦς· ἀμὴν ἀμὴν λέγω ὑμῖν, οὐ Μωϋσῆς δέδωκεν ὑμῖν τὸν ἄρτον ἐκ τοῦ οὐρανοῦ, ἀλλ᾽ ὁ πατήρ μου δίδωσιν ὑμῖν τὸν ἄρτον ἐκ τοῦ οὐρανοῦ τὸν ἀληθινόν·

6:33 ὁ γὰρ ἄρτος τοῦ θεοῦ ἐστιν ὁ καταβαίνων ἐκ τοῦ οὐρανοῦ καὶ ζωὴν διδοὺς τῷ κόσμῳ.

6:34 εἶπον οὖν πρὸς αὐτόν· κύριε, πάντοτε δὸς ἡμῖν τὸν ἄρτον τοῦτον.

6:35 εἶπεν αὐτοῖς ὁ Ἰησοῦς· ἐγώ εἰμι ὁ ἄρτος τῆς ζωῆς· ὁ ἐρχόμενος πρὸς ἐμὲ οὐ μὴ πεινάσῃ, καὶ ὁ πιστεύων εἰς ἐμὲ οὐ μὴ διψήσει πώποτε.

6:36 Ἀλλ᾽ εἶπον ὑμῖν ὅτι καὶ ἑωράκατέ [με] καὶ οὐ πιστεύετε.

6:37 πᾶν ὃ δίδωσίν μοι ὁ πατὴρ πρὸς ἐμὲ ἥξει, καὶ τὸν ἐρχόμενον πρὸς ἐμὲ οὐ μὴ ἐκβάλω ἔξω,

6:38 ὅτι καταβέβηκα ἀπὸ τοῦ οὐρανοῦ οὐχ ἵνα ποιῶ τὸ θέλημα τὸ ἐμὸν ἀλλὰ τὸ θέλημα τοῦ πέμψαντός με.

6:39 τοῦτο δέ ἐστιν τὸ θέλημα τοῦ πέμψαντός με, ἵνα πᾶν ὃ δέδωκέν μοι μὴ ἀπολέσω ἐξ αὐτοῦ, ἀλλὰ ἀναστήσω αὐτὸ [ἐν] τῇ ἐσχάτῃ ἡμέρᾳ.

6:40 τοῦτο γάρ ἐστιν τὸ θέλημα τοῦ πατρός μου, ἵνα πᾶς ὁ θεωρῶν τὸν υἱὸν καὶ πιστεύων εἰς αὐτὸν ἔχῃ ζωὴν αἰώνιον, καὶ ἀναστήσω αὐτὸν ἐγὼ [ἐν] τῇ ἐσχάτῃ ἡμέρᾳ.

6:32 Then Jesus said to them: amen, amen I say to you: Moses did not give you bread from heaven, but my Father gives you the true bread from heaven. [n. 907]

6:33 For the true bread is that which comes down from heaven and gives life to the world. [n. 910]

6:34 They therefore said to him: Lord, give us this bread always. [n. 911]

6:35 And Jesus said to them: I am the bread of life: he who comes to me shall not hunger, and he who believes in me shall never thirst. [n. 913]

6:36 But I said to you, that you also have seen me, and you do not believe. [n. 916]

6:37 All that the Father gives to me shall come to me, and he who comes to me, I will not cast out. [n. 917]

6:38 Because I came down from heaven, not to do my own will, but the will of him who sent me. [n. 922]

6:39 Now this is the will of the Father who sent me: that of all he has given to me, I should lose nothing but should raise it up again on the last day. [n. 924]

6:40 And this is the will of my Father who sent me: that every one who sees the Son and believes in him may have eternal life, and I will raise him up on the last day. [n. 927]

---

906. Posita Iudaeorum interrogatione, hic ponitur responsio Christi. Et

primo ostendit originem cibi spiritualis;

secundo probat eam, ibi *panis enim verus est qui de caelo descendit*.

907. Circa primum sciendum est, quod Iudaei duo proposuerant Christo circa originem cibi corporalis, quem Patres eorum habuerunt; scilicet datorem, qui fuit Moyses, et locum, quia de caelo; et ideo Dominus circa originem cibi spiritualis haec duo removens, ponit alium esse datorem cibi spiritualis, et alium locum. Unde dicit, removendo praedicta, *amen, amen dico vobis, non Moyses dedit vobis panem de caelo*. Alius est qui dat,

906. Having told us the question the Jews had asked Christ, the Evangelist now gives his answer.

First, Christ tells us of the origin of this spiritual food;

second, he proves what he has just said at *for the true bread is that which comes down from heaven*.

907. Concerning the first, we should note that the Jews had mentioned two things to Christ concerning the bodily food which had been given to their ancestors: the one who gave this food, Moses, and the place, that is, from heaven. Accordingly, when our Lord tells them about the origin of spiritual food, he does not mention these two, for he says that there is another who gives this food and another place. He says: *amen, amen, I say to you: Moses did not give you*

quia Pater meus, non panem corporalem, sed **panem verum de caelo**.

908. Sed contra. Numquid non vere panis fuit quem habuerunt patres in deserto?

Respondeo. Si accipiatur **verum** secundum quod dividitur contra falsum, sic panis ille verus fuit, non enim falsum erat miraculum de manna; si autem accipiatur **verum**, prout veritas dividitur contra figuram, sic panis ille non fuit verus, sed figura panis spiritualis, scilicet Domini nostri Iesu Christi, quem ipsum manna significabat, ut dicit Apostolus, I Cor. c. X, 3: *omnes eamdem escam spiritualem manducaverunt*.

909. Item contra hoc quod dicit **non dedit vobis panem de caelo**, est quod dicitur in Ps. LXXVII, 24: *panem caeli dedit eis*.

Respondeo. 'Caelum' accipitur tripliciter. Quandoque pro aere; Mt. XIII, 4: *volucres caeli comederunt illud*; et in Ps. XVII, 14: *intonuit de caelo Dominus*. Quandoque pro caelo sidereo, secundum illud Ps. CXIII, 16: *caelum caeli Domino*; et Mt. XXIV, 29: *stellae cadent de caelo*. Quandoque vero pro ipsis spiritualibus bonis; Mt. V, 12: *gaudete et exultate, quia merces vestra multa est in caelo*. Manna ergo **de caelo** fuit non sidereo seu spirituali, sed aereo. Vel dicitur **de caelo** inquantum erat figura veri panis caelestis Domini nostri Iesu Christi.

910. Consequenter cum dicit **panis enim verus est qui de caelo descendit, et dat vitam mundo**, probat quod sit de caelo et per effectum eius. Verum enim caelum est spiritualis naturae, cui per se convenit vita, et ideo per se vivificat; infra: **spiritus est qui vivificat**. Ipse autem Deus est auctor vitae. Ex hoc ergo cognoscitur quod panis iste spiritualis est de caelo, cum faciat proprium effectum, si dat vitam. Nam panis ille corporalis vitam non dabat, quia omnes qui manna manducaverunt, mortui sunt; iste autem dat vitam, et ideo dicit **panis verus est**, et non figuralis, **qui de caelo descendit**. Et hoc patet, quia **dat vitam mundo**. Nam Christus, qui est verus panis, quos vult vivificat; infra X, 10: **ego veni ut vitam habeant** etc. Ipse etiam de caelo descendit; supra III, 13: **nemo ascendit in caelum nisi qui descendit de caelo, filius hominis qui est in caelo**.

Si ergo Christus verus panis, vitam dat mundo ratione suae divinitatis, et descendit de caelo ratione humanae naturae. Nam, ut supra III dictum est, descendisse de caelo dicitur assumendo humanam naturam; Phil. II, 7: *exinanivit semetipsum, formam servi accipiens*.

911. **Dixerunt ergo**, etc. Hic agitur de adeptione cibi spiritualis, et

primo ponitur petitio ipsius cibi;

bread from heaven. There is another who gives to you, that is, my Father; and he gives, not, just bodily bread, but **the true bread from heaven**.

908. But was it not true bread that their ancestors had in the desert?

I answer that if you understand **true** as contrasted with false, then they had true bread, for the miracle of the manna was a true miracle. But if **true** is contrasted with symbolic, then that bread was not true, but was a symbol of spiritual bread, that is, of our Lord Jesus Christ, whom that manna signified, as the Apostle says: *all ate the same spiritual food* (1 Cor 10:3).

909. When it is said, *he gave them the bread of heaven* (Ps 77:24), this seems to conflict with, **Moses did not give youthe true bread from heaven**.

I answer that the word 'heaven' can be understood in three ways. Sometimes it can mean the air, as in *the birds of heaven ate them* (Matt 13:4); and also in, *the Lord thundered from heaven* (Ps 14:14). Sometimes heaven means the starry sky; as in, *the highest heaven is the Lord's* (Ps 113:16), and in, *the stars will fall from heaven* (Matt 24:19). Third, it can signify goods of a spiritual nature, as in *rejoice and be glad, because your reward is great in heaven* (Matt 5:12). So the manna was **from heaven**, not the heaven of the stars or of spiritual food, but from the air. Or, the manna was said to be **from heaven** insofar as it was a symbol of the true bread from heaven, our Lord Jesus Christ.

910. When he says, **for the true bread is that which comes down from heaven and gives life to the world**, he proves that it is from heaven by its effect. For the true heaven is spiritual in nature, and has life by its own essence; therefore, of itself, it gives life: **it is the spirit that gives life** (John 6:64). Now God himself is the author of life. Therefore, we know that this spiritual bread is from heaven when it produces its proper effect, if it gives life. That bodily bread used by the Jews did not give life, since all who ate the manna died. But this bread does give life, so he says: **the true bread**, not that symbolic bread, **is that which comes down from heaven**. This is clear, because it **gives life to the world**: for Christ, who is the true bread, gives life to whom he wills: **I have come that they may have life** (John 10:10). He also descended from heaven: **and no man has ascended into heaven, except he who descended from heaven** (John 3:13).

Thus Christ, the true bread, gives life to the world by reason of his divinity; and he descends from heaven by reason of his human nature, for as we said on the prior text, he came down from heaven by assuming human nature: *he emptied himself, taking the form of a servant* (Phil 2:7).

911. **They therefore said to him: Lord, give us this bread always**. Now he considers the acquisition of this spiritual food.

First, we see the Jews asking for it;

secundo ponitur expositio, ibi *dixit autem eis Iesus: ego sum panis vitae*, ubi ostendit modum adeptionis.

912. Sciendum est autem circa primum, quod Iudaei verba Domini carnaliter intelligebant; et ideo quia in desiderio carnalium erant, cibum carnalem petunt a Christo; unde dixerunt ad eum *Domine, semper da nobis hunc panem*, qui reficiat hoc modo. Et Samaritana verbum de aqua spirituali carnaliter intelligebat, et indigentia carere volens dixit: *Domine, da mihi hanc aquam*. Et licet isti verba Domini carnaliter de cibo intelligant, et carnaliter petant; tamen eorum petitio spiritualiter intellecta, nobis competit; Mt. VI, 11: *panem nostrum quotidianum da nobis hodie*: quia non possumus sine hoc pane vivere.

913. Consequenter cum dicit *dixit autem eis Iesus: ego sum panis vitae*, ostendit modum adeptionis, ostendens

primo quid sit iste panis;

secundo quomodo acquiratur, ibi *omne quod dat mihi pater, ad me veniet*.

Circa primum tria facit.

Primo ponit expositionem panis praedicti;

secundo expositionis rationem assignat, ibi *qui venit ad me, non esuriet*;

tertio exponendi necessitatem manifestat, ibi *sed dixi vobis* etc.

914. Dixit ergo eis Iesus *ego sum panis vitae*: nam, sicut supra dictum est, verbum sapientiae est specialis cibus mentis, quia eo mens sustentatur; Eccli. XV, 3: *cibavit illum pane vitae et intellectus*.

Dicitur autem panis sapientiae esse panis vitae, ad differentiam panis corporalis, qui est panis mortis, qui non competit nisi ad restaurandum defectum mortalitatis, unde et solum in hac vita mortali necessarius est. Sed panis sapientiae divinae est per se vivificativus, nec habet mortem contrariam. Item panis corporalis non dat vitam, sed tantum praeexistentem sustentat ad tempus; sed panis spiritualis ita vivificat quod dat vitam, nam anima incipit vivere per hoc quod adhaeret Verbo Dei; Ps. XXXV, 10: *apud te est fons vitae*. Quia ergo omne Verbum sapientiae derivatur a Verbo Dei unigenito, Eccli. I, 5: *fons sapientiae unigenitus Dei, residens in excelso*, ideo ipsum Dei Verbum principaliter dicitur panis vitae; et ideo Christus dicit *ego sum panis vitae*. Et quia caro Christi ipsi Verbo Dei unita est, habet etiam quod sit vivificativa, unde et corpus, sacramentaliter sumptum, vivificativum est: nam per mysteria quae Christus in carne sua complevit, dat vitam mundo; et sic caro Christi, propter Domini Verbum, panis est, non consuetae vitae, sed illius quae morte non reseratur. Et ideo

second, he shows the way it is acquired, at *and Jesus said to them: I am the bread of life*.

912. We should note with respect to the first, that the Jews understood what Christ said in a material way; and so, because they desired material things, they were looking for material bread from Christ. Hence they said to him, *Lord, give us this bread always*, which physically nourishes us. The Samaritan woman also understood what our Lord said about spiritual water in a material way, and wishing to slake her thirst, said, *Lord, give me this water* (John 4:15). And although these people understood what our Lord said about food in a material way, and asked for it this way, we are expected to ask for it as understood in a spiritual way: *give us this day our daily bread* (Matt 6:11), because we cannot live without this bread.

913. Then, at *and Jesus said to them: I am the bread of life*, he shows how this bread is acquired.

First, he shows what this bread is;

second, how to obtain it, at *all that the Father gives to me shall come to me*.

Concerning the first, he does three things.

First, he explains what this bread is, I am the bread of life;

second, he gives the reason for this, *he who comes to me shall not hunger*;

third, he shows why this had to be explained, at *but I said to you, that you also have seen me*.

914. Jesus said to them: *I am the bread of life*, for as we saw above, the word of wisdom is the proper food of the mind, because the mind is sustained by it: *he fed him with the bread of life and understanding* (Sir 15:3).

Now the bread of wisdom is called the bread of life to distinguish it from material bread, which is the bread of death, and which serves only to restore what has been lost by a mortal organism; hence material bread is necessary only during this mortal life. But the bread of divine wisdom is life-giving of itself, and no death can affect it. Again, material bread does not give life, but only sustains for a time a life that already exists. But spiritual bread actually gives life: for the soul begins to live because it adheres to the word of God: *for with you is the fountain of life* (Ps 35:10). Therefore, since every word of wisdom is derived from the only begotten Word of God—*the fountain of wisdom is the only begotten of God* (Sir 1:5)—this Word of God is especially called the bread of life. Thus Christ says, *I am the bread of life*. And because the flesh of Christ is united to the Word of God, it also is life-giving. Thus, too, his body, sacramentally received, is life-giving: for Christ gives life to the world through the mysteries which he accomplished in his flesh. Consequently, the flesh of Christ, because of the Word of the Lord, is not the bread of ordinary life, but of that life

caro Christi dicitur panis; Gen. penult., 20: *Aser, pinguis panis eius.*

Significatur etiam per manna, I Cor. X, 1 ss. ***Manna*** interpretatur *quid est hoc?* Quia Iudaei illud videntes admirabantur, dicentes unus ad alium quid est hoc? Sed nihil est admirabilius quam Filius Dei homo factus, ita ut cuilibet contingat quaerere quid est hoc? Idest, quomodo Filius Dei, Filius hominis est; quomodo ex duabus naturis fit una persona Christi? Is. IX, 6: *vocabitur nomen eius admirabilis.* Est etiam mirabile quomodo Christus sit sub sacramento.

915. Consequenter cum dicit **qui venit ad me, non esuriet**, assignat rationem expositionis, et hoc ex effectu istius panis. Panis enim corporalis comestus non in perpetuum famem aufert, cum corrumpatur et reficiat; et ideo exigitur ad nutrimentum; panis autem spiritualis dans per se vitam, numquam corrumpitur; et ideo homo semel comedens, numquam esurit. Et ideo dicit **qui venit ad me, non esuriet; et qui credit in me, non sitiet in aeternum**.

Hoc autem quod dicit, scilicet **qui venit** et **qui credit, non esuriet nec sitiet**, non differunt, secundum Augustinum, quia idem est venire ad eum, et credere in eum: quia ad Deum venimus non passibus corporis, sed mentis, quorum primus est fides. Idem est etiam comedere et bibere: utroque enim significatur aeterna satietas, ubi nulla est egestas. Mt. V, 6: *beati qui esuriunt et sitiunt iustitiam, quoniam ipsi saturabuntur*: ut sit idem cibus sustentans, et potus refrigerans.

Causa autem quare temporalia non auferunt sitim in perpetuum, una quidem est, quia non simul sumuntur, sed paulatim, et quasi cum motu, et ideo semper restat sumendum; et propter hoc, sicut congruit delectatio et satietas ex iam sumpto, ita et desiderium restat ex sumendo. Alia vero est, quia corrumpuntur, unde remanet memoria ex corrupto, et generatur iterato desiderium eorum. Spiritualia vero et simul sumuntur, et non corrumpuntur nec deficiunt; et ideo eorum satietas manet in perpetuum. Apoc. VII, 16: *non esurient neque sitient.* Ps. XV, 10: *adimplebis me laetitia cum vultu tuo, delectationes in dextera tua*, idest in spiritualibus bonis, *usque in finem*.

916. Consequenter cum dicit **sed dixi vobis** etc., ponitur exponendi necessitas.

Posset enim aliquis dicere: nos quaesivimus panem; sed tu non respondes: dabo vobis illum vel non dabo; sed potius dicis: **ego sum panis vitae**; et ideo non videtur bona responsio tua. Sed quod bona sit, ostendit Dominus dicens **dixi vobis quia et vidistis me, et non credidistis**: quod idem est ac si aliquis haberet panem coram se, ignorans illum et dicatur ei: ecce panis coram te est. Et ideo dicit **dixi vobis (ego sum panis vivus) et vidistis me, et non credidistis**; idest, desideratis panem,

which does not die. And so the flesh of Christ is called bread: *the bread of Asher is rich* (Gen 49:20).

His flesh was also signified by the manna. ***Manna*** means *what is this?* because when the Jews saw it they wondered, and asked each other what it was. But nothing is more a source of wonder than the Son of God made man, so that everyone can fittingly ask, what is this? That is, how can the Son of God be the Son of man? How can Christ be one person with two natures? *His name will be called Wonderful* (Isa 9:6). It is also a cause for wonder how Christ can be present in the sacrament.

915. Next, at **he who comes to me shall not hunger**, he gives the reason for this from the effect of this bread. When material bread is eaten, it does not permanently take away our hunger, since it must be destroyed in order to build us up; and this is necessary if we are to be nourished. But spiritual bread, which gives life of itself, is never destroyed; consequently, a person who eats it once never hungers again. Thus he says: **he who comes to me shall not hunger, and he who believes in me shall never thirst**.

According to Augustine, it is the same thing to say, **whoever comes**, as to say, **whoever believes**: since it is the same to come to Christ and to believe in him, for we do not come to God with bodily steps, but with those of the mind, the first of which is faith. To eat and to drink are also the same: for each signifies that eternal fullness where there is no want: *blessed are they who hunger and thirst for what is right, for they will be filled* (Matt 5:6); so that food which sustains and that drink which refreshes are one and the same.

One reason why temporal things do not take away our thirst permanently is that they are not consumed altogether, but only bit by bit, and with motion, so that there is always still more to be consumed. For this reason, just as there is enjoyment and satisfaction from what has been consumed, so there is a desire for what is still to come. Another reason is that they are destroyed; hence the recollection of them remains and generates a repeated longing for those things. Spiritual things, on the other hand, are taken all at once, and they are not destroyed, nor do they run out; and consequently the fullness they produce remains forever: *they will neither hunger nor thirst* (Rev 7:16); *your face will fill me with joy; the delights in your right hand* i.e., in spiritual goods *will last forever* (Ps 16:11).

916. Then, at **but I said to you, that you also have seen me**, we see why Christ had to explain these things.

For someone could say: we asked for bread; but you did not answer, that I will give it to you, or I will not. Rather, you say, **I am the bread of life**; and so your answer does not seem to be appropriate. But our Lord shows that it is a good answer, saying, **but I have said to you, that you also have seen me, and you do not believe**. This is the same as a person having bread right in front of him without his knowing it, and then being told: look! The bread is right before you. And so Christ says: **but I have said to you, (I am the bread**

et habetis illum coram vobis; et tamen non sumitis, quia non creditis. In quo eorum incredulitatem improperat eis; infra XV, 24: *sed viderunt, et oderunt me et Patrem meum*.

917. Consequenter cum dicit *omne quod dat mihi pater, ad me veniet*, ostendit quomodo acquiratur, et

primo ponit modum acquirendi;

secundo fidem perventionis, ibi *et eum qui venit ad me, non eiiciam foras*;

tertio manifestat quod dicit, ibi *quia descendi de caelo* etc.

918. Sciendum est circa primum, quod ipsum credere nostrum est nobis ex dono Dei. Eph. II, 8: *gratia salvati estis, et non ex vobis, Dei enim donum est*; Phil. I, 29: *vobis datum est ut non solum in illum credatis, sed ut etiam pro illo patiamini*. Dicitur autem quandoque Deus Pater dare Filio homines credentes, sicut hic *omne quod dat mihi Pater, ad me veniet*. Quandoque Filius dat Patri, sicut illud I Cor. XV, 24: *cum tradiderit regnum Deo et Patri*. Ex quo intelligimus quod sicut Pater dans non adimit sibi regnum, ita nec Filius. Pater autem Filio dat, inquantum facit hominem verbo suo adhaerere. I Cor. I, v. 9: *per quem*, scilicet Patrem, *vocati estis in societatem Filii eius*. Filius vero tradit Patri, inquantum Verbum est manifestativum ipsius Patris. Infra XVII, 6: *Pater, manifestavi nomen tuum hominibus*. Sic ergo dicit *omne quod dat mihi Pater, ad me veniet*; idest, qui in me credunt, quos Pater mihi facit adhaerere ex dono suo.

919. Sed diceret forte aliquis, quod non necessarium est quod aliquis dono Dei utatur: multi enim recipiunt donum Dei, qui non utuntur eo. Quomodo ergo dicit *omne quod dat mihi Pater, ad me veniet*?

Ad quod dicendum est, quod in datione ista non solum intelligitur habitus, qui est fides et huiusmodi, sed etiam interior instinctus ad credendum. Quidquid autem facit ad salutem, totum est ex dono Dei.

920. Sed restat quaestio: quia si omne quod dat Pater Christo, ad eum vadit, ut ipse dicit, illi soli ad Deum vadunt quos Pater dat ei; non ergo debet imputari illis qui non vadunt, cum non dentur ei.

Ad quod dicendum, quod non imputatur eis, si absque auxilio Dei ad fidem venire non possunt, sed hoc ei imputatur qui non venit, quia impedimentum praestat quod non veniat, avertens se a salute, cuius via quantum in se est, omnibus est aperta.

921. Finis autem perventionis ponitur cum dicit *et eum qui venit ad me non eiiciam foras*. Posset enim

of life) *that you also have seen me, and you do not believe*, i.e., you want bread, and it is right before you; and yet you do not take it because you do not believe. In saying this he is censuring them for their unbelief: *they have both seen and hated me and my Father* (John 15:24).

917. Then, at *all that the Father gives to me shall come to me*, he shows how this bread is acquired.

First, he mentions the way to acquire it;

second, the end attained by those who come to him, at *and he who comes to me, I will not cast out*;

third, he enlarges on this, at *because I came down from heaven*.

918. Concerning the first, we should note that the very fact that we believe is a gift of God to us: *you are saved by grace, through faith; and this is not due to yourself, for it is the gift of God* (Eph 2:8); it has been granted to you not only to believe in him, but also to suffer for him (Phil 1:29). Sometimes, God the Father is said to give those who believe to the Son, as here: *all that the Father gives to me shall come to me*. At other times, the Son is said to give them to the Father: *he will hand over the kingdom to God and the Father* (1 Cor 15:24). We can see from this that just as the Father does not deprive himself of the kingdom in giving to the Son, neither does the Son in giving to the Father. The Father gives to the Son insofar as the Father makes a person adhere to his word: *through whom* that is, the Father *you have been called into the fellowship of his Son* (1 Cor 1:9). The Son, on the other hand, gives to the Father insofar as the Word makes the Father known: *I have manifested your name to the men whom you have given me* (John 17:6). Thus Christ says: *all that the Father gives to me shall come to me*, i.e., those who believe in me, whom the Father makes adhere to me by his gift.

919. Perhaps some might say that it is not necessary for one to use God's gift: for many receive God's gift and do not use it. So how can he say: *all that the Father gives to me shall come to me*?

We must say to this that in this giving we have to include not only the habit, which is faith, but also the interior impulse to believe. So, everything which contributes to salvation is a gift of God.

920. There is another question. If everything which the Father gives to Christ comes to him, as he says, then only those come to God whom the Father gives him. Thus, those who do not come are not responsible, since they are not given to him.

I answer that they are not responsible if they cannot come to the faith without the help of God. But those who do not come are responsible, because they create an obstacle to their own coming by turning away from salvation, the way to which is of itself open to all.

921. Then, at *and he who comes to me, I will not cast out*, the end attained by those who come is mentioned. For

aliquis dicere: veniemus ad te; sed tu non recipies nos. Et ideo dicit, hoc excludens, *eum qui venit ad me*, passibus fidei et bonis operationibus, *non eiiciam foras*, in quo dat intelligere, esse se intus: illud est enim intus unde exitur foras.

Attendamus ergo quid sit istud intrinsecum, et quomodo inde eiiciantur.

Sciendum quidem igitur est, quod omnia visibilia cum dicantur esse quasi quaedam exteriora respectu spiritualium, quanto aliquid est magis spirituale, tanto magis est intrinsecum. Ergo duplex est intrinsecum. Unum est profundissimum, scilicet gaudium vitae aeternae, quod, secundum Augustinum, est magis penetrale et dulce secretum sine taedio, sine amaritudine malarum cogitationum, sine interpellatione tentationum et dolorum; de quo dicitur Matth. XXV, 21: *intra in gaudium Domini tui*. Et Ps. XXX, 21: *abscondes eos in abscondito faciei tuae*; idest, in plena visione tuae essentiae. Et ab hoc intrinseco nullus eiicietur. Apoc. III, 12: *qui vicerit faciam illum columnam in templo Dei vivi, et foras non egredietur amplius*, quia ut dicitur Matth. c. XXV, 46, *ibunt iusti in vitam aeternam*. Aliud intrinsecum est rectitudo conscientiae, quae est spirituale gaudium; et de hoc dicitur Sap. VIII, 16: *intrans in domum meam, conquiescam*. Et Cant. I, 3: *introduxit me rex in cellaria sua*. Et de isto aliqui eiiciuntur.

Et ideo quod Dominus dicit *non eiiciam foras*, potest dupliciter intelligi. Uno modo, ut illi dicantur ad ipsum venire qui sunt dati ei a Patre per aeternam praedestinationem; et de illis dicit *eum qui venit ad me*, praedestinatus a Patre, *non eiiciam foras*; Rom. XI, v. 2: *non repulit Deus plebem suam quam elegit*. Alio modo, quia illi qui egrediuntur, non tamquam a Christo eiecti egrediantur, sed causa eiectionis sit ex parte ipsorum, qui per infidelitatem et peccata, a secreto rectae conscientiae recedunt. Et sic dicitur *non eiiciam ego foras*, sed ipsi se eiiciunt; Ier. XXIII, 33: *vos estis onus, proiiciam vos, dicit Dominus*. Et hoc modo eiectus est foras qui ad nuptias intraverat non habens vestem nuptialem, ut dicitur Matth. XXII, 11 ss.

922. Rationem autem praemissorum assignat, cum dicit *quia descendi de caelo* etc., et

primo ponit propositum de implenda voluntate Patris;

secundo manifestat quae sit voluntas Patris, ibi *haec est voluntas eius qui misit me Patris*;

tertio ostendit finalem voluntatis impletionem, ibi *et ego resuscitabo eum in novissimo die*.

923. Circa primum sciendum est, quod littera ista potest legi dupliciter. Uno modo secundum Augustinum, alio modo secundum Chrysostomum.

some might say that we will come to you, but you will not receive us. To exclude this he says, *he who comes to me*, by steps of faith and by good works, *I will not cast out*. By this he lets us understand that he is already within, for one must be within before one can be sent out.

Let us consider, therefore, what is interior, and how one is cast out from it.

We should point out that since all visible things are said to be exterior with respect to spiritual things, then the more spiritual something is the more interior it is. What is interior is twofold. The first is the most profound, and is the joy of eternal life. According to Augustine, this is a sweet and most interior retreat, without any weariness, without the bitterness of evil thoughts, and uninterrupted by temptations and sorrows. We read of this: *share the joy of your Lord* (Matt 25:21); and, *you will hide them in the secret of your face*, that is, in the full vision of your essence (Ps 30:21). From this interior no one is cast out: *he who conquers, I will make him a pillar in the temple of the living God; and he will no longer leave it* (Rev 3:12), because *the just will go to everlasting life* (Matt 25:46). The other interior is that of an upright conscience; and this is a spiritual joy. We read of this: *when I enter into my house I will enjoy repose* (Wis 8:16); and *the king has brought me into his storerooms* (Song 1:3). It is from this interior, that some are cast out.

So, when our Lord says, *and he who comes to me, I will not cast out*, we can understand this in two ways. In one way, those who come to him are those who have been given to him by the Father through eternal predestination. Of these he says: *he who comes to me*, predestined by the Father, *I will not cast out*: *God has not rejected his people, the people he chose* (Rom 11:2). In a second way, those who do go out are not cast out by Christ, rather, they cast themselves out, because through their unbelief and sins they abandon the sanctuary of an upright conscience. Thus we read: *I will not cast out* such; but they do cast themselves out: *you are the burden, and I will cast you aside, says the Lord* (Jer 23:33). It was in this way that the man who came to the wedding feast without wedding clothes was cast out (Matt 22:13).

922. Next, at *because I came down from heaven*, he gives the reason for what he just said.

First, he mentions his intention to accomplish the will of the Father;

second, he states what the will of the Father is, at *and this is the will of the Father who sent me*; and

third, he shows the final accomplishment of this will, at *and I will raise him up on the last day*.

923. Concerning the first, we should note that this passage can be read in two ways: either as Augustine does, or following the interpretation of Chrysostom.

Secundum Augustinum quidem sic: *eum qui venit ad me, non eiiciam foras*, et hoc ideo, quia ille venit ad me qui meam humilitatem imitatur. Matth. XI, 28, cum diceret Dominus: *venite ad me, omnes, qui laboratis*, consequenter subdit: *discite a me, quia mitis sum et humilis corde*. Vera autem Filii Dei mititas in hoc est, quia voluntatem suam supposuit voluntati Patris. Et ideo dicit **non eiiciam, quia descendi de caelo non ut faciam voluntatem meam, sed voluntatem eius qui misit me**. Propterea anima a Deo exiit, quia superba erat; et ideo necesse est humilitate regredi veniendo ad Christum per imitationem suae humilitatis, quae in hoc est quod non facit voluntatem suam solum, sed Dei Patris.

Sciendum est autem, quod in Christo fuit duplex voluntas. Una secundum humanam naturam, quae est sibi propria, et natura, et voluntate Patris; alia secundum naturam divinam, quae est eadem cum voluntate Patris. Voluntatem ergo suam, scilicet humanam, ordinavit sub voluntate divina, quia obedientiam suam sub effectu Paternae voluntatis ostendit ipse, volens voluntatem Patris explere. Ps. XXXIX, 9: *ut faciam voluntatem tuam, Deus meus, volui*. Hanc voluntatem fieri in nobis petimus cum dicimus, Matth. VI, 10: *fiat voluntas tua*. Illi ergo non eiiciuntur foras, qui non faciunt voluntatem suam, sed voluntatem Dei. Nam diabolus volens facere voluntatem suam, quod est superbiae, eiectus est de caelo, et primus homo de Paradiso.

Secundum Chrysostomum vero sic. Ideo non eiicio foras eum qui venit ad me, quia ad hoc veni, ut impleam voluntatem Patris de salute hominum. Si ergo pro salute hominum incarnatus sum, quomodo debeo eos eiicere? Et hoc est quod dicit: ideo non eiicio, **quia descendi de caelo non ut faciam voluntatem meam**, scilicet humanam, ut proprium mihi acquiram; **sed voluntatem eius qui misit me**, Patris, *qui vult omnes homines salvos fieri*, ut dicitur I Tim. II, 4. Et ideo, quantum est ex me, nullum eiicio. Rom. V, 10: *si enim, cum inimici essemus, reconciliati sumus Deo per mortem Filii eius, multo magis, reconciliati, salvi erimus in vita ipsius*.

924. Quae autem sit voluntas Patris, exponit

primo, cum dicit **haec est enim voluntas eius qui misit me Patris** etc.;

secundo rationem assignat, ibi **haec est enim voluntas Patris mei** etc.

925. Dixit ergo: non eiiciam foras eos qui ad me veniunt, quia carnem assumpsi ut faciam voluntatem Patris. **Voluntas autem eius qui misit me Patris, haec est**, scilicet **ut non eiiciam foras**; et ideo non eiiciam. I Thess. c. IV, 3: *haec est voluntas Dei, sanctificatio vestra*. Et ideo dicit **ut omne quod dedit mihi, non perdam ex eo**; pater, idest, ut nihil perdam, quousque perveniat ad resurrectionem futuram, in qua aliqui perdentur, non tamen de illis qui dati sunt ei per aeternam

Augustine understands it this way: *the one who comes to me I will not cast out*; and this is because the one who comes to me imitates my humility. After our Lord said, *come to me, all you who labor*, he added, *learn from me, for I am gentle and humble of heart* (Matt 11:29). Now the true gentleness of the Son of God consists in the fact that he submitted his will to the will of the Father. Thus he says, **because I came down from heaven, not to do my own will, but the will of him who sent me**. Since a soul abandons God because of its pride, it must return in humility, coming to Christ by imitating his humility; and this humility of Christ was in not doing his own will, but the will of God the Father.

Here we should note that there were two wills in Christ. One pertains to his human nature, and this will is proper to him, both by nature and by the will of the Father. His other will pertains to his divine nature, and this will is the same as the will of the Father. Christ subordinated his own will, that is, his human will, to the divine will, because, wishing to accomplish the will of the Father, he was obedient to the Father's will: *my God, I desired to do your will* (Ps 39:9). We ask that this will be accomplished in our regard when we say, *your will be done* (Matt 6:10). Thus, those who do the will of God, not their own will, are not cast out. The devil, who wanted to do his own will out of pride, was cast from heaven; and so too the first man was expelled from paradise.

Chrysostom explains the passage this way. The reason I do not cast out one who comes to me is because I have come to accomplish the will of the Father concerning the salvation of men. So, if I have become incarnate for the salvation of men, how can I cast them out? And this is what he says: I do not cast out one who comes, **because I came down from heaven, not to do my own will**, my human will, so as to obtain my own benefit, **but the will of him who sent me**, that is, the Father, *he desires the salvation of all men* (1 Tim 2:4). And therefore, so far as I am concerned, I do not cast out any person: *for if, when we were enemies, we were reconciled to God by the death of his Son, now much more, having been reconciled, we will be saved by his life* (Rom 5:10).

924. He shows what the Father wills.

He does this first, at **and this is the will of my Father who sent me**,

and next, he explains why he wills it, at **and this is the will of my father**.

925. He says: I will not cast out those who come to me, because I have taken flesh in order to do the will of the Father: **and this is the will of him who sent me**, the Father, that those who come to me I will not cast out; and **so I will not cast them out**. *This is the will of God, your sanctification* (1 Thess 4:3). Therefore he says that **now this is the will of the Father who sent me: that of all he has given to me, I should lose nothing**, i.e., that I should lose nothing until the time of the resurrection. At this time some will be lost, the

praedestinationem, sed impii; Ps. I, 6: *iter impiorum peribit*. Illi vero qui usque tunc conservantur, non perdentur.

Per hoc autem quod dicit **non perdam**, non est intelligendum quod indigeat eorum, aut quod detrimentum sit ei, si pereunt. Sed dicit hoc propter affectum suum ad salutem illorum, et bonum illorum, quod reputat suum.

926. Sed contra est quod dicitur infra c. XVII, 12: **nemo ex eis**, scilicet quos dedisti mihi, **periit, nisi filius perditionis**. Ergo aliqui eorum qui dati sunt ei per aeternam praedestinationem, perduntur. Non est ergo verum hoc quod dicit **non perdam ex eo**.

Sed dicendum est, quod ex illis qui dati sunt ei per praesentem iustitiam perduntur; non autem de illis qui dati sunt per aeternam praedestinationem.

927. Rationem autem divinae voluntatis ponit cum dicit **haec est autem voluntas Patris mei** etc. Ratio quare Pater vult quod **non perdam ex eo quod dedit mihi**, est quia voluntas Patris est vivificare spiritualiter homines, quia ipse est fons vitae. Et quia aeternus est, quantum est de se, voluntatis eius est, ut omnis qui venit ad me habeat vitam aeternam. Et hoc est quod dicit **haec est voluntas Patris qui misit me, ut omnis qui videt Filium, et credit in eum, habeat vitam aeternam**.

Sed attendendum est quod supra V, 24, dixit: **qui videt Filium, et credit ei qui misit me, habet vitam aeternam**, hic vero dicit **qui credit in eum**: ut det intelligere eamdem divinitatem Patris et Filii, cuius visio per essentiam est ultimus finis noster, et obiectum fidei. Quod vero dicit **videt**, non intelligitur de visione per essentiam, quam praecedit fides, sed de visione corporali Christi, quae inducit ad fidem. Et ideo signanter dicit **qui videt Filium, et credit in eum**; supra V, 24: **qui credit in eum . . . non iudicatur, sed transiet a morte in vitam**; infra XX, 31: **haec autem scripta sunt, ut credatis quoniam Iesus Christus est Filius Dei, ut credentes vitam habeatis in nomine eius**.

928. Haec autem Patris voluntas similiter implebitur, et ideo subdit, **et ego resuscitabo eum in novissimo die**: quia ita vult ut non solum in anima, sed etiam in corpore habeat vitam aeternam (Dan. XII, 2: *de his qui in pulvere dormiunt evigilabunt alii in vitam aeternam, alii vero in opprobrium sempiternum*) sicut et Christus resurrexit; Rom. c. VI, 9: *Christus resurgens ex mortuis, iam non moritur* etc.

wicked; but none of those given to Christ through eternal predestination will be among them: *the way of the wicked will perish* (Ps 1:7). Those, on the other hand, who are preserved until then, will not be lost.

Now when he says, *lose nothing*, we should not understand this as implying that he needs such people or that he is damaged if they perish. Rather, he says this because he desires their salvation and what is good for them, which he regards as his own good.

926. What John later reports Christ as saying seems to conflict with this: *none of them*, that is, of those you have given me, *is lost but the son of perdition* (John 17:12). Thus, some of those given to Christ through eternal predestination are lost. Accordingly, what he says here, *that of all that he has given to me, I should lose nothing*, is not true.

We must say to this that some are lost from among those given to Christ through a present justification; but none are lost from among those given to him through eternal predestination.

927. Now he gives the reason for the divine will, at *and this is the will of my Father*. The reason why the Father wills that *of all he has given to me, I should lose nothing* is that the Father wills to bring men to life spiritually, because he is the fountain of life. And since the Father is eternal, he wills, absolutely speaking, that every one who comes to me should have eternal life. And this is what he says: *for this is the will of my Father, who sent me, that everyone who sees the Son and believes in him may have eternal life*.

Note that he said above: *he who hears my word, and believes him who sent me, has eternal life; and he will not come into judgment* (John 5:24), while here he says: *every one who sees the Son and believes in him*. We can understand from this that the Father and the Son have the same divine nature; and it is the vision of this, through its essence, that is our ultimate end and the object of our faith. When he says here, *sees the Son*, he is referring to the physical sight of Christ which leads to faith, and not to this vision through essence which faith precedes. Thus he expressly says, *every one who sees the Son and believes in him*: *he who believes him . . . will not come into judgment but passes from death to life* (John 5:24); *these things are written, so that you may believe that Jesus Christ is the Son of God, and so that believing you may have life in his name* (John 20:31).

928. This will of the Father will also be accomplished. So he adds: *and I will raise him up on the last day*, for he wills that we have eternal life not just in our soul alone, but also in our body, as Christ did at his resurrection: *many of those who sleep in the dust of the earth will awake: some to an everlasting life, and others to everlasting shame* (Dan 12:2); *Christ, having risen from the dead, will not die again* (Rom 6:9).

Lecture 5

6:41 Murmurabant ergo Iudaei de illo, quia dixisset: ego sum panis vivus, qui de caelo descendi, [n. 930]

6:42 et dicebant: nonne hic est filius Ioseph, cuius nos novimus patrem et matrem? Quomodo ergo dicit hic, quia de caelo descendi? [n. 931]

6:43 Respondit ergo Iesus, et dixit eis: nolite murmurare in invicem: [n. 932]

6:44 nemo potest venire ad me, nisi Pater, qui misit me, traxerit eum. Et ego resuscitabo eum in novissimo die. [n. 934]

6:45 Est scriptum in prophetis: erunt omnes docibiles Dei. Omnis qui audivit a Patre, et didicit, venit ad me. [n. 941]

6:46 Non quia Patrem vidit quisquam; nisi is qui est a Deo, hic vidit Patrem. [n. 947]

6:41 Ἐγόγγυζον οὖν οἱ Ἰουδαῖοι περὶ αὐτοῦ ὅτι εἶπεν· ἐγώ εἰμι ὁ ἄρτος ὁ καταβὰς ἐκ τοῦ οὐρανοῦ,

6:42 καὶ ἔλεγον· οὐχ οὗτός ἐστιν Ἰησοῦς ὁ υἱὸς Ἰωσήφ, οὗ ἡμεῖς οἴδαμεν τὸν πατέρα καὶ τὴν μητέρα; πῶς νῦν λέγει ὅτι ἐκ τοῦ οὐρανοῦ καταβέβηκα;

6:43 ἀπεκρίθη Ἰησοῦς καὶ εἶπεν αὐτοῖς· μὴ γογγύζετε μετ' ἀλλήλων.

6:44 οὐδεὶς δύναται ἐλθεῖν πρός με ἐὰν μὴ ὁ πατὴρ ὁ πέμψας με ἑλκύσῃ αὐτόν, κἀγὼ ἀναστήσω αὐτὸν ἐν τῇ ἐσχάτῃ ἡμέρᾳ.

6:45 ἔστιν γεγραμμένον ἐν τοῖς προφήταις· καὶ ἔσονται πάντες διδακτοὶ θεοῦ· πᾶς ὁ ἀκούσας παρὰ τοῦ πατρὸς καὶ μαθὼν ἔρχεται πρὸς ἐμέ.

6:46 οὐχ ὅτι τὸν πατέρα ἑώρακέν τις εἰ μὴ ὁ ὢν παρὰ τοῦ θεοῦ, οὗτος ἑώρακεν τὸν πατέρα.

6:41 The Jews therefore murmured at him, because he had said: I am the living bread, which came down from heaven. [n. 930]

6:42 And they said: is this not Jesus, the son of Joseph, whose father and mother we know? How can he then say, I came down from heaven? [n. 931]

6:43 Jesus therefore answered and said to them: do not murmur among yourselves. [n. 932]

6:44 No man can come to me, unless the Father, who has sent me, draws him; and I will raise him up on the last day. [n. 934]

6:45 It is written in the prophets: and they will all be taught about God. Every one who has heard of the Father and has learned, comes to me. [n. 941]

6:46 Not that any man has seen the Father, but he who is of God has seen the Father. [n. 947]

929. Posita doctrina Christi, hic excluditur contradictio praedictae doctrinae, et

primo quantum ad turbas murmurantes;

secundo quantum ad discipulos dubitantes, ibi **multi ergo audientes ex discipulis eius dixerunt** etc.

Circa primum duo facit.

Primo exprimit murmur turbarum de origine spiritualis cibi;

secundo mitigat eorum litigium de cibi spiritualis manducatione, ibi **litigabant ergo Iudaei**.

Circa primum duo facit.

Primo ponitur murmur turbarum;

secundo repressio murmuris, ibi **respondit ergo Iesus, et dixit eis**.

Circa primum duo facit.

Primo ponitur occasio murmuris;

secundo ponuntur murmurantium verba, ibi **nonne iste est filius Ioseph?**

930. Concludit ergo ex praemissis verbis Christi, quod quidam de quodam dictorum verborum murmurabant, quia scilicet dixerat: **ego sum panis vivus, qui de caelo descendi**; quem quidem spiritualem panem

929. Those opinions that conflict with the above teaching of Christ are now rejected.

First, those of the people, who were discontented;

second, those of the disciples, who were in a state of doubt, at **many therefore of the disciples, hearing it, said: this saying is hard** (John 6:61).

He does two things about the first.

First, we see the people grumble about the origin of this spiritual food;

second, we see Christ check the dispute which arose over the eating of this spiritual food, at **the Jews therefore quarreled among themselves** (John 6:53).

As to the first he does two things.

First, he mentions the grumbling of the people;

second, how it was checked, at **Jesus therefore answered and said to them**.

As to the first he does two things.

First, he shows the occasion for this complaining;

second, what those complaining said, at **is this not Jesus, the son of Joseph?**

930. He continues that some of the people were grumbling over what Christ had said, that is, because Christ had said, **I am the living bread, which came down from heaven**, a spiritual bread they did not understand or desire. And so

non capiebant nec desiderabant. Et ideo murmurabant, quia in spiritualibus mentem fundatam non habebant, et huius rei antiquam consuetudinem habebant, secundum illud Ps. CV, 25: *murmuraverunt in tabernaculis*; et I Cor. X, 10: *neque murmuraveritis, sicut quidam eorum murmuraverunt.* Ideo autem, ut Chrysostomus dicit, usque huc non murmurabant, quia semper sperabant se consecuturos corporalem escam: qua spe subtracta, statim murmurare incipiunt, licet aliam causam praetendant. Non autem manifeste contradicunt propter reverentiam quam adhuc habebant ad ipsum, ex memoria praecedentis miraculi.

931. Verba autem murmurantium ponit cum dicit **nonne hic est filius Ioseph?** Quia enim carnales erant, carnalem Christi generationem solam considerabant, ex qua impediebantur ne cognoscerent spiritualem et aeternam; et ideo de sola carnali loquuntur, secundum illud supra III, 31: **qui de terra est, de terra loquitur**, et spiritualem non capiunt; unde subdunt **quomodo ergo dicit hic, quia de caelo descendi?** Vocant autem eum filium Ioseph propter reputationem: quia nutritius eius erat, secundum illud Lc. III, 23: *ut putabatur filius Ioseph.*

932. Murmurationis autem repressio ponitur cum dicit **respondit ergo Iesus, et dixit eis**, et

primo reprimit ipsorum murmur;

secundo satisfacit dubitationi, ibi **amen, amen dico vobis: qui credit in me, habet vitam aeternam.**

Circa primum duo facit.

Primo cohibet eorum murmur;

secundo assignat causam murmuris eorum, ibi **nemo potest venire ad me** etc.

933. Cognoscens ergo Iesus eorum murmur, respondit; et comprimens ipsum murmur eorum, dixit eis **nolite murmurare** etc.

Hoc namque est salubre documentum: qui enim murmurat, ostendit mentem suam in Deo non esse firmatam, et ideo dicitur Sap. c. I, 11: *custodite vos a murmuratione, quia nihil prodest.*

934. Causa autem murmuris est infidelitas eorum; et ideo hanc ostendit dicens **nemo potest venire ad me** etc., ubi

primo ostendit necessariam esse Patris attractionem ad hoc ut veniatur ad Christum;

secundo ostendit modum attrahendi, ibi **est scriptum in prophetis** etc.

Circa primum tria facit.

Primo ponit humanae facultatis defectum;

secundo divini auxilii subsidium;

tertio auxilii finem, seu fructum.

---

they grumbled because their minds were not fixed on spiritual things. They were following in this case the custom of their ancestors: *they grumbled in their tents* (Ps 105:25); *do not grumble, as some of them did* (1 Cor 10:10). As Chrysostom says, they had not complained till now because they still hoped to obtain material food; but as soon as they lost that hope, they began to grumble, although they pretended that it was for a different reason. Yet they did not contradict him openly due to the respect they had for him arising from his previous miracle.

931. He says those who complained said: **is this not the son of Joseph?** For since they were earthly minded, they only considered Christ's physical generation, which hindered them from recognizing his spiritual and eternal generation. And so we see them speaking only of earthly things, **he who is of the earth is earthly, and he speaks of the earth** (John 3:31), and not understanding what is spiritual. Thus they said: **how can he then say, I came down from heaven?** They called him the son of Joseph as this was the general opinion, for Joseph was his foster father: *the son, as was supposed, of Joseph* (Luke 3:23).

932. Next, at **Jesus therefore answered and said to them: do not murmur among yourselves**, the grumbling of the people is checked.

First, Christ stops this complaining;

second, he clears up their difficulty, at **amen, amen I say to you: he who believes in me has eternal life** (John 6:47).

As to the first he does two things.

First, he checks their complaining,

second, he tells why they were doing it, at **no man can come to me.**

933. Jesus noticed that they were grumbling and checked them, saying, **do not murmur among yourselves.**

This was good advice, for those who complain show that their minds are not firmly fixed on God; and so we read: *keep yourselves from grumbling, for it does no good* (Wis 1:11).

934. The reason for their grumbling was their unbelief, and he shows this when he says, **no man can come to me, unless the Father, who has sent me, draws him.**

First, he shows that if one is to come to Christ, he has to be drawn by the Father.

Second, he shows the way one is drawn, at **it is written in the prophets: and they shall all be taught of God.**

As to the first he does three things.

First, he mentions that coming to Christ surpasses human ability;

second, the divine help we receive for this; and

third, the end or fruit of this help.

Est ergo humana facultas deficiens ad veniendum ad Christum per fidem; et ideo dicit **nemo potest venire ad me**. Secundo divinum auxilium est efficax ad subveniendum, unde subdit **nisi Pater, qui misit me, traxerit eum**. Sed finis, seu fructus est optimus; unde sequitur **et ego resuscitabo eum in novissimo die**.

935. Dicit ergo primo: non est mirum si murmuratis, quia nondum estis tracti a Patre ad me. Nam **nemo potest ad me venire**, in me credendo, **nisi Pater, qui misit me, traxerit eum**.

Sed hic est triplex quaestio. Prima est de hoc quod dicit **nisi Pater traxerit eum**. Cum enim ad Christum veniamus credendo, sicut supra eodem dictum est, venire ad Christum est credere in eum; credere autem nullus potest nisi volens. Cum ergo tractio importet violentiam quamdam, ergo qui tractus venit ad Christum, cogitur.

Respondeo dicendum, quod hoc quod hic dicitur de hac tractione Patris, non importat coactionem, cum non omne trahens faciat violentiam. Sic ergo multipliciter Pater trahit ad Filium, secundum multiplicem modum trahendi absque violentia in hominibus. Nam aliquis homo trahit aliquem persuadendo ratione; et hoc modo Pater trahit homines ad Filium, demonstrando eum esse Filium suum; et hoc dupliciter: vel per internam revelationem; Matth. XVI, 17: *beatus es, Simon Bariona, quia caro et sanguis non revelavit tibi*, scilicet Christum esse Filium Dei vivi, *sed Pater meus*; vel per miraculorum operationem, quam habet a Patre; supra V, 36: **opera quae dedit mihi Pater, ipsa testimonium perhibent de me**.

Item aliquis trahit alium alliciendo; Prov. VII, 21: *blanditiis labiorum suorum protraxit eum*. Et hoc modo illi qui attendunt ad Iesum propter auctoritatem Paternae maiestatis, trahuntur a Patre. Quicumque enim credit in Christum propter hoc quod credit eum Filium Dei, hunc Pater trahit ad Filium, idest Paterna maiestas. Hoc modo non trahitur Arius qui Christum non verum Dei Filium, nec de substantia Patris genitum credebat. Non sic tractus est Photinus, Christum purum hominem dogmatizans. Sic ergo trahuntur a Patre, sua maiestate allecti; sed trahuntur etiam a Filio, admirabili delectatione et amore veritatis, quae est ipse Filius Dei. Si enim, ut dicit Augustinus, *trahit sua quemque voluptas*, quanto fortius debet homo trahi ad Christum, si delectatur veritate, beatitudine, iustitia, sempiterna vita, quod totum est Christus? Ab isto ergo si trahendi sumus, trahamur per dilectionem veritatis; secundum illud Ps. XXXVI, 4: *delectare in Domino, et dabit tibi petitiones cordis tui*.

That we should come to Christ through faith surpasses our human ability; thus he says, **no man can come to me**. Second, divine help is effective in helping us to this; thus he says, **unless the Father, who has sent me, draws him**. The end or fruit of this help is the very best, so he adds, **and I will raise him up on the last day**.

935. He says first: it is not unexpected that you are grumbling, because my Father had not yet drawn you to me, for **no man can come to me**, by believing in me, **unless the Father, who has sent me, draws him**.

There are three questions here. The first is about his saying: **unless the Father draws him**. For since we come to Christ by believing, then, as we said above, to come to Christ is to believe in him. But no one can believe unless he wills to. Therefore, since to be drawn implies some kind of compulsion, one who comes to Christ by being drawn is compelled.

I answer that what we read here about the Father drawing us does not imply coercion, because there are some ways of being drawn that do not involve compulsion. Consequently, the Father draws men to the Son in many ways, using the different ways in which we can be drawn without compulsion. One person may draw another by persuading him with a reason. The Father draws us to his Son in this way by showing us that he is his Son. He does this in two ways. First, by an interior revelation, as in: *blessed are you, Simon Bar-Jona, for flesh and blood has not revealed this to you* that is, that Christ is the Son of the living God, *but it was done so by my Father* (Matt 16:17). Second, it can be done through miracles, which the Son has the power to do from the Father: *for the works that the Father has given to me . . . the works themselves, which I do, give testimony about me* (John 5:36).

Again, one person draws another by attracting or captivating him: *she captivated him with her flattery* (Prov 7:21). This is the way the Father draws those who are devoted to Jesus on account of the authority of the paternal greatness. For the Father, i.e., the paternal greatness, draws those who believe in Christ because they believe that he is the Son of God. Arius—who did not believe that Christ was the true Son of God, nor begotten of the substance of the Father— was not drawn in this way. Neither was Photinus—who taught that Christ was a mere man. So, this is the way those who are captivated by his greatness are drawn by the Father. But they are also drawn by the Son, through a wonderful joy and love of the truth, which is the very Son of God himself. For if, as Augustine says, *each of us is drawn by his own pleasure*, how much more strongly ought we to be drawn to Christ if we find our pleasure in truth, happiness, justice, eternal life: all of which Christ is? Therefore, if we would be drawn by him, let us be drawn through love for the truth,

Hinc sponsa dicebat, Cant. I, 3: *trahe me post te; curremus in odorem unguentorum tuorum.*

Sed quia non solum revelatio exterior, vel obiectum, virtutem attrahendi habet, sed etiam interior instinctus impellens et movens ad credendum, ideo trahit multos Pater ad Filium per instinctum divinae operationis moventis interius cor hominis ad credendum; Phil. II, 13: *Deus est qui operatur in nobis velle et perficere;* Oseae XI, 4: *in funiculis Adam traham eos in vinculis caritatis;* Prov. c. XXI, 1: *cor regis in manu Domini: quocumque voluerit inclinabit illud.*

936. Secunda quaestio est: quia cum dicatur quod Filius trahit ad Patrem, Matth. c. XI, 27: *nemo novit Patrem nisi Filius, et cui voluerit Filius revelare;* et infra XVII, 6: **Pater, manifestavi nomen tuum hominibus quos dedisti mihi:** quomodo hic dicitur, quod Pater trahit ad Filium?

Sed dicendum, quod ad hoc potest dupliciter responderi: nam de Christo possumus loqui aut secundum quod est homo aut secundum quod est Deus. Secundum autem quod homo, Christus est via; infra XIV, 6: **ego sum via:** et secundum quod est Christus, ducit ad Patrem, sicut via ad terminum seu finem. Pater vero trahit ad Christum hominem inquantum dat nobis suam virtutem, ut credamus in Christum; Eph. II, 8: *gratia salvati estis, et hoc non ex vobis, Dei enim donum est.* Inquantum est Christus, est Verbum Dei, et manifestativum Patris. Sic Filius trahit ad Patrem. Pater autem trahit ad Filium inquantum manifestat ipsum.

937. Tertia quaestio est de hoc quod dicit, quod nemo venire potest nisi tractus a Patre: quia secundum hoc, si nullus veniat ad Christum, non imputatur ei, sed ei qui non trahit eos.

Respondeo dicendum, quod vere nullus venire potest nisi tractus a Patre: nam sicut grave per naturam non potest per se sursum ferri nisi trahatur ab alio, ita cor humanum ex se ad inferiora tendens, non potest sursum elevari nisi tractus. Si vero non elevatur, non est defectus ex parte trahentis, qui quantum in se est, nulli deficit; sed est propter impedimentum eius qui non trahitur.

Aliter autem, quantum ad hoc pertinet, possumus loqui de hominibus in statu naturae integrae, et aliter in statu naturae corruptae; nam in natura integra non erat aliquod impedimentum prohibens ab hac tractione, unde tunc omnes homines huius tractionis poterant esse participes. Sed in natura corrupta omnes per impedimentum peccati aequaliter prohibentur ab hac tractione; et ideo omnes indigent trahi. Deus autem omnibus ad trahendum manum porrigit quantum in se est, et, quod plus est, non solum attrahit manum recipientis,

according to: *take delight in the Lord, and he will give you the desires of your heart* (Ps 36:4). And so the bride says: *draw me after you, and we will run to the fragrance of your perfume* (Song 1:4).

An external revelation or an object are not the only things that draw us. There is also an interior impulse that incites and moves us to believe. And so the Father draws many to the Son by the impulse of a divine action, moving a person's heart from within to believe: *it is God who is working in us, both to will and to accomplish* (Phil 2:13); *I will draw them with the cords of Adam, with bands of love* (Hos 11:4); *the heart of the king is in the hand of the Lord; he turns it wherever he wills* (Prov 21:1).

936. The second problem is this. We read that it is the Son who draws us to the Father: *no one knows the Father but the Son, and he to whom the Son wishes to reveal him* (Matt 11:26); **I have manifested your name to the men whom you have given me** (John 17:6). So how can it say here that it is the Father who draws us to the Son?

This can be answered in two ways: for we can speak of Christ either as a man, or as God. As man, Christ is the way: **I am the way** (John 14:6); and as the Christ, he leads us to the Father, as a way or road leads to its end. The Father draws us to Christ as man insofar as he gives us his own power so that we may believe in Christ: *you are saved by grace, through faith; and this is not due to yourself, for it is the gift of God* (Eph 2:8). Insofar as he is Christ, he is the Word of God and manifests the Father. It is in this way that the Son draws us to the Father. But the Father draws us to the Son insofar as he manifests the Son.

937. The third problem concerns his saying that no one can come to Christ unless the Father draws him. For according to this, if one does not come to Christ, it is not because of himself, but is due to the one who does not draw him.

I answer and say that, in truth, no one can come unless drawn by the Father. For just as a heavy object by its nature cannot rise up, but has to be lifted by someone else, so the human heart, which tends of itself to lower things, cannot rise to what is above unless it is drawn or lifted. And if it does not rise up, this is not due to the failure of the one lifting it, who, so far as lies in him, fails no one; rather, it is due to an obstacle in the one who is not drawn or lifted up.

In this matter we can distinguish between those in the state of integral nature, and those in the state of fallen nature. In the state of integral nature, there was no obstacle to being drawn up, and thus all could share in it. But in the state of fallen nature, all are equally held back from this drawing by the obstacle of sin; and so, all need to be drawn. God, in so far as it depends on him, extends his hand to every one, to draw every one; and what is more, he not only draws those who receive him by the hand, but even converts those who are turned away from him, according

sed etiam aversos a se convertit, secundum illud Thren. ult., 21: *converte nos, Domine, et convertemur*: et in Ps. LXXXIV, 7, secundum aliam litteram: *Deus, tu convertens vivificabis nos*. Ex quo ergo Deus paratus est dare omnibus gratiam, et ad se trahere, non imputatur ei, si aliquis non accipiat, sed ei qui non accipit.

938. Quare autem non omnes aversos trahit, sed aliquos, licet sint omnes aequaliter aversi: ratio quidem in generali potest assignari, ut scilicet in illis qui non trahuntur, appareat et refulgeat ordo divinae iustitiae; in illis autem qui trahuntur, immensitas divinae misericordiae. Quare autem in speciali trahat hunc, et illum non trahat, non est ratio aliqua, nisi beneplacitum voluntatis divinae. Unde dicit Augustinus: *quem trahat et quem non trahat, quare illum trahat et illum non trahat, noli velle iudicare, si non vis errare. Sed accipe, et intellige: nondum traheris, ora ut traharis.*

Hoc etiam ostendit potest per exemplum. Nam assignari potest ratio quare artifex ponit aliquos lapides inferius, et aliquos superius, et aliquos ex lateribus, ex dispositione domus, cuius complementum hoc exigit. Sed quare hos lapides hic ponat et hos ibi, dependet a sua simplici voluntate. Et inde est quod prima ratio dispositionis refertur ad voluntatem artificis. Sic ergo Deus ad complementum universi quosdam quidem trahit, ut in eis appareat sua misericordia; quosdam vero non trahit, ut ostendatur in eis sua iustitia. Sed hos trahit, illos non trahit secundum suum beneplacitum voluntatis. Similiter etiam quare in Ecclesia aliquos fecit apostolos, alios confessores, alios martyres, ratio est propter Ecclesiae decorem et complementum. Sed quare Petrum fecit apostolum, Stephanum martyrem et Nicolaum confessorem, non est alia ratio nisi voluntas sua.

Sic ergo patet humanae facultatis defectus, et auxilii divini subsidium.

939. Sequitur auxilii finis et fructus, cum dicit **et ego resuscitabo eum in novissimo die**, etiam inquantum homo: nam per ea quae Christus in carne sua gessit, consequimur resurrectionis fructum; I Cor. XV, 21: *sicut per hominem mors, ita et per hominem resurrectio mortuorum*. **Ego**, ergo, secundum quod homo, **resuscitabo eum**, non solum ad vitam naturae, sed etiam ad vitam gloriae, et hoc **in novissimo die**.

Tenet enim fides Catholica, quod status mundi innovabitur; Apoc. XXI, 1: *vidi caelum novum et terram novam*. Et inter alia quae ad hanc innovationem concurrent, credimus caeli motum cessare, et per consequens tempus; Apoc. X, 5: *et angelus quem vidi stantem super mare et super terram, levavit manum suam ad caelum*. Et infra: *quia tempus non erit amplius*. Quia ergo cessante tempore in resurrectione, cessabit etiam nox et dies,

to: *convert us, O Lord, to yourself, and we will be converted* (Lam 5:21); and *you will turn, O God, and bring us to life* (Ps 84:7). Therefore, since God is ready to give grace to all, and draw them to himself, it is not due to him if someone does not accept; rather, it is due to the person who does not accept.

938. A general reason can be given why God does not draw all who are turned away from him, but certain ones, even though all are equally turned away. The reason is so that the order of divine justice may appear and shine forth in those who are not drawn, while the immensity of the divine mercy may appear and shine in those who are drawn. But as to why in particular he draws this person and does not draw that person, there is no reason except the pleasure of the divine will. So Augustine says: *whom he draws and whom he does not draw, why he draws one and does not draw another, do not desire to judge if you do not wish to err. But accept and understand: if you are not yet drawn, then pray that you may be drawn.*

We can illustrate this by an example. One can give as the reason why a builder puts some stones at the bottom, and others at the top and sides, that it is the arrangement of the house, whose completion requires this. But why he puts these particular stones here, and those over there, this depends on his mere will. Thus it is that the prime reason for the arrangement is referred to the will of the builder. So God, for the completion of the universe, draws certain ones in order that his mercy may appear in them; and others he does not draw in order that his justice may be shown in them. But that he draws these and does not draw those, depends on the pleasure of his will. In the same way, the reason why in his Church he made some apostles, some confessors, and others martyrs, is for the beauty and completion of the Church. But why he made Peter an apostle, and Stepehen a martyr, and Nicholas a confessor, the only reason is his will.

We are now clear on the limitations of our human ability, and the assistance given to us by divine help.

939. He follows with the end and fruit of this help when he says, **and I will raise him up on the last day**, even as man; for we obtain the fruit of the resurrection through those things which Christ did in his flesh: *for as death came through a man, so the resurrection of the dead has come through a man* (1 Cor 15:21). So *I*, as man, **will raise him up**, not only to a natural life, but even too the life of glory; and this **on the last day**.

For the Catholic faith teaches that the world will be made new: *then I saw a new heaven and a new earth* (Rev 21:1), and that among the changes accompanying this renewal we believe that the motion of the heavens will stop, and consequently, time. *And the angel I saw standing on the sea and on the land, raised his hand to heaven* (Rev 10:5), and then it says that he swore that *time will be no more* (Rev 10:6). Since at the resurrection time will stop, so also will night

secundum illud Zac. XIV, 7: *erit dies una, quae nota est Domino, non dies neque nox*; ideo dicit **resuscitabo eum in novissimo die.**

940. Quare autem usque tunc caeli motus duret, et tempus, non minus vel amplius, sciendum est, quia illud quod est propter aliud, diversimode disponitur secundum diversam dispositionem eius propter quod est. Omnia autem corporalia propter hominem facta sunt; et ideo secundum diversam dispositionem hominis diversimode ea disponi oportet. Quia ergo in hominibus quando resurgent, inchoabitur status incorruptionis, secundum illud I Cor. XV, 54: *mortale hoc induet incorruptionem*, ideo cessabit tunc etiam corruptio in rebus; unde cessabit motus caeli, qui est causa generationis et corruptionis in rebus corporalibus; Rom. VIII, 21: *ipsa creatura liberabitur a servitute corruptionis in libertatem filiorum Dei*. Sic ergo patet quod ad fidem necessaria est nobis attractio Patris.

941. Consequenter cum dicit **est scriptum in prophetis** etc., determinat modum attrahendi, et

primo ponit attrahendi modum;

secundo attractionis efficaciam, ibi **omnis qui audivit a patre, et didicit, venit ad me**;

tertio excludit opinatum modum attractionis, ibi **non quia patrem vidit quisquam.**

942. Modus autem attrahendi est congruus, quia trahit revelando et docendo; et hoc est quod dicit **scriptum est in prophetis: erunt omnes docibiles Dei** etc. Beda dicit hoc esse scriptum in Ioel; sed non videtur expresse ibi esse, licet aliquid consonum dicitur; et Ioel. II, 22: *filii Sion, exultate in Domino Deo vestro, quia dabit vobis doctorem iustitiae*. Ideo autem, secundum Bedam, dicit **in prophetis**, ut det intelligere quod sensus iste potest colligi ex diversis dictis prophetarum. Sed expressius videtur hoc dici Is. LIV, 13: *ponam filios tuos universos doctos a Domino*. Dicitur etiam Ier. III, 15: *dabo vobis pastores iuxta cor meum, qui pascent vos scientia et doctrina.*

943. Hoc autem quod dicit **erunt omnes**, potest tripliciter intelligi. Uno modo ut ly **omnes** supponat pro omnibus hominibus mundi; alio modo ut supponat pro omnibus qui sunt in Ecclesia Christi; tertio modo pro omnibus qui erunt in regno caelorum.

Si autem dicatur primo modo, videtur non esse verum; nam statim subdit **omnis qui audivit a Patre et didicit, venit ad me**. Si ergo omnes de mundo erunt docibiles, ergo omnes venient ad Christum. Sed hoc est falsum, quia non omnium est fides.

Sed ad hoc tripliciter respondetur. Nam, secundum Chrysostomum, primo modo dicendum, hoc dictum

and day, according to *there will be one day, known to the Lord, not day and night* (Zech 14:7). This is the reason he says, **and I will raise him up on the last day**.

940. As to the question why the motion of the heavens and time itself will continue until then, and not end before or after, we should note that whatever exists for something else is differently disposed according to the different states of that for which it exists. But all physical things have been made for man; consequently, they should be disposed according to the different states of man. So, because the state of incorruptibility will begin in men when they arise—according to *what is mortal will put on incorruption* (1 Cor 15:54)—the corruption of things will also stop then. Consequently, the motion of the heavens, which is the cause of the generation and corruption of material things, will stop. *Creation itself will be set free from its slavery to corruption into the freedom of the children of God* (Rom 8:21). So, it is clear that the Father must draw us if we are to have faith.

941. Then, at **it is written in the prophets: and they will all be taught about God**, he considers the way we are drawn.

First, he states the way;

second, its effectiveness, at **every one who has heard of the Father and has learned, comes to me**;

and third, he excludes a certain way of being drawn, at **not that any man has seen the Father.**

942. The manner in which we are drawn is appropriate, for God draws us by revealing and teaching; and this is what he says: **it is written in the prophets: and they will all be taught about God**. Bede says that this comes from Joel. But it does not seem to be there explicitly, although there is something like it in: *O children of Zion, rejoice and be joyful in the Lord your God, because he will give you a teacher of justice* (Joel 2:23). Again, according to Bede, he says, **in the prophets**, so that we might understand that the same meaning can be gathered from various statements of the prophets. But it is Isaiah who seems to state this more explicitly: *all your children will be taught by the Lord* (Isa 54:13). We also read: *I will give you shepherds after my own heart, and they will feed you with knowledge and doctrine* (Jer 3:15).

943. That **they will all be taught about God**, can be understood in three ways. In one way, so that **all** stands for all the people in the world; in another way, so that it stands for all who are in the Church of Christ, and in a third way, so it means all who will be in the kingdom of heaven.

If we understand it in the first way, it does not seem to be true, for he immediately adds, **every one who has heard of the Father and has learned, comes to me**. Therefore, if every one in the world is taught, then every one will come to Christ. But this is false, for not every one has faith.

There are three answers to this. First, one could say, as Chrysostom does, that he is speaking of the majority: **all**,

esse de pluribus *erunt*, inquit, *omnes*, idest plurimi; secundum quem modum dicitur Matth. VIII, 11: *multi venient ab Oriente et Occidente*, etc.

Secundo, quod *omnes*, quantum est ex Deo, *erunt docibiles*; sed quod aliqui non doceantur, est ex parte eorum. Sol enim quantum est de se, omnes illuminat; potest autem ab aliquibus non videri, si claudant oculos, vel si sint caeci. Et hoc modo dicit Apostolus, I Tim. II, 4: *vult omnes homines salvos fieri, et ad agnitionem veritatis venire*.

Tertio modo, secundum Augustinum, quod haec est accommoda distributio, ut dicatur *omnes erunt docibiles Dei*; idest omnes qui docentur, a Deo docentur, sicut loquimur de aliquo litterarum magistro. Dicimus enim, si est in civitate: solus iste docet omnes pueros de civitate, quia nullus docetur in ea nisi ab illo. Et hoc modo dicitur supra I, 9: *erat lux vera, quae illuminat omnem hominem venientem in hunc mundum*.

944. Si autem exponatur de illis qui sunt in Ecclesia congregati, dicitur *erunt omnes*, scilicet qui sunt in Ecclesia, *docibiles Deo*; nam Is. LIV, 13, dicitur: *ponam universos Filios doctos a Domino* in quo quidem ostenditur sublimitas fidei Christianae, quae non inhaeret doctrinae humanae, sed doctrinae Dei.

Doctrina enim Veteris Testamenti data fuit per prophetas; sed doctrina Novi Testamenti est per ipsum Filium Dei; Hebr. I, 1: *multifarie multisque modis*, idest in Veteri Testamento, *Deus loquens patribus in prophetis, novissime diebus istis locutus est nobis in Filio*; et ibid. II, 3: *quae cum initium accepisset enarrari per Dominum, ab eis qui audierunt, in nos confirmata est*. Sic ergo omnes qui sunt in Ecclesia, sunt docti non ab apostolis, non a prophetis, sed ab ipso Deo. Et, secundum Augustinum, hoc ipsum quod ab homine docemur, est ex Deo, qui docet interius; Matth. c. XXIII, 10: *unus est magister vester Christus*. Nam intelligentia, quae necessaria est praecipue ad doctrinam, est nobis a Deo.

945. Si autem exponatur de his qui sunt in regno caelorum etc., tunc *omnes erunt docibiles Deo*, quia eius essentiam immediate videbunt; I Io. III, 2: *videbimus eum sicuti est*.

946. Attractio autem Patris efficacissima est: quia *omnis qui audivit a Patre, et didicit, venit ad me*. Ubi duo ponit: unum scilicet quod pertinet ad donum Dei, cum dicit *audivit*, scilicet Deo revelante; aliud quod pertinet ad liberum arbitrium, cum dicit *et didicit*, scilicet per assensum; et ista duo necessaria sunt in omni doctrina fidei.

Omnis qui audivit a Patre, docente et manifestante, *et didicit*, praebendo assensum, *venit ad me*; venit, inquam, tripliciter: per cognitionem veritatis, per amoris

i.e., very many *will be taught*, just as we find in Matthew: *many will come from the East and the West* (Matt 8:11).

Second, it could mean, *all*, so far as God is concerned, *will be taught*, but if some are not taught, that is due to themselves. For the sun, on its part, shines on all, but some are unable to see it if they close their eyes, or are blind. From this point of view, the Apostle says: *he desires the salvation of all men, and that all come to the knowledge of the truth* (1 Tim 2:4).

Third, we could say, with Augustine, that we must make a restricted application, so that *they will all be taught about God*, means that all who are taught, are taught by God. It is just as we might speak of a teacher of the liberal arts who is working in a city: he alone teaches all the boys of the city, because no one there is taught by anyone else. It is in this sense that it was said above: *he was the true light, which enlightens every man coming into this world* (John 1:9).

944. If we explain these words as referring to those who are gathered into the Church, it says: *they will all*, all who are in the Church, *be taught about God*. For we read: *all your children will be taught by the Lord* (Isa 54:13). This shows the sublimity of the Christian faith, which does not depend on human teachings, but on the teaching of God.

For the teaching of the Old Testament was given through the prophets; but the teaching of the New Testament is given through the Son of God himself. *In many and various ways* i.e., in the Old Testament *God spoke to our fathers through the prophets; in these days he has spoken to us in his Son* (Heb 1:1); and again: *it was first announced by the Lord, and was confirmed to us by those who heard him* (Heb 2:3). Thus, all who are in the Church are taught, not by the apostles nor by the prophets, but by God himself. Further, according to Augustine, what we are taught by men is from God, who teaches from within: *you have one teacher, the Christ* (Matt 23:10). For understanding, which we especially need for such teaching, is from God.

945. If we explain these words as applying to those who are in the kingdom of heaven, then *they will all be taught about God*, because they will see his essence without any intermediary: *we shall see him as he is* (1 John 3:2).

946. This drawing by the Father is most effective, because, *every one who has heard of the Father and has learned, comes to me*. Here he mentions two things: first, what relates to a gift of God, when he says, *has heard*, that is, through God, who reveals; the other relates to a free judgment, when he says, *and has learned*, that is, by an assent. These two are necessary for every teaching of faith.

Every one who has heard of the Father, teaching and making known, *and has learned*, by giving assent, *comes to me*. He comes in three ways: through a knowledge of the

affectum et per operis imitationem. Et in quolibet oportet quod audiat et discat.

Nam qui venit per cognitionem veritatis, oportet eum audire, Deo inspirante, secundum illud Ps. LXXXIV, 9: *audiam quid loquatur in me Dominus Deus*, et addiscere per affectum, ut dictum est. Qui vero venit per amorem et desiderium, ut dicitur infra VII, 37: **si quis sitit, veniat ad me, et bibat**, et hunc oportet audire Verbum Patris, et capere illud, ad hoc ut addiscat, et afficiatur. Ille enim discit Verbum qui capit illud secundum rationem dicentis; Verbum autem Dei Patris est spirans amorem: qui ergo capit illud cum fervore amoris, discit; Sap. VII, 27: *in animas sanctas se transfert, prophetas et amicos Dei constituit*. Per operis autem imitationem itur ad Christum, secundum illud Matth. XI, 28: *venite ad me, omnes qui laboratis et onerati estis, et ego reficiam vos*. Et hoc etiam modo quicumque discit, venit ad Christum: nam sicut conclusio se habet in scibilibus, ita et operatio in operabilibus. In scientiis autem quicumque perfecte discit, venit ad conclusionem: ergo in operabilibus qui perfecte verba discit, venit ad rectam operationem; Is. l, 5: *Dominus aperuit mihi aurem; ego autem non contradico*.

947. Sed quia aliqui possent opinari quod omnes homines visibiliter a Patre audirent et addiscerent, ideo ut hoc Dominus excludat, subdit **non quia Patrem vidit quisquam**, idest, aliquis homo vivens in hac vita non vidit Patrem in sua essentia, secundum illud Ex. XXXIII, 20: *non videbit me homo, et vivet, nisi is*, scilicet Filius, **qui est a Deo, hic vidit Patrem**, suum per essentiam. Vel *quisquam* non vidit Patrem, visione comprehensionis, qua visione nec homo nec angelus eum vidit unquam, nec videre potest, **nisi is qui est ex Deo**, idest Filius; Matth. XI, v. 27: *nemo novit Patrem nisi Filius*.

Cuius quidem ratio est, quia cum omnis visio sive cognitio fiat per aliquam similitudinem, secundum modum similitudinis, quem habent creaturae ad Deum, secundum hoc habent cognitionem ipsius. Unde et philosophi dicunt, quod intelligentiae cognoscunt primam causam, secundum hanc quam habent similitudinem eius. Omnis autem creatura participat quidem aliquam similitudinem Dei, sed in infinitum distantem a similitudine suae naturae et ideo nulla creatura potest ipsum cognoscere perfecte et totaliter, prout est in sua natura. Filius autem, quia perfecte totam naturam Patris accepit per aeternam generationem, ideo totaliter videt et comprehendit.

948. Sed attendendum ad congruum ordinem loquendi. Nam supra cum loqueretur de cognitione aliorum, usus est verbo auditus; hic vero cum loquitur de cognitione Filii, utitur verbo visionis: nam cognitio quae est per visum, est immediata et aperta; ea vero quae est per auditum, fit mediante eo qui vidit. Sic et nos

truth; through the affection of love; and through imitative action. And in each way it is necessary that one hear and learn.

The one who comes through a knowledge of the truth must hear, when God speaks within: *I will hear what the Lord God will speak within me* (Ps 84:9); and he must learn, through affection, as was said. The one who comes through love and desire—**if any man thirst, let him come to me and drink** (John 7:37)—must hear the word of the Father and grasp it, in order to learn and be moved in his affections. For that person learns the word who grasps it according to the meaning of the speaker. But the Word of the Father breathes forth love. Therefore, the one who grasps it with eager love, learns. *Wisdom goes into holy souls, and makes them prophets and friends of God* (Wis 7:27). One comes to Christ through imitative action, according to: *come to me, all you who labor and are burdened, and I will refresh you* (Matt 11:28). And whoever learns even in this way comes to Christ: for as the conclusion is to things knowable, so is action to things performable. Now whoever learns perfectly in the sciences arrives at the conclusion; therefore, as regards things that are performable, whoever learns the words perfectly arrives at the right action: *the Lord has opened my ear; and I do not resist* (Isa 50:5).

947. To correct the thought that some might have that every one will hear and learn from the Father through a vision, he adds: **not that any man has seen the Father**, that is, a person living in this life does not see the Father in his essence, according to: *man will not see me and live* (Exod 33:20), except the one, that is the Son, **who is of God has seen the Father**, through his essence. Or, not that any one has seen the Father, with a comprehensive vision: neither man nor angel has ever seen or can see in this way; **but the one who is of God**, i.e., the Son: *no one knows the Father except the Son* (Matt 11:27).

The reason for this, of course, is that all vision or knowledge comes about through a likeness: creatures have a knowledge of God according to the way they have a likeness to him. Thus the philosophers say that the intelligences know the First Cause according to this likeness which they have to it. Now every creature possesses some likeness to God, but it is infinitely distant from a likeness to his nature, and so no creature can know him perfectly and totally, as he is in his own nature. The Son, however, because he has received the entire nature of the Father perfectly, through an eternal generation, sees and comprehends totally.

948. Note how the words used are appropriate: for above, when he was speaking of the knowledge others have, he used the word 'heard'; but now, in speaking of the Son's knowledge, he uses the word 'seen', for knowledge which comes through seeing is direct and open, while that which comes through hearing comes through one who has seen.

cognitionem quam habemus de Patre, accepimus a Filio, qui vidit: ut sic nullus Patrem cognoscat nisi per Christum, qui eum manifestat, et nullus ad Filium veniat, nisi a Patre manifestante audierit.

And so we have received the knowledge we have about the Father from the Son, who saw him. Thus, no one can know the Father except through Christ, who makes him known; and no one can come to the Son unless he has heard from the Father, who makes the Son known.

Lecture 6

6:47 Amen, amen dico vobis: qui credit in me, habet vitam aeternam. [n. 950]

6:48 Ego sum panis vitae. [n. 951]

6:49 Patres vestri manducaverunt manna in deserto, et mortui sunt. [n. 952]

6:50 Hic est panis de caelo descendens, ut si quis ex ipso manducaverit, non moriatur. [n. 955]

6:51 Ego sum panis vivus, qui de caelo descendi. [n. 956]

6:52 Si quis manducaverit ex hoc pane, vivet in aeternum. Et panis quem ego dabo, caro mea est pro mundi vita. [n. 958]

6:47 ἀμὴν ἀμὴν λέγω ὑμῖν, ὁ πιστεύων ἔχει ζωὴν αἰώνιον.

6:48 Ἐγώ εἰμι ὁ ἄρτος τῆς ζωῆς.

6:49 οἱ πατέρες ὑμῶν ἔφαγον ἐν τῇ ἐρήμῳ τὸ μάννα καὶ ἀπέθανον·

6:50 οὗτός ἐστιν ὁ ἄρτος ὁ ἐκ τοῦ οὐρανοῦ καταβαίνων, ἵνα τις ἐξ αὐτοῦ φάγῃ καὶ μὴ ἀποθάνῃ.

6:51 ἐγώ εἰμι ὁ ἄρτος ὁ ζῶν ὁ ἐκ τοῦ οὐρανοῦ καταβάς·

6:52 ἐάν τις φάγῃ ἐκ τούτου τοῦ ἄρτου ζήσει εἰς τὸν αἰῶνα, καὶ ὁ ἄρτος δὲ ὃν ἐγὼ δώσω ἡ σάρξ μού ἐστιν ὑπὲρ τῆς τοῦ κόσμου ζωῆς.

6:47 Amen, amen I say to you: he who believes in me has eternal life. [n. 950]

6:48 I am the bread of life. [n. 951]

6:49 Your fathers ate manna in the desert, and they are dead. [n. 952]

6:50 This is the bread, which comes down from heaven, so that if any man eat of it, he will not die. [n. 955]

6:51 I am the living bread, which came down from heaven. [n. 956]

6:52 If any man eat of this bread, he will live for ever; and the bread that I will give is my flesh, for the life of the world. [n. 958]

---

949. Represso Iudaeorum murmure, consequenter Dominus satisfacit dubitationi quae orta erat in cordibus Iudaeorum de verbo quod dixerat, scilicet *ego sum panis, qui de caelo descendi*, ubi intendit probare hoc verum esse de se: et argumentatur sic. Ille panis descendit de caelo qui dat vitam mundo; sed ego sum panis dans vitam mundo: ergo ego sum panis qui de caelo descendi etc.

Circa hoc tria facit.

Primo ponit quasi minorem suae rationis, scilicet *ego sum panis vitae*;

secundo ponit maiorem, scilicet quod panis qui de caelo descendit, debet dare vitam, ibi *patres vestri manducaverunt manna in deserto, et mortui sunt*;

tertio ponit conclusionem, ibi *ego sum panis vivus*.

Circa primum duo facit.

Primo manifestat suum propositum;

secundo intentum quasi probatum inducit, ibi *ego sum panis vitae*.

950. Propositum suum est ostendere quod sit panis vitae. Panis autem vivificat inquantum sumitur. Constat autem quod qui credit in Christum, sumit eum intra seipsum, secundum illud Eph. III, 17: *habitare Christum per fidem in cordibus nostris*. Si ergo ille qui credit in Christum habet vitam, manifestum est quod manducando hunc panem vivificatur: ergo iste panis est panis vitae. Et hoc est quod dicit **amen, amen dico vobis, qui credit in me**, fide scilicet formata, quae non solum perficit

949. After our Lord quieted the grumbling of the Jews, he now clears up the doubt they had because of his saying, *I am the living bread, which came down from Heaven*, he intends to show here that this is true. This is the way he reasons: the bread which gives life to the world descended from heaven; but I am the bread that gives life to the world: therefore, I am the bread which descended from heaven.

He does three things concerning this.

First, he presents the minor premise of his reasoning, that is, *I am the bread of life*.

In the second place, he gives the major premise, that is, that the bread that descended from heaven ought to give life, at *your fathers ate manna in the desert, and they are dead*.

Third, we have the conclusion, at *I am the living bread, which came down from heaven*.

As to the first he does two things.

First, he states his point;

second, he expresses it as practically proved, at *I am the bread of life*.

950. His intention is to show that he is the bread of life. Bread is life-giving insofar as it is taken. Now one who believes in Christ takes him within himself, according to: *Christ dwells, in our hearts through faith* (Eph 3:17). Therefore, if he who believes in Christ has life, it is clear that he is brought to life by eating this bread. Thus, this bread is the bread of life. And this is what he says: *amen, amen, I say to you: he who believes in me*, with a faith made living by love, which not only perfects the intellect but the affections

intellectum, sed etiam affectum (non enim tenditur in rem creditam nisi ametur) **habet vitam aeternam**.

Christus autem est in nobis dupliciter: scilicet in intellectu per fidem, inquantum fides est; et in affectu per caritatem, quae informat fidem: I Io. IV, 16: *qui manet in caritate, in Deo manet, et Deus in eo*. Qui ergo credit sic in Christum ut in eum tendat, habet ipsum in affectu et in intellectu: et si addamus, quod Christus est vita aeterna, ut dicitur I Io. ult., c. 20: *ut simus in vero Filio eius Iesu Christo: hic est verus Deus et vita aeterna*; et supra I, 4: **in ipso vita erat**, possumus inferre, quod quicumque credit in Christum, habet vitam aeternam. Habet, inquam, in causa et in spe, quandoque habiturus in re.

951. Manifestato proposito, inducit intentum, cum dicit **ego sum panis vitae** idest dans vitam, ut evidenter sequitur ex praemissis. De isto pane Gen. penult., v. 20: *Aser, pinguis panis eius, praebebit delicias*, scilicet vitae aeternae, *regibus*.

952. Consequenter cum dicit **patres vestri manducaverunt manna in deserto, et mortui sunt**, ponit maiorem: scilicet quod dare vitam sit effectus panis de caelo descendentis. Et

primo praemittit manifestationem propositi;

secundo ponit intentum, ibi **hic est panis de caelo descendens**.

953. Propositum autem suum manifestat per contrarium. Dictum est enim supra, quod Moyses non dedit Iudaeis panem de caelo nisi aereo; omnis autem panis qui non est de vero caelo, non potest vitam sufficientem dare: ergo hoc est proprium panis caelestis quod det vitam. Et ideo panis Moysi, unde vos superbitis, non dat vitam: et hoc probat cum dicit **patres vestri manducaverunt manna in deserto, et mortui sunt**.

Ubi primo exprobrat eorum vitium, cum dicit **patres vestri** etc., quorum scilicet estis filii non solum secundum carnis originem, sed etiam secundum operum imitationem, quia estis murmuratores, sicut et ipsi *murmuraverunt in tabernaculis suis*, ut dicitur in Ps. CV, v. 25: et ideo dicebat eis, Matth. XXIII, 32: *implete mensuram patrum vestrorum*. Unde sicut Augustinus dicit, *de nulla re magis Deum offendisse populus dictus est, quam contra Deum murmurando*.

Secundo insinuat breve temporis spatium, cum dicit **in deserto**: non enim longum tempus fuit quo manna eis datum fuit, neque simul cum eis venit in terram promissionis, sed tantum in deserto, ut dicitur Iosue V, 12. Iste autem panis in perpetuum conservat et reficit.

Tertio manifestat cibi defectum, quia non conservabat vitam indeficientem; unde dicit **et mortui sunt**. Nam, sicut habetur Iosue V, omnes qui murmuraverunt, praeter Iosue et Caleb, mortui sunt in deserto. Unde, et haec fuit causa secundae circumcisionis, scilicet quod omnis

as well (for we do not tend to the things we believe in unless we love them), **has eternal life**.

Now Christ is within us in two ways: in our intellect through faith, so far as it is faith; and in our affections through love, which informs or gives life to our faith: *he who abides in love, abides in God, and God in him* (1 John 4:16). So he who believes in Christ so that he tends to him, possesses Christ in his affections and in his intellect. And if we add that Christ is eternal life, as stated in *that we may be in his true Son, Jesus Christ. This is the true God and eternal life* (1 John 5:20), and **in him was life** (John 1:4), we can infer that whoever believes in Christ has eternal life. He has it, I say, in its cause and in hope, and he will have it at some time in reality.

951. Having stated his position, he expresses it as, **I am the bread of life**, which gives life, as clearly follows from the above. We read of this bread: *the bread of Asher will be rich, he will furnish choice morsels*, of eternal life, *to kings* (Gen 49:20).

952. Then when he says, **your fathers ate manna in the desert, and they are dead**, he gives the major premise, namely, the bread that descended from heaven ought to have the effect of giving life.

First, he explains this;

second, he draws his point, at **this is the bread, which comes down from heaven**.

953. He explains his meaning through a contrasting situation. It was said above that Moses gave the Jews bread from heaven, in the sense of from the air. But bread that does not come from the true heaven cannot give adequate life. Therefore, it is proper to the heavenly bread to give life. So, the bread given by Moses, in which you take pride, does not give life. And he proves this when he says, **your fathers ate manna in the desert, and they are dead**.

In this statement he first reproaches them for their faults, when he says, **your fathers**, whose sons you are, not only according to the flesh, but also by imitating their actions, because you are grumblers just as *they grumbled in their tents* (Ps 105:25); this was why he said to them: *fill up, then, the measure of your fathers* (Matt 23:32). As Augustine says, *this people is said to have offended God in no matter more than by grumbling against God*.

Second, he mentions for how short a time this was done, saying, **in the desert**: for they were not given manna for a long period of time; and they had it only while in the desert, and not when they entered the promised land (Josh 5:12). But the other bread preserves and nourishes one forever.

Third, he states an inadequacy in that bread, that is, it did not preserve life without end; so he says, **and they are dead**. For we read that all who grumbled, except Joshua and Caleb, died in the desert (Josh 5). This was the reason for

populus qui egressus est ex Aegypto mortui sunt in deserto, ut ibidem dicitur.

954. Sed quaeritur de qua morte Deus hic loquitur. Nam si loquitur de morte corporali, nulla differentia erit inter panem illum qui fuit in deserto, et panem nostrum qui de caelo descendit: quia, etiam Christiani qui sumunt istum, corporaliter moriuntur. Si vero loquitur de morte spirituali, manifestum est quod hic et ibi quidam spiritualiter moriuntur, et quidam non. Nam Moyses, et multi qui Deo placuerunt, mortui non sunt, licet alii mortui sint. Similiter et qui istum panem indigne sumunt, moriuntur spiritualiter; I Cor. c. XI, 29: *qui enim manducat et bibit indigne, iudicium sibi manducat et bibit.*

Ad quod dicendum est, quod cibus ille cum cibo nostro spirituali convenit. Conveniunt quidem quantum ad hoc quod uterque idem significat: nam et ille et iste Christum signat, propter quod dicitur idem cibus; I Cor. X, 3: *omnes eamdem escam manducaverunt.* Eamdem dicit, quia utraque est figura spiritualis escae. Sed differunt, quia ille figurabat tantum, sed panis iste continet quod figurat, scilicet ipsum Christum.

Dicendum ergo, quod uterque ciborum istorum potest dupliciter sumi: vel quantum ad signum tantum, idest quod sumatur ut cibus tantum, non intellecto significato; et per hoc non tollitur mors spiritualis, seu corporalis. Vel quod sumatur quantum ad utrumque, idest quod ita sumatur cibus visibilis ut intelligatur cibus spiritualis, et spiritualiter gustetur, ut spiritualiter satiet: et hoc modo illi qui spiritualiter manducaverunt manna, mortui non sunt spiritualiter. Sed et qui Eucharistiam spiritualiter manducant, et absque peccato spiritualiter vivunt nunc, et corporaliter vivent in aeternum. Habet ergo plus cibus noster cibo illorum, quia in se continet quod figurat.

955. Manifestato ergo proposito, inducit intentum; unde dicit **hic est panis de caelo descendens.** Et secundum Glossam **hic** dicit demonstrando seipsum. Sed hic non est intellectus Domini, quia cum statim subdat **ego sum panis vivus qui de caelo descendi**, esset verborum inculcatio.

Dicendum est ergo, quod Dominus hoc intendit, ut scilicet dicat illum panem de caelo descendere qui hoc potest facere, scilicet dare vitam; sed ego sum talis: ergo ego sum panis de caelo descendens. Ideo autem de caelo descendens dat vitam indeficientem, quia omnis cibus nutrit secundum proprietatem suae naturae; caelestia autem incorruptibilia sunt: et ideo quia cibus ille caelestis est, non corrumpitur, quod quamdiu manet vivificat. Qui ergo manducaverit ex ipso, non morietur. Sicut si aliquis cibus corporalis numquam corrumperetur, dans nutrimentum, semper vivificaret. Et ideo panis iste significatus est per lignum vitae quod erat in medio

the second circumcision, as we see here, because all who had left Egypt died in the desert.

954. One might wonder what kind of death God is speaking of here. If he is speaking of physical death, there will be no difference between the bread the Jews had in the desert and our bread, which came down from heaven, because even Christians who share the latter bread die physically. But if he is speaking of spiritual death, it is clear that both then among the Jews and now among the Christians, some die spiritually and others do not. For Moses and many others who were pleasing to God did not die, while others did. Also, those who eat this bread unworthily, die spiritually: *he who eats and drinks unworthily, eats and drinks judgment upon himself* (1 Cor 11:29).

We may answer this by saying that the food of the Jews has some features in common with our spiritual food. They are alike in the fact that each signifies the same thing: for both signify Christ. Thus they are called the same food: *all ate the same spiritual food* (1 Cor 10:3). He calls them the same because each is a symbol of the spiritual food. But they are different because one was only a symbol; while this bread contains that of which it is the symbol, that is, Christ himself.

Thus we should say that each of these foods can be taken in two ways. First, as a sign only, i.e., so that each is taken as food only, and without understanding what is signified; and taken in this way, they do not take away either physical or spiritual death. Second, they may be taken in both ways, i.e., the visible food is taken in such a way that spiritual food is understood and spiritually tasted, in order that it may satisfy spiritually. In this way, those who ate the manna spiritually did not die spiritually. But those who eat the Eucharist spiritually, both live spiritually now without sin, and will live physically forever. Thus, our food is greater than their food, because it contains in itself that of which it is the symbol.

955. Having presented the argument, he draws the conclusion: **this is the bread, which comes down from heaven.** He says, **this**, the Gloss says, to indicate himself. But our Lord does not understand it this way as it would be superfluous, since he immediately adds, **I am the living bread, which came down from heaven.**

So we should say that our Lord wants to say that the bread which can do this, i.e., give life, comes from heaven; but I am that bread: thus, I am that bread that comes down from heaven. Now the reason why that bread which comes down from heaven gives a life which never ends is that all food nourishes according to the properties of its nature; but heavenly things are incorruptible: consequently, since this food is heavenly, it is not corrupted, and as long as it lasts, it gives life. So, he who eats it, will not die. Just as if there were some bodily food which never corrupted, then in nourishing it would always be life-giving. This bread was signified by the tree of life in the midst of Paradise, which somehow

Paradisi, quomodo dans vitam in perpetuum, secundum illud Gen. III, 22: *nunc ergo ne forte mittat manum suam, et sumat de ligno vitae, et comedat, et vivat in aeternum.* Si ergo iste sit effectus huius panis, ut scilicet qui manducat ex eo non moriatur; et ego sum talis: ergo etc.

956. *Ego sum panis vivus* etc. Circa hoc ergo duo facit.

Primo loquitur de seipso communiter;

secundo specialiter, ibi *et panis quem ego dabo, caro mea est*.

Circa primum duo facit.

Primo concludit originem sui ipsius.

Secundo ostendit eius virtutem, ibi *si quis manducaverit ex hoc pane, vivet in aeternum*.

957. Dixit ergo *ego sum panis vivus*, et ideo possum vitam dare. Panis enim corporalis non in perpetuum vivificat, quia non habet in se vitam; sed vivificat alteratus et conversus in nutrimentum virtute viventis. *Qui de caelo descendi*: hoc expositum est supra c. III, quomodo scilicet descenderit. Et per hoc excluduntur haereses dicentium Christum purum hominem, quia secundum hoc non descendisset de caelo.

958. Virtus autem eius est dare vitam aeternam; et ideo dicit *si quis manducaverit ex hoc pane*, spiritualiter scilicet, *vivet*, non tantum in praesenti per fidem et iustitiam, sed *in aeternum*; infra LI, 26: *omnis qui vivit et credit in me, non morietur in aeternum*.

959. Consequenter loquitur de corpore, cum dicit *et panis quem ego dabo, caro mea est*. Dixerat enim, quod erat panis vivus, et ne intelligatur quod hoc ei esset inquantum est Verbum, vel secundum animam tantum; ideo ostendit quod etiam caro sua vivificativa est: est enim organum divinitatis suae; unde, cum instrumentum agat virtute agentis, sicut divinitas Christi vivificativa est, ita ut Damascenus dicit et caro virtute Verbi adiuncti vivificat: unde Christus tactu suo sanabat infirmos. Sic ergo quod dixit supra, *ego sum panis vivus*, pertinet ad virtutem Verbi; hic vero quod subdit pertinet ad communionem sui corporis, scilicet ad Eucharistiae sacramentum.

960. Ubi possumus quatuor considerare circa ipsum sacramentum: scilicet speciem, instituentis auctoritatem, sacramenti veritatem, et eius utilitatem.

Species quidem sacramenti: *hic est panis*; Prov. IX, 5: *venite, et comedite panem meum.* Cuius ratio est, quia hoc est sacramentum corporis Christi; corpus autem Christi est Ecclesia, quae consurgit in unitatem corporis ex multis fidelibus: unde istud est sacramentum unitatis Ecclesiae; Rom. XII, 5: *omnes unum corpus sumus.* Quia ergo panis ex diversis granis conficitur, ideo est conveniens species sacramenti huius; ideo dicit *et panis quem ego dabo, caro mea est*.

gave life without end: *he must not be allowed to stretch out his hand and take from the tree of life and eat, and live forever* (Gen 3:22). So if the effect of this bread is that anyone who eats it will not die, and I am such: therefore etc.

956. *I am the living bread, which came down from heaven*. He does two things concerning this passage.

First, he speaks of himself in general;

second, in particular, *and the bread that I will give is my flesh*.

In regard to the first, he does two things:

first, he mentions his origin;

second his power, at *if any man eat of this bread, he will live forever*.

957. He said, *I am the living bread*; consequently, I can give life. Material bread does not give life forever, because it does not have life in itself; but it gives life by being changed and converted into nourishment by the energy of a living organism. *Which came down from heaven*: it was explained before how the Word came down. This refuted those heresies which taught that Christ was a mere man, because according to them, he would not have come down from heaven.

958. He has the power to give eternal life; thus he says, *if any man eat of this bread*, i.e., spiritually, *he will live*, not only in the present through faith and justice, but *forever. All who live and believe in me will never die* (John 11:26).

959. He then speaks of his body when he says, *and the bread that I will give is my flesh*. For he had said that he was the living bread; and so that we do not think that he is such so far as he is the Word or in his soul alone, he shows that even his flesh is life-giving, for it is an instrument of his divinity. Thus, since an instrument acts by virtue of the agent, then just as the divinity of Christ is lifegiving, so too his flesh gives life, as Damascene says, because of the Word to which it is united. Thus Christ healed the sick by his touch. So what he said above, *I am the living bread*, pertained to the power of the Word; but what he is saying here pertains to the sharing in his body, that is, to the sacrament of the Eucharist.

960. We can consider four things about this sacrament: its species, the authority of the one who instituted it, the truth of this sacrament, and its usefulness.

As to the species of this sacrament: *this is the bread*; *come, and eat my bread* (Prov 9:5). The reason for this is that this is the sacrament of the body of Christ; but the body of Christ is the Church, which arises out of many believers forming a bodily unity: *we are one body* (Rom 12:5). And so because bread is formed from many grains, it is a fitting species for this sacrament. Hence he says, *and the bread that I will give is my flesh*.

961. Auctor huius sacramenti Christus est: nam licet sacerdos consecret, tamen ipse Christus dat virtutem sacramento, quia etiam ipse sacerdos consecrat in persona Christi. Unde in aliis sacramentis utitur sacerdos verbis suis, seu Ecclesiae, sed in isto utitur verbis Christi: quia sicut Christus corpus suum propria voluntate dedit in mortem, ita sua virtute dat se in cibum; Matth. XXVI, 26: *accipiens panem, benedixit, ac fregit deditque discipulis suis, et ait: accipite et comedite: hoc est corpus meum.* Et ideo dicit **quem ego dabo**: et dicit **dabo**, quia nondum institutum erat hoc sacramentum.

962. Veritas autem huius sacramenti insinuatur cum dicit **caro mea est**. Non dicit autem carnem meam significat sed **caro mea est**; quia secundum rei veritatem hoc quod sumitur, vere est corpus Christi; Iob c. XXXI, 31: *si non dixerunt viri tabernaculi mei: quis det de carnibus eius ut saturemur?*

Sed cum in isto sacramento contineatur totus Christus, quare dixit tantum **caro mea est**?

Ad quod respondendo, sciendum est, quod in illo mystico sacramento totus Christus continetur secundum veritatem, sed corpus est ibi ex vi conversionis, divinitas vero et anima per naturalem concomitantiam. Dato enim per impossibile, quod divinitas separaretur a corpore Christi, iam non esset in sacramento divinitas. Similiter etiam si in triduo mortis suae aliquid consecrasset, non fuisset ibi anima Christi, sed tale corpus quale erat in cruce, seu in sepulcro. Ideo autem potius dicit **caro**, quia cum hoc sacramentum sit Dominicae passionis rememorativum, secundum illud I Cor. XI, 26: *quotiescumque manducabitis panem hunc, et calicem bibetis, mortem Domini annuntiabitis*, passio autem Christi fuit ex infirmitate, secundum illud II Cor. ult., v. 4: *mortuus est ex infirmitate* etc.: ut ergo insinuetur infirmitas ex qua mortuus est, potius dicit **caro mea est**: nam hoc nomen infirmitatem significat.

963. Utilitas autem huius sacramenti magna est, et universalis.

Magna quidem, quia efficit in nobis nunc vitam spiritualem, tandem aeternam, ut dictum est. Nam, ut ex supradictis apparet, cum hoc sacramentum sit Dominicae passionis, continet in se Christum passum: unde quidquid est effectus Dominicae passionis, totum etiam est effectus huius sacramenti. Nihil enim aliud est hoc sacramentum quam applicatio Dominicae passionis ad nos. Non enim decebat Christum secundum praesentiam suam semper esse nobiscum; et ideo voluit hoc supplere per hoc sacramentum. Unde manifestum est quod destructio mortis, quam Christus moriendo destruxit, et reparatio vitae, quam resurgendo effecit, est effectus huius sacramenti.

961. The author of this sacrament is Christ: for although the priest confers it, it is Christ himself who gives the power to this sacrament, because the priest consecrates in the person of Christ. Thus in the other sacraments the priest uses his own words or those of the Church, but in this sacrament he uses the words of Christ: because just as Christ gave his body to death by his own will, so it is by his own power that he gives himself as food: *Jesus took bread, he blessed it and broke it, and gave it to his disciples, saying: take and eat it, this is my body* (Matt 26:26). Thus he says, **that I will give**; and he says, **will give**, because this sacrament had not yet been instituted.

962. The truth of this sacrament is indicated when he says, **is my flesh**. He does not say, that this signifies my flesh, but it **is my flesh**, for in reality that which is taken is truly the body of Christ: *who will give us his flesh so that we may be satisfied?* (Job 31:31)

Since the whole Christ is contained in this sacrament, why did he just say, **is my flesh**?

To answer this, we should note that in this mystical sacrament the whole Christ is really contained: but his body is there by virtue of the conversion; while his soul and divinity are present by natural concomitance. For if we were to suppose whal is really inipossible, that is, that the divinity of Christ is separated from his body, then his divinity would not be present in this sacrament. Similarly, if someone had consecrated during the three days Christ was dead, his soul would not have been present there, but his body would have been, as it was on the cross or in the tomb. Thus, it is preferable to say **flesh**, ince this sacrament is the commemoration of our Lord's passion—according to *as often as you eat this bread and drink this cup, you proclaim the death of the Lord* (1 Cor 11:26)—and the passion of Christ depended on his weakness—according to *he was crucified through weakness* (2 Cor 13:4)—he rather says, **is my flesh**, to suggest the weakness through which he died, for **flesh** signifies weakness.

963. The usefulness of this sacrament is great and universal.

It is great, indeed, because it produces spiritual life within us now, and will later produce eternal life, as was said. For as is clear from what was said, since this is the sacrament of our Lord's passion, it contains in itself the Christ who suffered. Thus, whatever is an effect of our Lord's passion is also an effect of this sacrament. For this sacrament is nothing other than the application of our Lord's passion to us. For it was not fitting for Christ to be always with us in his own presence; and so he wanted to make up for this absence through this sacrament. Hence it is clear that the destruction of death, which Christ accomplished by his death, and the restoration of life, which he accomplished by his resurrection, are effects of this sacrament.

964. Universalis autem, quia vita quam confert, non solum est vita unius hominis, sed quantum in se est, totius mundi: ad quam sufficiens est mors Christi; I Io. II, 2: *ipse est propitiatio pro peccatis nostris, et non pro nostris tantum, sed etiam totius mundi.*

Notandum autem est, quod aliter est in isto sacramento, et aliter in aliis: nam alia sacramenta habent singulares effectus, sicut in baptismo solus baptizatus suscipit gratiam; sed in immolatione huius sacramenti est universalis effectus, quia non solum sacerdos effectum consequitur, sed etiam illi pro quibus orat, et Ecclesia tota, tam vivorum, quam mortuorum. Cuius ratio est, quia continetur in ipso ipsa causa universalis omnium sacramentorum, scilicet Christus. Nec tamen si laicus sumat hoc sacramentum, prodest aliis quantum est ex opere operato, inquantum consideratur ut perceptio, quamvis ex intentione operantis et percipientis, possit communicari omnibus ad quos dirigit suam intentionem.

Ex quo patet quod laici sumentes Eucharistiam pro his qui sunt in Purgatorio, errant.

964. The usefulness of this sacrament is universal because the life it gives is not only the life of one person, but, so far as concerns itself, the life of the entire world: and for this the death of Christ is fully sufficient. *He is the offering for our sins; and not for ours only, but also for those of the entire world* (1 John 2:2).

We should note that this sacrament is different from the others: for the other sacraments have individual effects: as in baptism, only the one baptized receives grace. But in the immolation of this sacrament, the effect is universal: because it affects not just the priest, but also those for whom he prays, as well as the entire Church, of the living and of the dead. The reason for this is that it contains the universal cause of all the sacraments, Christ. Nevertheless, when a lay person receives this sacrament it does not benefit others by its own power insofar as it is considered as a receiving. However, due to the intention of the person who is acting and receiving, it can be communicated to all those to whom he directs his intention.

It is clear from this that lay persons are mistaken when they receive the Eucharist for those in purgatory.

Lecture 7

6:53 Litigabant ergo Iudaei ad invicem, dicentes: quomodo potest hic nobis carnem suam dare ad manducandum? [n. 966]

6:54 Dixit ergo eis Iesus: amen, amen dico vobis: nisi manducaveritis carnem Filii hominis, et biberitis eius sanguinem, non habebitis vitam in vobis. [n. 967]

6:55 Qui manducat meam carnem, et bibit meum sanguinem, habet vitam aeternam: et ego resuscitabo eum in novissimo die. [n. 972]

6:56 Caro enim mea vere est cibus, et sanguis meus vere est potus. [n. 974]

6:57 Qui manducat meam carnem, et bibit meum sanguinem, in me manet, et ego in illo. [n. 976]

6:58 Sicut misit me vivens Pater, et ego vivo propter Patrem: et qui manducat me, et ipse vivet propter me. [n. 977]

6:59 Hic est panis, qui de caelo descendit. Non sicut manducaverunt patres vestri manna, et mortui sunt. Qui manducat hunc panem, vivit in aeternum. [n. 979]

6:60 Haec dixit in synagoga, docens in Capharnaum. [n. 982]

6:53 Ἐμάχοντο οὖν πρὸς ἀλλήλους οἱ Ἰουδαῖοι λέγοντες· πῶς δύναται οὗτος ἡμῖν δοῦναι τὴν σάρκα [αὐτοῦ] φαγεῖν;

6:54 εἶπεν οὖν αὐτοῖς ὁ Ἰησοῦς· ἀμὴν ἀμὴν λέγω ὑμῖν, ἐὰν μὴ φάγητε τὴν σάρκα τοῦ υἱοῦ τοῦ ἀνθρώπου καὶ πίητε αὐτοῦ τὸ αἷμα, οὐκ ἔχετε ζωὴν ἐν ἑαυτοῖς.

6:55 ὁ τρώγων μου τὴν σάρκα καὶ πίνων μου τὸ αἷμα ἔχει ζωὴν αἰώνιον, κἀγὼ ἀναστήσω αὐτὸν τῇ ἐσχάτῃ ἡμέρᾳ.

6:56 ἡ γὰρ σάρξ μου ἀληθής ἐστιν βρῶσις, καὶ τὸ αἷμά μου ἀληθής ἐστιν πόσις.

6:57 ὁ τρώγων μου τὴν σάρκα καὶ πίνων μου τὸ αἷμα ἐν ἐμοὶ μένει κἀγὼ ἐν αὐτῷ.

6:58 καθὼς ἀπέστειλέν με ὁ ζῶν πατὴρ κἀγὼ ζῶ διὰ τὸν πατέρα, καὶ ὁ τρώγων με κἀκεῖνος ζήσει δι᾽ ἐμέ.

6:59 οὗτός ἐστιν ὁ ἄρτος ὁ ἐξ οὐρανοῦ καταβάς, οὐ καθὼς ἔφαγον οἱ πατέρες καὶ ἀπέθανον· ὁ τρώγων τοῦτον τὸν ἄρτον ζήσει εἰς τὸν αἰῶνα.

6:60 Ταῦτα εἶπεν ἐν συναγωγῇ διδάσκων ἐν Καφαρναούμ.

6:53 The Jews therefore quarreled among themselves, saying: how can this man give us his flesh to eat? [n. 966]

6:54 Then Jesus said to them: amen, amen I say to you: unless you eat the flesh of the Son of man and drink his blood, you will not have life in you. [n. 967]

6:55 He who eats my flesh and drinks my blood has eternal life, and I will raise him up on the last day. [n. 972]

6:56 For my flesh is meat indeed, and my blood is drink indeed. [n. 974]

6:57 He who eats my flesh and drinks my blood abides in me, and I in him. [n. 976]

6:58 As the living Father has sent me, and I live because of the Father, so he who eats me will also live because of me. [n. 977]

6:59 This is the bread that came down from heaven. Unlike your fathers who ate manna and are dead, he who eats this bread will live forever. [n. 979]

6:60 These things he said teaching in the synagogue in Capernaum. [n. 982]

---

965. Supra repressit Dominus murmur Iudaeorum, quod ortum habuit de origine cibi spiritualis; hic reprimit eorum litigium, quod erat inter eos de sumptione huius cibi, et

primo ponit eorum litigium;

secundo Dominus comprimit illud, ibi **dixit ergo eis Iesus** etc.;

tertio Evangelista designat locum, ibi **haec dixit in synagoga, docens in Capharnaum**.

966. Circa primum sciendum est, quod Evangelista Iudaeorum litigium inducit per modum conclusionis, cum dicit **litigabant ergo Iudaei** etc. Et quidem satis congrue: nam, secundum Augustinum, Dominus locutus fuerat eis de cibo unitatis, quo qui reficiuntur, efficiuntur unanimes, secundum illud Ps. LXVII, v. 4: *iusti*

965. Above, our Lord checked the grumbling of the Jews over the origin of this spiritual food; here, he stops their dispute over the eating of this same food.

First, we see their dispute;

second, our Lord stops it, at **then Jesus said to them**: **amen, amen I say to you**;

third, the Evangelist mentions the place where all this happened, at **these things he said teaching in the synagogue in Capernaum**.

966. As to the first, note that the Evangelist brings in the dispute among the Jews in the form of a conclusion, saying, **the Jews therefore quarreled among themselves, saying: how can this man give us his flesh to eat?** And this is fitting: for according to Augustine, our Lord had just spoken to them about the food of unity, which makes into one those

epulentur, et exultent in conspectu Dei, et laetentur in laetitia, et sequitur, secundum aliam litteram: *qui habitare facit unanimes in domo*. Quia igitur Iudaei cibum concordiae non sumpserant, ideo ad invicem litigabant; Is. LVIII, 4: *ecce ad lites et contentiones ieiunatis*. Ex hoc autem quod litigabant cum aliis, se esse carnales ostendebant; I Cor. III, 3: *cum sit inter vos zelus et contentio, nonne carnales estis?* Et ideo haec verba Domini carnaliter intelligebant; scilicet quod caro Christi manducaretur sicut cibus carnalis; unde dicunt **quomodo potest hic carnem suam dare ad manducandum?** Quasi dicant: hoc est impossibile, sicut et patres eorum locuti sunt contra Dominum, Num. c. XXI, 5: *anima nostra nauseat super cibo isto levissimo*.

967. Sed hoc eorum litigium comprimitur a Domino; unde **dixit ergo eis Iesus** etc. Ubi

primo ponit virtutem sumptionis huius cibi;

secundo manifestat eam, ibi **qui manducat meam carnem, et bibit meum sanguinem, habet vitam aeternam**.

Circa primum tria facit.

Primo ponit carnis manducandae necessitatem;

secundo eius utilitatem, ibi **qui manducat carnem meam, et bibit meum sanguinem, habet vitam aeternam**;

tertio subdit eius veritatem, ibi **caro enim mea vere est cibus**.

968. Dixit ergo Iesus **amen, amen dico vobis: nisi manducaveritis carnem Filii hominis, et biberitis eius sanguinem, non habebitis vitam in vobis**, quasi dicat: vos reputatis impossibile et incongruum quod carnem meam manducetis; sed non solum non est impossibile, sed etiam est valde necessarium, intantum quod **nisi manducaveritis carnem Filii hominis, et biberitis eius sanguinem, non habebitis**, idest non poteritis habere, **in vobis vitam**, scilicet spiritualem. Nam sicut cibus corporalis ita est necessarius ad vitam corporalem, quod sine eo esse non possit Thren. I, v. 11: *dederunt pretiosa quaeque pro cibo*; et in Ps. CIII, 15: *panis cor hominis confirmet*: ita cibus spiritualis necessarius est ad vitam spiritualem, adeo quod sine ipso vita spiritualis sustentari non possit; Deut. VIII, 3: *non in solo pane vivit homo, sed in omni verbo quod egreditur de ore Dei*.

969. Notandum autem, quod haec sententia potest referri vel ad spiritualem manducationem, vel ad sacramentalem. Sed si referatur ad spiritualem, nullam dubitationem habet sententia. Ille enim spiritualiter carnem Christi manducat et sanguinem bibit qui particeps fit Ecclesiasticae unitatis, quae fit per caritatem; Rom. XII, 5: *omnes unum corpus estis in Christo*. Qui ergo non sic manducat, est extra Ecclesiam, et per

who are nourished on it, according to, *let those who are just feast and rejoice before God*, and then it continues, according to one reading, *God makes those who agree to live in one house* (Ps 67:4). And so, because the Jews had not eaten the food of harmony, they argued with each other: *when you fast, you argue and fight* (Isa 58:4). Further, their quarreling with others shows that they were carnal: *for while you are envious and quarreling, are you not carnal?* (1 Cor 3:3). Therefore, they understood these words of our Lord in a carnal way, i.e., as meaning that our Lord's flesh would be eaten as material food. Thus they say, **how can this man give us his flesh to eat?** As if to say: this is impossible. Here they were speaking against God just as their fathers did: *we are sick of this useless food* (Num 21:5).

967. Our Lord stops this argument at **Jesus therefore said to them: amen amen I say unto you**.

First, he states the power that comes from taking this food;

second, he expounds on it, at **he who eats my flesh and drinks my blood has eternal life, and I will raise him up on the last day**.

As to the first he does three things.

First, he states why it is necessary to eat this flesh;

second, its usefulness: **he who eats my flesh and drinks my blood abides in me, and I in him**; and

third, he adds something about its truth, at **for my flesh is meat indeed**.

968. Jesus said: **amen, amen, I say to you, unless you eat the flesh of the Son of man and drink his blood, you will not have life in you**. As if to say: you think it is impossible and unbecoming to eat my flesh. But it is not only possible, but very necessary, so much so that **unless you eat the flesh of the Son of man and drink his blood, you will not have**, i.e., you will not be able to have, **life in you**, that is, spiritual life. For just as material food is so necessary for bodily life that without it you cannot exist—*they exchanged their precious belongings for food* (Lam 1:11); *bread strengthens the heart of man* (Ps 103:15)—so spiritual food is necessary for the spiritual life to such an extent that without it the spiritual life cannot be sustained: *man does not live by bread alone, but by every word which comes from the mouth of God* (Deut 8:3).

969. We should note that this statement can refer either to eating in a spiritual way or in a sacramental way. If we understand it as referring to a spiritual eating, it does not cause any difficulty. For that person eats the flesh of Christ and drinks his blood in a spiritual way who shares in the unity of the Church; and this is accomplished by the love of charity: *you are one body, in Christ* (Rom 12:5). Thus, one who does not eat in this way is outside the Church, and consequently, without the love of charity. Accordingly, such

consequens extra caritatem; ideo non habet vitam in se-metipso; I Io. III, 14: *qui non diligit, manet in morte.*

Si vero referatur ad sacramentalem, dubium habet quod dicitur; nam supra III, 5, dicitur: **nisi quis renatus fuerit ex aqua et Spiritu, non potest introire in regnum caelorum.** Sed sicut proposita fuit illa sententia, ita est ista: **nisi manducaveritis carnem Filii hominis** etc. Cum ergo baptismus sit sacramentum necessitatis, videtur etiam quod Eucharistia. Sed hoc quidem Graeci concedunt, unde et pueris baptizatis dant Eucharistiam: et in hoc habent pro eis ritum Dionysii, qui dicit, quod perceptio cuiuslibet sacramenti debet consummari in communione Eucharistiae, quae est consummatio omnium sacramentorum. Sed hoc verum est in adultis, non autem in pueris: cum in sumente Eucharistiam exigatur actualis reverentia et devotio, quam illi qui non habent usum liberi arbitrii, sicut sunt pueri et amentes, habere non possunt; et ideo nullo modo eis est danda.

Dicendum ergo, quod sacramentum baptismatis est necessarium quantum ad omnes, ut realiter accipiatur, quia sine eo nullus regeneratur ad vitam: et ideo oportet quod ipsum habeatur in re vel in voto, quantum ad praeoccupatos; nam si contemptus in aliquo baptismum aquae excludat, neque baptismus flaminis nec sanguinis prodest ei ad vitam aeternam. Sacramentum vero Eucharistiae est necessitatis quantum ad adultos tantum, ita quod recipiatur re vel voto secundum Ecclesiae instituta.

970. Sed secundum hoc etiam dubitatur: quia per haec verba Domini, non solum manducatio corporis, sed etiam sumptio sanguinis est de necessitate salutis, praesertim cum perfecta refectio cibi non sit sine potu. Cum ergo consuetudo aliquarum Ecclesiarum sit quod solus sacerdos communicet de sanguine, alii vero communicant corpori tantum, videtur huic sententiae contrariari.

Respondeo dicendum, quod, secundum antiquae Ecclesiae consuetudinem, omnes sicut communicabant corpori, ita communicabant et sanguini; quod etiam adhuc in quibusdam ecclesiis servatur, ubi etiam ministri altaris continue et corpori et sanguini communicant. Sed propter periculum effusionis, in aliquibus ecclesiis servatur ut solus sacerdos communicet sanguini, reliqui vero corpori. Nec tamen est contra sententiam Domini, quia qui communicat corpori, communicat etiam sanguini, cum sub utraque specie totus Christus contineatur, etiam quantum ad corpus et sanguinem. Sed sub speciebus panis continetur corpus Christi ex vi conversionis, sanguis vero ex naturali concomitantia: sub speciebus vero vini continetur sanguis Christi ex vi conversionis, corpus vero ex concomitantia naturali. Sic ergo apparet necessitas sumendi hunc cibum spiritualem.

a one does not have life in himself: *he who does not love, remains in death* (1 John 3:14).

But if we refer this statement to eating in a sacramental way, a difficulty appears. For we read above: **unless a man is born again of water and the Holy Spirit, he cannot enter into the kingdom of God** (John 3:5). Now this statement was given in the same form as the present one: **unless you eat the flesh of the Son of man.** Therefore, since baptism is a necessary sacrament, it seems that the Eucharist is also. In fact, the Greeks think it is; and so they give the Eucharist to newly baptized infants. For this opinion they have in their favor the rite of Denis, who says that the reception of each sacrament should culminate in the sharing of the Eucharist, which is the culmination of all the sacraments. This is true in the case of adults, but it is not so for infants, because receiving the Eucharist should be done with reverence and devotion, and those who do not have the use of reason, as infants and the insane, cannot have this. Consequently, it should not be given to them at all.

We should say, therefore, that the sacrament of baptism is necessary for everyone, and it must be really received, because without it no one is born again into life. And so it is necessary that it be received in reality, or by desire in the case of those who are prevented from the former. For if the contempt within a person excludes a baptism by water, then neither a baptism of desire nor of blood will benefit him for eternal life. However, the sacrament of the Eucharist is necessary for adults only, so that it may be received in reality, or by desire, according to the practices of the Church.

970. But even this causes difficulty: because by these words of our Lord, it is necessary for salvation not only to eat his body, but also to drink his blood, especially since a repast of food is not complete without drink. Therefore, since it is the custom in certain Churches for only the priest to receive Christ's blood, while the rest receive only his body, they would seem to be acting against this.

I answer that it was the custom of the early Church for all to receive both the body and blood of Christ; and certain churches have still retained this practice, where even those assisting at the altar always receive the body and blood. But in some churches, due to the danger of spilling the blood, the custom is for it to be received only by the priest, while the rest receive Christ's body. Even so, this is not acting against our Lord's command, because whoever receives Christ's body receives his blood also, since the entire Christ is present under each species, even his body and blood. But under the species of bread, Christ's body is present in virtue of the conversion, and his blood is present by natural concomitance; while under the species of wine, his blood is present in virtue of the conversion, and his body by natural concomitance. It is now clear why it is necessary to receive this spiritual food.

971. Utilitas eius ostenditur cum dicit *qui manducat meam carnem, et bibit meum sanguinem, habet vitam aeternam*, et

primo quantum ad spiritum seu animam;

secundo quantum ad corpus, ibi *et ego resuscitabo eum in novissimo die*.

972. Est ergo utilitas huius manducationis magna, quia dat vitam aeternam; unde dicit *qui manducat meam carnem, et bibit meum sanguinem, habet vitam aeternam*. Nam cibus iste spiritualis est similis quidem corporali in hoc quod sine ipso vita spiritualis esse non potest, sicut nec sine corporali cibo vita corporalis, ut dictum est supra. Sed amplius habet ab eo, quia causat indeficientem vitam in sumente, quam cibus corporalis non efficit: non enim qui eum sumpserit, vivet; potest enim fieri, ut Augustinus dicit, ut *senio vel morbo, et aliquo casu plurimi qui eum sumpserunt, moriantur*. Qui vero hunc cibum et potum corporis et sanguinis Domini sumpserit, *habet vitam aeternam*: et ideo comparatur ligno vitae; Prov. III, 8: *lignum vitae est his qui apprehenderit eam*; unde dicitur panis vitae; Eccli. XV, 3: *cibavit illum pane vitae et intellectus*.

Et ideo dicit *vitam aeternam*: et hoc, quia qui manducat hunc panem, habet in se Christum, *qui est verus Deus, et vita aeterna*: ut dicitur I Io. ult., 20. Sed ille habet vitam aeternam, qui manducat et bibit, ut dicitur, non solum sacramentaliter, sed etiam spiritualiter. Ille vero sacramentaliter manducat et bibit, qui sumit ipsum sacramentum; spiritualiter vero, qui pertingit ad rem sacramenti; quae est duplex: una contenta et signata, quae est Christus integer, qui continetur sub speciebus panis et vini; alia res est signata et non contenta, et hoc est corpus Christi mysticum, quod est in praedestinatis, vocatis et iustificatis. Sic ergo spiritualiter manducat carnem et bibit sanguinem per comparationem ad Christum contentum et signatum, qui coniungitur ei per fidem et caritatem, ita quod transformatur in ipsum, et efficitur eius membrum: non enim cibus iste convertitur in eum qui sumit, sed manducantem convertit in se, secundum Augustinum, cum dicit: *cibus sum grandium: cresce, et manducabis me; nec tu me mutabis in te, sed tu mutaberis in me*. Et ideo est cibus hominem divinum facere valens, et divinitate inebrians. Item per comparationem ad corpus mysticum signatum tantum, si fiat particeps unitatis Ecclesiasticae. Qui ergo sic manducat, *habet vitam aeternam*. Et de primo per comparationem ad Christum iam satis patet. Similiter per comparationem ad corpus mysticum de necessitate habebit vitam aeternam, si perseveret. Nam unitas Ecclesiae fit per Spiritum Sanctum, Eph. IV, 4: *unus spiritus et unum corpus, qui est pignus hereditatis aeternae*, ut dicitur Eph. c. I, 14. Est ergo magna utilitas huius cibi, quia dat vitam aeternam

971. Next, the usefulness of this food is shown at *unless you eat the flesh of the Son of man and drink his blood, you will not have life in you*.

First, for the spirit or soul;

second, for the body, at *and I will raise him up on the last day*.

972. There is great usefulness in eating this sacrament, for it gives eternal life; thus he says, *he who eats my flesh and drinks my blood has eternal life*. For this spiritual food is similar to material food in the fact that without it there can be no spiritual life, just as there cannot be bodily life without bodily food, as was said above. But this food has more than the other, because it produces in the one who receives it an unending life, which material food does not do: for not all who eat material food continue to live. For, as Augustine says, *it can happen that many who do take it die because of old age or sickness, or some other reason*. But one who takes this food and drink of the body and blood of our Lord *has eternal life*. For this reason it is compared to the tree of life: *she is the tree of life for those who take her* (Prov 3:18); and so it is called the bread of life: *he fed him with the bread of life and understanding* (Sir 15:3).

Accordingly, he says, *eternal life*, because one who eats this bread has within himself Christ, who is *the true God and eternal life*, as John says (1 John 5:20). Now one has eternal life who eats and drinks, as it is said, not only in a sacramental way, but also in a spiritual way. One eats and drinks sacramentally or in a sacramental way, if he receives the sacrament; and one eats and drinks spiritually or in a spiritual way, if he attains to the reality of the sacrament. This reality of the sacrament is twofold: one is contained and signified, and this is the whole Christ, who is contained under the species of bread and wine. The other reality is signified but not contained, and this is the mystical body of Christ, which is in the predestined, the called, and the justified. Thus, in reference to Christ as contained and signified, one eats his flesh and drinks his blood in a spiritual way if he is united to him through faith and love, so that one is transformed into him and becomes his member: for this food is not changed into the one who eats it, but it turns the one who takes it into itself, as we see in Augustine, when he says: *I am the food of the robust. Grow and you will eat me. Yet you will not change me into yourself, but you will be transformed into me*. And so this is a food capable of making man divine and inebriating him with divinity. The same is true in reference to the mystical body of Christ, which is only signified, if one shares in the unity of the Church. Therefore, one who eats in these ways *has eternal life*. That this is true of the first way, in reference to Christ, is clear enough. In the same way, in reference to the mystical body of Christ, one will necessarily have eternal life if he perseveres: for the unity of the Church is brought about by the

animae; sed etiam magna est, quia dat vitam aeternam etiam corpori.

973. Et ideo subdit *et ego resuscitabo eum in novissimo die.* Sicut enim dictum est, ille qui spiritualiter manducat et bibit, fit particeps Spiritus Sancti, per quem unimur Christo unione fidei et caritatis, et per quem efficimur membra Ecclesiae. Resurrectionem autem facit mereri Spiritus Sanctus; Rom. IV, 24: *qui suscitavit Iesum Christum Dominum nostrum a mortuis, resuscitabit et mortalia corpora nostra propter inhabitantem Spiritum eius in nobis.* Et ideo dicit Dominus, quod eum qui manducat et bibit, resuscitabit ad gloriam, non ad condemnationem: quia haec resuscitatio non prodesset.

Et quidem satis congrue huiusmodi effectus sacramento Eucharistiae attribuitur, quia, ut dicit Augustinus, et dictum est supra, Verbum resuscitat animas, sed Verbum caro factum vivificat corpora. In hoc autem sacramento non solum est Verbum, secundum suam divinitatem, sed etiam secundum veritatem carnis: et ideo non est solum causa resurrectionis animarum, sed etiam corporum; I Cor. XV, 21: *per hominem mors, et per hominem resurrectio mortuorum.* Patet ergo utilitas huius manducationis.

974. Veritas autem eius ostenditur cum dicit *caro enim mea vere est cibus.* Posset enim aliquis credere, quod ea quae de carne dicta sunt et sanguine aenigma et parabola esset; et ideo hoc Dominus excludens, dicit *caro mea vere est cibus*; quasi dicat: non intelligatis quod figuraliter loquar; sed secundum veritatem caro mea continetur in cibo fidelium, et sanguis meus vere continetur in sacramento altaris; Matth. XXVI, 26: *hoc est corpus meum . . . et hic est sanguis meus Novi Testamenti.*

Vel aliter, secundum Chrysostomum, quia cibus et potus sumitur ad refectionem hominis. In homine autem sunt duae partes; principalis quae est anima, et secundaria quae est corpus. Illud autem quod est homo, est per anima, non per corpus: illud ergo est vere cibus hominis, qui est cibus animae; et hoc est quod Dominus dicit *caro enim mea vere est cibus*: quia non solum est cibus corporis, sed etiam animae. Similiter et sanguis. Ps. XXII, 2: *super aquam refectionis educavit me, animam meam convertit.* Quasi diceret: haec refectio specialiter ad animam ordinatur.

Vel aliter, secundum Augustinum. Illud vere dicitur esse aliquid quod facit effectum eius; effectus autem cibi est ut satiet: quod ergo vere facit satietatem, vere est cibus et potus. Hoc autem facit caro et sanguis Christi, qui ducit ad statum gloriae, ubi non est esuries neque sitis: Apoc. VII, 16: *non esurient nec sitient amplius*; et ideo

Holy Spirit: *one body, one Spirit . . . the pledge of our eternal inheritance* (Eph 4:4; 1:14). So this bread is very profitable, because it gives eternal life to the soul; but it is so also because it gives eternal life to the body.

973. And therefore he adds, **and I will raise him up on the last day**. For as was said, one who eats and drinks in a spiritual way shares in the Holy Spirit, through whom we are united to Christ by a union of faith and love, and through him we become members of the Church. But the Holy Spirit also merits the resurrection: *he who raised Jesus Christ our Lord form the dead, will raise our mortal bodies because of his Spirit, who dwells in us* (Rom 8:11). And so our Lord says that he will raise up to glory whoever eats and drinks; to glory, and not to condemnation, as this would not be for their benefit.

Such an effect is fittingly attributed to this sacrament of the Eucharist because, as Augustine says and as was said above, it is the Word who raises up souls, and it is the Word made flesh who gives life to bodies. Now in this sacrament the Word is present not only in his divinity, but also in the reality of his flesh; and so he is the cause of the resurrection not just of souls, but of bodies as well: *for as death came through a man, so the resurrection of the dead has come through a man* (1 Cor 15:21). It is now clear how profitable it is to take this sacrament.

974. We see its truth when he says, **for my flesh is meat indeed**. I some might think that what he was saying about his flesh and blood was just an enigma and a parable. So our Lord rejects this, and says, **my flesh is meat indeed**. As if to say: do not think that I am speaking metaphorically, for my flesh is truly contained in this food of the faithful, and my blood is truly contained in this sacrament of the altar: *this is my body . . . this is my blood of the New Covenant* (Matt 26:26).

Chrysostom explains this statement in the following way. Food and drink are taken for man's refreshment. Now there are two parts in man: the chief part is the soul, and the second is the body. It is the soul which makes man to be man, and not the body; and so that truly is the food of man which is the food of the soul. And this is what our Lord says: **my flesh is meat indeed**, because it is the food of the soul, not just of the body. The same is true of the blood of Christ. *He has led me to the waters that refresh* (Ps 22:2). As if to say: this refreshment is especially for the soul.

Augustine explains these words this way. A thing is truly said to be such and such a thing if it produces the effect of that thing. Now the effect of food is to fill or satisfy. Therefore, that which truly produces fullness is truly food and drink. But this is produced by the flesh and blood of Christ, who leads us to the state of glory, where there is

dicit *caro mea vere est cibus, et sanguis meus vere est potus*.

975. *Qui manducat*, etc. Hic probat Dominus cibi spiritualis virtutem supra positam, scilicet quod det vitam aeternam: et utitur tali argumento. Quicumque manducat meam carnem et bibit meum sanguinem, coniungitur mihi; sed qui coniungitur mihi, habet vitam aeternam: ergo qui manducat meam carnem et bibit meum sanguinem, habet vitam aeternam. Secundum hoc ergo tria facit.

Primo ponit maiorem;

secundo minorem, et probat eam, ibi *sicut misit me vivens Pater, et ego vivo propter Patrem*;

tertio infert conclusionem, ibi *hic est panis qui de caelo descendit*.

976. Sciendum est ergo quantum ad primum, quod si hoc quod dicit *qui manducat carnem meam* etc., referatur ad carnem et sanguinem mystice; nulla dubitatio est in verbo. Nam, sicut dictum est, ille manducat spiritualiter per comparationem ad rem signatam tantum, qui corpori mystico incorporatur per unionem fidei et caritatis: caritas autem facit Deum esse in homine, et e converso; I Io. IV, 16: *qui manet in caritate, in Deo manet, et Deus in eo*. Et hoc est quod facit Spiritus Sanctus; unde ibid. 13: *in hoc cognoscimus quoniam in Deo manemus, et Deus in nobis, quia de spiritu suo dedit nobis*.

Si vero referatur ad sumptionem sacramentalem; tunc quicumque manducat carnem et bibit sanguinem, manet in Deo: quia, sicut dicit Augustinus, est quidam modus manducandi illam carnem et bibendi illum sanguinem, quo qui manducat et bibit, in Christo manet, et Christus in eo. Sed hic est ille qui non sacramentaliter tantum, sed revera corpus Christi manducat, et sanguinem bibit.

Est et alius modus quo qui manducant, non manent in Christo, nec Christus in eis; hoc est qui in corde ficto ad illud accedunt: nullum enim effectum habet sacramentum in ficto. Fictus enim est, cum non respondet interius quod signatur exterius. In sacramento autem Eucharistiae exterius quidem signatur quod Christus incorporetur in eo qui percipit illud, et ipse in Christo. Qui ergo non habet in corde desiderium huius unionis, nec conatur ad removendum omne impedimentum ad hoc, est fictus. Et ideo Christus in eo non manet, nec ipse in Christo.

977. Hic ponit minorem: scilicet quod qui coniungitur Christo, habet vitam; et inducit hoc in manifestatione cuiusdam similitudinis, quae talis est. Filius propter unitatem quam habet ad Patrem recipit vitam a Patre: ergo qui unitur Christo, recipit vitam a Christo; et hoc est quod dicit *sicut misit me vivens Pater, et ego vivo propter Patrem*. Quae quidem verba possunt dupliciter

neither hunger nor thirst: *they will neither hunger nor thirst* (Rev 7:16). And so he says: *for my flesh is meat indeed, and my blood is drink indeed*.

975. *He who eats my flesh and drinks my blood has eternal life, and I will raise him up on the last day*. Here our Lord proves that this spiritual food has such power, that is, to give eternal life. And he reasons this way: whoever eats my flesh and drinks my blood is united to me, but whoever is united to me has eternal life: therefore, whoever eats my flesh and drinks my blood has eternal life. Here he does three things:

first, he gives his major premise;

second, the minor premise, which he proves, at *as the living Father has sent me, and I live because of the Father*; and

third, he draws his conclusion: *this is the bread that came down from heaven*.

976. We should note, with respect to the first, that if his statement, *he who eats my flesh and drinks my blood abides in me, and I in him*, is referred to his flesh and blood in a mystical way, there is no difficulty. For, as was said, that person eats in a spiritual way, in reference to what is signified only, who is incorporated into the mystical body through a union of faith and love. Through love, God is in man, and man is in God: *he who abides in love, abides in God, and God in him* (1 John 4:16). And this is what the Holy Spirit does; so it is also said, *we know that we abide in God and God in us, because he has given us his Spirit* (1 John 4:13).

If these words are referred to a sacramental reception, then whoever eats this flesh and drinks this blood abides in God. For, as Augustine says, there is one way of eating this flesh and drinking this blood such that he who eats and drinks abides in Christ and Christ in him. This is the way of those who eat the body of Christ and drink his blood not just sacramentally, but really.

And there is another way by which those who eat do not abide in Christ nor Christ in them. This is the way of those who approach with an insincere heart: for this sacrament has no effect in one who is insincere. There is insincerity when the interior state does not agree with what is outwardly signified. In the sacrament of the Eucharist, what is outwardly signified is that Christ is united to the one who receives it, and such a one to Christ. Thus, one who does not desire this union in his heart, or does not try to remove every obstacle to it, is insincere. Consequently, Christ does not abide in him nor he in Christ.

977. Now he presents his minor premise, that is, whoever is united to Christ has life. He mentions this to show the following similarity: the Son, because of the unity he has with the Father, receives life from the Father; therefore one who is united to Christ receives life from Christ. And this is what he says: *just as the living Father has sent me, and I live because of the Father*. These words can be explained

exponi de Christo, scilicet secundum humanam naturam, et secundum divinam.

Si enim exponantur de Christo Filio Dei, tunc ly *sicut* importat similitudinem Christi ad creaturam quantum ad aliquid, sed non quantum ad omnia, sed quantum ad hoc quod est esse ab alio. Nam hoc est commune Christo Filio Dei, et creaturae, quod sunt ab alio: sed quantum ad alium est dissimile. Quia Filius habet aliquid proprium, quia scilicet sic est a Patre quod tamen recipit totam plenitudinem divinae naturae, intantum quod quidquid est naturale Patri, sit etiam naturale Filio. Creatura vero accipit aliquam perfectionem et naturam particularem; supra V, 26: *sicut Pater habet vitam in semetipso, sic dedit et Filio vitam habere in semetipso*. Et hoc ostendit, quia non ait: *sicut manduco Patrem, et ego vivo propter Patrem*, cum loquatur de processione sua a Patre, sicut dixit *qui manducat me, et ipse vivet propter me*, cum loquitur de participatione corporis et sanguinis eius, qua nos efficimur meliores: nam manducatio quamdam participationem dicit. Sed Christus dicit se vivere propter Patrem, non quidem manducatum, sed generantem, sine aequalitatis detrimento.

Si vero exponatur de Christo homine, sic quantum ad aliquid ly *sicut* importat similitudinem inter Christum hominem et nos: in hoc scilicet quod sicut Christus homo accipit spiritualem vitam per unionem ad Deum, ita et nos accipimus spiritualem vitam in communione sacramenti. Sed tamen est dissimile: quia Christus homo accepit vitam per unionem Verbi, cui in persona unitur; sed nos unimur Christo per sacramentum fidei. Et ideo duo dicit *misit me* et *Pater*. Si ergo referatur ad Filium Dei, tunc dicit *vivo ego propter Patrem*: quia ipse Pater vivens est. Si vero referatur ad Filium hominis; tunc dicit *vivo ego propter Patrem*, quia *misit me*: idest, fecit me incarnari: missio enim Filii Dei est eius incarnatio; Gal. IV, 4: *misit Deus Filium suum factum ex muliere, factum sub lege*.

978. Per hoc ergo, secundum Hilarium, excluditur error Arii; nam si nos propter Christum vivimus, quia aliquid de natura sua habemus, ut ipse dicit: *qui manducat meam carnem, et bibit meum sanguinem, habet vitam aeternam*; ergo et Christus vivit propter Patrem, quia habet in se naturam Patris: non autem partem, quia simplex est et indivisibilis, ergo habet totam naturam Patris. Propter Patrem ergo vivit Filius, dum nativitas non alienam ei intulit diversamque naturam.

979. Consequenter cum dicit *hic est panis, qui de caelo descendit*, ponit duas conclusiones: nam de duobus litigabant, scilicet de origine spiritualis cibi, et de eius virtute.

Prima ergo conclusio est de origine;

---

in two ways about Christ: either in reference to his human nature, or in reference to his divine nature.

If they are explained as referring to Christ the Son of God, then the *as* implies a similarity of Christ to creatures in some respect, though not in all respects, which is, that he exists from another. For to be from another is common to Christ the Son of God and to creatures. But they are unlike in another way: the Son has something proper to himself, because he is from the Father in such a way that he receives the entire fullness of the divine nature, so that whatever is natural to the Father is also natural to the Son. Creatures, on the other hand, receive a certain particular perfection and nature. *For as the Father has life in himself, so he has also given to the Son to have life in himself* (John 5:26). He shows this because, when speaking of his procession from the Father, he does not say: *as I eat the Father, so I live because of the Father*, as he said, when speaking of sharing in his body and blood, *he who eats me, he also will live because of me*. This eating makes us better, for eating implies a certain sharing. Rather, Christ says that he lives because of the Father, not as eaten, but as generating, without detriment to his equality.

If we explain this statement as applying to Christ as man, then in some respect the *as* implies a similarity between Christ as man and us: that is, in the fact that as Christ the man receives spiritual life through union with God, so we too receive spiritual life in the communion or sharing in this Sacrament. Still, there is a difference: for Christ as man received life through union with the Word, to whom he is united in person; while we are united to Christ through the sacrament of faith. And so he says two things: *sent me* and *Father*. If we refer these words to the Son of God, then he is saying, *I live because of the Father*, because the Father himself is living. But if they are referred to the Son of man, then he is saying, *I live because of the Father*, because the Father *has sent me*, i.e., made me incarnate. For the sending of the Son is his incarnation: *God sent his Son, made from a woman* (Gal 4:4).

978. According to Hilary, this is a rejection of the error made by Arius. For if we live because of Christ, because we have something of his nature, as he says, *he who eats my flesh and drinks my blood has eternal life*, then Christ too lives because of the Father, because he has in himself the nature of the Father not a part of it, for it is simple and indivisible. Therefore, Christ has the entire nature of the Father. It is because of the Father, therefore, that the Son lives, because the Son's birth did not involve another and different nature.

979. Next, at *this is the bread that came down from heaven*, he presents his two conclusions. For they were arguing about two things: the origin of this spiritual food and its power.

The first conclusion is about its origin;

secunda est de virtute; et hanc principaliter intendit, ibi *qui manducat hunc panem vivet in aeternum*.

980. Sciendum est circa primum, quod Iudaei turbati fuerant, quia dixerat: *ego sum panis vivus qui de caelo descendit*, et ideo contra eos hoc iterum concludit ex hoc quod dicit *vivo propter Patrem*, cum dicit *hic est panis*. Nam descendere de caelo, est de caelo originem habere; sed Filius habet originem de caelo, quia vivit propter Patrem: ergo Christus est qui de caelo descendit. Et ideo dicit *hic est panis qui de caelo*, idest de vita Paterna, *descendit*, et hoc quantum ad divinitatem; vel *descendit* etiam quantum ad corpus: inquantum scilicet virtus formativa eius, quae fuit Spiritus Sanctus, de caelo fuit, ut virtus caelestis. Unde qui manducant hunc panem non moriuntur, quo modo mortui sunt Patres nostri, qui manducaverunt manna non de caelo: nec erat panis vivus, ut dictum est supra. Quomodo autem mortui sunt qui manna manducaverunt, ex praemissis manifestum est.

981. Secunda conclusio de virtute panis ponitur cum dicit *qui manducat hunc panem, vivet in aeternum*: quae sequitur ex hoc *qui manducat meam carnem*. Qui enim manducat hunc panem manet in me, et ego in illo; sed ego sum vita aeterna: ergo qui manducat hunc panem, ut debet, vivet in aeternum.

982. Locus autem ubi hoc dixit Iesus, fuit in synagoga, in qua Christus docebat in Capharnaum. Volens enim multitudinem attrahere, in templo et synagoga docebat, et ut ex multis saltem proficiant aliqui; Ps. XXXIX, 10: *annuntiavi iustitiam tuam in Ecclesia magna*.

the second is about its power: *he who eats this bread will have eternal life*.

980. With respect to the first, we should note that the Jews had been troubled because he had said, *I am the living bread, which came down from heaven* (John 6:51). Therefore, in opposition to them, he arrives at this same conclusion again, from his statement, *I live because of the Father*, when he says, *this is the bread that came down from heaven*. For to come down from heaven is to have an origin from heaven; but the Son has his origin from heaven, since he lives because of the Father: therefore, Christ is the one who has come down from heaven. And so he says, *this is the bread that came down from heaven*, i.e., from the life of the Father. *Came down*, in relation to his divinity; or *came down*, even in his body, so far as the power that formed it, the Holy Spirit, was from heaven, a heavenly power. Thus, those who eat this bread do not die; as our fathers died, who ate the manna that was neither from heaven, nor was living bread, as was said above. How those who ate the manna died is clear from what has been mentioned before.

981. The second conclusion, concerning the power of this bread, is given when he says, *if any man eat of this bread, he will live forever* (John 6:52). This follows from his statement, *he who eats my flesh and drinks my blood abides in me, and I in him*. For whoever eats this bread abides in me, and I in him. But I am eternal life. Therefore, whoever eats this bread, as he ought, shall live forever.

982. Jesus said this in the synagogue, in which he was teaching at Capernaum. He used to teach in the temple and in the synagogues in order to attract many, so that at least some might benefit: *I have proclaimed your justice in the great assembly* (Ps 39:10).

Lecture 8

6:61 Multi ergo audientes ex discipulis eius, dixerunt: durus est hic sermo, et quis potest eum audire? [n. 984]

6:62 Sciens autem Iesus apud semetipsum quia murmurarent de hoc discipuli eius, dicit eis: hoc vos scandalizat? [n. 985]

6:63 Si ergo videritis Filium hominis ascendentem ubi erat prius? [n. 988]

6:64 Spiritus est qui vivificat; caro non prodest quidquam. Verba quae ego locutus sum vobis, spiritus et vita sunt. [n. 992]

6:65 Sed sunt quidam ex vobis qui non credunt. Sciebat enim ab initio Iesus, qui essent credentes, et quis traditurus esset eum, [n. 994]

6:66 et dicebat: propterea dixi vobis, quia nemo potest venire ad me, nisi fuerit ei datum a Patre meo. [n. 997]

6:67 Ex hoc multi discipulorum eius abierunt retro, et iam cum illo ambulabant. [n. 998]

6:68 Dixit ergo Iesus ad duodecim: numquid et vos vultis abire? [n. 999]

6:69 Respondit ergo ei Simon Petrus: Domine, ad quem ibimus? verba vitae aeternae habes: [n. 1001]

6:70 et nos credimus, et cognovimus, quia tu es Christus Filius Dei. [n. 1004]

6:71 Respondit ei Iesus: nonne ego vos duodecim elegi, et ex vobis unus diabolus est? [n. 1005]

6:72 Dicebat autem de Iuda Simonis Iscariote: hic enim erat traditurus eum, cum esset unus ex duodecim. [n. 1009]

6:61 Πολλοὶ οὖν ἀκούσαντες ἐκ τῶν μαθητῶν αὐτοῦ εἶπαν· σκληρός ἐστιν ὁ λόγος οὗτος· τίς δύναται αὐτοῦ ἀκούειν;

6:62 εἰδὼς δὲ ὁ Ἰησοῦς ἐν ἑαυτῷ ὅτι γογγύζουσιν περὶ τούτου οἱ μαθηταὶ αὐτοῦ εἶπεν αὐτοῖς· τοῦτο ὑμᾶς σκανδαλίζει;

6:63 ἐὰν οὖν θεωρῆτε τὸν υἱὸν τοῦ ἀνθρώπου ἀναβαίνοντα ὅπου ἦν τὸ πρότερον;

6:64 τὸ πνεῦμά ἐστιν τὸ ζωοποιοῦν, ἡ σὰρξ οὐκ ὠφελεῖ οὐδέν· τὰ ῥήματα ἃ ἐγὼ λελάληκα ὑμῖν πνεῦμά ἐστιν καὶ ζωή ἐστιν.

6:65 ἀλλ᾽ εἰσὶν ἐξ ὑμῶν τινες οἳ οὐ πιστεύουσιν. ᾔδει γὰρ ἐξ ἀρχῆς ὁ Ἰησοῦς τίνες εἰσὶν οἱ μὴ πιστεύοντες καὶ τίς ἐστιν ὁ παραδώσων αὐτόν.

6:66 καὶ ἔλεγεν· διὰ τοῦτο εἴρηκα ὑμῖν ὅτι οὐδεὶς δύναται ἐλθεῖν πρός με ἐὰν μὴ ᾖ δεδομένον αὐτῷ ἐκ τοῦ πατρός.

6:67 Ἐκ τούτου πολλοὶ [ἐκ] τῶν μαθητῶν αὐτοῦ ἀπῆλθον εἰς τὰ ὀπίσω καὶ οὐκέτι μετ᾽ αὐτοῦ περιεπάτουν.

6:68 εἶπεν οὖν ὁ Ἰησοῦς τοῖς δώδεκα· μὴ καὶ ὑμεῖς θέλετε ὑπάγειν;

6:69 ἀπεκρίθη αὐτῷ Σίμων Πέτρος· κύριε, πρὸς τίνα ἀπελευσόμεθα; ῥήματα ζωῆς αἰωνίου ἔχεις,

6:70 καὶ ἡμεῖς πεπιστεύκαμεν καὶ ἐγνώκαμεν ὅτι σὺ εἶ ὁ ἅγιος τοῦ θεοῦ.

6:71 ἀπεκρίθη αὐτοῖς ὁ Ἰησοῦς· οὐκ ἐγὼ ὑμᾶς τοὺς δώδεκα ἐξελεξάμην; καὶ ἐξ ὑμῶν εἷς διάβολός ἐστιν.

6:72 ἔλεγεν δὲ τὸν Ἰούδαν Σίμωνος Ἰσκαριώτου· οὗτος γὰρ ἔμελλεν παραδιδόναι αὐτόν, εἷς ἐκ τῶν δώδεκα.

6:61 Many of his disciples, hearing it, said: this saying is hard, and who is able to accept it? [n. 984]

6:62 But Jesus, knowing that his disciples murmured at this, said to them: does this scandalize you? [n. 985]

6:63 What if you shall see the Son of man ascending to where he was before? [n. 988]

6:64 It is the spirit that gives life: the flesh profits nothing. The words that I have spoken to you are spirit and life. [n. 992]

6:65 But there are some of you who do not believe. For Jesus knew from the beginning who believed and who would betray him. [n. 994]

6:66 And he said: I therefore said to you, that no man can come to me, unless it is given to him by my Father. [n. 997]

6:67 After this many of his disciples departed and did not walk anymore with him. [n. 998]

6:68 Then Jesus said to the twelve: will you also go away? [n. 999]

6:69 And Simon Peter answered him: Lord, to whom shall we go? You have the words of eternal life. [n. 1001]

6:70 And we have believed and known, that you are the Christ, the Son of God. [n. 1004]

6:71 Jesus answered them: have I not chosen you twelve, and one of you is a devil? [n. 1005]

6:72 Now he meant Judas Iscariot, the son of Simon, who was about to betray him, since he was one of the twelve. [n. 1009]

---

983. Postquam compressit litigium Iudaeorum, et murmur, consequenter Dominus sedat scandalum discipulorum, et

primo agitur de scandalo discipulorum recedentium;

983. After our Lord put an end to the complaining and arguing among the Jews, he now removes the scandal given to his disciples.

First, we see the scandal of those disciples who left him;

secundo examinatur devotio remanentium, ibi *dixit ergo Iesus ad duodecim*.

Circa primum tria facit.

Primo ponitur scandalum discipulorum;

secundo benignitas Christi ad reprimendum ipsum, ibi *sciens autem Iesus* etc.;

tertio ponitur pertinacia et incredulitas recedentium, ibi *ex hoc multi discipulorum eius abierunt retro*.

984. Sciendum est ergo circa primum, quod multi erant in populo Iudaeorum qui adhaerebant Christo, credentes ei, et sequebantur eum non tamen relictis omnibus, sicut Duodecim, qui omnes dicebantur discipuli. Et de istis dicit, quod *multi*, scilicet in populo, qui ei credebant, *audientes*, quae supra dixit, *dixerunt: durus est hic sermo*. De istis dicitur Lc. VIII, 13: *ad tempus credunt, et in tempore tentationis recedunt*. Dicitur autem *multi*, quia, ut dicitur Eccle. I, v. 15, *stultorum infinitus est numerus*. Et Matth. XX, 16: *multi sunt vocati, pauci vero electi*.

Isti ergo dixerunt *durus est hic sermo*. Durum dicitur quod non facile dividitur, et resistentiam habet. Est ergo aliquis sermo durus, aut quia resistit intellectui, aut quia resistit voluntati; cum scilicet illum intellectu capere non possumus, aut voluntati non placet; et utroque modo erat istis durus sermo. Durus quidem intellectu, quia superexcedebat imbecillitatem intellectus eorum; cum enim carnales essent, non poterant capere quod dicebat, se carnem suam daturum eis ad manducandum. Voluntati autem, quia multa dixit de potentia suae divinitatis. Et licet isti crederent ei sicut prophetae, non tamen credebant eum Deum: et ideo videbatur eis quod loqueretur maiora seipso. II Cor. X, 10: *epistolae graves sunt*. Eccli. VI, 21: *aspera est nimium indoctis hominibus sapientia*. Et ideo sequitur *quis potest eum audire?* Haec dicunt ad excusationem suam. Nam ex quo dederant se ei, debebant eum audire: sed quia non docebat eos placentia, vellent aliquam occasionem quaerere recedendi; Prov. c. XVIII, 2: *non recipit stultus verba prudentiae, nisi ea dixeris quae versantur in corde suo*.

985. Consequenter cum dicit *sciens autem Iesus apud semetipsum quia murmurarent de hoc discipuli eius, dicit eis: hoc vos scandalizat?* ponitur benignitas Christi ad sedandum scandalum, et

primo denuntiat et manifestat scandalum;

secundo removet causam scandali, ibi *si ergo videritis filium hominis ascendentem ubi erat prius?*

Tertio innuit ipsam causam, ibi *sed sunt quidam ex vobis qui non credunt*.

986. Scandalum autem denuntiat, quia dixerant occulte *durus est hic sermo* ut ab illo non audirentur. Sed ille qui virtute suae divinitatis noverat quid dicebant,

second, the devotion of those who remained with him, at *then Jesus said to the twelve*.

Concerning the first, he does three things:

first, we see the scandal given to his disciples;

second, the kindly way Christ takes it away, at *but Jesus, knowing that his disciples murmured at this*, and

third, the stubbornness and unbelief of those who leave him, at *after this many of his disciples departed*.

984. We should note, with respect to the first, that there were many Jews who adhered to Christ, believed him and followed him. And although they had not left all things as the Twelve did, they were still all called his disciples. It is of these that he says, *many*, that is, many of the people who believed him, *hearing it*, what he had said above, *said, this saying is hard*. We read of these: *they believe for a while, and in the time of testing fall away* (Luke 8:13). He says, *many*, because *the number of fools is infinite* (Eccl 1:15); and, *many are called but few are chosen* (Matt 20:16).

They said: *this saying is hard*. Now that is said to be hard which is difficult to divide, and which offers resistance. Accordingly, a saying is hard either because it resists the intellect or because it resists the will, that is, when we cannot understand it with our mind, or when it does not please our will. And this saying was hard for them in both ways. It was hard for their intellects because it exceeded the weakness of their intellects: for since they were earthly minded, they were incapable of understanding what he said, namely, that he would give them his flesh to eat. And it was hard for their wills, because he said many things about the power of his divinity: and although they believed him as a prophet, they did not believe that he was God. Consequently, it seemed to them that he was making himself greater than he was. *His letters are strong* (2 Cor 10:10); *wisdom is exceedingly unpleasant to the unlearned* (Sir 6:21). And so it reads on. *Who is able to accept it?* They said this as an excuse: for since they had given themselves to him, they should have accepted what he said. But because he was not teaching them things that were pleasing to them, they were waiting for an occasion to leave him: *a fool does not accept words of wisdom unless You tell him what he desires* (Prov 18:2).

985. Next, at *but Jesus, knowing that his disciples murmured at this, said to them: does this scandalize you?*, we see the kindly way Christ dispelled their difficulty.

First, he takes notice of and mentions the scandal;

second, he removes its cause, at *what if you shall see the Son of man ascending to where he was before?*

Third, he mentions what the cause was, at *but there are some of you who do not believe*.

986. He had noticed that they were scandalized because they had said, although privately, so he could not hear, *this saying is hard*. But Christ, who in virtue of his divinity

hoc manifestat; et hoc est quod dicit *sciens autem Iesus apud semetipsum*, quod ipsi in semetipsis dicebant, scilicet *quia murmurarent de hoc discipuli eius* (supra II, 25: *non erat ei opus ut quis testimonium perhiberet de homine; ipse enim sciebat quid esset in homine*; Ps. VII, 10: *scrutans corda et renes Deus); dixit eis: *hoc vos scandalizat?* Quasi dicat: de hoc non debetis scandalizari. Vel potest legi remissive; quasi dicat: scio quod de hoc scandalizamini; Is. VIII, 4: *erit nobis*, scilicet in Christo credentibus, *quidem in sanctificationem; in lapidem autem offensionis duabus domibus Israel*, idest discipulis murmurantibus et turbis.

987. Sed cum doctores debeant vitare scandalum audientium, quare eis Dominus talia dogmata proponit, ut scandalizarentur et recederent?

Respondeo. Dicendum quod necessitas doctrinae exigebat ut Dominus eis talia proponeret. Institerant enim apud eum pro cibo corporali qui venerat ut duceret in appetitum cibi spiritualis; et ideo necesse erat ut eis proponeret doctrinam de cibo spirituali. Nec tamen scandalum eorum causabatur ex vitio doctrinae Christi, sed ex eorum infidelitate. Si enim verba Domini non intelligebant propter eorum carnalitatem, poterant Dominum interrogare, sicut apostoli alias fecerunt. Hoc autem, secundum Augustinum, Dominus dispensative permisit, ut bene docentibus causam patientiae et consolationis contra malignantes eorum dicta praeberet, cum discipuli etiam verbis Christi detrahere praesumerent.

988. Consequenter cum dicit *si ergo videritis Filium hominis ascendentem ubi erat prius?* Tollit occasionem scandali, quae quidem erat et de persona dicentis, et de verbis dictis, ut dicit Chrysostomus, et ideo

primo removet occasionem scandali quantum ad personam dicentis;

secundo quantum ad verba dicta, ibi *spiritus est qui vivificat.*

989. Occasio autem istorum fuit, quia audierant Dominum loqui de se divina: unde, quia ipsi credebant eum esse filium Ioseph, scandalizabantur ex hoc quod de se dicit. Et ideo hanc occasionem removens, ostendit eis Deus apertius suam divinitatem; unde dicit: vos turbamini de his quae de me dixi *si ergo videritis Filium hominis ascendentem ubi erat prius*; supple, quid dicetis? Quasi dicat: numquam potestis negare quin de caelo descenderim, quin sim dator vel doctor vitae aeternae. Simile fecit in Nathanaele: cum enim diceret: *tu es Rex Israel*, voluit eum ad perfectiorem cognitionem elevare; unde dixit ei: *maiora his videbis*. Et ideo istis aliquid maius futurum de se manifestat, dicens *si ergo videritis Filium hominis ascendentem ubi erat prius?* Ascendit autem in caelum videntibus discipulis, ut dicitur Act. I, 9. Si ergo ascendit ubi prius fuit, ergo prius fuit

knew that they had said this, mentions it. And this is what he says: *but Jesus, knowing that his disciples murmured at this*, that is, that his disciples were grumbling about this—*because he did not need anyone to give testimony of man: for he knew what was in man* (John 2:25); *God searches into the hearts and loins of men* (Ps 7:10)—said to them, *does this scandalize you?* As if to say: you should not be scandalized at this. Or, it can be understood less strongly, as meaning: I know that you are scandalized at this. *He will be our sanctification*, i.e., those who believe in Christ, but *a stumbling-stone to the two houses of Israel*, to the grumbling disciples and the crowds (Isa 8:4).

987. But since teachers should avoid creating difficulties for those who are listening to them, why did our Lord mention those things that would upset the people and have them leave?

I answer that Christ had to mention such things because his teaching required it. For they had pleaded with him for material food, when he had come to strengthen their desire for spiritual food; and so he had to make known to them his teaching on spiritual food. Nevertheless, their difficulty was not caused by any defect in what Christ was teaching, but by their own unbelief. For if they had not understood what our Lord was saying, because of their own earthly mindedness, they could have questioned him, as the apostles had done in similar circumstances. According to Augustine, however, our Lord purposely permitted this situation, to give teachers a reason for consolation and patience with those who belittle what they say, since even the disciples presumed to disparage what Christ said.

988. Then, at *what if you shall see the Son of man ascending to where he was before?* he takes away the occasion of their scandal so far as concerns the person speaking and what he said, as Chrysostom says.

First, he deals with the person who was speaking;

second, with what he said at *it is the spirit that gives life*.

989. The occasion for their scandal was when they heard our Lord say divine things about himself. And so, because they believed that he was the son of Joseph, they were upset at what he said about himself. God takes away this reason by showing them his divinity more openly, and says: you are upset over the things I have said about myself; *what if you should see the Son of man ascending to where he was before?* What would you say then? As if to say: You can never deny that I came down from heaven, or that I am the one who gives and teaches eternal life. He did the same thing before with Nathanael. When Nathanael said to him, *you are the King of Israel* (John 1:49) our Lord, wanting to lead him to more perfect knowledge, answered him: *you shall see greater things than these* (John 1:50). And here too, our Lord reveals to them something greater about himself which would happen in the future, saying,

in caelo; supra III, 13: *nemo ascendit in caelum nisi qui de caelo descendit*.

990. Sed attende quod etsi sit eadem persona Filii Dei et Filii hominis in Christo, quia tamen natura est alia, ideo aliquid convenit ratione humanitatis, scilicet ascendere, quod non convenit ei ratione divinitatis, secundum quam non habet quo ascendat, cum aeternaliter sit in summo rerum vertice, scilicet in Patre; sed secundum eam convenit ei ascendere *ubi erat prius*, scilicet in caelo, ubi non fuit secundum humanam naturam; quod est contra errorem Valentini dicentis, Christum attulisse corpus caeleste. Sic ergo ubi prius fuit secundum divinitatem, ascendit videntibus apostolis et propria virtute secundum humanitatem; infra XVI, 28: *exivi a Patre, et veni in mundum: iterum relinquo mundum, et vado ad Patrem*.

991. Sed, secundum Augustinum, aliter haec verba introducuntur: dicit enim, quod isti scandalizati sunt de hoc quod Dominus dixit quod daret eis carnem suam ad manducandum, quod intelligentes carnaliter, ac si eam ad litteram deberent comedere, ut carnes animalium, scandalizati sunt. Et hunc intellectum removens, dicit *si ergo videritis Filium hominis ascendentem*, integro corpore, *ubi erat prius*; supple: numquid dicetis quod sic daturus eram vobis carnem meam ad manducandum ut carnes animalium?

992. Consequenter cum dicit *spiritus est qui vivificat*, removet occasionem scandali ex parte verborum prolatorum, et, secundum Chrysostomum, primo distinguit duplicem intellectum ipsorum verborum; secundo ostendit quis eorum congruat ipsis verbis, ibi *verba quae ego loquor, spiritus et vita sunt*.

Sciendum est ergo quantum ad primum, quod verba Christi secundum duplicem sensum intelligi possunt, scilicet secundum spiritualem et secundum corporalem. Et ideo dicit *spiritus est qui vivificat* idest, si ea verba quae dixi, intelligatis secundum spiritum, idest secundum spiritualem sensum, vivificabunt; *caro non prodest quidquam* idest, si secundum carnalem sensum ea intelligatis, nihil vobis prosunt, immo nocent: quia, ut dicitur Rom. VIII, 13, *si secundum carnem vixeritis, moriemini*. Tunc autem verba Domini de carne sua manducanda, carnaliter intelliguntur, quando accipiuntur secundum quod verba exterius sonant, et ut natura carnis habet; et hoc modo ipsi intelligebant, ut dictum est. Sed Dominus dicebat daturum se eis sicut spiritualem cibum, non quin sit in sacramento altaris vera caro Christi, sed quia

what if you see the Son of man ascending to where he was before? Indeed, he did ascend into heaven in the sight of his disciples (Acts 1:9). If, therefore, he does ascend to where he was before, then he was in heaven before: *and no man has ascended into heaven, except he who descended from heaven* (John 3:13).

990. Let us note that Christ is one person: the person of the Son of God and the person of the Son of man being the same person. Still, because of his different natures, something belongs to Christ by reason of his human nature, that is, to ascend, which does not belong to him by reason of his divine nature, according to which he does not ascend, since he is eternally at the highest summit of things, that is, in the Father. It is according to his human nature that it belongs to him to ascend to *where he was before*, that is, to heaven, where he had not been in his human nature. This is in opposition to the teaching of Valentinus, who claimed that Christ had assumed a heavenly body. Thus, Christ ascended in the sight of his apostles to where he was before according to his divinity; and he ascended, by his own power, according to his humanity: *I came forth from the Father, and have come into the world: again I leave the world, and I go to the Father* (John 16:28).

991. Augustine understands this passage differently. He said that the disciples were scandalized when our Lord said that he would give him them his flesh to eat because they understood this in a material minded way, as if they were literally to eat this flesh, just like the flesh of an animal. Our Lord rejected this interpretation and said: *what if you shall see the Son of man ascending*, with his entire body, *to where he was before?* Would you say that I intended to give you my flesh to eat like you do the flesh of an animal?

992. Then, at *it is the spirit that gives life*, he settles the offense they took at what he said. And, as Chrysostom says, he distinguished two ways in which his words could be understood. And second, he showed which way was appropriate here, at *the words that I have spoken to you are spirit and life*.

With respect to the first, we should note that Christ's words can be understood in two senses: in a spiritual way, and in a material way. Thus he says, *it is the spirit that gives life*, that is, if you understand these words according to the spirit, i.e., according to their spiritual meaning, they will give life. *The flesh profits nothing*, that is, if you understand them in a material way, they will be of no benefit to you, they will, rather, be harmful, for *if you live according to the flesh you will die* (Rom 8:13). What our Lord said about eating his flesh is interpreted in a material way when it is understood in its superficial meaning, and as pertaining to the nature of flesh. And it was in this way that the Jews understood them. But our Lord said that he would give himself to them as spiritual food, not as though the true flesh of Christ is not present in this sacrament of the

quodam spirituali et divino modo manducatur. Sic ergo dictorum verborum congruus sensus est non carnalis, sed spiritualis.

Unde subdit *verba quae ego locutus sum vobis*, scilicet de carne mea manducanda, *spiritus et vita sunt*; idest, spiritualem sensum habent, et sic intellecta vitam dant. Nec mirum si habent spiritualem sensum, quia sunt a Spiritu Sancto; I Cor. XIV, 2: *Spiritus est qui loquitur mysteria.* Et ideo mysteria Christi vivificant; Ps. CXVIII, 93: *in aeternum non obliviscar iustificationes tuas, quia in ipsis vivificasti me.*

993. Secundum Augustinum vero aliter exponitur: nam hoc quod dixit *caro non prodest quidquam*, intelligitur de carne Christi. Manifestum est enim quod caro Christi, ut coniuncta Verbo et Spiritui, multum prodest per omnem modum: alioquin frustra Verbum caro factum esset, frustra ipsum Pater manifestasset in carne, ut dicitur I Tim. c. IV. Et ideo dicendum est quod caro Christi in se considerata non prodest quidquam, et non habet effectum proficuum, nisi sicut alia caro. Si enim per intellectum separetur a divinitate et Spiritu Sancto, non habet aliam virtutem quam alia caro; sed si adveniat Spiritus et divinitas, multis prodest, quia facit sumentes manere in Christo: est enim Spiritus caritatis per quem homo in Deo manet; I Io. IV, 13: *in hoc cognoscimus quia in Deo manemus et ipse in nobis, quoniam de Spiritu suo dedit nobis.* Et ideo dicit Dominus: hunc effectum, scilicet vitae aeternae quem ego promitto vobis, non debetis attribuere carni in se consideratae, quia *caro sic non prodest quidquam*; sed si Spiritui attribuatis, et divinitati coniunctae carni, sic praestat vitam aeternam; Gal. V, 25: *si Spiritu vivimus, Spiritu et ambulemus.* Et ideo subdit *verba quae locutus sum vobis, spiritus et vita sunt*; idest, referenda sunt ad Spiritum carni coniunctum; et sic intellecta, vita sunt, scilicet animae. Nam sicut corpus vivit vita corporali per spiritum corporalem, ita et anima vivit vita spirituali per Spiritum Sanctum; Ps. CIII, 30: *emitte Spiritum tuum, et creabuntur.*

994. Consequenter cum dicit *sed sunt quidam ex vobis qui non credunt*, demonstrat causam scandali, quae erat infidelitas eorum, quasi dicat: causa scandali vestri non est duritia sermonis quem ego locutus sum vobis, sed infidelitas vestra. Et ideo

primo ostendit eorum infidelitatem;
secundo excludit falsam opinionem;
tertio manifestat causam infidelitatis eorum.

995. Infidelitatem quidem eorum ostendit Dominus cum dicit *sunt quidam ex vobis qui non credunt*. Non autem dixit qui non intelligunt sed, quod plus est, causam quare non intelligunt insinuat: ex hoc enim non intelligebant, quia non credebant; Is. VII, 9, secundum aliam litteram: *nisi credideritis, non intelligetis.* Et dixit

altar, but because it is eaten in a certain spiritual and divine way. Thus, the correct meaning of these words is spiritual, not material.

So he says, *the words that I have spoken to you*, about eating my flesh, *are spirit and life*, that is, they have a spiritual meaning, and understood in this way they give life. And it is not surprising that they have a spiritual meaning, because they are from the Holy Spirit: *it is the Spirit who tells mysteries* (1 Cor 14:2). And therefore, the mysteries of Christ give life: *I will never forget your justifications, because through them you have brought me to life* (Ps 118:93).

993. Augustine explains this passage in a different way, for he understands the statement, *flesh profits nothing*, as referring to the flesh of Christ. It is obvious that the flesh of Christ, as united to the Word and to the Spirit, does profit very much and in every way; otherwise, the Word would have been made flesh in vain, and the Father would have made him known in the flesh in vain (1 Tim 4). And so we should say that it is the flesh of Christ, considered in itself, that profits nothing and does not have any more beneficial effect than other flesh. For if his flesh is considered as separated from the divinity and the Holy Spirit, it does not have different power than other flesh. But if it is united to the Spirit and the divinity, it profits many, because it makes those who receive it abide in Christ, for man abides in God through the Spirit of love: *we know that we abide in God and God in us, because he has given us his Spirit* (1 John 4:13). And this is what our Lord says: the effect I promise you, that is, eternal life, should not be attributed to my flesh as such, because understood in this way, *flesh profits nothing*. But my flesh does offer eternal life as united to the Spirit and to the divinity. *If we live by the Spirit, let us also walk by the Spirit* (Gal 5:25). And so he adds, *the words that I have spoken to you are spirit and life*, i.e., they must be understood of the Spirit united to my flesh; and so understood they are life, that is, the life of the soul. For as the body lives its bodily life through a bodily spirit, so the soul lives a spiritual life through the Holy Spirit: *send forth your Spirit, and they will be created* (Ps 103:30).

994. Then, at *but there are some of you who do not believe*, he indicates the reason why they were upset, that is, their unbelief. As if to say: the cause of your difficulty is not the hardness of what I have just said, but your own unbelief.

And so first, he mentions their unbelief;
second, he excludes an incorrect interpretation; and
third, he gives the reason for their unbelief.

995. Our Lord indicated their infidelity when he said, *but there are some of you who do not believe*. He did not say, who do not understand. He did more than this, for he gave the reason why they did not understand: they did not understand because they did not believe. *If you do not believe, you will not understand*, as we read in another version

quidam, ut excipiat discipulos; II ad Thess. III, 2: *non omnium est fides*; ad Rom. X, 16: *non omnes obediunt Evangelio*; Ps. CV, 25: *non crediderunt verbis eius*.

996. Falsam suspicionem excludit Evangelista, cum subdit *sciebat enim*, quasi dicat: non ideo dixit Iesus Sunt quidam ex vobis qui non credunt, quasi de novo hoc ei innotuisset; sed quia sciebat ab initio, mundi scilicet, *qui essent credentes et quis esset traditurus eum*; Hebr. IV, 13: *omnia nuda et aperta sunt oculis eius*; et Eccli. XXIII, 29: *Domino Deo nostro nota sunt omnia antequam fiant*.

997. Causa autem infidelitas eorum assignat Dominus consequenter, quae est ex remotione gratiae attrahentis; unde dicebat *propterea ego dixi vobis*; quasi dicat: ideo necessarium fuit ut vobis praedicta dicerem, *quia nemo potest venire ad me*, scilicet per fidem, *nisi fuerit ei datum a Patre meo*. Ex quo sequitur, secundum Augustinum, quod etiam ipsum credere datur nobis a Deo.

Cur autem non omnibus detur, ostensum est supra, eodem ubi quasi eadem verba Dominus dixit. Repetit tamen ea hic propter duo: ut ostendat quod hoc quod recepit eos ad fidem, magis erat eis ad beneficium et utilitatem quam Christo; Phil. I, 29: *vobis datum est ut in ipsum credatis*; quasi dicat: bonum vestrum est quod credatis; et ideo dicit Augustinus: *magnum quidem est credere: gaude quia credidisti*. Secundo, ut ostendat se non esse filium Ioseph, ut ipsi putabant, sed Dei: nam Deus Pater est qui attrahit homines ad Filium, sicut ex praemissis apparet.

998. Consequenter cum dicit *ex hoc multi, discipulorum eius abierunt retro*, ponitur ipsorum discipulorum pertinacia. Nam licet Dominus reprehenderit eos, et causam scandali, quantum est ex parte sua, removerit, nihil ominus tamen perseverant in infidelitate: et ideo dicit, quod *multi discipuli eius abierunt retro*. Non dixit recesserunt sed, *abierunt retro*, a fide, quam secundum virtutem habebant, et praecisi a corpore Christi, vitam perdiderunt, quia forte nec in corpore fuerunt, ut dicit Augustinus. Sunt enim aliqui qui simpliciter vadunt retro: illi scilicet qui sequuntur diabolum, cui dictum est, Matth. IV, 10: *vade retro, satana*. Et de quibusdam feminis dicitur I Tim. V, 15: *quaedam conversae sunt retro post satanam*. Non sic vadit retro Petrus, sed post Christum; Matth. XVI, 23: *vade retro me, satana*. Isti autem abierunt post satanam.

Unde sequitur *et iam non cum illo ambulabant*: scilicet quamvis a nobis requiratur ut cum Iesu ambulemus; Mich. VI, 8: *iudicabo tibi, homo, quid sit bonum*, et sequitur: *sollicite ambulare cum Deo tuo*.

999. Consequenter cum subditur *dixit ergo Iesus ad duodecim: numquid et vos vultis abire?* Examinat Dominus discipulos remanentes, et

(Isa 7:9). He said, *some*, in order to exclude his disciples: *all do not have faith* (2 Thess 3:2); *all do not obey the Gospel* (Rom 10:16); *they did not believe what he said* (Ps 105:24).

996. The Evangelist then rejects an incorrect interpretation when he adds, *for Jesus knew*. As if to say: Jesus did not say, that there are some of you who do not believe, because he just recently learned it, but because Jesus knew from the beginning, i.e., of the world, those *who believed and who would betray him*. *All things are naked and open to his eyes* (Heb 4:13); *all things were known to the Lord God before they were created* (Sir 23:29).

997. Our Lord next mentioned the cause of their infidelity which was the withdrawal of attracting grace. Thus he said: *I therefore said to you*. As if to say: thus it was necessary to tell you what I told you before: that *no man can come to me*, i.e., through faith, *unless it is given to him by my Father*. It follows from this, according to Augustine, that the act of believing itself is given to us by God.

Why it is not given to everyone we discussed above, where our Lord used almost the same words (John 6:44). They are repeated here for two reasons. First, to show that Christ received them in the faith more for their advantage and benefit than for his own: *it has been granted to you to believe in him* (Phil 1:29). As if to say: it is good for you to believe. Thus Augustine says: *it is a great thing to believe: rejoice, because you have believed*. Second, to show that Christ was not the son of Joseph, as they thought, but of God, for it is God the Father who draws men to the Son, as is clear from what has been said.

998. Then, at *after this many of his disciples departed*, we see the stubbornness of the disciples: for although our Lord had rebuked them and had taken away the cause of their difficulty so far as it concerned himself, they still would not believe. Thus he says, *after this many of his disciples departed*. He did not say, that they left, but they *departed*, i.e., from the faith, which they had in a virtuous way; and cut off from the body of Christ, they lost life, because perhaps they were not in the body, as Augustine says. There are some who turn back in an absolute way, that is, those who follow the devil, to whom our Lord said, *go back, satan* (Matt 4:10). We also read of certain women that *some turned back after satan* (1 Tim 5:15). But Peter did not turn back in this way; he rather turned after Christ: *follow after me, satan* (Matt 16:23). But the others followed after satan.

Then follows: *and did not walk anymore with him*, that is, even though we are required to walk with Jesus: *I will show you man what is good*, and then it continues on, *to walk attentively with your God* (Mic 6:8).

999. Then, at *then Jesus said to the twelve: will you also go away?* our Lord examined those disciples who remained with him.

primo ponitur examinatio discipulorum ex interrogatione Christi;

secundo subditur devotio remanentium ex responsione Petri, ibi **respondit ergo Simon Petrus**;

tertio corrigitur Petri responsio, ibi **respondit ei Iesus**.

1000. Examinat autem Dominus Duodecim qui remanserant an velint persistere; et ideo **dixit ad Duodecim**, scilicet apostolos: **numquid et vos vultis abire?** Et hoc propter duo. Primo ne hoc quod isti, aliis recedentibus, remanserant, propriae iustitiae ascribentes, superbirent, existimantes se gratiam fecisse Christo, eum non relinquendo: et ideo, ostendens se non indigere eorum sequela, magis eos detinet et confirmat. Iob XXXV, 7: *porro, si iuste egeris, quid donabis ei, aut quid de manu tua accipiet?*

Secundo, quia contingit quod aliquando aliquis habet voluntatem recedendi ab aliquo, et tamen verecundia retinetur; et ideo nolens eos verecundia coarctari apud eum remanere (quia idem est invite servire quod penitus non servire), aufert etiam verecundiam et necessitatem remanendi, ponens in eorum arbitrio, an vellent remanere, an abire, quia *hilarem datorem diligit Deus*, ut dicitur II Cor. IX, 7.

1001. Sequitur devotio remanentium ex responsione Petri: nam ipse fratrum amator, et amici conservator, et specialem affectum gerens ad Christum, respondet pro toto collegio, dicens **Domine, ad quem ibimus? Verba vitae aeternae habes, et nos credimus**.

Ubi tria facit.

Primo extollit Christi excellentiam;

secundo commendat eius doctrinam; et

tertio profitetur fidem.

1002. Excellentiam quidem extollit cum dicit **Domine, ad quem ibimus?** Quasi dicat: repellis nos a te; da nobis alium meliorem te, ad quem eamus. Sed certe *nullus similis tui in fortibus, Domine*: Ex. XV, 11, et in Ps. LXXXVIII, 7: *quis similis Deo?* Et ideo non dimittemus te; Ps. CXXXVIII, 7: *quo ibo a spiritu tuo?* Et, secundum Chrysostomum, verbum Petri multum amicitiae est ostensivum: iam enim Christus eis erat honorabilior quam patres et matres.

1003. Doctrinam vero commendat cum dicit **verba vitae aeternae habes**. Moyses autem habuit verba Dei, similiter et prophetae, sed raro verba vitae aeternae; tu vero promittis vitam aeternam, quid ergo aliud maius quaerimus? Supra: **qui credit in me, habet vitam aeternam**; et Sup. III, 39: **qui credit in Filium Dei, habet vitam aeternam**.

1004. Fidem autem confitetur cum subdit **et nos credimus e cognovimus quia tu es Christus Filius Dei**. In

First, we see this in the question he asked them;

second, Peter's answer shows the devotion of those who remained, at **and Simon Peter answered him**; and

third, our Lord corrects Peter's answer, at **Jesus answered them: have not I chosen you twelve?**

1000. Our Lord examined the Twelve who remained as to their willingness to stay on; and **then Jesus said to the Twelve** that is, to the Apostles, **will you also go away?** He asked them this for two reasons. First, so that they would not take pride, thinking it was due to their own goodness, in the fact that they stayed on while the others left, and think that they were doing Christ a favor. And so he showed that he did not need them by holding them off, but still giving them strength: *if you live rightly, what do you give him, or what does he receive from your hand?* (Job 35:7).

Second, it sometimes happens that a person would really prefer to leave another but is kept from doing so by shame or embarrassment. Our Lord did not want them to stay with him because they were forced to do so out of embarrassment (because to serve unwillingly is not to serve at all), and so he took away any embarrassment in their leaving or necessity for their staying, and left it to their own judgment whether they wanted to stay with him or leave, because *God loves a cheerful giver* (2 Cor 9:7).

1001. Then, from Peter's answer, we see the devotion of those who did not leave. For Peter—who loved the brethren, who guarded his friendships, and had it special affection for Christ—answered for the whole group, and said, **Lord, to whom shall we go? You have the words of eternal life. And we have believed.**

Here he did three things.

First, he extolled the greatness of Christ;

second, he praised his teaching; and

third, he professed his faith.

1002. He extolled the greatness of Christ when he said, **Lord, to whom shall we go?** As if to say: are you telling us to leave you? Give us someone better to whom we can go. But then, *there is no one like you among the strong, O Lord* (Exod 15:11); *who is like God* (Ps 88:7). And so you will not tell us to go. *Where can I go that is away from your spirit?* (Ps 138:7). Further, according to Chrysostom, Peter's words show great friendship; for to him, Christ was more worthy of honor than father or mother.

1003. He praised his teaching when he said, **you have the words of eternal life.** Now Moses, and the prophets, also spoke the words of God; but they rarely had the words of eternal life. But you are promising eternal life. What more can we ask? **He who believes in me has eternal life** (John 6:47); **he who believes in the Son has eternal life** (John 3:36).

1004. He professed his faith when he said, **and we have believed and known, that you are the Christ, the Son of**

fide enim nostra duo principaliter credenda sunt, scilicet mysterium Trinitatis et incarnationis: quae duo hic Petrus confitetur. Mysterium quidem Trinitatis, cum dicit **tu es Filius Dei**. In hoc enim quod dicit eum Filium Dei, facit mentionem de persona Patris et Filii, simul etiam et Spiritus Sancti, qui est amor Patris et Filii, et nexus utriusque. Mysterium vero incarnationis, cum dicit **tu es Christus**, *Christus* enim Graece, Latine *unctus* dicitur, oleo scilicet invisibili Spiritus Sancti; sed non secundum divinam naturam, quia qui ungitur Spiritu Sancto ipsa unctione melior efficitur, sed, secundum quod Deus, Christus non efficitur melior: ergo est unctus secundum quod homo.

Dicit autem **credimus et cognovimus**, quia prius est credere quam cognoscere: et ideo si prius cognoscere quam credere vellemus, non cognosceremus, nec credere valeremus, ut dicit Augustinus. Is. VII, 9, secundum aliam litteram: *nisi credideritis, non intelligetis*.

1005. Responsionem autem Petri Dominus corrigit cum dicit **nonne ego vos duodecim elegi, et ex vobis unus diabolus est?** Et

primo ponitur responsio Domini;

secundo expositio Evangelistae, ibi **dicebat autem de Iuda**.

1006. Quia Petrus largus fuit in responsione sua omnes includendo, sic dicens **et nos credimus, et cognovimus quia tu es Christus Filius Dei**, per quod videbatur quod omnes perventuri essent ad vitam aeternam, ideo Dominus de collegio credentium excepit Iudam. Sed haec quidem in Petro commendabilis erat confidentia, quod nullum de socio malum suspicabatur: sed in Domino admiranda est sapientia, qui occulta videbat. Et ideo dicit **nonne ego vos duodecim elegi, et unus ex vobis diabolus est**? Non per naturam, sed per imitationem diabolicae malitiae. Sap. II, 24: *invidia diaboli mors introivit in orbem terrarum: imitantur autem illum qui sunt ex parte illius*; infra XIII, 27: **post buccellam introivit in eum satanas**, quia scilicet factus est conformis malitiae eius.

1007. Sed si Christus elegit Iudam, et ipse factus est malus, videtur quod erraverit in electione.

Ad quod respondetur primo, secundum Chrysostomum, quia hoc non dicitur de electione praedestinationis, sed ad aliquod officium, et ad statum praesentis iustitiae, ad quem aliquando aliquis eligitur non secundum futurum, sed secundum quod nunc est in re: quia per hanc electionem non aufert arbitrii libertatem, nec aufert possibilitatem peccandi; unde, dicitur I Cor. X, 12: *qui existimat stare, videat ne cadat*. Sic ergo Dominus

God. For in our faith there are two things above all that must be believed: the mystery of the Trinity, and the incarnation. And these two Peter professed here. He professed the mystery of the Trinity when he said, **you are the Son of God**: for in calling Christ the Son of God he mentioned the person of the Father and that of the Son, along with the person of the Holy Spirit, who is the love of the Father and of the Son, and the bond or nexus of both. He professed the mystery of the incarnation when he said, **you are the Christ**: for in Greek, the word **Christ** means *anointed*; anointed, that is, with the invisible oil of the Holy Spirit. He was not anointed according to his divine nature, because one who is anointed by the Holy Spirit is made better by that anointing. But Christ, so far as he is God, is not made better. Thus, Christ was anointed as man.

He said, **we have believed and known**, because believing comes before knowing. And therefore, if we wanted to know before believing, we would neither know nor be able to believe, as Augustine says, and as in another version of Isaiah: *if you do not believe, you will not understand* (Isa 7:9).

1005. Our Lord corrected Peter's answer when he said, **have I not chosen you twelve, and one of you is a devil?**

First, we have the Lord's reply:

second, the Evangelist's explanation of it, at **and he meant Judas Iscariot**.

1006. Because Peter was great-hearted and included all in his answer, **we have believed and known, that you are the Christ, the Son of God**, it seemed that all of them would arrive at eternal life. And so our Lord excluded Judas from this community of believers. This trust was commendable in Peter, who did not suspect any evil in his companions; but we must also admire the wisdom of our Lord, who saw what was hidden. Thus he says, **have I not chosen you twelve**, a**nd one of you is a devil**; not by nature, but by imitating the devil's malice: *death came into the world by the envy of the devil; his disciples imitate him* (Wis 2:24); **after the morsel, satan entered into him** (John 13:27), because Judas became like him in malice.

1007. But if Christ chose Judas, who was later to become evil, it seems that our Lord made a mistake in choosing him.

First, we might answer this as Chrysostom does, and say that this choice was not for predestination, but for some task, and in reference to a condition of present justice. Sometimes a person is chosen this way, not in relation to the future, but according to present realities; for being chosen in this way does not destroy one's free choice or the possibility of sinning: hence we read, *let him who thinks that he stands, take heed so he will not fall* (1 Cor 10:12). And so

elegit Iudam non tamquam malum tunc, nec tamen per electionem ablata est ei possibilitas peccandi.

Secundo respondetur, secundum Augustinum, quod Dominus elegit Iudam malum: et quia boni est ut malo utatur in bonum, licet sciret eum malum, malo eius bene est usus Deus, dum tradi se pertulit ut nos redimeret.

Vel dicendum quod electio Duodecim apostolorum non refertur hic ad personas, sed ad numerum; quasi dicat: ego elegi in vobis duodenarium numerum. Hic enim numerus congrue consecratur eis qui fidem sanctae Trinitatis per quatuor mundi cardines praedicaturi erant; qui quidem numerus non periit, quia in locum pereuntis proditoris surrogatus est Mathias.

Vel, secundum Ambrosium, ideo elegit Iudam malum, ut consolaretur infirmitatem nostram, si aliquando contigerit nos ab amicis prodi, cum legimus a discipulo proditum Dominum et magistrum.

1008. Sed quaeritur hic, quare cum dicit Dominus *unus ex vobis diabolus est*, nihil dicunt discipuli; et postea cum dicit, infra XIII, 21, *unus ex vobis me tradet*, dixerunt, *numquid ego sum, Domine?*

Respondeo dicendum, quod huius ratio est, quia hic Dominus generaliter locutus est, dicens, unum ex eis esse diabolum, quod potest referri ad quamcumque malitiam, et ideo non sunt commoti: ibi vero tantum facinus audientes, proditionem scilicet magistri, se continere non valent.

Vel dicendum ad hoc, quod cum Dominus haec verba dixit, quilibet eorum de sua virtute confidebat, et ideo non timebant de se. Sed quando Petrus audivit: *vade post me, satana*, territi sunt, et infirmiora de se senserunt: et ideo vacillantes dicebant: *numquid ego sum, Domine?*

1009. Hanc autem responsionem, quam Dominus occulte fecerat, Evangelista exponit, dicens *dicebat autem de Iuda*, ut rei probavit eventus, ut patet infra, XIII.

our Lord did choose Judas, but not as evil at that time; and being so chosen did not take away his possibility of sinning.

Second, we could answer with Augustine, who said that our Lord did chose Judas as evil. And although he knew that he was evil, because it is characteristic of a good person to use evil for good, God made good use of this evil in allowing himself to be betrayed in order to redeem us.

Or, we could say that the choice of the Twelve does not refer here to the persons, but rather to the number; as if to say: I have chosen Twelve. For this number is fittingly set apart for those who would preach the faith of the Holy Trinity to the four corners of the world. And indeed, this number did not pass away, because Matthias was substituted for the traitor.

Or, according to Ambrose, Jesus chose Judas as evil so that when we read that our Lord and Master was betrayed by his disciple, we might be consoled if sometimes our friends betray us.

1008. We could ask here why the disciples did not say anything after our Lord said, *one of you is a devil*; for later on, when he says, *one of you will betray me* (John 13:21), they reply, *is it I, Lord?* (Matt 26:22).

I answer that the reason for this is that our Lord was speaking here in a general way when he said that one of them was a devil; for this could mean any kind of malice, and so they were not disturbed. But later on, when they heard of such a great crime, that their Master would be betrayed, they could not keep quiet.

Or, we could say that when our Lord said this, each of them had confidence in his own virtue, and so none feared for himself; but after he said to Peter, *follow after me, satan* (Matt 16:23), they were afraid, and realized their own weakness. That is why they asked in that indecisive way, *is it I, Lord?* (Matt 26:22).

1009. Finally, what our Lord had just said privately is explained by the Evangelist when he says, *now he meant Judas Iscariot*, as events proved and which will be clear below (John 13).

CHAPTER 7

Lecture 1

7:1 Post haec autem ambulabat Iesus in Galilaeam: non enim volebat in Iudaeam ambulare, quia quaerebant eum Iudaei interficere. [n. 1011]

7:2 Erat autem in proximo die festus Iudaeorum Scenopegia. [n. 1013]

7:3 Dixerunt autem ad eum fratres eius: transi hinc, et vade in Iudaeam, ut et discipuli tui videant opera tua quae facis: [n. 1014]

7:4 Nemo quippe in occulto quid facit, et quaerit ipse in palam esse: si haec facis, manifesta teipsum mundo. [n. 1016]

7:5 Neque enim fratres eius credebant in eum. [n. 1017]

7:6 Dixit ergo eis Iesus: tempus meum nondum advenit; tempus autem vestrum semper est paratum. [n. 1018]

7:7 Non potest mundum odisse vos; me autem odit: quia ego testimonium perhibeo de illo, quia opera eius mala sunt. [n. 1020]

7:8 Vos ascendite ad diem festum hunc; ego autem non ascendam ad diem festum istum, quia meum tempus nondum impletum est. [n. 1022]

7:1 Καὶ μετὰ ταῦτα περιεπάτει ὁ Ἰησοῦς ἐν τῇ Γαλιλαίᾳ· οὐ γὰρ ἤθελεν ἐν τῇ Ἰουδαίᾳ περιπατεῖν, ὅτι ἐζήτουν αὐτὸν οἱ Ἰουδαῖοι ἀποκτεῖναι.

7:2 Ἦν δὲ ἐγγὺς ἡ ἑορτὴ τῶν Ἰουδαίων ἡ σκηνοπηγία.

7:3 εἶπον οὖν πρὸς αὐτὸν οἱ ἀδελφοὶ αὐτοῦ· μετάβηθι ἐντεῦθεν καὶ ὕπαγε εἰς τὴν Ἰουδαίαν, ἵνα καὶ οἱ μαθηταί σου θεωρήσουσιν σοῦ τὰ ἔργα ἃ ποιεῖς·

7:4 οὐδεὶς γάρ τι ἐν κρυπτῷ ποιεῖ καὶ ζητεῖ αὐτὸς ἐν παρρησίᾳ εἶναι. εἰ ταῦτα ποιεῖς, φανέρωσον σεαυτὸν τῷ κόσμῳ.

7:5 οὐδὲ γὰρ οἱ ἀδελφοὶ αὐτοῦ ἐπίστευον εἰς αὐτόν.

7:6 λέγει οὖν αὐτοῖς ὁ Ἰησοῦς· ὁ καιρὸς ὁ ἐμὸς οὔπω πάρεστιν, ὁ δὲ καιρὸς ὁ ὑμέτερος πάντοτέ ἐστιν ἕτοιμος.

7:7 οὐ δύναται ὁ κόσμος μισεῖν ὑμᾶς, ἐμὲ δὲ μισεῖ, ὅτι ἐγὼ μαρτυρῶ περὶ αὐτοῦ ὅτι τὰ ἔργα αὐτοῦ πονηρά ἐστιν.

7:8 ὑμεῖς ἀνάβητε εἰς τὴν ἑορτήν· ἐγὼ οὐκ ἀναβαίνω εἰς τὴν ἑορτὴν ταύτην, ὅτι ὁ ἐμὸς καιρὸς οὔπω πεπλήρωται.

7:1 After these things, Jesus walked in Galilee, for he did not want to walk in Judea, because the Jews sought to kill him. [n. 1011]

7:2 Now the Jewish feast of Tabernacles was at hand. [n. 1013]

7:3 And his brethren said to him: pass from here and go into Judea so that your disciples also may see the works that you do. [n. 1014]

7:4 For there is no man who does anything in secret, and he himself seeks to be known openly. If you do these things, manifest yourself to the world. [n. 1016]

7:5 For neither did his brethren believe in him. [n. 1017]

7:6 Then Jesus said to them: my time is not yet come, but your time is always here. [n. 1018]

7:7 The world cannot hate you, but it hates me, because I give testimony against it, that its works are evil. [n. 1020]

7:8 Go up to this festival day, but I will not go up to this festival day, because my time is not yet completed. [n. 1022]

1010. Postquam Dominus egit de vita spirituali et nutrimento, hic consequenter agit de instructione seu doctrina, quae est necessaria spiritualiter regeneratis, ut dictum est supra, et

primo ostendit originem suae doctrinae;

secundo manifestat eius utilitatem ab octavo capitulo, et deinceps.

Circa primum tria facit.

Primo ponitur locus ubi originem suae doctrinae manifestavit;

secundo ponuntur occasiones eam manifestandi, ibi *Iudaei ergo quaerebant eum* etc.;

1010. After our Lord considered the spiritual life and its food, he now treats of his instruction or teaching, which, as mentioned above, is necessary for those who are spiritually reborn.

First, he shows the origin of his teaching;

second, its usefulness (John 8).

As to the first, he does three things.

First, he mentions the place where he revealed the origin of his teaching;

second, the occasion for revealing this, at *the Jews sought to kill him*; and

tertio ponitur ipsa manifestatio, ibi *respondit eis Iesus, et dixit: mea doctrina non est mea* etc.

Circa primum tria facit.

Primo ponitur incitatio Christi ad eundum ad locum, ubi publicavit originem suae doctrinae;

secundo ponitur recusatio Domini, ibi *dicit ergo eis Iesus* etc.;

tertio subditur quomodo Christus ad locum illum pervenit, ibi *haec cum dixisset, ipse mansit in Galilaea*.

Circa primum duo facit.

Primo ponit occasiones quare Christum incitabant ad eundum;

secundo subdit ipsam incitationem, ibi *dixerunt autem ad eum fratres eius*.

Ex tribus autem movebantur ut incitarent Christum ad eundum in Iudaeam:

primo quidem ex mora eius;

secundo ex proposito;

tertio ex congruitate temporis.

1011. Ex mora quidem eius in Galilaea, in qua ostendebat Christus se velle morari: et ideo dicit *post haec*, verba scilicet quae dicta sunt in Capharnaum, *ambulabat Iesus in Galilaeam*; scilicet, acceperat iter de Capharnaum, quae erat metropolis Galilaeae, ut discurreret per Galilaeam.

Ideo autem Dominus in Galilaea frequentius moratur, ut ostendat nobis transmigrandum esse de vitiis ad virtutes; Ez. XII, 3: *tu ergo, fili hominis, fac tibi vasa transmigrationis, et transmigrabis per diem coram eis.*

1012. Ex proposito autem Christi, qui forte eis per verba innotuit; et ideo dicit *non enim volebat in Iudaeam ambulare*. Cuius ratio est *quia quaerebant eum Iudaei interficere*; supra V, 18: *quaerebant eum Iudaei interficere: quia non solum solvebat Sabbatum, sed et Patrem suum dicebat Deum, aequalem se faciens Deo.*

Sed numquid non poterat illuc ire, et ambulare inter Iudaeos, et ab eis non occidi, sicut fecit infra VIII, 59?

Respondeo dicendum, quod ad hoc triplex ratio assignatur. Prima ab Augustino: quia futurum erat ut aliquis fidelis Christi absconderet se ne a persecutoribus inveniretur. Ne ergo illi fuga obiiceretur pro crimine, voluit Dominus ad consolationem nostram hoc in se praecessisse ostendere: quod etiam et verbo docuit. Matth. X, 23: *si vos persecuti fuerint in una civitate, fugite in aliam.*

Alia quidem ratio est, quia scilicet Christus Deus erat et homo, et ideo virtute divinitatis poterat non laedi a persecutoribus. Sed hoc noluit continue facere, quia sic fuisset declarata eius divinitas, quod tamen humanitas eius venisset in dubium. Et ideo fugiens quandoque persecutores ut homo, asserit suam humanitatem,

third, his actual statement is given, at *Jesus answered them and said: my doctrine is not mine* (John 7:16).

Three things are done about the first.

First, we see Christ invited to go to the place where he revealed the origin of his teaching;

second, we see our Lord refuse, at *then Jesus said to them: my time is not yet come*; and

third, how Jesus finally did go, at *when he had said these things, he himself stayed in Galilee* (John 7:9).

As to the first, he does two things.

First, he gives the reasons why they encouraged Christ to go to Judea;

second, he adds their exhortation, at *and his brethren said to him*.

They were influenced by three things to encourage Christ to go to Judea:

first, by his delay,

second, by his intention and

third, by the appropriateness of the time.

1011. They were influenced by Christ's delaying in Galilee, which showed that he wanted to stay there. Thus he says, *after these things*, after teaching in Capernaum, *Jesus walked in Galilee*, i.e., he set out from Capernaum, a city of Galilee, with the intention to journey throughout this region.

Our Lord lingered on so often in Galilee to show us that we should pass from vices to virtues: *so you, son of man, prepare your belongings for exile, and go during the day in their sight* (Ezek 12:13).

1012. Then they were influenced by Christ's intention, which he perhaps told them; hence he says, *for he did not want to walk in Judea*, the reason being, *because the Jews sought to kill him*. As above: *therefore the Jews sought the more to kill him, because he did not only break the Sabbath, but also said that God was his Father, making himself equal to God* (John 5:18).

But could not Christ still have gone among the Jews without being killed by them, as he did later, *but Jesus hid himself, and went out of the temple* (John 8:59)?

Three answers are given to this question. The first is given by Augustine, who says that Christ did this because the time would come when some Christians would hide from those who were persecuting them. And so they would not be criticized for this, our Lord wanted to console us by setting a precedent himself in this matter. He also taught this in word, saying: *if they persecute you in one town, flee to another* (Matt 10:23).

Another answer is that Christ was both God and man. By reason of his divinity, he could prevent his being injured by those persecuting him. Yet, he did not want to do this all the time, for while this would have shown his divinity, it might have cast doubt on his humanity. Therefore, he showed his humanity by sometimes fleeing, as man, those

ut confundat omnes eum non verum hominem fuisse dicentes. Quandoque autem transiens illaesus per eos, ostendit suam divinitatem, confundens omnes eum hominem purum esse dicentes. Et ideo Chrysostomus habet aliam litteram, *scilicet non enim habebat potestatem, si vellet, in Iudaeam ambulare*: quod dicitur secundum modum humanum; sicut si dicatur: aliquis non potest aliquo ire, si vellet, propter insidias.

Tertia ratio est, quia nondum passionis aderat tempus: futurum enim erat ut Pateretur in Pascha, quando immolabatur agnus, ut sic victima succederet victimae; infra XIII, v. 1: *sciens Iesus quia venit hora eius ut transeat ex hoc mundo ad Patrem.*

1013. Ex congruitate vero temporis, quia erat tempus congruum ad eundum in Ierusalem: et hoc est quod dicit **erat autem in proximo die festus Iudaeorum Scenopegia.** *Scenopegia* autem Graecum est, compositum ex scenos, quod est umbra, et phagim, quod est comedere; quasi dicat: erat tempus in quo comedebant in tabernaculis. Dominus enim mandavit filiis Israel, Lev. XXIII, 41, quod mense septimo per septem dies habitarent in tabernaculis, in memoriam quod quadraginta annis habitaverunt in tabernaculis in deserto. Et hoc festum tunc celebrabant Iudaei.

Commemorat autem hoc Evangelista, ut ostendat quod multum tempus praetermisit ab eo tempore quo praemissa de cibo spirituali dicta fuerunt usque ad istud tempus. Nam quando fecit miraculum de panibus, erat prope dies Paschae; hoc autem festum Scenopegiae est multo post Pascha; et sic nihil eorum quae in quinque mensibus intermediis per Dominum facta sunt, recitat hic Evangelista: ut detur intelligi quod licet indeficienter signa faceret, ut patet infra ultimo, illa praecipue studuerunt Evangelistae dicere pro quibus aut querela aut contradictio a Iudaeis subsequebatur.

1014. Consequenter cum dicit **dixerunt autem ad eum fratres eius,** ponitur incitatio fratrum Domini, et

primo ponitur eorum admonitio;

secundo assignatur admonitionis ratio, ibi **ut discipuli tui videant opera tua**;

tertio ab Evangelista assignatur causa talis rationis, ibi **neque enim fratres eius credebant in eum.**

1015. Circa primum primo ponuntur incitantes; unde dicit **dixerunt autem ad eum fratres eius,** non carnales et uterini, ut Elvidius blasphemavit, quod abhorret fides Catholica, quod sanctissimus ille virgineus uterus qui Deum protulit et hominem, protulisset postmodum alium hominem mortalem. Fratres ergo eius erant cognatione, quia erant consanguinei Beatae Mariae virginis; haec enim est consuetudo Scripturae, consanguineos appellare fratres, secundum illud Gen. c. XIII, 8: *non sit, quaeso, iurgium inter me et te . . . fratres enim sumus*; cum

who were persecuting him, to silence all those who would say that he was not a true man. And he showed his divinity by sometimes walking among them unharmed, thus refuting all those who say he was only a man. Thus, Chrysostom has another text, which reads: *he could not, even if he wanted to, walk about Judea.* This is expressed in our human way, and is the same as saying: due to the danger of treachery, a person cannot go anywhere he might wish.

The third answer is that it was not yet the time for Christ's passion. The time would come when Christ would suffer, at the feast of the Passover, when the lamb was sacrificed, so that victim would succeed victim: **Jesus knowing that his hour was come, that he should pass out of this world to the Father** (John 13:1).

1013. They were also influenced by the suitableness of the time, for it was a time for going to Jerusalem. **Now the Jewish feast of Tabernacles was at hand. Tabernacles** is a Greek word, composed of 'scenos,' which means shade, or tent, and 'phagim,' which means to eat. As if to say: it was the time in which they used to eat in their tents. For our Lord (Lev 23:41) had ordered the children of Israel to stay in their tents for seven days during the seventh month, as a reminder of the forty years they had lived in tents in the desert. This was the feast the Jews were then celebrating.

The Evangelist mentions this in order to show that some time had already passed since the previous teaching about spiritual food. For it was near the Passover when our Lord performed the miracle of the loaves, and this feast of Tabernacles is much later. The Evangelist does not tell us what our Lord did in the intervening five months. We can see from this that although Jesus was always performing miracles, as the last chapter says, the Evangelist was mainly concerned with recording those matters over which the Jews argued and with which they disagreed.

1014. Then, at **and his brethren said to him,** our Lord is urged on by his brethren.

First, we are given their advice;

second, the reason for it, at **so that your disciples also may see your works**; and

third, the Evangelist mentions the cause of this reason, at **for neither did his brethren believe in him.**

1015. As to the first, the ones who urge Christ are mentioned; hence he says, **and his brethren said to him.** These were not brothers of the flesh or of the womb, as the blasphemous opinion of Elvidius would have it. It is, indeed, offensive to the Catholic faith that the most holy virginal womb, which bore him who was God and man, should later bear another mortal man. Thus, they were his brothers or brethren in the sense of relatives, because they were related by blood to the Blessed Virgin Mary. For it is the custom in Scripture to call relatives *brothers: let us not quarrel, for*

tamen Lot nepos esset Abrahae. Et, ut Augustinus dicit, sicut in sepulcro ubi positum fuerat corpus Domini, nec ante nec postea iacuit corpus, sic uterus Mariae nec ante nec postea quidquam mortale concepit. Sed quia aliqui de consanguineis beatae virginis erant apostoli, sicut filii Zebedaei, et Iacobi Alphaei, et alii, ideo non est intelligendum quod fuerunt de illis qui incitaverunt Christum, sed illi fuerunt alii propinqui eius, qui Christum non diligebant.

Secundo ponitur monitio eorum, cum dicunt *transi hinc*, scilicet de Galilaea, *et vade in Iudaeam*, ubi est Ierusalem locus solemnis, doctoribus conveniens; Amos VII, 12: *qui vides, gradere in terram Iuda, et ibi comedes panem tuum, et prophetabis ibi*.

1016. Rationem autem subdunt, dicentes *ut et discipuli tui videant opera tua*, ubi ostendunt se primo inanis gloriae cupidos; secundo suspiciosos, et tertio incredulos.

Cupidos quidem inanis gloriae ostendunt se, cum dicunt *ut et discipuli tui videant opera tua*. Patiebantur enim aliquid humani ad Christum, et volebant captare gloriam de honore humano, qui Christo exhiberetur a turbis; et ideo inducebant eum ut faceret opera sua in publico. Est enim proprium inanis gloriae cupidi ut quidquid gloriosum sui vel suorum fuerit, ostendatur in publico; Matth. VI, 5: *amant in synagogis et in angulis platearum stantes orare ut videantur ab hominibus*; de quibus dicitur infra XII, 43: *dilexerunt magis gloriam hominum quam Dei*.

Suspiciosos autem ostendunt se et primo de formidine Christum notant; unde dicunt ei *nemo quippe in occulto aliquid facit*, quasi dicant: tu dicis te facere miracula, sed facis in occulto et hoc ex timore, alioquin ires in Ierusalem et faceres ea ibi coram multitudine. Sed tamen Dominus dicit infra XVIII, v. 20: *in occulto locutus sum nihil*.

Secundo notant eum de amore gloriae; unde dicunt *et quaerit ipse in palam esse*, quasi dicant: tu quaeris gloriam de his quae facis, et tamen propter timorem abscondis te. Hoc est proprium malorum, ut credant alios similes eis animi passiones habere. Vide quam irreverenter prudentia carnis Verbum carnem factum arguebat: contra quos dicit Iob IV, 3: *arguis eum qui non est similis tibi, et loqueris quod tibi non expedit*.

Incredulos ostendunt se esse, cum dicunt *si haec facis, manifesta teipsum mundo*; quasi sub dubio ponunt an ipse miracula faciat; Is. XXI, 2: *qui incredulus est, infideliter agit*.

1017. Causam autem quare sic loquebantur, subdit Evangelista cum dicit *neque enim fratres eius credebant in eum*. Contingit enim quod carnales consanguinei maxime adversantur suis, et invident de bonis spiritualibus,

we are brothers (Gen 13:8), although Lot was the nephew of Abraham. And, as Augustine says, just as in the tomb in which our Lord's body had been placed no other body was placed either before or after, so the womb of Mary conceived no other mortal person either before or after Christ. Although some of the relatives of the Blessed Virgin were apostles, such as the sons of Zebedee, and James of Alpheus, and some others, we should not think that these were among those who were urging Christ; this was done by other relatives who did not love him.

Second, we see their advice when they say: *pass from here*, that is, Galilee, *and go into Judea*, where you will find Jerusalem, a sacred place, well-suited to teachers. *Seer, go, flee to the land of Ridah. There eat your bread and there prophesy* (Amos 7:12).

1016. They give their reason when they say: *so that your disciples also may see your works*. Here they show, first, that they are hungry for an empty glory; second, that they are suspicious; and third, do not believe.

They show that they are hungry for an empty glory when they say, *so that your disciples also may see your works*. For they allowed something human to Christ and wanted to share the glory of the human honor that the people would show him. And so, they urged him to perform his works in public: for it is a characteristic of one who is seeking human glory to want publicly known whatever of his own or of his associates can bring glory. *They like to pray at street comers, so people can see them* (Matt 6:5). We read of such people: *for they loved the glory of men, more than the glory of God* (John 12:43).

They reveal that they themselves are suspicious, and first of all remark on Christ's fear, saying: *for there is no man who does anything in secret*. As if to say: you say that you are performing miracles. But you are doing them secretly because of fear; otherwise you would go to Jerusalem and do them before the people. Nevertheless, our Lord says below: *I have spoken nothing in secret* (John 18:20).

Second, they refer to his love of glory, saying: *and he himself seeks to be known openly*. As if to say: you want glory because of what you are doing, yet you are hiding because you are afraid. Now this attitude is characteristic of those who are evil: to think that other people are experiencing the same emotions as they are. Notice the disrespect with which the prudence of the flesh reproached the Word made flesh. Job says against them: *you reproach him who is not like you, and say what you should not* (Job 4:3).

They show they do not believe when they say: *if you do these things, manifest yourself to the world*, doubting whether he did perform miracles. *He who does not believe is unfaithful* (Isa 21:2).

1017. The Evangelist tells why they said this when he says, *for neither did his brethren believe in him*. For sometimes blood relatives are very hostile to one of their own, and are jealous of his spiritual goods. They may even

et contemnunt eum. Unde dicit Augustinus: *Christum consanguineum habere potuerunt, credere autem in eum in ipsa propinquitate fastidierunt.* Mich. VII, 6: *inimici hominis domestici eius*; Iob XIX, 13: *fratres meos longe facit a me, et noti mei quasi alieni recesserunt a me: dereliquerunt me proximi mei, et qui me noverant, obliti sunt mei.*

1018. Consequenter cum dicit **dixit ergo eis Iesus: tempus meum nondum advenit** etc., ponitur Christi responsio, et

primo designat temporis ad ascendendum indispositionem;

secundo assignat dictorum rationem, ibi **non potest mundus odisse vos**;

tertio ponit ascendendi recusationem, ibi **vos ascendite ad diem festum hunc** etc.

1019. Sciendum est autem quod tota sequens littera aliter exponitur secundum Augustinum, et aliter secundum Chrysostomum.

Nam, secundum Augustinum, fratres Domini invitabant eum ad humanam gloriam. Est autem tempus quo sancti perveniunt ad gloriam, scilicet tempus futurum, ad quam perveniunt per passiones et tribulationes. Sap. c. III, 6: *tamquam aurum in fornace probavit illos, et quasi holocausti hostiam accepit illos, et in tempore erit respectus illorum.* Aliud vero est tempus quo mundani gloriam suam acquirunt, scilicet tempus praesens. Sap. c. II, 7: *non praetereat nos flos temporis: coronemus nos rosis antequam marcescant, nullum pratum sit quod non pertranseat luxuria nostra* etc. Voluit ergo Dominus ostendere quod non quaerebat gloriam huius temporis; sed ad celsitudinem gloriae caelestis per passionem et humilitatem suam volebat pervenire. Lc. ult., 26: *oportuit Christum pati, et ita intrare in gloriam suam.* Et ideo dicit eis, scilicet fratribus, **tempus meum**, idest tempus gloriae meae, **nondum venit**: quia oportet quod tristitia convertatur in gaudium. Rom. VIII, 18: *non sunt condignae passiones huius temporis ad futuram gloriam quae revelabitur in nobis.* Sed **tempus vestrum**, idest mundi gloria, **semper est paratum.**

1020. Rationem huius diversitatis temporis assignat cum dicit **non potest mundus odisse vos; me autem odit.** Ideo enim mundani habent tempus gloriae paratum, quia eadem amant quae mundus amat, et mundo consentiunt. Sancti vero qui quaerunt gloriam spiritualem, non habent hoc tempus paratum, quia quaerunt quae mundo displicent, scilicet paupertatem, luctum, esuriem et huiusmodi. Vituperant etiam quae mundus amat: immo ipsum mundum contemnunt; Gal. ult., v. 14: *mihi mundus crucifixus est, et ego mundo.* Et ideo dicit **non potest mundus odisse vos**; quasi diceret: ideo paratum est tempus gloriae vestrae, quia mundus non odit vos, qui convenitis cum eo, et omne animal diligit sibi simile.

despise him. Thus Augustine says: *they could have Christ as a relative, but in that very closeness they refused to believe in him.* A man's enemies are in his own house (Mic 7:6); *he has put my brethren far from me, and my acquaintances, like strangers, have gone from me. My relatives have left me, and those who knew me have forgotten me* (Job 19:13).

1018. Then, at **then Jesus said to them: my time is not yet come, but your time is always here**, Christ's answer is given.

First, he mentions that the time was not appropriate for going to Jerusalem;

second, the reason for this, at **the world cannot hate you**; and

third, we see Christ deciding not to go, at **go up to this festival day, but I will not go up to this festival day**.

1019. We should note that all of the following text is explained differently by Augustine and by Chrysostom.

Augustine says that the brethren of our Lord were urging him to a human glory. Now there is a time, in the future, when the saints do acquire glory, a glory they obtain by their Sufferings and troubles. *He has tested them like gold in a furnace, and he accepted them as the victim of a holocaust. At the time of their visitation they will shine* (Wis 3:6). And there is a time, the present, when the worldly acquire their glory. *Let not the flowers of the time pass us by; let us crown ourselves with roses before they wither* (Wis 2:7). Our Lord, therefore, wanted to show hat he was not looking for the glory of this present time, but that he wanted to attain to the height of heavenly glory through his passion and humiliation. *It was necessary for Christ to suffer, and so enter into his glory* (Luke 24:26). So Jesus says to them, i.e., his brethren: **my time**, i.e., the time of my glory, **has not yet come**, because my sorrow must be turned into joy: *the sufferings of this present time are not worthy to be compared with the glory to come, which will be revealed in us* (Rom 8:18); but **your time**, i.e., the time of the glory of this world, **is always here**.

1020. He gives the reason why these times are different when he says, **the world cannot hate you, but it hates me.** The reason why the time for the glory of the worldly is here is that they love the same things the world loves, and they agree with the world. But the time for the glory of the saints, who are looking for a spiritual glory, is not here, because they want what is displeasing to the world, that is, poverty, afflictions, doing without food, and things like that. They even disparage what the world loves; in fact, they despise the world: *the world has been crucified to me, and I to the world* (Gal 6:14). And so he says, **the world cannot hate you**. As if to say: thus, the time of your glory is here, because the world does not hate you, who are in agreement

Sed me odit; et ideo tempus meum non semper est paratum. Et ratio odii est, *quia ego testimonium perhibeo de illo*, scilicet mundo, quia *opera eius mala sunt*; idest, non praetermitto mundanos homines redarguere, licet sciam ex hoc odium incurrere et mortem intentari. Amos c. V, X: *odio habuerunt corripientem in porta*, illi scilicet qui amant malitiam. Et Prov. IX, 8: *noli arguere derisorem*.

1021. Sed numquid non mundani aliqui odio habentur a mundo, idest ab alio mundano?

Responsio. Dicendum, quod in particulari mundanus quidem unus habetur odio ab alio, inquantum habet ea quae ipse vellet habere, vel impedit eum in his quae sunt de gloria mundi; sed inquantum mundanus, nullus oditur a mundo. Sancti vero universaliter odiuntur a mundo, quia contrariantur ei: et si aliquis de mundo eos diligat, hoc non est inquantum est de mundo, sed inquantum est in eo aliquid spirituale.

1022. Recusat autem Dominus ascendere, cum dicit *vos ascendite ad diem festum hunc; ego autem non ascendam*. Sicut enim sunt duae gloriae, ita duo diversa festa. Mundani enim habent festa temporalia, scilicet gaudere et epulari, et huiusmodi exteriores delicias. Is. XXII, 12: *vocavit Dominus ad lamentum et ad planctum, ad calvitium et ad cingulum sacci: et ecce gaudium et laetitia occidere vitulos, et iugulare arietes, comedere carnes, et bibere vinum*; ibid. I, 14: *solemnitates vestras odivit anima mea*. Sancti vero habent festa spiritualia, quae in delectationibus spiritus consistunt. Is. XXXIII, 20: *respice Sion civitatem solemnitatis vestrae*. Et ideo dicit *vos*, qui gloriam mundi quaeritis, *ascendite ad diem festum hunc*, idest ad festa laetitiae temporalis; *ego autem non ascendam ad diem festum istum*, sed ad diem festum solemnitatis aeternae; et hoc, *quia meum tempus*, scilicet gloriae verae, quod erit permanens in aeternum gaudium sine fine, aeternitas sine labore, claritas sine nube, *nondum impletum est*.

1023. Secundum Chrysostomum, servata eadem divisione, exponitur sic: scilicet quod fratres Domini conspiraverant in mortem Christi cum Iudaeis, unde inducebant eum ad eundum, volentes eum prodere et tradere Iudaeis. Et ideo dicit *tempus meum*, scilicet crucis et mortis, *nondum advenit*, ut vadam in Iudaeam, et occidar; *tempus autem vestrum semper est paratum*, quia sine periculo conversari poteritis cum eis. Et huius ratio est, quia non possunt odire vos, zelantes eadem et amantes cum eis: *me autem odit: quia ego testimonium perhibeo de illo, quia opera eius mala sunt*. Per quod patet quod Iudaei non propter solutionem sabbati, sed propter publicam redargutionem me odiunt. *Vos ergo ascendite ad diem festum hunc* scilicet ad principium festi (nam septem diebus celebrabatur, ut dictum est),

with it; and every animal loves its like. *But it hates me*, and so my time is not always here. And the reason it hates me is *because I give testimony against it*, that is, the world, *that its works are evil*; that is, I do not hesitate to reprimand those who are worldly, even though I know that they will hate me for it and threaten me with death. *They*, that is, those who love evil, *hate the one who rebukes at the city gate* (Amos 5:10); *do not rebuke one who mocks, lest he hate you* (Prov 9:8).

1021. But cannot a person of the world be hated by the world, i.e., by another person of the world?

I answer that, in a particular case, one worldly person can hate another insofar as the latter has what the first wants, or prevents him from obtaining what relates to the glory of this world. But precisely insofar as a person is of the world, the world does not hate him. The saints, however, are universally hated by the world because they are opposed to it. And if anyone of the world does love them, it is not because he is of the world, but because of something spiritual in him.

1022. Our Lord refuses to go when he says, *go up to this festival day, but I will not go up to this festival day*. For just as there are two kinds of glory, so there are two different feasts. Worldly people have temporal feasts, that is, their own enjoyments and banquets and such exterior pleasures. *The Lord called for weeping and mourning . . . and look at the rejoicing and gladness* (Isa 22:12); *I hate your feasts* (Isa 1:14). But the saints have their own spiritual feasts, which consist in the joys of the spirit: *look upon Zion, the city of your feasts* (Isa 33:20). So he says: *you* yourselves, who are looking for the glory of this world, *go up to this festival day*, i.e., to the feasts of temporal pleasure; *but I will not go up to this festival day*, for I will go to the feast of an eternal celebration. I am not going up now because *my time*, that is, the time of my true glory, which will be a joy that lasts forever, an eternity without fatigue, and a brightness without shadow, *is not yet completed*.

1023. Chrysostom keeps the same division of the text, but explains it this way. He says that these brethren of our Lord joined with the Jews in plotting the death of Christ. And so they urged Christ to go to the feast, intending to betray him and hand him over to the Jews. That is why he says: *my time*, that is, the time for my cross and death, *is not yet completed*, to go to Judea and be killed. *But your time is always here*, because you can associate with them without danger. And this is because they cannot hate you: you who love and envy the same things they do. *But it hates me, because I give testimony against it, that its works are evil*. This shows that the Jews hate me, not because I broke the sabbath, but because I denounced them in public. *Go up to this festival day*, that is, for its beginning (for it lasted seven days, as was said), *but I will not go up to this festival*

ego autem non ascendam ad diem festum istum, scilicet vobiscum, scilicet ad principium festi, *quia nondum tempus meum est impletum*, in quo patiar: nam in futuro Pascha crucifigendus erat. Ideo autem non ascendit cum eis, ut posset magis latere etc.

day, that is, with you, and when it first begins: *because my time is not yet completed*, when I am to suffer, for he was to be crucified at a future Passover. Accordingly, he did not go with them then in order to remain out of sight, and so forth.

Lecture 2

7:9 Haec cum dixisset, ipse mansit in Galilaea. [n. 1025]

7:10 Ut autem ascenderunt fratres eius, tunc et ipse ascendit ad diem festum, non manifeste, sed quasi in occulto. [n. 1026]

7:11 Iudaei ergo quaerebant eum in die festo, et dicebant: ubi est ille? [n. 1028]

7:12 Et murmur multus erat in turba de eo: quidam enim dicebant, quia bonus est; alii autem dicebant: non, sed seducit turbas. [n. 1030]

7:13 Nemo tamen palam loquebatur de illo propter metum Iudaeorum. [n. 1032]

7:14 Iam autem die festo mediante, ascendit Iesus in templum, et docebat. [n. 1033]

7:15 Et mirabantur Iudaei dicentes: quomodo hic litteras scit, cum non didicerit? [n. 1035]

7:16 Respondit autem Iesus, et dixit: mea doctrina non est mea, sed eius qui misit me. [n. 1037]

7:17 Si quis voluerit voluntatem eius facere, cognoscet de doctrina utrum ex Deo sit, an ego a meipso loquar. [n. 1038]

7:18 Qui a semetipso loquitur, gloriam propriam quaerit: qui autem quaerit gloriam eius qui misit eum, hic verax est, et iniustitia in illo non est. [n. 1040]

7:19 Nonne Moyses dedit vobis legem? Et nemo ex vobis facit legem. [n. 1041]

7:20 Quid me quaeritis interficere? Respondit turba, et dixit: daemonium habes: quis te quaerit interficere? [n. 1043]

7:21 Respondit Iesus, et dixit eis: unum opus feci, et omnes miramini. [n. 1044]

7:9 ταῦτα δὲ εἰπὼν αὐτὸς ἔμεινεν ἐν τῇ Γαλιλαίᾳ.

7:10 Ὡς δὲ ἀνέβησαν οἱ ἀδελφοὶ αὐτοῦ εἰς τὴν ἑορτήν, τότε καὶ αὐτὸς ἀνέβη οὐ φανερῶς ἀλλὰ [ὡς] ἐν κρυπτῷ.

7:11 οἱ οὖν Ἰουδαῖοι ἐζήτουν αὐτὸν ἐν τῇ ἑορτῇ καὶ ἔλεγον· ποῦ ἐστιν ἐκεῖνος;

7:12 καὶ γογγυσμὸς περὶ αὐτοῦ ἦν πολὺς ἐν τοῖς ὄχλοις· οἱ μὲν ἔλεγον ὅτι ἀγαθός ἐστιν, ἄλλοι [δὲ] ἔλεγον· οὔ, ἀλλὰ πλανᾷ τὸν ὄχλον.

7:13 οὐδεὶς μέντοι παρρησίᾳ ἐλάλει περὶ αὐτοῦ διὰ τὸν φόβον τῶν Ἰουδαίων.

7:14 Ἤδη δὲ τῆς ἑορτῆς μεσούσης ἀνέβη Ἰησοῦς εἰς τὸ ἱερὸν καὶ ἐδίδασκεν.

7:15 ἐθαύμαζον οὖν οἱ Ἰουδαῖοι λέγοντες· πῶς οὗτος γράμματα οἶδεν μὴ μεμαθηκώς;

7:16 ἀπεκρίθη οὖν αὐτοῖς [ὁ] Ἰησοῦς καὶ εἶπεν· ἡ ἐμὴ διδαχὴ οὐκ ἔστιν ἐμὴ ἀλλὰ τοῦ πέμψαντός με·

7:17 ἐάν τις θέλῃ τὸ θέλημα αὐτοῦ ποιεῖν, γνώσεται περὶ τῆς διδαχῆς πότερον ἐκ τοῦ θεοῦ ἐστιν ἢ ἐγὼ ἀπ᾽ ἐμαυτοῦ λαλῶ.

7:18 ὁ ἀφ᾽ ἑαυτοῦ λαλῶν τὴν δόξαν τὴν ἰδίαν ζητεῖ· ὁ δὲ ζητῶν τὴν δόξαν τοῦ πέμψαντος αὐτὸν οὗτος ἀληθής ἐστιν καὶ ἀδικία ἐν αὐτῷ οὐκ ἔστιν.

7:19 Οὐ Μωϋσῆς δέδωκεν ὑμῖν τὸν νόμον; καὶ οὐδεὶς ἐξ ὑμῶν ποιεῖ τὸν νόμον. τί με ζητεῖτε ἀποκτεῖναι;

7:20 ἀπεκρίθη ὁ ὄχλος· δαιμόνιον ἔχεις· τίς σε ζητεῖ ἀποκτεῖναι;

7:21 ἀπεκρίθη Ἰησοῦς καὶ εἶπεν αὐτοῖς· ἓν ἔργον ἐποίησα καὶ πάντες θαυμάζετε.

7:9 When he had said these things, he himself stayed in Galilee. [n. 1025]

7:10 But after his brethren had gone up, then he also went up to the feast, not openly, but, as it were, in secret. [n. 1026]

7:11 The Jews therefore looked for him on the festival day and said: where is he? [n. 1028]

7:12 And there was much murmuring among the multitude concerning him. For some said: he is a good man. And others said: no, but he seduces the people. [n. 1030]

7:13 Yet no man spoke openly about him for fear of the Jews. [n. 1032]

7:14 Now on the middle feast day, Jesus went up into the temple and taught. [n. 1033]

7:15 And the Jews wondered, saying: how does this man know letters, when he has never learned? [n. 1035]

7:16 Jesus answered them and said: my doctrine is not mine but his who sent me. [n. 1037]

7:17 If any man wants to do his will, he will know of the doctrine, whether it is from God or whether I speak from myself. [n. 1038]

7:18 He who speaks of himself seeks his own glory, but he who seeks the glory of him who sent him is true, and there is no injustice in him. [n. 1040]

7:19 Did not Moses give you the law, and yet none of you keep the law? [n. 1041]

7:20 Why do you seek to kill me? The multitude answered and said: you have a devil: who seeks to kill you? [n. 1043]

7:21 Jesus answered and said to them: I have done one work, and you all wonder: [n. 1044]

7:22 Propterea Moyses dedit vobis circumcisionem, non quia ex Moyse est, sed ex patribus. Et in Sabbato circumciditis hominem. [n. 1046]

7:23 Si circumcisionem accipit homo in Sabbato, ut non solvatur lex Moysi: mihi indignamini, quia totum hominem sanum feci in Sabbato? [n. 1049]

7:24 Nolite iudicare secundum faciem, sed iustum iudicium iudicate. [n. 1050]

7:22 διὰ τοῦτο Μωϋσῆς δέδωκεν ὑμῖν τὴν περιτομήν — οὐχ ὅτι ἐκ τοῦ Μωϋσέως ἐστὶν ἀλλ' ἐκ τῶν πατέρων — καὶ ἐν σαββάτῳ περιτέμνετε ἄνθρωπον.

7:23 εἰ περιτομὴν λαμβάνει ἄνθρωπος ἐν σαββάτῳ ἵνα μὴ λυθῇ ὁ νόμος Μωϋσέως, ἐμοὶ χολᾶτε ὅτι ὅλον ἄνθρωπον ὑγιῆ ἐποίησα ἐν σαββάτῳ;

7:24 μὴ κρίνετε κατ' ὄψιν, ἀλλὰ τὴν δικαίαν κρίσιν κρίνετε.

7:22 Therefore, Moses gave you circumcision, not because it is of Moses but of the fathers; and you circumcise a man on the Sabbath day. [n. 1046]

7:23 If a man receives circumcision on the Sabbath, that the law of Moses may not be broken, why are you angry at me because I have healed a whole man on the Sabbath? [n. 1049]

7:24 Do not judge according to the appearance, but judge according to just judgment. [n. 1050]

1024. Postquam egit Evangelista de incitatione qua cognati Domini inducebant Christum ut ascenderet in Iudaeam, et posuit

Christi responsionem, hic consequenter agit de ascensu eius, et

primo ponitur dilatio ascensus Christi;

secundo ordo eius;

tertio ascensionis modus.

1025. Dilatio quidem ponitur cum dicit *haec cum dixisset*, scilicet quae respondit, *mansit ipse in Galilaea*, non ascendens cum cognatis ad diem festum, ut verificaretur verbum suum, quod dixerat: *ego non ascendam ad diem festum istum*. Num. c. XXIII, 19: *non est Deus ut homo, ut mentiatur, neque ut filius hominis, ut mutetur.*

1026. Ordo vero eius ponitur cum dicit *ut autem ascenderunt fratres eius*, idest cognati, *tunc et ipse ascendit* etc.

Sed hoc videtur contra illud quod supra dixit: *ego autem non ascendam*; cum Apostolus dicat II Cor. I, 19: *Christus Iesus qui in vobis praedicatus est per nos . . . non fuit in illo est et non, sed est in illo fuit.*

Respondeo dicendum primo, quod festum Scenopegiae septem diebus agebatur, ut dictum est. Dominus autem dixit supra: *ego autem non ascendam ad diem festum hunc*, idest ad principium festi. Hoc autem quod hic dicitur *ad diem festum*, intelligendum est quantum ad intermedios dies, unde et sequitur: *iam autem die festo mediante*. Et sic patet quod factum Christi non contrariatur eius dicto. Secundo vero, ut Augustinus dicit, isti volebant quod Christus ascenderet in Iudaeam, ut quaesiturus gloriam temporalem, et sic dixit eis: *non ascendam ad diem festum hunc*, hoc modo sicut vos vultis. Sed ipse ascendit ad diem festum, quasi docturus turbas et instructurus de gloria sempiterna. Tertio, secundum Chrysostomum, quia supra dixit *non ascendam ad diem festum hunc*, passurus et moriturus, ut ipsi volebant; et tamen ipse ascendit ad diem festum non ut pateretur, sed ut alios erudiret.

1024. After the Evangelist mentioned how our Lord's relatives urged him to go to Judea, he also tells what

Christ replied to them, he then tells us of his journey.

First, of his delay in going into Judea;

second, of the order of the events; and

third, the way Christ went up.

1025. He mentions our Lord's delay in going when he says, *when he had said these things*, in answer to his relatives, *he himself stayed in Galilee*. He did this to keep to his word: *I will not go up to this festival day* (John 7:8). As we read: *God is not like man, a liar, nor as the son of man, that he should be changed* (Num 23:19).

1026. He gives the order of events when he says, *but after his brethren had gone up*, that is, his relatives, had gone up, *he also went up to the feast*.

This seems to conflict with what he had said before: *I will not go up* (John 7:8), for the Apostle says, *Jesus Christ, whom we preached among you . . . was not 'yes' and 'no,' but only 'yes.'* (2 Cor 1:19).

I answer, first, that the festival of Tabernacles lasted for seven days, as was mentioned. Now our Lord first stated, *but I will not go up to this festival day* (John 7:8), that is, for its beginning (John 7:8). When it says here that he himself went *up to the feast*, we should understand this to refer to the middle of the feast. This is why we read a little further on: *now on the middle feast day*. So it is clear that Christ was not breaking his word. Second, as Augustine says, his relatives wanted him to go to Jerusalem to try for a temporal glory. So he said to them: *but I will not go up to this festival day* (John 7:8), for the purpose you want me to. But he did go to the festival to teach the people and to tell them about an eternal glory. Third, as Chrysostom says, our Lord said, *but I will not go up to this festival day* (John 7:8), to suffer and die, as they wished; but he did go, not in order to suffer, but to teach others.

1027. Modus ascensus ostenditur *non in manifesto, sed quasi in occulto*.

Et huius ratio triplex est. Una, secundum Chrysostomum, ne magis suam divinitatem denudans, incarnatio eius minus certa esset, ut dictum est supra, et ut auferat verecundiam latendi iustis hominibus, quando non possunt persecutores suos publice detinere; et ideo dicit *quasi in occulto*, ut ostendat hoc esse dispensatione factum. Is. XLV, 15: *vere tu es Deus absconditus*.

Alia, secundum Augustinum, ut scilicet daretur intelligi quod Christus occultus est in figuris Veteris Testamenti. Is. VIII, 17: *expectavi Dominum, qui abscondit faciem*, idest manifestam notitiam, *suam a domo Iacob: unde et usque in hodiernum diem velamen habent positum super cor eorum*, ut dicitur II Cor. III, 15. Ideo omnia quae dicta sunt antiquo populo illi, umbrae fuerunt futurorum bonorum, ut dicitur Hebr. X, 1. Ut ergo ostendat quod etiam ipsum festum esset figura, ideo ascendit in occulto. *Scenopegia*, ut dictum est, erat festum tabernaculorum. Ille ergo hoc festum celebrat qui se in mundo isto intelligit peregrinum.

Alia ratio est, ut doceat nos bona quae facimus occultare debere, non quaerentes favorem hominum, nec pompas stipantium turbarum desiderantes, secundum illud Matth. c. VI, 1: *attendite ne iustitiam vestram faciatis coram hominibus, ut videamini ab eis*.

1028. Consequenter cum dicit *Iudaei ergo quaerebant eum in die festo* ponit occasionem manifestandi originem doctrinae spiritualis, et ponit duas occasiones

unam causatam ex dissensione turbarum,

aliam ex admiratione earum, ibi *iam autem die festo mediante, ascendit Iesus in templum* etc.

Dissensio turbarum erat circa opinionem de Christo; unde circa hoc tria facit.

Primo proponit id in quo omnes conveniebant;

secundo illud in quo differebant, ibi *et murmur multus erat in turba de eo*;

tertio quorum opinio inter eos praevalebat, ibi *nemo tamen palam loquebatur de illo propter metum Iudaeorum*.

1029. Conveniebant autem omnes in hoc quod *quaerebant eum in die festo, et dicebant: ubi est ille?* Patet quod ex multo odio et inimicitia neque eum nominare volebant. Gen. XXXVII, 4: *oderant eum, nec poterant ei quidquam pacifice loqui*.

1030. Differebant autem, quia quidam quaerebant desiderio addiscendi, secundum illud Ps. LXVIII, 33: *quaerite eum, et vivet anima vestra*; alii quaerebant eum desiderio malignandi, secundum illud Ps. XXXIX, 14: *quaerunt animam meam ut auferant eam*. Et ideo *murmur erat multus in turba*, de contentione quae erat *de eo*

1027. The way he went was *not openly, but, as it were, in secret*.

There are three reasons for this. The first, given by Chrysostom, is so that he would not call more attention to his divinity, and so perhaps make his incarnation less certain, as was said above; and so that those who are virtuous would not be ashamed to hid from those who are persecuting them when they cannot openly restrain them. Thus he says, *in secret*, to show that this was done according to plan: *truly, you are a hidden God* (Isa 45:15).

Augustine gives us another reason: to teach us that Christ was hidden in the figures of the Old Testament: *I will wait for the Lord, who has hidden his fact* (i.e., clear knowledge) *from the house of Jacob* (Isa 8:17); so, *even to this day . . . a veil is over their hearts* (2 Cor 3:15). Thus everything that was said to this ancient people was a shadow of the good things to come (Heb 10:1). So our Lord went up in secret to show that even this feast was a figure. *Scenopegia*, as we saw, was the feast of Tabernacles; and the one who celebrates this feast is the one who understands that he is a pilgrim in this world.

Another reason why our Lord went up in secret was to teach us that we should conceal the good things we do, not looking for human approval or desiring the applause of the crowd: *take care not to perform your good actions in the sight of men, in order to be seen by them* (Matt 6:1).

1028. Then, at *the Jews therefore looked for him on the festival day*, he mentions the opportunity Christ had to show the origin of his spiritual teaching. He mentions two such opportunities:

one was due to the disagreement among the people;

the other to their amazement, at *now on the middle feast day, Jesus went up into the temple and taught*.

The people disagreed in what they thought of Christ. He does three things concerning this.

First, he shows what they had in common;

second, how they differed, at *and there was much murmuring*; and

third, whose opinion prevailed, *yet no man spoke openly about him for fear of the Jews*.

1029. What they had in common was that they *looked for him on the festival day and said: where is he?* It is obvious that they did not even want to mention his name because of their hatred and hostility: *they hated him and could not speak civilly to him* (Gen 37:4).

1030. They differed, however, because some looked for him because they wished to learn: *seek him, and your soul will live* (Ps 68:33); others were looking for him in order to harm him: *they seek my soul to carry it away* (Ps 39:15). And so *there was much murmuring among the multitude concerning him*, because of their disagreements. And although

in turba. Et licet *murmur* sit generis neutri, tamen Hieronymus ponit in masculino, quia hoc habebat antiqua grammatica, vel ut ostendat divinam Scripturam non subiacere regulis Prisciani. Et erat dissensio, quia *quidam*, de turba, illi scilicet qui habebant rectum cor, *dicebant*, de Christo, *quia bonus est*. Ps. LXXII, 1: *quam bonus Israel Deus his qui recto sunt corde*. Thren. c. III, 25: *bonus est Dominus sperantibus in eum, animae quaerenti illum*. *Alii*, scilicet qui erant male dispositi, *dicebant, non*, scilicet non est bonus. Datur autem per hoc intelligi, quod multitudo opinabatur eum bonum; sed principes sacerdotum opinabantur eum malum, et ideo dicunt *sed seducit turbas*. Lc. XXIII, 2: *hunc invenimus subvertentem gentem nostram*; Matth. XXVII, 63: *recordati sumus quod seductor ille dixit* etc.

1031. Sciendum est autem, quod seducere est seorsum ducere: potest autem homo duci seorsum vel a veritate, vel a falsitate; et utroque modo potest dici aliquis seductor. Vel inquantum seorsum ducit a veritate; et hoc modo non competit Christo, quia ipse est veritas etc., infra XIV, 6. Vel a falsitate; et hoc modo Christus seductor dicitur; Ier. XX, 7: *seduxisti me, Domine, et seductus sum: fortior me fuisti, et invaluisti*. Et utinam sic omnes seductores vocemur et simus, ut dicit Augustinus. Magis autem seductor dicitur qui a veritate seducit et decipit: quia ille dicitur seorsum duci, qui trahitur a via communi. Veritas autem communis via est; haeresis vero et via malorum, diverticula quaedam sunt.

1032. Praevalet autem opinio malorum, scilicet principum sacerdotum, unde sequitur *nemo tamen palam loquebatur*. Et hoc, quia turbae comprimebantur propter metum principum sacerdotum; quia, ut dicitur infra IX, v. 22, *si quis confiteretur ipsum esse Christum, extra synagogam fiebat*.

Ex quo patet eorum qui principabantur malitia, qua Christo insidiabantur, et eorum qui subiiciebantur, scilicet plebis, quia non habebant libertatem dicendi quod sentiunt.

1033. Consequenter cum dicit *iam autem die festo mediante, ascendit Iesus in templum*, ponitur secunda occasio manifestandi doctrinam, quae sumitur ex admiratione turbarum: et primo ponitur admirationis materia; secundo ipsa admiratio; et tertio admirationis ratio.

1034. Materia quidem admirationis est doctrina Christi; unde et circa hanc ponitur et tempus et locus.

Tempus, cum dicit *iam autem die festo mediante*; idest cum illius festi tot dies remansissent quot effluxerant, unde cum septem diebus ageretur festum, dicitur hoc fuisse quarto die. Et quidem in hoc quod se

murmuring is neuter in gender, Jerome makes it masculine because he was following the custom of the older grammarians, or else to show that divine Scripture is not subject to the rules of Priscian. There was disagreement: *for some* of the people, that is, those who were right in heart, *said*, of Christ, that *he is a good man. How good God is to Israel, to those whose heart is right* (Ps 72:1); *the Lord is good to those who hope in him, to the one who seeks him* (Lam 3:25). While *others*, that is, those who were badly disposed, *said: no*, i.e., he is not a good man. We can see from this that it was the people who thought that he was a good person, while he was considered evil by the chief priests; so they say, *he seduces the people*: *we found this man leading our people astray* (Luke 23:2); *we have remembered that that seducer said . . .* (Matt 27:63).

1031. Here we should note that to seduce is to lead away. Now a person can be led away either from what is true or from what is false. And in either way a person can be called a seducer: either because he leads one away from the truth, and in this sense it does not apply to Christ, because he is the truth (John 14:6); or because he leads one away from what is false, and in this sense Christ is called a seducer: *you seduced me, O Lord, and I was seduced. You were stronger than I, and you have won* (Jer 20:7). Would that all of us were called and were seducers in this sense, as Augustine says. But we call a person a seducer primarily because he leads others away from the truth and deceives them: because a person is said to be led away if he is drawn from the common way. But the common way is the way of truth; heresies, on the other hand, and the way of the wicked, are detours.

1032. It was the opinion of the evil, that is, of the chief priests, that finally won out. Thus he continues, *yet no man spoke openly about him for fear of the Jews*. This was because the people were held back by their fear of the chief priests: *if any man should confess him to be Christ, he should be put out of the synagoge* (John 9:22).

This reveals the wickedness with which the leaders plotted against Christ; and it shows that those who were subject to them, i.e., the people, were not free to say what they thought.

1033. Next, at *now on the middle feast day, Jesus went up into the temple*, we see the second opportunity Christ had to present his teaching, that is, the amazement of the people. First, we see the object of their amazement; second, their amazement itself, and third, the reason why they were amazed.

1034. The object of their amazement is the doctrine or teaching of Christ. Both the time and the place of this teaching are given.

The time is mentioned when he says, *now on the middle feast day*, that is, when as many days were left of the feast as had passed. Thus, since the feast lasted some seven days, this took place on the fourth day. As we said, when Christ

occultavit, humanitatis Christi est indicium, et nostrae virtutis documentum, ut dictum est; hoc autem quod se propalavit, nec eum tenere potuerunt, divinitatis est ostensivum. Ideo autem in medio festivitatis tempore ascendit, quia in principio festi omnes magis attenti sunt his quae festi sunt. Boni quidem ad cultum Dei, alii vero ad vanitates et lucra. Sed circa medium temporis, his quae festi sunt expeditis, magis parati sunt ad doctrinam. Ut ergo eos attentiores et paratiores ad doctrinam inveniret, non in primis diebus ascendit. Similiter etiam quia hoc congruit ordini doctrinae Christi: quia non in fine mundi, nec in principio, sed in medio tempore venit instruere homines de regno Dei, secundum illud Habac. III, 2: *in medio annorum notum facies*.

Locus autem doctrinae ostenditur cum dicit **in templum**, ubi docebat propter duo; scilicet ut ostenderet se docere veritatem quam calumniari non poterant, et quae erat omnibus necessaria: infra XVIII, 20: **ego in occulto locutus sum nihil**; secundo vero quia templum, cum sit locus sacer, conveniens est doctrinae Christi sanctissimae. Is. II, 3: *venite, ascendamus ad montem Domini, et ad domum Dei Iacob; et docebit nos vias suas, et ambulabimus in semitis eius*.

Quid autem doceret Christus, praetermittit Evangelista; quia, ut dictum est, non omnia facta et verba Domini exprimunt evangelistae, sed ea quae commotionem et contradictionem in populo faciebant. Et ideo hic mentionem facit de commotione populi ex ipsa doctrina: quia scilicet qui ante dixerant **seducit turbas**, postea ex ipsa doctrina admiratione moventur.

1035. Et ideo consequenter cum dicit **et mirabantur Iudaei**, ponitur ipsorum admiratio. Nec mirum, quia hoc dicitur in Ps. CXVIII, 129: *mirabilia testimonia tua*. Verba enim Christi verba sunt sapientiae divinae.

Ratio autem admirationis subditur cum dicit **quomodo hic litteras scit cum non didicerit?** Sciebant enim Iesum filium esse pauperis mulieris; et putabatur filius fabri, qui de labore suo vivens, non insisteret studio litterarum, sed potius operi manuali; secundum illud Ps. LXXXVII, 16: *pauper sum ego, et in laboribus a iuventute mea*. Et ideo cum audiunt eum docere et disputare, mirantur dicentes **quomodo hic litteras scit, cum non didicerit?** Simile habetur Matth. XIII, 54: *unde huic sapientia et virtutes? Nonne hic est filius fabri?*

1036. Posito loco et occasionibus manifestandi doctrinae spiritualis originem, hic consequenter ipsius doctrinae originem manifestat, et

primo ostendit originem spiritualis doctrinae esse a Deo;

---

hid himself, it was a sign of his humanity, and an example of virtue for us. But when he did come before them, and they could not suppress him, this showed his divinity. Further, our Lord went when the feast was half over, because at the beginning everyone would be occupied with matters relating to the feast: the good, with the worship of God, and others with trivialities and financial profit; but when it was half over, and such matters had been settled, the people would be better prepared to receive his teaching. Thus our Lord did not go to the first several days of the feast so that he would find them more attentive and better prepared for his teaching. Similarly, Christ's going to the feast at this time paralled the arrangement of his teaching: for Christ came to teach us about the kingdom of God, not at the beginning of the world, nor at its ending, but during the intervening time. *You will make it known in the intervening years* (Heb 3:2).

The place where our Lord taught is mentioned when he says, **into the temple**. He taught there for two reasons. First, to show that he was teaching the truth, which they could not depricate, and which was necessary for all: **I have spoken nothing in secret** (John 18:20). Second, because the temple, since it was a sacred place, was appropriate for the very holy teaching of Christ: *come! Let us go up the mountain of the Lord, and to the house of the God of Jacob. And he will teach us his ways, and we will walk in his steps* (Isa 2:3).

The Evangelist does not mention what Christ taught, for, as was said, the evangelists do not report everything our Lord did and said, but those which excited the people or produced some controversy. And so here he mentions the excitement his teaching produced in the people: that is, that those who had said before, **he seduces the people**, were now amazed at his teaching.

1035. He mentions this amazement when he says, **and the Jews wondered**. And this is not surprising, for *your testimony is wonderful* (Ps 118:129). For the words of Christ are the words of divine wisdom.

He adds the reason why they were amazed when he says, **how does this man know letters, when he has never learned?** For they knew that Jesus was the son of a poor woman and he was considered the son of a carpenter; as such, he would be working for a living and devoting his time, not to study, but to physical work, according to *I am poor, and have labored since my youth* (Ps 87:16). And so when they hear him teach and debate, they are amazed, and say, **how does this man know letters when he has never learned?** Much the same is said: *where did he acquire this widsom, and these great works? Isn't he the son of the carpenter?* (Matt 13:54).

1036. Having been told of the place and opportunity which Christ had to reveal the origin of his spiritual teaching, we now see the origin of this teaching.

First, he shows them that God is the source of this spiritual teaching;

secundo invitat ad susceptionem eius, ibi *in novissimo magnae festivitatis die stabat Iesus et clamabat.*

Circa primum duo facit.

Primo ostendit originem doctrinae;

secundo originem docentis, ibi *dicebant ergo quidam ex Ierosolymis* etc.

Circa primum duo facit.

Primo ostendit originem doctrinae;

secundo excludit obiectionem, ibi *nonne Moyses dedit vobis legem?*

Circa primum duo facit.

Primo ostendit originem doctrinae;

secundo probat, ibi *si quis voluerit voluntatem eius facere, cognoscet de doctrina.*

1037. Dicit ergo *respondit eis Iesus et dixit*, quasi dicat: vos admiramini unde habeam scientiam; sed ego dico, quod *mea doctrina non est mea.*

Si dixisset doctrina quam ego dico, non est mea nulla esset quaestio; sed quod dicit *mea non est mea*, videtur contradictionem implicare.

Sed hoc solvitur, quia hoc dici potest multipliciter. Unde sua doctrina aliquo modo potest dici sua, et aliquo modo non sua. Si enim intelligatur de Christo Filio Dei, sic cum doctrina uniuscuiusque nihil aliud sit quam Verbum eius, Filius autem Dei sit Verbum eius: sequitur ergo quod doctrina Patris sit ipse Filius. Idem autem Verbum est sui ipsius per identitatem substantiae. Quid enim tuum est nisi tu ipse? Est autem non suum per originem. *Quid enim non tuum quam tu, si alicuius es, quod es?* Ut Augustinus dicit. Hoc ergo breviter videtur dixisse *mea doctrina non est mea*; ac si diceret: ego non sum a meipso.

In quo haeresis Sabelliana confunditur, qui dicere ausi sunt ipsum esse Filium qui est Pater.

Vel *mea doctrina*, quam ego pronuntio verbo creato, *non est mea, sed eius qui misit me*, Patris; idest, non est mihi a me ipso, sed a Patre, quia etiam cognitionem Filius per aeternam generationem habet a Patre; Matth. II, 27: *omnia tradita sunt mihi a Patre meo.*

Si vero intelligatur de Christo Filio hominis, tunc dicit *mea doctrina*, quam ego habeo secundum animam creatam, et profero corporis ore, *non est mea*, idest, non est mihi a meipso, sed a Deo: quia omne verum, a quocumque dicatur, a Spiritu Sancto est.

Sic ergo, secundum Augustinum I *de Trin.*, secundum aliquid suam dixit doctrinam, et secundum aliquid non suam: secundum formam Dei suam, secundum

second, he invites them to accept it, at *and on the last and great day of the festivity, Jesus stood and cried* (John 7:37).

As to the first, he does two things.

First, he shows the origin of this teaching;

second, the origin of the one teaching it, at *therefore, some of Jerusalem said: is this not he whom they seek to kill?*

He does two things about the first.

First, he shows the origin of this teaching;

second, he answers an objection, at *did not Moses give you the law?*

In regard to the first he does two things.

First, he shows the origin of this teaching;

second, he proves that it comes from God, at *if any man wants to do his will, he will know of the doctrine.*

1037. He says, *Jesus answered them and said.* As if to say: you are wondering where I gained my knowledge; but I say, *my doctrine is not mine.*

If he had said: the doctrine that I am presenting to you is not mine, there would be no problem. But he says: *my doctrine is not mine*; and this seems to be a contradiction.

However, this can be explained, for this statement can be understood is several ways. Our Lord's doctrine can in some sense be called his own, and in some sense not his own. First, we can understand Christ as the Son of God. Then, since the doctrine of anyone is nothing else than his word, and the Son of God is the Word of God, it follows that the doctrine of the Father is the Son himself. But this same Word belongs to himself through an identity of substance. What does belong to you, if not you yourself? *However, he does not belong to himself through his origin.* As Augustine says. If you do not belong to yourself, because you are from another, what does? This seems to be the meaning, expressed in summary fashion, of *my doctrine is not mine.* As if to say: I am not of myself.

This refutes the Sabellian heresy, which dared to say that the Son is the Father.

Or, we could understand it as meaning that *my doctrine*, which I proclaim with created words, *is not mine but his who sent me*, i.e., it is the Father's; that is, my doctrine is not mine as from myself, but it is from the Father: because the Son has even his knowledge from the Father through an eternal generation. *All things have been given to me by my Father* (Matt 11:27).

Second, we can understand Christ as the Son of man. Then he is saying: *my doctrine*, which I have in my created soul, and which my lips proclaim, *is not mine*, i.e, it is not mine as from myself, but from God: because every truth, by whomever spoken, is from the Holy Spirit.

Thus, as Augustine says in *The Trinity* (Bk 1), our Lord called this doctrine his own from one point of view, and not his own from another point of view. According to his

formam servi non suam. Ex quo habemus exemplum, quod omnem cognitionem nostram cum gratiarum actione recognoscamus a Deo; I Cor. IV, 7: *quid habes quod non accepisti? Si autem accepisti, quid gloriaris, quasi non acceperis?*

1038. Consequenter cum dicit *si quis voluerit voluntatem eius facere, cognoscet de doctrina* etc., probat suam doctrinam esse a Deo: et hoc dupliciter.

Primo ex iudicio recte sentientium;

secundo ex sua intentione, ibi *qui a semetipso loquitur, gloriam propriam quaerit.*

1039. Circa primum sciendum est, quod iudicio illius standum est, utrum aliquis bene operetur in aliqua arte, qui est expertus in arte illa: sicut an aliquis bene loquitur Gallice, standum est iudicio eius qui est peritus in lingua Gallica. Secundum hoc ergo dicit Dominus: illius iudicio standum est, an doctrina mea sit a Deo, qui est expertus in rebus divinis, talis enim recte potest de his iudicare; I Cor. II, 14: *animalis homo non percipit ea quae sunt spiritus Dei, spiritualis autem iudicat omnia.* Et ideo dicit: quia vos alienati estis a Deo, ideo non cognoscitis de doctrina utrum ex Deo sit. Sed *si quis voluerit voluntatem eius*, idest Dei, *facere*, iste potest cognoscere utrum doctrina haec sit a Deo, *an ego a meipso loquar*. Ille quidem a seipso loquitur qui falsum dicit; quia, sicut dicitur infra VIII, 44, *cum loquitur mendacium, ex propriis loquitur.*

Vel aliter, secundum Chrysostomum. Voluntas enim Dei est pax, caritas et humilitas nostra; unde Matth. V, 9, dicitur: *beati pacifici, quoniam filii Dei vocabuntur.* Studium autem contentionis frequenter pervertit mentem hominis, intantum ut verum aestimet falsum. Unde deposito contentionis spiritu, rectius habetur certitudo veritatis; Iob. VI, 29: *respondete, obsecro, absque contentione, et loquentes id quod iustum est, iudicate.* Et ideo dicit Dominus: si quis vult recte de doctrina mea iudicare, faciat voluntatem eius; idest, deponat iram, invidiam et odium quod sine causa in me habet. Et nihil est quod prohibeat eum cognoscere, *utrum ex Deo sit an ego a meipso loquar*, idest quod Dei verba sunt quae loquor.

Vel aliter, secundum Augustinum. Voluntas Dei est ut faciamus opera eius, sicut voluntas patrisfamilias est ut operarii faciant opus eius. Opus autem Dei est ut credamus in eum quem ipse misit; supra VI, 29: *hoc est opus Dei ut credatis in eum quem ille misit*. Ideo dicit *si quis voluerit facere voluntatem eius*, scilicet Dei, idest credere in me, iste *cognoscet an doctrina mea sit ex*

form of God, it was his own; but according to his form of a servant, it was not his own. This is an example for us, that we should realize that all our knowledge is from God, and thank him for it: *what do you have which you have not been given? And if you have been given it, why do you glory as if you have not been given it?* (1 Cor 4:7).

1038. Then, at *if any man wants to do his will, he will know of the doctrine, whether it is from God or whether I speak from myself*, he proves that his doctrine is from God. And he does this in two ways:

first, from the judgment of those who correctly understand such matters; and

second, from his own intention, at *he who speaks of himself seeks his own glory*.

1039. With respect to the first, we should note that when there is a question whether someone is performing well in some art, this is decided by one who has experience in that art; just as the question whether someone is speaking French well should be decided by one who is well versed in the French language. With this in mind, our Lord is saying: the question whether my doctrine is from God must be decided by one who has experience in divine matters, for such a person can judge correctly about these things. *The sensual man does not perceive those things that pertain to the Spirit of God. The spiritual man judges all things* (1 Cor 2:14). Accordingly, he is saying: because you are alienated from God, you do not know whether a doctrine is from God. *If anyone wants to do his will*, that is, the will of God, he can know whether this doctrine is from God, *or whether I speak from myself*. Indeed, one who is speaking what is false is speaking on his own, because *when he speaks a lie, he speaks of his own* (John 8:44).

Chrysostom explains this text in another way. The will of God is our peace, our love, and our humility: *happy are the peacemakers, because they will be called sons of God* (Matt 5:9). But the love of controversy often distorts a person's mind to such an extent that he thinks that what is really true is false. Thus, when we abandon the spirit of controversy, we possess more surely the certitude of truth. *Answer, I entreat you, without contention, and judge, speaking what is just* (Job 6:29). So our Lord is saying: if anyone wishes to judge my doctrine correctly, let him do the will of God, i.e., abandon the anger, the envy and the hatred which he has for me without reason. Then, nothing will prevent him from knowing whether this doctrine is from God, *or whether I speak from myself*, i.e., whether I am speaking the words of God.

Augustine explains it this way. It is the will of God that we know his works, just as it is the will of a head of a household that his servants do his works. The work of God is that we believe in him whom he has sent: *this is the work of God, that you believe in him whom he has sent* (John 6:29). Thus he says: *if any man wants to do his will*, that is, God's will, which is to believe in me, *he will know of the doctrine,*

Deo. Is. c. VII, 9, secundum aliam litteram: *nisi credideritis, non intelligetis*.

1040. Consequenter cum dicit **qui a semetipso loquitur, gloriam propriam quaerit**, probat idem ex sua intentione. Et ponit duplicem intentionem per quam intelligitur duplex origo doctrinae.

Dictum est autem aliquos loqui a se, aliquos vero loqui non a se. Loquitur autem non a se quicumque studet loqui veritatem. Omnis veritatis cognitio ab alio est: vel per modum quidem disciplinae, ut a magistro; vel per modum revelationis, ut a Deo; vel per inventionem, ut ab ipsis rebus, quia, ut dicitur Rom. I, 20: *invisibilia Dei per ea quae facta sunt, intellecta conspiciuntur*. Sic ergo quocumque istorum modorum cognitio aliqua habeatur, non est homini a se.

A se autem loquitur qui ea quae dicit nec a rebus nec ex doctrina humana accepit, sed de corde suo; Ier. XXIII, 16: *visionem cordis sui loquuntur*; Ez. XIII, 3: *vae prophetis insipientibus qui vaticinantur de corde suo*. Sic ergo confingere aliquid a se ipso, est propter humanam gloriam: quia, sicut Chrysostomus dicit, qui aliquam propriam vult instruere doctrinam, propter nihil aliud hoc vult quam ut gloriam acquirat. Et hoc est quod Dominus dicit, probans doctrinam suam a Deo esse. **Qui a semetipso loquitur**, de certa cognitione veritatis quae est ab alio, iste **quaerit gloriam propriam** propter quam et proptem superbiam, haereses et falsae opiniones introducuntur. Et hoc competit Antichristo; II Thess. II, 4: *qui adversatur, et extollitur supra omne quod dicitur Deus aut quod colitur*.

Sed **qui quaerit gloriam eius qui misit illum**, sicut ego quaero, (infra VIII, v. 50: **ego gloriam meam non quaero**) **hic verax est, et iniustitia in illo non est**. Verax sum, quia doctrina mea continet veritatem; iniustitia in me non est, quia alterius gloriam non usurpo. Et, ut dicit Augustinus, *magnum nobis praebuit humilitatis exemplum, dum habitu inventus ut homo, quaerit gloriam Patris, non suam: quod tu homo facere debes. Quando aliquid boni facis, gloriam tuam quaeris; quando aliquid mali facis, Deo calumniam meditaris*. Patet autem quod gloriam suam non quaerebat; quia si non fuisset adversarius principibus sacerdotum, non fuissent eum persecuti.

Sic ergo Christus, et quicumque gloriam Dei quaerit, habet quidem in intellectu cognitionem, Matth. XX, 16: *magister, scimus quia verax es*, et ideo dicit **hic verax est**: in effectu autem rectam intentionem, unde dicit **et iniustitia in illo non est**. Iniustitia enim est quod homo usurpet sibi alienum; gloria autem est propria solius Dei: qui ergo sibi quaerit gloriam, iniustus est.

whether it is from God: *if you do not believe, you will not understand* (Isa 7:9), as the other version says.

1040. Then when he says, **he who speaks of himself seeks his own glory**, he proves the same thing from his intention. And he presents two intentions through which we can recognize the two sources of a doctrine.

Some are said to speak on their own, and others not on their own. Now whoever strives to speak the truth does not speak on his own. All our knowledge of the truth is from another: either from instruction, as from a teacher; or from revelation, as from God; or by a process of discovery, as from things themselves, for *the invisible things of God are clearly known by the things that have been made* (Rom 1:20). Consequently, in whatever way a person acquires his knowledge, he does not acquire it on his own.

That person speaks on his own who takes what he says neither from things themselves, nor from any human teaching, but from his own heart: *they proclaim a vision taken out of their own hearts* (Jer 23:16); *woe to those foolish prophets who prophesy out of their own hearts* (Ezek 13:3). Accordingly, when a person devises a doctrine on his own he does it for the sake of human glory: for, as we see from Chrysostom, a person who wishes to present his own private doctrine does so for no other purpose than to acquire glory. And this is what our Lord says, proving that his doctrine is from God: **he who speaks of himself**, about a certain knowledge of the truth, which is really from another, **seeks his own glory**. It is for this reason, and because of pride, that various heresies and false opinions have arisen. And this is a characteristic of the antichrist *who opposes and is exalted above all that is called God, or is worshipped* (2 Thess 2:4).

But **the one who seeks the glory of him who sent him**, as I do—**I do not seek my own glory** (John 8:50)—**is true, and there is no injustice in him**. I am truthful because my doctrine contains the truth; there is no injustice in me because I do not appropriate the glory of another. As Augustine says: *he gave us a magnificent example of humility when, in the form of a man, he sought the glory of the Father, and not his own. O man, you should do the same! When you do something good, you seek your glory; when you do something evil, you insult God*. It is obvious that he was not looking for his own glory, because if he had not been an enemy of the chief priests, he would not have been persecuted by them.

So Christ, and everyone who is looking for the glory of God, has knowledge in his intellect, *master, we know that you are truthful* (Matt 22:16), thus he says, **is true**. And he has the correct intention in his will: thus he says, **and there is no injustice in him**. For a person is unjust when he takes for himself what belongs to another; but glory is proper to God alone; therefore, he who seeks glory for himself is unjust.

1041. Consequenter cum dicit *nonne Moyses dedit vobis legem?* Excludit obiectionem.

Posset enim aliquis dicere Christo, quod ideo doctrina sua non esset a Deo, quia Sabbatum solvit, secundum illud infra IX, 16: *non est hic homo a Deo, qui Sabbatum non custodit.* Et hoc intendit excludere; unde circa hoc tria facit.

Primo excusat se, arguendo ex parte accusantium;

secundo ostenditur eorum iniqua responsio, ibi *respondit turba* etc.;

tertio excusat se per rationem, ibi *respondit Iesus, et dixit eis: unum opus feci, et omnes miramini.*

1042. Dicit ergo: dato, ut vos dicitis, quod doctrina mea non sit a Deo, quia legem non servo, sabbatum solvens; tamen vos non habetis causam accusandi, cum sitis in simili delicto. Unde dicit *nonne Moyses dedit vobis,* idest populo vestro, *legem?* Et tamen *nemo ex vobis facit,* idest servat, legem; Act. VII, 53: *accepistis legem in dispositione angelorum, et non custoditis.* Unde et Petrus, Act. XV, 10: *hoc est onus quod neque nos, neque patres nostri portare potuerunt.* Si ergo non servatis legem, quare propter transgressionem eius vultis me interficere? Non enim propter hoc facitis, sed propter odium: alioquin si propter zelum legis faceretis, ipsi vos servaretis eam; Sap. II, 12: *circumveniamus iustum, quoniam inutilis est nobis, et contrarius est operibus nostris, et improperat nobis peccata legis*; et sequitur: *morte turpissima condemnemus eum.* Vel dicendum, quod non servatis legem quam Moyses dedit vobis: et hoc patet in eo quod me vultis interficere, quod est contra legem; Ex. XX, 13: *non occides.* Vel aliter, secundum Augustinum: *non facitis legem, quia in lege ipse contineor*; supra V, 46: *si credideritis Moysi, crederetis forsitan et mihi: de me enim ille scripsit.* Sed vos vultis me interficere.

1043. Consequenter ponitur iniqua responsio turbae, cum dicit *respondit turba, et dixit: daemonium habes.* Vero autem turba respondet non pertinentia ad ordinem, sed ad perturbationem, ut dicit Augustinus: eum enim dicunt Daemonium habere qui Daemones expellit, Matth. XII, 24.

1044. Et ideo consequenter cum dicit *unum opus feci, et omnes miramini,* Dominus in sua veritate tranquillus, confutat eos, excusans se per rationem, et

primo commemorat eis factum propter quod turbantur;

secundo ostendit eos non debere turbari, ibi *propterea Moyses dedit vobis circumcisionem*;

1041. Then, at *did not Moses give you the law?* he answers an objection.

For someone could tell Christ that his doctrine was not from God because he broke the sabbath, according to, *this man is not of God, who does not keep the Sabbath* (John 9:16). This is what he intends to answer; and he does three things.

First, he clears himself, by arguing from the actions of those who are accusing him;

second, we see their vicious reply at *the multitude answered*; and

third, he vindicates himself with a reasonable explanation, at *Jesus answered and said to them: I have done one work, and you all wonder*.

1042. He says: even granting, as you say, that my doctrine is not from God because I do not keep the law, breaking the sabbath, nevertheless, you do not have any reason to accuse me since you do the same thing. Thus he says: *did not Moses give you the law?* i.e., did he not give it to your people? *And yet none of you keep the law. You received the law through the angels, and have not kept it* (Acts 7:53). This is why Peter says: *a yoke, which neither our fathers nor we were able to bear* (Acts 15:10). Therefore, if you do not keep the law, why do you want to kill me for not keeping it? You are not doing this because of the law, but out of hatred. If you were acting out of devotion for the law, you would keep it yourselves. *Let us lie in wait for the just man, because he is unfavorable to us, and against our works, and he reproaches us for breaking the law* (Wis 2:12); and a little further on we read: *let us condemn him to a most shameful death* (Wis 2:20). Or, it could be explained this way: you do not keep the law that Moses gave you; and this is obvious from the fact that you want to kill me, which is against the law: *you shall not kill* (Exod 20:13). Another explanation, following Augustine, is: *you do not keep the law because I myself am included in the law*; *if you believed Moses, you would perhaps believe me also, for he wrote of me* (John 5:46). But you want to kill me.

1043. Then we see the vicious reply of the crowd, when he says, *the multitude answered and said: you have a devil!* As Augustine says, their reply indicates disorder and confusion, rather than any order: for they are saying that the one who casts out devils has one himself (Matt 12:24).

1044. Then when he says, *I have done one work, and you all wonder*, our Lord, at peace in his own truth, answers them, and justifies himself with a reasonable explanation.

First, he recalls the incident that is troubling them;

second, he shows that this should not bother them, at *therefore, Moses gave you circumcision*; and

tertio inducit eos ad iustum iudicium, ibi *nolite iudicare secundum faciem* etc.

1045. *Respondit ergo Iesus, et dixit eis: unum opus feci, et omnes miramini.* Non reddit convicio convicium, nec repulit, quia *cum malediceretur, non maledicebat*: sed eis opus commemorat de curatione paralytici, de quo omnes admirabantur, non admiratione devotionis, secundum illud Is. LX, 5: *videbis, et afflues, et mirabitur, et dilatabitur cor tuum*, sed admiratione turbationis, secundum illud Sap. V, v. 2: *videntes turbabuntur timore horribili, et mirabuntur in subitatione insperatae salutis.* Si ergo propter unum opus miramini, idest cum turbatione turbamini, quid faceretis si omnia opera mea videretis? Nam, ut dicit Augustinus, *ipsius opera erant quae in mundo videbant: omnes etiam infirmi per eum sanantur*; Ps. CVI, 20: *misit verbum suum, et sanavit eos*; Sap. XVI, 12: *nec herba nec malagma sanavit eos; sed tuus, Domine, sermo, qui sanat omnia.* Ideo ergo turbamini, quia unum tantum opus videtis, et non omnia.

1046. Consequenter cum dicit *propterea Moyses dedit vobis circumcisionem*, convincit eos de iniusta turbatione, et

primo ponit mandatum eis datum a Moyse;
secundo opus eorum; et
tertio arguit ex utroque.

1047. Mandatum autem Moysi est de circumcisione; et ideo dicit *propterea*, idest ad significandum mea opera, *Moyses dedit vobis circumcisionem.* Nam circumcisio in signum data est, ut habetur Gen. XVII, 2: *erit vobis in signum foederis inter me et vos*: significabat enim Christum; et ideo semper data est in membro generationis, quia ex Abraham secundum carnem descensurus erat Christus, qui spiritualem circumcisionem, idest mentis et corporis, facit. Vel ideo in ipso membro fiebat, quia data est contra peccatum originale.

Quod autem Moyses dederit circumcisionem, expresse non habetur, nisi Ex. XVII, 44: *omnis servus emptitius circumcidetur.* Et licet Moyses dederit circumcisionem, non tamen quasi eam instituens: quia non ipse primus accepit circumcisionis mandatum, sed Abraham, ut habetur Gen. XVII, 10.

1048. Factum autem Iudaeorum est quia in Sabbato circumcidebant; et hoc est quod dicit *et Sabbato circumciditis* etc. Et hoc ideo, quia Abrahae mandatum est, ut octavo die circumcideretur puer; Gen. XXI, 4: *circumcidit eum die octavo, sicut praeceperat ei Deus.* A Moyse autem praeceptum erat eis quod nihil operis facerent in die Sabbati. Contingebat autem aliquando quod octavus dies necessitatis veniret in die Sabbati; et sic circumcidentes puerum ipso die, mandatum Moysi solvebant, propter mandatum patrum.

third, he shows the way to a judgment that is just, at *do not judge according to the appearance, but judge according to just judgment*.

1045. *Jesus answered and said to them: I have done one work, and you all wonder.* He does not trade one insult for another, nor rebuff it, because *when he was derided, he did not deride in return* (1 Pet 2:23). He rather recalls for them his cure of the paralytic, which was the cause of their amazement. But their amazement was not one of devotion, as in *your heart will be amazed and expanded* (Isa 60:5), but a kind of agitation and disturbance, as in *those who see it will be afflicted with terrible fear, and will be amazed* (Wis 5:2). So, if you are amazed over one of my works, i.e., if you are disturbed and troubled, what would you do if you saw all of my works? For, as Augustine says, *his works were those which they saw in the world: even all the sick are healed by him. He sent his word, and healed them* (Ps 106:20); *it was neither a herb nor a poultice that healed them, but your word, O Lord, which heals all* (Wis 16:12). Thus, the reason why you are disturbed is that you have seen only one of my works, and not all of them.

1046. Then, at *therefore, Moses gave you circumcision*, he shows that there is no reason why they should be disturbed.

First, he recalls the command given to them by Moses; second, he states their customary behavior; and third, he presents an argument based on the first two.

1047. The command of Moses was about circumcision; so he says: *therefore*, i.e., to signify my works, *Moses gave you circumcision.* For circumcision was given as a sign, as we read, *it will be a sign of the covenant between me and you* (Gen 17:11). For it signified Christ. This is the reason why it was always done on the genital organ, because Christ was to descend, in his human nature, from Abraham; and Christ is the one who spiritually circumcises us, i.e., both in mind and body. Or, it was done to the genital organ because it was given in opposition to original sin.

We do not find it explicitly stated that Moses gave circumcision, unless at *every slave who is bought shall be circumcised* (Exod 12:44). And although Moses did tell them to circumcise, he was not the one who established this practice, because he was not the first one to receive the command to circumcise; this was Abraham (Gen 17:10).

1048. Now it was the custom among the Jews to circumcise on the sabbath. And this is what he says: *you circumcise a man on the Sabbath day.* They did this because Abraham was told that a boy should be circumcised on the eighth day: *he circumcised him on the eighth day, as God had commanded him* (Gen 21:4). On the other hand, they were told by Moses not to do any work on the sabbath. But it sometimes happened that the eighth day was a sabbath. And so, in circumcising a boy on that day, they were breaking a command of Moses for a command of the patriarchs.

1049. Et ideo ex his arguit Dominus cum dicit *si circumcisionem accipit homo in Sabbato, ut non solvatur lex Moysi; mihi indignamini, quia totum hominem sanum feci in Sabbato?*

Ubi notandum est, quod hoc argumentum efficaciam habet ex his tribus considerationibus, quarum duae sunt expressae, sed tertia subintelligitur. Videmus enim primo, quod quamvis mandatum Abrahae prius fuerit, tamen mandatum Moysi de observatione sabbati non praeiudicabat priori, scilicet mandato de circumcisione; Gal. III, 17: *dico autem, testamentum confirmatum a Deo, quae post quadringentos et triginta annos facta est lex, non irritum facit.* Et ideo ex hoc arguit: quia licet in humanis legibus posteriora praeiudicent prioribus, tamen in divinis priora sunt maioris auctoritatis. Et ideo praecepto facto Abrahae de circumcisione non praeiudicat praeceptum Moysi de observatione sabbati. Multo ergo minus praeiudicat mihi, qui facio quod dispositum est a Deo ante mundi constitutionem de salute hominum in sabbato figurata.

Alia consideratio est, quia Iudaei mandatum habebant ut non operarentur in Sabbato; et tamen Iudaei operabantur quae ad salutem particularem erant. Dicit ergo: si vos, quibus mandatum est ut nihil operemini in Sabbato, circumcisionem accipitis ipso die, quae est quaedam particularis salus (unde et in membro particulari fiebat), et hoc facitis, *ut non solvatur lex Moysi* (ex quo patet, ea quae ad salutem pertinent in Sabbato praetermittenda non esse): ergo multo magis debet homo facere ipso die ea quae sunt ad universalem salutem. Non ergo debetis mihi indignari, *quia totum hominem sanum feci in Sabbato*.

Tertia consideratio est, quia utrumque mandatum fuit figura: nam *omnia in figura contingebant illis,* I Cor. X, 11. Si ergo figura, scilicet mandatum de observatione sabbati, non praeiudicat figurae, scilicet mandato circumcisionis, multo minus praeiudicat veritati. Nam circumcisio ipsum Dominum figurabat, ut dicit Augustinus. Ideo autem dicit *totum hominem,* quia, cum Dei perfecta sint opera, curatus est ut sanus esset in corpore, et credidit ut sanus esset in anima.

1050. Consequenter cum dicit *nolite iudicare secundum faciem* etc., reducit eos ad iustum examen sui: ut scilicet non secundum faciem iudicent, sed iustum iudicium. Dicitur autem quis iudicare secundum faciem dupliciter. Nam iudex iudicat secundum allegata; I Reg. XV, 7: *homines vident ea quae apparent.* Sed in hoc potest esse deceptio; et ideo dicit *nolite iudicare secundum faciem,* idest secundum illud quod statim apparet, sed diligenter inquirite; Iob XXIX, 16: *causam quam*

1049. Our Lord is arguing from those facts when he says: *if a man receives circumcision on the Sabbath, that the law of Moses may not be broken, why are you angry at me because I have healed a whole man on the Sabbath?*

We should note here that three things make this argument effective: two of these are explicit, and the other implied. First, although the command given to Abraham was the first to be given, it was not canceled by the command given to Moses concerning observing the sabbath. *I say that the covenant, confirmed by God, is not canceled by the law, which came four hundred and thirty years later* (Gal 3:17). And so Christ is arguing from this: although when dealing with human laws, the later ones cancel the earlier laws, in the case of divine laws, the earlier ones have greater authority. And so the command given to Moses about observing the sabbath does not cancel the command which was given to Abraham concerning circumcision. Therefore, much less does it interfere with me, who am only doing what was decided by God before the creation of the world, for the salvation of mankind; and this salvation was symbolized by the sabbath.

Another point is that the Jews were commanded not to work on the sabbath; yet they did do things that were related to the salvation of the individual. So Christ is saying: if you people, who were commanded not to work on the sabbath, circumcise on that day (and this concerns the salvation of the individual, and thus it was done to an individual organ) and you do this so *that the law of Moses may not be broken* (from which it is clear that those things that pertain to salvation should not be omitted on the sabbath), it follows with greater reason that a man should do on that day those things that pertain to the salvation of everyone. Therefore, you should not be indignant with me *because I have healed a whole man on the Sabbath.*

The third point is that each command was a symbol: for *all these things happened to them in symbol* (1 Cor 10:11). Thus, if one symbol, i.e., the command to observe the sabbath, does not cancel the other symbol, i.e., the command to circumcise, much less does it cancel the truth. For circumcision sybolized our Lord, as Augustine says. Finally, he says, *a whole man,* because, since God's works are perfect, the man was cured so as to be healthy in body, and he believed so as to be healthy in soul.

1050. Then when he says, *do not judge according to the appearance, but judge according to just judgment,* he guides them to a fair consideration of himself, so that they do not judge him according to appearances, but give a judgment which is just. There are two ways in which one is said to judge according to appearances. First, a judge may reach his decision relying on the allegations: *men see the things that are evident* (1 Kgs 15:7). But this way can lead to error; thus he says, *do not judge according to the appearance,*

nesciebam diligenter investigabam; Is. XI, 3: *non secundum visionem oculorum iudicabit.*

Vel aliter **nolite iudicare secundum faciem**, idest nolite accipere personam in iudicio: hoc enim est prohibitum omnibus iudicantibus; Ex. XXIII, 6: *non accipiens personam pauperis in iudicio*; Mal. II, 9: *faciem accipitis in iudicio.* Accipere autem personam in iudicio est praetermittere iustum iudicium propter amorem, seu reverentiam, seu timorem, seu conditionem personae, quae non faciunt ad causam. Dicit ergo **nolite iudicare**, quasi dicat: non quia Moyses apud vos habet maiorem gloriam quam ego, ex personarum dignitate feratis sententiam, sed a rerum natura: quia ea quae ego facio, maiora sunt quam ea quae fecit Moyses.

Sed notandum, secundum Augustinum, quod ille non iudicat partialiter, qui aequaliter diligit. Non enim cum homines diverso modo pro suis gradibus honoramus, timendum est ne personam accipiamus.

i.e., by what is immediately evident, but examine the matter diligently: *I diligently investigated the stranger's cause* (Job 29:16); *he will not judge by appearances* (Isa 11:3).

In the second way, **do not judge according to the appearance**, i.e., do not show partiality or favoritism in your judgment: for all judges are forbidden to do this. *You will not show favoritism when judging a person who is poor* (Exod 23:6); *you have shown partiality in your judgment* (Mal 2:9). To show partiality in a judgment is not to give a judgment that is just because of love, or deference, or fear, or the status of a person, which things have nothing to do with the case. So he says: **do not judge according to the appearance**, but with a just judgment, as if to say: just because Moses is more honored among you than I am, you should not base your decision on our reputations, but on the nature of the facts: because the things I am doing are greater than what Moses did.

But it should be noted, according to Augustine, that one who loves all equally does not judge with partiality. For when we honor men differently according to their rank, we must beware of showing partiality.

Lecture 3

7:25 Dicebant ergo quidam ex Ierosolymis: nonne hic est quem quaerunt interficere? [n. 1052]

7:26 Ecce palam loquitur, et nihil ei dicunt. Numquid vere cognoverunt principes quia hic est Christus? [n. 1053]

7:27 Sed hunc scimus unde sit: Christus autem cum venerit, nemo scit unde sit. [n. 1055]

7:28 Clamabat ergo Iesus in templo docens, et dicens: et me scitis, et unde sim scitis. Et a me ipso non veni; sed est verus, qui misit me, quem vos nescitis. [n. 1057]

7:29 Ego scio eum: et si dixero, quia nescio eum, ero similis vobis, mendax. Sed scio eum, quia ab ipso sum, et ipse me misit. [n. 1061]

7:30 Quaerebant ergo eum apprehendere; et nemo misit in illum manus, quia nondum venerat hora eius. [n. 1066]

7:31 De turba autem multi crediderunt in eum, et dicebant: Christus cum venerit, numquid plura signa faciet quam quae hic facit? [n. 1070]

7:32 Audierunt Pharisaei turbam murmurantem de illo haec: et miserunt principes et Pharisaei ministros, ut apprehenderent Iesum. [n. 1071]

7:25Ἔλεγον οὖν τινες ἐκ τῶν Ἱεροσολυμιτῶν· οὐχ οὗτός ἐστιν ὃν ζητοῦσιν ἀποκτεῖναι;

7:26 καὶ ἴδε παρρησίᾳ λαλεῖ καὶ οὐδὲν αὐτῷ λέγουσιν. μήποτε ἀληθῶς ἔγνωσαν οἱ ἄρχοντες ὅτι οὗτός ἐστιν ὁ χριστός;

7:27 ἀλλὰ τοῦτον οἴδαμεν πόθεν ἐστίν· ὁ δὲ χριστὸς ὅταν ἔρχηται οὐδεὶς γινώσκει πόθεν ἐστίν.

7:28 ἔκραξεν οὖν ἐν τῷ ἱερῷ διδάσκων ὁ Ἰησοῦς καὶ λέγων· κἀμὲ οἴδατε καὶ οἴδατε πόθεν εἰμί· καὶ ἀπ' ἐμαυτοῦ οὐκ ἐλήλυθα, ἀλλ' ἔστιν ἀληθινὸς ὁ πέμψας με, ὃν ὑμεῖς οὐκ οἴδατε·

7:29 ἐγὼ οἶδα αὐτόν, ὅτι παρ' αὐτοῦ εἰμι κἀκεῖνός με ἀπέστειλεν.

7:30 Ἐζήτουν οὖν αὐτὸν πιάσαι, καὶ οὐδεὶς ἐπέβαλεν ἐπ' αὐτὸν τὴν χεῖρα, ὅτι οὔπω ἐληλύθει ἡ ὥρα αὐτοῦ.

7:31Ἐκ τοῦ ὄχλου δὲ πολλοὶ ἐπίστευσαν εἰς αὐτὸν καὶ ἔλεγον· ὁ χριστὸς ὅταν ἔλθῃ μὴ πλείονα σημεῖα ποιήσει ὧν οὗτος ἐποίησεν;

7:32 ἤκουσαν οἱ Φαρισαῖοι τοῦ ὄχλου γογγύζοντος περὶ αὐτοῦ ταῦτα, καὶ ἀπέστειλαν οἱ ἀρχιερεῖς καὶ οἱ Φαρισαῖοι ὑπηρέτας ἵνα πιάσωσιν αὐτόν.

7:25 Therefore, some of Jerusalem said: is this not he whom they seek to kill? [n. 1052]

7:26 And behold, he speaks openly, and they say nothing to him. Have the rulers truly known that this is the Christ? [n. 1053]

7:27 But we know where this man comes from: but when the Christ comes, no man knows where he comes from. [n. 1055]

7:28 Jesus, therefore, teaching in the temple, cried out, saying: you know me, and you know from where I come. And I have not come from myself, but he is true who sent me, whom you do not know. [n. 1057]

7:29 I know him, and if I said, I do not know him, then I would be like you, a liar. I know him, because I am from him, and he has sent me. [n. 1061]

7:30 They sought therefore to apprehend him, and no man laid hands on him, because his hour had not yet come. [n. 1066]

7:31 But of the people many believed in him, and they said: when the Christ comes, will he do more miracles than what this man does? [n. 1070]

7:32 The Pharisees heard the people murmuring these things concerning him, and the rulers and Pharisees sent officers to apprehend him. [n. 1071]

1051. Postquam egit de origine doctrinae, consequenter agit de origine docentis, et

primo Christus ostendit suum principium a quo procedit;

secundo suum finem ad quem vadit, ibi *adhuc modicum tempus vobiscum sum*.

Circa primum tria facit.

Primo proponitur dubitatio turbarum de origine;

secundo ponitur doctrina ipsius originis, ibi *clamabat ergo Iesus in templo*;

tertio ponitur effectus doctrinae, ibi *quaerebant ergo eum apprehendere*.

1051. Having considered the origin of his doctrine, he now tells us about the origin of its teacher.

First, Christ shows his source, from which he comes

second, he shows his end, to which he goes, at *yet a little while I am with you* (John 7:33).

He does three things concerning the first.

First, we see the doubt of the people about his origin;

second, we have Christ's teaching concerning his origin, at *Jesus, therefore, teaching in the temple, cried out*; and

third, we see the effect this teaching had, at *they sought therefore to apprehend him*.

Circa primum tria facit.

Primo ponitur admiratio turbae;

secundum eorum suspicio, ibi **numquid vere cognoverunt principes quia hic est Christus?**

Tertio inducit eorum obiectio contra ea quae suspicabantur, ibi **sed scimus**, etc.

Admiratio autem turbarum consurgit ex duobus.

Primo ex iniquo proposito principum:

secundo ex publica doctrina Christi, ibi **ecce palam loquitur**.

1052. Dictum est autem supra, quod Christus ut ostenderet infirmitatem humanae naturae, latenter ascendit ad diem festum; sed ut ostenderet suae divinitatis personam, publice docet in templo, et a persequentibus teneri non potest. Et sic, ut ait Augustinus, apparet potestas quae putabatur timiditas. Et ideo **dicebant quidam ex Ierosolymis**, quasi admirantes, nam ipsi sciebant qua saevitia quaerebatur a principibus, utpote eius familiares, et Ierosolymis existentes. Unde Chrysostomus dicit: *omnibus miserabiliores erant, qui divinitatis signum videntes maximum, omnia iudicio corruptorum principum permittentes, Christum minus reverebantur, secundum illud* Eccli. X, 2: *qualis rector civitatis, tales et inhabitantes in ea.* Sed tamen mirabantur qua potentia non tenebatur; unde et dicebant **nonne hic est quem** Iudaei **quaerunt**, idest principes, secundum illud supra V, 16, *propterea persequebantur eum Iudaei*, idest principes, **quia haec faciebat in Sabbato**; Dan. c. XIII, 5: *egressa est iniquitas a senioribus populi, qui videbantur regere populum.*

Apparet autem per hoc veritas sermonum Christi, et falsitas principum. Supra enim cum Dominus diceret eis **quid me quaeritis interficere?** Negaverunt, dicentes: **daemonium habes: quis te quaerit interficere?** Sed ecce quod principes negabant, isti confitentur cum dicunt **quem Iudaei quaerunt interficere.** Sic ergo admirantur ex iniquo proposito principum.

1053. Similiter etiam ex publica doctrina Christi: unde dicunt **ecce palam loquitur**, docens, scilicet Christus, quod est indicium securae veritatis; infra XVIII, 20: **ego palam locutus sum; et** tamen **nihil ei dicunt**, quasi repressi virtute divina. Haec est enim propria Dei virtus quod malorum corda ab impetu suae malitiae reprimit; Prov. XVI, 7: *cum placuerint Domino viae hominis, inimicos eius quoque convertet ad pacem.* Et alibi; *cor regum in manu Dei: quocumque voluerit inclinabit illud.*

1054. Suspicio eorum ponitur cum dicit **numquid vere cognoverunt principes quia hic est Christus?** Quasi dicant: ante quaerebant eum interficere, modo invenerunt, et tamen nihil ei dicunt; non tamen mutati a

He does two things about the first.

First, we see the amazement of the people;

second, their conjecture, at **have the rulers truly known that this is the Christ?**

third, he brings their objection against those who are suspicious, at **but we know where this man comes from.**

The people were amazed over two things:

first, at the unjust statements of their leaders

and at the public teaching of Christ, at **behold, he speaks openly**.

1052. As we said before, Christ went up to this feast in secret to show the weakness of his human nature; but he publicly taught in the temple, with his enemies being unable to restrain him, to show his divinity. And so, as Augustine remarks, what was thought to be a lack of courage turned out to be strength. Accordingly, **some of Jerusalem said**, in amazement, for they knew how fiercely their leaders were looking for him, as they lived with them in Jerusalem. Thus Chrysostom says: *the most pitiable of all were they who saw a very clear sign of his divinity and, leaving everything to the judgment of their corrupt leaders, failed to show Christ reverence. As the ruler of a city is, so are its inhabitants* (Sir 10:2). Yet they were amazed at the power he had which kept him from being apprehended. So they said: **is this not he whom they**, the Jews, **seek**, i.e., the leaders, according to what was said before: **therefore the Jews**, the leaders, **persecuted Jesus, because he did these things on the Sabbath** (John 5:16); *evil has come out of the elders of the people, who ruled them* (Dan 13:5).

This also shows that Christ spoke the truth, while what their leaders said was false. For above, when our Lord asked them: **why do you seek to kill me?** they denied it and said: **you have a devil: who seeks to kill you?** (John 7:20) But here, what their leaders had denied, these others admit when they say, **is this not he whom they seek to kill?** Accordingly, they are amazed, considering the evil intentions of their leaders.

1053. Again, they were amazed that Christ was openly teaching; so they said: **and behold, he speaks openly**, i.e., Christ was teaching, an indication of the secure possession of the truth, **I have spoken publicly** (John 18:20), **and they say nothing to him**, held back by divine power. For it is a characteristic of God's power that he prevents the hearts of evil men from carrying out their evil plans. *When the Lord is pleased with the way a man is living he will make his enemies be at peace with him* (Prov 16:7); and again, *the heart of the king is in the hand of the Lord; he turns it wherever he wills* (Prov 21:1).

1054. We see their conjecture when he says, **have the rulers truly known that this is the Christ?** As if to say: before, they sought to kill him; but now that they have found him, they do not say anything to him. Still, the leaders had

propria sententia, quia, ut dicitur I Cor. II, 8: *si enim cognovissent, numquam Dominum gloriae crucifixissent*: sed repressi a virtute divina.

1055. Obiectio autem eorum contra suspicionem subditur *sed hunc scimus unde sit*, quasi hoc modo arguentes: Christus debet habere occultam originem; sed iste habet originem manifestam: ergo non est Christus. In quo apparet eorum amentia, quia supposito quod quidam etiam principes crederent Christo, non tamen eorum sententiam sequuntur, sed aliam corruptam proferunt; Ez. V, 5: *ista est Ierusalem, in medio gentium posui eam*. Sciebant enim Christum esse ex Maria secundum originem, sed tamen eius modum ignorabant; Mt. XIII, 55: *nonne pater eius est Ioseph, et mater eius dicitur Maria?*

1056. Sed cum dicatur Mich. V, 2: *ex te exiet dux, qui regat populum meum Israel*: quare dicunt **Christus cum venerit, nemo scit unde sit?**

Respondeo. Dicendum quod hoc habent ex verbo Is. LIII, 8: *generationem eius quis enarrabit?* Sic ergo et ex prophetis habent ut sciant unde sit, secundum humanam originem; et ex eis habent quod nesciant, secundum divinam generationem.

1057. Consequenter cum dicit **clamabat ergo Iesus in templo**, manifestat suam originem, et

primo ostendit secundum quid sua origo sit nota, et secundum quid sit ignota;

secundo docet quomodo ad eius notitiam possumus pervenire, ibi *ego scio eum* etc.

Circa primum duo facit.

Primo ostendit quid de origine eius sciebant;

secundo quid circa ipsum ignorabant, ibi *et a meipso non veni*.

1058. Noverant autem de Iesu originem suam: et ideo dicit **clamabat Iesus**. Clamor autem ex magnitudine affectus procedit. Et ideo quandoque importat turbulentiam animi interius concitati: et hoc modo non competit Christo, de quo scriptum est Is. XLII, 2: *non clamabit, nec accipiet personam, nec audietur vox eius foris*; Eccle. IX, 17: *verba sapientium audiuntur in silentio*. Quandoque importat magnitudinem devotionis, secundum illud Ps. CXIX, 1: *ad Dominum, cum tribularer, clamavi*. Quandoque vero cum hoc magnitudinem dicendorum, secundum illud Is. VI, v. 3: *Seraphim clamabant alter ad alterum, et dicebant: sanctus, sanctus, sanctus Dominus Deus exercituum*; Prov. VIII, 1: *numquid non sapientia foris clamitat, et prudentia dat vocem suam?* Et sic praedicatores clamare monentur Is. LVIII, 1: *clama, ne cesses, quasi tuba exalta vocem tuam*. Et sic clamabat hic Dominus, **docens in templo, et dicens**, hoc scilicet **me scitis**, secundum faciem noscitis, et **unde sim scitis**, scilicet corporaliter; Bar. III, v. 38: *post haec in terris*

not changed their opinion about Christ: *if they had known, they would never have crucified the Lord of glory* (1 Cor 2:8), but were restrained by divine power.

1055. Their objection to this conjecture is then added: **but we know where this man comes from**. As if to argue: the Christ should have a hidden origin; but the origin of this man is known; therefore, he is not the Christ. This shows their folly, for granted that some of their leaders believed Christ, they did not follow their opinion, but offered another, which was false. *This is Jerusalem; I have set her in the midst of the nations* (Ezek 5:5). For they knew that Christ took his origin from Mary, but they did not know the way this came about: *isn't Joseph his father, and Mary his mother?* (Matt 13:55).

1056. Why did they say, **but when the Christ comes, no man knows where he comes from**, since it is said: *out of you will come a leader, who will rule my people Israel?* (Mic 5:2).

I answer that they took this opinion from Isaiah, who said: *who will make known his origin?* (Isa 53:8). Thus, they knew from the prophets where he was from, according to his human origin; and they also knew from them that they did not know it, according to his divine origin.

1057. Then, at **Jesus, therefore, teaching in the temple, cried out**, he shows his origin.

First, he shows in what sense his origin is known, and in what sense it is not known; in the

second place, he shows how we can acquire a knowledge of his origin, at **I know him, and if I said, I do not know him, then I would be like you, a liar**.

He does two things about the first.

First, he shows what they knew about his origin;

second, what they did not know about it, at **I have not come from myself**.

1058. They did know the origin of Jesus; and so he says that he **cried out**. Now a cry comes from some great emotion. Sometimes it indicates the upheaval of a soul in interior distress; and in this sense it does not apply to Christ: *he will not cry out* (Isa 42:2); *the words of the wise are heard in silence* (Eccl 9:17). Sometimes it implies great devotion, as in, *in my trouble I cried to the Lord* (Ps 119:1). And sometimes, along with this, it signifies that what is to be said is important, as in, *the seraphim cried to each other and said: holy, holy, holy, is the Lord God of hosts* (Isa 6:3); and in, *does not wisdom cry out?* (Prov 8:1). This is the way preachers are encouraged to cry out: *cry out, do not stop! Raise you voice like a trumpet* (Isa 58:1). This is the way Christ cried out here, **teaching in the temple, saying**. And he said: **you know me**, according to appearances, **and you know from where I come**, that is, as to my bodily existence: *after this he was seen on earth* (Bar 3:38). For they knew that he was born from Mary in Bethlehem, and brought up in Nazareth; but they did not know about the virgin birth, and that he had

visus est. Sciebant enim, quod ex Maria natus erat in Bethlehem, et nutritus in Nazareth; sed nesciebant virginis partum, et quod per Spiritum Sanctum conceptus esset, ut dicit Augustinus. Excepto virginis partu, totum noverant in Iesu, quod ad hominem pertinet.

1059. Nesciebant autem de ipso originem occultam: unde dicit *et a me ipso non veni*, et primo insinuat suam originem; secundo ostendit eam eis esse occultam.

Origo autem sua est a Patre ab aeterno: unde dicit *a me ipso non veni*, quasi dicat: ante fui secundum divinitatem, quam in mundo venirem per humanitatem; infra VIII, 58: *antequam Abraham fieret, ego sum.* Alias non conveniret ei venire, nisi ante fuisset; et tamen hoc ipsum quod veni, *non veni a me ipso*: quia Filius non est a se, sed a Patre; infra XVI, 28: *exivi a Patre, et veni in mundum.* Praenuntiata autem fuit eius origo a Patre, qui eum promisit mittere; Ex. IV, 13: *obsecro, Domine, mitte quem missurus es*; Is. c. XIX, 20: *mittam eis salvatorem et propugnatorem qui liberet eos.* Et ideo dicit *sed est verus qui misit me*, quasi dicat: non aliunde veni, sed ab eo qui promisit, et promissum adimplevit, quia verus est; Rom. III, v. 4: *est autem Deus verax*, et ideo docet me veritatem loqui, quia a vero missus sum.

Est autem eis occulta, quia nesciunt eum qui misit me; unde dicit *quem vos nescitis.*

1060. Sed cum omnis homo, licet in carne natus, sit a Deo, videtur quod possit dicere: ego sum a Deo, et per consequens: me scitis unde sim.

Responsio. Dicendum, secundum Hilarium, quod Filius aliter est *a* Deo quam alii homines, quia sic est a Deo quod etiam est Deus: unde Deus est principium eius consubstantiale. Alii vero sic sunt a Deo quod tamen non sunt ex illo. Sic ergo Filius unde sit ignoratur, quia natura ex qua est, nescitur; sed homines unde sint non ignoratur, quia unde sit ignorari non potest quidquid subsistit ex aliquo.

1061. Consequenter cum dicit *ego scio eum*, docet quomodo perveniri possit ad notitiam eius a quo est. Ab illo enim oportet nos addiscere aliquid qui scit illud; solus autem Filius novit Patrem, et ideo dicit: si vultis notitiam eius qui misit me habere, oportet quod habeatis a me, quia *ego* solus *scio eum*. Et ideo

     primo ostendit suam scientiam;

     secundo scientiae suae perfectionem;

     tertio scientiae suae rationem.

1062. Suam scientiam ostendit cum dicit *ego scio eum* etc. Verum est autem, quod *omnes homines vident eum*, ut dicitur Iob c. XXXVI, 25, sed tamen diversimode, quia homines in vita ista vident eum per creaturas; Rom. I, 20: *invisibilia Dei per ea quae facta sunt, intellecta*

been conceived through the Holy Spirit, as Augustine says. With the exception of the virgin birth, they knew everything about Jesus that pertained to his humanity.

1059. They did not know his hidden origin; and so he says: *and I have not come from myself.* First, he gives his origin; and second, he shows that it is hidden from them.

His origin is from the Father, from eternity. And so he says: *I have not come from myself*, as if to say: before I came into the world through my humanity, I existed according to my divinity; *before Abraham was made, I am* (John 8:58). For he could not have come unless he already was. And although I have come, *I have not come from myself*, because the Son is not of himself, but from the Father. *I came forth from the Father, and have come into the world* (John 16:28). Indeed, his origin was foretold by the Father, who promised to send him: *I beg you, O Lord, send him whom you are going to send* (Exod 4:13); *I will send them a savior and a defender, to free them* (Isa 19:20). And so he says: *the one who sent me is truthful*, as if to say: I have not come from another but from him who promised and kept his promise, as he is truthful: *God is truthful* (Rom 3:4). Consequently, he teaches me to speak the truth, because I have been sent by one who is truthful.

But they do not know this, because they do not know him who sent me; and so he says: *whom you do not know.*

1060. But since every man, although born in a bodily condition, is from God, it seems that Christ could say that he is from God; and consequently, that they do know where he comes from.

I answer, according to Hilary, that the Son is *from* God in a different way than others: for he is from God in such a way that he is also God; and so God is his consubstantial principle. But others are from God, but in such a way that they are not out of him. Thus, it is not known where the Son is from because the nature out of which he is, is not known. But where men are from is not unknown: for if something exists out of nothing, where it is from cannot be unknown.

1061. Then when he says, *I know him*, he teaches us how to know him from whom he is. For if a thing is to be learned, it must be learned from one who knows it. But only the Son knows the Father. And so he says: if you wish to know him who sent me, you must acquire this knowledge from me, because *I* alone *know him.*

     First, he shows that he knows him;

     second, he shows the perfection of his knowledge; and

     third, the nature of his knowledge.

1062. He shows that he knows him when he says, *I know him.* Now it is true that *all men see him* (Job 36:25), but they do not see him in the same way, for in this life we see him through the intermediary of creatures: *the invisible things of God are clearly known through the things that have*

conspiciuntur. Ideo dicitur I Cor. XIII, 12: *videmus nunc per speculum in aenigmate.* angeli vero et beati in Patria, vident eum immediate per essentiam; Matth. XVIII, 10: *angeli eorum in caelis semper vident faciem Patris mei qui in caelis est*; I Io. III, 2: *videbimus eum sicuti est.* Sed Filius Dei videt eum excellentius omnibus, scilicet visione comprehensionis; supra I, 18: **Deum nemo vidit unquam**, scilicet comprehendendo; **unigenitus Filius, qui est in sinu Patris, ipse enarravit**; Matth. XI, 27: *neque Patrem quis novit nisi Filius.* Et de hac visione loquitur hic, dicens **ego scio eum**, scilicet notitia comprehensionis.

1063. Perfectionem vero scientiae suae ostendit dicens **si dixero quia nescio eum, ero similis vobis, mendax.** Quod quidem introducit propter duo: nam creaturae intellectuales sciunt eum, sed longe, et imperfecte, quia *unusquisque intuetur eum procul*, ut dicitur Iob XXXVI, 25. Veritas enim divina excedit omnem cognitionem; I Io. III, 20: *Deus maior est corde nostro.* Quicumque ergo Deum cognoscit, potest absque mendacio dicere **nescio eum**: quia non cognoscit eum quantum cognoscibilis est. Filius autem Deum Patrem perfectissime cognoscit, sicut perfectissime ipse se novit: unde non potest dicere **nescio eum**.

Item quia cognitio Dei, et maxime quae est per gratiam, potest perdi; secundum illud Ps. CV, 21: *obliti sunt Deum qui redemit eos*, unde possunt dicere **nescio eum**, quamdiu sunt in vita ista: quia nemo scit utrum odio vel amore dignus sit. Filius autem inamissibilem notitiam habet de Patre, unde non potest dicere **nescio eum**.

In hoc autem quod dicit **ero similis vobis, mendax**, debet accipi similitudo per contrarium. Non enim essent mendaces, si dicerent se nescire Deum; sed potius si dicerent se Deum cognoscere, cum eum ignorent. Si autem Christus diceret se eum non nosse, cum noscat, esset mendax. Est ergo sensus verbi **si dixero quia nescio eum**, cum sciam eum, **ero similis vobis, mendax**, qui dicitis vos cognoscere eum, cum tamen ipsum ignoretis.

1064. Sed numquid non poterat Christus dicere **nescio eum**? Videtur quod sic, quia poterat movere labia, et proferre verba huiusmodi: ergo potest esse mendax.

Sed dicendum, quod Christus huiusmodi verba protulit, et tamen non fuit mendax: quod intelligendum est sic: si dixero: **nescio eum**, cum assertione, ita scilicet quod corde credam quod profero ore. Asserere autem falsum pro vero, ex duplici defectu contingit. Scilicet ex defectu cognitionis in intellectu; et hic defectus non poterat esse in Christo, cum sit Dei sapientia, ut dicitur I Cor. I, 30. Item ex defectu rectae voluntatis in affectu; qui similiter in Christo esse non poterat, cum sit Dei virtus, ut ibidem dicitur. Unde non poterat dicere

been made (Rom 1:20). Thus we read: *now we see in a mirror, in an obscure manner* (1 Cor 13:12). But the angels and the blessed in heaven see him through his essence:—*their angels in heaven always see the face of my Father who is in heaven* (Matt 18:10): *we shall see him as he is* (1 John 3:2). The Son of God, on the other hand, sees him in a more excellent way than all, that is, with a comprehensive or all-inclusive vision: **no one has ever seen God**, i.e., in a comprehensive way; **the only begotten Son, who is in the bosom of the Father, has made him known** (John 1:18); *no one knows the Father but the Son* (Matt 11:27). It is of this vision that he is speaking of here, when he says: **I know him**, with a comprehensive knowledge.

1063. He shows the perfection of his knowledge when he says: **and if I said, I do not know him, then I would be like you, a liar.** This is mentioned for two reasons. Intellectual creatures do know God, though from a distance and imperfectly, for *all men see him, from a distance* (Job 36:25). For divine truth transcends all our knowledge: *God is greater than our hearts* (1 John 3:20). Therefore, whoever knows God can say without lying: **I do not know him**, because he does not know him to the full extent that he is knowable. But the Son knows God the Father most perfectly, just as he knows himself most perfectly. Thus he cannot say: **I do not know him**.

Again, because our knowledge of God, especially that which comes through grace, can be lost—*they forgot God, who saved them* (Ps 105:21)—men can say, **I do not know him**, as long as they are in this present life: because no one knows whether he deserves love or hatred. The Son, on the other hand, has a knowledge of the Father that cannot be lost; so he cannot say: **I do not know him**.

We should understand, **I would be like you**, as a reverse likeness. For they would not be lying if they said they did not know God; but they would be if they said that they did know him, since they did not know him. But if Christ said that he did not know him, he would be lying, since he did know him. So the meaning of this statement is this: **if I said, I do not know him**, then since I really do know him, **I would be like you, a liar**, who say that you know him, although you do not.

1064. Could not Christ have said: **I do not know him**? It seems he could, since he could have moved his lips and said the words. And so he could have lied.

I reply that Christ did say this and still was not lying. We should explain it this way: if he were to say, **I do not know him**, declaratively, meaning, I believe in my heart what I profess by my lips. Now to say as the truth what is false comes from two defects: from a defect of knowledge in the intellect; and Christ could not have this since he is the wisdom of God (1 Cor 1:30); or it could come from a defect of right will in the affections; and this could not be in Christ either since he is the power of God, according to the same text. Thus he could not say the words **I do not know him**,

asserendo *nescio eum*. Nec tamen conditionalis est falsa, quamvis antecedens sit impossibile, et consequens.

1065. Ratio autem singularis et perfectae scientiae Christi ponitur, cum dicit *sed ego scio eum, quia ab ipso sum, et ipse me misit*. Omnis enim cognitio est per aliquam similitudinem, cum nihil cognoscatur nisi prout similitudo cogniti est in cognoscente; omne autem quod procedit ab aliquo, habet eius similitudinem a quo procedit, unde omnes vere cognoscentes, secundum diversum gradum processionis eorum a Deo, habent diversimode eius cognitionem. Anima autem rationalis, Dei cognitionem habet, secundum quod similitudinem eius participat imperfectiori quodam modo ab aliis creaturis intellectualibus. angelus, quia expressiorem Dei similitudinem habet, cum sit signaculum similitudinis, manifestius Deum cognoscit. Filius autem perfectissimam Patris similitudinem habet, cum sit eiusdem essentiae et virtutis cum ipso; et ideo perfectissime cognoscit, ut dictum est. Et ideo dicit *sed ego scio eum*, scilicet quantum cognoscibilis est. Et huius ratio est *quia ab ipso sum*, quasi habens eamdem naturae essentiam cum ipso per consubstantialitatem. Unde, sicut ipse perfecte se novit per essentiam suam, ita et per eamdem essentiam *ego scio eum*, perfecte. Sed ne hoc referatur ad missionem qua venit in mundum, continuo subiecit *et ipse me misit*: ut sic quod dicit *ab ipso sum*, referatur ad aeternam generationem, per quam consubstantialis est Patris. Ex quo habetur proprietas cognitionis de proprietate generationis.

Per hoc vero quod dicit *ipse me misit*, insinuat Patrem auctorem incarnationis; Gal. IV, v. 4: *misit Deus Filium suum factum ex muliere, factum sub lege*. Sicut autem per hoc quod Filius est a Patre, perfectam Patris cognitionem habet; ita etiam per hoc quod anima Christi singulariter est unita Verbo, habet singularem et excellentiorem prae aliis creaturis cognitionem Dei, licet eum non comprehendat. Et ideo potest Christus secundum humanam naturam dicere: scio eum excellentius prae omnibus creaturis, non tamen comprehendendo.

1066. Consequenter cum dicit *quaerebant ergo eum apprehendere*, agitur de effectu doctrinae, et

primo quantum ad turbas;

secundo quantum ad Pharisaeos, ibi *audierunt Pharisaei turbam murmurantem*.

Circa primum duo facit.

Primo ponit effectum doctrinae in turbis malevolis;

secundo in turbis devotis, ibi *de turba autem multi crediderunt in eum*.

Circa primum tria facit.

Primo innuit turbarum iniquum propositum;

declaratively. Yet this entire conditional statement is not false, although both its parts are impossible.

1065. The reason for this singular and perfect knowledge of Christ is given when he says: *I do know him, because I am from him, and he has sent me*. Now all knowledge comes about through some likeness, since nothing is known except insofar as there is a likeness of the known in the knower. But whatever proceeds from something has a likeness to that from which it proceeds; and so, all who truly know have a varied knowledge of God according to the different degrees of their procession from him. The rational soul has a knowledge of God insofar as it participates in a likeness to him in a more imperfect way than other intellectual creatures. An angel, because it has a more explicit likeness to God, being a stamp of resemblance, knows God more clearly. But the Son has the most perfect likeness to the Father, since he has the same essence and power as he does; and so he knows him most perfectly, as was said. And so he says: but *I know him*, that is, to the extent that he is knowable. And the reason for this is *because I am from him*, having the same essence with him through consubstantiality. Thus, just as he knows himself perfectly through his essence, so *I know him* perfectly through the same essence. And so that we do not understand these words as referring to his being sent into this world, he at once adds, because *he has sent me*. Consequently, the statement, *I am from him*, refers to his eternal generation, through which he is consubstantial with the Father.

But then when he says, *because he has sent me*, he is saying that the Father is the author of the incarnation: *God sent his Son, made from a woman, made under the law* (Gal 4:4). Now just as the Son has a perfect knowledge of the Father because he is from the Father, so because the soul of Christ is united to the Word in a unique way, it has a unique and more excellent knowledge of God than other creatures, although it does not comprehend him. And so Christ can say, according to his human nature: I know him in a more excellent way than other creatures do, but without comprehending him.

1066. Then, at *they sought therefore to apprehend him*, he considers the effect of his teaching.

First, on the people;

then on the Pharisees, at *the Pharisees heard the people murmuring*.

He does two things with the first.

First, he shows the effect of this teaching on those of the people who were ill-willed;

second, on those who were favorable, at *but of the people many believed in him*.

He does three things concerning the first.

First, he mentions the evil intention of the people;

secundo propositi implendi impedimentum; et

tertio impedimenti rationem.

1067. Iniquitas autem propositi manifestatur cum dicit *quaerebant ergo eum apprehendere*. Quia enim dixerat Dominus *quem vos nescitis*, irati sunt Iudaei quasi simularent eum scire, et ideo iniqua proponebant, scilicet eum apprehendere, ad crucifigendum et occidendum, secundum illud Ps. LXX, 11: *persequimini, et comprehendite eum*.

Sunt autem aliqui qui Christum in se habentes, quaerunt tamen pie apprehendere; Cant. VII, 8: *ascendam in palmam, et apprehendam fructus eius*. Unde et Apostolus dicebat, Phil. III, 12: *sequor, si quo modo apprehendam, in quo et comprehensus sum a Christo Iesu*.

1068. Impedimentum propositi ponit cum dicit *nemo misit in illum manus*. Invisibiliter enim eorum furor refrenatus est et repressus. Per quod patet quod voluntas nocendi est unicuique a se, sed nocendi potestas a Deo, quod patet Iob I et II, ubi satan non potuit Iob affligere nisi quantum permissum est sibi a Deo.

1069. Ratio impedimenti assignatur *quia nondum venerat hora eius*.

Unde sciendum est, quod, secundum illud Eccle. VIII, 6: *omni negotio tempus est et opportunitas*. Tempus autem unicuique rei ex sua causa determinatur. Quia ergo corporalium effectuum causa sunt corpora caelestia, ideo in his quae corporaliter aguntur, hora determinatur ex corporibus caelestibus; anima vero, cum secundum intellectum et rationem nullis corporibus caelestibus subiaceat, cum quantum ad hoc temporales causas transcendat, non habet horas determinatas ex corporibus caelestibus; sed ex causa eius, scilicet Deo, qui dispensat quid quo tempore sit faciendum; Eccli. XXXIII, 7: *quare dies diem superat; et iterum lux lucem, et annus annum a sole? A Domini scientia separati sunt, facto sole, et praeceptum custodiente*. Multo ergo minus in Christo determinatur hora ab ipsis corporibus.

Sic ergo intelligenda est hora eius, non ex necessitate fatali, sed a tota Trinitate praefinita: nam, ut dicit Augustinus, *hoc nec de te credendum est; quanto magis de illo per quem factus es? Si tua hora voluntas illius est, scilicet Dei; hora illius, quae est nisi voluntas sua? Non ergo horam dixit qua cogeretur mori, sed qua dignaretur occidi*. Supra II, 4: *nondum venit hora mea*; infra XIII, v. 1: *sciens Iesus quia venit hora eius ut transeat ex hoc mundo ad Patrem* etc.

1070. Consequenter cum dicit *de turba autem multi crediderunt in eum*, ponit effectum doctrinae in turbis devotis. Et

second, that they were hindered in carrying out their plan; and

third, he mentions the reason why they were hindered.

1067. He presents their evil intention when he says, *they sought therefore to apprehend him*. Because our Lord said to them, *whom you do not know*, they became angry, feigning that they did know him. And so they formed the evil plan of seizing him, so that they could crucify and kill him: *go after him, and seize him* (Ps 70:11).

Yet there are some who have Christ within themselves, and still seek to seize him in a reverent manner: *I will go up into the palm tree and seize its fruit* (Song 7:8). And so the Apostle says: *I will go after it to seize it, wherein I am also apprehended by Christ Jesus* (Phil 3:12).

1068. He mentions that they were hindered in their plans when he says, but *no man laid hands on him*: for their rage was invisibly checked and restrained. This shows that a person has the will to inflict injury from himself, while the power to inflict injury is from God. This is clear from the first chapters of Job, where satan was unable to torment Job except to the extent that he was permitted to do so by God.

1069. The reason they were hindered was because *his hour had not yet come*.

Here we should note that *there is a time and fitness for everything* (Eccl 8:6). However, the time for anything is determined by its cause. Therefore, because the heavenly bodies are the cause of physical effects, the time for those things that act in a physical way is determined by the heavenly bodies. The soul, on the other hand, since it is not subject to any heavenly body in its intellect and reason, for in this respect it transcends temporal causes, does not have times determined by the heavenly bodies; rather, its times are determined by its cause, that is, God, who decrees what is to be done and at what time: *why is one day better than another? . . . they are differentiated by the knowledge of the Lord* (Sir 33:7). Much less, therefore, is Christ's time determined by these bodies.

Accordingly, his hour must be regarded as fixed not by fatal necessity, but by the entire Trinity. For as Augustine says: *you should not believe this about yourself; and how much less should you believe it about he who made you? If your hour is his will, that is, God's, what is his hour but his own will? Therefore, he was not speaking here of the hour in which he would be forced to die, but rather of the hour in which he thought it fitting to be killed. My hour has not yet come* (John 2:4); *Jesus knowing that his hour was come, that he should pass out of this world to the Father* (John 13:1).

1070. Then, at *but of the people many believed in him*, he mentions the effect his teaching had on those who were favorable.

primo ponitur eorum fides, *quia multi de turba crediderunt in eum*. Non dicit de principibus: quia quanto maiores erant, tanto magis erant elongati, et ideo in eis sapientia locum non habebat, quia, ut dicitur Prov. XI, v. 2: *ubi humilitas, ibi sapientia*. Turba autem, quia suam aegritudinem cito vidit, Domini medicinam sine dilatione cognovit; Mt. c. XI, 25: *abscondisti haec a sapientibus et prudentibus, et revelasti ea parvulis*. Et propter hoc in principio humiles et pauperes conversi sunt ad Christum; I Cor. I, 28: *ignobilia et contemptibilia mundi elegit Deus, et ea quae non sunt, ut ea quae sunt destrueret*.

Secundo ponit motivum ad fidem cum dicit *Christus cum venerit, numquid plura signa faciet quam quae hic facit?* Prophetatum enim erat quod Christus in adventu suo miracula multa esset facturus; Is. XXXV, 4: *Deus ipse veniet, et salvabit nos: tunc aperientur oculi caecorum, et aures surdorum patebunt* etc. Et ideo videntes miracula quae Christus faciebat, inducebantur ad fidem eius. Sed tamen fides eorum infirma erat, quia non a doctrina, sed a signis moventur ad credendum ei; cum tamen ipsi, qui fideles iam erant, et per legem instructi, magis a doctrina moveri debuissent, nam ut dicitur I Cor. XIV, 22: *signa data sunt infidelibus, prophetiae autem non infidelibus, sed fidelibus*. Secundo quia adhuc videntur alium Christum expectare; unde dicunt *Christus cum venerit, numquid plura signa faciet quam quae hic facit*? Unde patet quod non credebant in Christum, sicut in Deum, sed sicut in aliquem iustum virum, seu prophetam. Vel, secundum Augustinum, syllogizant: *Christus cum venerit, numquid plura signa faciet*? Quasi dicant: Christus promittitur venturus, sed ipse non plura signa faciet quam hic facit: ergo vel ipse est Christus, vel erunt plures Christi.

1071. Consequenter cum dicit *audierunt Pharisaei turbam murmurantem de illo haec*, ponitur effectus in Pharisaeis. Et, ut Chrysostomus dicit, Christus multa dixit, et tamen non sunt moti contra eum. Quando autem vident turbam ei acquiescere, statim concitantur contra eum, et insanientes, eum occidere cupiebant. Ex quo patet quod sabbati solutio non erat vera causa odii eorum sed hoc eos maxime mordebat quod turbae Christum glorificabant. Et hoc patet infra c. XII, 19: *videtis quia nihil proficimus? Ecce totus mundus post eum vadit*. Quia vero ipsi Christum capere non audebant, timentes periculum, ministros mittunt, tamquam periculis expositos.

First, he shows their faith: *but of the people many believed in him*. He does not say, of the leaders, because the higher their rank, the further away they were from him. So there was no room in them for wisdom: *where there is humility, there is wisdom* (Prov 11:2). But the people, because they were quick to see their own sickness, immediately recognized our Lord's medicine: *you have hidden these things from the wise and the prudent, and have revealed them to little ones* (Matt 11:25). This is why in the beginning, it was the poor and the humble who were converted to Christ: *God chose what is lowly and despised in the world, and things that are not, to destroy those things that are* (1 Cor 1:28).

Second, he gives the motive for their faith when he says, *when the Christ comes, will he do more miracles than what this man does?* For it had been prophesied that when the Christ came, he would work many miracles: *God himself will come, and save us. Then the eyes of the blind will be opened, and the ears of the deaf will hear* (Isa 35:4). And so when they saw the miracles Christ was accomplishing, they were led to believe. Yet their faith was weak, because they were led to believe him not by his teaching, but by his miracles; whereas, since they were already believers, and instructed by the law, they should have been influenced more by his teaching: *signs were given to unbelievers; while prophecies were given to believers, not to unbelievers* (1 Cor 14:22). Second, their faith was weak because they seemed to be expecting another Christ; thus they say: *when the Christ comes, will he do more miracles than what this man does?* From this it is obvious that they did not believe in Christ as in God, but as in some just man or prophet. Or, according to Augustine, they were reasoning this way: *when the Christ comes, will he do more miracles than what this man does?* As if to say: we were promised that the Christ would come. But he will not work more signs than this man is doing. Therefore, either he is the Christ, or there will be several Christs.

1071. Then when he says, *the Pharisees heard the people saying these things concerning him*, we see the effect this had on the Pharisees. And as Chrysostom says, Christ said many things, and yet the Pharisees were not aroused against him. But when they saw that the people were accepting him, they were immediately fired up against him; and in their madness they wanted to kill him. This shows that the real reason why they hated him was not that he broke the sabbath; what provoked them the most was the fact that the people were honoring Christ. And this is clear below: *do you see that we accomplish nothing? Behold, the whole world is gone after him* (John 12:19). Because they were afraid of the danger they did not dare to seize Christ themselves, but they sent their officers, who were used to such things.

Lecture 4

7:33 Dixit ergo eis Iesus: adhuc modicum tempus vobiscum sum: et vado ad eum qui me misit. [n. 1073]

7:34 Quaeretis me, et non invenietis. Et ubi ego sum, vos non potestis venire. [n. 1076]

7:35 Dixerunt ergo Iudaei ad semetipsos: quo hic iturus est, quia non inveniemus eum? Numquid in dispersionem gentium iturus est, et docturus gentes? [n. 1079]

7:36 Quis est hic sermo quem dixit: quaeretis me, et non invenietis: et ubi sum ego, vos non potestis venire? [n. 1082]

7:33 εἶπεν οὖν ὁ Ἰησοῦς· ἔτι χρόνον μικρὸν μεθ᾽ ὑμῶν εἰμι καὶ ὑπάγω πρὸς τὸν πέμψαντά με.

7:34 ζητήσετέ με καὶ οὐχ εὑρήσετέ [με], καὶ ὅπου εἰμὶ ἐγὼ ὑμεῖς οὐ δύνασθε ἐλθεῖν.

7:35 εἶπον οὖν οἱ Ἰουδαῖοι πρὸς ἑαυτούς· ποῦ οὗτος μέλλει πορεύεσθαι ὅτι ἡμεῖς οὐχ εὑρήσομεν αὐτόν; μὴ εἰς τὴν διασπορὰν τῶν Ἑλλήνων μέλλει πορεύεσθαι καὶ διδάσκειν τοὺς Ἕλληνας;

7:36 τίς ἐστιν ὁ λόγος οὗτος ὃν εἶπεν· ζητήσετέ με καὶ οὐχ εὑρήσετέ [με], καὶ ὅπου εἰμὶ ἐγὼ ὑμεῖς οὐ δύνασθε ἐλθεῖν;

7:33 Jesus therefore said to them: yet a little while I am with you, and then I am going to him who sent me. [n. 1073]

7:34 You will seek me and will not find me; and where I am, you are not able to come. [n. 1076]

7:35 The Jews therefore said among themselves: where will he go that we will not find him? Will he go to the dispersed among the gentiles and teach the gentiles? [n. 1079]

7:36 What is this saying that he has said: you will seek me and will not find me; and where I am, you are not able to come? [n. 1082]

1072. Postquam posuit Dominus originis suae principium, hic consequenter insinuat suum terminum, quo scilicet iturus est per mortem, et

primo insinuatur terminus viae Christi;

secundo ponitur admiratio turbarum de sermonibus eius, ibi *dixerunt ergo Iudaei ad semetipsos* etc.

Circa primum tria facit.

Primo insinuat suae vitae terminum;

secundo praenuntiat futurum turbarum desiderium, ibi *quaeretis me, et non invenietis*;

tertio subdit eorum defectum, ibi *et ubi sum ego, vos non potestis venire*.

Circa primum duo facit.

Primo praenuntiat mortis suae dilationem;

secundo innuit quo iturus est per mortem, ibi *et vado ad patrem* etc.: et sic in primo ostendit suam potestatem; in secundo patiendi voluntatem.

1073. Potestatem quidem suam ostendit in dilatione mortis, quia, licet Iudaei quaererent eum apprehendere, non tamen hoc possunt, nisi Christus velit; infra X, 18: *nemo tollit animam meam; sed ego pono eam*. Et ideo *dixit eis Iesus: adhuc modicum tempus vobiscum sum*; quasi dicat: vultis me interficere, sed hoc non est positum in voluntate vestra, sed in voluntate mea: et ego determino quod *adhuc modicum tempus vobiscum sum*; et ideo parum expectate tempus. Hoc quod vultis modo facere, facturi estis: *adhuc* enim *modicum tempus vobiscum sum*. In quo quidem Dominus satisfacit primo quidem turbae quae eum reverebatur, faciens eam magis

1072. After our Lord told the principle of his origin, he then mentions his end, i.e., where he would go by dying.

First, the end of Christ's life is given;

second, we see that the people are puzzled by what he says, at *the Jews therefore said among themselves: where will he go that we will not find him?*

As to the first he does three things.

First, the end of his life is mentioned;

second, he predicts what they will desire in the future, at *you will seek me and will not find me*; and

third, he mentions one of their deficiencies, at *and where I am, you are not able to come*.

He does two things about the first.

First, he predicts the delay of his death until later; and

second, he states where he will go by dying, at *I go to the Father, and you shall see me no more* (John 16:5). And so, in the first, he shows his power; and in the second, his will to suffer.

1073. Our Lord shows his power by the delaying of his death until later; because, although the Jews wanted to seize him, they could not do this until Christ willed. *No man takes it away from me, but I lay it down of myself* (John 10:18). And so Jesus said: *yet a little while I am with you*. As if to say: you want to kill me; but this does not depend on your will, but on my will. And I have decided that *yet a little while I am with you*; so wait a while. You will do what you want to do, for *yet a little while I am with you*. These words of our Lord first of all satisfied those people who honored him, and made them more eager to listen to him because there was only a short time left to receive his

avidam ad audiendum, quasi parvo tempore derelicta, in quo possent hac doctrina potiri, ut Chrysostomus dicit. Infra XII, v. 36: *dum lucem habetis, credite in lucem.* Secundo vero turbae quae eum persequebatur, quasi dicat: non diu differtur desiderium vestrum de morte mea, unde patienter sustinete: quia *adhuc modicum.* Implere enim debeo dispensationem meam; praedicando scilicet, et miracula faciendo, et sic pervenire ad passionem; Lc. XIII, 32: *ite, et dicite vulpi illi, quia hodie et cras operor, et tertia die consummor.*

1074. Est autem triplex causa, quare Christus modico tempore voluit praedicare. Prima ad demonstrandum suam virtutem, quod in tam modico tempore totum mundum immutaret; Ps. LXXXIII, 11: *melior est dies una in atriis tuis super millia.*

Secunda est ad excitandum desiderium discipulorum, ut scilicet magis eum desiderarent quem modico tempore corporali praesentia habituri erant; Lc. XVII, 22: *venient dies in quibus desiderabitis unam diem Filii hominis.*

Tertia est ad augmentandum discipulorum spiritualem profectum. Cum enim Christi humanitas sit nobis via tendendi in Deum, ut dicitur infra XIV, 6: *ego sum via, veritas et vita,* non debemus in ea quiescere ut in termino, sed per eam debemus in Deum tendere. Ne ergo corda discipulorum ad Christum carnaliter affecta, in eo ut in homine quiescerent ideo Christus corporalem sui praesentiam ab eis cito subtraxit: unde dicebat, infra XVI, 7: *expedit vobis ut ego vadam;* II Cor. V, 16: *et si Christum secundum carnem novimus,* tunc scilicet quando corporaliter nobiscum erat, *sed nunc iam non novimus.*

1075. Voluntatem suae passionis ostendit cum dicit *et vado ad eum qui me misit,* quia spontaneus, scilicet per passionem; Is. c. LIII, 7: *oblatus est, quia ipse voluit;* Eph. c. V, 2: *obtulit semetipsum hostiam Deo in odorem suavitatis.* **Vado,** inquam, *ad Patrem qui misit me.* Et hoc convenienter: nam quaelibet res naturaliter redit ad suum principium; Eccle. I, 7: *ad locum unde exeunt flumina, revertuntur.* Infra XIII, 3: *sciens quia a Deo exivit, et ad Deum vadit.* Et iterum c. XVI, 5: *vado ad eum qui misit me.*

1076. Consequenter cum dicit *quaeretis me, et non invenietis,* praenuntiat Iudaeorum desiderium, quasi dicat: modicum est quod potestis mea doctrina frui; sed hoc modicum, quod modo respuitis, quandoque quaeretis, et non invenietis; Is. LV, 6: *quaerite Dominum dum inveniri potest;* et in Ps. LXVIII, 33: *quaerite Dominum,* scilicet in praesenti, *et vivet anima vestra.*

1077. Hoc autem quod dicit *quaeretis me, et non invenietis,* potest intelligi vel de inquisitione corporali Christi, vel de spirituali.

teaching, as Chrysostom says. *While you have the light, believe in the light* (John 12:36). Second, he satisfied those who were persecuting him. As if to say: your desire for my death will not be delayed long; so be patient, because it is a *little while.* For I must accomplish my mission: to preach, to perform miracles, and then to come to my passion. *Go and tell that fox that I will work today and tomorrow, and on the third day I will finish my course* (Luke 13:32).

1074. There are three reasons why Christ wished to preach for only a short time. First, to show his power, by transforming the entire world in such a brief time: *one day in your courts is better than a thousand elsewhere* (Ps 83:11).

Second, to arouse the desire of his disciples, i.e., to desire him more, him whose physical presence they would have for only a short time: *the days will come when you will desire to see one day of the Son of man* (Luke 17:22).

Third, to accelerate the spiritual progress of his disciples. For since the humanity of Christ is our way to God, as it says below, *I am the way, and the truth, and the life* (John 14:6), we should not rest in it as a goal, but through it tend to God. And so that the hearts of his disciples, which were moved by the physical presence of Christ, would not rest in him as man, he quickly took his physical presence from them; thus he said: *it is expedient to you that I go* (John 16:7); *if we knew Christ according to the flesh* i.e., when he was physically present to us *now we no longer know him in this way* (2 Cor 5:16).

1075. He shows his desire for his passion when he says, *then I am going to him who sent me* (John 16:5), that is, willingly, by my passion: *he was offered because it was his own will* (Isa 53:7); *he gave himself for us, an offering to God* (Eph 5:2). *Now I go,* I say, to the Father, *to him who sent me* (John 16:5). And this is appropriate, for everything naturally returns to its principle: *rivers return to the place from which they come* (Eccl 1:7); *knowing . . . that he came from God, and was going to God* (John 13:3). And again: *I am going to him who sent me* (John 16:5).

1076. When he says, *you will seek me and will not find me,* he is predicting what the Jews will desire in the times to come. As if to say: you can enjoy my teaching for a short time; but this brief time, which you are now rejecting, you will look for later, and you will not find it: *search for the Lord while he can be found* (Isa 55:6); and *seek the Lord* at the present time, *and your soul will live* (Ps 68:33).

1077. This statement, *you will seek me and will not find me,* can be understood either as a physical search for Christ or as a spiritual search.

Si vero intelligatur de corporali, sic, secundum Chrysostomum, quaesierunt eum quando filiae Ierusalem, scilicet mulieres, plangebant super eum, ut dicitur Lc. XXIII, 27, et credibile est hoc tunc multos alios passos esse. Nec est etiam a veritate remotum, quia imminente tribulatione Iudaeis, et praecipue cum civitas caperetur, memores Christi et miraculorum eius, desiderarent eius praesentiam, qua liberarentur; et secundum hoc dicendum est *quaeretis me*, idest meam praesentiam corporalem, *et non invenietis*.

Si vero intelligatur de spirituali, dicendum est, secundum Augustinum, quod eum quem noluerunt cognoscere praesentem, tunc postea quaesierunt cum videntes multitudinem credentem, compuncti de scelere mortis Christi, dixerunt Petro, Act. II, 37: *quid faciemus, viri fratres?* Sic ergo quaesierunt Christum quando crediderunt in eum suis sceleribus ignoscentem, quem viderunt ipsorum scelere morientem.

1078. Consequenter cum dicit *et ubi ego sum, vos non potestis venire*, ostendit eorum defectum. Nec dicit quo vado, quod esset magis consequens ad praemissa, scilicet *vado ad Patrem qui me misit*; sed dicit *ubi ego sum*, ut ostendat se Deum et hominem. Hominem quidem, inquantum vadit, infra XVI, 5: *vado ad eum qui me misit*, sed inquantum semper ibi erat Christus quo fuerat rediturus, ostendit se Deum; supra III, 13: *nemo ascendit in caelum nisi qui descendit de caelo*. Sic ergo, secundum Augustinum, *sicut Christus rediit ut nos non relinqueret, sic ad nos per assumptionem visibilis carnis descendit ut secundum invisibilem maiestatem etiam esset in caelo.*

Non autem dicit non invenietis, quia aliqui ituri erant; sed dicit *non potestis venire*, quamdiu scilicet sic dispositi estis. Nullus enim ad hereditatem caelestem pervenire potest, nisi sit heres Dei. Heres autem Dei aliquis efficitur per fidem Christi; supra I, 12: *dedit eis potestatem filios Dei fieri, his qui credunt in nomine eius*. Iudaei autem nondum in eum credebant; et ideo dicit *non potestis venire*. In Ps. XXIII, 3, requirit: *quis ascendet in montem Domini?* Et respondetur: *innocens manibus, et mundo corde*. Iudaei autem non erant mundo corde, nec innocentes manibus, quia volebant Christum interficere, ideo dicit: *non potestis* ascendere in montem Domini.

1079. Consequenter cum dicit *dixerunt ergo Iudaei ad semetipsos*, ponitur Iudaeorum admiratio, qui licet carnaliter de Christo saperent, tamen ex parte credebant.

Et tria faciunt.

Primo admirantur;

If we understand it as a physical search, then, according to Chrysostom, this is the way he was sought by the daughters of Jerusalem, i.e., the women who cried for him (Luke 23:27); and no doubt many others were affected at the same time. It is not unreasonable to think that when trouble was near, especially when their city was being captured, the Jews remembered Christ and his miracles and wished that he were there to free them. And in this way, *you will seek me*, i.e., for me to be physically present, *and will not find me*.

If we understand this as a spiritual search for Christ, then we should say, as Augustine does, that although they refused to recognize Christ while he was among them, they later looked for him, after they had seen the people believe and had themselves been stung by the crime of his death; and they said to Peter: *brothers, what shall we do?* (Acts 2:37). In this way, they were looking for Christ whom they saw die as a result of their crime when they believed in him who forgave them.

1078. Then when he says, *and where I am, you are not able to come*, he points out one of their deficiencies. He does not say, and where I am going, which would be more in keeping with the earlier thought, *I am going*, to the Father, *to him who sent me* (John 16:5). He says rather, *where I am*, to show that he is both God and man. He is man insofar as he is going: *I am going to him who sent me* (John 16:5). But insofar as Christ had always been where he was about to return, he shows that he is God: *and no man has ascended into heaven, except he who descended from heaven* (John 3:13). And so, as Augustine says, *just as Christ returned in such a way as not to leave us, so he came down to us, when he assumed visible flesh, but in such a way as still to be in heaven according to his invisible greatness.*

He does not say, you will not find, because some were about to go; but he does say, *you are not able to come*, i.e., as long as you keep your present attitude; for no one can obtain the eternal inheritance, unless he is God's heir. And one becomes an heir of God by faith in Christ: *he gave them power to be made the sons of God, to those who believe in his name* (John 1:12). But the Jews did not yet believe in him; and so he says, you will not be able to come. In the Psalm it is asked: *who will ascend the mountain of the Lord?* And the answer given is: *those whose hands are innocent and whose hearts are clean* (Ps 23:3). But the hearts of the Jews were not clean, nor were their hands innocent, because they wanted to kill Christ. And so he says: *you are not able* to ascend the mountain of the Lord.

1079. Then, at *the Jews therefore said among themselves*, we see that this was bewildering to the Jews, who, although they thought of Christ in a worldly way, still did believe to a certain extent.

And three things happen here.

First, they are astonished;

secundo suspicantur; et

tertio contra suspicionem argumentantur.

1080. Admirantur quidem cum dicunt ad semetipsos *quo iturus est hic, quia non invenerimus eum?* Ut enim dictum est, hoc carnaliter intelligebant; I Cor. II, 14: *animalis homo non percipit ea quae sunt spiritus Dei.*

1081. Et ideo quod esset iturus, non quidem per mortem, sed corporaliter, ad aliquem locum quo eis non liceret ascendere, suspicantur super hoc, dicentes *numquid in dispersionem gentium iturus est, et docturus gentes?* Nam gentes alienatae erant a conversatione Iudaeorum; Eph. II, 12: *hospites testamentorum eratis alienati a conversatione Israel, promissionis spem non habentes, et sine Deo in hoc mundo.* Et ideo quasi eis exprobrantes, dicunt *in dispersionem gentium,* quae scilicet ubique disseminatae erant, et imperfecte ad invicem permixtae; Gen. X, 32: *hae sunt familiae Noe iuxta populos et nationes suas, et ab his divisae sunt gentes in terra post diluvium.* Sed populus Iudaeorum collectus erat loco, et cultu unius Dei, et observatione legis; Ps. CXLVI, 2: *aedificans Ierusalem Dominus, dispersiones Israelis congregabit.*

Nec dicunt quod iturus sit ad gentes quasi gentilis futurus, sed tamquam eas reducturus: unde subdunt *et docturus gentes.* Quod forte sumpserunt ex Is. XLIX, 6: *parum est mihi ut sis mihi servus ad suscitandas tribus Iacob, et faeces Israel convertendas: dedi te in lucem gentium, ut sis salus mea usque ad extremum terrae.* Quamvis autem isti non intelligerent ea quae dicunt, sicut nec Caiphas intellexit cum dixit: *expedit vobis ut unus homo moriatur, et non tota gens pereat,* tamen verum dicunt, et salutem gentium praedixerunt, ut Augustinus dicit, quod iturus esset ad gentes, non praesentia corporis, sed pedibus suis, scilicet apostolis. Misit enim ad nos membra sua, et fecit nos sua membra; infra X, 16: *alias oves habeo quae non sunt ex hoc ovili, et illas oportet me adducere . . . et fiet unum ovile, et unus pastor.* Et ideo Is. II, 3, dicitur in persona gentium: *docebit nos vias suas.*

1082. Obiiciunt autem contra ea quae suspicantur, dicentes *quis est hic sermo quem dixit: quaeretis me?* Quasi dicant: si dixisset quaeretis me, et non invenietis, et ubi sum ego, vos non potestis venire, poterat quidem intelligi quod iturus esset ad gentes; sed per hoc quod addidit *ubi ego sum non potestis venire,* videtur excludere hunc intellectum. Non enim impossibile est nobis ad gentes ire etc.

second, they form an opinion, and

third, they argue against their own opinion.

1080. They are perplexed when they say to each other: *where will he go that we will not find him?* For, as was said, they understood this in a physical way: *the sensual man does not perceive those things that pertain to the Spirit of God* (1 Cor 2:14).

1081. And so they came to the opinion that Christ was going to go in a physical way, not by dying, to some place where they would not be permitted to go. Thus they say: *will he go to the dispersed among the gentiles and teach the gentiles?* For the gentiles were separated from the way of life of the Jews: *separated from Israel's way of life, strangers to the covenants, without hope in the promise, and without God in this world* (Eph 2:12). And so they said, in a way reproaching him, to those dispersed among the gentiles, who had settled in many different places: *these are the families of Noah . . . and they settled among the nations on the earth after the flood* (Gen 10:32). But the Jewish people were united by place, by their worship of the one God, and by the observance of the law: *the Lord builds up Jerusalem, and he will gather the dispersed of Israel* (Ps 146:2).

They did not say that he would go to the gentiles to become a gentile himself, but to bring them back; and so they said, *and teach the gentiles.* They probably took this from Isaiah: *I have given you to be a light to the gentiles, to be my salvation to the ends of the earth* (Isa 49:6). However, even though they did not understand what they were saying just as Caiphas did not understand his own words: *it is expedient for you that one man should die for the people and that the whole nation should not perish* (John 11:50), what they said was true, and they were predicting the salvation of the gentiles, as Augustine says, for Christ would go to the gentiles, not in his own body, but by his feet, i.e., his apostles. For he sent his own members to us to make us his members. *And other sheep I have that are not of this fold: those also I must bring, and they will hear my voice, and there will be one fold and one shepherd* (John 10:16). And so Isaiah says, speaking for the gentiles: *he will teach us his ways* (Isa 2:3).

1082. Finally, they saw an objection to their own opinion when they said: *what is this saying that he has said: you will seek me?* As if to say: if he had said only, you will look for me, and you will not find me, we could think that he was going to the gentiles. But he seems to exclude this when he adds, *where I am, you are not be able to come,* for we can go to the gentiles.

Lecture 5

7:37 In novissimo autem die magno festivitatis stabat Iesus, et clamabat, dicens: si quis sitit, veniat ad me, et bibat. [n. 1084]

7:38 Qui credit in me, sicut dicit Scriptura, flumina de ventre eius fluent aquae vivae. [n. 1089]

7:39 Hoc autem dixit de Spiritu, quem accepturi erant credentes in eum. Nondum enim erat Spiritus datus, quia Iesus nondum erat glorificatus. [n. 1091]

7:40 Ex illa ergo hora turba cum audissent hos sermones eius, dicebant: hic est vere propheta. [n. 1098]

7:41 Alii dicebant: hic est Christus. Quidam autem dicebant: numquid a Galilaea venit Christus? [n. 1099]

7:42 Nonne Scriptura dicit: quia ex semine David, et de Bethlehem castello, ubi erat David, venit Christus? [n. 1101]

7:43 Dissensio itaque facta est in turba propter eum. [n. 1102]

7:44 Quidam autem ex ipsis volebant apprehendere eum; sed nemo misit super eum manus. [n. 1104]

7:45 Venerunt ergo ministri ad pontifices et Pharisaeos, et dixerunt eis illi: quare non adduxistis illum? [n. 1106]

7:46 Responderunt ministri: numquam sic locutus est homo, sicut hic loquitur. [n. 1108]

7:47 Responderunt ergo eis Pharisaei: numquid et vos seducti estis? [n. 1109]

7:48 Numquid ex principibus aliquis credidit in eum, aut ex Pharisaeis? [n. 1111]

7:49 Sed turba haec quae non novit legem, maledicti sunt. [n. 1112]

7:50 Dixit Nicodemus ad eos, ille qui venit ad eum nocte, qui unus erat ex ipsis: [n. 1113]

7:37Ἐν δὲ τῇ ἐσχάτῃ ἡμέρᾳ τῇ μεγάλῃ τῆς ἑορτῆς εἱστήκει ὁ Ἰησοῦς καὶ ἔκραξεν λέγων· ἐάν τις διψᾷ ἐρχέσθω πρός με καὶ πινέτω.

7:38 ὁ πιστεύων εἰς ἐμέ, καθὼς εἶπεν ἡ γραφή, ποταμοὶ ἐκ τῆς κοιλίας αὐτοῦ ῥεύσουσιν ὕδατος ζῶντος.

7:39 τοῦτο δὲ εἶπεν περὶ τοῦ πνεύματος ὃ ἔμελλον λαμβάνειν οἱ πιστεύσαντες εἰς αὐτόν· οὔπω γὰρ ἦν πνεῦμα, ὅτι Ἰησοῦς οὐδέπω ἐδοξάσθη.

7:40 Ἐκ τοῦ ὄχλου οὖν ἀκούσαντες τῶν λόγων τούτων ἔλεγον· οὗτός ἐστιν ἀληθῶς ὁ προφήτης·

7:41 ἄλλοι ἔλεγον· οὗτός ἐστιν ὁ χριστός, οἱ δὲ ἔλεγον· μὴ γὰρ ἐκ τῆς Γαλιλαίας ὁ χριστὸς ἔρχεται;

7:42 οὐχ ἡ γραφὴ εἶπεν ὅτι ἐκ τοῦ σπέρματος Δαυὶδ καὶ ἀπὸ Βηθλέεμ τῆς κώμης ὅπου ἦν Δαυὶδ ἔρχεται ὁ χριστός;

7:43 σχίσμα οὖν ἐγένετο ἐν τῷ ὄχλῳ δι' αὐτόν·

7:44 τινὲς δὲ ἤθελον ἐξ αὐτῶν πιάσαι αὐτόν, ἀλλ' οὐδεὶς ἐπέβαλεν ἐπ' αὐτὸν τὰς χεῖρας.

7:45 Ἦλθον οὖν οἱ ὑπηρέται πρὸς τοὺς ἀρχιερεῖς καὶ Φαρισαίους, καὶ εἶπον αὐτοῖς ἐκεῖνοι· διὰ τί οὐκ ἠγάγετε αὐτόν;

7:46 ἀπεκρίθησαν οἱ ὑπηρέται· οὐδέποτε ἐλάλησεν οὕτως ἄνθρωπος.

7:47 ἀπεκρίθησαν οὖν αὐτοῖς οἱ Φαρισαῖοι· μὴ καὶ ὑμεῖς πεπλάνησθε;

7:48 μή τις ἐκ τῶν ἀρχόντων ἐπίστευσεν εἰς αὐτὸν ἢ ἐκ τῶν Φαρισαίων;

7:49 ἀλλὰ ὁ ὄχλος οὗτος ὁ μὴ γινώσκων τὸν νόμον ἐπάρατοί εἰσιν.

7:50 λέγει Νικόδημος πρὸς αὐτούς, ὁ ἐλθὼν πρὸς αὐτὸν [τὸ] πρότερον, εἷς ὢν ἐξ αὐτῶν·

7:37 And on the last and great day of the festivity, Jesus stood and cried out, saying: if any man thirst, let him come to me and drink. [n. 1084]

7:38 He who believes in me, as the Scripture says, out of his heart shall flow rivers of living water. [n. 1089]

7:39 Now this he said concerning the Spirit, whom they who believed in him would receive: for the Spirit was not yet given, because Jesus was not yet glorified. [n. 1091]

7:40 Of that multitude, therefore, when they had heard his words, said: truly, this is the prophet. [n. 1098]

7:41 Others said: this is the Christ. But some said: is it possible that the Christ comes out of Galilee? [n. 1099]

7:42 Does not the Scripture say that the Christ comes from the seed of David and from Bethlehem, the town where David was? [n. 1101]

7:43 So there arose dissension among the people because of him. [n. 1102]

7:44 And some of them wanted to apprehend him, but no man laid hands on him. [n. 1104]

7:45 The ministers therefore came to the chief priests and the Pharisees. And they said to them: why have you not brought him? [n. 1106]

7:46 The ministers answered: never has a man spoken like this man. [n. 1108]

7:47 The Pharisees therefore answered them: have you also been seduced? [n. 1109]

7:48 Has any one of the rulers or the Pharisees believed in him? [n. 1111]

7:49 But these people, who do not know the law, are accursed. [n. 1112]

7:50 Nicodemus said to them, he who came to him by night, who was one of them: [n. 1113]

7:51 numquid lex nostra iudicat hominem, nisi prius audierit ab ipso, et cognoverit quid faciat? [n. 1115]

7:51 μὴ ὁ νόμος ἡμῶν κρίνει τὸν ἄνθρωπον ἐὰν μὴ ἀκούσῃ πρῶτον παρ' αὐτοῦ καὶ γνῷ τί ποιεῖ;

7:51 does our law judge any man, unless it first hear him and know what he does? [n. 1115]

7:52 Responderunt, et dixerunt ei: numquid et tu Galilaeus es? Scrutare Scripturas, et vide quia a Galilaea propheta non surgit. [n. 1116]

7:52 ἀπεκρίθησαν καὶ εἶπαν αὐτῷ· μὴ καὶ σὺ ἐκ τῆς Γαλιλαίας εἶ; ἐραύνησον καὶ ἴδε ὅτι ἐκ τῆς Γαλιλαίας προφήτης οὐκ ἐγείρεται.

7:52 They answered and said to him: are you also a Galilean? Search the Scriptures and see that, out of Galilee, a prophet does not rise. [n. 1116]

7:53 Et reversi sunt unusquisque in domum suam. [n. 1117]

7:53 Καὶ ἐπορεύθησαν ἕκαστος εἰς τὸν οἶκον αὐτοῦ,

7:53 And every man returned to his own house. [n. 1117]

1083. Postquam Dominus egit de origine suae doctrinae et docentis nec non de termino eius, hic consequenter invitat ad ipsam doctrinam, et

primo ponitur Christi invitatio;

secundo turbarum dissensio, ibi *ex illa autem hora* etc.

Circa primum tria facit.

Primo ponit invitandi modus;

secundo ipsa invitatio, ibi *si quis sitit, veniat ad me*;

tertio subditur expositio, ibi *hoc autem dixit de Spiritu*.

Modus autem invitandi attenditur quantum ad tria;

scilicet quantum ad tempus invitationis;

quantum ad situm invitantis;

quantum ad conatum vocantis.

1084. Quantum ad tempus, quia *in novissimo die magno festivitatis*: nam, ut dictum est, festum illud celebrabatur septem diebus, et primus et ultimus dies solemniores erant, sicut et apud nos primus dies festi et octavus solemnis est magis. Hoc ergo quod hic Dominus fecit, non fecit primo die, quia nondum ascenderat Ierusalem, nec intermediis diebus, sed in novissimo; et hoc ideo, quia pauci sunt qui festa spiritualiter celebrant: et ideo non eos a principio ad doctrinam invitat, ne per vanitates sequentium dierum festorum aboleretur de cordibus eorum, quia, ut dicitur Lc. VIII, 7 verbum Domini suffocatur a spinis, sed in ultimo die eos invitat, ut tenacius eorum cordibus imprimatur.

1085. Quantum ad situm autem quia *stabat Iesus*.

Ubi sciendum est, quod Christus docuit sedens, et stans. Sedens, quidem docuit discipulos, Matth. V, 1; stans autem turbas, sicut hic. Et ideo ex hoc inolevit consuetudo in Ecclesia, ut turbis praedicetur stando, religiosis vero et clericis sedendo. Cuius ratio est, quia cum praedicatio ad turbas sit quasi ad eas convertendas, fit per modum exhortationis; sed cum praedicatio ad clerum fit, quasi iam ad existentes in domo Dei, est ut quaedam commemoratio.

1083. After our Lord told them about the origin of his doctrine and of the teacher, as well as his end, he now invites them to accept his teaching itself.

First, we see Christ's invitation;

second, the dissension among the people, at *of that multitude therefore, when they had heard his words*.

He does three things about the first.

First, he tells us the manner of this invitation;

second, we see the invitation itself, at *if any man thirst, let him come to me*; and

third, he explains what it means, at *now this he said concerning the Spirit*.

The manner of the invitation is described in three ways:

by its time;

by the posture of the one inviting;

and by his efforts.

1084. As to the time, we see that it was *on the last and great day of the festivity*. For as we saw before, this feast was celebrated for seven days, and the first and the last day were the more solemn; just as with us, the first day of a feast and its octave are the more solemn. Therefore, what our Lord did here he did not do on the first day, as he had not yet gone to Jerusalem, nor in the intervening days, but on the last day. And he acted then because there are few who celebrate feasts in a spiritual way. Consequently, he did not invite them to his teaching at the beginning of the festival so that the trifles of the following days would not drive it from their hearts; for we read that the word of the Lord is choked by thorns (Luke 8:7). But he did invite them on the last day so that his teaching would be more deeply impressed on their hearts.

1085. As to his posture, *Jesus stood*.

Here we should note that Christ taught both while sitting and standing. He taught his disciples while sitting (Matt 5:1); while he stood when he taught the people, as he is doing here. It is from this that we get the custom in the Church of standing when preaching to the people, but sitting while preaching to religious and clerics. The reason for this is that since the aim in preaching to the people is to convert them, it takes the form of an exhortation; but when preaching is directed to clergy, already living in the house of God, it takes the form of a reminder.

1086. Quantum ad conatum vero vocantis quia *clamabat*, ut scilicet ostenderet suam securitatem; Is. XL, 9: *exalta in fortitudine vocem tuam . . . exalta, noli timere*. Et ut ab omnibus audiretur; Is. LVIII, 1: *clama, ne cesses, quasi tuba exalta vocem tuam*. Et ut ostendat magnitudinem dicendorum; Prov. VIII, v. 6: *audite me, quia de rebus magnis locutura sum*.

1087. Consequenter cum dicit *si quis sitit, veniat ad me*, ponitur invitatio, et

primo ostendit qui invitentur;

secundum quis sit fructus invitationis.

1088. Invitantur quidem sitientes; unde dicit *si quis sitit, veniat ad me, et bibat*. Is. LV, 1: *omnes sitientes, venite ad aquas*. Ideo enim sitientes vocat, quia tales sunt qui desiderant Deo servire. Deus autem coacta servitia non acceptat; II Cor. IX, 7: *hilarem datorem diligit Deus*. Et propter hoc dicebat Ps. LIII, 8: *voluntarie sacrificabo*. De istis dicitur Matth. V, 6: *beati qui esuriunt et sitiunt iustitiam*. Quos quidem Dominus non partialiter vocat, sed omnes; unde dicit *si quis sitit*, quasi dicat, quicumque est ille; Eccli. XXIV, 26: *transite ad me, omnes qui concupiscitis me, et a generationibus meis implemini*; I Tim. II, 4: *vult omnes homines salvos fieri*.

Invitat autem ad potandum; unde dicit *et bibat*. Potus enim iste est spiritualis refectio in cognitione divinae sapientiae et veritatis; etiam in impletione desideriorum. Is. LXV, 13: *servi mei bibent, et vos sitietis*; Prov. IX, 5: *venite, et comedite panem meum, et bibite vinum quod miscui vobis*; Eccli. XV, 3: *aqua sapientiae salutaris potabit illum*.

1089. Fructus autem huius invitationis est redundantia bonorum in alios; unde dicit *qui credit in me, sicut dicit Scriptura, flumina de ventre eius fluent aquae vivae*. Quod quidem, secundum Chrysostomum, legendum est sic: *qui credit in me, sicut dicit Scriptura*, hic subdistingue punctando; et postea subsequitur *flumina de ventre eius fluent aquae vivae*. Nam si dicis qui credit in me, et postea subsequatur sicut dicit Scriptura, flumina, etc., non videtur conveniens, quia hoc quod dicitur *flumina de ventre eius fluent aquae vivae*, non invenitur in aliquo libro Veteris Testamenti. Hoc ergo modo dicatur *qui credit in me, sicut dicit Scriptura*; idest, secundum Scripturae documenta; supra v. 39. *Scrutamini Scripturas . . . ipsae sunt quae testimonium perhibent de me*. Et tunc *flumina de ventre eius fluent aquae vivae*. Et dicit *qui credit in me*, cum supra dixerit *qui venit ad me*; quia idem est credere et venire; Ps. XXXIII, 6: *accedite ad eum, et illuminamini*.

Secundum Hieronymum vero, aliter punctatur sic: *qui credit in me*, et postea subditur sicut dicit Scriptura, *flumina de ventre eius fluent aquae vivae*. Quod, ut ipse dicit, de proverbiis sumptum est; Prov. V, 15: *bibe aquam*

1086. As to his effort we read that *and cried*, in order to show his own assurance: *raise up your voice with strength . . . raise it up, and do not be afraid* (Isa 40:9); and so that all would be able to hear him: *cry out, and do not stop; raise your voice like a trumpet* (Isa 58:1); and to stress the importance of what he was about to say: *listen to me, for I will tell you about great things* (Prov 8:6).

1087. Next, at *if any man thirst, let him come to me*, we see Christ's invitation:

first, those who are invited;

second, the fruit of this invitation.

1088. It is the thirsty who are invited. Thus he says: *if any man thirsts, let him come to me and drink*; *come to the waters, all you who thirst* (Isa 55:1). He calls the thirsty because such people want to serve God. For God does not accept a forced service: *God loves a cheerful giver* (2 Cor 9:7). So we read: *I will sacrifice freely* (Isa 53:8). And such people are described in Matthew this way: *blessed are they who hunger and thirst for what is right* (Matt 5:6). Now our Lord calls all of these people, not just some; and so he says: *if any man thirsts*, as if to say: whoever it is. *Come to me, all you who desire me, and be filled with my fruits* (Sir 24:26); he desires the salvation of all (1 Tim 2:4).

Jesus invites them to drink; and so he says, *and drink*. For this drink is spiritual refreshment in the knowledge of divine wisdom and truth, and in the realization of their desires: *my servants will drink, and you will be thirsty* (Isa 65:13), *come and eat my bread, and drink the wine I have mixed for you* (Prov 9:5), *she will give him the water of saving wisdom to drink* (Sir 15:3).

1089. The fruit of this invitation is that good things overflow upon others; thus he says: *he who believes in me, as the Scripture says, out of his heart shall flow rivers of living water*. According to Chrysostom, we should read this as follows: *he who believes in me, as the Scripture said*. And then a new sentence begins: *out of his heart shall flow rivers of living water*. For if we say: whoever believes in me, and follow this with, as the Scriptures say, *out of his heart shall flow rivers of living water*, it does not seem to be correct, for the statement, out of his heart shall flow rivers of living water, is not found in any book of the Old Testament. So we should say: *whoever believes in me, as the Scriptures say*; that is, according to the teaching of the Scriptures. *Search the Scriptures . . . they give testimony about me* (John 5:39). And then there follows: *out of his heart shall flow rivers of living water*. He says here, *he who believes in me*, while before he said, *he who comes to me* (John 6:35), because to believe and to come are the same thing: *come to him and be enlightened* (Ps 33:6).

But Jerome punctuates this in a different way. He says that after *he who believes in me*, there follows, as the Scriptures say, *out of his heart shall flow rivers of living water*. And he says that this phrase was taken from Proverbs: *drink*

de cisterna tua, et fluenta putei tui: deriventur fontes tui foras.

1090. Sciendum est autem, secundum Augustinum, quod flumina procedunt de fontibus sicut a principio. Qui autem bibit potum corporalem, non habet in se nec fontem, nec flumen, quia particulam aquae gustat: sed qui bibit credendo in Christum, haurit fontem aquae, quo hausto, vivescit conscientia, quae est venter interioris hominis, et etiam ipsa fons erit. Unde dicitur supra IV, v. 13: *qui biberit ex hac aqua, fiet in eo fons aquae salientis.* Hic autem fons qui hauritur, est Spiritus Sanctus, de quo dicitur in Ps. XXXV, 10: *apud te est fons vitae.* Qui ergo bibit ita quod soli sibi proficit, dona gratiarum, quae per flumina signantur, non fluent aquae vivae de ventre eius; sed qui proximo festinat consulere, et diversa dona gratiarum recepta a Deo aliis communicare, de ventre eius fluent aquae vivae. Propter quod dicit Petrus: *unusquisque sicut accepit gratiam, in alterutrum illam administrantes.*

Dicit autem *flumina*, ad significandum spiritualium donorum abundantiam fidelibus repromissam; Ps. LXIV, 10: *flumen Dei repletum est aquis.* Iterum eorum impetum; Is. c. XXVII, 6: *qui ingredientur impetu a Iacob, florebit et germinabit Israel, et implebunt faciem orbis semine;* et in Ps. XLV, 5: *fluminis impetus laetificat civitatem Dei.* Unde, quia ex instinctu et fervore Spiritus Sancti movebatur Apostolus, dicebat: *caritas Christi urget nos;* et Rom. VIII, 14: *qui spiritu Dei aguntur, hi filii Dei sunt.* Item donorum Spiritus Sancti divisionem: quia, ut dicitur I ad Cor. XII, 10: *alii genera linguarum, alii genera sanitatum* etc. Huiusmodi autem flumina sunt *aquae vivae*, quia sunt continuatae suo principio, scilicet Spiritui Sancto inhabitanti.

1091. Consequenter cum dicit *hoc autem dixit de Spiritu*, exponit quae dixit, et

primo ponitur expositio;

secundo assignatur ratio expositionis, ibi *nondum enim erat Spiritus datus*.

1092. Dicit ergo dixit, quod *flumina de ventre eius fluent aquae vivae.* Sed hoc intelligendum esse Evangelista dicit *de Spiritu quem accepturi erant credentes in eum*, quia ipse est fons vitae et fluvius. Fons, de quo dicitur in Ps. XXXV, 10: *apud te est fons vitae, et in lumine tuo videbimus lumen.* Fluvius vero, quia a Patre et Filio procedit. Apoc. ult., 1: *ostendit mihi angelus fluvium aquae vivae splendidum tamquam crystallum, procedentem de sede Dei et agni;* Is. XLII, v. 1: *dedit spiritum,* scilicet obedientibus sibi.

the water from your own cistern, and from the streams of your own well. Let your fountains flow far and wide (Prov 5:15).

1090. We should note, with Augustine, that rivers come from fountains as their source. Now one who drinks natural water does not have either a fountain or a river within himself, because he takes only a small portion of water. But one who drinks by believing in Christ draws in a fountain of water; and when he draws it in, his conscience, which is the heart of the inner man, begins to live and it itself becomes a fountain. So we read above: *but the water that I will give to him will become in him a fountain of water, springing up into eternal life* (John 4:14). This fountain which is taken in is the Holy Spirit, of whom we read: *with you is the fountain of life* (Ps 35:10). Therefore, whoever drinks the the gifts of the graces, which are signified by the rivers, in such a way that he alone benefits, will not have living water flowing from his heart. But whoever acts quickly to help others, and to share with them the various gifts of grace he has received from God, will have living water flowing from his heart. This is why Peter says: *according to the grace each has received, let them use it to benefit one another* (1 Pet 4:10).

He says, *rivers*, to indicate the abundance of the spiritual gifts which were promised to those who believe: *the river of God is full of water* (Ps 64:10); and also their force or onrush: *when they rush to Jacob, Israel will blossom and bud, and they will fill the surface of the earth with fruit* (Isa 27:6); and again, *the rush of the rivers gives joy to the city of God* (Ps 45:5). Thus, because the Apostle was governed by the impulsive force and fervor of the Holy Spirit, he said: *the love of Christ spurs us on* (2 Cor 5:14); and *those who are led by the Spirit of God are the sons of God* (Rom 8:14). The separate distribution of the gifts of the Holy Spirit is also indicated, for we read, *to one the gift of healing . . . to another the gift of tongues* (1 Cor 12:10). These gifts are *rivers of living water* because they flow directly from their source, which is the indwelling Holy Spirit.

1091. Then, at *now this he said concerning the Spirit*, he explains what he said.

First we see the explanation;

second, the reason behind this explanation, at *for the Spirit was not yet given*.

1092. Christ had said: *out of his heart shall flow rivers of living water.* The Evangelist tells us that we should understand this *concerning the Spirit, whom those who believed in him would receive*, because the Spirit is the fountain and river of life. He is the fountain of which we read: *with you is the fountain of life; and in your light we will see light* (Ps 35:10). And the Spirit is a river because he proceeds from the Father and the Son: *the angel then showed me the river of the water of life, clear as crystal, coming from the throne of God and of the Lamb* (Rev 22:1). *He gave the Spirit*, that is, to those who obey him (Isa 42:1).

1093. Huius expositionis rationem assignat, dicens *nondum enim erat Spiritus datus*; et dicit duo: scilicet quod *nondum erat Spiritus datus*, et quod *Christus nondum erat glorificatus.*

Circa primum est duplex opinio. Chrysostomus enim dicit, quod Spiritus Sanctus non fuit datus apostolis, quantum ad dona prophetica et miraculorum, ante resurrectionem Christi. Unde gratia huius, quae dabitur prophetis a terra defecerat usque ad adventum Christi, nec postmodum alicui data est usque ad praedictum tempus. Et si dicitur quod apostoli eiiciebant Daemonia ante resurrectionem, intelligendum est quod haec non spiritu eiiciebantur, sed ea quae a Christo erat potestate. Quando enim mittebat eos, non dicitur dedit eis Spiritum Sanctum sed *dedit eis potestatem*: Matth. X, 1.

Sed hoc videtur contra illud quod Dominus dicit Lucae XI, 19: *si ego in Beelzebub eiicio Daemonia, filii vestri in quo eiiciunt?* Sed constat quod ipse in Spiritu Sancto eiiciebat Daemonia, et filii, idest apostoli: unde manifestum est eos accepisse Spiritum Sanctum.

Et ideo dicendum est, secundum Augustinum, quod ante resurrectionem apostoli habuerunt Spiritum Sanctum etiam quantum ad dona prophetica et miraculorum. Et hic quod dicitur *nondum enim erat Spiritus datus*, intelligendum de abundanti datione, et visibilibus signis; sicut datus fuit eis post resurrectionem et ascensionem in linguis igneis.

1094. Sed cum Spiritus Sanctus sanctificet Ecclesiam, et etiam modo accipiatur a fidelibus, quare nemo loquitur linguis omnium gentium sicut tunc?

Dicendum ad hoc, quod non est necessarium, ut Augustinus dicit. Quia iam universalis Ecclesia linguis gentium loquitur, quia per Spiritum Sanctum datur caritas; Rom. V, v. 5: *caritas Dei diffusa est in cordibus nostris, et haec, faciens omnia communia, facit quemlibet cuilibet loqui. Unde dicit: si amas unitatem, etiam tibi habet quisquis in illa (idest Ecclesia) aliquid habet. Tolle invidiam, et tuum est quod habeo: livor separat, caritas iungit: ipsam habeto, et cuncta habebis.* In principio autem antequam Ecclesia per mundum dilataretur, quia pauci erant, oportebat quod linguis omnium loquerentur, ut sic Ecclesiam in omnibus fundarent.

1095. Circa secundum, sciendum est, secundum Augustinum, quod hoc quod dicit *Iesus nondum fuerat glorificatus*, intelligendum est de gloria resurrectionis; quasi dicat: nondum a mortuis resurrexerat, nondum ad caelos ascenderat. De qua dicitur Io. XVII, 5: *clarifica me, Pater*. Et causa quare sic voluit prius glorificari quam daret Spiritum Sanctum, assignatur, quia Spiritus

1093. He gives the reason behind this explanation, saying, *for the Spirit was not yet given*. And he says two things, namely that *the Spirit was not yet given*, and that *Jesus was not yet glorified*.

There are two opinions about the first of these. For Chrysostom says that before the resurrection of Christ the Holy Spirit was not given to the apostles with respect to the gifts of prophecy and miracles. And so this grace, which was given to the prophets, was not to be found on earth until Christ came, and after that it was not given to anyone until the above mentioned time. And if anyone objects that the apostles cast out devils before the resurrection, it should be understood that they were cast out by that power which was from Christ, not by the Spirit; for when he sent them out, we do not read that he gave them the Holy Spirit, but rather that *he gave them power over unclean spirits* (Matt 10:1).

However, this seems to conflict with what our Lord says in the Gospel of Luke: *if I cast out devils by Beelzebub, by whom do your children cast them out?* (Luke 11:19). But it is certain that our Lord cast out devils by the Holy Spirit, as the children did also, that is, the apostles. Therefore, it is clear that they had received the Holy Spirit.

And so we must say, with Augustine, that the apostles had the Holy Spirit before the resurrection, even with respect to the gifts of prophecy and miracles. And when we read here that *for the Spirit was not yet given*, we should understand this to refer to a more abundant giving, and one with visible signs, as the Spirit was given to them in tongues of fire after the resurrection and ascension.

1094. But since the Holy Spirit sanctifies the Church and is even now received by those who believe, why does no one speak in the languages of all nations as then?

My answer is that it is not necessary, as Augustine says. For now the universal Church speaks the languages of all the nations, because the love of charity is given by the Holy Spirit: *the love of God is poured out into our hearts by the Holy Spirit* (Rom 5:5); and this love, making all things common, makes everyone speak to everyone else. As Augustine says: *if you love unity, then you have everything that anyone else has in it (i.e., in the Church). Give up your envy, and what I have is also yours; ill-will divides, the love of charity unites. If you have this love, you will have everything.* But at the beginning, before the Church was spread throughout the world, because it had few members, they had to speak the languages of all so that they could establish the Church among all.

1095. With regard to the second point, we should note that Augustine thinks the statement, *Jesus was not yet glorified*, should be understood as the glory of the resurrection. As if to say: Jesus had not yet risen from the dead or ascended into heaven. We read about this below: *glorify me, O Father* (John 17:5). And the reason why Christ willed to be glorified before he gave the Holy Spirit is that

Sanctus ad hoc datur nobis, ut erigat corda nostra ab amore saeculi in resurrectionem spiritualem et totaliter currant in Deum. Quia ergo vitam aeternam promisit Spiritus Sancti caritate ferventibus, ubi non moriemur, ubi nihil timebimus. Ideo ipsum Spiritum Sanctum noluit dare nisi dum esset glorificatus, ut in corpore ostenderet vitam quam in resurrectione speramus.

1096. Secundum Chrysostomum vero, hoc non intelligitur de gloria resurrectionis, sed de glorificatione passionis: de qua, imminente passionis hora, Dominus dicit infra c. XIII, 31: *nunc glorificatus est Filius hominis*. Et secundum hoc Spiritus Sanctus tunc primum datus est quando post passionem dixit apostolis: *accipite Spiritum Sanctum* etc. Ideo autem non ante passionem datus est Spiritus Sanctus, quia, cum sit donum, non debuit dari inimicis, sed amicis. Nos autem inimici eramus. Oportebat ergo prius offerri hostiam in ara crucis et inimicitiam in carne solvi, ut sic per mortem Filii eius reconciliaremur Deo, et tunc facti amici, donum Spiritus Sancti reciperemus etc.

1097. Posita ergo Christi ad spiritualem potum invitatione, hic consequenter agit Evangelista de turbarum dissensione, et

    primo ponitur dissensio turbarum ad invicem;

    secundo dissensio in principibus, ibi *venerunt ergo ministri*.

    Circa primum duo facit.

    Primo ponuntur diversa dissidentium verba;

    secundo ponitur ipsa dissensio, ibi *dissensio itaque facta est in turba*.

Diversitas autem verborum turbarum ex diversitate opinionum turbarum de Christo proveniebat, et ideo ponit tres opiniones turbarum: duas quidem iam accedentium ad spiritualem potum, tertiam vero resilientium.

1098. Prima autem opinio erat quod dicebant Christum prophetam esse; et ideo dicit *ex illa ergo hora*, quando scilicet in magno festivitatis die talia dixerat, *turba cum audissent hos sermones eius, dicebant*, illi scilicet qui iam illam aquam spiritualiter haurire coeperant, *hic est vere propheta*. Non solum prophetam eum dicunt, sed etiam verum, idest quasi antonomastice, intelligentes hunc esse de quo Moyses praedixit, Deut. c. XVIII, 15: *prophetam suscitabit vobis Deus de fratribus vestris: ipsum tamquam me audietis*.

1099. Alia opinio erat quia quidam dicebant *hic est Christus*: isti enim magis ad potum accedebant, et sitim infidelitatis magis deposuerant. Et hoc etiam Petrus confessus est, Matth. XVI, 16: *tu es Christus Filius Dei vivi*.

the Holy Spirit is given to us so that we might raise our hearts from the love of this world in a spiritual resurrection, and turn completely to God. To those who are afire with the love of the Holy Spirit, Christ promised eternal life, where we will not die, and where we will have no fear. And for this reason he did not wish to give the Holy Spirit until he was glorified, so that he might show in his body the life for which we hope in the resurrection.

1096. For Chrysostom, however, this statement does not refer to the glory of the resurrection, but to the glorification of the passion. When his passion was near, our Lord said: *now the Son of man is glorified* (John 13:31). So, according to this view, the Holy Spirit was first given after the passion, when our Lord said to his apostles: *receive the Holy Spirit* (John 20:22). The Holy Spirit was not given before the passion because, since it is a gift, it should not be given to enemies, but to friends. But we were enemies. Thus it was necessary that first the victim be offered on the altar of the cross, and enmity be destroyed in his flesh, so that by this we might be reconciled to God by the death of his Son; and then, having been made friends, we could receive the gift of the Holy Spirit.

1097. The Evangelist, having shown us Christ's invitation to a spiritual drink, now presents the disagreement of the people.

    First, the disagreement among the people themselves;

    second, that of their leaders, at *the ministers therefore came*.

    He does two things about the first.

    First, he states what those who disagreed said;

    second, he states the fact that there was a disagreement, at *so there arose dissension among the people*.

What the people said varied according to their different opinions about Christ. And he gives three of their opinions: two of these were the opinions of those who were coming for spiritual drink; and the third was held by those who shrank from it.

1098. The first opinion was that Christ was the Prophet. So he says, *of that multitude, therefore, when they had heard his words*, i.e., from the time Christ had spoken on the great day of the feast, *said*, i.e., those who had now begun to drink that water spiritually, *truly, this is the prophet*. They did not just call him a prophet, but the prophet, thinking that he was the one about whom Moses foretold: *the Lord your God will raise up a prophet for you from your brothers . . . you will listen to him* (Deut 18:15).

1099. Another opinion was of those who said, *this is the Christ*. These people had drawn closer to that drink, and had slaked the thirst of unbelief to a greater extent. This is what Peter himself professed: *you are the Christ, the Son of the living God* (Matt 16:16).

1100. Tertia opinio est referentium contraria prae-dictis. Et primo obiiciunt contra opinionem dicentium eum esse Christum; secundo obiectionem auctoritate confirmant.

Dicit ergo *quidam autem*, in suae infidelitatis aridi-tate permanentes, *dicebant: numquid a Galilaea venit Christus?* Noverant enim, prophetas, Christum a Ga-lilaea venturum, non praedixisse: et ideo credentes in Nazareth eum natum fuisse (ignorabant enim suae nati-vitatis locum esse Bethlehem), hoc dicunt. Manifestum enim erat eum in Nazareth nutritum, sed paucis notus erat nativitatis locus. Quamvis tamen Scriptura non di-cat Christum in Galilaea nasciturum, praedixit tamen il-luc eum primo declinaturum. Is. c. IX, 1: *primo tempore alleviata est terra Zabulon et terra Nephthali, et novissi-mo aggravata est via maris trans Iordanem Galilaeae gen-tium. Populus gentium qui ambulabat in tenebris, vidit lucem magnam, et habitantibus in regione umbrae mortis lux orta est eis.* Praedixit etiam quod de Nazareth proces-surus esset. Is. XI, 1: *flos de radice eius ascendet*: ubi in Hebraeo habetur: *Nazarenus de radice est* etc.

1101. Confirmant obiectionem auctoritate Scriptu-rae, cum dicunt *nonne Scriptura dicit, quia ex semine David et de Bethlehem castello, ubi erat David, venit Christus?* Quod autem de semine David venturus esset Iesus, dicitur Ierem. XXIII, 5: *suscitabo David germen iu-stum.* Et II Reg. XXIII, 1, dicitur de David: *dixit vir cui constitutum est de Christo Dei.* Quod vero de Bethlehem, dicitur Mich. V, 1: *et tu, Bethlehem, terra Iuda: ex te mihi egredietur qui sit dominator in Israel.*

1102. Consequenter cum dicit *dissensio itaque facta est in turba propter eum*,

primo ponitur ipsa dissensio;

secundo conatus quorumdam ex eis contra Chri-stum;

tertio conatus repressio.

1103. *Dissensio autem facta est propter eum*, scilicet Christum, *in turba*. Frequenter enim contingit quod in cordibus malorum ex manifestatione veritatis causatur dissensio et turbatio. Unde et hoc in persona Christi di-citur Ier. XV, 10: *vae mihi, mater mea, ut quid me genuisti virum rixae, virum discordiae in universa terra?* Propter hoc dicebat Dominus, Mt. X, 34: *non enim veni mittere pacem, sed gladium.*

1104. Conatus autem, scilicet aliquorum, erat ad eum apprehendendum; unde dicit *quidam autem ex eis*, scilicet qui dixerant: *numquid a Galilaea venit Christus?* etc., *voluerunt apprehendere eum*, scilicet ex inimicitia ad occidendum; Ps. LXX, 2: *persequimini et comprehendite*; Ex. XV, 9: *dixit inimicus: persequar et comprehendam.* Sed tamen boni et fideles volunt Chri-stum apprehendere, ut eo fruantur; Cant. VII, 8: *ascen-dam in palmam, et apprehendam fructus eius.*

1100. The third opinion conflicts with the other two. First, those who hold this disagree with those who say that Jesus is the Christ; second, they support their opinion with an authority.

So he says: *but others said*, those remaining in the dry-ness of unbelief, *is it possible that the Christ comes out of Galilee?* For they knew that it was not predicted by the prophets that the Christ would come from Galilee. And they said what they did because they thought that Jesus had been born in Nazareth, not knowing that it was really in Bethlehem: for it was well known that he had been brought up in Nazareth, but only a few knew where he was born. Nevertheless, although the Scripture does not say that the Christ would be born in Galilee, it did foretell that he would first start out from there: *the people who walked in darkness saw a great light, and on those who lived in the region of the shadow of death, a light has risen* (Isa 9:1). It even foretold that the Christ would come from Nazareth: *a flower will rise up from his roots* (Isa 11:1), where the Hebrew version reads: *a Nazarene will rise up from his roots.*

1101. They support their objection by the authority of Scripture when they say, *does not the Scripture say that the Christ comes from the seed of David and from Bethlehem, the town where David was?* We read that Jesus would come from the seed of David: *I will raise up a just branch for Da-vid* (Jer 23:5). And we see that David was *the anointed of God* (2 Sam 23:1). We also read that Jesus would come from Bethlehem: *and you, Bethlehem, land of Judah: from you there will come forth, for me, a ruler of Israel* (Mic 5:2).

1102. Then, at *so there arose dissension among the peo-ple because of him*,

the disagreement among the people is mentioned;

second, the attempt of some of them to seize Christ; and

third, the failure of their attempt.

1103. And *so there was dissension among the people because of him*, that is, Christ. For it often happens that when the truth is made known, it causes dissensions and uneasiness in the hearts of the wicked. So Jeremiah says, representing Christ: *woe is me, my mother! Why did you give birth to me as a man of strife and dissension for all the earth* (Jer 15:10). And our Lord said: *I have not come to send peace, but the sword* (Matt 10:34).

1104. Some of them attempted to seize Christ; so he says, *some of them*, that is, those who had said, *is it possible that the Christ comes from Galilee? wanted to apprehend him*, to kill him out of hatred: *pursue and seize him* (Ps 70:11); *the enemy said: I will pursue and seize* (Exod 15:9). On the other hand, those who are good and those who believe want to seize Christ to enjoy him: *I will go up into the palm tree and seize its fruit* (Song 7:8).

1105. Repressio autem conatus est ex potestate Christi: et ideo dicit *sed nemo misit super illum manus*, quia scilicet Christus nolebat. In potestate sua erat hoc; infra X, v. 18: *nemo tollit a me animam meam; sed ego pono eam a me ipso.* Unde et quando voluit pati, non eos expectavit, sed ipse se eis obtulit; infra XVIII, 4: *processit, et dixit ad eos, quem quaeritis?*

1106. Consequenter cum dicit *venerunt ergo ministri ad pontifices et Pharisaeos*, ponitur dissensio principum, et

primo ponitur dissensio eorum ad ministros;

secundo dissensio eorum ad invicem, ibi *dixit Nicodemus.*

Circa primum tria facit.

Primo ponitur redargutio principum ad ministros;

secundo testimonium latum de Christo a ministris;

tertio reprehensionis conatus principum ad ministros.

1107. In primo attende principum iniquitatem, cum dicunt, scilicet pontifices et Pharisaei, ministris *quare non adduxistis eum?* Adeo enim mali erant, quod eis non poterant satisfacere ministri, nisi Christo nocumentum inferrent; Pro. IV, 16: *rapitur somnus ab oculis eorum, nisi supplantaverint.*

Sed hic incipit quaestio litteralis: quia cum supra dictum est, quod ministri missi fuerunt ad capiendum Iesum die festo mediante, idest quarto die; et hic ponatur reditus eorum post septimum diem, quando dixit: *in novissimo autem die* etc., videtur quod intermediis diebus vacaverunt.

Ad quod est duplex responsio. Una quod Evangelista anticipavit murmur turbarum. Vel dicendum, quod forte tunc redierunt; sed hoc nunc commemorat, ut manifestet causam dissensionis inter principes.

1108. In secundo attende ministrorum bonitatem in commendabili testimonio quod perhibuerunt de Christo, dicentes *numquam sic locutus est homo, sicut hic loquitur.* Ubi redduntur commendabiles ex tribus. Primo ex admirationis causa: quia non propter miracula, sed propter doctrinam Christum mirabantur, ex quo propinquiores efficiuntur veritati, et recedunt a consuetudine Iudaeorum, qui signa quaerunt, ut dicitur I Cor. I, 22. Secundo ex conversionis facilitate: quia ad pauca verba Christi, capti sunt, et allecti ad eius amorem. Tertio ex animi securitate: quia ipsis Pharisaeis, qui Christo adversabantur, talia dicunt de Christo *numquam sic locutus est homo.*

Et hoc rationabiliter: quia non solum homo erat, sed etiam Dei Verbum; et ideo verba sua erant virtuosa ad

1105. But they were frustrated by the power of Christ. So he says: *no man laid hands on him*, that is, because Jesus was not willing that they do so, for this depended on his power: *no man takes it away from me, but I lay it down of myself* (John 10:18). Accordingly, when Christ did will to suffer, he did not wait for them, but he offered himself to them: *Jesus stepped forward and said to them: 'whom are you looking for?'* (John 18:4).

1106. Then, at *the ministers therefore came to the chief priests and the Pharisees*, we see the dissension of the leaders of the people:

first, their disagreement with their officers; and

second, the disagreement among themselves, at *Nicodemus said.*

He does three things about the first:

first, he shows the leaders rebuking their officers;

second, the testimony the officers gave about Christ; and

third, we see the leaders reprimanding their own officers.

1107. As to the first, let us note the evil of the leaders, that is, the chief priests and Pharisees, when they say to their officers: *why have you not brought him?* For their evil was so great that their own officers could not please them unless they injured Christ: *they cannot sleep unless they have done something evil* (Prov 4:16).

There is a problem here about the literal meaning of the text. For since it was said before that the officers were sent to apprehend Jesus when the festival was half over, that is, on the fourth day, and here we read that they returned on the seventh day, at *and on the last and great day of the festivity*, it seems that the Evangelist overlooked the days in between.

There are two answers to this: either the Evangelist anticipated the disagreement among the people, or the officers had returned before, but it is just mentioned now to show the reason why there was dissension among the leaders.

1108. As to the second point, let us realize how good these officers were in giving this praiseworthy testimony about Christ, saying: *never has a man spoken like this man.* They deserve our praise for three reasons. First, because of their admiration: for they admired Christ because of his teachings, not his miracles. And this brought them nearer to the truth, and further from the custom of the Jews, who looked for signs (1 Cor 1:22). Second, we should praise them because of the ease with which they were won over: because with just a few words, Christ had captivated them and had drawn their love. Third, because of their confidence: because it was to the Pharisees, who were the enemies of Christ, that they said: *never has a man spoken like this man.*

And these things are to be expected, for Jesus was not just a man, but the Word of God; and so his words had

commovendum; Ier. c. XXIII, 29: *numquid non verba mea quasi ignis sunt, dicit Dominus, et quasi malleus conterens petram?* Et ideo dicitur Mt. VII, 29, quod *erat docens sicut potestatem habens.* Erant etiam sapida ad dulcorandum; Cant. II, v. 14: *sonet vox tua in auribus meis, vox enim tua dulcis;* Ps. CXVIII, 103: *quam dulcia faucibus meis eloquia tua.* Erant utilia ad retinendum, quia promittebant bona aeterna; supra VI, 69: **Domine, ad quem ibimus? Verba vitae aeternae habes;** Is. XLVIII, 17: *ego Dominus docens te utilia.*

1109. In tertio attende detestari Iudaeorum perfidiam, qua conantur ministros a Christo retrahere, unde **responderunt eis,** scilicet ministris, **numquid et vos seducti estis?** Ubi tria faciunt.

Primo arguunt aestimatum ministrorum errorem;

secundo proponunt exemplum principum;
tertio excludunt exemplum turbarum.

1110. Arguunt autem eos, cum dicunt **numquid et vos seducti estis?** Quasi dicant: videmus vos delectatos esse in sermone illius. Et revera laudabiliter seducti erant, qui dimisso malo infidelitatis, ad veritatem fidei sunt adducti: de qua dicitur Ier. XX, 7: *seduxisti me, Domine, et seductus sum.*

1111. Exemplum autem principum proponunt, ut magis eos avertant: unde dicit **numquid ex principibus aliquis credidit in eum?** Ex duobus enim aliqui fide digni redduntur: scilicet ex auctoritate et ex religione. Unde haec duo contra Christum adducunt, quasi dicant: si Christus esset acceptandus, utique acceptassent eum principes, in quibus est auctoritas, et Pharisaei, in quibus apparebat religio; sed nullus istorum credidit in eum: ergo nec vos debetis in eum credere. In his ergo impletur quod dicitur in Ps. CXVII, v. 22: *lapidem quem reprobaverunt aedificantes,* scilicet principes et Pharisaei, *hic factus est in caput anguli,* idest in cordibus populorum. *Sed a Domino factum est istud:* quia bonitas eius praeponderat malitiae hominum.

1112. Testimonium autem turbae excludunt, quia eorum malitiam confutant; et ideo dicunt **sed turba haec quae non novit legem, maledicti sunt;** et ideo non est standum cum eis. Hoc autem scriptum est, Deut. c. XXVII, 27: *maledictus qui non permanserit in lege, nec eam opere perfecerit.* Sed hoc male intelligebant, quia etiam illi qui non habent scientiam legis, et opera legis faciunt, magis permanent in lege quam habentes legis scientiam, et non servantes eam: de quibus dicitur Mt. XV, 8: *populus hic labiis me honorat, cor autem eorum longe est a me;* Iacob V: *estote factores verbi, et non auditores tantum.*

power to affect people. *Are not my words like fire, says the Lord, and like a hammer breaking a rock?* (Jer 23:29). And so Matthew says: *he was teaching them as one who had authority* (Matt 7:29). And his words were sweet to contemplate: *let your voice sound in my ears, for your voice is sweet* (Song 2:14); *how sweet are your words to my tongue!* (Ps 118:103). And his words were useful to keep in mind, because they promised eternal life: **Lord, to whom shall we go? You have the words of eternal life** (John 6:69); *I am the Lord, who teaches you things that are useful* (Isa 48:17).

1109. As to the third point, see the treachery of the Jews in living to alienate the officers from Christ; **the Pharisees therefore answered them,** to the officers, **have you also been seduced?** Here they do three things.

First, they attack what they consider a mistake of their officers;

second, they hold up their leaders as an example; and
third, they reject the example of the people.

1110. They attack the officers when they say, **have you also been seduced?** As if to say: we see that what he said was pleasing to you. As a matter of fact, they had been seduced, but in an admirable way, because they left the evil of unbelief and were brought to the truth of the faith. We read about this: *you seduced me, O Lord, and I was seduced* (Jer 20:7).

1111. Then they appeal to their rulers as an example, to turn the officers further from Christ, saying: **has any one of the rulers or the Pharisees believed in him?** There are two reasons why a person should be believed: either because of some authority or because of a religious disposition. And they say that none of these are found with Christ. As if to say: if Christ were worthy to be received, then our rulers, who have authority, would have accepted him; and so would the Pharisees, who have a religious disposition. But none of these believe in him; and so neither should you believe in him. This fulfills the Psalm: *the stone that the builders,* that is, the rulers and the Pharisees *rejected has become the cornerstone* that is, in the hearts of the people. *The Lord has done this,* because his goodness is greater than man's evil (Ps 117:22–23).

1112. They reject the statements of the people because they are a rebuke to their own evil. So they say: **but these people, who do not know the law, are accursed;** therefore, you should not agree with them. This thought was found in Deuteronomy: *accursed are they who do not live within the law and do not act according to it* (Deut 27:26). But they did not understand this correctly, because even those who do not have a knowledge of the law but act in harmony with it, live more within the law than those who do have a knowledge of the law yot do not keep it. It is said about such people: *this people honors me with their lips, but their heart is far from me* (Matt 15:8); *be a doer of the word, and not just a hearer* (Jas 1:22).

1113. Consequenter cum dicit *dixit Nicodemus ad eos*, ponitur dissensio principum ad invicem, et

primo ponitur Nicodemi exhortatio;

secundo principum contradictio, ibi *responderunt et dixerunt*;

tertio dissensionis terminatio.

Circa primum duo facit.

Primo praemittit quaedam de Nicodemo;

secundo ponit eius exhortationem.

1114. Praemittit autem tria de eo: quorum duo ostendunt intentionem dicendi, et tertium nequitiam principum.

Primum ergo pertinet ad fidem Nicodemi; unde dicit *dixit ille qui venerat ad eum*, idest crediderat: idem enim est venire ad Christum, et credere in eum.

Secundum pertinet ad fidei suae imperfectionem, quia *nocte venit*. Si enim perfecte credidisset, non pertimuisset. Infra XII, 42: *multi ex principibus crediderunt in eum; sed propter Pharisaeos non confitebantur, ut e synagoga non eiicerentur*; de quibus unus erat Nicodemus.

Tertium pertinet ad principum falsitatem. Dixerunt enim, quod nullus ex principibus et Pharisaeis in Christum credidit, et ideo dicit *qui erat unus ex ipsis*; quasi dicat: si Nicodemus, qui est unus ex principibus, credidit in eum, manifestum est falsum esse quod principes et Pharisaei dicunt, scilicet quod nullus ex principibus credidit in eum. Ier. c. XVI, 19: *vere mendacium locutus est.*

1115. Exhortatio autem Nicodemi ponitur cum dicit *numquid lex nostra iudicat hominem, nisi prius audierit ab ipso et cognoverit quid faciat?* Nam secundum leges civiles debet praecedere diligens inquisitio sententiam. Unde dicitur Act. XV, 16: *non est Romanis consuetudo damnare aliquem hominem, priusquam is qui accusatur, praesentes habeat accusatores, locumque defendendi accipiat ad abluenda crimina*. Unde Iob XXIX, 16: *causam quam ignorabam, diligenter investigabam.* Propter hoc in lege Moysi, Ex. XXIII, 7, dicitur: *innocentem et iustum non condemnabis, quia aversor impium.*

Haec autem verba ideo dicit, quia cum fidelis esset, volebat eos ad Christum convertere. Quia tamen timidus erat, occulte hoc faciebat. Credebat enim, quia si tantummodo Christum vellent audire, quod verbum Christi esset tantae efficaciae quod forte similes fierent illis qui missi fuerant ad Iesum, et ad verba eius conversi sunt in facto eo ad quod missi fuerant.

1116. Contradictio principum ponitur cum dicit *responderunt et dixerunt ei* etc. Ubi primo comprehendunt eum quasi seductum; secundo quasi legis ignarum.

1113. Next, at *Nichodemus said to them*, we see the dissension among the rulers.

First, the advice of Nicodemus is given;

second, the opposition of the rulers, at *they answered and said*; and

third, the outcome of the whole affair.

The Evangelist does two things about the first:

first, he tells us something about Nicodemus;

second, he gives his advice.

1114. He tells us three things about Nicodemus: the first two show us the attitude of Nicodemus himself; and the second reveals the malice of the rulers.

The first concerns the faith of Nicodemus, and he says: Nicodemus, *he who came to him*, i.e., who believed, for to come to Christ is the same as to believe in him.

The second shows the imperfection of his faith, because *he who came to him by night*. For if he had believed perfectly, he would not have been fearful, for *many of the chief men also believed in him; but because of the Pharisees they did not confess him, that they might not be cast out of the synagogue* (John 12:42). And one of these was Nicodemus.

The third thing the Evangelist tells us shows us that the rulers did not speak the truth: for they said that none of the rulers, or of the Pharisees, believed in Christ. And so the Evangelist says about Nicodemus that he *was one of them*: as if to say: if Nicomedus, who was one of the rulers, believed in Christ, then the rulers and Pharisees are speaking falsely when they say that none of the rulers believed in him. *Truly, a lie was spoken* (Jer 16:19).

1115. The advice of Nicodemus is given when he says: *does our law judge any man, unless it first hear him and know what he does?* For according to the civil laws, a judgment was only to be given after a complete investigation. This is why we read: *it is not the custom of the Romans to condemn any man before he has his accusers face him, and can defend himself from the charges* (Acts 25:16). *I diligently investigated the stranger's cause* (Job 29:16). And so the law of Moses says: *do not condemn one who is innocent and just, because I hate the wicked* (Exod 23:7).

Nicodemus said what he did because he believed in Christ and wanted to convert them to Christ; yet because he was afraid, he did not act very candidly. He thought that if they would only listen to Christ, the words of Christ would be so effective that perhaps they would be changed like those whom they sent to Jesus, and who, when they heard Christ, were turned aside from the very act for which they had been sent.

1116. We see the opposition of the rulers to Nicodemus when he says, *they answered and said to him: are you also a Galilean?* First, they think that he has been seduced; and second, that he does not know the law.

Quantum ad primum dicunt *numquid et tu Galilaeus es*, idest, a Galilaeo seductus. Arbitrantur enim Christum Galilaeum ex conversatione in Galilaea: et ideo omnes qui Christum confitebantur, quasi in opprobrium Galilaeos vocant; Mt. XXVI, 69: *respondit ancilla Petro: et tu Galilaeus es?* Infra IX, v. 27: *numquid et vos vultis discipuli eius fieri?*

Quantum ad secundum dicunt *scrutare Scripturas, et vide, quia a Galilaea propheta non surgit*; cum tamen esset legis doctor, nec de novo scrutari indigebat. Quasi dicant: licet tu sis doctor, tamen hoc ignoras: sicut supra dictum est III, 10, *tu es magister in Israel, et haec ignoras?* Licet autem non habeatur expresse in Scriptura Veteris Testamenti quod de Galilaea propheta surgeret, hoc tamen habetur quod inde exire debeat Dominus prophetarum, secundum illud Is. II, 1: *flos*, idest Nazarenus, *de radice eius ascendet, et requiescet super eum Spiritus Domini.*

1117. Sed terminatio dissensionis ostenditur infructuosa; unde dicit *et reversi sunt unusquisque*, quasi infecto negotio, *in domum suam*, idest in propria, vacui fide, et fraudati a malo desiderio suo. Iob V, 13: *consilium pravorum dissipat*; Ps. XXXII, 10: *Dominus reprobat consilia principum, et cogitationes populorum dissipat.* Vel, *in domum suam*, idest in malitiam infidelitatis et impietatis suae; Apoc. II, 13: *scio ubi habitas, ubi sedes est satanae: et tenes nomen meum, et non negasti fidem meam.*

As to the first, they say: *are you also a Galilean?* that is, one who has been seduced by this Galilean. For they considered Christ a Galilean because he lived in Galilee. And so anyone who followed Christ they derisively called a Galilean. *The girl servant said to Peter: you are a Galilean, are you not?* (Matt 26:69). *Will you also become his disciples?* (John 9:27).

About his ignorance of the law, they say: *search the Scriptures and see that, out of Galilee, a prophet does not rise*. But since Nicodemus was a teacher of the law, he did not have to look again. It is as if they were saying: Although you are a teacher, you do not know this. Something like this was said before: *you are a teacher in Israel, and you do not know these things?* (John 3:10). Now even though the Old Testament does not explicitly say that a prophet will come from Galilee, it does say that the Lord of the prophets would come from there, according to: *a flower* (i.e., a Nazarene) *will arise from his root . . . and the Spirit of the Lord will rest upon him* (Isa 11:1).

1117. The outcome of this dissension is seen to be useless. So he says: *and every man returned*, leaving the matter unfinished, *to his own house*, i.e., to what belonged to him, empty of faith and frustrated in his evil desires. *He frustrates the plans of the wicked* (Job 5:13); *God destroys the plans of rulers, and frustrates the schemes of the people* (Ps 32:10). Or, each returned *to his own house*, i.e., to the evil of his unbelief and irreverence. *I know where you live: where the throne of satan is. You hold to my name, and you have not denied my faith* (Rev 2:13).

CHAPTER 8

Lecture 1

8:1 Iesus autem perrexit in montem Oliveti, [n. 1119]

8:2 et diluculo iterum in templum. Et omnis populus venit ad eum, et sedens docebat eos. [n. 1120]

8:3 Adducunt autem Scribae et Pharisaei mulierem in adulterio deprehensam, et statuerunt eam in medio. [n. 1123]

8:4 Et dixerunt ei: Magister, haec mulier modo deprehensa est in adulterio. [n. 1125]

8:5 In lege autem Moyses mandavit nobis huiusmodi lapidare. Tu ergo quid dicis? [n. 1127]

8:6 Haec autem dicebant, tentantes eum, ut possent accusare eum. Iesus autem inclinans se deorsum, digito scribebat in terra. [n. 1130]

8:7 Cum ergo perseverarent interrogantes, erexit se, et dixit eis: qui sine peccato est vestrum, primus in illam lapidem mittat. [n. 1132]

8:8 Et iterum se inclinans scribebat in terra. [n. 1134]

8:9 Audientes autem haec, unus post unum exibant, incipientes a senioribus, et remansit solus Iesus, et mulier in medio stans. [n. 1135]

8:10 Erigens autem se Iesus, dixit ei: mulier, ubi sunt qui te accusabant? nemo te condemnavit? [n. 1136]

8:11 Quae dixit: nemo, Domine. Dixit autem Iesus: nec ego te condemnabo. Vade, et iam amplius noli peccare. [n. 1138]

8:1 Ἰησοῦς δὲ ἐπορεύθη εἰς τὸ ὄρος τῶν ἐλαιῶν.

8:2 Ὄρθρου δὲ πάλιν παρεγένετο εἰς τὸ ἱερὸν καὶ πᾶς ὁ λαὸς ἤρχετο πρὸς αὐτόν, καὶ καθίσας ἐδίδασκεν αὐτούς.

8:3 Ἄγουσιν δὲ οἱ γραμματεῖς καὶ οἱ Φαρισαῖοι γυναῖκα ἐπὶ μοιχείᾳ κατειλημμένην καὶ στήσαντες αὐτὴν ἐν μέσῳ

8:4 λέγουσιν αὐτῷ· διδάσκαλε, αὕτη ἡ γυνὴ κατείληπται ἐπ᾽ αὐτοφώρῳ μοιχευομένη·

8:5 ἐν δὲ τῷ νόμῳ ἡμῖν Μωϋσῆς ἐνετείλατο τὰς τοιαύτας λιθάζειν. σὺ οὖν τί λέγεις;

8:6 τοῦτο δὲ ἔλεγον πειράζοντες αὐτόν, ἵνα ἔχωσιν κατηγορεῖν αὐτοῦ. ὁ δὲ Ἰησοῦς κάτω κύψας τῷ δακτύλῳ κατέγραφεν εἰς τὴν γῆν.

8:7 ὡς δὲ ἐπέμενον ἐρωτῶντες αὐτόν, ἀνέκυψεν καὶ εἶπεν αὐτοῖς· ὁ ἀναμάρτητος ὑμῶν πρῶτος ἐπ᾽ αὐτὴν βαλέτω λίθον.

8:8 καὶ πάλιν κατακύψας ἔγραφεν εἰς τὴν γῆν.

8:9 οἱ δὲ ἀκούσαντες ἐξήρχοντο εἷς καθ᾽ εἷς ἀρξάμενοι ἀπὸ τῶν πρεσβυτέρων καὶ κατελείφθη μόνος καὶ ἡ γυνὴ ἐν μέσῳ οὖσα.

8:10 ἀνακύψας δὲ ὁ Ἰησοῦς εἶπεν αὐτῇ· γύναι, ποῦ εἰσιν; οὐδείς σε κατέκρινεν;

8:11 ἡ δὲ εἶπεν· οὐδείς, κύριε. εἶπεν δὲ ὁ Ἰησοῦς· οὐδὲ ἐγώ σε κατακρίνω· πορεύου, [καὶ] ἀπὸ τοῦ νῦν μηκέτι ἁμάρτανε.

8:1 And Jesus went to the Mount of Olives. [n. 1119]

8:2 And early in the morning he came again into the temple. All the people came to him, and sitting down, he taught them. [n. 1120]

8:3 And the scribes and the Pharisees brought to him a woman caught in adultery, and they set her in the midst. [n. 1123]

8:4 And said to him: Master, this woman was just now caught in adultery. [n. 1125]

8:5 Now Moses commanded us in the law to stone such a woman. But what do you say? [n. 1127]

8:6 And they said this tempting him, that they might accuse him. But Jesus, bending down, wrote with his finger on the ground. [n. 1130]

8:7 When they continued asking him, he lifted himself up and said to them: he who is without sin among you, let him first cast a stone at her. [n. 1132]

8:8 And again bending down, he wrote on the ground. [n. 1134]

8:9 But hearing this, they left one by one, beginning with the eldest. And Jesus alone remained, and the woman standing in the midst. [n. 1135]

8:10 Then Jesus, lifting himself up, said to her: woman, where are they who accused you? Has no man condemned you? [n. 1136]

8:11 She said: no one, Lord. And Jesus said: neither will I condemn you. Go, and sin no more. [n. 1138]

1118. Postquam egit Evangelista de origine doctrinae Christi, hic consequenter agit de eius virtute. Habet

1118. After having treated of the origin of the doctrine of Christ, the Evangelist here considers its power. Now the

autem doctrina Christi virtutem illuminativam et vivificativam, quia verba eius spiritus et vita sunt.

Primo ergo agit de virtute doctrinae Christi illuminativa;

secundo de virtute vivificativa, infra X, *amen, amen dico vobis, qui non intrat per ostium in ovile ovium, sed ascendit aliunde, ille fur est et latro.*

Ostendit autem illuminativam virtutem doctrinae Christi, primo verbo;

secundo miraculo, ibi *et praeteriens Iesus, vidit hominem caecum a nativitate.*

Circa primum duo facit.

Primo introducit Christum docentem;

secundo ponit doctrinae Christi virtutem, ibi *iterum ergo locutus est eis Iesus.*

Ad officium autem doctoris duo pertinent. Primo ut devotos instruat; secundo ut adversarios repellat.

Primo ergo Christus instruit populum devotum;

secundo repellit adversarios, ibi *adducunt autem Scribae* etc.

Circa primum tria facit. Primo describitur locus doctrinae; secundo auditor; tertio doctor.

Locus autem doctrinae est templum. Unde primo ponit recessum ab eo; secundo reditum.

1119. Recessus quidem, cum dicit *Iesus autem perrexit in Montem oliveti.* Nam Dominus hanc sibi consuetudinem fecerat ut per diem quando erat Ierosolymis in diebus festis, praedicaret in templo, signa et miracula faceret, et in sero revertebatur in Bethaniam, et apud sorores Lazari Mariam et Martham hospitabatur, quae erat in Monte oliveti. Secundum igitur hunc morem dicit, quod cum in novissimo magnae festivitatis die Iesus stetisset in templo, et praedicasset, de sero *perrexit in Montem oliveti*, ubi erat Bethania.

Et hoc convenit mysterio: nam, ut dicit Augustinus, *ubi decebat Christum docere et suam misericordiam manifestare nisi in Monte oliveti, in Monte unctionis et chrismatis?* Oliva autem misericordiam signat: unde et in Graeco *oleos* idem est quod misericordia. Lc. X, 34, dicitur de Samaritano, quod infudit oleum et vinum, secundum misericordiam et severitatem iudicii. Item oleum sanativum est; Is. I, 6: *vulnus et livor et plaga tumens non est circumligata medicamine, neque fota oleo.* Signatur etiam medicina spiritualis gratiae, quae ad nos derivata est. Ps. XLIV, 8: *unxit te Deus, Deus tuus, oleo laetitiae prae consortibus tuis.* Et alibi: *sicut unguentum in capite quod descendit in barbam.*

doctrine of Christ has the power both to enlighten and to give life, because his words are spirit and life.

So first, he treats of the power of Christ's doctrine to enlighten;

second, of its power to give life: *amen, amen I say to you: he who does not enter by the door into the sheepfold but climbs in another way is a thief and a robber* (John 10:1).

He shows the power of Christ's doctrine to enlighten, first by words; and

second, by a miracle: *and Jesus, passing by, saw a man blind from birth* (John 9:1).

As to the first, he does two things:

first, he presents the teaching of Christ;

second, he shows the power of his teaching, at *Jesus spoke to them again* (John 8:12).

There are two things that pertain to the office of a teacher: to instruct the devout or sincere, and to repel opponents.

So first, Christ instructs those who are sincere; and

second, he repels his opponents, at *and the scribes and Pharisees brought to him a woman caught in adultery.*

The Evangelist does three things with respect to the first: first, he mentions the place where this teaching takes place; second, he mentions those who listened to it; and third, the teacher.

This teaching took place in the temple; so he first mentions that Jesus left the temple, and then that he returned.

1119. He mentions that Jesus left the temple when he says, *and Jesus went to the Mount of Olives.* For our Lord made it his practice, when he was at Jerusalem on the festival days, to preach in the temple and to work miracles and signs during the day, and when evening came, he would return to Bethany, which was on the Mount of Olives as the guest of Lazarus' sisters, Martha and Mary. With this in mind, the Evangelist says that since Jesus had remained in the temple and preached on the last day of the great feast, in the evening, *and Jesus went to the Mount of Olives*, where Bethany was located.

And this is appropriate to a mystery: for as Augustine says, *where was it appropriate for Christ to teach and show his mercy, if not on the Mount of Olives, the mount of anointing and of grace.* The olive signifies mercy; so also in Greek, *oleos* is the same as mercy. And we are told that the Samaritan applied oil and wine, which correspond to mercy and the stringency of judgment (Luke 10:24). Again, oil is healing: *wounds and bruises and swelling sores are not bandaged or dressed, or soothed with oil* (Isa 1:6). It also signifies the medicine of spiritual grace which has been transmitted to us by Christ: *God, your God, has anointed you with the oil of gladness above your fellows* (Ps 44:8); and again, *like the precious ointment on the head which ran down upon the beard* (Ps 132:2).

1120. Reditus autem ad locum ponitur tempestivus; unde dicit *et iterum diluculo venit in templum.* Per quod signatur quod cognitionem et manifestationem gratiae suae in templo suo, scilicet fidelibus suis, manifestaturus erat, Ps. XLVII, 10: *suscepimus, Deus, misericordiam tuam in medio templi tui.*

Quod autem diluculo rediit, exortum lumen novae gratiae designat; Os. VI, 3: *quasi diluculum praeparatus est egressus eius.*

1121. Auditor autem doctrinae est populus devotus; et ideo dicit *et omnis populus venit ad eum*; Ps. VII, 8: *synagoga populorum circumdabit te.*

1122. Doctor autem introducitur sedens, unde dicit *et sedens,* idest condescendens, ut eius doctrina facilius caperetur. Sessio enim humilitatem incarnationis significat; Ps. CXXXVIII, 1: *tu cognovisti sessionem meam et resurrectionem meam.* Quia per susceptam humanitatem visibilis apparens, coeperunt de divinis facilius edoceri; et ideo dicit, quod *sedens docebat eos,* idest simplices, et sermonem eius admirantes; Ps. XXIV, 9: *docebit mites vias suas, et diriget mansuetos in iudicio*; Is. II, 3: *docebit nos vias suas.*

1123. Consequenter cum dicit *adducunt autem Scribae et Pharisaei mulierem in adulterio deprehensam,* repellit adversarios, et

primo ponitur calumniae tentatio;

secundo calumniantium repulsio, ibi *Iesus autem inclinans se deorsum, digito scribebat in terra.*

Circa primum tria facit.

Primo ponitur tentationis occasio;

secundo describitur ipsa tentatio, ibi *dixerunt ei: Magister, haec mulier modo deprehensa est in adulterio*;

tertio tentatorum intentio, ibi *haec autem dicebant tentantes eum.*

1124. Occasio autem tentationis ponitur adulterium a muliere perpetratum: et ideo primo aggravant culpam; secundo praesentant personam peccantem.

Dicit ergo quantum ad primum *adducunt autem Scribae et Pharisaei mulierem in adulterio deprehensam.* Ut enim Augustinus dicit, tria in Christo praeeminebant: scilicet veritas, mansuetudo et iustitia. De ipso quippe fuerat praedictum: *procede, et regna, propter veritatem et mansuetudinem et iustitiam.* Nam veritatem attulit ut doctor, et hanc perceperant Pharisaei et Scribae dum doceret. Infra eodem: *si veritatem dico vobis, quare non creditis mihi?* Nullum enim falsum in verbis et doctrina eius deprehendere poterant; et ideo calumniari de hoc cessaverant.

Mansuetudinem vero attulit ut liberator; et hanc cognoverunt dum adversus inimicos et persecutores non

1120. Christ's return to the temple is described as being early; thus he says, ***and early in the morning he came again into the temple.*** This signifies that he was about to impart knowledge and manifest his grace in his temple, that is, in his believers: *we have received your mercy, O God, in the middle of your temple* (Ps 47:10).

The fact that he returned early in the morning signifies the rising light of new grace: *his going forth is as sure as the dawn* (Hos 6:3).

1121. Those who listened to his teaching were the sincere among the people; thus he says, ***all the people came to him***: *the assembly of the people will surround you* (Ps 7:8).

1122. Their teacher is presented as seated, ***and sitting down***, that is, going down to their level, so that his teaching would be more easily understood. His sitting down signifies the humility of his incarnation: *you knew when I sat down, and when I rose* (Ps 138:1). Because it was through the human nature that our Lord assumed that he became visible, we began to be instructed in the divine matters more easily. So he says, ***sitting down, he taught them***, that is, the simple, and those who respected his teaching: *he will teach his ways to the gentle, and will guide the mild in judgment* (Ps 24:9); *he will teach us his ways* (Isa 2:3).

1123. Then, at ***and the scribes and Pharisees brought to him a woman caught in adultery***, our Lord wards off his opponents.

First, we see him tested, so that he can then be accused; and

second, he checks his accusers, at ***but Jesus, bending down, wrote with his finger on the ground***.

As to the first, the Evangelist does three things:

first, he mentions the occasion for the test;

second, he describes the test itself, at ***and said to him: Master, this woman was just now caught in adultery***;

and third, the purpose of those who were testing our Lord, at ***and they said this tempting him***.

1124. The occasion for the test is a woman's adultery. And so first, her accusers detail the crime; and also exhibit the sinner.

As to the first, the Evangelist says, ***then the scribes and Pharisees brought in a woman caught in adultery***. As Augustine says, three things were noteworthy about Christ: his truth, his gentleness, and his justice. Indeed, it was predicted about him: *Go forth and reign, because of truth, gentleness, and justice* (Ps 44:5). For he set forth the truth as a teacher; and the Pharisees and scribes noticed this while he was teaching: *if I say the truth to you, why do you not believe me?* (John 8:46). Since they could find nothing false in his words or his teachings, they had ceased their accusations on that score.

He showed his gentleness as a liberator or savior; and they saw this when he could not be provoked against his

commoveretur; I Petr. II, v. 23: *cum malediceretur, non maledicebat*. Unde dicebat, Mt. XI, 29: *discite a me, quia mitis sum, et humilis corde*. Et ideo de hoc etiam non calumniabantur.

Iustitiam autem attulit ut cognitor, et hoc quia nondum nota erat Iudaeis, maxime in iudiciis: ideo in ea scandalum posuerunt, volentes scire utrum a iustitia propter misericordiam recederet. Et ideo proponunt ei crimen notum et confusione dignum, scilicet adulterium; Eccli. IX, 10: *omnis mulier fornicaria quasi stercus in via conculcabitur*. Consequenter personam peccantem repraesentant, ut magis commoveant. Unde *et statuerunt eam in medio*; Eccli. XXIII, 34: *hic in medio adducetur, et inter filios Dei* etc.

1125. Consequenter cum dicit *et dixerunt ei: Magister, haec mulier modo deprehensa est in adulterio*, prosequuntur ipsam tentationem, et

primo manifestant culpam;

secundo allegant legis iustitiam;

tertio exquirunt sententiam.

1126. Culpam quidem manifestant cum dicunt *haec mulier modo deprehensa est in adulterio*: quam quidem culpam exaggerant ex tribus, quae Christum commovere deberent a sua mansuetudine. Et primo ex culpae novitate; unde dicunt *modo*: nam quando est antiqua, non tantum movet, quia forte praecessit correctio.

Secundo ex eius evidentia; unde dicunt *deprehensa est*, ita quod non possit se excusare, quod est consuetudinis mulierum, secundum illud Prov. XXX, 20: *tergit os suum, dicens: non sum operata malum*.

Tertio ex culpae enormitate; unde dicunt *in adulterio*, quod est grave facinus et malorum multorum causa; Eccli. IX: *omnis mulier quae adulteratur peccabit*, primo quidem in lege Dei sui.

1127. Legis iustitiam allegant cum dicunt: *in lege autem*, scilicet Lev. et Deut. XXII, *Moyses mandavit huiusmodi lapidare*.

1128. Sententiam autem exquirunt cum subdunt: *tu ergo quid dicis?* Calumniosa est interrogatio; quasi dicant: si eam dimitti censuerit iustitiam non tenebit. Sed, absit ut qui venerat quaerere et salvum facere quod perierat, eam condemnaret; supra III, 17: *non enim misit Deus Filium suum in mundum ut iudicet mundum, sed ut salvetur mundus per ipsum*. Lex etiam quod iniustum erat iubere non poterat. Et ideo non dicit absolvatur ne contra legem facere videretur.

1129. Et ideo consequenter subditur perversa tentantium intentio, cum dicit *haec autem dicebant tentantes eum*. Credebant enim, quod Christus ne mansuetudinem perderet, eam dimitti debere dicturus esset;

enemies and persecutors: *when he was reviled, he did not revile* (1 Pet 2:23). Thus: *learn from me, for I am gentle and humble of heart* (Matt 11:29). Thus they did not accuse him on this point.

And he exercised justice as its advocate; he did this because it was not yet known among the Jews, especially in legal proceedings. It was on this point that they wanted to test him, to see if he would abandon justice for the sake of mercy. So they present him with a known crime, deserving denunciation, adultery: *every woman who is a harlot will be walked on like dung on the road* (Sir 9:10). Then they present the sinner in person to further influence him: *and they set her in the midst. This woman will be brought into the assembly, and among the sons of God* (Sir 23:24).

1125. The Evangelist, at *and said to him: Master, this woman was just now caught in adultery*, shows them proceeding with their test.

First, they point out the woman's fault;

second, they state the justice of the case according to the law;

third, they ask him for his verdict.

1126. They point out the woman's fault when they say *this woman was just now caught in adultery*. They detail her fault in three ways, calculated to deflect Christ from his gentle manner. First, they mention the freshness of her fault, saying *just now*; for an old fault does not affect us so much, because the person might have made amends.

Second, they note its certainty, saying, *caught*, so that she could not excuse herself. This is characteristic of women: *she wipes her mouth and says: I have done no evil* (Prov 33:20).

Third, they point out that her fault is great, *in adultery*, which is a serious crime and the cause of many evils. *Every woman who is adulterous will sin* (Sir 9), and first of all against the law of her God.

1127. They appeal to the justice contained in the law when they remark, *in the law*, that is, in Leviticus (Lev 20:10) and in Deuteronomy (Deut 22:21), *Moses commanded us to stone such a woman*.

1128. They ask Jesus for his verdict when they say, *but what do you say?* Their question is a trap, for they are saying in effect: if he decides that she should be let go, he will not be acting according to justice, yet he cannot condemn her because he came to seek and to save those who are lost: *for God did not send his Son into the world to judge the world, but that the world might be saved through him* (John 3:17). Now the law could not command anything unjust. Thus, Jesus does not say, let her go, lest he seem to be acting in violation of the law.

1129. The Evangelist reveals the malicious intention behind those who were questioning Jesus when he says, *they said this tempting him, that they might accuse him*. For they thought that Christ would say that she should be let

et sic accusarent eum tamquam legis praevaricatorem. I Cor. X, 9: *neque tentaveritis Christum, sicut illi tentaverunt.*

1130. Consequenter cum dicit *Iesus autem inclinans se deorsum, digito scribebat in terra*, repellit adversarios sua sapientia. Nam Pharisaei de duobus eum tentabant: scilicet de iustitia et de misericordia. Et utrumque in respondendo servavit, et ideo

primo ostendit quomodo servavit;

secundo quod non recessit a misericordia, ibi *erigens autem se Iesus dixit ei* etc.

Circa primum duo facit.

Primo proponit sententiam iustitiae;

secundo subditur effectus sententiae, ibi *audientes autem haec, unus post unum exibant.*

Circa primum tria facit.

Primo describit sententiam;

secundo pronuntiat eam;

tertio perseverat iterum in scribendo sententiam.

1131. Sententiam autem describit in terra digito; unde dicit Iesus *autem inclinans se deorsum, digito scribebat in terra*. Scribebat autem secundum quosdam illud quod dicitur Ier. XXII, 29: *terra terra, audi . . . scribe iustum virum sterilem.* Secundum alios vero, et melius, dicitur quod scripsit eadem quae protulit, scilicet: *qui sine peccato est vestrum, primus in illam lapidem mittat.* Neutrum tamen certum est.

Sed in terra quidem scribebat triplici ratione. Una quidem, secundum Augustinum, ut ostendat eos qui eum tentabant in terra describendos esse; Ier. XVII, 13: *Domine, recedentes a te in terra scribuntur.* Iusti autem, et discipuli qui eum sequuntur, in caelo scribuntur; Lc. X, 20: *gaudete et exultate, quia nomina vestra scripta sunt in caelo.* Item ut ostendat se quod signa faceret in terra: qui enim scribit, signa facit. Scribere ergo in terra, est signa facere: et ideo dicit quod *inclinavit se*, scilicet per incarnationis mysterium, ex quo in carne assumpta miracula fecit. Tertio, quia lex vetus in tabulis lapideis scripta erat, ut habetur Ex. XXXI, et II Cor. III. Per quod signatur eius duritia: quia *irritam quis faciens legem Moysi, absque ulla miseratione occidebatur*, ut dicitur Hebr. c. X, 28. Terra autem mollis est. Ut ergo signaret dulcedinem et mollitiem novae legis per eum traditae, in terra scribebat.

Ex quo tria in sententiis debemus attendere. Primo benignitatem in condescendendo puniendis: unde dicit *inclinans se*; Iac. II, 13: *iudicium sine misericordia ei qui non fecit misericordiam*; Gal. ult., 1: *si praeoccupatus fuerit aliquis in aliquo delicto, vos, qui spirituales estis, huiusmodi instruite in spiritu lenitatis.* Secundo discretionem in discernendo; unde dicit *digito scribebat*, qui propter

go, so as not to be acting contrary to his gentle manner; and then they would accuse him of acting in violation of the law: *let us not test Christ as they did* (1 Cor 10:9).

1130. Then, at *but Jesus, bending down, wrote with his finger on the ground*, Jesus checks his enemies by his wisdom. The Pharisees were testing him on two points: his justice and his mercy. But Jesus preserved both in his answer.

First, the Evangelist shows how Jesus kept to what was just; and

second, that he did not abandon mercy, at *he lifted himself up and said to them*.

As to the first, he does two things:

first, he mentions the sentence in accordance with justice;

second the effect of this sentence, at *but hearing this, they left one by one.*

About the first he does three things:

first, we see Jesus writing his sentence;

then pronouncing it; and

third, continuing again to write it down.

1131. Jesus wrote his sentence on the earth with his finger: *but Jesus, bending down, wrote with his finger on the ground*. Some say that he wrote the words: *O earth, earth, listen . . . write down this man as sterile* (Jer 22:29). According to others, and this is the better opinion, Jesus wrote down the very words he spoke, that is, *he who is without sin among you, let him first cast a stone at her*. However, neither of these opinions is certain.

Jesus wrote on the earth for three reasons. First, according to Augustine, to show that those who were testing him would be written on the earth: *O Lord, all who leave you will be written on the earth* (Jer 17:13). But those who are just and the disciples who follow him are written in heaven: *rejoice, because your names are written in heaven* (Luke 10:20). Second, he wrote on earth to show that he would perform signs on earth, for he who writes make signs. Thus, to write on the earth is to make signs. And so he says that Jesus was *bending down*, by the mystery of the incarnation, by means of which he performed miracles in the flesh he had assumed. Third, he wrote on the earth because the old law was written on tablets of stone (Exod 31; 2 Cor 3), which signify its harshness: *a man who violates the law of Moses dies without mercy* (Heb 10:28). But the earth is soft. And so Jesus wrote on the earth to show the sweetness and the softness of the new law that he gave to us.

We can see from this that there are three things to be considered in giving sentences. First, there should be kindness in lowering oneself before those to be punished; and so he says, *Jesus, bending down: there is judgment without mercy to him who does not have mercy* (Jas 2:13); *if a man is overtaken in any fault, you who are spiritual instruct him in a spirit of mildness* (Gal 6:1). Second, there should be

flexibilitatem discretionem significat; Dan. c. V, 5: *apparuerunt digiti quasi manus hominis scribentis contra candelabrum.* Tertio certitudinem in pronuntiando: unde dicit **scribebat**.

1132. Sententiam autem profert ad eorum instantiam; unde dicit **cum autem perseverarent interrogantes eum, erexit se, et dixit eis: qui sine peccato est vestrum, primus in illam lapidem mittat**. Pharisaei enim transgressores legis erant, tamen nitebantur Christum de transgressione legis accusare, et mulierem condemnare: et ideo Christus sententiam proponit iustitiae, dicens **qui sine peccato est vestrum**, quasi dicat: puniatur peccatrix, sed non a peccatoribus: impleatur lex, sed non a praevaricatoribus legis, quia, ut dicitur Rom. II, 1: *in quo enim alium iudicas, teipsum condemnas.* Aut ergo istam dimittite, aut cum illa poenam legis excipite.

1133. Hic incidit quaestio utrum iudex in peccato existens, peccet ferendo contra alium sententiam qui in eodem peccato existit. Et licet manifestum sit, quod iudex si publice in peccato existens sententiam ferat, peccat scandalizando; nihilominus tamen hoc idem videtur, si sit in peccato occulto. Nam Rom. II, 1: *in quo alium iudicas, teipsum condemnas.* Constat autem, quod nullus condemnat se nisi peccando: ergo videtur quod iudicando alium peccet.

Respondeo dicendum, quod in hoc uti oportet duplici distinctione. Aut enim iudex perseverat in proposito peccandi, aut poenitet se peccasse. Item aut punit ut legis minister, aut motu proprio. Et si quidem poenitet se peccasse, iam peccatum non est in eo; et sic absque peccato sententiam posset ferre. Si autem est in proposito peccandi: aut profert sententiam ut legis minister, et sic non peccat ex hoc quod sententiam profert, quamvis peccet ex hoc quod talia facit, quibus dignus est contra se similem sententiam recipere; si autem proprio motu, dico, quod proferendo sententiam peccat, cum non moveatur ad hoc amore iustitiae, sed ex aliqua mala radice; alias primo in se puniret quod animadvertit in alio; quia hoc dicitur in Prov. c. XVIII, 17: *iustus prior accusator est sui.*

1134. Perseverant autem in scribendo, quia **iterum se inclinans scribebat**: primo quidem ut ostendat suae scientiae firmitatem; Num. XXIII, 19: *non est Deus ut homo, ut mentiatur, et ut filius hominis, ut mutetur.*

Secundo ut ostendat eos sua visione indignos. Unde cum eos zelo iustitiae percussisset, non dignatus est eos attendere, sed avertit ab eis obtutum.

Tertio ut eorum verecundiae consulens, daret eis exeundi liberam facultatem.

1135. Effectus autem iustitiae est eorum confusio; unde dicit **audientes autem haec, unus post unum exibant**: tum quia gravioribus peccatis erant impliciti, et

discretion in determining the judgment and so he says that Jesus **wrote with his finger**, which because of its flexibility signifies discretion: *the fingers of a man's hand appeared, writing* (Dan 5:5). Third, there should be certitude about the sentence given; and so he says, **Jesus wrote**.

1132. It was at their insistence that Jesus gave his sentence; and so the Evangelist says, **when they continued asking him, he lifted himself up and said to them: he who is without sin among you, let him first cast a stone at her**. The Pharisees were violators of the law; and yet they tried to accuse Christ of violating the law and were attempting to make him condemn the woman. So Christ proposes a sentence in accord with justice, saying, **he who is without sin**. He is saying in effect: let the sinner be punished, but not by sinners; let the law be accomplished, but not by those who break it, because *when you judge another you condemn yourself* (Rom 2:1). Therefore, either let this woman go, or suffer the penalty of the law with her.

1133. Here the question arises as to whether a sinful judge sins by passing sentence against another person who has committed the same sin. It is obvious that if the judge who passes sentence is a public sinner, he sins by giving scandal. Yet, this seems to be true also if his sin is hidden, for we read: *when you judge another you condemn yourself* (Rom 2:1). However, it is clear that no one condemns himself except by sinning. And thus it seems that he sins by judging another.

My answer to this is that two distinctions have to be made. For the judge is either continuing in his determination to sin, or he has repented of his sins; and again, he is either punishing as a minister of the law or on his own initiative. Now if he has repented of his sin, he is no longer a sinner, and so he can pass sentence without sinning. But if he continues in his determination to sin, he does not sin in passing sentence if he does this as a minister of the law; although he would be sinning by doing the very things for which he deserves a similar sentence. But if he passes sentence on his own authority, then I say that he sins in justice, but from some evil root; otherwise he would first punish in himself what he notices in someone else, because *a just person is the first to accuse himself* (Prov 18:17).

1134. Jesus continued to write, **and again bending down, he wrote**. He did this, first, to show the firmness of his sentence, *God is not like a man, who may lie, or like a son of man, so that he may change* (Num 23:19).

Second, he did it to show that they were not worthy to look at him. Because he had disturbed them with his zeal for justice, he did not think it fit to look at them, but turned from their sight.

Third, he did this out of consideration for their embarrassment, to give them complete freedom to leave.

1135. The effect of his justice is their embarrassment, **but hearing this, they left one by one**, both because they had been involved in more serious sins and their conscience

magis eos conscientia remordebat; Dan. XIII, 5: *egressa est iniquitas a senioribus iudicibus, qui videbantur regere populum*; tum etiam quia melius cognoscebant aequitatem prolatae sententiae; Ier. V, 5: *ibo ergo ad optimates, et loquar eis: ipsi enim cognoverunt viam Domini, et iudicium Dei sui*. **Et remansit solus Iesus, et mulier stans**, scilicet misericordia et miseria. Ideo autem solus remansit, quia ipse solus sine peccato erat. Nam, ut dicitur in Ps. XIII, 1: *non est qui faciat bonum, non est usque ad unum*, scilicet Christum. Et ideo forte mulier territa est, et ab illo se puniendam credebat.

Sed si remansit solus, quomodo dicit *in medio stans*? Et dicendum, quod mulier stabat in medio discipulorum, et sic ly *solus* excludit extraneos, non discipulos. Vel *in medio*, idest in dubio, utrum absolvenda esset, vel condemnanda. Sic ergo patet quod Dominus in respondendo iustitiam servavit.

1136. Consequenter cum dicit **erigens autem se Iesus, dixit ei** etc. ostendit quod a misericordia non recessit, dando sententiam misericordiae, et

primo examinat;

secundo absolvit;

tertio admonet;

1137. examinat autem eam de accusatoribus; unde dicit, quod **erigens se Iesus**, scilicet faciem suam a terra, in qua scribebat, ad mulierem convertens, **dixit ei: mulier, ubi sunt qui te accusabant?** Item de condemnatione; unde quaerit **nemo te condemnavit?** Et illa respondit: **nemo, Domine**.

1138. Absolvit autem eam; unde dicit **dixit ei Iesus: nec ego te condemnabo**, a quo te forte damnari timuisti, quia in me peccatum non invenisti. Nec mirum, **quia non misit Deus Filium suum in mundum, ut iudicet mundum, sed ut salvetur mundus per ipsum**; supra III, 17; Ez. XVIII, 32: *nolo mortem peccatoris*.

Absolvit autem eam a culpa, non imponendo ei aliquam poenam: quia cum absolvendo exterius iustificaret interius, bene potuit eam adeo immutare interius per sufficientem contritionem de peccatis, ut ab omni poena immunis efficeretur. Nec tamen trahendum est in consuetudinem ut aliquis exemplo domini absque confessione et poenae inflictione quemquam absolvat; quia Christus excellentiam habuit in sacramentis, et potuit conferre effectum sine sacramento, quod nullus purus homo potest.

1139. Admonet vero eam cum dicit **vade, et iam noli peccare**. Duo enim erant in muliere ista: scilicet natura et culpa. Et utrumque poterat Dominus condemnare. Puta naturam, si iussisset eam lapidare; et culpam, si non absolvisset. Poterat etiam utrumque absolvere, puta si dedisset licentiam peccandi, dicens vade, vive ut vis, esto

gnawed them more: *iniquity came out from the elder judges who were seen to rule the people* (Dan 13:5), and because they better realized the fairness of the sentence he gave: *I will go therefore to the great men and speak to them: for they have known the way of the Lord and the judgment of their God* (Jer 5:5). **And Jesus alone remained, and the woman standing in the midst**, that is, mercy and misery. Jesus alone remained because he alone was without sin; as the Psalm says: *there is no one who does what is good not even one*, except Christ (Ps 13:1). So perhaps this woman was afraid, and thought she would be punished by him.

If only Jesus remained, why does it say that the woman was standing there **in the midst**? I answer that the woman was standing in the center of the disciples, and so the word **alone** excludes outsiders, not the disciples. Or, we could say, **in the midst**, that is, in doubt whether she would be forgiven or condemned. And so it is clear that our Lord's answer preserved justice.

1136. Then, at **then Jesus lifting himself up, said to her**, he shows that Jesus did not abandon mercy, but gave a merciful sentence.

First, Jesus questions the woman;

then forgives her;

and finally, cautions her.

1137. Jesus questioned her about her accusers; thus he says that **Jesus, lifting himself up**, that is, turning from the ground on which he was writing and looking at the woman, **said to her: woman, where are they who accused you?** He asks about her condemnation saying, **has no man condemned you?** And she answers, **no one, Lord**.

1138. Jesus forgives her; and so it says, **then Jesus said: neither will I condemn you**, I who perhaps you feared would condemn you, because you saw that I was without sin. This should not surprise us for **God did not send his Son into the world to judge the world, but that the world might be saved through him** (John 3:17); *I do not desire the death of the sinner* (Ezek 18:23).

And he forgave her sin without imposing any penance on her because since he made her inwardly just by outwardly forgiving her, he was well able to change her so much within by sufficient sorrow for her sins that she would be made free from any penance. This should not be taken as a precedent for anyone to forgive another without confession and the assigning of a penance on the ground of Christ's example, for Christ has power over the sacraments, and could confer the effect without the sacrament. No mere man can do this.

1139. Finally, Jesus cautions her when he says, **go, and sin no more**. There were two things in that woman: her nature and her sin. Our Lord could have condemned both. For example, he could have condemned her nature if he had ordered them to stone her, and he could have condemned her sin if he had not forgiven her. He was also able

de mea liberatione secura; ego, quantumcumque peccaveris, etiam a Gehenna et ab inferni tortoribus liberabo. Sed Dominus culpam non amans, peccatis non favens, ipsam damnavit culpam, non naturam, dicens **amplius noli peccare**: ut sic appareat quam dulcis est Dominus per mansuetudinem, et rectus per veritatem.

to absolve each. For example, if he had given her license to sin, saying: go, live as you wish, and put your hope in my freeing you. No matter how much you sin, I will free you even from Gehenna and from the tortures of hell. But our Lord does not love sin, and does not favor wrongdoing, and so he condemned her sin but not her nature, saying, **go, and sin no more**. We see here how kind our Lord is because of his gentleness, and how just he is because of his truth.

Lecture 2

8:12 Iterum ergo locutus est eis Iesus, dicens: ego sum lux mundi. Qui sequitur me, non ambulat in tenebris. Sed habebit lumen vitae. [n. 1141]

8:13 Dixerunt ergo ei Pharisaei: tu de teipso testimonium perhibes: testimonium tuum non est verum. [n. 1146]

8:14 Respondit Iesus, et dixit eis: et si ego testimonium perhibeo de meipso, verum est testimonium meum, quia scio unde veni, et quo vado. Vos autem nescitis unde venio, aut quo vado. [n. 1148]

8:15 Vos secundum carnem iudicatis. Ego non iudico quemquam. [n. 1150]

8:16 Et si iudico ego, iudicium meum verum est, quia solus non sum; sed ego, et qui misit me Pater. [n. 1153]

8:17 Et in lege vestra scriptum est, quia duorum hominum testimonium verum est. [n. 1155]

8:18 Ego sum qui testimonium perhibeo de meipso, et testimonium perhibet de me, qui misit me Pater. [n. 1157]

8:19 Dicebant ergo ei: ubi est pater tuus? Respondit Iesus: neque me scitis, neque Patrem meum: si me sciretis, forsitan et Patrem meum sciretis. [n. 1158]

8:20 Haec verba locutus est Iesus in gazophylacio, docens in templo; et nemo apprehendit eum, quia necdum venerat hora eius. [n. 1163]

8:12 Πάλιν οὖν αὐτοῖς ἐλάλησεν ὁ Ἰησοῦς λέγων· ἐγώ εἰμι τὸ φῶς τοῦ κόσμου· ὁ ἀκολουθῶν ἐμοὶ οὐ μὴ περιπατήσῃ ἐν τῇ σκοτίᾳ, ἀλλ᾽ ἕξει τὸ φῶς τῆς ζωῆς.

8:13 εἶπον οὖν αὐτῷ οἱ Φαρισαῖοι· σὺ περὶ σεαυτοῦ μαρτυρεῖς· ἡ μαρτυρία σου οὐκ ἔστιν ἀληθής.

8:14 ἀπεκρίθη Ἰησοῦς καὶ εἶπεν αὐτοῖς· κἂν ἐγὼ μαρτυρῶ περὶ ἐμαυτοῦ, ἀληθής ἐστιν ἡ μαρτυρία μου, ὅτι οἶδα πόθεν ἦλθον καὶ ποῦ ὑπάγω· ὑμεῖς δὲ οὐκ οἴδατε πόθεν ἔρχομαι ἢ ποῦ ὑπάγω.

8:15 ὑμεῖς κατὰ τὴν σάρκα κρίνετε, ἐγὼ οὐ κρίνω οὐδένα.

8:16 καὶ ἐὰν κρίνω δὲ ἐγώ, ἡ κρίσις ἡ ἐμὴ ἀληθινή ἐστιν, ὅτι μόνος οὐκ εἰμί, ἀλλ᾽ ἐγὼ καὶ ὁ πέμψας με πατήρ.

8:17 καὶ ἐν τῷ νόμῳ δὲ τῷ ὑμετέρῳ γέγραπται ὅτι δύο ἀνθρώπων ἡ μαρτυρία ἀληθής ἐστιν.

8:18 ἐγώ εἰμι ὁ μαρτυρῶν περὶ ἐμαυτοῦ καὶ μαρτυρεῖ περὶ ἐμοῦ ὁ πέμψας με πατήρ.

8:19 ἔλεγον οὖν αὐτῷ· ποῦ ἐστιν ὁ πατήρ σου; ἀπεκρίθη Ἰησοῦς· οὔτε ἐμὲ οἴδατε οὔτε τὸν πατέρα μου· εἰ ἐμὲ ᾔδειτε, καὶ τὸν πατέρα μου ἂν ᾔδειτε.

8:20 Ταῦτα τὰ ῥήματα ἐλάλησεν ἐν τῷ γαζοφυλακίῳ διδάσκων ἐν τῷ ἱερῷ· καὶ οὐδεὶς ἐπίασεν αὐτόν, ὅτι οὔπω ἐληλύθει ἡ ὥρα αὐτοῦ.

8:12 Jesus spoke to them again, saying: I am the light of the world: he who follows me does not walk in darkness but will have the light of life. [n. 1141]

8:13 The Pharisees therefore said to him: you give testimony about yourself, but your testimony is not true. [n. 1146]

8:14 Jesus answered and said to them: although I give testimony about myself, my testimony is true: for I know where I came from and where I go, but you do not know where I come from or where I go. [n. 1148]

8:15 You judge according to the flesh; I do not judge any man. [n. 1150]

8:16 And if I do judge, my judgment is true, because I am not alone, but there is me and the Father who sent me. [n. 1153]

8:17 And in your law it is written that the testimony of two men is true. [n. 1155]

8:18 I am one who gives testimony about myself, and the Father who sent me gives testimony about me. [n. 1157]

8:19 They therefore said to him: where is your father? Jesus answered: you know neither me nor my Father: if you did know me, perhaps you would also know my Father. [n. 1158]

8:20 These words Jesus spoke in the treasury, teaching in the temple, and no man laid hands on him, because his hour had not yet come. [n. 1163]

1140. Postquam Evangelista introduxit Christum docentem, hic consequenter

primo ostendit doctrinae ipsius illuminativam virtutem;

secundo manifestat quae de ea dicit, ibi **dixerunt ergo ei Pharisaei: tu de te ipso testimonium perhibes.**

Circa primum tria facit.

1140. The Evangelist has presented Christ as teaching; now he shows,

first, the power which this teaching has to give light, and

second, what Christ himself said about it, at **the Pharisees therefore said to him: you give testimony about yourself.**

With respect to the first he does three things:

Primo ponit spiritualis lucis privilegium;

secundo eius effectum, ibi *qui sequitur me, non ambulat in tenebris*;

tertio eius fructum, ibi *sed habebit lumen vitae*.

1141. Privilegium autem spiritualis lucis ponitur quantum ad Christum, qui est lux; et quantum ad hoc dicit *iterum locutus est eis Iesus dicens: ego sum lux mundi*. Quod potest uno modo continuari ad immediate dictum. Quia enim dixit: *nec ego condemnabo te* etc., absolvens eam a crimine, ideo ne aliqui dubitarent utrum ipse absolvere posset, et peccata dimittere, dignatur apertius divinitatis suae potentiam demonstrare, dicens se esse lucem, qui peccati tenebras pellit.

Alio modo potest continuari ad illud quod supra VII, 52 dixit: *scrutare Scripturas, et vide quia propheta a Galilaea non surgit*. Quia enim eum aestimabant Galilaeum, et quasi ex loco determinato dependentem, doctrinam eius repudiabant; ideo Dominus ostendit se totius mundi esse lucem universalem, dicens *ego sum lux mundi*, non Galilaeae, neque Palaestinae, neque Iudaeae.

1142. Manichaei autem, ut Augustinus dicit, hoc falso intelligebant. Quia enim imaginatio eorum erat solum de sensibilibus, ideo non valebant se ad intellectualia et spiritualia extendere, credebant enim supra corporalia nihil esse in rerum natura, unde dicebant Deum esse corpus et lucem quamdam infinitam, et solem istum oculis carnis visibilem, Christum Dominum esse putaverunt: et propter hoc ipsum dixisse *ego sum lux mundi*.

Sed hoc stare non potest et Ecclesia Catholica improbat tale figmentum. Sol enim iste corporalis est lux quam sensus attingere potest: et ideo non est suprema lux, quam intellectus solus attingit, quae est lux intelligibilis propria rationalis creaturae. Hic de ea dicit Christus *ego sum lux mundi*. De ista dicitur supra I, 9: *erat lux vera quae illuminat omnem hominem venientem in hunc mundum*.

Lux autem ista sensibilis, imago quaedam est illius lucis intelligibilis: nam omne sensibile est quasi quoddam particulare, intellectualia autem sunt quasi totalia quaedam. Sicut autem lux ista particularis habet effectum in re visa, inquantum colores facit actu visibiles, et etiam in vidente, quia per eam oculus confortatur ad videndum, sic lux illa intelligibilis intellectum facit cognoscentem. Quia quidquid luminis est in rationali creatura, totum derivatur ab ipsa suprema luce; supra I, 9: *illuminat omnem hominem venientem in hunc mundum*. Item facit res omnes actu intelligibiles, inquantum ab ipsa derivantur omnes formae, per quas res habent quod cognoscantur, sicut omnes formae artificiatorum derivantur ab arte et ratione artificis; Ps. CIII, 24: *quam magnificata sunt opera tua, Domine. Omnia in sapientia fecisti*. Et ideo recte dicit *ego sum lux mundi*: non sol factus, sed per

first, he states Christ's prerogative concerning spiritual light;

second, the effect of this prerogative, *he who follows me does not walk in darkness*; and

third, its fruit, *but will have the light of life*.

1141. He says, concerning the prerogative of Christ, who is the light, to the spiritual light, *Jesus spoke to them again, saying: I am the light of the world*. We can relate this statement with what went before in this way. Christ had said, when forgiving the woman's sin, *neither will I condemn you* (John 8:11). And so they would have no doubt that he could forgive and pardon sins, he saw fit to show the power of his divinity more openly by saying that he is the light which drives away the darkness of sin.

Or, we could connect this statement with what the Pharisees said before: *search the Scriptures and see that, out of Galilee, a prophet does not rise* (John 7:52). For they thought of him as a Galilean and linked to a definite place, and so they rejected his teaching. So our Lord shows them that he is in the universal light of the entire world, saying, *I am the light of the world*, not just of Galilee, or of Palestine, or of Judea.

1142. The Manicheans, as Augustine relates, misunderstood this: for since they judged by their imagination, which does not rise to intellectual and spiritual realities, they believed that nothing but bodies existed. Thus they said that God was a body; and a certain infinite light. Further, they thought that the sun that we see with our physical eyes was Christ the Lord. And that is why, according to them, Christ said, *I am the light of the world*.

However, this opinion cannot be held and the Catholic Church rejects such a fiction. For this physical sun is a light which can be perceived by sense. Consequently, it is not the highest light, which intellect alone grasps, and which is the intelligible light characteristic of the rational creature. Christ says about this light here: *I am the light of the world*. And above we read: *he was the true light, which enlightens every man coming into this world* (John 1:9).

Since perceptible light, however, is a certain image of spiritual light, for every sensible thing is something particular, whereas intellectual things are a kind of whole. Just as particular light has an effect on the thing seen, inasmuch as it makes colors actually visible, as well as on the one seeing, because through it the eye is conditioned for seeing, so intellectual light makes the intellect to know because whatever light is in the rational creature is all derived from that supreme light *which enlightens every man coming into the world*. Furthermore, it makes all things to be actually intelligible inasmuch as all forms are derived from it, forms which give things the capability of being known, just as all the forms of artifacts are derived from the art and reason on the artisan: *how magnificent are your works, O Lord! You have made all things in wisdom* (Ps 103:24). Thus Christ truly says here: *I am the light of the world*; not the

quem sol factus est. Tamen, ut Augustinus dicit, lumen quod solem fecit, sub sole factum est, et carnis nube tegitur, non ut obscuretur, sed ut temperetur.

1143. Excluditur etiam per hoc haeresis Nestorii dicentis, quod Filius Dei erat unitus homini per inhabitationem tantum.

Constat enim quod qui haec verba proferebat, scilicet *ego sum lux mundi*, homo erat. Nisi ergo ipse qui loquebatur et videbatur homo, personaliter esset Filius Dei, non dixisset *ego sum lux mundi*, sed in me habitat lux mundi.

1144. Effectus autem huius lucis est expellere tenebras; unde dicit *qui sequitur me, non ambulat in tenebris*. Et quia lux ista est universalis, ideo universaliter tenebras omnes expellit.

Sunt autem triplices tenebrae, scilicet ignorantiae; Ps. LXXXI, 5: *nescierunt neque intellexerunt: in tenebris ambulant*. Et hae sunt rationis secundum seipsam, inquantum per seipsam obnubilatur. Item culpae; Eph. V, 8: *eratis aliquando tenebrae, nunc autem lux in Domino*. Et istae sunt rationis humanae non ex se, sed ex appetitu, inquantum male dispositus per passiones vel habitum, appetit aliquid ut bonum, quod tamen non est vere bonum. Item tenebrae damnationis aeternae; Matth. c. XXV, 30: *inutilem servum eiicite in tenebras exteriores*. Sed duae primae sunt in vita ista; tertiae vero sunt in termino viae. *Qui* ergo *sequitur me, non ambulat in tenebris*, ignorantiae, quia *ego sum veritas*, nec culpae, quia *ego sum via*, neque damnationis aeternae, quia *ego sum vita*.

1145. Et ideo consequenter subdit fructum doctrinae, scilicet *sed habebit lumen vitae*: nam qui hoc lumen habet, est extra tenebras damnationis.

Dicit autem *qui sequitur*, quia sicut quicumque non vult errare in tenebris, oportet ut sequatur eum qui lumen portat; ita quicumque vult salvari, oportet quod sequatur Christum, qui est lux, credendo et amando; et sic apostoli secuti sunt eum, Matth. IV, 20. Quia vero lux corporalis deficere potest per occasum, contingit quia qui sequitur eam, tenebras incurrit. Lux vero ista, quae nescit occasum, numquam deficit: et ideo qui sequitur eam, habet lumen indeficiens, scilicet vitae. Lumen enim visibile non dat vitam, sed coadiuvat exterius operationes vitae corporalis; lumen vero istud vitam dat, quia vivimus inquantum intellectum habemus, qui est quaedam participatio illius lucis. Quando autem lux illa perfecte irradiabit, tunc habebimus vitam perfectam; Ps. XXXV, 10: *apud te est fons vitae, et in lumine tuo videbimus lumen*; quasi dicat: tunc ipsam vitam perfecte habebimus quando ipsum lumen per speciem videbimus.

sun which was made, but the one who made the sun. Yet as Augustine says, the light which made the sun was himself made under the sun and covered with a cloud of flesh, not in order to hide but to be moderated.

1143. This also eliminates the heresy of Nestorius, who said that the Son of God was united to human nature by a mere indwelling.

For it is obvious that the one who said, *I am the light of the world*, was a human being. Therefore, unless the one who spoke and appeared as a human being was also the person of the Son of God, he could not have said, *I am the light of the world*, but the light of the world dwells in me.

1144. The effect of this light is to expel darkness; and so he says, *he who follows me does not walk in darkness*. Because this light is universal, it universally expels all darkness.

Now there are three kinds of darkness. There is the darkness of ignorance: *they have neither known nor understood; they walk in darkness* (Ps 81:5); and this is the darkness reason has of itself, insofar as it is darkened of itself. There is the darkness of sin: *you were at one time darkness, but now you are light in the Lord* (Eph 5:8). This darkness belongs to human reason not of itself, but from the affections which, by being badly disposed by passion or habit, seek something as good that is not really good. Further, there is the darkness of eternal damnation: *cast the unprofitable servant into the exterior darkness* (Matt 25:30). The first two kinds of darkness are found in this life; but the third is at the end of life. Thus, *he who follows me does not walk in darkness*: the darkness of ignorance, because *I am the truth*; nor the darkness of sin, because *I am the way*; nor the darkness of eternal damnation, because *I am the life*.

1145. He next adds the fruit of his teaching, *but will have the light of life*, for one who has the light is outside the darkness of damnation.

He says, *he who follows me*, because just as one who does not want to stumble in the dark has to follow the one who is carrying the light, so one who wants to be saved must, by believing and loving, follow Christ, who is the light. This is the way the apostles followed him (Matt 4:20). Because physical light can fail because it sets, it happens that one who follows it meets with darkness. But the light we are talking about here does not set and never fails; consequently, one who follows it has an unfailing light, that is, an unfailing light of life. For the light that is visible does not give life, but gives us an external aid because we live insofar as we have understanding, and this is a certain participation in this light. And when this light completely shines upon us we will then have perfect life: *with you is the fountain of life, and in your light we will see the light* (Ps 35:10). This is the same as saying: we will have perfectly or completely when we see this light as it is. Thus we read further on: *this is*

Unde dicitur Io. XVII, 3: *haec est vita aeterna, ut cognoscant te solum verum Deum, et quem misisti Iesum Christum.*

Sed attendendum, quod hoc quod dicit *qui sequitur me*, pertinet ad meritum; quod vero dicit *habebit lumen vitae*, ad praemium.

1146. Consequenter cum dicit *dixerunt ergo ei Pharisaei* etc., manifestat haec tria quae de se dicit, et

primo primum;

secundo secundum, ibi *dicit ergo iterum, eis Iesus*;

tertio tertium, ibi *amen, amen dico vobis, si quis sermonem meum servaverit, mortem non videbit in aeternum.*

Primum autem quod dixit, est *ego sum lux mundi*, quod Iudaeos turbabat, et ideo

primo ponit Iudaeorum contradictionem;

secundo eorum confutationem, manifestando veritatem sui dicti, ibi *respondit Iesus, et dixit eis* etc.

1147. Manifestum est autem circa primum, quod illa quae dixit in templo, dixit in conspectu turbarum, hic autem coram Pharisaeis. Et ideo dixerunt ei ipsi Pharisaei: *tu de teipso testimonium perhibes, testimonium tuum non est verum*; quasi dicant: ex hoc ipso quod tu de teipso testificaris, testimonium tuum non est verum.

In hominibus enim nec acceptum nec congruum est quod homo se laudet; Prov. XXVII, v. 2: *laudet te alienus, et non os tuum*: quia non ex hoc commendabilis redditur, sed si a Deo commendatur; II Cor. X, 18: *non enim qui seipsum commendat, ille probatus est, sed quem Deus commendat*: quia solus Deus perfecte eum cognoscit. Deum autem nullus potest sufficienter commendare, nisi ipse seipsum, et ideo oportet quod ipse de seipso testificetur, et etiam de hominibus; Iob XVI, 20: *ecce in caelo testis meus*. Et ideo Iudaei decipiebantur.

1148. Consequenter cum dicit *respondit Iesus, et dixit eis* etc., Dominus repellit eorum contradictionem, et

primo auctoritate Patris;

secundo removet contradictionem exortam de Patre, ibi *dicebant ergo ei: ubi est pater tuus?*

Contradictio autem Iudaeorum erat per quamdam consequentiam, et ideo

primo ostendit eorum consequentiam non tenere;

secundo probat suum testimonium verum esse, ibi *ego non iudico quemquam* etc.

Circa primum duo facit.

Primo ostendit consequentiae falsitatem;

eternal life: *that they may know you, the only true God, and Jesus Christ, whom you have sent* (John 17:3).

Note that the phrase, *he who follows me*, pertains to our merits; while the statement, *will have the light of life*, pertains to our reward.

1146. At *the Pharisees therefore said to him*, the Evangelist mentions three things that Jesus says about himself.

First concerning the first;

second, the second, at *again Jesus said to them: I go and you will seek me* (John 8:21); and

third, the third, at *amen, amen I say to you: if any man keep my word, he will never see death* (John 8:51).

The first thing he said was, *I am the light of the world*; and this troubled the Jews.

So first, he shows their opposition;

second, how Jesus proved that they were wrong by showing what he said was true, at *Jesus answered and said to them: although I give testimony about myself.*

1147. With respect to the first, it is obvious that what Jesus said in the temple, he said in the presence of the people. But now he is speaking before the Pharisees, and so they said to him: *you give testimony about yourself, but your testimony is not true*. They were saying in effect: because you are bearing witness to yourself, your testimony is not true.

Now in human affairs it is neither acceptable nor fitting that a person praise himself: *let another praise you, and not your own mouth* (Prov 27:2), because self-praise does not make a person commendable, but being commended by God does: *it is not he who commends himself who is approved, but he whom God commends* (2 Cor 10:18), because only God perfectly knows a person. But no one can really sufficiently commend God except God himself; and so it is fitting that he bear witness to himself, and also to men: *my witness is in heaven* (Job 16:20). Thus the opinion of the Jews was mistaken.

1148. Next, at *Jesus answered and said to them: although I give testimony about myself*, our Lord rejects their opposition:

first, by the authority of his Father;

second, by answering their rejection, which arose concerning his Father, at *they therefore said to him: where is your father?*

The opposition of the Jews arose from a certain conclusion which they drew: and so

first he shows that their conclusion is not true;

second, he proves that his own testimony is true, at *I do not judge any man.*

He does two things concerning the first:

first, he shows that their conclusion is false;

secundo subdit deceptionis ipsorum causam, ibi *vos autem nescitis unde venio, aut quo vado*.

1149. Consequentia autem istorum erat quod ex hoc ipso quod Christus de se testimonium perhibebat, testimonium eius non erat verum. Sed Dominus dicit contrarium, scilicet quod ex hoc verum est. Unde respondit, *et dixit eis: si ego testimonium perhibeo de meipso, testimonium meum verum est*: et hoc ideo, quia *ego scio unde veni, et quo vado*; quasi dicat, secundum Chrysostomum, quia ex Deo sum, et Deus, et Dei Filius. *Est autem Deus verax*: Rom. III, 4.

Dicit autem *scio unde veni*, idest cognosco meum principium, *et quo vado*, scilicet ad Patrem, quem nullus perfecte scire potest nisi Filius Dei; Matth. XI, 27: *nec Patrem quis novit nisi Filius, et cui voluerit Filius revelare*. Non autem quicumque scit affectu et intellectu, unde veniat et quo vadat, non potest nisi verum dicere, nam a Deo venit, et ad Deum vadit; Deus autem veritas est: quanto ergo magis Filius Dei, qui perfecte scit unde venit et quo vadit, verum dicit?

1150. Consequenter cum dicit *vos autem nescitis unde venio aut quo vado*, ostendit causam erroris, quae est ignorantia divinitatis Christi; quia enim ipsam ignorabant, iudicabant de eo secundum humanitatem.

Sic ergo duplex causa erroris erat in eis. Una, quia eius divinitatem ignorabant; alia, quia de eo secundum humanitatem tantum iudicabant. Et ideo quantum ad primum dicit *vos nescitis unde venio*, idest aeternum meum processum a Patre, *aut quo vado*. Supra: *est verax qui misit me, et ego quae audivi ab eo, haec loquor in mundo*; Iob XXVIII, 20: *unde ergo venit sapientia?* Is. LIII, 8: *generationem eius quis enarrabit?*

Quantum ad secundum dicit *vos secundum carnem iudicatis*, scilicet de me, solum carnem esse putantes, non autem Deum. Vel secundum carnem, idest male et iniuste. Sicut enim secundum carnem vivere est male vivere, ita et secundum carnem iudicare, est male iudicare.

1151. Consequenter cum dicit *ego non iudico quemquam*, ostendit testimonium suum esse verum, et falsum esse quod ipse solus de se testimonium perhibeat. Et quia de iudicio mentio facta est, ostendit

primo se non esse solum in iudicando;

secundo se non esse solum in testificando, ibi *et in lege vestra scriptum est* etc.

Circa primum tria facit.

Primo ponit iudicii dilationem;

secundo iudicii veritatem; et

tertio veritatis rationem.

second, he adds the reason for their error, at *but you do not know where I come from or where I go*.

1149. Their conclusion was that the testimony of Christ was not true, because he bore witness to himself. But our Lord says the opposite, namely, that because of this it is true. Jesus replied: *although I give testimony about myself, my testimony is true*; and it is true because *I know where I came from and where I go*. It is like saying, according to Chrysostom, my testimony is true because I am from God, and because I am God, and because I am the Son of God: *God is truthful* (Rom 3:4).

He says, *I know where I came from*, that is, my origin, *and where I go*, that is to the Father, whom no one but the Son can know perfectly: *no one knows the Father except the Son, and he to whom Son wishes to reveal him* (Matt 11:27). This does not imply that anyone who knows, by love and understanding, where he comes from and where he is going can speak only the truth, for we all come from God and are going to God. But God is truth: how much more, then, does the Son of God speak the truth, he who knows perfectly where he comes from and where he is going.

1150. Then when he says, *but you do not know where I come from or where I go*, he shows the reason for their error, which was their ignorance of the divinity of Christ. For it was because they did not know this that they judged him according to his human nature.

Thus, there were two reasons for their error. One, because they did not know his divinity; the other, because they judged him only by his human nature. And so he says, with respect to the first, *you do not know where I come from*, that is, my eternal procession from the Father, *or where I go*. It says below: *he who sent me is truthful, and the things that I have heard from him are the same that I speak to the world* (John 8:26); *from where, then, does wisdom come?* (Job 28:20); *who will state his origin?* (Isa 53:8).

As for the second reason for their error, he says, *you judge according to the flesh*, that is, you judge me thinking that I am merely flesh and not God. Or, we could say, according to the flesh, that is, wickedly and unjustly. For just as to live according to the flesh is to live wickedly, so to judge according to the flesh is to judge unjustly.

1151. Then, at *I do not judge any man*, he shows that his testimony is true, and that it is false to say that he alone is bearing witness to himself. Because mention was now made about judging, he shows,

first, that he is not alone in judging; and

second, that he is not alone in bearing witness, at *and in your law it is witten that the testimony of two men is true*.

He does three things about the first:

first, he says that his judgment is deferred;

second, that his judgment is true; and

third, he gives the reason why his judgment is true.

1152. Dilationem quidem iudicii ponit cum dicit *ego non iudico quemquam*; quasi dicat: vos iudicatis male, sed *ego non iudico quemquam*; supra III, 17: *non enim misit Deus Filium suum in mundum ut iudicet mundum, sed ut salvetur mundus per ipsum.* Vel *non iudico quemquam*, scilicet secundum carnem, sicut vos iudicatis; Is. XI, 3: *non secundum visionem oculorum iudicabit, neque secundum auditum aurium arguet.*

1153. Sed tamen quandoque iudicabo; quia *Pater omne iudicium dedit Filio*; supra c. V, 22. Et tunc *iudicium meum verum est*, idest iustum; Ps. XCV: *iudicabit orbem terrae in aequitate*; Rom. II, 2: *scimus quia iudicium Dei est secundum veritatem in eos qui talia agunt.* In quo ostenditur iudicii veritas.

1154. Rationem veritatis ostendit, cum dicit *quia non sum solus*. Quod autem dicit supra V, 22, *Pater non iudicat quemquam*, intelligendum est seorsum a Filio, vel quia non visibiliter Pater apparebit omnibus in iudicio; et ideo dicit *non sum solus*, quia non derelictus ab ipso, sed simul cum ipso; infra XIV, v. 10: *ego in Patre, et Pater in me est.*

Hoc autem verbum excludit errorem Sabellii dicentis unam esse personam Patris et Filii, nec differre nisi secundum nomina. Si enim hoc esset, non dixisset *non sum solus, sed ego, et qui misit me*, sed dixisset: ego sum Pater, et ego ipse sum Filius. Distingue ergo personas, et cognosce Filium esse alium a Patre.

1155. Consequenter cum dicit *et in lege vestra scriptum est* etc., ostendit quod non est solus in testificando; nec tamen differt testimonium, sicut iudicium: unde non dicit, testimonium non perhibeo.

Primo ergo introducit legem;

secundo concludit propositum, ibi *ego sum qui testimonium perhibeo de meipso.*

1156. Dicit ergo *in lege vestra*, et vobis data, Eccli. XXIV, 23: *legem mandavit Moyses: scriptum est*, Deut. XIX, *quia duorum hominum testimonium verum est*: sic enim est ibi: *in ore duorum aut trium stabit omne verbum.*

Sed, secundum Augustinum, habet magnam quaestionem quod dicit *duorum hominum testimonium verum est*. Fieri enim potest quod duo mentiantur. Nam Susanna casta duobus falsis testibus urgebatur, ut habetur Dan. XIII, 5 ss. Universus etiam populus mentitus est contra Christum.

Responsio. Hoc quod dicit *duorum hominum testimonium verum est*, intelligendum est quod pro vero in iudicio est habendum. Cuius ratio est, quia in actibus humanis vera certitudo haberi non potest; et ideo

1152. He mentions that his judgment is deferred when he says, *I do not judge any man.* He is saying in effect: you judge wickedly, but *I do not judge any man.* As it says above: *for God did not send his Son into the world to judge the world, but that the world might be saved through him* (John 3:17). Or, we could say, *I do not judge any man*, according to the flesh, as you judge: *he will not judge by the sight of his eyes, or reprove by what his ears hear* (Isa 11:3).

1153. Yet, I will judge at some time, because *he has given all judgment to the Son* (John 5:22). And then, *my judgment is true*, that is, just: *he will judge the people with justice* (Ps 95:10); *we know that the judgment of God is according to the truth* (Rom 2:2). This shows that his judgment is true.

1154. He gives the reason for its truth when he says, *because I am not alone.* What Christ said before, *neither does the Father judge any man* (John 5:22), should be understood to refer to the Father in isolation from the Son. Or, again, he said this because the Father will not appear visibly to all at the judgment. Thus he says, *I am not alone*, because he is not left alone by the Father, but is with him: *I am in the Father, and the Father is in me* (John 14:10).

This statement rejects the error of Sabellius, who said that the Father and the Son were the same person, the only difference between them being in their names. But if this were true, Christ would not have said: *I am not alone, but there is me and the Father who sent me.* He would rather have said: I am the Father, and I am the Son. We should, therefore, distinguish between the persons, and realize that the Son is not the Father.

1155. Then, at *and in your law it is written that the testimony of two men is true*, he shows that he is not alone in bearing witness. He does not defer bearing witness, as he does his judging. Thus he does not say, I do not bear witness.

First, he mentions the law;

second, he gives his conclusion, at *I am one who gives testimony about myself.*

1156. He says, *and it is written in your law*, the law which was given to you—*Moses imposed a law* (Sir 24:33)—*that the testimony of two men is true*; for it is written: *by the mouth of the two or three witnesses the issue will be settled* (Deut 19:15).

According to Augustine the statement that *the testimony of two men is true*, involves a great difficulty. For it could happen that both of them would be lying. Indeed, the chaste Susanna was harassed by two false witnesses (Dan 13:5 ff), and all the people lied about Christ.

I answer that statement, *the testimony of two men is true*, means that such testimony should be regarded as true when giving a verdict. The reason for this is that true certitude cannot be obtained when human acts are in question,

accipitur inde id quod certius haberi potest, quod est per multitudinem testium: magis enim est probabile quod unus mentiatur, quam quod multi; Eccle. IV, 12: *funiculus triplex difficile solvitur.*

Nihilominus tamen per hoc quod dicit: *in ore duorum aut trium testium stabit omne verbum*, reducit nos, secundum Augustinum, in considerationem Trinitatis, in qua est perpetua stabilitas veritatis, a qua omnes veritates derivantur. Dicit autem *duorum vel trium*, quia in Scriptura sacra quandoque nominantur tres, quandoque duae personae, cum quibus etiam intelligitur Spiritus Sanctus, qui est nexus duorum.

1157. Si ergo duorum hominum testimonium verum est vel trium, testimonium meum verum est, quia et ego *testimonium perhibeo de meipso, et testimonium perhibet de me qui misit me Pater*; supra V, 36: *ego testimonium habeo maius Ioanne.*

Sed hoc non videtur ad propositum pertinere. Primo quidem, quia Pater Filii Dei non est homo; cum ipse dicat **duorum hominum testimonium verum est.** Secundo vero, quia tunc sunt duo testes alicuius quando testificantur de aliquo tertio; sed si unus testificatur de uno, non sunt duo testes. Cum ergo Christus testificetur de se, et similiter Pater de Christo, videtur quod non sunt duo testes.

Sed dicendum, quod Christus hic arguit per locum a minori. Manifestum est enim quod veritas Dei maior est quam veritas hominis. Si ergo credunt testimonio hominum, multo magis credendum est testimonio Dei. I Io. V, 9: *si testimonium hominum accipitis, testimonium Dei maius est.* Item hoc dicit, ut ostendat se consubstantialem Patri, et non indigentem alieno testimonio, ut dicit Chrysostomus.

1158. Consequenter cum dicit **dicebant ergo ei: ubi est pater tuus?** Removet exortam quaestionem de Patre, et

primo ponit quaestionem Iudaeorum;

secundo ponit responsionem Christi;
tertio innuit securitatem respondentis.

1159. Quaestio autem Iudaeorum proposita Christo est de Patre, ubi esset: unde dicebant ei **ubi est pater tuus?** Intelligebant enim Christum habere Patrem hominem sicut ipsi habent; et ideo, quia audierunt eum dicere: **solus non sum, sed ego et qui misit me Pater**, et hic viderant eum solum, dicunt **ubi est pater tuus?**

Vel dicendum, quod loquuntur hic cum quadam ironia et contumelia; quasi dicant: quid frequenter Patrem tuum nobis inducis? Numquid est tantae virtutis, ut eius testimonio credatur? Ignotus enim est, et ignobilis. Intelligebant hoc de Ioseph; nihilominus tamen Patrem

and so in its place one takes what can be considered the more certain, that is, what is said by a number of witnesses: for it is more probable that one person might lie than many: *a threefold cord is not easily broken* (Eccl 4:12).

When we read, *by the mouth of two or three witnesses the issue will be settled* (Deut 19:15), we are led, as Augustine says, to a consideration of the Trinity, in which truth is permanently established, from which all truths are derived. It says, *of two or three*, because in Sacred Scripture sometimes three persons are enumerated and at other times two persons, in which is implied the Holy Spirit, who is the bond of the other two.

1157. If, therefore, the testimony of two or three is true, my testimony is true, because ***I am one who gives testimony about myself, and the Father who sent me who gives testimony about me***; as above: ***but I have a greater testimony than that of John*** (John 5:36).

But this does not seem to be to the point. First, because the Father of the Son of God is not a man, while Christ says, ***the testimony of two men is true.*** Second, because there are two witnesses to someone when they are testifying about a third person; but if one testifies to one of the two, there are not two witnesses. Thus, since Christ is testifying about himself, and the Father is also testifying about Christ, it does not seem that there are two witnesses.

To answer this we must say that Christ is here arguing from the lesser to the greater. For it is clear that the truth of God is greater than the truth of a man. So, therefore, if they believe in the testimony of men, then they should believe the testimony of God much more. *If you receive the testimony of men, the testimony of God is greater* (1 John 5:9). In addition, he says this to show that he is consubstantial with the Father, and does not need outside testimony, as Chrysostom says.

1158. Next, at ***they said therefore to him: where is your father?*** we see the question arising about Christ's Father.

First, the Evangelist mentions the question asked by the Jews;
then Christ's answer; and
third, he intimates the security of Christ.

1159. The question which the Jews had for Christ was about his Father, where his Father was. ***They said to him: where is your father?*** for they thought that the Father of Christ was a man, just like their own fathers. Because they heard him say, ***I am not alone, but there is me and the Father who sent me***, and since they saw that he was now alone, they asked him, ***where is your father?***

Or, we could say that they were here speaking with a certain irony and contempt, saying in effect: why do you speak to us so often about your Father? Is he so great that his testimony should be believed? For they were thinking of Joseph, who was an unknown, and a person of low status;

ignorabant. Ps. CXIII, 2: *ne quando dicant gentes: ubi est Deus eorum?*

1160. Responsio autem Christi est occulta, ibi: *respondit Iesus: neque me scitis, neque Patrem meum*. Quia enim non studio addiscendi, sed malignandi quaerebant, ideo Christus non aperit eis veritatem; sed ostendit primo quidem ipsorum ignorantiam; secundo quomodo possint ad veritatis cognitionem pervenire.

Ignorantiam quidem ipsorum ostendit cum dicit *neque me scitis*; quasi dicat: non quaeratis de Patre, quia me nescitis. Quia enim me hominem putatis, ideo Patrem meum hominem quaeritis; sed quia me non noscitis, neque Patrem cognoscere potestis.

1161. Sed contra. Supra VII, 28, dixit: *et me scitis, et unde sim scitis*.

Est dicendum quod sciebant eum secundum humanitatem, sed non secundum divinitatem.

Sciendum autem, secundum Origenem, quod ex hoc verbo aliqui sumentes occasionem erroris, dixerunt Patrem Christi non fuisse Deum Veteris Testamenti; nam ipsum Iudaei cognoscebant, secundum illud Ps. LXXV, 1: *notus in Iudaea Deus*.

Sed ad hoc est quadruplex responsio. Prima, quia ideo dicit Dominus Iudaeos Patrem ignorare, quia ad modum ignorantium se habent, inquantum mandatum eius non servant. Et haec responsio pertinet ad actum. Secundo dicuntur Deum ignorare, quia non adhaerent ei spiritualiter per amorem: qui enim aliquid cognoscit, ei adhaeret. Tertio, quia etsi cognoscerent eum per fidem, non tamen habebant de eo plenam scientiam. Supra I, v. 18: *Deum nemo vidit unquam. Unigenitus Filius, qui est in sinu Patris, ipse enarravit*. Quarto, quia in Veteri Testamento innotuit Pater sub ratione Dei omnipotentis, Ex. VI, 3: *ego apparui eis in Deo omnipotente, et nomen meum Adonai non indicavi eis*, non autem sub ratione Patris; unde licet scirent eum ut Deum, non tamen ut Patrem Filii consubstantialis.

1162. Viam autem perveniendi ad cognitionem Patris dicit se esse: unde dicit *si me sciretis*, quasi dicat: quia Patrem meum loquor occultum, opus prius est ut me noveritis, et tunc *Patrem meum forsitan scietis*. Nam Filius est via cognitionis Paternae. Infra XIV, 7: *si cognovissetis me, et Patrem meum utique cognovissetis*. Nam, secundum Augustinum, quid est *si me sciretis*, nisi *ego et Pater unum sumus*? Quotidiana locutio est, quando vides aliquem alicuius similem, ut dicas: si hunc vidisti, illum vidisti, non tamen quod Pater sit Filius, sed quia sit Patri similis.

and they were ignorant of the Father: *so the gentiles will not say: where is their God* (Ps 113:2).

1160. Christ's answer is mysterious: *you know neither me nor my Father*. Christ does not reveal the truth to them because they were questioning him not because they desired to learn, but in order to belittle him. Rather, he first shows them that of which they were ignorant; second how they may be able to attain knowledge of the truth.

He shows them their ignorance when he says, *you know neither me*. He is saying: you should not be asking about my Father, because you do not know me. For since you regard me as a man, you are asking about my Father as though he were a man. But because you do not know me, neither can you know my Father.

1161. This seems to conflict with what he said above: *you know me, and you know from where I come* (John 7:28).

The answer to this is that they did know him according to his humanity, but not according to his divinity.

We should note, according to Origen, that some have misunderstood this, and they said that the Father of Christ was not the God of the Old Testament: for the Jews knew the God of the Old Testament, according to *God is known in Judea* (Ps 75:1).

There are four answers to this. First, our Lord says that the Jews did not know his Father because insofar as they do not keep his commandments they are acting like those who do not know him. This answer refers to their conduct. Second, they are said not to know God because they did not cling to him spiritually by love: for one who knows something adheres to it. Third, because although they did know him through faith, they did not have a full knowledge of him: *no one has ever seen God: the only begotten Son, who is in the bosom of the Father, has made him known* (John 1:18). Fourth, because in the Old Testament the Father was known under the aspect of God Almighty: *I appeared to Abraham, to Isaac and to Jacob as God Almighty, but my name, Lord, I did not show them* (Exod 6:3), that is, under the aspect of Father. Thus, although they knew him as God Almighty, they did not know him as the Father of a consubstantial Son.

1162. Christ says that he is the way to arrive at a knowledge of the Father, *if you did know me*. He is saying in effect: because I speak of my Father, who is hidden, it is first necessary that you know me, *perhaps you would also know my Father*. For the Son is the way to the knowledge of the Father: *if you had known me, you would without doubt have known my Father also* (John 14:7). As Augustine says, what does, *if you did know me* mean, except, *I and the Father are one* (John 10:30). It is customary when you see someone who is like someone else to say: if you have seen one, you have seen the other; not that the Son is the Father, but he is like the Father.

Dicit autem *forsitan*, non dubitative, sed increpative, velut si indigneris servo tuo, et dicas: contemnis me? Considera quod forsitan dominus tuus sum.

1163. Securitatem autem Christi respondentis ostendit Evangelista, cum dicit *haec verba locutus est Iesus in gazophylacio*. Et primo quidem ex loco ubi docebat, quia in gazophylacio et in templo. *Gaza* enim, Persica lingua, dicuntur divitiae, *phylaxe* vero servare: unde 'gazophylacium' ponitur in Scriptura pro arca, ubi divitiae conservantur; et hoc modo accipitur IV Reg. XII, 9, quod *tulit Ioiada sacerdos gazophylacium unum, aperuitque foramen desuper, et posuit illud iuxta altare ad dexteram ingredientium domum Domini, mittebantque in eo sacerdotes qui custodiebant ostia, omnem pecuniam quae deferebatur ad templum Domini.* Aliquando autem pro domo ubi divitiae conservantur; et hoc modo accipitur hic.

Secundo, ex hoc quod illi qui missi fuerant ad eum apprehendendum, hoc facere non potuerunt, quia ipse nolebat: unde dicit *et nemo apprehendit eum, quia nondum venit hora eius*, in qua pateretur; non fatalis, sed sua voluntate ab aeterno praedestinata. Unde dicit Augustinus *nondum venerat hora eius, non qua cogeretur mori, sed qua dignaretur occidi.*

1164. Sed nota, secundum Origenem, quod quandocumque designatur locus in quo Dominus aliquid fecit, hoc fit propter mysterium. In gazophylacio ergo, qui est locus divitiarum, Christus docuit, ut daret intelligi, quod numismata, id est verba suae doctrinae, imaginem regis magni impressam habent.

Nota etiam, quod quando docebat, *nemo apprehendit eum*, quia sermones eius fortiores erant his qui eum capere volebant: quando vero voluit crucifigi, tacuit.

He says, *perhaps*, not to indicate a doubt, but as a rebuke. It would be like being irritated with your servant and saying to him: have you no respect for me? Just remember that I might be your master.

1163. The Evangelist shows the security with which Christ answered when he says, *these words Jesus spoke in the treasury*. We see the first from the place where he taught, that is, in the treasury and in the temple. For *gaza* is the Persian word for riches, and *philaxe* for keep. Thus 'gazophylacium' is the word used in Sacred Scripture for the chest in which riches are kept. It is used in this sense: *and Jehoiada the priest took a chest and bored a hole in its top, and put it by the altar, to the right of those coming into the house of the Lord. And the priests who kept the doors put into it all the money that was brought to the temple of the Lord* (2 Kgs 12:9). Sometimes, however, it was used to indicate the building where riches were kept; and this is the way it was used here.

We can also see Christ's security from the fact that those who had been sent to arrest him could not do so, because he was not willing. Thus the Evangelist says, *and no man laid hands on him, because his hour had not yet come*, that is, the time for him to suffer, an hour not fixed by fate, but predetermined from all eternity by his own will. Thus Augustine says: *his hour had not yet come, not in which he would be forced to die, but in which he would not refuse being killed.*

1164. We may note, according to Origen, that whenever the place where our Lord did something is mentioned, this is done because of some mystery. Thus Christ taught in the treasury, the place where riches were kept, to signify that the coins, that is, the words of his teaching, are impressed with the image of the great King.

Note also that when Christ was teaching, *no man laid hands on him*, because his words were stronger than those who wanted to seize him; but when he willed to be crucified, then he became silent.

Lecture 3

8:21 Dicit ergo iterum eis Iesus: ego vado, et quaeretis me, et in peccato vestro moriemini. Quo ego vado, vos non potestis venire. [n. 1166]

8:22 Dicebant ergo Iudaei: numquid interficiet semetipsum, quia dicit: quo ego vado, vos non potestis venire? [n. 1172]

8:23 Et dicebat eis: vos de deorsum estis, ego de supernis sum. Vos de mundo hoc estis, ego non sum de hoc mundo. [n. 1174]

8:24 Dixi ergo vobis quia moriemini in peccatis vestris. Si enim non credideritis quia ego sum, moriemini in peccato vestro. [n. 1177]

8:25 Dicebant ergo ei: tu quis es? Dixit eis Iesus: principium, qui et loquor vobis. [n. 1180]

8:26 Multa habeo de vobis loqui, et iudicare; sed qui me misit, verax est: ego quae audivi ab eo, haec loquor in mundo. [n. 1185]

8:27 Et non cognoverunt quia Patrem eius dicebat Deum. [n. 1189]

8:28 Dixit ergo eis Iesus: cum exaltaveritis Filium hominis, tunc cognoscetis. Quia ego sum, et a meipso facio nihil; sed sicut docuit me Pater, haec loquor. [n. 1191]

8:29 Et qui me misit, mecum est, et non reliquit me solum, quia ego quae placita sunt ei, facio semper. [n. 1192]

8:30 Haec illo loquente, multi crediderunt in eum. [n. 1193]

8:21 Εἶπεν οὖν πάλιν αὐτοῖς· ἐγὼ ὑπάγω καὶ ζητήσετέ με, καὶ ἐν τῇ ἁμαρτίᾳ ὑμῶν ἀποθανεῖσθε· ὅπου ἐγὼ ὑπάγω ὑμεῖς οὐ δύνασθε ἐλθεῖν.

8:22 ἔλεγον οὖν οἱ Ἰουδαῖοι· μήτι ἀποκτενεῖ ἑαυτόν, ὅτι λέγει· ὅπου ἐγὼ ὑπάγω ὑμεῖς οὐ δύνασθε ἐλθεῖν;

8:23 καὶ ἔλεγεν αὐτοῖς· ὑμεῖς ἐκ τῶν κάτω ἐστέ, ἐγὼ ἐκ τῶν ἄνω εἰμί· ὑμεῖς ἐκ τούτου τοῦ κόσμου ἐστέ, ἐγὼ οὐκ εἰμὶ ἐκ τοῦ κόσμου τούτου.

8:24 εἶπον οὖν ὑμῖν ὅτι ἀποθανεῖσθε ἐν ταῖς ἁμαρτίαις ὑμῶν· ἐὰν γὰρ μὴ πιστεύσητε ὅτι ἐγώ εἰμι, ἀποθανεῖσθε ἐν ταῖς ἁμαρτίαις ὑμῶν.

8:25 ἔλεγον οὖν αὐτῷ· σὺ τίς εἶ; εἶπεν αὐτοῖς ὁ Ἰησοῦς· τὴν ἀρχὴν ὅ τι καὶ λαλῶ ὑμῖν;

8:26 πολλὰ ἔχω περὶ ὑμῶν λαλεῖν καὶ κρίνειν, ἀλλ᾽ ὁ πέμψας με ἀληθής ἐστιν, κἀγὼ ἃ ἤκουσα παρ᾽ αὐτοῦ ταῦτα λαλῶ εἰς τὸν κόσμον.

8:27 οὐκ ἔγνωσαν ὅτι τὸν πατέρα αὐτοῖς ἔλεγεν.

8:28 εἶπεν οὖν [αὐτοῖς] ὁ Ἰησοῦς· ὅταν ὑψώσητε τὸν υἱὸν τοῦ ἀνθρώπου, τότε γνώσεσθε ὅτι ἐγώ εἰμι, καὶ ἀπ᾽ ἐμαυτοῦ ποιῶ οὐδέν, ἀλλὰ καθὼς ἐδίδαξέν με ὁ πατὴρ ταῦτα λαλῶ.

8:29 καὶ ὁ πέμψας με μετ᾽ ἐμοῦ ἐστιν· οὐκ ἀφῆκέν με μόνον, ὅτι ἐγὼ τὰ ἀρεστὰ αὐτῷ ποιῶ πάντοτε.

8:30 Ταῦτα αὐτοῦ λαλοῦντος πολλοὶ ἐπίστευσαν εἰς αὐτόν.

8:21 Again Jesus said to them: I go, and you will seek me, and you will die in your sin. Where I go, you cannot come. [n. 1166]

8:22 The Jews therefore said: will he kill himself, because he said: where I go, you cannot come? [n. 1172]

8:23 And he said to them: you are from below, and I am from above. You are of this world, and I am not of this world. [n. 1174]

8:24 Therefore I said to you that you will die in your sin. For if you do not believe that I am he, you will die in your sin. [n. 1177]

8:25 They therefore said to him: who are you? Jesus said to them: the source, who also speaks to you. [n. 1180]

8:26 Many things I have to say and to judge about you. But he who sent me is truthful, and the things that I have heard from him are the same that I speak to the world. [n. 1185]

8:27 And they did not understand why he called God his Father. [n. 1189]

8:28 Jesus therefore said to them: when you have lifted up the Son of man, then you will know that I am he and that I do nothing of myself, but as the Father has taught me, these things I speak: [n. 1191]

8:29 and he who sent me is with me, and he has not left me alone, for I always do the things that please him. [n. 1192]

8:30 When he spoke these things, many believed in him. [n. 1193]

1165. Postquam Dominus manifestavit de se privilegium lucis, hic consequenter manifestat lucis effectum, scilicet quod liberat a tenebris, et

primo ostendit quod ipsi in tenebris detinentur;

secundo docet remedium quo ab eis liberentur, ibi ***dicebant ergo Iudaei: numquid interficiet semetipsum*** etc.

1165. After our Lord showed his special position with respect to light, he here reveals the effect of this light, that is, that it frees us from darkness.

First, he shows that the Jews are imprisoned in darkness;

second he teaches the remedy which can free them, at ***the Jews therefore said: will he kill himself?***

Circa primum tria facit.

Primo denuntiat Dominus suum recessum;

secundo ostendit Iudaeorum studium perversum;

tertio ipsorum defectum.

1166. Recessum autem suum dicit Dominus esse per mortem; et ideo dicit **ego vado**: in quo duo dat intelligere. Primo, quod voluntarie moritur, scilicet vadens, et non ab alio ductus. Infra XVI, 5: **vado ad eum qui me misit**; infra X, 18: **nemo tollit a me animam meam: sed ego pono eam a meipso**. Et secundum hoc recte continuatur ad praecedentia. Dixit enim: **nemo apprehendit eum** etc. Et quare? Quia per se vadit sponte.

Secundo ostendit quod mors Christi erat quaedam profectio illuc unde venerat et unde non discesserat: sicut enim qui vadit in anteriora proficit, ita Christus per mortem pervenit ad gloriam exaltationis. Phil. II, 8: *factus est obediens usque ad mortem, mortem autem crucis; propter quod et Deus exaltavit illum*; infra XIII, 3: **sciens quia a Deo exivit, et ad Deum vadit**.

1167. Perversum eorum studium ostendit in dolosa inquisitione Christi: et quantum ad hoc dicit **quaeretis me**. Quidam autem quaerunt Christum pie ex caritate; et hanc inquisitionem sequitur vita; Ps. LXVIII, v. 33: *quaerite Dominum, et vivet anima vestra*. Sed isti impie quaerunt, et odio ad persequendum; Ps. XXXVII, 13: *vim faciebant qui quaerebant animam meam*. Et sic dicit **quaeretis me**, scilicet persequentes post mortem quidem infamia; Matth. XXVII, 63: *recordati sumus quod seductor ille dixit adhuc vivens: post tres dies resurgam*. Item in membris meis; Act. IX, 4: *Saule, Saule, quid me persequeris?*

1168. Et hanc sequelam sequitur mors; et ideo subdit ipsorum defectum, quem eis praenuntiat dicens **et in peccato vestro moriemini**, et

primo praenuntiat defectum qui consistit in mortis damnatione;

secundo defectum qui consistit in eorum a gloria exclusione, ibi **quo ego vado, vos non potestis venire**.

1169. Dicit ergo: quia inique me quaeritis, ideo **in peccato vestro**, scilicet permanentes, **moriemini**. Quod potest intelligi uno modo de morte corporali: et sic in peccatis suis moritur qui usque ad mortem perseverat in eis. Et sic per hoc quod dicit **in peccato vestro moriemini**, exaggerat eorum obstinatam pertinaciam. Ier. VIII, 6: *non est qui poenitentiam agat de peccato suo dicens, quid feci?* Ez. XXXII, 27: *descenderunt cum armis ad Inferna*.

Alio modo de morte peccati, de qua dicitur in Ps. XXXIII, 21: *mors peccatorum pessima*. Et sicut mortem corporalem praecedit infirmitas corporis, ita et hanc mortem infirmitas quaedam praecedit. Quamdiu enim peccatum remediabile est, tunc est quasi quaedam infirmitas quae praecedit Ps. VI, 3: *miserere mei, Domine,*

He does three things concerning the first:

first, our Lord tells them he is going to leave;

second, he reveals the perverse plans of the Jews, and

third, he mentions what they will be deprived of.

1166. Our Lord says that he is going to leave them by his death, **I go**. We can see two things from this. First, that he is going to die voluntarily, that is, as going, and not as one led by someone else: **I go to him who sent me** (John 16:5); **no man takes it away from me, but I lay it down of myself** (John 10:18). And so this appropriately follows what went before: for he had said, **and no man laid hands on him** (John 8:20). Why? Because he is going willingly, on his own.

Second, we can see that the death of Christ was a journey to that place from which he had come, and which he had not left, for just as one who walks heads toward what is ahead, so Christ, by his death, reached the glory of exaltation: *he became obedient unto death, even the death of the cross. Because of this God exalted him* (Phil 2:8); **knowing... that he came from God, and was going to God** (John 13:3).

1167. We see their sinful plans by their deceitful search for Christ; he says, **you will seek me**. Some look for Christ in a devout way through charity, and such a search results in life: *seek the Lord, and your soul will live* (Ps 68:7). But they wickedly searched for him out of hatred, to persecute him: *the one who sought my soul used violence* (Ps 37:13). He says, **you will seek me**, by attacking me after my death with your accusations: *we remembered that while still living the seducer said: after three days I will rise* (Matt 27:63). And they will also seek out my members: *Saul, Saul, why are you persecuting me?* (Acts 9:4).

1168. This will be followed by their death, and so he adds what they will be deprived of, foretelling to them, **and you will die in your sin**.

First, he foretells that deprivation which consists in the condemnation of death;

second, that deprivation which consists in their exclusion from glory, **where I go, you cannot come**.

1169. He is saying: because you will wickedly search for me, **you will die in your sin**. We can understand this in one way as applying to physical death: and then one dies in his sins who keeps on sinning up to the time of his death. And so in saying, **you will die in your sin**, he emphasizes their obstinacy: *there is no one who does penance for his sin, saying: what have I done?* (Jer 8:6); *they went down to the lower regions with their weapons* (Ezek 32:2).

In another way, we can understand this as applying to the death of sin, about which the Psalm says, *the death of sinners is the worst* (Ps 33:22). And just as a physical weakness precedes physical death, so a certain weakness precedes this kind of death. For as long as sin can be remedied, it is a kind of weakness which precedes death: *have mercy*

quoniam infirmus sum. Sed quando est irremediabile, vel simpliciter, sicut post hanc vitam, vel quod ad ipsum, sicut est peccatum in Spiritum Sanctum; tunc causat mortem; I Io. V, 16: *est peccatum ad mortem, non pro illo dico, ut roget quis.* Et secundum hoc praenuntiat eis Dominus infirmitatem peccatorum esse ad mortem.

1170. Defectum qui consistit in eorum exclusione a gloria ostendit cum dicit **quo ego vado, vos non potestis venire.** Quo vadit Dominus, vadunt et isti per mortem; sed Dominus sine peccato, isti vero cum peccatis, quia in peccato suo moriuntur, et ideo non perveniunt ad gloriam Paternae visionis. Et ideo dicit **quo ego vado,** scilicet sponte per passionem meam, scilicet ad Patrem et ad suam gloriam, **vos non potestis venire,** quia non vultis. Si enim voluissent, et non potuissent, non rationabiliter dicetur eis **in peccato vestro moriemini.**

1171. Sed notandum quod aliqui impediuntur ne possint ire quo Christus vadit, dupliciter.

Uno modo ratione contrarietatis, et sic impediuntur peccatores: et de hoc loquitur hic; et ideo simpliciter perseverantibus in peccato dicit **quo ego vado, vos non potestis venire.** Ps. c, 7: *non habitabit in medio domus meae qui facit superbiam;* Is. XXXV, 8: *via sancta vocabitur, et pollutus non transibit per eam;* Ps. XIV, 1: *quis habitabit in tabernaculo tuo? Innocens manibus et mundo corde.*

Alio modo ratione imperfectionis, seu indispositionis: et hoc modo impediuntur iusti quamdiu sunt in corpore; II Cor. V, 6: *quamdiu sumus in corpore, peregrinamur a Domino.* Et talibus non dicit Dominus simpliciter **quo ego vado, non potestis venire,** sed addit determinationem temporis: infra XIII, 37: **quo ego vado, non potes me modo sequi.**

1172. Consequenter cum dicit **dicebant ergo Iudaei** etc., agit de remedio per quod a tenebris liberentur, et

primo proponit remedium tenebras evadendi;

secundo inducit rationes ad hoc remedium impetrandum, ibi **dicebant ergo eis: tu quis es?**

Tertio praenuntiat modum ad hoc perveniendi, ibi **dixit ergo eis Iesus: cum exaltaveritis filium hominis, tunc cognoscetis.**

Circa primum duo facit.

Primo ponitur verborum Christi occasio;

secundo ponuntur ea quibus causatur remedii insinuatio, ibi **vos de deorsum estis.**

1173. Occasio autem verborum Christi sumitur ex persona, vel intellectu Iudaeorum. Cum enim carnales essent, verba domini quae dixerat **quo ego vado, vos non**

on me, O Lord, for I am weak (Ps 6:3). But when sin can no longer be remedied, either absolutely, as after this life, or because of the very nature of the sin, as a sin against the Holy Spirit, it then causes death: *there is a sin that leads to death; I do not say that one should pray for that* (1 John 5:16). And according to this, our Lord is foretelling them that the weakness of their sins results in death.

1170. He shows the deprivation which consists in their exclusion from glory when he says, **where I go, you cannot come.** Our Lord goes by death, and so also do they. But our Lord goes without sin, while they go with their sins, because they are dying in their sin, and so do not come to the glory of the vision of the Father. So he says, **where I go,** willingly, by my passion, to the Father and to his glory, **you cannot come,** because you do not want to. For if they had wanted to and had not been able to do so, it could not have reasonably been said to them, **you will die in your sin.**

1171. Note that one can be hindered from going where Christ goes in two ways.

One way is by reason of some contrary factor, and this is the way that sinners are hindered. This is what he is speaking of here; and so to those who are absolutely continuing in their sin he says, **where I go, you cannot come.** *He who is proud will not live in my house* (Ps 100:7); *it will be called a holy way, and the unclean will not pass over it* (Isa 35:8); *who will dwell in your tent? He who walks without blame* (Ps 14:1).

One is hindered in another way by reason of some imperfection or indisposition. This is the way the just are hindered as long as they live in the body: *while we are in the body, we are absent from the Lord* (2 Cor 5:6). To persons such as these our Lord does not say absolutely, **where I go, you cannot come,** but he adds a qualification as to the time: **where I go, you cannot follow me now** (John 13:36).

1172. Then, at **the Jews therefore said: will he kill himself?** he treats of the remedy which can set them free from the darkness.

First, he gives the remedy for escaping the darkness;

second, he shows the efficacy of the remedy, at **they therefore said to him: who are you?**

Concerning the first, he does three things: first, he indicates what is the unique remedy for escaping the darkness; second, he states the reasons why they should ask for this remedy; and third, we see Christ foretelling the means of obtaining it, at **Jesus therefore said to them: when you have lifted up the Son of man, then will you know.**

As for the first, he does two things:

first, he gives the circumstances for Christ's words; and

second, the reason why Christ can propose the remedy, at **you are from below.**

1173. The circumstances surrounding Christ's words was the perverse understanding of the Jews. For since they were carnal, they understood what Christ said, **where I go,**

potestis venire, carnaliter intelligebant; I Cor. II, 14: *animalis homo non percipit ea quae sunt spiritus Dei.* Unde dicunt Iudaei **numquid interficiet semetipsum?** Quae quidem, secundum Augustinum, stulta opinio est. Numquid enim non poterant venire quo Christus perrexit, si interficeret semetipsum? Poterant quidem et ipsi seipsos interficere. Sic ergo mors non erat terminus quo iturus erat Christus, sed via qua ibat ad Patrem. Unde non dixit quod non possent ire ad mortem, sed quod per mortem non poterant ire ad locum quo per eam Christus exaltabatur, ad dexteram scilicet Dei.

Secundum Origenem autem, forte non sine causa Iudaei hoc dicunt. Habebant enim ex traditionibus quod Christus voluntarie esset moriturus, sicut ipse dixit, infra X, 18: **nemo tollit animam meam, sed ego pono eam a meipso.** Quod specialiter videntur habuisse ex Is. LIII, 12: *pro eo quod tradidit animam suam in mortem, ideo dispertiam ei plurimos, et fortium dividet spolia.* Quia ergo aliqualem suspicionem habebant de Iesu quod esset Christus, ideo, cum dixit **ego vado** etc., introduxerunt hanc opinionem, quod ipse semetipsum voluntarie morti traderet. Sed contumeliose hoc proferunt, dicentes **numquid interficiet se?** Alias dixissent: numquid anima eius, cum ipsi placuerit, egredietur relicto corpore? Quod nos non possumus facere. Et propter hoc ait **quo ego vado, vos non potestis venire.**

1174. Consequenter cum dicit **vos de deorsum estis** etc., proponit remedium tenebras evadenti, et

primo praemittit suam et illorum originem;

secundo ex hoc concludit propositum, ibi **dixi ergo vobis** etc.

1175. Circa primum autem diversificat originem suam ab illorum origine dupliciter. Primo, quia ipse est de supernis, et isti deorsum. Secundo, quia isti sunt de hoc mundo, de quo non est Christus. Sed, sicut Origenes dicit, aliud est esse deorsum, et aliud de hoc mundo; nam **sursum** et **deorsum** sunt differentiae situs. Ne ergo per hoc quod dixit se esse de supernis intelligant eum esse de superiori parte mundi huius, ideo hoc excludens, dicit se non esse de hoc mundo. Quasi dicat: ita de supernis sum, quod tamen totaliter sum supra totum mundum istum.

1176. Et quidem eos esse de hoc mundo et de deorsum manifestum est; sed Christum esse de supernis, et non de hoc mundo, sane indiget intellectu.

Nam quidam ponentes omnia visibilia creata esse a diabolo, sicut Manichaei, dixerunt Christum etiam quantum ad corpus non esse de hoc mundo visibili, sed de mundo alterius creationis, scilicet invisibili. Valentinus etiam hoc male suscipiens, dixit, Christum attulisse corpus caeleste. Quod autem hic non sit verus intellectus apparet, quia ipsis apostolis Dominus dicit, infra XV, 19: **vos non estis de hoc mundo.**

you cannot come, in a carnal way: *the sensual man does not perceive those things that pertain to the Spirit of God* (1 Cor 2:14). Thus the Jews said, **will he kill himself?** As Augustine says, this is indeed a foolish notion. For if Christ was going to kill himself, couldn't they go where he was going? For they could kill themselves also. Thus, death was not the term of Christ's going: it was the way he was going to the Father. Accordingly, he did not say that they could not go to death but that they could not go through death to the place where Christ, through his death, would be exalted, that is, at the right hand of God.

According to Origen, however, perhaps the Jews did have a reason why they said this. For they had learned from their traditions that Christ would die willingly, as he himself said: **no man takes it away from me, but I lay it down of myself** (John 10:18). They seem especially to have gathered this from the saying: *I will give him many things, and he will divide the spoils of the strong, because he delivered himself to death* (Isa 53:12). And so because they suspected that Jesus was the Christ, when he said, **where I go, you cannot come**, they understood it according to this opinion that he would willingly deliver himself to death. But they interpreted this in an insulting way, saying, **will he kill himself?** Otherwise they would have said: is his soul going to depart, leaving his body when he wishes? We are unable to do this, and this is the reason for his saying, **where I go, you cannot come**.

1174. Then, at **you are from below**, he proposes the remedy for escaping from the darkness.

First, he mentions his own origin, and then theirs;

second, he concludes to his point, at **therefore I said to you that you will die in your sin**.

1175. With respect to the first, he distinguishes his own origin from theirs in two ways. First, because he is from above, and they are from below. Second, because they are of this world, and Christ is not. As Origen says, to be from below is not the same as to be of this world, for **above** and **below** refer to differences in place. Thus, so that they do not understand the statement that he is from above as meaning that he is from a part of the world which is above, he excludes this by saying that he is not of this world. He is saying in effect: I am from above, but in such a way that I am entirely above the entire world.

1176. It is clear that they are of this world and from below. But we have to understand correctly how Christ is from above and not of this world.

For some who thought that all visible created realities were from the devil, as the Manicheans taught, said that Christ was not of this world even with respect to his body, but from some other created world, an invisible world. Valentine also incorrectly interpreted this statement, and said that Christ assumed a heavenly body. But it is obvious that this is not the true interpretation, since our Lord said to his apostles: **you are not of the world** (John 15:19).

Dicendum est ergo, quod potest intelligi de Christo Filio Dei, et de Christo homine. Nam Christus secundum quod Filius Dei, est de supernis; infra XVI, 28: *exivi a Patre, et veni in mundum*. Et similiter non est de hoc mundo sensibili, scilicet, qui consistit in rebus sensibilibus, sed de mundo intelligibili, qui est in mente Dei, quia est ipsum Verbum Dei, prout est summa sapientia. Omnia enim in sapientia facta sunt. Unde de eo dicitur supra, I, 10: *mundus per ipsum factus est*.

Secundum autem quod homo, Christus est de supernis, quia non habuit affectum ad mundana et infima, sed ad superiora, in quibus anima Christi conversabatur, secundum illud Phil. III, 20: *nostra conversatio in caelis*; Matth. VI, 21: *ubi est thesaurus tuus, ibi est et cor tuum*. Et e converso isti qui deorsum sunt, originem infimam habent, et de hoc mundo, quia habent affectum circa terrena; I ad Cor. XV, 47: *primus homo de terra terrenus*.

1177. Consequenter cum dicit *dixi ergo vobis, quia moriemini in peccatis vestris*, concludit propositum, et

primo manifestat ea quae dixit de eorum defectu;

secundo ostendit eis remedium, ibi *si enim non credideritis* etc.

1178. Sciendum autem circa primum, quod unumquodque in suo progressu sequitur conditionem suae originis; unde ea quae habent originem infimam, si sibi relinquantur, naturaliter deorsum tendunt. Et nihil naturaliter tendit sursum nisi quod superiorem originem habet; Sup. III, 13: *nemo ascendit in caelum nisi de caelo descendit*.

Dicit ergo Dominus: haec est causa quare non potestis venire quo ego vado, quia cum sitis de deorsum, quantum in vobis est, non potestis nisi cadere; et ideo quod dixi, quia *moriemini in peccatis vestris*, verum est, nisi mihi adhaereatis.

1179. Et ideo ut non totaliter excludat spem salutis, ponit remedium, dicens *si enim non credideritis quia ego sum, moriemini in peccato vestro*; quasi dicat: nati estis in originali peccato, a quo non potestis absolvi nisi per fidem meam, quia *si non credideritis quia ego sum, moriemini in peccato vestro*.

Et dicit *ego sum*, non autem quid sim, ut rememoret quod dictum est Moysi, Ex. III, v. 14: *ego sum qui sum*: nam ipsum esse est proprium Dei. In qualibet enim alia natura a divina differt esse et quod est, cum quaelibet natura creata participet suum esse ab eo quod est ens per essentiam, scilicet ipso Deo, qui est ipsum suum esse, ita quod suum esse sit sua essentia. Unde ipse solus denominatur ab eo. Et ideo dicit *nisi credideritis quia ego sum*, idest quia sum vere Deus, qui habet esse per essentiam, *moriemini in peccato vestro*.

Dicit enim *quia ego sum*, ut ostendat suam aeternitatem. In omnibus enim quae incipiunt est mutabilitas

We must say, therefore, that this passage can be understood of Christ as the Son of God, and of Christ as human. Christ, as Son of God, is from above: *I came forth from the Father, and have come into the world* (John 16:28). Likewise, he is not of this sensible world, that is, this world which is made up of sense perceptible things, but he is of the intelligible world, because he is the very Word of God, being the supreme wisdom. For all things were made in wisdom. Thus we read of him: *through him the world was made* (John 1:10).

Christ, as human, is from above, because he did not have any affection for worldly and weak things, but rather for higher realities, in which the soul of Christ was at home, as in *our home is in heaven* (Phil 3:20); *where your treasure is, there is your heart also* (Matt 6:21). On the other hand, those who are from below have their origin from below, and are of this world because their affections are turned to earthy things: *the first man was of the earth, earthly* (1 Cor 15:47).

1177. Then, at *therefore I said to you that you will die in your sins*, he concludes his point.

First, he explains what he said about their deprivation;

second, he points out its remedy, at *for if you do not believe that I am he, you will die in your sin*.

1178. We should note with respect to the first, that everything in its development follows the condition of its origin. Thus, a thing whose origin is from below naturally tends below if left to itself. And nothing tends above unless its origin is from above: *no man has ascended into heaven, except he who has descended from heaven* (John 3:13).

Thus our Lord is saying: this is the reason why you cannot come where I am going, because since you are from below, then so far as you yourself are concerned, you can only go down. And so what I said is true, that *you will die in your sin*, unless you adhere to me.

1179. Then, in order not to entirely exclude all hope for their salvation, he proposes the remedy, saying, *for if you do not believe that I am he, you will die in your sin*. He is saying in effect: you were born in original sin, from which you cannot be absolved except by my faith: because, *if you do not believe that I am he, you will die in your sin*.

He says, *I am he*, and not what I am, to recall to them what was said to Moses: *I am who am* (Exod 3:14), for existence itself is proper to God. For in any other nature but the divine nature, existence and what exists are not the same: because any created nature participates its existence from that which is being by its essence, that is, from God, who is his own existence, so that his existence is his essence. Thus, this designates only God. And so he says, *for if you do not believe that I am he*, that is, that I am truly God, who has existence by his essence, *you will die in your sin*.

He says, *that I am he*, to show his eternity. For in all things that begin, there is a certain mutability, and a potency

quaedam, et aliqua potentia ad non esse, unde est invenire in eis quoddam praeteritum et futurum: et ideo non est ibi verum esse per se. Sed in Deo nulla est potentia ad non esse, nec esse incepit; et ideo est ipsum esse, quod proprie per tempus praesens designatur.

1180. Consequenter cum dicit *dicebant ergo ei: tu quis es?* Ponit rationes inducentes ad fidem, et

primo ponitur Iudaeorum interrogatio;

secundo Christi responsio, ibi *dixit eis Iesus: principium, qui et loquor vobis*;

tertio intellectus eorum excaecatio, ibi *et non cognoverunt* etc.

1181. Quia enim Dominus dixerat *nisi credideritis quia ego sum*, restabat adhuc quaerere quis esset; et ideo dicebant ei *tu quis es?* Quasi dicant: unde es, ut tibi credere debeamus?

1182. Et ideo consequenter cum dicit *principium, qui et loquor vobis*, respondet, inducens eos ad credendum, et

primo ex suae naturae sublimitate;

secundo ex iudiciaria sua potestate, ibi *multa habeo de vobis loqui et iudicare*;

tertio ex Paterna veritate, ibi *sed qui misit me, verax est*.

1183. Inducit quidem eos ad credendum Christo, naturae eius sublimitas, quia ipse est principium. Unde dixit eis Iesus: *principium, qui et loquor vobis*. Principium in Latino est neutri generis: unde dubium est, utrum sit hic nominativi, vel accusativi casus. In Graeco autem est feminini generis, et in hoc loco est accusativi casus. Unde, secundum Augustinum, non est legendum: ego sum principium, sed, principium me credite, ne moriamini in peccatis vestris.

Dicitur etiam Pater *principium*. Et uno quidem modo nomen principii commune est Patri et Filio, inquantum scilicet sunt unum principium Spiritus Sancti per communem spirationem; et tres personae simul sunt principium creaturae per creationem. Alio modo est proprium Patris, inquantum scilicet Pater est principium Filii per aeternam generationem. Non tamen plura dicimus principia, sicut nec plures deos; Ps. CIX, 3: *tecum principium in die virtutis tuae* etc. Hic autem dicit Dominus se principium respectu totius creaturae: nam quod est per essentiam tale, est principium et causa eorum quae sunt per participationem. Esse autem per essentiam, ut dictum est, est esse suum. Sed quia Christus non solum habet in se divinam naturam, sed etiam humanam, ideo subdit *qui et loquor vobis*: nam vocem Dei immediate homo ferre non potest, quia, secundum Augustinum, *infirma corda intelligibile Verbum sine voce sensibili audire non possunt*. Ex. c. XX: *quid est homo, ut audiat vocem Domini Dei sui?* Ad hoc ergo quod immediate ipsum divinum Verbum audiremus, carnem assumpsit, cuius

to nonexistence; thus we can discern in them a past and a future, and so they do not have true existence of themselves. But in God there is no potency to non-existence, nor has he begun to be. And thus he is existence itself, which is appropriately indicated by the present tense.

1180. Next, at *they therefore said to him: who are you?* we are given the reasons that can lead them to believe.

First, we see the question asked by the Jews;

second, the answer of Christ, at *Jesus said to them: the source, who also speaks to you*; and

third, the blindness of their understanding, at *and they did not understand why he called God his Father*.

1181. Since our Lord had said, *if you do not believe that I am he*, it was left to them to ask who he was. And so they said to him, *who are you?* As if to say: where are you from, so that we may believe?

1182. When he says, *the source, who also speaks to you*, he gives an answer which can lead them to believe:

first, because of the sublimity of his nature;

second, because of the power he has to judge, at *many things I have to say and to judge about you*; and

third, because of the truthfulness of his Father, at *but he who sent me is truthful*.

1183. Indeed, the sublimity of Christ's nature can lead them to believe in him, because he is the source. Wherefore Jesus said to them: *the source, who also speaks to you*. In Latin the word for 'source' is neuter in gender, and so there is a question whether it is used here in the nominative or accusative case. In Greek, it is feminine in gender and is used here in the accusative case. Thus, according to Augustine, we should not read this as *I am the source*, but rather as *believe that I am the source, lest you die in your sins*.

The Father is also called the *source* or beginning. In one sense the word 'source' is common to the Father and the Son, insofar as they are the one source of the Holy Spirit through a common spiration. Again, the three persons together are the source of creatures through creation. In another way, the word 'source' is proper to the Father, insofar as the Father is the source of the Son through an eternal generation. Yet, we do not speak of many sources, just as we do not speak of many gods: *the source is with you in the day of your power* (Ps 109:3). Here, however, our Lord is saying that he is the source or beginning with regard to all creatures: for whatever is such by essence is the source and the cause of those things which are by participation. But, as was said, his existence is an existence by his very essence. Yet because Christ possesses not only the divine nature but a human nature as well, he adds, *who also speaks to you*. Man cannot hear the voice of God directly, because as Augustine says: *weak hearts cannot hear the intelligible word without a sensible voice. What is man that he may hear the voice of the Lord his God* (Exod 20). So, in order for us to

organo locutus est nobis: unde dicit *qui et loquor vobis*; idest, humilis propter vos factus, ad ista verba descendi. Ad Hebr. I, 1: *multifarie multisque modis olim Deus loquens Patribus in prophetis, novissime locutus est nobis in Filio*; supra I, 18: *unigenitus, qui est in sinu Patris, ipse enarrabit vobis*.

1184. Vel aliter, secundum Chrysostomum, ut per hoc quod dicit *principium, qui et loquor vobis*, reprehendat tarditatem intellectus Iudaeorum. Nam post multa signa quae ab eo viderant fieri, adhuc indurati, quaerunt a Domino *tu quis es?* etc. Et ideo Iesus respondit ego sum *principium*, idest qui locutus sum vobis a principio; quasi dicat: non habetis opus adhuc quaerere quis ego sum, cum iam deberet esse manifestum. Hebr. V, 12: *cum deberetis esse magistri propter tempus, rursum indigetis ut vos doceamini, quae sint elementa exordii sermonum Dei.*

1185. Secundo inducit eos ad credendum Christo iudiciaria eius auctoritas; et ideo subdit *multa habeo de vobis loqui et iudicare*; quasi dicat: habeo auctoritatem vos iudicandi.

Sed sciendum, quod aliud est loqui nobis, et aliud loqui de nobis. Nobis enim loquitur Christus ad nostram utilitatem, scilicet ut ad se trahat; et sic loquitur nobis, dum vivimus, praedicando, inspirando et huiusmodi faciendo. Loquitur autem de nobis non ad nostram utilitatem, sed ad suam iustitiam ostendendam; et hoc modo loquetur de nobis in iudicio futuro.

1186. Sed contra. Supra III, 17: *non enim misit Deus Filium suum in mundum ut iudicet mundum, sed ut salvetur mundus per ipsum.*

Responsio. Dicendum, quod aliud est iudicare, et aliud habere iudicare. Iudicare dicit actum iudicii; et hoc non pertinet ad primum adventum Domini, ut supra dixit: *ego non iudico quemquam*, scilicet ad praesens. Sed habere iudicare dicit iudicii potestatem; et hanc habet Christus; supra V, 22: *Pater omne iudicium dedit Filio*; Act. X, 42: *ipse est qui constitutus est a Deo iudex vivorum et mortuorum.* Et ideo signanter dicit *multa habeo de vobis loqui et iudicare*, sed in futuro iudicio.

1187. Inducit etiam ad credendum Christo veritas Paterna; et quantum ad hoc dicit *sed qui misit me, verax est*; quasi dicat: Pater est verus; ego autem loquor consona ei: ergo loquor vera, ergo debetis mihi credere.

Dicit ergo *qui misit me*, scilicet Pater, *verax est*, non participative, sed ipsa essentia veritatis; alias, cum Filius sit ipsa veritas, esset maior Patre; Rom. III, 4: *est autem Deus verax.* *Et ego quae audivi ab eo*: non auditu humano, sed per generationem aeternam accepi, *haec loquor.*

hear the divine Word directly, the Word assumed flesh, and spoke to us with a mouth of flesh. Thus he says, *who also speaks to you*, that is, I, who was humbled for your sakes, have come down to speak these words: *in many and various ways God spoke to our fathers through the prophets; in these days he has spoken to us in his Son* (Heb 1:1); *the only begotten Son, who is in the bosom of the Father, has made him known* (John 1:18).

1184. Chrysostom explains this a little differently, so that in saying, *the source, who is also speaking to you*, our Lord is reproving the Jews for their slowness to understand. For in spite of the many signs which they had seen our Lord perform, they were still impenetrable, and asked our Lord, *who are you?* Our Lord then answers: I am the *beginning*, that is, the one who has spoken to you from the beginning. It is the same as saying: you should not have to ask who I am, because it should be clear to you by now: *for although you should be masters by this time, you have to be taught again the first rudiments of the world of God* (Heb 5:12).

1185. Second, they can be led to believe in Christ by his judicial authority; and so he says, *many things I have to say and to judge about you*, which means in effect: I have authority to judge you.

Let us note that it is one thing to speak to us, and another to speak about us. Christ speaks to us for our benefit, that is, to draw us to himself; and he speaks to us this way while we are living, by means of preaching, by inspiring us, and by things like that. But Christ speaks about us, not for our benefit, but for showing his justice, and he will speak about us this way at the future judgment.

1186. This seems to conflict with what was said above: *for God did not send his Son into the world to judge the world, but that the world might be saved through him* (John 3:17).

I answer by saying that it is one thing to judge, and another to have judgment. For to judge implies the act of judging, and this does not belong to the first coming of our Lord, as he said above: *I do not judge any man* (John 8:15), that is, at present. But to have judgment implies the power to judge; and Christ does have this: *he*, the Father, *has given all judgment to the Son* (John 5:22); *it is he who was appointed by God to be the judge of the living and of the dead* (Acts 10:42). And so he says, explicitly, *many things I have to say and to judge about you*, but at a future judgment.

1187. The truthfulness of the Father can also lead them to believe in Christ, and as to this he says, *but he who sent me is truthful*. He is saying in effect: the Father is truthful; but what I say is in agreement with him; therefore, you should believe me.

Thus he says, *he who sent me*, that is, the Father, *is truthful*, not by participation, but he is the very essence of truth; otherwise, since the Son is truth itself, he would be greater than the Father: *God is truthful* (Rom 3:4). *The things that I have heard from him*, what I have received, not by my

Is. XXI, 10: *quae audivi a Domino exercituum Deo Israel, annuntiavi vobis*; supra V, 19: **non potest Filius a se facere quidquam**.

1188. Hoc autem quod dixit **qui misit me, verax est**, dupliciter continuatur ad praecedentia. Uno modo sic. Dico quod *habeo de vobis iudicare*. Sed iudicium meum verum erit, quia **qui misit me, verax est**. Rom. c. II, 2: *iudicium Dei est secundum veritatem*.

Alio modo, secundum Chrysostomum, dico quod **habeo de vobis iudicare**; sed hoc differo, non ex impotentia, sed ut obediam voluntati Paternae: nam **qui misit me, verax est**. Unde cum promiserit salvatorem et propugnatorem, misit me nunc ad salvandum; et ego quia non loquor nisi quae audivi ab eo, ideo loquor vobis salutaria.

1189. Consequenter cum dicit **et non cognoverunt quia Patrem eius dicebat Deum**, reprehendit tarditatem intellectus ipsorum: nondum enim oculos cordis apertos habebant, quibus Patri et Filii aequalitatem intelligerent, et hoc quia carnales erant; I Cor. II, 14: *animalis homo non percepit ea quae sunt spiritus Dei*.

1190. Hic primo praenuntiat Christus per quod pervenire debeant ad fidem, quod est remedium contra mortem; et circa hoc duo facit.

Primo ostendit per quid venturi sunt ad fidem;

secundo docet quid sit de se ipso credendum, ibi **quia ego sum**.

1191. Dicit ergo primo quod ad fidem pervenire debebant per passionem eius. Unde **dixit eis Iesus: cum exaltaveritis Filium hominis, tunc cognoscetis**; quasi dicat: modo non cognoscitis Patrem meum esse Deum; sed **cum exaltaveritis Filium hominis**, idest cum me ligno crucis affixeritis, **tunc cognoscetis**, scilicet aliqui ex vobis per fidem; infra c. XII, 32: *ego, si exaltatus fuero a terra, omnia traham ad me ipsum*.

Ideo autem, secundum Augustinum, crucis commemorat passionem, ut det spem peccatoribus, ut scilicet nullus desperet a quocumque scelere, et male sibi conscius, quando ipsi crucifigentes Christum per sanguinem Christi liberantur a peccatis. Nullus est enim adeo peccator qui per sanguinem Christi liberari non possit.

Vel, secundum Chrysostomum, **cum exaltaveritis Filium hominis**, scilicet in cruce, **tunc cognoscetis**, idest cognoscere poteritis, qualis sim, non solum per gloriam resurrectionis meae, sed etiam per poenam captivitatis et destructionis vestrae.

human sense of hearing, but by my eternal generation, **are the same that I speak**. *What I have heard from the Lord of hosts, the God of Israel, I have announced to you* (Isa 21:10); **the Son cannot do anything of himself** (John 5:19).

1188. The statement, **he who sent me is truthful**, can be connected in two ways with what went before. One way is this: I say that I have much to judge about you; but my judgment will be true, because **he who sent me is truthful**: *the judgment of God is according to the truth* (Rom 2:2).

The other way of relating this to what went before is from Chrysostom, and is this: I say that **I have much to judge about you**; but I am not doing so now, not because I lack the power, but out of obedience to the will of the Father. For **he who sent me is truthful**: thus, since he promised a savior and a defender, he sent me this time as savior. And since I only say what I have heard from him, I speak to you about life-giving things.

1189. When he says, **and they did not understand why he called God his Father**, he reproves their slowness to understand: for they had not yet opened the eyes of their hearts by which they could understand the equality of the Father and the Son. The reason for this was because they were carnal: *the sensual man does not perceive those things that pertain to the Spirit of God* (1 Cor 2:14).

1190. Here, for the first time, Christ foretells how they are to come to the faith, which is the remedy for death. He does two things:

first: he shows what will lead them to the faith; and

second, he teaches what must be believed about himself, at **that I am he**.

1191. He says, first, that they ought to come to the faith by means of his passion: **Jesus therefore said to them: when you have lifted up the Son of man, then you will know**. He is saying in effect: you do not know now that God is my Father, but **when you have lifted up the Son of man**, that is, when you have nailed me to the wood of the cross, **then you will know**, that is, some of you will understand by faith. **And I, if I am lifted up from the earth, will draw all things to myself** (John 12:32).

And so, as Augustine says, he recalls the sufferings of his cross to give hope to sinners, so that no one will despair, no matter what his crime, or think that he is too evil, since the very people who crucified Christ are freed from their sins by Christ's blood. For there is no sinner so great that he cannot be freed by the blood of Christ.

Chrysostom's explanation is this: **when you have lifted up the Son of man**, on the cross, **then you will understand**, that is, you will be able to understand what I am, not only by the glory of my resurrection, but also by the punishment of your captivity and destruction.

1192. Quantum autem ad secundum, tria docet de se credenda. Primo divinitatis maiestatem; secundo suam originem a Patre; tertio sui a Patre inseparabilitatem.

Maiestatem quidem divinitatis, cum dicit *quia ego sum*; idest, habeo in me naturam Dei, et sum ille qui locutus est Moysi, dicens: *ego sum qui sum.*

Sed quia ad ipsum esse pertinet tota Trinitas, ideo ne excludatur personarum distinctio, consequenter docet credere originem a Patre, cum dicit *et a me ipso facio nihil: sed sicut docuit me Pater, haec loquor.* Sed quia coepit Iesus facere et docere, ideo in duobus originem suam a Patre designat: scilicet in his quae facit, unde dicit *et a me ipso facio nihil*, supra V, 19: *non potest Filius a se facere quidquam*, et in his quae docet: unde dicit *sed sicut docuit me Pater*; idest, tradidit scientiam generando me scientem. Quia cum sit simplex natura veritatis, hoc est Filio esse, quod nosse; et sic quemadmodum Pater dedit Filio gignendo ut esset, sic gignendo dedit ei ut nosset; supra VII, 16: *mea doctrina non est mea.*

Et ne intelligatur quod sit missus a Patre quasi ab eo distinctus, ideo tertio docet credere eius a Patre inseparabilitatem, cum dicit *et qui misit me*, scilicet Pater, *mecum est*, per essentiae unitatem; infra XIV, 10: *ego in Patre, et Pater in me est.* Item per amoris coniunctionem; supra V, 20: *Pater diligit Filium, et omnia demonstrat ei quae ipse facit.* Et sic ita Pater misit Filium quod non recessit ab eo. Unde sequitur *et non reliquit me solum*, quia affectus eius est circa me. Sed cum ambo simul sint, unus tamen est missus, et alter misit: quia missio incarnatio est, quae quidem Filii tantum est, et non Patris.

Quod autem non reliquit me, patet ex signo, *quia quae placita sunt ei, facio semper*: quod quidem non ponitur pro causa meritoria, sed pro signo; quasi dicat: hoc ipsum quod ego facio semper, sine initio, sine fine, *quae placita sunt ei*, est signum quod semper mecum est, et non reliquit me; Prov. VIII, v. 30: *cum eo eram cuncta componens.* Vel aliter: *non reliquit me*, scilicet hominem, protegendo, *quia quae placita sunt ei facio semper.* Et secundum hoc dicit causam meritoriam.

1193. Consequenter cum dicit *haec illo loquente, multi crediderunt in eum*, ponitur effectus doctrinae, qui est conversio multorum ad fidem ex auditu doctrinae Christi; Rom. X, 17: *fides ex auditu; auditus autem per verbum Christi.*

1192. With respect to the second, he teaches three things that must be believed about himself: first, the greatness or grandeur of his divinity; second, his origin from the Father; third, his inseparability from the Father.

He mentions the greatness of his divinity when he says, *that I am he*, that is, that I have in me the nature of God, and that it is I who spoke to Moses, saying: *I am who am* (Exod 3:14).

But because the entire Trinity pertains to existence itself, and so that we do not overlook the distinction between the Persons, he teaches that his origin from the Father must be believed, saying, *I do nothing of myself; but as the Father taught me, these things I speak.* Because Jesus began both to do and to teach, he indicates his origin from the Father in these two respects. As regards those things he does, he says, *I do nothing of myself*; as above: *the Son cannot do anything of himself* (John 5:19). And as regards what he teaches, he says, *as the Father taught me*, that is to say, he gave me knowledge by generating me as one who knows. Since he is the simple nature of truth, for the Son to exist is for him to know. And so, just as the Father, by generating, gave existence to the Son, so he also, by generating, gave him knowledge: *my doctrine is not mine* (John 7:16).

So that we do not think that the Son was sent by the Father in such a way as to be separated from the Father, he teaches, third, that they must believe that he is inseparable from the Father when he says, *he who sent me*, the Father, *is with me*, by a unity of essence: *I am in the Father, and the Father in me* (John 14:10). And the Father is also with me by a union of love, *the Father loves the Son, and shows him all things that he himself does* (John 5:20). And so the Father sent the Son in such a way that the Father did not separate himself from the Son; and so the text continues, *he has not left me alone*, because I am the object of his love. For although both are together, one sends and the other is sent: for the sending is the incarnation, and this pertains only to the Son, and not to the Father.

That he has not deserted me is clear from this sign: *for I always do the things that please him.* We should not understand this to indicate a meritorious cause, but a sign; it is the same as saying: the fact that I always do, without beginning and without end, *the things that please him*, is a sign that he is always with me and has not deserted me, *I was with him forming all things* (Prov 8:30). Another interpretation would be this: *and he has not left me alone*, that is, as man, protecting me, *for I always do the things that please him.* In this interpretation it does indicate a meritorious cause.

1193. Then when he says, *when he spoke these things, many believed in him*, he shows the effect of his teaching, which is the conversion of many of them to the faith because they had heard Christ's teaching: *faith comes by hearing, and what is heard by the word of Christ* (Rom 10:17).

Lecture 4

8:31 Dicebat ergo Iesus ad eos qui crediderunt ei, Iudaeos: si vos manseritis in sermone meo, vere discipuli mei eritis: [n. 1195]

8:32 et cognoscetis veritatem, et veritas liberabit vos. [n. 1198]

8:33 Responderunt ei: semen Abrahae sumus, et nemini servivimus unquam. Quomodo tu dicis, liberi eritis? [n. 1200]

8:34 Respondit eis Iesus: amen, amen dico vobis, quia omnis qui facit peccatum, servus est peccati. [n. 1203]

8:35 Servus autem non manet in domo in aeternum; filius autem manet in aeternum. [n. 1205]

8:36 Si ergo vos Filius liberaverit, vere liberi eritis. [n. 1207]

8:37 Scio quia filii Abrahae estis. Sed quaeritis me interficere: quia sermo meus non capit in vobis. [n. 1211]

8:38 Ego quod vidi apud Patrem meum, loquor. Et vos quae vidistis apud patrem vestrum, facitis. [n. 1216]

8:31 ἔλεγεν οὖν ὁ Ἰησοῦς πρὸς τοὺς πεπιστευκότας αὐτῷ Ἰουδαίους· ἐὰν ὑμεῖς μείνητε ἐν τῷ λόγῳ τῷ ἐμῷ, ἀληθῶς μαθηταί μού ἐστε

8:32 καὶ γνώσεσθε τὴν ἀλήθειαν, καὶ ἡ ἀλήθεια ἐλευθερώσει ὑμᾶς.

8:33 ἀπεκρίθησαν πρὸς αὐτόν· σπέρμα Ἀβραάμ ἐσμεν καὶ οὐδενὶ δεδουλεύκαμεν πώποτε· πῶς σὺ λέγεις ὅτι ἐλεύθεροι γενήσεσθε;

8:34 ἀπεκρίθη αὐτοῖς ὁ Ἰησοῦς· ἀμὴν ἀμὴν λέγω ὑμῖν ὅτι πᾶς ὁ ποιῶν τὴν ἁμαρτίαν δοῦλός ἐστιν τῆς ἁμαρτίας.

8:35 ὁ δὲ δοῦλος οὐ μένει ἐν τῇ οἰκίᾳ εἰς τὸν αἰῶνα, ὁ υἱὸς μένει εἰς τὸν αἰῶνα.

8:36 ἐὰν οὖν ὁ υἱὸς ὑμᾶς ἐλευθερώσῃ, ὄντως ἐλεύθεροι ἔσεσθε.

8:37 Οἶδα ὅτι σπέρμα Ἀβραάμ ἐστε· ἀλλὰ ζητεῖτέ με ἀποκτεῖναι, ὅτι ὁ λόγος ὁ ἐμὸς οὐ χωρεῖ ἐν ὑμῖν.

8:38 ἃ ἐγὼ ἑώρακα παρὰ τῷ πατρὶ λαλῶ· καὶ ὑμεῖς οὖν ἃ ἠκούσατε παρὰ τοῦ πατρὸς ποιεῖτε.

8:31 Then Jesus said to those Jews who believed him: if you remain in my word, you will truly be my disciples. [n. 1195]

8:32 And you will know the truth, and the truth will set you free. [n. 1198]

8:33 They answered him: we are the seed of Abraham, and we have never been slaves to anyone: how can you say, you will be free? [n. 1200]

8:34 Jesus answered them: amen, amen I say to you: whoever commits sin is the slave of sin. [n. 1203]

8:35 Now the servant does not abide in the house forever, but the son abides forever. [n. 1205]

8:36 If therefore the Son makes you free, you will truly be free. [n. 1207]

8:37 I know that you are the sons of Abraham, but you seek to kill me, because my word has no place in you. [n. 1211]

8:38 I speak that which I have seen with my Father, and you do the things that you have seen with your father. [n. 1216]

1194. Posito remedio evadendi tenebras, hic consequenter ostendit ipsius remedii efficaciam, et

primo ponitur remedii efficacia;

secundo introducitur remedii indigentia, ibi **responderunt ei Iudaei**.

Circa primum duo facit:

primo ostendit quid exigitur ab eis quibus remedium confertur, quod pertinet ad meritum;

secundo quid eis pro eo redditur, quod pertinet ad praemium, ibi **vere discipuli mei eritis**.

1195. Dicit ergo primo: dictum est quod multi crediderunt in eum; et ideo dicit eis, scilicet qui crediderunt in eum, Iudaeis, quid ab eis requiratur, hoc scilicet quod maneant in sermone eius: unde dicit **si vos manseritis in sermone meo, vere discipuli mei eritis**. Quasi dicat: non propter hoc quod creditis superficie tenus, eritis discipuli mei, sed **si manseritis in sermone meo**.

Exiguntur autem a nobis tria circa verbum Dei: scilicet sollicitudo ad audiendum, Iac. I, v. 19: *sit autem*

1194. After he had shown the remedy for escaping from the darkness, he now shows the effectiveness of this remedy.

First, he shows the effectiveness of this remedy;

then their need for remedy, at **they answered him, we are the seed of Abraham**.

He does two things about the first.

First, he shows what is required from those to whom the remedy is granted, and this concerns merit;

second, he shows what is given for this, and this concerns their reward, at **you will truly be my disciples**.

1195. He says first: it was said that many believe in him, and so he told them, the Jews who believed in him, what they had to do, which was to remain in his word. So he says, **if you remain in my word, you will truly be my disciples**. He is saying in effect: you will not be my disciples if you just believe superficially, but **if you remain in my word**.

We need three things with respect to the word of God. A concern to hear it: *let every man be quick to hear*

omnis homo velox ad audiendum etc., fides ad credendum, Rom. X, v. 17: *fides ex auditu*, constantia ad perma-
nendum, Eccli. VI, 21: *quam aspera est nimium indoctis
hominibus sapientia. Et non permanebit in illa excors*. Et
ideo dicit *si manseritis*, scilicet per fidei stabilitatem, per
continuam meditationem, Ps. I, 2: *in lege eius meditabitur die ac nocte*; et ferventem affectionem: *in lege Domini
fuit voluntas eius*. Unde dicit Augustinus quod illi in verbis Domini permanent qui nullis tentationibus cedunt.

1196. Primum autem quod persistentibus redditur,
ostendit cum dicit *vere discipuli mei eritis*, et hoc quantum ad tria: scilicet quantum ad discipulatus Christi
sublimationem, quantum ad veritatis cognitionem, et
quantum ad libertatis adeptionem.

1197. Et quidem magnae dignitatis est privilegium,
esse discipulum Christi; Ioel. II, v. 23: *filii Sion, exultate,
et laetamini in Domino Deo vestro, quia dedit vobis doctorem iustitiae*. Et quantum ad hoc dicit *vere discipuli mei
eritis*: quanto enim magister est maior, tanto discipuli
eius sublimiores sunt; Christus autem excellentissimus
et summus magister est: discipuli ergo eius excellentis-
simi sunt.

Tria autem requiruntur ex parte discipulorum.
Primum est intellectus ad capiendum verba magistri;
Matth. XV, 16: *adhuc et vos sine intellectu estis?* Solus autem Christus potest aperire aurem intelligentiae; Lc. ult.,
45: *aperuit illis sensum, ut intelligerent Scripturas*. Et ideo
dicebat Is. l, 5: *Dominus aperuit mihi aurem*. Secundum
est assensus ad credendum sententiae magistri: nam, ut
dicitur Lc. VI, 40, *non est discipulus super magistrum*, et
ideo non debet ei contradicere. Unde dicitur Eccli. IV, 30:
non contradicas verbo veritatis ullo modo. Et ideo subdit
Isaias: *ego autem non contradico*. Tertio stabilitas ad per-
manendum; supra VI, 67, dicitur, quod *multi discipuli
abierunt retro, et iam non cum illo ambulabant*. Et ideo
subdit Isaias: *retrorsum non abii*.

1198. Sed maius est veritatem cognoscere, cum sit
finis discipuli. Et hoc etiam Dominus credentibus reddit; unde dicit *cognoscetis veritatem*, scilicet doctrinae,
quam ego doceo; infra XVIII, 37: *in hoc natus sum, et ad
hoc veni, ut testimonium perhibeam veritati*. Item gratiae quam facio; supra, VIII, v. 17: *gratia et veritas per
Iesum Christum facta est*. Et dicitur gratia veritatis per
comparationem ad figuras veteris legis. Item aeternitatis
in qua permaneo; Ps. CXVIII, 89: *in aeternum, Domine,
permanet verbum tuum, in generatione et generatione veritas sua*.

1199. Sed maximum est libertatis adeptio, quam efficit cognitio veritatis in credentibus; unde dicit *et veritas
liberabit vos*.

(Jas 1:19). Then we need faith to believe it: *faith comes by
hearing* (Rom 10:17). And also perseverance in continuing
with it: *how exceedingly bitter is wisdom to the unlearned.
The foolish will not continue with her* (Sir 6:21). And so he
says, *if you remain*, that is, by a firm faith, through continual meditation: *he will meditate on his law day and night*
(Ps 1:2); and by your ardent love: *his will is the law of the
Lord* (Ps 1:2). Thus Augustine says that those who remain
in the word of our Lord are those who do not give in to
temptations.

1196. He mentions what will be given to those who do
remain when he says, *you will truly be my disciples*, and
with three characteristics. First, they will have the excellence of being disciples of Christ; second, they will have a
knowledge of the truth; and then, they will be free.

1197. Indeed, it is a great privilege to be a disciple of
Christ: *children of Zion, rejoice and delight in the Lord your
God, because he has given you a teacher of justice* (Joel 2:23).
Concerning this he says, *you will truly be my disciples*; for
the greater the master, the more honorable or excellent it is
to be his disciple. But Christ is the greatest and most excellent of teachers; therefore, his disciples will be of the highest dignity.

Three things are required to be a disciple. The first is
understanding, to grasp the words of the teacher: *are you
also still without understanding?* (Matt 15:16). But it is only
Christ who can open the ears of the understanding: *then
he opened their minds so that they could understand the
Scriptures* (Luke 24:45); *the Lord opened my ears* (Isa 50:5).
Second, a disciple needs to assent, so as to believe the doctrine of his teacher, for *the disciple is not above his teacher*
(Luke 6:40), and thus he should not contradict him: *do not
speak against the truth in any way* (Sir 4:30). And Isaiah
continues in the same verse, *I do not resist*. Third, a disciple
needs to be stable, in order to persevere. As we read above:
*after this many of his disciples departed and did not walk
anymore with him* (John 6:67); and Isaiah adds: *I did not
turn back* (Isa 50:5).

1198. But it is a greater thing to know the truth, since
this is the end of a disciple. And our Lord also gives this
to those who believe; thus he says, *and you will know the
truth*, the truth, that is of the doctrine that I am teaching:
*for this I was born, and for this I came into the world, that
I should give testimony to the truth* (John 18:37); and they
will know the truth of the grace that I produce: *grace and
truth came through Jesus Christ* (John 1:17)—in contrast
to the figures of the old law—and they will know the truth
of the eternity in which I remain: *O Lord, your word remains forever, your truth endures from generation to generation* (Ps 118:89).

1199. Yet the greatest thing is the acquisition of freedom, which the knowledge of the truth produces in those
who believe. Thus he says, *and the truth will set you free*.

Liberare autem, in hoc loco, non importat exceptionem a quacumque angustia, prout in Latino sonat, sed proprie dicit liberum facere. Et hoc a tribus: quia veritas doctrinae liberabit ab errore falsitatis; Prov. VIII, 7: *veritatem meditabitur guttur meum, et labia mea detestabuntur impium*; veritas gratiae, liberabit a servitute peccati; Rom. VIII, 2: *lex autem spiritus vitae in Christo Iesu, liberabit me a lege peccati et mortis*; sed veritas aeternitatis, in Christo Iesu, liberabit nos a corruptione; Rom. VIII, 21: *ipsa creatura liberabitur a servitute corruptionis.*

1200. Consequenter cum dicit *responderunt ei: semen Abrahae* etc., ostendit remedii necessitatem Iudaeis inesse, et

primo exaggeratur Iudaeorum praesumptio, se tali remedio indigere negantium;

secundo ostenditur quomodo remedio indigent, ibi *respondit eis Iesus: amen, amen dico vobis.*

1201. Praesumptio autem Iudaeorum ostenditur in quadam praesumptuosa interrogatione; unde *responderunt ei Iudaei: semen Abrahae sumus, et nemini servivimus unquam. Quomodo tu dicis, liberi eritis?* In qua quidem primo aliquid affirmant; secundo aliquid negant; et tertio interrogant.

Affirmant quidem se esse semen Abrahae, unde dicunt *semen Abrahae sumus*: in quo ostenditur eorum inanis gloria, quia de sola carnis origine gloriantur; Matth. III, 9: *ne coeperitis dicere: Patrem habemus Abraham*. Simile faciunt qui de carnali nobilitate extolli quaerunt; Oseae IX, 11: *omnis gloria eorum a partu, ab utero et conceptu.*

Negant autem servitutem, unde dicunt *nemini servivimus unquam*: in quo se hebetes ostendunt, et mendaces. Hebetes quidem, quia quod Dominus de spirituali libertate loquitur, ipsi intelligunt de corporali; I Cor. II, 14: *animalis homo non percipit ea quae sunt spiritus Dei*. Mendaces autem, quia si hoc quod dicunt *nemini servivimus unquam*, intelligunt de servitute carnali, aut loquuntur universaliter quantum ad totum genus Iudaeorum, aut specialiter quantum ad seipsos. Si quidem universaliter, manifeste mentiuntur: nam Ioseph venumdatus est, et patres eorum servierunt in Aegypto, ut patet Gen. XL et Ex. I. Unde Augustinus dicit: *o ingrati, quid est quod assidue vobis imputat Deus quod vos de domo servitutis liberavit, si nemini servistis?* Dicitur enim Deut. VI, 13: *eduxi vos de Aegypto, de domo servitutis* etc. Si autem de seipsis loquuntur, non possunt etiam a mendacio excusari: nam et ipsi tunc temporis Romanis tributa solvebant; unde dicebant, Matth. c. XXII, 17: *si licet tributum dari Caesari, an non?*

Interrogant autem libertatis modum; unde dicunt *quomodo tu dicis, liberi eritis?* Dominus eis duo promiserat: scilicet libertatem et veritatis cognitionem, cum

In this context, to free does not mean a release from some confinement, as the Latin language suggests, but rather a being made free; and this is from three things. The truth of this doctrine will free us from the error of falsity: *my mouth will speak the truth; my lips will hate wickedness* (Prov 8:7). The truth of grace will free us from the slavery to sin: *the law of the Spirit of life in Christ Jesus has freed me from the law of sin and of death* (Rom 8:2). And the truth of eternity, in Christ Jesus, will free us from corruption: *the creature will be freed from its slavery to corruption* (Rom 8:21).

1200. Next, at *they answered him: we are the seed of Abraham*, he shows that the Jews need this remedy.

First, he amplifies on their presumption in denying that they need any such remedy;

second, he shows in what respect they need this remedy, at *Jesus answered them: amen, amen I say to you.*

1201. The presumption of the Jews is shown by their disdainful question: *they answered him: we are the seed of Abraham, and we have never been slaves to anyone: how can you say, you will be free?* First, they affirm one thing; then deny another; and third, pose their question.

They assert that they are the descendants of Abraham: *we are of the seed of Abraham*. This shows their vainglory, because they glory only in the origin of their flesh: *do not think of saying: we have Abraham as our Father* (Matt 2:9). Those who seek to be praised for their noble birth act in the same way: *their glory is from their birth, from the womb and from their conception* (Hos 9:11).

Further, they deny their slavery; thus they say, *and we have never been slaves to anyone*. This reveals them as dull in mind and as liars. It shows them as dull because while our Lord is speaking of spiritual freedom, they are thinking of physical freedom: *the sensual person does not perceive what pertains to the Spirit of God* (1 Cor 2:14). It shows them as liars because if they mean their statement as, *we have never been the slaves of anyone*, to apply to physical slavery, then they are either speaking generally of the entire Jewish people, or in particular of themselves. If they are speaking generally, they are obviously lying: for Joseph was sold into slavery and their ancestors were slaves in Egypt (Gen 40; Exod 3). Thus Augustine says: *ungrateful! Why does the Lord so often remind you that he freed you from the house of bondage, if you have never been slaves to anyone?* For we read: *I have called you out of Egypt, from the house of your slavery* (Deut 13:10). But even if they are speaking of themselves, they are still guilty of lying, because they were at that time paying taxes to the Romans. Thus they asked: *is it lawful to pay taxes to Caesar or not?* (Matt 22:17).

They ask him about the kind of freedom he is talking about when they say, *how can you say, you will be free?* Our Lord had promised them two things: freedom and

dixit: *cognoscetis veritatem, et veritas liberabit vos*. Per quod Iudaei intelligebant, se servos et ignaros a Domino reputari. Et licet magis iniuriosum sit deficere a cognitione quam a libertate; quia tamen carnales erant, neglecta veritate, modum libertatis inquirunt; Ps. XVI, 12: *oculos suos statuerunt declinare in terram*.

1202. Hic Dominus eorum praesumptionem excludens, eos remedio praedicto indigere convincit, et

primo agit de eorum servitute;

secundo de eorum liberatione, ibi *servus autem non manet in domo in aeternum*;

tertio de eorum origine, ibi *scio quia filii Abrahae estis*.

1203. Convincit autem eos de servitute, non carnali, qualem illi intelligebant, sed spirituali, scilicet peccati, ad quam exaggerandam duo praemittit: scilicet ingeminatum iuramentum; unde dicit *amen, amen dico vobis*. *Amen* est nomen Hebraeum, quod interpretatur *vere*, vel *fiat*. Quod, secundum Augustinum, nec Graecus interpres, nec Latinus ausus est interpretari, ut honorem haberet velamento secreti, non ut esset ligatum, sed ne vilesceret nudatum; et specialiter propter reverentiam Domini, qui frequenter ipso usus est. Ponit ergo hic Dominus quasi quoddam iuramentum: quod ideo geminatur, ut suam sententiam magis firmam ostendat; ad Hebr. c. VI, 17: *interposuit iusiurandum, ut per duas res immobiles, quibus impossibile est mentiri Deum, fortissimum solatium habeamus*.

Secundo universalem locutionem, cum dicit *omnis*, sive Iudaeus sive Graecus, dives aut pauper, imperator vel mendicus; Rom. III, 23: *non est distinctio Iudaei et Graeci; omnes enim peccaverunt, et egent gloria Dei*. Servitutem etiam proponit dicens *qui facit peccatum, servus est peccati*.

1204. Sed contra. Servus non movetur proprio arbitrio suo, sed domini; qui autem facit peccatum, movetur proprio arbitrio suo: ergo non est servus.

Responsio. Dicendum, quod unumquodque est illud quod convenit ei secundum suam naturam: quando ergo movetur ab aliquo extraneo, non operatur secundum se, sed ab impressione alterius; quod est servile. Homo autem secundum suam naturam est rationalis. Quando ergo movetur secundum rationem, proprio motu movetur, et secundum se operatur, quod est libertatis; quando vero peccat, operatur praeter rationem, et tunc movetur quasi ab alio, retentis terminis alienis: et ideo *qui facit peccatum, servus est peccati*; II Petr. II, 19: *a quo quis superatus est, eius servus addictus est*. Sed quanto quis movetur ab extraneo, tanto magis in servitutem redigitur; et tanto magis vincitur a peccato, quanto minus habet de proprio motu, scilicet rationis, et magis efficitur

knowledge of the truth, when he said, *you will know the truth, and the truth will set you free*. The Jews took this to mean that our Lord regarded them as ignorant slaves. And although it is more harmful to lack knowledge than freedom, yet because they were carnal they pass over the truth part and ask about the kind of freedom: *they have set their eyes, lowering themselves to the earth* (Ps 16:11).

1202. Our Lord ignores their presumption and shows them that they do need the remedy he mentioned.

First, he mentions their slavery;

second, he treats of their freedom, at *now the servant does not abide in the house forever*; and

third, of their origin, at *I know that you are the sons of Abraham*.

1203. He shows that they are slaves, not in the physical sense they thought he meant, but spiritually, that is, slaves of sin. And in order to make this clear he starts with two things. The first is a solemn affirmation that he repeats, saying, *amen, amen, I say to you*. *Amen* is a Hebrew word which means *truly*, or *may it be this way*. According to Augustine, neither the Greeks nor the Latins translated it so that it might be honored and veiled as something sacred. This was not done to hide it, but to prevent it from becoming commonplace if its meaning were stated. It was done especially out of reverence from our Lord who frequently used it. Our Lord makes use of it here as a kind of oath, and he repeats it to reinforce his statement: *he interposed an oath, so that by two immutable things, in which it is impossible for God to lie, we might have the strongest comfort* (Heb 6:17).

Second, he makes a general statement when he says, *whoever*, whether Jew or Greek, rich or poor, emperor or beggar: *there is no difference between Jews and Greeks: all have sinned* (Rom 3:22). He mentions slavery when he says, *whoever commits sin is the slave of sin*.

1204. But one might argue against this in the following way: a slave does not act by his own judgment, but by that of his master; but one who commits sin is acting by his own judgment; therefore, he is not a slave.

I answer by saying that a thing is whatever is appropriate to it according to its nature, it acts of itself; but when it is moved by something exterior, it does not act of itself, but by the influence of that other: and this is a kind of slavery. Now according to his nature, man is rational. And thus when he acts according to reason, he is acting by his own proper motion and is acting of himself; and this is a characteristic of freedom. But when he sins, he is acting outside reason; and then he is moved by another, being held back by the limitations imposed by that other. Therefore, *whoever commits sin is a slave of sin*: *whatever overcomes a person, is that to which he is a slave* (2 Pet 2:19). And to the extent that someone is moved by something exterior, to that extent he is brought into slavery; and the more one is overcome by

servus. Unde quanto aliqui liberius peragunt perversa quae volunt, et minori difficultate, tanto peccati servitio obnoxius obligantur, ut Gregorius dicit. Quae quidem servitus gravissima est, quia vitari non potest: nam quocumque homo vadat, peccatum intra se habet, licet actus et delectatio eius transeat; Is. XIV, 3: *cum requiem dederit tibi Deus . . . a servitute tua dura,* scilicet peccati, *qua antea servisti.* Servitus autem corporalis, saltem fugiendo, evadi potest; unde dicit Augustinus: *o miserabilis servitus* (scilicet peccati). *Servus hominum, aliquando sui domini duris imperiis fatigatus, fugiendo requiescit; servus peccati secum trahit peccatum, quocumque fugerit: peccatum enim quod fecit, intus est, voluptas transit; peccatum* (idest actus) *transit: praeteriit quod delectabat, remansit quod pungat.*

1205. Consequenter cum dicit **servus autem non manet in domo in aeternum**, agit de liberatione a servitute: quia enim omnes peccaverunt, omnes erant servi peccati. Sed imminet vobis liberationis spes ab eo quia liber est a peccato; et hic est Filius.

Unde circa hoc tria facit.

Primo praemittit servi conditionem, ut distinguatur liber a servo;

secundo ostendit conditionem Filii a servo diversam;

tertio concludit potestatem Filii in liberando.

1206. Est ergo conditio servi transitoria et instabilis; unde dicit **servus non manet in domo in aeternum**. Domus ista est Ecclesia; I Tim. III, 15: *ut scias quomodo oporteat te conversari in domo Dei, quae est Ecclesia Dei vivi.* In qua quidem domo aliqui spiritualiter servi ad horam tantum permanent, sicut in domo patrisfamilias corporaliter servi manent ad tempus; non tamen in aeternum: quia licet modo mali non sint separati numero a fidelibus, sed merito tantum, in futuro tamen separabuntur utroque modo; Gal. IV, 30: *eiice ancillam et filium eius: non enim erit heres filius ancillae cum filio liberae.*

1207. Conditio vero Filii est aeterna et stabilis; unde dicit **Filius autem**, idest Christus, **permanet in aeternum**, scilicet in Ecclesia, tamquam in domo sua; Heb. III, 6, dicitur quod Christus, tamquam Filius in domo sua etc. Et quidem ipse per seipsum in domo manet in aeternum, quia ipse immunis est a peccato; nos autem sicut per ipsum a peccato liberamur, ita et per ipsum in domo manemus.

1208. Liberationis autem potestatem habet Filius; unde subdit **si igitur Filius vos liberaverit, vere liberi eritis**; Gal. IV, 31: *non sumus ancillae Filii, sed liberae, qua libertate Christus nos liberavit.* Nam, ut Apostolus

sin, the less he acts by his own proper motion, that is, by reason, and the more he is made a slave. Thus, the more freely one does the perverse things he wills, and the less the difficulty he has in doing them, the more he is subjected to the slavery of sin, as Gregory says. This kind of slavery is the worst, because it cannot be escaped from: for wherever a person goes, he carries his sin with him, even though its act and pleasure may pass: *God will give you rest from your harsh slavery* (that is, to sin) *to which you were subjected before* (Isa 14:3). Physical slavery, on the other hand, can be escaped, at least by running away. Thus Augustine says: *what a wretched slavery* (that is, slavery to sin). *A slave of man, when worn out by the harsh commands of his master, can find relief in flight; but a slave of sin drags his sin with him, wherever he flees: for the sin he did is within him. The pleasure passes, the sin* (the act of sin) *passes; what gave pleasure has gone, what wounds have remained.*

1205. Then, at **now the servant does not abide in the house forever**, he considers their liberation from slavery; for since all have sinned, all were slaves to sin. Now the hope of liberation is held out by the one who is free of sin, and this is the Son.

Thus he does three things with respect to this.

First, he mentions the status of a slave as distinguished from that one who is free;

second, he shows that the status of the Son is different from that of a slave; and

third, he concludes that the Son has the power to set us free.

1206. The status of a slave is transient and unstable; so he says, **the servant does not abide in the house forever**. This house is the Church: *so you may know how to act in the house of God, which is the Church of the living God* (1 Tim 3:15). In this house some who are spiritually slaves remain only for a time, just as in a household those who are physically slaves remain only for a while. But the former will not remain forever, for although those who are evil are not now separated from the faithful in a separate group, but only by merit, in the future they will be separated in both ways: *cast out the slave and her son: for the son of the slave woman will not inherit with the son of the free woman* (Gal 4:30).

1207. On the other hand, the status of the Son is everlasting and stable; so he says, **but the Son**, that is, Christ, **abides forever**, namely, in the Church, as in his own house. Christ is described as a son in his own house (Heb 3:6). And indeed, it is of himself that Christ remains in his house forever, because he is immune from sin. As for us, just as we are freed from sin through him, so it is through him that we remain in his house.

1208. The Son has the power to free us; so he adds, **if therefore the Son makes you free, you will truly be free**: *we are not the children of the slave woman, but of the free, by whose freedom Christ has freed us* (Gal 4:31). For as the

dicit, ipse pretium dedit non argentum, sed sanguinem suum: venit enim in similitudinem carnis peccati, nullum omnino habens peccatum; et ideo factum est verum sacrificium pro peccato: unde per eum liberamur non a barbaris, sed a diabolo.

1209. Et nota, quod est multiplex libertas. Scilicet perversa, quando quis abutitur ea ad peccandum; et haec est libertas a iustitia, quam nullus cogitur servare; I Petr. c. II, 16: *quasi liberi, et non quasi velamen habentes malitiae libertatem.* Vana, quae est temporalis, seu carnalis, Iob III, 19: *servus liber a domino suo.* Vera et spiritualis, quae est libertas gratiae, quae est scilicet carere criminibus; quae est imperfecta, quia caro concupiscit adversus spiritum, ut non ea quae volumus faciamus, Gal. V, 17. Gloriae, et perfecta atque plena, quae erit in patria; Rom. VIII, 21: *ipsa creatura liberabitur a servitute*: et hoc erit, quia nihil erit ibi inclinans ad malum, nihil opprimens, quia ibi erit libertas a culpa et a poena.

1210. Chrysostomus autem hoc aliter introducit. Quia enim dixerat: *qui facit peccatum, servus est peccati*, ne praecurrant Iudaei, et dicant: licet simus servi peccati, tamen possumus liberari per sacrificia et caeremonias legis, propterea Dominus ostendit, quod per ea liberari non possunt, sed solum per Filium. Unde dicit *servus*, idest Moyses et pontifices Veteris Testamenti, *non manet in domo in aeternum*; Hebr. III, 5: *Moyses sicut famulus in omni domo sua.* Et caeremoniae etiam aeternae non sunt; et ideo non possunt conferre libertatem aeternam.

1211. Consequenter cum dicit *scio quia filii Abrahae estis*, agit de eorum origine: et primo confitetur eorum originem carnis; secundo inquirit originem spiritus, ibi *sed quaeritis me interficere* etc.

1212. Originem autem carnis ipsorum dicit esse Abraham. *Scio* inquit *quia filii Abrahae estis*, origine carnis tantum, non similitudine fidei; Is. LI, 2: *attendite ad Abraham patrem vestrum, et ad Saram, quae peperit vos.*

1213. Spiritualem originem inquirit dicens *sed quaeritis me interficere*, et

primo ostendit eos originem spiritualem habere;

secundo excludit originem praesumptam, ibi *responderunt, et dixerunt ei: pater noster Abraham est*;

tertio ostendit originem eorum veram, ibi *vos ex patre diabolo estis.*

Circa primum duo facit.

Primo ponit eorum culpam;

secundo concludit eorum spiritualem originem, ibi *vos quae vidistis apud patrem vestrum, facitis.*

Apostle says, he paid a price not in silver, but of his own blood, for he came in the likeness of sinful flesh although he had no sin; and so he became a true sacrifice for sin. Thus, through him, we are freed, not from barbarians, but from the devil.

1209. Note that there are several kinds of freedom. There is a perverted freedom, when one abuses his freedom in order to sin; there is a freedom from justice, a freedom that no one is compelled to keep: *be free, and do not make your freedom a cloak for evil* (1 Pet 2:16). Then there is a vain freedom, which is temporal or bodily: *a slave, free from his master* (Job 3:19). Then we have true and spiritual freedom, which is the freedom of grace, and consists in the absence of sin. This freedom is imperfect because the flesh lusts against the spirit, and we do what we do not want to do (Gal 5:17). Then there is the freedom of glory; this is a perfect and full freedom, which we will have in our homeland: *the creature will be delivered from its slavery* (Rom 8:21), and this will be so because there will be nothing there to incline us to evil, nothing to oppress us, for then there will be freedom from sin and punishment.

1210. Chrysostom explains this in another way: since he had said, *whoever commits sin is a slave to sin*, then lest the Jews anticipate him and say, that even though we are slaves to sin, we can be freed by the sacrifices and ceremonies of the law, our Lord shows that they cannot be freed by these, but only by the Son. Hence he says, *a slave*, i.e., Moses and the priests of the Old Testament, *does not remain in the household forever*: *Moses was faithful in all God's house as a servant* (Heb 3:5). Furthermore, the ceremonies are not eternal; therefore they cannot confer a freedom which will continue forever.

1211. Then he considers their origin, at *I know that you are the sons of Abraham*. First, he gives their origin according to the flesh; second, he inquires into their origin according to the spirit, at *but you seek to kill me*.

1212. He traces their origin in the flesh to Abraham. *I know that you are sons of Abraham*, by carnal origin only, and not by resembling him in faith: *look to Abraham your father and to Sarah who bore you* (Isa 51:2).

1213. He inquires into their spiritual origin when he says, *but you seek to kill me*.

First he shows that they have a spiritual origin;

second, he rejects what they presume to be their origin, at *they answered him and said to him: Abraham is our father* (John 8:39);

third, he shows them their true origin, at *you are of your father the devil* (John 8:44).

As to the first he does two things:

first, he points out their guilt;

second, he infers their spiritual origin, at *and you do the things that you have seen with your father*.

Circa primum tria facit.

Primo imponit eis culpam homicidii;

secundo crimen infidelitatis;

tertio aufert eis excusationis viam.

1214. Ostendit ergo eos Dominus spiritualiter ex mala radice procedere, et ideo signanter arguit eos de peccato; et dimissis omnibus aliis, quibus Iudaei multipliciter irretiti erant, hoc illis tantum commemorat quod iugiter in mente habebant, scilicet peccatum homicidii, quia, ut dictum est supra, volebant eum occidere. Et ideo dicit *sed quaeritis me interficere*; quod est contra legem vestram; Ex. XX, 13: *non occides*; infra XI, 53: **ab illo ergo die cogitabant interficere eum.**

1215. Sed possent dicere quia occidere aliquem ex culpa non est peccatum, et ideo Dominus dicit causam homicidii esse non quidem culpam Christi, nec eorum iustitiam, sed ipsorum infidelitatem; quasi dicat: *quaeritis me interficere*, non propter iustitiam, sed propter vestram infidelitatem, **quia sermo meus non capit in vobis**; Matth. XIX, 11: *non omnes capiunt verbum istud, sed quibus datum est.*

Utitur autem Dominus hoc modo loquendi primo quidem ad ostendendum sui sermonis excellentiam; quasi dicat: sermo meus superexcedit capacitatem vestram, nam ipse de spiritualibus est, vos autem intellectum carnalem habetis; et ideo ipsum non capitis; I Cor. II, 14: *animalis homo non percipit ea quae sunt spiritus Dei.* Secundo vero propter similitudinem quamdam. Nam, ut Augustinus dicit, sic est sermo Dei infidelibus, tamquam piscibus hamus, qui non capit nisi capiatur. Et ideo dicit *sermo meus non capit in vobis*, idest in cor vestrum, quia non recipitur in vobis eo modo quo Petrus captus erat; supra VI, 69: **Domine, ad quem ibimus? Verba vitae aeternae habes.** Nec tamen fit iniuria eis qui capiuntur: ad salutem quippe, non ad perniciem capit. Nam dicitur Deut. XVIII, 20 quod propheta qui loquitur ex ore Domini ea quae Dominus non dixit, debet interfici.

1216. Unde, ne Iudaei dicerent eum interficiendum fore, eo quod a seipso et non ex ore Domini loquebatur, inducit subdens **ego quae vidi apud Patrem meum, loquor**; quasi dicat: non potest imponi mihi quod loquor quae non audivi, quia non solum audita, sed, quod plus est, visa loquor. Alii enim prophetae locuti sunt ea quae audierunt, sed ego quae vidi haec loquor; supra c. I, 18: **Deum nemo vidit unquam unigenitus Filius qui est in sinu Patris, ipse enarravit**; I Io. I: *quod vidimus et audivimus, annuntiamus vobis.*

Est autem hoc intelligendum de visione certissimae cognitionis, quia Filius Patrem cognoscit sicut ipse seipsum novit: de quo dicitur Matth. ii, 27: *Nemo novit Patrem nisi Filius.*

As to the first he does three things:

first, he lays on them the guilt of murder;

second, the sin of unbelief; and

third, he anticipates an excuse they might give.

1214. Our Lord shows that they have their spiritual origins from an evil root. Hence he expressly accuses them of sin and passing over all the other crimes in which the Jews were implicated, he mentions only the one which they continued to nurture in their minds, the sin of murder, because, as was said, they wished to kill him. This is why he says, *you seek to kill me*, which is against your law: *you shall not kill* (Exod 20:13); **from that day forward they devised to put him to death** (John 11:53).

1215. Because they might say that to kill someone for his crime is not a sin, our Lord says that the cause of this murder is not any crime committed by Christ or their own righteousness, but rather their unbelief. As if to say: *you seek to kill me* not because of your own righteousness but because of your unbelief: **because my word has no place in you**: *not all men can receive this message, but only those to whom it is given* (Matt 19:11).

Our Lord uses this way of speaking, first of all, to show the excellence of his message. As if to say: my message transcends your ability, for it is concerned with spiritual things, whereas you have a sensual understanding, that is why you do not grasp it: *the sensual man does not perceive the things that are of the Spirit of God* (1 Cor 2:14). He speaks this way also to recall a certain similarity: for as Augustine says, the Lord's message to unbelievers is what a hook is to a fish, it does not grasp unless it is grasped. And so he says **my word has no place in you** because his message does not grasp them in their hearts, because it is not grasped by them, as Peter was grasped: **Lord, to whom shall we go? You have the words of eternal life** (John 6:69). Yet it does not harm those who are grasped, for they are grasped to salvation, and left uninjured. We read that a prophet who speaks, as coming from the mouth of the Lord, things that the Lord did not say, should be killed (Deut 18:20).

1216. So, lest the Jews say that he should be killed for speaking from himself, and not from the mouth of the Lord, he adds, **I speak that which I have seen with my Father**. As if to say: I cannot be accused of speaking things that I have not heard, for I speak not only what I have heard, but what is more, I speak of what I have seen. Other prophets spoke the things they heard, whereas I speak the things I have seen: **no man has ever seen God: the only begotten Son, who is in the bosom of the Father, has made him known** (John 1:18); *that which we have seen and heard we proclaim also to you* (1 John 1:3).

This must be understood of a vision which gives the most certain knowledge, because the Son knows the Father as he knows himself: *no one knows the Father except the Son* (Matt 11:27).

1217. Spiritualem autem eorum originem concludit, dicens *et vos quae vidistis apud patrem vestrum, facitis*; quasi dicat: ego ea loquor quae meae origini conveniunt; vos autem illa facitis quae sunt apud patrem vestrum, scilicet diabolum, cuius filii erant, secundum Augustinum, non inquantum homines, sed inquantum mali erant. Ea, inquam, quae vidistis, diabolo suggerente; Sap. c. II, 24: *invidia diaboli mors introivit in orbem terrarum.*

Secundum Chrysostomum, est alia littera *vos quae vidistis apud Patrem vestrum, facite*; quasi dicat: sicut ego verbis in veritate Patrem meum ostendo, ita vos ostendite operibus Patrem vestrum origine, scilicet Abraham; unde dicit: facite quae apud Patrem vestrum vidistis, docti per legem et prophetas.

1217. He then infers their spiritual origin when he says, *and you do the things that you have seen with your father*. As if to say: I speak things that are in accord with my origin; but you do the things that are done by your father, namely, the devil, whose children they were, according to Augustine, not insofar as they were men, but insofar as they were evil. You do those things, I say, which you see, at the devil's suggestion: *through the devil's envy death entered the world* (Wis 2:24).

Chrysostom uses another text: *do what you have seen with your father*. As if to say: just as I reveal my Father in truth by my words, so you, reveal the father of our origin, namely, Abraham, by your deeds. Thus he says: do what you see your father doing, you who are taught by the law and the prophets.

Lecture 5

8:39 Responderunt, et dixerunt ei: pater noster Abraham est. Dicit eis Iesus: si filii Abrahae estis, opera Abrahae facite. [n. 1219]

8:40 Nunc autem quaeritis me interficere, hominem, qui veritatem vobis locutus sum, quam audivi a Deo. Hoc Abraham non fecit. [n. 1226]

8:41 Vos facitis opera patris vestri. Dixerunt itaque ei: nos ex fornicatione non sumus nati. Unum Patrem habemus Deum. [n. 1230]

8:42 Dixit ergo eis Iesus: si Deus Pater vester esset, diligeretis utique me: Ego enim ex Deo processi, et veni. Neque enim a meipso veni, sed ille me misit. [n. 1233]

8:43 Quare loquelam meam non cognoscitis? Quia non potestis audire sermonem meum. [n. 1238]

8:39 ἀπεκρίθησαν καὶ εἶπαν αὐτῷ· ὁ πατὴρ ἡμῶν Ἀβραάμ ἐστιν. λέγει αὐτοῖς ὁ Ἰησοῦς· εἰ τέκνα τοῦ Ἀβραάμ ἐστε, τὰ ἔργα τοῦ Ἀβραὰμ ἐποιεῖτε·

8:40 νῦν δὲ ζητεῖτέ με ἀποκτεῖναι ἄνθρωπον ὃς τὴν ἀλήθειαν ὑμῖν λελάληκα ἣν ἤκουσα παρὰ τοῦ θεοῦ· τοῦτο Ἀβραὰμ οὐκ ἐποίησεν.

8:41 ὑμεῖς ποιεῖτε τὰ ἔργα τοῦ πατρὸς ὑμῶν. εἶπαν [οὖν] αὐτῷ· ἡμεῖς ἐκ πορνείας οὐ γεγεννήμεθα, ἕνα πατέρα ἔχομεν τὸν θεόν.

8:42 εἶπεν αὐτοῖς ὁ Ἰησοῦς· εἰ ὁ θεὸς πατὴρ ὑμῶν ἦν ἠγαπᾶτε ἂν ἐμέ, ἐγὼ γὰρ ἐκ τοῦ θεοῦ ἐξῆλθον καὶ ἥκω· οὐδὲ γὰρ ἀπ᾽ ἐμαυτοῦ ἐλήλυθα, ἀλλ᾽ ἐκεῖνός με ἀπέστειλεν.

8:43 διὰ τί τὴν λαλιὰν τὴν ἐμὴν οὐ γινώσκετε; ὅτι οὐ δύνασθε ἀκούειν τὸν λόγον τὸν ἐμόν.

8:39 They answered and said to him: Abraham is our father. Jesus said to them: if you are the sons of Abraham, do the works of Abraham. [n. 1219]

8:40 But now you seek to kill me, a man who has spoken the truth to you, which I have heard from God: Abraham did not do this. [n. 1226]

8:41 You do the works of your father. They said therefore to him: we were not born of fornication: we have one God, the Father. [n. 1230]

8:42 Jesus therefore said to them: if God were your Father, you would indeed love me, for I proceeded and came forth from God; for I came not of myself, but he sent me. [n. 1233]

8:43 Why do you not know my speech? Because you are not able to hear my word. [n. 1238]

1218. Postquam Dominus ostendit Iudaeos aliquam spiritualem originem habere, hic excludit ab eis origines quas sibi praesumptuose attribuebant, et

primo excludit originem, quam se traxisse dicebant ab Abraham;

secundo originem, quam se putabant habere a Deo, ibi *dixerunt itaque ei: nos ex fornicatione non sumus nati*.

Circa primum duo facit.

Primo ponit opinionem Iudaeorum de eorum origine;

secundo excludit eam, ibi *si filii Abrahae estis opera Abrahae facite*.

1219. Sciendum est autem circa primum, quia Dominus dixerat eis *quae vidistis apud patrem vestrum, facitis*, ideo gloriantes se de carnali generatione, transferunt se ad Abraham. Unde dicunt *pater noster Abraham est*, quasi dicant: si spiritualem originem habemus, boni sumus, quia Abraham pater noster bonus est; Ps. CIV, 6: *semen Abraham servi eius*. Et, ut dicit Augustinus, nitebantur eum provocare, ut aliquid male diceret de Abraham, et esset eis occasio facere quod cogitabant, scilicet occidendi Christum.

1220. Sed Dominus, consequenter cum dicit *si filii Abrahae estis, opera Abrahae facite*, excludit hanc ipsorum opinionem tamquam falso prolatam, et proponit

1218. After showing that the Jews had a certain spiritual origin, our Lord here rejects certain origins which they had presumptuously attributed to themselves.

First, he rejects the origin they claimed to have from Abraham;

second, the origin they thought they had from God, at *they said therefore to him: we were not born of fornication*.

As to the first he does two things:

first, he gives the opinion of the Jews about their origin;

second, he rejects it, at *if you are the sons of Abraham, do the works of Abraham*.

1219. It should be noted with respect to the first, that our Lord had said to them, *you do the things that you have seen with your father* (John 8:38), and so, glorying in their carnal descent, they aligned themselves with Abraham. Thus they said, *Abraham is our father*. This is like saying: if we have a spiritual origin we are good, because our father Abraham is good: *O offspring of Abraham his servant* (Ps 105:6). And as Augustine says, they tried to provoke him to say something against Abraham and so give them an excuse for doing what they had planned, namely, to kill Christ.

1220. Our Lord rejects this opinion of theirs as false, at *if you are the sons of Abraham, do the works of Abraham*.

primo signum debitum filiationis Abrahae;

secundo ostendit, hoc signum in Iudaeis non esse, ibi *nunc autem quaeritis me interficere*;

tertio concludit propositum, ibi *vos facitis opera patris vestri*.

1221. Signum quidem filiationis alicuius est quod assimiliter ei cuius filius est: sicut enim filii carnales ut plurimum parentibus carnalibus assimilantur, ita et filii spirituales (si sint vere filii) debent spirituales parentes imitari; Eph. V, 1: *estote imitatores Dei, sicut filii carissimi*. Et quantum ad hoc dicit *si filii Abrahae estis, opera Abrahae facite*; quasi dicat: hoc signum esset quod essetis filii Abrahae, si eum imitaremini; Is. LI, 2: *attendite ad Abraham patrem vestrum, et ad Saram quae peperit vos*.

1222. Sed dubitatur hic, quod videtur quidem eos negare esse filios Abrahae, dubitative loquens *si filii Abrahae estis*, quod tamen affirmavit superius, dicens: *scio quod filii Abrahae estis*.

Ad quod dupliciter respondetur. Uno modo, secundum Augustinum, quod supra affirmavit eos esse filios Abrahae secundum carnem; hic autem negat eos filios secundum imitationem operum, et praecipue fidei. Caro ergo illorum ex ipso erat, sed vita non erat; Gal. III: *qui ex fide sunt, hi reputantur in semine*.

Alio modo, secundum Origenem, quod utrumque referatur ad spiritualem originem. Sed ubi nos habemus: *scio quod filii Abrahae estis*, in Graeco habetur: *scio quod semen Abrahae estis*; hic vero dicit *si filii Abrahae estis, opera Abrahae facite*; quia Iudaei quidem, spiritualiter loquendo, semen Abrahae erant, sed non eius filii. Differentia est inter semen et filium: nam semen est quid informe, et tamen habet in seipso rationes eius cuius est semen; filius autem, transmutato semine per virtutem informativam ab agente in appositam sibi materiam a muliere, superinducto nutrimento, similitudinem generantis habet. Eodem modo et Iudaei semen quidem Abrahae erant inquantum in eis aliqua ratio eorum quae Deus in Abraham infuderat apparebat; sed quia non ad perfectionem Abrahae pervenerant, ideo filii eius non erant: et propter hoc dicit eis *si filii Abrahae estis, opera Abrahae facite*; idest, ad perfectam imitationem operum eius satagite.

1223. Ex hoc autem quod dicit *opera Abrahae facite*, videtur quod quaecumque ipse fecit, et nos facere debemus. Ergo debemus plures uxores accipere, et ad ancillam accedere, sicut Abraham fecit.

Respondeo. Dicendum quod praecipuum opus Abrahae est fides, per quam iustificatus est apud Deum; Gen. XV, 6: *credidit Abraham Deo, et reputatum est illi*

First, he gives the true sign of being a child of Abraham;

second, he shows that this sign is not verified in the Jews, at **but now you seek to kill me**;

third, he draws his conclusion, **you do the works of your father**.

1221. The sign of anyone being a child is that he is like the one whose child he is; for just as children according to the flesh resemble their parents according to the flesh, so spiritual children (if they are truly children) should imitate their spiritual parents: *be imitators of God, as beloved children* (Eph 5:1). And as to this he says, **if you are the sons of Abraham, do the works of Abraham**. This is like saying: if you imitated Abraham, that would be a sign that you are his children: *look to Abraham your father and to Sarah who bore you* (Isa 51:2).

1222. Here a question arises, for when he says, **if you are the sons of Abraham**, he seems to be denying that they are the children of Abraham, whereas just previously he had said, **I know that you are the sons of Abraham** (John 8:37). There are two ways of answering this. The first, according to Augustine, is that before he said that they were children of Abraham according to the flesh, but here he is denying that they are children in the sense of imitating his works, especially his faith. Therefore, they took their flesh from him, but not their life: *it is men of faith who are the sons of Abraham* (Gal 3:7).

For Origin, who has another explanation, both statements refer to their spiritual origin. Where our text reads, **I know that you are the sons of Abraham**, the Greek has, **I know that you are the seed of Abraham** (John 8:37). But Christ says here, **if you are the sons of Abraham, do the works of Abraham**, because the Jews, spiritually speaking, were the seed of Abraham, but were not his children. There is a difference between a seed and a child: for a seed is unformed, although it has in it the characteristics of that of which it is a seed. A child, however, has a likeness to the parent after the seen has been modified by the informing power infused by the agent acting upon the matter which has been furnished by the female. In the same way, the Jews were indeed the seed of Abraham, insofar as they had some of the characteristics which God had infused into Abraham; but because they had not reached the perfection of Abraham, they were not his children. This is why he said to them, **if you are the sons of Abraham, do the works of Abraham**, i.e., strive for a perfect imitation of his works.

1223. Again, because he said, **do the works of Abraham**, it would seem that whatever he did, we should do. Consequently, we should have a number of wives and approach a maidservant, as Abraham did.

I answer that the chief work of Abraham was faith, by which he was justified before God: *he believed the Lord; and he reckoned it to him as righteousness* (Gen 15:6). Thus, the

ad iustitiam. Et ideo intelligendum est **opera Abrahae facite**, idest, ad similitudinem Abrahae credite.

1224. Sed contra hoc est, quia fides non videtur posse dici opus, cum contra opera distinguatur; Iac. II, 26: *fides sine operibus mortua est.*

Respondeo. Dicendum, quod fides opus dici potest, secundum illud supra VI, 29: **hoc est opus Dei, ut credatis in eum quem misit ille.** Verum opus interius non est manifestum hominibus, sed soli Deo, secundum illud I Reg. c. XVI, 7: *homines vident ea quae apparent; Deus autem intuetur cor.* Inde est quod communius ea quae exterius sunt, consuevimus opera nominare. Fides ergo distinguitur non ab omnibus operibus, sed ab exterioribus tantum.

1225. Sed numquid omnia opera Abrahae debemus facere?

Ad hoc dicendum, quod opus potest considerari dupliciter: vel secundum speciem operis eius, et sic omnia opera eius non sunt imitanda; vel secundum radicem eorum, et sic opera Abrahae imitanda sunt: quia quidquid fecit, ex caritate fecit. Unde dicit Augustinus, quod caelibatus Ioannis non praefertur coniugio Abrahae, cum eadem fuerit radix utriusque. Vel dicendum, quod omnia opera Abrahae imitanda sunt quantum ad signationem, quia *omnia in figura contingebant illis,* ut dicitur I Cor. X, 11.

1226. Consequenter cum dicit **nunc autem quaeritis me interficere**, ostendit, praedictum filiationis signum in eis non esse, et

primo ponuntur Iudaeorum opera;

secundo ostendit ea esse Abrahae operibus dissimilia, ibi **hoc Abraham non fecit.**

1227. Ostenduntur autem Iudaeorum prava opera esse et perversa, quia homicidae erant; unde dicit **nunc autem quaeritis me interficere**; Is. I, 21: *quomodo facta est meretrix civitas fidelis, plena iudicii? Iustitia habitavit in ea, nunc autem homicidae.* Sed hoc homicidium inaestimabile peccatum erat contra personam Filii Dei. Unde quia, ut dicitur I Cor. II, 8, *si cognovissent, numquam Dominum gloriae crucifixissent,* ideo Dominus non dicit eos Filium Dei quaerere interficere, sed hominem: quia etsi Filius Dei dicatur passus et mortuus propter unitatem suppositi, hoc non est inquantum Filius Dei, sed propter infirmitatem humanam, quia, ut dicitur II Cor. ult., 4, *si crucifixus est ex infirmitate nostra, sed vivit ex virtute Dei.*

1228. Et ut magis eorum homicidium exaggeret, ostendit, eos nullam mortis causam adversus eum habere; unde subdit **qui veritatem locutus sum vobis, quam audivi a Deo.** Ista veritas est quod dicebat se aequalem Deo; supra V, 18: **quaerebant eum Iudaei interficere, quia non solum Sabbatum solvebat, sed Patrem suum dicebat Deum, aequalem se faciens Deo.** Hanc veritatem

meaning is, **do the works of Abraham** i.e., believe according to the example of Abraham.

1224. One might say against this interpretation that faith should not be called a work, since it is distinguished from works: *faith apart from works is dead* (Jas 2:26).

I answer that faith can be called a work according to what was said above: **this is the work of God: that you believe in him whom he has sent** (John 6:29). An interior work is not obvious to man, but only to God, according to, *the Lord sees not as man sees; man looks on the outward appearance, but the Lord looks on the heart* (1 Sam 16:7). This is the reason we are more accustomed to call exterior action works. Thus, faith is not distinguished from all works, but only from external works.

1225. But should we do all the works of Abraham?

I answer that works can be considered in two ways. Either according to the kind of works they are, in which sense we should not imitate all his works; or, according to their root, and in this sense we should imitate the works of Abraham, because whatever he did, he did out of charity. Thus Augustine says that the celibacy of John was not esteemed above the marriage of Abraham, since the root of each was the same. Or, it might be said that all of Abraham's works should be imitated as to their symbolism, because *all these things happen to them in figure* (1 Cor 10:11).

1226. Then, at **but now you seek to kill me**, he shows that they do not have the above mentioned sign of being children.

First, the conduct of the Jews is given;

second, he shows that it does not resemble the conduct of Abraham, at **Abraham did not do this.**

1227. The conduct of the Jews is shown to be wicked and perverse, because they were murderers; so he says, **now you seek to kill me**: *how the faithful city has become a harlot, she that was full of justice! Righteousness lodged in her, but now murderers* (Isa 1:21). This murder was an unfathomable sin against the person of the Son of God. But because it is said, *if they had understood, they would not have crucified the Lord of glory* (1 Cor 2:8), our Lord does not say that they sought to kill the Son of God, but a man. For although the Son of God is said to have suffered and died by reason of the oneness of his person, this suffering and death was not insofar as he was the Son of God, but because of his human weakness, as it says: *for he was crucified in weakness, but lives by the power of God* (2 Cor 13:4).

1228. In order to further elucidate this murder, he shows that they have no reason to put him to death; thus he adds, **a man who has spoken the truth to you, which I have heard from God.** This truth is that he said that he is equal to God: **therefore, the Jews sought the more to kill him, because he did not only break the Sabbath, but also said that God was his Father, making himself equal to**

audivit a Deo inquantum ab aeterno per generationem aeternam accepit a Patre eamdem naturam quam ipse habet; supra V, 26: *sicut Pater habet vitam in semetipso, sic dedit et Filio habere vitam in semetipso*.

Excludit autem duas causas propter quas prophetae mandabantur occidi in lege. Primo quidem propter mendacium, Deut. XIII, 5 ubi praecipitur, quod si aliquis propheta surrexerit loquens mendacium, aut fictor somniorum, interficiatur: et hoc a se Dominus excludit, dicens *qui veritatem locutus sum vobis*; Prov. c. VIII, 7: *veritatem meditabitur guttur meum*. Secundo vero si aliquis propheta locutus fuerit ex nomine falsorum deorum, vel ex nomine Dei quod ipse non praecepit, occidi debebat, ut habetur Deut. XIII, 5. Et hoc Dominus excludit a se, cum dicit *quam audivi a Deo*.

1229. Consequenter cum dicit *hoc Abraham non fecit*, ostendit eorum opera dissimilia esse operibus Abrahae, quasi dicat: in hoc probatis vos non esse filios Abrahae, quia facitis opera contraria operibus eius: nam de eo legitur Eccli. XLIV, 20, *quod servavit legem Altissimi, et fuit in testimonio cum illo*.

Sed aliqui superflue obiiciunt, quod Christus ante Abraham nondum erat, et ideo Abraham hoc non fecit: non enim occidi potuisset qui non erat.

Sed dicendum, quod Abraham non commendatur ex hoc quod non fecit in Christo, sed ex eo quod non fecit in simili persona, idest in his qui tunc veritatem dicebant.

Vel dicendum, quod si Christus non venerat tempore Abraham in carnem, venerat tamen in mentem, secundum illud Sap. VII, 27: *in animas sanctas per nationem se transfert*, quem tamen Abraham non interfecit mortaliter peccando: de quo dicitur ad Hebr. VI, 6: *rursum crucifigentes Filium Dei, et ostentui habentes*.

1230. Consequenter cum dicit *vos facitis opera patris vestri*, concludit propositum; quasi dicat: ex quo non facitis opera Abrahae, ergo habetis aliquem alium patrem, cuius opera facitis. Simile habetur Matth. XXIII, v. 32: *vos implete mensuram patrum vestrorum*.

1231. Consequenter cum dicit *dixerunt itaque ei: nos ex fornicatione non sumus nati*, ostendit eos non habere originem a Deo: quia enim iam ex verbis Domini cognoscebant eum non de carnali generatione loqui, ideo ad spiritualem generationem se transferunt, dicentes *nos ex fornicatione non sumus nati* etc. Ubi

primo eorum opinionem proponunt;

secundo eam Dominus excludit, ibi *dixit ergo eis Iesus* etc.

1232. In eorum autem opinione Iudaei unum negant et aliud asserunt. Negant se ex fornicatione natos: quod quidem, secundum Origenem, quasi improperando,

God (John 5:18). He heard this truth from God inasmuch as from eternity he received from the Father, through an eternal generation, the same nature that the Father has: *for as the Father has life in himself, so he has also given to the Son to have life in himself* (John 5:26).

Furthermore, he excludes the two reasons for which the law commanded that prophets were to be killed. First of all, for lying, for Deuteronomy commands that a prophet should be killed for speaking a lie or feigning dreams (Deut 13:5). Our Lord excludes this from himself, saying, *a man who has spoken the truth to you*: my mouth will utter truth (Prov 8:7). Second, a prophet ought to be killed if he speaks in the name of false gods, or says in the name of God things that God did not command (Deut 13:5). Our Lord excludes this from himself when he says, *which I have heard from God*.

1229. Then when he says, *Abraham did not do this*, he shows that their works are not like those of Abraham. He is saying in effect: because you act contrary to Abraham, you show that you are not his children, for it is written about him: *he kept the law of the Most High, and was taken into covenant with him* (Sir 44:20).

Some frivolously object that Christ did not exist before Abraham and therefore that Abraham did not do this, since one who did not exist could not be killed.

I answer that Abraham is not commended for something he did not do to Christ, but for what he did not do to anyone in like circumstances, i.e., to those who spoke the truth in his day.

Or, it might be answered that although Christ had not come in the flesh during the time of Abraham, he nevertheless had come into his mind, according to: *in every generation she passes into souls* (Wis 7:27). And Abraham did not kill wisdom by sinning mortally. Concerning this we read: *they crucify the Son of God* (Heb 6:6).

1230. Then when he says, *you do the works of your father*, he draws his conclusion. It was like saying: from the fact that you do not do the works of Abraham, it follows that you have some other father whose works you are doing. A similar statement is made: *fill up, then, the measure of your fathers* (Matt 23:32).

1231. Then when he says, *they said to him: we were not born of fornication*, he shows that they do not take their origin from God, for since they knew from our Lord's words that he was not speaking of carnal descent, they turn to spiritual descent, saying, we were not born of fornication, saying, *we were not born of fornication*.

First, they give their own opinion;

second, our Lord rejects it, at *Jesus therefore said to them: if God were your Father*.

1232. According to some, the Jews are denying one thing and affirming another. They are denying that they were born of fornication. According to Origin, they said

Christo proponunt, latenter designantes, ipsum ex adulterio productum fore; quasi dicant nos ex fornicatione non sumus nati, sicut tu.

Sed melius potest dici, quod sponsus animae spiritualiter Deus est, Oseae II, 19: *sponsabo te mihi.* Sicut autem fornicatur sponsa cum praeter sponsum suum carnalem, alium virum admittit; ita, in Scripturis, Iudaea fornicari dicebatur quando Deum verum deserens, idolis adhaerebat; Oseae I, 2: *fornicans fornicabitur terra a Domino.* Dicunt ergo Iudaei **nos ex fornicatione non sumus nati**; quasi dicant: si aliquando mater nostra synagoga a Deo recedens fornicata est cum idolis, nos tamen non recessimus, nec cum idolis fornicati sumus; Ps. XLIII, 18: *nec obliti sumus te, et inique non egimus in testamento tuo, et non recessit retro cor nostrum;* Is. LVII, 3: *ascendite huc, filii fornicatricis, semen adulteri et fornicariae.*

Affirmant autem se esse filios Dei: quod videbatur sequi ex quo non credebant se natos ex fornicatione; unde dicunt **unum Patrem habemus Deum**; Mal. II, 10: *nonne unus est Pater omnium nostrum?* Ier. III: *Patrem vocabis me.*

1233. Consequenter cum dicit **dixit ergo eis Iesus** etc., confutatur eorum opinio a Domino, et

primo proponit divinae filiationis signum;

secundo assignat rationem signi, ibi **ego enim a Deo veni** etc.;

tertio ostendit eos a praedicto signo deficere, ibi **quare loquelam meam non cognoscitis?**

1234. Sciendum est autem circa primum, quod supra signum carnalis filiationis dixit esse opera exteriora, quae homines exterius operantur; hic autem signum filiationis divinae ponit interiorem affectionem. Nam filii Dei efficimur per communicationem Spiritus Sancti; Rom. VIII, 15: *non accepistis spiritum servitutis iterum in timore, sed spiritum adoptionis.* Spiritus autem sanctus causa est amoris Dei, quia *caritas Dei diffusa est in cordibus nostris per Spiritum Sanctum, qui datus est nobis:* Rom. V, 5. Signum ergo speciale divinae filiationis est dilectio; Eph. V, 1: *estote imitatores Dei sicut filii carissimi, et ambulate in dilectione.* Et ideo dicit **si Deus Pater vester esset, diligeretis utique me**; Ps. c. XXIV, 21: *innocentes et recti*, qui sunt filii Dei, *adhaeserunt mihi.*

1235. Rationem autem signi assignat, dicens **ego enim ex Deo processi et veni**, et

primo ponit veritatem;

secundo excludit errorem, ibi **neque enim a meipso veni**.

1236. Veritas autem, quam proponit, est quod a Deo processit et venit.

this tauntingly to Christ, with the unspoken suggestion that he was the product of adultery. It was like saying: we were not born of fornication as you were.

But it is better to say that the spiritual spouse of the soul is God: *I will betroth you to me forever* (Hos 2:19), and just as a bride is guilty of fornication when she admits a man other than her husband, so in Scripture Judea was said to be fornicating when she abandoned the true God and turned to idols: *for the land commits great harlotry by forsaking the Lord* (Hos 1:2). And so the Jews said: **we were not born of fornication**. It was like saying: although our mother, the synagogue, may now and then have departed from God and fornicated with idols, yet we have not departed or fornicated with idols: *we have not forgotten thee, or been false to thy covenant. Our heart has not turned back* (Ps 44:17); but you, *draw near hither, sons of the sorceress, offspring of the adulterer and the harlot* (Isa 57:3).

Further, they affirm that they are children of God; and this seems to follow from the fact that they did not believe that they were born of fornication. Thus they say, **we have one God, the Father**: *have we not all one father?* (Mal 2:10); *and I thought you would call me, my Father* (Jer 3:19).

1233. Next, at **Jesus therefore said to them: if God were your Father**, our Lord refutes their opinion:

first we see the sign of being a child of God;

second, the reason for this sign is given, at **for I proceeded and came forth from God**; and

third, we see that the Jews lack this sign, at **why do you not know my speech?**

1234. With respect to the first it should be noted that above he had said that the sign of being a child according to the flesh was in the exterior actions that a person performs; but here he places the sign of being a child of God in one's interior affections. For we become children of God by sharing in the Holy Spirit: *you did not receive the spirit of slavery to fall back into fear, but you have received the spirit of sonship* (Rom 8:15). Now the Holy Spirit is the cause of our loving God, because *God's love has been poured into our hearts through the Holy Spirit which has been given to us* (Rom 5:5). Therefore, the special sign of being a child of God is love: *be imitators of God, as beloved children. And walk in love* (Eph 5:1). Therefore he says, **if God were your Father, you would indeed love me**: *the innocent and the right in heart*, who are the children of God, *have clung to me* (Ps 21:4).

1235. Then, at **for I proceeded and came forth from God**, he gives the reason for this sign.

First, he states the truth;

second, he rejects an error, at **for I came not of myself**.

1236. The truth he asserts is that he proceeded and came forth from God.

Sed sciendum est, quod omnis amicitia in coniunctione fundatur; unde et fratres se diligunt inquantum ex eisdem parentibus principium sumunt. Dicit ergo Dominus: vos dicitis quod filii Dei estis; sed si hoc esset, *diligeretis me, quia a Deo processi et veni*. Qui ergo non me diligit, non est filius Dei. *Processi*, inquam, *a Deo*, ut unigenitus ab aeterno, de substantia Patris; Ps. CIX, 3: *ante Luciferum genui te*; supra I: *in principio erat Verbum*. *Veni* autem, ut *Verbum caro factum est*, et missus a Deo per incarnationem; infra XVI, 28: *exivi a Patre*, ut Verbum ab aeterno, *et veni in mundum*, ut caro, factum in tempore.

1237. Errorem autem excludit cum dicit *neque enim a meipso veni*: et primo excludit errorem Sabellii, qui Christum non ab alio originem habuisse dicit, sed idem esse Patrem et Filium in persona finxit. Et quantum ad hoc dicit *neque enim a meipso veni*; idest, secundum Hilarium, ego veni non a meipso existens, sed quasi ab alio missus, scilicet a Patre, unde subdit *sed ille me misit*; Gal. IV, 4: *misit Deus Filium suum natum ex muliere, factum sub lege*.

Secundo vero errorem Iudaeorum, qui dicebant Christum non esse missum a Deo, sed falsum prophetam: de quibus dicitur: *non mittebam eos, sed ipsi currebant*. Et quantum ad hoc dicit, secundum Origenem, *neque enim a meipso veni, sed ille me misit*. Hunc petebat Moyses: *obsecro, Domine, mitte quem missurus es*.

1238. Ostendit autem eos ab hoc signo deficere, cum dicit *quare loquelam meam non cognoscitis?* Nam, sicut dictum est supra dilectio Christi est signum filiationis divinae: isti autem Christum non diligebant: unde manifestum est eos ab hoc signo deficere. Quod autem non diligunt, manifestant per effectum: nam effectus dilectionis alicuius est quod diligens libenter audit verba dilecti. Unde Cant. II, 14: *sonet vox tua in auribus meis; vox enim tua dulcis*. Et Cant. ult., 13: *fac me audire vocem tuam: amici auscultant te*. Quia ergo isti Christum non diligebant, durum videbatur eis etiam vocem eius audire; supra VI, 61: *durus est hic sermo: quis potest eum audire?* Sap. II, 15: *gravis est nobis etiam ad videndum*.

Contingit autem quod aliquis non libenter audit verba alicuius, quia ea examinare non potest nec per consequens cognoscere, et ideo eis contradicunt; Iob VI, 29: *respondete, obsecro, absque contentione . . . et non invenietis in lingua mea iniquitatem*. Et ideo dicit *quare loquelam meam non cognoscitis?* Dicentes et interrogantes: quid est hoc quod dixit: *quo ego vado vos non potestis venire?* Et hoc ideo, inquam, non cognoscitis, quia non potestis audire sermonem meum; idest, ita durum cor habetis ad me, quod nec sermonem meum audire vultis.

It should be noted that all friendship is based on union, and so brothers love one another inasmuch as they take their origin from the same parents. Thus our Lord says: you say that you are the children of God; but if this were so, *you would indeed love me, for I proceeded and came forth from God*. Therefore, any one who does not love me is not a child of God. I say *I proceeded from God* from eternity as the Only Begotten, of the substance of the Father: *from the womb before the daystar I begot you* (Ps 109:4); *in the beginning was the Word* (John 1:1). And I *came forth* as *the Word* who *was made flesh*, sent by God through incarnation. *I came forth from the Father*, from eternity, as the Word, *and have come into the world* when I was made flesh in time (John 16:28).

1237. He rejects an error when he says, *I came not of myself*. And first, he rejects the error of Sabellius, who said that Christ did not have his origin from another, for he said that the Father and the Son were the same in person. In regard to this he says, *I came not of myself*, i.e., according to Hilary, I came, not existing of myself, but in a way as sent by another, that is, the Father. Thus he adds, *but he sent me*: God sent forth his Son, born of woman, born under the law (Gal 4:4).

Second, he rejects an error of the Jews who said that Christ was not sent by God, but was a false prophet, of whom we read: *I did not send the prophets, yet they ran* (Jer 23:21). And in regard to this he says, according to Origen, *I came not of myself, but he sent me*. Indeed, this is what Moses prayed for: *I beseech thee, Lord send whom thou wilt send* (Exod 4:13).

1238. He shows that they lack this sign when he says, *why do you not know my speech?* For as was stated above, to love Christ is the sign of being a child of God; but they did not love Christ; therefore it is obvious that they did not have this sign. That they do not love Christ is shown by the effect of love: for the effect of loving someone is that the lover joyfully hears the words of the beloved; thus we read: *let me hear your voice, for your voice is sweet* (Song 2:14). And again, *my companions are listening for your voice; let me hear it* (Song 8:13). Therefore, because they did not love Christ, it seemed tedious to them even to hear his voice: *this saying is hard, and who is able to accept it?* (John 6:61); *the very sight of him is a burden to us* (Wis 2:15).

It sometimes happens that a person is not glad to hear the words of another because he cannot weigh them and for that reason does not understand them, and so he contradicts them: *answer, I beseech you, without contention . . . and you shall not find iniquity on my tongue* (Job 6:29). Therefore he says, *why do you not know my speech?* For you asked ealier, what is this that he said, *where I go, you cannot come?* (John 8:21). I say that you do not understand because you cannot bear to hear my word, i.e., your heart is so hardened against me that you do not even want to hear me.

Lecture 6

8:44 Vos ex patre diabolo estis, et desideria patris vestri vultis facere. Ille homicida erat ab initio, et in veritate non stetit, quia non est veritas in eo: cum loquitur mendacium, ex propriis loquitur, quia mendax est, et pater eius. [n. 1239]

8:44 ὑμεῖς ἐκ τοῦ πατρὸς τοῦ διαβόλου ἐστὲ καὶ τὰς ἐπιθυμίας τοῦ πατρὸς ὑμῶν θέλετε ποιεῖν. ἐκεῖνος ἀνθρωποκτόνος ἦν ἀπ᾽ ἀρχῆς καὶ ἐν τῇ ἀληθείᾳ οὐκ ἔστηκεν, ὅτι οὐκ ἔστιν ἀλήθεια ἐν αὐτῷ. ὅταν λαλῇ τὸ ψεῦδος, ἐκ τῶν ἰδίων λαλεῖ, ὅτι ψεύστης ἐστὶν καὶ ὁ πατὴρ αὐτοῦ.

8:44 You are of your father the devil, and you will do the desires of your father. He was a murderer from the beginning, and he did not stand in the truth, because the truth is not in him. When he speaks a lie, he speaks of his own: for he is a liar and the father of lies. [n. 1239]

1239. Postquam Dominus Iudaeos ostendit originem aliquam spiritualem habere et exclusit ab eis originem praesumptam, hic astruit veram, ascribens eis paternitatem diaboli, et

     primo proponit intentum;

     secundo rationem eis assignat, ibi *et desideria patris vestri vultis facere*;

     tertio positam rationem manifestat, ibi *ille homicida erat ab initio*.

1240. Dicit ergo *vos facitis opera diaboli, ergo vos ex patre diabolo estis*, scilicet per imitationem; Ez. XVI, 3: *pater tuus Amorrhaeus, et mater tua Cethaea*.

Cavenda est hic haeresis Manichaeorum, qui dicunt esse quamdam naturam 'mali,' et gentem quamdam tenebrarum cum principibus suis, a qua corruptibilia omnia originem trahunt; et secundum hoc omnes homines secundum carnem ex diabolo processisse. Ponebant autem quasdam animas ad bonam creationem pertinere, et quasdam ad malam; unde dicebant hoc dictum a Domino *vos ex patre diabolo estis*, quia ab eo secundum carnem processistis, et animae vestrae sunt de mala creatione.

Sed, ut Origenes dicit, introducere duas naturas propter differentiam boni et mali, simile videtur ei qui diceret alteram esse oculi videntis substantiam, alteram caligantis vel se avertentis. Quemadmodum enim oculi sani et lippi non differunt substantia, sed quaedam contingit causa deficiens, scilicet quae facit eum caligare; ita eadem est substantia et natura rei, sive sit bona, seu habeat in se defectum, quod est peccatum voluntatis. Non ergo Iudaei ut mali, dicuntur filii diaboli natura, sed imitatione.

1241. Consequenter cum dicit *et desideria patris vestri vultis facere*, rationem assignatam exponit; quasi dicat: non estis filii diaboli tamquam ab eo creati, et in esse producti sed quia eum imitantes, *desideria patris vestri vultis facere*, quae quidem mala sunt: nam sicut ille invidit homini, et occidit, Sap. II, 24: *invidia diaboli mors intravit in orbem terrarum*, ita et vos mihi invidentes,

1239. After showing that the Jews had a certain spiritual origin, and after rejecting the origin they presumed they had, our Lord here gives their true origin, ascribing their fatherhood to the devil.

First, he makes his statement;

second, he gives its reason; at *and you will do the desires of your father*;

third, he explains this reason, at *he was a murderer from the beginning*.

1240. He says: *you are of your father the devil, and you will do the desires of your father*, that is, by imitating him: *your father was an Amorite, and your mother a Hittite* (Ezek 16:3).

Here one must guard against the heresy of the Manicheans who claim that there is a definite nature called 'evil,' and a certain race of darkness with its own princes, from which all corruptible things derive their origin. According to this opinion, all men, as to their flesh, have come from the devil. Further, they say that certain souls belong to that creation which is good, and others to that which is evil. Thus they said that our Lord said, *you are of your father the devil*, because they came from the devil according to the flesh, and their souls were part of that creation which was evil.

But as Origen says, to suppose that there are two natures because of the difference between good and evil seems to be like saying that the substance of an eye which sees is different from that of an eye that is clouded or crossed. For just as a healthy and bleary eye do not differ in substance, but the bleariness is from some deficient cause, so the substance and nature of a thing is the same whether it is good or has a defect in itself, which is a sin of the will. And so the Jews, as evil, are not called the children of the devil by nature, but by reason of their imitating him.

1241. Then when he says, *and you will do the desires of your father*, he gives the reason for this, for their being of the devil. It is like saying: you are not the children of the devil as though created and brought into existence by him, but because by imitating him *you will do the desires of your father*. And these desires are evil, for as he envied and killed man—*through the devil's envy death entered the world*

quaeritis me interficere hominem, qui veritatem locutus sum vobis.

1242. Consequenter cum dicit *ille homicida erat ab initio*, positam rationem manifestat, et

primo ponit diaboli quam imitantur conditionem;

secundo ostendit eos esse imitatores conditionis illius, ibi *ego autem si veritatem dico, non creditis mihi.*

Sciendum est circa primum, quod in diabolo duplex peccatum maxime pollet: scilicet peccatum superbiae ad Deum, et invidiae ad hominem, quem occidit. Sed ex peccato invidiae ad hominem quo infert nocumenta hominibus, cognoscitur a nobis peccatum superbiae et ideo

primo ponit peccatum Daemonis contra hominem;

secundo peccatum eius contra Deum, ibi *et in veritate non stetit.*

1243. Peccatum autem invidiae contra hominem est quod occidit eum; unde dicit: *ille*, scilicet diabolus, *homicida erat ab initio.*

Ubi sciendum est quod non ferro accinctus diabolus occidit hominem, sed mala persuasione; Sap. II, 24: *invidia diaboli mors introivit in orbem terrarum.* Et primo quidem introivit mors peccati, Ps. XXXIII, 22: *mors peccatorum pessima*, deinde vero mors corporalis, Rom. V, 12: *per unum hominem peccatum intravit, et per peccatum mors.* Et, ut dicit Augustinus, *noli putare te non esse homicidam, quando fratri tuo mala persuades.*

Attendendum est autem, secundum Origenem, quod ille homicida dicitur non propter aliquem singulariter tantum, sed pro toto genere, quod peremit in Adam, in quo cuncti moriuntur, ut dicitur I ad Cor. XV, 22. Unde antonomastice homicida dicitur; et hoc *ab initio*, ex quo scilicet fuit homo, qui occidi poterat, ex quo potuit fieri homicidium: non enim posset occidi homo, nisi prius homo fieret.

1244. Consequenter cum dicit *et in veritate non stetit*, ponit peccatum Daemonis contra Deum, quod consistit in hoc quod avertit se a veritate, quae Deus est, et

primo ostendit eum a veritate aversum;

secundo ostendit eum veritati contrarium, ibi *dum loquitur mendacium, ex propriis loquitur.*

Circa primum duo facit.

Primo ostendit eum a veritate aversum;

secundo manifestat quod dixit, ibi *quia veritas in eo non est.*

1245. Dicit ergo *et in veritate non stetit.*

Unde sciendum est, quod duplex est veritas: scilicet vocis et operis. Veritas quidem vocis est qua quis profert ore quod gerit corde, et est in rerum natura; Eph. IV, 25: *deponentes mendacium, loquimini veritatem unusquisque cum proximo suo*; Ps. XIV, 3: *qui loquitur veritatem cum proximo suo, qui non egit dolum in lingua sua.*

(Wis 2:24)—so you too envy me and *but now you seek to kill me, a man who has spoken the truth to you* (John 8:40).

1242. Then when he says, *he was a murderer from the beginning*, he explains the reason he gave.

First, he mentions the characteristic of the devil that they imitate;

second, he shows that they are truly imitators of that, at *but if I say the truth, you do not believe me* (John 8:45).

With respect to the first it should be noted that two sins stand out in the devil: the sin of pride towards God, and of envy towards man, whom he destroys. And from the sin of envy towards man, because of which he injures him, we can know his sin of pride. And so

first, he mentions the devil's sin against man;

second, his sin against God, *he did not stand in the truth.*

1243. His sin of envy against man lies in the fact that he kills him. So he says, *he*, that is, the devil, *was a murderer from the beginning.*

Here it should be noted that the devil kills man not with the sword, but by persuading him to do evil. *Through the devil's envy death entered the world* (Wis 2:24). First, the death of sin entered: *the death of the wicked is very evil* (Ps 33:22); then came bodily death: *sin came into the world through one man and death through sin* (Rom 5:12). As Augustine says: *do not think that you are not a murderer when you lead your brother into evil.*

However, it should be noted with Origen, that the devil is not called a murderer with respect to only some particular person, but with respect to the whole race, which he destroyed in Adam, in whom all die (1 Cor 15:22). Thus he is called a murderer because that is a chief characteristic, and he is so indeed *from the beginning*, that is, from the time that a man existed who could be killed, who could be murdered; for one cannot be murdered unless he first exists.

1244. Then when he says, *he did not stand in the truth*, he mentions the devil's sin against God, which consists in the fact that he turned away from the truth, which is God.

First, he shows that he is turned from the truth;

second, he shows that he is contrary to the truth, at *when he speaks a lie, he speaks of his own.*

As to the first he does two things:

first, he shows that the devil is turned from the truth;

second, he explains what he has said, because there is no truth in him, at *because the truth is not in him.*

1245. He says, *he did not stand in the truth.*

Here it should be noted that truth is of two kinds, namely, the truth of word and the truth of deed. The truth of word consists in a person saying what he feels in his heart and what is in reality: *therefore, putting away falsehood, let every one speak the truth with his neighbor* (Eph 4:25); *he who speaks truth from his heart, who does not slander with*

Veritas iustitiae, quando scilicet quis agit quod convenit sibi secundum ordinem suae naturae: de qua supra III, 21, dicit: *qui fecerit veritatem, veniet ad lucem, ut manifestentur opera eius, quia in Deo sunt facta*. De hac ergo veritate Dominus loquens dicit *et in veritate*, scilicet iustitiae, *non stetit*, quia deseruit ordinem suae naturae, qui erat ut Deo subiiceretur, et per eumdem beatitudinem suam et naturalis desiderii complementum consequeretur. Unde dum hoc per se consequi voluit, a veritate cecidit.

1246. Hoc autem quod dicit *in veritate non stetit*, potest dupliciter intelligi: vel quod numquam in veritate steterit; vel quod aliquando steterit, sed in ea non permansit.

Sed hoc quod numquam fuerit in veritate iustitiae, potest habere duplicem sensum. Unum quidem secundum Manichaeos, qui dicunt diabolum naturaliter malum esse: ex quo sequitur quod semper malus fuerit. Nam quod inest naturaliter, semper inest. Sed hoc est haereticum, quia in Ps. CXLV, 6, dicitur, quod *Deus fecit caelum et terram, mare et omnia quae in eis sunt*. Ergo omne ens est a Deo; omne autem quod est a Deo, inquantum est, bonum est.

Et ideo alii dixerunt, quod Daemon ex sui natura bonus est a Deo creatus, sed in primo instanti factus est malus per liberum arbitrium. Et differunt isti a Manichaeis: quia illi dicunt Daemones semper fuisse malos, et naturaliter; isti vero semper malos, sed per liberum arbitrium.

Sed posset alicui videri quod quia angelus non est malus per naturam, sed per peccatum propriae voluntatis, peccatum autem est actus quidam, potuit fieri ut angelus in principio actus fuerit bonus, sed in termino actus mali fuerit malus effectus. Manifestum est autem quod actus peccati in Daemone est creatione posterior, terminus autem creationis est ipsum esse angeli: terminus vero operationis peccati est quod sint mali. Et sic ex hac ratione volunt quod impossibile sit quod in primo instanti quo angelus esse coepit, fuerit malus.

Sed haec ratio non videtur sufficiens, habet enim locum in motibus temporalibus tantum, qui successive aguntur, non autem in motibus instantaneis. Nam in motibus successivis aliud est instans in quo incipit actio, et aliud in quo terminatur: sicut si motus localis sequitur ad alterationem, non potest in eodem instanti terminari motus localis et alteratio. Sed in mutationibus instantaneis, simul et in eodem instanti potest esse terminus primae et secundae mutationis; sicut in eodem instanti quo illuminatur luna a sole, illuminatur aer a luna. Manifestum est autem quod creatio est instantanea, et similiter motus liberi arbitrii in angelis, cum non indigerent collatione et discursu rationis; unde nihil prohibet simul

his tongue (Ps 15:3). The truth of deed, on the other hand, is the truth of righteousness, i.e., when a person does what befits him according to the order of his nature. Concerning this it says above: *but he who practices truth comes to the light, so that his works may be made manifest, because they are done in God* (John 3:21). Speaking of this truth our Lord says, *in the truth*, namely, the truth of righteousness, *he did not stand*, because he abandoned the order of his nature, which was that he be subject to God, and through him acquire his happiness and the fulfillment of his natural desire. And so, because he wanted to obtain this through himself, he fell from the truth.

1246. The statement, *he did not stand in the truth*, can be understood in two ways. Either he never had anything to do with the truth, or that he once did, but did not continue in it.

Now never to have anything to do with the truth of righteousness has two meanings. One is according to the Manicheans, who say that the devil is evil by nature. From this it follows that he was always evil, because whatever is present by nature is always present. But this is heretical, for we read: *God made heaven and earth, the sea, and all that is in them* (Ps 146:6). Therefore, every being is from God; but everything which is from God, insofar as it is, is good.

Consequently, others have said that the devil was created good in his nature by God, but became evil in the first instant by his own free choice. And this opinion differs from that of the Manicheans who say that the devils were always and by nature evil, whereas this opinion claims that they were always evil by free choice.

Someone might suppose that since an angel is not evil by nature but by a sin of his own will—and sin is an act—it is possible that at the beginning of the act the angel was good, and at the end of the evil act he became evil. For it is plain that the act of sin in the devil is subsequent to his creation, and that the terminus of creation is the existence of an angel; but the terminus of the act of sin is that he is evil. Consequently, according to this explanation, they conclude that it is impossible that an angel be evil in the first instant in which the angel came to exist.

But this explanation does not seem to be sufficient, because it is true only in motions that occur in time and that are accomplished in a successive manner, not in instantaneous motions. For in every successive motion the instant in which an act begins is not the one in which the action is terminated; thus, if a local motion follows upon an alteration, the local motion cannot be terminated in the same instant as the alteration. But in changes that are instantaneous, the terminus of a first and of a second change can occur together and in the same instant. Thus, in the same instant that the moon is illumined by the sun, the air is illumined by the moon. Now it is clear that creation is instantaneous, and likewise the act of free choice in the angels,

et in eodem instanti esse terminum creationis, in quo fuit bonus, et iterum terminum liberi arbitrii, in quo fuit malus.

Et hoc aliqui concedunt; sed dicunt hoc non fuisse, licet esse potuerit: et hoc propter auctoritatem Scripturae. Dicitur enim sub figura regis Babylonis de diabolo, Is. XIV, 12: *quomodo cecidisti, Lucifer, qui mane oriebaris?* Ez. XXVIII, 13, dicitur sub persona regis Tyri: *in deliciis Paradisi Dei fuisti.* Et ideo dicunt, quod non fuit in principio suae creationis malus, sed quandoque bonus fuit, et per liberum arbitrium cecidit.

Sed dicendum est, quod in primo instanti suae creationis non potuit esse malus. Cuius ratio est, quia nullus actus habet rationem peccati, nisi inquantum est praeter rationem naturae agentis voluntarii. In quolibet autem ordine actuum prius est actus naturalis; sicut in intelligendo, primo intelliguntur prima principia, et per ipsa intelliguntur alia, et, in volendo similiter, primo volumus ultimam perfectionem et ultimum finem, cuius appetitus naturaliter nobis inest, et propter ipsum appetimus alia. Quod autem secundum naturam fit, non est peccatum. Impossibile est ergo quod primus actus diaboli fuerit malus. Fuit ergo diabolus in aliquo instanti bonus, *sed in veritate non stetit*, idest, non permansit.

Ad illud autem quod dicitur I Io. III, 8: *diabolus ab initio peccavit*, dicendum, quod ab initio quidem peccavit; quia ex quo incepit peccare, numquam desiit.

1247. Consequenter cum dicit *quia non est veritas in eo*, manifestat quod dixit. Quae quidem manifestatio intelligitur dupliciter.

Uno quidem modo, secundum Origenem, ut sit manifestatio communis per specialem, sicut si vellem manifestare quod Socrates est animal per hoc quod est homo. Quasi dicat *in veritate non stetit*, sed cecidit; et hoc *quia non est veritas in eo*. Est autem duplex gradus non stantium in veritate. Aliqui enim in veritate non stant, quia non firmatur in ea, sed dubitant Ps. LXXII, 2: *mei autem pene moti sunt pedes, pene effusi gressus mei.* Aliqui autem quia totaliter a veritate resiliunt. Et sic diabolus in veritate non stetit, sed ab ea recessit per aversionem.

Sed numquid nulla veritas est in eo? Et quidem si nulla veritas sit, neque semetipsum intelliget, neque aliquid, cum intellectus non sit nisi verorum: quod est inconveniens.

Dicendum est ergo, in Daemonibus esse aliquam veritatem, sicut aliquod verum. Nullum enim malum totaliter corrumpit bonum, cum ad minus, subiectum in

since they do not go through the weighings and discoursings of reason. Thus, in the case of an angel there is nothing to prevent the same instant from being the terminus of creation, in which he was good, and the terminus of a free decision in which he was evil.

Some admit this, although they do not say that it so happened, but that it could have so happened. And they base themselves on the authority of Scripture, for under the figure of the king of Babylon it is said of the devil: *how have you fallen from heaven, O Lucifer, who did rise in the morning?* (Isa 14:12); and under the person of the king of Tyre it says: *you were in the pleasures of the paradise of God* (Ezek 28:13). Accordingly, they say that he was not evil at the first instant of his creation, but that he was once good, and fell through his free choice.

But it must be said that he could not be evil at the first instant of his creation. The reason for this is that no act is sinful except insofar as it is outside the nature of the voluntary agent. But in order of acts, the natural act is first: thus in understanding, first principles are understood first, and through them other things are understood; and in willing, we likewise first will the ultimate perfection and ultimate end, the desire for which is naturally in us, and on account of this we seek other things. Now that which is done according to nature is not sin. Therefore, it is impossible that the first act of the devil was evil; consequently, at some instant the devil was good. But *he did not stand in the truth*, i.e., he did not remain in it.

Concerning the statement, *the devil has sinned from the beginning* (1 John 3:8), one may say that he did indeed sin from the beginning in the sense that once he began to sin he never stopped.

1247. Then when he says, *because the truth is not in him*, he explains what he has said. And this explanation can be understood in two ways.

In one way, according to Origen, so that it is an explanation of the general by the particular, as when I explain that Socrates is an animal by the fact that he is a man. It is then like saying: *he did not stand in the truth*, but fell from it, and this *because the truth is not in him*. Now there are two classes of those that do not stand in the truth: some do not stand in the truth because they are not convinced, but waiver: *my feet had almost stumbled, my steps had well nigh slipped* (Ps 73:2); others, on the other hand, because they have entirely recoiled from the truth. And this was the way the devil did not stand in the truth, but turned away from it in aversion.

But is there no truth at all in him? For if there is no truth in him, we would not understand himself or anything else, since understanding is concerned only with things that are true.

I answer that there is some truth in the evil spirits, just as there is something true. For no evil utterly destroys a good thing, since at least the subject in which evil is found

quo malum est, sit bonum. Ideo Dyonisius dicit, quod in Daemonibus manent integra naturalia bona. Sic igitur aliqua veritas est in eis, sed non completiva, a qua aversi sunt, scilicet a Deo, qui est veritas et sapientia completiva.

1248. Secundo vero modo manifestatio ista est per signum, ut Augustinus dicit. Quia videtur quod potius debuisset contrarium dici. Ideo scilicet *veritas non est in eo*, quia *in veritate non stetit*. Sed sicut causa aliquando manifestatur per effectum, ita Dominus voluit ostendere quod *in veritate non stetit* per hoc quod *veritas non est in eo*: esset enim in eo, si in veritate stetisset. Similis modus loquendi habetur in Ps. XVI, 6: *ego clamavi quoniam exaudisti*; quasi, ex hoc apparet quod clamavit, quia fuit exauditus.

1249. Consequenter cum dicit *cum loquitur mendacium, ex propriis loquitur*, ostendit quod diabolus est contrarius veritati, et

primo ponit intentum;

secundo manifestat propositum, ibi *quia mendax est, et pater eius*.

1250. Veritati autem contrarium est falsum et mendacium; diabolus autem est veritati contrarius, quia *loquitur mendacium*: et ideo dicit dum loquitur, *mendacium loquitur*.

Ubi sciendum est, quod quicumque praeter Deum loquitur ex propriis, mendacium loquitur quamvis non quicumque mendacium loquitur, ex propriis loquatur. Solus autem Deus loquendo ex propriis, loquitur veritatem. Veritas enim est illuminatio intellectus; Deus autem est ipsum lumen, et ab ipso omnes illuminantur, supra I, 9: *erat lux vera, quae illuminat omnem hominem venientem in hunc mundum*: unde et est ipsa veritas, et alii non loquuntur veritatem nisi inquantum ab ipso illuminantur. Unde, sicut Ambrosius dicit, *omne verum a quocumque dicatur, a Spiritu Sancto est*. Sic ergo diabolus cum loquitur ex propriis, loquitur mendacium; homo etiam, cum ex propriis loquitur, mendacium loquitur; sed cum a Deo loquitur, tunc loquitur veritatem; Rom. III, 4: *est autem Deus verax, omnis autem homo mendax*, quantum est in se. Sed non omnis homo qui loquitur mendacium, loquitur ex propriis, quia quandoque hoc ab alio accipit: non quidem a Deo, qui est verax, sed ab eo qui in veritate non stetit et primo mendacium adinvenit. Et ideo ipse singulariter cum loquitur mendacium, ex propriis loquitur; III Reg. ult., 22: *egrediar, et ero spiritus mendax in ore omnium prophetarum eius*; Is. XIX, 14: *Dominus immiscuit*, idest miscere permisit *in medio eius spiritum erroris*.

1251. Propositum autem manifestat cum dicit *quia mendax est, et pater eius*. Quod quidem Manichaei male intelligentes, ponebant Daemonum generationes, putantes diabolum patrem habere. Unde dicebant, quod

is good. Thus Dionysius says that the natural goods remain intact in evil spirits. Thus there is some truth in them, but not the fulfilling truth from which they have turned, namely, God, who is fulfilling truth and wisdom.

1248. In a second way, this explanation is understood as a sign, as Augustine says. For it seems that he should rather have said the converse, namely, that there is not truth in him, because *he did not stand in the truth*. But just as a cause is sometimes shown by its effect, so our Lord wished to show that *the truth is not in him* because *he did not stand in the truth*; for truth would have been in him had he stood in the truth. A similar pattern of speech is found in *I cried because you heard* (Ps 16:6); as if to say that it is evident that I cried because you heard me.

1249. Then he shows that the devil is contrary to the truth, when he lies, *he speaks of his own*.

First, he makes this point;

second, he explains it, at *for he is a liar and the father of lies*.

1250. The contrary of truth is falsity and a lie. The devil is contrary to the truth because *he speaks a lie*. Thus he says that when he speaks, *he speaks a lie*.

Here we should note that, God excepted, whoever speaks on his own speaks a lie; although not everyone who speaks a lie speaks on his own. God alone, when speaking on his own, speaks the truth, for truth is an enlightenment of the intellect, and God is light itself and all are enlightened by him: *he was the true light, which enlightens every man coming into this world* (John 1:9). Thus he is truth itself, and no one speaks the truth except insofar as he is enlightened by him. So Ambrose says: *every truth, by whomsoever spoken, is from the Holy Spirit*. Thus the devil, when he speaks on his own, speaks a lie; man, too, when he speaks on his own, speaks a lie; but when he speaks from God, he speaks the truth: *let God be true though every man be false* (Rom 3:4). But not every man who tells a lie speaks on his own, for sometimes he gets this from someone else, not indeed from God, who is truthful, but from him who did not stand in the truth and who first invented lying. So in a unique way when the devil tells a lie, he is speaking on his own: *I will go forth and will be a lying spirit in the mouth of all prophets* (1 Kgs 22:22); *the Lord mingled* (that is, allowed to mingle) *a spirit of error in their midst* (Isa 19:14).

1251. He explains this statement when he says, *for he is a liar and the father of lies*. The Manicheans did not understand this, and placed some kind of procreation in the evil spirits, with the devil as their father. They said that the devil

diabolus *mendax est, et pater eius*, idest diabolus. Quod quidem non sic est intelligendum. Nam Dominus dixit, quod diabolus est mendax, et pater eius, idest mendacii: non enim omnis qui mentitur, pater est sui mendacii. Nam, ut Augustinus dicit, *si ab alio mendacium accepisti, et dixisti; tu quidem mentitus es, sed pater mendacii non es*. diabolus vero, quia aliunde non accepit mendacium, quo tamquam veneno hominem occideret, pater mendacii est, sicut Deus pater est veritatis. diabolus enim primo mendacium invenit, cum scilicet mulieri mentitus est: *nequaquam moriemini*, Gen. III, 4. Quod qualiter verum fuerit, rei eventus postmodum comprobavit.

1252. Sciendum est autem, quod haec verba ab illo loco **vos ex patre diabolo estis**, in libro *de quaestionibus novi et Veteris Testamenti* exponuntur de Cain, hoc modo: secundum quod ille dicitur diabolus qui facit opera diaboli, et vos eum imitamini. Cain **homicida erat ab initio**, ex quo scilicet Abel fratrem suum occidit, **et in veritate non stetit, quia veritas non est in eo**. Et hoc apparet, quia cum Dominus quaereret ab eo (Gen. IV, 9): *ubi est Abel frater tuus?* Respondit dicens: *nescio, Domine; numquid custos fratris mei sum ego?* Unde ipse *mendax est et pater eius*, scilicet diabolus, qui est pater eius impressione. Prima tamen expositio melior est.

is a liar and the father of lies. It should not be understood this way, as our Lord said that the devil is a liar and its father, the father of lies. Not everyone who lies is the father of his lie. As Augustine says, *if you have learned a lie from someone else and you repeat it, you have indeed lied, but you are not the father of that lie*. But the devil, because he did not learn from someone else the lie by which he destroyed humankind as with poison, is the father of the lie, just as God is the father of truth. The devil was the first to invent the lie, namely, when he lied to the woman: *you will not die* (Gen 3:4). Just how true this statement was, was proved by the outcome.

1252. Here we should note that the book *Questions of the New and Old Testament* takes the words **you are of your father the devil**, and applies them to Cain, in the sense that one is called a devil who performs the works of the devil, and you are imitating him; hence **you are of your father the devil**, that is, of Cain, who did the work of the devil, and you are imitating him. Cain **was a murderer from the beginning**, because he killed his brother Abel. And he **did not stand in the truth, because the truth is not in him**. This is obvious because when the Lord asked him, *where is Abel your brother?* he said, *I do not know; am I my brother's keeper?* (Gen 4:9). Thus he is a liar. But the first explanation is better.

Lecture 7

8:45 Ego autem si veritatem dico, non creditis mihi. [n. 1254]

8:46 Quis ex vobis arguet me de peccato? Si veritatem dico, quare non creditis mihi? [n. 1255]

8:47 Qui ex Deo est, verba Dei audit: propterea vos non auditis, quia ex Deo non estis. [n. 1258]

8:48 Responderunt ergo Iudaei, et dixerunt: nonne bene dicimus nos, quia Samaritanus es tu, et daemonium habes? [n. 1262]

8:49 Respondit Iesus: ego daemonium non habeo; sed honorifico Patrem meum, et vos inhonorastis me. [n. 1263]

8:50 Ego autem non quaero gloriam meam: est qui quaerat, et iudicet. [n. 1268]

8:45 ἐγὼ δὲ ὅτι τὴν ἀλήθειαν λέγω, οὐ πιστεύετέ μοι.

8:46 τίς ἐξ ὑμῶν ἐλέγχει με περὶ ἁμαρτίας; εἰ ἀλήθειαν λέγω, διὰ τί ὑμεῖς οὐ πιστεύετέ μοι;

8:47 ὁ ὢν ἐκ τοῦ θεοῦ τὰ ῥήματα τοῦ θεοῦ ἀκούει· διὰ τοῦτο ὑμεῖς οὐκ ἀκούετε, ὅτι ἐκ τοῦ θεοῦ οὐκ ἐστέ.

8:48 Ἀπεκρίθησαν οἱ Ἰουδαῖοι καὶ εἶπαν αὐτῷ· οὐ καλῶς λέγομεν ἡμεῖς ὅτι Σαμαρίτης εἶ σὺ καὶ δαιμόνιον ἔχεις;

8:49 ἀπεκρίθη Ἰησοῦς· ἐγὼ δαιμόνιον οὐκ ἔχω, ἀλλὰ τιμῶ τὸν πατέρα μου, καὶ ὑμεῖς ἀτιμάζετέ με.

8:50 ἐγὼ δὲ οὐ ζητῶ τὴν δόξαν μου· ἔστιν ὁ ζητῶν καὶ κρίνων.

8:45 But if I say the truth, you do not believe me. [n. 1254]

8:46 Who among you will convict me of sin? If I say the truth to you, why do you not believe me? [n. 1255]

8:47 He who is of God hears the words of God. Therefore, you do not hear them, because you are not of God. [n. 1258]

8:48 The Jews therefore answered and said to him: are we not right in saying that you are a Samaritan and have a demon? [n. 1262]

8:49 Jesus answered: I do not have a demon, but I honor my Father, and you have dishonored me. [n. 1263]

8:50 I do not seek my own glory, but there is one who seeks and judges. [n. 1268]

1253. Postquam posuit diabolicam conditionem, hic consequenter ostendit Iudaeos esse diabolicae conditionis imitatores. Duas autem malitiae conditiones Dominus diabolo ascripsit, homicidium scilicet et mendacium. Sed de homicidio quidem, in quo isti diabolum imitabantur, reprehendit eos; supra eodem: *nunc autem quaeritis me interficere, hominem, qui veritatem vobis locutus sum, quam audivi a Deo*. Et ideo, hoc praetermisso, redarguit eos de aversione eorum a veritate, et

    primo ostendit eos esse aversos a veritate;

    secundo causam quam allegare poterant, excludit, ibi *quis ex vobis arguet me de peccato?*

    Tertio veram causam aversionis concludit, ibi *si veritatem dico, quare non creditis mihi?*

1254. Dicit ergo primo: dictum est, quod diabolus *mendax est, et pater eius*, quem quidem vos imitamini, quia veritati non vultis adhaerere. Unde dicit *ego autem si veritatem dico vobis, non creditis mihi*. Lc. XXII, 67: *si autem dixero, non credetis mihi*; supra III, 12: *quomodo si dixero vobis caelestia, credetis?* Unde et Is. LIII, 1, conqueritur dicens: *Domine, quis credidit auditui nostro?*

1255. Causa autem suae infidelitatis, quam poterant Iudaei allegare est peccatum in Christo; nam peccatori etiam in veritate non de facili creditur. Unde Ps. XLIX, 16: *peccatori autem dixit Deus: quare tu enarras*

1253. After mentioning some characteristics of the devil, he then shows that the Jews are imitating these. Our Lord ascribed two kinds of evil to the devil, murder and lying. He reproved them before for their imitation of one of these, namely, murder: *but now you seek to kill me, a man who has spoken the truth to you, which I heard from God* (John 8:40). Then passing from this, he reproves them for turning away from the truth:

    first, he shows that they are turned away from the truth;

    second, he rejects a certain reason they might give for this, at *who among you will convict me of sin?*

    Third, he concludes to the true reason for their being turned away from the truth, at *if I say the truth to you, why do you not believe me?*

1254. He says first: it was said that the devil *is a liar and the father of lies* (John 8:44), and you are imitating him because you do not wish to adhere to the truth. Thus he says, *if I say the truth to you, why do you not believe me? If I tell you, you will not believe* (Luke 22:67); *if I have spoken to you of earthly things, and you do not believe, how will you believe if I speak to you of heavenly things?* (John 3:12). And Isaiah complains: *who has believed what we have heard?* (Isa 53:1).

1255. The reason which the Jews might allege for their unbelief is that Christ is a sinner, for it is not easy to believe a sinner even when he is telling the truth. Thus we read: *but to the wicked God says: what right have you to recite my*

iustitias meas? Poterant ergo dicere: non credimus, quia peccator es.

Et ideo hanc causam excludit, dicens **quis ex vobis arguit me de peccato?** Quasi dicat: non habetis iustam causam quare mihi veritatem dicenti non creditis, cum in me nullum peccatum inveniri possit; I Petr. II, 22: *qui peccatum non fecit, nec inventus est dolus in ore eius.*

Secundum Gregorium, pensanda est Dei mansuetudo, qui non dedignatur ex ratione ostendere se peccatorem non esse, qui ex virtute divinitatis poterat peccatores iustificare; Iob XXXI, 13: *si contempsi subire iudicium meum cum servo meo et ancilla mea, cum disceptarent adversum me.*

Admiranda est etiam Christi singularis puritatis excellentia, quia, ut Chrysostomus dicit, hoc nullus hominum fiducialiter potuit dicere **quis ex vobis arguet me de peccato?** Nisi solus Deus noster, qui peccatum non fecit; Prov. XX, 9: *quis potest dicere: mundum est cor meum, purus sum a peccato?* Quasi dicat, nullus nisi solus Deus. Et in Ps. XIII, v. 3: *omnes declinaverunt, simul inutiles facti sunt: non est qui faciat bonum, non est usque ad unum,* idest Christum.

1256. Veram autem causam aversionis concludit, dicens **si veritatem dico, quare non creditis mihi?** Et

primo ponit eam;

secundo Iudaeorum contradictionem excludit, ibi **responderunt ergo Iudaei** etc.

Circa primum tria facit.

Primo ponit quaestionem;

secundo assumit rationabilem propositionem;

tertio infert intentam conclusionem.

1257. Dicit ergo primo: ex quo ergo non potestis dicere, quod ideo non creditis mihi quia peccator sum, nunc restat quaerere quare **si veritatem dico, non creditis mihi,** ex quo non sum peccator; quasi dicat: si me, quem exosum habetis, non potestis arguere de peccato, manifestum est quoniam propter veritatem me odio habetis, quoniam dico me Filium Dei; Prov. XVIII, 2: *non recipit stultus verba prudentiae, nisi ea dixerit quae versantur in corde eius.*

1258. Rationabilem autem propositionem et veram assumit, dicens **qui ex Deo est, verba Dei audit.** Ut enim dicitur Eccli. c. XIII, 19, *omne animal diligit sibi simile,* quicumque ergo est ex Deo, inquantum huiusmodi, similitudinem habet horum quae sunt Dei, et eis inhaeret. Unde **qui ex Deo est, verba Dei** libenter **audit;** infra XVIII, 37: *omnis qui est ex veritate, audit meam vocem.* Praecipue autem verbum Dei libenter audiri debet ab his qui ex Deo sunt, cum ipsum sit semen per quod in filios Dei generamur; infra X, 35: **illos dixit deos ad quos sermo Dei factus est.**

statutes? (Ps 50:16). So they might have said: we do not believe you since you are a sinner.

Accordingly, he excludes this reason when he says, **who among you will convict me of sin?** As if to say: you have no good reason for not believing me when I speak the truth, since you can find no sin in me: *he committed not sin; no guile was found on his lips* (1 Pet 2:22).

According to Gregory, we are invited to consider the mildness of God, who did not consider it beneath himself to show by rational grounds that he who can justify sinners by the power of his divinity is not a sinner: *if I have rejected the cause of my manservant or my maidservant, when they brought a complaint against me; what then shall I do when God rises up?* (Job 31:13).

We should also honor the unique greatness of Christ's purity, for as Chrysostom says, no mere man could have confidently said, **who among you will convict me of sin?** Only God, who had no sin, could say this: *who can say, I have made my heart clean; I am pure from my sin?* (Prov 20:9)—this is like saying: no one but God alone. *They have all gone astray, they are all alike corrupt; there is none that does good, no, not one,* except Christ (Ps 14:3).

1256. Next, at **if I say the truth to you, why do you not believe me?** he concludes to the real reason they have turned away from the truth.

First, he mentions the reason;

second, he rejects their rejoinder, at **the Jews therefore answered: are we not right?**

As to the first he does three things:

first, he asks a question;

second, he begins with a reasonable starting point;

third, he draws from his conclusion.

1257. First, he says: since you cannot say that you do not believe me because I am a sinner, one can ask why **if I say the truth to you, why you do not believe me,** since I am not a sinner? This is like saying: if you cannot convict me, whom you hate, of sin, it is obvious that you hate me because of the truth, that is, because I say that I am the Son of God: *a fool takes no pleasure in understanding, but only in expressing his opinion* (Prov 18:2).

1258. He then begins with a reasonable and true starting point, saying, **he who is of God hears the words of God.** For we read: *every creature loves its like* (Sir 13:15). Therefore, whoever is of God, to that extent possesses a likeness to the things of God and clings to them. Thus, **he who is of God** gladly **hears the words of God;** as it says below: **every one who is of the truth hears my voice** (John 18:37). The word of God ought to be heard gladly by those, above all, who are of God, since it is the seed by which we are made the children of God: **he called them gods to whom the word of God was spoken** (John 10:35).

1259. Et ideo ex hoc intentam conclusionem infert, dicens *propterea vos non auditis, quia ex Deo non estis*; quasi dicat: non ergo peccatum meum est causa incredulitatis vestrae, sed malitia vestra; Eccli. VI, v. 21: *quam aspera est nimium indoctis hominibus sapientia*. Et, ut dicit Augustinus, ex Deo quidem sunt secundum naturam, sed ex Deo non sunt vitio et prava affectione: nam eis hoc verbum dictum est qui non solum peccato vitiosi erant, hoc enim commune omnibus erat, sed etiam praecogniti quod non fuerant credituri ea fide qua possent a peccatorum obligatione liberari.

1260. Notandum est autem, quod triplex est gradus male affectorum, ut dicit Gregorius. Nam quidam sunt qui praecepta Dei nec aure corporis, idest exteriori auditu, dignantur audire: de quibus dicitur in Ps. LVII, 5: *sicut aspidis surdae, obturantis aures suas*. Quidam vero sunt qui haec quidem corporis aure percipiunt, sed nullo ea mentis desiderio complectuntur, non habentes voluntatem implendi: Ez. XXXIII, 31: *audiunt sermones, et non faciunt eos*. Quidam autem sunt qui libenter verba Dei suscipiunt, ita ut etiam in fletibus compungantur; sed post lacrymarum tempus, vel tribulationibus oppressi, aut allecti deliciis, ad iniquitatem redeunt; cuius exemplum habetur Matth. XIII, 18 ss., et Lc. VIII, 11 ss., de verbo a sollicitudinibus suffocato. Ez. III, 7: *domus Israel nolunt audire te, quia nolunt audire me*. Est ergo signum quod homo sit a Deo, si libenter audit verba Dei, sed qui recusant audire affectu vel effectu, ex Deo non sunt.

1261. Hic excludit Iudaicam contradictionem, et

primo ponit Evangelista Iudaeorum contradictionem;

secundo Domini exclusionem, ibi *respondit Iesus: ego daemonium non habeo*.

1262. Duo autem imponunt Iudaei Christo in eorum contradictione. Primo quidem quod sit Samaritanus, cum dicunt *nonne bene dicimus nos, quia Samaritanus es?* Secundo vero quod daemonium habeat; unde subdunt *et daemonium habes*.

In hoc autem quod dicunt *nonne bene dicimus nos?* Datur intelligi quod hoc verbum frequenter domino improperabant. Et quidem de secundo quod sit daemoniacus, legimus Matth. IX, 34; et XII, 24, cum dicebant: *in Beelzebub principe Daemoniorum eiicit Daemones*. Sed quod dixerunt eum Samaritanum, nusquam nisi hic in Evangelio invenitur, licet forte hoc multoties dixerunt: multa enim dicta et facta sunt erga Iesum et a Iesu quae non sunt scripta in Evangeliis, ut dicitur infra XX, 25.

Duplex autem causa assignari potest quare Iudaei hoc Christo dicebant. Una quidem, quia Samaritani gens odiosa erat pro populo Israelitico, eo quod decem tribus in captivitatem ductis, terram eorum possidebant; supra IV, 9: *non enim coutuntur Iudaei Samaritanis*.

1259. He draws his conclusion from this saying, *therefore, you do not hear them, because you are not of God*. This is like saying: the reason for your unbelief is not my sin, but your own wickedness; as it is said: *wisdom seems very harsh to the uninstructed* (Sir 6:21). Augustine says about them that as to their nature, they are of God, indeed; but by reason of their vice and evil affection they are not of God. For this statement was made to those who were not just sinful, for this was common to all; it was made to those of whom it was foreknown that they would not believe with that faith by which they could have been set free from the chains of their sins.

1260. It should be noted, as Gregory says, that there are three degrees of being badly disposed in one's affections. Some refuse to physically hear God's precepts. Of these we read: *like the deaf adder that stops its ear* (Ps 58:4). Others hear them physically, but they do not embrace them with the desire of their heart, since they do not have he will to obey them: *they hear what you say, but they will not do it* (Ezek 33:32). Finally, there are those who joyfully receive the words of God and even weep with tears of sorrow; but after the time of crying is past and they are oppressed with troubles or allured by pleasures, they return to their sins. An example of this is given, where we read of the word being choked by cares and anxieties (Matt 13:18 ff and Luke 8:11 ff). *But the house of Israel will not listen to you; for they are not willing to listen to me* (Ezek 3:7). Consequently, a sign that a person is of God is that he is glad to hear the words of God, while those who refuse to hear, either in affection or physically, are not of God.

1261. Next he rejects the rejoinder made by the Jews. First, the Evangelist mentions this rejoinder; and

second, our Lord's rejection of it, at *Jesus answered: I do not have a demon*.

1262. In their response the Jews charge Christ with two things: first, that he is a Samaritan, when they say, *are we not right in saying that you are a Samaritan?* Second, that he has a demon, when they add, *and have a demon?*

In saying, *are we not right?* we can infer that they often reproached Christ this way. In fact, concerning the second, that he has a demon, *it is only by Beelzebul, the prince of demons, that he casts out demons* (Matt 12:24). But this is the only place where it is recorded that they called him a Samaritan, although they probably said it often: for many of the things that were said and done about Christ and by Christ were not written in the Gospels (John 21:25).

Two reasons can be given why the Jews said this about Christ. First, because the Samaritans were hateful to the people of Israel, for when the ten tribes were led into captivity, they took their land: *the Jews do not communicate with the Samaritans* (John 4:9). Thus, because Christ

Quia ergo Christus Iudaeos arguens, credebatur a Iudaeis quod hoc ex odio faceret, ideo eum Samaritanum et quasi adversarium reputabant etc. Alia ratio, quia Samaritani partim quidem servabant ritus Iudaicos, partim vero non. Videntes ergo Iudaei Christum in aliquo legem servantem, et in aliquo dissolventem, utpote Sabbatum, vocabant eum Samaritanum.

Similiter autem duplici de causa dicebant eum Daemonium habere. Una quidem, quia miracula quae faciebat, et cogitationes eorum quas revelabat, non attribuebant virtuti divinae in Christo; sed arte Daemonum ipsum ea facere suspicabantur. Unde dicebant: *in Beelzebub principe Daemoniorum eiicit Daemones.* Alia vero ratio est propter eius sermones transcendentes capacitatem humanam, dicens, Deum Patrem suum esse, et descendisse de caelo etc. Consuetudo autem rudium est, quod cum talia audiunt, diabolica reputant: et sic isti credebant quod Christus quasi Daemonio plenus loqueretur; infra X, 20: *alii dicebant: daemonium habet, et insanit; quid eum auditis?* Dicunt autem haec verba, ut arguant de peccato, contra illud quod dixerat: *quis ex vobis arguet me de peccato?*

1263. Consequenter cum dicit *respondit Iesus: ego daemonium non habeo,* repellit Dominus Iudaeorum contradictionem. Duo autem imposuerant Christo: scilicet quod Samaritanus esset, et quod Daemonium haberet. Et de primo quidem Dominus non se excusat; et hoc duplici de causa. Una quidem, secundum Origenem, quia Iudaei semper volebant se a gentilibus separare. Iam autem venerat tempus quo removenda erat distinctio gentilium et Iudaeorum, et omnes ad viam salutis revocandi: et ideo Dominus, ut ostendat se venisse pro salute omnium ut, magis quam Paulus, omnia factus, omnes nanciscatur, I Cor. IX, ideo non negavit se esse Samaritanum. Alia ratio est, quia **Samaritanus** interpretatur *custos:* et quia ipse praecipue custos noster est, secundum illud Ps. CXX, 4: *ecce non dormitabit neque dormiet qui custodit Israel:* ideo se Samaritanum esse non negavit.

Negat autem se daemonium habere, dicens *ego daemonium non habeo,* et

primo quidem repellit illatam iniuriam;

secundo arguit iniuriantium pertinaciam, ibi *et vos inhonorastis me.*

Circa primum duo facit.

Primo repellit illatam iniuriam;

secundo manifestat hoc per oppositum, ibi *sed honorifico Patrem meum.*

1264. Notandum est autem circa primum, quod Dominus Iudaeos corrigendo, frequenter eis dure locutus est: *vae vobis, Scribae et Pharisaei hypocritae:* et multa quae leguntur in Evangeliis. Sed non invenitur, quod

reproved the Jews, they believed that he did it out of hatred, so that they regarded him as a Samaritan, an adversary, as it were. Another reason was that the Samaritans observed the Jewish rites in some things and not in others. Therefore, the Jews, seeing that Christ observed the law in some matters and broke it in others, for example, the law of the Sabbath, called him a Samaritan.

Again, there are two reasons why they said he had a demon. First, because they did not attribute the miracles he worked, and their thoughts that he revealed, to a divine power in Christ; rather, they suspected that he did these things by some demonic art. Thus they said: *it is only by Beelzebul, the prince of demons, that he casts out demons* (Matt 12:24). The other reason was based on the fact that his words exceeded human understanding, such as his statements that God was his Father, and that he had come down from heaven. And when uneducated people hear such things they usually regard them as diabolical. Accordingly, they believed that Christ spoke as one possessed by a demon: *many of them said: he has a devil and is mad: why do you hear him?* (John 10:20) Furthermore, they said these things in an attempt to accuse him of sin, to dispute what he had said: *who among you will convict me of sin?*

1263. Then when he says, *Jesus answered: I do not have a demon,* our Lord rejects the response of the Jews. Now they had taxed Christ with two things, that he was a Samaritan and that he had a demon. Concerning the first, our Lord makes no apology, and this for two reasons. First, according to Origen, because the Jews always wanted to keep themselves apart from the gentiles. But the time had now come when the distinction between Jews and gentiles was to be removed, and everyone was to be called to the way of salvation. Accordingly, our Lord, in order to show that he had come for the salvation of all, made himself all things to all men, more so than Paul, so that he might win all (1 Cor 9:22); and so he did not deny that he was a Samaritan. The other reason was that **Samaritan** means *keeper,* and because he especially is our keeper, as we read, *he who keeps Israel will neither slumber nor sleep* (Ps 121:4), so he did not deny that he was a Samaritan.

But he did deny that he had a demon, saying, *I do not have a demon.*

First, he rejects the insult;

second, he reproves the insulters for the obstinacy, at *and you have dishonored me.*

As to the first he does two things:

first, he rejects the insult;

second, he shows that the opposite is true, *but I honor my Father.*

1264. It should be noted with respect to the first that when correcting the Jews our Lord often spoke harshly to them: *woe to you, Scribes and Pharisees* (Matt 23:14), and many other instances are recorded in the Gospels. But there

Dominus Iudaeis sibi dura verba vel facta inferentibus, iniuriose vel dure locutus fuerit; sed, ut dicit Gregorius, iniuriam suscipiens Deus, non contumeliosa verba respondet, sed simpliciter dicit *ego daemonium non habeo*. Ex qua re quid nobis innuitur, nisi ut eo tempore quo a proximis ex falsitate contumelias accipimus, etiam eorum verba mala taceamus, ne ministerium iustae correctionis in arma vertatur furoris? Et quod quae ad Deum pertinent, vindicare debemus; quae vero ad nos, despicere.

Hoc autem verbum, scilicet *ego daemonium non habeo*, solus Christus dicere potest, ut Origenes dicit: nam ille nihil quod Daemonis est, leve videlicet, aut grave, in se habet; unde infra XIV, 30: *venit princeps huius mundi, et in me non habet quidquam*; II Cor. VI, 15: *quae conventio Christi ad Belial?*

1265. Manifestat autem hoc quod dixit, per oppositum dicens *sed honorifico Patrem meum.* diabolus enim honori Dei resistit: qui ergo quaerit Dei honorem, alienus est a diabolo. Christus ergo qui honorificat Patrem suum, scilicet Deum, Daemonium non habet. Est autem proprium Christo et singulare quod honorificet Patrem suum, ut dicitur Mal. I, 6: *Filius honorificat Patrem.* Christus autem singulariter est Dei Filius .

1266. Consequenter cum dicit *et vos inhonorastis me*, arguit iniuriantium pertinaciam, et

primo arguit iniuriantes;

secundo excludit causam inopinatam arguitionis;

tertio praedicit eis debitam damnationem.

1267. Dicit ergo primo: *ego honorifico Patrem meum, et vos inhonorastis me*; quasi dicat: ego facio quod debeo; vos facitis quod non debetis; immo in hoc quod inhonorastis me, inhonoratis Patrem meum; supra V, 23: *qui non honorificat Filium, non honorificat Patrem, qui misit illum.*

1268. Sed quia possent dicere: nimis durus es, nimis de gloria tua curas, sic nos arguens; ideo hoc excludens, subdit loquens inquantum est homo, *ego gloriam meam non quaero.* Solus enim Deus est qui potest gloriam suam absque culpa quaerere; alii autem non nisi in Deo; II Cor. X, 17: *qui gloriatur, in Domino glorietur*; infra (hoc cap.): *si ego glorifico meipsum, gloria mea nihil est.*

Sed numquid Christus inquantum homo non habet gloriam? Immo magnam per omnem modum: quia licet ipse eam non quaerat, *est tamen qui quaerat*, scilicet Pater. Nam dicitur in Ps. VIII, 7: *gloria et honore coronasti eum*, scilicet Christum hominem. Et alibi, XX, 6: *gloriam et magnum decorem imposuisti super eum.*

is no record that our Lord spoke harsh or injurious words in answer to their harsh words or deeds against himself. Rather, as Gregory said, God accepted their insults, and did not answer with insulting words, but simply said, *I do not have a demon*. And what does this suggests to us if not that when we are falsely attacked by our neighbor with railing words, we should keep silence, even about his abusive words, so as not to pervert our ministry of correcting in a just manner into a weapon of our anger. However, while we should not value our own goods, we should vindicate the things that are of God.

As Origen says, Christ alone is capable of claiming, *I do not have a demon*, for he has nothing, either slight or serious, of the devil in him; thus he says: *the prince of this world comes, and in me he has not anything* (John 14:30). *What accord has Christ with Belial?* (2 Cor 6:15).

1265. He supports his stand by saying the opposite: *but I honor my Father*. Now the devil hinders honor being given to God; therefore, any person who seeks God's honor is a stranger to the devil. Thus, Christ, who honors his Father, that is, God, has not a demon. Furthermore, it is a proper and singular mark of Christ that he honor his Father, as we read: *a son honors his father* (Mal 1:6). And Christ is most singularly the Son of God.

1266. Next, at *and you have dishonored me*, he reproves the impudence of those insulting him.

First, he reproves them;

second, he rejects the supposed reason for their reproof; and

third, he foretells their deserved condemnation.

1267. He says first, *I honor my Father, and you have dishonored me*. This is like saying: I do what I ought, but you do not do what you ought. Indeed, by dishonoring me you dishonor my Father: *he who does not honor the Son, does not honor the Father, who has sent him* (John 5:23).

1268. But they could say: you are too severe, you are too concerned for your own glory, and so you reprove us. He rejects this, and speaking as man, says, *I do not seek my own glory*. For it is God alone who can seek his own glory without fault; others must seek it in God: *let him who glories, glory in the Lord* (2 Cor 10:17); *if I glorify myself, my glory is nothing.*

But does not Christ as man have glory? He does indeed, and it is great in every respect, because, although he does not seek it, nevertheless, *there is one who seeks*, that is, the Father; for we read: *thou dost crown him with glory and honor* (Ps 8:5), referring to Christ in his human nature. And in another place: *glory and great beauty shalt thou lay upon him.* (Ps 20:6)

1269. Et non solum gloriam meam quaeret in operantibus vivas veritatis causas, sed et puniet et condemnabit contradicentes gloriae meae; unde subdit *et iudicet*.

Sed contra; supra V, 22, dicitur: *Pater non iudicat quemquam; sed omne iudicium dedit Filio*.

Respondeo. Pater non iudicat quemquam seorsum a Filio: quia etiam hoc iudicium quod faciet de eo quod iniuriamini mihi per Filium faciet. Vel dicendum, quod iudicium quandoque pro condemnatione accipitur; et hoc iudicium Pater dedit Filio, quia ipse solus apparebit in forma visibili in iudicium, ut dictum est supra. Quandoque accipitur pro discretione; et de hoc loquitur hic. Unde dicit in Ps. XLII, 1: *iudica me, Deus, et discerne causam meam*; quasi dicat: est Pater qui gloriam meam a vestra discernet. Vos enim, pro saeculo gloriari, discernit, et gloriam Filii sui, quem unxit prae participibus suis, et qui sine peccato est; vos vero homines cum peccato.

1269. Not only will he seek my glory in those who accomplish works of great virtue, but he will punish and condemn those who speak against my glory thus he adds: *and judges*.

This, however, seems to conflict with the statement above: *for neither does the Father judge any man, but he has given all judgment to the Son* (John 5:22).

I answer that the Father does not judge anyone apart from the Son, because even that judgment which he will make concerning the fact that you insult me, he will make through the Son. Or, one might say that judgment is sometimes taken for condemnation, and this judgment the Father has given to the Son, who alone will appear in visible form in judgment, as has been said. Sometimes, however, it is understood as meaning to distinguish one from another; and this is the way it is used here. Thus we read: *judge me, O God, and distinguish my cause* (Ps 42:1). It is like saying: it is the Father who will distinguish my glory from yours, for he discerns that you glory in the world; and he sees the glory of his Son, whom he has anointed above his fellows and who is without sin. But you are men with sin.

Lecture 8

8:51 Amen, amen dico vobis: si quis sermonem meum servaverit, mortem non videbit in aeternum. [n. 1271]

8:52 Dixerunt ergo Iudaei: nunc cognovimus quia daemonium habes. Abraham mortuus est, et prophetae, et tu dicis: si quis sermonem meum servaverit, non gustabit mortem in aeternum. [n. 1272]

8:53 Numquid tu maior es patre nostro Abraham, qui mortuus est? Et prophetae, mortui sunt. Quem teipsum facis? [n. 1274]

8:54 Respondit Iesus: si ego glorifico meipsum, gloria mea nihil est. Est Pater meus qui glorificat me, quem vos dicitis, quia Deus vester est. [n. 1276]

8:55 Et non cognovistis eum: ego autem novi eum. Et si dixero, quia non scio eum, ero similis vobis mendax. Sed scio eum, et sermonem eius servo. [n. 1280]

8:56 Abraham pater vester exultavit, ut videret diem meum: vidit, et gavisus est. [n. 1287]

8:57 Dixerunt ergo Iudaei ad eum: quinquaginta annos nondum habes, et Abraham vidisti? [n. 1288]

8:58 Dixit eis Iesus: amen, amen dico vobis, antequam Abraham fieret, ego sum. [n. 1290]

8:59 Tulerunt ergo lapides, ut iacerent in eum, Iesus autem abscondit se, et exivit de templo. [n. 1291]

8:51 Amen, amen I say to you: if any man keep my word, he will never see death. [n. 1271]

8:52 The Jews therefore said: now we know that you have a demon. Abraham is dead, and the prophets, and you say, if any man keep my word, he will never taste death. [n. 1272]

8:53 Are you greater than our father Abraham, who is dead? And the prophets are dead. Who do you make yourself to be? [n. 1274]

8:54 Jesus answered: if I glorify myself, my glory is nothing. It is my Father who glorifies me, of whom you say that he is your God. [n. 1276]

8:55 And you have not known him, but I know him. And if I said that I do not know him, I would be like you, a liar. But I do know him and keep his word. [n. 1280]

8:56 Your father Abraham rejoiced that he might see my day: he saw it and was glad. [n. 1287]

8:57 The Jews therefore said to him: you are not yet fifty years old, and you have seen Abraham? [n. 1288]

8:58 Jesus said to them: amen, amen I say to you, before Abraham was made, I am. [n. 1290]

8:59 They therefore took up stones to cast at him. But Jesus hid himself and went out of the temple. [n. 1291]

1270. Supra Dominus duo promiserat eum sequentibus: scilicet liberationem a tenebris, et adeptionem vitae, dicens: *qui sequitur me, non ambulat in tenebris, sed habebit lumen vitae.* Et de primo quidem dictum est supra; nunc autem agitur de secundo, scilicet de adeptione vitae per Christum, et

primo proponit veritatem;

secundo repellit Iudaeorum contradictionem, ibi *dixerunt ergo Iudaei: nunc cognovimus* etc.

1271. Sciendum est autem, quod quamvis Christus lacessitus esset iniuriis et opprobriis, non tamen destitit

1270. Above, our Lord had promised two things to his followers: liberation from darkness and the attainment of life, saying, *he who follows me does not walk in darkness but will have the light of life* (John 8:12). The first of these has been treated above; so we are now concerned with the second, the obtaining of life through Christ.

First, he states the truth;

second he counters its denial by the Jews, at *the Jews therefore said: now we know that you have a demon.*

1271. It should be noted that although Christ had been loaded down with insults and criticisms, he did not stop his

a doctrina; sed postquam habere Daemonium dictus est, praedicationis suae beneficia largius impendit, dicens *amen, amen dico vobis* etc. In quo datur nobis exemplum, quod cum malorum perversitas crescit, et per opprobria hominum conculcantur qui convertuntur, non solum praedicatio frangi non debet, sed etiam augeri; Ez. II, 6: *tu ergo, fili hominis, ne timeas eos, neque sermones eorum metuas*; II Tim. IX: *laboro usque ad vincula quasi male operans; sed verbum Dei non est alligatum.*

Duo autem facit Dominus in his verbis. Unum quidem est quod requirit, aliud quod promittit. Requirit quidem sermonis sui observationem; unde dicit *si quis sermonem meum servaverit*. Nam sermo Christi veritas est; ideo debemus ipsum servare, primo quidem per fidem, et iugem meditationem; Prov. IV, 6: *serva eam et servabit te*; secundo vero per operis impletionem; infra XIV, 21: *qui habet mandata mea, et servat ea, ille est qui diligit me.*

Promittit autem mortis liberationem; unde dicit *mortem non videbit in aeternum*, idest non experietur; Eccli. XXIV, 30: *qui operantur in me*, scilicet in divina sapientia, *non peccabunt; et qui elucidant me, vitam aeternam habebunt.* Et congrue tali merito debetur tale praemium. Nam vita aeterna praecipue in divina visione consistit; infra XVII, 3: *haec est vita aeterna ut cognoscant te solum verum Deum, et quem misisti Iesum Christum.* Huius autem visionis quoddam seminarium et principium in nobis fit per verbum Christi; Lc. VIII, 11: *semen est verbum Dei.* Sicut ergo ille qui servat semen alicuius plantae vel arboris ne corrumpatur, pervenit ad perceptionem fructus; ita qui servat verbum Dei; pervenit ad vitam aeternam; Lev. XVIII, v. 5: *quae fecerit homo, vivet in eis.*

1272. Consequenter cum dicit *dixerunt ergo Iudaei* etc., ponitur contradictionis Iudaeorum confutatio. Contradicunt autem Christo tripliciter.

Primo quidem falsitatis arguendo;

secundo irridendo, ibi *dixerunt ergo Iudaei ad eum: quinquaginta annos nondum habes, et Abraham vidisti?*

Tertio persequendo, ibi *tulerunt ergo lapides, ut iacerent in eum.*

Circa primum duo faciunt.

Primo conantur eum redarguere praesumptionis;

secundo ad quaedam eorum quae dicta sunt Christus respondet, ibi *si ego glorifico meipsum, gloria mea nihil est.*

Circa primum tria faciunt.

Primo irrogant improperium;

secundo proponunt factum, ibi *Abraham mortuus est* etc.;

teaching; indeed, after being accused of having a demon, he offers the benefits of his teachings more generously, saying: *amen, amen, I say to you, if any man keeps my word, he will never see death*. He is here giving us an example that when the malice of wicked men increases, and those that are converted are abused with insults, preaching, so far from being curtailed, should be increased: *and you, son of man, be not afraid of them, nor be afraid of their words* (Ezek 2:6); . . . *the Gospel for which I am suffering and wearing fetters like a criminal. But the word of God is not fettered* (2 Tim 2:9).

In this statement our Lord does two things: he requires something, and he promises something. What he requires is that his words be kept, *if any man keep my word*—for the word of Christ is the truth. Therefore, we should keep it, first of all, by faith and continual meditation: *do not forsake her, and she will keep you* (Prov 4:6); second, by fulfilling it in action: *he who has my commandments and keeps them, he it is who loves me* (John 14:21).

What he promises is freedom from death; thus he says, *he will never see death*, that is, experience it: *they who act by me* i.e., by divine wisdom *shall not sin; they who explain me shall have life everlasting* (Sir 24:30). Such a reward suits such merit, for life everlasting consists especially in the divine vision: *this is eternal life: that they may know you, the only true God, and Jesus Christ, whom you have sent* (John 17:3). Now the seedbed and source of this vision comes into us by the word of Christ; *the seed is the word of God* (Luke 8:11). Therefore, just as a person who keeps the seed of some plant or tree from being destroyed succeeds in obtaining its fruit, so the person who keeps the word of God attains to life everlasting: *keep my statutes and my ordinances by doing which a man shall live* (Lev 18:5).

1272. Next, at *the Jews therefore said: now we know that you have a demon*. We see the opposition of the Jews being repelled. They oppose Christ in three ways:

first, by accusing him of making a false statement;

second, by their derision, at *the Jews therefore said to him: you are not yet fifty years old, and you have seen Abraham?* and

third by assaulting him, at *they therefore took up stones to cast at him.*

As to the first, there are two things:

first, they try to accuse him of presumption;

second, Christ answers some of their retorts, at *if I glorify myself, my glory is nothing.*

As to the first they do three things:

first, they insult Christ;

second, they state a certain fact, at *Abraham is dead*;

tertio interrogant, ibi *numquid tu maior es patre nostro Abraham?*

1273. Irrogaverunt autem improperium mendacii, cum dicunt *nunc cognovimus quia daemonium habes.* Et hoc ideo dixerunt, quia notum est apud Iudaeos quod adinventor peccatorum est diabolus, et praecipue mendacii, secundum illud Reg. ult., 22, *egrediar, et ero spiritus mendax in ore omnium prophetarum eius.* Quia autem videbatur eis hoc quod Dominus dixit, scilicet *si quis sermonem meum servaverit, mortem non videbit in aeternum,* apertum mendacium esse, nam ipsi tamquam carnales intelligebant de morte corporali, quod de spirituali et aeterna morte dixerat, et praecipue, quia contrariatur auctoritati Sacrae Scripturae, Ps. LXXXVIII, 49: *quis est homo qui vivit, et non videbit mortem, eruet animam suam de manu Inferi?* Ideo dicunt ei *daemonium habes,* quasi dicant: ex instinctu Daemonis mendacium loqueris.

1274. Et ut convincant eum de mendacio, duo faciunt. Primo quidem proponunt mortem antiquorum; secundo vero repetunt verba Christi, ibi *et tu dicis* etc.

Dicunt ergo: vere falsum est quod loqueris: *si quis sermonem tuum* etc., nam *Abraham,* homo, *mortuus est,* ut patet Gen. c. XXV. Similiter *et prophetae mortui sunt*; II Reg. XIV, 14: *omnes morimur, et quasi aquae dilabimur in terram, quae non revertuntur.* Et quidem licet mortui sint corporaliter, non tamen mortui sunt spiritualiter; Matth. XXII, 32, dicit Dominus: *ego sum Deus Abraham, et Deus Isaac, et Deus Iacob.* Postea sequitur: *non est Deus mortuorum, sed vivorum.* Mortui ergo sunt corpore, sed vivunt spiritu, quia sermonem Dei servaverunt, et vixerunt ex fide. Et de ea morte Dominus intelligebat, non de corporali.

Verbum autem Christi repetunt cum subdunt *et tu dicis: si quis sermonem meum servaverit, non gustabit mortem in aeternum.* Velut incauti et maligni auditores, Dominicum sermonem confundentes, non repetunt eadem verba. Nam Dominus dixit *mortem non videbit* ipsi vero protulerunt *mortem non gustabit.* Sed quantum ad eorum intentionem idem est: quia per utrumque ipsi intelligunt, quod mortem, scilicet corporalem, non experietur in aeternum. Sed quantum ad verum intellectum differt, ut Origenes dicit, inter mortem gustare et videre: nam videre mortem est eam perfecte experiri; gustare autem est aliquem mortis gustum seu participationem habere. Sicut autem est plus ad poenam videre mortem quam gustare, ita plus est ad gloriam non gustare mortem quam non videre. Illi enim non gustant qui in alto sunt cum Christo, scilicet in intellectuali loco statum observant: de quibus dicitur Matth. XVI, 28: *sunt de hic stantibus, qui non gustabunt mortem, donec videant Filium hominis venientem in regno suo.* Aliqui tamen sunt qui si non videant mortem mortaliter peccando, tamen

and third, they ask a question, at *are you greater than our father Abraham?*

1273. They reproached him for lying when they said, *now we know that you have a demon.* They said this because the Jews knew that the inventor of sin, and especially of lying, was the devil: *I will go forth and will be a lying spirit in the mouth of his prophets* (1 Kgs 22:22). It seemed to them that our Lord's statement, *if any man keep my word, he will never see death,* was an obvious lie—for since they were carnal minded, they understood of physical death what he said about spiritual and eternal death; and especially also because it was contrary to the authority of Sacred Scripture, which says, *what man can live and never see death? Who can deliver his soul from the power of Sheol?* (Ps 89:48). For these reasons they said to him: *you have a demon.* It was like saying: you are lying because prompted by the devil.

1274. Further, they do two things to convict him of lying: first, they mention the death of the ancients; second, they quote Christ's own words, at *and you say, if any man keep my word, he will never taste death.*

So they say: what you say, *if any one keeps my word, he will never see death,* is obviously false, for *Abraham is dead* (Gen 25); *and the prophets are dead*; *we must all die, we are like water split on the ground, which cannot be gathered up again* (2 Sam 14:14). But although they are dead in the bodily sense, they are not dead spiritually, for our Lord says: *I am the God of Abraham and the God of Isaac and the God of Jacob* (Matt 22:32), and then he adds, *he is not God of the dead, but of the living.* Thus, they were dead as to the body, but they were living in the spirit, because the Lord was speaking of, and not bodily death.

However, they repeat the words of Christ and add *and you say, if any man keep my word, he will never taste death.* But they were careless and evil listeners and so garbled our Lord's words and did not repeat them exactly. For our Lord had said, *he will never see death,* but they quote it as *he will never taste death.* However, as far as their understanding was concerned, it was all the same, because in both cases they understood that they would never experience a bodily death. But as Origen tells us, there is a real difference between seeing death and tasting death: for to see death is to experience it completely; while to taste it is to have some taste or share in death. Now, just as it is a greater punishment to see death than to taste it, so not to taste death is more of a glory than not to see death. For the ones who do not taste death are those who are on high with Christ, i.e., who remain in an intellectual order: *there are some standing here who will not taste death before they see the Son of man coming in his kingdom* (Matt 16:28). And there are others who, if they do not see death by sinning mortally, nevertheless taste it, because they have a slight

aliquid gustant per aliquam levem terrenorum affectionem. Et ideo Dominus, ut habetur in Graeco, et Origenes etiam exponit, dixit, ***mortem non videbit in aeternum***: quia qui sermonem Christi acceperit et custodierit, etsi gustet aliquid, non tamen videbit mortem.

1275. Interrogant autem cum dicunt ***numquid tu maior es patre nostro Abraham, qui mortuus est?*** Et primo quidem quaerunt de comparatione ipsius ad antiquos patres: ***numquid*** inquiunt ***tu maior es patre nostro Abraham?*** Poterant, ut Chrysostomus dicit, secundum carnalem eorum intellectum, altius quaerere: numquid scilicet ut maior es Deo? Nam Abraham et prophetae mandata Dei servaverunt, et tamen corporaliter mortui sunt. Sic ergo si qui sermonem tuum servaverit non morietur, videtur quod sis maior Deo. Sed contenti sunt hac redargutione, quia putabant eum minorem quam Abraham; cum tamen sit scriptum in Ps. LXXXV, 8: *non est similis tui in diis, Domine*; et Ex. XV, 11: *quis similis tui in fortibus, Domine?* Quasi dicat nullus.

Secundo quaerunt de sua aestimatione, quem scilicet seipsum facit; quasi dicant: si tu es maior istis, scilicet Abraham et prophetis, videtur per hoc intelligi quod sis altioris naturae, puta angelus, vel Deus. Sed hoc non aestimamus de te. Et ideo non dicunt, tu quis es; sed quem te ipsum facis? Quia quidquid dicitur supra istis, non recognoscentes de te, reputabimus, quod tu illud fingas. Similiter dicebant infra X, 33: ***de bono opere non lapidamus te, sed de blasphemia: quia tu homo cum sis, facis teipsum Deum.***

1276. Consequenter cum dicit ***respondit Iesus*** etc., ponitur responsio Domini, et

primo respondet secundae quaestioni;

secundo vero primae, ibi ***Abraham pater vester exultavit ut videret diem meum.***

Circa primum tria facit Dominus.

Primo excludit falsitatem quam intendebant;

secundo docet veritatem, quam ignorabant, ibi ***est pater meus qui glorificat me***;

tertio manifestat utrumque quod proponebant, ibi ***et non cognovistis eum.***

1277. Dicit ergo: quaeritis me dicentes: ***quem teipsum facis?*** Ac si gloriam quam non habeo, mihi usurpem. Sed supervacua fuit haec prolatio, quoniam non me facio id quod sum, sed ex Patre recepi: nam ***si ego glorifico meipsum, gloria mea nihil est.*** Quod secundum hunc modum posset intelligi de Christo secundum quod est Filius Dei, ut dicatur cum praecisione ***si ego***, scilicet solus, ***glorifico meipsum***, idest attribuam mihi gloriam, quam Pater mihi non attribuat, ***gloria mea nihil est***: nam gloria Christi secundum quod est Deus, est gloria Verbi et Filii Dei; Filius autem nihil habet nisi natus, idest quod nascendo ab aliquo recepit: si ergo detur

affection for earthly things. Consequently, our Lord, as it is written in the Greek, and as Origen explains it, said, ***he will never see death***, because the person who has accepted and kept the words of Christ will not see death, even though he might taste something of it.

1275. Then they ask their question, saying, ***are you greater than our father Abraham, who is dead?*** They are asking, first of all, about a comparison between him and their fathers of old: ***are you***, they ask ***greater than our father Abraham?*** But as Chrysostom says, in their carnal understanding they could have asked something higher, that is, are you greater than God? For Abraham and the prophets kept God's commands, yet they died in the bodily sense. Therefore, if any one who keeps your word will never die, it seems that you are greater than God. Yet they were satisfied with their retort, because they considered him less than Abraham, in spite of the fact that we read: *there is none like thee among the gods, O Lord* (Ps 86:8); and *who is like thee, O Lord, among the gods?* (Exod 15:11); as if to say: no one.

Second, they ask about his estimate of himself, i.e., who does he take himself to be? As if to say: if you are greater than them, namely, Abraham and the prophets, it seems to imply that you are of a higher nature, say an angel or God. But we do not think you are. So they do not ask, who are you? but who do you claim to be? For whatever you say in this matter, we who know will regard it as a fiction. They spoke in a similar fashion below: ***we do not stone you for a good work but for blasphemy, and because you, being a man, make yourself God*** (John 10:33).

1276. Then, at ***Jesus answered: if I glorify myself, my glory is nothing***, our Lord's answer is given.

First, he answers the second question;

second, the first question, at ***your father Abraham rejoiced that he might see my day.***

As to the first, he Lord does three things:

first, he rejects their error;

second, he teaches them a truth which they did not know, at ***it is my Father who glorifies me***; and

third, he clarifies both of these things, at ***and you have not known him.***

1277. He says, you ask me, ***who do you make yourself to be?*** As if I am usurping a glory that I do not have. But this is a false assumption on your part, because I do not make myself what I am, but I have received it from the Father: for ***if I glorify myself, my glory is nothing***. Now this could be understood of Christ according as he is the Son of God, as though saying in precise language; ***if I***, namely, myself alone, ***glorify myself***, that is, ascribe to myself a glory which the Father does not give me, ***my glory is nothing***. For the glory of Christ according as he is God is the glory of the Word and the Son of God. But the Son has nothing except being begotten, i.e., what he has received from another by being begotten. Therefore, assuming the impossible, if his

per impossibile quod gloria sua non esset ab alio, non esset gloria Filii.

Melius tamen videtur quod dicatur de Christo secundum quod homo. Nam quicumque attribuit sibi gloriam quam non habet a Deo, gloria illa est falsa: nam quidquid veritatis est, a Deo est; quod autem est veritati contrarium, falsum est, et per consequens, nihil. Gloria ergo quae a Deo non est, nihil est; Hebr. V, 5, dicitur de Christo, quod *non seipsum clarificavit ut pontifex fieret*; II Cor. X, 18: *non enim qui seipsum commendat, ille probatus est, sed quem Deus commendat*. Sic ergo patet Iudaeorum falsitas.

1278. Veritatem autem, quam intendit docere, ponit dicens *est Pater meus qui glorificat me*, quasi dicat: non ego meipsum glorifico, sicut vos fingitis; sed alius est qui me glorificat, scilicet *Pater meus*: quem quidem describit ex proprietate, et ex natura.

Ex proprietate quidem Paternitatis; unde dicit *est Pater meus*, et non ego.

Ex quo quidem verbo, ut Augustinus dicit, calumniantur Ariani fidei nostrae, dicentes maiorem esse Patrem Filio: nam maior est, qui glorificat, eo qui glorificatur ab ipso. Si ergo Pater glorificat Filium, Pater maior est Filio.

Sed dicendum quod apparentiam quidem haberet argumentum, nisi inveniretur e converso quod Filius glorificet Patrem: dicit enim Filius, infra XVII, 1: **Pater, venit hora, clarifica Filium tuum, ut Filius tuus clarificet te**. Et in eodem *ego te clarificavi super terram*. In Graeco autem idem est glorifica et clarifica; et, secundum Ambrosium, *gloria est clara cum laude notitia*.

Hoc autem quod dicit **est Pater meus qui glorificat me**, potest referri ad Christum, et secundum quod est Filius Dei, et secundum quod est Filius hominis. Secundum quidem quod est Filius Dei, Pater glorificat eum gloria divinitatis, ab aeterno eum sibi aequalem generando; Hebr. I, 3: *qui cum sit splendor gloriae et figura substantiae eius . . . sedet ad dexteram Maiestatis in excelsis*; Phil. II, 11: *omnis lingua confiteatur quia Dominus Iesus Christus in gloria est Dei Patris*. Secundum vero quod homo, habuit gloriam per redundantiam divinitatis in ipsum, et gratiae et gloriae singularis; supra I, 14: **videbimus gloriam eius, gloriam quasi unigeniti a Patre, plenum gratiae et veritatis**.

1279. Ex natura vero divinitatis describit eum, cum dicit **quem vos dicitis quia Deus vester est**. Ne autem alium Patrem putes quam Deum, dicit se glorificari a Deo; infra XIII, 31: **nunc clarificatus est Filius hominis, et Deus clarificatus est in eo. Si Deus clarificatus est in eo, et Deus clarificabit eum in semetipso**.

Sed, secundum Augustinum, hoc verbum est contra Manichaeos, qui dicunt annuntiatum non esse in Veteri

glory were not from another, it would not be the glory of the Son.

However, it seems better to suppose that this is said of Christ according as he is man, because anyone who ascribes to himself a glory he does not have from God, has a false glory. For whatever is true is from God, and whatever is contrary to the truth is false, and consequently, nothing. Therefore, a glory which is not from God is nothing. We read of Christ: *Christ did not exalt himself to be made a high priest* (Heb 5:5); and *it is not the man who commends himself that is accepted, but the man whom the Lord commends* (2 Cor 10:18). Thus the error of the Jews is obvious.

1278. He sets down the truth he intends to teach and says: *it is my Father who glorifies me*. It is like saying: I do not glorify myself, as you think; but it is another who glorifies me, namely, **my Father**, whom he describes by his proper characteristic and by his nature.

He describes him by his proper characteristic of fatherhood; thus he says that *it is my Father* and not I.

As Augustine says, the Arians use this statement to injure our faith, and they claim the Father is greater than the Son, for one who glorifies is greater than the one glorified by him. If, therefore, the Father glorifies the Son, the Father is greater than the Son.

Now this argument would be valid unless it were found that, conversely, the Son glorifies the Father. But the Son says: **Father, the hour has come, glorify your Son, that your Son may glorify you** (John 17:1); and **I have glorified you on earth** (John 17:4). In the Greek however, glorify and clarify are the same; and, according to Ambrose, *glory is clarity with praised notice*.

It is my Father who glorifies me, can be applied to Christ both according as he is the Son of God, and also as the Son of man. As the Son of God, the Father glorifies him with the glory of the divinity, generating him from eternity as equal to himself: as we read, *he reflects the glory of God and bears the very stamp of his nature . . . he sat down at the right hand of the Majesty on high* (Heb 1:3); *and every tongue confess that Jesus Christ is Lord, to the glory of God the Father* (Phil 2:11). But as man, he had glory through an overflowing into him of the divinity, and overflowing of unique grace and glory: **we saw his glory, the glory as it were of the only begotten of the Father, full of grace and truth** (John 1:14).

1279. He describes the Father by his nature, that is, by his divinity, when he says, **of whom you say that he is your God**. But lest anyone suppose that his Father is other than God, he says that he is glorified by God: **now is the Son of man glorified, and God is glorified in him; if God is glorified in him, God will also glorify him in himself** (John 13:31–32).

According to Augustine, these words are against the Manicheans, who say that the Father of Christ was not

Testamento Patrem Christi, sed esse aliquem ex principibus malorum angelorum. Constat autem quod Iudaei non dicunt alium Deum suum esse quam Deum Veteris Testamenti. Ergo Deus Veteris Testamenti est Pater Christi glorificans eum.

1280. Manifestat autem utrumque, scilicet Iudaeorum falsitatem, et suam veritatem, cum dicit **et non cognovistis eum**. Manifestat autem dupliciter.

Primo quidem ostendendo Iudaeorum ignorantiam; secundo suam notitiam, ibi **ego autem cognovi eum**.

1281. Circa primum sciendum, quod possent Iudaei dicere: tu dicis quod glorificaris a Deo; sed nobis nota sunt iudicia eius, secundum illud Ps. CXLVII, 20: *non fecit taliter omni nationi, et iudicia sua non manifestavit eis*. Ergo si verum est quod dicis, nos utique sciremus hoc: cum ergo nos lateat, constat quod non est verum. Et ideo concludens, dicit **et non cognovistis eum**; quasi dicat: non mirum est si non cognoscitis gloriam qua me glorificat Pater meus, quem dicitis Deum vestrum, quia nec ipsum Deum cognoscitis.

1282. Sed contra Ps. LXXV: *notus in Iudaea Deus*.

Respondeo: ut Deus, sed non ut Pater, notus est ab eis; unde supra dixit: **est Pater meus qui glorificat me**. Vel dicendum, quod non cognovistis eum affectu: quia carnaliter colitis qui spiritualiter colendus est; supra IV, 24: **spiritus est Deus, et eos qui adorant eum, in spiritu et veritate oportet adorare**. Item affectu, quia mandata eius adimplere contempsistis; ad Tit. I, 16: *confitentur se nosse Deum; factis autem negant*.

1283. Sed quia possent dicere: esto quod nos non cognoscamus gloriam tuam, quomodo cognoscis tu gloriam te a Deo Patre habere? Ideo subiungit notitiam suam, dicens **ego autem novi eum**, et

primo ponit suam notitiam;

secundo ostendit necessitatem huius notitiae proferendae, ibi **et si dixero quia non scio eum, ero similis vobis mendax**;

tertio exponit quod dicit, ibi **sed scio eum**.

1284. Dicit ergo: ideo scio me habere gloriam a Deo Patre, quia ego novi eum, ea scilicet notitia quae ipse novit seipsum, et nullus alius nisi Filius; Matth. XI, 27:

nemo novit Filium nisi Pater, nec Patrem quis novit nisi Filius, scilicet cognitione perfecta comprehensionis. Et quia omne imperfectum a perfecto initium sumit, inde est quod omnis nostra cognitio a Verbo derivatur: unde sequitur: *et cui voluerit Filius revelare*.

1285. Sed quia, secundum carnem iudicantibus, posset Christo ad arrogantiam ascribi dicenti se nosse Deum, ideo subdit necessitatem dicti sui, cum subiungit **et si dixero quia non scio eum, ero similis vobis mendax**.

proclaimed in the Old Testament, but rather it was one of the princes of the evil angels. However, it is plain that the Jews do not say that their God is any other than the God of the Old Testament. Therefore, the God of the Old Testament is the Father of Christ and the One who glorifies him.

1280. Then he shows both these things, that is, the error of the Jews, and his own truth, when he says, **and you have not known him**. He shows these in two ways:

first, by pointing out the ignorance of the Jews;

second, his own knowledge, at **but I know him**.

1281. With respect to the first it should be noted that the Jews could say: you say that you are glorified by God; but his judgments are known by us, according to: *he has not dealt thus with any other nation; they do not know his ordinances* (Ps 147:20). Therefore, if what you say is true, we would certainly know it; but since we do not know of it, it is obviously not true. Christ concludes saying, but **you have not known him**. This is like saying: it is not strange if you do not know about the glory with which my Father, who you say is your God, glorifies me, for you do not know God.

1282. This seems to conflict with what is said: *in Judah God is known* (Ps 76:1).

I answer that he was known by them as God, but not as the Father; thus he said above: **it is my Father who glorifies me**. Or, one might answer that you have not known him with affection, because you adore him in a bodily way, whereas he should be adored spiritually: **God is spirit, and they who adore him ought to worship him in spirit and in truth** (John 4:24). And there is no affection because you are reluctant to keep his commandments: *they profess to know God; but they deny him by their deeds* (Titus 1:16).

1283. But they might say: granted that we do not know about your glory, how do you know that you have glory from God the Father? For this reason Christ speaks of his own knowledge, saying, **but I know him**.

First, he mentions his own knowledge;

second, he shows the need for mentioning it, at **and if I said that I do not know him, I would be like you, a liar**; and

third, he explains what he said, at **but I do know him**.

1284. He says: I know that I have glory from God the Father, because I know him, namely, with that knowledge with which he knows himself; and no one else except the Son knows him:

No one knows the Father except the Son (Matt 11:27), i.e., with a perfect and comprehensive knowledge. And because every imperfect thing derives from the perfect, all our knowledge is derived from the Word; thus Christ continues, *and any one to whom the Son chooses to reveal him*.

1285. Now because some who judge in a carnal manner might attribute arrogance to Christ for saying that he knows God, he mentions why his statement is necessary. For, according to Augustine, arrogance should not be so

Nam, secundum Augustinum, non est sic arrogantia vitanda ut relinquatur veritas et incurratur mendacium. Ideo dicit *si dixero*; quasi diceret: sicut vos dicentes scire eum, mentimini; ita ego *si dixero* me nescire, cum sciam eum, *ero similis vobis mendax*. Unde haec similitudo sequitur a contrario, ut sit similitudo in mendacio; quia sicut isti mentiuntur dicentes se scire eum quem nesciunt; ita Christus esset mendax, si diceret se nescire quem novit. Sed dissimilitudo est in cognitione: quia isti non cognoscunt, Christus vero scit eum.

Sed numquid potuisset Christus hoc dicere? Potuisset quidem verba proferre materialiter, sed non intendere exprimere falsitatem: quia hoc non potuisset fieri nisi per inclinationem voluntatis Christi ad falsum, quod erat impossibile, sicut impossibile erat eum peccare. Nihilominus tamen conditionalis est vera, licet antecedens et consequens sit impossibile.

1286. Quod autem Patrem cognoscat, manifestat subdens *sed scio eum*: et cognitione speculativa, cum dicit *scio*, intellectualiter per dictam cognitionem, *eum*, scilicet Patrem; item cognitione affectiva, scilicet per consensum voluntatis ad ipsum: unde dicit *et sermonem eius servo*; supra VI, 38: *descendi de caelo, non ut faciam voluntatem meam, sed voluntatem eius qui misit me*.

1287. Consequenter cum dicit *Abraham pater vester exultavit ut videret diem meum*, respondet primae quaestioni quam fecerunt ei Iudaei, dicentes *numquid tu maior es patre nostro Abraham?* Ostendens se maiorem, tali ratione.

Quicumque enim expectat bonum ab aliquo, et perfectionem suam, est minor eo a quo expectat, sed Abraham totam spem suae perfectionis et sui boni habuit in me: ergo est me minor. Et quantum ad hoc dicit *Abraham pater vester*, de quo scilicet gloriamini, *exultavit ut videret diem meum*. Ubi ponit duplicem visionem et duplex gaudium, sed alio et alio ordine.

Nam primo praemittit gaudium exultationis, dicens *exultavit*, et subdit visionem, dicens *ut videret*. Deinde praemittit visionem, dicens *vidit*, et subdit gaudium, dicens *et gavisus est*. Et sic gaudium consistit inter duas visiones, procedens ab una, et tendens in aliam: quasi dicat vidit, et gavisus est ut videret diem meum.

Primo ergo videndum quid sit iste dies quem vidit, et exultavit ut videret. Est autem duplex dies Christi: scilicet aeternitatis, de quo in Ps. II, 7: *ego hodie genui te*. Item dies incarnationis et humanitatis, de quo infra IX, 4: *me oportet operari . . . donec dies est*; Rom. XIII, 12: *nox praecessit, dies autem appropinquavit*.

guarded against that the truth is neglected and a lie committed. Thus Christ says: *and if I said that I do not know him, I would be like you, a liar*. Thus he says *if I said*; this is like saying: just as you are lying when you say that you know him, so *if I said that I do not know him*, whereas I do, *I would be like you, a liar*. There is a similarity here in the fact of lying: as they lie in saying that they know him whom they do not know, so Christ would be a liar were he to say that he does not know him whom he knows. But there is a lack of similarity because they do not know him, whereas Christ does.

But could Christ say these things, *I do not know him* and *I would be like you, a liar*? He could, indeed, have spoken the words materially, but not so as to intend expressing a falsehood, because this could be done only by Christ's will inclining to falsehood, which was impossible, just as it was impossible for him to sin. However, the conditional statement is true, although both antecedent and consequent are impossible.

1286. When he continues he shows that he knows the Father, both with speculative knowledge when he says *I know*, and intellectually through saying *him*. And I also know him with affective knowledge, by consenting to him with my will: thus he says, *and I keep his word*: as it said above: *for I have come down from heaven, not to do my own will, but the will of him who sent me* (John 6:38).

1287. Then when he says, *your father Abraham rejoiced that he might see my day*, he gives his answer to the first question asked by the Jews: *are you greater than our father Abraham?* He shows that he is greater for the following reason:

whoever awaits for someone as for his good and perfection is less than the one he waits for; but Abraham placed the entire hope of his perfection and good in me; therefore, he is less than I. In regard to this he says, *your father Abraham*, in whom you glory, *rejoiced that he might see my day*; he saw it and was glad. He is stating two visions and two joys, but the second vision and its joy is mentioned first.

In the first part of the statement, he first mentions the joy of exultation when he says, *Abraham rejoiced*, and then adds the vision, saying that *he might see my day*. Then in the second part he first mentions the vision, saying, *he saw it*, my day, and adds the joy, *and was glad*. Thus a joy lies between two visions, proceeding from the one and tending to the other. He is saying in effect: he saw my day, and rejoiced that he was to see my day.

First of all, let us examine what that day is which he saw, and also what that day is which he rejoiced that he was to see. Now the day of Christ is twofold: the day of eternity, *today I have begotten you* (Ps 2:7); and the day of his incarnation and humanity, *I must do the works of him who sent me while it is day* (John 9:4); *the night is passed, and*

Utroque ergo modo dicimus, quod Abraham vidit primo diem Christi, scilicet aeternitatis, et incarnationis per fidem; Gen. XV, 6: *credidit Abraham Deo, et reputatum est illi ad iustitiam.* Et quod vidit diem aeternitatis, manifestum est: alias enim non fuisset iustificatus a Deo, quia, ut dicitur Hebr. II, 6, *accedentem ad Deum oportet credere quia est, et inquirentibus se remunerator sit.*

Quod autem viderit diem incarnationis, manifestatur ex tribus: scilicet ex iuramento quod exegit a servo, nam Gen. XXIV, 2, ait servo suo quem mittebat: *pone manum subter femore meo, et iura mihi per Deum caeli.* Ex quo, ut dicit Augustinus, signabatur, quod de femore eius processurus esset Deus caeli. Secundo, ut Gregorius dicit, cum in figura summae Trinitatis tres angelos hospitio suscepit. Tertio quando cognovit praefiguratam passionem Christi in oblatione arietis et Isaac; Gen. XXII.

Sic ergo ex hac visione gavisus est; sed non quievit in ea, immo ex hac exultavit in aliam visionem, scilicet apertam et per speciem, quasi totum gaudium suum in ea ponens. Unde dicit **exultavit ut videret** aperta visione, **diem meum**, scilicet divinitatis et humanitatis meae; Lc. X, 24: *multi reges et prophetae voluerunt videre quae vos videtis, et non viderunt.*

1288. Consequenter cum dicit **dixerunt ergo Iudaei ad eum** etc., ostendit quomodo Iudaei irrident verba Christi, et

primo ponitur irrisio verborum Christi a Iudaeis ad confutandum;

secundo subditur manifestatio ipsorum verborum a Christo, ad irrisionem vitandam, ibi **dixit ergo Iesus: amen, amen dico vobis** etc.

1289. Quia ergo Christus dixerat quod Abraham exultavit ut videret diem suum, Iudaei carnalem mentem habentes, et in eo solum carnis aetatem pensantes, irrident dictum, et dicunt **quinquaginta annos nondum habes**. Vere quinquaginta annos non habebat, nec etiam quadraginta, sed circa trigesimum annum erat; Lc. III, 23: *erat Iesus incipiens quasi annorum triginta.*

Quod autem dicunt **quinquaginta annos nondum habes**, ideo forte est, quia apud Iudaeos annus iubilaeus in maxima reverentia habebatur, quasi per eum omnia computantes, in quo et captivos manumittebant, et emptitiis cedebant possessionibus. Quasi dicant: tu nondum excessisti spatium unius iubilaei, et Abraham vidisti? Quamvis Dominus non dixerit quod viderit Abraham, sed quod Abraham diem eius vidit.

1290. Et ideo Dominus ut irrisionem vitet, respondens Iudaeis, verba sua exponit, dicens **amen, amen dico vobis, antequam Abraham fieret, ego sum**: in quibus verbis Dominus duo de se notabilia et efficacia contra Arianos dicit. Unum est, quia, ut dicit Gregorius, coniungit simul verbum praesentis temporis et praeteriti. Ante enim significat praeteritum; sum temporis

the day is at hand (Rom 13:12). We say that Abraham saw, by faith, each day of Christ: the day of eternity and the day of the incarnation: *he believed the Lord; and he reckoned it to him as righteousness* (Gen 15:6). It is clear that he saw the day of eternity, for otherwise he would not have been justified by God, because: *whoever would draw near to God must believe that he exists and that he rewards those who see him* (Heb 11:6).

That he saw the day of the incarnation is clear from three things. First, from the oath he exacted from his servant. For he said to his servant: *put your hand under my thigh, and I will make you swear by the Lord* (Gen 24:2). This signified, as Augustine says, that the God of heaven was to come out of his thigh. Second, as Gregory says, when he showed hospitality to the three angels, a symbol of the most high Trinity. Third, when he knew the passion of Christ as prefigured in the offering of the ram and of Isaac (Gen 22).

So he was glad over this vision, but he did not rest in it. Indeed, from it he rejoiced in another vision, namely, the direct face-to-face vision, as though placing all his joy in this. Thus he says, **Abraham rejoiced that he might see** by revealed vision, **my day**, the day of my divinity and of my human nature; *many prophets and kings have desired to see the things that you see, and have not seen them.*

1288. Then: **the Jews therefore said to him: you are not yet fifty years old, and you have seen Abraham?** he shows how the Jews ridiculed Christ's words:

first, we have their ridicule, in an attempt to belittle what Christ said;

second, Christ clarifies what he said in order to counteract this ridicule, at **Jesus said to them: amen, amen I say to you, before Abraham was made, I am**.

1289. Because Christ had said that Abraham rejoiced that he was to see his day, the Jews, having a carnal mind and considering only his physical age, ridiculed him and said, **you are not yet fifty years old**. Indeed, he was not yet fifty years old, or even forty, but closer to thirty: *and Jesus, when he began his ministry, was about thirty years of age* (Luke 3:23).

The Jews said, **you are not yet fifty years old**, probably because they held the year of Jubilee in the greatest reverence and computed everything in terms of it—it was a time for freeing captives and giving up certain possessions. They were saying in effect: you have not yet lived beyond the span of a Jubilee, and have you seen Abraham? However, our Lord did not say that he saw Abraham, but that Abraham saw his day.

1290. To counteract their ridicule, our Lord answers the Jews by explaining his words, saying, **amen, amen I say to you, before Abraham was made, I am**. These words of our Lord mention two things about himself that are noteworthy and efficacious against the Arians. One is that, as Gregory says, he combines words of present and past time, because before signifies the past, and am signifies

praesentis est. Ut ergo ostenderet se esse aeternum, et esse suum esse aeternitatis insinuet, non ait ante Abraham ego fui sed *ante Abraham ego sum* nam esse aeternum non novit tempus praeteritum et futurum, sed in uno indivisibili includit omne tempus. Unde dici potest illud Ex. III, 14: *qui est misit me ad vos*; et *ego sum qui sum*. Ante ergo vel post Abraham habuit esse, qui et accedere potuit per exhibitionem praesentis, et recedere per cursum vitae.

Aliud est, secundum Augustinum, quia cum loqueretur de Abraham, qui creatura est, non dixit antequam Abraham esset sed *antequam fieret*. Sed loquens de se, ut ostendat quod non est factus ut creatura, sed ab aeterno de essentia Patris genitus, non dicit, ego fio, sed *ego sum*, qui *in principio erat Verbum*; supra I Prov. VIII, 25: *ante omnes colles generavit me Dominus*.

1291. Consequenter cum dicit *tulerunt ergo lapides ut iacerent in eum*, ponitur intentio Iudaeorum contra Christum: et primo ponitur Iudaeorum persecutio; secundo Christi evasio. Sed persecutio Iudaeorum procedit ex infidelitate. Nam mentes infidelium aeternitatis verba sustinere non valentes, nec intelligere ea, reputabant blasphemiam; et ideo, secundum legis mandatum, eum tamquam blasphemum lapidare volentes, *tulerunt lapides, ut iacerent in eum* etc. Et, ut dicit Augustinus, *tanta duritia lapidum, quo curreret nisi ad lapides?* Inf. X, 33: *de bono opere non lapidamus te*. Simile faciunt qui ex duritia cordis non intelligentes veritatem aperte prolatam, blasphemant proferentem, unde dicitur in canonica Iudae: *quaecumque non noverunt, blasphemant*.

1292. Evasio autem Christi est ex eius potestate: unde sequitur *Iesus autem abscondit se*, qui scilicet si divinitatis suae potentiam exercere voluisset in suis actibus, eos ligaret, aut in poenas subitae mortis obrueret.

Abscondit autem se, specialiter propter duo. Primo ut daret fidelibus suis exemplum declinandi persecutores suos; Matth. X, 23: *si vos persecuti fuerint in una civitate, fugite in aliam*. Secundo, quia non elegerat hoc genus mortis, sed potius in ara crucis voluit immolari; et quia nondum impletum erat tempus, adhuc fugit. Sic ergo tamquam homo a lapidibus fugit. Non autem abscondit se sub lapide vel in angulo, sed potestate suae divinitatis, invisibilem se eis exhibens, exivit, et recessit de templo. Simile fecit, Lc. IV, 29, quando voluerunt eum praecipitare de supercilio montis. Per quod, ut Gregorius dicit, datur intelligi quod illis ipsa veritas absconditur, qui eius verba sequi contemnunt. Eam quippe quam non invenit humilem veritas fugit mentem; Is. VIII, 17: *qui abscondit faciem suam a domo Iacob*. Et similiter etiam quia debebat eos, correctionem et veritatem non suscipientes,

the present. Therefore, in order to show that he is eternal, and to indicate that his existence is an eternal existence, he does not say, before Abraham, I was, but *before Abraham, I am*. For eternal existence knows neither past nor future time, but embraces all time in one indivisible instant. Thus it could be said: *he who is, sent me to you*, and *I am who am* (Exod 3:14). Jesus had being both before Abraham and after him, and he could approach him by showing himself in the present and be after him in the course of time.

The other point, according to Augustine, is that when speaking of Abraham, a creature, he did not say, before Abraham was, but *before Abraham was made*. Yet when speaking of himself, in order to show that he was not made as a creature is, but was eternally begotten from the essence of the Father, he does not say, I came to be, but *I am* he who *in the beginning was the Word* (John 1:1); *before the hills, I was brought forth* (Prov 8:25).

1291. Then, at *they therefore took up stones to cast at him*, we see the attitude of the Jews towards Christ: first, their harassment of him; second, Christ's escape. The harassment of the Jews came from their unbelief: for the minds of unbelievers, being unable to tolerate words of eternity, or understand them, regard them as blasphemy. *They*, according to the command of the law, they decided to stone Christ as a blasphemer: *therefore took up stones to throw at him*. As Augustine remarks: *what hardness of heart! To what could it resort except the hardness of stones?* The Jews therefore respond: *we do not stone you for a good work but for blasphemy* (John 10:33). And they act in the same way who from the hardness of their own hearts, failing to understand the clearly stated truth, blaspheme the one who speaks it; for we read: *these men revile whatever they do not understand* (Jude 1:10).

1292. Jesus escapes from them by his own power; he continues, *but Jesus hid himself*—he, who, if he had wished to exercise his divine power in his acts, could have bound or delivered them to the punishment of a sudden death.

Jesus hid himself for two main reasons. First, as an example to his followers to avoid those who persecute them: *when they persecute you in one town, flee to the next* (Matt 10:23). Second, because he had not chosen this form of death, but rather wanted to be sacrificed on the altar of the cross. He also fled because his time had not yet come. Thus, as man, he avoids their stoning. But he did not conceal himself under a rock or in a corner, but made himself invisible by his divine power and left the temple. He acted in a similar way when they wanted to throw him from the top of a hill (Luke 4:29). As Gregory says, this leads us to understand that the truth is hidden from those who disdain to follow his words. Indeed, the truth shuns a mind that it does not find to be humble: *the Lord is hiding his face from the house of Jacob* (Isa 8:17). Finally, he hid himself because it was fitting that he leave them because they

relinquere, et ire ad gentes; Matth. XXIII, 38: *ecce relinquetur vobis domus vestra deserta.*

refused to accept correction and the truth, and that he go to the gentiles: *behold your house is forsaken and desolate* (Matt 23:38).